1980

# A
# *SHORT HISTORY*
# *OF*
# OPERA

ONE-VOLUME EDITION

# A
# *SHORT HISTORY*
# *OF*
# OPERA

SECOND EDITION

By *DONALD JAY GROUT*

*Given Foundation Professor of Musicology*
*Cornell University*

Columbia University Press
*New York*

A.M.D.G.

# PREFACE TO
# THE SECOND EDITION

The present edition aims to incorporate the results of recent research and to bring the history of opera forward to about 1960. As in the first edition, the main divisions are chronological and based primarily on considerations of musical style. Revisions, more or less extensive, have been made in all chapters; a few judgments have been revised; new illustrations and musical examples have been provided.

The bibliography has been subdivided in accordance with the larger subdivisions of the text. Books that cover more than one chronological period are listed either in the "general" section or under the earliest period with which they deal. Dates of operas refer to first performance unless otherwise specified. Modern editions of operas before 1800 are listed on pages 769 to 786; some of these editions contain, in addition to the music, valuable critical or historical essays.

Grateful acknowledgment is made to the Graduate School of Cornell University and to the American Council of Learned Societies for grants in aid of research.

I am indebted to many friends and colleagues for help at various stages in the preparation of this edition. Particular thanks are due to Professor Anna Amalie Abert of Kiel for advice, to Mr. Harold Rosenthal of London for illustrations, and to Mr. James Bossert of Ithaca for assistance in reading proof.

Acknowledgment is made to the following publishers for permission to use copyrighted material in the musical examples added for this edition : Boosey & Hawkes, Ltd., London (Exs. 114, 116, 123); J. & W. Chester, Ltd., London (Ex. 107); Heugel et Cie, Paris (Ex. 121);

Möseler Verlag, Wolfenbüttel and Zurich (Exs. 38 and 40); G. Ricordi
& Co., Milan (Exs. 101 and 117); B. Schott's Soehne, Mainz, and
Associated Music Publishers Inc., New York (Ex. 126); Universal
Editions, A.G., Vienna (Exs. 115, 119, 124, 127); Edizioni Suvini
Zerboni, Milan (Ex. 125).

DONALD JAY GROUT

*Ithaca, New York*
*September 15, 1963*

# *PREFACE TO*
# *THE FIRST EDITION*

✧

Volumes almost beyond counting have been written about opera, but no systematic historical survey since the publication of Hermann Kretzschmar's *Geschichte der Oper* in 1919. This work, though valuable for the early periods of opera history, ends to all intents and purposes with Wagner; moreover, it has never been translated. Most books in English which profess to deal historically with opera are either mere collections of plot synopses strung on a thin thread of continuity, or else obvious bids for popular success without serious pretensions to accuracy or thoroughness. There are a few excellent books which treat of opera in a nonhistorical manner, among which may be especially mentioned Edward J. Dent's *Opera* (New York, Penguin Books, 1940). But the bulk of serious writing about opera at the present time is in the form of specialized studies of limited scope and is read for the most part only by specialists.

Recognizing this fact, it would seem that there might be room for a book which has for its purpose to offer a comprehensive report on the present state of our knowledge about the history of opera. In compressing such a long and diversified history into the compass of a single book it is obvious that many things must be omitted. The reader will not find here, for example, many synopses of opera plots or much gossip about the personal affairs of composers and singers; no attempt has been made to furnish complete statistical information about the output of composers or complete records of performances; biographies have been treated summarily; and digressions on the relation of opera to contemporary production in literature and the other arts, to politics, economics, and the *Zeitgeist* generally have been regretfully held to a minimum. On the other hand, a conscientious effort has been made to present the essential points in the history of opera clearly, fairly, in proper proportion, and with constant reference to the music. Musical examples have been provided, especially for the earlier periods from which scores are not readily available, and some technical analysis of important representative works or passages is included. The bibliographical material has been made full enough, it is hoped, to provide the student with adequate information for beginning research on almost any desired special topic. An elementary acquaintance on the reader's part with the history of music is assumed, though this is perhaps not essential; knowledge of music theory will be found necessary for understanding some of the technical analyses.

Generous help has been given by many friends in the course of preparation of this work. The author wishes especially to express his thanks to the Trustees of the Wesley Weyman Fund, Harvard University, for a grant of one thousand dollars for aid in research. Professor Otto Kinkeldey kindly read the manuscript and made many suggestions which are gratefully acknowledged. Advice on various special topics has been most cheerfully given by Mr. Gilbert Chase, Professor Archibald T. Davison, Mr. Richard S. Hill, Professor Scott Goldthwaite, Dr. Henry L. Clarke, Dr. Walter Rubsamen, Professor Chase Baromeo, and many others. To Mr. Lawrence Apgar, Mr. Leonard Burkat, and their helpers, thanks are due for skilled and devoted labor on bibliographical problems, and to Mr. John Scabia for preparation of the musical examples. Lastly to my wife, who typed most of the manuscript and who has been both a patient sufferer and an encouraging companion throughout the entire labor, a special debt of gratitude must always stand.

Acknowledgment is made to the following publishers for permission to use copyrighted material in the musical examples : Edwin Arnold & Co., London (Ex. 59); E. de Boccard, Paris (Ex. 30); Choudens, Editeur, Paris (Ex. 83); Durand & Cie., Paris (Exs. 57, 100, 110, 111); Novello & Co., Ltd., London (Exs. 48, 49, 50, 81, 91, 92); G. Schirmer, Inc., New York (Ex. 93); and Joseph Williams, Ltd., London (Exs. 45, 46, 47).

It is perhaps not out of order to warn the reader against the delusion that the history of any kind of music can be learned simply by reading a book. The principal use of any book about music is to serve as an introduction to the music itself, which must always be the central object of study. If beyond this essential point it is possible to suggest some of the implications of the music, some of its relation to the culture of which it is a part and some of its significance for our own time, so much the better. The landscape of history is not alone the solid earth of fact; above must spread the rolling cloudbanks of imagination.

DONALD JAY GROUT

*Skaneateles Lake, New York*
*September 1, 1947*

# CONTENTS

PART 3

*The Eighteenth Century*

PART 4

*The Nineteenth Century*

PART 5

## The Twentieth Century

# LIST OF ABBREVIATIONS

| | | | |
|---|---|---|---|
| AfMf | *Archiv für Musikforschung* | MD | *Musica disciplina* |
| AfMw | *Archiv für Musikwissen-schaft* | Mf | *Musikforschung* |
| | | MfMg | *Monatshefte für Musik-geschichte* |
| AMZ | *Allgemeine musikalische Zeitung* | MGG | *Musik in Geschichte und Gegenwart* |
| art. | article | | |
| B&H | Breitkopf & Härtel | M&L | *Music & Letters* |
| C.E. | Collected Edition (Gesamtausgabe) | MLA Notes | *Music Library Association Notes* |
| C.F. | *Chefs-d'oeuvre de l'opéra français* | MM | *Mercure musical* |
| | | MMus | *Modern Music* |
| DdT | *Denkmäler deutscher Tonkunst* | MMR | *Monthly Musical Record* |
| | | MQ | *Musical Quarterly* |
| DTB | *Denkmäler der Tonkunst in Bayern* | MR | *Music Review* |
| | | MTNA | *Proceedings of the Music Teachers National Association* |
| DTOe | *Denkmäler der Tonkunst in Oesterreich* | | |
| ed. | edition, editor, edited by | MuG | *Musik und Gesellschaft* |
| EMTA | *Echo Muzyczne, Teatralne i Artystyczne* | mus. | music (by) |
| | | NM | *Nuestra musica* |
| HAM | *Historical Anthology of Music*, Vol. II (Davison and Apel) | NOHM | *New Oxford History of Music* |
| | | NZfM | *Neue Zeitschrift für Musik* |
| JAMS | *Journal of the American Musicological Society* | OeM | *Oesterreichische Musik-zeitschrift* |
| JMP | *Jahrbuch der Musik-bibliothek Peters* | OHM | *Oxford History of Music* |
| | | perf. | performed, performance |
| K | Köchel, *Chronologisch-thematisches Verzeichnis sämtlicher Tonwerke Wolfgang Amade Mozarts*, 3d ed., rev. Einstein | PMA | *Proceedings of the Royal Musical Association* (London) |
| | | RassM | *Rassegna musicale* |
| | | RBM | *Revue belge de musicologie* |
| M | *Musica* (Kassel, 1947–   ) | RdM | *Revue de musicologie* |
| MA | *Musical Antiquary* | rev. | revised |

RHCM    *Revue d'histoire et de critique musicales* (with No. 10 of Vol. II, 1902, became SIM *Revue musicale*)

RIdM    *Revue internationale de musique*

RM    *Revue musicale* (Paris, 1920– )

RMI    *Rivista musicale italiana*

SB    Schering, *Geschichte der Musik in Beispielen*

SchwM    *Schweizerische Musikzeitung*

SIM    Société internationale de musique

SIMG    *Sammelbände der internationalen Musikgesellschaft*

STM    *Svensk Tidskrift för Musikforskning*

SzMw    *Studien zur Musikwissenschaft* (Beihefte der DTOe)

VfMw    *Vierteljahrsschrift für Musikwissenschaft*

ZfMw    *Zeitschrift für Musikwissenschaft*

ZIMG    *Zeitschrift der internationalen Musikgesellschaft*

*That day the sky was cloudless; the
wind blew softly where we sat. Above
us stretched in its hugeness the vault
and compass of the World; around us
crowded in green newness the myriad
tribes of Spring. Here chimed around
us every music that can soothe the ear;
was spread before us every color that
can delight the eye. Yet we were sad.
For it is so with all men: a little while
(some by the fireside talking of
homely matters with their friends,
others by wild ecstasies of mystic
thought swept far beyond the boundaries of carnal life) they may be easy
and forget their doom. But soon their
fancy strays; they grow dull and list-
less, for they are fallen to thinking that
all these things which so mightily
pleased them will in the space of a
nod be old things of yesterday.*

WANG HSI-CHI (A.D. 353)

*A SHORT HISTORY OF OPERA*

# INTRODUCTION

The custom of using music in connection with dramatic presentations is universal. It is found throughout the history of all cultures and among primitive and civilized peoples alike. This is perhaps because the desire to add music to drama is really part of the dramatic instinct itself. The motives may be either religious or secular: drama with music may have as its end either edification or entertainment. Of religious dramatic music we know today such forms as the cantata, the oratorio, and the Passion; the two last (aside from their subject matter) differ from opera essentially only in that they include some narrative portions and that they do not require scenery, costumes, or stage action. Even this difference is little more than a historical accident; it arises from the traditional antipathy between church and theatre which has existed especially since the period of the Renaissance. The dramatic impulse is retained in these types of sacred music but divested of those external trappings most closely associated with its secular manifestations. The opera itself is, with rare exceptions, a secular form. Its aim is like that of all the secular arts: the enrichment and embellishment of civilized life.

The first work now known as an "opera" was performed in 1597. The word itself, however, was not used in its present sense before 1634. It means literally a "work" (compare "opus") and is a shortened form of the Italian *opera in musica*, that is, a "work of music." Dozens of other designations have been used at different times and places, and new ones are still being invented. The earliest Italian operas were called *favola* ("fable"), *tragedia* ("tragedy"), or *dramma*, usually with a qualifying word: *favola in musica*, *favola pastorale*, *dramma per musica* ("drama by means of music"), or the like. The word "opera" came into general use first in England (from 1656); it was not common in France or Germany until the eighteenth century, and is still relatively infrequent in Italy.[1]

It is a remarkable fact that not only had both music and the theatre existed for hundreds of years before an opera was written, but also that both music and drama have since flourished during periods and in countries in which opera has shown no comparable vitality. In eighteenth-century Italy, on the other hand, the production of operas far exceeded, in both quantity and quality, that of other musical or dramatic forms. It seems necessary, therefore, to consider what special inherent features of opera may account for such anomalies.

The first is undoubtedly its luxuriousness. Opera is an expensive affair because it is so difficult to stage and perform. It involves the cooperation of a large number of experts, from the librettist and composer through the conductor, the singers, the orchestra, the stage designers, managers, technicians, and so on. All these people must be persuaded or compelled to work together harmoniously, and they must be paid. A large theatre, with all kinds of special equipment, has to be maintained. Since there have seldom been enough persons in any community who are both able and willing to pay the high admission prices necessary to make opera self-supporting, some form of patronage is necessary. The patron may be a wealthy noble maintaining an opera company for the amusement of himself and his friends; or it may be a private association of individuals who attempt with greater or less success to sell opera to the public by exploiting it both as an art work and as a prestige symbol; or again, the state may be the patron, supporting opera by means of subsidies from the public funds. In any case the result is the same : opera is conditioned poetically, musically, scenically, and to the last detail by the ideals and desires of those upon whom it depends, and this to a degree and in a manner not true of any other musical form. The opera is the visible and audible projection of the power, wealth, and taste of the society that supports it. For this reason, the study of its history is of value for the light it sheds on the history of culture in general.

Another inherent feature of opera is its artificiality, or stylization. Opera is always laden with certain conventions, which people agree to

---

[1] A list of designations used for operas in the seventeenth and eighteenth centuries is given in Haas, "Geschichtliche Opernbezeichnungen," in *Festschrift . . . Kretzschmar*, pp. 43–45. See also Dent, "The Nomenclature of Opera."

accept while at the same time acknowledging them to be unnatural or even ridiculous. Take for example the practice of singing instead of talking. Nothing could be more "unnatural," yet it is accepted as a matter of course, as the equally "unnatural" blank verse is accepted as the form of speech in Shakespeare's tragedies. Not only are there such timeless conventions in opera, but every age has a set of them peculiar to itself, which the second or third generation following begins to find old-fashioned and the next generation finds insupportable. And so all the music and poetry which were tied to these conventions suffer their fate and are forgotten. Nothing in music dates more quickly than an opera. Handel's oratorios are still widely performed, but, except for an occasional historical revival, do we ever hear a Handel opera? Shakespeare's plays are still produced at a profit, but what modern opera house has ventured to stage commercially Monteverdi's *Orfeo*, which was written during Shakespeare's lifetime? It is not that the music of these operas is inferior, but that it is bound up with a hundred details which interfere with our understanding it—operatic conventions which, passing out of knowledge, all too often carry the music with them to oblivion.

All of this points to the necessity for approaching the study of an opera, particularly one of a past period, with especial care. An opera score must be studied with imagination as well as attention. It will not do merely to read the music as if it were a symphony or a series of songs accompanied by an orchestra. One must at the same time imagine the work as it appears in performance, with the stage action, the costumes, and the scenery; and one must be aware of the operatic conventions by which the librettist and composer were governed, so as not to judge them according to the conventions of a different period, committing the absurdity (for example) of condemning an opera of Lully or Handel merely because it is not like the operas of Verdi or Wagner, or some other familiar composer.

The luxuriousness and stylization of opera have always provoked reactions. Just as every age has its own kind of opera, so every age has its own humbler counterparts of the form, designed to appeal to persons of less wealth or less cultivation. These stepchildren of opera have been known by many different names: *opera buffa, opéra comique*, ballad opera, "intermezzo," comic opera, vaudeville, operetta, musical comedy, and so on. Whatever the name, all have certain common features: they are less expensive than the opera, their social standing is lower, their tone is more familiar, and many of them caricature or parody the serious opera. They are the poor man's opera, even (as the title of one of the most famous of them has it) the *Beggar's Opera*. So far as artistic merit goes they may be equal or even superior to the more pretentious form and must certainly be considered along with it in any historical treatment.

What is an opera ? Briefly defined, it is a *drama in music* : a dramatic action, exhibited on a stage with scenery by actors in costume, the words conveyed entirely or for the most part by singing, and the whole sustained and amplified by orchestral music. The term "opera" is further restricted in ordinary usage to a form peculiar to Western civilization, having a definite historical beginning about the year 1600.

Is there any essential difference between a good opera libretto and a good play? Evidently so; if there were not, conceivably any of Shakespeare's tragedies could be set to music exactly as it stands—a feat which has probably never been attempted. The difference is one of emphasis. A play centers about characters and a plot; it may contain episodes which could be omitted without damaging its unity or continuity, but if this is the case, it is, strictly speaking, a defect in the structure. An opera libretto, on the other hand, may almost be said to center about the episodes; at least, it admits and even requires many portions which contribute little or nothing to characterization or to development of the action, such as dances, choruses, instrumental or vocal ensembles, and spectacular stage effects. Even the solo songs (arias) are often, from the dramatic point of view, mere lyrical interruptions of the plot; they correspond, in a way, to soliloquies in spoken drama. All these things, which (on a comparable scale at least) would be out of place in a spoken drama, are the very life blood of opera. Composers may accept them frankly as episodes or may try to make them contribute in a greater or less degree to the depiction of character or the development of the dramatic idea; but they are so much a part of opera that it is difficult to find an example which does not include them to some extent, even among the so-called realistic operas of the late nineteenth and twentieth centuries.

On the other hand, plot and characterization in an opera libretto are likely to be sketched in broad outline rather than in detail. The action is usually simpler than in a play, with fewer events and less complex interconnections among them. Subtle characterization, if it exists at all, is accomplished by means of music rather than dialogue. Most important of all, the entire dramatic tempo is slower, so as to allow time for the necessary episodic scenes and especially for the deployment and development of the musical ideas.

There is another kind of difference between a play and a libretto, one which has to do with the poetic idiom employed, the choice of words and images. It is a commonplace that not all poetry is suitable for music; it would require a composer of genius equal to Shakespeare's to add music to such lines as

> The cloud-capp'd towers, the gorgeous palaces,
> The solemn temples, the great globe itself,
> Yea, all which it inherit, shall dissolve
> And, like this insubstantial pageant faded,
> Leave not a rack behind.

But consider the following :

> When I am laid in earth, [may] my wrongs create
> No trouble in thy breast. Remember me, but ah !
>     Forget my fate.

Judged merely as poetry this passage, from Nahum Tate's *Dido and Aeneas*, could hardly merit high praise. Yet it is excellent poetry for music. It suggests in simple terms the image of a woman desolated by an emotion which the words by themselves cannot completely convey, an emotion so overpowering that only with the aid of music can it be given full expression. Moreover, the passage has a maximum of the appropriate dark vowel sounds and liquid consonants, with few sibilants. The important words (laid, earth, wrongs, trouble, remember, fate) are not only well adapted for singing but also are full of emotional suggestion. The very imperfections of the passage considered purely as poetry are its great merit, so strongly do they invite completion by means of music.

Making due allowance for the special requirements of the form, an opera libretto will usually reflect the prevailing ideas of its time with regard to drama. Similarly, opera music will be, in general, very much like other music of the same period. It must be remembered that in an opera, music is only one of several factors. It is necessarily always a kind of program music, in that it must (even if only to a slight degree) adapt itself to the dramatic and scenic requirements instead of developing in accordance with purely musical principles. As a rule it is somewhat simpler, more popular in style than contemporary larger forms of non-dramatic music, more tuneful, more obvious in its rhythms, less contra-puntal in texture—though there are some exceptions to this, notably the music dramas of Wagner. On the other hand, an opera score is apt to be more varied and original in instrumental color, partly because an opera is so long that more variety is needed, and partly in consequence of the composer's constant search after new dramatic effects by means of instrumentation. Thus the trombones had been used in opera two hundred years before they were admitted to symphonic combinations; the devices of string tremolo and pizzicato were first used in dramatic music; Wagner introduced a whole new group of instruments, the so-called Wagner tubas, in his *Ring*.

Neither the poetry nor the music of an opera is to be judged as if it existed by itself. The music is good not if it happens to make a successful concert piece but primarily if it is appropriate and adequate to the particular situation in the opera where it occurs, and if it contributes something which the other elements cannot supply. If it sounds well in concert form, so much the better, but this is not essential. Similarly, the poetry is good not because it reads well by itself but primarily if, while embodying a sound dramatic idea, it furnishes opportunity for effective musical and scenic treatment. Both poetry and music are to be under-stood only in combination with each other and with the other elements of the work. True, they may be considered separately, but only for purposes of analysis. In actuality they are united as the elements of hydrogen and oxygen are united in water. "It is . . . not simply the combination of elements that gives opera its peculiar fascination; it is the fusion produced by the mutual analogy of words and music—a union further enriched and clarified by the visual action." [2]

Throughout the history of opera, in all its many varieties, two funda-mental types may be distinguished : that in which the music is the main issue, and that in which there is more or less parity between the music

[2] Edward T. Cone, "Music : A View from Delft," MQ XLVII (1961) 447. Cf. R. Leibowitz: "La musique dramatique ne reproduit nullement l'action pour l'élever . . . sur un plan symbolique, mais le son qui pénètre l'action signifie que celle-ci se trouve absorbée par celui-là." "Alban Berg et l'essence de l'opéra," *L'Arche*, March, 1946 (no. 13 4e année) 164. On this whole subject, see also the introductory chapter of Kerman's *Opera as Drama*.

and the other factors. The former kind is sometimes called "singer's opera," a term to which some undeserved opprobrium is attached. Examples of this type are the operas of Rossini, Bellini, Verdi, and indeed of most Italian composers; Mozart's *Magic Flute* also is a singer's opera, in which a complicated, inconsistent, and fantastic libretto is redeemed by some of the most beautiful music ever written. On the other hand, such operas as those of Lully, Rameau, and Gluck, not to mention the music dramas of Wagner, depend for their effect on a balance of interest among many different factors of which music is only one, albeit the most important.

Theoretically it would seem that there should be a third kind of opera, one in which the music is definitely subordinated to the other features. As a matter of fact, the very earliest operas were of this kind; but it was found that their appeal was limited and that it was necessary to admit a fuller participation of music in order to establish the form on a sound basis. Consequently an opera is not only a drama but also a type of musical composition, and this holds even for those works which include spoken dialogue. The exact point at which such a work ceases to be an opera and becomes a play with musical interludes is sometimes difficult to determine; no rule can be given except to say that if the omission of the music makes it impossible to perform the work at all, or alters its fundamental character, then it must be regarded as an opera.

Throughout its career opera has been both praised and censured in the strongest terms. It was lauded by its creators as "the delight of princes," "the noblest spectacle ever devised by man." [3] On the contrary, Saint-Evremond, a French critic of the late seventeenth century, defined an opera as "a bizarre affair made up of poetry and music, in which the poet and the musician, each equally obstructed by the other, give themselves no end of trouble to produce a wretched work." [4] Opera has been criticized on moral as well as on aesthetic grounds; the respectable Mr. Haweis in 1872 regarded it "musically, philosophically, and ethically, as an almost unmixed evil." [5] Despite both enemies and friends, however, it has continued to flourish and indeed shows every sign of vitality at the present time; there is every reason to expect that opera, in one shape

[3] Marco da Gagliano, preface to *Dafne*. In Solerti, *Origini del melodramma*, p. 82.

[4] Saint-Evremond, *Œuvres* (ed. 1740) III, 249.

[5] Haweis, *Music and Morals*, p. 423.

or another, will be with us for a long time to come. Like all other forms of art, it contains many things today which cannot be understood without a knowledge of its history. It is hoped that this book will not only serve as an introduction to the opera of the past but may thereby contribute as well to understanding the opera of the present.

PART I


MUSIC AND DRAMA
TO THE END
OF THE
SIXTEENTH CENTURY

CHAPTER 2

# THE LYRIC THEATRE
# OF THE GREEKS

It is indispensable for a student of the history of opera to know something of the history, literature, and mythology of the ancient world, if only because so many opera subjects have been drawn from these sources. The myth of Orpheus and Eurydice has been used for over thirty operas, the story of Iphigenia (first dramatized by Euripides toward the end of the fifth century B.C.) for at least fifty, and the myth of Hercules for probably twice as many. Over half of the ninety-four operas of J. A. Hasse (1699–1783) are on classical themes. Berlioz's masterpiece, *Les Troyens*, is an outstanding nineteenth-century example. More recently there have been such works as Richard Strauss's *Elektra* (1909), Fauré's *Pénélope* (1913), Wellesz's *Alkestis* (1924), Milhaud's *Médée* (1939), Malipiero's *Ecuba* (1941), and Orff's *Antigonae* (1948), though on the whole the preference for classical subjects is now much less pronounced than in former times.

Greek drama, however, is of particular interest to us for the reason that it was the model on which the creators of modern opera at the end of the sixteenth century based their own works; it was the supposed music of Greek tragedy which they sought to revive in their "monodic style." Unfortunately, they did not know (nor do we) just how this music sounded. The only surviving specimen of Greek dramatic music is a very short mutilated fragment of unison melody from a chorus of Euripides' *Orestes* (408 B.C.),[1] and even this was not known to the early Florentine opera composers.

[1] A reproduction of the papyrus fragment (which itself is at least four centuries later than the time of Euripides) and transcription of the melody may be found in

That music did play an important part in Greek tragedy we may learn from Aristotle's definition in the *Poetics*, written about a century later than the works of Sophocles and Euripides, which still served as models :

Tragedy, then, is an imitation of some *action* that is *important, entire*, and of a proper *magnitude*—by language, embellished and rendered *pleasurable*, but by different *means* in different parts. . . .

By *pleasurable language*, I mean language that has the embellishments of rhythm, melody, and metre. And I, add, by *different means in different parts*, because in some parts metre alone is employed, in others, melody.[2]

The last sentence of this passage would seem to indicate that the tragedies were not sung in their entirety, as has sometimes been stated. It is believed, however, that some kind of musical declamation was employed for at least part of the dialogue, and the fact that the plays were given in large open-air theatres makes this probable on acoustical grounds, if for no other reason. Such declamation may have been a kind of sustained, semimusical speech, perhaps like the *Sprechstimme* of Schoenberg's *Pierrot Lunaire* or Berg's *Wozzeck*, but moving within a more limited range of pitch. It is also probable that regular melodic settings were used in certain places.

Whatever may have been the manner of performing the dialogue, there can be no doubt that the choruses were really sung, and not merely musically declaimed. When Greek drama developed out of the earlier Bacchus-worship ceremonies, it took over from them the choral songs (dithyrambs) and solemn figured choral dances which have such an important place in the tragedies. The role of the chorus in these works is largely that of the "articulate spectator," voicing the audience's response to the events portrayed in the action, remonstrating, warning, or sympathizing with the hero. Formally, the choruses are generally so placed as to divide the action into parts, corresponding to the division of a modern play into acts or scenes, resulting in an alternation of drama with the comparatively static or reflective choral portions. It is significant that this same formal arrangement is characteristic of opera in the seventeenth and eighteenth centuries, with its clear distinction between the dramatic action (recitative or spoken dialogue) and the lyrical or

Sachs, *Musik der Antike*, pp. 17–18; see also Mountford, "Greek Music in the Papyri and Inscriptions," in *New Chapters in the History of Greek Literature*, pp. 168–69; Reinach, *La Musique grècque*, pp. 175–76.

[2] Aristotle, *Poetics* (tr. Twining) 1449b20.

decorative scenes (arias, choruses, ballets) to which the action gives rise. The typical use of the chorus in Greek drama is best seen in the tragedies of Sophocles (495–406 B.C.) and Euripides (484–407 B.C.), the choruses of the latter's *Iphigenia in Tauris* being particularly beautiful examples. In Aeschylus (525–456 B.C.) the choruses are more numerous, and sometimes serve to narrate preceding events (*Agamemnon*) or take a direct part in the action (*Eumenides*).

All the actors in Greek tragedy were men, and the chorus was no exception. Although in later ages it numbered no more than twelve or fifteen singers, in Periclean times it was undoubtedly larger;[3] the chorus of Furies in Aeschylus' *Eumenides* numbered fifty, whose singing and dancing were said to have had such a terrifying effect that children in the audience were thrown into convulsions from fright. The leader of the chorus (*choregos, choryphaios*) was chosen from among the wealthiest and most prominent citizens of the community. The position was regarded as a distinction, but since the leader had to train and equip the chorus at his own expense he sometimes found himself ruined by the honor, which the satirists listed among the possible calamities of life, like lawsuits and taxes.

The choral songs were unison melodies (like all Greek music), one note to a syllable, with accompaniment of instruments of the kithara or aulos type. The kithara was an instrument like the lyre, the strings being plucked either with the fingers or with a plectrum. The aulos was a double-reed wind instrument, the tone of which probably resembled that of the oboe but with a more piercing character. These instruments may have played short introductions and interludes to the choral songs. The "accompaniments" consisted in either doubling the voices at the unison or embellishing the vocal melody, a practice known as "heterophony." Theorists prescribed certain modes or types of melody as appropriate for certain kinds of scene, the Dorian being generally favored for majestic verses and the Mixolydian for lamentations in dialogue between the chorus and a soloist. Such dialogues are quite frequent; there are also dialogues between the choregos and one of the actors, and occasionally (as in the *Alcestis* of Euripides) various members of the chorus have short solo parts. The choruses occasionally have a refrain, a passage recurring several times in "ritornello" fashion (Aeschylus, *Eumenides*).

No composers are mentioned, but poets are sometimes stated to have

[3] Cf. Hamilton, "The Greek Chorus," *Theatre Arts Monthly* XVII (1933) 459.

composed the music for their own plays. This does not mean so much as it would in the present day, for it is probable that the declamatory solo portions of the drama were for the most part improvised, only slight general indications of the rise and fall of the voice being given by the poet; the choruses may possibly have employed certain standard melodies (*nomoi*), though on occasion new melodies might be composed.

The Greek comedy assigned to music a much less important role than did the tragedy, although Aristophanes (*ca.* 448–385 B.C.) has choruses of Clouds, Wasps, Birds, and Frogs. In keeping with the general satirical spirit of the comedies, the chorus was dressed in fantastic costumes and indulged in imitation of animal and bird sounds. There was probably very little if any solo singing in the comedies.

By the second century B.C. the chorus had disappeared from Greek drama altogether. Aristotle in the fourth century already speaks of its decline and complains that the poets of that day introduce choral songs which "have no more connection with their subject, than with that of any other Tragedy : and hence, they are now become detached pieces, inserted at pleasure." [4] Solo singing still remained a feature of the Roman drama, as we learn from a passage in Lucian's dialogue "On the Dance," written about A.D. 165, describing an actor in tragedy

bawling out, bending forward and backward, sometimes actually singing his lines, and (what is surely the height of unseemliness) melodising his calamities. . . . To be sure, as long as he is an Andromache or a Hecuba, his singing can be tolerated; but when he enters as Hercules in person and warbles a ditty . . . a man in his right mind may properly term the thing a solecism. [5]

There are still many unanswered questions about the way in which Greek drama was performed, but we may be certain that, although it was not precisely like a modern opera, neither was it entirely in spoken dialogue like a modern play. The function of music was that of an embellishment, though a very important one. [6] It was this conception which Gluck expressed as his theory of the relation of music to drama, namely, that its purpose should be to "animate the figures without altering their contours."

[4] Aristotle, *Poetics*, 1456a25.
[5] Lucian (tr. Harmon) V, 240.
[6] Cf. Aristotle: "Music . . . of all the pleasurable accompaniments and embellishments of tragedy, the most delightful." (*Poetics*, 1450b15.)

# CHAPTER 3

# MEDIEVAL DRAMATIC MUSIC[1]

The history of the theatre during the Middle Ages is obscure. Ancient drama seems to have disappeared, although it is possible that traces of Roman comedy may have been retained in the popular farces and other pieces performed by strolling bands of players and (later) by the jongleurs. So far as our actual knowledge goes, however, the significant theatre of the Middle Ages is religious. It develops within the liturgy and emerges only partially from the church in the fifteenth century. In the West, two stages of this religious theatre are to be distinguished : the liturgical drama (from the eleventh to the thirteenth century and later) and the mysteries (chiefly from the fourteenth to the sixteenth century, with later survivals). We shall give first a brief summary of their course and then a somewhat more detailed description of the features of each.

The origin of the religious theatre appears to have been the practice of performing certain portions of the service dramatically, that is, the officiating priests actually representing the characters rather than merely narrating the events. This technique was first applied to the story of the Resurrection, and soon after to that of the Nativity. Around the original kernel there was a steady growth by accretion : in the Resurrection dramas the episode of the two Marys at the tomb of Christ (Matthew 28 : 1–7) was preceded by the scene of the buying of the ointment and followed by scenes representing the appearance of the risen Christ to the women and later to the apostles; the story was extended backward

---

[1]The two leading works in English on this period are Chambers, *The Medieval Stage*, and Young, *The Drama of the Medieval Church* (on liturgical dramas only). See also Mantzius, *A History of Theatrical Art* II.

to include the Crucifixion, the trial, and eventually all the events of Passion Week. Similarly in the Nativity dramas the scene of the shepherds worshiping at the manger was expanded by taking in the Annunciation, the flight into Egypt, the Massacre of the Innocents, and so on. Before this process of accretion was completed, the drama had been removed from its primitive position as part of the church service and reserved as a special feature of feast days, often coming as the climax of a procession and being performed on the church porch or steps, still however with priests and clerics as the actors, though the people might take part as a chorus. Next, the vernacular began to replace Latin; stage properties and costumes grew more elaborate; and with the constantly increasing size of the spectacle, the charge of the performances was finally given over to guilds of professional actors, and the arena of the action changed from the church to the market place. This transformation of the liturgical drama from an ecclesiastical to a municipal function was completed by about the middle of the fourteenth century and led into the mysteries, the typical late medieval form of sacred drama. But alongside the latter, the tradition of the older, simpler form survived; its traces are to be found in such works as the "school dramas" (plays on sacred subjects performed in schools and colleges), the oratorio, and certain aspects of opera in the seventeenth century, especially in Rome and northern Germany.

THE LITURGICAL DRAMA. Like Greek tragedy, the liturgical drama grew out of religious ceremonies. The origin of the principal group of these, the Resurrection dramas, is found in a trope (that is, a passage added to the regular liturgy) [2] of the tenth century which was prefixed to the Introit of the Mass for Easter Sunday:

> Int.   Quem quaeritis in Sepulcro, o cristicolae?
> Resp.  Jesum-Nazarenum crucifixum, o celicolae.

[2] It has been suggested that, since the tropes never formed a part of the liturgy, the name "liturgical drama" applied to plays developed from tropes is inappropriate; however, since this term is well established there seems little point in attempting to replace it by the more accurate designation "ecclesiastical drama" or "church drama." Cf. Reese, *Music in the Middle Ages*, pp. 185–86, 193–97; Smoldon, "The Music of the Medieval Church Drama." Modern editions of liturgical dramas with the music include: Coussemaker, *Drames liturgiques du moyen âge*; G. Vecchi, *Uffici drammatici padovani*; E. Krieg, *Das lateinische Osterspiel von Tours*; Kühl, "Die Bordesholmer Marienklage"; *Sacre rappresentazioni nel manoscritto 201 della Bibliothèque municipale di Orléans*, ed. Tintori and Monterosso; Smits van Waesberghe, "A Dutch Easter Play"; Smoldon, "The Easter Sepulchre Music-Drama"; Greenberg, *The Play of Daniel*.

As these phrases were sung, music was retained in the scenes which grew up around them. In the earliest liturgical dramas, everything was sung; the further these plays grew away from the church, the more speaking and the less music they included, thus approaching in form the later mysteries. The music of the liturgical dramas is of two kinds: (1) Nonmetrical plainsong of a simple though not purely syllabic type. For texts taken from the liturgy or the tropes the existing melodies were usually retained, either intact or in a "mosaic" made by selecting and combining fragments of the traditional chants. For the added portions other melodies were selected or composed. (2) Songs of a more or less distinctly metrical character, either hymn melodies or perhaps tunes of popular origin. These are less common, but they tend to occur more frequently in the later dramas. Their rhythm is not evident from the original notation but is apparent from the metrical form and presence of a rhyme scheme in the texts. The latter are usually strophic, with two to fifteen or more stanzas, and may be either in Latin or in the vernacular. It is possible that some of these songs were sung by the congregation.

There are songs for both soloists and chorus. In the earlier dramas they may have been accompanied by the organ; occasionally other instruments are mentioned and it is probable that instruments of many kinds were used much more extensively in performance than the manuscripts themselves indicate.[3] Most of the music is written as single-line melody, though there are occasional passages in two or more parts. The term "conductus," which sometimes occurs, refers not to a musical form but to the procession from one part of the stage to another, marking the division of the drama into scenes.

Over two hundred liturgical dramas have been preserved; twenty-two are published in Coussemaker's *Drames liturgiques du moyen âge*. The subjects of these cover a wide range: the Resurrection, the Nativity, miracles of saints, the prophets (for example, *Daniel*), a melodrama with a kidnaping (*Le Fils de Guédron*), and a comedy (*Le Juif volé*). Adolphe Didron has pointed out how the liturgical drama must have represented for the medieval church a visible embodiment of the sacred stories commemorated in the statues and stained glass windows of the cathedrals, as though the figures in these monuments "descended from their niches and panes . . . to play their drama in the nave and choir of the vast edifice." [4] There is about them certainly an air of profound and simple

---

[3] See Bowles, "The Role of Musical Instruments in Medieval Sacred Drama."
[4] Coussemaker, *Drames*, p. ix.

piety, a naïve blending of sacred and profane without the least sense of incongruity, which is one of the most engaging features of medieval art.

THE MYSTERIES. The mysteries (the word is probably derived from the Latin *ministerium*, "service") flourished during the fifteenth and sixteenth centuries. They differed considerably from the earlier liturgical dramas. Although the church still collaborated and the bishop's permission was necessary for a performance, the sponsor was the community as a whole and the actors were recruited from professional guilds, such as the Confrérie de la Passion in France and the Compagnia del Gonfalone in Italy. National differentiations are evident, and the vernacular is used consistently. The Italian works of this class were known as *sacre rappresentazioni*,[5] and are generally regarded as forerunners of the oratorio, though their influence is apparent in some seventeenth-century Italian operas as well. The subjects of the mysteries are sacred but of much greater scope than those of the liturgical dramas; thus there was the *Mystery of the Old Testament*, which ran for twenty-five days consecutively,[6] and the *Mystery of the Acts of the Apostles* performed at Bourges in 1536, which lasted forty days. The performance was usually on a large outdoor stage, using the principle of "simultaneous décor," that is, with all the scenes disposed in various places about the stage and each being used as required. Paradise was always placed at a higher level, and it was here that the singers and players were stationed, whence the hauntingly beautiful recurrent phrase in the stage directions, "Adoncques se doit resonner une melodye en Paradis" ("Now shall a melody be sounded in Paradise"). The middle level was for Earth, and there might be a still lower stage to represent Hell. The walls of Jerusalem, Herod's palace, Noah's Ark, the hill of Golgotha, the Garden of Eden, limbo, purgatory, and scores of other scenes were represented. All the miracles had to be shown visibly: descents and ascents of angels, Lucifer on a fire-breathing dragon, Aaron's rod blossoming, the souls of Herod and Judas carried off by devils, water changed to wine, eclipses, earthquakes, the Deluge, even tortures and beheadings took place on the

---

[5] For the other Italian names for these pieces, and a general account of them in Italy, see D'Ancona, *Origini del teatro italiano* I, 370 ff.; Becherini, "La musica nelle 'Sacre rappresentazioni' Fiorentine"; examples in V. de Bartholomaeis, ed., *Laude drammatiche e rappresentazioni sacre*; D'Ancona, *Sacre rappresentazioni*; Bonfantini, *Le sacre rappresentazioni italiane*.

[6] Modern edition by Rothschild, 6 vols.

stage.[7] The juxtaposition of sacred scenes and crude displays no longer gives the impression of naïve piety, as in the liturgical dramas, but rather of almost blasphemous incongruity; the large number of characters, the grotesque, disorderly crowding of episodes, all make of the mysteries a typically Gothic spectacle, reminiscent of the sprawling confusion of incidents and personages in the medieval epics and romances. There were also comic insertions, improvised antics or farces, often of an indecent nature. Finally the mysteries went so far as to permit mockery of the church and priests and the introduction of pagan deities on the stage. The awakened conscience of the church, together with the revival of classic ideals of the drama, eventually led to the condemnation of the mysteries on both moral and aesthetic grounds. By the end of the sixteenth century they were virtually extinct, though some remnants of the medieval love of profusion and grotesquerie survived in the operas and ballets of the seventeenth century.

Music in the mysteries was less extensive than in the liturgical dramas. In most cases its function was incidental, and since little of it has come down to us we learn of its existence only by references in the stage directions and from other indirect sources. Hymns and other parts of the liturgy were sung, as in the *Mystery of the Resurrection* (fifteenth century) where at the moment when Christ descends into Hell all the spirits sing "Veni creator spiritus." [8] Most of these selections were probably simple plainsong, but there were occasionally pieces in polyphonic style. In the *Mystery of the Passion* (Angiers, 1486), the voice of God is represented by three singers, soprano, tenor, and bass [9]—this doubtless being intended to symbolize the Trinity. Sometimes the angels in Paradise sing three-part motets, as in the *Mystery of the Incarnation* (Rouen, 1474). In addition to music of this kind the mysteries included popular airs, in the singing of which the audience joined. In Germany, where the Nativity plays were especially cultivated, one such song was the well-known "In dulci jubilo." [10]

[7] Dr. Charles Burney describes a scene of this character which he witnessed in the performance of a popular mystery play near Florence in 1770 (*The Present State of Music in France and Italy*, entry for Tuesday, September 4).

[8] Jubinal, *Mystères inédits du quinzième siècle* II, 339.

[9] "Et est à noter que la loquence de Dieu le père se doit pronuncer entendiblement et bien atraict en trois voix cest assavoir ung hault dessus, une hault contre et une basse contre bien accordées et en cest armonie se doit dire toute la clause qui s'ensuit . . ." (quoted in Cohen, *Histoire de la mise en scène*, p. 140).

[10] Moser, *Geschichte der deutschen Musik*, 5th ed., I, 320; Hoffmann von Fallersleben, *In dulci jubilo . . . ein Beitrag zur Geschichte der deutschen Poesie*.

There was also a considerable amount of instrumental music in the mysteries. Before the performance there would be a procession (*monstre*) through the town, with music by pipe and tabor. Entrances of important personages were announced by a *silete*, similar to the "flourish of trumpets" in Shakespeare. Instrumental music accompanied the procession of the actors to a different scene on the stage. Angels played concerts of harps—or rather pretended to play them while musicians concealed behind the scenes furnished the music. Instruments were also played for dancing: in the *Mystery of the Passion* Herod's daughter dances a *moresca* to the accompaniment of a tambourine; in Italy we learn of morescas, galliards, pavanes, and many other dances in these spectacles, which frequently concluded with a general dance. For the monstre of the *Mystery of the Acts of the Apostles* there was an orchestra of flutes, harps, lutes, rebecs, and viols. Trumpets, *bucinae*, bagpipes, cornemuses, drums, and organs are also mentioned; in the *Mystery of the Passion* the march of Jesus to the Temple is accompanied by "a soft thunder of one of the large organ pipes," and in the *Mystery of the Resurrection* the descent of the Holy Ghost is similarly signalized.[11]

There was at least one mystery in which music, instead of being merely incidental, was used throughout. This was the *Festa d'Elche*, a Spanish mystery performed in the sixteenth century, which had instrumental pieces, unaccompanied plainsong solos, and a number of three- and four-part choruses by the Spanish composers Ribera, Pérez, and Lluis Vich.[12] This instance of continuous music in the mysteries is probably not unique. Some of the Italian sacre rappresentazioni and similar pieces of the fifteenth century seem to have been sung throughout.[13]

The medieval liturgical dramas and mysteries, although they did not lead directly into the opera, are more than merely isolated precursors of the form. The Italian sacre rappresentazioni were the models from which the first pastoral dramas with music were derived. We shall have occasion later to see how the traditions and practices of such works manifest themselves in some of the operas of the seventeenth century. But their music was completely unsuited to modern dramatic expression.

[11] Cohen, *Histoire*, pp. 136, 159.

[12] Ambros, *Geschichte der Musik*, 3d ed., IV, 274; Pedrell,"*La Festa d'Elche*"; Trend, "The Mystery of Elche."

[13] Rolland, "L'Opéra avant l'opéra," in his *Musiciens d'autrefois*, p. 24; Becherini, "La musica nelle 'Sacre rappresentazioni' Fiorentine."

The immediate predecessors of the opera must be sought in the secular theatre of the late Middle Ages and the Renaissance.

SECULAR DRAMATIC MUSIC. Aside from the dramas of antiquity, the earliest known secular play with music is Adam de la Hâle's *Li Gieus de Robin et de Marion*, performed probably at the court of the king of Naples in 1283 or 1284.[14] Although this work is sometimes called "the first opéra comique," it actually has no historical connection with the latter form, and indeed differs in no way from other *pastourelles* of its period, except that Adam chose to omit the customary narrative portions and make it simply a little pastoral comedy, in which the spoken dialogue is interspersed with a score of short songs or refrains, a number of dances, and some instrumental music. It is probable that Adam himself wrote neither the words nor the music of the songs, but simply selected them from a current common repertoire.[15] Their charmingly naïve character is illustrated in Example 1.

*Li Gieus de Robin et de Marion* is an early example of the use of

### Li Gieus de Robin et de Marion

EXAMPLE 1                                                    ADAM DE LA HÂLE

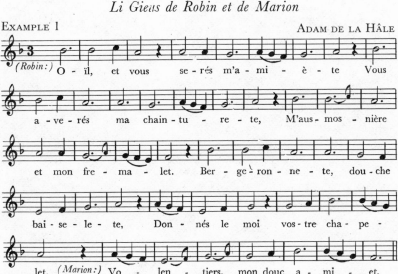

(Robin:) O - il, et vous se - rés m'a - mi - è - te Vous a - ve - rés ma chain - tu - re - te, M'aus - mos - nière et mon fre - ma - let. Ber - ge - ron - ne - te, dou - che bai - se - le - te, Don - nés le moi vos - tre cha - pe - let. (Marion:) Vo - len - tiers, mon douc a - mi - et.

[14] *Œuvres complètes du trouvère Adam de la Halle*, ed. Coussemaker (1872); other modern editions by E. Langlois (1896), G. Cohen (1935), and K. Varty (1960). See also H. Guy, *Essai sur la vie et les œuvres littéraires du trouvère Adan de la Hale* (1898).

[15] Chailley, "La Nature musicale du *Jeu de Robin et Marion*," in *Mélanges d'histoire du théâtre ... offerts à Gustave Cohen*, pp. 111-17.

chansons in a dramatic framework. Chansons, for the most part of popular nature and uncertain origin, were frequently inserted in moralities, farces, *sotties*, and like entertainments of the fifteenth and early sixteenth centuries in France.[16]

[16] H. M. Brown, *Music in the French Secular Theater, 1400–1550*; G. Cohen, *Recueil de farces françaises inédites du XVe siècle.*

# CHAPTER 4

# THE IMMEDIATE FORERUNNERS OF OPERA

With the coming of the Renaissance, interest in all forms of nonchurchly music increased. Throughout the fifteenth and sixteenth centuries music was a feature of courtly entertainments, banquets, tourneys, festivals, triumphal entrances, and similar brilliant occasions.[1] This music cannot properly be called "dramatic," since it did not serve to carry on the action of a drama; nevertheless, its connection with the history of opera is important, for these courtly displays of the Renaissance established the practice of bringing together many different artistic resources—singing, playing, dancing, scenery, costumes, stage effects—in a single spectacle calculated to appeal equally to the eye, the ear, and the imagination. Scenes of this kind, nondramatic displays with accompaniment of music, came into opera very early in the seventeenth century and have remained characteristic of opera ever since. In the sixteenth century the most important of the many types of entertainment in which music served were the ballet and the *intermedio*.

THE BALLET. The ancestor of the ballet was the *mascarade* (Italian *mascherata*, English masque). Originally a popular spectacle associated with carnival time, the Italian mascherata had developed into a favorite court amusement which was imitated by the French and English in the

[1] See Nolhac and Solerti, *Il viaggio in Italia di Enrico III, re di Francia* [1574], for some notable instances. Comparatively little of this music has been preserved (some examples are published in Ghisi, *Feste musicali della Firenze Medicea*). The most comprehensive general treatment of all this preoperatic music is in Ambros, *Geschichte der Musik*, 3d ed., IV (revised by H. Leichtentritt), 161–346.

sixteenth century. The French mascarades frequently formed part of the ceremonies of welcome to a distinguished personage, as on the occasion of a visit of Charles IX to Bar-le-Duc in 1564, when actors representing the four elements, the four planets, and various allegorical and mythological personages, including the god Jupiter, united in a fulsome ceremony of homage to the king. Mascarades of this sort later became the models for the French opera prologues. By the sixteenth century, as these mascarades show, aristocratic poetry had taken over the whole panoply of ancient pagan deities, demigods, nymphs, satyrs, and heroes, together with scores of figures from the pages of medieval epics and romances; all these were freely introduced on the stage, usually more lavishly than logically. In those mascarades where the purpose was the entertainment of an entire company rather than the complimenting of an illustrious guest, dancing was the chief attraction, and it was from mascarades of this sort that the characteristic French form of the ballet was derived. The English masque, somewhat similar to the mascarade, developed later in the sixteenth century, and its heyday was the time of James I and Charles I (1603–49). The French word *ballet* comes from the Italian *balletto*, the diminutive of *ballo* (dance): The most famous ballet of the period was *Circe, ou le Ballet comique de la reine*, performed at the Petit-Bourbon palace in Paris, October 15, 1581, on the occasion of the marriage of Mademoiselle de Vaudemont, the queen's sister, to the Duc de Joyeuse. A complete account of this incredibly lavish production (it cost nearly half a million dollars) was published with the score in the following year.[2] The principal author and director, Balthasar de Beaujoyeulx, explains in his introduction that the word "comique" refers to the fact that here for the first time an attempt was made to unify all the elements of the ballet by means of a coherent plot (*comédie*), a simple dramatic framework which gave occasion for the introduction of many different stage settings and dances. Slight as it was, this introduction of a dramatic action into the ballet might have led at once to the creation of French opera if only the musicians had undertaken to solve the problem of setting dramatic dialogue, thereby making continuous music possible. But neither their interest nor that of their audiences lay in this direction. The dramatic ballet survived for a few

[2] Yates, *The French Academies of the Sixteenth Century*, chap. xi; *idem*, "Poésie et musique pour les magnificences . . . 1581," in *Musique et poésie au XVIe siècle*, pp. 241–64.

decades in France, but by 1620 all pretense of a unified plot was abandoned, and the ballet reverted to a mere diversified spectacle for the amusement of the court. The music of the *Ballet comique de la reine* was by Lambert de Beaulieu and Jacques Salmon. It consists of six choruses, two dialogues with choral refrains, two solos, and two sets of instrumental dances. The choruses are strictly homophonic and rather dull, partly because their musical rhythm is slavishly bound to that of the words, with long and short notes for the "long" and "short" syllables according to the principles of *musique mesurée à l'antique*. The bass solos, as was customary in the period, simply follow the bass of the harmony. Some of the soprano airs are highly ornamented—a style of writing frequently found in solo madrigals and also used by Monteverdi for one aria in his *Orfeo*. The most interesting pieces are the dances, with their formal, stately, geometrical rhythms. One of them, "Le Son de la clochette," is still played today (Example 2).

*Ballet comique de la reine* (1582)

EXAMPLE 2

Both the ballet and the masque exercised a strong influence on the formation of the respective French and English national operas, as we shall see later.

THE INTERMEDIO. It will be observed that in such pieces as the mascarades and ballets the function of music is essentially that of adjunct to a visual spectacle. There is another class of sixteenth-century works in which the role of music was to offer diversion in connection with a

regular spoken play. As is well known, one of the features of the Renaissance was the revival of secular drama. The movement began in Italy
toward the end of the fifteenth century with performances of Latin
plays, in the original or in translation, under courtly auspices, at various
centers, of which Ferrara, Rome, Florence, Mantua, and Venice were
particularly prominent. Many new plays were written, in Latin or
Italian, imitated from classical models. Practically all these plays made
use of music to a greater or less extent, though in a subordinate, decorative fashion.[3] There were occasional solos or duets, choruses (these especially in tragedies based on Greek originals), madrigals, and instrumental
pieces. The general tendency was to separate the musical numbers from
the play itself by placing them in the prologue and at the ends of the
acts, so that each appeared as an "intermezzo" or "intermedio," that is,
something "intermediate" in the action of the play. Their subjects were,
as a rule, connected in some allegorical way with the subject of the
drama : "that which is enacted by the Gods in the fable of the Inter-
medii, is likewise enacted—as it were, under constraint of a higher
power—by the mortals in the comedy." [4] On especially festive occasions,
such as princely marriages, the intermedi might be very elaborate. Those
performed at Florence in 1539 at the marriage of Cosimo I and Eleonora
of Toledo, with music by Francesco Corteccia, included three solo songs
and four madrigals for four to eight voices with varied instrumental
accompaniment.[5] The intermedi by Corteccia and A. Striggio for
D'Ambra's *La cofanaria* (Florence, 1565) had solos, madrigals, and
other ensemble pieces, with accompaniments by large and varied
orchestral groups.[6] Striggio's intermedi for *L'amico fido* (Florence, 1569)
were presented with a pomp of staging and music that foreshadowed
many seventeenth-century operas.[7] Other composers of intermedi include Alfonso della Viola (Giraldi's *Orbecche,* Ferrara, 1541, and
several others), Antonio dal Cornetto (Giraldi's *Eglè*, Ferrara, 1545),

[3] See Rubsamen, *Literary Sources of Secular Music,* chap. vi; Einstein, *The
Italian Madrigal,* pp. 161, 234, 250, 283 f., 301, 550, *et passim.*
[4] Il Lasca, foreword to the intermedi *Psyche ed Amore,* reprinted in Sonneck,
"[The] Intermedi *Psyche and Amor,*" in his *Miscellaneous Studies,* pp. 269–86; also
MA III (1911), 40–53.
[5] See Schering, "Zur Geschichte des begleiteten Sologesangs"; *idem, Aufführungspraxis alter Musik,* p. 67. The instrumentation mentioned is found in a later edition
of the comedy: *Il commodo, commedia d'Antonio Landi con i suoi intermedi* [etc.]
(1566), p. 95.
[6] Sonneck, "[The] Intermedi *Psyche and Amor,*" pp. 276–86.
[7] See description by Balduccini in Ambros, *Geschichte* IV, 245–51.

and Claudio Merulo (Dolce's *Marianna*, Venice, 1565, *Troiana*, 1566, and others). Andrea Gabrieli's settings of four of the choruses in an Italian translation of Sophocles' *Oedipus Rex* (Vicenza, 1585) were long famous.[8] Perhaps the most elaborate intermedi of the sixteenth century were those for Bargagli's comedy *La pellegrina*, performed at Florence in May of 1589 as part of the festivities attending the wedding of the Grand Duke Ferdinand de' Medici and Christine of Lorraine.[9] The six intermedi were planned by Count Giovanni Bardi; some of the texts were by Ottavio Rinuccini, and the music was by several different composers, including Luca Marenzio, Emilio de' Cavalieri, and Cristofano Malvezzi. Forty-one of the most celebrated musicians of the time took part in the performance. There were five- and six-part madrigals, double and triple choruses, and a final madrigal calling for seven different vocal ensembles in a total of thirty parts, each part sung by two voices. These songs were accompanied by various groups of instruments, which also played a number of "sinfonie." The orchestra included organs, lutes, lyres, harps, viols, trombones, cornetts,[10] and other instruments, used in different combinations for each number. The style of orchestration is like that in Monteverdi's *Orfeo*.[11] Three of the six solos are in ordinary madrigal style with the lower voices played on instruments. The others exemplify the florid solo style of the sixteenth century, the voice ornamenting a melodic line which is given simultaneously in unornamented form in the accompaniment. Example 3, for soprano with accompaniment of a *chitarrone* (bass lute), is by Cavalieri.

With intermedi on such a scale as this, we can well imagine that the audience must have had little attention to give to the play itself, and this was no doubt often the case with such performances in Italy in the sixteenth century. "For the majority of the audience the dances and pageants formed the chief attraction. It is therefore no marvel if the

---

[8] See Schrade, *La Représentation d'Edipo Tiranno*.

[9] See Solerti, *Musica, ballo e drammatica alla corte Medicea*, pp. 12–22; *idem, Gli albori del melodramma* II, 15–42; *Atti dell' accademia del R. Istituto musicale di Firenze, Anno XXXIII* (1895), pp. 103 ff.; Einstein, *The Italian Madrigal*, p. 730. The two principal source documents differ in some details as to the composers.

[10] The cornett (It. *cornetto*, Ger. *Zinke*) is not to be confused with the modern cornet. See Karstädt, "Zur Geschichte des Zinken."

[11] Unlike most sixteenth-century intermedi, the music of these was printed (Venice, 1591). See D. P. Walker, "La Musique des intermèdes florentins de 1589," and Ghisi, "Un Aspect inédit des intermèdes de 1589," both in *Les Fêtes de la Renaissance* (Paris, 1956).

drama, considered as a branch of high poetic art, was suffocated by the growth of its mere accessories." [12]

It must not be imagined that the coming of opera at once put an end to the intermedi and similar spectacles. On the contrary, they remained popular at Italian courts well into the seventeenth century; the opera eventually took over many features of the earlier form, and eventually supplanted it. The intermedio is important as a forerunner of opera for two reasons : first, because it kept alive in the minds of Italian poets and musicians the idea of close collaboration between drama and music; and second, because in these works, as in the French dramatic ballet, the external form of the future opera is already outlined—a drama with interludes of music, dancing, splendid scenery, and spectacular stage effects. As soon as the drama itself could be set to music and sung instead of spoken, opera would be achieved.

It is evident that the theatre music of the sixteenth century, far from being a mere tentative and imperfect experiment, was a well-developed, essential feature of the entire Renaissance movement. The academies of Italy and France quite naturally interested themselves in music as one aspect of their interest in the revival of ancient art and letters. The texts of the ballets and intermedi imply a degree of familiarity with Greek mythology on the part of their audiences which is hardly conceivable at the present day; while mingled with this, as a heritage from the Middle Ages, is a pervasive, subtle use of allegory and personification. Yet these

*Intermedio VI*

EXAMPLE 3

CAVALIERI

Voice

Go - di— tur-ba—————mor - tal fe- - -

Chitarrone

---

[12] Symonds, *The Renaissance in Italy: Italian Literature* II, 143.

(Example 3 continued)

li - ce e lie - ta go - - - di di tan -

- - - to do - no E col can - to e col suo -

- - noi fa - ti - co - sì tuoi tra - va - gli ac - que - ta

ac - - - ta - - - que - ta.

works were not intended only for the erudite. They were a common part
of the luxurious, pleasure-loving court life of cultivated persons. Princes
and nobles, poets, painters, and musicians, amateur and professional
alike, all participated in their composition and performed in them side
by side. The music itself, as has been said, was not dramatic; all the
action and passion of the drama were in spoken dialogue, leaving for
music only the adornment of the spectacular, reflective, or lyrical scenes.
But in these, the important musical forms of the sixteenth century found
their place : instrumental dances, airs, madrigals, choruses, chansons,
canzonets—everything that music had to offer, with one tremendous
exception : the learned contrapuntal art of the Netherlanders. By the
last decade of the sixteenth century Europe was on the verge of opera.
It remained only to transform the relation between drama and music
from a mere association into an organic union. For this end, two things
were necessary : a kind of drama which should be suitable for continuous music, and a kind of music capable of dramatic expression. The
former was found in the pastorale, and the latter in the monodic recitative of the Florentine composers Peri and Caccini.

THE PASTORALE. Toward the middle of the sixteenth century the
pastorale began to displace all other types of dramatic poetry in Italy.
So complete did its dominance become that Angelo Ingegneri, the foremost writer on the theatre in the latter part of the century, remarked
that "if it were not for the pastorales, it might almost be said that the
theatre was extinct." [13] A dramatic pastorale is a poem, lyric in substance
but dramatic in form, intended for either reading or stage presentation,
with shepherds, shepherdesses, and sylvan deities for the chief characters,
and with a background of fields, forests, or other idyllic and pleasant
natural scenes. The dramatic action is restricted to mild love adventures
and a few incidents rising out of the circumstances of pastoral life and
usually ends happily. The attraction of the pastorale consisted, therefore,
not in the plot but in the scenes and moods, the sensuous charm of the
language, and the delicately voluptuous imagery, at which the Italian
Renaissance poets excelled. The sources of the pastoral ideal lay partly
in literary studies (Theocritus, Vergil), but it was redeemed from affecta-
tion by the sincere and profound Italian feeling for the beauties of
"nature humanized by industry."

[13] Ingegneri, *Della poesia rappresentativa*, p. 8.

The vision of a Golden Age idealized man's actual enjoyment of the country, and hallowed, as with inexplicable pathos, the details of ordinary rustic life. Weary with courts and worldly pleasures, in moments of revolt against the passions and ambitions that wasted their best energies, the poets of that century, who were nearly always also men of state and public office, sighed for the good old times, when honor was an unknown name, and truth was spoken, and love sincere, and steel lay hidden in the earth, and ships sailed not the sea, and old age led the way to death unterrified by coming doom. As time advanced, their ideal took form and substance. There rose into existence, for the rhymsters to wander in, and for the readers of romance to dream about, a region called Arcadia, where all that was imagined of the Golden Age was found in combination with refined society and manners proper to the civil state.[14]

The earliest pastoral play was Poliziano's *Orfeo*, performed sometime between 1472 and 1483 at Mantua, with music consisting of at least three solo songs and one chorus, interspersed with the spoken dialogue.[15] The pastoral poem was firmly established by Sannazaro's *Arcadia* (1504), but the real beginning of the pastoral drama is usually dated from the performance of Agostino Beccari's *Sacrificio d'Abramo* at Ferrara in 1554. The music of this work, by Alfonso della Viola, has been reprinted by Solerti.[16] In the third scene of Act III occurs a strophic monologue for bass, with a choral refrain. The solo part is a kind of psalmodic recitative on the bass notes of the harmonies, which were undoubtedly filled in (improvised?) by a lute or similar instrument (Example 4).

The finest examples of the pastorale, and indeed two of the most beautiful poems in all sixteenth-century Italian literature, are Torquato Tasso's *Aminta* (Ferrara, 1583) and Battista Guarini's *Pastor fido* (written at Ferrara between 1581 and 1590).[17] The pastorales lent themselves naturally to musical treatment not only because of their preponderantly lyric content, their brevity, and their use of choruses, songs,

---

[14] Symonds, *Renaissance* II, 196–97 (paraphrased in part from Tasso's *Aminta*, the closing chorus of Act I, which in turn is paraphrased from Ovid, *Metamorphoses* I, verses 89–112).

[15] Poliziano, *Le stanze, l'Orfeo e le rime*, pp. 369–507; see also Symonds, *Renaissance* I, 409–15, and Henderson, *Some Forerunners of the Italian Opera*, chaps. 4–9.

[16] See his "Precedenti del melodramma" and *Gli albori del melodramma* I, 12–13. Cf. also Schering, "Zur Geschichte des begleiteten Sologesangs."

[17] See Solerti, *Vita di Torquato Tasso*; and, on the significance of Ferrara and the ducal family of the Este in the history of Italian sixteenth-century music, the same author's *Ferrara e la corte Estense*. See also Neri, "Gli intermezzi del *Pastor fido*."

### Il Sacrificio d'Abramo

and dances, but also because of the very language, "flowery and sweet . . . so that one may even admit that it has melody in its every part, since there are shown deities, nymphs, and shepherds from that most remote age when music was natural and speech like poetry." [18] In *Aminta* the words are hovering on the edge of song at every moment; every phrase is filled with that unheard music which Tasso himself called "the sweetness and, so to speak, the soul of poetry." [19] Tasso, like all the Italian artists and poets of his time, was an amateur of music and particularly admired Gesualdo, who made settings of a number of his madrigals. He was a friend of Cavalieri, who composed the incidental music for a performance of *Aminta* at Florence in 1590.[20] Rinuccini, the librettist of the first operas, was a disciple of Tasso, and his poems *Dafne* and *Euridice*, as well as Striggio's *Orfeo* (composed by Monteverdi in 1607) and many of the other early operas, are simply pastorales on the model of Tasso's and Guarini's works.

Great tragedy and great comedy were denied to the Italians. But they produced a novel species in the pastoral drama, which testified to their artistic originality, and led by natural transitions to the opera. Poetry was on the point of expiring; but music was rising to take her place. And the imaginative medium prepared by the lyrical scenes of the Arcadian play, afforded just that generality and aloofness from actual conditions of life, which were needed by the new art in its first dramatic essays. . . . *Aminta*

[18] Doni, "Trattato della musica scenica," cap. 6 (quoted in Solerti, *Origini del melodramma*, p. 203).

[19] "La dolcezza, e quasi l'anima della poesia." *Dialoghi* III, 111.

[20] The music of two other pastorales by this composer—*Il satiro* and *La disperazione di Fileno* (Florence, 1590)—has not been preserved. According to Doni ("Trattato della musica scenica," cap. 9), the pastorales were not in recitative style.

and the *Pastor fido* . . . complete and close the Renaissance, bequeathing in a new species of art its form and pressure to succeeding generations.[21]

THE MADRIGAL COMEDY. In any study of sixteenth-century Italian music as a whole, attention is usually concentrated on two fields: the sacred polyphonic music stemming from the Netherlands tradition and brought to its culmination by Palestrina, and the polyphonic madrigal, represented at its height by Marenzio, Gesualdo, and Monteverdi. With the great body of sixteenth-century church music the history of opera has simply nothing to do. With the madrigal, however, the case is different. The experiments of the latter part of the century include a number of works [22] now known as madrigal comedies, which represent attempts to adapt the madrigal to dramatic requirements. The most famous of these was Orazio Vecchi's *Amfiparnaso*, published in 1597.[23] The *Amfiparnaso* was not staged, but only sung as a madrigal cycle. Vecchi's pupil, Adriano Banchieri, in the preface to his madrigal comedy *La saviezza giovanile* (1598), gives directions which indicate that in this work the singers and players were placed behind the scenes, while the actors on the stage mimed their parts. (It is not clear whether there was also spoken dialogue by the actors.) The *Amfiparnaso* and similar works show clearly in their plots, character types (Pantalone, Pedrolino, Isabella, and the like), and use of dialect their derivation from the *commedia dell' arte*. In the *Amfiparnaso* there are eleven dialogues and three monologues, the same kind of musical setting being used for all, namely five-part (one four-part) madrigal ensembles. In the monologues, all five voices sing; in the dialogues, the differentiation of persons is commonly suggested by contrasting the three highest with the three lowest voices (the *quinto* or middle part thus being in both groups), though at times all five are used even here. The music of the comic characters is mostly in simple note-against-note style, with a fine sense of the animation of comic dialogue. On the other hand, some of the five-voice pieces are beautiful examples of the serious Italian madrigal style.

The madrigal comedies were an early attempt to combine farce comedy with music, to exploit the lively, popular commedia dell' arte as

[21] Symonds, *Renaissance* II, 241, 245.

[22] Solerti in his "Primi saggi del melodramma giocoso" reprints a famous predecessor of these works: Striggio's *Cicalamento delle donne* (1567).

[23] See Dent, "Notes on the *Amfiparnaso*"; *idem*, "The *Amfiparnaso*"; Hol, "Horatio Vecchi et l'évolution créatrice"; Ronga, "Lettura storica dell' *Amfiparnaso*"; Camillucci, "*L'Amfiparnaso*."

against the languid, aristocratic pastorales. But they were suites of madrigals, not theatre music. So far as their contribution to opera is concerned, their chief usefulness may have been to prove that madrigals alone were not suitable for dramatic purposes. It has even been surmised that Vecchi intended the *Amfiparnaso* (the title has been freely translated "The Lower Slopes of Parnassus") as a satire on the early attempts at operatic music. In the hands of Banchieri and other later composers the madrigal comedies soon declined and eventually disappeared.

THE FLORENTINE "CAMERATA" AND THE MONODIC RECITATIVE. There can be no doubt that the first composers of dramatic recitative at Florence toward the end of the sixteenth century believed they were renewing a musical practice of the ancient Greeks, and that in so doing they were accomplishing something of revolutionary importance. Yet the mere singing of solos to instrumental accompaniment was nothing revolutionary. Even in the performance of polyphonic madrigals it was not uncommon for one part to be sung while the others were played, perhaps by the singer himself, in a simplified version on a lute. The prevalence of solo singing in sixteenth-century Italy has the character of a national reaction against the Netherlands polyphony which had been implanted there in the early part of the century. It is a manifestation of certain deep-rooted Italian traits which have remained constant throughout the musical history of that nation : hatred of complexity and obscurity, a profound feeling for melody as constituting the essence of music, and (this partly as a result of the whole mental attitude of the Renaissance) a preference for the individual artist as against the communal group represented by the church choir or the madrigal vocal ensemble.

Now it is a fact provable by many examples in the history of music that the establishment of a new practice, particularly if it be in conflict with an older practice, sooner or later inevitably calls forth a theory by which the new practice is sought to be justified. In the present case the development of the theory, as well as its practical applications, was the work of a group of scholars, poets, musicians, and amateurs in Florence. The group, commonly known as the "Florentine Camerata," [24] was a

[24] Martin, "La 'Camerata' du Comte Bardi"; Pirrotta, "Temperaments and Tendencies in the Florentine Camerata"; *idem*, "Tragédie et comédie dans la 'Camerata fiorentina'," in *Musique et poésie au XIVe siècle*, pp. 287–97; Palisca, "Girolamo Mei : Mentor to the Florentine Camerata"; *idem*, "Vincenzo Galilei and Some Links between 'Pseudo-Monody' and Monody."

species of academy or *ridotto*, of which many were established in Italy during the Renaissance. Its leading spirit in the beginning was Count Giovanni Bardi di Vernio (1534–1612), a distinguished patron of arts and letters, in whose house the members met. Among them was Vincenzo Galilei (1533–91), father of the famous astronomer and himself a singer and a composer of lute music and madrigals.[25] Galilei, having become interested in the study of ancient Greek music, applied for enlightenment on certain questions to a Roman scholar, Girolamo Mei (1519–94). In a series of letters [26] and conversations between 1572 and 1581 Mei communicated to Galilei his discoveries and conclusions about Greek music and musical theory. Galilei embodied these in a "Dialogue about Ancient and Modern Music" published under his own name at Florence in 1581 or 1582.[27] This work, containing among other matters an explicit "declaration of war against counterpoint," became the basis of all the later theory and practice of the Camerata.

After 1592, when Bardi was called to Rome, the patron of the group was another nobleman and amateur composer, Jacopo Corsi. His principal associates were the poet Ottavio Rinuccini (1562–1621) and the composers Emilio de' Cavalieri (*ca.* 1550–1602), Jacopo Peri (1561–1633), and Giulio Caccini (*ca.* 1546–1618). Rinuccini wrote the librettos of *Dafne* (composed by Peri before 1597 and by Marco da Gagliano in 1608), *Euridice* (composed by both Peri and Caccini in 1600), and *Arianna* (composed by Monteverdi in 1608). Cavalieri composed and produced at Rome in 1600 the *Rappresentazione di anima e di corpo* ("The Spectacle of the Soul and the Body"), a work commonly but erroneously known as the "first oratorio." Peri was a singer, organist, and director of the ducal chapel. Caccini was a famous virtuoso singer and teacher; two of his daughters were also well-known singers, and one of them, Francesca, was a composer as well.

In the writings of Galilei and other members of the Camerata the theory of the "new music" was fully developed.[28] And since the music is, to some extent, the result of the theory, it will be well to outline the latter before proceeding to a study of the music itself. Like most Renaissance

[25] See F. Fano, ed., *La camerata fiorentina: Vincenzo Galilei.*

[26] Published with introduction and annotations by Claude V. Palisca: *Girolamo Mei, Letters on Ancient and Modern Music* (Rome, 1960).

[27] *Dialogo della musica antica, et della moderna.* Facsimile reprint, Rome, 1934; excerpts in Strunk, *Source Readings*, pp. 302–22.

[28] For a list of these writings see Ambros, *Geschichte* IV, 292, note 1. The most important documents are reprinted in Solerti, *Origini del melodramma.*

philosophers, the Camerata appealed for authority to the ancient Greeks. But the actual Greek music was unknown to them; Galilei had published three examples in his *Dialogo* but had not been able to transcribe them. Consequently, it was necessary to deduce the character of the music from such writings of the ancients as were available. Long study and discussion of these writings led to the formulation of a basic principle, namely, that the secret of Greek music lay in the perfect union of words and melody, a union to be achieved by making the former dominate and control the latter. "Plato and other philosophers . . . declare that music is none other than words and rhythm, and sound last of all, and not the reverse." [29] From this principle three corollaries followed. First, *the text must be clearly understood* : therefore the performance must be by a solo voice with the simplest possible accompaniment, preferably a lute or similar instrument played by the singer himself. There must be no contrapuntal writing, for this distracts the mind and produces confusion owing to different words being heard at the same time with different rhythms in different parts, leading to distortion of pronunciation (in Caccini's phrase, "laceramento della poesia"), and in general appealing not to the intelligence at all but only to the sense of hearing. (This wholesale condemnation of counterpoint was due rather to the exigencies of the theory than to ignorance or lack of appreciation and need not be taken altogether seriously.) The second corollary was that *the words must be sung with correct and natural declamation*, as they would be spoken, avoiding on the one hand the regular dancelike metres of popular songs such as the villanelle, and on the other the textual repetitions and subservience to contrapuntal necessities found in madrigal and motet writing.

The idea came to me [says Caccini] to introduce a kind of music whereby people could as it were speak in tones (*in armonia favellare*), using therein . . . a certain noble negligence of melody (*sprezzatura di canto*), now and then running over some dissonant tones (*false*), but holding firmly to the chord in the bass.[30]

---

[29] Caccini, Foreword to *Le nuove musiche*. Solerti, *Origini del melodramma*, p. 56; entire foreword translated in Strunk, *Source Readings*, pp. 377–92.

[30] Caccini, *Le nuove musiche* (Solerti, *Origini del melodramma*, p. 57). Similarly in the dedicatory letter to his *Euridice* Caccini writes : "Nella quale maniere di canto, ho io usata una certa sprezzatura, che io ho stimato, che habbia del nobile, parendomi con essi di essermi appressato quel più alla natural favella." The entire letter is translated in Strunk, *Source Readings*, pp. 370–72.

Peri is even more explicit :

I believed that the ancient Greeks and Romans (who, according to the opinion of many, sang their tragedies throughout) used a kind of music more advanced than ordinary speech, but less than the melody of singing, thus taking a middle position between the two.[31]

The third and final corollary had to do with the relation between music and words. *The melody must not depict mere graphic details in the text but must interpret the feeling of the whole passage,* by imitating and intensifying the intonations and accents proper to the voice of a person who is speaking the words under the influence of the emotion which gives rise to them.[32] This pronouncement was, of course, directed against certain aspects of textual treatment in the sixteenth-century madrigals and motets.

It was in these aesthetic principles and their practical consequences, not in the mere employment of the solo voice, that the revolutionary character of the Florentine reform consisted. They formed the necessary foundation for true dramatic music and thus made possible the creation of opera. Tentative experiments in the new style were made by Galilei as early as 1582, when he composed a setting of Ugolino's monologue from Dante's *Inferno* (Canto XXIII, verses 4–75), which he sang to the accompaniment of four viols; neither this music nor his setting of part of the Lamentations of Jeremiah from about the same date has been preserved. It seems that the new ideas must have made their way very slowly at first, for no trace of them is to be found in the music of the famous intermedi of 1589, most of which was written by members of the Camerata. In 1595 a little pastorale by Cavalieri, *Il giuoco della cieca,* [33] was performed at Florence, a work which probably made use of the new style of singing. Early in 1597 [34] the first opera, *Dafne*—Rinuccini's text set to music by Peri, with some parts by Corsi—was played before a small audience in Corsi's palace and repeated annually with changes and additions for two or three years following. In view of the great historical interest of this score it is singularly unfortunate that

[31] Foreword to *Euridice*. Solerti, *Origini del melodramma*, pp. 45–46; translated entire in Strunk, *Source Readings*, pp. 373–76.
[32] Galilei, *Dialogo*, pp. 88–89; Strunk, *Source Readings*, pp. 315–19.
[33] Cf. Solerti, "Laura Guidiccioni."
[34] Probably not in 1594, as is sometimes stated. The exact date is uncertain. See Sonneck, "*Dafne*, the First Opera," SIMG XV (1913–14) 102–10 (also in Library of Congress, *Catalogue of Opera Librettos*, pp. 340–45.

none of the music has survived, with the exception of four tiny fragments.

The earliest extant examples of Florentine monody are undoubtedly some of the songs in Caccini's *Nuove musiche* [35] which, although not published until 1601, were composed at least ten years previously. The collection consists of "arias" and "madrigals" for solo voice with accompaniment of a lute or other stringed instrument. The music is in the *stile recitativo* ("reciting style") which, unlike the *stile rappresentativo* ("theatre style") of the operas,[36] permits a more symmetrical organization of phrases and a certain amount of textual repetition and vocal embellishment—in other words, a free *arioso* type of melody. The arias, which are strophic in form, have simpler and more regular rhythms than the madrigals.

One other early work must be mentioned before going on to a discussion of the first operas. Cavalieri's *Rappresentazione di anima e di corpo*,[37] performed before the Congregazione dell' Oratorio at Rome in 1600, is one of the first attempts to apply the principle of monody in a sacred composition. The text, with its moralizing purpose and allegorical figures (Soul, Body, Pleasure, Intellect, and the like), shows its connection with the sacred dramas and morality plays of the sixteenth century. The chorus is used more extensively than in the earliest operas, and several of the solo songs are not in monodic recitative but are distinctly tuneful and popular in character. Dances and instrumental interludes also occur. The prologue is spoken; the alternation of speaking and singing, as in the medieval mysteries, remained during the first half of the seventeenth century a characteristic feature of the sacred dramas which flourished at Rome and Florence.[38]

The "new music" immediately found imitators all over Italy and soon spread to other countries. The older contrapuntal art of the sixteenth century did not, of course, disappear; but the first half of the seventeenth century witnessed a gradual modification of the language

[35] *Le nuove musiche di Giulio Caccini detto Romano* (Florence, 1601–2). See also Francesco Mantica, *Prime fioriture del melodramma italiano* II.

[36] This distinction between "reciting" and "theatre" styles was first made explicit about 1635 by Doni in his "Trattato della musica scenica," cap. 11. (See his *Lyra Barberina* II, 28–30.)

[37] The text was written by Padre Agostino Manni, a disciple of San Filippo Neri; see Alaleona, "Su Emilo de' Cavalieri."

[38] For a theoretical justification of this practice see Doni, "Trattato," cap. 4–6, and the two "Lezioni" following cap. 49 of the same work.

of music owing to the interaction of the new monodic idea with the older contrapuntal principles, and the efforts of composers to find a means of reconciling the two. For a long time they existed side by side. Christoph Bernhard in his *Tractatus compositionis* (written about 1648) distinguished between the *stylus gravis* or *antiquus* (marked by slow notes, little use of dissonance, "music mistress of poetry") and *stylus luxurians* or *modernus* (some fast notes, unusual skips, more dissonance, more ornamentation, more tuneful melody); the latter in turn he subdivided into *communis* (poetry and music of equal importance) and *theatralis*, in which poetry was the "absolute mistress" of music.[39] The integration of monody with the traditional practices of music and the earliest adaptation of the resultant new style to opera were achieved during the first half of the seventeenth century.

[39] *Die Kompositionslehre Heinrich Schützens in der Fassung seines Schülers Christoph Bernhard,* ed. J. Müller-Blattau (1926).

PART 2


*THE
SEVENTEENTH
CENTURY*

# CHAPTER 5

# THE BEGINNINGS

The earliest opera of which the music has survived is *Euridice*. Two complete settings of Rinuccini's poem exist, one by Peri and one by Caccini. Peri's version, with some added numbers by Caccini, was performed on October 6, 1600, at the Pitti Palace in Florence as part of the festivities attending the wedding of Henri IV of France and Marie de' Medici; it was published four months later. Caccini's setting was published at about the same time, but not performed in its entirety until 1602.[1] The poem is a pastorale on the myth of Orpheus and Eurydice— a favorite subject for operas, owing not only to the fact that the mythical hero is himself a singer, but also to the combination of a simple action with a variety of emotional situations (love, death, suspense, rescue from danger) and possibilities for striking scenic effects. In the classic version of the myth, it will be remembered, the condition of the rescue of Eurydice from Hades is that Orpheus shall not look back or speak to his wife until they arrive at the upper world; but in his anxiety he looks back and Eurydice is returned to death irredeemably. Poets have invented all sorts of expedients to avoid this tragic outcome. Rinuccini's solution is simplicity itself : no condition at all is attached to the rescue, and Eurydice is happily restored to life. The divisions of Rinuccini's poem are as follows :

*Prologue.* "Tragedy," in a solo of seven strophes, announces the subject and makes flattering allusions to the noble auditors.

*Rejoicings.* Shepherds and nymphs celebrate the wedding day of Orpheus and Eurydice. Choruses; entrance of Eurydice; at her invitation

---

[1] See Solerti, *Musica, ballo e drammatica*; Ehrichs, *Caccini*; and *Commemorazione della riforma melodrammatica* (*Atti dell' accademia del R. Istituto musicale di Firenze, Anno XXXIII*, 1895); Strunk, *Source Readings*, pp. 363–76.

all join in a dance ("Al canto, al ballo"). Entrance of Orpheus (solo "Antri, ch'a miei lamenti") with his friends Arcetro and Tirsi.

*Death of Eurydice.* As usual in pastoral poetry, this is not enacted on the stage but narrated by a Messenger (represented in Peri's version of 1600 by a boy soprano).

*Lamentations.* A long scene, beginning with a solo by Orpheus and climaxing in a choral threnody with a recurring phrase ("Sospirate, aure celeste").

*Epiphany.* Arcetro as Messenger relates how Orpheus in his grief wished to kill himself; but the goddess Venus came down from heaven to console him and encourage him to demand Eurydice from Pluto in Hades.

*Descent into Hell* (change of scene). After a brief dialogue between Orpheus and Venus, there follows a solo by Orpheus ("Funeste piagge"). Then, supported by some of the deities of Hades, he argues and pleads with Pluto until the latter yields. The scene closes with a solemn antiphonal chorus of the infernal spirits.

*Resurrection* (return to the opening scene). A Messenger (Aminta) announces the happy return of Orpheus and Eurydice. Solo by Orpheus ("Gioite al canto mio"); closing choruses and dances.

The two versions of Peri and Caccini are similar. Peri is somewhat more forceful in tragic expression, whereas Caccini is more tuneful, excels in elegiac moods, and gives more occasion for virtuoso singing. Neither score has an overture, and there is almost no independent instrumental music. At the first performance of Peri's work, as we learn from his foreword, there were at least four accompanying instruments, placed behind the scenes: a *gravicembalo* (harpsichord), *chitarrone* (bass lute), *lira grande* (large lyre, a bowed chord-instrument with as many as twenty-four strings), and *liuto grosso* (literally "large lute," that is, probably a theorbo). Doubtless these continuo instruments alternated or were used in various combinations, making possible a considerable variety of tonal color. What notes did they play? The score gives only the bass, with a few figures,[2] below the melody of the solo part; the exact realization of the bass is a matter about which editors have differed, and it is essential to keep this in mind when dealing with modern editions of early operas. In the case of Peri and Caccini, the probability is that the harmonies were simple, with few nonharmonic tones or chromatics;

[2] On the figuring of the basses and their realization in the early monodists, see Arnold, *The Art of Accompaniment from a Through-Bass*, Part I, secs. 5–8. Cf. also Wellesz, "Die Aussetzung des Basso Continuo in der italienischen Oper"; Torchi, "L'accompagnamento degli istrumenti nei melodrammi italiani della prima metà del Seicento"; Goldschmidt, "Die Instrumentalbegleitung der italienischen Musikdramen."

certainly the basses do not suggest many contrapuntal possibilities in the texture of the inner parts. The bass has no importance as a line, as may be recognized not only by its stationary, harmonic character but also by the absence of any sustaining bass instrument in the orchestra.

The action in both *Euridice* operas is carried on by solo voices in the new Florentine theatre style (stile rappresentativo), consisting of a melodic line not so formal as an aria or even an arioso, yet on the other hand not at all like the recitative [3] of eighteenth- and nineteenth-century Italian opera, which is characterized by many repeated notes and an extremely rapid delivery. The operatic monody of Peri and Caccini is different from all these. Its basis is an absolutely faithful adherence to the natural rhythms, accents, and inflections of the text,[4] following it in these respects even to the extent of placing a full cadence regularly at the end of every verse. Occasionally a solo will be given musical form by using the same bass for two or more strophes, and long scenes are commonly unified by means of choral ritornellos. But the prevailing impression in the solo portions is one of almost rhapsodic freedom, as though the melodic line existed solely to add the ultimate fulfillment of song to a poetic language already itself more than half music. Rarely—too rarely —the song will rise to picturesque and pathetic expression, as at the end of the Messenger's narration of the death of Eurydice in Caccini's setting (Example 5) or the heartbroken exclamation of Orpheus in Peri's version (Example 6).

In contrast with the free-rhythmed portions are a few songs in regular metre, either solos or solos alternating with chorus. These songs are in the nature of lyrical interludes in the action; they are placed usually at the ends of scenes, where the effect of dropping into a metrical pattern is similar to the effect produced by a pair of rhymed verses at the end of a scene in Shakespeare, contrasting with the preceding blank verse. One such air is the well-known "Gioite al canto mio" of Peri's setting, sung by Orpheus in the closing scene.

The "chorus"—consisting of probably not more than ten or twelve persons—is on stage during nearly all of the action, and plays an important part both dramatically and musically. From time to time it engages in the dialogue, but its principal functions are to lend unity to a

[3] See Neumann, *Die Aesthetik des Rezitativs: Zur Theorie des Rezitativs im 17. und 18. Jahrhundert.*
[4] Cf. Paoli, "Difesa del primo melodramma."

EXAMPLE 5

*Euridice*

CACCINI

E vol - ti gl'oc-chi al cie - lo Sco-lo - ri-to il bel vi - so, e'

bei sem-bian - ti Re - stò tan-ta bel-lez-za im-mo - bil ge - lo.

EXAMPLE 6

*Euridice*

PERI

Las - sa, che di spa - ven-to e di pie - ta - de

Ge-la-mi il cor nel se - no Mi - se - ra - bil bel-ta - te

Co-m'in un pun-to ohi - mè ve - ni - sti me - no

EXAMPLE 7               *Euridice*               CACCINI

scene (as already mentioned) by means of short phrases in refrain and to provide sonorous and animated climaxes, with combined singing and dancing. Such a climax occurs, for example, with the choral ballet "Al canto, al ballo" after the first entrance of Eurydice (Example 7).

Another notable early opera is *Dafne* by Marco da Gagliano (*ca.* 1575–1642),[5] first performed at Mantua in 1608 and at Florence two

[5] Vogel, "Marco da Gagliano."

years later. The libretto of this work is adapted from Rinuccini's poem of 1594, which in turn had been taken in part from one of the intermedi of 1589. The action is divided into two parts: Apollo slays the Python with his arrows but is himself in turn wounded by the arrows of Love; he vainly pursues the nymph Daphne, who is changed into a laurel tree just as he is about to seize her. The latter episode does not take place on the stage, but is narrated by a messenger. The prologue is sung by Ovid, from whose *Metamorphoses* the story is taken. The music is essentially like that of the Florentine monodists, to whose doctrines Gagliano professes adherence, but is more animated in the melodic line and supported by more logical basses and richer harmonies. The free monody occasionally alternates with aria-like sections, and it is possible to see in certain places the outline of the future "recitative and aria" grouping. An "echo song" exemplifies a musical and poetic conceit which long remained popular in opera. Some of the arias have instrumental ritornellos, and there is an instrumental dance (ballo) at the end as in Peri's *Euridice*. There is no overture, but Gagliano in his preface states that a "sinfonia of the various instruments which accompany the choruses and play the ritornellos" should be played before the prologue—a direction which suggests that similar introductory pieces may have been performed before the earlier operas of Peri and Caccini. The chorus is very prominent in Gagliano's work, sometimes associated with the action and sometimes in purely contemplative passages. Solos, duets, and short instrumental interludes lend variety to the choral numbers. The whole score, in sum, shows abundant musical resources, drawing on the tradition of the old intermedi as well as the new monodic recitative. An air with choral refrain is illustrated in Example 8.

Gagliano wrote two other operas for Florence: *Il Medoro* (1619), the music of which is lost; and, in collaboration with Peri, *La Flora* (1628). Another Florentine opera, or rather opera-ballet, was *La liberazione di Ruggiero* by Francesca Caccini (1588–*ca.* 1640), performed in 1625.[6] With these exceptions, the city that saw the birth of opera played little part in its subsequent history until after the middle of the seventeenth century.[7]

[6] See Silbert, "Francesca Caccini." Other Florentine theatre music of the early seventeenth century may be found in *Smith College Archives* XIII (1957).

[7] For a list of musical spectacles in Florence see Solerti, *Musica, ballo e drammatica alla corte Medicea*, and Weaver, "Florentine Comic Operas of the Seventeenth Century," Appendix II.

The defects of Peri's and Caccini's operas, which came to be recognized as soon as the novelty of the stile rappresentativo had worn off, were the weakness of characterization, the limited range of emotions expressed, the lack of clear, consistent musical organization, and above all the monotony of the solo style. Especially for this last reason G. B.

EXAMPLE 8        *Dafne*        GAGLIANO

Doni, the foremost opera theorist of the early seventeenth century, not only advocated the plentiful use of arias and choruses to relieve the "tedium" of the recitative, but as late as 1635 argued that the ideal dramatic work was one in which music alternated with spoken dialogue.[8]

Opera in the beginning was the outgrowth of a limited musical theory applied to an artificial, stylized poetic form. There were no first-rate musicians among the founders but only noble amateurs, poets, and singers, all actuated by an enthusiastic misconception of antiquity. They have often been compared to Columbus, who set out to find the East

[8] "Trattato," cap. iv–vi.

Indies and accidentally discovered a new continent : so the Florentines, seeking to revive Greek drama, opened the way to modern opera. Like all pioneers, they were soon outdistanced; it was left to others to exploit and develop the new form. The first composer fully to realize its possibilities was Monteverdi.

# CHAPTER 6

# *MONTEVERDI'S* ORFEO

Claudio Monteverdi (1567–1643),[1] the greatest composer of the early seventeenth century, is perhaps better entitled than either Peri or Caccini to be called the founder of opera. At his hands the new form passed out of the experimental stage, acquiring a wealth of musical resource, a power and depth of expression, that make his music dramas still living works after more than three hundred years. Of his nineteen dramatic or semidramatic compositions only six, including three operas, have been preserved in their entirety. *Orfeo*, his first opera, was performed at Mantua in 1607. The poem, by Alessandro Striggio (*ca.* 1560–after 1628), is on the same subject as Rinuccini's *Euridice* but considerably expanded and with a different ending.

*Prologue.* Five strophes, sung by "Music" : a significant contrast to Rinuccini's prologue, sung by "Tragedy."

*Rejoicings* (Act I and first half of Act II). Broadly arched poetic and musical structures, combining solo arias, recitatives, duets, choruses, and orchestral ritornellos.

*Death of Eurydice* (this and the next section comprise the second half of Act II). Introductory recitatives, narration by the Messenger (Silvia).

*Lamentations.* Solo of Orpheus ("Tu se' morta"); orchestral interlude; finale, duets with choral refrain ("Ahi, caso acerbo").

*Epiphany* (this and the next section comprise Act III). "Hope" consoles and encourages Orpheus.

---

[1] The fundamental work on Monteverdi as an opera composer is A. Abert's *Claudio Monteverdi und das musikalische Drama*, which also includes analyses of most of the operas by other composers contemporary with Monteverdi. See also articles by Pannain in RassM, 1958–61, and Ronga in RMI, 1958. Important recent studies are those of Redlich, Schrade, and Sartori (see bibliography). References to Monteverdi's works will be to the complete edition by Malipiero, Vols. XI (*Orfeo*), XII (*Il ritorno d'Ulisse*), and XIII (*L'incoronazione di Poppea*).

*Descent into Hell*. Aria of Orpheus ("Possente spirto"); recitatives, orchestral interludes, closing chorus.

*Resurrection* (first half of Act IV). Orpheus and the infernal deities (recitatives).

*Second death of Eurydice* (second half of Act IV). Scena: recitatives by Orpheus, with short phrases by others. Solemn reflective closing chorus.

*Second Lamentation* (first part of Act V). Solo scena, Orpheus (with an "echo" song).

*Ascent into Heaven* (last part of Act V). Apollo takes Orpheus with him to dwell forever in heaven. Duet ("Saliam cantando"), short closing chorus and ballet (moresca).

In his original libretto Striggio had followed the ancient form of the myth according to which Orpheus met his death by being torn to pieces by a band of women in a Dionysiac frenzy. For obviously good dramatic reasons Monteverdi changed this ending; he also shortened Striggio's choruses at the close of the second and fourth acts, and probably made other changes as well. At any rate, the resulting "favola in musica" is a work of extraordinary and impressive symmetry. All the essential dramatic action takes place in Acts II–IV; Act I is a prelude, Act V an epilogue. The musical and dramatic center of the whole is Orpheus' aria "Possente spirto" in Act III where he opens his way into the underworld by the charm of music.

Equal care for the grand lines of symmetry is evident in each separate act and subdivision. The first part of Act I, for example, is shaped this way :

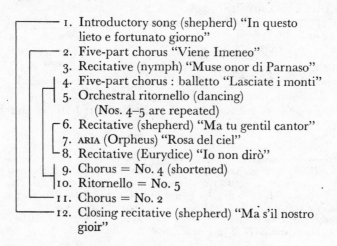

```
┌──── 1. Introductory song (shepherd) "In questo
│           lieto e fortunato giorno"
├──── 2. Five-part chorus "Viene Imeneo"
│     3. Recitative (nymph) "Muse onor di Parnaso"
│  ┌─ 4. Five-part chorus : balletto "Lasciate i monti"
│  │  5. Orchestral ritornello (dancing)
│  │        (Nos. 4–5 are repeated)
│  ┌─ 6. Recitative (shepherd) "Ma tu gentil cantor"
│  │  7. ARIA (Orpheus) "Rosa del ciel"
│  └─ 8. Recitative (Eurydice) "Io non dirò"
│     9. Chorus = No. 4 (shortened)
│    10. Ritornello = No. 5
├──── 11. Chorus = No. 2
└──── 12. Closing recitative (shepherd) "Ma s'il nostro
            gioir"
```

The music of *Orfeo* was greeted by contemporaries as a new example of the Florentine style, and indeed the general plan of the opera—a pastorale, with monodic declamation—justified this view. Nevertheless, the differences are fundamental. Monteverdi was a musician of genius, soundly trained in technique, concerned very much with musical and dramatic truth and very little with antiquarian theories. He combined the madrigal style of the late sixteenth century with the orchestral and scenic apparatus of the old intermedi and a new conception of the possibilities of monodic singing. *Orfeo* represents the first attempt to apply the full resources of the art of music to opera, unhampered by artificial limitations.

The imposing list of orchestral instruments at the front of the score gives an idea of the extent and importance of the instrumental music of *Orfeo*. The similarity of this orchestra to those of the earlier intermedi may be seen by a glance at the table on p. 54.[2] The great number and variety of "fundament" (chord-playing) instruments is characteristic of the sixteenth century. Of course, not all the instruments were used at once, and undoubtedly many of the players doubled, so that there were not so many performers as there were different instruments. All the players united for certain numbers (for example, the opening toccata, some of the sinfonie, accompaniments of some of the choruses), but at many places Monteverdi indicated in the score precisely what instruments were to be used, his choice obviously being dictated not only by the desire to secure variety of color but to help characterize the dramatic situation as well. A detailed study of the score in this respect is extremely interesting. For example, in Act III the voice of Charon, the ferryman of the Styx, is accompanied by the *regale*, or organ with reed pipes; Orpheus' aria "Possente spirto" has with each strophe a different set of instruments; Charon's slumber is depicted by the strings with organ of wood pipes, playing "very softly"; the same organ alone accompanies Orpheus' song as he crosses the Styx; and the final chorus of infernal spirits (two altos, tenor, two basses) is accompanied by a combination of reed and wood organs, five trombones, two bass gambas, and contrabass viol—this in accordance with the traditional usage in the sixteenth-century intermedi for such scenes.[3]

[2] The exact nature of all these instruments and of the various combinations is not yet definitely established. Cf. Goldschmidt, *Studien* I, 132–38; Westrup, "Monteverdi and the Orchestra"; Collaer, "L'orchestra di Claudio Monteverdi."

[3] See Weaver, "Sixteenth-Century Instrumentation."

# MONTEVERDI'S ORCHESTRA AND ITS PREDECESSORS

| | MONTEVERDI'S "Orfeo," 1607 | INTERMEDI of 1589 | "Ballet comique," 1581 | "Psyche ed Amore," 1565 |
|---|---|---|---|---|
| *Fundament instruments* | 2 clavicembalos<br>1 double harp (one more needed in performance?)<br>2 chitarrones (one more called for in score)<br>2 bass cithers (not listed, but called for in score)<br>3 bass gambas<br>2 organs with wood (flute) pipes<br>1 organ with reed pipes (*regale*) | 1 small cembalo<br>2 harps<br>6 lutes<br>2 chitarrones<br>2 guitars<br>1 psaltery<br>1 cither<br>1 mandola<br>1 viola bastarda<br>2 lyres<br>1 organ with wood pipes<br>1 *organo di pivette* (probably a *regale*) | lutes<br>lyres<br>harps<br>organ with wood pipes | 4 clavicembalos<br>4 lutes<br>1 lyre<br>1 bass lyre<br>1 small rebec |
| *Stringed instruments* | 2 small violins *alla francese*<br>10 viole da braccio (i.e., a string ensemble, possibly 4 violins, 4 violas, 2 violoncellos)<br>2 contrabass viols | 1 small violin (*sopranino di viola*)<br>1 *violino*<br>3 tenor viols<br>2 bass viols<br>1 contrabass viol (and perhaps additional viols) | *violons* (generic name for all bowed instruments) | 1 soprano viol<br>4 "bowed viols"<br>4 bass viols<br>1 contrabass viol |
| *Wind instruments* | 4 trombones (one more called for in score)<br>2 cornetts<br>1 *flautino alla Vigesima seconda* (i.e. a high recorder: one more(?) called for in score)<br>1 high trumpet (*clarino;* possibly referring to use of high range of ordinary trumpet)<br>3 soft trumpets (*trombe sordine*) | 4 trombones<br>2 cornetts<br>1 traverse flute<br>1 (or more) tenor oboes<br>bassoons | trombones<br>cornetts<br>flutes<br>oboes | 4 trombones<br>1 large cornett<br>2 soft-toned cornetts<br>2 recorders<br>4 traverse flutes<br>2 tenor flutes<br>1 tenor oboe<br>5 (!) serpents |
| *Percussion instruments* | None | None | None | 2 drums |

The overture to *Orfeo*—called "toccata" (compare English "tucket")
—is probably a dressed-up version of the customary opening fanfare; it
consists of a brilliant flourish on the chord of C major, played three times
by the full orchestra. In addition, the score contains ten short instrumental pieces called "ritornello" and five called "sinfonia"; most of
these pieces recur one or more times at different places. The distinction
between the two types is not always clear, nor are the designations consistent, in early opera.[4] In principle a ritornello is, as the name suggests,
a recurring interlude in connection with a song. Thus the prologue to
*Orfeo* opens with a ritornello (Example 9) which is repeated in shortened

## *Orfeo*, Ritornello from prologue

EXAMPLE 9                                                             MONTEVERDI

form after each stanza and in its original form at the end of the prologue.
Moreover, Monteverdi brings in the same ritornello at the end of Act II,

[4] See Abert, *Monteverdi*, pp. 254, 260, 304; Heuss, *Die Instrumental-Stücke des
Orfeo*, Appendix 3; Wellesz, "Cavalli."

the turning-point of the drama, and again at the end of Act IV, the close of the significant dramatic action—thus making it a species of leitmotif symbolizing the "power of music," the central idea of the opera as announced in the prologue :

> Io la musica son, ch'ai dolci accenti
> so far tranquillo ogni turbato core.

A *sinfonia*, on the other hand, is generally a more or less independent instrumental piece serving as introduction or postlude, or for depicting events on the stage. The sinfonie in *Orfeo* are serious, solidly chordal pieces, with occasional short points of imitation, full texture, and much crossing of parts. The ritornellos are more lightly scored, sequential in structure, and more contrapuntal in texture.

The aria "Possente spirto" in Act III is a remarkable example of the florid solo style of the period. It has six strophes, of which all but the fifth are melodic variations over an essentially identical bass. For each of the first four strophes Monteverdi wrote out a different set of vocal embellishments which he incorporated in the score on an additional staff; these embellishments are doubtless similar to those an accomplished singer of the time would have been expected to add to a plain melodic line. The practice of having solo instruments "concertize"—that is, collaborate and compete—with the voice, as Monteverdi does here, was one destined to become important in later seventeenth- and eighteenth-century opera arias. The employment of such elaborate vocal and instrumental effects at this place is not merely for purposes of display but is calculated to suggest the supreme effort of Orpheus to overcome the powers of Hades by all the strength of his divine art; at the same time, the wild, fantastic figures of the music seem to depict the supernatural character of the scene.

Quite different kinds of songs are found in the first part of Act II. The act begins with a little air by Orpheus in periodic phrasing and three-part form—a miniature *da capo* aria. This whole scene is a lyric interlude, containing no dramatic action; and appropriate to the joyous pastoral atmosphere are the duet of the shepherds ("In questo prato adorno"), with its ritornellos for two high recorders played behind the scenes, and Orpheus' strophic solo "Vi ricorda, o boschi ombrosi," with its effect of alternating 6/8 and 3/4 metres (Example 10).[5]

[5] This is Jeppesen's "type A" of Laude melodies (*Die Mehrstimmige italienische Laude*, p. xxxi) and is common also in *frottole* (Einstein, *The Italian Madrigal*, p. 80).

### *Orfeo*, Act II

EXAMPLE 10                                                        MONTEVERDI

Vi ri - cor - da o bos-chi om - bro - si Vi ri - cor - da o bos-chiom-
- bro - si de' miei lungh' as - pri tor - men - ti

Songs of this sort, which show the traits of popular style, establish the background for the abrupt contrast at the entrance of the messenger with the news of Eurydice's death. Nowhere is Monteverdi's superiority to the early Florentine composers more manifest than in the startling change of mood which he achieves at this place and in the dialogue immediately following, with the alternating E major and G minor harmonies at Orpheus' exclamations (Example 11). The harmonic contrast here was undoubtedly underlined by contrast of tone color in the accompanying instruments.

### *Orfeo*, Act II

EXAMPLE 11                                                       MONTEVERDI

Messenger:
A te ne ven-go Or - feo mes-sag-ge-ra in-fe - li - ce di

ca - so più in-fe - li - ce e più fu - ne - sto, la tua bel-la Eu - ri - di -

Orpheus:                    Messenger:                          Orpheus:
- ce, Ohi-mè che o - do? La tua di-let-ta spo-sa è mor-ta. Ohi-mè.

The ending of the messenger's account (Example 12) may be compared with the corresponding passage in Caccini's *Euridice* (Example 5),
as showing Monteverdi's grasp of the dramatic possibilities of the
monodic style.[6]

### *Orfeo*, Act II

EXAMPLE 12                                                    MONTEVERDI

The choruses of *Orfeo* are more numerous and important than those
in the early Florentine operas. Some are intended to accompany
dancing, such as the chorus "Lasciate i monti" in Act I; others are in
madrigal style, such as the ritornello chorus "Ahi, caso acerbo" at the
end of the second act. The choruses of spirits at the end of the third and
fourth acts exploit the somber color of the lower voices in a thick texture,
supported by the trombones.

[6] As a warning of the way in which editors can make practically two different
pieces out of the same given bass and melody, the reader is invited to compare
Leichtentritt's realization of Examples 11 and 12 (Ambros, *Geschichte der Musik*
[3d ed.] IV, 564, 567) with that of Malipiero (C.E. XI, 59, 61). An equally instructive comparison may be made between two versions of Orpheus' "Tu se' morta" by
Riemann (*Musikgeschichte* II, Part 2, 200 ff.) and Malipiero (C.E. XI, 62–64).

Perhaps the most remarkable feature of *Orfeo* is Monteverdi's sense of form, of a logically articulated, planned musical structure. This is apparent not only in the use of such devices as strophic songs and instrumental ritornellos and in the broad symmetrical structure of the large units, but even in the monodic portions, such as the entire recitative of the messenger in Act II from which Example 12 is quoted. Such places in Peri and Caccini were nearly formless vocal rhapsodies; here they are organized into musical units in which the freedom of declamation is admirably balanced by the careful plan of the passage as a whole.

Monteverdi's second opera, *Arianna* (Mantua, 1608) was on the same large scale as *Orfeo*, insofar as can be judged from the libretto. The only music that has been preserved is the famous "lament" of the heroine.[7] This song was probably the most celebrated monodic composition of the early seventeenth century and was declared by Gagliano to be a living modern example of the power of ancient (that is, Greek) music, since it "visibly moved the entire audience to tears." Monteverdi later arranged it as a five-part madrigal and used the music again for a sacred text.

In 1613 Monteverdi received an appointment as choirmaster of St. Mark's at Venice, in which city he remained for the rest of his life. Of his dozen or so operas after *Arianna* only the last two have been preserved; these will be considered later (see Ch. 8). One other work, the dramatic cantata *Il combattimento di Tancredi e Clorinda* (performed at Venice in 1624), may be briefly mentioned here because of its significance in the development of a new type of musical expression and because of its use of two new devices of instrumental technique. In the preface to his *Madrigali guerrieri ed amorosi* ("Madrigals of War and Love," the collection in which the *Combattimento* was first published in 1638) Monteverdi explains that music hitherto has not developed a technique for the expression of anger or excitement, and that he has supplied this need by the invention of the *stile concitato* ("agitated style"), based on the metre of the pyrrhic foot (two short syllables).[8] This is a typical Renaissance theory to justify the use of rapidly reiterated sixteenth notes on one tone—in modern parlance, a tremolo of the strings. Monteverdi claims credit for the discovery of this device, as well

[7] C.E. XI. See Epstein, "Dichtung und Musik in Monteverdi's *Lamento d'Arianna*."
[8] Kreidler, *Heinrich Schütz und der Stile concitato von Claudio Monteverdi.*

as for the pizzicato, which he likewise uses in this work to depict the clashing of weapons in combat. The orchestra of the *Combattimento* consists of only strings and continuo, an instance of the trend during the early seventeenth century toward reducing the number and variety of the older instrumental groups and centering interest on the strings.

# CHAPTER 7

# OTHER ITALIAN COURT OPERAS OF THE EARLY SEVENTEENTH CENTURY

Marco da Gagliano called opera "the delight of princes." For the first four decades of its existence it was exclusively that; indeed, up to the end of the eighteenth century some operas continued to be produced that were primarily for the delectation or glorification of rulers, nobles, or other wealthy patrons and only incidentally if at all for the entertainment of the public. The majority of such operas between 1610 and 1650 appeared at Rome. Most of them, like the earlier operas at Florence and Mantua, were created as special events for festal occasions, and hence were mounted with little regard for expense. The scores were usually printed and have come down to us, so that this period of opera is fairly well known to historians.[1] Moreover, the available financial resources permitted elaborate stage effects and a sufficiently large cast to allow for ballets and extensive musical ensembles. These ensembles—called "choruses," though they were in reality madrigal-like pieces for a comparatively small group of singers—are characteristic of the so-called Roman opera of the early seventeenth century.

The monodic style was introduced at Rome in 1600 with Cavalieri's *Rappresentazione di anima e di corpo* and soon found adherents, notably Agostino Agazzari, whose *Eumelio*, a pastorale with moralizing

[1] The fundamental book in this field is Goldschmidt's *Studien zur Geschichte der italienischen Oper im 17. Jahrhundert* I (1901), which contains numerous musical examples. Cf. Rolland's review in SIM *Revue musicale* II (1902) 20–29. Additional information may be found in Ademollo's *I teatri di Roma nel secolo decimosettimo*.

aim, was given in 1606. The first secular opera to be performed at Rome was *La morte d'Orfeo* ("The Death of Orpheus", 1619) by Stefano Landi (*ca.* 1581–*ca.* 1650),[2] which introduces large "scene-complexes," carefully organized with solos and choral ensembles, at the close of each act, and the largest one of all at the end of Act V. There had been scene-complexes of this sort, of course, in the Florentine *Euridice* operas and in Monteverdi's *Orfeo*, but there they were essentially connected with the drama; in Landi's *Morte d'Orfeo* and the later operas at Rome, on the other hand, the big finales do not as a rule grow organically out of the plot, but seem rather like intermedi, spectacular visual and vocal displays only loosely related to the action.

Still further departure from the Florentine ideal is evident in Domenico Mazzocchi's (1592–1665) *Catena d'Adone* ("The Chain of Adonis"), which was presented at Rome in 1626.[3] The libretto, based on an episode in Marino's epic *Adone*, tells the story of the rescue of Adonis by Venus from the wiles of the enchantress Falsirena. (According to the "allegory" printed at the end of the score, this is supposed to symbolize the rescue of Man by heavenly grace from the bonds of sensuality and error.) The various mythological personages on the stage are no longer the statuesque and serious figures of early Florentine opera but conduct themselves like characters in a bedroom farce; the complicated intrigue is bolstered by all kinds of magic tricks and particularly by the use of disguises—credulity in this respect knowing no bounds in opera from this early day to the present—sudden transformations of scene, conjurations, descents of gods, and by the familiar pastoral background. The typical later baroque opera plot, with its multitude of characters, fantastic scenes, and incongruous episodes, is already foreshadowed in this work. Musically, *La catena d'Adone* is important for its many vocal ensembles and also for its embryonic line of demarcation between monodic recitatives and songs of a more definite melodic profile and musical form. The term "aria" appears for the first time in the history of opera in this score, being applied however not only to solo songs but also to duets and larger ensembles. Some of the solo "arias" are hardly different from the monodic recitative; others, however, are organized into clear-cut sections with distinct melodic contours. An aria of Falsirena in the finale of Act I, over a bass in steady movement of

[2] Carfagno, "The Life and Dramatic Music of Stefano Landi."
[3] Cf. Finney, "*Comus.*"

## Aria from *La catena d'Adone*, Act I, sc. 3

EXAMPLE 13

D. MAZZOCCHI

EXAMPLE 14          *Sant' Alessio,* Act II, sc. 7

(Recitative) Angel:          S. LANDI

Bre-ve sa-rà l'in-du-gio: pren-di ri-sto-ro, e spe-me; E giun-to all' ho-re e-stre-me Non pa-ven-tar di Mor-te il var-co om-bro-so, Che à chi pe-ne sof-fri, Mor-te è ri-po-so

quarter-notes ("walking bass"), introduces coloratura passages for the expression of joy (Example 13).

The leading patrons of opera at Rome were the powerful family of the Barberini, princes of the church. Their palace had a theatre with a capacity of over three thousand, which was opened in 1632 [4] with one of the most important operas of the Roman school, Landi's *Sant' Alessio.* The poem was by Giulio Rospigliosi, friend of the Barberini family, distinguished man of letters, papal secretary, later cardinal, and finally Pope under the name of Clement IX from 1667 to 1669.[5] *Sant' Alessio* was the first opera to be written about the inner life of a human character: it is based on the legend of the fifth-century Saint Alexis; but the persons and scenes, both serious and comic, are obviously drawn from

[4] Rolland, "La Première Représentation du *Sant Alessio* . . . à Rome." See also Pastor, *History of the Popes* XXIX, 408–544. There is some evidence for a previous performance of *Sant' Alessio* at Rome in 1631.

[5] Biographical sketch in Ademollo, *Teatri di Roma,* chap. VIII; Salza, "Drammi inediti di Giulio Rospigliosi"; Pastor, *History of the Popes* XXXI, 314–37.

EXAMPLE 15     *Sant' Alessio*                    S. LANDI

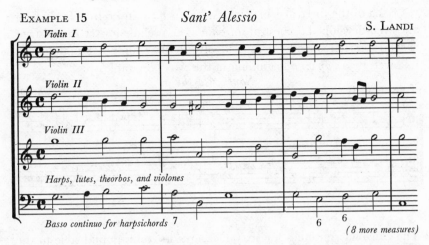

Violin I

Violin II

Violin III

Harps, lutes, theorbos, and violones

*Basso continuo for harpsichords* 7                    6   6
                                                           *(8 more measures)*

the contemporary life of seventeenth-century Rome. The recitative begins to show its characteristic later features with many repeated notes and frequent cadences (Example 14); but on the whole it is rather solemn and oratorio-like, rather than warm and passionate as in *La catena d'Adone*. There are few distinct solo arias, but many ensemble and choral scenes, among which the finale of the last act is particularly impressive.

The extremely high range of Alessio's part is typical of many roles in early seventeenth-century opera for male sopranos. Such singers (*castrati*) had first appeared on the operatic stage in Monteverdi's *Orfeo*, and despite efforts to abolish the custom it became increasingly prevalent, especially in Italy, throughout the seventeenth century.[6]

In the orchestra of *Sant' Alessio* the old-fashioned viols are replaced throughout by violins (in three parts) and violoncellos. Harps, lutes, and theorbos go for the most part with the strings, but the harpsichords have a separate staff in many of the instrumental numbers. It will be noted that the outlines of the modern orchestra are here distinct; only the number and variety of fundament instruments remind us of the earlier practice, and these will remain in the orchestra, though in decreasing numbers, until the time of Haydn and Mozart. The wind and percussion instruments will become from now on ever less conpicuous, being used in opera only for special effects or in full subordination to the string group.

[6] Maugars, "Response faite à un curieux."

Each of the three acts of *Sant' Alessio* is introduced by a fairly long and well-developed orchestral *sinfonia*. The prelude to Act I consists of a solid chordal introduction, evidently in slow tempo (Example 15), followed by a *canzona* beginning in this way (Example 16):

EXAMPLE 16        *Sant' Alessio*        S. LANDI

The canzona continues for sixty measures in contrapuntal style to the end, with the exception of one more homophonic section consisting of alternating *forte* and *piano* phrases and one interlude in the rhythm of a saraband, in strict note-against-note writing. The piece is then brought to a close with a stretto-like passage in eighth notes and a final broad cadence in G major.[7] The formal resemblance of this canzona overture to the later *sonata da chiesa* is obvious; and it has further historical importance as being the model for the type of "French overture" perfected about thirty years later by Lully. The prelude to the second act of *Sant' Alessio* is likewise a canzona in three movements but without a slow introduction, thus giving it a superficial resemblance to the later "Italian overture" pattern (fast-slow-fast).

Conditions at Rome on the whole did not favor the growth of serious opera on secular themes. The influence of the church tended rather to the cultivation of the oratorio or similar quasi-dramatic forms, or at most permitted operas of a pious allegorical or moralizing nature, such as *Sant' Alessio* or *La vita humana* (1656) by Marco Marazzoli (*ca.* 1602–62), one of the last operas to be produced at the Barberini theatre. Secular productions were represented chiefly by the harmless, diverting genre of the pastorale. *Erminia sul Giordano* ("Erminia at the Jordan") by Michelangelo Rossi (fl. 1620–60) was performed in 1633. The libretto,

---

[7] The overture to Francesca Caccini's ballet *La liberazione di Ruggiero* (1624) begins with a theme in canzona rhythm but does not have the fugal entrances. An overture similar to that of *Sant' Alessio* is Michelangelo Rossi's "sinfonia" to *Erminia sul Giordano* (1633). See DeLage, "The Overture in Seventeenth-Century Italian Opera."

by Rospigliosi, is based on the sixth and seventh cantos of Tasso's *Gerusalemme liberata* with episodes from other parts of the poem. *Erminia* consists of an imperfectly connected series of scenes featuring elaborate stage settings and machines. The music, including a hunting chorus with echo effects and a chorus of soldiers on a trumpet-like motif to the words "All' armi," shows on the whole no significant advances in style.

*La Galatea* (1639), with words and music by the castrato Loreto Vittori [8] (1604–70), is almost the last Italian pastorale of this period. Musically it is a superior work, and Romain Rolland calls it "the finest lyric drama of the first half of the seventeenth century." [9] The arias show progress in the direction of formal organization based on a clear system of tonal relationships; the recitatives include occasional expressive dissonances but on the whole tend toward the *secco* style. Some of the finest music of this opera is found in its ensembles (Example 17).

The last important Roman composer of serious opera in this period was Luigi Rossi (*ca.* 1598–1653), a singer who also composed oratorios and over 400 cantatas and songs. [10] Only two operas by Rossi are known: *Il palazzo incantato* ("The Enchanted Palace," Rome, 1642) [11] and *Orfeo*, given in Italian at Paris in 1647. This Paris performance was the consequence of political changes at Rome resulting in the election of Pope Innocent X in 1644, which forced the Barberini family to emigrate. At the invitation of Cardinal Mazarin many of their musicians, including Rossi, came with them to Paris to give the French public a taste of Italian opera. [12] The poem of *Orfeo*, though based faithfully on the ancient myth, introduces many more or less irrelevant episodes, resulting in a hodgepodge of serious and comic scenes intermingled with ballets and spectacular stage effects. The only way a composer can deal with such a libretto is to ignore the drama (or lack of it) and concentrate on the musical opportunities offered by each scene. The score of *Orfeo* is as variegated as its poem, and is especially remarkable as being the first

[8] Rau, *Loreto Vittori.*

[9] Rolland, "L'Opéra au XVIIe siècle en Italie," in Lavignac, *Encyclopédie,* Part I, Vol. II, p. 711.

[10] See Ghislanzoni, *Luigi Rossi* (1954), which contains analyses of Rossi's two operas with many short musical examples.

[11] In some sources this work is entitled *Il palazzo d'Atlante.* See Prunières, "Les Représentations du *Palazzo d'Atlante* à Rome."

[12] Rolland, "Le Premier Opéra joué a Paris: 'L'Orfeo' de Luigi Rossi," in his *Musiciens d'autrefois,* pp. 55–105; Pastor, *History of the Popes* XXX, 48–72.

EXAMPLE 17

*La Galatea*, Act III, sc. 3

VITTORI

*(Example 17 continued)*

EXAMPLE 18

L. ROSSI

Uc - ci - de - te - mi, uc - ci - de - te - mi, ò pe - ne

e men - tre vò con di - spe - ra - ti passi per quest'hor - ri - di sas - si

cer - can - do ah com' io pe - ra à voi

più ch'ad un an - gue e ad u - na fe - ra co - sì spie

to - sa glor - ia sì con - vie - ne uc - ci - de -

*(Example 18 continued)*

-te - mi   uc - ci - de - te - mi      ò   pe -      ne.

uc - ci - de - te - mi   voi      perch' al - la      mor - te es - sen-do no - to

ch'Eu - ri - di - ce   so - la      e - ra   la   vi - ta      mi - a      che più

vivo hora io   sia   non   gli sov - vie -   ne      Uc - ci - de -

- te - mi   uc - ci - de - te - mi      ò      pe -   ne.

opera in which the arias outnumber the recitatives. There are strophic arias over an *ostinato* bass, two-part arias, *buffo* (comic) arias, and da capo arias as well as many ensembles of different kinds. The music is distinguished by that grace and perfection of style, that refinement of sensuous effect, for which its composer, along with Carissimi and Cesti, was so greatly admired in the seventeenth century. Eurydice's aria "Mio ben" in Act II is an excellent example of a "lament," with long-breathed, mournful coloraturas streaming above a repeated descending bass figure. Another "lament" in Act III is built, like the celebrated one from Monteverdi's *Arianna*, in an expressive monodic recitative with a refrain—slightly varied at each recurrence—on the words "Uccidetemi, ò pene" ("Kill me, O sorrows" : Example 18).

With all its beauty of detail, however, Rossi's *Orfeo* as a whole is no more a dramatic entity than Berlioz's *Damnation de Faust*; it is a succession of lyrical and scenic moments in which the beauty of music and *décor* successfully conceals the lack of any serious dramatic purpose. As such, it illustrates the extent to which opera in the course of forty years had moved away from the early Florentine ideal in the direction of the formal exterior of the later baroque.

THE FIRST COMIC OPERAS. There were no comic scenes in the earliest operas. Italian popular comedy at this period was represented by the commedia dell' arte, which found its musical counterpart in the madrigal comedies of Vecchi and Banchieri. There are some comic episodes of the sort common to Italian pastorales in Landi's *Morte d'Orfeo* and Giacinto Cornacchioli's *Diana schernita* ("Diana Ridiculed," 1629), and more realistic comic characters are found in *Sant' Alessio*. But the creation of comic opera as a separate form, the foundation of the long Italian opera buffa tradition which was to culminate in Mozart and Rossini, was the work of a future Pope, Giulio Rospigliosi. Rospigliosi's opera poems include *Sant' Alessio, Il palazzo incantato, Erminia sul Giordano*, and several others, in addition to the two comedies *Chi soffre, speri* ("Who Suffers May Hope") and *Dal male il bene* ("Good from Evil"). *Chi soffre, speri*, with music by Virgilio Mazzocchi (1597–1646) and Marco Marazzoli, was performed at the Barberini palace in 1637 and, in a second version (the only one of which the music is now known), in 1639.[13] It has a romantic plot, with comic scenes featuring character types of the commedia dell' arte and figures from the common walks of

[13] See Reiner, "Collaboration in *Chi soffre speri*."

Italian life, in the manner established by Michelangelo Buonarroti with his comedies *La Tancia* (1612) and *La Fiera* (1618), and already used by Rospigliosi in his own opera *Sant' Alessio*. The dialogue of *Chi soffre, speri* is conveyed in a kind of recitative which differs essentially from the quasi-melodic monody of the Florentines; it is, in short, the style which later came to be called *recitativo secco* : a quick-moving, narrow-ranged, sharply accented, irregularly punctuated, semimusical speech, with many repeated notes sustained only by occasional chords—a style for which the Italian language alone is perfectly adapted and which has

EXAMPLE 19        *Chi soffre, speri,* Act I, sc. 1

Segue ogn' un sua va-ghez-za pur ch'io lie to mi vi-va in que-sta ombro-sa ri-va ov' il mio ge-ni-tor vi-ci-no a mor-te à me pro-mi-se (ah ve-ri sian gl'au-spi-ci) di suc--ces-si fe-li-ci in-a-spet-ta-ta sor-te.

always been a familiar feature of Italian opera. Although tendencies toward this type of recitative were manifest in earlier Roman works, the necessity of finding a musical setting for realistic comic dialogue led to its fuller development here (Example 19).

Apart from the recitative and one lively ensemble scene (in an intermezzo which depicts the bustle of a fair), the music of *Chi soffre, speri* offers few points of special interest. In quality of both libretto and songs it is surpassed by *Dal male il bene*, with music by Marco Marazzoli (Act II) and Antonio Maria Abbatini (Acts I and III),[14] performed in 1653 after the return of the Barberini to Rome, to which event the title alludes. Rospigliosi, who had served as papal legate in Madrid from 1646 to 1653, showed in the construction of this work some influence of the Spanish playwright Calderón de la Barca, especially the latter's *La dama duende* (1629). *Dal male il bene* is a romantic comedy in which, after complications and mis-understandings, two pairs of lovers are happily united. The servant characters are evidently drawn from life, except for one of them, the comic servant Tabacco, who is obviously taken over from the commedia dell' arte masks. This character type, incidentally, appears again and again in operas of the seventeenth and eighteenth centuries; Leporello in *Don Giovanni* is probably the most familiar example. The music of *Dal male il bene* is notable for the skill of the recitatives and for another feature which later became characteristic of the opera buffa, namely the solo ensembles, especially the trio at the end of Act I and the sextet which forms the finale of the opera. Tabacco's aria "In che dà?" from Act I shows a well-developed tonal and formal scheme, together with a good sense of comic style (Example 20).

Another excellent comic opera is Andrea Moniglia's *La Tancia, overo il podestà di Colognole* ("Tancia, or the Mayor of Colognole"), with music by Jacopo Melani (1623–76), performed in 1657 at Florence.[15] Among the ensembles of this work is a parody of the famous incantation scene from Cavalli's *Giasone*, which had been first performed at Venice eight years before. *La Tancia* contains many more arias in proportion to the recitative than did the earlier comic works, and it is possible to observe some of the standardized forms into which the

[14] On Abbatini (1597–1680) see biography by Coradini.
[15] See Weaver, "Florentine Comic Operas of the Seventeenth Century"; Ademollo, *I primi fasti del teatro della Pergola.*

*Dal male il bene*, Act I, sc. 7

EXAMPLE 20

A. M. ABBATINI

*(Ritornello: strings and continuo)*

Aria

In che dà, in che dà il cer-car con tan-to af-fa-no tut-to l'an-no di sa-per quel ch'al-tri fa? In che dà, in che dà? in che dà? Mi par pro - pio fre - ne - si-a lam-bi - car sem pre il cer--vel-lo per in-ten-der quel che si - a hor di que-sto e hor di quel-lo

(7#6)

4#3

4#3

(7) (4#3)

4#3

*(15 more measures, followed by the Ritornello and a ''2a parte'' = last 20 measures of part one)*

aria, in both serious and comic opera, was settling down during the latter half of the seventeenth century. These forms divide themselves, with few exceptions, into three groups :

1) *Strophic songs*, in which the solo part may be either literally repeated for each stanza or more or less varied. The style in many of these is light and simple, frequently showing traces of popular song-types or dance metres. Others are more serious in mood. There is usually an orchestral ritornello or a short section of recitative between the stanzas. (Example : Tancia's "S'io miro il volto," Act I, scene 9, Goldschmidt, *Studien* I, 357.)

2) *Through-composed arias*. These show a wide variety of types, both serious and comic, but all have a broader formal pattern and are less regular in melodic and rhythmic structure than the strophic songs. They consist of a number of sections, each ending with a full cadence in the tonic or a related key, and separated by orchestral ritornellos. (Examples : Isabella's "Son le piume acuti strali," Act I, scene 1, Goldschmidt, *Studien* I, 349; Leandro's "Sovra il banco di speranza," Act I, scene 8, Goldschmidt, *Studien* I, 355). The basic form of these arias is two-part, without marked contrast of thematic material. Sometimes, however, the second section may be more contrasting, followed by a repetition of the first, resulting in a three-part form. (Example : Lisa's "Se d'amore un cor legato," Act I, scene 1, Goldschmidt, *Studien* I, 352.)

Arias of this second group represent the main channel of development of operatic style in the later seventeenth century. In the course of time the formal scheme is expanded, the orchestra enters into the accompaniment proper as well as at the ritornellos, concertizing instruments appear, a fully developed da capo form gradually replaces the simple two-part structure, and eventually a number of stereotypes develop—arias of definite categories, each distinguished by certain stylistic procedures and appearing in the opera in a more or less rigidly fixed order of succession. This final degree of stylization, however, is not achieved until the early part of the eighteenth century.

3) *Arias over an ostinato bass*. Most arias of this group are serious in mood and belong to a recognized type known as the *Lamento*. (Example : Isabella's "Lungi la vostra sfera," Act I, scene 20, Goldschmidt, *Studien* I, 360.) They are most often in triple metre, with slow tempo, and the usual bass figure is the passacaglia theme consisting of a diatonic or chromatic stepwise descent of a fourth from the tonic to the dominant, or some variant of this.[16]

Apart from the three works which we have mentioned and a few others, little is known about the history of comic opera as a separate

[16] A familiar example of this kind of aria is the lament of Dido, "When I am laid in earth," from Purcell's *Dido and Aeneas*.

genre in the seventeenth century.[17] There was a school of comic and satirical opera at Venice after 1650.[18] Comic scenes persisted in serious opera until after the end of the century, and the incongruous mingling of the two moods is one of the typical features of baroque opera.

By the middle of the seventeenth century opera had come a long way from its beginnings as a pastoral play with monodic singing based on a supposed imitation of ancient Greek drama. Extensive ensemble numbers, typical of the earliest operas, survived after 1650 only in works destined for special aristocratic or state occasions. More significant historically, therefore, were the steps taken in the early seventeenth century toward establishing the main outlines of the structure of opera as a whole, founded on the separation of recitative from aria and the working out of musical forms for the latter, with distinct tonal relationships. Along with this formal progress went the discovery of new types of expression : the comic opera began its career, with its secco recitative and solo ensemble numbers, while for serious opera the possibility of successful musical treatment of other subject matter than the conventional pastorale was demonstrated by Rospigliosi and Landi. Finally, the modern orchestra, centering around violin instruments and continuo, was established, and an important type of overture originated. Changes already begun in the first few decades were accelerated as opera moved out of the shelter of aristocratic salons onto the stage of public theatres.

[17] D'Arienzo, "Origini dell' opera comica."
[18] Wolff, *Die venezianische Oper in der zweiten Hälfte des 17. Jahrhunderts,* pp. 107–41.

CHAPTER 8

# ITALIAN OPERA
# IN THE LATER
# SEVENTEENTH CENTURY
# I. IN ITALY[1]

Although the beginning of opera is commonly reckoned from the Florentine performances of 1600, it would be almost more appropriate to date it from the opening of the first public opera house in Venice in 1637. Itinerant troupes of singers, rivaling the troupes of the commedia dell' arte and borrowing from them many features of both libretto and music, had begun to circulate in Italy before this date; but the destined center of the new kind of musical drama, based on a combination of broad popular support and prestige appeal to the upper social classes, was Venice. Court operas of the early seventeenth century had always kept a certain reserve, a refinement, almost a preciosity of form and content. After 1640, as opera became increasingly a public spectacle,

[1] Bibliography: *Mercure galant* (Paris, 1672–74, 1677–1714); Solerti, "I rappresentazioni musicali di Venezia dal 1571 al 1605" (intermedi, pastorales, etc., at the ducal court; no music preserved): Wiel, *I codici musicali contariniani*; Groppo, *Catalogo*; [Salvioli] *I teatri musicali di Venezia nel secolo XVII*; Kretzschmar, "Die venetianische Oper"; *idem*, "Beiträge zur Geschichte der venetianischen Oper"; Wellesz, "Cavalli und der Stil der venetianischen Oper"; Prunières, *Cavalli et l'opéra vénitien au XVIIe siècle*; Worsthorne, *Venetian Opera in the Seventeenth Century*; Abert, *Monteverdi*, chaps. 2 and 3; Wolff, *Die venezianische Oper*; Rolland, "L'Opéra populaire à Venise: Francesco Cavalli"; Prunières, "I libretti dell' opera veneziana nel secolo XVII"; Pirrotta, "'Commedia dell' arte' and Opera"; Rommel, *Die Alt-Wiener Volkskomödie*; Westrup, "The Cadence in Baroque Recitative."

changes were inevitable. The popularity of the new form of entertainment at Venice was amazing. Between 1637 and the end of the century, 388 operas were produced in seventeen theatres in Venice itself and probably at least as many more by Venetian composers in other cities. Nine new opera houses were opened during this period; after 1650 never fewer than four were in operation at once, and for the last two decades of the century this city of 125,000 people supported six opera troupes continuously, the usual seasons filling from twelve to thirty weeks of the year. Citizens were admitted on payment of about fifty cents, and wealthy families rented loges by the season.

The transformation which took place in the character of both libretto and music is attributable in part to these new circumstances; yet signs of the change had already become apparent in Rome, and the whole movement was part and parcel of the changing literary and musical tastes of the time. The genuine Renaissance interest in antiquity being exhausted, only the shell of classical subject matter remained, and even this was frequently abandoned in favor of episodes from medieval romances, especially as embodied in the epics of Ariosto and Tasso. Moreover, the outlines of history or legend were overlaid with so-called *accidenti verissimi*—incidents invented and added by the poets—to the point of being no longer recognizable. Perseus, Hercules, Medea, Alcestis, Scipio, Leonidas, Tancred and Clorinda, Rinaldo and Armida were, in these operas, not so much human (or superhuman) persons as mere personified passions, moving through the drama with the stiff, unreal air of abstract figures (despite the vehemence with which their emotions were expressed), preoccupied with little more than their eternal political or amorous intrigues and caricatured in comic episodes which might fill half the opera. Mistaken identity—a device rendered somewhat less implausible by the presence of castrati in male roles—was a dramatic stock in trade. The Aristotelian unities gave way before a bewildering succession of scenes, sometimes as many as fifteen or twenty in a single act, full of strong feeling and suspense, abounding in sharp contrast and effects of all kinds. Lavish scenic backgrounds added to the spectacle. Pastoral idylls, dreams, oracles, incantations, spectral apparitions, descents of gods, shipwrecks, sieges, and battles filled the stage. In particular the machines, ingenious mechanical contrivances for the production of sudden miraculous changes and supernatural appearances, attained a degree of development never since surpassed. Heritage of the medieval mysteries, beloved adjunct of the Renaissance intermedi and the seventeenth-century court spectacles, the machines formed an indispensable part of opera in this period, though their magnificence declined before the end of the century.[2]

A striking feature of the scores after about 1645 is the virtual disappearance of the chorus. There are a few choruses in operas from around this time, and occasional indications that more were planned but apparently never composed. The mystery of these missing choruses has not yet been satisfactorily solved, but it is possible that they were replaced by ballets the music of which was written by some other composer and consequently not included in the regular score. At any rate, the absence of a chorus was primarily a matter of aesthetic propriety, for the stately, antique choral group of the Florentine pastorales had no place in the lusty melodrama of later seventeenth-century opera. Moreover, the public cared little for choral singing on the stage, preferring to hear soloists. Bontempi, in the preface of his opera *Il Paride* (Dresden, 1662), stated bluntly that the chorus belonged only in the oratorio,[3] and the managers soon found that the money it cost to maintain such a large body of singers could be more advantageously spent for other purposes. Only in festival operas, for which extraordinary sums were available, did the chorus remain. Its place was taken by ensemble solo voices, particularly in the prologues and epilogues, where divinities and allegorical figures of all kinds came forward to sing greetings to distinguished spectators or make general moral observations and topical allusions to events of the day. The decline of the chorus was followed by the rise of a typical operatic phenomenon, the virtuoso soloist, for whose sake numerous songs having no connection with the drama were interpolated in the score.

Along with these external changes, the music of Italian opera in the course of the seventeenth century developed some fundamentally new features of style. The works of the Florentines and early Romans were essentially chamber operas : relatively short, with a limited range of musical effects, sophisticated in feeling and declamation, calculated

---

[2] Sabbattini, *Pratica di fabricar scene, e machine ne' teatri*; Haas, *Musik des Barocks, passim; idem, Aufführungspraxis*, pp. 163 ff.; see also Burnacini's stage designs in the edition of Cesti's *Pomo d'oro* (DTOe III², IV²); *Denkmäler des Theaters*, Part II; Kinsky, *History of Music in Pictures*; Zucker, *Theaterdekoration des Barock.*

[3] Kretzschmar, "Die venetianische Oper," p. 22.

to appeal to invited guests of aristocratic tastes and education. The later operas, on the other hand, were destined for performance in public theatres before a mixed audience who had paid admission. Box-office appeal was essential. Broad effects by simple means, direct and vivid musical characterization, continual sharp contrasts of mood were required. Tuneful melodies, unmistakable major-minor harmonies, a solid but uncomplicated texture, strong rhythms in easily grasped patterns, above all a clear formal structure founded on the sequential repetition of basic motifs—these became the elements of a new operatic style.

MONTEVERDI.[4] A glance at the scores of the two Venetian operas of Monteverdi which have been preserved, *Il ritorno d'Ulisse in patria* ("The Return of Ulysses to His Country," 1641) and *L'incoronazione di Poppea* ("The Coronation of Poppea," 1642), shows what striking changes had taken place in the generation since his *Orfeo.* The recitative in *Il ritorno d'Ulisse* is no mere rhapsodic declamation of the text, with dramatic high points underlined by startling shifts of harmony; it is constantly organized into patterns, with sequences and canonic imitation between the solo voice and the bass. Sections of free "parlando" on a single note alternate with melodic phrases at the cadences. The recitative frequently gives way to short arias, mostly in triple metre and strophic form. There are several arias on a ground bass. The parts of the gods and goddesses are filled with elaborate coloraturas. Ensembles, particularly duets, are abundant. Conventional word painting is evident —long-held notes over a moving bass for words like "costanza," melismatic runs on "lieto," long coloratura phrases on "aria," and the like. Serious, comic, and spectacular scenes follow one another closely. Every possible occasion for emotional effect is exploited. From beginning to end one senses the effort to be immediately understood, along with an almost nervous dread of monotony, of that *tedio del recitativo* which had been so severely criticized in the early Florentine operas. There is little instrumental music : a few sinfonie which recur in the same fashion as the ritornellos in *Orfeo,* and one *sinfonia da guerra* to depict the combat between Ulysses and the suitors at the end of Act II. The high points of the opera are undoubtedly the monologue of Penelope in the first scene of Act I (reminiscent of the famous lament of Arianna) and the opening solo of Ulysses in the seventh scene of this act. At the beginning of Act III there is a comic lament, a clever parody of this favorite type

4 See W. Osthoff, *Das dramatische Spätwerk Claudio Monteverdis.*

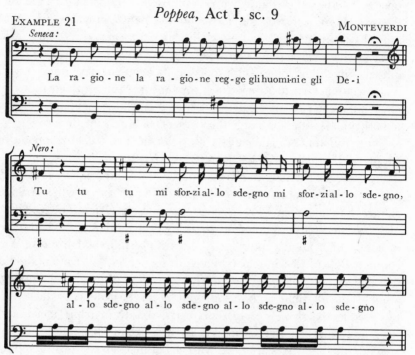

EXAMPLE 21     *Poppea*, Act I, sc. 9     MONTEVERDI

of scene. Some of the little strophic songs in popular style, such as Minerva's "Cara, cara e lieta" (Act I, scene 8), are very attractive.

On the whole, however, *Il ritorno d'Ulisse* is not to be compared with Monteverdi's next (and last) opera, *L'incoronazione di Poppea*,[5] a masterpiece of the composer's old age paralleled only by the last two operas of Verdi. The libretto of this work, by Francesco Busenello, deals with the love of the Roman emperor Nero for Poppea, the wife of Nero's general Ottone; Nero banishes Ottone and divorces his own wife Ottavia in order to make Poppea his empress. This rather sordid subject is handled by the poet with consistency, good taste, and dramatic insight. Monteverdi altered many details of the libretto in the course of composition, for the sake of more effective musical treatment. The music is not spectacular; there are no display scenes and few ensembles except duets.

[5] C.E. XIII; Goldschmidt, *Studien* II; see also Kretzschmar's analysis in VfMw X (1894) 483 ff. On the interpretation of the time values in Malipiero's edition of the score, see Redlich, "Notationsprobleme," and cf. Osthoff, *Das dramatische Spätwerk Claudio Monteverdis*, pp. 211 ff.

The composer's greatness lies in his power of interpreting human character and passions—a power which ranks him among the foremost musical dramatists of all times. Take for example the dialogue between Nero and Seneca in Act I, scene 9, where the grave admonitions of the philosopher contrast with the petulant outbursts of the willful young emperor (Example 21).

The delineation of comic characters is delightful. The song of the page boy (*valletto*) has a naïveté comparable to Mozart's music for Cherubino (Example 22).

EXAMPLE 22      *Poppea,* Act II, sc. 5

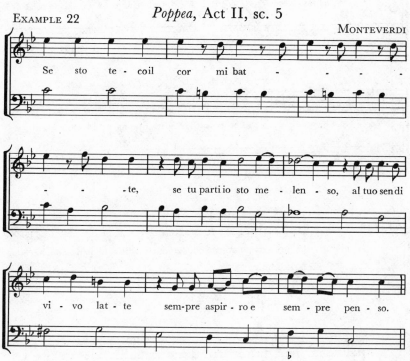

MONTEVERDI

Not less remarkable is the power of pathetic expression, as in the profound grief of Ottavia's lament "Disprezzata regina" (Act II, scene 5), or the noble resignation of Ottone's "E pur io torno," the characteristic motif of which is deliberately recalled in scene 12 and again in Act II, scene 11. The love passages in *Poppea* can only be compared to Wagner's *Tristan* or Verdi's *Otello*. The frankly sensuous passion of

Nero and Poppea is matched by a voluptuous, incandescent music, as in
the closing duet (a da capo form over a passacaglia bass), or in the third
and tenth scenes of the first act, which are in a free mixture of recitative
and arioso (Example 23).

*Poppea*, Act I, sc. 10

EXAMPLE 23

MONTEVERDI

No operatic score of the seventeenth century is more worthy of study
and revival than *Poppea*, as recent modern performances have amply
shown. In it Monteverdi applied the full resources of a mature technique

to a dramatically valid subject, creating in a great variety of musical forms and effects a unified, moving whole. The perfect balance between drama and music here achieved was soon to be upset by a trend toward musical elaboration at the expense of dramatic truth and consistency. Yet the influence of the work was far-reaching. Just as *Orfeo* marked the climax of the old-style pastorale, so *Poppea* marked a definitive step (already foreshadowed ten years earlier in Landi's *Sant' Alessio*) in the establishment of modern opera, centering about the personalities and emotions of human characters instead of the artificial figures of an ideal world.

CAVALLI.[6] The leading figure in the first period of opera at Venice was Monteverdi's pupil Pier Francesco Caletti-Bruni, who (following a common practice of the time) took the name of his patron, Cavalli. About forty of his operas appeared at different Venetian theatres between 1639 and 1669. Cavalli's fame during his lifetime is attested by the fact that many of his works were performed also in other cities, including Paris. His best-known opera was *Giasone* (1649), based on the legend of Jason, Medea, and the Golden Fleece.

In the works of Cavalli and later Venetian composers a standard type of overture developed, consisting of a solemn, pompous, chordal opening movement followed by one or more movements in contrasting tempo [7] which occasionally introduced themes that would reappear in the prologue or elsewhere in the opera. In addition to the overtures and a few descriptive sinfonie, the orchestra accompanied some of the songs or played short ritornellos between sections of them.

Solo arias were of course a regular feature of opera by this time, and they grew constantly more numerous in proportion to the whole as the century went on. At first, arias were given mainly to secondary personages; they were usually quite short, easily singable, mostly in triple metre with rhythmic patterns characteristic of popular dances or songs. Some were elegiac, minor in tone, with gently curving melodic lines, as in the beautiful "Delizie contente" from the first act of Cavalli's *Giasone*. Others were more lively, sometimes introducing trumpet-like motives for expression of rejoicing (Example 24).

[6] On Cavalli (1602–76) see literature listed on p. 78 (note 1) and Goldschmidt, "Cavalli als dramatischer Komponist" (many musical examples); Wiel, "Cavalli"; Hjelmborg, "Aspects of the Aria."

[7] Cf. Heuss, *Die Venetianischen Opern-Sinfonien*, pp. 85, 118, 120; Wolff, *Die venezianische Oper*, Anhang No. 67; Worsthorne, *Venetian Opera*, pp. 106 ff.

## Aria from *Egisto* (1643), Act III, sc. 7

EXAMPLE 24

CAVALLI

(Allegro)

Strings

Voice

Continuo

Ral-le- gra-te-vi, ral-le- gra-te-vi ral-le-

- gra - - - - te-vi

me-co Al- ber - ghi a-ma - ti sol di lie-te

(*Example 24 continued*)

sol di lie-ti, di lie-ti, di lie-ti ar-mo-ni-e rim-bom-ba-te, rim-bom-

-ba-te, rim-bom-ba-te, rim-bom-ba-te, rim-bom-ba-te, ca-no-ri, a me

Li-dio ri-tor-na e la-scia Clo-ri.

* This broadening at the final cadence — a "built-in" *ritardando* — was a common device in baroque music in triple metre. It was usually notated, as here, by "blackening" the notes affected, resulting in a change from 2 × 3 to 3 × 2 beats $\left(\frac{3}{4} \ \flat \ \flat \flat \flat = \frac{3}{2} \ \flat \ \flat \ \flat \right)$ but without change of duration of the individual notes.

Many arias of these and other types were strophic in form, with orchestral ritornellos. Another favorite form was the lament on a ground bass (Example 25) in which the contrast of passionate expression with

EXAMPLE 25    Aria from *Egisto*, Act II, sc. 6

one of the most rigid of musical forms gives rise to a typically baroque species of tension. Toward the end of the century, as arias came to be assigned more and more frequently to principal characters in the drama, the three-part da capo form became more common and more arias were written in difficult virtuoso style.

Certain traits of style peculiar to Cavalli may be especially mentioned. His comic scenes are marked by robustness, even crudity. Quite unlike the badinage of Monteverdi's page boy and maid in waiting is the scene in *Giasone* between Orestes and Demo, who is a stutterer—a typical farce figure, one of many such characters which were always welcomed on the Venetian stage. Cavalli's characteristic way of establishing a mood is to reiterate one striking figure, as in the conjuration scene from *Giasone* where the motif ♩ ♩ ♩ | ♩ is repeated twenty-one times with hardly a break, using (except at the cadences) only the chords of E minor and C major (Example 26). This scene from *Giasone* remained famous for a long time; it was parodied at Venice as late as 1677 in Legrenzi's *Totila*.

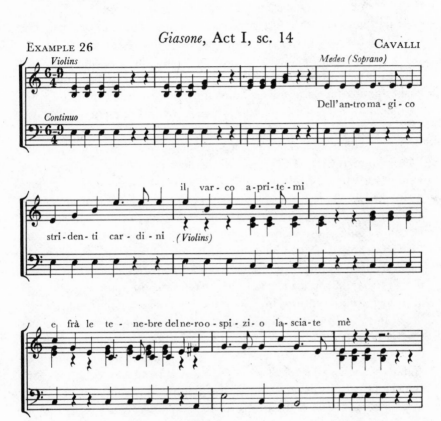

EXAMPLE 26                *Giasone*, Act I, sc. 14                CAVALLI

Despite the presence of well-marked arias and distinct sections of recitative, the formal separation of the styles is by no means complete in the operas of Cavalli. Most of the scenes are a mixture, or rather a free alternation of the two, as in Monteverdi, except that the arias in Cavalli form a somewhat larger proportion of the whole than is the case with the older composer. The method is not fixed; the form arises in each case out of the dramatic requirements. A typical example is the scene from *Ormindo* (1644) reprinted in Schering's *Geschichte der Musik in*

*Beispielen*[8] which consists of (*a*) a dialogue in recitative, C minor, eighteen measures; (*b*) an eight-measure solo revitative, ending in G minor; (*c*) a lament on a ground bass, in E flat major, fifty-six measures; and (*d*) a closing solo recitative in G minor, thirteen measures. The constant use of "scene-complexes" of this sort (that is, scenes made up of different musical elements freely assembled) shows that opera in Cavalli's time had not yet altogether sacrificed dramatic values to the demands of abstract, symmetrical musical form. Cavalli, while not critical of details, had a sound judgment for choosing dramatically effective librettos. He was not an artist of Monteverdi's caliber, but his music has virility and a kind of elemental directness in dramatic expression comparable to Mussorgsky—qualities which justify his position in history as the first great popular composer of opera.

CESTI. The most celebrated composer of opera after Cavalli was Pietro Antonio Cesti (1623–69),[9] whose dozen or so extant operas were written for various Italian and South German cities between 1649 and 1669. They include *Orontea* (Venice, 1649), *La Dori* (Florence, 1661), and *Il pomo d'oro* ("The Golden Apple," Vienna, 1667). Compared to Cavalli, Cesti's music is more facile, less vigorous, more feminine; he excels in the setting of idyllic, tender scenes; his melodies are clearly defined and graceful; his harmony is more conventional than Cavalli's—that is to say, it sounds less bold and experimental, more like the style of the eighteenth century; his rhythmic patterns are more regular, sometimes almost stereotyped. In his operas the already growing fissure between recitative and aria is noticeably widened: the center of musical interest shifts from the former, reserving the chief attention of composer and audience for the lyrical songs. The latter, by way of compensation, achieve larger proportions and clearer outlines, blossoming forth in an unprecedented variety of forms and types, offering frequent opportunities for vocal display. Thus the whole outline of the future singer's opera begins to come into focus in the works of Cesti.

This step, involving as it did a complete reorientation of operatic ideals, was of capital importance for the future. The doctrines of the Camerata had emphasized poetic values at the expense of music. Monteverdi, by means of organizing the recitative, deepening its content, and

---

[8] No. 200; see also a similar scene in HAM, No. 206.

[9] See Coradini, "P. Antonio Cesti"; Wellesz, "Zwei Studien"; Sandberger, "Beziehungen der Königin Christine . . . zur italienischen Oper."

introducing arioso or aria forms at critical points in the action, had made the music an equal partner with the text, thus restoring the balance. But now by the middle of the century, as composers were becoming more familiar with the new musical idiom, their interest in problems of form began to outweigh their concern for dramatic propriety. It must be said in their defense that the type of libretto which the poets supplied in some measure justified this attitude. As audiences demanded more and more music, they cared less and less about the poetry. The trend was hastened, moreover, by another influence, namely the cantata, a genre in which both Cesti and his teacher, Carissimi, excelled. The cantata, although semidramatic in form and employing recitatives and arias like the opera,[10] was not theatre music. Designed for performance before a small audience, the cantata was a vehicle for fine singing rather than for dramatic expression. Its virtues were those appropriate to the chamber : symmetrical forms, correctly balanced phrases, pleasing melodies, unadventurous harmonies; logic, clarity, elegance, and moderation. It was a musical style founded on these ideals, a style for which the widespread popularity of the cantata had already prepared both composers and audiences, which Cesti introduced into the opera.[11] With him may be said to begin the reign of the composer over the dramatist, and of the virtuoso singer over both, which was to characterize Italian opera for the next hundred years.

Cesti's *Pomo d'oro* is the most famous example of a baroque court opera in the grand style. It was composed for the wedding of the Emperor Leopold I of Austria with the Infanta Margherita of Spain, and performed at Vienna early in 1667 with a magnificence of staging appropriate to an imperial court desirous of not being outdone by the royal festivals of Louis XIV at Versailles.[12] The five acts included sixty-six scenes, in the course of which twenty-four different stage sets were

[10] "Eine Cantata siehet aus, wie ein Stück aus einer Opera." Hunold, *Die allerneueste Art, zur reinen und galanten Poesie zu gelangen* (1707), p. 285.

[11] Rolland, "L'Opéra au XVIIe siècle en Italie," in Lavignac, *Encyclopédie,* Part I, Vol. II, p. 722; Dent, "Italian Chamber Cantatas."

[12] See Wellesz, "Ein Bühnenfestspiel aus dem 17. Jahrhundert" (in translation : "A Festival Opera of the Seventeenth Century," in *Essays on Opera*, pp. 54–81). *Il pomo d'oro* was one of nine new operas performed at Vienna in 1667 (including Draghi's *Monarchia latina trionfante*) and was said to have run continuously for a year, three performances a week—a doubtful claim. A less well known but equally magnificent festival opera of the same period was *Il Paride* by G. A. Bontempi (1624–1705), performed at the court theatre in Dresden in 1662. See Briganti, *Gio. Andrea Angelini-Bontempi.*

required, some of them involving exceedingly elaborate machines. There were several ballets in each act and a grand triple ballet at the end. Ballets, a constant feature of Italian opera, were of course staged with especial magnificence in court spectacles. Often the music was written by a different composer.[13]

The story of *Il pomo d'oro* was based on the myth of Paris and the golden apple; in the epilogue (*licenza*) the god Jupiter presents this prize of beauty to the new empress, as being more worthy than the goddesses whose contention for it had brought about the Trojan War. In addition to the chorus there were forty-eight roles, though not necessarily this number of singers, since doubling was customary. All the gods of Olympus, as well as a host of heroes and other legendary personages, were represented in the cast. All the parts were sung by men, with the quaint consequence that some of the male characters in the opera have higher voices than the female ones—a situation not uncommon in Italian seventeenth-century opera even when there were women singers, for the composers favored the woman's alto voice and commonly reserved the soprano roles for castrati. The orchestra consisted of six violins, twelve viols (alto, tenor, and bass), two flutes (for pastoral scenes), trumpets in two parts (used chiefly in sinfonie and choruses), a *gravicembalo* (harpsichord), which was occasionally replaced by a *graviorgano* (a theatre organ, that is, probably a *positiv* or one-manual organ with wood pipes), and other continuo instruments (lutes, theorbo). There was also a special group of instruments for infernal scenes, consisting of two cornetts, three trombones, a bassoon, and a *regale*.

The prologue and each act are opened by stately instrumental "sonatas," and there are also many short sinfonie and ritornellos in the course of the opera. Choruses, found chiefly in the prologue, epilogue, and ballet scenes, are of comparatively little musical interest. The recitatives are for the most part mere perfunctory settings of dialogue, with the usual continuo accompaniment; there are, however, a few very beautiful accompanied recitatives (continuo and strings), notably that of Aurindo in Act I, which show what Cesti could do in the expressive

[13] For some of the ballets in the Vienna court operas, see DTOe XXVIII[2], and cf. Nettl, "An English Musician at the Court of Charles VI."

style when he had occasion.[14] The recitatives in *La Dori* are on the whole more flexible and expressive, more closely related to the earlier style of Cavalli, than those of *Il pomo d'oro*.

The favorite ensemble medium in seventeenth-century Italian opera was the duet. With Monteverdi and (to a lesser degree) Cavalli, the duet, when not merely a recitative dialogue, showed, by its imitative style, the derivation from the older madrigal. In Cesti, the contrapuntal feature is less favored, often being only suggested in the opening phrase and then giving way to melismatic passages in thirds or sixths. The opening measures of "Se perfido Amore" from *La Dori* (Example 27) are typical of this graceful, amiable style.

Cesti's arias are not usually of large dimensions, but they show a remarkable variety of types and much care in planning the order in which these occur. There are serene, long-breathed, noble Handelian melodies; playful airs with graceful and piquant rhythms such as Arsete's "Non scherzi con amore" from *La Dori*, a complete da capo form with the ritornello repeated between the first and second parts and again at the end; martial airs with strong rhythms and much bravura passage work; and buffo arias, lively, moving by wide intervals, exploiting the virtuoso powers and comic possibilities of the bass voice (Example 28).

The traditional strophic air is also represented in Cesti's operas; the characteristic form of each strophe in these airs is two-part, frequently with the second part repeated (a–b–b). Arias on a ground bass are also used, and there is a considerable number of complete da capo arias. Yet the forms are not stereotyped; subtleties of detail abound. One feature of Cesti's melody, found typically in slow-moving airs of an elegiac character, is the melodic interval of the diminished third at cadences—or, harmonically expressed, the Neapolitan sixth followed by the dominant (Example 29).[15]

[14] DTOe III², 97, 100 ff. Also in Lavignac, *Encyclopédie*, Part I, Vol. II, pp. 729–31.

[15] "Les italiens en mettant Bemol au ton favory [i.e., by flatting the supertonic in the melody at a ii–V–VI cadence] évitent la fausse relation [e.g., *d* soprano—*A-flat* bass, which with the flat becomes *d-flat*—*A-flat*] mais c'est pour exprimer les douleurs ou la faiblesse des moribonds." (M.-A. Charpentier, MS treatise on the rules of composition, ca. 1692. Quoted in Crussard, "Marc-Antoine Charpentier théoricien," p. 53.)

EXAMPLE 27    *La Dori*, Act I, sc. 9

EXAMPLE 28    *Il pomo d'oro*, Act I, sc. 11

EXAMPLE 29    *La Dori*, Act I, sc. 9

LATER ITALIAN COMPOSERS. Although Venice remained the most flourishing center for opera during the second half of the seventeenth century, public opera theatres were opened in many other Italian cities [16] soon after 1650; the style developed by Cavalli, Cesti, and their followers soon came to be a national and even an international possession. The leading composers in this period who worked principally at Venice were Antonio Sartorio (ca. 1620–81), Giovanni Legrenzi (1626–90),[17] Pietro Andrea Ziani (ca. 1620–84), Giovanni Domenico Freschi (1640–90), and Carlo Francesco Pollarolo (1653–1722). Sartorio's chief work was the serious "heroic opera" Adelaide (1672). Legrenzi excelled in the genre of the "heroic-comic" opera, which intermingled serious and comic scenes; and he was noted for the unusual care he gave to the orchestra, both in independent instrumental numbers and in accompaniments. His principal operas were Totila (1677) and Il Giustino (1683). At the hands of the later composers the trend was toward comedy or parody, with lightening of the musical texture, lessening musical importance of the recitative, increasing dominance of the aria, and larger use of the orchestra for accompaniments.

The songs of the earliest operas had been accompanied only by the continuo instruments, improvising in a more or less elaborate texture over a figured bass. Orchestral ritornellos, first used on an extensive scale by Monteverdi in Orfeo, were eventually brought into close relation with the vocal part by the simple device of using the same thematic material in both.[18] A further step was taken when the orchestral instruments, instead of being confined to the pauses between sections or stanzas of the aria, played with the voice, either as a continuous supporting accompaniment [19] or constantly alternating with the vocal phrases in echoes or imitations. During the latter part of the seventeenth century the simple continuo accompaniment of arias diminished in favor. In Cavalli's Giasone (1649) only nine out of twenty-seven arias had been accompanied by the orchestra; in Cesti's La Dori (1661) only five out of thirty-two; in Stradella's Floridoro (ca. 1680?) the proportion is sixteen to thirty-seven; in his Forza d'amor paterno (1678) thirty-five to fifty-one; in Steffani's Servio Tullio (1686) twenty-three to fifty-two; in Pallavicino's Gerusalemme

[16] For a list of the local histories dealing with these theatres see Bustico, Bibliografia delle storie e cronistorie dei teatri italiani.

[17] See Fogaccia, Giovanni Legrenzi.

[18] Landi's Sant' Alessio (Goldschmidt, Studien I, 211); Rossi's Orfeo (Goldschmidt, Studien I, 301); Monteverdi's Ritorno (finale of Act III) and Incoronazione (see Wellesz, "Cavalli," p. 32).

[19] See for example Oronte's aria "Renditimi il mio bene," in Act I of Cesti's La Dori, in Eitner, Publikationen XII, 129 ff.

*Il schiavo di sua moglie*, Act I, sc. 8

EXAMPLE 30

Largo

PROVENZALE

(Strings and continuo)

La - scia - te - mi

La - scia - te - mi mo - rir        stel - le cru - de - li

liberata (1687) eleven to fifty-one. The number varied according to circumstances; the Vienna opera had a large orchestra, and we consequently find many orchestral accompaniments in Draghi. The later Venetians, especially Pollarolo, introduced the orchestra more frequently, while Handel in his *Agrippina* (Venice, 1709) has thirty-one of the forty arias accompanied by the orchestra, and Scarlatti in *Telemaco* (Rome, 1718) dispenses with the continuo-accompanied arias altogether.[20] Mattheson in

[20] Haas, *Musik des Barocks*, p. 202.

1744 laments the passing of the continuo arias, which he says had long since gone out of fashion.[21]

Many operas of the Venetian composers were given also in other cities—Freschi's, for example, at Bologna; Cesti's *Argia* (Innsbruck, 1655) at Rome, Naples, Venice, Milan, Siena, Genoa, Reggio, and Udine; Cavalli's *Giasone* (1649) in at least fourteen other Italian cities within eighteen years; and so on. In addition to the composers already named there were others in this period who had little or no connection with Venice. Carlo Pallavicino (1630–88) began at Venice but later worked principally at Dresden. The first Neapolitan composers of importance were Francesco Cirillo (1623–56),[22] whose works were performed at Naples from 1654; and Francesco Provenzale (1627–1704),[23] the music of whose two extant operas shows a fine quality of expressiveness and a subtle use of chromatic harmony comparable to the best Italian style of the late seventeenth century (Example 30).

Another notable late seventeenth-century composer was Alessandro Stradella (1644–82),[24] whose roving and adventurous life has furnished the subject of operas by Flotow (1844) and others. His own thirteen operas and other stage works as well as some two hundred and fifty cantatas show a facility and sensuous grace of melodic invention that justify his position in history as an important predecessor of Scarlatti and the Italian school of the eighteenth century. Stradella's best-known stage works are *La forza d'amor paterno* (Genoa, 1678) and the comic opera *Trespolo tutore* (?1679; Example 31).

Although Venice by no means had a monopoly of opera in the latter half of the seventeenth century, it was preeminent among Italian cities, and always kept a certain glamour for foreign visitors interested in opera. Some of their observations make interesting reading. John Evelyn wrote in 1645 :

This night, having . . . taken our places, we went to the Opera, where comedies and other plays are represented in recitative music, by the most excellent musicians, vocal and instrumental, with variety of scenes painted

---

[21] *Die neueste Untersuchung der Singspiele*, p. 162.

[22] See Prota-Giurleo, *Francesco Cirillo e l'introduzione del melodramma a Napoli.*

[23] Goldschmidt, "Francesco Provenzale als Dramatiker."

[24] Giazotto, *Vita di Alessandro Stradella*; Hess, *Zur Geschichte des musikalischen Dramas im Seicento: Die Opern Alessandro Stradellas*; other studies by Allam, Gentili, Richard, Catelani, Roncaglia, and Della Corte.

EXAMPLE 31

STRADELLA

and contrived with no less art of perspective, and machines for flying in the air, and other wonderful motions; taken together, it is one of the most magnificent and expensive diversions the wit of man can invent. The history was, Hercules in Lydia; [25] the scenes changed thirteen times.[26]

In 1680 the French traveller Limojon de St. Didier reported as follows:

At Venice they Act in several Opera's at a time: The Theaters are Large and Stately, the Decorations Noble, and the Alterations of them good: But they are very badly Illuminated: The Machines are sometimes passable and as often ridiculous. . . . These Opera's are long, yet they would divert the Four Hours which they last, if they were composed by better Poets, that were a little more conversant with the Rules of the Theater. . . . The Ballets or Dancings between the Acts are generally so pittiful, that they would be much better omitted; for one would imagine these Dancers wore Lead in their Shoes, yet the Assembly bestow their Applauses on them, which is meerly for want of having seen better.

The Charms of their Voices do make amends for all imperfections: These Men without Beards [that is, the castrati] have delicate Voices (*des voix argentines*) besides which they are admirably suitable to the greatness of the Theater. They commonly have the best Women Singers of all *Italy*. . . . Their Airs are languishing and touching; the whole composition is mingl'd with agreeable Songs (*chansonettes*) that raise the Attention; the Symphony [orchestra] is mean[,] inspiring rather Melancholy than Gaiety: It is compos'd of Lutes, Theorbos and Harpsichords, yet they keep time to the Voices with the greatest exactness imaginable. . . .

They that compose the Musick of the Opera, endeavor to conclude the Scenes of the Principal Actors with Airs that Charm and Elevate, that so they may acquire the Applause of the Audience, which succeeds so well to their intentions, that one hears nothing but a Thousand *Benissimo's* together; yet nothing is so remarkable as the pleasant Benedictions and the Ridiculous Wishes of the *Gondoliers* in the Pit to the Women-Singers . . . for those impudent Fellows (*canailles*) say whatever they please, as being assured to make the Assembly rather Laugh than Angry.[27]

Ten years later Maximilien Misson, obviously no enthusiastic devotee, had this to say about the Venetian opera:

The Habits are poor, there are no Dances, and commonly no fine Machines, nor any fine Illuminations; only some Candles here and there, which deserve not to be mentioned . . . they have most excellent Ayres . . .

[25] *Ercole in Lidia*, music by G. Rovetta.
[26] *Diary* I, 202.
[27] *La Ville et la république de Venise*, English translation, 1699, Part III, pp. 61–63.

but I cannot forbear telling you, that I find a certain Confusion and Unpleasantness in several Parts of their Singing in those Opera's : They dwell many times longer on one Quavering, than in singing Four whole Lines; and oftentimes they run so fast, that 'tis hard to tell whether they Sing or Speak, or whether they do neither of the Two and both together. . . . The Symphony is much smaller than at *Paris*; but perhaps, it is never the worse for that. There is also one Thing which charms them, which I believe would not please you; I mean those unhappy Men who basely suffer themselves to be maimed, that they may have the finer Voices. The silly Figure! which, in my Opinion, such a mutilated Fellow makes, who sometimes acts the Bully, and sometimes the Passionate Lover, with his Effeminate Voice, and wither'd Chin[,] is such a thing to be endured? . . . There are at present Seven several Opera's at *Venice*, which Strangers, as we are, are in a manner oblig'd to frequent, knowing not, some times, how to spend an Evening any where else.[28]

[28] *A New Voyage to Italy,* I, 269–70.

# CHAPTER 9

# ITALIAN OPERA IN THE LATER SEVENTEENTH CENTURY II. IN GERMANY

The South German courts were not slow to import Italian opera. Performances are recorded in Salzburg as early as 1618; Vienna and Prague soon followed (1626, 1627). Cesti's works were performed at Innsbruck from 1655 to 1665, and there was Italian opera at Regensburg and Munich from 1653. The chief center, as might be expected, was Vienna.[1] Monteverdi, Cavalli, and Cesti were heard here at the middle of the century; subsequent composers included Antonio Bertali (1605–69), Giovanni Felice Sances (*ca.* 1600–1679), Pietro Andrea Ziani (*ca.* 1620–84), the Emperor Leopold I (reigned 1658–1705), and the most prolific of all, Antonio Draghi (1635–1700), who between 1663 and 1699 contributed some one hundred and seventy dramatic pieces of various kinds to the Viennese repertoire.[2] Draghi, his librettist Nicolo Minato, and the court architect Ludovico Burnacini were the leaders of opera at Vienna during the last three decades of the century. Draghi was

---

[1] Bibliography: Köchel, *Die kaiserliche Hofmusikkapelle in Wien von 1543 bis 1867*; Nettl, "Zur Geschichte der kaiserlichen Hofkapelle von 1636–1680"; *idem,* "Exzerpte aus der Raudnitzer Textbüchersammlung"; Weilen, *Zur Wiener Theatergeschichte; idem, Geschichte des Wiener Theaterwesens*; Haas, *Die Wiener Oper;* Adler, "Die Kaiser . . . als Tonsetzer"; Wellesz, "Die Opern und Oratorien in Wien"; *idem, Essays on Opera,* Nos. II–V; Bauer, *Opern und Operetten in Wien.*

[2] Neuhaus, "Antonio Draghi" (with catalogue of works and many musical examples).

a court composer of skill and facility, if not of distinction. The airs of his early works are usually short and in strophic form, typically with the first part returning after a middle section in the dominant (or relative major), either with or without thematic contrast. In his later works this is evolved into a full da capo form, with much textual repetition and extremely difficult bravura passages. His recitatives are of the parlando variety, generally barren of musical interest, though occasionally a few measures of arioso are introduced, as in the older Venetian style. His overtures also follow the Venetian model and frequently have dance movements at the end.

A style similar to Draghi's is found in later works of Pallavicino, director of the first permanent opera theatre at Dresden from 1686. About twenty of Pallavicino's operas had been performed at Venice before he composed his *Gerusalemme liberata* for Dresden in 1687.[3] The libretto of this work combines three episodes from Tasso with a number of newly invented incidents in considerable confusion, but with opportunity for several of the favorite spectacular scenes. Comic episodes are less conspicuous than in most contemporary operas; each of the three acts ends with a ballet. Despite readiness of melodic invention and surety of style, the music gives a total impression of monotony. With the exception of two duets, everything is for solo voice. The sixty-six arias are for the most part very short and preponderantly in da capo form; the orchestral ritornello, played either at the beginning or end, is based on a motif from the aria itself. Certain mannerisms obtrude: phrases are constantly repeated in echo style,[4] whether or not the text justifies such a procedure (Example 32). The device of sequence is ever present; there

*Gerusalemme liberata*, Act II, sc. 12

EXAMPLE 32                                                              PALLAVICINO

[3] See H. Abert's introduction to the edition of this work in DdT LV.
[4] Cf. Kretzschmar, "Einige Bemerkungen über den Vortrag alter Musik."

are many passages of brilliant coloratura, especially in the larger arias accompanied by the full orchestra. On the other hand, many of the smaller arias are in simple, popular style including examples of the barcarole and siciliano types. The formal balance is always clear, the middle section of the da capo arias being shorter than the first part and usually offering contrast of key, material, phrase structure, and general design (Example 33).

There are three accompanied recitatives and two ostinato bass arias. One of the latter (Act I, scene 1), in genuine passacaglia style, is nevertheless in a–b–a form, the third and last variation being a literal repetition of the first—a striking instance of the imposition of the da capo idea on the older form, recalling the combination of chaconne and sonata-allegro in the finale of Brahms's Fourth Symphony.

One feature of the instrumental music in Pallavicino is the frequent repetition of phrases. Sometimes this is merely the echo effect common in the songs, but the repetition may involve also a contrast of instrumentation. The second movement of the overture, for example, consists only of five two-measure phrases, each of which is first played by the continuo instruments alone and then immediately repeated by the full orchestra. Similar places are found in many of the ritornellos : usually (as in the overture) a mere antiphony of short phrases between different instrumental groups, but occasionally a more freely developed concerto-like structure in miniature.[5] Essentially, of course, this procedure amounts to no more than taking over into the instrumental field a practice already established in the orchestrally accompanied arias, with their interplay of solo voice and orchestra. Yet it is worth noting that the appearance of the concerto principle in the instrumental music of opera at this time coincides with the earliest independent compositions for string orchestra in concerto style. The trumpet concerto, a favorite of a slightly earlier period, is represented in the overture to Pallavicino's *Diocletiano* (Venice, 1675) and in a sinfonia from the first act of M. A. Sartorio's *Adelaide* (Venice, 1672).[6]

One of the leading Italian composers in Germany was Agostino Steffani (1654–1728), most of whose eighteen operas were written between 1681 and 1696. Steffani was at Munich in the years 1667–72 and

[5] See also the overture to *L'amazone corsara* (1688) in Heuss, *Venetianischen Opern-Sinfonien*, p. 121.

[6] Cf. Schering, *Geschichte des Instrumentalkonzerts*, pp. 27 ff.

EXAMPLE 33

PALLAVICINO

* These six measures are repeated.

1674–88, after which he went to Hanover. He was the principal intermediary between the Italian opera of the late seventeenth century and the German operas of Keiser and Handel, so that even apart from his own achievements as a composer his historical position is an important one.[7]

The librettos of Steffani's operas differ from those of Pallavicino and other contemporary Italian composers only in their use of subjects from German history and a diminished emphasis on mythological and spectacular elements; in form, there is the usual regular alternation of recitative and aria, relieved only by an occasional accompanied recitative or duet. But the contraputal texture of the music marks a profound break with the prevailing tendencies in Italy, which were toward the homophonic style. Steffani's basses in the continuo arias are independently moving contrapuntal lines. In the orchestrally accompanied arias the voice is treated as one instrument among several, yet without ever sacrificing its position as "chief among equals" or taking on any nonvocal traits. Concertizing instruments (solo flutes, oboes, violins, bassoon, or trumpet) weave strands of melody about the vocal part, while the full orchestra joins in at the cadences. The characteristic arias are lyrical rather than dramatic, noble and serious in expression—long-breathed, leisurely melodies, effortlessly flowing (Example 34).

Attention must be called in Example 34 to the way in which the voice makes a false start, beginning the first phrase of the aria only to abandon it during a short instrumental interlude, after which the phrase is begun again and continued normally. This peculiarity—called by German writers *Devise* and often rendered in English as the "motto beginning" [8]—first came prominently into operatic music with Legrenzi: twenty-six of the arias in his *Eteocle e Polinice* (Venice, 1675) begin in this way. Instances may be found also in Cesti and earlier; it was very commonly used by Pallavicino and P. A. Ziani and by the end of the century had become an almost unconscious mannerism of style, constantly present in the arias of Steffani, Handel, Fux, and other composers. In many of Scarlatti's arias the first word or phrase of the text

---

[7] Bibliography: Chrysander, *Händel* I, 309–73; Fischer, *Musik in Hannover*; Untersteiner, "Agostino Steffani"; De Rensis, "Un musicista diplomatico"; Werner, "Steffanis Operntheater in Hannover"; A. Einstein, "Agostino Steffani"; Baxter, "Agostino Steffani."

[8] See G. F. Schmidt, *Die frühdeutsche Oper* II, 382–97 for a critical definition, history, and examples of this device.

EXAMPLE 34 *Alcibiade*, Act I, sc. 3

Orchestra: *Strings and Winds* STEFFANI

*(Example 34 continued)*

will be repeated but with different music—the first statement being like a mere prelude or announcement whereas the second is the real beginning of the song.

The fundamental simplicity of Steffani's arias does not exclude melismatic passages, many of which have no particular justification in the text but seem to well forth as the natural completion of the musical idea (Example 35).

EXAMPLE 35    *Tassilone* (1709), Act III, sc. 6

STEFFANI

Tut-ta tre - mo e per le ve-ne___ Fred-do scor-re un gel mor-

ta- - - - - - - - - le.

The bravura aria is less characteristic of Steffani, though it was a favorite of Cesti, P. A. Ziani, Sartorio, and other Italian composers. Written for texts of stirring or martial character,[9] these airs abounded in virtuoso passage work; trumpet-like figures in the melody or the addition of trumpet obbligato rendered the effect even more brilliant (Example 36).

Steffani's arias are nearly all in da capo form. In keeping with the contrapuntal character of his music, there is an unusually high proportion of arias on a ground bass, which sometimes itself determines the form but more often is simply incorporated in the da capo pattern. In many instances the ostinato principle is modified, leaving a bass consisting of a steady movement in quarter or eighth notes (walking bass), or of a characteristic rhythmic motif constantly repeated.[10] In the accompanied recitatives, with their flexible structure and free mingling of declamatory and arioso phrases, the old Monteverdi-Cavalli ideal of purely dramatic song is recalled. It was customary in the Venetian opera to accompany scenes of a supernatural character (especially the appearance of specters, the *ombra* scenes) with the full string orchestra; an

[9] Cf. Bücken, *Der heroische Stil in der Oper.*
[10] Cf. Riemann, "*Basso ostinato* und *Basso* quasi *ostinato*," in *Festschrift Liliencron*, pp. 193–202.

## *Tassilone,* Act IV, sc. 8

EXAMPLE 36

STEFFANI

echo of this tradition is heard in the string accompaniment to the recitatives of Christ in Bach's *Passion According to St. Matthew.*

Steffani's overtures are obviously modeled on those of Lully, with whose music he had become acquainted on a visit to Paris in 1678–79. Steffani is credited with being the first to introduce trio sections in the fast movement of the overture—short interludes for solo instruments, contrasting with the *tutti* in the manner of the *concerto grosso*.

Steffani is one of the culminating points of operatic style at the end of the seventeenth century. He was a spontaneous genius on the order of Mozart or Schubert rather than a dramatist like Cavalli or Handel, and his works represent in perfection the goal of musical opera toward which the whole century had been moving. In his music at last is achieved the reconciliation of the monodic principle with the contrapuntal tradition. Steffani's operas, like the (contemporary) trio sonatas of Corelli, exemplify that balanced classical style of the late baroque which led the way in the next generation to the monumental achievements of Bach and Handel. The aristocratic, dignified, musically serious opera of Steffani found successors in the early eighteenth century only in the works of a few exceptional northern composers, for example, Johann Christoph Pez (1664–1716) at Munich and Bonn, but more notably in the works of Keiser and Handel. In Italy it was a stranger; there the demand for simplicity and melody, always immanent in the Italian temperament as well as in the nature of opera itself as a large public spectacle, led ineluctably to the *galanteries* of the eighteenth century.

Echoes of the older style are heard in the ceremonial operas or *feste teatrali* of Johann Josef Fux (1660–1741),[11] court music director at Vienna from 1713, composer of eighteen operas and much church music, and author of a famous treatise on counterpoint, the *Gradus ad Parnassum. Costanza e fortezza* ("Constancy and Fortitude") was performed at Prague in 1723 to celebrate at the same time the coronation of the Emperor Charles VI and the birthday of the Empress. Like Fux's other operatic works of the 1720s, *Costanza e fortezza* is filled with elaborate scenic effects, machines, and choruses—all the apparatus, in short, appropriate to festival occasions. The nature of these occasions, as well as Fux's official position, dictated a conservative, somewhat stiff, old-fashioned style in his music; yet he was not without progressive traits. His earlier operas consist almost entirely of solo numbers. Even in the later ceremonial works the arias and ensembles are in the full da capo form characteristic of the eighteenth century; contrapuntal elements are present but not predominant, and general baroque severity is lightened by graceful melodies and dancelike rhythms.

[11] Köchel, *Johann Josef Fux*; Van der Meer, *Johann Josef Fux als Opernkomponist.*

# CHAPTER 10

# *EARLY GERMAN OPERA*

The early history of opera in Germany is not one of a comparatively unified development, as in France or England, or even of a comparatively consistent musical style evolution, as in Italy. The numerous political subdivisions of Germany in the seventeenth century, with many different cultural traditions, the conflicting elements in both the dramatic and the musical background, and the extremely strong infusion of foreign styles (chiefly Italian, but some French) to different degrees in different parts of the country—all combine to produce a complicated task for the historian. Abstractly speaking, a purely "German" opera is one written for performance by German artists for German audiences, with an original libretto in the German language and on a German (or, at least, not a typically foreign) subject, composed by a German, and with music in a German (or, at least, not predominantly foreign) style. In actuality, there are few, if any, operas of the early period which correspond to this admittedly narrow abstract definition. In actuality, we find foreign conductors and singers performing before German courts whose tastes are often formed on Italian and French models, librettos in Italian or German translations or paraphrases of Italian or French texts, Italian composers, German composers aping the Italian manner, and all possible permutations and combinations of these factors. Add to these conditions the fact that many composers were active in different places; that frequently the same opera poem appeared under different names, or different poems under the same name; that composers habitually used music from their own earlier works or inserted music from other sources in their scores; and add finally that the scores themselves, a study of which alone could resolve many of the problems, are in the great majority of cases utterly lost or survive only in fragments—and it will be readily seen that a complete history of German opera in the seventeenth and early eighteenth centuries is, if not quite impossible, at least far beyond the scope of the present work. It has seemed best, therefore, in this chapter to begin with a brief survey of the political and social conditions under which German opera was composed and of the dramatic and musical factors which entered into it, to indicate some of the principal developments at important centers, and then to concentrate on the most distinctive of the many local schools, that of Hamburg.[1]

Germany in the seventeenth century was not a nation but a loose confederation of some 1,700 more or less independent states; most of these were petty "knights' dominions," but there were also fifty-one free imperial cities (of which the chief were Hamburg, Bremen, Frankfurt am Main, Nuremberg, Augsburg, Ulm, and Strassburg), sixty-three ecclesiastical holdings, and nearly two hundred secular principalities and counties, a few of which were of considerable size and importance. The semblance of unity arising from an ill-defined allegiance to the Holy Roman Empire was disrupted by the Thirty Years War (1618–48), a calamity which left the country economically prostrated and bereft of almost all pride in its national heritage. Like a body weakened by illness, German culture was invaded by foreign elements. The language became filled with French and Spanish words; French became the common tongue of polite society;[2] the little local courts, narrow, paternalistic, and extravagant, aspired to imitate the glories of Versailles. Italian opera thus made its appearance as a courtly show, particularly in southern

---

[1] The conditions of early German opera are reflected in the fact that the great majority of the studies in this field are in the form of local or regional histories, embodying chronicles and statistics. References to this extensive literature will be found in the three chief general surveys of the period: Kretzschmar, "Das erste Jahrhundert der deutschen Oper," in his *Geschichte der Oper*, pp. 133–57, also SIMG III (1901–2) 270–93; Moser, "Die frühdeutsche Oper," in his *Geschichte der deutschen Musik* II, Book II, chap. 3; and Schiedermair's *Deutsche Oper*, Part I. See also Bolte, *Die Singspiele der englischen Komödianten*; Haas, "Die Oper in Deutschland bis 1750," in Adler's *Handbuch*; Schletterer, *Das deutsche Singspiel*; G. F. Schmidt, "Zur Geschichte, Dramaturgie und Statistik"; Schreiber, *Dichtung und Musik der deutschen Opernarien*; Huber, *Das Textbuch der frühdeutschen Oper*. A bibliography of regional and local histories of German music will be found in MGG III, *s.v.* "Deutschland," cols. 364–90. Biographies of many composers are to be found in Mattheson's *Ehrenpforte* (1740).

[2] A proverb at the Brunswick court in the latter part of the seventeenth century ran: "Wer nicht französisch kann, Der kommt bei Hof nicht an" (Hartmann, *Sechs Bücher Braunschweigischer Theatergeschichte*, p. 85). See also *Braunschweigischer Magazin* IX (1903) 116–17.

Germany, where we have already traced some of its manifestations at Vienna, Dresden, and Munich. Other centers of Italian opera were Hanover (Steffani's operas from 1689 to 1696), Düsseldorf, and Bonn. Yet many courts tried at first to encourage German talent. The early Italian operas at Vienna occasionally had German songs inserted. The "first German opera" was performed at Torgau in 1627 at the marriage of Princess Luise of Saxony and Landgraf Georg von Hessen-Darmstadt. This work was the old *Dafne* of Rinuccini, translated and adapted by the leading German poet of the time, Martin Opitz, with music by Heinrich Schütz (1585–1672). Since the score has not survived, it is impossible to say whether Schütz composed a new setting or merely arranged Gogliano's music and added a ballet.[3] Before the opening of the Italian opera in 1686, Dresden had a few works in German; one of these, *Dafne* (1671), with music by Bontempi and M. G. Peranda (*ca.* 1600–1675), is the earliest German opera still extant in full score.[4]

The German equivalent of the term "opera" was *Singspiel*, a literal translation of the Italian *dramma per musica*.[5] Ayrer's comedies on popular song-tunes at Nuremberg (from 1598) bear the designation *singets Spil*; the first operas at Hamburg were called *Sing-Spiele*. The term was applied in the seventeenth and early eighteenth centuries both to works sung in their entirety and to those having some spoken dialogue. In the second half of the eighteenth century its meaning was restricted to pieces of the latter type. (It may be added that, in the absence of scores, it is not always possible to ascertain in the case of some seventeenth-century German operas whether the recitatives were sung or spoken.) The word "opera" does not often occur in German scores before 1720.[6]

At Brunswick the court opera employed native poets, subjects, and composers (Erlebach, Philipp Krieger, Bronner, Kusser, Keiser), but with the opening of a public theatre in 1690 the demand for foreign goods became so strong that French and Italian works had to be added to the repertoire. A temporary revival of native opera in the early

[3] A *Ballet von der Zusammenkunft und Wirkung der sieben Planeten* (Dresden, 1678), formerly attributed to Schütz, has been ascribed on the basis of internal evidence to his pupil, Christoph Bernhard (Bittrich, *Ein deutsches Opernballett des siebzehnten Jahrhunderts*).

[4] Engländer, "Zur Frage der *Dafne*."

[5] Cf. Hunold: "Eine *Opera* oder ein Sing-Spiel ist gewiss das galanteste Stück der Poesie, so man heut zutage æstimieren pfleget" (*Die allerneueste Art* [1707], p. 394).

[6] See G. F. Schmidt, *Die frühdeutsche Oper*, II, 45–54.

eighteenth century was led by Georg Caspar Schürmann, one of the most significant of the German composers, whose dignified, serious musical style has much in common with Keiser, Handel, and Bach. Schürmann (*ca.* 1672–1751) composed about forty operas which were given at Wolfenbüttel and Hamburg, but only eleven scores have been preserved. His chief work was *Ludwig der Fromme* ("Louis the Pious," 1726).[7]

At Leipzig, where operas were played during the Fair seasons from 1693 to 1720, the texts were mostly translations of Venetian librettos; poets and composers, players and singers were largely recruited from the students of St. Thomas's, and so successfully that Kuhnau in 1709 complained that church music suffered from the competition.[8] The general enthusiasm for opera at Leipzig was such that even J. S. Bach did not altogether escape its influence.[9] Another center of German opera was Weissenfels; here the leading composer was Johann Philipp Krieger (1649–1725), whose opera songs were in the simple German "lied" tradition. The subject matter of the Weissenfels operas, however, was not distinctively German; the repertoire shows a strong preponderance of mythological dramas and ballets. A similarly ambiguous picture is presented at many of the lesser courts—German elements struggling against an increasing tide of Italian opera, which by the fourth decade of the eighteenth century had won the field everywhere.

The characteristic German forerunner of opera was the school drama, a play in Latin or German, usually of a moral or religious nature, didactic in aim, performed by the students of a school or seminary. Many of these dramas in the sixteenth century included instrumental dances, solo odes, and choral pieces.[10] In the early seventeenth century the musical portions became even more extensive. Although the Thirty Years War put an end to the most flourishing era of the school drama, its influence may be seen in the earliest German

[7] See Schmidt, *Die frühdeutsche Oper.*

[8] Spitta, *Johann Sebastian Bach* (4th ed.) II, 854.

[9] The most obviously dramatic work of Bach is *Phoebus und Pan* (composed for the Leipzig Collegium Musicum in 1731), which one contemporary called a Gesprächspiel" (Spitta, *Bach* II, 740). Several of the secular cantatas, so called, actually bear the designation "Drama" or "Drama per Musica," and others (e.g., the "Coffee Cantata") are semidramatic—not to mention the Passions and oratorios, in which the influence of dramatic forms is clearly evident.

[10] See Flemming, *Geschichte des Jesuitentheaters*; Liliencron, "Die Chorgesänge des lateinischen-deutschen Schuldramas"; Schünemann, *Geschichte der deutschen Schulmusik*, pp. 67 ff., 137.

opera whose music has been preserved : *Seelewig*, a "spiritual pastorale" by Philipp Harsdörffer, set to music by Sigmund Theophil Staden (1607–55), and published at Nuremberg in 1644 in a family periodical.[11] As with the first Hamburg opera, nearly thirty-five years later, the subject matter of this work is religious. The form is allegorical. "Seelewig" is the soul; the villain of the piece is one Trügewalt, who attempts to ensnare Seelewig with the help of other characters representing Art, the Senses, and so on, while Wisdom and Conscience act as her defenders. The final triumph of virtue is celebrated by an invisible chorus of angels. This highly moral drama is placed in a fashionable pastoral setting : the sylvan scenes are described in poetry filled with moral symbolism; Seelewig's companions are nymphs and shepherds, while Trügewalt is figured as a satyr. Each of the three acts is introduced by a symphony, and there are a few other short instrumental pieces, together with the composer's direction that more may be added if necessary in order to avoid pauses during the changing of the scenery. In the solo songs, which comprise most of the music, there is evidence of some effort to write in the recitative style, but Staden has not acquired the knack; consequently, most of the songs are short melodies, and nearly all are in strophic form. Perhaps the best is Seelewig's outburst of thanksgiving in the closing scene (Example 37).

*Seelewig* was not the only effort of Harsdörffer along operatic lines. If there he showed himself a follower of the Italian pastorale, in *Die Tugendsterne* ("The Stars of Virtue")[12] he sought to turn to moral purposes another favorite genre, the ballet with machines; still another play, *Von der Welt Eitelkeit* ("Of Worldly Vanity"),[13] consists of four allegorical scenes, each representing a worldly Vanity, with an epilogue sung by Death. No doubt such works are exceptional, as being designed primarily for reading rather than performance; but they show what kind of stage spectacles presumably interested the good citizens of Nuremberg at this period. A later Nuremberg composer, Johann

[11] *Frauenzimmer Gesprechspiele* IV, 31–165, 489–622. Cf. Narciss, *Studien zu den Frauenzimmergesprächspielen*, pp. 93–96; Tittmann, *Kleine Schriften zur deutschen Literatur und Kulturgeschichte*, Theil I; E. Schmitz, "Zur musikgeschichtlichen Bedeutung der Harsdörfferschen 'Frauenzimmergesprächspiele,' " in *Festschrift Liliencron*, pp. 254–77.

[12] *Frauenzimmer Gesprechspiele* V, 280–310; see also Haar, "Astral Music in Seventeenth-Century Nuremberg."

[13] *Frauenzimmer Gesprechspiele* III, 170–242. A nearly complete reprint, with the music, by Eugen Schmitz in *Festschrift Liliencron*, pp. 264–75.

### *Seelewig*, Act III, sc. 6

EXAMPLE 37

STADEN

Ach wun-der star - ker Gott der du durch man-
- che Nacht mich gnä-dig - lich ___ ge- führ - et. Es ist kein
Un- ge-lück kein Aug-undHert-zen-blickda ich mich wol re - gi - ret.

*( Three more stanzas)*

Löhner (1645–1705), is represented for us by some surviving arias but no complete scores.

With the increase of Italian opera everywhere in the South, the native school found a home not in one of the courts but in the free imperial North German city of Hamburg. Here for sixty years (1678–1738) flourished with varying fortunes a public opera house, the first in Europe outside Italy, where German composers were able for a time to combine contributions from Italian and French sources with their own genius to make an original, truly national form.[14]

The earliest Hamburg operas show the influence of the school

[14] Bibliography: H. C. Wolff, *Die Barockoper in Hamburg* (the basic work; the second volume consists entirely of musical examples. Cf. review by H. Becker in *Die Musikforschung* XIII [1960] 211 ff.); Flemming, *Die Oper*, introduction; Lindner, *Die erste stehende deutsche Oper*; Chrysander, articles on the Hamburg opera (1678–1706) in *Allgemeine musikalische Zeitung* XII (1877)—XV (1880), *passim*; Kleefeld, "Das Orchester der Hamburger Oper"; Moller, *Cimbria literata*.

drama. The first one presented the story of Adam and Eve, under the title *Der erschaffene, gefallene und wieder aufgerichtete Mensch* ("The Creation, Fall, and Redemption of Man"), with music by Schütz's pupil Johann Theile;[15] many similar titles appeared in the first few years. Such material was not only traditional but was also useful in retaining the good will of the Lutheran church authorities and providing a defense of the opera against frequent attacks on the ground of its worldly and immoral character. Despite sporadic opposition, secular operas soon gained the ascendancy; composers and poets began to introduce subjects from the Italian and French stages—chiefly translations or adaptations from Venetian librettists (especially Minato), but also occasionally from Corneille (*Andromeda und Perseus,* 1679), from Quinault (*Alceste,* 1680), and from Italian comedies; a few foreign operas were performed in French or Italian (Lully's *Acis et Galatée,* 1689; Colasse's *Achille et Polyxène,* 1692; Cesti's *Schiava fortunata* [in M. A. Ziani's revision?], 1693; Pallavicino's *Gerusalemme liberata,* 1693; and others). Many of Steffani's works were presented in German translation, and a number of German composers chiefly associated with other cities or courts were represented in the Hamburg repertoire, notably J. S. Kusser (Brunswick), Johann Philipp Krieger (Weissenfels), and G. C. Schürmann (Wolfenbüttel). So far as their literary quality is concerned, the Hamburg librettos were on the average neither worse nor better than those of contemporary Italian opera, on which they were modeled. As in Venice, the machines played a conspicuous role. The leading poets were Christian Heinrich Postel (1658–1705), Friedrich Christian Bressand (*ca.* 1670–99; also active at Brunswick), Lucas von Bostel (1649–1716), and Barthold Feind (1678–1721), the last of whom in the eighteenth century took the lead in cultivating caricature and parody.

The chief composers of the period were Nikolaus Adam Strungk (1640–1700),[16] the Nuremberger Johann Wolfgang Franck (1644–*ca.* 1710),[17] and Johann Philipp Förtsch (1652–1732).[18]

[15] Zelle, *Johann Theile und Nikolaus Adam Strungk.*
[16] Berend, *Nicolaus Adam Strungk.*
[17] Zelle, *Johann Wolfgang Franck*; Barclay Squire, "J. W. Franck in England"; Sachs, "Die Ansbacher Hofkapelle"; G. F. Schmidt, "Johann Wolfgang Francks Singspiel *Die drey Töchter Cecrops*"; Günther Schmidt, *Die Musik am Hofe der Markgrafen von Brandenburg-Ansbach*; Klages, *Johann Wolfgang Franck.*
[18] Zelle, *Johann Philipp Förtsch*; Wiedemann, *Leben und Wirken des Johann Philipp Förtsch.*

EXAMPLE 38     Aria from *Cara Mustapha* (1686)

J. W. FRANCK

*(Example 38 continued)*

Franck composed fifteen operas for Hamburg between 1679 and 1686. His music is serious in tone and shows a fine feeling for long-breathed expressive lines (Example 38) as well as for melodies in a lighter, more popular vein (Example 39). He writes arias in a variety of

### Die drey Töchter Cecrops, Act V, sc. 4

EXAMPLE 39                                                                FRANCK

Wenn man sei - nen Zweck er - hält, muss man sich um nich- tes

küm-mern, und da-durch sein Glück ver-schlim-mern, das doch, eh' man's meynt, ver-

fällt, _____          das doch,    eh' man's meynt, ver-fällt.

musical forms, including the da capo. He uses a wide range of keys and —exceptionally for this time—his scores seem to show evidence of consciously designed tonal architecture. Franck's recitative is more melodic, slower in tempo, and altogether of more musical significance than that of contemporary Italian opera; its style rather resembles the recitative of German seventeenth-century church composers, half declamation and half arioso, measured and dignified in tone, composed with great care for both the rhythm and the expressive content of the text. Altogether, Franck's is a full-textured, stiff-rhythmed baroque music, unmistakably Italian in inspiration but tinged with the serious, heavy formality of Lutheran Germany.

A more cosmopolitan style was represented at Hamburg by Johann Sigismund Kusser (1660–1727),[19] who had acquired a taste for French music from his studies under Lully during a sojourn of eight years at Paris. Operas of Kusser's were performed at Brunswick and Stuttgart as well as at Hamburg, where he worked from 1694 to 1696. His *Erindo* (1694) is a pastorale on the model of Guarini's *Pastor fido*—a choice of libretto attributable perhaps to the composer's French background, since pastorales were uncommon in Italian opera at this period. Kusser's music, as far as can be judged from the only two sets of opera airs that have survived, is distinguished by attractive *cantabile* melodies, clear formal and tonal schemes, skillful use of concertizing instruments, and numerous little songs in French dance rhythms, such as the passepied (Example 40), minuet, or gavotte. His importance for the history of

EXAMPLE 40        Duet from *Erindo*, Act III                    KUSSER

German opera, however, is apparently due less to his standing as a composer than to his influence as conductor and impresario. By making the German public better acquainted with French and Italian music he was instrumental in preparing the way for the international style of Mattheson, Keiser, and Handel, the leading composers of opera at Hamburg in the early part of the eighteenth century.

[19] Scholz, *Johann Sigismund Kusser*. (Note that the name is sometimes spelled Cousser.)

# CHAPTER II

# LULLY AND THE OPERA
# IN FRANCE[1]

French opera as a continuous institution began only in 1671. This late date is surprising if we reflect that throughout the first part of the seventeenth century (that is, during the reigns of Henri IV, Louis XIII, and the minority of Louis XIV, who assumed power on the death of Mazarin in 1661) close political and cultural relations existed between Italy and the French court. But opera was not congenial to the Gallic spirit, with its rationalistic bias and its quick awareness of absurdities; furthermore, the French for many years held that their language was not suited to recitative, which is the foundation of musical drama. They preferred their drama unadulterated and regarded music in the theatre as only an auxiliary to dancing and spectacle. Having their tragedy and their ballet, each the best of its kind in the world, they were of no mind to risk spoiling both by trying to combine them in the form of opera. Yet once launched, the French opera was the only national school in Europe able to maintain itself unbroken through the eighteenth century in the face of Italian competition.

The explanation of this is to be found partly in political circumstances but chiefly in the extraordinary personality of the founder of the French school, Jean-Baptiste Lully (1632–87).[2] Italian by birth, Lully

[1] General works: Blaze, *De l'opéra en France*; Chouquet, *Histoire de la musique dramatique en France*; Lajarte, *Bibliothèque musicale du théâtre de l'opéra*; Campardon, *L'Académie royale de musique au XVIIIe siècle*; Borland, "French Opera before 1750"; Vallas, *Un Siècle de musique et de théâtre à Lyon;* Liuzzi, *I musicisti in Francia.* See also works cited below.

[2] See biographies by La Laurencie and Prunières, in which references to sources and other bibliographical material will be found; see also RM, *Numéro Spécial* (Jaunary, 1925); Rolland, "Notes sur Lully," in his *Musiciens d'autrefois,* pp. 107–202; Lavignac, *Encyclopédie,* Part I, Vol. III, pp. 1343–1425; Borrel, *Jean-Baptiste Lully.*

came to Paris at the age of fourteen. Having been trained as a ballet dancer and violinist, he rapidly developed into a skillful conductor and composer; a combination of musical talent, ruthlessness, commercial shrewdness, and obsequious manners assured him a brilliant career under the patronage of Louis XIV. In establishing the fundamental pattern of French opera, Lully created a type which incorporated elements from every musical and dramatic form that had already proved itself in France. Those forms were the French classical tragedy as exemplified by the works of Corneille and Racine, the pastorale, the Italian opera, and the French ballet.[3]

Lully's librettist, Philippe Quinault,[4] had begun his career as a playwright. In general form and dramatic framework his operas are similar to contemporary French tragedies. The subject matter, however, is restricted to mythology or legend, including three works (*Roland, Amadis, Armide*) derived from romantic sources. The pastorale genre, which had remained popular in France long after its decline in Italy, and which Lully had used with success in some of his early works, came into his operas especially in the prologues, though in *Isis* and *Roland* there are long pastoral scenes in the body of the opera as well.

Italian opera was known in France [5] from a half-dozen works performed at Paris by visiting troupes between 1645 and 1662, including L. Rossi's *Orfeo* (1647) and Cavalli's *Egisto* (1646), *Serse* (1660), and *Ercole amante* ("Hercules in Love," 1662). The last-named work showed evidence of Cavalli's efforts to adapt his music to French taste both in the style of the melodies and recitatives and in the inclusion of many ballet scenes, the music of which was furnished by Lully and other French composers. Italian opera, however, was not a success in France. Undoubtedly audiences were intrigued by the discovery that an entire drama could be set to music; they enjoyed the ballets; but their real enthusiasm was for the machines invented by Giacomo Torelli,[6] the like of which had not been seen on such a scale in France since the sixteenth century. The influence of Italian opera was therefore indirect : it stimulated the French to emulate the Italians by trying to create an opera of

[3] Schletterer, *Vorgeschichte* . . . *der französischen Oper*; Grout, "Some Forerunners of the Lully Opera."

[4] Gros, *Philippe Quinault*.

[5] Prunières, *L'Opéra italien en France*.

[6] On Torelli, see works by Bragaglia and Torrefranca listed in bibliography; also Nicoll, *The Development of the Theatre*, pp. 215–28.

their own, and it probably led them to favor a large proportion of machine scenes.

The determining factor in the background of French opera, however, was the ballet, which had flourished in France steadily since the famous *Ballet comique de la reine* of 1581.[7] The accession of the young Louis XIV stimulated a revival of the ballet under Benserade [8] and Lully from 1653 to 1668, as well as a series of "comedy ballets" which Lully wrote in collaboration with Molière, including *Georges Dandin* in 1668, *Monsieur de Pourceaugnac* in 1669, *Les Amants magnifiques* and *Le Bourgeois gentilhomme* in 1670, and *Psyché* (by Molière, Quinault, and Corneille) in 1671. During these years Lully perfected all the elements of his mature style; indeed, some of the later ballets and comedy ballets had such elaborate musical and scenic interludes as to be little short of full operas, lacking only a continuous dramatic action developed musically, that is, in recitative.

The official existence of French opera dates from the founding of the Académie Royale de Musique in 1669, under the direction of Pierre Perrin and Robert Cambert (*ca.* 1628–77). They staged two operas, or rather pastorales, with music by Cambert, before going bankrupt three years later. Lully, who had hitherto loudly maintained that opera in French was impossible, changed his opinion when his favor with the king enabled him to seize control of the Academy and establish a monopoly of operatic performances in France.[9] From 1673 until his death he produced an opera nearly every year.[10] These works, all perfectly consistent in form and style, established a type of French national opera destined to endure for a hundred years, essentially unchanged by Rameau and hardly dethroned by Gluck himself.

The nature of opera as conceived by Lully is expressed in his designa-

[7] Prunières, *Le Ballet de cour en France avant Benserade et Lully*; Lacroix, *Ballets et mascarades de cour*; Ménestrier, *Des Ballets anciens et modernes.*

[8] Silin, *Benserade and His Ballets de Cour.*

[9] See La Laurencie, *Les Créateurs de l'opéra français*; Nuitter and Thoinan, *Les Origines de l'opéra français*; the account by Pougin (*Les Vrais Créateurs de l'opéra français*) makes Lully out more of a scoundrel than he really was in this matter, according to Prunières.

[10] The following is a complete list of Lully's operas (librettos are by Quinault unless otherwise indicated): *Cadmus et Hermione*, 1673; *Alceste*, 1674; *Thésée*, 1675; *Atys*, 1675; *Isis*, 1677; *Psyché*, 1678 (Fontenelle); *Bellérophon*, 1679 (T. Corneille); *Proserpine*, 1680; *Persée*, 1682; *Phaëton*, 1683; *Amadis de Gaule*, 1684; *Roland*, 1685; *Armide et Renaud*, 1686; *Acis et Galatée*, 1686 (Campistron); *Achille et Polyxène*, 1687 (Campistron; Act I by Lully, score completed after his death by Colasse).

tion of the form as a *tragédie en musique*, that is, a tragedy first and foremost, which is then set to music. Interest in the poem of an opera, and insistence that it be of respectable dramatic quality, was one of the basic differences between the French and Italian viewpoints in the seventeenth and eighteenth centuries and indeed (though perhaps to a lesser degree) since. Contemporary French criticism was directed fully as much to Quinault's texts as to Lully's music. The operas, divided into five acts, always had a prologue devoted to the glorification of Louis XIV, with allusions to important recent events of his reign. The action, unrolling with majestic indifference to realism, presented a series of personages discoursing lengthily on *l'amour* or *la gloire* in the intervals of all kinds of improbable adventures. There were no comic figures, except in *Cadmus* and *Alceste*; everything was stately, formal, and detached from ordinary life—the kingly opera par excellence, designed not for a general public as in Venice, not even for an aristocracy as in Rome and Florence, but for a single individual who was conceived to embody the perfection of national artistic taste and whose approbation alone was sufficient to guarantee success: what Louis approved, few dared to condemn.

The music was in keeping with this ideal. Its fundamental character may be described by the word "conventional": aspiring not to be new or different but to create the accepted effects supremely well. There were no startling intervals, chords, or modulations; everything was kept within moderate bounds, avoiding violence or passion. At its best, therefore, early French opera was impressive, noble, rich, and dignified; at its worst, barren, stereotyped, pale, and thin. Considered solely as music, it is likely to be less appealing to modern ears than contemporary Italian scores; but considered as opera, and in its proper setting, the French school stands comparison with the Italian very well.

One of Lully's achievements was the creation of musical recitative suited to the French language. His model for the recitative is said to have been the declamation employed in tragedies at the Comédie Française.[11] Almost strictly syllabic, it often falls into monotony of rhythmic and melodic patterns; yet where the feeling of the text permits, the recitative may display extraordinary variety and naturalness, necessitating for its notation continual changes of time signature. The relatively more complex notation of French recitative has sometimes led to an

[11] Le Cerf de la Viéville, *Comparaison* III, 188.

exaggerated view of the contrast between it and the Italian recitative. To a considerable degree this is a matter of notation rather than of actual sound, although naturally the difference in accent and tempo of the two languages determines the characteristics of the recitative in each case. Modern singers need to be cautioned against taking Lully's recitative too slowly and songfully, forgetting the composer's dictum "mon récitatif n'est fait que pour parler." [12]

Occasionally, at points where the emotion expressed by the words is more lofty or concentrated, the usual recitative will give way to a melodic phrase, which may recur several times in rondo fashion—a procedure analogous to that of Monteverdi or Cavalli, welding recitative and arioso into a unified and expressive whole. A beautiful example of this is the lament in *Persée*, in which the recurring vocal phrase is first announced in the orchestral introduction (Example 41).

EXAMPLE 41         *Persée*, Act V, sc. 1         LULLY

A word is necessary on the interpretation of the time signatures in Lully. The signs 2 (=2/2) and ₵ are two-beat measures, in which theoretically the beat is *half as fast* as in C (a four-beat measure). Thus where the signatures alternate in the same piece, in changing from 2 or ₵ to C, two quarter notes in the latter would have the same value as one half note in the former. The same holds true if the change is from 2 or ₵ to 3 (=3/4), or from 3/2 to 3 or C. In other words, the duration of a quarter note is theoretically the same whether the measure is divided into two beats or four, the different signatures being indications of different metres rather than different tempos. Nevertheless, the signatures do serve in some degree as tempo indications, especially in instrumental pieces. [13] In the above example the half notes after 2/2 obviously must not be quite twice as long as the preceding quarters; the change of signature is a way of indicating an *allargando* effect at the cadence rather than an abrupt shift to a slower tempo.

[12] *Ibid.*

[13] See Georg Muffat's *Florilegium*, Part II, Introduction, sections reprinted in Vol. I of Prunières' edition of Lully's ballets, with notes by A. Tessier.

The vocal airs in Lully's operas differ considerably from Italian arias. As a rule, they are not strongly set apart as separate numbers, but are continually interspersed in a scene along with recitatives, duets, choruses, and dances. For the most part these airs are short, narrow in range, and subject to piquant irregularities of phrasing. They do not use coloratura, except for conventional short passages on such picture words as *lancer, briller*, and the like, though the vocal line is ornamented by a multitude of *agréments* (short trills, grace notes, passing tones, and so on). These are seldom indicated in the score, unless by a little *t* or cross above the note affected, which signifies only that some kind of agrément is expected without specifying what one. Their correct choice and placing were largely a matter of custom and taste, both for singers and for instrumentalists.[14] Thus for the French singer less technical vocal cultivation was required than for the Italian, but a clearer enunciation and a more intelligent grasp of the text. A favorite type of air in Lully, derived in part from the French popular chanson and in part from instrumental dance music, is illustrated in Example 42. Part A of this example is from the edition in full score of 1689; Part B shows the same air as notated in an edition of 1720. It will be seen that the latter, besides giving fuller directions for realization of the bass and correcting what is probably an error in measure eight, is careful to indicate precisely to which notes the agréments are to be applied. This tune was one of many from Lully's operas that passed into the repertoire of popular chansons and remained familiar to the public for many years (*cf.* Ex. 71a). Dance rhythms are common in Lully's airs, as is the rondo-like recurrence of the opening phrase in the middle and again at the end of the song.

A more serious type of air goes back to the French air de cour, culti-vated in the early and middle seventeenth century by such composers as Antoine Boesset and Michel Lambert.[15] The well-known "Bois épais" from *Amadis* (Example 43) and the equally famous "Plus j'observe ces lieux" from *Armide*, both occurring in pastoral scenes, show this style at its best.

Lully's operas are filled with long scenes having nothing to do with furthering the action but existing solely to furnish pleasure to eye and

[14] See Aldrich, "The Principal Agréments of the Seventeenth and Eighteenth Centuries" (Harvard Dissertation, 1942); Goldschmidt, *Die Lehre von der vokalen Ornamentik.*
[15] Gérold, *L'Art du chant en France au XVIIe siècle.*

EXAMPLE 42a    *Atys*, Act I

ear—pastoral episodes, sacrifices, combats, descents of gods, infernal
scenes, funeral and triumphal processions. These pompous displays are
the heritage of the seventeenth-century ballet, and the generic French
term *divertissement* well describes their place in the scheme of the opera.
They give occasion for most of the choruses, instrumental numbers, and
dances which are so prominent in Lully. The choruses are generally
homophonic and massive; those sung to accompany dancing are charac-

EXAMPLE 42 b

*Atys*, Act I

LULLY

Quand le pé - ril est a - gré - a - ble Le moy-

-en de s'en al - lar - mer; Est-ce un grand mal de trop ay-

mer, Ce que l'on trouve ay - ma - ble! Est-ce un grand

mal de trop ay - mer Ce que l'on trouve ai - ma - ble.

terized by strongly marked rhythms. Scenes with choruses are particularly numerous in *Bellérophon*.

Lully's orchestra consists chiefly of the strings (in five parts), which play the ritornellos, double the chorus parts, and occasionally accompany solos. Flutes or oboes are used especially in pastoral scenes, either in combination with the strings or playing short episodes in trio style with continuo. Bassoons may be added to the ensemble, and the martial scenes employ trumpets and drums. The orchestra of the Paris opera, carefully selected and strictly drilled by Lully himself, achieved a quality of performance that made it celebrated throughout Europe.

Instrumental ritornellos are usually placed at the opening of acts or scenes, and descriptive symphonies (for example, the "Songes agré-ables" in *Atys*, Act III, scene 4) are common. For the ballets there are dances and airs. The most frequent dances are the minuet, gavotte, and

EXAMPLE 43         *Amadis*, Act II, sc. 4                    LULLY

chaconne; and instrumental "air" in French ballet or opera of this period is a piece played to accompany any dance or other movement on the stage which does not fall into one of the standard dance categories.

The overture, descended from the older canzona, the sonata da chiesa, and the early Venetian overture, and first definitively established by Lully,[16] is a large two-part (not three-part) form. The introductory section, in duple metre, is slow, sonorous, and majestic, marked always by dotted rhythms and usually by suspensions; it cadences on the dominant and is repeated. The second section, the theme of which may be derived from the introduction, is lively and in either triple or duple metre; it begins with imitative entries in the manner of a canzona, but once the voices have come in all pretence of systematic imitation is abandoned, though a pseudocontrapuntal texture is maintained throughout, with much sequential treatment (Example 44). This part, which is also usually repeated, may conclude with a broad *allargando* somewhat in the style of the opening section, though not necessarily having any thematic resemblance to it. The French overture form was one of the most influential musical patterns of the late baroque period, being taken over into the oratorio and the instrumental suite. Later opera composers (for example, Handel), borrowing in turn from the suite, often introduced one or more dance movements at the end of a French overture.

Lully's operas continued to be performed at Paris for many years after his death. *Thésée* and *Amadis* were revived as late as 1779 and 1771 respectively, and nearly all the others lasted until the middle of the eighteenth century. Every successful French opera in this period called forth comic parodies or burlesques at the popular theatres of Paris. *Roland* accumulated ten of these satellites between 1685 and 1755; *Atys*, *Amadis*, and *Armide* each had nine.

The dignified, formal splendor of Lully's works, veritable embodiments of the glory of the age of Louis XIV, offered a model to be imitated at lesser European courts. The serious quality of the librettos, the careful composition of the recitative, the prominence of instrumental music, and the importance of chorus and ballet—all contrasting with the prevailing tendencies in Italy—helped to characterize a distinctive national type of opera which eventually made its influence felt on composers of other countries.

In France itself, Lully established the opera as an institution of the state. This was a source at once of weakness and of strength: of weakness, because it tended to perpetuate forms which, whatever meaning they may have had during the great days of the Sun King, became mere

[16] In the ballet *Alcidiane*, 1658. Cf. Prunières, "Notes sur les origines de l'ouverture française."

EXAMPLE 44

*Phaëton*, Overture

(Largo)

LULLY

[etc.]

(Allegro)

empty show when that triumphal age was past; yet of strength, for without such a foundation French opera might never have survived the series of second-rate composers and the general relaxation of taste which set in toward the end of the century.

One of Lully's first successors was his pupil Pascal Colasse (1649–1708). Colasse's best opera was *Thétis et Pélée* (1689), which remained in the repertoire at Paris until 1754. The *Médée* of Marc-Antoine Charpentier (1634–1704),[17] produced in 1693, was never revived, though contemporary critics wrote favorably of it. André-Cardinal Destouches (1672–1749) was distinguished for *Issé*, a "pastorale heroïque" produced at Fontainebleau in 1697, and for the opera *Omphale* (1700), the last revival of which in 1752 set off a notorious literary quarrel known as the "guerre des bouffons." [18] Another opera composer of this period was Marin Marais (1656–1728); his *Alcyone* (1706) contains an orchestral representation of a "tempête," one of the early examples of this kind of musical realism in opera.[19]

The period between the death of Lully in 1687 and the first opera of Rameau in 1733 was marked by a gradual change from the grave pomp and formality of the age of Louis XIV toward the *galanteries* of the Regency (1713–23) and the reign of Louis XV. The dramatic integrity of Lully's and Quinault's tragédie lyrique was undermined by the growing popularity of the pastorale and by the rise of a new form, the *opéra-ballet*. The latter differed from the traditional *ballet de cour* in that it was purely a spectators' show with professional performers and was set to music throughout. It had no consistent dramatic action, though each act (*entrée*) might have a self-contained little plot and all be vaguely connected by some central idea. [20] Thus the first important opéra-ballet, *L'Europe galante* by André Campra (1660–1744),[21] given at Paris in 1697, had its four entrées set in the four European countries France, Spain, Italy, and Turkey. Even so tenuous a bond of unity disappeared from many later opéra-ballets, in which the poem existed only to provide occasion for dances, airs, choruses, and scenic effects. At the

[17] Crussard, *Un Musicien française oublié.*
[18] See below, p. 256.
[19] Barthélemy, "Les Opéras de Marin Marais." Earlier examples of "storm" music in opera are found in Locke's *Macbeth* and Colasse's *Thétis et Pélée.*
[20] ". . . un spectacle composé d'actes détachés quant à l'action, mais réunis sous une idée collective, comme les Sens, les Élémens. . . ." Marmontel, *Élémens de littérature* (*s.v.* "Prologue") V, 528.
[21] Barthélemy, *André Campra.*

same time the tragédie lyrique itself became invaded by irrelevant ballet and display scenes to an extent never imagined by Lully.

Another sign of change in this period was the infiltration of Italian characteristics—a tendency stoutly opposed by conservative critics, who remained loyal to the pure tradition of French opera as represented by Lully. The conflict between French and Italian styles flared up many times in the course of the eighteenth century and led to a tremendous amount of polemical writing.[22] The Italian taste was represented by the use of Italian background in scenes of operas and ballets (for example, Campra's *Festes vénitiennes*, 1710), by the insertion of whole Italian arias and cantatas or of "ariettes" with French words set to music of Italian style, by occasional use of the da capo form, and more particularly by certain harmonic innovations foreign to the idiom of Lully but common in the music of Scarlatti and other Italian composers, such as freer modulations, a more liberal use of appoggiaturas, seventh chords (especially the diminished seventh), chromatic alterations, and more florid or expressive vocal writing.[23]

[22] The two chief polemical essays of the early part of the century were Raguenet's *Parallèle des Italiens et des Français* (1702) and Le Cerf de la Viéville's *Comparaison de la musique italienne et de la musique françoise* (1705–6); see translations in Strunk, *Source Readings*, pp. 473–507.

[23] Examples in the music of Campra and especially Destouches. See La Laurencie in Lavignac, *Encyclopédie*, Part I, Vol. III, pp. 1374, 1382–84.

# CHAPTER 12

# ENGLISH OPERA[1]

As in France opera grew out of the ballet, so in England it was rooted in the masque. English opera, like the French, developed late in the seventeenth century into a distinct national type retaining many traces of the parent form. Unlike the French, however, English national opera succumbed to Italian taste soon after 1700. The untimely death of its master, Henry Purcell, is symbolic of its own fate—"a spring never followed by summer."

The English masque was an entertainment something like the French court ballet, allegorical in character, with the main interest in costumes and spectacle, but including spoken dialogue, songs, and instrumental music.[2] The principal author of masques in the early seventeenth-century period was Ben Jonson, and one of his colleagues was Inigo Jones, who designed costumes and scenery. None of the great Elizabethan composers wrote masque music, but the form became a proving ground for experiments in solo singing soon after the beginning of the seventeenth century. It may be recalled that this was also the age of the solo ayre, beginning with the publication of John Dowland's first collection in 1597. Among the earliest composers of masques were Alfonso Ferrabosco (*ca.* 1575–1628) and Thomas Campion (1567–1620), but the first recitative in England was probably written by Nicolas

[1] Dent, *Foundations of English Opera*; White, *The Rise of English Opera*; Parry, *The Music of the Seventeenth Century* (OHM III); Forsyth, *Music and Nationalism.*

[2] Reyher, *Les Masques anglais*; Herford, "Jonson," in *Dictionary of National Biography* X (1917), 1069–79; Mark, "The Jonsonian Masque"; Noyes, *Ben Jonson on the English Stage*; Cutts, "Le Rôle de la musique dans les masques de Ben Jonson"; Lawrence, "Notes on a Collection of Masque Music"; H. A. Evans, *English Masques*; W. M. Evans, *Ben Jonson and Elizabethan Music*; Prendergast, "The Masque of the Seventeenth Century"; Gombosi, "Some Musical Aspects of the English Masque"; Finney, "*Comus*, Dramma per musica."

Lanier (1588–1666) in his music (now lost) for Ben Jonson's *Lovers Made Men* in 1617. This and similar efforts to adapt the new Italian *stile recitativo* to English words were of no immediate importance for English music, which in the course of the seventeenth century developed its own style in the airs and songs, preferring to leave most of the rest of the masque (that is, those portions which in an Italian opera would have made up the recitative) in spoken dialogue. The songs, being simply inserted pieces and not organically connected with recitative as were the early Italian arias, retained a simple and even popular flavor which gave a distinctive national stamp to English masque music and, by inheritance, to later English opera.[3]

The masque flourished especially during the reigns of James I (1603–25) and Charles I (1625–49). Under the Commonwealth (1649–60), there were few public masques, though some were still given privately, for example, Shirley's *Cupid and Death* (1643) with music by Matthew Locke (*ca.* 1630–77) and Christopher Gibbons (1615–76). Masques were also performed in schools during this period. The professional theatre flourished briefly under the management of William D'Avenant, who in 1656 presented a five-act work entirely in music, *The Siege of Rhodes*. The music (which has not been preserved) included recitatives and arias; it was written by a number of different composers, among whom were Locke and Henry Lawes (1596–1662). Apparently in order to avoid trouble with the Puritan authorities, the acts were called "entries" and the whole spectacle was known not as an opera (which word, in any case, was still new in England at the time) but "A Representation by the art of Prospective in Scenes and the Story sung in Recitative Musick." In spite of this subterfuge, however, *The Siege of Rhodes* was actually the "first English opera." Though successful, it was not followed up, for the Restoration soon brought influences to bear which gave a different direction to English dramatic music.

The Puritans had not aimed to suppress secular music, but they did oppose the theatre,[4] and this resulted in an attempt to evade their prohibition by disguising a theatrical spectacle as a musical concert. English opera, therefore, as represented by *The Siege of Rhodes*, was born four years before the return of Charles II in 1660. Paradoxically, the result

[3] Parry in OHM III, 196–97. The song "Back, shepherd, back" in Henry Lawes's setting of Milton's *Comus* (perf. 1634) is typical of this style.

[4] Scholes, *The Puritans and Music*, chap. XIII *et passim*; Bannard, "Music of the Commonwealth."

of that event was to put a stop to opera by removing the prohibition against stage plays. English audiences preferred spoken drama, and once this was permitted they no longer had any interest in maintaining a form which to them represented only a makeshift, called forth by special circumstances. Theatre music, to be sure, was composed after the Restoration, but not in the form of opera; it was confined for the most part to masques and incidental music for plays, and the style in both these fields was affected by foreign influences.

The English tendency to underrate their own music in comparison with that of continental composers has been a bane of their musical history ever since Elizabethan times. That a true English style in dramatic music survived as long as it did—that is, until the end of the seventeenth century—was due partly to the strength of the old tradition, partly to the Commonwealth (which had decidedly not welcomed continental artists), and partly to the genius of a very small number of English composers who were either conservative enough or of sufficiently original genius to resist foreign domination. In the sixteenth and early seventeenth centuries the predominant foreign influence had been Italian; a number of Italian musicians appeared in the first years of the Restoration: there were Italian operas at the court in 1660; G. B. Draghi arrived in 1667;[5] Nicola Matteis about 1672 introduced the works of the Italian school of violin composers in England;[6] a celebrated castrato, Giovanni Francesco Grossi (known as "Siface"), tarried briefly in London in 1687 and probably introduced there some of the music of Scarlatti.[7] But Charles II, who had learned to admire French music at the court of Versailles during his exile, and who soon after his restoration organized a band of twenty-four violins (that is, a string orchestra) in emulation of the *vingt-quatre violons* of Louis XIV, showed himself disposed to encourage French composers rather than Italian. Thus in 1666 a Frenchman, one Louis Grabu, was appointed Master of the King's Music, the highest official musical post in England. Grabu was undoubtedly a better courtier than composer, if we may judge by his chief work, a setting of Dryden's *Albion and Albanius* (1685) in three acts, along the lines of a French opera prologue. The music, a feeble imitation of Lully, dealt the death blow to this "monument of

[5] Pepys, *Diary*, Feb. 12, 1667.
[6] Cf. Evelyn, *Diary*, Nov. 19, 1674.
[7] *Ibid.*, Jan. 30 and April 19, 1687; Dent, *Alessandro Scarlatti*, p. 37.

stupidity"[8] as far as public success was concerned. King Charles tried to lure Lully from Paris but failing in the attempt was obliged to be content with Cambert, who found himself out of employment in Paris when Lully took over the Académie de Musique in 1672. Cambert was in London from 1673 until his death in 1677, and two of his operas were performed there in 1674.[9] In addition to these and other importations, Charles sent a number of young English musicians, among them Pelham Humfrey (1647–74), to acquire a French polish under Lully at Paris.[10]

In spite of foreign influences, however, the vitality of English music was preserved in the latter part of the seventeenth century by three composers : Matthew Locke, John Blow, and Henry Purcell.

Locke, the eldest of the three, had received his training during the Commonwealth and was at the height of his powers during the early years of the Restoration. He composed portions of the music for revivals of Shakespeare's *Macbeth* in 1672 and *The Tempest* in 1674.[11] These and similar Shakespearean performances were decked out with machines and added songs, ballets, and instrumental pieces; the language was altered, the order of scenes changed, prologues and even new episodes and characters were added to make an operatic entertainment of a sort frequently burlesqued in the popular theatres. Nevertheless, this tradition of plays with music is important, since it was for such productions that Purcell later wrote most of his dramatic compositions. Another work for which Locke furnished some of the music was *Psyche* (?1674), an adaptation by Shadwell of Lully's "tragi-comedy-ballet" of the same name. The music of *Psyche* was published in 1675 under the title "The English Opera." It is of interest as showing the strong French influence in English theatre music at this time and for the skillful setting of English recitative; but on the whole it lacks distinction and is generally regarded as inferior to Locke's earlier dramatic pieces or his instrumental works.

Although he produced only one complete work for the stage, John Blow (1649–1708) [12] is the most important English dramatic composer

[8] Dent, *Foundations of English Opera*, p. 165.
[9] *Ariane ou le mariage de Bacchus* (probably with revisions by Grabu) and *Pomone*. See Tessier, "Robert Cambert à Londres"; Flood, "Cambert et Grabu à Londres."
[10] Pepys, *Diary*, Nov. 15, 1667.
[11] McManaway, "Songs and Masques in *The Tempest*."
[12] Clarke, "Dr. John Blow" (Harvard Dissertation, 1947).

before Purcell. His *Venus and Adonis* (1684 or 1685), although sub-
titled "a masque," is really a little pastoral opera, with the simplest
possible plot and continuous music. The first act, after a long dialogue
between Venus and Adonis, ends with a chorus of huntsmen and a
dance. The entire second act is an interlude: first a scene in which
Cupid instructs all the little Cupids (in the form of a spelling lesson) in
the art of causing the wrong people to fall in love with each other; then
a half-serious conversation between Venus and Cupid, ending with a
dance of Cupid and the three Graces. The farewell of Venus and Adonis,
and the latter's death, are set to pathetic strains in the third act; Venus
bids Cupid bear Adonis to heaven, and the chorus calls on Echo and
the Nymphs to mourn his death.

In its musical style and proportions, *Venus and Adonis*, like Purcell's
*Dido and Aeneas*, shows the influence of the Italian cantata rather than
the opera; certain details, however, suggest that Blow was well
acquainted with Cambert's works and with at least the instrumental
portions of Lully's. The overture is on the French pattern, though with
a rather more contrapuntal style and an individual harmonic idiom.
The prologue, like many of Lully's, introduces allegorical figures discoursing on love in general terms, and ends with an "entry," that is, a
ballet. Little coloratura phrases on descriptive words in the recitatives
and songs are reminiscent of the French practice, as is also the common

*Venus and Adonis*, Act II

EXAMPLE 45                                                                    BLOW

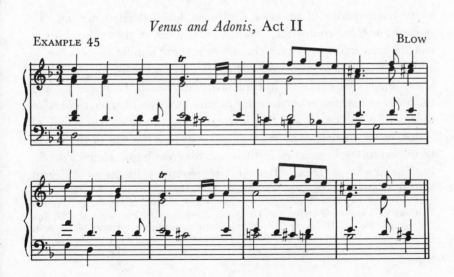

device of echoing the final phrase of a chorus or solo. An important part is given to ballets and choruses, and there is a relatively large amount of instrumental music, including particularly a "ground" (that is, a passacaglia) in the finale of Act II and a lovely "sarabrand" in the same scene, beginning with a descending chromatic bass (Example 45).

Typically English are the forthright melodies, such as the duet "O let him not from hence remove" in Act I (Example 46). Above all, Blow's

EXAMPLE 46                   *Venus and Adonis*, Prologue                   BLOW

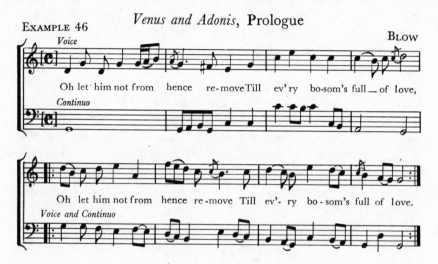

music has a quality of sincerity, directness, and independence, an "air of owing nothing to anyone," [13] which lifts it out of the realm of mere courtly show and gives to his characters a living human likeness beside which the conventional figures of French opera seem like puppets. The lamenting cry of Venus on hearing of Adonis' death (Example 47) and the nobly elegiac final chorus exemplify this quality which has marked so much of English music, whether in the national folk songs, the motets of Tallis, or the madrigals of Wilbye, and which at the end of the seventeenth century is incarnated in Blow and his great pupil, Henry Purcell.

The music of Henry Purcell [14] represents a fusion of different

[13] H. Watkins Shaw in *Grove's Dictionary* [5], *s.v.* "Blow."

[14] Biography by J. A. Westrup (1937, 1949); R. E. Moore, *Henry Purcell and the Restoration Theatre*; Rolland, in Lavignac, *Encyclopédie*, Part I, Vol. III, pp. 1881–94; I. Holst, ed., *Henry Purcell*; relevant sections in the histories of Hawkins (IV, 495–539), Burney, and Parry (OHM III); last three chapters of Dent's *Foundations of English Opera*; Barclay Squire's bibliographical study, "Purcell's Dramatic Music."

EXAMPLE 47  *Venus and Adonis*, Act III  BLOW

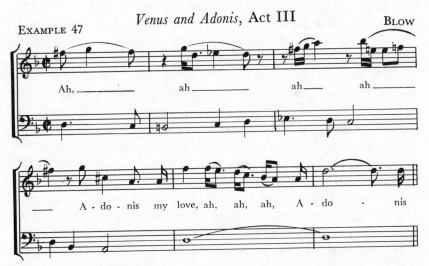

Ah,_____ ah_____ ah___ ah_____

_____ A - do - nis my love, ah, ah, ah, A - do - nis

national style qualities. His early training under Captain Henry Cooke, master of the boys of the Royal Chapel, made him familiar with the English musical tradition; from Pelham Humfrey he undoubtedly learned something of the French manner of composition, and from Blow the Italian, but these elements were always dominated by a genius essentially individual and imbued with national feeling. The dramatic work of Purcell includes only one opera in the strict sense—that is, sung throughout—namely *Dido and Aeneas*. Composed for performance at a girls' school in 1689, it is on the scale of a chamber opera rather than a full stage work, though exquisite in detail and effective in performance. The rest of Purcell's theatre music consists of overtures, interludes, masques, songs, dances, choruses, and other music for plays;[15] but in some cases the extent and importance of the musical numbers are so great that the works may rightly be considered operas, and indeed were commonly so called in England at the time.[16]

It will readily be seen that such productions are similar to the Renaissance Italian plays with intermedi and the French dramatic ballets, though of course their immediate forebears are the masque and the comedy-ballets of Molière and Lully. It is remarkable how long it

[15] The principal ones are: *Dioclesian*, 1690; *King Arthur*, 1691; *The Fairy Queen*, 1692; *The Indian Queen*, 1695; *The Tempest*, 1695; *Bonduca*, 1695; and the masque in *Timon of Athens*, 1694.

[16] Cf. Locke's preface to *Psyche*, 1675.

took before poets and composers worked out fully the implications of the ideal of *dramma per musica*, drama carried on wholly by means of music. To be sure, in Italian opera all the dialogue was sung and, at least with composers like Monteverdi and Cavalli, often sung in appropriately flexible and expressive recitative. Nevertheless the Italian tendency, as we have seen, was constantly toward sharpening the contrast in musical style between action dialogue on the one hand and verses expressing emotion on the other. Even their arias, solos and duets in regular closed musical forms with periodic melody, were at first treated almost like interpolations and given only to subordinate characters, while larger musical units involving choruses and dances were held quite distinct from the development of the action itself. By and large, this was the state of affairs in Lully's *tragédies lyriques* also. But early German opera often, the French comedy-ballet always, and early English opera with only two or three exceptions, kept the distinction absolute : spoken dialogue for the action, music only for "set numbers."

When we examine Purcell's music, we are impressed first of all by the fresh, engaging quality of his melodies, so like in feeling to English folk songs. The air "Pursue thy conquest, love" from Act I of *Dido and Aeneas*, with its horn-call figures and constant lively echoing between melody and bass, suggests the sounds and bustle of the chase. In *King Arthur* the martial "Come if you dare" shows an English adaptation of the popular trumpet aria of Italian opera, with two of these instruments concertizing in the introduction and interlude, and the characteristic rhythmic motif ♩ ♩ common in French music and so appropriate to the declamation of English words (Example 48).

## *King Arthur*, Act I

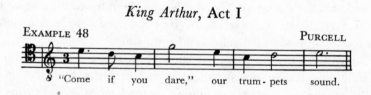

EXAMPLE 48                                                        PURCELL

"Come  if  you  dare,"  our  trum - pets  sound.

The duet "Fear no danger" from Act I of *Dido and Aeneas* is similar in rhythm and style to the duets of Lully. No less characteristic, though in a different mood, is an aria such as "Charon the peaceful shade invites" from *Dioclesian* (Example 49), with the two concertizing flutes,

## *Dioclesian*, Act II

EXAMPLE 49

PURCELL

the three- and six-measure phrases, the delicate cross relations, and the word painting on "hastes." There are also many fine comic airs and duets, particularly in the lesser theatre pieces.[17] Da capo arias are not frequent in Purcell, but he uses most effectively the older form of the passacaglia or ground, the best example of which is Dido's "When I am laid in earth" from the last act of *Dido and Aeneas*, one of the most affecting expressions of tragic grief in all opera. Another air of this kind is the "plaint" ("O let me weep") from Act V of *The Fairy Queen*.

Purcell's recitative is found at its best in *Dido and Aeneas*, the only one of his operas that gives opportunity for genuine dramatic dialogue. The treatment, as Dent points out,[18] has nothing in common with the Italian recitativo secco; rather, the style is that of free arioso, admitting expressive florid passages, and always maintaining a clear rhythmic, formal, and harmonic organization, yet without sacrificing correctness of declamation or expressive power. The dialogue in the parting scene between Dido and Aeneas (Act III) and the beautiful arioso phrase which introduces Dido's last aria show what can be done by way of dramatic musical setting of the English language, that despised tongue which has been so often condemned as "unsuitable for opera." In Purcell's other works there are isolated examples of recitative phrases, including one from *The Indian Queen* which Dr. Burney called "the best piece of recitative in our language" [19] (Example 50).

The overtures to Purcell's operas are in the same general form as the French overtures of Lully; one of the finest examples is found in *Dioclesian*. Other instrumental music includes "act tunes" (that is, interludes or introductions), and there are some interesting examples of the canzona and other forms.[20] There are dance pieces of all kinds, including the hornpipe, *paspe* (French *passepied*), canaries, and special descriptive dances as in Lully; a favorite type (also common in French opera) is the chaconne or ground, which is often placed for climax toward the end of a scene, and in which dancing is combined with solo and choral singing as well as with instrumental accompaniment.[21] Descriptive symphonies

[17] Examples: "Dear pretty youth" (*The Tempest*), "Celia has a thousand charms" (*The Rival Sisters*), "I'll sail upon the dogstar" (*A Fool's Preferment*), "Celimene pray tell me" (*Oroonoko*), and the song of the drunken poet "Fi-fi-fi-fill up the bowl" (*The Fairy Queen*, Act I).

[18] *Foundations of English Opera*, pp. 188–92.

[19] *History* (2d ed.) II, 392.

[20] *Indian Queen*, Acts II and III; *Fairy Queen*, Act IV; *King Arthur*, Act V.

[21] Examples in *King Arthur*, Act III; *Dioclesian*, Act III (in canon form).

## The Indian Queen, Act III

EXAMPLE 50                                                    PURCELL

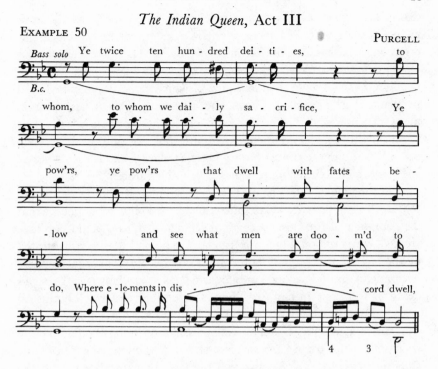

occur, such as the introduction to the song "Ye blustering bretheren" in Act V of *King Arthur* or the famous "Cold" symphony and chorus "See, see, we assemble" from Act III—a scene perhaps suggested by the chorus of *trembleurs* in Lully's *Isis*.

The choruses in Purcell's operas contain some of his best music. Such numbers as "Sing Io's" from Act II of *Dioclesian*, with stately vigorous rhythms, brilliant voice groupings, orchestral interludes, and passages of harmony contrasting with contrapuntal sections, foreshow the broad, sonorous choral movements in Handel's oratorios. Other choruses in Purcell are more like those of Lully, in strict chordal style with piquant rhythms;[22] still others show the influences of the English madrigal tradition.[23] Finally, there are the choruses of lamentation, such as "With drooping wings," from *Dido and Aeneas*, which (like many other features of this opera) has a worthy predecessor in the closing number of Blow's *Venus and Adonis*. Except for *Dido and Aeneas*, where the

[22] E.g., " 'Tis love that hath warmed us," from *King Arthur*, Act III.
[23] "In these delightful pleasant groves," from *The Libertine*.

chorus has a part in the action, Purcell's choral numbers usually occur in scenes devoted to spectacle or entertainment, corresponding to the ceremonies, ballets, and the like in French opera. There are scenes of this kind in *Bonduca* (Act III), *King Arthur* (Acts I and III), and *The Indian Queen* (Act V). The masques, of which examples may be found particularly in *Timon of Athens* and *The Fairy Queen*, also contain many choruses and dances; for parallels to these masques, with their fantastic settings and characters, we must look not only in the French opera but also in the contemporary popular plays of the Italian Theatre at Paris, which contain many scenes of a similar nature.[24]

On the whole, it is difficult to accept Romain Rolland's estimate [25] of Purcell's genius as "frail" or "incomplete." It is difficult to believe that the composer of the closing scenes of *Dido and Aeneas* could not have created a true national opera in England if he had not been frustrated by the lack of an adequate librettist and by his apparently inescapable servitude to an undeveloped public taste.[26] As it was, however, Purcell's death in 1695 put an end to all hope for the future of English musical drama. London was even then full of Italian musicians; audiences became fascinated with Italian opera, and English composers did no more than follow the trend. The success of M. A. Bononcini's *Trionfo di Camilla, regina de' Volsci* in 1706 marked the capitulation, and the fashion was completely established by the time of Handel's arrival and the performance of his *Rinaldo* in 1711.

There was at least one Englishman who viewed this state of operatic affairs with regret. Joseph Addison in the *Spectator* frequently alluded to the absurdities of Italian opera in England and in one issue [27] wrote a long essay in criticism of Italian recitative, with acute observations on the relation of language to national style in music and an exhortation to English composers to emulate Lully by inventing a recitative proper to their own language: "I would allow the *Italian* Opera to lend our *English* Musick as much as may grace and soften it, but never entirely to annihilate and destroy it." That this was a vain hope, Addison had virtually admitted in an earlier letter which so well sums up the situation of opera in England at the beginning of the eighteenth century that it deserves to be quoted at length :

[24] Gherardi, *Théâtre italien*.
[25] In Lavignac, *Encyclopédie*, Part I, Vol. III, p. 1894.
[26] Cf. the preface to *The Fairy Queen*.
[27] No. 29, Tuesday, April 3, 1711.

It is my Design in this Paper to deliver down to Posterity a faithful Account of the Italian Opera, and of the gradual Progress which it has made upon the English Stage : For there is no Question but our great Grand-children will be very curious to know the Reason why their Fore-fathers used to sit together like an Audience of Foreigners in their own Country, and to hear whole Plays acted before them in a Tongue which they did not understand.

*Arsinoe* [28] was the first Opera that gave us a Taste of Italian Musick. The great Success which this Opera met with, produced some Attempts of forming Pieces upon Italian Plans, that should give a more natural and reasonable Entertainment than what can be met with in the elaborate Trifles of that Nation. This alarm'd the Poetasters and Fiddlers of the Town, who were used to deal in a more ordinary Kind of Ware; and therefore laid down as an established Rule, which is receiv'd as such to this very day, *That nothing is capable of being well set to Musick, that is not Nonsense.*

This Maxim was no sooner receiv'd, but we immediately fell to trans-lating the Italian Operas; and as there was no great Danger of hurting the Sense of those extraordinary Pieces, our Authors would often make Words of their own, that were entirely foreign to the Meaning of the Passages which they pretended to translate. [Here Addison gives some instances of inept translations, and continues :] By this Means the soft Notes that were adapted to Pity in the Italian, fell upon the Word Rage in the English; and the angry Sounds that were turn'd to Rage in the Original, were made to express Pity in the Translation. It oftentimes happen'd likewise, that the finest Notes in the Air fell upon the most insignificant Words in the Sentence. I have known the word *And* pursu'd through the whole Gamut, have been entertain'd with many a melodious *The*, and have heard the most beautiful Graces Quavers and Divisions bestow'd upon *Then*, *For*, and *From*; to the eternal Honour of our English Particles.

The next Step to our Refinement, was the introducing of Italian Actors into our Opera; who sung their Parts in their own Language, at the same Time that our Countrymen perform'd theirs in our native Tongue. The King or Hero of the Play generally spoke in Italian, and his Slaves answer'd him in English : The Lover frequently made his Court, and gain'd the Heart of his Princess in a Language which she did not understand. One would have thought it very difficult to have carry'd on Dialogues after this Manner, without an Interpreter between the Persons that convers'd together; but this was the State of the English Stage for about three Years.

At length the Audience grew tir'd of understanding Half the Opera, and therefore to ease themselves intirely of the Fatigue of Thinking, have

---

[28] *Arsinoe* was performed in 1706; the text was a translation from the Italian, the music by Thomas Clayton. See Burney, *History* (2d ed.) II, 655; Fassini, "Gli albori del melodramma italiano a Londra"; Nicoll, "Italian Opera in England."

so order'd it at Present that the whole Opera is perform'd in an unknown Tongue. We no longer understand the Language of our own Stage. . . .

It does not want any great Measure of Sense to see the Ridicule of this monstrous Practice; but what makes it the more astonishing, it is not the Taste of the Rabble, but of Persons of the greatest Politeness, which has establish'd it. . . .

At present, our Notions of Musick are so very uncertain, that we do not know what it is we like, only, in general, we are transported with anything that is not English : so if it be of a foreign Growth, let it be Italian, French, or High-Dutch, it is the same thing. In short, our English Musick is quite rooted out, and nothing yet planted in its stead.[29]

[29] *The Spectator*, No. 18, Wednesday, March 21, 1711. See also two essays from *The Spectator* in Strunk, *Source Readings*, pp. 511–17; and cf. the accounts quoted in Lowens, "*The Touch-Stone* (1728): A Neglected View of London Opera."

PART 3

*THE
EIGHTEENTH
CENTURY*

# CHAPTER 13

# MASTERS OF THE EARLY EIGHTEENTH CENTURY

During the early part of the eighteenth century the younger librettists and composers in Italy were gradually evolving a new type of serious opera that was to dominate the scene for over a hundred years. This new Italian *opera seria* will be the subject of our next chapter. For the present, our concern is with certain composers of the first half of the century who in the main kept to types of opera already long established, and whose works include some of the best dramatic music of the period. The principal composers of this group are Keiser in Germany, Handel in England, Rameau in France, and A. Scarlatti in Italy.

KEISER. Reinhard Keiser (1674–1739)[1] was the most talented of the Hamburg composers. He is reputed to have written over one hundred and twenty operas, of which, however, only twenty-five have been preserved. Writing with a sureness of style and fertility of invention which remind one of Mozart, Keiser completed the process begun by Franck and Kusser, taking over a full measure of contemporary Italian and French operatic achievements but uniting them in a highly individual way with fundamental German qualities. A worldly, adventurous, impulsive, energetic personality, a musician who commanded the deepest respect of other musicians, Keiser was important historically not only for his own work but also for his direct influence on Handel, whose early Hamburg success stung the older composer at one time to open rivalry.[2] Keiser in the course of his works traversed the road from

[1] H. C. Wolff, *Die Barockoper in Hamburg*; Leichtentritt, *Reinhard Keiser in seinen Opern*; Voigt, "Reinhard Keiser"; Lindner, *Die erste stehende deutsche Oper*.

[2] Chrysander, *Händel* I, 129–34. For a list of some of Handel's thematic "borrowings" from Keiser, see the preface to the Händelgesellschaft edition of *Octavia*.

the heavy-textured music of the late baroque toward the light, thin, and playful *style galant* of the eighteenth century. His career was thus an epitome of an age of transition. It was also, unfortunately, an epitome of the declining fortunes of the Hamburg opera. The librettos of his later works (*Prinz Jodelet* may serve as an example) show an increasing tendency toward the burlesque, the trivial, the vulgar, and the indecent; unskillful poets, pandering to the lowest tastes of an ignorant public, led the way to extinction of German opera, while Keiser lacked either the will or the greatness of soul to fight against the current. Yet at its best the music of Keiser will stand comparison with that of the greatest of his contemporaries—Purcell, Steffani, Scarlatti, even Handel. The influence of Lully and the French school may be traced in his choruses, ballets, and instrumental pieces. He made no fundamental changes in opera, but his work is remarkable for three features: the flexibility of form in the arias, the skill and elaborateness of the orchestral accompaniments, and the mastery of effect in lyrical and tragic scenes. The da capo does not predominate in Keiser's arias, as it did in those of his Italian contemporaries; when used, it is often modified in subtle ways which suggest the freedom of the earlier Venetian period.[3] In addition, there are many shorter types—arioso melodies, German lieder—occurring at places where the dramatic situation requires something other than the da capo pattern. On the whole, Keiser's melodic lines, although certainly not unvocal, do not show that instinctive adaptation to the qualities and limitations of the voice which is the gift of nearly all Italian composers: there are more wide intervals, angular phrases, and instrumental idioms. The characteristic mood is more energetic and aggressive than in Steffani. No composer of opera demands a higher degree of virtuosity in bravura-type arias; this is especially true in those arias with Italian texts which are often found in the midst of otherwise German operas—a peculiar practice beginning with *Claudius* in 1703 and increasing in the later works, and for which parallels may be found in both France and England at the same period. There are some arias with simple continuo accompaniment and a very few in which the continuo instruments are omitted from the orchestra. A special effect is created in the arias *all' unisono*, where the violins or violas in unison (sometimes with an oboe added), or all the strings in octaves, concertize with the voice, while the continuo fills in the harmonies. Accompaniments of this sort were

[3] See for example the aria "Hoffe noch" in *Croesus*, Act I, sc. 2.

fashionable in Italian opera around 1700; examples may be found in the works of Scarlatti and Handel. Sometimes with Keiser the vocal line will be doubled at the unison by a solo instrument or by all the strings. Repeated chords or broken-chord figures are frequent in the orchestral accompaniments. The orchestral parts are particularly noteworthy in the many arias with obbligato solo instruments, which appear sometimes in novel combinations (for example, four bassoons or three oboes), produc-

## *Octavia*, Act II, sc. 6

EXAMPLE 51

ing great richness and variety of texture. Instruments are used effectively for descriptive touches, as in Octavia's aria "Wallet nicht zu laut" (Example 51).

Keiser's recitative is somewhat short breathed, cadencing frequently; it is no mere colorless declamation of text, however, but freely introduces expressive phrases and arioso passages, thus harking back to the older Venetian practice. Such phrases are sometimes used in recurring fashion to give point to the dramatic situation, for example in *Octavia*, Act I, scene 4 (Example 52. Note the descent from the third at the

### *Octavia*, Act I, sc. 4

EXAMPLE 52                                            KEISER
(Performed)

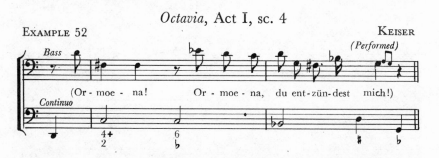

(Or-moe-na!    Or-moe-na, du ent-zün-dest    mich!)

cadence, which is characteristic). The vitality of Keiser's treatment of the text is well summed up by Mattheson : "I believe assuredly that in the time he flourished there was no composer who . . . had set words to music so richly, naturally, flowingly, attractively, or (above all) so distinctly, understandably, and eloquently."[4]

Keiser's chief opera is *Der hochmütige, gestürtzte und wieder erhabene Croesus* ("Croesus Haughty, Overthrown, and Again Raised Up"), on one of the most popular librettos of the Venetian poet Minato, translated and arranged by Von Bostel.[5] The plot is an amusing hodgepodge of impossible melodramatic situations, but it has the operatic virtue of providing many opportunities for strong expression of moods (*Affekten*) as well as for pastoral scenes in the second act. There are two versions of this work, one from 1710 and the other a revision by Keiser for a revival in 1730. The two versions show some interesting differences in detail, aside from the generally higher quality of music in the latter. For example, the ballets were omitted in 1730. In the original version, the overture was on the French pattern; in 1730, an overture of the

---

[4] *Ehrenpforte*, p. 129.
[5] See Beare, *The German Popular Play Atis and the Venetian Opera.*

Italian type was substituted : a fanfare-like opening movement in simple texture, with musical material and formal treatment like the first movement of an early symphony; a short adagio consisting of broken-chord figures over a sequential series of seventh chords; and a "third" movement which is nothing but a da capo repetition of the first.

Examples of Keiser's lyrical and tragic power are plentiful in *Croesus* : the spontaneous charm of Elmira's "Sobald dich nur mein Auge sah," with the clever cadence at which Atis (a mute personage in this scene) responds to her question by a gesture on the chord of resolution, is unequaled (Example 53); the pastoral solo and duet "Mein

*Croesus*, Act I, sc. 6

EXAMPLE 53

Kätchen ist ein Mädchen" (Act II, scene 3) is in the purest German lied style; Croesus' aria "Götter, übt Barmherzigkeit," over a recurring bass motif, is filled with noble pathos (Example 54). Altogether, there is ample justification in the music for Mattheson's punning laudatory

EXAMPLE 54   *Croesus*, Act III, sc. 12

reference to the composer as "ein Kaiser des Gesangs" ("an emperor of song").[6]

The Hamburg composers after Keiser need not detain us long. Johann Mattheson (1681–1764)[7] is more important as a theorist and historian than as a composer. Christoph Graupner (1683–1760) is noted more for his church works and instrumental pieces than for his operas.[8] G. C. Schürmann, Handel, and K. H. Graun all appear in the Hamburg list, but their work chiefly centered elsewhere. The change in musical style announced by Keiser's *Prinz Jodelet* and other later works was completed by Georg Philipp Telemann,[9] whose fabulous productivity included some twenty operas for the Hamburg stage in addition to an even larger number for Leipzig and other cities. Telemann was the most progressive German composer of his day and was far more renowned than Bach. His music belongs fully to the rococo period of the eighteenth century. In opera he excelled in the comic style; his intermezzi *Pimpinone* [10] (Hamburg, 1725; the text a mixture of Italian and German) are a model of Italian opera buffa style, strikingly similar in both subject and musical idiom to the more famous *Serva padrona* of Pergolesi which appeared eight years later.

The closing of the Hamburg opera in 1738 marked the end of German opera for nearly half a century; although scattered native companies held on for a few years in other cities, the creative impulse that had called them into being was long since spent. The spirit of common-sense rationalism, the decline of the court-centered life of the wealthy bourgeoisie, and the rise of a commercially-minded middle class, all contributed to this outcome. As in England, so in Germany, opera became an exotic; national opera was abandoned in favor of the imported product from Italy.

[6] *Ehrenpforte*, p. 133.

[7] Autobiography in his *Ehrenpforte*; Cannon, *Johann Mattheson*; Meinardus, "Mattheson und seine Verdienste um die deutsche Tonkunst"; H. Schmidt, *Johann Mattheson*; Haberl, "Johann Mattheson."

[8] See Noack, "Die Opern von Christoph Graupner in Darmstadt."

[9] Autobiography in Mattheson's *Ehrenpforte*; Rolland, "L'Autobiographe d'un illustre oublié"; Ottzen, *Telemann als Opernkomponist*; Valentin, *Georg Philipp Telemann*; Schering, *Musikgeschichte Leipzigs* II, 437–71; Menke, *Das Vocalwerk Georg Philipp Telemanns*; T. W. Werner, "Zum Neudruck von . . . *Pimpinone*."

[10] German title: *Die ungleiche Heyrath oder Das herrsch-süchtige Camer Mädgen*. This work may not be entirely Telemann's: he may have incorporated or adapted music from a *Pimpinone* (Venice, 1708) by Tomaso Albinoni (1671–1750), only setting the German recitatives and adding a few German arias. (Loewenberg, *Annals*, 2d ed., col. 152.)

HANDEL.[11] Handel's operas do not loom large in the estimation of most of his present-day admirers. Passage of time and changes in operatic style have thrust them into ill-deserved oblivion; modern revivals,[12] while revealing a multitude of beauties, at the same time have raised many questions with regard to the proper "adjustment" of these works for twentieth-century audiences. They conform to the conventions of their time, and the music, much of which was composed under extremely unfavorable conditions, is not always at the highest level of inspiration. Nevertheless, the best of Handel in this field is not only superior to anything his contemporaries were writing but also forms historically a culminating point which makes the works of Steffani and Keiser seem almost like preliminary stages. Like Bach at Leipzig, Handel in London worked in comparative isolation from the so-called advanced currents of the day—an isolation due not to ignorance but to independence; and though his later operas make some concessions to the fashionable modern style, he never capitulated to it entirely and indeed abandoned opera for oratorio when it became evident that his own way of writing could not hold the favor of the London opera-going public against the combined competition of the new ballad operas on the one hand and the modern Italian music of Porpora, Hasse, and Galuppi on the other.

Handel's first opera, *Almira*, was performed at Hamburg in 1705. The poem, a typical Hamburg libretto with comic scenes and ballets, is a mixture of German and Italian, and the music shows many traces of Keiser's influence. A visit to Italy from 1707 to 1709 resulted in the Italian operas *Rodrigo* (Florence, 1707) and *Agrippina* (Venice, 1709), and also a number of other stage works and Italian cantatas. In 1710 Handel accepted a position as director of music at the court of Hanover.

[11] On the operas of George Frideric Handel (1685–1759) see the standard biographies by Mainwaring, Chrysander, Leichtentritt (with plot synopses of all the operas), Rolland, Dent, Rockstro, Flower, and Siegmund-Schultze; Burney, *History* (2d ed.) II, 672–835 *et passim*; Hawkins, *History* (1776) Vol. V, Book III, chaps. 6–7; Mattheson, *Ehrenpforte*, pp. 93–101; Deutsch, *Handel: A Documentary Biography*; Dean, *Handel's Dramatic Oratorios and Masques*; Poladian, "Handel as an Opera Composer"; Dent, "The Operas," in Abraham, ed., *Handel: A Symposium*; Powers, "*Il Serse trasformato*"; articles in the Händel-Jahrbuch, *passim*.

[12] Notably in Germany since the 1920s; see H. C. Wolff, *Die Händel-Oper auf der modernen Bühne*; Loewenberg, *Annals* (2d ed.), col. 152; Steglich, articles in ZfMw and *Zeitschrift für Musik*, 1920–27, *passim*; *idem*, "Die neue Händel-Opern-Bewegung"; *Die Göttinger Händel-Festspiele* (1953); *Festschrift zur Händel-Ehrung* (1959).

The maturity of style evident in *Agrippina*, where Handel showed himself fully capable of assimilating the art of the Italian masters Legrenzi and Scarlatti, came to even fuller realization in *Rinaldo* (1711), the work by which he was first introduced to London, and one of the most popular of all his operas.[13] The London visit was so successful that Handel obtained permission from his master, the elector of Hanover, to return in 1712; and this time, whether by intention or negligence, he overstayed his leave. With the sudden death of Queen Anne in 1714 the elector ascended the English throne as George I, and the famous "reconciliation" between king and composer took place shortly afterwards.[14] Between 1712 and 1741, Handel produced thirty-six operas in London, of which the most notable were *Radamisto* (1720), *Ottone* (1723), *Giulio Cesare* and *Tamerlano* (1724), and *Rodelinde* (1725). The later works (for example, *Orlando*, 1733; *Serse*, 1738, his only comic opera) show a tendency toward a more facile kind of music, influenced to some extent by the newer Italian style with which Handel had refreshed his acquaintance on a trip to Italy in 1728–29. During much of the time in London, Handel was not only composer and conductor but manager and impresario as well, with all the troubles incident to such a position. The Royal Academy of Music, which had been opened in 1720, was for a time highly successful but finally had to close its doors in 1728. A new company, founded under Handel's direction the following year, soon fell into difficulties; reorganized in 1733, it was opposed by a rival group (the "Opera of the Nobility"), and both undertakings ended in complete bankruptcy four years later. A breakdown in health forced Handel to retire from active work for some months, and his last operas were produced in London between 1738 and 1741 by the Swiss impresario Heidegger. A blow to the prosperity of Italian opera in London was the fabulous success of the *Beggar's Opera* (1728) and its numerous offspring, with their satirical tendencies, evidencing a reaction in England against the "foreign growth" of which Addison had complained twenty years earlier. Wearied by the material difficulties and discouraged by the waning fortunes of opera, Handel had already begun in the 1730s

---

[13] *Rinaldo* was revised in 1731. On the original London performances see the *Spectator*, No. 5 (March 6, 1711; in Strunk, *Source Readings*, pp. 511–14) and No. 14 (March 16, 1711; both essays in Deutsch, *Handel*, pp. 35–37). Cf. Babcock, "Francis Coleman's 'Register of Operas.' "

[14] The story (possibly apocryphal) of the reconciliation and the composition of the "Water Music" is told by Mainwaring in his *Memoirs* (1760), pp. 89–92.

to turn his attention to oratorio; *Saul* and *Israel in Egypt* were performed in 1739, and in the following years came the other masterpieces by which the composer is best known today.

Handel's operas will not be understood if they are regarded merely as examples of an outworn operatic formula, composed because such was the fashionable thing to do or the best way to make money, and unworthy of remembrance except for a few arias to be sung in modern recital programs. Such views have been advanced by persons who should know better; unqualified acceptance of them can be founded only on ignorance of the nature of this type of opera, on insufficient knowledge of the scores, or on a misunderstanding of Handel's character. These operas, as Leichtentritt has pointed out,[15] are based on the presentation of moods not mixed and modified as in "real" life, but each pure, so that a character at any given moment of expression is for the time being simply the incarnation of a certain state of mind and feeling; thus the complete picture of the character is to be obtained by the synthesis of all these expressive moments rather than, as in modern drama, by the analysis of a complex of moods expressed in a single aria or scene. For such an aesthetic, the questions of consistency and plausibility in the plot are secondary : it is of little importance what a situation is or how it comes about, provided that it gives occasion for expression of a mood. On the other hand, music, being free to devote itself to its peculiar function of unmixed emotional expression, expands freely into forms conditioned only by its own nature, unrestricted by requirements of so-called naturalness on the stage. Once this fundamental idea is grasped —and its difficulty is due only to the fact that it happens to be different from modern dramatic principles—then it is easy to perceive that the form of a Handel opera, with its continual succession of recitative and aria, its ubiquitous da capos, and all the other apparently artificial features, is in reality a musical structure of perfect artistic validity, whose restrictions, far from being arbitrary, exist only to assure freedom in essential matters.[16]

Handel was not a revolutionist in opera; he accepted the forms he found but filled them with his own inimitable genius. The subject matter is conventional, drawn from history (*Tolomeo*), mythology (*Admeto*), or romantic legend (*Orlando*). The chief librettists were Nicola Haym

[15] *Händel*, pp. 592 ff.; *Music, History, and Ideas*, pp. 150–51.
[16] Cf. H. Abert, "Händel," in *Gesammelte Schriften*, pp. 232–63.

(*Radamisto, Giulio Cesare, Ottone, Tamerlano*, and others) and Paolo Rolli (*Floridante, Scipione, Deidamia*, and others); Handel set only three of Metastasio's texts: *Siroe, Poro* (from *Alessandro nell' Indie*), and *Ezio*.

The overtures are for the most part of the French type, frequently with added movements after the allegro. One of the best overtures is that to *Agrippina*; in *Ottone* the allegro is followed by a gavotte, and then closes with a fast movement in concerto grosso style with solo passages for two oboes. The sinfonie, marches, and the like, which are used to introduce an act or scene or to accompany some stage business, are neither numerous nor distinctive, and the same may be said of the choruses as a general rule; dramatic use of the chorus—as in the pastorale *Acis and Galatea* and the operas *Ariodante* and *Alcina*—is exceptional. Ballets are few and of little importance.[17] The favorite ensemble form is the duet, in which Handel learned much from the example of Steffani.

The recitatives are remarkable for the richness and variety of their harmonic patterns, taking full advantage of modulatory possibilities and of the expressive quality of chords such as the Neapolitan sixth and the diminished seventh to underline the dramatic situation. In the comparatively rare accompanied recitatives (see Example 56) and even occasionally in the recitativo secco, the dramatic element is more prominent.[18] At times the recitative encloses distinct arioso passages or is combined with an aria in a free manner which relieves the prevailing regular alternation between the two styles [19] and recalls the scene-complex technique of Cavalli and other seventeenth-century composers.

With few exceptions, Handel's opera arias follow the da capo pattern, but within this framework there is inexhaustible variety.[20] The principle of musical development is the unified working out of one or two basic motives, by voice and instruments jointly, in a continuous flow, within which the various periods are organized by a clear key scheme and a systematic use of sequences. In many of the longer arias, a fairly distinct binary form may be perceived in the principal section. The middle section most often uses the same or similar thematic material,

[17] Roth, "Händel's Ballettmusiken."

[18] E.g., *Agrippina*, Act II, sc. 4.

[19] E.g., in *Poro*, Act I, sc. 9; *Serse*, Act I, sc. 2; and (on a greater scale) *Tamerlano*, Act III, sc. 10.

[20] Flögel, "Studien zur Arientechnik in den Opern Händels."

though it is usually shorter than the first section and somewhat contrasting in mood, accompaniment, and tonality. Even where at first glance the middle part of a da capo aria appears to be in complete contrast with the first, often subtle thematic relationships may be discovered. In sum, the whole formal treatment of the aria in Handel may be regarded as a climax of perfection in a style of which Steffani and Keiser were the forerunners. For details, one can only refer the student to the scores themselves, a careful study of which will be found to be both fascinating and rewarding.

The orchestra in Handel's operas is important chiefly (aside from the overtures) for its part in the accompaniment of the solo voice. Here it functions, as in Steffani and Keiser, as an equal partner with the singer. The basic instrumental group is formed by the strings and continuo, to which various instruments are frequently joined for obbligato parts (for example, solo violin, flutes, oboes, bassoons). The principle of opposition between *ripieno* and *concertino* is retained; accompaniments during the singing are entrusted to the smaller group, while the full orchestra joins in at cadences and for the ritornellos. Horns, trumpets, and trombones are used only with the chorus or for special effects. Many of the shorter arias are accompanied only by the continuo and one or two solo instruments, or by continuo and unisono violins. A few have accompaniment by continuo alone. In general, the cembalo parts are very sparsely indicated in the originals, since Handel usually played this instrument himself and needed notes only as a reminder. There are even occasionally some blank measures, marked only "cembalo" in the score, at which places we are to understand that the composer improvised.

Handel's use of tonality is a subject which has received considerable attention. Of the importance of the tonal scheme as a formal element within the aria there can be no doubt. Leichtentritt [21] has also emphasized the composer's tendency to associate certain keys with certain moods, as F major with calm, pastoral, or idyllic sentiments, G major for arias of cheerful character, F-sharp minor for the expression of suffering, and so on. Similar concepts were fairly widespread in the eighteenth century. [22] But an interesting question is raised by what

[21] See "Handel's Harmonic Art."

[22] Cf. Borrel, "Un Paradoxe musical au XVIIIe siècle"; Crussard ("Marc-Antoine Charpentier théoricien") gives Charpentier's and Rameau's tables of the qualities of the various major and minor keys, with reference to similar tables by Zarlino (1558), Mersenne (1627), Gantez (1643), Parran (1646), De Gouz (1650),

often looks like evidence of a tonal plan extending over not merely a single aria or scene but entire acts and even entire operas. The first act of *Amadigi* has a symmetrical tonal structure which it is difficult to believe could be accidental.[23] Many of the operas show a preference for one tonality which is established in the overture or at the beginning of the first act, returns briefly perhaps somewhere in the second, and is strongly confirmed in the finale.[24] A similar procedure is found in Keiser's *Croesus*, where the overture and first chorus are in D major, and each of the three acts ends in the same key. Purcell's *Dioclesian* seems to be in C major; his *Dido and Aeneas* is not unified in this way, though there is an evident tonal plan for each act.[25] But these observations, whatever significance they may have, are far from establishing any kind of general rule. Indeed, it seems hardly probable that we should find consistent, conscious tonal architecture throughout many operas of this period, where the choice of key for a given number was so often dictated by external considerations, such as the limitations of wind instruments, the presence of a certain singer, the transference of whole numbers from earlier compositions, or the mood suggested by the text. Nevertheless, the question remains open; a comprehensive study of operas, oratorios, and other large composite works of the late seventeenth and early eighteenth centuries from this point of view might lead to more definite conclusions.[26]

One trait which Handel shares with all composers of his epoch is the constant use of tone painting and musical symbolism. This ranges all

Masson (1705), Saint-Lambert (1707), and later ones by Grétry, Le Sueur, Lacombe, and J.-J. Rousseau.

[23] Leichtentritt, *Händel*, p. 643; *idem, Music, History, and Ideas*, p. 145; Steglich, "Händels Opern," in Adler, *Handbuch* II, 663–67.

[24] Examples: *Almira* (B-flat), *Scipione* (G), *Alessandro* (D), *Alcina* (B-flat, with instrumental pieces and chorus in G at the end, corresponding to similar forms in the same key in the second scene of Act I), *Atalanta* (D), *Silla* (G, with closing chorus in D), *Floridante* (A minor and major, closing chorus in D), *Flavio* (B-flat), *Ottone* (B-flat), *Tolomeo* (F), *Ricardo* (D), *Siroe* (F), *Ezio* (F), *Arianna* (D minor and major), *Ariodante* (G minor and major).

[25] Act I: C–F; Act II: D–A; Act III: B-flat–G minor. Cf. Dent, *Foundations of English Opera*, pp. 180–83.

[26] Cf. G. F. Schmidt, *Die frühdeutsche Oper* II, 315–17; Lorenz, after an exhaustive examination of A. Scarlatti's operas, could find no evidence of a consistently applied tonal plan, though in certain works (especially among the earlier ones) there are traces of it (*Scarlatti's Jugendoper*, p. 177 *et passim*). Gerber (*Der Operntypus Johann Adolf Hasses*, pp. 39–42) finds no evidence whatever in Hasse. The evidence for Rameau has been examined in a doctoral dissertation by E. G. Ahnell (1957), likewise with inconclusive results as far as a definite over-all tonal structure is concerned.

the way from naïve, playful imitation of natural sounds [27] through the brilliant trumpet arias [28] to such awe-inspiring effects as Claudio's "Cade il mondo" ("Let the world fall") in *Agrippina* (Act II, scene 4) with its downward plunge through two octaves to the low bass D (Example 55).

*Agrippina*, Act II, sc. 4

EXAMPLE 55                                    HANDEL

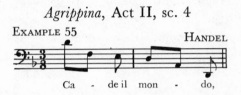

Ca   -   de il   mon   -   do,

Such places show the play of fancy, now whimsical, now earnest, on the surface of baroque musical forms, but they are no mere externals. All these picturesque or conventional figures are part of the music itself, inseparable from the structure they adorn—so much so that though, as in the London performance of *Rinaldo*, live birds may be released to flutter about the stage while flutes twitter in the orchestra, and the unreflecting person may hear only that the music is imitating the birds, yet the musician feels that this is not so, but rather that it is the birds who are imitating the music. Handel's art, like that of Bach, has the power of glorifying the apparently trivial by showing it to be a manifesation of the eternal; as the rhythm of walking feet becomes in Bach's chorale prelude the rhythm of the soul's march to Heaven, so in Handel the song of the birds is a magic window opening on a glimpse of pastoral Eden.

This universal quality is, of course, most apparent in those arias that are pure expression of moods, with few or no picturesque external details. The number and variety of these arias is so great, and the power of capturing the most subtle nuances of feeling so astounding, that one is tempted to believe there is no emotion of which humanity is capable that has not found musical expression somewhere in Handel's operas. Referring the reader once more to the only adequate source of information, the scores themselves, let us call attention to a half-dozen examples : (1) the famous "Ombra mai fù" (*Serse*, Act I, scene 1), known universally (in transcriptions, alas) as the "Largo from Xerxes"; (2) the nobly mournful "Lascio ch'io pianga" (*Rinaldo*, Act II, scene 4); (3) the deeply moving "Cara sposa" (*Rinaldo*, Act I, scene 7), "one of the best airs in that style that was ever composed by [Handel] or any other

[27] E.g., *Rinaldo*, Act I, sc. 6, "Augelletti, che cantate."
[28] E.g., *Radamisto*, Act I, sc. 3, "Stragi, morti."

master; and by many degrees the most pathetic song, and with the richest accompaniment, which had been then heard in England";[29] (4) a whole class of arias of the siciliano type, adopted by Handel from the example of Scarlatti and other Italian composers, elegant in contour, elegiac in feeling, moving in languorous 12/8 metre (example: "Con saggio tuo consiglio," from *Agrippina*, Act I, scene 1); (5) the idyllic arias, musical pastorales, and landscapes of tranquil charm, filled with sunlight (example: "Se in un fiorito ameno prato," from *Giulio Cesare*, Act II, scene 2); (6) the light, playful, "Un cenno leggiadretto" (*Serse*, Act I, scene 15), representative of a less numerous class of arias appropriate to the comic style; in a similar category may be mentioned also the bass songs of Polyphemus in *Acis and Galatea*.

A fine example of the energetic, passionate, displayful aria is Radamisto's "Perfido" (*Radamisto*, revised version, Act I, scene 6), with its recurring rhythmic figure (♩. ♪ ♪) curiously prophetic of the motif of the Scherzo in Beethoven's Ninth Symphony. Coloratura passages such as we find in this aria are frequent in Handel; often they were composed to show off a particular singer, and Handel's mastery of his craft is evident in the virtuosity of this vocal writing. Yet he seldom employed such passages solely for display; they spring naturally from the tension of the music or from some obvious image in the text and are strictly organized within the musical structure. Occasionally occurs a melismatic passage that recalls the softer style of Steffani.[30]

Surely one of the most beautiful of Handel's arias is Cleopatra's "Se pietà di me non senti" (*Giulio Cesare*, Act II, scene 8), which is preceded by an accompanied recitative (notable for its wide range of modulations) and introduced by an orchestral ritornello, from which the characteristic "drooping" motif of the obbligato violin is derived (Example 56).

It must be emphasized that in every case the realization not only of mood but also of personality comes from the music. Caesar in Haym's libretto is a stage hero in the manner of the early eighteenth century; only through Handel's music does his character receive those qualities which make him a truly dramatic figure. Caesar and Cleopatra, Radamisto and Zenobia, Bajazet (in *Tamerlano*), and others of Handel's

[29] Burney, *History* II, 674.
[30] See Example 56, end; also the beautiful closing cadence of the first part of "Forte e lieto" (*Tamerlano*, Act I, sc. 1).

EXAMPLE 56

HANDEL

Che sen-to? oh Di - o! mor - rà Cleo-pa-tra an-co - ra.

A - ni - ma vi - le, che par - li mai? deh,

[etc.]

ta - ci! a - vrò, per ven - di - car - mi in

*(Example 56 continued)*

*(Example 56 continued)*

giu - sto ciel     io mo - ri- rò,     giu - sto ciel,

io mo - ri- rò,     io mo - ri - rò. —

dramatic creations are universal, ideal types of humanity, moving and thinking on a vast scale, the analogue in opera of the great tragic personages of Corneille. This quality is more than the reflection of a certain musical style or a consummate technique; it is the direct emanation of Handel's own spirit, expressed in music with an immediacy that has no parallel outside Beethoven. It is the incarnation of a great soul. If his characters suffer, the music gives full, eloquent expression to their sorrows—but it never whines; there is not a note in it of self-pity. We are moved by the spectacle of suffering, but our compassion is mingled with admiration at suffering so nobly endured, with pride that we ourselves belong to a species capable of such heroism.

RAMEAU. Conditions in France were not favorable for serious musical drama in the early eighteenth century. The tendency, as has already been mentioned, was toward the nondramatic entertainment spectacle of the opéra-ballet. A glance at the statistics of new works staged at the Paris Opéra [31] shows this: from 1700 to 1715 there were twenty-seven new tragédies lyriques and ten new ballets; from 1716 to 1740 there were twenty-one new tragédies lyriques and forty-one new ballets of various kinds. Not only were the ballet pieces becoming more numerous; they were always more popular as well. Among the hits of the early eighteenth century were Les Fêtes de Thalie (1714), a ballet with music by Jean-Joseph Mouret (1682–1738),[32] which enjoyed revivals until 1764 and was parodied; and a "ballet héroïque,"[33] Les Fêtes grecques et romaines (1723) by Colin de Blamont (1690–1760) which lasted till 1770. The only opera of this period that approached such popularity was Jephté (1732), on the biblical subject with music by Michel Pignolet de Montéclair (1667–1737).

Jean-Philippe Rameau (1683–1764) [34] was already known as an organist, theorist, and composer of keyboard music before he presented his tragédie lyrique Hippolyte et Aricie in 1733. Over twenty other works for the theatre followed, the most important of which were the operas Castor et Pollux (1737), Dardanus (1739), and Zoroastre (1749) and the opéras-ballets Les Fêtes d'Hébé (1739), Platée (1745), and Zaïs (1748). In general, these works do not depart from the fundamental outlines established by Lully and Quinault: mythological or legendary subject matter, frequent large display scenes with choruses and ballets, and carefully notated recitative intermingled with short airs. Nevertheless, Rameau's operas immediately raised a storm of controversy. He was

[31] Chouquet, Histoire de la musique dramatique en France, pp. 327–42.

[32] Viollier, Jean-Joseph Mouret, le musicien des grâces.

[33] Ballet héroïque, pastorale héroïque, comédie lyrique, comédie ballet, and similar designations were used in France at this time for works partaking of the character of both opera and ballet; to avoid unnecessary complexity we shall refer to such works under the generic name "opéra-ballet." For the distinctions, see Masson, L'Opéra de Rameau, pp. 20 ff.

[34] Biographies by La Laurencie and Girdlestone; La Laurencie, "La Musique française de Lulli à Gluck," in Lavignac, Encyclopédie, Part I, Vol. III, pp. 1362–1562; Masson, L'Opéra de Rameau; Leclerc, "Les Indes galantes."

hailed by progressives as the savior of French opera, and condemned by conservatives as a hopeless pedant, a *distillateur d'accords baroques*, whose capitulation to Italian style was tantamount to musical treason. The reasons for this criticism are not to be sought in the outward aspects of his operas but rather in the music itself, which represents the late baroque style in France as Bach represented it in Germany and Handel in England. Tonalities are absolutely clear, often being emphasized by Rameau's predilection for outlining triads in the melody; large-scale forms are common, supported by definite modulatory schemes with systematic use of secondary sevenths (a particularly fine example is the great chaconne in the finale of *Castor et Pollux*). The whole style is more contrapuntal than Lully's though not so much so as that of Bach. Some of Rameau's longer airs are formally set apart from the recitative, and the Italian-inspired ariettes in particular make use of coloratura passages.[35] Other large arias occasionally foreshadow the profound, serious moods of Gluck (Example 57).

The contrast between Lully and Rameau is particularly evident in the choruses, which are more numerous and varied in the latter and often extremely brilliant, recalling the style of Handel (for example, "Brillant soleil" in *Les Indes galantes*, Act II, scene 5). In his use of the chorus for dramatic purposes (as in the impressive opening of Act I of *Castor et Pollux*) Rameau showed the way for developments which were to culminate in the later operas of Gluck.

Above all, Rameau is distinguished for the instrumental music in his operas. The Paris opera orchestra in 1756 numbered forty-seven players, comprising two flutes, four oboes, five bassoons, one trumpet, and percussion, in addition to the strings and continuo instruments;[36] extra players were hired when needed for musettes, horns, and clarinets (from 1749). The three main types of instrumental pieces in Rameau are the overtures, the descriptive symphonies, and the dances.

The overtures of the earlier operas are in the conventional form, but in certain cases Rameau, unlike Lully, connects the overture with the particular opera for which it is written. Thus the opening theme of the overture to *Castor et Pollux*, in G minor, reappears in the finale in A major for the scene of the apotheosis of the two heroes. *Zoroastre* has a program overture aiming to summarize the main outlines of the plot

[35] See examples in the closing scenes of *Hippolyte et Aricie* and *Castor et Pollux*.
[36] Masson, *L'Opéra de Rameau*, p. 513.

EXAMPLE 57

**Prélude**
Gravement
*Violins*

*Dardanus*, Act IV, sç. 1

RAMEAU

*(Example 57 continued)*

of the opera. In his later works Rameau experimented with different overture forms : that of *Zoroastre* is in three movements (fast-slow-fast), approaching not only in general outline but also in many details—the texture of the music, the nature of the themes, the form of the last two movements, the rhythms, methods of motivic development, use of devices like parallel thirds, unison passages, and echoes—the style of the early classical symphony.

The descriptive symphonies are short instrumental pieces intended to depict in music certain scenes or happenings on the stage. They are typical of an age whose music aesthetic was based on the ideal of imitation of nature, thus leading to a whole conventional language of musical images [37] for conveying landscapes, sunrises, babbling brooks, thunderstorms, earthquakes, or other natural phenomena. Rameau never wrote a piece of nature music more perfectly expressive of pastoral tranquillity than the slumber scene in Lully's *Armide*, but he excelled in more violent episodes, of which the earthquake in the second entrée of *Les Indes galantes* is a good example. There are in his operas also many short symphonies for filling awkward pauses in the action (such as descents of celestial beings) or suggesting off-stage battles.

Most numerous of all are the dances, which comprise all types from the simple minuet to the elaborate chaconne, with an astounding variety, freshness, and fertility of rhythmic invention. These are a noble flowering of the oldest instrumental tradition in France, a line descending from the sixteenth-century ballet through Chambonnières, Lully, François Couperin, and many other distinguished composers. In Rameau perhaps more than in any other of his countrymen the music has the strange power of vividly suggesting the movements of the dancers; it is in truth "gesture made audible."

The common dance types in duple metre are: gavotte, *bourrée, rigaudon,* tambourin, *contredanse*; in triple metre: saraband, *chaconne,* minuet, *passepied*; in compound metre: *loure, forlane, gigue*; others, variable in metre and form: musette, march, *entrée,* air (the last usually qualified by a descriptive term, as *air majestueux* or *grave, air pour les Fleurs, pour les Ombres,* and so on). The principal forms are: two-part, rondo, chaconne. Many of these dances are sung by solo, ensemble, or chorus as well as played by the orchestra. Examples are too numerous and varied to warrant mention of any in particular. Only a study of the scores can give an idea of Rameau's inexhaustible richness in this field.

Rameau is not to be regarded as a mere way station between Lully and Gluck; any conception of him as no more than a composer of graceful dance trifles is completely false. On the contrary, he is one of the very few first-rank composers whose work happens to fall largely in the realm of opera. If he is less consistently a dramatist than Lully, the fault is that of the age in which he worked; as a musician, he is by far

[37] Du Bos, *Critical Reflections,* Part I, sec. xlv.

Lully's superior. His limited success in France is to be attributed to the poor quality of his librettos (for which his own indifference was partly responsible) and to the fact that in his day the old French opera itself, encumbered by so many conventions of a bygone era, was on its way toward decline, and Rameau's music went down to obscurity with it. Today it stands as a classic example of great music forgotten because it cannot be detached from a dead operatic style—for Rameau's opera cannot be revived as a living art without reviving the age of Louis XV. Yet by means of the requisite knowledge and imagination, one can in some measure learn to hear and see it as it lived in Paris under the *ancien régime* and thereby alone arrive at a just estimate of its greatness.

SCARLATTI. Alessandro Scarlatti (1660–1725) [38] has usually figured in the history of opera as the founder of the so-called Neapolitan school of the eighteenth century. Recent investigations, however, tend to show that his importance in this connection was considerably less than has been supposed and that he is probably better to be understood as one of the last masters of an older tradition than as the initiator of a new movement. Scarlatti was in Naples from 1685 to 1702 and again for shorter periods after 1709; he wrote operas not only for Naples but also for Rome (including some of his most important works), Venice, and Florence. It is not known exactly how many operas he produced; about eighty-five are traceable, of which number a little more than half are extant, some incompletely.

Scarlatti began work in the style of Legrenzi and Stradella; their influence is apparent in his first operas performed at Rome previous to 1684. The small forms, the free mixture of recitative and aria passages, and the use of the ground-bass are all characteristic of this period. It was during his first stay in Naples that Scarlatti began to develop more individual characteristics. The presence of comic characters (as in the Venetian librettos) led to his custom of ending each of the first two acts of a serious opera with a comic duet in lively style, clearly the ancestor of the later opera buffa finale. By 1700 Scarlatti had definitely established the new Italian overture with its quick opening movement, short slow interlude, and closing movement in two-part form with marked dance rhythms. During this period also there is evident a growing differentiation between Scarlatti's cantata and opera styles. *La Rosaura*

[38] Dent, *Alessandro Scarlatti*; Lorenz, *Alessandro Scarlatti's Jugendoper*; studies by Van den Borren and Prota-Giurleo.

(1690) has many details that suggest the cantata. Most of the arias are of small dimensions, and the harmonies are often intricate and subtle. The recitatives, carefully composed, are far from mere stereotypes, and there are many scenes in which recitative, arioso, and aria passages are freely intermingled. The music shows to perfection that quality of pleasure in sensuous effect which is such a strong characteristic of the Italian composers. The moods range from tender melancholy to charming playfulness, occasionally touching vehement grief on the one hand or outright broad comedy on the other. The whole is suffused with an aristocratic elegance, avoidance of excess, and perfect understanding of the powers of the solo voice for dramatic expression.

In contrast to *La Rosaura*, *La Statira* (performed at Rome in the same year) is "a very fine example of the grand manner";[39] some of the arias are on a broad scale, impressive in their rhythms, showy and effective in a masterful way, with copious use of coloratura passages after an opening phrase in long notes with wide melodic intervals. This eminently theatrical style is further exemplified in *Eraclea* (1700), *La principessa fedele* (Naples, 1710), and *Tigrane* (Naples, 1715), the last-named work being also remarkable for its comic scenes. In contrast to this popularizing tendency is *Mitridate Eupatore*, composed for Venice in 1707. This work, with its dignified, deeply expressive music, shows Scarlatti as a worthy representative of the serious Italian opera in late baroque style (Example 58). The recitative "O Mitridate mio" from Act IV is a remarkable example of passionate declamation, supported by skillful chromatic harmonies with sudden, though always appropriate, modulations (Example 59). The aria in B minor which follows ("Cara tomba") is marked by many suspensions between the voice and concertizing solo violin; in its mood of mingled pathos and resignation it is similar to many of the lyrical effusions of Steffani and equally beautiful.[40]

The popular or folk element in Scarlatti is represented by the realistic dialogue in the comic scenes of his serious works, as well as his comic opera, *Il trionfo dell' onore* (1718). In addition, there are many tunes which in their strongly characteristic rhythms and melodic turns are clearly of popular derivation. Perhaps the most common of these are the

---

[39] Dent, *Scarlatti*, p. 63.
[40] Both recitative and aria are reprinted (incomplete) in Dent, *Scarlatti*, pp. 109–12.

## Mitridate Eupatore, Act II, sc. 1

EXAMPLE 58

A. SCARLATTI

*(Example 58 continued)*

il mio do - lor._____ fau - sti u - di - te_____

_____ il mio do - lor._____ u - di - te u-

di - te il mio do - lor _____ il mio do - lor.

*(con cembalo)*

(Example 58 continued)

poi che fo - ste nell' im - pre - se si pro -

pi - zi-i agl' a - vi mie - i virtù da - te a chi si pre - ste di pu -

ni -re un tra - di - tor, un tra-di-tor_____ un tra-di - tor, di pu-ni-re un tradi-

*(Example 58 continued)*

tor,   un tra - di-tor,                    *(Dal Segno al Fine)*

EXAMPLE 58

*(con cembalo)*                            *(·senza cembalo)*

rather insinuating, languid, minor melodies in 12/8 metre to which the name "siciliano" [41] is generally applied, though it is notable that Scarlatti himself restricts this term to those airs in which the flatted supertonic is a prominent feature. This note and its harmonization by means of the Neapolitan sixth are not confined to the siciliano-type airs but form a conspicuous mannerism of Scarlatti's style.[42]

The later operas show an increasing emphasis on vocal ensembles (especially in *Griselda*, 1721) and growth in the size and importance of the orchestra. In *Tigrane* the horns are introduced for the first time. The orchestra of *Telemaco* (1718) is large, and in this work there is not a single aria with simple continuo accompaniment. The beginning of the overture to *Griselda* shows evidence not only of a homophonic style in orchestral writing but also of the typical later classical division between strings and winds according to function—the strings having arpeggios and tremolandos while oboes and trumpets reinforce with chords on the strong beats.[43] An even more significant development in the later works is the accompanied recitative, which evinces a growing recognition of the essential feature of this style, namely antiphonal dialogue effects between voice and orchestra, in free declamatory rhythms and irregu-

[41] This type of melody is not new in Scarlatti. One is found in Monteverdi's *Orfeo*, and there are many in P. A. Ziani's *Galatea* (1660). Their predecessors may be found in the slower, 3/2 metre, barcarole arias typical of Steffani and Pallavicino (cf. DdT LV, Introduction, p. ix).

[42] Dent, *Scarlatti*, pp. 146–47.

[43] Music in Dent, *Scarlatti*, p. 171.

## Mitridate Eupatore, Act IV

EXAMPLE 59

A. SCARLATTI

larly recurring motifs. An interesting example of the influence of the accompanied recitative on the aria itself is found in Act II of *Griselda*, where the aria "Figlio! Tiranno," although accompanied throughout in steady rhythm of eighths or sixteenths, is nevertheless so broken and interjectional, with its phrases alternately echoed by the strings or interrupted by rushing scale passages, as to give almost the impression of being a recitative—an original and highly dramatic treatment.[44] In *Attilio regolo* (1719), toward the end of Act I the arias "Finiscila ragazza" and "Da fine al disprezzo" are both interrupted by recitatives. The scene closes with a dialogue-duet for alto and bass, which has been immediately preceded by a dramatic soliloquy-recitative and a big aria "Son qual nave." This entire scene, though not altogether unrelated to the plot of the opera, nevertheless functions as a kind of comic pendant to the first act.

Fundamentally, Scarlatti in his operas remained a conservative composer, though not altogether unaffected by the current of the times. Like his contemporaries, he came to use the full da capo pattern almost exclusively in his arias. Yet there is much evidence to show that he deplored the extremes toward which music, especially in Italy, was then tending. That evidence is found not only in the scores themselves but also in the attitude of Scarlatti's noble patrons (who were forever urging him to write down to the level of his audience) and in the significant fact that for the last four years of his life, during which he resided at Naples, he wrote no operas, but only cantatas and church music. His fate, like Bach's, was to be outmoded before his death, "a great man . . . forgotten by his own generation." His influence, except on Handel and Hasse, was only partial and indirect. His own happy combination of strength and sweetness, of passion and humor, was not to be heard again in music until the time of Mozart.

Two Italian contemporaries of Scarlatti must be briefly mentioned here. Antonio Lotti (1667–1740),[45] a pupil of Legrenzi, produced about twenty operas at Venice and others at Dresden and Vienna. Antonio Vivaldi (?1678–1741),[46] celebrated for his orchestral concertos, was also the composer of about forty-four operas which were popular at Venice between 1713 and 1739.

[44] See music in Dent, *Scarlatti*, pp. 165–67.

[45] Spitz, *Antonio Lotti*; *idem*, "Die Opern *Ottone* von Händel und *Teofane* von A. Lotti."

[46] Biography by Pincherle; Rowell, "Four Operas of Antonio Vivaldi."

# CHAPTER 14

# THE OPERA SERIA

We have seen how, from its earliest beginnings at Florence and Rome,
Italian opera in the course of the seventeenth century passed out of the
experimental stage. Radiating from Venice with its public opera houses,
it established itself on a firm basis of public interest and support which
made it by the end of the century the most widespread and most popular
of all musical forms. We have also seen how, in the course of this
development, three important national schools of opera rose outside
Italy. One of these, the French, maintained its existence and individuality; the English school died with Purcell, while the German
gradually lost its identity by absorption into the Italian style. At the
beginning of the eighteenth century, therefore, it is possible practically
to perceive one single operatic type which dominated all western Europe
except France—a type which, despite variations in different countries
and composers, showed certain fundamental common features everywhere. From the standpoint of the libretto, we identify this type as the
opera of moods or *Affects*.[1] Its intention was to present a series of discrete
expressive moments, each devoted exclusively to a particular mood; in
order to call forth the necessary variety and intensity of moods, situations
were contrived with little attention to unity or consistency of plot, and
with corresponding indifference to realism either in subject matter or in
details of dramatic development. The form in which this intention was
realized was one which we may call the "aria opera"; musically speaking, that is to say, it consisted of a series of arias separated by passages of
recitative. Throughout the latter half of the seventeenth century the
tendency had been more and more to differentiate these two styles and,
in general, to concentrate the musical interest more and more on the

[1] Kretzschmar, "Allgemeines und Besonderes zur Affektenlehre."

aria. Ensembles, ballets, and instrumental pieces were of only incidental importance.

Within this general type of Italian opera two distinct directions were perceptible by the end of the seventeenth century. These have been designated by German historians as respectively "aristocratic" and "democratic"; we may also refer to them, in terms corresponding to the usual divisions of music history, as the "late baroque" and the "pre-classical" styles of opera. The distinction involves many criteria, apply-ing to both libretto and music.[2] The aim of baroque opera had been to excite admiration and astonishment, to overwhelm, *far stupire* : hence the machines and marvels, the multitude of characters, the sensational disorderly plots, extravagant language, and comic episodes. The newer style came to be refined, polished, regulated; poets envisioned the drama as a school of virtue, teaching devotion to duty and loyalty to the higher impulses of man's nature. They eschewed supernatural interventions and miracles; comic scenes were abolished; the cast was reduced to six stereotyped personages; plots became orderly and formalized, emotions restrained, language conventional and courtly. Not less sweeping were the differences in the music. In the older style the harmony was com-paratively rich and changeable, the bass lines fairly active, the melody spun out in long phrases of variable length (except in pieces based on dance rhythms), and the forms still somewhat free despite the tendency toward exclusive use of the da capo pattern. In the newer style, harmony was simplified to a few fundamental chords with the bass changing relatively seldom and the whole texture functioning solely as a support for the melody; the latter came to be organized in symmetrical short phrases, though with considerable variety of rhythmic patterns within the phrase; variety of form gave way to the almost exclusive dominance of the full five-part da capo scheme.[3] The older style admitted the orchestra as a more nearly equal partner with the voice, aiming at a contrapuntal kind of bass and, in the case of composers like Steffani, Keiser, or Handel, sometimes interweaving the vocal line with one or more strands of instrumental melody; the newer style tended to relegate the orchestra to a servile position, with a bass whose function was

[2] See Edward O. D. Downes, "The Operas of Johann Christian Bach," Vol. I. I am indebted to Dr. Downes for an extended loan of a typescript of this disser-tation, which contains the most thorough survey yet made of Italian *opera seria* between 1720 and 1780.

[3] See below, p. 211, for description of the da capo form.

entirely harmonic, concentrating all musical attention on the singer. Mattheson remarks on the contrast in this respect between his own time and the seventeenth century;[4] in the earlier period "hardly anyone gave a thought to melody, but everything was centered simply on harmony." Quantz laments that, though most Italian composers of the present day (that is, 1752) are talented, they start writing operas before they have learned the rules of musical composition; that they do not take time to ground themselves properly; and that they work too fast.[5] To these criticisms, with their implications of frivolousness and lack of counterpoint in Italy, may be opposed, as representing the Italian viewpoint, Galuppi's classic definition of good music: "Vaghezza, chiarezza, e buona modulazione," which Dr. Burney translates "beauty, clearness, and good modulation,"[6] though there are really no words in English capable of conveying the exact sense of the original.

The older opera was represented by Legrenzi, Steffani, Keiser, Handel, and, to a considerable extent, Scarlatti; the newer tendencies were developed in the works of most Italian composers after 1700 and became dominant by 1720. One way to illustrate the distinction is to consider the contrasting types of operatic overture associated with each of the two schools. The older type was the French *ouverture*, first outlined by the early Venetians, given definitive form by Lully, and adopted in its essential features by Steffani, Keiser, and Handel; the newer type was the Italian *sinfonia*, first established by Scarlatti about 1700, and gradually ousting the French overture everywhere as the eighteenth century went on. The difference between these two kinds of overture is usually stated in terms of the order of movements—the French beginning (and often also ending) in slow tempo, whereas the Italian began fast, had a slow movement in the middle, and ended with an allegro or presto. This distinction, however, is superficial; the essential difference was a matter of musical texture. The French overture was a creation of the late baroque, having a rich texture of sound, some quasi-contrapuntal independence of the inner voices, and a musical momentum bound to the nonperiodic progression of the bass and harmonies. The Italian overture was a characteristic preclassical form, light in texture, with busy activity of the upper voices accom-

[4] *Ehrenpforte*, p. 93.
[5] *Versuch*, XVIII. Hauptstück, par. 63.
[6] *The Present State of Music in France and Italy*, p. 177.

panied by simple, standardized harmonic formulas. The French overture looked to the past, the Italian to the future; the latter represented those principles of texture, form, nature of thematic material, and methods of motivic development which were to lead eventually to the style of the classical symphony.[7]

Both the older and the newer type of Italian opera existed in the early part of the eighteenth century, but the former was obviously on the decline as far as popularity was concerned. The general change in the language of music which characterized the middle of the century, and which led through the rococo or gallant style to the later classical idiom, was evident in opera as everywhere else. The growing taste for simplicity, ease, lightness of texture, tuneful melody, and facile ornamentation brought to the fore a kind of opera, Italian in origin but international in practice, that has often been called "Neapolitan." This term came into use originally because many of the composers associated with early eighteenth-century opera lived or were trained at Naples. But the implications of "Neapolitan," when used to denote a certain type or style of opera, lead to confusion;[8] so altogether it seems best to abandon the use of the word as a descriptive term, at least until further research shall show whether a strictly Neapolitan kind of opera (as distinct from Venetian or Roman, for example) actually existed in the eighteenth century.

One division within the general field of eighteenth-century Italian opera, however, must be kept in mind, namely that between the serious opera (*opera seria*) and the comic opera (*opera buffa*). The latter is, at least in the beginning, a quite distinct form and will be treated later. At present we are concerned exclusively with the *opera seria*, the characteristic type of the age, cultivated in all countries by imported Italians as well as by native composers and singers imitating the Italian style, maintaining itself throughout the eighteenth century, and continuing its influence far into the nineteenth. We shall attempt first to give a general idea of this operatic type and, if possible, to dispose of certain misconceptions regarding it; afterwards, we shall study the music of

[7] On the early history of the Italian overture cf. Heuss, *Die venetianischen Opern-Sinfonien*, pp. 88–92. Wellesz's designation of Cavalli's overture to *Ercole* ("Cavalli," pp. 53–54) as an early example of the Italian type seems to rest on questionable assumptions.

[8] See articles by Hucke and Downes in Vol. I of the *Report of the Eighth Congress of the International Musicological Society*, pp. 253–84.

particular composers. The latter undertaking is still hampered by the paucity of available scores. Almost none of this music was printed; hundreds of manuscripts have been lost, and hundreds of others exist only in rare copies; only an infinitesimal fraction of it is accessible in modern editions.

THE LIBRETTO.[9] The foundation of the eighteenth-century *opera seria* goes back to the reform of the seventeenth-century libretto. First steps in this direction were taken by Silvio Stampiglia (1664–1725), but the two poets chiefly associated with the reform were Apostolo Zeno (1668–1750)[10] and Pietro Metastasio (1698–1782).[11] Zeno, under the influence of the French dramatists, favored historical subject matter and sought to purge the opera of erratically motivated plots, reliance on supernatural interventions, machines, irrelevant comic episodes, and the bombastic declamation which had reigned in the seventeenth century.[12] This movement was brought to fulfillment by Metastasio, the guiding genius of eighteenth-century Italian opera and a literary figure of such stature that his compatriots seriously compared him with Homer and Dante. Metastasio became court poet at Vienna in 1730, succeeding Stampiglia and Zeno who had held that position since 1705 and 1718 respectively. His twenty-seven *drammi per musica* and other theatre works were given over a thousand musical settings in the eighteenth century, some of them being composed as many as seventy times. The composers chiefly associated with his works were Leo, Vinci, and Hasse. A modern reader is apt to find Metastasio's plays mannered and artificial, elegant rather than powerful; his characters seem more like eighteenth-century courtiers than ancient Romans; "sentimental quandaries" make up most of the situations in these dramas of amorous and political intrigue; there is almost always a *lieto fine*, a happy ending,

[9] Giazotto, *Poesia melodrammatica e pensiero critico nel Settecento*; *idem*, "Apostolo Zeno, Pietro Metastasio e la critica del Settecento"; Burt, "Opera in Arcadia"; Vetter, "Deutschland und das Formgefühl Italiens."

[10] See biographies by Negri and Fehr; Wotquenne, *Alphabetisches Verzeichnis der Stücke in Versen aus den dramatischen Werken von Zeno, Metastasio und Goldoni.*

[11] See Burney, *Memoirs of the Life and Writings of the Abate Metastasio*; De' Calsabigi, "Dissertazione"; Mattei, *Memorie*; Stendhal, *Vies de Haydn, de Mozart et de Métastase*; Callegari, "Il melodramma e Pietro Metastasio"; Rolland, "Métastase, précurseur de Gluck," in his *Voyage musical*, pp. 153–70, and also in MM VIII, No. 4 (1912) 1–10; Della Corte, "Appunti sull' estetica musicale di Pietro Metastasio"; Gerber, *Der Operntypus Hasses*, chap. I.

[12] Metastasio, letter to Fabroni, December 7, 1767; in Burney, *Memoirs* III, 19. See also Wellesz, Introduction to Fux's *Costanza e fortezza*, DTOe XXXVII, xiii.

and the stock figure of the magnanimous tyrant is often in evidence. Yet in spite of all this, if one is willing to allow for the dramatic conventions of the time, some of Metastasio's plays may still be read with pleasure. His achievement consisted in the creation of a consistent dramatic structure conforming to the rationalistic ideals of the period, but incorporating lyrical elements suited for musical setting in such a way as to form an organic whole.

As an example of the Metastasian libretto, let us take *Attilio regolo* (1740). Attilio, having been taken captive by the Carthaginians, is offered his freedom if he will use his influence with the Roman Senate to obtain certain advantages for Carthage. Under parole to return if unsuccessful, he is permitted to go to Rome; but once there, he urges the Senate to stand firm, scorning to purchase his own life by betraying the interests of his country. Resisting the entreaties of his friends and family, of the Senate (who are willing to make national sacrifices to save him), and of the entire populace, he voluntarily boards the ship which will take him back to captivity and death. This tragic ending was something of an innovation with Metastasio; it appears in only two of his other works: *Didone* (1724) and the original version of *Catone in Utica* (1727), and is exceedingly rare in earlier Italian opera—Busenello's *Didone* of 1641 (music by Cavalli) being one instance.

Now we may well ask where, in such a drama as *Attilio regolo*, there is any place for lyricism. The answer is to be found in the peculiar construction of the scenes. In seventeenth-century opera, recitatives, arioso passages, and arias were intermingled according to the composer's fancy or the requirements of the action. There was no standard procedure; very often a scene might end with a recitative. Metastasio standardized the form. In his operas a typical scene consists of two distinct parts: first, dramatic action in recitative; and second, expression of sentiments by the chief actor in an aria. In the first part of the scene, the actor is a character in the drama, carrying on dialogue with other actors; in the second part, he is a person expressing his emotions or conveying some general sentiments or reflections appropriate to the current situation—not to his fellows on the stage but to the audience. While this goes on, the progress of the drama usually comes to a complete stop. Consequently, the play is made up of regularly alternating periods of movement and repose, the former representing the rights of the drama (recitative) and the latter the rights of the music (aria): the former occupying the larger part of the scene in the libretto, but the latter far exceeding it in the score, by reason of the extended musical structure of the aria being built usually on only two stanzas of four lines each. There results from this scheme an endlessly repeated pattern of tension and release, each recitative building up an emotional situation which finds outlet in the following aria. "The recitative loads the gun, the aria fires it." [13] This is the classical compromise operatic form, in which drama and music each yield certain rights and thereby find a means of living together compatibly. It permits free development of both elements within conventional limits. So long as these limits were tolerable (as they were to the early and middle eighteenth century), the form was found satisfactory; it lost favor only when other ideals of drama began to prevail. Moreover, the stiffness of the scheme was mitigated in Metastasio's operas by the naturalness of the transition from recitative to aria, by the musical quality of the language in the recitative, and by the variety of verse forms in the aria.

It may be remarked that, whereas with respect to the dramatic action tension is greatest in the recitative and least in the aria, with respect to the music the exact opposite obtains. Musical tension is at a minimum in recitative and becomes strongest in the aria. Thus the two forces, drama and music, tend to cancel one another and the result is a certain neutrality, a remoteness or *generality* of expression in these works, which agrees well with the highly formal pattern of their design.

One paramount fact emerges : the central position of the aria as a musical unit. Musically speaking, that is to say, an opera is a succession of arias; other elements—recitatives, ensembles, instrumental numbers —are nothing but background. From this fact stem certain consequences : (1) the variety and degree of stylization of aria types, (2) a corresponding looseness of structure in the opera as a whole, and (3) the importance of the singer not only as an interpreter but also as a creative partner of the composer.

ARIA TYPES. Eighteenth-century writers on opera classify arias into certain well-defined types, having distinct characteristics. Thus the Englishman John Brown mentions five traditional varieties :

*Aria cantabile,*—by pre-eminence so called, as if it alone were Song : And, indeed, it is the only kind of song which gives the singer an oppor-

---

[13] Flemming, *Die Oper*, p. 58. See also the admirably clear exposition of this aesthetic in Grimm's essay "Poëme lyrique" in Diderot's *Encyclopédie* (1765).

tunity of displaying at once, and in the highest degree, all his powers. . . .
The proper subjects for this Air are sentiments of tenderness.

*Aria di portamento* . . . chiefly composed of long notes, such as the
singer can dwell on, and have, thereby, an opportunity of more effectually
displaying the beauties, and calling forth the powers of his voice. . . . The
subjects proper to this Air are sentiments of dignity.

*Aria di mezzo carattere* . . .a species of Air, which, though expressive
neither of the dignity of this last, nor of the pathos of the former, is,
however, serious and pleasing.

*Aria parlante,*—speaking Air, is that which . . . admits neither of long
notes in the composition, nor of many ornaments in the execution. The
rapidity of motion of this Air is proportioned to the violence of the passion
which is expressed by it. This species of Air goes sometimes by the name of
*aria di nota e parola,* and likewise of *aria agitata.* . . .

*Aria di bravura, aria di agilita,*—is that which is composed *chiefly,*
indeed, too often, *merely* to indulge the singer in the display of certain
powers in the execution, particularly extraordinary agility or compass of
voice.[14]

A less scientific tabulation is given by the Frenchman Charles de
Brosses, writing from Rome about 1740 :

The Italians . . . have airs of great agitation, full of music and harmony,
for brilliant voices; others are of a pleasant sound and charming outlines,
for delicate and supple voices; still others are passionate, tender, affecting,
truly following the natural expression of emotions, strong or full of feeling
for stage effect and for bringing out the best points of the actor. The
"agitato" airs are those presenting pictures of storms, tempests, torrents,
thunderclaps, a lion pursued by hunters, a war-horse hearing the sound
of the trumpet, the terror of a silent night, etc.—all images quite appropriate to music, but out of place in tragedy. [This is the so-called comparison aria, the stock-in-trade of eighteenth-century opera.] This kind of air
devoted to large effects is almost always accompanied by wind instruments
—oboes, trumpets, and horns—which make an excellent effect, especially
in airs having to do with storms at sea. . . .

Airs of the second kind are madrigals, pretty little songs with ingenious
and delicate ideas or comparisons drawn from pleasant objects, such as
zephyrs, birds, murmuring waves, country life, etc. . . .

As to airs of the third kind, which express only feeling, Metastasio takes
great care to place them at the most lively and interesting point of his
drama, and to connect them closely with the subject. The musician then
does not seek for embellishments or passage-work, but tries simply to por-
tray the feeling, whatever it may be, with all his power. . . . I should also

---

[14] *Letters on the Italian Opera* (2d ed., 1791), pp. 36–39.

place in this class the airs of spectres and visions, to which the music lends a surprising power.[15]

It goes without saying that these and similar classifications cannot always be applied in all their details to the actual music; but their very existence is of interest as showing the high degree of organization—of stylization—which the aria reached in this period. There were other conventions as well, notably the one which decreed that practically every aria must be in the da capo form. Even the order and distribution of the different types were prescribed : every performer was to have at least one aria in each act, but no one might have two arias in succession; no aria could be followed immediately by another of the same type, even though performed by a different singer; the subordinate singers must have fewer and less important arias than the stars; and so on.[16] At first glance, the whole system seems artificial to the point of absurdity; later in the century, in fact, it was attacked on this very ground. Yet, granted the postulates of early eighteenth-century opera aesthetic, it was quite logical, and justification could be found for every rule. (Moreover, the composers did not hesitate to break the rules if it suited their purposes to do so.) It was one of the secrets of Metastasio's success that he could construct a drama which met these rigid requirements without being too obviously constrained by them.

THE "PASTICCIO." A second consequence of overconcentration on the aria was a certain looseness of structure in the opera as a whole. With few exceptions, the composer's responsibility for formal unity was limited to each single number. Apart from the libretto, there was nothing to bind these into a larger musical unit except the general requirements as to variety and the custom of placing the two most important arias at the end of each of the first two acts. To use a familiar comparison, the arias were not like figures in a painting, each fulfilling a certain role in the composition and each in some measure conditioned by the others; rather they were like a row of statues in a hall, symmetrically arranged but lacking any closer bond of aesthetic union. The conception corresponded to the baroque ideal of dynamics, where the various degrees of loudness or softness were distinct, without transitions of crescendo or

[15] *Lettres familières sur l'Italie* (1931) II, 348–51. (Author's translation.)
[16] Hogarth, *Memoirs of the Opera* II, chap. 3; Goldoni, *Mémoires*, chap, 28. Cf. also the letter of the Abate Giuseppe Riva to Muratori in 1725, on the requirements for a London libretto, quoted in Streatfeild, "Handel, Rolli"; see also Hucke, "Neapolitanische Tradition," pp. 262 ff.

diminuendo; or to forms such as the sonata and concerto, in which each movement was a complete, thematically independent unit. The arias were like Leibniz's monads, each closed off from the others, and all held together only by the "preestablished harmony" of the libretto. Thus their order could be changed, new numbers added, or others taken away, without really doing violence to the musical plan of the opera as a whole —though, needless to say, the drama might suffer. Composers therefore freely substituted new arias for old in revivals of their works, or for performances with a different cast. A composer at Rome, for example, who had orders to revise a Venetian opera to suit the taste of the Roman singers and public, would have no compunction about replacing some of the original composer's arias with some of his own, perhaps taken from an earlier work where they had been sung to different words. Indeed, it was exceptional for an opera to be given in exactly the same form in two different cities.

This working of new materials into old garments, if carried far enough, resulted in a kind of opera known as a *pasticcio*—literally, a "pie," but perhaps translatable more expressively for modern readers a "patchwork." There were two distinct kinds of pasticcio. One is illustrated by the opera *Muzio Scevola* (London, 1721), the first act of which was composed by F. Mattei, the second by Giovanni Bononcini, and the third by Handel. But the typical pasticcio was the result of a more haphazard process; it was an opera which had migrated from city to city, undergoing patching and alteration at every stage, until it might one day arrive at London (its usual final home) with a libretto in which Metastasio shared honors with "Zeno, Goldoni, Stampiglia, Rossi, and other librettists," while "Gluck, Ciampi, Galuppi, Cocchi, Jommelli, Latilla, Handel and several more might be pasted together" in the same musical score.[17]

THE SINGERS. A third effect—which operated at the same time as a cause—of the importance of the aria was the glorification of the singer. The virtuoso singer was to the eighteenth century what the virtuoso pianist was to the nineteenth, or the virtuoso conductor to the twentieth. The operatic songbirds of that age have been so often and so unsparingly condemned that it seems worth while to try to correct this judgment by quoting a passage from Vernon Lee's *Studies of the Eighteenth Century*

[17] Cf. Sonneck, "Ciampi's *Bertoldo*"; Walker, "*Orazio*: The History of a Pasticcio."

*in Italy*, a book naïve in many of its musical opinions and perhaps too uncritical in its enthusiasm for everything Italian, but which nevertheless states the case for the singer with sympathy and insight :

The singer was a much more important personage in the musical system of the eighteenth century than he is now-a-days. He was not merely one of the wheels of the mechanism, he was its main pivot. For in a nation so practically, spontaneously musical as the Italian, the desire to sing preceded the existence of what could be sung : performers were not called into existence because men wished to hear such and such a composition, but the composition was produced because men wished to sing. The singers were therefore not trained with a view to executing any peculiar sort of music, but the music was composed to suit the powers of the singers. Thus, ever since the beginning of the seventeenth century, when music first left the church and the palace for the theatre, composition and vocal performance had developed simultaneously, narrowly linked together; composers always learning first of all to sing, and singers always finishing their studies with that of composition; Scarlatti and Porpora teaching great singers, Stradella and Pistocchi forming great composers; the two branches . . . acting and reacting on each other so as to become perfectly homogeneous and equal. . . .

The singer, therefore, was neither a fiddle for other men to play upon, nor a musical box wound up by mechanism. He was an individual voice, an individual mind, developed to the utmost; a perfectly balanced organization; and to him was confided the work of embodying the composer's ideas, of moulding matter to suit the thought, of adapting the thought to suit the matter, of giving real existence to the form which existed only as an abstraction in the composer's mind. The full responsibility of this work rested on him; the fullest liberty of action was therefore given him to execute it. Music, according to the notions of the eighteenth century, was no more the mere written score than a plan on white paper would have seemed architecture to the Greeks. Music was to be the result of the combination of the abstract written note with the concrete voice, of the ideal thought of the composer with the individuality of the performer. The composer was to give only the general, the abstract; while all that depended upon individual differences, and material peculiarities, was given up to the singer. The composer gave the unchangeable, the big notes, constituting the essential, immutable form, expressing the stable, unvarying character; the singer added the small notes, which filled up and perfected that part of the form which depended on the physical material, which expressed the minutely subtle, ever-changing mood. In short, while the composer represented the typical, the singer represented the individual.[18]

We read much about abuses on the part of the eighteenth-century

[18] Vernon Lee, *Studies of the Eighteenth Century in Italy*, pp. 117–18.

opera singers, but we are seldom told why these abuses were tolerated, being tacitly allowed to infer that audiences and composers were either blind to the evil or too supine to resent it. This was not so. The abuses were recognized, but they were endured because they seemed to be inseparable from the system out of which they grew and because, on the whole, people liked the system. The principle of absolute dominance of the aria in the form entailed the absolute dominance of the singer in performance; and in their submission to this principle audiences, composers, and poets alike allowed excesses on the part of the singers which would not have been endured in another age. Only rarely was even an autocrat like Handel (who had the incidental advantage of combining the offices of composer and manager in one person) able to control them, and then only by an extraordinary combination of tact, patience, humor, personal force, and even threats of physical violence. But usually the singers reigned supreme. Metastasio might insist all he pleased that poetry should be the "dictator" in opera, and complain of the mutilation of his dramas by "those ignorant and vain vocal heroes and heroines, who having substituted the imitation of flageolets and nightingales to human affections, render the Italian stage a national disgrace," [19] but he was powerless to alter a situation which his own works had contributed so much to bring about.

A lively, though unquestionably exaggerated, picture of the singers may be drawn from the critical and satirical writings of the seventeenth and early eighteenth centuries.[20] The most famous satire was Marcello's *Teatro alla moda* ("The Fashionable Theatre"), which first appeared in 1720.[21] Marcello's work is in the form of ironically worded counsels to everyone connected with opera, from the poets and composers down to the stagehands and singing teachers. Thus, he says, the composer

---

[19] Burney, *Memoirs* II, 325; III, 43.

[20] Salvator Rosa, "La musica"; Adimari, "Satira quarta"; Muratori, *Della perfetta poesia*, Lib. III, Cap. V (refutation of Muratori is undertaken by Mattheson in his *Neueste Untersuchung der Singspiele*); memoirs of Casanova, Da Ponte, Goldoni, and others; Jommelli's comic opera *La critica*, 1766 (H. Abert, *Jommelli*, p. 426) and similar works (cf. H. Abert, *Mozart* I, 415, note). See also "Die Oper und ihre Literatur bis 1752," in Goldschmidt, *Musikästhetik des 18. Jahrhunderts*, pp. 272–87; Cametti, "Critiche e satire"; Frati, "Satire"; Monnier, *Venise au XVIIIe siècle*, pp. 48 ff.

[21] Modern editions in Italian (E. Fondi, 1913; A. D'Angeli, 1927), French (E. David, 1890), German (A. Einstein, 1917), and English (R. Pauly, 1948); selections in Strunk, *Source Readings*, pp. 518–31. See also Pauly, "Benedetto Marcello's Satire"; biography of Marcello by D'Angeli.

will hurry or slow down the pace of an aria, according to the caprice of the singers, and will conceal the displeasure which their insolence causes him by the reflection that his reputation, his solvency, and all his interest are in their hands.[22]. . . The director will see that all the best songs go to the *prima donna*, and if it becomes necessary to shorten the opera he will never allow her arias to be cut, but rather other entire scenes.[23]

If a singer

has a scene with another actor, whom he is supposed to address when singing an air, he will take care to pay no attention to him, but will bow to the spectators in the loges, smile at the orchestra and the other players, in order that the audience may clearly understand that he is the *Signor Alipi Forconi, Musico*, and not the Prince Zoroaster, whom he is representing.[24]

All the while the ritornello of his air is being played the singer should walk about the stage, take snuff, complain to his friends[25] that he is in bad voice, that he has a cold, etc., and while singing his aria he shall take care to remember that at the cadence he may pause as long as he pleases, and make runs, decorations, and ornaments according to his fancy; during which time the leader of the orchestra shall leave his place at the harpsichord, take a pinch of snuff, and wait until it shall please the singer to finish. The latter shall take breath several times before finally coming to a close on a trill, which he will be sure to sing as rapidly as possible from the beginning, without preparing it by placing his voice properly, and all the time using the highest notes of which he is capable.[26]

The cadenzas and ornaments to which Marcello here alludes were carefully prepared beforehand :

If [a singer] have a role in a new opera, she will at the first possible moment take all her arias (which, in order to save time she has had copied without the bass part) to her Maestro *Crica* so that he may write in the passages, the variations, the beautiful ornaments, etc.—and Maestro Crica, without knowing the first thing about the intentions of the composer either with regard to the tempo of the arias, or the bass, or the instrumentation, will write below them in the empty spaces of the bass staff everything he can think of, and in very great quantity, so that the *Virtuosa* may be able to sing her song in a different way at every performance . . . and if her variations have nothing in common with the bass, with the violins which

[22] *Il teatro alla moda*, pp. 19–20.
[23] *Ibid.*, p. 23.
[24] *Ibid.*, p. 26.
[25] This is an allusion to the eighteenth-century custom of seating spectators on the stage.
[26] Marcello, *Il teatro*, pp. 26–27.

are to play in unison with her, or with the concertizing instruments, even if they are not in the same key, that will be of no consequence, since it is understood that the modern opera director is both deaf and dumb.[27]

The more serious critics viewed with alarm the overemphasis on vocal virtuosity, as attracting attention at the expense of both drama and music. Thus Metastasio writes,

The singers of the present times wholly forget, that their business is to imitate the speech of man, with numbers and harmony : on the contrary, they believe themselves more perfect, in proportion as their performance is remote from human nature. . . . When they have played their Symphony with the throat, they believe they have fulfilled all the duties of their art. Hence the audience keep their hearts in the most perfect tranquillity, and expect the performers merely to tickle their ears

—to which Dr. Burney adds, "If, forty years ago, Metastasio speaks with so much indignation of the abuse of execution, which has been increasing ever since, what would he say now ?"[28]

The technique of singing seems to have reached a level in the eighteenth century that has never since been equaled. In the nature of things it is difficult to find out much about the details of this art in specific cases, for the singers' greatest displays of skill were improvised, and consequently no record remains in the scores. In general, however, it may be said that there were two related practices, one having to do with ornamentation of the given melodic line (coloratura), and the other with the insertion of improvised passages at the cadences (cadenzas).

Ornamentation of the melodic line by solo singers was a custom inherited from the Renaissance and carried on through the whole baroque period.[29] It rose to special prominence in the latter part of the seventeenth century in Italy, when the aria came into its commanding position and the accompaniment suffered a corresponding lapse of importance. The climax was reached in the eighteenth century, the age of the great Italian singing schools. Particularly on the da capo repetition of the first part of an aria the singer was expected to show his full powers:

Among the Things worthy of Consideration, the first to be taken Notice of, is the Manner in which all *Airs* divided into three Parts are to be sung.

[27] *Ibid.*, pp. 39, 41.

[28] Burney, *Memoirs* II, 135–36.

[29] For a general survey of this subject see Haas, *Aufführungspraxis*; see also Aldrich, "The Principal Agréments," which gives full reference to the sources; and Goldschmidt, *Die Lehre von der vokalen Ornamentik*.

In the first they require nothing but the simplest Ornaments, of a good Taste and few, that the Composition may remain simple, plain, and pure; in the second they expect, that to this Purity some artful Graces be added, by which the Judicious may hear, that the Ability of the Singer is greater; and, in repeating the *Air*, he that does not vary it for the better, is no great Master.[30]

In the rapid bravura arias, opportunity for improvised ornamentation was less than in those arias in slower tempo. The well-known "Largo" from Handel's *Serse* would probably have been ornamented by the singer somewhat as shown in Example 60.[31]

The practice of improvising cadenzas likewise originated in the sixteenth-century solo song, and was revived in the eighteenth-century opera. Examples are found in Scarlatti. The natural place for a cadenza was on the 6–4 chord of an important cadence, just as we find it commonly in the concertos of the classical period. Inserted in arias, where they served par excellence for the display of the singers' powers, the cadenzas were often extended to ridiculous lengths. Ange Goudar quotes a burlesque petition supposed to have been presented to the management of the Paris Opéra "by the Italian eunuchs" [the castrati] which includes the statement "A cadenza, to be according to the rules, must last seven minutes and thirty-six seconds, all without drawing breath; for the whole of this must be done in one breath even though the actor should faint on the stage." [32] Tosi criticizes the cadenzas in these words:

Every *Air* has (at least) three *Cadences,* that are all three final. Generally speaking, the Study of the Singers of the present Times consists in terminating the *Cadence* of the first Part with an overflowing of *Passages* and *Divisions* at Pleasure, and the *Orchestre* waits; in that of the second the Dose is encreased, and the *Orchestre* grows tired; but on the last Cadence, the Throat is set a going, like a Weather-cock in a Whirlwind, and the *Orchestre* yawns.[33]

Examples of cadenzas sung by Farinelli in Giacomelli's *Merope* (Venice, 1734) have been preserved in a manuscript dedicated to the

[30] Tosi, *Observations on the Florid Song*, pp. 93–94.

[31] For examples of elaborate bravura arias, see Haböck, *Die Gesangskunst der Kastraten*; Burney, *History* II, 833–37; OHM IV, 221–32. For the realization of the ornamented melodic line in Example 60 I am indebted to Dr. Putnam Aldrich.

[32] "Une cadenza, pour être dans les regles, doit durer sept minutes & trente-six seconds, le tout sans prendre respiration; car il faut que toute cette tirade soit d'une seule haleine, l'acteur en dût crever sur la scene" (*Le Brigandage de la musique italienne*, 1777, p. 127).

[33] Tosi, *Florid Song*, pp. 128–29.

EXAMPLE 60

*Serse*, Act I, sc. 1

## Cadenza in Giacomelli's *Merope*

EXAMPLE 61

FARINELLI

Spie - ga del fa - to la cru - del - tà,

la cru - - -

- del - tà,

Empress Maria Theresa and now in the Vienna library; one of them well illustrates the remarks of Tosi quoted above (Example 61).[34]

All this outburst of virtuosity was bound up with the peculiar seventeenth- and eighteenth-century Italian institution of the castrato.[35] There are many references to the presence of eunuchs among the singers of Italian and German chapels of the sixteenth century; they are found at Florence in 1534, in the Papal Chapel at Rome by 1562. By the end of the seventeenth century they were a usual feature in Italian churches, despite periodic pronouncements by the Popes against the custom. They came into opera first in Monteverdi's *Orfeo*; seventeenth-century Italian operas made use of them to the almost total exclusion of women singers. Castrato singers flourished especially during the period 1650–1750, both male and female roles in the opera being entrusted to them. Their popularity began to decline in the latter part of the eighteenth century, and the last Italian opera castrato died in 1861.[36] Their extraordinary vogue was due in part to the shortage of women singers after the first few years of the seventeenth century, coupled with the fact that for a long time (especially at Rome) women were forbidden to appear on the public stage;[37] even where women did take part in opera, as at Paris (there were no castrati in the French opera), they were generally regarded as morally outside the pale of respectable society. But the castrati held their ground even in the eighteenth century, a period when there was no dearth of first-rate women singers (such as Faustina Bordoni, wife of the composer Hasse), by reason of sheer superiority in their art. Educated as they were from early childhood in the famous conservatories of the Italian cities, their long training gave them a solid grounding in musicianship in addition to developing a miraculous vocal technique. Their voices (known as *voci bianche*, literally "white voices") were more powerful and flexible,

---

[34] An autograph manuscript page of Mozart's cadenzas and ornaments to arias from the operas of J. C. Bach (K. 293e), formerly preserved in the Mozarteum at Salzburg, disappeared during the Second World War. Fortunately, it had previously been photographed by Edward Downes, who reproduces and transcribes Mozart's embellishments for the aria "Cara la dolce fiamma" from Bach's *Adriano in Siria* (London, 1765). ("The Operas of Johann Christian Bach," Appendix B.)

[35] Haböck, *Die Kastraten und ihre Gesangskunst*; Raguenet, *Paralele des Italiens et des François*; Villeneuve, *Lettre sur le méchanisme de l'opéra italien* (1756); Lalande, *Voyage d'un françois en Italie* VI, chap. XVI; Parini, "La evirazione (La musica)" (1769); Foscolo, *Dei sepolcri* (1807), vv. 73–74; Rogers, "The Male Soprano"; Heriot, *The Castrati in Opera*.

[36] Parolari, "Giambattista Velluti." Cf. also Hogarth, *Memoirs* II, 306–13.

[37] Cf. Lalande, *Voyage en Italie* V, 179.

if less sweet and expressive, than those of women, and the quality often remained unimpaired after as many as forty years of singing. So great were the rewards of a successful career that even the slightest sign of a promising voice was often sufficient to induce hopeful parents to offer a boy for emasculation, with the inevitable result that (according to Dr. Burney) in every great town in Italy could be found numbers of these pathetic creatures "without any voice at all, or at least without one sufficient to compensate for such a loss." [38]

Of all the Italian castrati, the most renowned was Carlo Broschi (1705–82), known as Farinelli, who had a legendary career in Europe. Brilliantly successful as a singer in every country, the friend of princes and emperors, for twenty-four years the confidant of two successive Spanish kings and virtually prime minister of Spain, the hero of popular tales, and the subject of an opera, he was a figure in the public imagination of the eighteenth century comparable to Liszt or Paganini in the nineteenth. [39]

COMPOSERS AND AUDIENCES. The amount of music written by eighteenth-century opera composers testifies to the popularity of this entertainment. [40] A tabulation of forty leading composers of the period shows nearly two thousand works, or an average of about fifty operas apiece. The sum total of the production of all composers would, of course, be much greater. One reason for this was that audiences insisted on new music each season, though they welcomed the old familiar librettos year after year. [41] Then, too, the writing out of the score was not the time-consuming process that it is in modern days, since so much was left to be improvised. The score was really little more than a memorandum of the composer's intentions, to be filled in by the performers. A composer commonly completed a score in a month or six weeks, and received for it a sum amounting to $100 or $150, plus the price of the first copy of the arias—in manuscript usually, though favorite airs of popular operas were often published in London. Once the first copy was

---

[38] *The Present State of Music in France and Italy*, p. 303. See also Lalande, *Voyage* VI, chap. 16 *passim*, and Parini, "La evirazione."

[39] For an account of Farinelli, see Burney, *Present State of Music in France and Italy*, pp. 202–17. See also Monaldi, *Cantanti evirati celebri*; Haböck, *Die Gesangskunst der Kastraten*.

[40] Cf. Monnier, *Venise au XVIIIe siècle*, chap. VI; Grosley, *New Observations on Italy, passim*; Villeneuve, *Lettre sur le méchanisme de l'opéra italien*.

[41] Lalande, *Voyage* VI, 352.

sold, the composer's income from his work ended, for there was no copyright protection for him.

Contemporary audiences, far from regarding the opera as a serious dramatic spectacle, looked upon it merely as an amusement. De Brosses reports that the performances in Rome began at eight or nine in the evening and lasted to midnight. Everyone of any consequence had a box, which was a social gathering place for friends. "The pleasure these people take in music and the theatre is more evidenced by their presence than by the attention they bestow on the performance." After the first few times, no one listened at all, except to a few favorite songs. The boxes were comfortably furnished and lighted so that their occupants could indulge in cards and other games. "Chess is marvellously well adapted to filling in the monotony of the recitatives, and the arias are equally good for interrupting a too assiduous concentration on chess." [42] Dr. Burney mentions the faro tables at the Milan opera;[43] at Venice, where the pit was usually filled with gondoliers and workmen, "there is a constant noise of people laughing, drinking, and joking, while sellers of baked goods and fruit cry their wares aloud from box to box";[44] at Florence it was the custom to serve hot suppers in the boxes during the performance.[45]

Some understanding of the circumstances under which these operas were performed will explain why we of today often fail to see what there was in the music to arouse enthusiasm on the part of the audiences. We must realize that those things which were the very life of the performance were just the things which could never be written in the score —the marvelous, constantly varied embellishments by the singers, the glamour of famous names, the intoxication of the lights and scenery, above all the gay, careless society of the eighteenth century, the game of chess during the recitatives, and the gabble of conversation, hushed only for the favorite aria and the following rapturous applause.

OTHER ELEMENTS OF OPERA SERIA. Although the arias were the chief musical feature, there were a few other elements. The chorus was limited to occasional interjections, or at most to short recurring phrases which could be memorized without difficulty. The only theatre works that used

[42] De Brosses, *Lettres . . . sur l'Italie* II, 36 *et passim*. But see also Lalande, *Voyage* V, chap. X.
[43] *Present State of Music in France and Italy*, pp. 81–82.
[44] Maier, *Beschreibung von Venedig* II, 284.
[45] Doran, *"Mann" and Manners at the Court of Florence*.

choruses at all extensively were of the type known as *festa teatrale*, not regular operas but pieces written for special occasions, like the festival operas of the earlier period. Hardly more important practically was the overture, since the composer knew there would be too much noise in the house for it to be heard. The orchestra [46] in accompaniments, however, was carefully managed, so as to support the singer without obscuring him. The first violins frequently played in unison with the voice—or rather, they played the simple written version of the melody which the singer was ornamenting. Ensembles were few; in the early part of the century there was usually no more than a perfunctory closing number for all the singers, but later this feature took on more importance, largely under the influence of the comic opera ensembles. Duets were more common, though even here much of the writing was a mere alternation rather than a combination of the two voices; a duet would be placed, like an aria, at the close of a scene, and was practically always in da capo form.

Two distinct types of recitative in eighteenth-century opera were inherited from the preceding age. The *recitativo semplice* ("simple"), later called *recitativo secco* ("dry"), was accompanied only by the continuo instruments.[47] Its function was to carry on the action in dialogue with the slightest possible musical accompaniment. Although audiences as a rule gave it little attention, the secco recitative was not altogether a perfunctory matter. Certain conventions of harmony and certain melodic formulas appear in it regularly, according with the fluctuating emotions of the text; and since the singers allowably took all sorts of rhythmic and melodic liberties with the score in the interest of "natural" expression, it is probable that the secco recitative had in performance considerably more dramatic impact than the bare written notes suggest.

The other kind of recitative was the *recitativo accompagnato* or *stromentato* ("accompanied recitative"), so called because it was accompanied either by the strings or the full orchestra in addition to the continuo. These recitatives were reserved for the two or three most dramatic points in the opera, for monologues expressing strong emotion at the climaxes of the action. The voice, declaiming in flexible, varied,

[46] See diagram of the Dresden Opera orchestra under Hasse in Rousseau, *Dictionnaire de musique, s.v.* "Orchestre."

[47] On the performance of the accompaniment in the eighteenth century, see Schneider, "Die Begleitung des Secco-Rezitativs um 1750"; Downes, "*Secco* Recitative in Early Classical Opera Seria."

and expressive phrases, alternated with orchestral outbursts of chords, tremolando figures, or rhythmic motifs. Sudden changes of mood, abrupt modulations, were featured. The essential function of the orchestra, indeed, was not so much to accompany the singer as to express, during the pauses of his song, the emotions which words were insufficient to convey—to suggest, in combination with the attitudes and gestures of the actor, those further depths of feeling which only music and movement, transcending the too definite ideas and images of a text, could adequately render.[48] The close union between words and music, together with the natural freedom of form, gave these places great dramatic power, and all contemporaries speak of them with enthusiasm. They were almost the only relief from the monotony of the recitativo secco on the one hand and the strict formality of the aria on the other, and it is significant that the accompanied recitative was especially cultivated by the later composers Hasse, Graun, and Terradellas, above all by Jommelli, Gluck, and Traetta, who were striving to break down the rigidity of the old operatic framework.

## THE COMPOSERS

Naples in the eighteenth century [49] was preeminent for its music as Venice had been in the seventeenth century. Lalande wrote in 1769 :

Music is the special triumph of the Neapolitans. It seems as if in that country the membranes of the eardrum are more taut, more harmonious, more sonorous than elsewhere in Europe. The whole nation sings; gesture, tone of voice, rhythm of syllables, the very conversation—all breathe music and harmony. Thus Naples is the principal source of Itàlian music, of great composers and excellent operas; it is there that Corelli, Vinci,. Rinaldo [di Capua], Jommelli, Durante (learned in harmony above all the rest), Leo, Pergolesi, Galuppi, Perez, Terradeglias, and so many other famous composers have brought forth their masterpieces.[50]

[48] Cf. Rousseau, "Récitatif obligé," in his *Dictionnaire de musique.*

[49] Florimo, *La scuola musicale di Napoli* (the basic work, a thoroughgoing study of the Neapolitan conservatories, teachers, composers, and singers to the middle of the nineteenth century); Croce, *I teatri di Napoli*; Roberti, "La musica in Italia nel secolo XVIII"; Grosley, *New Observations on Italy* (1769); Schletterer, "Die Opernhäuser Neapels."

[50] Lalande, *Voyage d'un françois en Italie* VI, 345. Of the composers named, all but two (Corelli and Durante) were famous chiefly for operas. Francesco Durante (1684–1755), though he wrote no operas himself, was the teacher of many of the most important Italian opera composers of the eighteenth century.

## Aria from *Artaserse*, Act III, sc. 1

Example 62

L. Vinci

(24 measures introduction)

(*Violin I colla voce*)

Violin II

Voice

L'on-da del mar di - vi-sa ba - gna la val - le, il

Violas and Continuo

(*Horns:*)

mon - te, và pas-sag-gie - ra in fiu - me và pri-gio-

(*1st and 2nd violins*)

-nie - ra in fon - te mar-mo - ra sem-pre, e ge - me

*(Example 62 continued)*

Among the opera composers active at Naples immediately after the time of Alessandro Scarlatti were Leonardo Vinci (1690–1730) [51] and Leonardo Leo (1694–1744).[52] Vinci was among the earliest composers of comic opera in Neapolitan dialect. He is also one of the first in whose music the traits of the new opera seria are fully apparent. Example 62 shows the beginning (after an orchestral introduction) of a da capo aria from his *Artaserse* (1730), typical for its fresh, clear melody, simple harmonic vocabulary, and thin texture in the string orchestra, colored by a few passages from the horns, doubtless suggested by the rural landscape depicted in the text. Leo was also important for his comic operas. The most successful of his serious operas was *Demofoonte* (Naples, 1735). The immensely facile Nicola Porpora (1686–1768) [53] worked at Naples and Venice, and at various times also in London, Dresden, and Vienna. Porpora was the greatest singing teacher of his time. Dr. Burney remarked about one of his arias that it seemed to have been composed "in a shivering fit," [54] so full was it of vocal pyrotechnics; but this probably does injustice to Porpora, whose music, if not especially distinguished, is workmanlike and no more extreme in its demands on the singers than that of other composers of the time.

The only Neapolitan composer of operas in this period whose name is at all well known today was Giovanni Battista Pergolesi (1710–36).[55] Though remembered now chiefly for his *Stabat Mater* and his comic intermezzi, Pergolesi in his short lifetime produced also one of the finest *opere serie* of the early eighteenth century. This was *Olimpiade* (Rome, 1735), one of Metastasio's most popular dramas. An aria from this opera (Example 63) illustrates the "tenderness of sentiment . . . noble, attractive, enthusiastic feeling, an innocent, touching, childlike quality" [56] that characterizes Pergolesi's music. Note particularly the use of "Lombardic rhythm" in the melody at measure four and elsewhere, also the triplet divisions of the eighth-note beat, both typical characteristics of the style of this period. Pergolesi's serious operas, despite their

[51] On Vinci, see Silva, *Illustri musicisti calabresi*; Dent, "Notes on Leonardo Vinci."

[52] Biography by G. Pastore (1957); earlier studies by G. Leo (see bibliography).

[53] See Villarosa, *Memorie dei compositori*; Di Giacomo, *Il conservatorio dei poveri*; idem, *Il conservatorio di Sant' Onofrio*; Fassini, *Il melodramma italiano a Londra*.

[54] *History* II, 842.

[55] Biography by Radiciotto. See also below, p. 248.

[56] Kretzschmar, *Geschichte der Oper*, p. 172.

## L'Olimpiade, Act I, sc. 8

EXAMPLE 63

PERGOLESI

(Example 63 continued)

merit (or, perhaps, because of it), procured him no popular success among his compatriots.

One of the remarkable phenomena of the eighteenth century was the way Italian opera, both serious and comic, spread to every country of Europe. This movement involved the importation not only of scores and singers but frequently of composers as well. Italian-born or Italian-trained composers would go for a season, or for a few years, to a foreign city or court, where they would conduct their operas and compose new ones tailored to local requirements. Thus Attilio Ariosti (1666–*ca.* 1740) [57] of Modena worked at Vienna, Berlin, and London; Giovanni Bononcini (1670–1747) of Bologna and his brother Marc Antonio Bononcini (1677–1726) [58] also worked at Vienna and London. The latter's *Trionfo di Camilla, regina de' Volsci* ("The Triumph of Camilla, Queen of the Volsci"), first given at Naples in 1696, was one of the most popular works of the early eighteenth century; it was heard in Italian cities as late as 1715 and held the stage in London for a total of 113 performances (most of them in English translation) from 1706 to 1728. [59]

As in the seventeenth century so in the eighteenth, the South German courts attracted many of the best Italian opera composers. At Vienna, the principal successors of Fux were Antonio Caldara (1670–1736) [60] and Francesco Conti (1681–1732), in whose music the change from baroque to preclassical traits is manifest, though the Vienna opera always retained somewhat of the formal style, the magnificence of staging, and the participation of chorus and ballet which we have already noticed in Fux's ceremonial operas. [61] Caldara, a Venetian by birth, was a pupil of Legrenzi; Conti, born at Florence, came to Vienna in 1701. The most successful of his operas was *Don Chisciotte* (1719), a "tragicommedia per musica" on a libretto by Zeno after Cervantes.

The most thoroughly representative composer of Italian opera around the middle of the eighteenth century was not an Italian but a German, Johann Adolph Hasse (1699–1783). [62] Hasse began his musical

---

[57] Ebert, *Attilio Ariosti in Berlin*; Frati, "Attilio Ottavio Ariosti."

[58] Valdrighi, *I Bononcini da Modena*.

[59] Loewenberg, *Annals*, 1696.

[60] See Gmeyner, "Die Opern M. A. Caldaras."

[61] See Lady Mary Wortley Montagu, *Letters* (3d ed.) I, 239, Sept. 14 (O.S.), 1716.

[62] Gerber, *Der Operntypus Johann Adolf Hasses*; Mennicke, *Hasse und die Brüder Graun als Sinfoniker; idem,* "Johann Adolph Hasse"; Zeller, *Das recitativo accompagnato in den Opern Johann Adolf Hasses*; Burney, *The Present State of Music in Germany* I, *passim.*

career as a tenor singer at the Hamburg and Brunswick opera houses. His first opera was produced at the latter city in 1721. He studied then at Naples under Porpora and A. Scarlatti, and had several works performed there before moving to Venice in 1727. Here he met and married a famous singer, Faustina Bordoni, and their two careers were joined from then on. In 1731 Hasse was appointed musical director of the Dresden opera, with his wife the *prima donna*. He continued to hold his position at Dresden until 1763 while taking frequent travel leaves in order to present his operas elsewhere—at London, Warsaw, Vienna, and various Italian cities. Between 1721 and 1771 Hasse wrote more than fifty operas, the majority of them on librettos of Metastasio, with whom he enjoyed a close friendship. The joint works of these two men exemplify the type of eighteenth-century *opera seria* that we have described in the first part of this chapter. Hasse had so thoroughly assimilated the Italian spirit that he was known familiarly in that country as "il caro Sassone"—"the beloved Saxon." His operas were given all over Europe; during his prime he was generally acclaimed as the greatest living master of vocal music,[63] though he had the misfortune to outlive the period of his greatest fame. His style is marked by an easy flow of elegant, tasteful, and singable melody. No doubt there is much in his music to justify criticism that he was merely another composer gifted with facility and understanding of the voice but without dramatic insight and uninterested in the instrumental parts of his operas; nevertheless, such criticism must be tempered by remembrance of the operatic ideals of his time and of the peculiar qualities of the Metastasian librettos. These qualities Hasse completely understood; and he wrote music to correspond to them, untroubled by any revolutionary impulses. His arias are models of that musical feeling which transmutes everything into beautiful melody, flowering naturally into long smooth curves of coloratura—superficial perhaps, but with a surface of such perfection that it seems captious to demand more (Example 64). Yet even within this style, Hasse is not without certain traits here and there which foreshadow a change in operatic ideals. His arias, though always in the prevailing da capo form, are well constructed, with a feeling for real development rather than mere repetition of the themes. In the later works, even the da capo form itself becomes more plastic. His respect for the integrity of the drama is in contrast to the carelessness of some

[63] See Burney, *Present State of Music in Germany* I, 234.

*Didone abbandonata*, Act II, sc. 10

EXAMPLE 64

HASSE

Ta - ce - rò se tu lo bra - mi ma fai tor - to al - la mia fe - de se mi chia - mi tra - di - tor, se mi chia - - - - - mi se mi chia - mi tra - di - tor, se mi chia - mi tra - di - tor.

earlier Italians in this regard; he is no slave to the conventional pattern of regular alternation of arias and secco recitatives but will on occasion freely intermingle passages in different styles as the situation demands. His handling of the orchestra is above the general level of opera composers of his time. Moreover, and particularly in the accompanied recitatives for which he was so celebrated, he sometimes shows a depth of expression which may be attributable to his Germanic origin (as German historians are fond of pointing out), but which in any case is not a quality for which most Italian composers of the early eighteenth century, except Scarlatti, were distinguished.

The typical full or five-part da capo aria as found at its highest point of development in Hasse has the following scheme :

A (first four-line stanza) : ritornello I; first section, cadencing on the dominant or relative major; ritornello II; second section, in the nature of a development of the material of the first, with extended coloratura passages, modulating back to the tonic and sometimes with a return of the theme of the first section; cadenza; ritornello III.

B (second four-line stanza) : in one section, shorter than A, in a related key, and with material either (1) continuing and developing that of A, or (2) contrasting with A; ending with cadenza, then ritornello IV (usually = ritornello I).

A da capo (usually without ritornello I), with additional improvised coloraturas and a longer cadenza.

The above scheme is frequently shortened in later composers (for example, Di Majo) by omitting a portion of part A in the da capo, or by setting both stanzas in a one-movement ABA' form. The da capo aria in one shape or another, however, persists through the whole eighteenth-century opera seria, along with other aria forms.

Another Italianized German, contemporary with Hasse, was Karl Heinrich Graun (1704–59),[64] the official composer of Frederick the Great of Prussia. This monarch, who supervised with the closest interest all musical productions at his court, was enamored of Hasse's operas, and as a natural consequence Graun's music for the Berlin opera was similar in style to that of his famous compatriot. The libretto of Graun's *Montezuma* (1755), written by King Frederick himself in French prose and translated into Italian verse by the court poet, is remarkable as being one of the comparatively rare modern subjects in eighteenth-century opera—the conquest of Mexico by Cortez. On the strength of this background the ballets even make some attempt at local color, though with rather feeble results. The chief historical importance of *Montezuma* is the preponderance (in the ratio of about two to one) of the "cavatina" over the traditional da capo aria.

The word "cavatina"[65] comes from the Italian *cavare*, "to draw out, to excavate"; hence one meaning of *cavata* is that of something buried or

[64] See A. Mayer-Reinach, "Carl Heinrich Graun als Opernkomponist"; *idem*, "Zur Herausgabe des *Montezuma*"; Yorke-Long, *Music at Court*, chap. iv; Strunk, *Source Readings*, pp. 699–710.

[65] On the history and significance of "cavatina" see Pirrotta, "Falsirena e la più antica delle cavatine."

concealed. Thus in vocal compositions of the fifteenth and sixteenth centuries there were *soggetti cavati*, for example, themes (in the tenor) which "concealed" a name, each vowel of which was represented by a note (a by *fa*, e by *re*, i by *mi*, and so on). Walther's *Lexikon* (1732) defines cavata as a short arioso passage, occurring usually at the end of a recitative, in which the mood or meaning of the recitative is concentrated or drawn forth. Cavatina (the diminutive of cavata) is used in the eighteenth century as opposed to aria in the sense of a vocal number which "gathers together" an aria (that is, a da capo aria) in shorter and simpler form, without much text repetition or coloratura. In general, the word defines a *type* of song rather than any particular formal scheme. In the nineteenth-century opera it signifies merely a song of a lyric nature, usually forming part of a larger *scena.*

The cavatinas in *Montezuma* are in two-part form without repeats and with the following key scheme : Tonic → Dominant‖Dominant → (modulations) → Tonic, the ending of the second part repeating that of the first more or less exactly but in the tonic key. Thus the scheme is that already exemplified in the principal section of many of the large-scale da capo arias in the works of Vinci, Schürmann, and Hasse, corresponding to the typical contemporary instrumental sonata· first-movement form. It may be regarded as a truncated da capo aria : an elaborate first section, but without the traditional middle (contrasting) section or the traditional recapitulation of Part A. The· decline of the da capo had already begun in Germany by the 1730s; many of the German scores of that period bear the direction *senza da capo* at the end of the arias.[66]

It is uncertain whether the large proportion of cavatinas in *Montezuma* is due to the librettist or the composer. Graun had used the form in earlier works, but Frederick claims the credit in this instance :

As for the cavatinas, I have seen some by Hasse which are infinitely more beautiful than the arias [that is, da capo arias]. . . . There is no need of repetition, except when the singers know how to make variations [note that "except" !]; but it seems to me, in any case, that it is an abuse to repeat the same thing four times. Your actors . . . were never obliged to do such a stupid thing.[67]

This statement is interesting not only as the comment of an intelligent contemporary on one of the conventions of eighteenth-century opera but also as a presentiment of the theories of Gluck on the same subject.

Graun's music is in typical mid-eighteenth-century style. The over-

[66] See G. F. Schmidt, *Die frühdeutsche Oper* II, 397 ff.
[67] In a letter to his sister May 4, 1754, quoted in DdT XV, Introduction, p. ix.

ture [68] is of the Italian type, in three movements, with homophonic texture, short themes, a simple harmonic vocabulary, many repetitions and sequential patterns, broken-chord figures, and the "Lombardic

[68] On the overtures to Graun's other operas see Mennicke, *Hasse und die Brüder Graun*, chaps. III and IV.

## Montezuma, Act III, sc. 1

EXAMPLE 65                                                         GRAUN

Sen - za   pe - na ab - ban-do-no u - na gran-dez-za, che fra-gil troppo e

(strings and continuo)

va - na ò  co - no-sciu - ta,   e   sen-za in - su - per-bir-ne ò pos-se-

du - ta.                         Sem-pre a la - sciar quei be - ni

(*Example 65 continued*)

on - de la dee pri - va - re un di    la    mor - te, pron-taes-ser de - ve    un' al-ma

gran-de    e    for- te.

*f*        *poco piano e lento*

Ma    tu,    spo - sa    fe - de - le!

*p*

rhythm" ( ♪♩.), a device very common in the music of this period.[69]
The arias are well written, though occasionally, as in Keiser, there are

[69] Quantz (*Versuch*, ed. Schering, p. 241) says this rhythm was introduced
"about the year 1722." Burney (*History* II, 847) complains of its abuse in operas
sung at London in 1748.

figures which suggest the instrumental rather than the vocal idiom. The secco recitatives show some harmonic variety and are enlivened by the use of deceptive cadences. (Musical improvement of the secco recitative is a noticeable feature in the work of many composers by the middle of the century.) The accompanied recitatives are excellent examples of this style (Example 65).

Among the Italianized German composers after Hasse and Graun we may mention Johann Gottlieb Naumann (1741–1801) [70] of Dresden, a celebrity in his time and a typical representative of the *Empfindsamkeit* of the late eighteenth century. Curiously enough, the best-remembered opera of Naumann is *Cora och Alonzo*, composed on a Swedish text in 1779 and performed for the inauguration of a new opera house at Stockholm in 1782. This work was frequently revived at Stockholm until 1832, and also appeared on many German stages in translation.

## THE LATER EIGHTEENTH CENTURY [71]

Certain writers in the past have tended to regard everything in eighteenth-century opera before Gluck as being somewhat in the nature of a necessary but regrettable episode, declining about the middle of the century to a hopelessly low state of affairs, which Gluck, practically singlehanded, redeemed through his so-called reforms—the very word carrying with it an aura of moral uplift, implying that something bad was replaced by something better. This point of view—a relic of the evolutionary philosophy of history—has had the consequence of leading to the neglect of early and middle eighteenth-century Italian opera composers, a failure to appreciate their real merits and the qualities of their music in relation to its period and the circumstances for which it was composed. The situation has been aggravated by the fact that Italian scholars, who of all people should be most concerned to set this matter in its true light, have so far not made much of the music of their own composers available in modern editions. The German musicologists, as is only natural, have concerned themselves chiefly with either composers of German birth or composers who were active in Germany, and even here they have been more attentive to those aspects of the music which appeal to Germans—more serious quality of expressiveness, richer

[70] Breitholtz, *Studier i operan Gustaf Wasa.*

[71] Several operas by composers mentioned in this section are discussed and analyzed in Part II of Heinse's novel *Hildegard von Hohenthal.* Cf. Lauppert, *Die Musikästhetik Wilhelm Heinses.*

texture, greater importance of the orchestra—than to the fundamentally vocal and melodic traits characteristic of Italy. The result is that the importance of Gluck, great as it unquestionably is, has been exaggerated by an inadequate idea both of the real nature of the situation against which he was striving and of the contributions of other composers who to some extent anticipated his doctrines.[72]

The reform of opera was no new thing with Gluck. Opera is always being reformed; that is to say, it is always changing, and one is presumably entitled to call any marked change which he regards as being in the right direction, a reform. A more objective viewpoint is neatly stated by Martin Cooper :

Opera is constructed of three elements—the musical, the literary, and the spectacular; and at different times each of these three elements has in fact gained an undue supremacy over the other two. For this reason the history of opera is the history of a series of reformations and counter-reformations, no two countries and no two epochs agreeing on the role that each element should ideally play in the constitution of the whole. Neither evolutionary nor unified, it is the history of perpetually recurring schools of thought, one never victorious over the other, though occasionally gaining the majority of popular opinion.[73]

Granting, then, that in much of the Italian opera of the early eighteenth century the elements of melody and display of singers' virtuosity had usurped too large a place in the scheme, it was natural that a reaction should take place calculated to restore the balance. Then, too, by the middle of the century there was a general turning away from the frivolities of the age of the Regency, and with this went a desire to make music more serious and expressive. The new Empfindsamkeit, which was at first nothing more than an infusion of a tender and pretty sentimentality into the fabric of rococo music, prepared the way for the classical style of the later eighteenth century. A deepening of the texture, an increased attention to harmonic variety and to the inner voices in the composition, were natural concomitants of this change. French opera, with its informal mingling of recitative and aria and its emphasis on ballet, chorus, and spectacle, began to exert some influence on composers in other countries. Finally, the comic opera, constantly increasing in popularity, acted as a goad through parody and satire and at the same

[72] Goldschmidt, "Die Reform der italienischen Oper des 18. Jahrhunderts."
[73] *Gluck* (New York, Oxford University Press, 1935), p. 4. Quoted by permission of the publisher.

time provided a living example of the effects to be gained through simplicity and variety of style with new types of subject matter, forcing the creators of serious opera to take stock and adapt themselves to a new generation of audiences.

Not all the influences came from the side of music. The rise of the sentimental novel (Richardson) and above all the cult of naturalness popularized by Rousseau wrought such changes in literary thought and expression that the opera libretto, and consequently opera music, could not possibly remain aloof. But as these changes are to be more clearly observed in the field of comic opera (through which in large measure their effects were transmitted to the serious opera), we shall defer a more detailed consideration of them until later.

We have already intimated that Gluck was not the only reformer in the eighteenth century. As a matter of fact, there was hardly a composer of serious opera after 1750 who was not touched by the general movement of reaction against the older type. As in all such changes, there were moderates and radicals. The radical reform movement took place almost wholly outside Italy and, as far as its consequences for Italian opera went, was short-lived. We shall deal with the radical reformers later; at present we are concerned with the moderate or evolutionary changes that came into opera seria everywhere after the middle of the eighteenth century.

These changes affected both the libretto and the music.[74] It was typical of the more moderate composers that they continued to use Metastasio's librettos, although he himself wrote only four new ones between 1754 and his death in 1782. But in the settings of the later eighteenth century the Metastasian librettos were altered : many recitatives and arias were deleted; ensembles and occasionally choruses were added. The whole tendency was to make an opera a less regular but more organic whole, with arias and ensembles more often carrying on the action instead of being merely static moments in its flow. The distinction between recitative and aria was still maintained; but accompanied recitatives became longer and more elaborate and some scenes were composed in a free alternation of recitative, arioso, aria, and ensemble. The old five-part da capo aria virtually disappeared in favor of various more compact versions of the basic da capo scheme; other

[74] For a detailed treatment of this topic, with musical examples, see Downes, "The Operas of Johann Christian Bach," Vol. I.

aria forms were also used, among them a two-movement form, generally in the order slow–fast. Within the general pattern, the music came to be organized in longer and more complex phrases. More attention was given to the orchestra : the texture was enriched; greater variety of color and more thematic independence were sought. All three movements of the Italian overture became longer and more elaborate; occasionally overtures might be in one movement, usually a sonata-allegro form. Moreover, in the last part of the century, and especially after Gluck had set the example in his first "reform" works, it became increasingly common to relate the overture to the particular opera introduced, sometimes only by foreshadowing the general mood, sometimes by using themes that would later appear in the body of the opera.[75] This was a contrast to the practice of the early eighteenth century when as a rule the overture was a neutral, independent composition that might have served equally well for almost any opera.

Among the moderate reformers in the eighteenth century we may certainly class Hasse and Graun, the extent of whose innovations has already been noted. A slightly younger and more progressive group includes Davide Pérez (1711–68), whose scores are remarkable for their wealth of feeling as well as for the skill of their instrumental music. His most important opera was *Solimano*, first performed at Lisbon in 1757. Another Spanish composer active in Italy, Domingo Terradellas (1713–51),[76] was noted for his depiction of violent emotions and for the daring quality of his modulations. His principal work was a setting of Metastasio's *Artaserse* (Venice, 1744).

Three composers of a later generation may be briefly mentioned here. Gian Francesco di Majo (1732–70) ranks with Pérez and Terradellas as one who brought into the regular tradition of Italian opera certain individual qualities, particularly in the expression of sorrowful emotions and in the fineness and elegance of his style, of which the aria "Se mai più saro geloso" from *Alessandro* (Naples, 1767) is an example.[77] Other important operas of Majo are *Cajo Fabricio* (Naples, 1760) and *Ifigenia in Tauride* (1764), which comes close to the advanced reform

---

[75] See Botstiber, *Geschichte der Ouvertüre*, chaps. 5–7; Mennicke, *Hasse und die Brüder Graun*, chap. VI.

[76] Carreras y Bulbena, *Domenech Terradellas* (contains musical examples); Volkmann, "Domenico Terradellas"; Mitjana, "Les Espagnols italianisants," in Lavignac, *Encyclopédie*, Part I, Vol. IV, pp. 2195–2209.

[77] Printed in Bücken, *Rokoko und Klassik*, p. 115.

ideals of Gluck. (It may be noted that this work was composed not for an Italian audience but for the German court of Mannheim.) Johann Christian Bach (1735–82),[78] known as the "Milan" or the "London" Bach, was the youngest surviving son of the great Johann Sebastian. Having moved to Milan shortly after his father's death, he turned Catholic and became as completely Italianized in his music as Graun or Hasse. Bach was one of the most popular of the later composers in the Italian style. Among his operas are *Alessandro nell' Indie* (Naples, 1762), *Lucio Silla* (Mannheim, 1774), *La clemenza di Scipione* (London, 1778), and one on a revised version of Quinault's *Amadis de Gaule* (Paris, 1779), in which he endeavored to adapt his style to the French requirements. Bach's music, elegant and expressive though seldom profoundly emotional, clear in form, expert in detail, most characteristic in lyrical moods and cantabile melodies, was much admired by the young Mozart.[79] Dr. Burney states that in his arias "the richness of the accompaniments perhaps deserve [*sic*] more praise than the originality of the melodies; which, however, are always natural, elegant, and in the best taste of Italy at the time he came over." [80]

One of the last composers of opera seria in the eighteenth-century tradition was Giuseppe Sarti (1729–1802),[81] whose career, like that of many of his contemporaries, took him to foreign courts : Copenhagen for most of the period 1755–75, and St. Petersburg from 1784 to the end of his life. The most successful of his serious operas was *Giulio Sabino* (Venice, 1781), but he was longer remembered for his works in lighter vein, particularly for the opera buffa *Fra due litiganti il terzo gode*, from which Mozart quoted a phrase in *Don Giovanni*. Sarti's serious operas show, along with many traditional features, some influence of newer ideas, especially in their powerful accompanied recitatives. His graceful melodies and the profusion of his ideas often suggest the style of Mozart.

An Italian contemporary of Mozart was Nicola Antonio Zingarelli (1752–1837), one of the last of the eighteenth-century Neapolitan composers. His principal opera, *Giulietta e Romeo*, with a libretto based on

---

[78] Downes, "The Operas of Johann Christian Bach"; Terry, *Johann Christian Bach* (see also review in ZfMw XVI [1934] 182–88); Schwarz, "Johann Christian Bach"; H. Abert, "Johann Christian Bach's italienische Opern"; Geiringer, *The Bach Family.*

[79] Abert, *Mozart* I, 58, 242–49; cf. Köchel, *Verzeichnis* (3d ed.), No. 293e.

[80] *History* II, 866.

[81] See Scudo, *Le Chevalier Sarti*, and the sequel "Frédérique," *Revue des deux mondes* (1863–64); Rivalta, *G. Sarti*; Mooser, *Annales* II, 415–50, 463–79.

Shakespeare, was performed at Milan in 1796 and continued to be played for more than twenty-five years. Most of Zingarelli's dramatic works were serious, but he also had some success with a comic opera, *Il mercato di Monfregoso* (Milan, 1792).

The radical reform movement in eighteenth-century opera, as we have already noted, took its course mainly outside Italy. The two Italian composers chiefly associated with this movement were Niccolò Jommelli (1714–74) and Tommaso Traetta (1727–79). Jommelli [82] produced a large number of operas, both serious and comic, in Italy beginning in 1737. His earliest works were quite in traditional style, but signs of change and experimentation became evident by 1750. Perhaps unfortunately, in 1749 Jommelli became acquainted with Metastasio at Vienna and remained under his spell ever thereafter, with the result that he was never moved to make a fundamental break with the older type of opera libretto. Two of his most successful works were settings of Metastasian texts: *Demofoonte* (Padua, 1743) and *Didone abbandonata* (Rome, 1747). The climax of Jommelli's life was his period of service (1753–69) as chapelmaster to the Duke of Württemberg at Stuttgart—a German court, but one in which French taste was an important factor. It was in the works written in Germany that Jommelli's innovations were most marked, and particularly in *Fetonte* (Ludwigsburg, 1768), on a libretto by M. Verazi. His last operas, written after he had returned to Naples in 1769, were received coldly by his countrymen, who found his new style "too German." So strong was the admixture of northern elements in his music that he has been called "the Italian Gluck."

Traetta,[83] by both temperament and circumstances, was led to even greater departure from the accepted Italian models of his time. Like Jommelli, he began with successes in Italian theatres, including two operas on librettos of Metastasio: *Didone abbandonata* (Venice, 1757) and *Olimpiade* (Verona, 1758). An important influence in Traetta's career was his term of service from 1758 to 1765 at the court of Parma, which was dominated by French ideas of opera. Some of his most important later works were written for the German stage: *Armida* (1761)

[82] H. Abert, *Niccolo Jommelli als Opernkomponist*; *idem*, "Zur Geschichte der Oper in Württemberg"; Alfieri, *Notizie biografiche*; Yorke-Long, *Music at Court*.

[83] On Traetta, see studies by Nuovo, Damerini, Raeli, Casavola, and Schlitzer; also Yorke-Long, *Music at Court*; Mooser, *Annales* II, 87–132.

and *Ifigenia in Tauride* (1763) for Vienna, *Sofonisba* (1762) for Mannheim. From 1768 to 1775 Traetta was at the court of St. Petersburg.

What are the qualities in the operas of Jommelli and Traetta—qualities most strongly evident in the works for non-Italian theatres—that have caused their composers to be numbered among the reformers in the eighteenth century?

The first is their international character. Earlier Italian composers, though they traveled a great deal, always took with them the Italian tradition and preserved it untouched by foreign musical influences, even of those countries in which they worked. At this time there was only one school of opera in Europe outside Italy, namely that of France, which had been preserved by virtue of almost complete isolation from Italian music in the first half of the century. By 1750 the French opera had begun, though slightly, to make itself felt by composers in those courts and cities which in other respects also were touched by French culture —meaning, in effect, the German courts and a few in northern Italy. French influence was still strong on German life throughout the eighteenth century to the time of Lessing, Herder, and Goethe, as witness in literature the doctrines of Gottsched (1700–1766) and in manners Frederick the Great of Prussia (1712–86), the great friend of Voltaire, who habitually spoke and wrote French and despised German as "the language of boors." It happened that both Jommelli and Traetta came into this French orbit, the former at Stuttgart and the latter at Parma. The very subjects of some of Traetta's operas are significant, for example, *I tintaridi* (1760), a translation of Rameau's *Castor et Pollux*; *Le Feste d'Imeneo* (1760), a *festa teatrale* or opéra-ballet similar to Rameau's *Fêtes d'Hébé* of 1739; and *Ippolito ed Arice* (1759), the same subject as Rameau's *Hyppolite et Aricie*. Traetta's principal librettists, Marco Coltellini (*ca.* 1740–75) and Carlo Frugoni (1692–1768), were well acquainted with Rameau's works. Coltellini was a pupil of Calsabigi; in 1765 he was engaged to prepare the libretto of *Telemacco* for Gluck, and in 1772 Calsabigi designated him as his successor at the Vienna court. The importance of the ballets in both Jommelli's and Traetta's operas is another sign of French influence. At Stuttgart the ballet master was Jean-Georges Noverre (1720–1810), author of a celebrated treatise [84] and later ballet master at the Paris Opéra, who

[84] *Lettres sur la danse et les ballets*, 1760. See H. Abert, "J. G. Noverre," in *Gesammelte Schriften*, pp. 264–86.

advocated a return to Greek ideals of the dance, with naturalness of movements, simplicity of costume, and emphasis on the dramatic content of the ballet rather than on abstract figures or virtuosity of the dancers. Another evidence of French taste in Traetta and Jommelli is the greater prominence of the spectacular element in their operas, as in Traetta's *Sofonisba*, with temple scenes, battle scenes, the submarine palace of Thetis, the transformations of Proteus—all reminiscent of Lully and Rameau. Equally French are the pictorial details in the music, touches of that imitation of nature so dear to eighteenth-century aestheticians : storms, battles, pastoral idyls, even the rhythm of a horse's galloping imitated in the second violins throughout an aria,[85] or the realistic direction *urlo francese* ("French howl"), a cry rather than a musical note, literally imitating the sound of the voice under stress of emotion.[86]

The German influence on Jommelli and Traetta is seen in their treatment of the orchestra, in a greater complexity of texture and increased attention to idiomatic use of the instruments. The orchestra was the medium through which German music in the eighteenth century began its conquering career in Europe; the Mannheim orchestra was famous by 1745, while those of Dresden under Hasse and Stuttgart under Jommelli (there were forty-seven players for his *Fetonte* in 1768) were hardly less celebrated. Likewise due to German influence is the greater richness and variety of the harmonies in both Jommelli and Traetta, as compared with their Italian contemporaries.

Another aspect of the operas of Jommelli and Traetta is the way in which they consistently aim at a closer coordination of music and drama. One sign of this is the decreased proportion of secco recitative, a style which by its very nature excludes any thorough participation of music in the action. To a greater extent than ever before, secco recitatives are replaced by the accompanied variety. In the second act of Jommelli's *Demofoonte* only two of the eleven scenes are secco, all the rest being accompanied by full orchestra; this is an extreme instance, but it illustrates the whole tendency of the century which culminates in the later works of Gluck, where the secco recitative is abolished altogether. Among the accompanied recitatives in these operas are some splendid examples of dramatic power, such as the tenth scene of Act III of

---

[85] "Quel destriere" in Jommelli's *Olimpiade*.
[86] Traetta's *Sofonisba*.

Traetta's *Sofonisba*. The treatment of the aria also undergoes a change: many are so contrived as to further the action rather than interrupt it as in the older Italian opera; the melodic style is more expressive and covers a wider range of emotions. A distinctly Mozartean quality is apparent in some of the cantabile arias, such as "Non piangete" from Traetta's *Antigona* (1772) (Example 66). A sense of climax and proportion, a sure

*Antigona*, Act III, sc. 2

EXAMPLE 66                                                    TRAETTA

grasp of the principles of musical form and their adaptation to the dramatic situation, are everywhere evident.[87] The tendency is constantly toward greater fluidity, toward breaking down the old hard-and-fast boundaries between recitative and aria. We often find long scene-complexes in which accompanied recitative, arioso, aria, ensemble, and chorus all participate freely. Even the conventional da capo pattern of the arias is artfully concealed: more prominence is given to the middle (contrasting) section, especially in Traetta; on repetition, the principal section is shortened or otherwise altered; changes of mood, of metre, and of tempo are incorporated; declamatory (recitative) sections occur in the midst of an aria; or an accompanied recitative and the following aria will use the same thematic material—all changes from the old order, some of which had, however, been anticipated by earlier composers.

The changing conception of the overture is another eighteenth-century tendency which finds reflection in the works of Jommelli and

[87] See for example Jommelli's *Fetonte*, Act II, scs. 8–9.

Traetta. One of the points of Gluck's reform manifesto of 1769 is a statement of the new ideal of an overture which should be specifically connected with the drama following; though neither Jommelli nor Traetta consistently aimed at this ideal, their operas do show certain interesting features. Thus in Traetta's *Sofonisba* the theme of the slow movement of the overture recurs in a quintet in the last scene of the opera—a device similar to that employed by Rameau in *Castor et Pollux* twenty-five years earlier—and the finale leads without pause directly into the first scene of Act I. Both here and in Jommelli's *Fetonte* the overture evidently suggests the general course of the drama—as in Rameau's *Zoroastre* of 1749. In *Fetonte*, the very short first movement of the overture leads at once into the first scene of the opera (an andante solo with chorus), which replaces the usual second movement; then follows the "third" movement, a musical depiction of an earthquake (as in many French operas), after which, with the second scene of Act I, the opera proper begins. The overture to Majo's *Ifigenia in Tauride* is a similar compromise between the old Italian concert overture and the later nineteenth-century program type, which was first exemplified in Gluck's *Iphigénie en Aulide* (1772) and brought to full realization in Beethoven's *Fidelio* (1806).

The French example, and the departure from the Italian norm, are most clearly evidenced in Jommelli and Traetta by the return of the chorus to an important place in their operas not written for Italian performance. Choruses are numerous and often of large dimensions; they do not merely appear in the spectacle scenes but also form part of the action. Perhaps the most notable instance is the fourth scene of Act II of Traetta's *Ifigenie in Tauride*, in which the pleadings of Orestes are interrupted by outbursts of the Chorus of Furies. Although the librettos are not the same, an interesting comparison may be made between this and the parallel scene in Gluck's *Iphigénie en Tauride* (Act II), written twenty years later. In spite of their impressive scale and appearance, the choruses in Traetta never attain the real solemnity and impact of the great choral scenes of Rameau and Gluck, or of Mozart's *Idomeneo*. The eighteenth-century Italians apparently lacked feeling for the full dramatic possibilities of the chorus.

In sum, while the operas of Jommelli and Traetta show many important differences from what may be called the orthodox Italian opera seria of the eighteenth century, they still do not make a complete break with it. In Jommelli particularly, and in Traetta to a lesser degree, the old type of libretto still prevails. The old duality of poem and music is weakened but not overcome. In spite of all changes in detail, the works remain singers' operas, with the old virtuoso display, improvised embellishments, and cadenzas. Furthermore, and by comparison with Gluck, the style of the music itself is still essentially rococo : it is, for the most part, elegant and polished rather than simple and passionate; attention is directed to a smooth surface rather than to depth; melody is still the chief issue, not harmony; the rhythms are restless, nervous, almost as though the composer felt the audience would go to sleep if not constantly titillated by new and unexpected turns. The whole is, from the standpoint of a genuine classicism, overornamented; it is full of merely decorative short notes, trills, graces, snaps, runs, and appoggia-turas—a frilly, lace-valentine texture, related to that of Gluck as a courtier's dress to a simple peasant costume.

# CHAPTER 15

# THE OPERAS OF GLUCK[1]

Christoph Willibald Gluck was born in 1714, the son of a Bohemian forester. After acquiring some knowledge of music in the elementary schools, he went to Prague, where he remained from 1732 to 1736. After a short spell at Vienna as a chamber musician in the employ of Prince Ferdinand Philip Lobkowitz, he was sent by another noble patron to study with Sammartini at Milan. No details of his early musical education are known for certain; he must have become acquainted in Prague with the current Italian opera as represented by Hasse, while at Vienna he would have heard the older style of Caldara. At Vienna likewise he met Metastasio, whose poetry appealed to him as to every other opera composer; seventeen of Gluck's operas were on Metastasian librettos. His studies with Sammartini opened to him the new world of modern symphonic music. His first ten operas were successfully performed at Milan and other Italian cities between 1741 and 1745. They are distinguished from those of contemporary Italian composers by a certain melodic freedom and individual energy of expression, but they show no traces of the revolutionary principles for which he later became famous.[2] In the season of 1745–46 Gluck visited London, where he

---

[1] Of Gluck's approximately one hundred dramatic works, about half have been preserved either wholly or in part. For editions, see list (p. 776) and Hopkinson's *Bibliography*. The leading biographies are those of Schmid (1854), Marx (1863), Arend (1921), and Gerber (1950). There is a thematic catalogue of Gluck's works by Wotquenne (supplement by Liebeskind, additions and corrections by Arend). Important material is found in the publications of the Gluck-Gesellschaft (4 vols., 1913–18). See Wortsmann, *Die deutsche Gluckliteratur* (1914) for additional bibliography. The best books in English are those of Einstein (translated by Eric Blom), Newman, and Cooper.

[2] For a technical study of all the operas before *Orfeo*, with musical examples, see Kurth, "Die Jugendopern Glucks"; cf. also H. Abert, "Glucks italienische Opern," *Gluck-Jahrbuch II* (1915) 1–25, and the same author's introduction to *Le nozze d'Ercole e d'Ebe* in DTB XXVI.

presented two operas with no particular success and drew upon himself the oft-quoted remark of Handel to the effect that "he [Gluck] knows no more of counterpoint than Waltz, my cook." Nevertheless, Gluck made friends with the older composer and was undoubtedly impressed by his music,[3] though the influence exerted itself only considerably later and then indirectly, in the form of an ideal of grandeur which Gluck embodied in his own particular way in the reform operas. The two years following the visit to London were spent in touring Germany as conductor with a traveling opera company. *Le nozze d'Ercole e d'Ebe* ("The Marriage of Hercules and Hebe"), a serenata [4] performed at a wedding in Pillnitz (near Dresden) in 1747, shows Gluck as an accomplished composer in a rather pretty, trifling Italian style. In this work, as indeed in all his operas, Gluck followed the eighteenth-century custom of borrowing numbers from his own previous works or even from those of other composers; several arias are from earlier Gluck operas, and the first movement of the overture is taken from a symphony of Sammartini, with only slight alterations. The aria "Così come si accese," from the epilogue, is typical of the graceful, tuneful, Pergolesi-like melody in which this work abounds (Example 67).

*Le nozze d'Ercole*

EXAMPLE 67

GLUCK

Co - sì co - me si ac - ce - se la ___ vo - stra fiam - ma

bel - la nel - la na - ti - va stel - la, nel - la na - ti - va

stel - la, co - sì ri - splen - de - rà, ri - splen - de - rà.

In 1750 Gluck was married at Vienna. The substantial dowry his wife brought him undoubtedly encouraged a certain independence

---

[3] Cf. Kelly, *Reminiscences* I, 255.

[4] "Serenata" is the eighteenth-century name for a small opera or dramatic cantata, often of a pastoral nature and employing few characters, composed for a special occasion (such as a birthday or wedding) in a patron's household.

which Gluck began to manifest about this time. Concrete evidence of the new attitude is found in the scores of *Ezio* (Prague, 1750) and *La clemenza di Tito* ("The Mercy of Titus," Naples, 1752), both on librettos of Metastasio. In carefulness of orchestral writing, nobility of melody, and seriousness of expression these works surpass not only the earlier operas but also most of the Italian ones of the next ten years. The characteristic vigor which had always been remarked in Gluck's music, and the growing individuality of his methods, may have been what caused Metastasio about this time to describe him as a composer of "surprising fire, but . . . mad." [5] It was the cry of the conservative, instinctively recognizing the presence of a force inimical to the settled state of affairs. Yet it was to be ten years before Gluck composed *Orfeo*; and during this time he still produced some works in the old manner, as well as a sparkling one-act comic piece, *Le cinesi* ("The Chinese Ladies"), on a libretto of Metastasio, for the entertainment of the imperial court in 1754. The success of this work was instrumental in securing for him the position of official court composer of theatre and chamber music under the superintendency of Count Durazzo, whose influence and encouragement played a large part in determining the new artistic ideals which were then developing in Gluck's mind. Their first collaborative work, the one-act *Innocenza giustificata* ("Innocence Vindicated," 1755), although apparently conforming to the Metastasian type of libretto, is in actuality a forerunner of the monumental simplicity of *Orfeo*, with the musical resources (including a chorus) largely subordinated to the dramatic aims. This work was revised by Gluck in 1768 under the title *The Vestal*; it is the same subject as that of Spontini's opera of 1807.

Another important influence on Gluck in the years immediately preceding the composition of *Orfeo* was his contact with the French *opéra comique*.[6] This distinctive national form of comic opera had grown up at Paris, at first using only popular melodies to which poets fitted their words but coming toward the middle of the century to make use of more and more original music and at the same time improving in poetic quality and musical interest. The Viennese court being curious to hear these pieces, Durazzo arranged for some to be sent from Paris. Gluck was charged with the duty of conducting the performances, which entailed arranging the music and composing new numbers where it was thought

[5] Letter to Farinelli, Nov. 16, 1751; in Burney, *Metastasio* I, 402.
[6] Haas, *Gluck und Durazzo*; Holzer, "Die komische Opern Glucks."

the original melodies might not be suited to the Viennese taste. These performances of opéras comiques at Vienna began in 1755, and it is noteworthy that the proportion of new music steadily increased, until in the last of them, *La Rencontre imprévue* ("The Unexpected Meeting," 1764), not one of the original French airs was retained, the entire text having been newly composed by Gluck. Thus, as it were by accident, the composer in his forties went to school to the French opéra comique, learning a syllabic style of text setting, a melodic restraint, a freedom of phrase structure, and a close adaptation of music to poetry which contrasted with the typical Italian arias in an extreme degree. How thoroughly he assimilated the French musical idiom may be gathered not only from the scores but also from the testimony of the French poet and manager Favart, who speaks with highest praise of Gluck's settings of his librettos: "They leave nothing to be desired in the expression, the taste, the harmony, even in the French prosody." [7]

A final stage of preparation for *Orfeo* was the composition of Angiolini's ballet *Don Juan* in 1761,[8] a work which seems as though designed to illustrate the new principles outlined by Noverre in his book on the dance, published only a year previously. As in the opéras comiques Gluck had learned to subordinate music to text, so here he adapted his art to the service of pantomime. There is in this music something of Rameau's wonderful power of depicting gesture in sound; and, as in the older opera, the score is divided into many short numbers, each complete in itself. But the music is more than mere accompaniment to patterns of motion; it enters into the action and becomes a partner of the drama figured forth by the dancers. Part of the closing scene between Don Juan and the Statue will serve to show this quality and also to suggest how Mozart must have remembered, perhaps unconsciously, the music of Gluck when composing his own *Don Giovanni* (Example 68). Indeed, comparison between the two works is almost inevitable, though it is not in superficial thematic resemblances but rather in the whole spirit of the music that Mozart's indebtedness to the older composer is evident.

With the composition of *Don Juan* Gluck stood at the parting of the ways; having begun with the conventional Italian operatic formulas and

---

[7] Letter to Durazzo, Nov. 19, 1763; in Favart, *Memoires et correspondances* II, 169.

[8] Haas, "Die Wiener Ballet-Pantomime im 18. Jahrhundert."

## Don Juan, No. 30

EXAMPLE 68

GLUCK

having reached the point of instilling into this framework a new breath of dramatic life, he might have continued along the lines of Jommelli and Traetta, toward the type of opera which Mozart eventually brought to unsurpassable heights. That Gluck's genius now took a different turn was not owing to any inner compulsion of Gluck the musician but rather

to a quite unexpected development of Gluck the dramatist—a development for which at this moment external forces were largely responsible.
These forces were immanent in the whole intellectual and artistic atmosphere of the later eighteenth century.[9] Fundamental was the profound
yearning for free, simple, unaffected expression of human feelings. The
baroque had been an age of order, authority, and formality, to which the
early eighteenth century had reacted with the critical and skeptical
philosophy of rationalism, summed up in the works of Voltaire. Into the
vacuum created by this essentially negative criticism there rushed the
earlier manifestations of mannered sentimentality and capricious, superficial ornamentation, extending through all the details of life, and mirrored in music of the gallant style. But mere caprice was not enough. To
the gallant ideal succeeded that of naturalness, whose great prophet was
Jean-Jacques Rousseau with his *Nouvelle Héloïse* (1760) and *Emile*
(1762), the fountains of the romantic movement in literature. Yet
naturalness, however valid as an ideal, was too vague to furnish by itself
a sure foundation for art; not only an ideal but a form as well was
needed, and the form, the regulating, ordering principle without which
great artistic creation is impossible, was sought now, as it had been at
the time of the Renaissance, in the models of the classical age of ancient
Greece. In 1764 a German archaeologist, Johann Joachim Winckelmann, published his *Geschichte der Kunst des Alterthums* ("History of
Ancient Art"), embodying the fruits of nearly twenty years of study and
meditation; from this publication may be said to date the epoch known
par excellence in the history of European art as the classical period.
Winckelmann's work was not only a history but a philosophy of art,
which served in some degree to counteract the dangers of unrestrained
individualism implicit in the doctrines of Rousseau. Beauty, according
to this philosophy, can be attained only when individual, characteristic
details are subordinated to the general plan of the whole, thus creating
an ideal, suprapersonal work marked by harmonious proportions and a
certain repose in the total effect—in Winckelmann's phrase, "noble
simplicity and calm greatness." [10]

[9] Cf. Abert, "Gluck, Mozart und der Rationalismus," in his *Gesammelte Schriften*, pp. 311–45.
[10] Winckelmann, "Gedanken über die Nachahmung der griechischen Werke,"
¶ 79. He may have obtained the phrase from Gottsched: "Man sollte in der
Opernmusik mehr auf eine edle Einfalt sehen, als auf die unförmlichen Aus-
schweifungen der Italiener" (*Kritische Dichtkunst* III, 1734; quoted by Reichel in
"Gottsched und Johann Adolf Scheibe," p. 665).

It may be doubted whether Gluck ever read either Rousseau's or Winckelmann's books, though he probably had met Winckelmann at Rome in 1756. In any case, the question is not important, for the ideas which both men expressed were so much in the air at this time that no thinking person could possibly have escaped them. With regard to the classic models, of course, the same difficulty was present as in the Renaisance, namely the lack of actual specimens of ancient music. But theorists in the eighteenth century did not trouble to speculate, as the Florentine Camerata had done, on the nature of Greek music; rather, they attacked the problem of opera at its root, advocating fundamental changes in the libretto and in the relations among composer, poet, and performing artists. The most influential writer in this field was the Italian Francesco Algarotti, a highly esteemed philosopher, a friend of Voltaire and Frederick the Great, and artistic adviser to the court of Parma where Traetta was stationed. His *Saggio sopra l'opera in musica* ("Treatise on the Opera"), first issued in 1755, became the manifesto of operatic reform, influencing even in details both the practice and the theory of Gluck.[11] The resemblance between Algarotti's book and Gluck's preface to *Alceste* (1769) leaves no room for doubt on this point.

The fundamental impulse, the suggestion of a model, and the aesthetic theory were thus present. And at this moment appeared the poet Ranieri de' Calsabigi (1714–95),[12] from whose collaboration with Gluck *Orfeo* and *Alceste* resulted. Calsabigi was the real standard-bearer of the revolt against Metastasio,[13] in spite of the fact that he had earlier brought out at Paris an edition of the latter's works which in the preface he characterized as "perfect tragedies." He had led an adventurous life in Italy, Paris, and elsewhere; he was known as a literary amateur and aesthetician and was an admirer of Shakespeare. Gluck handsomely acknowledged his indebtedness to Calsabigi:

If my music has had some success, I think it my duty to recognize that I am beholden for it to him. . . . However much talent a composer may have, he will never produce any but mediocre music, if the poet does not awaken

---

[11] See Strunk, *Source Readings*, pp. 657–72. A summary of Algarotti's teachings, with copious quotations, will be found in Newman, *Gluck and the Opera*, Part II, chap. II.

[12] Michel, "Ranieri Calzabigi," *Gluck-Jahrbuch* IV (1918) 99–171.

[13] Cf. Einstein, "Calzabigi's 'Erwiderung' von 1790," *Gluck-Jahrbuch* II (1915) 56–102; III (1917) 25–50.

in him that enthusiasm without which the productions of all the arts are but feeble and drooping.[14]

Calsabigi even went so far as to claim, and without contradiction from Gluck, that it was he who had taught the composer exactly how to write his recitatives and had persuaded him to banish both coloratura passages and the secco accompaniment of recitative from his operas.[15]

*Orfeo ed Euridice*,[16] the first joint work of Calsabigi and Gluck, was performed at Vienna October 5, 1762. Thus the new reform began with the same subject as that of the first Florentine operas of 1600. Aside from two incongruous features—the irrelevant overture and the artificial happy ending (both due to the festive occasion for which the opera was written, where too much tragedy would have been out of place)— the work is a profound contrast to the contemporary Italian operas. On the title page of the libretto for the first production, as well as in the first engraved edition of the score, it is called an "azione teatrale"—a designation commonly used with eighteenth-century Italian works which, unlike the regular *dramma per musica*, make large use of the chorus. The plot is simplified to the verge of austerity; it is presented in a series of tableaux rather than as a connected story. Eurydice has died before the action begins, and the curtain rises to show Orpheus and the chorus lamenting about her bier; this was a favorite type of scene in French opera, the *tombeau*, a fine example of which may be found at the opening of Act I of Rameau's *Castor et Pollux*. The choral lament is intensified by Orpheus' moving cries of "Euridice!" There follows a short recitative and a ballo, that is, a solemn dance, after which the chorus is resumed. At its conclusion Orpheus sings his aria "Chiamo il mio ben così" ("Thus I call my beloved"), in F major, three strophes separated by short recitatives, a simple expression of grief made more poignant through echo repetitions of the closing phrases by a second orchestra behind the scenes. A final outburst of sorrow is interrupted by the appearance of the God of Love, who in pity directs Orpheus to seek his departed wife in the realms of the dead. The second act opening shows the Furies guarding the gates of the underworld; their fierce denials Orpheus overcomes by the magic power of his singing. A gradual lessen-

---

[14] Letter in the *Mercure de France*, 1781; quoted in Einstein, *Gluck* (English ed.), pp. 67–68.
[15] Letter in the *Mercure de France*, August, 1784, p. 135.
[16] See Tiersot, "Étude sur *Orphée*."

ing of tension leads naturally into the next scene of the Elysian Fields, where a mood of bright, serene happiness is sustained throughout with remarkable consistency. This scene is introduced by the famous "Ballet of the Happy Spirits" and the lovely aria "Che puro ciel" ("What pure sky"), with its delicately pictorial accompaniment. Eurydice appears, conducted by a train of Blessed Spirits. Everything moves with a still, unearthly, dreamlike motion. With the third act, the mood is abruptly broken; we suddenly find ourselves watching a human-interest drama. The first part of this act is less interesting musically, though it brings the catastrophe of the action. Orpheus, no longer able to withstand the pleadings of Eurydice, looks back; and her death is followed by that ideal, classic outpouring of grief "Che faro senza Euridice?" ("What shall I do without Eurydice? Whither shall I go without my beloved?"), which in its profoundly simple feeling is matched in opera only by the closing solo of Purcell's *Dido and Aeneas*. Here the action properly concludes; but since the occasion required a happy ending, the God of Love once more appears and restores Eurydice to life. General rejoicings, with ballets and chorus, furnish the closing scene, which thus, with the overture, frames this antique myth for presentation to a European court of the eighteenth century.

In no other work did Gluck realize so consciously and so fully the effect of classic, statuesque repose as in *Orfeo*. The music, like the libretto, is denuded of all unnecessary ornament; nothing in it calls attention to itself. The forms are clearly perceived but freely intermingled and always appropriate to the moods and situations; the extremes of secco recitative on the one hand and of coloratura aria on the other are abolished; always the simplest means are used, and yet these produce an effect apparently out of all proportion to their simplicity. It can hardly be said that the music is in any degree suppressed in favor of poetry, even in the recitatives, which are certainly more musical and expressive than those of Lully or Rameau.[17] Rather, the music is purified; it is as though Gluck, by voluntarily abandoning the outward charms of Italian operatic melody, stimulated the sources of inward beauty. *Orfeo* was performed at Paris in 1774 with a French libretto, some added ballets, and a change of the role of Orpheus from contralto to tenor, which also involved some changes in the key scheme. The full score was printed at

[17] See Meyer, *Die Behandlung des Rezitatives in Glucks italienischen Reform-opern.*

Paris in 1764—one of the very few Italian operas to be published since 1639. Its popularity may be inferred both from this fact and from the number of parodies which appeared in the latter half of the eighteenth century.[18]

The five years after *Orfeo* were filled with the composition of two other Italian operas and a number of lesser works. On December 26, 1767, occurred the performance of the second opera in which Gluck and Calsabigi collaborated, *Alceste*. Here is another Greek subject, first dramatized by Euripides. Like *Orfeo*, the opera exists in both the original form and a revision made for Paris in 1777. The differences between the two versions are more extensive than in *Orfeo*, and, as in the earlier work, it is hardly possible to decide which is superior. Both have certain faults of dramatic construction, chiefly the artificial ending. King Admetus lies at the point of death; an oracle decrees his life may be spared if another will die in his stead. His wife, Alcestis, offers herself as the victim but is rescued and restored to Admetus—in Calsabigi's poem by Apollo, and in the Paris version by Hercules. The latter accords with the Greek original, but in both librettos the interference has the character of a mere arbitrary act of magnanimity on the part of a conventional eighteenth-century *deus ex machina* instead of being motivated, as in Euripides, by a feeling of gratitude for hospitality. Still, as Einstein points out, the strength of this motive, however it may have been appreciated by the Athenians, could not have been made clear to a modern audience, for whom the spectacle of Alcestis' sacrificial devotion was bound to overshadow all other interests. Thus the opera centers around the heroine, in comparison with whom the other figures count for little.

Gluck had called *Orfeo* an "azione teatrale"; *Alceste* he designated as a "tragedia per musica." The entire action is on a grander scale than in *Orfeo*. It is organized, in a manner similar to Traetta, into monumental scene-complexes with large choruses, which are the most prominent features of the score. The first act is the most unified and satisfactory, from the truly tragic overture which leads directly into the opening outburst of the chorus, the announcement by the herald of Admetus' impending death, the choruses of mourning, proceeding in unbroken crescendo of interest through the pronouncement of the oracle, and climaxing with Alcestis' heroic resolve and her famous aria "Divinités du Styx." The second act (in the Paris version) opens with

[18] Cucuel, "Les Opéras de Gluck dans les parodies du XVIIIe siècle."

the needed contrast, the dances and choruses of rejoicing over Admetus' recovery; the dramatic entrance of Alcestis, and the revelation to the king of the identity of his rescuer, lead to some remarkable recitative dialogue, ending with Alcestis' cavatina "Ah! malgré moi," the agitated second part of which is broken by a short choral interlude. The third act is dramatically an anticlimax, the action remaining for a long while just where it was at the end of Act II; but the music is notable for the choruses, the strangely calm and yet moving aria of Alcestis, "Ah, divinités implacables," and a fine passionate aria of Admetus, "Alceste, au nom des Dieux." [19] After a banal final chorus, the opera closes with the customary suite of ballets.

When the score of *Alceste* was published at Vienna in 1769 it contained a dedicatory preface which is the clearest and fullest statement of Gluck's and Calsabigi's new ideals for opera. This preface has been reproduced so many times, and is so easily accessible in translation,[20] that it does not seem necessary to quote it in full here. Like many history-making documents, it embodied no ideas that had not been stated before; it was a defense of a *fait accompli* rather than a program for the future. It voiced the usual arguments against the caprice and vanity of singers and against the domination of musical stereotypes over the requirements of the text; it set forth the purpose of the overture in much the same way that Algarotti had done; most significantly, it enunciated Gluck's musical aesthetic in a famous simile:

I have striven to restrict music to its true office of serving poetry by means of expression and by following the situations of the story, without interrupting the action or stifling it with a useless superfluity of ornaments; and I believed that it should do this in the same way as telling colors affect a correct and well-ordered drawing; by a well-assorted contrast of light and shade, which serves to animate the figures without altering their contours.[21]

Such self-abasement would have been inconceivable to an Italian composer of the old school, for whom the story existed only as a pretext for the music. In the preface to *Paride et Elena* (1770), Gluck (or Calsabigi) was even more explicit: "He who is concerned with truthfulness must model himself to his subject, and the noblest beauties of harmony and

---

[19] The aria of Hercules, "C'est en vain que l'enfer," was probably arranged (by Gossec) from an aria in Gluck's *Ezio*.

[20] Strunk, *Source Readings*, pp. 673–75.

[21] As translated in Einstein, *Gluck*, pp. 98–99.

melody become serious faults if they are misplaced." [22] Such a theory strongly suggests the later doctrines of Wagner, and it has sometimes been cited as evidence of the latter's ignorance of operatic history, or of his egoistic jealousy, that he failed to recognize the fundamental kinship of Gluck's ideas with his own when he proclaimed that "the famous revolution of Gluck . . . really consisted only in the revolt of the composer against the arbitrariness of the singer." [23] But Wagner was right inasmuch as he was judging by results, not by professed intentions; for Gluck did not fully carry out the implications of his own theories. How far the comparative simplicity of his music was the result of his aesthetic beliefs, and how far the beliefs were *ex post facto* attempts to justify his practice, is not easy to say. He was not a great technician; and though he probably did know more about counterpoint than Handel's cook, he certainly was not a match for either Hasse or Jommelli in facility of invention or power of sustained thematic development in long arias. Moreover, the art of singing was already on the decline; there were no more artists of the caliber of Farinelli, even if Gluck could or would have written for them. By way of compensation, orchestral technique was steadily improving. One cannot therefore totally exclude the possibility that Gluck's ideas of the subordination of music, of formal freedom, plainness of diction, and importance of orchestration were, if not actually inspired, at least supported by very practical considerations. At any rate, they had a certain measure of success. When Dr. Burney visited Vienna in 1772 he reported the operatic situation in these words :

Party runs as high among poets, musicians, and their adherents, at Vienna as elsewhere. Metastasio, and Hasse, may be said, to be at the head of one of the principal sects; and Calzabigi and Gluck of another. The first, regarding all innovations as quackery, adhere to the ancient form of the musical drama, in which the poet and musician claim equal attention from an audience; the bard in the recitatives and narrative parts; and the composer in the airs, duos, and choruses. The second party depend more on theatrical effects, propriety of character, simplicity of diction, and of musical execution, than on, what *they* style, flowery descriptions, superfluous similes, sententious and cold morality, on one side, with tiresome symphonies, and long divisions, on the other [24] . . . . the chevalier Gluck is simplifying music . . . he tries all he can to keep his music chaste and

[22] Quoted in Cooper, *Gluck*, p. 143.
[23] "Oper und Drama, Erster Theil," in *Gesammelte Schriften* III, 237.
[24] Paraphrased from the preface to *Alceste*.

sober, his three operas of *Orfeo, Alceste,* and *Paride* are proof of this, as they contain few difficulties of execution, though many of expression.[25]

I cannot quit Hasse and Gluck, without saying that it is very necessary to use discrimination in comparing them together. Hasse may be regarded as the Raphael, and . . . Gluck the Michael Angelo of living composers. If the affected French expression of *le grand simple* can ever mean anything, it must be when applied to the productions of such a composer as Hasse, who succeeds better perhaps in expressing, with clearness and propriety, whatever is graceful, elegant, and tender, than what is boisterous and violent; whereas Gluck's genius seems more calculated for exciting terror in painting difficult situations, occasioned by complicated misery, and the tempestuous fury of unbridled passions.[26]

Reading between the lines it is easy to see that Dr. Burney's sympathies are temperamentally with Hasse rather than with Gluck; and this lends added weight to his testimony as to the enthusiasm with which both *Orfeo* and *Alceste* were received at Vienna. By comparison *Paride ed Elena,* the next production of Gluck and Calsabigi, was a failure, and whether for this reason or another, they collaborated no more. Gluck remained dissatisfied. His new style met with no understanding and but little attention outside the Vienna circle. Durazzo meanwhile had gone as ambassador to Venice in 1764, and Calsabigi left in 1771. Gluck's native tenacity rebelled at the prospect of only an incomplete triumph. Moreover, he had suffered financial reverses and doubtless felt the need to recoup his fortunes. Only one city in Europe offered the possibilities he sought, and his inclination to try his luck in Paris was strengthened by the fact that the new dauphine of France, Marie Antoinette, who had formerly been his singing pupil at the imperial court, was still interested in his career. Fortunately also, the situation in Paris was favorable for him. The old French opera, incurably conservative, had declined steadily in prestige since the middle of the century and was under constant critical attack from the partisans of Italian music, led by Jean-Jacques Rousseau. Although Gluck himself was probably not well known in Paris, the works of the German symphonists had been favorably received there for many years. In 1772 Gluck began the composition of *Iphigénie en Aulide,* a "tragédie opéra" on a libretto adapted from Racine's tragedy by Du Roullet, a member

[25] *The Present State of Music in Germany* II, 232–33, 237.
[26] *Ibid.,* II, 349–50.

of the French embassy staff at Vienna. By a combination of skillful diplomacy and the powerful intercession of Marie Antoinette the score was accepted; Gluck directed the carefully rehearsed first performance at Paris on April 19, 1774, and the work had an immediate success.

The chief thing which distinguishes *Iphigénie en Aulide* from *Orfeo* and *Alceste* is the greater rapidity and decisiveness of the action; it is a drama of events rather than a series of comparatively static pictures. As a consequence, the rhythm is more animated, the declamation more pointed, and the musical units shorter, more continuous, more completely intermingled, less self-sufficient than in the earlier works. When Dr. Burney visited Gluck at Vienna, the composer sang for him almost the whole of *Iphigénie*, which he had (according to his custom) already composed in his mind, though not yet set down on paper; and it was doubtless this work which led Burney to remark that "it seldom happens that a single air of his operas can be taken out of its niche, and sung singly, with much effect; the whole is a chain, of which a detached single link is but of small importance." [27] Gluck himself expressed the same idea : lamenting the insufficiency of melody and even of harmony for the expression of certain emotions, and speaking particularly of Achilles' air "Calchas, d'un trait mortel percé" from *Iphigénie en Aulide*, he said, "My magic consists only in the nature of the song that precedes this and the choice of instruments that accompany it." [28] Burney's observation is especially applicable to the great scene at the end of Act II, where Agamemnon, wavering between his supposed duty to his country and his love for his daughter, in a magnificent monologue finally resolves to save Iphigenia's life. Gluck's power as a dramatist in this scene is surpassed only by some of the pages of his own later *Iphigénie en Tauride*. Another beautiful place is the farewell of Iphigenia in the third act ("Adieu ! conservez dans votre âme"), surely, as Newman says, "one of the most perfect emotional utterances of the eighteenth century." [29] The overture to *Iphigénie en Aulide*, Gluck's finest instrumental composition, still holds a place on symphonic programs.

The triumph of *Iphigénie en Aulide* was followed by Paris performances of the revised versions of *Orfeo* (1774) and *Alceste* (1776), as well as by unsuccessful revivals of two of Gluck's French opéras

[27] *Ibid.*, II, 262.
[28] Reported in *Le Journal de Paris*, No. 234, August 21, 1788, p. 1010; quoted in Downes, "The Operas of Johann Christian Bach" I, 202.
[29] *Gluck and the Opera*, p. 128.

comiques. Meanwhile the inevitable happened. A group of literati, headed by Marmontel, determined to furnish Paris the spectacle of a musical combat between the new lion and a representative of the Italian school. Their chosen champion was Niccolò Piccinni (1728–1800),[30] a prolific composer of Italian operas, trained at Naples, and famous throughout Europe for his comic opera *La buona figliuola*.[31] Piccinni lent himself in all innocence to the proposed competition and came out of the affair a distressed and chastened man.[32] The excitement in Paris over the "Quarrel of the Gluckists and Piccinnists," as over that of the Bouffonists twenty-five years earlier, manifested a side of the Gallic temperament that usually leaves the Anglo-Saxon cold. Benjamin Franklin, then commissioner of the United States of America in Paris, was moved to satire in the manner of Swift:

We had been shown numberless skeletons of a kind of little fly, called an ephemera, whose successive generations, we were told, were bred and expired within the day. I happened to see a living company of them on a leaf, who appeared to be engaged in conversation. You know I understand all the inferior animal tongues. . . . I listened through curiosity to the discourse of these little creatures; but as they, in their national vivacity, spoke three or four together, I could make but little of their conversation. I found, however, by some broken expressions that I heard now and then, they were disputing warmly on the merit of two foreign musicians, one a *cousin*, the other a *moscheto*; in which dispute they spent their time, seemingly as regardless of the shortness of life as if they had been sure of living a month. Happy people! thought I, you live certainly under a wise, just, and mild government, since you have no public grievances to complain of, nor any subject of contention but the perfections and imperfections of foreign music.[33]

Franklin's badinage is less withering than the straight-faced observation of Symonds: "At times when politics have been dull, theology dormant, and science undemonstrative, even music has been found sufficient to excite a nation."[34]

---

[30] Cametti, "Saggio cronologico"; H. Abert, "Piccinni als Buffokomponist," in his *Gesammelte Schriften*, pp. 346–64; biographies and studies by Pascazio, Guingené, Della Corte, La Rotella.

[31] See below, p. 250.

[32] For details see Desnoiresterres, *Gluck et Piccinni*; Strunk, *Source Readings*, pp. 676–83.

[33] "The Ephemera," a "bagatelle" written in 1778; in *Writings*, ed. Smith (New York, Macmillan, 1907) VII, 207. Quoted by permission of the publisher.

[34] *The Revival of Learning* (New York, 1883), p. 244.

The pleasant idea was conceived of having both Gluck and Piccinni compose music for the same libretto, Quinault's *Roland*. When Gluck found that Piccinni was already working on such a project, he refused and produced instead a setting of Quinault's *Armide*, which was performed in September, 1777, four months before Piccinni was ready with his *Roland*. The latter had a better reception than its composer had hoped, though his reputation in French opera was not made secure until later. Meanwhile, Gluck's *Armide* was received with enthusiasm by his friends and disparagement by his enemies. The score is indeed uneven, partly because of the old-fashioned five-act libretto which included many scenes not capable of stimulating the composer to his best efforts. Comparisons with Lully were to be expected, and verdicts were freely rendered in favor of one or the other according to the prepossessions of the critic. The most remarkable feature of the music is its idyllic, sensuous charm, giving a foretaste of the romantic style. This may be heard particularly in the air "Plus j'observe ces lieux" (Act II, scene 3) and in the scene of parting between Armide and Renaud (Act V, scene 1), a surprisingly passionate love duet for the eighteenth century. The chaconne in the following scene is one of Gluck's noblest instrumental creations, a worthy companion to the chaconne in Rameau's *Castor et Pollux*.

The last important work of Gluck, and his masterpiece, was *Iphigénie en Tauride*, first performed at Paris May 18, 1779. The libretto, written by Guillard on the model of Euripides, is the best poem Gluck ever set, and the entire work, a real drama in music, probably comes as close as possible to the ideal of a modern revival of the spirit of Greek tragedy. It is an extraordinary and happy mixture of ancient and modern motifs. The sense of an inexorable Fate which drives human beings on to catastrophe is combined with vivid, contrasting characterization and masterly depiction of emotion: the noble pathos of Iphigenia, the sullen, superstitious cruelty of Thoas, the fearful remorse of Orestes, the friendship between him and Pylades, and the mysterious brother-sister love between Orestes and Iphigenia. All these were things calculated to call forth Gluck's highest powers. These are displayed in the accompanied recitative near the beginning of the first act "Cette nuit j'ai revu le palais de mon père," where Iphigenia relates her dream which obscurely prefigures the course of the entire tragedy and serves in a manner as a substitute for the prologue of Euripides. It is not difficult to see in the music of these pages the source and model for nineteenth-century composers of similar scenes—Cherubini, Weber, Berlioz, even Wagner and Richard Strauss. Equally powerful is the gloomy air of Thoas, "De noirs pressentiments," with its heavy dotted rhythm and rising arpeggio figures in the bass reaching up "like tentacles of the underworld." [35] The choruses intensify by contrast the outlines of these individual characters. Unlike *Alceste* and the earlier *Iphigénie*, the chorus here takes no direct part in the action, except for a moment at the climax of the last act; the priestesses of Diana (sopranos and altos) furnish an immobile, neutral-colored background for Iphigenia; the chorus of Scythians (tenors and basses) is little else than spectacle, closely connected with a series of ballets whose descent from the exotic scenes of the traditional French ballet is obvious despite the conventional "Turkish" instruments of the late eighteenth century; the chorus of the Eumenides in Act II is the personification of Orestes' conscience, haunting him in a symbolic and terrible dream.

*Iphigénie en Tauride* has no formal overture, but rather an introduction depicting first "the calm," then a "storm"—no mere tour de force of nature painting (as often in earlier French opera) but a prelude leading naturally into the first scene, which opens with the cry of Iphigenia and the chorus "Grands dieux! soyez-nous secourables!" Of the many fine details of the orchestral accompaniment in the course of the opera, one in particular may be mentioned: Orestes, left alone after his friend Pylades has been arrested by the temple guards, falls in a half stupor; in pitiable self-delusion he tries to encourage the feeling of peace which descends upon him momentarily, singing "Le calme rentre dans mon cœur." But the accompaniment, with a subdued, agitated sixteenth-note reiteration of one tone, and with a *sforzando* accent at the first beat of every measure, betrays the troubled state of his mind, from which he cannot banish the pangs of remorse for his past crime. It is perhaps the first occurrence in opera of this device of using the orchestra to reveal the inward truth of a situation, in distinction from, even in contradiction to, the words of the text—a practice which Wagner was later to incorporate in a complete system.

One feature of this opera is the way in which Gluck returns to long-breathed, purely musical, even lyrical forms in the arias. It is as though

---

[35] Marx, *Gluck* II, 273. This rising broken-chord figure in the bass is characteristic of Gluck for the suggestion of the supernatural.

the extreme of revolt against the dominance of music over poetry had passed, and the two were coming together again on equal terms. It is an example of the final stage of artistic revolutions, which usually end by taking over much of that which at first they had rejected. We are accustomed to regard Monteverdi, Gluck, and Wagner as three revolutionary figures in the history of opera; but we tend too much to emphasize what each rejected of the past and to lose sight of the fact that the end result in every case was an enrichment of the musical substance of opera by the incorporation of many earlier musical achievements, though in a new guise or with new significance. Gluck, as we have already mentioned, often used numbers from his earlier operas when composing a new score; borrowings of this sort are especially frequent in his reform operas, and we are thus confronted with the realization that the works in which he is supposed to have renounced the ways of Italian opera are, to a considerable degree, made up of music from his own Italian operas of earlier date. The opening of the overture and of the aria "Diane impitoyable" in *Iphigénie en Aulide* comes from an aria of *Telemacco*, which work likewise supplied the overture to *Armide* and the opening chorus of *Alceste*; "Che puro ciel" of *Orfeo* is a final version of an aria used in three previous works; in *Iphigénie en Tauride* the chorus of the Eumenides is taken from *Semiramide* (1748), Iphigenia's aria "O malheureuse Iphigénie" from *La clemenza di Tito*, and other portions from *Telemacco*. The reversion to musical opera, however, is more than a matter of a few borrowed numbers. The whole score of *Iphigénie en Tauride*, particularly the arias, shows a tendency toward gathering the music into longer, more continuous, and more highly developed units. Even the old da capo appears in Orestes' "Dieux qui me poursuivez," a fine instance of the dramatically appropriate use of this form; and two of the other arias have the same pattern. Altogether, we may see in this work a reconciliation of the two elements, words and music, the conflict of which had so much occupied the thoughts of Gluck and his contemporaries.

Gluck's last opera, *Echo et Narcisse* (1779), was not a success at Paris in spite of some beautiful individual numbers, and he took the disappointment badly. He returned at once to Vienna, where he died in 1787.

It is difficult to define Gluck's true significance for the history of opera. His essential achievement was the restoration of a more even balance between music and poetry, between what we may call the audible surface of opera and its dramatic content. His task was to elevate the drama to a more important place and to reduce the musical excrescences of the preceding period. Paradoxically, he accomplished this by simplifying the libretto and enriching the music, by replacing the intricacies of Metastasian intrigue with the elemental actions of Greek drama, the roulades and ornaments of Hasse with his own harmonically conceived, orchestrally supported, oratorically molded melody, for which he obtained many suggestions from French opera. Gluck had a genius for achieving effects of sublimity by apparently simple means. At the same time, he enriched opera by bringing into it elements from both the ballet and the oratorio and by utilizing all resources of the operatic style in long complex scenes held together by broad principles of musical form.[36] His reform works combined the simplicity of the opéra comique, the grandeur of the tragédie lyrique, the vocal charm of Italian opera seria, and the symphonic achievements of the Italian and German schools in an international, or rather supranational, opera, which corresponded at once to the demand of his contemporaries for naturalness, their interest in classical forms, and their passion for art with the moral aim of offering great models of heroism for contemplation. His success was due not only to his fiery temperament and his powers as a musician but also to his intellectual grasp of the moving ideas of his age, his gift for taking practical advantage of the means at hand, his willingness to compromise when necessary, and a certain peasantlike obstinacy in the pursuit of his fundamental aims.

Nothing could be more misleading on the subject of Gluck than his own oft-quoted statement to the effect that when composing an opera he endeavored above all things to forget that he was a musician. Such a remark has all the characteristics of an epigram for the benefit of the French literary critics whom it was his interest to conciliate. Even if he himself by any chance believed there was an atom of meaning in it, there is no reason for us to take it seriously. On the contrary, he never forgot he was a musician; but he also never forgot that it was a drama he was composing, and, so far as the later works are concerned, he composed it so carefully, his settings were so uniquely right, that he marks the beginning of the end of that era that regarded any libretto as any composer's property and saw nothing extraordinary in seventy different

[36] Similar constructions are found in operas and oratorios earlier in the eighteenth century: see for example Handel's *Semele* (1744), Act I, scenes 1–4.

settings of the same poem, all, if not perhaps equally good, at least equally suitable to the words. Gluck's operas survive not because of their poems, or of anyone's theories, but because of Gluck's music; and his music survives while that of many cleverer composers is forgotten because it is in itself the drama, not a mere fashionable dress to cover a text.

The influence of Gluck on later composers was largely indirect. Something of his spirit may be sensed in Mozart's *Idomeneo* of 1780 and Haydn's *Armida* of 1784, but only at Paris did his operas become part of the regular repertoire. Here too were presented some works by other composers in a style clearly derived from Gluck. Such were Piccinni's *Didon* (1783); two operas—*Les Danaïdes* (1784) and *Tarare* (1787)— by Antonio Salieri (1750–1825),[37] an Italian composer chiefly resident at Vienna; and *Oedipe à Colone* (1786) by another Italian, Antonio Sacchini (1730–86),[38] who worked at Paris after 1781. We may trace the influence of Gluck in the French operas of Méhul, Cherubini, and Spontini, to the greatest of his nineteenth-century spiritual descendants, Berlioz. But the line, particularly as regards Berlioz, is through similarity of dramatic aims and ideals rather than actual musical idiom. Outside France, Gluck made little permanent impression. Italy practically ignored him; there were a few performances of his later works in Germany in the eighteenth century but on the whole that country remained under the Italian spell until a national opera began to develop with the approach of romanticism. Gluck was, like Handel, the end of an epoch rather than the beginning. He sums up the classical age of serious opera as Handel does that of the late baroque. The qualities of sincerity, uprightness, and honest dealing with the art of music are common to both men.

[37] Jullien, *La Cour et l'opéra sous Louis XVI*; biographies by Von Mosel (1827) and Magnani (1934).
[38] Jullien, *La Cour et l'opéra sous Louis XVI*.

CHAPTER 16

# EIGHTEENTH-CENTURY
# COMIC OPERA

In the seventeenth-century opera, comic episodes of all kinds were regularly mingled with serious scenes. One of the reforms of Zeno and Metastasio was the abolition of the comic as being irrelevant to the plot and incongruous with the tragic style. In the first part of the eighteenth century, therefore, we find a complete separation of the two types, which flourished for a long time side by side without much mutual influence. Comic opera grew up independently in each country, developing a number of quite diverse national forms, such as the Italian opera buffa, the French opéra comique, and the English ballad opera; after the middle of the century arose the German Singspiel and the Spanish *tonadilla*. Certain features were common to all these works in the early stages of their history: all showed signs of their humble origin in the choice of light or farcical subjects and the preference for scenes, personages, and dialogue taken from familiar popular comedies or from the everyday life of the common people (if fantasy was present, it was treated comically); all were performed by comparatively unskilled singers, often by inferior actors with whom music was, to say the least, only an avocation;[1] all except the Italian opera buffa used spoken dialogue; all occasionally parodied the serious opera; and all cultivated a simple, easily grasped musical style in which national popular idioms played a decisive part. Finally, in the course of the eighteenth century, all underwent a radical change in character from low-class farce to middle-class comedy of various sorts, acquiring in the process so many new features, both in the

---

[1] The castrato, that symbol of opera seria, appeared only rarely in comic opera, but male roles were sometimes sung by women.

libretto and in the music, that by the end of the century the original distinction of serious and comic opera no longer had much meaning. Comic opera in its beginning was a "low-brow" entertainment, regarded by operagoers as something about on the level of a circus midway show; within a little over fifty years it became of equal respectability and importance with serious opera; in less than fifty years more it dominated the stage, having supplanted or absorbed the old opera seria almost completely. Mozart is the representative of comic opera at the end of the eighteenth century as Scarlatti was of opera seria at the beginning of that period.

OPERA BUFFA.[2] The term "opera buffa" is used somewhat loosely as a general designation for Italian operas of the early and middle eighteenth century that do not come under the heading of opera seria. Two distinct kinds of comic opera existed in Italy at the beginning of the century. First, there were regular operas on nonserious libretti, works like *Dal male il bene* and other comic and pastoral pieces which had been produced, though not in large numbers, all through the seventeenth century. Scarlatti's *Trionfo d'onore* (Naples, 1718), his only comic opera, is an eighteenth-century example; and most composers of Italian opera seria also produced works in the comic genre. Around the beginning of the eighteenth century a special type of "comedy in music" appeared at Naples, using Neapolitan dialect and drawing some of its character types from the commedia dell' arte, with music in simple style. Vinci and Leo each produced a half-dozen or more pieces of this sort in the 1720s.

The other kind of Italian comic opera at the beginning of the eighteenth century is in the form of *intermezzi*, that is, short pieces in one act, intended to be performed between the acts of a serious opera. These eighteenth-century intermezzi are, in a way, the descendants of the comic scenes which we commonly find scattered at random through the plots of seventeenth-century operas. When the reforms of Zeno and Metastasio banished comic episodes from the opera seria libretto, the comic element found refuge in the intermezzi. Intermezzi are recorded from Naples as early as 1683, and from Venice and other cities, both in Italy and elsewhere, from the early years of the

[2] D'Arienzo, "Le origini dell' opera comica"; Della Corte, *L'opera comica italiana nel 1700*; Scherillo, *L'opera buffa napoletana*; H. Abert, *Mozart* I, 400–58; Roncaglia, *Il melodioso settecento italiano*.

eighteenth century.[3] The custom grew up of making the two intermezzi which were required for a three-act opera form a continuous plot, so that performances in effect consisted of two operas, one serious and one comic, in alternation. Understandably, foreigners sometimes complained of the resultant confusion.[4] Sometimes the intermezzi were performed at the end of the opera as an afterpiece, thus becoming to all intents and purposes an independent work, retaining a vestige of their origin in the division into two acts instead of the three customary in full-length operas. Of the hundreds of intermezzi produced by famous as well as obscure composers in the first half of the eighteenth century, Pergolesi's *La serva padrona* ("The Maid Mistress," 1733) has deservedly maintained its popularity to our own time. It is characteristic of such works in its economy of musical resources—only two singers (soprano and bass) and a third mute character, with orchestra of strings and continuo. The musical style is likewise typical: prevailingly major, rapid in movement, having much repetition of short motifs, a disjunct melodic line, comic effects produced by sudden offbeat accents, wide skips, and an infectious gaiety and vigor of utterance, offering much to the tone and gesture of the actor (Example 69). Beside the more common allegro arias there is

*La serva padrona*, Act I

EXAMPLE 69                                                                    PERGOLESI

found in the intermezzi a slower, cantabile style, sometimes in minor, which often features chromatic melodies and harmonies for mock-pathetic effects. Folk-songish canzonettas and bass-buffo patter songs

---

[3] See Loewenberg, *Annals*, General Index *s.v.* "Intermezzo."

[4] Cf. Wright, *Some Observations Made in Travelling Through France, Italy, &c*, p. 85.

frequently appear. Throughout the scores, one is impressed by the absolute fidelity of music to text; the singing seems to be simply a highly flexible, sensitive, melodic declamation of the words, preserving and heightening every detail that might contribute to the comic effect. At the same time, there is never a suggestion that the words impede the spontaneous flow of the music; textual repetition is a constant feature but somehow never gives the impression of artificiality. One consequence of this perfect union of text and music is the extraordinary variety of forms in the arias of the intermezzi, in marked contrast to the stock da capo pattern of the contemporary opera seria.

Around 1740 the two previously distinct kinds of Italian comic opera began to lose their peculiar characteristics and merge in a common type. This process was facilitated because the intermezzi gradually became detached from their original connection with serious operas and came to be regarded as a separate and independent form. One traditional characteristic of the intermezzi had been the use of the bass voice, which practically never appeared in opera seria. The presence of basses along with the higher voices made possible one of the most distinctive features of Italian comic opera, namely the ensembles, particularly those at the end of each act.[5] Opera seria, with its emphasis on solo singing, had not developed the ensemble forms, with the exception of the duet. A composer who is reputed to have made important contributions to the ensemble finale is Nicola Logroscino (1698–after 1765);[6] he produced a considerable number of comic operas at Naples in the 1740s and 1750s, but so little of his music has been preserved that it is difficult to know how far his reputation as the founder of the "buffo finale" is deserved. The ideal aim in these comic operas was an ensemble finale which should not be a mere closing set-piece, but which should carry on the action of the drama while at the same time evolving a satisfactory musical form. Although this aim was not to be fully achieved before Mozart, some progress was made toward it after the middle of the century. One of the most prolific composers was Baldassare Galuppi (1706–85),[7] called "Il

[5] M. Fuchs, "Die Entwicklung des Finales in der italienischen Opera Buffa vor Mozart"; Dent, "Ensembles and Finales in 18th Century Italian Opera."

[6] See Kretzschmar, "Zwei Opern Nicolo Logroscinos," JMP XV (1908) 47–68 (also in *Gesammelte Aufsätze* II, 374–400), and biography by Prota-Giurleo.

[7] Wotquenne, "Baldassare Galuppi . . .: Étude bibliographique"; Piovano, "Baldassare Galuppi: Note biobibliografiche"; Bollert, *Die Buffoopern Baldassare Galuppis*; Della Corte, *Baldassare Galuppi: Profilo critico*; Mooser, *Annales* II, 69–86.

Buranello" from the name of his birthplace, an island near Venice. Galuppi's operas, nearly a hundred in number, both serious and comic, were presented for the most part at Venice, but he was famous all over Europe and worked at the court of St. Petersburg from 1765 to 1768. Galuppi frequently composed the finales of his comic operas in the form of a chain of short sections, by means of which he was able to relate the music closely to the ongoing action.

About the middle of the century began Galuppi's association with the dramatist Carlo Goldoni (1707–93)[8] at Venice; one of the most successful of their joint productions was *Il filosofo di campagna* ("The Peasant Philosopher") in 1754. Goldoni was the leading figure in the reform of Italian drama in the eighteenth century. His comedies, rejecting the stock character types and plots as well as the improvised dialogue of the old commedia dell' arte, are models of natural characterization and spontaneous action. His influence on the libretto marked a turning point in the history of the opera buffa, which from this time on became more dignified, more orderly in structure, and more refined in action and language. New kinds of comic opera librettos began to appear— works which must be called dramas rather than farces, and which were often sentimental or even pathetic in character. These newer tendencies did not, of course, replace the old comic elements altogether but rather existed side by side or intermingled with them, so that the comic opera libretto in the second half of the eighteenth century was distinctly varied and, on the whole, much more interesting than that of the opera seria.

One of the best and most popular comic operas of this period was Goldoni's *Buona figliuola* ("The Good Girl"), composed by Piccinni in 1760 for Rome. It enjoyed a two-year run there and soon became known all over Europe. The story was taken from Richardson's *Pamela; or, Virtue Rewarded*,[9] which had become the favorite novel of readers in every country since its publication in 1740. Piccinni's score is remarkable for the long, complex, and carefully planned finales of each act. Piccinni was probably the first composer to try to unify these sections by means of a recurring musical theme ("rondo finale"), thus taking a step toward the highly organized symphonic finale which was to be perfected by Mozart. In other ways also, for example, in the assigning of

[8] See Goldoni's *Mémoires*, which are important for the history of the theatre and of opera in the eighteenth century; biographies and studies by Chatfield-Taylor, Della Torre, Spinelli, Rabanay.

[9] Cf. Holmes, "Pamela Transformed."

independent motifs to the orchestra and in the relatively greater continuity and self-sufficiency of the instrumental parts, Piccinni advanced the style of opera buffa.

As the century went on, the music of comic opera grew more ambitious, broadening its range of expression in accordance with the broadening subject matter of the librettos. One notable work of the 1770s was *L'incognita perseguitata* ("The Persecuted Incognita," Rome, 1773) by Piccinni's pupil Pasquale Anfossi (1727–97). A more important composer of the late eighteenth century was Giovanni Paisiello (1740–1816),[10] who worked principally at Naples except for a period at St. Petersburg from 1776 to 1784. *Il Rè Teodoro in Venezia*, first given at Vienna in 1784, had many performances over the next thirty years and was revived at New York in 1961; the most remarkable features of this opera are the lively ensemble finales. Paisiello's *Barbiere di Siviglia* (1782) remained such a favourite in Italy that even in 1816 Rossini had to overcome popular prejudice against the presumption of any other composer attempting to set the same libretto. *Socrate immaginario* ("The Man Who Thought He Was Socrates," Naples, 1775) is an example of parody, a frequent resource of comic opera librettists. The objects in this case are the classicist movement in general and Gluck's *Orfeo* in particular—the scene between Orpheus and the Furies being burlesqued in broad, though clever, fashion. In *La molinara* ("The Maid of the Mill," Naples, 1788) Paisiello displays many of those expressive qualities and turns of phrase which we are accustomed to associate with Mozart, while his *Nina* (Naples, 1789) is one of the best examples of sentimental comedy in this whole period (Example 70). Paisiello was a master of musical characterization, perhaps the most important figure in eighteenth-century opera buffa next to Mozart himself, and one who exercised a strong influence on the musical style of the latter. Paisiello's gifts are apparent in his orchestral writing, which is more varied and more important dramatically than in any earlier buffo composer. In his finales, Paisiello rivaled the achievements of Piccinni both in scope and in the skill with which musical forms were adapted to the action of the text. He also was one of the first composers to introduce ensemble finales in serious opera.

[10] See H. Abert, "Paisiello's Buffokunst," in his *Gesammelte Schriften*, pp. 365–96 (also in AfMw I); biographies and studies by Della Corte, Pupino-Carbonelli, Speziale, and Faustini-Fasini; Cortese, "Un' autobiografia inedita di Giovanni Paisiello"; Mooser, *Annales* II, 191–244, 355–62.

EXAMPLE 70        *Nina*        PAISIELLO

An immediate forerunner of Mozart at Vienna was Florian Leopold
Gassmann (1729–74),[11] whose two most celebrated comic operas were
*L'amore artigiano* ("Love among the Laborers," 1767) and *La contessina* ("The Countess," 1770), both on librettos by Goldoni. Gassmann's
ensemble finales are remarkable for the way in which the orchestra
carries on the music in continuous fashion, giving unity and direction
to the entire scene. The orchestral part is important also in the arias,
sometimes even having greater melodic interest than the voice.

Also active in Austria as a composer of Italian operas was Franz
Joseph Haydn (1732–1809),[12] though his works for the theatre are

[11] Donath, "Gassmann als Opernkomponist."
[12] Larsen, *Die Haydn-Ueberlieferungen*; Geiringer, *Joseph Haydn*; Wirth, *Joseph
Haydn als Dramatiker; idem*, "The Operas of Joseph Haydn before *Orfeo*," in
*Joseph Haydn, Orfeo ed Euridice . . . Analytical Notes* (Boston, Haydn Society
[1951]), pp. 12–48; Lawner, "Form and Drama in the Operas of Joseph Haydn";

little known today in comparison with his symphonies, quartets, and oratorios. Yet one of Haydn's prime concerns during his long years of service under Prince Esterházy was the preparation and conducting of operas, the composition of new arias to be inserted in others' operas performed at Esterháza, and the composition of new operas of his own. Nor did he lack success: more performances of Haydn's operas took place during his lifetime than of Mozart's during *his* lifetime.

The music of Haydn's six German Singspiels and of two of his four pieces for marionettes is no longer extant. The rest of his operatic output, all on Italian librettos, consists of eight comic operas; four others of serious or semiserious character, the most successful of which was *Armida* (1784); and one dramma per musica, *Orfeo ed Euridice* (also known as *L'anima del filosofo*), composed for London in 1791 but not performed.[13] *Orfeo* contains some beautiful music, but the libretto (by C. F. Badini) is certainly one of the worst specimens of its kind in the whole history of opera—no mean distinction. More satisfactory as far as balance of interest between text and music goes are Haydn's operatic works of the 1760s and 1770s, from *Lo speziale* (1768) to *L'infedeltà delusa* ("Infidelity Deluded," 1773), *L'incontro improvviso* ("The Unexpected Meeting," 1775), and *Il mondo della luna* ("The World of the Moon," 1777). The *dramma giocoso La vera costanza* ("True Constancy," *ca.* 1776) is a particularly good example of the way in which Haydn could combine comic and serious elements in the new kind of mixed musical drama that was gradually replacing both the strictly comic opera buffa and the old-fashioned opera seria everywhere in the last three decades of the eighteenth century.

The comic opera in Italy at the end of the eighteenth century is best represented by Domenico Cimarosa (1749–1801),[14] a prolific composer of some eighty operas. Like many of his compatriots, Cimarosa was called for a time to St. Petersburg (1787–91); on his return he stopped over at Vienna and there produced his masterpiece, *Il matrimonio segreto* ("The Secret Marriage"), in 1792. The success of this work was

Bartha and Somfai, *Haydn als Opernkapellmeister*; Hárich, "Das Repertoire des Opernkapellmeisters J. Haydn in Eszterháza"; Robbins Landon, "Haydn's Marionette Operas."

[13] The score was reconstructed and the opera recorded by the Haydn Society in 1950.

[14] Biographies by Vitale and Tibaldi Chiesa; see also essays in *Per il bicentenario della nascita di Domenico Cimarosa*, especially F. Schlitzer's "Annali delle opere," pp. 73–148; Chailly, *Il matrimonio segreto*; Mooser, *Annales* II, 451–55.

immediate and has continued to the present day. Cimarosa's music fairly rivals Mozart's in tunefulness and spontaneity, though lacking Mozart's profundity and musical constructive power. But profundity was far from being an Italian ideal in this field; the qualities of wit, liveliness, and melodic flow, a never-ending vein of loquacity and good humour, constituted the charm of Cimarosa as of his Italian confreres. He continued the tradition of Paisiello and the other eighteenth-century buffo composers in that inimitable musical style which led in the nineteenth century to Rossini, Donizetti, and (ultimately) Verdi's *Falstaff*.

OPÉRA COMIQUE.[15] The founders of the French comic opera were Molière and Lully, whose comedy ballets, pieces in which spoken dialogue alternated with songs and dances, were presented before Louis XIV during the 1660s.[16] When Lully assumed control of the Academy of Music in 1672 his monopoly cut off all but the barest musical resources from other Paris theatres, and the death of Molière in the following year put an end to the first stage of the comedy ballet. At this juncture an Italian Theatre, which had been established on a permanent basis at Paris in 1661, began to intermingle French scenes, including music, with its improvised Italian comedies. In the course of the next two decades, the French language gradually replaced Italian: eventually the "Italian" troupe gave nothing but comedies and farces (of a rather low sort) in French, which still retained many traces of their commedia dell' arte predecessors, and which were embellished by fanciful displays with ballets and songs.[17] After the Italians were expelled from Paris in 1697 their repertoire was taken over, in a still cruder form, by various small popular theatres which played a few weeks in each year at the two large fairs of Paris. Practical exigencies forced these groups to simplify their music to an extreme degree. They used for the most part little popular tunes ("vaudevilles"—Example 71) to which the authors adapted new words—a process known technically as "parody." Little by little the fortunes of the Fair Theatres improved, until in 1715 they were brought

[15] Cucuel, *Les Créateurs de l'opéra-comique*; idem, "Sources et documents"; Genest, *L'Opéra-comique*; Campardon, *Les Comédiens du roi de la troupe italienne*; idem, *Les Spectacles des foires*; La Laurencie, "L'Opéra-comique," in Lavignac, *Encyclopédie*, Part I, Vol. III, pp. 1457 ff.; Grout, "Origins of the Opéra-comique"; Cooper, *Opéra comique*.

[16] Tiersot, *La Musique dans la comédie de Molière*; Böttger, *Die "Comédie-Ballet" von Molière-Lully*.

[17] Parfaict, *Histoire de l'ancien théâtre italien*; Du Gérard, *Tables*; Gherardi, *Théâtre italien*; Grout, "The Music of the Italian Theatre at Paris, 1682–1697"; idem, "Seventeenth Century Parodies of French Opera."

Vaudeville Airs from *Théâtre de la Foire*, Vol. I

EXAMPLE 71

a. No. 5

Quand le péril    est agreable

b. No. 13

Joconde

c. No. 39

Faire    l'amour    la    nuit et    le    jour.

d. No. 66

Dondaine,    dondaine

under one management and formally established as the Théâtre de l'Opéra-comique. For a long time they continued giving popular comedies in which the vaudevilles were the principal source of music [18] and burlesque of the serious opera a frequent device.[19] As a competitor, they had the so-called New Italian Theatre, which had been reestab-

[18] Carmody, *Le Repertoire de l'opéra-comique en vaudevilles*; Parfaict, *Mémoires*; Le Sage, *Théâtre de la foire*; Barberet, *Lesage et le théâtre de la foire*; Calmus, *Zwei Opernburlesken*.

[19] Cf. Cucuel, "La Critique musicale"; Grannis, *Dramatic Parody in Eighteenth Century France*.

lished in Paris after the death of Louis XIV in 1715.[20] Among the literary talents attracted to the latter theatre was Charles-Simon Favart, who during the 1740s raised the vaudeville comedy to its highest level and at the same time encouraged the introduction of new music—airs parodied from operas and even some originally composed songs—in place of the old-fashioned vaudevilles.[21] From 1752 to 1754 the performance at Paris of a dozen Italian buffo operas (including Pergolesi's *Serva padrona*) by a visiting troupe gave rise to a famous quarrel, the "War of the Bouffons," [22] in the course of which the relative merits of French and Italian music were argued *ad nauseam*. One of the peculiar features of this quarrel was that no one seemed to realize that all the comparisons were being made between French *serious* opera and Italian *comic* opera, and therefore the real point at issue was missed. However, the results of the Italians' visit were important, for they led a new generation of French composers to create a national comic opera with original music, in which the native popular idiom of the vaudeville was overlaid and enriched by a more refined, varied, and expressive style.

A forerunner of this new opéra comique was Jean-Jacques Rousseau's *Devin du village* ("The Village Soothsayer"),[23] which was performed at the Academy of Music in 1752 and remained in the repertoire for sixty years. This charming little work is Italian in form—that is, it has continuous music, with recitatives—but French in style and feeling. The melodies show kinship with both the vaudeville and the popular romances of the day, while the harmonizations are amusingly

[20] *Le Nouveau Théâtre italien; Les Parodies du nouveau théâtre italien* (with *Supplément*); Geulette, *Notes et souvenirs*; Desboulmiers, *Histoire anecdotique*; Origny, *Annales du théâtre-italien*; Cucuel, "Notes sur la comédie italienne de 1717 à 1789."

[21] Favart, *Théâtre; idem, Mémoires et correspondances*; Monnet, *Mémoires*; Font, *Favart*; Iacuzzi, *The European Vogue of Favart*.

[22] Richebourg's *Contribution à l'histoire de la "Querelle des Bouffons"* contains a bibliography of the principal documents in this affair. See especially Grimm, "Lettre sur Omphale"; *idem, Le Petit Prophète de Boemischbroda; idem, Correspondance littéraire*; Kretzschmar, "Die *Correspondance littéraire*," in *Gesammelte Aufsätze* II, 210–25, also in JMP X (1903) 77–92; Rousseau, *Lettre sur la musique française*; Diderot, *Le Neveu de Rameau*; La Laurencie, "La Grande Saison italienne de 1752"; Hirschberg, *Die Enzyklopädisten und die französische Oper*; Boyer, *La Guerre des bouffons*; Oliver, *The Encyclopedists as Critics of Music*; Strunk, *Source Readings*, pp. 619–55.

[23] Tiersot, *Jean-Jacques Rousseau*; Masson, "Les Idées de Rousseau sur la musique"; Pougin, *Jean-Jacques Rousseau musicien*; Arnheim, "*Le Devin du village*."

naïve. Rousseau's attempt to found a French comic opera had no immediate results; he himself, with typical inconsistency, declared in the
following year that "the French have no music and never can have any
—or if they ever do, so much the worse for them." [24] Yet after a few
years of experimentation, the new French comic opera came to full
growth in the works of three composers: Egidio Romoaldo Duni
(1709–75), an Italian who came to Paris in 1757 after having tried his
hand at French comic operas at the court of Parma; François-André
Danican Philidor (1726–95),[25] the last of a distinguished family of
musicians and equally renowned as a chess master; and Pierre-Alexandre Monsigny (1729–1817),[26] who, though not a trained musician,
succeeded on the strength of his natural melodic gift, which lay in the
direction of tender and sentimental expression. While these three composers were writing opéras comiques at Paris, Gluck was producing a
series of similar pieces at Vienna.

The new opéra comique differed in many ways from both the
earlier vaudeville comedies and the Italian opera buffa. The form was
known as a *comédie mêlée d'ariettes*, a "comedy [in spoken dialogue]
mingled with songs." The term "ariette" was used as the diminutive of
the Italian "aria" to distinguish a newly composed song from the traditional vaudeville melodies. The subject matter was varied: Gluck's
*Rencontre imprévue* ("The Unexpected Meeting"), given at Vienna in
1764, was a romantic comedy in an oriental setting; Duni's *Isle des
Foux* ("The Island of Madmen," 1760) and *La Fée Urgèle* (1765) were
respectively farce and fairy tale; Philidor's *Tom Jones* (1764) was based
on Fielding's picaresque novel; Monsigny in *On ne s'avise jamais de tout*
("You Never Know All," 1761) produced an intrigue comedy of the
Italian sort and in *Le Déserteur* (1769), his best work, a sentimental
drama. An important class of opéras comiques were those with scenes
and characters representing an idealized peasantry, with a naïve heroine
(a character type inherited from Favart) and a manly young hero who,
oppressed by a wicked noble, are finally saved either by virtue of their
own innocence and honesty or by the intervention of a more powerful
noble or the king himself. Monsigny's *Le Roi et le fermier* ("The King

[24] End of his *Lettre sur la musique française*.
[25] Bonnet, *Philidor et l'évolution de la musique française*; Carroll, "François-
André Danican-Philidor."
[26] Pougin, *Monsigny et son temps*. Cf. also Arnoldson, *Sedaine et les musiciens
de son temps*.

and the Farmer," 1762) and Duni's *Caprice amoureux* ("The Whim of Love," 1755) were of this type, and the same motif entered into many other opéras comiques. The "advanced" ideas of the day, the currently fashionable criticism of the social order, the doctrines of Rousseau and the other encyclopedists, were reflected, though in a harmless enough fashion, in these works.

The music of the opéra comique was seldom profound but often tuneful and charming (see Example 72). Ensembles, especially duets,

### *Le Déserteur*, Act I, sc. 1

EXAMPLE 72

MONSIGNY

Peut-on af-fli-ger ce qu'on ai-me? Pour-quoi cher-cher à le fâ-cher? Peut-on af-fli-ger ce qu'on ai-me? C'est bien en vou-loir à soi mê-me, c'est bien en vou-loir à soi mê-me.

were common, though the French never developed the dramatic ensemble finale to the extent the Italians did. Short descriptive orchestral background pieces were frequent—a heritage from Lully and Rameau. Most opéras comiques ended with a "vaudeville final," a strophic song with refrain, the tune either a popular vaudeville or in imitation of that style. The form of the vaudeville final established itself not only in the later French opéra comique but in other countries as well; the finales of Gluck's *Orfeo*, Mozart's *Entführung*, and Rossini's *Barbiere di Siviglia* are of this type.

The leading composer of opéras comiques in the latter part of the eighteenth century was André Ernest Modeste Grétry (1741–1813).[27] Grétry was a Belgian who, after studying at Rome, came to Paris in 1767 and there produced over forty opéras comiques, of which the chief are *Le Tableau parlant* ("The Talking Picture," 1769), *Zémire et Azor* (1771), and especially *Richard Coeur-de-Lion* (1784). Grétry's music happily combines the melodic grace of Italy with the delicate imagination, simplicity, lyricism, and rhythmic finesse of the French. *Richard Coeur-de-Lion* is a landmark of early romantic opera, based on the legend of the rescue of King Richard from prison by his faithful minstrel Blondel. The rescue plot was a favorite in operas of the late eighteenth and early nineteenth centuries, blending the emotions of suspense, personal loyalty, and triumph of virtue over evil in an effective dramatic pattern, familiar to us still through Beethoven's *Fidelio*. By way of added romantic color, Grétry introduced in *Richard* an imitation of a simple troubadour song, which pervades the work almost like a leitmotif. The ballad "Que le sultan Saladin" in Act I, introduced simply as a song external to the action, is the type of many such interpolations in later opera. Blondel's air "O Richard, O mon roi" ("O Richard, O my king," Act I), by its elevated, earnest, and ardent expression, lifts this opéra comique into the realm of serious romantic drama, setting an ideal to which many later composers paid homage (Example 73).

The opéra comique continued to flourish during the revolution and the early years of the nineteenth century,[28] though it had no composers comparable to Grétry either in ability or popularity until the success of Boieldieu's *Jean de Paris* in 1812. Like the Italian opera buffa, the French opéra comique in the course of the eighteenth century had undergone a transformation from low popular comedy to varied, semi-serious human drama, from the music of popular song to the effort of able composers. It was destined for greater triumphs in the nineteenth century and for such further changes of style and subject matter as to leave the designation "comique" merely a memento of its origin and a conventional indication of one vestige of its early days, the use of spoken dialogue.

BALLAD OPERA.[29] When Addison in 1711 complained that "our

---

[27] On Grétry, see his *Mémoires* and *Réflexions d'un solitaire*; Strunk, *Source Readings*, pp. 711–27; bibliography in Lavignac, *Encyclopédie*, Part I, Vol. III, p. 1481; biographies by Clercx, Bobillier, and De Curzon.

[28] Pougin, *L'Opéra-comique pendant la révolution*.

[29] Tufts, "Ballad Opera"; Squire, "An Index of Tunes in the Ballad-Operas"; Gagey, *Ballad Opera*.

EXAMPLE 73

GRÉTRY

English Musick is quite rooted out," he uttered no more than the melancholy truth, so far as the theatre was concerned. Yet the enthusiasm for Italian opera which prevailed during the first quarter of the eighteenth century eventually provoked a reaction. The English, unable to compete with foreign opera seria on its own ground, took revenge by creating the ballad opera, which at the same time ridiculed Italian music and originated a national comic type as distinctive and popular for the British as opera buffa was for the Italians or opéra comique for the French. The best-known of these works, and one which has survived to our own time, was *The Beggar's Opera*, written by John Gay with music arranged by John Christopher Pepusch (1667–1752) [30] and first performed at London in 1728. The characters are pickpockets, bawds, jailbirds, and similar gentry (in keeping with Swift's suggested title "The Newgate Pastoral"), the language is low and racy, and the play is full of satirical thrusts both at the absurdities of Italian opera and at the reigning Whig politicians of the day. The songs, which alternate with spoken dialogue, are for the most part familiar ballad tunes (Example 74), though there

*The Beggar's Opera*, **Air XVI**
Over the Hills and Far Away

EXAMPLE 74

are some borrowings from other sources (for example, the march from Handel's *Rinaldo*). The motifs of political and musical satire are particularly congenial to the English in comic opera, as witness Gilbert and

[30] Burney, *History* (2d ed.) II, 985–90; Hughes, "John Christopher Pepusch"; Calmus, *Zwei Opernburlesken*; studies of Gay and *The Beggar's Opera* by Benjamin, Kidson, Schultz, and Berger.

Sullivan; neither in the eighteenth nor the nineteenth century were the Londoners inclined to take opera seria with complete seriousness.

The success of *The Beggar's Opera* struck a blow at the fortunes of Handel and marked the beginning of the decline of Italian opera in England. A spate of ballad operas followed during the next ten years, and they continued to be produced throughout the century. The form underwent an evolution similar to that of the vaudeville comedy in France: people tiring of the same old tunes, composers turned to other sources or began to introduce their own songs into the scores, though keeping in general to the ballad style. Indeed, the typical English comic opera of the later eighteenth century is such a hodgepodge of popular tunes, songs from favorite operas, and original music that the elements are hard to disentangle, though the genuine folk ballads of the early days gradually disappeared. The influence of the opera buffa and opéra comique is increasingly apparent after the middle of the century, not only in the outright appropriation of both librettos and music but also in the whole trend from broad comedy and burlesque toward a semiserious, sentimental type of plot with simple half-Italian, half-English music—a singularly innocent, naïve kind of entertainment which was tremendously popular in its day and is still not without a certain appeal.[31]

One of the composers of comic opera was Dr. Thomas Augustine Arne (1710–78), the most eminent English composer of his generation. Arne's *Thomas and Sally* (1760), on a libretto by Isaac Bickerstaffe, was one of his most successful comic operas and has had frequent revivals up to our own time. *Love in a Village* (1762), also with words by Bickerstaffe, was a typical pasticcio of the period, drawing on music by sixteen different composers; Arne, besides arranging the work, contributed six new airs of his own. Dr. Arne, incidentlly, was the composer of the only successful English serious opera of the eighteenth century: *Artaxerxes* (1762), on a libretto translated and adapted by the composer from Metastasio. The music of *Artaxerxes* is quite a fair specimen of the current Italian style; the opera continued to be performed in England through the early years of the nineteenth century and was revived in London in 1962.

A popular comic opera of the eighteenth century was *The Duenna*

---

[31] The basic study of English opera in the second half of the eighteenth century is Winesanker, "The Record of English Musical Drama, 1750–1800." See also Kelly, *Reminiscences* II, 36, 66, *et passim*; Graves, "English Comic Opera: 1760–1800."

(1775), Sheridan's comedy with music arranged and in part composed by his father-in-law, Thomas Linley, Sr. (1733–95). The principal later composers of English comic opera were Charles Dibdin (1745–1814), William Shield (1748–1829), and Stephen Storace (1763–96).[32] The most successful of Dibdin's operas were *Lionel and Clarissa* (1768), *The Padlock* (1768), *The Waterman* (1774), *The Quaker* (1775), and *The Seraglio* (1776). Shield was the most gifted, though not the most popular, of these three composers. His *Rosina* (1782) is an excellent example of English comic opera in this period. Shield's librettos, like those of Storace (*The Haunted Tower*, 1789; *The Pirates*, 1792; *The Cherokee*, 1794), show an expansion of subject matter to include popular supernatural and adventurous tales in the early romantic taste. Storace's music betrays to some extent the influence of Mozart, especially in the use of the concerted finale (as in Act I of *The Pirates*). The comic opera was continued in the early nineteenth century by Sir Henry Rowley Bishop (1786–1855), of whose 120 dramatic compositions or arrangements nothing is known to present-day audiences but a setting of Shakespeare's "Lo, here the gentle lark" and the melody of "Home, sweet home," from the comic opera *Clari, the Maid of Milan* (1823).

English opera, unlike that of either Italy or France, remained a local development, without influence on the course of serious opera anywhere. In the American colonies it flourished for a time, but with no important historical consequences. In a century which, to speak mildly, was not the Golden Age of British music, the ballad opera appeared as a vigorous but solitary gesture of revolt against foreign musical domination; but it lacked the principle of growth within itself, nor did external conditions favor the rise of an independent serious national opera on the basis of the popular comic-opera style.

THE SINGSPIEL.[33] The collapse of German opera in the first half of the eighteenth century discouraged any systematic attempt at native musical drama for many years. Even the regular theatre, though spurred on by the reforms of Gottsched, did not succeed in shaking off its baroque crudities and its later subservience to French tragedy until after

[32] Sear, "Charles Dibdin"; Hauger, "William Shield"; Fiske, "The Operas of Stephen Storace." See also Kelly's *Reminiscences*, which gives many interesting details on the state of the English stage at the end of the eighteenth century. Dibdin published a five-volume *History of the Stage* (1795), as well as memoirs and several novels.

[33] Schletterer, *Das deutsche Singspiel*; Eitner, "Die deutsche komische Oper"; Lüthge, *Die deutsche Spieloper*.

the middle of the century. As for opera, with a few insignificant exceptions, nothing corresponding to the Italian opera seria or the French tragédie lyrique ever appeared. Yet the seeds of a new growth were present, and the soil in which they were to flourish was the same that had nurtured comic opera in Italy, France, and England—namely, the theatre of the common people. Bands of strolling players discovered that they could attract larger audiences by mingling music with their plays, and so the new German Singspiel arose, somewhat like the French opéra comique, as a spoken comedy with interspersed lyrical songs. The latter, since they were to be performed by actors not skilled in music, had to be of the simplest possible kind. A model was at hand in the new German lied, which, from the publication of Sperontes's collection *Die Singende Muse an der Pleisse* (1736–45), entered upon a revival destined to continue uninterruptedly through the century and eventually lead up to the works of Schubert.[34]

Although there were earlier isolated instances of popular comic music in cantatas, school dramas, and intermezzi,[35] the first definite impulse to the new Singspiel came from England. In 1743 a ballad opera, *The Devil to Pay; or, The Wives Metamorphos'd* (*Der Teufel ist los; oder, Die verwandelten Weiber*), was performed at Berlin, in German translation but with the original English music; in a new arrangement by Christian Felix Weisse, and with new music by J. C. Standfuss,[36] it was given again at Leipzig in 1752 with great success. Another Singspiel by the same two men, likewise based on a ballad opera, *The Merry Cobbler* (*Der lustige Schuster*), was presented at Lübeck in 1759. The music of Standfuss is fresh and jolly, with the true breath of German folk song. His successor, and the most important early composer of the Singspiel, was Johann Adam Hiller (1728–1804),[37] who was the first conductor of the famous *Gewandhaus* concerts at Leipzig and editor of an important musical periodical, the *Wöchentliche Nachrichten*, as well as composer of a dozen Singspiels. The latter were produced in collaboration with Weisse at Leipzig, beginning with a new

[34] Friedländer, *Das deutsche Lied im 18. Jahrhundert*; Kretzschmar, *Geschichte des neuen deutschen Liedes*.

[35] Cf. Moser, *Geschichte der deutschen Musik* II, 371; Schering, "Zwei Singspiele des Sperontes."

[36] Calmus, *Die ersten deutschen Singspiele von Standfuss und Hiller*; Rubsamen, "Mr. Seedo, Ballad Opera, and the Singspiel." Biography of Weisse by Minor.

[37] On Hiller see his autobiography; biography by Peiser; Calmus, *Die ersten deutschen Singspiele von Standfuss und Hiller*.

version of *Der Teufel ist los* in 1766 and climaxing with *Die Jagd* ("The Hunt") in 1770, the most popular German opera before Weber's *Freischütz*. Although Hiller's early works show some Italian influence, the music of *Die Jagd* is characteristically German; the score is filled with melodies of the purest folk-song type, contrasting (as in all his Singspiels) with the intentionally more elaborate and Italianate arias which Hiller considered appropriate for kings and other highly placed characters. Some of the songs, without departing from the prevailing simple style, have a sweep of line which almost reminds one of Beethoven (Example 75). There are nine ensembles, including three with chorus,

*Die Jagd*, Act II

EXAMPLE 75                                   HILLER

O dass mich noch sein Her - ze lieb-te so wie mein Herz, so wie mein Herz ihn liebt!

and an orchestral "storm" in addition to the usual three-movement overture.

The success of Hiller's Singspiels was not due alone to the music. Weisse's librettos, adapted nearly every one from contemporary French opéras comiques,[38] reflected the same preoccupation with scenes and characters from common life, the same touches of romantic fancy, the same exaltation of sentiment and glorification of the peasantry, the same inevitable triumph of simple virtue over the wickedness of the nobles, and the same motif of devotion to the king as protector and father of the innocent—in short, all those ideas which made such a deep appeal to the feelings of the people in this prerevolutionary period, and which made the comic opera of both nations a genuine popular manifestation. The folk basis is even more pronounced in Germany than in

---

[38] The derivation of the principal librettos is as follows: *Lisuart und Dariolette* (1766) from Favart's *Fée Urgèle, ou Ce qui plaît aux dames*, mus. Duni, 1765; *Lottchen am Hofe* (1767) from Favart's *Ninette à la cour*, mus. pasticcio, 1755; *Die Liebe auf dem Lande* (1768) from Mme Favart's *Annette et Lubin*, mus. mostly vaudevilles, 1762, and Anseaume's *Clochette*, mus. Duni, 1766; *Die Jagd* (1770) from Sedaine's *Roi et le fermier*, mus. Monsigny, 1762; *Der Dorfbarbier* (1771) from Sedaine's *Blaise le savetier*, mus. Philidor, 1759.

France; many of Hiller's melodies became national folk songs.[39] French opéras comiques, or translations and imitations, with the original music or in new settings by German composers, appeared in Germany by scores after 1770.[40] The growth of the Singspiel went hand in hand with the ever-increasing popularity of the lied; authors and composers, professional and amateur alike, all over the country, joined in a universal outpouring of song; for sheer quantity it was one of the most productive periods in the history of German music.

Two distinct branches of the Singspiel developed. In the North, where the influence of Weisse and Hiller predominated, the literary framework remained that of the idyllic, sentimental, lyrical comedy on the model of the French opéra comique, with music of a simple melodic type closely allied to folk song. The adherence to a national musical language and the increase of romantic elements in the libretto [41] led naturally in the nineteenth century to the romantic German opera of Weber.

Of the many North German composers after Hiller we may mention particularly Georg Benda (1722–95),[42] who was noted not only for his Singspiels but also for his "melodramas." A melodrama is a stage piece without singing, but with action and speaking by one or two performers accompanied by or alternating with the orchestra (there may also be choral interludes). Rousseau had already written a melodrama *Pygmalion* (performed 1770, with music by Coignet),[43] but Benda's *Ariadne auf Naxos* (1775) was the first important German work in this form and had many successors.[44] The chief historical importance of the melodrama lay in the effective use made of the style by later composers for special scenes in opera : the grave-digging scene in *Fidelio* and the Wolf's Glen scene in *Der Freischütz* are familiar examples; Beethoven has a melo-

[39] Burney, *The Present State of Music in Germany* I, 84; Hoffman von Fallersleben, *Unsere volkstümlichen Lieder*, Nos. 48, 265, 304, 947.

[40] *Theater-Kalendar* (Reichard), *passim*.

[41] E.g., Kunzen's *Holger Danske* (Copenhagen, 1789) from Wieland's *Oberon*; cf. Leopold Schmidt, *Geschichte der Märchenoper*.

[42] Studies by Hodermann and Brückner; see also Istel, *Die Entstehung des deutschen Melodrams*; musical examples in Martens, *Das Melodram*.

[43] On the debated question of Rousseau's music for his *Pygmalion* see Istel, *Studien zur Geschichte des Melodrams. I. Jean Jacques Rousseau als Komponist seiner lyrischen Szene Pygmalion*, and (*contra*) Hirschberg, *Die Enzyklopädisten*, pp. 88–90; cf. also Mason, "The Melodrama in France."

[44] Schletterer, *Das deutsche Singspiel*, p. 225; Subirá, *El compositor Iriarte y el cultivo español del melólogo (melodrama)*.

drama in his music to *King Stephen*, and Schubert makes good use of the technique in his operas *Die Zauberharfe* (1820) and *Fierrabras* (1823).

Other notable North German Singspiels include *Die Dorfgala* ("The Village Festival," 1772) by Anton Schweitzer (1735–87);[45] *Das tartarische Gesetz* ("The Law of the Tartars," 1789) by Johann André (1741–99); and *Die Apotheke* ("The Apothecary," 1771) by Christian Gottlob Neefe (1748–98),[46] pupil of Hiller and teacher of Beethoven. Johann Friedrich Reichardt (1752–1814), Goethe's favorite composer and an important figure in the history of German song, invented a new form which he called the *Liederspiel*, a comedy with familiar popular songs, similar to the early French vaudeville comedy or English ballad opera. Reichardt was also of some importance for the development of opera at Berlin; his *Claudine von Villa Bella* (Goethe's text) and his Italian opera *Brenno* were presented there in 1789. A revival of the latter, in translation and in concert form, in 1798 was the first occasion on which opera was sung at Berlin with German words.

A Danish branch of the Singspiel [47] had as its leading composers Johann Abraham Peter Schulz (1747–1800) and Friedrich Ludwig Aemilius Kunzen (1761–1817). Two other composers prepared the way for Danish national opera in the nineteenth century: Christoph Ernst Friedrich Weyse (1774–1842) and Friedrich Kuhlau (1786–1832).

In South Germany the Singspiel took on a different character, owing in part to the strong influence of Italian opera buffa. The Viennese [48] found the quiet, lyrical melodies of the North "too Lutheran" and demanded more liveliness and display. The librettos tended to be gay and farcical, with not a hint of any social significance; the supernatural, which in the North was an accepted means of romantic expression, here became usually an object of spectacle or of ridicule. A national opera theatre, founded at Vienna by the Emperor Josef II, was opened in

---

[45] Maurer, *Schweitzer als dramatischer Komponist.*
[46] Leux, *Christian Gottlob Neefe.*
[47] Krogh, *Zur Geschichte des dänischen Singspiels*; Behrend, "Weyse und Kuhlau"; Thrane, *Danske Komponister.*
[48] On the history of the Singspiel at Vienna, see R. Haas, introduction to Umlauf's *Bergknappen* in DTOe XVIII, Part 1; *idem*, "Die Musik in der Wiener deutscher Stegreifkomödie"; *idem*, "Wiener deutsche Parodieopern um 1730"; Helfert, "Zur Geschichte des Wiener Singspiels." For examples of the music see (in addition to works of separate composers) *Deutsche Komödienarien 1754–1758* (DTOe XXXIII) and *Wiener Komödienlieder aus 3 Jahrhunderten*, ed. Glossy and Haas (Vienna, 1924).

1778 with a performance of *Die Bergknappen* ("The Miners") by Ignaz Umlauf (1746–96), and Mozart's *Entführung* was performed there four years later. The leading Viennese Singspiel composer, however, was Karl Ditters von Dittersdorf (1739–99),[49] composer of fifteen Italian and twenty-nine German comic operas as well as a huge amount of symphonic and other instrumental music. Dittersdorf's Singspiels show traces of the Italian comic style in their vivacious rhythms, bravura passages, chromatic touches, short-phrased interjectional melodic lines, long ensembles which continue the action, and lively comic details of all sorts. Yet Dittersdorf is no mere imitator of the Italians; many of his melodies are unmistakably Viennese (Example 76). His facility, energy, and humor, together with his melodic gift, his imaginative use of the orchestra, and his grasp of formal structure, make it easy to understand the success of his works at Vienna and show him as a composer of comic opera not unworthy to be named along with Mozart.

Later Viennese Singspiel composers include Johann Schenk (1753–1836),[50] whose *Dorfbarbier* ("The Village Barber," 1796) looks forward to the comic style of Lortzing; and Wenzel Müller (1767–1835),[51] in whose works there is apparent an increasing popularization of both libretto and musical idiom, in a manner destined to lead to the nineteenth-century Viennese operetta. The operetta is, indeed, the natural successor of the lighthearted, melodious Singspiel of the eighteenth century.

EARLY SPANISH OPERA : THE "ZARZUELA" AND THE "TONADILLA." [52]
From its beginnings in the fifteenth century the Spanish secular theatre, like the Italian, called on music to adorn and supplement the spoken dialogue of its dramas. Most of the plays of Juan del Encina (1469?–

[49] See Dittersdorf's autobiography; also Krebs, *Dittersdorfiana* (with thematic catalogue); Holl, *Dittersdorfs Opern*; Riedinger, "Dittersdorf als Opernkomponist."
[50] Autobiography in SzMw XI (1924) 75–85.
[51] See studies by Krone and Raab.
[52] Soriano Fuertes, *Historia de la música española*; Chavarri, *Historia de la música*; Mitjana, "La Muisque en Espagne" (with many musical examples), in Lavignac, *Encylopédie de la musique*, Part I, Vol. IV, pp. 2003–17 (madrigals), 2027–35 (sixteenth-century theatre), 2052–71 (seventeenth-century zarzuela), 2108–14 (late seventeenth century), 2123–28 (Italian opera in Spain), 2150–80 (eighteenth-century theatre), 2195–2209 (Spanish composers of Italian opera), 2227–57 (tonadilla); idem, *Histoire du développement du théâtre dramatique et musical en Espagne*; Pedrell, *Teatro lírico español* (many musical examples); Reiff, "Die Anfänge der Oper in Spanien"; Subirá, *La música en la casa de Alba*; idem, "Le Style dans la musique théâtrale espagnole"; idem, *Historia de la música teatral en España*; Chase, *The Music of Spain*.

EXAMPLE 76

*Das rote Käppchen,* Act II, finale

DITTERSDORF

1. Herr Schultz auf ein Wort warum bleibt er zu
2. Ich dan - ke fürs Es - sen, ich dan - ke fürs

Haus, und will nicht er - schei-nen beim heu - ti - gen Schmaus?
Trin-ken, wenn Män - ner be - trunk-en vom Stuhl her-ab sinken.

Da

*Orch.*

mögt' es wohl ü - bel den Wei - bern er - geh'n,

mögt' es ü - bel den Wei - bern schon geh'n, doch

bleibt man zu Hau - se, da kann nichts ge - scheh'n

*ca.* 1529) end with a *villancico*, a little song for four voices somewhat similar to the Italian *frottola*, which was both sung and danced.[53] The plays of Gil Vicente (d. 1557) and Diego Sánchez de Badajoz (1479–*ca.* 1550) also commonly used music, not only at the beginning and end but sometimes intermingled with the action. In the sixteenth century also flourished the *ensalada* (literally "salad," that is, "hodgepodge"), a humorous type of piece reflecting popular scenes and character types, and having many features in common with the Italian madrigal comedy.[54]

During the Golden Age of Spanish drama, the seventeenth century, there arose the characteristic national "zarzuela." [55] The name comes from the "Palace of the Zarzuela" near Madrid, where these pieces were first performed. The zarzuela of this period, of which Calderón's *El laurel de Apolo* (1658) is a typical example, was in two acts, often on pastoral or mythological subjects, and with emphasis on elaborate scenic effects; it was in spoken dialogue but included much music, in the form of choruses, dialogues, and solos. In general plan it corresponded most closely to the contemporary comedy ballet of Molière and Lully, but its vitality and significance were greater. All the great Spanish playwrights of the seventeenth century interested themselves in the zarzuela and similar forms, such as the *comedia harmónica* (comedy with music), the *egloga* (pastorale), or the *auto sacramentale* (a religious play). Most of the musical scores of these plays seem to have been lost, and if we may judge from the published examples of those that survive, it is a loss greatly to be regretted. The zarzuela attained the height of its development toward the end of the seventeenth century. Its historical career is strikingly parallel to that of the national English and German operas of the same period, for in the course of the eighteenth century it was abandoned owing to the popularity of Italian opera, which first came to Spain in 1703.[56]

Among the zarzuelas of the seventeenth century a few were sung throughout. The earliest was Lope de Vega's pastorale *La selva sin amor*

[53] Examples of music in Barbieri, *Cancionero musical de los siglos XV y XVI.* Cf. Subirá, *La participación musical en el antiguo teatro español*; Livermore, "The Spanish Dramatists and Their Use of Music"; Beau, "Die Musik im Werk des Gil Vicente."

[54] See Mateo Flecha, *Las Ensaladas* (1581), ed. Anglès.

[55] Cotarelo, *Historia de la zarzuela.*

[56] Cotarelo, *Orígenes y establecimento de la ópera en España*; Carmena, *Crónica de la ópera italiana en Madrid*; Virella, *La ópera en Barcelona.*

("The Forest without Love," 1629), the music of which is not known.[57] In 1662 was performed a *fiesta cantada, Celos aun del aire matan,* by Calderón, with music by Juan Hidalgo; the music of the first of the three acts has been published.[58] This music consists for the most part of simple solo songs in dancelike triple metre, with frequently recurring themes connected by recitatives; there are also a few short choruses. Other similar works, often designated as *zarzuelas a la italiana,* appeared in the eighteenth century; but they were few in number, too much under the influence of Italian style, or too insignificant dramatically to establish a genuine Spanish opera in this period.

The different musical numbers in the zarzuelas and plays of the seventeenth and early eighteenth centuries appeared in various forms, some of which developed considerable importance of their own.[59] Among these was the *entremés* (intermezzo), which was usually performed as an interlude between the acts of a play. Frequently the entremés ended with a song, called a *tonadilla* (diminutive of *tonada,* a word applied in the seventeenth century to a solo song with accompaniment). About the middle of the eighteenth century this finale of the entremés, this tonadilla, began to be expanded to include two or more separate numbers, and even a little dramatic framework. Eventually the tonadilla, thus expanded, was detached from the entremés and launched on a career of its own; it flourished especially at Madrid throughout the second half of the eighteenth century as the national Spanish form corresponding to the English ballad opera or the French opéra comique.[60] One of the earliest composers, though not the originator, of the tonadilla was Luis Misón (d. 1766), who established the independence of the form and the use of the orchestra for accompaniments. The chief later composers were Pablo Esteve y Grimau (d. 1794) and Blas de Laserna (1751-1816).[61]

[57] There is some doubt also as to whether *La selva sin amor* was really sung throughout. Cf. Chase, "Origins of the Lyric Theater in Spain."

[58] Barcelona, 1933, ed. J. Subirá. The title means literally "Jealousy, even from the air, kills." See Ursprung, "*Celos* usw."

[59] Cotarelo, *Colección de entremeses, loas, bailes, jácaras y mojingangas desde fines del siglo XVI á mediados del XVII.*

[60] The chief study of the tonadilla is Subirá's *Tonadilla escénica,* which contains many musical examples; further examples in the same author's *Tonadillas teatrales inéditas* and *Los maestros de la tonadilla escénica,* also in Nin's modern editions (*Sept Chants lyriques; Sept Chansons picaresques*) and Pedrell's *Cancionero musical popular español* (Vol. IV).

[61] See biographical study by J. Gómez.

*Una mesoñera y un arriero*
*Tonadilla a duo* (?1757)

EXAMPLE 77

Vivo

Soprano and Tenor

MISÓN

Vá - mo-nos a la ven - ta, vá - mo-nos a la

ven - ta, ca - ri - ño

mi - o, ca - ri - ño mi - o.

The tonadilla was usually performed between the first and second acts of a comedy; it was seldom more than twenty minutes long and consisted almost entirely of solo songs or dialogues, sometimes with dancing, and with occasional short spoken phrases. The later tonadillas became longer and had a larger proportion of spoken parts, though they still kept to the basic plan of a series of songs in contrasting tempos, with occasional duets or ensembles. There were no independent instrumental pieces, though a full orchestra was nearly always used for accompaniments. The cast of singers might comprise one to six persons, or even more in the *tonadilla generale*. The solo tonadillas were mostly on satirical or narrative texts; the others usually consisted of a short comic episode, with scenes and character types from familiar daily life, ending (especially in the later period) with a general moral reflection. In form, the tonadilla was divided into three parts, the *introducción, coplas,* and *final,* the last usually consisting of *seguidillas* of various types, which might be both sung and danced; seguidillas were also sometimes inserted in the coplas, the body of the tonadilla, by way of interludes.

The music of the early tonadillas was simple, tuneful, and with marked dancelike rhythms, closely derived from folk song (Example 77). Later it became slightly more sophisticated, often giving evidence of the popularity of Italian opera at Madrid by the inclusion of recitatives and arias in Italian style and even with Italian texts. By the nineteenth century the national Spanish element had practically disappeared, being replaced by an imitation of Italian opera buffa music. Tonadillas were still produced during the first half of the nineteenth century, but the form finally gave way to a new type of zarzuela about 1850.

CHAPTER 17

# MOZART[1]

✧

Most opera composers have been specialists; Mozart was one of the few whose greatness was manifested equally in opera and in other branches of composition. His genius and training led him to conceive of opera as essentially a musical affair, like a symphony, rather than as a drama in which music was merely one means of dramatic expression. In this conception he was at one with the Italian composers of the day, and his work may be regarded in a sense as the ideal toward which the whole eighteenth-century Italian opera had been striving. He overtopped his predecessors not by a changed approach to opera but by the superior beauty, originality, and significance of his musical ideas, by his greater mastery of counterpoint, by his higher constructive powers, and by his ability to write music which not only perfectly portrayed a dramatic situation but at the same time could develop freely in a musical sense, without appearing to be in the least hampered by the presence of a text. The variety of musical forms in Mozart's operas, which can only be appreciated by an analysis of the scores, is paralleled by the skill with which these forms are adapted to the dramatic aims. In this rare combination of dramatic truth and musical beauty, there can be no doubt that the music is the important thing. Without it none of the operas,

[1] For a survey of the Mozart bibliography see the article in MGG. Only the basic books and those most important for Mozart's operas are listed here: Köchel, *Chronologisch-thematisches Verzeichnis*; H. Abert, *Mozart* (7th ed.); Wyzewa and Saint-Foix, *W.-A. Mozart*; Einstein, *Mozart*; *Mozart, die Dokumente seines Lebens*; *Mozart und seine Welt in zeitgenössischen Bildern*; E. Anderson, ed., *The Letters of Mozart and His Family*; *Mozart: Briefe und Aufzeichnungen*, ed. Bauer and Deutsch; articles in the *Mozart-Jahrbuch* (two series) and *Neues Mozart-Jahrbuch*; Lert, *Mozart auf dem Theater*; Conrad, *Mozarts Dramaturgie der Oper*; Dent, *Mozart's Operas* (both editions); Abraham, "The Operas," in *The Mozart Companion*; Szabolcsi, "Mozart et la comédie populaire." For other titles see subsequent footnotes and the bibliography.

except possibly *Figaro*, would be intelligible; with it, even *The Magic Flute* makes sense. So completely does the music absorb the drama, and so perfect is the music itself, that Mozart today not only holds the stage but offers the phenomenon of one composer whose operas are universally enjoyed, by operagoers and music lovers alike.

It is no disparagement of Mozart to remark that, like many another great man, he was born at the right time. Everywhere there were producers ready to stage new operas and audiences ready to listen to them; the classical orchestra and orchestral style were well beyond the experimental stage; the art of singing, though beginning to decline, was still at a high level of virtuosity; the opera itself had the advantage of an established form within which recent developments—the innovations of Gluck, the vitality of opera buffa, and the growing interest in the German Singspiel—offered stimulating possibilities to a composer. Mozart's operas were, on the whole, successful; if they did not obtain for him all the reward or recognition which their merits deserved, and for which he hoped, the fault lay not in the conditions of the time so much as in the fact that Mozart personally was always unfortunate in his adjustments to the patronage system, and that the Viennese public, who might have sustained him, were not yet capable of appreciating those qualities which set him above Dittersdorf and other popular Singspiel composers. In other words, Mozart was slightly in advance of his age; but he was no more a conscious revolutionist in opera than was . Handel. His twenty-two dramatic works include school dramas, serenatas, and Italian serious operas, but the important part of his output lies in the two fields most cultivated in the later eighteenth century, the Italian opera buffa and the German Singspiel.

THE ITALIAN OPERAS. The predominance of Mozart's Italian background is natural, since Italian music was the international standard of his time. The strong early influence of J. C. Bach (London, 1764–65), the three Italian journeys of his boyhood, and the course of contrapuntal studies with Padre Martini in 1770, all strengthened this tendency. Among Mozart's childhood works was an Italian opera buffa, *La finta semplice* ("The Pretended Simpleton"), composed for Vienna in 1768 but not performed until the following year at Salzburg. At the age of fourteen he composed his first opera seria, *Mitridate, rè di Ponto* ("Mithridates, King of Pontus"), which was performed at Milan in December, 1770. Two years later another work of the same type, *Lucio*

*Silla*, was also produced at Milan. Both are on librettos of the conventional type established by Metastasio and are more remarkable as examples of Mozart's extraordinary precocity than for anything else. His aim, and the aim of his father who still closely supervised his compositions, was to produce successful operas according to the current Italian standard. We marvel at the degree to which Mozart had assimilated the operatic manner of his time, but the whole effect is similar to that produced by any performance of a child prodigy : brilliant but inappropriate coloratura passages abound in these early scores; there is little individuality of melody, nothing of the later variety of forms or, except in a few places, true characterization of the text. One aria in *Mitridate* [2] foreshadows the Mozartean pathetic style; in *Lucio Silla* the ombra scene with chorus (Act I, scenes 7–8) is an imaginative and even powerful treatment of the situation, while Cecilio's aria, "Quest' improvviso tremito" (No. 9), with the preceding accompanied recitative, is an unusually dramatic solo in the grand style. The success of these early works was not great, and, though his interest in the form continued, it was nearly ten years before Mozart had the opportunity to compose another opera seria.

*La finta giardiniera* ("The Pretended Gardener"), produced at Munich in 1775, was an Italian opera buffa with a libretto by Calsabigi which unhappily combined the new sentimental motif of Goldoni's *Buona figliuola* with a complicated and cumbersome array of secondary characters, disguises, mistaken identity, and farcical episodes inherited from the older Italian comedy. The music is only too faithful to the text, with the consequence that it not merely lacks dramatic continuity but presents the same characters at different moments in contradictory aspects. Tragedy and comedy rub shoulders, but there is no sign of the synthesis of the two which is so characteristic of Mozart's later dramatic works. Thus the heroine Sandrina in Act I (No. 4) is presented as a superficial young girl of the usual comic-opera type, but in Act II (Nos. 21, 22) as a tragic figure appropriate to opera seria. Aside from such inconsistencies, which were so common in this period, the score of *La finta giardiniera* is extraordinarily attractive. The musical material is individual and is treated with imagination and humor. The serious portions mark an important advance in Mozart's handling of this type of expression, however out of place they are dramatically. Another notable

[2] Aspasia's "Nel sen mi palpitar," No. 4.

feature is the finale of Act I, where the development of the action is combined with character differentiation and musical continuity, giving a foretaste of the finales of *Figaro* and *Don Giovanni*.[3]

The remaining early Italian works may be briefly noticed here. The serenata *Ascanio in Alba* (Milan, 1771) is notable chiefly for its choruses. The serenata *Il sogno di Scipione* ("The Dream of Scipio," Salzburg, 1772) and the festival opera *Il rè pastore* ("The Shepherd King," Salzburg, 1775) offer nothing of particular interest or significance in Mozart's development. They were occasional pieces composed as part of his duties in the service of the archiepiscopal court and (like many of their kind) were adequate but uninspired—with the exception of one aria with a solo violin obbligato, "L'amerò, sarò costante," in Act II of *Il rè pastore*, which is a lovely example of Mozart's lyrical powers.

The influence of Italian opera in Mozart's dramatic career was balanced and modified by his interest in symphonic music. Stemming from Italy and based to a large extent originally on the musical idiom and forms of Italian opera, the preclassical German symphony was at a flourishing stage when Mozart visited one of its chief centers, Mannheim, in 1777-78. Before this date he had already composed many symphonies, two of which especially (K. 183, 201) showed a sure grasp of the form; the works of Johann Stamitz and the Mannheim school were among the models which most influenced him in his mature years. His close association with Christian Cannabich (1731-98), Stamitz's successor as conductor of the famous Mannheim orchestra at the time of Mozart's visit, led to a deeper appreciation of the symphonic style and of the possibilities of orchestral manipulation in general. This is not the place to speak of Mozart as a symphonist, except to point out that his lifelong interest in and mastery of the larger instrumental forms are reflected on every page of his operas—in the way in which voices and instruments are adjusted to one another, in the texture and treatment of the orchestral parts (particularly the independence of the wood winds), in the broadly symphonic overtures, and in the unerring sense of musical continuity extending over long and complex sections of the score.

At Mannheim also Mozart came into contact with German opera—

---

[3] *La finta giardiniera* was revised by Mozart in 1780 for a performance in German, and probably again in 1789. It is possible that some of the stylistic inconsistencies in the score as we now have it may be due to these revisions. The autograph MS of Act I has been lost, and since in the German versions the secco recitatives were replaced by spoken dialogue, the music of these portions cannot be recovered.

not the Singspiel but the new German opera, raising its head again after a forty years' sleep. In 1773 Wieland's *Alceste*, with music by Anton Schweitzer, was performed at Mannheim with such success that in January, 1777, a second German opera, this time actually on a subject from German history, was presented : *Günther von Schwarzburg*, composed by Ignaz Holzbauer (1711–83). Mozart wrote enthusiastically of Holzbauer's music, which is indeed fiery and spirited, though both it and the libretto show all too plainly the outlines of Italian opera seria. Neither Schweitzer nor Holzbauer was able to bring about a permanent awakening in Germany; the time was not ripe, and their works, although performed at Mannheim and in several other cities, remained only an episode in the history of national opera. Yet the ideal persisted; Mozart's *Magic Flute*, which has strains reminiscent of *Günther*, was the first effective step toward its realization.

From Mannheim, Mozart journeyed to Paris, arriving (March, 1778) in the midst of the Gluck-Piccinni controversy. An unknown young foreign musician, he attracted little attention—a disappointing contrast to his reception fifteen years before as a child prodigy. His temperament, coinciding with the anxious advice of his father, kept him aloof from the current quarrel. Moreover, the whole tone of musical life and society in Paris was discouraging to him, with its endless theorizing and debating about matters which he himself either understood quite simply as a musician or else felt to be of no importance. He had no sympathy for French opera and could not abide French singing; the opéra comique apparently did not interest him, and he does not seem to have made the acquaintance of Grétry. Plans for a French opera came to nothing, and the only theatre music of this period was part of a ballet, *Les Petits Riens* (K. Suppl. 10), arranged by Noverre and performed in connection with one of Piccinni's operas. Mozart's joy over the success of his "Paris" Symphony (K. 297) was turned to sadness by the death of his mother; he left Paris in September and returned to Salzburg no richer in either money or prospects than when he had left. Yet the Paris visit was not without importance, for it helped to make Mozart for the first time more fully conscious of his own artistic aims and of his position as a composer in relation to the ideals of Gluck and the French school.

In 1780 came a welcome commission to furnish an opera seria for Munich. The result was *Idomeneo, rè di Creta* ("Idomeneus, King of

Crete"), the first opera which shows Mozart in the fullness of his powers. The libretto, on a subject first used by the French composer Campra in 1712, was written by the Abbé G. B. Varesco of Salzburg; it is of the old-fashioned Metastasian type, on a classical subject with amorous intrigues, but including some large choral scenes in the newer style of Coltellini and Frugoni. In some external details the music also is old-fashioned; there is the conventional framework of recitatives alternating with arias, one of the principals is a male soprano, and there are many brilliant coloratura songs with improvised cadenzas, such as Idomeneo's comparison aria "Fuor del mar" in Act II or Electra's "Tutte nel cor vi sento" in Act I, which is especially notable for the striking effect made by the return of the first theme in C minor after the original statement in D minor. Ensembles are few : two duets, one trio, and one quartet. In accordance with later eighteenth-century practice, there is relatively little secco recitative but a large number of accompanied recitatives; one of the best of these is the highly dramatic recognition scene between Idomeneo and his son Idamante in Act I ("Spietatissimi Dei"), a master-piece of psychological perception and effective harmonic treatment. Like the operas of Jommelli, Traetta, and Gluck, *Idomeneo* is filled with large scene-complexes built around recitative, with free musical and dramatic handling, often combined with spectacular effects—for example, the oracle scene in Act III. Many of these scenes introduce ballets,[4] marches, and choruses. The extent and importance of the choral portions are reminiscent of Gluck and Rameau : the last scene of Act I has a march and chorus (*ciacona*) which is similar to the choral scenes of older French operas, as is also the well-known "Placido è il mar, andiamo" in Act II. More like ancient Greek usage is the scene in Act III between Idomeneo and the chorus, where the latter comments, warns, and expostulates. The most dramatic choral scene is that at the end of the second act, where the repeated cries of the chorus, "Il reo qual è ?" ("Who is the guilty one ?"), with the feeling of terror enforced by the strange, swiftly changing tonalities of the music, the tumult of the storm in the orchestra, Idomeneo's anguished confession, and the final dispersal and flight of the people all form a great and powerful finale equal in force to anything of Gluck and surpassing Gluck in fertility of musical invention.

---

[4] Contrary to the usual practice, Mozart himself composed the ballet music for *Idomeneo*.

Mozart's understanding of the style of opera seria is seen in his treatment of the most traditional of operatic forms, the aria, of which we may single out two examples for special mention. Ilia's "Se il padre perdei" ("Though I have lost my father," Act II) is a splendid example of Mozart's sensitiveness to details of the text, of his ability to unite many different aspects of feeling in one basic mood, and of his imaginative use of orchestral accompaniment for subtle psychological touches. Ilia's third aria, "Zeffiretti lusinghieri" ("Gentle Zephyrs," Act III), brings a commonplace conceit of eighteenth-century opera in a setting which simply transfigures the faded sentiments of the poem by the freshness of the music.

Nowhere in his operas did Mozart lavish more care on the orchestral writing than in *Idomeneo*. This is seen especially in the independence of the wood winds and their frequent employment for the most subtle touches of color and expression.[5] The overture at once sets the tone of lofty seriousness which prevails throughout the opera. At the end, the music dies away with a tonic pedal point, over which we hear in the wood winds a series of repetitions of a characteristic descending phrase which recurs several times during the opera, alternating with rising scale-passages; the final chord of D major, owing to the plagal harmonies, has the effect of a dominant in G, thus leading into the G minor accompanied recitative with which the first act opens.

It is perfectly clear that in writing *Idomeneo* Mozart had before his mind not only the most recent developments in the Italian opera seria but likewise the French operas of Gluck. Since *Idomeneo* was Mozart's last opera seria, except for the unfortunate *Clemenza di Tito* of 1791, it is appropriate at this point to establish his position in the history of this form and his relation both to the Italian school and to Gluck.

In many respects *Idomeneo* is the finest opera seria of the late eighteenth century; it shows that Mozart had fully appreciated the

[5] See for examples: the recurrent descending fifth in the oboes and bassoons in Ilia's aria "Padre, germani" (No. 1); the arpeggio figure for the flute in Electra's "Tutte nel cor vi sento" (No. 4); the many expressive interludes for wood winds in Ilia's "Se il padre perdei" (No. 11), which seem to envelop the solo as if with phrases of consolation; the spirited interplay of the voice with flutes and oboes in the coloratura passages of Idomeneo's "Fuor del mar" (No. 12); the repetition of the climactic phrases of the chorus "Qual nuovo terrore" (No. 17) by the brasses and wood winds; the solemn chorus of the trombones and horns accompanying the voice of the Oracle (No. 28) and the effective contrast of the dominant seventh chord for flutes, oboes, and bassoons which introduces the recitative immediately following.

advances made by Jommelli, Traetta, and Sarti and thus marks an important stage in his own development over his youthful dismissal of Jommelli's *Armide* as "too serious and old-fashioned for the theatre." [6] Mozart surpassed Jommelli not only in spontaneity, variety, and richness of invention but even more in his grasp of the emotional content of the text and in his incomparable power of musically characterizing both persons and situations. To the mastery of traditional outward forms he added the quality of psychological insight and the genius for expressing this insight in musical terms. Observing his treatment of the opera seria we are made aware that a miracle is taking place: the plane figures of the old dramma per musica suddenly take on a new dimension, and we see them in depth and perspective. Yet all this did not amount to a fundamental reform. *Idomeneo* was not the starting point of a new evolution in opera seria but rather the last great example of a form which was already on the decline and in which Mozart himself never produced anything more of significance.

The presence of choral scenes in *Idomeneo* does not indicate acceptance of Gluck's reform theories. Mozart simply adapted for his own purposes certain practices by which the leading Italian composers of the time were seeking to rejuvenate the opera seria. To regard him in any sense as a disciple of Gluck is to misunderstand both men. As a matter of fact, the contrast between two contemporary opera composers could hardly be greater. Gluck, at least so far as *Orfeo* and later works are concerned, was an artist to whom the conscious perception of aims and rational choice of means were necessary preliminaries to musical creation; every detail of his scores was the result of a previously thought out plan, and he was always ready to justify his procedures by reference to his intentions. He could claim that when he composed an opera he endeavored before all else to forget that he was a musician. Mozart, on the contrary, was no philosopher; thought and realization were to him indivisible parts of the same creative process; his music was no less logical than Gluck's, but it was the logic of music, not something capable of being detached and discussed in relation to extramusical conceptions. For him, "in an opera poetry must be altogether the obedient daughter of the music." [7] With Gluck the idea of the drama as a whole came first, and the music was written as part of the means through which the idea

[6] Anderson, *Letters* I, 211; but cf. *ibid.*, p. 208.
[7] *Ibid.*, III, 1150.

was realized; with Mozart the idea took shape immediately and completely as music, the mental steps involved in the process being so smooth and so nearly instantaneous that he has often been called an "instinctive" composer. This is incorrect, unless we choose to denote by the word "instinct" that sureness, clarity, and speed of reasoning which is characteristic of genius.

In addition to this difference of temperament, there was a fundamental difference between Gluck's and Mozart's conceptions of drama. Gluck's characters are generalized and typical rather than individual; they have a certain classic, superhuman stature; and as they are at the beginning of an opera, so they remain to the end. But Mozart's characters are human persons, each uniquely complex and depicted variously in changing moods rather than statically as a fixed bearer of certain qualities. It is for this reason that Mozart's operas seem to us modern while Gluck's seem old-fashioned; Gluck's dramatic psychology is that of the eighteenth century, while Mozart's is that of our own time. The symbols of the contrast are the Gluck chorus, in which the individual is submerged in the typical, and the Mozart ensemble, in which the individual is all the more sharply defined by means of interaction with other individuals.

Finally, Gluck's music, quite apart from any technical inferiority to Mozart's, is intentionally austere. Its appeal is not to the senses and emotions primarily, but to the entire "rational" man as the eighteenth century conceived him. Much of it therefore (though we must make important exceptions to this statement, especially in *Orfeo*) lacks those qualities of ease and spontaneity which are never absent from Mozart even in his least inspired moments. To appreciate Gluck, one needs to know something about the eighteenth century, but no comparable background is required in the case of Mozart.

With the exception of two unfinished pieces of 1783, Mozart's next Italian opera was *Le nozze di Figaro* ("The Marriage of Figaro"),[8] performed at Vienna May 1, 1786. During the five years between *Idomeneo* and *Figaro*, Mozart had become acquainted with the music of Bach and Handel; he had written *Die Entführung*, the "Haffner" Symphony, the six "Haydn" quartets, and many of the great piano concertos. He was now a mature artist, at the height of his powers. Moreover, he had a libretto which combined comedy with excellent possibilities for char-

[8] Levarie, *Mozart's Le Nozze di Figaro: A Critical Analysis.*

acter delineation. Beaumarchais's play *Le Mariage de Figaro* had been written in 1778 but owing to difficulties with the censorship at Paris was not performed until 1784. It was an immediate success, in part because the author had seasoned his comedy with the fashionable revolutionary doctrines of the time. The adaptation for Mozart's libretto was made by Lorenzo da Ponte (1749–1838),[9] then imperial court poet at Vienna and a past master of the craft of writing for the theatre. The story is a sequel to Beaumarchais's *Barbier de Seville*, which had been so popular in Paisiello's setting four years previously. Needless to say, the subversive aspects of the plot were not unduly emphasized by Da Ponte or Mozart in an opera intended for Vienna, where Beaumarchais's play was still forbidden. The first performance was a great success,[10] and it was therefore all the more disappointing to Mozart that *Figaro* was soon displaced in the affections of the public by newer works—Dittersdorf's *Doktor und Apotheker* and *Una cosa rara* by the popular Spanish-Italian composer Vicente Martín y Soler (1754–1806),[11] which also had a libretto by Da Ponte.

No characters in any opera give more strongly the impression of being real persons than do Figaro and Susanna, the Count and Countess, Cherubino, and even the lesser figures of this score. It is therefore important to point out that this vividness of characterization is not due to Da Ponte or Beaumarchais but to Mozart, whose imagination conceived his characters not as stock figures in opera buffa going through a set of conventional antics travestied from the superficial aspects of current daily life, nor yet as social types in an eighteenth-century political pamphlet, but as human beings, each feeling, speaking, and behaving under certain vital circumstances very much as any other human being of like disposition would under similar conditions whether in the eighteenth century or the twentieth. Just how music succeeds in making us aware of this timeless quality is not easy to describe, but no one who has read the libretto and then heard the opera will deny that it does so. It is not merely that the words are sung, or that through his control of tempo, pitch, and accent the composer can suggest the inflections of speech necessary to a given character at a given moment. The secret is rather in

[9] On the checkered career of Da Ponte, including the last thirty-three years of his life in the United States, see his *Memoirs* (not always reliable) and Fitzlyon, *The Libertine Librettist*.

[10] See Kelly, *Reminiscences* I, 258 ff.

[11] Mooser, "Un Musicien espagnol en Russie"; *idem, Annales* II, 455–61.

the nature of music itself, in the form created by the extension of a melodic line in time, and in the simultaneous harmonic combinations, rhythms, and colors of the supporting instruments—all of which somehow (given a composer like Mozart) convey to us just those things inexpressible in words yet infinitely important which make the difference between a lifeless figure and a living being. Take for example the Countess's "Porgi amor" or Cherubino's "Non so più" or "Voi che sapete" : note how little the words alone tell us about the person, and how much the music.[12] Indeed, it seems that with Cherubino (significant name!) Mozart has achieved in music what Guillaume de Lorris is said to have achieved in poetry, "that boy-like blending . . . of innocence and sensuousness which could make us believe for a moment that paradise had never been lost." [13]

One of the most remarkable things about the character delineation in *Figaro* is that more of it is done in ensembles than in solo arias. Nearly half the numbers in the score are ensembles, a higher proportion than in the usual Italian opera buffa. The technique of differentiating the persons is extremely subtle, depending on details of rhythm, harmony, accompaniment, the register or even the tone of the voice, rather than on obviously contrasting melodic lines. Moreover, it all takes place without causing the slightest impediment to the music, which continues to develop in its natural way all the time while carrying on the drama.

The highest examples of Mozart's skill are to be found in the ensembles finales, in which no other composer before or since has equaled him. This characteristic feature of the opera buffa had attained by Mozart's time such a high degree of development that Da Ponte could describe it quite correctly as "a sort of little comedy in itself," [14] a section in which all the lines of the action were brought together and driven more and more swiftly to a climax or to the final solution of the plot, involving the appearance on the stage of all the characters, singly and in various combinations, but in increasing numbers and excitement as the end of the act approached. Mozart's music appropriately follows the general pattern indicated, but it differs from that of the typical Italian opera buffa in two important particulars. Whereas the Italian

[12] Cf. also Levallois and Souriau, "Caractérologie musicale (les personnages du *Don Juan* de Mozart)."

[13] C. S. Lewis, *The Allegory of Love* (New York, 1958), p. 135.

[14] *Memoirs* (Philadelphia, 1929), p. 133. Cf. the tonadilla, which was "a little comedy in itself," growing out of a finale.

composers as a rule were concerned only with suggesting bustle and
activity and exploiting in every way the often crude farcical elements
of the finale, Mozart never loses sight of the individuality of his persons;
humor is there in abundance, but it is a finer, more penetrating humor
than that of the Italians, a humor of character more than of situations,
with that intermingling of seriousness which is the mark of all great
comedy. Then too, Mozart's music in these finales is not merely a succession of pieces in appropriate tempi but is truly symphonic—that is, a
Mozart finale is a composition for voices and orchestra in several movements, with variety of texture within each movement, with the musical
material developed by essentially the same technique as in a symphony,
with a definite relation between principal and subordinate elements, and
with continuity and unity arising from an over-all plan of tempo succes-
sions and key relationships.

The tonal plan of the finale as a whole in Mozart is an interesting
study. In the first finale of *Figaro* the principal keys are :

E-flat    B-flat          G C F          B-flat    E-flat

In the last finale, the scheme is :

D G          E-flat    B-flat          G D

The last finale of *Così fan tutte* is more complicated both dramatically and
tonally; it begins and ends in C, with the tonality strongly enforced by the
dominant-tonic relation of the last two movements, but dwells on the minor
mediant (E-flat) and related keys, with an excusion to E, A, and D in the
middle. The first finale of *Don Giovanni* is tonally in rondo form, thus:
Tonic (C)—Subdominant—Tonic—Dominant—Tonic. The second finale
is similar : Tonic (D)—Minor Mediants—Tonic (minor → major)—Subdominant—Tonic. The first finale of *The Magic Flute* has the key succes-
sions C, G, C, F, C, but with many connecting recitative passages and
passing modulations; the second finale (E-flat) is remarkable for having no
movement in the dominant, the emphasis instead being on the mediant
keys of C and G. Incidentally it may be noted that in every opera of
Mozart from *Mitridate* on (with the exception of *Il rè pastore* and *Die
Entführung*) the last finale is in the same key as the overture.

The unity within each single movement of a finale comes from its
key scheme and from the use of a few simple rhythmic motifs throughout, generally in the orchestra. Forms within these movements are infinitely varied, but each is usually a complete unit; only exceptionally
(for example, in the first finale of *Figaro*) is a particular theme or motif

carried over from one movement to another. Each finale is a unique form, resulting from the translation of a dramatic action into symphonically conceived music by a master of that style. They are, consequently, invaluable sources for study of the principles—as distinct from the patterns—of symphonic form in the classical period.[15]

Although *Figaro* did not have a long run in Vienna, it met with an enthusiastic reception at Prague the following winter, and this resulted in a commission to Mozart for a new opera for that city. Da Ponte furnished the libretto of *Il dissoluto punito, ossia: Il Don Giovanni* ("The Libertine Punished, or : Don Juan"), a *dramma giocoso* in two acts, performed at Prague October 29, 1787. The ancient Don Juan legends have been used by playwrights and poets since the early seventeenth century—by Tirso de Molina, Molière, Shadwell, Goldoni, Byron, Lenau (whose poem furnished inspiration to R. Strauss), and Shaw, among others. Da Ponte took his version largely from a one-act comic opera, *Il convitato di pietra* ("The Stone Guest"), by Giovanni Bertati with music by Giuseppe Gazzaniga (1743–1818), which had been first performed at Venice early in 1787.[16] This was the most recent of some half-dozen musical settings of the story in the eighteenth century before Mozart's.

It may seem strange that an action whose catastrophe shows divine vengeance overtaking a libertine and blasphemer should have been treated as a comedy; the reason lies not only in the obvious comic possibilities of the great lover's adventures but fully as much in the grotesque and fanciful aspects of the statue scenes and the final spectacular punishment of the hero. The legend has a dramatic weakness similar to that of Orpheus in that it is impossible to find a satisfactory ending : moral considerations require that the Don be punished, but unfortunately the spectators either feel so sternly about the matter that the customary lighthearted merrymaking of a closing buffo scene would be improper or else sympathize too strongly with the hero to rejoice at his fate. Da Ponte and Mozart compromised by using a device common in the opéra

[15] This applies only to the Italian operas. The ensembles in *The Magic Flute* are, musically speaking, more in the nature of medleys than symphonic compositions. Cf. Lorenz, "Das Finale in Mozarts Meisteropern"; H. Engel, "Die Finali der Mozartschen Opern," in *Mozart-Jahrbuch 1954* (Salzburg, 1955), pp. 113–34; Rossell, "The Formal Construction of Mozart's Operatic Ensembles and Finales."

[16] See Chrysander, "Die Oper *Don Giovanni*," and cf. Heuss, "Mozarts *Idomeneo*"; see also Jouve, *Le Don Juan de Mozart*.

comique, a "closing moral," sung by the entire surviving cast, to the effect that the death which overtakes the wicked is a fit end to their misdeeds.[17]

Another weakness of the Don Juan subject matter is that the only really necessary scenes are those in which the hero and the Commander are brought together—the duel, the cemetery scene, and the banquet. To fill out the opera the librettist has to bring in a great deal of nonessential material, which, however, Mozart turns to advantage by writing some of his most effective numbers, such as Leporello's "catalogue aria," Don Giovanni's "champagne aria" and serenade ("Deh vieni alla finestra"), Ottavio's "Dalla sua pace" (a later addition to the score, which is unfortunately sometimes omitted in performance), Donna Anna's brilliant "Or sai chi l'onore," or Zerlina's "Batti, batti"—to mention only a few of the outstanding arias in a score particularly rich in unforgettable melodies. The ensembles are less important than in *Figaro*. It is significant that not only the duet ("Là ci darem la mano"), the serenade trio ("Ah taci, ingiusto core"), and most of the great sextet in Act II (which Dent conjectures may have been originally intended for one of the finales in a three-act version), but even considerable portions of both finales belong to the class of static ensembles; they are like the quintet in the third act of *Die Meistersinger* or the canon in *Fidelio*, where the singing, instead of carrying on the action, is devoted to comment on or contemplation of the current situation, developing its significance by means of music in a manner not possible in ordinary drama but eminently suitable to opera. One amusing touch in the last finale, comparable to the practice of representing actual persons among the figures of an imagined group in a painting, is the brief quotation of three melodies from popular operas of the day—Sarti's *Fra due litiganti il terzo gode*, Martín's *Cosa rara*, and Mozart's own *Figaro*. These inserts, for wind instruments, make a formal counterpart to the little dances in the first finale, which are played by strings.

Although it is misleading to regard *Don Giovanni* as a romantic opera in the nineteenth-century sense, nevertheless we cannot ignore one quality in the music which reveals Mozart in a different light from the all too common misconception of him as a merely elegant and graceful

[17] On the romantic interpretations of *Don Giovanni* and various "improvements" of the closing scene, see Dent, *Mozart's Operas*, pp. 265 ff. (1st ed.), 177 ff. (2d ed.); E. T. A. Hoffmann's essay on *Don Giovanni*; Kirkegaard, "The Immediate Stages of the Erotic."

artificer in tones. The very opening measures of the overture—that "sound of dreadful joy to all musicians"—suggest at once the idea of the inexorable, superhuman power which opposes itself to the violent human passion of the hero. The overture does not outline the course of the action, nor does it aim to depict the details of Don Giovanni's character; it simply presents in monumental contrast the two opposing principles whose conflict is the essence of the drama. The daemonic element of Mozart's genius [18] is even more strongly evident in the cemetery scene and in the terrifying apparition of the Commander's statue in the last finale. At these places Mozart follows a long tradition of opera by introducing the trombones. The irruption of this peculiar daemonic quality in many of Mozart's late works—it is heard in some scenes of *The Magic Flute* and is even more striking in the *Requiem*—suggests interesting speculations as to the possible course of his artistic development had he lived long enough to be fully exposed to the forces which brought about the romantic movement in music in the early nineteenth century.

Mozart's last comic opera was *Così fan tutte; osia la Scuola degli amanti* ("Thus Do They All; or The School for Lovers"), on an original libretto by Da Ponte, first performed at Vienna January 26, 1790. It is an opera buffa in the Italian manner, with two pairs of lovers, a plot centering about mistaken identities, and a general air of lighthearted confusion and much ado about nothing, with a satisfactorily happy ending. The music is appropriately melodious and cheerful, rather in the vein of Cimarosa, with a large proportion of ensemble numbers. Nowhere does the music suggest that Mozart felt constrained by the somewhat commonplace, old-fashioned libretto; rather it is as though he were playing with the traditional types and combinations of the opera buffa, making out of them a masterpiece of musical humor lightly touched with irony, avoiding vapid superficiality but never introducing a tone of inappropriate seriousness. The last fianale is an especially fine example of his art, an apotheosis of the whole spirit of eighteenth-century comic opera.

If *Così fan tutte* was the very incarnation of opera buffa, *La clemenza di Tito* was only a shadow of the old opera seria, a form and style which Mozart had long outgrown when he was commissioned to compose Metastasio's libretto (with revisions by C. Mazzolà) for the

[18] Cf. Heuss, "Das dämonische Element in Mozarts Werken"; Clive, "The Demonic in Mozart."

coronation of Leopold II at Prague on September 6, 1791. The first performance was a failure, though the opera later attained some degree of popularity. The whole score had been put together within eighteen days, at a time when Mozart was preoccupied with work on *The Magic Flute* and the *Requiem*, when he was suffering under financial distress, worried about the health of his wife, and himself already ill. The wonder is that under such circumstances he could summon enough of his old powers of adaptability to produce music such as these arias and duets— music which, however lacking in high inspiration, yet has a certain stiff, old-fashioned nobility, appropriate to the formality of the occasion and of the libretto.[19] Of the ensembles (most of which were introduced by Mazzolà) the finale of Act I is the most dramatic and is incidentally interesting on account of the use of the chorus as background for the soloists—a device which Mozart had not hitherto employed.

THE GERMAN OPERAS. Mozart's first Singspiel was *Bastien und Bastienne*, composed at the age of twelve on a German translation of Favart's vaudeville comedy of 1753 (which in turn had been parodied from Rousseau's *Devin du village*) and first performed at Vienna in the garden of Dr. Anton Mesmer, the famous hypnotist. The charming song-like melodies and the simplicity of the style, in which some influence of the French opéra comique composers is discernible, have kept this little work alive, and it is still occasionally heard. Mozart had no further occasion to compose theatre music to German words until 1779, from which year we have the unfinished Singspiel *Zaïde*, evidently intended for performance at Salzburg, and three choruses and five entr'actes for Gebler's play *Thamos, König in Aegypten* ("Thamos, King of Egypt"). Both these works are notable for employing the device of melodrama, which Benda had recently introduced in Germany. *Zaïde*, in both subject matter and musical style, is like a preliminary study for *Die Entführung*. Mozart himself was particularly fond of the *Thamos* choruses, which have a dignity comparable to Gluck and Rameau. The same religious and mystical mood is heard again in the second act of *The Magic Flute*, which deals with similar subject matter. *Der Schauspieldirektor* ("The Impresario," Vienna, 1786) was a little one-act comedy with music on the model of some of the early French opéras comiques, in which a rehearsal scene serves as a pretext to show off the paces of two rival women singers, who then fall to quarreling while a

[19] See for example Sesto's aria "Deh, per questo istante solo" in Act II.

tenor tries to make peace. The closing number is a vaudeville final (strophic solos with refrain), like the finale of Die Entführung. This piece also is occasionally revived.

That which Mozart had done for the opera seria in Idomeneo and for the opera buffa in Così fan tutti he did for the German Singspiel in Die Entführung aus dem Serail ("The Elopement from the Seraglio"), which was performed at Vienna July 16, 1782, with immediate success. The libretto, arranged by Stephanie the Younger from C. F. Bretzner, makes use of the Turkish background which was so popular in eighteenth-century opera, both serious and comic.[20] It is not remarkable for originality but offers sufficient possibilities for effective musical setting, especially in the character of Osmin, to whom Mozart required Stephanie to give a much more conspicuous role than he had in Bretzner's original libretto, and for whom he wrote two of the best comic bass arias in the whole realm of opera.[21] The music is somewhat inconsistent in style; the hero and heroine sing big arias of the Italian sort, while their two servants have simpler liedlike melodies—a division of labor quite in accordance with the theories of J. A. Hiller. Pedrillo's "romanza" (No. 18), a strophic ballad inserted in the action like "Quand le Sultan Saladin" in Grétry's Richard, has curious modulations by which Mozart perhaps intended to suggest oriental atmosphere. Other concessions to local color are found in the theme of the first chorus and in the addition of "Turkish" instruments (that is, piccolo, triangle, cymbals, and bass drum) to the orchestra for the overture, one duet, and two choruses of Janizaries. The ensembles are not to be compared in either dramatic or musical importance with those of the later Italian comic operas, since the action of Die Entführung takes place almost entirely in spoken dialogue. On the whole, the melodic line is less ornate than in the Italian operas, and the phrases are noticeably shorter and more regular, in conformity with the less flexible construction of the German poetry.

What Mozart accomplished in Die Entführung was to raise the Viennese Singspiel at one stroke from a comparatively amateur level to a

---

[20] E.g., Gluck's Rencontre imprévue, the plot of which is almost identical with Die Entführung. See also Engländer, "Glucks Cinesi und Orfano della China," in Gluck-Jahrbuch I (1913) 54–81; Preibisch, "Quellenstudien zu Mozart's Entführung"; Szabolcsi, "Exoticisms in Mozart."

[21] See Mozart's remarks about these arias and other numbers in Die Entführung in a letter to his father dated September 26, 1781 (No. 426 in Anderson's edition).

complex work of dramatic art, taking in (though, to be sure, not always fully assimilating) elements of Italian serious and comic opera and of French opéra comique, as well as the warmth and earnestness of German song. Moreover he created a work which, whatever its stylistic inconsistencies, is fresh and youthful in inspiration, filled with vitality and beauty which have not faded to this day.

We come now to Mozart's last dramatic composition, that sphinx among operas, *Die Zauberflöte* ("The Magic Flute"), first performed on September 30, 1791. It was an immediate and lasting success in Vienna, thus realizing one of Mozart's deepest desires; unfortunately he did not live to enjoy the triumph for long. The libretto at first sight presents probably the most extraordinary jumble of persons and incidents ever brought together on the operatic stage since the seventeenth century. The explanation of this state of affairs is somewhat complicated and has been further complicated by various widespread but apocryphal stories about the circumstances under which the work was written.

The author (even this point has been disputed) was Emanuel Schikaneder (1751–1812),[22] an actor and manager whom Mozart had met at Salzburg in 1780. Schikaneder was in charge of a theatre (the Theater auf der Wieden) just outside the city walls of Vienna, where he offered to the public a mixed fare of Singspiels and plays. Included in these were plots of fairy tales and magic adventure in exotic settings, featuring spectacular tableaux and scene-transformations, the whole often spiced with allusions to current events and personalities in Viennese life. When Schikaneder proposed the subject of *The Magic Flute,* Mozart accepted it as an opportunity to create a real German opera; in the manuscript it is called not a Singspiel (despite its spoken dialogue) but a "grosse Oper," something that might be translated as "grand opera" if that particular term had not been preempted by historians for a different use.[23]

An extraordinary mixture of material went into *The Magic Flute.* Schikaneder, a typical literary magpie, filched characters, scenes, incidents, and situations from others' plays and with Mozart's assistance crammed them into a libretto that ranges all the way from buffoonery to high solemnity, from childish faërie to sublime human aspiration— from the circus to the temple, in short, and never neglecting an oppor-

[22] See biography by Komorzynski (1951).
[23] See below, chap. 19.

tunity for effective theatre along the way. One of the more puzzling features of this work is the way in which the "good" characters apparently change into "bad" ones, and vice versa, beginning at the closing scene of Act I. The explanation usually assumed is that Schikaneder and Mozart at this point suddenly decided, for no evident good reason, to reverse the plot and transform the entire character of the opera. But there is good weight of authority now to discredit this explanation, or at least to restrict its scope.[24] In the first place, the inconsistencies between the earlier and later parts of the libretto are not so great as they appear at first sight, and not greater than might be expected in a plot that moves altogether in an atmosphere of magic and the marvelous. In the second place, there is no evidence in Mozart's music that he felt a complete reversal of moral values was occurring at the end of Act I. It is rather as though the first part of the opera takes place in a neutral, one might say a premoral, realm; the appearance of Sarastro and the priests signifies the coming of higher, specifically human obligations, the transition from childhood to adulthood. Whether this new element came in as the result of a deliberate change of plan or whether it had been tacitly foreseen from the beginning is a question that probably never will be finally answered.

One thing, however, is certain. Mozart and Schikaneder resolved to depict the realm of moral duties and virtues by means of Masonic symbols. Masonry was a force of great influence and considerable political importance in eighteenth-century Europe, counting among its members such distinguished men as Frederick the Great, Voltaire, Goethe, and Haydn. Both Mozart and Schikaneder were members of the Masonic order, and there is evidence in Mozart's correspondence and his music of the deep impression its teachings had made upon him.[25] So the second act of *The Magic Flute* carries its hero Tamino and heroine Pamina through various solemn ordeals, undoubtedly veiled representations of the degrees of Masonic initiation, which they undergo successfully with the help of the priests, and are finally united.

[24] The arguments on this point and other matters concerning the tangled history of *The Magic Flute* may be read in Dent's *Mozart's Opera The Magic Flute*, *Mozart's Operas* (2d ed.), pp. 209 ff., and "Emanuel Schikaneder"; and in Komorzynski's books on Mozart (1955) and Schikaneder (1951) and his articles in the *Neues Mozart-Jahrbuch* I (1941) and *Mozart-Jahrbuch* for 1952, 1953, and 1955.

[25] K. 468, 471, 477, 483, 484, 619, 623. Anderson, *Letters* III, 1351. See also H. Abert, *Mozart* (7th ed.) II, 56–64; Deutsch, *Mozart und die Wiener Logen*; Nettl, *Mozart and Masonry*.

One cannot hope to understand the libretto of *The Magic Flute* unless he is willing to accept its externals as in some sense symbolical of profounder meanings. That such meanings exist is suggested by the respect this opera has always claimed from poets and philosophers as well as musicians. Goethe, for example, not only praised its theatrical effectiveness but also compared it with the second part of his *Faust* as a work "whose higher meaning will not escape the initiated." [26] Was this a reference simply to its Masonic features? Attempts have been made to interpret the opera in detail as representing not merely Masonic doctrines but actual persons and events associated with the lodges of Vienna in Mozart's time.[27] But such an interpretation, even if true, would not by itself account for the peculiar quality of the music. Equally inadmissible is the assumption that Mozart simply poured forth great music in serene disregard of the inconsistencies or frivolous details of the libretto. Such a view can only ignore his whole career as an opera composer, for he was never uncritical of his texts and was always making changes suggested by his own dramatic instinct or experience of the theatre.[28] It is more reasonable to conclude that he saw in *The Magic Flute* an expression, partly in the guise of a fairy story and partly by means of Masonic or pseudo-Masonic symbols, of the same great ethical ideal of human ennoblement through enlightened striving in brotherhood which exercised such power over men's minds at the time of the French Revolution and which later inspired Beethoven's Ninth Symphony and the second part of Goethe's *Faust*. The exact interpretation of the significance of each person and event of the opera in this general plan must be largely a subjective matter. What concerns us here is that the idea itself operated so powerfully on Mozart that it not only enabled him to fuse all sorts of contradictory elements into unity—a trait which had always been fundamental to his genius—but furthermore compelled him to seek a new musical language for the stage. With the creation of that language,

---

[26] Eckermann, *Gespräche* I, 175; II, 18. Goethe's "Second Part" of *The Magic Flute* was left unfinished for lack of a suitable composer; many of the ideas it contains reappear in Part II of *Faust*, which, itself strongly influenced by the form and style of opera, may be regarded historically as the link between *The Magic Flute* and Wagner's music dramas.

[27] Zille, *Die Zauberflöte*.

[28] See for example the letters exchanged between Mozart and his father during the composition and rehearsals of *Idomeneo* (Anderson, *Letters* II, 978–1051, *passim*).

modern German opera was born. The way lay open to *Fidelio, Der Freischütz*, and the *Ring*.

When we look over the score of *The Magic Flute* we are struck by the variety of musical types : simple, folklike, strophic songs, elaborate coloratura arias, ensembles, choruses, a chorale, and long accompanied recitatives—a diversity corresponding to the diversity of characters and scenes in the story. Yet in hearing the opera we are conscious that it is a unit. This homogeneity results not only from the fundamental dramatic idea but also from musical factors. If one excepts the two arias for the Queen of the Night, in which the style of opera seria is adopted for dramatic reasons, the music is essentially German rather than Italian. Little attention is paid to merely picturesque details of the text, and sensuous appeal is treated not as an end in itself but as a means of expression. German folk-song quality is most apparent in the solos of Papageno (Nos. 2, 20), in his duet with Pamina (No. 7), in the dance of the slaves (Finale I), and in the duet ("Wir wandelten durch Feuergluten") sung by Pamina and Tamino in the last finale. Less naïve in language, more varied in form, richer in harmony, and filled with that combination of German fervor and Italian melodic charm which we recognize as peculiarly Mozartean are airs like Tamino's "Dies' Bildnis ist bezaubernd schön" (No. 3),[29] Sarastro's "In diesen heil'gen Hallen" (No. 15), and Pamina's "Ach, ich fühl's" (No. 17). The dignified, earnest mood is especially felt in the march at the opening of Act II, the immediately following aria "O Isis und Osiris" with its choral refrain, and above all the choruses of the priests, to which the trombones lend a characteristic somber color. The dark tone-color of the trombones and bassett horns (tenor clarinets) is a striking feature of this score. A contrasting, though equally original, color effect is heard in the trios for boys' voices at the beginning of each finale and in No. 16. In the duet of the armed men in the second finale we have the chorale "Ach Gott vom Himmel sieh' darein" sung in octaves and in a strict contrapuntal setting—a style novel in opera and producing here a climax of solemnity. In the recitatives Mozart solved a problem which the Singspiel had hitherto avoided, namely, that of finding an appropriate musical

[29] An instructive comparison may be made between this aria and one in the same key on a similar text in *La finta giardiniera*, "Welch ein Reiz in diesem Bilde" (Act I, No. 6). The resemblance of melodic outline in the themes makes the contrast in treatment all the more striking—Italian-style coloratura against simple German melody.

declamation for German dialogue. In the long scene between Tamino and the High Priest in the first finale we hear how the melodic line— now declamatory, now breaking forth in arioso phrases—is fitted to the accents and rhythm of the language and at the same time suggests most vividly the contrasted feelings of the two interlocutors. Not a note is wasted; there are no meaningless formulae; every phrase plays its part in the dramatic structure of the dialogue, to which the harmonic progressions also contribute a significant share.[30] Such recitative had not been heard in Germany since the time of Bach.

The unity arising from the pervasive national quality of the music is reinforced by various technical means, chief among which is the key scheme. The tonality of the opera as a whole is E-flat, and the principal related keys are the dominant, its dominant, and the two mediants. The first act begins and ends in C, with the middle section (Nos. 3–7) in E-flat; the second act is divided, tonally, into three parts : Nos. 9–13, C and its dominants; Nos. 14–18, distant keys; Nos. 19–21, returning to E-flat. The second finale is almost an epitome of the whole tonal plan : E-flat—c— F—C—G—C—G—c—E-flat.

Particular dramatic significance, as Abert points out,[31] attaches to certain keys : E-flat is consistently the tonality of the basic dramatic idea of the opera, G major that of the comic persons, and G minor of the expression of pain. F major is the tonality of the "world of the priests," but also of Papageno's merry song "Ein Mädchen oder Weibchen"; C minor is the key of the "inimical dark powers" but also of the chorale.

Several motifs recur at different places in the opera and thus contribute to the effect of unity. Most conspicuous is the symbolic "threefold chord" of the overture, which we hear again at particularly solemn moments in connection with Sarastro and the ceremonies of initiation. The dotted rhythm of these chords in some form or other is always associated with the priests, though dotted rhythms are also employed in situations of danger for the expression of fear or excitement. Phrases from Sarastro's "O Isis und Osiris" appear in the Quintet No. 5 (at "O Prinz, nimm dies' Geschenk" and "Zauberflöten sind zu eurem Schutz vonnöthen") and in the Duet No. 7 (at "Wir leben durch die Lieb' allein"). The opening phrase of "Dies' Bildnis ist bezaubernd schön" turns up at a half-dozen unexpected places in the second finale. These and similar melodic reminiscences are not to be regarded as leitmotifs in the Wagnerian sense but as partly unconscious echoes of musical ideas which were in Mozart's mind throughout the composition of the opera. Such reminiscences, not only within a single

[30] This recitative may be compared with that preceding the Queen of the Night's first aria (No. 4), which is in the conventional Italian style.

[31] *Mozart* II, 687, note 4; see also E. Schmitz, "Formgesetze in Mozart's *Zauberflöte*."

opera but also from one opera to another, are not infrequent in Mozart; they seem to be motivated by corresponding resemblances of dramatic ideas or situations. Certain stylistic details in *The Magic Flute*—the large proportion of themes built on notes of the triad, the frequent use of first inversions, deceptive cadences, and the melodic interval of the seventh— may be further mentioned as characteristic.[32]

In Mozart's operas the eighteenth and nineteenth centuries meet. He brought into the inherited traditions, forms, and musical language a new conception, that of the individual as the proper subject for operatic treatment. His characters are viewed from the point which most strongly emphasizes their individuality, namely their love relationships. No composer has ever sung of human love in such manifold aspects or with such psychological penetration; and in every instance it is the person, not the abstract emotion, that is central. The change from the expression of an affect to the portrayal of a person is symbolized in the disappearance of the castrato, in the replacement of this impersonal instrument by the natural human voice. It is this shift of emphasis from the typical to the individual that most clearly separates Mozart from earlier opera composers of the eighteenth century and establishes his kinship with the romantics. When finally, as in *The Magic Flute*, sexual love is subordinated to a mystic ideal and the individual begins to be a symbol as well as a person, we may well feel that a path has been opened which will lead ultimately to the music drama of Wagner.

[32] See Chantavoine, *Mozart dans Mozart*; A. H. King, "The Melodic Sources and Affinities of 'Die Zauberflöte,'" in *Mozart in Retrospect*, chap. 9; E. Werner, "Leading or Symbolic Formulas in *The Magic Flute*"; E. Schmitz, "Formgesetze in Mozarts *Zauberflöte*."

PART 4

# *THE*
# *NINETEENTH*
# *CENTURY*

# CHAPTER 18

# THE TURN OF THE CENTURY

⚬⚬⚬

During the first half of the nineteenth century Paris was virtually the European capital of opera. Not only did many composers of eminence live there, but even those residing elsewhere did not feel they had arrived until they had had a Paris success. The origin of this dominance goes back to the time of Gluck. Although Gluck's later operas had but a slow success in Germany and none at all in Italy, their style was so congenial to the French that it attracted disciples, through whom this style of opera maintained itself through the Revolutionary period and blossomed anew in the days of the First Empire.

French fondness for public spectacles was gratified during the Revolution by the inauguration of magnificent national festivals, for which music was provided by composers such as Gossec, Méhul, Catel, Lesueur, and Cherubini, largely in the form of huge choral numbers and "hymns" to be sung by the entire populace.[1] These festivals kept alive the demand for operas with similar large musical numbers and in this way formed a historical link between old French opera and the grand opera of the nineteenth century. Interest in classical subjects did not wane during the Revolution; it is manifest in one of the operas of Luigi Cherubini (1760–1842),[2] a Florentine who had studied under Sarti and had produced a number of serious and comic operas in Italy and London before settling permanently at Paris in 1788. Cherubini's *Médée* (1797)

---

[1] Pierre, *Hymnes et chansons de la révolution.*

[2] See biographies of Cherubini by Bellasis, Hohenemser, and Schemann; Confalonieri, *Prigionia di un artista*; Stomne, "The French Operas of Luigi Cherubini"; Kretzschmar, "Ueber die Bedeutung von Cherubinis Ouvertüren und Hauptopern für die Gegenwart."

is strongly reminiscent of Gluck in general plan and treatment, though in a musical idiom which is on the dividing line between classicism and romanticism, often suggesting the early style of Beethoven. This opera did not fare particularly well at Paris, but was given frequently in Germany during the nineteenth century. It was heard in Italy for the first time only in 1909; in an Italian version, with recitatives added in place of the original spoken dialogue, *Médée* has recently been revived with considerable success. Like the composer's other operas, it is notable for long instrumental introductions and important instrumental obbligatos in the arias. Cherubini was a master of counterpoint and an important composer of church music; one of the criticisms voiced about his operas, particularly about *Médée*, was that the music was "overdeveloped," too heavy in texture—"too much accompaniment," Napoleon complained—and too slow in dramatic pace to be fully effective in the theatre. Still, Cherubini was one of the most influential composers of the early nineteenth century; a conservative by nature, an admirer of Mozart, distrusting Weber, and having apparently no understanding whatever for the later Beethoven, he was nevertheless almost universally admired by his professional contemporaries.

Aside from *Médée*, Cherubini's importance for the history of opera rests chiefly on three works : *Lodoïska* (1791), *Les Deux Journées* ("The Two Days," 1800), and *Faniska*, presented at Vienna in 1806, three months after the first performance of Beethoven's *Fidelio*. All three, like *Médée*, have spoken dialogue, and all three are of the type known as "rescue" operas, an earlier example of which we have already met in Grétry's *Richard*. The natural popular taste for this kind of plot was strengthened in the disturbed times of the Revolution, when hairbreadth escapes through the loyalty of friends or servants were of frequent actual occurrence. The violent events and feelings of this period naturally stimulated the demand for plays and operas exploiting danger, suspense, and the thrilling last-minute rescue; and the emotion accumulated by all these events was discharged in impassioned appeals for the Rights of Man against tyranny and oppression. Thus *Les Deux Journées*, for example, is filled with outbursts of the most exemplary sentiments of loyalty, kindness, and general devotion to the ideals of "humanity," with which the "good" characters of the libretto are fully identified.

This infusion into the libretto of a new spirit of urgency, of direct concern with the sentiments and the fate of recognizably "real" people,

EXAMPLE 78

CHERUBINI

*(Example 78 continued)*

*(Example 78 continued)*

**Ending:**

que j'ai souf-ferts, la fin des maux

La fin des maux que j'ai souf - ferts.

making the plot not a remote play of fancy to be enjoyed with detachment but something to grip a contemporary auditor's feelings by making him think "this might happen, even to me," and by voicing emotions that appealed to masses of people caught up in the excitement of revolutionary times—this kind of plot called for a new kind of musical expression. French critics tend to see in *Lodoïska* a landmark of early romantic style in opera, a work that "opened the way to Méhul, Lesueur, and Spontini"[3] (Example 78).

*Les Deux Journées* had a successful run in Paris, and was received even more warmly in Germany, where for many years it was played, in translation, under the title of *Der Wasserträger* ("The Water-Carrier"). Weber wrote enthusiastically about this opera and Beethoven was much impressed when he heard it at Vienna in 1803. The music consists mostly of ensemble numbers, which are developed usually at some length with more regard for musical than dramatic considerations. The chorus of soldiers at the beginning of Act II was one of the favorite numbers of the opera, and the bridal chorus in Act III has a folklike quality similar to the bridal chorus in Weber's *Freischütz*. The principal solo is the romance of Anton in Act I ("Un Pauvre Petit Savoyard"), the refrain of which (Example 79) recurs several times in the course of the opera like

*Les Deux Journées*, Act I

EXAMPLE 79

CHERUBINI

Bon Fran - cais, Dieu te re - com - pen - se, Un bien-fait

n'est ja - mais per - du.

---

[3] Clément and Larousse, *Dictionnaire lyrique, s.v.* "Lodoïska."

Blondel's song in *Richard Coeur-de-Lion*. Anton's song is a forerunner of numberless romances and ballads in nineteenth-century opera, including Senta's ballad in *The Flying Dutchman*, which has the same two-part structure and is even in the same key (G minor-major). The overture, like most of Cherubini's, is a full movement in sonata form with a slow introduction. The device of melodrama is effectively used in several scenes.

One of the most typical rescue operas was *La Caverne* by Jean-François Lesueur (1760–1837),[4] performed at Paris in 1793, the most terrible year of the Revolution. The eminently romantic nature of the plot—it includes a band of picturesque brigands and their mysterious and magnanimous chief—was to find an echo in many operas of the nineteenth century. Lesueur is remembered now chiefly as the teacher of Berlioz and his forerunner in the use of program music and great masses of performers. His predilection for romantic subjects is evident in some of his other operas, notably *Ossian, ou Les Bardes* (1804), a work highly praised by Napoleon but not overly successful with the critics and public of Paris. His other principal operas were *Télémaque* and *Paul et Virginie* (both 1794).

Another composer of the Revolutionary period was Etienne Nicolas Méhul (1763–1817),[5] who first turned to dramatic composition on the advice of Gluck. During the two decades 1790–1810 he produced about twenty-five opéras comiques which show a wide variety of styles and many interesting experiments in orchestration. His *Euphrosine, ou Le Tyran corrigé* ("Euphrosine; or, The Tyrant Rebuked," 1790) was highly praised by Grétry; this work and *Stratonice* (1792) were important in establishing the type of opéra comique on serious subjects, approaching the musical style of ordinary opera in all respects save for the use of spoken dialogue. The chief works of the following years were *Ariodant* (1799), especially notable for its chromatic harmonies and for its systematic use of a musical leitmotif associated with the central idea of the opera and recurring throughout the work in different scenes;[6] *Une Folie* (1802), Méhul's most popular work in purely comic vein; and *Uthal* (1806), on a subject from Ossian.

[4] See Fouque, "Le Sueur comme prédécesseur de Berlioz," in *Les Révolutionnaires de la musique*, pp. 1–183; also biographies by Buschkötter and Lamy.

[5] Biographies by Pougin and Brancoeur; H. Strobel, "Die Opern von E. N. Méhul."

[6] See Bücken, *Der heroische Stil in der Oper*, pp. 81–83.

Méhul's most celebrated opera was *Joseph* (1807), one of the rare examples in the history of opera of a biblical subject treated with good taste and at the same time with real dramatic force. It has no feminine characters, though the part of Benjamin is sung by a soprano and women's voices are heard in many of the choruses. The most noticeable characteristic of the music is the happy combination of classical severity, as in the overture and the chorus "Dieu d'Israël" (on a plainsong motif), with a simple and touching melodic expressiveness in the solos, especially in the two romances of Joseph and Benjamin. Many of the harmonic and rhythmic patterns recall the style of Gluck, but there is throughout a certain personal, direct quality, a rather naïve appeal to the tender emotions, which makes this score an interesting example of the transitional period between classicism and romanticism in music.

Opera in the grand manner attained a climax under the First Empire with the works of Napoleon's favorite composer, Gasparo Spontini (1774–1851),[7] whose masterpiece, *La Vestale* ("The Vestal"), triumphed at Paris in 1807 and has remained in the repertoire of opera companies almost to the present day. The success of *La Vestale* was due in part to a brilliant libretto by Etienne Jouy, which combined the old rescue motif and a passionate love story with the solemnity of the tragédie lyrique on a huge scale, adding a strong touch of the melodramatic. The many spectacular crowd scenes are climaxed in the third act, where a bolt of lightning rekindles the fire on the altar of Vesta to establish the innocence of Julia, the heroine, and lead to the happy ending. The music, which Spontini revised many times during the rehearsals, was at first condemned by the Opéra jury as "bizarre, defective, and noisy," and the personal intervention of the Empress Josephine was required to bring about the performance. It is one of the most effective operas ever written from the theatrical point of view, every opportunity offered by the libretto being exploited to the utmost. The score abounds in beautiful solos and ensembles, the choral numbers are built on a massive scale, and the orchestration is full of fine details. That the music now seems so old-fashioned may be explained in part by the rather stodgy harmonic structure, ponderously swinging between tonic and dominant, while the melodic line flows above in regular, often

---

[7] See biographies by Ghislanzoni and Fragapane; Belardinelli, *Documenti Spontiniani inedite*; Wagner, "Erinnerungen an Spontini," in *Gesammelte Schriften* V, 86–104.

singsong rhythms, dividing by triplets or dotted figures, with a strong
beat invariably at the beginning of each measure. "Expressive" appoggiaturas, often on chromatic tones, are a constant feature. Even where
the harmonic rhythm is quickened, as in passages of excitement, the
rising sequential phrases and the usual diminished seventh chord at the
climax are devices which have lost much of their effect for modern ears.

The second act of *La Vestale* contains the most celebrated numbers
of the opera, among which may be mentioned especially Julia's aria
"Impitoyables Dieux" (No. 9), Licinius' "Les Dieux prendront pitié"
(No. 10), and Julia's solo at the beginning of the finale, "O des infor-
tunés." The finale itself attains a thrilling climax by sheer weight of
numbers and volume of sound, intensified at the close by a stretto, that
is, an acceleration of the tempo—an effect then new, though later
overworked in the operas of Meyerbeer.

The success of *La Vestale* was not equaled two years later by
*Fernand Cortez*, which Spontini revived with important changes in
1817. The libretto is not so good as that of *La Vestale*, and the musical
style is less even; there are some passages of real distinction (Example
80) but also many trivial tunes where the poverty of melodic and

*Fernand Cortez*, Act III

EXAMPLE 80                                                        SPONTINI

Tris - tes pres-sen - ti - ments!    Vous ne me trom-pez pas, —

vous ne me trom - pez    pas, —    mon sort    est dé - ci - dé

harmonic invention suggests nineteenth-century Italian opera at its
worst. A third work, *Olympie* (1819), long in composition and subjected

to many revisions, was slow in making its way at Paris, though it found some favor at Berlin, where Spontini was conductor of the Opera and a consequential figure in German musical life from 1819 to 1841. During this time his only important dramatic composition was *Agnes von Hohenstaufen* (1827, revised 1837), his last completed opera.

Spontini was the last of the great opera composers in whose music the dramatic methods of Gluck were still of living force. Although his works, particularly *Fernand Cortez*, may be regarded as the starting point of the Meyerbeer type of grand opera, Spontini has by comparison a certain restraint, an artistic integrity which keeps sensational elements within bounds and never allows the dramatic purpose to be overwhelmed by irrelevant theatrical or musical effects. His style, despite its pompous rhetoric, has a unity, a massiveness, and a fundamental simplicity which are closer to the classic than to the romantic spirit.

In what sense can the French operas of the period 1790–1815 be called "romantic"?[8] In considering this question it is important to remember three related social factors: first, the breakdown or at least the radical transformation of many old traditions under the impact of Revolutionary ideas; second, the rapid increase of middle-class audiences for opera; and third, the general intensification of emotion in a long-continued atmosphere of national excitement. To these may be added, under the Empire, the position of Napoleon as patron, toward whom Spontini had much the same sort of relation that Lully had had toward Louis XIV. The grandiose sentiments and the colossal style in French opera of this whole period were largely motivated by the desire to glorify the Revolution, the nation, or the Empire, using for this purpose the traditional form of opera with huge spectacular and choral scenes, a form already long established in France by Lully, Rameau, and Gluck. But the grandiose, whether in sentiment or in outward form, was not the only characteristic of French opera around the turn of the century. More specifically romantic was the intermixture, in both libretto and music, of elements formerly thought to be incongruous. We have already seen how everywhere in the latter part of the eighteenth century the comic and the serious opera tended to approach one another in style and eventually to merge, as in Mozart's "dramma giocoso" *Don Giovanni* or in *The Magic Flute*, which is a synthesis of many apparently discordant elements. So likewise in French opera of the

[8] Cf. Dent, "The Rise of the Romantic Opera," chaps. I–VII, XII.

1790s we find similar incongruities : the form of the opéra comique (that is, spoken dialogue instead of recitative) used for deadly serious plots—which, however, admit occasional comic scenes and characters; musical numbers in the grand style of the tragédie lyrique side by side with the simple popular song types of the *romance* and *couplets*;[9] magic happenings involving ordinary people and being mixed up with everyday occurrences instead of being relegated to a realm of pure make-believe as in the eighteenth century; and Christian religious ceremonies and prayers brought onto the stage as a means of theatrical effect. (The prayer in Act III of Méhul's *Mélidor et Phrosine* [1794] is one of the first of a long line of *preghiera* scenes stretching through the opera of the nineteenth century.) Some elements in the librettos of late eighteenth-century French opera that we may be inclined to think of as particularly romantic—forests, caverns, wild landscapes, storms—are in fact equally common in operas of the seventeenth and early eighteenth centuries; the difference is that in the earlier period they were mere decorative background, whereas now they are an essential ingredient in the setting of the plot. The same applies to exoticisms and "local color." An example of the latter was the Swiss mountain setting of Cherubini's *Elisa ou Le Voyage au Mont-Bernard* (1794); Grétry had used the same background in his *Guillaume Tell* of 1791, and Rossini was to make the most of it in his own opera of the same title in 1829.

It is evident from the foregoing that one cannot easily isolate any single element of the libretto in French opera of the period 1790–1815 and simply say of it "this is romantic." It is in the peculiar combination of the elements and the peculiar function of each in the whole pattern that the romantic quality consists. Much the same may be said of the music. The mixture of musical styles has already been mentioned; popular idioms had long been familiar in comic opera of the eighteenth century, and the only difference now was that these idioms were incorporated into serious opera and in consequence came to be regarded as serious music. Their presence may also be explained in part by reference to the new middle-class audience for opera. This factor, however, is more important in explaining one feature of the music, especially of

[9] *Romance* : "Petit morceau de chant ou de musique instrumentale, d'un caractère naïf et gracieux."

*Couplets* : originally, verses (spoken or sung) inserted in spoken prose dialogue; hence, a song in popular style, more sophisticated than a *romance*, usually strophic with a refrain, inserted as a separate number in an opera.

Cherubini's music, that has become a common subject of present-day criticism, which alleges that the musical ideas are spread too thin, that too much time is taken up with reiterating the obvious and repeating musical clichés. Such criticism is natural to us because we have long since become accustomed to the more concentrated musical style of Mozart and Beethoven, beside whom Cherubini seems unbearably diffuse. But to audiences of the 1790s, for many of whom listening to music of any complexity at all must have been an unfamiliar experience, the thinner, spread-out style of Cherubini and his operatic contemporaries was well adapted; indeed, the very concentration of Mozart's and Beethoven's language was probably one of the factors that operated against an immediate popular success for *Don Giovanni* and *Fidelio*. Certain features in the French opera of this period may be pointed out as romantic at least in the sense that they were imitated by later nineteenth-century composers. One of these is the large proportion of ensembles and choruses. The former, of course, came from the Italian opera buffa and the latter from the French serious opera of Rameau and Gluck; but the choruses in the newer operas were not those monumental affairs, reminiscent of Greek tragedy, that we find in Gluck and in Mozart's *Idomeneo*, but rather were like the "picturesque" choruses of nineteenth-century romantic opera—bands of peasants, sailors, soldiers, priests, brigands, or gypsies, singing music that is clearly intended to be correspondingly picturesque and colorful. It is significant that the most admired numbers in these operas were more often ensembles and choruses than solos. The solos are, in fact, usually conventional, often declamatory in style, lacking both the melodic suavity and the coloratura embellishments of Italian arias, but intended to be sung with intense feeling, a manner of delivery suggested by the occasional directions "très-concentré" or "voix concentrée" in the score of Lesueur's *Télémaque*. Another romantic trait in these operas is the presence of long descriptive instrumental "symphonies" for scenes of battle, storms, conflagrations, and the like; these descriptive symphonies are a heritage from earlier French opera, but they become much more extensive and important toward the end of the century. More particularly romantic in the scores of Cherubini and Méhul are occasional touches of special orchestral color—long solo phrases for flute or horn, *cantabile* melodies for the clarinet, the ensemble of harps in Lesueur's *Ossian*, or the string section without violins of Méhul's *Uthal*. Finally may be mentioned occasional premonitions of romantic harmony, in the shape of chromaticisms or unexpected modulations—although some of Lesueur's strange harmonies are probably due to his thinking he was writing in the Greek modes.

It must be recalled that the French operas we have been considering were not confined to France; they never reached Italy but most of them were much more widely known and more often performed in German cities than in Paris. The influence of Cherubini, Méhul, and Spontini on the development of German romantic opera was considerable; in particular, the rescue opera of the French Revolutionary period was the model for the only opera written in the first decade of the nineteenth century that has survived to the present day.

BEETHOVEN'S "FIDELIO." [10] When Cherubini's operas came to Vienna Beethoven was, as usual, in search of a libretto for himself. There was, in fact, hardly a year between 1800 and 1815 that he did not dally with some operatic proposal. In 1803 he had begun work on a libretto by Schikaneder, *Vestas Feuer* ("The Vestal Fire"), some of the music of which he later incorporated in *Fidelio*. His continued interest in the theatre is evidenced not only by this and other abortive projects but also by such works as the ballet *Prometheus* (1801) and the incidental music to plays (*König Stephan, Egmont, Coriolanus*). His aptitude for dramatic writing was proved in the oratorio *Christus am Ölberg* (1803). But Beethoven was a difficult man to please. He could not bring himself to compose music to the usual buffo libretto and constantly refused any drama which did not conform to his own high standards of the proper subject matter for serious works. He rejected in principle all "magic" subjects and condemned on moral grounds the texts of *Don Giovanni* and *Figaro*. In his opinion the two best opera librettos were *La Vestale* and *Les Deux Journées*.

This preference brings into relief one characteristic of Beethoven's which is important for the understanding of *Fidelio*. We have already mentioned among the effects of the French Revolution on opera the popularization of the grand style and the demand for dramatic tension, suspense, and strong feeling which brought the typical rescue plot into such favor. But another, even more far-reaching effect came from the

[10] Bibliography: Thayer, *Life of Ludwig van Beethoven*; Braunstein, *Beethovens Lenore-Ouvertüren*; Kufferath, *Fidelio*; Hess, *Beethovens Oper Fidelio*. See further Kastner, *Bibliotheca Beethoveniana;* monographs in *Neues Beethoven Jahrbuch*.

tremendous liberation of humanitarian idealism all over Europe at this period. The theories of the eighteenth-century Enlightenment suddenly ceased to be playthings of philosophers, orators, and dramatists and became explosive realities of life, ideas to which powerful emotions were attached, capable of inspiring enthusiasm. Their effect on the music of the early nineteenth century in general and that of Beethoven in particular cannot possibly be ignored. *Fidelio*, with its themes of unselfish love, loyalty, courage, sacrifice, and heroic endurance, appealed so strongly to the idealism of Beethoven that he was perhaps blind to the technical faults of the drama. The original French libretto, by Jean Nicolas Bouilly (author of *Les Deux Journées*), under the title *Léonore, ou l'Amour conjugale* ("Leonora, or Married Love"), was composed by Pierre Gaveaux in 1798. The German version for Beethoven was prepared by Joseph Ferdinand Sonnleithner and was first performed November 20, 1805, at Vienna. It was a comparative failure, partly owing to disturbed political conditions and partly because it was too long and not well arranged. Beethoven was persuaded to make some cuts and changes, and the opera was produced again the following spring, but the composer withdrew it after only a few performances. In 1814 the libretto was completely revised by G. F. Treitschke, and in this final setting began its successful career.

The outline of the plot, said to be based on an actual event of the French Revolution, is as follows : Florestan has been unjustly imprisoned. His wife Leonora, disguised as a man under the name of Fidelio, obtains the post of assistant to Rocco, the jailer. There are two subsidiary characters : the jailer's daughter Marzelline and her lover, the porter Jaquino. Pizarro, governor of the prison, has been warned that Don Fernando, the minister of state, is coming to investigate the cases of the prisoners. Pizarro therefore determines to murder Florestan, but Leonora prevents him. At that instant Don Fernando arrives, sets Florestan free, and punishes Pizarro.

*Fidelio* is thus a rescue opera, and the customary touch of horror is introduced by means of an episode where Rocco and Fidelio are depicted digging a grave for the doomed prisoner (Beethoven opens this scene very effectively with a melodrama). The whole of the dungeon scene in which Leonora saves Florestan's life, with the superbly theatrical detail of the trumpet call announcing the arrival of Fernando, realizes to the full the suspense and excitement which all opera composers of the time sought. Even the spoken dialogue, so often a stumbling block, is turned to good account. The entrance of Jaquino, the porter, at the climax of this scene, with his excited words, provides an element of almost comic relief after the unbearable tension of the preceding action —one of Beethoven's Shakespearean effects, comparable to the introduction of the Turkish music in the finale of the Ninth Symphony. The characters of Marzelline and Jaquino are descendants of the servant lover pair of eighteenth-century comic operas, and in Fernando we have an echo of the magnanimous king of Metastasio. The significant characters are three: Pizarro, the thoroughly wicked man; Florestan, the just man suffering undeserved cruelty; and above all Leonora, the devoted and courageous wife, one of the truly great heroines of opera. It is obvious from the music that it was these three persons, and the situations rising from their interrelations, that chiefly fired Beethoven's imagination.

The music of *Fidelio* is unique in opera. Every measure bears the stamp of Beethoven's high purpose and painstaking care in composition. The score was a labor of love, but a labor nonetheless, as the four overtures and the endless revisions testify; the introduction to Florestan's aria at the beginning of Act II, for example, was changed at least eighteen times before reaching its final form. All this is a striking contrast to the facility of a composer like Mozart, not to mention the Italian opera composers of both the eighteenth and nineteenth centuries. To be sure, Beethoven was notorious for revising and working over his material, and the composition of any important work was a struggle with him; but *Fidelio* gave him even more trouble than usual. Part of the difficulty was no doubt due to Beethoven's lack of experience with opera; still more rose from the fact that he was not a natural opera composer. It was only by an effort that his mind could concern itself with details of action or characterization that did not form part of the larger ethical and musical plan of the work. Take for example Rocco's aria in Act I, "Hat man auch nicht Geld beineben," the burden of which is that money is more necessary than love for a happy marriage. To this banal proposition Beethoven did his best to write a comic bass aria in the general style of the Viennese Singspiel. It cannot be denied that he succeeded, but the effect on the listener is, in a peculiar way, painful, like the spectacle of a profound thinker with no gift of small talk trying to enter cheerfully into a conversation on trivial topics. To save himself from boredom, and because he cannot help it, he pursues and develops ideas in a manner so superior to that of the company in which he finds himself that he remains, despite the most conscientious effort, an outsider. Thus the music of Rocco's aria, with its fine rhythmic details, its individual harmonic scheme, its welding of three short movements into the strophe, and the little canon between voice and violins in the coda, is perfectly good Beethoven, and much too good for the commonplace text, which could have been better suited by someone like Dittersdorf. The case is much the same with the famous quartet "Mir ist so wunderbar" (No. 3). Here, where the dramatic situation is not significant, Beethoven simply writes a four-part canon in G major which is so beautiful that the words are quite superfluous.

The whole approach changes, however, when the drama really gets under way. In the arias of Pizarro, Florestan, and Leonora, the ensembles of Act II, and both finales, Beethoven wrestles with the text, using it as a springboard for the loftiest flights of imagination, setting to music not so much the actual words as their implications, the abstract ideas of wickedness, devotion, endurance, courage, and the final triumph of right. It is in these numbers that we are aware of Beethoven the poet, the idealist, the musician for whom opera is only a vehicle for expression of his own towering conceptions, in comparison with which the outward dramatic form is of only secondary importance. In all this music Beethoven, as usual when his "raptus'" was upon him, is merciless in his demands on the singers. The thought simply transcends complete expression, and the glory of the music lies not so much in what it says as in its suggestion of things too great for utterance. In *Fidelio,* as in the Mass and the Ninth Symphony, there are passages which cannot be adequately sung by human beings, though they are nonetheless worthy to be sung by the angels. *Fidelio* is not merely an opera—and this "not merely" is the source of its defects—but, in the last analysis, a hymn to the heroism of Leonora, and (like the Third Symphony, composed at about the same time) to heroism in general.

# CHAPTER 19

# GRAND OPERA[1]

During the eight years after Spontini's *Olympie* (1819) no significant new works were produced at the Paris Opéra. In 1828 occurred the first performance of Auber's serious opera *La Muette de Portici* ("The Dumb Girl of Portici," known also as *Masaniello*, after the name of its hero). This was followed less than a year later by Rossini's French opera, *Guillaume Tell*. In 1831 appeared Meyerbeer's *Robert le Diable* ("Robert the Devil"), in 1835 Halévy's *La Juive* ("The Jewess"), and the following year Meyerbeer's *Huguenots*. These works established a type of musical drama which has come to be generally known under the name of "grand opera." Before considering specific examples, let us attempt to define the essential features of this style.

The term "grand opera" was originally used in contrast to "opéra comique," and involved the technical distinction already mentioned, namely, that in the former the musical numbers were connected by recitatives and in the latter by spoken dialogue. But the adjective "grand" had other evident implications: such works were on serious subjects of a heroic nature, treated in grandiose proportions and employing the utmost resources of singing, orchestral music, and staging. Grand opera was in the line of descent from Lully, Rameau, Gluck, and Spontini, but in its most flourishing period—the 1830s and 1840s—the traditional features were infused with romantic conceptions in such a way as to give it a special character. Subjects were chosen no more from classical antiquity, but from medieval or modern history, with strong emphasis on local color and often with pointed application to contemporary issues (*Guillaume Tell*); religious motifs were introduced (*Les Hugue-*

[1] Crosten, *French Grand Opera*; Lang, "Grand Opera," in *Music in Western Civilization*, pp. 825–34; Abry, *Histoire illustrée de la littérature française*, chaps. 51–58.

*nots*), and actions of violence and passion were favored (*La Juive*). Some parallels in the field of literature may be briefly indicated : the romantic treatment of religious themes by Chateaubriand; the historical novels of Scott and Dumas *père*; and the romantic dramas of Dumas (*Henri III et son cour*, 1829) and Victor Hugo (*Hernani*, 1830; *Le Roi s'amuse*, 1832; *Ruy Blas*, 1838; *Les Burgraves*, 1843).

French grand opera was the creation of three men : the director and entrepreneur Louis Véron (1798–1867), who reigned over the Paris Opéra from 1831 to 1835; the librettist Eugène Scribe (1791–1861), author of *La Muette de Portici, La Juive, Robert le Diable*, and *Les Huguenots*; and the composer Giacomo Meyerbeer (1791–1864),[2] in whose works all the best and worst features of grand opera were exemplified. The elements were ready to hand, having been developed in French opera of the late eighteenth and early nineteenth centuries; they were combined under the stimulus of a commercial undertaking that had to pay its own way—and did so, with a little help from the government— by appealing to the *haute bourgeoisie* of Paris in the early days of Louis Philippe. Sheer spectacle, on a scale surpassing anything before attempted, was a basic ingredient in that appeal; but this was amply supported by the nature of the drama and music that went with it. Plots aiming to stimulate excitement through sudden, often grotesque, contrasts and shocks were well adapted for music and indeed required it for their full realization. Scores became longer and more complex than ever before in the history of opera. All kinds of novel orchestral effects were exploited. Ballets became larger and more elaborate. Choruses and crowd scenes abounded. The Mozartean ensemble, with its careful preservation of the individuality of each character, was transformed into a brilliant chorus for solo voices. Solo parts expanded in range, tone color, and expression; coloratura arias, impassioned dramatic outbursts, appeared side by side with simple ballads and romances. Musical forms and idioms were mingled in a luxuriant eclecticism, the object being to dazzle popular audiences who demanded thrills and for whom the aristocratic restraints of the eighteenth century had no meaning. The inevitable consequence was an inflated style of "effects without causes," [3]

[2] On Meyerbeer, see biography by J. Kapp; *Briefwechsel*, ed. H. Becker; H. Abert, "Giacomo Meyerbeer,'" in his *Gesammelte Schriften*, pp. 397–420; H. Heine, "Uber die französische Bühne . . . neunter Brief," in his *Sämtliche Werke* (Leipzig, Insel-Verlag, 1913) VIII, 99–116; H. Becker, *Der Fall Heine-Meyerbeer*.

[3] Wagner's phrase; see *Oper und Drama*, Part I, chap. VI.

of striking and brilliant musical numbers inadequately motivated by the dramatic situation. In short, composers and librettists acted on three principles that are still perfectly familiar : (1) give the public what it wants; (2) if a little is good, more is better; and (3) the whole (that is, the complete opera) is equal to the sum of its parts (that is, the several musical styles of which the opera is composed). The result, while undeniably successful at the time and of great influence on the future course of opera, was not one that can now be contemplated with unmixed admiration.

Auber's *Muette* is his only work in the serious style of grand opera. The plot is based on a historical event, the revolution at Naples in 1647 which was led by Masaniello, a fisherman; for good measure, another event—the eruption of Mt. Vesuvius in 1631—is brought in at the climax of the opera. This work has the distinction of having triggered a revolution; a performance of *La Muette* at Brussels on August 25, 1830, touched off the popular uprising which resulted the next year in the constitution of Belgium as an independent state. A novelty in the score is that the heroine is a mute personage, who expresses herself only in pantomime to orchestral accompaniment—an interesting and possibly unique use of the melodrama technique. The music is on a typical grand-opera scale, filled with choruses, crowd scenes, processions, ballets, and huge finales. There are a few lighter numbers for contrast, such as the barcarole in the finale of Act II and the vivacious market-place chorus in Act III, but the mood is for the most part serious, pervaded with romantic enthusiasm, rising to patriotic fervor in the celebrated duet of Act II, "Mieux vaut mourir" (Example 81)—incidentally a good specimen of the "military band" rhythm of the accompaniment that was a common feature in many nineteenth-century operas, a steady four staccato chords per measure in march-time, with a whang on the second beat at the cadences.

In spite of its grandiose qualities, the music of *La Muette* seems appropriate to and justified by the libretto; Auber does not fall into the error of striving after effects merely for their own sake. The same observation holds for Rossini's *Guillaume Tell* (1829), which exploits a similar patriotic-revolutionary theme in a spectacular, though dramatically weak, arrangement of Schiller's drama by Etienne Jouy and Hippolyte Bis (with revisions by Rossini himself). The success of *Guillaume Tell* was not great at first, but the work has remained in the repertoire

EXAMPLE 81          *La Muette de Portici*, Act II, no. 8                    AUBER

almost to the present day, and the score, the masterpiece of one of the most original geniuses of nineteenth-century opera, has always held the respect of musicians. Undoubtedly it is uneven in quality and, by modern standards, too long. The overture has a vitality which years of playing by military bands has failed to quench. The first act is well planned to furnish contrast between the pastoral music at the beginning, in which Rossini employed many authentic Alpine horn motifs (*Ranze des vaches*), and the magnificent finale, ending with an exciting *Veloce* movement in 3/4 rhythm. Act II is the most nearly perfect both in general arrangement and in the details : Mathilde's recitative and aria "Sombres forêts," the following duet, and above all the trio for men's voices "Ces jours, qu'ils ont osé proscrire." The third act is taken up by long, very dull ballets, by the too-often-parodied scene of the apple, and by many uninspired choruses. Both the third and fourth acts contain long arid stretches, relieved by occasional numbers of great beauty, such as the introduction to Act IV and Arnold's aria "Asile héréditaire," the canonic trio for women's voices "Je rends à votre amour" (very like the canon in *Fidelio*), and the final hymn to freedom.

One French grand opera that still holds the stage is *La Juive* (1835) by Jacques-François-Fromental-Elie Halévy (1799–1862),[4] distinguished composer of some thirty-seven operas of which the most successful, along with *La Juive*, were *L'Eclair* (1835) and *La Reine de Chypre* (1841). The longevity of *La Juive* is probably due to the fact that by making copious cuts it is possible to eliminate not only much of the repetition which was such a feature of grand opera but also many of the more commonplace melodies, thereby discovering a score which, in originality of musical ideas, consistency of style, orchestral coloring, and harmonic interest, is distinctly superior to any of its contemporaries, except possibly *Tell*. *La Juive* has all the characteristic devices of grand opera— the big ensembles, the processions and crowd scenes, the ballets (which were staged at the first performances with unusual magnificence), and the emotional tension. Among the many effects may be mentioned the use of church style in the Te Deum of Act I (with organ accompaniment) and in the striking choral prayer of the last finale—examples of the common practice in romantic opera of employing religious ceremonial for sentimental or theatrical purposes. All the solo roles are expertly written to display the best qualities of the singers. The chief fault of this opera is its monotony of mood, owing to the succession of melodramatic situations almost unrelieved by lighter touches; the choruses and ballets which offer variety in this respect are musically among the weakest numbers of the score. Halévy's style in this and other operas was often criticized as too heavy and learned for the theatre, but it has been admired and studied by musicians.

Meyerbeer is the composer who more than any other fixed the distinguishing traits of grand opera. German by birth, he was a fellow pupil with C. M. von Weber of the famous organist and teacher Georg Joseph ("Abbé" or "Abt") Vogler (1749–1814). Meyerbeer had written two German operas before going, at Salieri's suggestion, to Venice for

[4] Halévy, *Souvenirs et portraits* (1861) and *Derniers Souvenirs et portraits* (1863); biography by A. Pougin; Curtiss, "Fromental Halévy."

further study in 1815. There he soon mastered the Italian style of composition, at that time chiefly represented by Rossini, and had considerable success with a number of Italian operas, especially *Il crociato in Egitto* ("The Crusade in Egypt") at Venice in 1824. But Paris was the goal of his ambition, and after going there to supervise the preparation of *Il crociato* for a performance in 1826, he undertook a systematic study of French opera scores. Assimilating this style also, he achieved his own mature idiom in which German harmony, Italian melody, and French declamation were all represented. Meyerbeer's first French opera, *Robert le Diable*, produced at Paris in 1831, was a sensational triumph. It was followed five years later by *Les Huguenots*, which is generally regarded as his masterpiece. His other two grand operas were *Le Prophète* (first performed at Paris, after many revisions, in 1849) and *L'Africaine*, posthumously produced in 1865. Other notable works of Meyerbeer include two opéras comiques, *L'Etoile du nord* ("The North Star," 1854) and *Le Pardon de Ploermel* ("The Pardon of Ploermel," also know as "Dinorah," 1859). The librettos of all except the last-named work were by Scribe.

Few compasors in history have been subject to such diverse and strongly held judgments as Meyerbeer.[5] The extraordinary fascination he exercised over many generations of opera audiences has led with the passage of time to a reaction, so that the very qualities that ensured his success are those for which he is now most strongly condemned. Whatever opinion one may hold of Meyerbeer's music, there can be no doubt that his and Scribe's operas corresponded to the taste of the time and consequently are, at the very least, important documents for a phase of European culture of the nineteenth century. *Robert le Diable*, for example, that jumble of medieval legends, romantic passions, grotesque superstitions, and fantastic confrontations, could hardly have been endured save by a generation nourished on the gothic novels of Mrs. Radcliffe and the tales of E. T. A. Hoffmann. Historical subject matter in opera has always been transmuted to suit contemporary ideas; the perversions of history in *Les Huguenots* and *Le Prophète*—based respectively on the French religious wars of the late sixteenth century and the career of John of Leyden (d. 1536)—are no worse than similar

---

[5] Instances in H. Becker, ed., *Briefwechsel*, Introduction, pp. 23–24. I am indebted to Prof. Becker also for suggestions leading to what I hope is a more objective view of Meyerbeer than was expressed in the first edition of this book.

distortions in librettos of the seventeenth and eighteenth centuries, and no less characteristic of their own period.

Meyerbeer's music likewise must be judged in its historical context. He was an exceptionally gifted and versatile composer, one who as a dramatic craftsman has had few equals in the history of opera. A master of effect, he labored conscientiously to realize to the uttermost all the scenic and emotional possibilities of his librettos. His music is tuneful and highly competent technically, his rhythms vigorous, his harmony often original, his orchestration, choral writing, and treatment of the solo voices uniformly brilliant. Moreover his operas are not lacking in numbers that are beautiful, moving, and worthy of all respect : for example, in *Robert le Diable*, the aria "Robert, toi que j'aime"; in *Les Huguenots*, the duet in Act IV (particularly the portion from the words "Tu m'aimes?" to the final stretto) and the *scena* and trio in Act V; in *Le Prophète*, the famous aria "Ah! mon fils"; and in *L'Africaine*, the entire finale of Act II. Nevertheless, Meyerbeer's work is uneven. Numbers like those just mentioned will be found side by side with tunes that can only be described as trivial, no matter how well covered by orchestral color and stage action. Meyerbeer was primarily a composer for the theatre, interested equally in music, scenery, stage management, and choreography; his aim was to present theatrically effective scenes and he never proposed—as Wagner later did—to undertake a fundamental reformation of opera.[6] Moreover, change in fashion, that nemesis of all opera, has borne particularly hard on Meyerbeer. The very length of the scores, the irrelevant ballets and spectacular scenes, the repetitions, the monotony of phrase structure, the overworked device of the sequence, unmotivated coloratura passages, languishing cadenzas—in short, all those features which were practically obligatory in an opera of this period have become stale through familiarity, outmoded musical gestures.

Meyerbeer's last work, *L'Africaine*, evidences a more sober and more consistent musical style, even though its composition extended over a period of twenty years—a style purged of many of the earlier excesses, rich in melodic beauties, and containing some interesting harmonic refinements (Example 82); its musical exoticism was not without influence on Verdi when he undertook the composition of *Aida* five years later.

[6] Cf. Becker: "Wagner vertonte Dichtungen, Meyerbeer komponierte Libretti." (*Briefwechsel*, Introduction, p. 25.)

### L'Africaine, Act II, finale

The high reputation which Meyerbeer enjoyed, and his long-continued influence on the opera everywhere, were not due merely to two or three ephemeral successes in the 1830s. It has been well said that "Meyerbeer's faults remained in his own works; his virtues were transmitted to his successors." [7] His harmony and especially his treatment of the orchestra [8] influenced many later composers. The ideal of grand opera, which he did more than anyone else to embody in concrete form, is evident in Verdi's *Vêpres siciliennes*, *Don Carlos*, and *Aida*, as well as in numberless other operas of the nineteenth and even the twentieth century. One of Meyerbeer's most notable, if ungrateful, disciples was Wagner, whose *Rienzi* (Dresden, 1842), originally designed for Paris audiences, frankly aimed to surpass Meyerbeer and Scribe on their own ground. All the familiar dramatic and scenic apparatus of grand opera was employed in Wagner's libretto, and the music, with its tunes so often repeated, its monotony of phraseology, its massive choruses and ensembles, and its generally huge proportions, is startlingly like Meyerbeer's. Thus Wagner, like Gluck, began his career by demonstrating his mastery of a style of which he later became the most vociferous opponent.

[7] Dauriac, *Meyerbeer*, p. 182.
[8] Lavoix, *Histoire de l'instrumentation*, pp. 384–416, especially pp. 402 ff.

Although he cannot be regarded as in any sense a follower of Meyer-beer, the contributions of Hector Berlioz (1803–69) [9] to opera may be considered here, since his chief work, *Les Troyens* ("The Trojans," composed 1856–58), is in form a grand opera and in content and spirit a worthy successor to the musical dramas of Gluck and the romantic operas of Lesueur. Berlioz wrote a few other operatic works. The general plan of *Benvenuto Cellini* (1838) is a chain of broadly conceived episodes rather than a plot developed in full detail. Its form, therefore, is somewhat like that of Mussorgsky's *Boris Godunov*, and the treatment of the crowd scenes foreshadows both that work and Wagner's *Meistersinger*. The overture is one of Berlioz's best short instrumental pieces. *Béatrice et Bénédict* (1862), based on Shakespeare's *Much Ado about Nothing*, is in many places rather lyrical, almost melancholy in mood; it is full of the most exquisite detail, though perhaps too fine in its workmanship for the requirements of the theatre.[10] *La Damnation de Faust* (1846; based on Goethe's drama), though sometimes given as an opera, is perhaps better defined as a symphonic drama. As in *Cellini*, here also Berlioz sets to music only those scenes that he regards as most suitable for musical treatment, omitting unessential connecting episodes. In this music Berlioz's fantastic imagination and orchestral virtuosity are at their height, and it is these things rather than any specifically operatic qualities that have made *Faust* one of his best-known works.

The libretto of *Les Troyens* is by Berlioz himself, after the second and fourth books of Vergil's *Aeneid*. Part I, comprising the first two acts, is entitled *La Prise de Troie* ("The Capture of Troy") and Part II, comprising the last three acts, *Les Troyens à Carthage* ("The Trojans at Carthage"). The second part was performed exactly twenty-one times at Paris in 1863; the first part never saw the stage until 1890, at Karlsruhe. A number of revivals, some complete but more in partial or shortened versions, have occurred since 1920, but performances are still very rare. Yet *Les Troyens* is incomparably the most important French opera of the nineteenth century, the Latin counterpart of Wagner's

---

[9] The tempestuous life and opinions of Berlioz can best be followed in his own *Mémoires* (translated into English and annotated by Ernest Newman, 1932), supplemented by his letters and other writings (the only complete single edition is the German one of B&H). See biographical studies by Boschot; Barzun, *Berlioz and the Romantic Century* (with copious bibliography); *idem*, ed., *New Letters of Berlioz*.

[10] See especially the duet "Vous soupirez Madame" (Act I) and Beatrice's recitative and aria "Dieu! Que viens-je d'entendre?" (Act II).

Teutonic *Ring*; its strange fate is paralleled by nothing in the history of music unless it be the century-long neglect of Bach's *Passion According to St. Matthew*. One can account for this in the case of Berlioz's work: it is long, it is extremely expensive to stage, and its musical idiom is so original, so different from the conventional operatic style, that managers (no doubt with reason) have felt unable to take the redoubtable financial risks involved in mounting it. There is no overwhelming public in any country for Berlioz as there is for Wagner, Verdi, or Puccini; and not even all connoisseurs are agreed about *Les Troyens*.[11] But, public or no public, the work ought to be produced regularly at state expense until conductors, singers, and audiences are brought to realize its greatness.

Even the full score has never been published in authentic form—a serious matter in the case of a composer like Berlioz, whose music is conceived in terms of specific instruments and of whom it may be said, as of Delacroix, that "the color creates the design." The piano-vocal reduction is the work of Berlioz himself and is full of most pathetic suggestions as to how scenes might be cut and the cost of staging and the performance time reduced. How deeply the failure of the work affected him may be seen in his foreword: "O ma noble Cassandre, mon heroïque vierge, il faut donc me résigner, je ne t'entendrai jamais!" [12]

In form, *Les Troyens* is a number opera with many large choral and ballet scenes. With these features its resemblance to the typical grand opera ends. Its plot revolves not about individuals' fates but about the great historic-legendary motifs: the fall of Troy, the flight of Aeneas, the sojourn at Carthage, the departure of the Trojans for Italy, and the death of Dido. The individuals appear as agents in a cosmic drama, not as persons concerned only with dramatizing their own woes and posturing before a picturesque historical background. Since the average operagoer is not accustomed to associate dramatic emotion with impersonal issues, he is prone to regard a work like *Les Troyens* as an epic (that is, a long and boring narrative relieved by occasional spectacular interludes), especially since he has never been given the opportunity of realizing that here is the one opera of the nineteenth century in which

[11] See for example Lang, *Music in Western Civilization*, pp. 850–51. I shall never forget my astonishment at hearing Vaughan Williams describe *Les Troyens* as "the second most boring opera in the world." (Of course I immediately asked him which was the first.)

[12] "O my noble Cassandra [the heroine of Part I], my heroic virgin, I must then be resigned, I shall never hear thee!"

## *Les Troyens*, Act V

EXAMPLE 83

BERLIOZ

the epic has been successfully dramatized.[13] So strong is this supra-personal, antique character that the appearance of the god Mercury at

[13] Wagner's music dramas are not epics, but myths. The only comparable works are from the twentieth century (for example, Milhaud's *Christophe Colomb*); but the dramatic technique here is completely different from that of *Les Troyens*.

(*Example 83 continued*)

the end of Act IV or the specters of Priam, Hector, and other Trojan warriors in Act V seems actually natural and convincing.

Berlioz's melodic line is in the best French tradition of utter fidelity to the text. It contains not a trace of Italian operatic opulence; nothing is brought out merely to gratify the singer or tickle the ear of the listener.

The rhythmic patterns are novel, subtle, and extraordinarily varied. Most notable in *Les Troyens* is the quality of classic restraint, that purification and concentration of style characteristic of the maturity of genius (Example 83). The harmony occasionally drops into the commonplace (there is unquestionably too much reliance on the chord of the diminished seventh, for example); one remarkable feature is the almost total absence of suspensions and appoggiaturas, making an extreme contrast with the characteristic later Wagnerian style. The chromaticism is much more restrained than in Berlioz's earlier works. There are occasional dull passages, though certainly no more in proportion to the whole than in Wagner. Yet these are surely redeemed by such places as the lament of Cassandra (Act I), the March of the Trojans (Act III, and recurring at various times), the choruses "Dieux de la ville éternelle" (Act I) and "Gloire, gloire à Didon" (Act III), the song of the sailor (Act V, scene 1), and the magnificent final scene of Dido's immolation—all music that can hardly be excelled in beauty by any score of the nineteenth century.

The principal interlude is the scene of the hunt (Act III), a complete symphonic poem in Berlioz's most brilliant orchestral style, accompanied by a fantastic pantomime on the stage with wordless vocalizing calls and distant cries of "Italie!"—the recurring motif of the drama, the command of the gods to Aeneas to lead his Trojan warriors to Italy and there found the empire destined to rule the world.

Comparison of Berlioz with Wagner is inevitable and leaps to the mind again and again when studying the score of *Les Troyens*. It is well to remember that *Tristan* had not yet been heard when Berlioz wrote the marvelously delicate and sensuous love music at the end of Act IV: the septet and chorus "Tout n'est que paix et charme" and the duet "Nuit d'ivresse et d'extase infinie!," the dialogue form of which is imitated from Act V, scene 1, of *The Merchant of Venice*. The change from G-flat to D at the entrance of Mercury, who strikes Aeneas' shield and utters the solemn warning word "Italie!," and the final dark, unexpected cadence in the remote key of E minor make an effect absolutely unparalleled in tragic power.

In view of the current conception of Berlioz (based on his earlier works and autobiographical writings) as an irrational extremist, a composer who "believed in neither God nor Bach," [14] it should be pointed

[14] F. Hiller, cited in Berlioz, *Mémoires*, p. 103.

out that he never ceased to emphasize the independence of music from literary associations and expressed the hope that even his *Symphonie fantastique*, when performed as an orchestral work in the concert hall, would "on its own merits and irrespective of any dramatic aim, offer interest in the musical sense alone." He was no Wagnerian. He cared for none of Wagner's music later than *Lohengrin*, found the *Tristan* prelude incomprehensible, and had only the vaguest notion of Wagner's musico-dramatic theories. He wrote, after outlining what he thought were the doctrines of the "music of the future" : "If such is this new religion, I am far from being a devotee; I have never been, I am not, I never shall be. I raise my hand, and I swear : 'non credo.' " [15]

Berlioz had an apostle in Félicien David (1810–76),[16] one of the earliest orientalists in French nineteenth-century music, whose symphonic ode *Le Désert* caused a sensation at Paris in 1844. His opera *La Perle du Brésil* ("The Pearl of Brazil," 1851) has many points of resemblance to Meyerbeer's *Africaine*; another opera, *Herculanum* (1859), won a state prize in 1867. But David's most successful stage work was his two-act opéra comique *Lalla-Roukh* (1862), which held the stage in Paris till the end of the century and even received some performances outside France. David's orientalism was an early example of those exotic tendencies in French romanticism which were to become more prominent in opera of the seventies and eighties.

[15] *A Travers Chants* (1872), p. 315.
[16] Biography by Brancour; Combarieu, *Histoire* III, 111–17.

# CHAPTER 20

# OPÉRA COMIQUE, OPERETTA, AND LYRIC OPERA[1]

༺ ❀ ༻

Even before the French Revolution, two distinct tendencies had become apparent in the opéra comique. On the one hand there were those works, such as Monsigny's *Déserteur*, Philidor's *Tom Jones*, and Grétry's *Richard*, in which the comic features were secondary to sentimental or romantic elements. Other early composers who contributed pieces of this type were Dezède (*ca.* 1740–92),[2] who produced about fifteen opéras comiques at Paris, including *Les Trois Fermiers* ("The Three Farmers," 1777), and Nicolas Dalayrac (1753–1809),[3] an unusually prolific and popular composer whose *Nina* (1786) furnished the libretto for Paisiello's work of the same title and whose *Deux Petits Savoyards* ("The Two Little Savoyards," 1789) made its way all over Europe and lasted well into the nineteenth century. During the Revolution and afterwards this vein of romantic comedy was still cultivated, but it had a strong rival in the many horror and rescue pieces of the same period, to which allusion has already been made. There were also, of course, many operas and opéras comiques on patriotic subjects which were of only ephemeral interest. To the composers of opéra comique who have already been

---

[1] Chouquet, *Histoire de la musique dramatique*, chaps. 8–9; Pougin, "La Première Salle Favart"; Soubies, *Histoire de l'opéra-comique: La seconde Salle Favart, 1840–[1887]*; idem, *Histoire du théâtre-lyrique, 1851–1870*; idem, *Le Théâtre-italien de 1801 à 1913*; "L'Opéra-comique au XIX^e siècle."

[2] Biography by Pougin in his *Musiciens français du XVIIIe siècle*.

[3] Biography by Pougin; see also Cucuel, *Les Créateurs de l'opéra-comique*, chap. 8, and Lavignac, *Encyclopédie*, Part I, Vol. III, pp. 1600–1604.

mentioned we need add only the names of Daniel Steibelt (1765–1823), with *Roméo et Juliette* (1793), and Henri-Montan Berton (1767–1844), a pupil of Salieri, the most successful of whose forty-seven operas were *Montano et Stéphanie, Le Délire* (both 1799), and *Aline, reine de Golconde* (1803). All these works, while never losing the popular touch or pretending to be as grand and formal as the regular opera, assumed a more or less serious attitude toward the subject matter, which in turn was reflected in the style of the music. Cherubini's *Médée* and Méhul's *Joseph* are examples of this combination of serious themes with the old opéra comique practice of alternating singing with spoken dialogue, a combination found likewise in Germany with Mozart's *Magic Flute* and Beethoven's *Fidelio*. Thus the opéra comique approached more closely the style of the regular opera, the distinction between the two in many cases resting almost entirely on the technical point of spoken dialogue in the one as against continuous music (with recitatives) in the other.

The *rapprochement* between the two forms is illustrated by the fact that practically all the opera composers were at least equally active in the field of opéra comique. The old Academy of Music, founded under Lully and made illustrious in the eighteenth century by the productions of Rameau and Gluck, was maintained as a national institution by the Revolutionary governments and strongly supported by Napoleon. Its leading composers during this period were Cherubini, Lesueur, Méhul, and Spontini. Lesser figures included François-Joseph Gossec (1734-1829),[4] Belgian by birth and better known as a composer of symphonies and quartets; Jean-Baptiste Lemoyne (1751–96), a disciple of Piccinni and Sacchini; Rodolphe Kreutzer [5] (1766–1831; the violinist to whom Beethoven dedicated his "Kreutzer" Sonata), who composed a *Lodoïska* opera in competition with Cherubini's in 1791 but whose *Aristippe* (1808) and *Abel* (1810) were more successful; Charles-Simon Catel (1773–1830),[6] author of a textbook on harmony; and Louis Luc Loiseau de Persuis (1769–1819), whose most important opera was *Jérusalem delivrée* (1812).

Along with the opera and the serious opéra comique there continued a lighter type of comic opera with librettos based on amusing intrigues

---

[4] Biographies by Hédouin (1852), Hellouin (1903), Dufrane (1927), and Prod'homme (1949).

[5] Biography by J. Hardy.

or developments of improbable farcical situations, coupled with music of extreme simplicity and popular appeal, largely in the style of the vaude-villes and romances. Among the specialists in this field may be mentioned François Devienne (1759–1803; *Les Visitandines,* 1792); Jean-Pierre Solié (1755–1812; *Le Secret,* 1796); Pierre-Antoine-Dominique Della Maria (1769–1800), pupil of Paisiello and composer of extraordinary facility, who wrote his chief work, *Le Prisonnier* (1798), in eight days; and especially Nicolo Isouard (1775–1818),[7] a prolific composer who was also endowed with a remarkable flair for effective theatre music. Isouard excelled in ensemble writing. The most successful of his earlier works was *Les Rendez-vous bourgeois* (1807); his style gradually developed along more serious lines, and his best works (*Cendrillon,* 1810; *Joconde,* 1814; *Jeannot et Colin,* 1814) were composed under the stimulus of rivalry with Boieldieu, of whom he was the principal forerunner.

François-Adrien Boieldieu (1775–1834)[8] represents the French opéra comique of the nineteenth century in what may be termed its classical phase. Inadequately trained in youth, he nevertheless attracted favorable attention with some of his early opéras comiques. After a sojourn in St. Petersburg (1803–11) he returned to Paris where *Jean de Paris* (1812) established his fame. Later works included *Le Petit Chaperon rouge* ("Little Red Riding Hood," 1818) and his masterpiece, *La Dame blanche* ("The White Lady," 1825), which had a thousand performances within forty years. To Boieldieu is due the merit of having upheld the national French comic opera almost singlehanded for a long time against the blandishments of the Italian opera of Rossini. His music is neither learned nor brilliant; it may easily be criticized for its frequent monotony of phraseology and excessive textual repetition. But withal it has to a superlative degree the characteristic French traits of clarity, restraint, and simplicity, "de la grâce, de l'esprit, des motifs charmants, une harmonie élégante"[9] (see Example 84). In *La Dame blanche* these qualities are applied to a libretto by Scribe derived from Scott's *Lady of the Lake,* *The Monastery,* and *Guy Mannering,* combining a long-lost hero, a haunted castle, buried treasure, and similar appurtenances in the

---

6 Biographies by Carlez and Hellouin.
7 Biography by Wahl.
8 Excellent biography and study of Boieldieu's works by G. Favre.
9 Clément, *Dictionnaire lyrique,* p. 375.

## Jean de Paris, Act I (no. 5) Duo

EXAMPLE 84

BOIELDIEU

(Tenor)

Res - ter à la gloire fi - dè - le des dames ché-rir les at-

traits_____ voi - là voi-là ce qui s'ap-pel- le a - gir

Soprano

Res - ter à la gloi - re fi - dè - le des

Tenor

en che - va - lier fran - çais res - ter a la

*(Example 84 continued)*

best romantic tradition. In honor of the Scottish background of the story the composer introduced the tune "Robin Adair" in the last act.

With the works of Daniel-François-Esprit Auber (1782–1871) [10] we enter a new phase of the opéra comique, marked by sophistication in the librettos instead of the earlier naïve romantic fantasy and by increasing presence of Italian characteristics in the melodies. The

[10] See biographies by Kohut and Malherbe; Longyear, "Auber: A Chapter in French Opéra Comique."

latter may undoubtedly be traced from the performance at Paris in 1828 of Rossini's *Comte Ory*, an event that considerably affected the subsequent course of French opéra comique. Both Auber and his usual librettist, Scribe, were thorough Parisians, and their work has a certain smartness, an air of the boulevards, an alert, nervous, often lightly mocking quality which is one of its principal charms. Their first pronounced success was *Le Maçon* ("The Mason," 1825), followed by a long series of works of which *Fra Diavolo* (1830) and *Le Domino noir* ("The Black Domino," 1837) were especially popular. Auber's musical style is well suited to comic opera, being for the most part light-textured, tuneful, piquant, and unpretentious. The most characteristic melodies are built on one salient motif in dotted or 6/8 rhythm, which is repeated over and over without undergoing anything like a musical development (Example 85). Less common are lyrical melodies of elegant contour,

### Les Diamants de la couronne (1841)

EXAMPLE 85

lightly seasoned with chromatics (Example 86). The favorite solo forms are strophic, as in the frequent couplets, romances, and the like. There are many duets and trios, though the larger ensembles (for example, the finales) are not so extensively developed either musically or dramatically as in Boieldieu. The chorus is used freely, most often in combination with soloists. Instrumental numbers are relatively unimportant, consisting only of the overtures (generally a mere medley of tunes from the opera), entr'actes, and occasional dances or marches.

With Louis-Joseph-Ferdinand Herold (1791–1833) [11] the Italian traits evident in Auber's music become more conspicuous. Herold was a brilliant young composer who won the Prix de Rome in 1812 and produced an opera buffa, *La gioventù di Enrico Quinto* ("The Youth

---

[11] Biographies by Jouvin (1868) and Pougin (1906); according to the latter, the name should be spelled Herold, not Hérold as usually found.

## La Part du Diable, Act III (1843)

EXAMPLE 86                                                                      AUBER

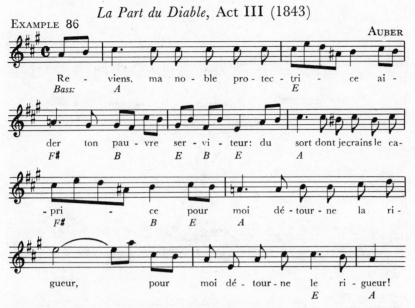

Re - viens, ma no - ble pro - tec - tri - ce ai -
Bass:        A                                    E

der ton pau - vre ser - vi - teur: du    sort dont je crains le ca-
F#      B            E   B     E          A

- pri - ce pour moi dé - tour - ne la ri -
F#        B    E     A

gueur,      pour moi dé - tour - ne le ri - gueur!
                          E           A

of Henry V"), at Naples in 1815. Endowed with a real gift for
theatrical style, he nevertheless had no enduring success in French opera
until toward the end of his short life, with *Zampa* (1831) and *Le Pré
aux clercs* ("The Field of Honor," 1832). The former work, on a melodramatic and confused libretto, and with a wide variety of musical
expression, was long a favorite in Germany. *Le Pré aux clercs,* more
consistent and unified in both text and music, equaled the popularity
of Boieldieu's *Dame blanche,* with a thousand performances at Paris in
the first forty years of its existence. Herold's style is a good illustration
of his own axiom: "Remember that *rhythm* does everything." [12] His
music is more virile than that of Auber; the melodies, most of which begin
on the first beat of the measure, are strongly accented and abound in
syncopations, chromatic appoggiaturas, and sudden shifts to the minor
submediant or even remoter keys (Example 87). Every effect is repeated
many times, as if to make sure that the listener shall not possibly miss it.
There is some coloratura writing. A common device—found also in
Rossini [13] and the early works of Auber—is for the voice to declaim rapid
syllables on a single tone while the melody is heard in the orchestra.

[12] Pougin, *Herold,* p. 32.
[13] See for example the aria with chorus "Dans ce lieu solitaire" in Act II of *Le
Comte Ory.*

EXAMPLE 87 *Le Pré aux clercs*, Act I

HEROLD

Lyrical melodies are exceptional in Herold, though a beautiful example is found in the duet in Act III of *Zampa,* in the form of a barcarole, a type of song almost as popular in early nineteenth-century opera as the siciliano had been a century previous.

THE OPERETTA. Boieldieu's pupil Adolphe-Charles Adam (1803–56),[14] in his *Postillon de Longjumeau* (1836) and some fifty other works for the theatre, continued the trend toward a more frivolous type of opéra comique which, growing in popularity during the next two decades, prepared the way for the flourishing of the operetta in the favorable atmosphere of the Second Empire (1852–70). It is hard to draw a definite dividing line between the lighter opéra comique and the operetta : both have spoken dialogue, both deal with pleasant subjects and have comic elements, both cultivate a comparatively restricted and simple musical style, and both aim at charm, lightness, and *esprit.* If there is any principle of difference, it is that in the opéra comique the audience is expected to lend a certain amount of credence and sympathy to the story; some appeal is made to the feelings of the spectators, some trace of sentiment exists. In the operetta and similar genres, on the other hand, the aim is simply to amuse, and the means are wit, parody, and satire. Opéra comique, as we have already seen, is a broad term, admitting at one extreme frivolous, operetta-like pieces, but at the other extreme admitting sentimental and serious works which in some cases cannot be called "comic" at all. The mid-nineteenth-century version of this serious opéra comique in France is exemplified by such composers as A. Thomas and Gounod, with whom we shall deal later. Meanwhile the composers of lighter types, in France and elsewhere, claim our attention.

Among the many French composers of popular stage works in the 1850s we may recall the names of Albert Grisar (1808–69) with *Bonsoir, M. Pantalon* (1851) and Antoine-Louis Clapisson (1808–66) with *La Fanchonette* (1856). A longer day of fame was allotted to Victor Massé (1822–84) for his sentimental *Galatée* (1852) and *Les Noces de Jeannette* ("Jeannette's Wedding," 1853); the latter had received a thousand performances by 1895 and is still given occasionally. A more serious work, *Paul et Virginie* was produced in 1876 with some success. *Les Dragons de Villars* by Louis Maillart (1817–71) and *Maître Pathelin* by

---

[14] Adam, *Souvenirs d'un musicien* and *Derniers souvenirs d'un musicien*; biography by Pougin.

François Bazin (1816–78), both produced in 1856, were popular for some years, though Bazin's greatest success came with *Le Voyage en Chine* in 1865. The works of Florimond Ronger, called Hervé (1825–92), represent the French operetta of the 1860s in characteristic fashion (*L'Oeil crevé*, 1867; *Chilpéric*, 1868; *Le Petit Faust*, 1869, a parody of Gounod's opera). But one name overtops all others in this field : Jacques Offenbach (1819–80),[15] whose witty, melodious, and cleverly orchestrated operettas had a tremendous vogue in the Paris of the Second Empire and have in large part maintained their popularity to this day. The principal ones are *Orphée aux enfers* ("Orpheus in the Underworld," 1858, revised 1874), *La Belle Hélène* (1864), *La Vie parisienne* (1866), and *La Périchole* (1868). *Les Contes d'Hoffmann*, his only opera to be sung throughout, was posthumously produced in 1881. In his operettas Offenbach revived the gay spirit of the eighteenth-century vaudeville comedies and Italian buffo operas, signalizing the connection by using the designation *opéra bouffe*.

The influence of French opéra comique was felt in other countries, setting the tone for light opera everywhere for a long period. It was reflected in Germany in the works of C. Kreutzer, Lortzing, and Flotow, and in Great Britain in the two most popular romantic operas to English texts of the nineteenth century, both the work of Irish composers : *The Bohemian Girl* (1843) by Michael William Balfe (1808–70)[16] and *Maritana* (1845) by William Vincent Wallace (1812–65).[17] The apparently immortal operettas of W. S. Gilbert and Arthur Seymour Sullivan (1842–1900)[18] were to London of the eighties what Offenbach's works had been to Paris twenty years earlier (*H.M.S. Pinafore*, 1878; *The Pirates of Penzance*, 1880; *The Mikado*, 1885).

Other composers of English opera in the middle nineteenth century were John Barnett (1802–90), whose *Mountain Sylph* (1834) was sung throughout, thereby earning the distinction of being the "first English opera since Arne's *Artaxerxes*"; Edward James Loder (1813–65), whose *Night Dancers* (1846) was highly praised by Hogarth;[19] Sir George Alexander Macfarren

[15] See the composer's own *Offenbach en Amérique: Notes d'un musicien en voyage*; also Kracauer, *Orpheus in Paris*; Decaux, *Offenbach, roi du second empire*.
[16] Biography by W. Barrett; *Memoir* by Kenney.
[17] *Memoir* by W. H. Grattan Flood.
[18] The literature on Gilbert and Sullivan is extensive. Some titles are listed in the bibliography under Dunhill, Goldberg, Pearson, G. Hughes, H. Sullivan, Baily, and others; see especially A. Williamson's *Gilbert & Sullivan Opera: A New Assessment* (1955).
[19] *Memoirs of the Opera* II, 375–76.

(1813–87), with twelve operas of which the most successful was *Robin Hood* (1860); and Sir Julius Benedict (1804–85), whose *Lily of Killarney* (1862) is still remembered.

A distinct branch of the operetta stemmed from Offenbach and flourished at Vienna from about 1870.[20] The leading composers of this school were Franz von Suppé (1819–95),[21] whose overtures, in arrangement, used to be the delight of amateur orchestras and village bands; Johann Strauss the Younger, "The Waltz King" (1825–99),[22] of whose numerous operettas *Die Fledermaus* ("The Bat," 1874) and *Der Zigeunerbaron* ("The Gypsy Baron," 1885) are still heard with pleasure; Karl Millöcker (1842–99) with *Der Bettelstudent* ("The Beggar Student," 1882); Richard Genée (1823–95) with *Der Seekadett* ("The Naval Cadet," 1876); Karl Zeller (1842–98) with *Der Vogelhändler* ("The Bird Dealer," 1891); and Richard Heuberger (1850–1914), conductor and critic [23] as well as composer of *Der Opernball* ("The Opera Ball," 1898) and other operettas.

LYRIC OPERA. If the opéra comique turned on the one hand in the direction of the operetta, composers were still not lacking who, in the middle decades of the nineteenth century, preferred to cultivate the more serious and lyrical aspects of this characteristic French form of dramatic music and thereby continue the tradition of Cherubini and Boieldieu. Between the pompous grand opera and the merry operetta there was room for a type of piece less heavy and pretentious than the former yet more serious than the latter—a kind of opera that should give scope to the French national genius for measured and refined lyrical expression of serious (or, at all events, not exclusively comic) subject matter, combined with a certain amount of ballet and similar stage entertainment. Such works, although they grew up within the fold of the opéra comique with spoken dialogue, are nevertheless better described by the term "lyric opera." Of course in one sense all opera is lyric, since by definition it is sung poetry. But the word "lyric" is especially applicable to the kind of opera we are now considering, which is, by comparison with grand opera, more inward in the emotions expressed,[24] smaller in dimen-

[20] See Keller, *Die Operette in ihrer geschichtlichen Entwicklung*; Hadamowsky, *Die Wiener Operette*.

[21] Keller, *Franz von Suppé*.

[22] On Strauss see studies by Decsey, Jaspert, H. Jacob, and Schenk.

[23] See bibliography for Heuberger's collected essays.

[24] Cf. Hegel's distinction between lyric and epic poetry, in his *Aesthetik*, *Sämtliche Werke* (Stuttgart, 1927) XIV, 419 ff.

sions, and more unified in mood. The leading composers of this kind of opera in France before 1870 were Ambroise Thomas (1811–96) and Charles Gounod (1818–93).[25]

Thomas was a pupil of Lesueur and a teacher of Massenet, thus linking the late eighteenth and late nineteenth centuries in French music. He began his career as an opera composer auspiciously with the opéra comique *La Double Echelle* ("The Double Ladder") in 1837, but his subsequent works obtained no favor until *Le Caïd* (1849), followed in the next year by *Le Songe d'une nuit d'été*, the libretto of which has hardly anything to do with *A Midsummer Night's Dream* though Shakespeare himself appears in it as one of the principal characters. Thomas's most famous works are the opéra comique *Mignon* (1866; derived from Goethe's *Wilhelm Meister*) and the opera *Hamlet* (1868). *Mignon* had attained its sixteen-hundredth performance at the Opéra-comique by 1927.[26] Its music—clear, correct, melodious, and elegantly expressive—is a splendid example of these eminently French qualities as descended from the eighteenth century through the line of Monsigny, Grétry, and Boieldieu. Thomas's talents were hardly equal to the exigencies of tragic drama, and although *Hamlet* has remained in the repertoire, it is rather for the sake of its lyrical virtues than for its adequacy to the Shakespearean subject.

Gounod, the most thoroughly representative French composer of the mid-nineteenth century, was an eclectic yet individual musician, an ingratiating melodist, capable of a certain profundity, endowed with a fine ear for the effects of harmony and color in music, and exceptionally sensitive to the qualities of a text. Familiarity has tended to breed contempt for Gounod's music, which is sometimes unfairly compared with that of later nineteenth-century composers; it is amusing to note that after the production of *Faust* Gounod was accused of Wagnerism and of obscurity traceable to his fondness for the later Beethoven quartets, "that muddy spring whence have issued all the bad musicians of modern Germany." [27] Such criticisms can be understood only when we remember the opera music which Parisians were accustomed to hearing in 1860. Gounod's style is in fact admirably logical and well proportioned,

[25] See Gounod's *Mémoires* and the standard biography by Prod'homme. On *Faust* in particular, see Chorley, *Recollections*, pp. 302 ff.; Soubies and De Curzon, *Documents inédits*; Landormy, *Faust*.

[26] Loewenberg, *Annals of Opera*.

[27] See quotations in Combarieu, *Histoire* III, 371.

truly French but tinged to some degree by Italianate feeling, and with occasional touches of solemnity which remind us that he was a composer for the church as well as the theatre. His dramatic masterpiece, *Faust*, was staged as an opéra comique in 1859. Recitatives were soon substituted for spoken dialogue, and in the new form *Faust* became the most popular French opera ever written, attaining its two-thousandth Paris performance in 1934 and having been given besides in at least forty-five different countries and twenty-four different languages.[28]

The legend of Faust received numerous musical treatments in the nineteenth century, including Spohr's opera (1816), Berlioz's *Damnation*, Schumann's *Szenen aus Goethes Faust*, Liszt's "Faust" Symphony, and Boito's opera *Mefistofele* (1864).[29] The libretto prepared for Gounod by Jules Barbier and Michel Carré is based only on Part I of Goethe's drama—damnation being a more fascinating subject in the theatre than salvation—and consequently the Germans rightly insist on calling this opera *Margarete*, after the name of its heroine. It is well that the subject was limited in this way, for it is hardly conceivable that Gounod could have risen to an appropriate treatment of the second part. Berlioz, unusually for him, highly praised Gounod's music, singling out especially Faust's aria "Salut, demeure chaste et pure" and the closing portion of the love duet (Act III); yet nearly every number of the score is famous.

Of Gounod's other operas the most popular were *Mireille* (1864) and *Roméo et Juliette* (1867), though the latter called down renewed criticisms of lack of tunefulness (!) and undue subjection to the influence of Meyerbeer and Wagner. A word should be added about the lighter comic operas of Gounod (especially *Philémon et Baucis*, 1860); these are filled with charming melodies which it would be a pleasure to hear more often on concert programs.

Whatever the present verdict on the music of Gounod, it must be remembered that in the decade before the Franco-Prussian War it was he who, almost alone, maintained characteristic French qualities in serious dramatic music. Maurice Ravel has thus estimated his importance for the later French school: "The musical renewal which took place with us towards 1880, has no more weighty precursor than Gounod."[30]

---

[28] Loewenberg, *Annals of Opera*.
[29] Hoechst, *Faust in Music*; Butler, *The Fortunes of Faust*.
[30] Quoted in E. B. Hill, *Modern French Music*, p. 45.

CHAPTER 21

# *ITALIAN OPERA:*
# *VERDI*

᧞

In the early part of the eighteenth century Italian opera had been predominant in every country of Europe except France; by the end of the
century it was one among several national schools. Composers of
Italian birth who worked mainly outside their own country—men like
Sacchini, Salieri, Cherubini, and Spontini—tended to merge their
national characteristics in an international style of which the most conspicuous examples were the works of Gluck's followers in France and, in
a later line of development, the French grand opera. Alongside this
cosmopolitan opera were the various national types, especially the
French opéra comique and the German Singspiel, all taking on renewed
life from about 1815 and destined for an honorable growth during the
remainder of the nineteenth century.

The two decades from 1790 to 1810, which saw the production of
*The Magic Flute* and *Fidelio* at Vienna and of Cherubini's *Deux
Journées*, Spontini's *Vestale*, and Méhul's *Joseph* at Paris, were in Italy
a time of relative stagnation—not in point of quantity, to be sure, but
insofar as progress through acceptance of new ideas was concerned.
Cimarosa had to all intents and purposes ended his career with *Il matrimonio segreto* in 1792; Zingarelli never produced anything better than
his *Giuletta e Romeo of* 1796. Ferdinando Paër (1771–1839),[1] one of
the most talented Italians of this period, spent most of his productive
life in Germany and France. His *Camilla, ossia il sotterano* ("Camilla;
or, The Tunnel"), based on one of the French Revolutionary "horror"

[1] Della Corte, *L'opera comica* II, 199 ff.; Engländer, "Paërs *Leonora* und
Beethovens *Fidelio*."

operas, was presented at Vienna in 1799, his *Leonora* (the same subject as Beethoven's *Fidelio*) at Dresden in 1804, and an opéra comique, *Le Maître de chapelle*, at Paris in 1821. Various minor masters in Italy supplied the demand for light entertainment with their comic operas, especially a characteristic one-act type, the *farsa in un atto*, an example of which is *Adelina* (Venice, 1810) by Pietro Generali (1773–1832). But the opera seria in Italy held conservatively to the old traditions until signs of change began to appear after 1800 with the works of Simon Mayr (1763–1845).[2]

Mayr was a Bavarian who came to Italy at an early age and, after studies at Venice, settled at Bergamo where he directed music in the church of Santa Maria Maggiore and became head of the conservatory. The most important of his seventy operas were *Lodoiska* (1800), *Ginevra di Scozia* (1801), *Adelasia ed Aleramo* (1806), *La rosa rossa e la rosa bianca* ("The Red Rose and the White," 1813), and *Medea in Corinto* (1813). Mayr was a thoroughly italianized German, like Hasse and J. C. Bach, but he was able to accomplish something that Jommelli had vainly attempted fifty years earlier, namely, to induce the Italian public to accept some changes in the forms and style of serious opera music. Like Traetta, Mayr drew often on French sources for his librettos, and this necessarily led him to include a considerable number of ensembles and choruses—a practice to which Mayr introduced one of his later librettists, Felice Romani, who carried it on in the librettos he afterwards wrote for Mercadante, Bellini, and Donizetti. The use of the chorus— sometimes as a set piece, sometimes as part of the dramatic action, sometimes as background to a solo—was only one aspect of the generally greater flexibility of form which began to characterize Italian opera in the early nineteenth century. The old Metastasian opera seria had in principle permitted only three types of solo song—recitativo secco, recitativo accompagnato, and aria—and the three were kept separate. A soloist was seldom interrupted in the course of an aria, and when he had finished he made his exit, thereby bringing that scene to an end. Metastasio's formal pattern, from which eighteenth-century composers of opera seria departed only exceptionally, gradually in nineteenth-century Italian opera came to be modified at will by a more or less thorough intermingling, in the same scene, of several soloists and differ-

---

[2] Kretzschmar, "Die musikgeschichtliche Bedeutung Simon Mayrs," in his *Gesammelte Aufsätze* II, 226–41; Schiedermair, *Beiträge zur Geschichte der Oper.*

ent types of solo song, perhaps also with ensembles, choruses, and orchestral passages, the whole being organized on a broad musical-dramatic plan. Something of this kind, of course, had already taken place in the opera buffa ensemble finales in the eighteenth century, as well as in the operas of Gluck and his followers in France and Germany; but the idea penetrated only slowly to the more conservative opera seria in Italy. Another eventual new form in nineteenth-century Italian opera was the so-called *scena ed aria* for a single soloist, which consisted usually of a recitativo accompagnato followed by an aria, the whole in contrasting tempi and of a dramatic rather than lyrical or reflective character.

These formal developments were certainly foreshadowed in the works of Mayr, but their full realization was reserved for his successors. A more immediately important innovation of his was to make the orchestra richer in sonority and texture, and to use the wood winds and brasses, not only in the overtures and set pieces but also in accompaniments, to an extent hitherto unheard-of in Italian opera. The variety of instrumental color and the sometimes sheerly overpowering sound of the Italian opera orchestra of the nineteenth century—as in Verdi's *Aida*, for example—go back ultimately to the example of Mayr.

That example is evident in the work of Saverio Mercadante (1795–1870),[3] Neapolitan and pupil of Zingarelli, one of the most popular composers in Italy in the 1820s and 1830s. Mercadante's best operas were *Il giuramento* ("The Oath," 1837) and *La Vestale* (1840). An example from the latter (see Example 88) will illustrate the full-bodied, rich texture and lusty melodic sweep of his style, as well as another new trait in nineteenth-century Italian opera, namely the frequent use of the more remote flat keys.

Other Italian composers were soon put in the shade when a brilliant young genius, Gioacchino Rossini (1792–1868),[4] began his meteoric career with the one-act *Inganno felice* ("The Fortunate Stratagem") at Venice in 1812, followed in the same year by the "farsa" *La scala di seta* ("The Silken Ladder") at Venice and the opera buffa *La pietra del paragone* ("The Touchstone") at Milan. European fame began with *Tan-*

---

[3] Florimo, *La scuola musicale di Napoli*; Notarnicola, *Saverio Mercadante* (two titles); and (by way of antidote) F. Walker, "Mercadante and Verdi."

[4] Biographies by Radiciotti and Toye; Stendhal, *Vie de Rossini* (untrustworthy for facts but lively reading). See also Strunk, *Source Readings*, pp. 808–26; G. M. Gatti, *Le Barbier de Seville*; Moutoz, *Rossini et son Guillaume Tell.*

La Vestale, Act II, finale

MERCADANTE

EXAMPLE 88

(Example 88 continued)

(*Example 88 continued*)

(*Example 88 continued*)

(*Example 88 continued*)

(*Example 88 continued*)

(Example 88 continued)

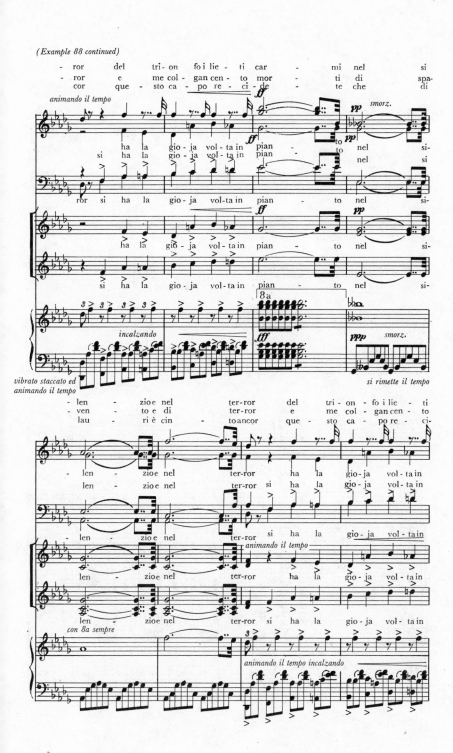

*(Example 88 continued)*

*credi*, an opera seria, and *L'italiana in Algeri* (both 1813) and was confirmed for all time by the world-wide success of *Almaviva o sia L'inutile precauzione* ("Almaviva; or, The Useless Precaution")—better known by its later title *Il barbiere di Siviglia*—following the spectacular failure of its first performance at Rome in 1816. *Otello*, produced at Naples in the same year, was given frequently until it fell into oblivion after Verdi's *Otello* came out in 1887. Although the libretto is an incredibly silly caricature of Shakespeare, Rossini's opera contains— especially in the third act—some of the most beautiful music he ever wrote.

Very few composers have equaled Rossini in rhythmic *élan* and sheer tunefulness. It is difficult to analyze the patent charm of these apparently effortless, seemingly artless Rossinian melodies that well forth in a ceaseless stream from his operas. Held within the frame of a persistent rhythmic motif (typically with dotted notes or in 6/8 metre), cast in short regular phrases of narrow range which are often immediately repeated, crystal clear in their harmonic implications, punctuated by occasional emphasized chromatic notes, and sometimes modulating in their second period to the rather remote mediant key instead of the familiar dominant, they seem to gather up in themselves the whole national genius for pure vocal melody as the elemental mode of musical expression. (See Example 89, the celebrated cavatina from

## Aria "Di tanti palpiti," *Tancredi*, Act I

*Tancredi*, which is said to have been adopted as a favorite melody by the gondoliers of Venice.) Such tunes require the lightest possible texture in the accompaniment, and they will not enter into contrapuntal combinations; in places where Rossini gives a melody to the orchestra, the voice will be kept in the musical background, having perhaps detached interjections or a patter of words in monotone.

There is some coloratura ornamentation of the melodic line in Rossini, but it is not excessive for the period. In all his operas after 1815 Rossini sought to curb the abuse of ornamentation by writing out the ornaments and cadenzas instead of leaving them to be improvised by the singers as had been the former practice; and it is one of the minor ironies of musical history that he has sometimes been accused of introducing excessive coloratura into opera, simply because his scores are *in appearance* more florid than those of his predecessors. Moreover, it must be remembered that in Italian serious operas of the nineteenth century coloratura passages were not intended to be taken at high speed by a light voice but were to be sung rather slowly and expressively by a dramatic coloratura—a type of singer with which the present generation is not familiar. Rossini was the last important composer to write castrato roles and also one of the first to appreciate the value of contralto or mezzo-soprano voices in leading parts, as in *L'italiana, Il barbiere,* and *Semiramide* (1823).

Already in *Tancredi* Rossini had introduced an unusual number of large ensembles; in *Elisabetta regina d'Inghilterra* (1815) and *Otello* he took the further step of having all the recitatives accompanied by the orchestra. His technique of ensemble writing is best exemplified, of course, in the comic operas, above all in *Il barbiere.* His ensembles are always lively, realistic, and full of contrasts; musically they are kaleidoscopic rather than symphonic as in Mozart. Their principle of unity is mainly that of steadily mounting excitement, sometimes assisted by the famous Rossinian crescendo. This is a deceptively simple device (and one easily abused), consisting in many repetitions of a passage, each time at a higher pitch and with fuller orchestration; the classic example is the "Calunnia" aria in *Il barbiere.*

Rossini's treatment of the orchestra, though criticized by some of his contemporaries as noisy and obtrusive, seems to us now a model of clarity, economy of means, and deft choice of instrumental color. Always kept tactfully subordinate when accompanying solos, it comes into its own in the ensembles and especially in the overtures, many of which are still played today while the operas to which they were originally attached are all but forgotten.

Rossini's first opera of importance after *Otello* was *La Cenerentola* (1817), a semicomic treatment of the tale of Cinderella, abounding in melodies from the inexhaustible Rossinian treasure-house, an excellent specimen of that hedonistic manner once described by Stendhal as "seldom sublime, but never tiresome." An equally attractive work is *La gazza ladra* ("The Thieving Magpie," 1817), now remembered chiefly for its overture. *Mosè in Egitto,* a "tragic sacred drama" (1818), is especially notable for the stirring *preghiera con coro* near the end of Act III; this opera, in the extensively revised version given at Paris in 1827, with its generally elevated style and many choral scenes, clearly foreshadows the more famous *Guillaume Tell* of 1829. *La donna del lago* ("The Lady of the Lake," 1819) has a romantic libretto adapted from Scott's poem, but the few romantic touches in the music itself are evidently only skin-deep. The last opera for Italy was *Semiramide* (1823), a "tragic melodrama" with a huge score including one of Rossini's finest overtures (built for the most part on themes from the opera itself), many ensembles and large choruses, and arias in a great variety of forms with much coloratura—all in all, a good illustration of the progress of Italian opera since the beginning of the century. One innovation in *Semiramide* that was frequently to be imitated by later Italian composers was the introduction of a military band on the stage.

After one short season in London Rossini in 1824 moved to Paris, where he remained for most of the rest of his life. Here he presented, among other operas of his own, the above-mentioned French version of *Moïse en Egypte* and *Le Siège de Corinthe* ("The Siege of Corinth," 1826), the latter also being an extensively revised form of one of his Italian operas, *Maometto II* (1820). As *Moïse* and *Le Siège de Corinthe* were important steps toward the formation of French grand opera, so *Le Comte Ory* (1828), an original and sparkling opéra comique, demonstrated Rossini's mastery of the French comic style and in turn exercised a strong influence on the later course of French opéra comique and operetta. With *Guillaume Tell* Rossini reached the climax of both his art and his fame. He was then thirty-seven. Whether from distrust of his own powers, disgust at the new direction of public taste as evinced in the rage for Meyerbeer, or a combination of these and other motives, he wrote no more operas—though the *Stabat Mater* of 1842 showed that he had not forgotten how to be dramatic in music. But he had carried Italian opera, as Beethoven had carried the symphony, through the transition from the eighteenth to the nineteenth century; he had furnished in *Il barbiere* an immortal masterpiece of opera buffa and in *Tell* one of the finest examples of grand opera of the early nineteenth century.

The main stream of the history of Italian opera from Rossini to Verdi is summed up in the work of Gaetano Donizetti (1797–1848) and Vincenzo Bellini (1801–35). Donizetti,[5] a pupil of Simon Mayr, was a composer of almost incredible fecundity whose 73 operas make up only a fraction of his total musical output. His first important opera was *Anna Bolena* (1830), followed two years later by the romantic comedy *L'elisir d'amore* ("The Elixir of Love"), a work that is still in the repertoire. The idyllic, sentimental charm of the familiar aria "Una furtiva lagrima" is all the more effective in this opera by contrast with the prevailing lighthearted character of the rest of the music.

*Lucrezia Borgia* (1833) and *Lucia di Lammermoor* (1835) may be taken as typical of the more violent sort of romantic Italian operas of this period. *Lucrezia* was adapted from Hugo's drama, *Lucia* from Scott's novel. Both are full of melodramatic situations well adapted to Donizetti's style, and it is undeniable that his music at its best has a primitive dramatic power even when its substance is only rudimentary, as in the closing scene of *Lucrezia*. The score of *Lucia* is worked out with more critical care and its effects are less often marred by trivial melodic episodes; the famous sextet from Act II and the "Mad Scene" in Act III are excellent examples of Donizetti's art. He had a Midas gift of turning everything into the kind of melody which people could remember and sing, or at least recognize when they heard it sung next day in the streets. His tunes have a robust swing, with catchy rhythms reinforced by frequent sforzandos on the offbeats. A common musical form for arias (and sometimes duets) in Donizetti, as in all Italian opera of his time and later in the nineteenth century, is the *cavatina*, an expressive melodious slow movement followed usually by a fiery allegro (called the *cabaletta*) with virtuoso vocal effects and a climactic close; recitative dialogue and even phrases for the chorus might intervene between the two parts of such an aria, thereby bringing it into connection with the ongoing dramatic action. Frequent ensembles and choruses were the rule in opera by Donizetti's time; he keeps the chorus onstage a great

[5] Biographies by Weinstock, Donati-Pettini, and Zavadini; Barblan, *L'opera di Donizetti*.

deal of the time, not always for dramatic reasons but sometimes simply to add volume and color to the musical background. Another common device, heard sometimes in Spontini and increasingly often in Rossini, Donizetti, and later composers, is the declaiming of a salient melodic phrase in unison or octaves by both singers of a duet or by a whole ensemble or chorus—an electrifying effect at high moments in a scene.

Like Rossini and Bellini before him, Donizetti was invited to compose for the Paris theatres. Of his five operas originally written to French texts the most important were the opéra comique *La Fille du regiment* and the opera *La Favorite* (both 1840). The former, still popular in France, shows traces of both Rossini and Boieldieu in some of its melodies and rhythms. *La Favorite* is uneven, though the third act is very fine both musically and dramatically. Donizetti's last two serious operas were both written for Vienna : *Linda di Chamounix* (1842) and *Maria di Rohan* (1843). *Linda*, the better of the two, is an "opera semiseria" with mingled comic, romantic, and pathetic scenes, matched with unaffectedly expressive music (Example 90).

Donizetti's opera buffa *Don Pasquale* (Paris, 1843) is worthy to be named with Rossini's *Barbiere di Siviglia* and Verdi's *Falstaff* among the masterpieces of nineteenth-century comic opera. The comedy of *Don Pasquale* is delightful in itself, but it is also touched with deeper feeling and thus lifted above the level of mere amusement; this is particularly evident in the duet of Norina and Don Pasquale in Act III, a poignant juxtaposition of buffoonery and pathos.

The music of Donizetti's serious operas represents the more hearty, extrovert qualities in romanticism, that of Bellini's[6] the more inward and lyrical qualities. Bellini's principal early operas were *Il pirata* ("The Pirate," 1827) and *La straniera* ("The Stranger," 1829). His European fame began with the production of *La sonnambula* ("The Sleepwalker") and the masterwork *Norma* at Milan in 1831. Bellini's last opera, *I puritani di Scozia*, was written for Paris and performed there in 1835.

When Bellini died at the age of thirty-four he had written nine operas. At the same age Rossini had written thirty-four operas and Donizetti thirty-five. One reason for this difference in the rate of production is evident from a glance at the autograph score of *Norma*, which

[6] On Bellini, see *Epistolario*, ed. Cambi; Pizzetti, "La musica di Vincenzo Bellini," in *La musica italiana dell' Ottocento*, pp. 149–228; *idem, Vincenzo Bellini*; biography by Policastro; Pastura, *Bellini secondo la storia*; Pannain, *Ottocento musicale italiano*, pp. 16–48.

EXAMPLE 90

## *Linda di Chamounix*, Act II

is full of cancellations and emendations. Bellini worked more slowly because he was more particular about his librettos and more fully dedicated to an ideally perfect union of words and music. He had a loyal collaborator in Felice Romani, who furnished the librettos for all his important operas except *I puritani*. One consequence of Bellini's sensitiveness to the text is that his recitative not only is more correct, musical, and flexible than that of his contemporaries, but also at the right dramatic moments rises to extraordinary intensity of expression, as in the marvelous scene that opens the second act of *Norma*.

Bellini's melodies are of incomparable elegance, evolving in long lines usually without much obvious repetition of motifs but sometimes with subtle irregularities in the length of the phrases. The elegiac, melancholy character of some of Bellini's music (Example 91) has often been

### *La sonnambula*, Act II, finale

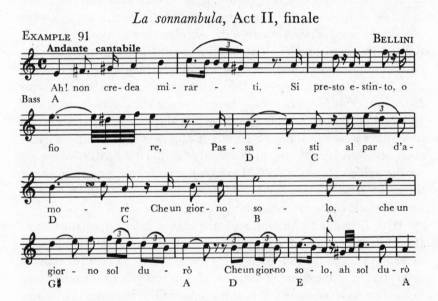

compared to Chopin's, and indeed the two composers are similar not only in this respect but also in that both require a sympathetic interpreter to do them justice. It must never be forgotten in dealing with Italian opera of this period that everything depends on the singers. Composers most often wrote their parts with certain singers in mind, and many a melody which looks banal enough on the page become luminous with meaning when sung by one who understands the Italian *bel canto* and the traditions of this type of opera. This is especially true of Bellini, in whose works the whole drama is concentrated in melody to a degree surpassing even Rossini, Donizetti, and Verdi. Yet Bellini's harmony, while never calling attention to itself, is considerably more varied and interesting than that of Donizetti, and his treatment of the orchestra, particularly in the later works, is by no means negligible. The principal place of instrumental music (aside from the overture) in the operas of these two composers is in the introduction to a *scena*; comparison of any such orchestral passages in Donizetti with the introduction to the first act of Bellini's *Norma* will strikingly demonstrate the latter's superiority. In the accompaniments Bellini's orchestra is, of course, completely subordinated to the singer. Like all his contemporaries, he frequently gives the melody to both voice and instruments, ornamented for one and plain for the other; or he may realize the melody in unbroken continuity in the orchestra while the voice joins in with fragmentary phrases—but it is always one and the same melody. Another device, found equally in Rossini, Donizetti, and Verdi, is the announcement of an aria by playing the first phrase or two in the orchestra before the singer begins. This has a superficial resemblance to the "false start" of seventeenth- and eighteenth-century opera arias, where the voice sings an opening phrase and then breaks off to begin again, but the difference between the two procedures is significant: in Scarlatti or Handel the beginning is like a sonorously proclaimed title; in Donizetti or Bellini it is a seductive appeal for the audience's attention. It has also the practical purpose of giving the singer time to disengage himself from the business of the preceding recitative and come downstage into position for his aria.

With Bellini, as with Donizetti, the chorus is an important factor. It is most conspicuous in *I Puritani*, where Bellini was adapting himself to grand opera on the scale required at Paris, but it is also used effectively in *Norma*, as in the opening scene—a chorus was practically obligatory in the first scene of an opera at this time—and in the cavatina "Casta diva," where the chorus forms part of the quiet musical background for Norma's solo. A few choral scenes in Bellini's earlier operas, notably those in the second act of *La sonnambula*, suggest in some inexplicable way the feeling of Greek drama or the early Florentine *favola in musica*.

None of the changes in Italian opera from 1800 to 1840 had overturned the foundations already established. Starting from the axiom that music should prevail over drama, the Italians had always held to two principles of opera : the solo voice, therefore *melody*, as the essential vehicle of musical expression; and division into distinct numbers, mainly recitatives and arias, as the governing rule of the musical structure. Beginning with Mayr and Rossini, composers in the nineteenth century made the orchestra more colorful and gave it more to do but they never questioned the supremacy of melody in the total musical scheme; instead they tried to make the melody more expressive and thus to bring it, with the aid of harmony, rhythm, and instrumental color, into closer relation with the drama. Similarly, while loosening the formal structure of opera by giving prominence to ensembles and choruses, they never renounced the general principle of separate numbers; instead they made the numbers longer and more diversified within themselves, combining soloists and chorus, replacing the three-part da capo aria by the two-part cavatina-cabaletta with recitative between the two sections, or the old recitative-aria combination with the more ample and varied *scena ed aria*. The first impulse toward the expansion of the orchestra came from Germany through Simon Mayr; the model for the greater flexibility of form was French opera, but French opera as developed mainly by foreigners resident at Paris—Gluck, Cherubini, Spontini, Paër, Rossini, Meyerbeer —who had brought into French opera certain traits from their own countries. Thus opera in Italy, which at the turn of the century had been a rather local affair, gradually began to assume a more cosmopolitan character, though without sacrifice of its individuality. This process of adjustment, already well advanced in Donizetti and Bellini, was to be carried to its final stage by Verdi.

*Don Pasquale*, Donizetti's last important work, was produced in 1843. For the next fifty years [7] the history of Italian opera is dominated by a single figure, that of Giuseppe Verdi (1813–1901).[8] Verdi began where his countrymen left off, brought the older Italian opera to its

[7] Lists of Italian opera composers of the early and middle nineteenth century may be found in Adler, *Handbuch* II, 908, 912–14. The most important are : P. A. Coppola, 1793–1877 (*La pazza per amore*, 1835); G. Pacini, 1796–1867 (*Saffo*, (1840); the brothers L. and F. Ricci (1805–59, 1809–87), whose best work was the jointly composed *Crispino e la comare*, 1850; A. Cagnoni, 1828–96 (*Don Bucefalo*, 1847); E. Petrella, 1813–77 (*Marco Visconti*, 1854; *Jone*, 1858); and F. Marchetti, 1831–1902 (*Ruy Blas*, 1869).

[8] See bibliography in Toye, *Giuseppe Verdi* (the principal authority in English); biographies by Gatti and Abbiati (includes many of Verdi's letters); Walker, *The Man Verdi*; for other titles, see bibliography.

greatest height, and finally in his own person embodied the change from that style to the more subtle and sophisticated manner of the later nineteenth century. An Italian of the Italians, faithful to the instincts of his race, a clear-sighted and indomitable artist, he maintained almost singlehanded the cause of Italian opera against the tide of enthusiasm for Wagner and in the end vindicated the tradition of Scarlatti and Rossini alongside that of Keiser and Weber. The old struggle between Latin and German, southern and northern music in opera—the singer against the orchestra, melody against polyphony, simplicity against complexity—was incarnate in the nineteenth century in the works of Verdi and Wagner, who represented the two ideals in all their irreconcilable perfection.

With the exception of *Falstaff* (1893) and one early unsuccessful work, all Verdi's operas are serious. His first triumph was achieved at Milan in 1842 with the biblical opera *Nabucodonosor* (generally known as *Nabucco*), followed a year later by *I Lombardi alla prima crociata* ("The Lombards at the First Crusade")—both works which in their large choruses and melodramatic situations recall Meyerbeer's *Robert le Diable*. International fame began with *Ernani* (1844), on a libretto arranged by Francesco Piave from Victor Hugo's drama. The music of these early operas showed Verdi as a composer with a sure feeling for the theatre and a melodic gift in which the facility of Donizetti was combined with greater breadth of phrase and ferocious energy of expression (Example 92). Verdi was immensely popular in Italy because he brought to the accepted forms and idiom of opera just that touch of dynamic individuality which was needed; but there was a further reason only indirectly connected with the music itself. Italy during the *risorgimento* (1820–70) was seething with revolution, and Verdi's operas came to play an important part in the patriotic movements of the 1840s and 1850s. Though their scenes and characters ostensibly had no connection with contemporary events, the librettos were filled with conspiracies, political assassinations, appeals to liberty, and exhortations against tyranny, all of which were of course understood in the intended sense by sympathetic audiences. *Nabucco*, *I Lombardi*, *Ernani*, *I due Foscari* ("The Two Foscari," 1844), *Giovanna d'Arco* (1845), and especially *Attila* (1846) and the occasional opera *La battaglia di Legnano* ("The Battle of Legnano," Rome, 1849) all gave rise to fervent demonstrations and made Verdi's name a rallying-cry for Italian patriots. Even

## *Ernani*, Act III

EXAMPLE 92

VERDI

*Rigoletto* (1851), based on a very good adaptation by Piave of Victor Hugo's *Le Roi s'amuse*, was attacked by the censorship, and the names of historical characters (especially King Francis I of France) as well as several other details had to be changed before production was permitted. A similar situation arose with regard to *Un ballo in maschera* ("A

Masked Ball") at Naples in 1859, where the authorities insisted on the transformation of the original Gustavus III of Sweden into an imaginary Earl of Warwick and the locale of this fantastic and bloody melodrama to the Puritan city of Boston in New England ! It was during the popular demonstrations attending the preparation of this opera that crowds in front of his hotel shouted "Viva Verdi"—a cry of double meaning, for the letters of the composer's name formed the initials of "Vittorio Emanuele Re D'Italia," and thus he came to be identified with the cause of Italian national unity as a symbol.

With the production of *Il trovatore* ("The Troubadour") and *La traviata* ("The Erring Woman") in 1853 a climax of Verdi's work in the purely Italian opera was reached. We may therefore pause here to indicate some of the essential characteristics of the style by which Verdi was known and loved in his own land at this time.

Verdi's principal librettists were T. Solera (*Oberto, Nabucco, I Lombardi, Giovanna d'Arco, Attila*), Francesco Piave (*Ernani, I due Foscari, Macbeth, Il corsaro, Stiffelio, Rigoletto, La traviata, Aroldo, Simon Boccanegra,* and *La forza del destino*), and Cammarano (*Luisa Miller, Il trovatore*). The literary sources of the librettos were various : from Schiller came *Giovanna d'Arco, Luisa Miller* (*Kabale und Liebe*), *I masnadieri* (*Die Räuber*), and *Don Carlos*; from Victor Hugo, *Ernani* and *Rigoletto*; from Dumas the Younger, *La traviata* (*La Dame aux camélias*); from Scribe, *Les Vêpres siciliennes* and *Un ballo in maschera*; from Byron, *I due Foscari* and *Il corsaro*; from the Spanish dramatist Gutierrez came *Il trovatore* and *Simon Boccanegra,* and from another Spaniard, the Duke of Rivas, *La forza del destino*; from Shakespeare, Verdi took *Macbeth, Otello,* and *Falstaff* (the last two arranged by Arrigo Boito), as well as the projected, but never completed, *King Lear* and *Hamlet*.

The plots (except for *Falstaff*) are all serious, gloomy, and violent; the earlier works especially are typical examples of the blood-and-thunder romantic melodrama, marked by situations of strong passion in rapid succession, giving vivid contrasts and a theatrically effective sweep to the action, however questionable the details may be from a dramatist's viewpoint. The ancestor of this type of plot is the French Revolutionary horror opera, the influence of which may be traced through Meyerbeer in France and through Mayr, Mercadante, and Donizetti in Italy; but whereas in the French operas the horror served to reinforce the humanitarian message, now it is being used for its own sake. The obscurity of many of Verdi's plots is due largely to the extreme condensation upon which the composer insisted, and often a careful reading of the libretto is necessary in order to understand the action. Whatever may be thought of the subject matter, it cannot be denied that it always offers the kind of opportunity which Verdi needed to exercise his special gifts.

The essence of his early style is a certain primitive directness, an uninhibited vigor and naturalness of utterance. This results often in melodies of apparent triviality, which are nevertheless patently sincere and almost invariably appropriate to the dramatic situation. His effects are always obtained by means of voices. His orchestration grew constantly more expert and original from the earliest to the latest operas, but the orchestra never has the symphonic significance or the polyphonic texture of Wagner's. Only two of the overtures (*Luisa Miller* and *Les Vêpres siciliennes*) are important, and many operas begin with only a short orchestral prelude. The ballet music is seldom distinguished, and most of the instrumental music for ball scenes, marches, and the like (often performed by a military band on the stage) is trite. Nature painting and the depiction of the fantastic, so important in contemporary German romantic opera, find little place in Verdi. His interest is in the expression of human passions in song, to which all else is subordinated; and through that medium he creates a musical structure of sensuous beauty and emotional power, basically simple and uncomplicated by philosophical theories, with an appeal so profound, so elemental, that it can hardly be conveyed or even intelligibly discussed in any other language than that of music itself.

The heart of the melodramatic, romantic Verdi is to be found in three works: *Ernani, Rigoletto,* and *Il trovatore.* The last is particularly rich in traits that mark the composer's works of this period: the roaring unison of the "anvil chorus"; the unbelievable contrast of moods in the "miserere" scene; the nostalgic sentiment of Azucena's "Ai nostri monti"; Manrico's lusty bravura aria "Di quella pira"—these and other melodies from this opera are so well known that citation or comment is superfluous. *Rigoletto*, almost equally agonizing in its plot and situations, is a more unified whole and superior in character delineation, besides containing the famous quartet, one of the finest serious dramatic ensembles in all opera.

Beside the naked brutality of *Rigoletto, Il trovatore,* and some of the other early works, *La traviata* is a refined drawing-room tragedy; its

more restrained, almost intimate musical style had already been foreshadowed in *Luisa Miller* (1849). Several details in *La traviata* are
significant in the light of Verdi's future development. The orchestra is
of relatively greater dramatic importance : in the ballroom scene of
Act I it furnishes a continuous background of dance music against which
a conversation is carried on;[9] the opening strain of the prelude, with its
pathetic minor harmonies in the divided violins, recurs most effectively
at the beginning of Act III to set the mood for the closing scenes of the
opera. Then, too, there is an occasional vocal phrase which demonstrates
a greater freedom in the melodic line, a beginning of emancipation from
the usually all-too-regular patterns of the early Verdi (Example 93); the

*La traviata,* Act II

EXAMPLE 93                                                      VERDI

entire scene which culminates in this beautiful passage is a fine example
of moving dramatic declamation.

Several of Verdi's operas make systematic use of recurring themes.
Mere repetition of previously heard themes was not at all uncommon in
operas of the first half of the nineteenth century, and instances may also
be found in Mozart, Grétry, and Monteverdi. Verdi's procedure should
not be confused either with the simple earlier practice or with Wagner's
system of leitmotifs;[10] it consists rather in introducing a musical phrase
already associated with a certain dramatic situation into a later situation

[9] Cf. also the last scene of *Un ballo in maschera,* and the waltzes in Strauss's
*Rosenkavalier.*
[10] See below, p. 409.

with the purpose of underlining the similarity—and also perhaps, by implication, the contrast—between the two.[11] Thus in *Ernani* the motif of the pledge, and in *Rigoletto* that of Monterone's curse, recur at appropriate moments in the opera; *I due Foscari* offers further examples, as do also *Il trovatore* and especially *La traviata*. The use of recurring themes in *Aida* and *Otello* is thus only a continuation and refinement of Verdi's earlier practice and of course has nothing to do with any alleged Wagnerian influence.

With regard to the ensembles in Verdi, one can do little but refer the reader to the scores. Telling declamation, perfect dramatic timing, and an infallible sense of climax mark them all; perhaps the most remarkable feature is the composer's endless inventiveness in sound combinations, his reveling in sweet and powerful sonorities. The *sotto voce* ensembles, such as those in the Paris version of *Macbeth*, have an indescribably mysterious, suggestive quality.

Verdi was not a composer who studied the scores of his rivals with a view to excelling them on their own ground; secure in his own musical and dramatic instincts, he pointedly avoided too close acquaintance with other composers' music. Almost the only specific non-Italian influence which can be traced in his works is that of Meyerbeer, for whom he had considerable admiration. *Il trovatore*, in its bewildering array of incidents and musical effects, is very reminiscent of Meyerbeer, and the character of Azucena, the gypsy mother, has often been compared to that of Fidès, the mother of John of Leyden in Meyerbeer's *Prophète*. The magic attraction of Paris for Italian composers was still strong, and it is not surprising that Verdi should have aspired, like Cherubini, Spontini, Rossini, Bellini, and Donizetti before him, to the satisfaction of a Paris success. He made some essays in the grand-opera style in his early career, especially in *Giovanna d'Arco*. *I Lombardi* had been adapted and successfully performed at Paris in 1847, under the title *Jérusalem*. An even more thorough adoption of grand-opera style occurred in 1855 when Verdi composed music for a five-act libretto by Scribe, *Les Vêpres siciliennes* ("The Sicilian Vespers"), on the historical subject of the massacre of the French by the Sicilians in 1282. The story reads almost like a travesty of all the devices for which Verdi's operas were famous; the music, with the exception of the overture, is in general

[11] Cf. Roncaglia, "Il 'temo-cardine' nell' opera di Giuseppe Verdi"; Kerman, *Opera as Drama*, pp. 155 ff.

inferior to Verdi's usual style. A better success was obtained with *Don Carlos* (Paris, 1867), another work along grand-opera lines, excessively long in the original version but containing many fine individual numbers.

Other operas of the period between *La traviata* and *Aida* include *Simon Boccanegra*, which failed at its first appearance (1857) but was successful in a thoroughly revised version in 1884.[12] *Un ballo in maschera* (1859) is remarkable both for certain experimental details in the instrumental writing (for example, the canonic treatment of one of the themes in the prelude) and for the beginning of Verdi's later buffo style in the music given to Oscar, the page—a new idiom which is carried through the role of Fra Melitone in *La forza del destino* and reaches fruition in the pages of *Falstaff*. *La forza del destino* ("The Power of Destiny," St. Petersburg, 1862) is a somber melodrama distinguished by a score in which we can trace still further the progress of Verdi toward that long-breathed, broadly rhythmed, infinitely expressive melody which we associate with the composer's later style.

Early in 1870 Verdi accepted a commission to write a work for a new opera house at Cairo, to be produced as a festival performance in connection with the opening of the Suez Canal. The plot of *Aida*, based on a story by the French Egyptologist Mariette, was sketched by Verdi and his friend Du Locle and put into poetic shape by Antonio Ghislanzoni. Ghislanzoni's share really amounted to little more than turning Verdi's ideas into verse, for the composer himself dictated the layout of scenes and even details of the dialogue, on the basis of his long experience with the theatre.[13] The libretto is even more effective theatrically than those of Verdi's earlier operas, since the details of the plot are clearer, the psychology of the characters more lifelike, and the action simpler and more straightforward. The first performance at Cairo in December of 1871 was followed by an equally successful one at La Scala in Milan two months later.

*Aida* was in every respect the culmination of Verdi's art up to that time, uniting the melodic exuberance, the warmth and color of the Italians with the pageants, ballets, and choruses of grand opera. *Aida* is

---

[12] See Toye's *Verdi*, pp. 342–49, for many interesting details of the composer's revisions.

[13] For details, see the *Copialettere*, pp. 631–75; Werfel, ed., *Verdi: The Man in His Letters*, pp. 278–87.

Italian opera made heroic, grand opera imbued with true human passion, a fusion of two great nineteenth-century styles. Verdi here surpassed himself in his own domain : he had never written better solo arias than Radames' "Celeste Aida" or Aida's soliloquy "Ritorna vincitor"; the finale of Act II excels in splendor anything from the earlier operas; and the closing scene is a climax in the expression of that mood of tragic poignancy of which Verdi had always been a master. But beyond such matters as these are still more significant advances. Music and drama are more tightly interwoven, and this in turn affects the form as a whole: for while *Aida* is still a number opera, the score possesses more continuity than any of Verdi's previous works. This is due in part, but not entirely, to two devices : (1) the use of recurring themes, more extensively and systematically than in any of the other operas; and (2) a pervasive, subtle exoticism. The latter is not the product of borrowed Egyptian native tunes but of Verdi's own sensitiveness to color, expressed not only in melodies of modal turn, with chromatic intervals, but also in original harmonies and many details of instrumentation (see for example the introduction to Act III). Even the ballet music, usually rather perfunctory with Verdi, here has a richness of harmony and scoring, a freshness of melodic and rhythmic invention, which make it of equal interest with the rest of the opera.

In a word, the production of *Aida* saw Verdi, then aged fifty-eight, at the summit of his career, wealthy, successful, the acknowledged master of Italian opera, the idol of his countrymen, a world-famous figure. Had he never written another note, his high position in the history of opera would have been secure. After the triumphal reception of the *Requiem* (1874) he himself felt that his active days as a composer were over. A mood of depression gripped him in the years around 1880, due to both political and musical conditions in Italy at the time. Wagnerian music and Wagnerian philosophy were threatening the very foundations of Italian art, and while Verdi was far from feeling envy toward Wagner, he could not but be alarmed at what he felt was a false course on the part of many of his countrymen.

Our young Italians are not patriots [he wrote]. If the Germans, basing themselves on Bach, have culminated in Wagner they act like good Germans, and it is well. But we, the descendants of Palestrina, commit a musical crime in imitating Wagner, and what we are doing is useless, not to say harmful.[14]

Although Verdi sensed the "irrepressible conflict" between German and Italian opera, he hesitated long before committing himself to battle. He was weary, haunted with distrust of his own powers, and apprehensive of public failure. For sixteen years after *Aida* no new opera came from his pen. It was not until 1887, when the composer was over seventy years old, that *Otello* appeared, the greatest Italian tragic opera of the nineteenth century and the triumphant answer of Italian art to the threat of German domination.

Verdi chose to counter the Nordic myth as operatic subject matter with a return to purely human drama, and from his favorite dramatist, Shakespeare, he chose the subjects of *Otello* and *Falstaff*. The arrangement of the librettos was the work of Boito, to whose skill and devotion much of the credit for both works must be given. Boito's adaptations of Shakespeare are excellent. In *Otello*, especially, the delicate problem of shortening the poetry so as to leave scope for the development of the music is handled with skill, and the action of the original is followed closely. Boito altered only a few details and added only the verses of Iago's "Credo" in Act II.[15]

As to the music of *Otello*, we must beware of regarding it as a complete break with Verdi's earlier style. It is rather the culminating point of an evolution. Not all the older practices are abandoned : there are precedents for the storm at the opening of Act I (compare *Rigoletto*); the drinking song and chorus in the same act; the serenade in the garden scene of Act II, with its accompaniment of bagpipes, mandolins, and guitars; the duets, conventional enough in their placing at the end of Acts I and II; the ensembles, especially the magnificent one at the end of Act III; and the superb theatrical close of this act, with Iago's melodramatic "Ecco il Leone !,'" which is in the best tradition of Italian opera. There are recitatives and arias (for example, Iago's "Credo," Otello's "Ora e per sempre addio !," Desdemona's "Salce" and "Ave Maria." But all these forms and styles in *Otello* have a finish and perfection, a

[14] Letter to Franco Faccio, 1889, quoted in Toye, *Verdi*, pp. 196 f. The sentiments here expressed dated from many years previous. See also Franz Werfel's novel, *Verdi*, for an imaginative treatment of this phase of the composer's life.

[15] See Kerman, "Verdi's *Otello*, or Shakespeare Explained"; Roncaglia, *L'Otello di Giuseppe Verdi*.

close connection with the drama, surpassing anything previous. Moreover, certain procedures are definitely new with this work. Perhaps the most obvious of these is the continuity of the music throughout each act, that is, the absence of separate numbers as in the earlier operas. But closer attention shows that this does not involve a radical change in structure: the divisions are still there, only their boundaries are a little less distinct; instead of a double bar, there is an interlocking or a transition. The sense of unity is also strengthened by the magnificent use Verdi makes of the recurring motif of "the kiss," first heard in the orchestra near the end of the love duet in Act I and returning twice with indescribably poignant effect in the closing scene of the opera.

Much of the continuity of style in *Otello* must also be attributed to the libretto, which offers few opportunities for numbers of the traditional sort, being made up for most part of scenes of continuing action which are more appropriately set to a different kind of music—a flexible, dramatically powerful, sensitive, and infinitely varied melody, supported by the orchestra with characteristic rhythmic motifs for each scene and organized in long periods by means of the harmonic structure: "dramatic declamation in strict time substituted for classical recitative on the one hand and Wagnerian polyphony on the other." [16] This declamation includes both strict recitative (used especially effectively for the dialogue between Otello and Emilia at the end of the scene of Desdemona's murder in Act IV) and melodic phrases of the most pronounced arioso character, with extreme compression of emotion. No such free, passionate, long-spun melodic line had been heard in Italian opera since Monteverdi's *Poppea*. It is clearly enough the model for Puccini and other later Italian composers, who constantly aimed at, but seldom attained, the pathos of Verdi in this style (Example 94).

Even within the more or less formal arias, the melody is a long way removed from the singsong, regularly patterned tunes of some of the early operas. It is no less expressive than these, no less vocal, but nobler, more plastic, more richly interwoven with the orchestra, more intimately wedded to the harmony. In the harmonic idiom itself, Verdi never went to Wagnerian lengths of chromaticism, though no composer was more alive to the effectiveness of a few judicious chromatic alterations. He was aware of the broadening conceptions of tonality which prevailed at

[16] From a criticism of the first performance in *Secolo*, quoted in Toye, *Verdi*, p. 191.

Otello, Act IV

EXAMPLE 94                                                                  *pp*  VERDI

this time, as witness the freedom of his harmonic vocabulary and the range of his modulations.[17]

Inasmuch as it has been claimed that Verdi in his later operas was imitating the Wagnerian music drama, it may be well not only to emphasize again the continuity of the musical style of *Otello* with that of Verdi's preceding works but also to point out certain fundamental differences which remain between the two composers. In the first place, *Otello* and *Falstaff* are both singer's operas; in spite of the greater independence of the orchestra, it is never made the center of the picture, and the instrumental music does not have either the self-sufficiency or the symphonic range of development that it has in Wagner. Second, Verdi never adopted a system of leading motifs; the formal unity of his operas is like that of the classical symphony rather than the romantic tone poem, that is, a union of relatively independent individual numbers with

[17] Cf. for example the tonal scheme of the duet at the end of Act I : G-flat – F – C – E – D-flat.

themes recurring only in a few exceptional cases. Third, Verdi's operas are human dramas, not myths. Their librettos have no hidden world, no symbolism, no set of meanings below the surface. They are free of any trace of the *Gesamtkunstwerk* or other theories. And finally, there is about Verdi's music a simplicity, a certain Latin quality of serenity, which the complex German soul of Wagner could never encompass. It is a classic, Mediterranean art, self-enclosed within limits which by their very existence make possible its perfection.

As *Otello* was the climax of tragic opera, so *Falstaff* (1893) is the transfiguration of opera buffa. Written on a libretto arranged by Boito from Shakespeare's *Merry Wives of Windsor*, it is not only a remarkable achievement for an octogenarian but a magnificent final crescendo of a great career. Excelling all earlier works in brilliancy of orchestration, wealth of spontaneous melody, and absolute oneness of text and music, it is a technical tour de force, abounding in the most subtle beauties which often pass so quickly that only a close acquaintance with the score enables the listener to perceive them all. Because of this very fineness of workmanship and perhaps also because of the profound sophistication of the ideas underlying the music, *Falstaff* has never become so popular with the public as any of the other three comic operas with which alone it can be compared—Mozart's *Figaro*, Rossini's *Barbiere*, and Wagner's *Meistersinger*. *Falstaff* is the kind of comedy that can be imagined only by an artist who is mature enough to know human life and still be able to laugh. Verdi parodied himself in the conspiracy scene at the end of the first part of Act III and took his leave of opera with a jest at the whole world, including the art of music : *Falstaff* ends with a fugue, that most learned of all forms of composition, to the words "Tutto nel mondo è burla"—"All the world's a joke."

Two of Verdi's younger contemporaries may be briefly noticed here. Arrigo Boito (1842–1918),[18] novelist, poet, and composer, had been an ardent Italian disciple of Wagner, but was converted to Verdi by the music of *Aida* and the *Requiem*. Boito's own opera *Mefistofele* (1868, revised 1875), of which he wrote both libretto and music, holds much closer to the model of Goethe's *Faust* than either Berlioz's or Gounod's settings. The score includes many marginal Wagner-like disquisitions on

---

[18] Biographies by Ballo and Nardi; collected writings, ed. Nardi; Borriello, *Mito, poesia e musica nel Mefistofele di Arrigo Boito*; Walker, *The Man Verdi*, chap. ix.

the characters and events of the drama. Boito's music is interesting and original in many respects but, although *Mefistofele* is still fairly often performed, it has never become as great a popular success as Gounod's more conventional work. *Nerone*, Boito's last opera, was left unfinished at his death but was given in 1924 in a version completed by Toscanini and V. Tommasini.

Boito was a leader among the "advanced" Italian composers of the 1860s. The chief figure in the conservative group, which found its ideal in the operas of Verdi's middle period, was Amilcare Ponchielli (1834–86);[19] his most famous opera, *La Gioconda* (1876), is an old-fashioned melodramatic work which still holds the stage in Italy and is occasionally revived elsewhere.

[19] Biography by De Napoli.

# CHAPTER 22

# THE ROMANTIC OPERA
# IN GERMANY[1]

❧

The rise of nationalism in music, one of the outstanding features of the nineteenth century, is nowhere more striking than in the rapid growth of the romantic opera in Germany. Before 1820 German opera was known outside its own country only through *The Magic Flute* and a few Singspiels. A truly national opera came into existence with the performance of Weber's *Freischütz* at Berlin in 1821 and ensuing developments culminated in the world-wide triumph of Wagner's music dramas fifty years later. Since Germany displays more clearly and completely than any other country the effects of the romantic doctrines on opera, it will be convenient to summarize here those features of romanticism which come to light particularly in German opera from 1800 to 1870.

Many of those features are evident also, if to a lesser degree, in other countries. If we were to search for the most general principle of difference between the opera of the eighteenth and that of the nineteenth century, we should probably find it in the contrast between the idea of distinctness on the one hand and that of coalescence on the other. The contrast begins with the relation of the composer to his music. The eighteenth-century composer was a craftsman who stood outside the art works which he created; the nineteenth-century composer thought of

[1] General bibliography: Dent, "The Rise of the Romantic Opera"; Chantavoine and Gaudefroy-Demombynes, *Le Romantisme dans la musique européenne*; Istel, *Die Blütezeit der musikalischen Romantik in Deutschland*, chap. V: Kraus, "Das deutsche Liederspiel in den Jahren 1800–1830"; Goslich, *Beiträge zur Geschichte der deutschen romantischen Oper*; *Almanach der deutschen Musikbücherei auf das Jahr 1924/25*; Schmitz, "Zur Geschichte des Leitmotivs in der romantischen Oper"; Daninger, *Sage und Märchen im Musikdrama*; Ehrenhaus, *Die Operndichtung der deutschen Romantik*; Strunk, *Source Readings*, pp. 782–97.

music rather as a means of self-expression, a projection of his own feelings and ideas. His music has consequently a certain subjective quality which demands that the hearer shall place himself in sympathy with the composer, failing which he may fail to understand the music. Moreover, the music itself is directed more to the listener's emotions and less to his intellect than in the eighteenth century. The horror and rescue operas, the works of Weber, Meyerbeer, Donizetti, Verdi, and Wagner, all make a direct assault on the nerves and feelings of the audience in a manner which to Hasse, Gluck, or Mozart would have been inconceivable. In pursuit of this aim, and emancipated by the authority of individual freedom from the old restrictions, the nineteenth century proceeded to create a new aesthetic and a new set of musical procedures for opera, all of which, as said before, were dominated by the idea of coalescence as against the eighteenth-century idea of distinctness.

Let us look for example at the relation between libretto and music in each of the two periods. We have already seen how in the eighteenth-century opera seria these two elements were harnessd together in a kind of marriage of convenience which, provided certain conventions were observed, left each to a great extent free and unimpeded; the same libretto might receive many different musical settings, and the same music might be used for different words. This conception was no longer prevalent in the nineteenth century even in Italy. Everywhere, and to an increasing degree, the ideal, express or implicit, came to be a complete union of words and music in one perfect whole. But this ideal, especially in Germany, was carried in theory even further to advocate generally the amalgamation of music, poetry, and all the other arts in one supreme art which should be greater than the sum of its individual constituents. The ideal took various and sometimes fantastic forms; thus Schlegel: "The arts should be brought together again, and bridges sought from one to another. Perhaps columns shall come to life as paintings, paintings become poems, poems become music." [2] Poets and

---

[2] Quoted in Adler, *Handbuch* II, 865. Cf. Schelling's well-known definition of architecture as "frozen music" (*Philosophie der Kunst*, pp. 576, 593), and Goethe's similar statement (Eckermann, *Gespräche* I, 261, March 23, 1829). Such conceptions were not peculiar to the nineteenth century. In 1643 Harsdörffer, at the end of his "Spiel von der Welt Eitelkeit" (*Frauenzimmer Gesprechspiele* III. Theil, p. 242), wrote: "Hieraus erhellet wie alle Künste gleichsam also in einer Ketten aneinander hangen / deren ein Glied in das andere geschlossen / und absonderlich zwar ihre volkommene Rundungen / jedoch ohne so dienstliche Stärkleistung / haben. Die Reimkunst ist ein Gemälde / das Gemälde eine ebenstimmige Music / und diese

painters saw in music the ideal toward which the other arts were striving
—immediate in its expression of feeling, limited in its power to depict
the world of objects, but by this very indefiniteness supporting all the
more strongly that flight from the outer to the inner world, toward those
"somber longings, depressions and joyous elation without any recognizable cause" [3] which are typical of certain romantic temperaments. The
arts were united not only in ideal but also in practice : poets and painters
composed music, musicians wrote essays, novels, and poetry. The ultimate stage as far as opera was concerned came with Wagner's theory
and realization of the *Gesamtkunstwerk*, the total, all-inclusive work of
art.

In the librettos of many German romantic operas we find also that
the eighteenth-century distinction between man and nature, and between nature and the supernatural, is broken down. In the eighteenth
century, nature appears in opera only as scenery in the background, and
so the music that depicts nature is of an imitative or descriptive sort,
such as bird-song arias, comparison arias, orchestral storms, and the
like. The supernatural in eighteenth-century opera is either a dramatic
convention (as in Rameau and Gluck) or else a source of farce (Dittersdorf) or pageantry (*The Magic Flute*). But in much German opera of
the nineteenth century, both nature and the supernatural are closely
identified with the moods of man, nature becoming as it were a vast
soundingboard for the murmurs of the unconscious soul, and the "invisible world of spirits" constantly impinging for good or evil on the affairs
of everyday life. The storms in Mozart's *Idomeneo* are only incidental;
the storm in Wagner's *Fliegende Holländer* is the whole mood of the
drama. In Weber's *Freischütz* both the natural background and the
supernatural happenings must be taken seriously or the plot is meaningless; yet here we have scarcely emerged from the fairy-tale stage. In
*Tannhäuser* and *Lohengrin* the supernatural begins to have symbolic importance. Finally, in the *Ring*, both nature and humanity become ab-
gleichsam eine beseelte Reimkunst." This may be compared with an eighteenth-
century view (Mattheson, *Neueste Untersuchung der Singspiele*, 1744, pp. 86–87)
which notably does not assert the identity of the arts but only their cooperation :
"Meines wenigen Erachtens ist ein gutes Operntheater nichts anders, als eine hohe
Schule vieler schönen Wissenschaften, worinn zusammen und auf einmal Architectur,
Perspective, Mahlerey, Mechanik, Tanzkunst, *Actio oratoria*, Moral, Historie, Poesie,
und vornehmlich Musik, zur Vergnügung und Erbauung vornehmer und ver-
nünftiger Zuschauer, sich aufs angenehmste vereinigen, und immer neue Probe
geben."

[3] Berlioz, program of *Symphonie fantastique*.

sorbed into a supernatural and superhuman realm ruled by transcendent moral forces, so that the whole action takes place on a symbolic, mythical plane.

All this fairy tale, legend, and myth in German romantic opera is national in character, as opposed to the earlier use of Greek mythology, medieval epic, or Roman history. The emphasis on national subject matter in opera followed the movement in literature which had begun in England with the publication of Macpherson's "edition" of Ossian and Percy's *Reliques of Ancient English Poetry* in the 1760s. In Germany Herder's cosmopolitan *Stimmen der Völker in Liedern* (1778–79) was followed in the years 1805–8 by an exclusively German collection, Arnim and Brentano's *Des Knaben Wunderhorn*. Interest in German legends and medieval literature was revived by the brothers Grimm (*Kinder- und Hausmärchen*, 1812–15; *Deutsche Mythologie*, 1835). Folk tales, fairy tales, patriotic odes, historical novels and dramas were produced by many authors. Much of this literature was not only national but also popular, that is, "of the folk." Glorification of "the folk," of humble scenes and pleasures and the instincts of simple people, is common in the early romantic period; and the imprint of these features remained on German opera even after 1830, when new influences were at work in literature.

Turning now to the music of romantic opera, we find likewise a coalescing of formerly distinct factors. Thus in the eighteenth century the functions of voice and orchestra were clearly defined. The orchestra accompanied the singers; it was heard by itself only on specified occasions, as in the overture, the ritornellos, and the ballets, marches, or descriptive pieces. In the nineteenth century the orchestra not only creates moods and provides exotic suggestion but enters intimately into the pattern of the drama itself. Eventually it becomes a continuous web of instrumental sound, thereby freeing the voice for more realistic, varied, and pointed declamation of the text. The overture achieves a close connection, both thematic and structural, with the opera itself. Improvement of the brass and wood-wind instruments, and the introduction of new instruments, make possible an enormously enlarged and variegated color scheme in operatic music. With increasing emphasis on the inner voices and increasing chromaticism in the harmony, the orchestra becomes more and more dominant in the musical texture. Curt Sachs has pointed out how this growth in importance of the orchestra in opera coincides with the rise of non-Italian schools—"the eternal antithesis between the playing North and the singing South." [4] The climax comes with Wagner's music dramas, in which the orchestra develops the entire action in a polyphonic tissue of sound.

Still another contrast between eighteenth- and nineteenth-century opera is seen with respect to musical forms. The older opera consisted of a series of distinct numbers, without thematic interconnection. The tendency throughout the romantic period, as we have already observed, is for the separate numbers to coalesce into larger units, and this process is finally carried to a point where the music flows uninterruptedly from the beginning of an act to the end. This continuity may be simply a matter of concealing the joints, as in late Verdi, or it may be the kind of organic unity in Wagner's music dramas, with a number of musical motifs used continually and systematically throughout a whole act, or a whole opera, or even several different operas. What is true of the form as a whole is true also of the details : distinction between aria and recitative becomes less marked; recitatives, arias, ensembles, and choruses combine freely in large form-complexes. In harmony, the boundaries of tonality become less definite, modulations more frequent and to more distant keys; chromatic alterations, progressions motivated by chromatically moving inner voices, become characteristic. In the later works of Wagner even distinct cadences are avoided, so that the music seems never to come to a full stop but to move on in an endless melody. Finally dissonance, especially in the form of suspension or appoggiatura, takes on new and special importance as a leading means of expression, and the indefinite postponement of its final resolution becomes a symbol of the eternal romantic longing after the unattainable.

The actual historical course of opera in early nineteenth-century Germany was affected by a number of factors which tended to interfere with the steady development of a truly national type. The original inspiration of German romantic opera, both for the poetry and for the music, came from France—in part directly from late eighteenth- and early nineteenth-century opéra comique and in part indirectly through the Singspiel, which, as we have seen, was largely dependent in the beginning on French models. There being no national center of opera in Germany, the Singspiel developed in relatively isolated localities, pre-

[4] "The Road to Major," p. 403.

serving everywhere however two traditional characteristics of the form : the choice, indifferently, of either serious or comic subject matter (or of a mixture of the two) and the use of spoken dialogue. One factor that constantly hampered the growth of a national opera was the rooted public favor for foreign works, or works of essentially foreign cast, so that composers who might otherwise have devoted their full energies to the building of German opera felt often induced to write in imitation of French or Italian models. Beethoven's *Fidelio*, for example, was a French Revolutionary rescue opera; later, it was the French grand opera or the Italian opera of Rossini, Bellini, and Donizetti that offered the fatal attraction to German composers. Nevertheless, the native Singspiel continued to flourish in a modest way, and to make progress during the first two decades of the nineteenth century.

Two general types of libretto are discernible in the Singspiel at the beginning of the century. One type, specializing in familiar, homely scenes and characters idyllically or sentimentally treated, is illustrated in *Die Schweitzerfamilie* ("The Swiss Family"), first given at Vienna in 1809. The music, by Joseph Weigl (1766–1846),[5] has some romantic orchestral coloring and makes use of Swiss themes and of reminiscence motifs. *Die Schweitzerfamilie* continued to be played in Germany and abroad throughout the nineteenth century; one aria was long a favorite showpiece for soprano singers. The other type of Singspiel libretto in the early nineteenth century emphasized legendary or magic elements, strange happenings to men and women living in a "real" world but ever subject to the mysterious intervention of unseen spiritual powers. It was this eminently romantic kind of subject matter that was to furnish the material of German romantic opera.

Romantic motifs came increasingly into the libretto of the Singspiel around the turn of the century, as the mere titles of some works of this time show : *Oberon, Titania, Das Donauweibchen* ("The Nixie"), *Die Geisterinsel* ("The Isle of Spirits" = Shakespeare's "Tempest"), *Der Kobold, Die Sylphen, Der Unsichtbare* ("The Invisible"), and others similar. The first "Faust" opera based on Goethe's poem had appeared in 1797;[6] two works inspired by Mozart's *Magic Flute* were given at Vienna in 1797 and 1798 respectively : *Babilons Piramiden* and *Das Labirint, oder Der Kampf mit den Elementen* ("The Labyrinth; or, The

---

[5] De Eisner-Eisenhof, "Giuseppe Weigl."
[6] Spitta, "Die älteste Faust-Oper," in his *Zur Musik*, pp. 199–234.

Battle with the Elements"), both on librettos of Schikaneder with music by Peter Winter (1754–1825) [7]—who, however, had had his greatest success with *Das unterbrochene Opferfest* ("The Interrupted Sacrifice") in 1796.

Composers of the other works named above were : Paul Wranitzky (1756–1808; *Oberon*, 1790); Georg Christoph Grosheim [8] (1764–1841; *Titania*, 1792); Ferdinand Kauer (1751–1831; *Das Donauweibchen*, 1798, was very successful and inspired numerous imitations); Friedrich Heinrich Himmel[9] (1765–1814; *Die Sylphen*, 1806, and *Der Kobold*, 1813; but his most popular work was *Fanchon das Leiermädchen*, 1804); and Carl David Eule (1776–1827; *Der Unsichtbare*, 1809). *Die Geisterinsel* was set to music twice in 1798 : by Johann Rudolf Zumsteeg (1760–1802) at Stuttgart and J. F. Reichardt at Berlin.

A decisive stage in the creation of German romantic opera came with two works first performed in 1816 : *Undine*, by E. T. A. Hoffmann at Berlin, and *Faust* by Ludwig Spohr at Prague. Hoffmann (1776–1822),[10] the famous romantic author, is important in the history of German opera for both his writings and his music. In *Undine*, his best opera, the earlier merely fanciful play with fairy elements is given a feeling of human significance, thus achieving some dramatic force in spite of a complex and fantastic plot. The music suffers from some technical faults, but the romantic mood of Weber's *Freischütz* is distinctly foreshadowed, especially in the scenes depicting supernatural beings and in the many folklike melodies and choruses. The more ambitious arias are less successful. Hoffmann shows a sensitiveness for the effect of key contrasts, though the actual results do not always come up to his evident intentions.

Spohr (1784–1859) [11] is now remembered chiefly for his oratorios and violin music, but *Faust* and his other important opera *Jessonda* (1823) are typical of the early romantic musical style. *Faust* makes con-

[7] Frensdorf, *Peter Winter als Opernkomponist*; Moser, *Geschichte der deutschen Musik* II, 5 f.

[8] *Selbstbiographie*, ed. G. Heinrichs.

[9] Odendahl, *Friedrich Heinrich Himmel.*

[10] Hoffmann's literary works are published in an edition by Griesebach; his writings on music separately, ed. Istel. See biography by Kroll; Greeff, *E. T. A. Hoffmann als Musiker und Musikschriftsteller*; Strunk, *Source Readings*, pp. 801–7 (Weber's essay on Hoffmann's *Undine*). The edition of his musical works by G. Becking (1922–23) does not include the operas.

[11] *Selbstbiographie* (to 1838); Wassermann, *Ludwig Spohr als Opernkomponist*; Salburg, *Ludwig Spohr*; Spitta, "Jessonda," in his *Zur Musik*, pp. 237–66.

siderable use of reminiscence motifs, and the idiom, like that of Hoffmann's *Undine*, points toward Weber's *Freischütz*. Spohr's music,
though less masculine and forceful than Weber's, is interesting for its
freedom of key relationships and chromatic progressions;[12] expressive
suspensions and upward-resolving appoggiaturas often suggest the style
of Wagner, although it must be confessed that the romanticism of Spohr
is mostly a matter of such details as these rather than of a fundamentally
new approach. It is somewhat surprising that Spohr was unsympathetic
to the music of Weber and late Beethoven, but he was one of the earliest
champions of Wagner in Germany, and in his own *Kreuzfahrer* ("The
Crusaders," 1845) attempted to write a national romantic opera after
the model of *Der fliegende Holländer* and *Tannhäuser*.

The operatic production of Franz Schubert (1797–1828)[13] extends
from 1814 to 1823 and includes sixteen works (counting those that have
been preserved incomplete), only three of which ever reached performance during the composer's lifetime. These were: the one-act
Singspiel *Die Zwillingsbrüder* ("The Twin Brothers," 1819); the melodrama *Die Zauberharfe* ("The Magic Harp," 1820), Schubert's first big
work for the stage, consisting of choruses and some particularly beautiful
orchestral numbers in a fantastic play by G. E. von Hoffmann; and the
well-known incidental music for Helmine von Chézy's drama *Rosa-
munde von Cypern* (1823). But Schubert's principal dramatic works
were the two large operas *Alfonso und Estrella* (composed 1822, first
performed 1854) and *Fierrabras* (composed 1823, first performed 1897).
*Fierrabras* has some spoken dialogue, but *Alfonso und Estrella*—exceptionally for German opera in this period—is sung throughout. Schubert
had hoped to see this opera staged at Berlin, but it was rejected because
of the alleged difficulty of the music and because the libretto was found
"unsuitable." The score contains a wealth of arias in great variety, a
large proportion of choruses, and a tremendously big finale—altogether
a work in the grand romantic style, with characteristic Schubertian
harmony and orchestral colors. *Fierrabras* is equally rich in large scene-
complexes with intermingled arias, dramatic accompanied recitatives,
and choruses, and in addition contains many instances of recurring

[12] See for example the passage from the first finale of *Jessonda* quoted in Bücken,
*Die Musik des 19. Jahrhunderts*, p. 88.

[13] Krott, *Die Singspiele Schuberts*; A. H. King, "Music for the Stage," in *The
Music of Schubert*, ed. G. Abraham; Deutsch, *Schubert: Thematic Catalogue* and
other books on Schubert; M. J. E. Brown, *Schubert: A Critical Biography*.

themes in the orchestra, a device used here with consummate skill and effect. Outstanding numbers in this score are the lovely duet for two sopranos "Weit über Glanz und Erdenschimmer" and the four-part unaccompanied men's chorus "O theures Vaterland" in Act II; the melodrama scene near the end of this act; and the finale-complex at the end of Act I. It is indeed tragic that Schubert never had the opportunity to hear these two operas in the theatre, for he might then have gone on, with that experience as a guide and with the help of better librettos, to adapt his great lyric genius more fully to the practical requirements of the stage [14] and attain in this field the success that always just eluded him.

Two other romantic composers also attempted opera without much success. Mendelssohn's *Hochzeit des Camacho* ("Camacho's Wedding") was withdrawn after a few performances at Berlin in 1827; he composed a half-dozen smaller stage pieces (of which only the one-act Singspiel *Son and Stranger* was published) and left unfinished a large opera, *Loreley*.[15] Schumann's *Genoveva* was performed at Leipzig in 1850 under the composer's direction, but neither then nor since has it obtained enduring public favor.[16] Its libretto is poorly constructed and the music lacks genuine dramatic directness and characterizing power, though there are many beautiful passages (see for example near the beginning of Act IV, Genoveva's recitative and aria from the words "Die letzte Hoffnung schwindet"). Schumann's *Szenen aus Goethes Faust*, for chorus, soloists, and orchestra, is intended for concert performance; it is perhaps, of all *Faust* music, the most appropriate to Goethe's drama and ranks equal with the composer's better-known cantata *Paradise and the Peri*.

Hoffmann and Spohr had prepared the way, but the real founder and hero of German romantic opera was Carl Maria von Weber (1786–1826).[17] Weber's father was a theatre director and the boy was reared in an atmosphere of the stage. His own experience as impresario and

---

[14] Cf. Liszt's essay on *Alfonso und Estrella*, in his *Gesammelte Schriften* III, 1, pp. 68–78.

[15] Schünemann, "Mendelssohns Jugendopern."

[16] H. Abert, "Robert Schumann's *Genoveva*"; Abraham, "The Dramatic Music," in *Schumann: A Symposium*, chap. vii.

[17] On Weber, see his own writings and the biographies by his son M. M. von Weber (1864), E. Kroll (1934), and H. Schnoor (1953); the best life of Weber in English is L. and R. Stebbins's *Enchanted Wanderer* (1940), which contains a copious and well-organized bibliography; further bibliography in Dünnebeil, *Schrifttum über Carl Maria von Weber* (4th ed., 1957). See further Dünnebeil, *C. M. von Weber, ein Brevier*; thematic catalogue by Jähns. The edition of Weber's works (ed. J. H. Moser) begun in 1926 includes the operas *Das Waldmädchen, Peter Schmoll* (Vol. I); *Rübezahl, Silvana* (Vol. II); *Preciosa* (Vol. III).

conductor at Breslau (1804–6) and Prague (1813–17) gave him a still firmer knowledge of the essentials of dramatic style. At Prague he staged works by Spontini, Méhul, and Cherubini, Grétry's *Richard*, Mozart's *Figaro*, *Don Giovanni*, and *Titus*, Beethoven's *Fidelio*, and other leading operas of the current repertoire. The influence of Weber's principal teacher, the Abbé Vogler, as well as the whole intellectual milieu of his life, inclined him strongly toward romanticism, and in 1814 his settings of ten songs from Körner's *Leyer und Schwert* ("Lyre and Sword") made him the idol of the patriotic youth of Germany. Weber's first extant dramatic work was a Singspiel, *Das stumme Waldmädchen* ("The Dumb Girl of the Forest," 1800), which was not successful; parts of the music were incorporated in *Silvana* (1810, revised 1812). Two comic Singspiels, *Peter Schmoll und seine Nachbarn* ("Peter Schmoll and His Neighbors," 1803) and *Abu Hassan* (1811), and an unfinished romantic work, *Rübezahl* (*ca.* 1805),[18] complete the list of Weber's earlier dramatic compositions. Though he showed in these works an original talent for instrumentation, a gift for comic writing and characterization, and a natural feeling for the quality of German folk melody, there is little in the music to suggest the romantic power later to be unloosed in *Der Freischütz*. *Abu Hassan* may be regarded as a forerunner of *Oberon*, and the medieval-romantic *Silvana* anticipates some features of *Euryanthe*.

Early in the year 1817 Weber, who had just been appointed director of the German opera at Dresden, persuaded his friend Friedrich Kind to write for him a libretto based on a tale by J. A. Apel (1810) and a "romantic tragedy" *Der Freischütz* (1812) by Franz Xavier von Caspar.[19] The legend itself was at least a hundred years older, and some of its motifs belong to still more ancient folklore. The title is difficult to translate: it means literally "The Free Marksman," but the usual English title "The Charmed Bullet" is sufficiently descriptive and certainly more graceful. Weber's music was not completed until 1820, and still another year elapsed before the first performance, at Berlin, on June 18, 1821. The work was fabulously successful from the start and spread like wildfire all over Germany. After its reception in Vienna Weber wrote in his

---

[18] "Rübezahl" is the name of a mountain spirit of the Riesengebirge, a prominent figure in the folklore of Silesia, the subject of many folk tales, plays, and operas. Weber's overture is still occasionally played, in a revised form, under the title "The Ruler of the Spirits."

[19] Mayerhofer, *Abermals vom Freischützen*.

diary, "Greater enthusiasm there cannot be, and I tremble to think of the future, for it is scarcely possible to rise higher than this." [20] His words were unconsciously prophetic, as the fate of *Euryanthe* was to prove; but with *Der Freischütz* he had set German romantic opera on its road and dealt a blow to the century-long Italian reign in the German theatres. The popularity of *Der Freischütz* was due not only to the music but also to the libretto, which, for Germany in the early romantic period, literally had everything.[21] Most of its elements were inherited from the late eighteenth-century Singspiel: a background of nature and a foreground of humble and happy village life; a pure heroine and a well-intentioned but credulous hero; a villain caught in his own trap; the supernatural in many picturesque and shuddery forms; and finally the time-tested figure of the magnanimous prince as righteous judge and father of his people. But though the ingredients were old, the mixture was new. For the first time in opera all these details were convincingly presented as aspects of something important; the trial of marksmanship took on the character of Armageddon, the ultimate battle of good against evil, one sustained by the power of the church and the other aided by the maleficent spirits of ancient heathendom, and the triumph of good was felt as the triumph of the German soul. Thus the national appeal of *Der Freischütz* was not limited to the romantic period but has remained equally strong to this day. "There never was an opera, and there is no likelihood that there ever will be one, so intimately bound up with the loves, feelings, sentiments, emotions, superstitions, social customs, and racial characteristics of a people." [22]

Weber's overture is a model of its kind. Although made up entirely, except for the opening horn theme, of melodies from the opera, it is not a mere medley but a finished composition in symphonic first-movement form. The mysterious last twelve measures of the introduction (diminished sevenths with low clarinets, strings tremolo, pizzicato basses and kettledrums on the afterbeats) are the quintessence of romanticism in music, and so, in a different way, is the clarinet melody in E-flat of the *vivace* movement. The return of the closing triumph theme in C major,

[20] Quoted by Philipp Spitta in his article on Weber in *Grove's Dictionary* (4th ed.) V, 652.

[21] For a synopsis the reader is referred to any opera handbook; many editions of the music do not give the spoken dialogue, which is essential to the understanding of the plot.

[22] Krehbiel, *A Book of Operas*, p. 207.

heralded by a recurrence of the last part of the introduction and three impressive "general pauses," is electrifying. In the larger arias the music of *Der Freischütz* approaches grand opera, and it is natural to find in Caspar's "Der Hölle Netz" (end of Act I) a resemblance to Italian style, or in the opening section of Max's "Durch die Wälder" a mild echo of Méhul. Both this aria and Agathe's "Leise, leise" are complex musical structures, splendidly dramatic and of Beethovenian amplitude. Aennchen's "Kommt ein schlanker Bursch gegangen," with its polacca rhythm, is in keeping with the Singspiel tradition of differentiating the social standing of the characters by means of different musical styles and forms. The contrast between Agathe and Aennchen, mistress and maid, so neatly established in their duet at the beginning of Act II, is confirmed and emphasized in their two following arias.

Parts of the score which did much to endear it to the public were those which glorified the songs and dances of the people : the hunters' and bridesmaids' choruses, the march and waltzes in Act I, and the shorter pieces (lied, romance, cavatina) in popular form. In *Der Freischütz* Weber succeeded as no other composer had done in raising the music of the folk to the dignity of serious opera and combining it skillfully with more pretentious elements. The most celebrated part of the opera has always been the finale of the second act, the "Wolf's Glen" scene, one of the most effective evocations of supernatural thrills ever created for the stage. Among the devices Weber uses may be pointed out the mysterious harmonies (tremolo strings) at the beginning, the monotone choruses of the spirits (note the unison of tenors, altos, and sopranos on a'), the dialogue between the singing Caspar and the speaking Samiel, and the melodrama for the casting of the magic bullets, a Walpurgisnacht of legendary phantoms of the dark forest. The C minor themes of the overture, associated throughout the opera with the demonic powers, are much in evidence. The systematic recurrence of these motifs and others, especially the triumph motif (overture, in E-flat and C major; Agathe's aria, E major; last finale again in C major), contributes much to the feeling of unity which is one of the outstanding qualities of the work. The overture gives the musical plan of the whole as it were in embryo, and the structure thus sketched is fully expanded in the course of the three acts.

Weber's incidental music to P. A. Wolff's play *Preciosa* (adapted from a novel by Cervantes) was composed immediately after *Der*

*Freischütz* and came sooner to performance (Berlin, March 14, 1821). At about the same time he started, but did not finish, a comic opera on another Spanish subject, *Die drei Pintos* ("The Three Pintos").[23]

*Euryanthe* was first performed at Vienna October 25, 1823. The source of the plot was a thirteenth-century *fabliau* which had been employed by Boccaccio in the *Decameron* (Day II, Story 9) and Shakespeare in *Cymbeline*; Schlegel had published a version in 1804 under the title "Die Geschichte der tugendsamen Euryanthe von Savoyen" ("The History of the Virtuous Euryanthe of Savoy"). Helmine von Chézy, after many revisions and with considerable help from Weber, produced a libretto. In planning the work Weber, in accordance with his lifelong habit, deliberately tried to correct the faults that critics had found in *Der Freischütz*. The criticisms had been mainly to the effect that the work was deficient in large, highly developed musical forms; that is, that it was too much of a Singspiel and not enough of an opera. Spontini, whose *Olympie* had been thrown into the shade by *Der Freischütz* at Berlin, was particularly bitter, and even Weber's friend, the romantic poet Tieck, was not persuaded. *Euryanthe*, therefore, Weber set to music throughout (it is the only opera of his that does not have spoken dialogue), and on a greater scale than any of his other works. However, he did not wish to make the music dominant as in Italian opera, but conceived rather a kind of Gesamtkunstwerk, "a purely dramatic attempt, aiming to create its effect by means of the combined effects of all the sister arts."[24] Unfortunately the results did not correspond to this ideal, nor did the success of the opera come up to Weber's hopes and expectations. It has never become a public favorite, but its interest for musicians is shown by numerous attempts to promote it in revised forms. There can be no doubt that it includes some of Weber's greatest music (for example, the overture); the arias are broad and powerful,[25] and the way the chorus is used in the drama reminds one of Gluck. Weber's usual skillful handling of the orchestra is evident, as well as the same tasteful use of folklike motifs as in *Der Freischütz*. Contrast of key is used as an aid to characterization, and there is a

[23] It was completed, partly from Weber's sketches and partly from other works of the composer, by Gustave Mahler and performed at Leipzig in 1888.

[24] Quoted in Moser, *Geschichte der deutschen Musik* III, 73, note 1.

[25] See especially Lysiart's aria at the beginning of Act II and Euryanthe's aria with chorus "Zu ihm, und weilet nicht" in Act III.

significant employment of reminiscence motifs. All in all, *Euryanthe* is a grand opera both in form and in loftiness of conception, a landmark in the history of German opera between *Fidelio* and *Lohengrin*, and a work that deserves to be performed more frequently.

Weber's last opera, *Oberon*, was composed to an English libretto by J. F. Planché and first performed under the composer's direction at London, April 12, 1826. The fatigue of the journey and labor of the production hastened Weber's death, which occurred at London on June 4. In some ways *Oberon* was a backward step: the story, a rambling oriental fantasy with numberless scene changes, gave only limited occasion for development of character or genuine human emotion; there were many nonsinging actors, and so much of the action took place in spoken dialogue that the music was reduced almost to an incidental position. Weber intended to rearrange the work for German theatres, and though he did not live long enough to do so, many more or less thoroughgoing revisions and additions have been made (some in accordance with Weber's plan) by later musicians. *Oberon* is historically important chiefly because of its fairy music, such as the opening chorus of Act I, the finales of the second and third acts, and above all the beginning of the overture, with its magic horn call, muted strings, and swift figure in the wood winds. Such music was in the air: Mendelssohn's octet with its scherzo had appeared the year before, and the *Midsummer Night's Dream* overture was composed in the summer of 1826. The more vigorous, ardent, stormy romanticism of Rezia's aria "Ocean, thou mighty monster" (the closing theme of which had appeared in the overture) is also well represented in *Oberon*.

Weber died in mid-career. Had he lived to complete his work, the history of German opera for the next twenty years might have been one of steady development. As it was, although *Der Freischütz* continued its triumphal course, no German work was produced for nearly a generation that could match it either in popularity or in musical worth. The early romantics had created a world of opera in which the lives of simple human beings were felt to be so intertwined with the processes of nature, and both man and nature so informed and governed by all-encompassing spiritual powers, that the three realms seemed as one. This original unity was lost after *Der Freischütz*, with unfortunate results for both libretto and music. Poets and composers began to exploit the supernatural for mere sensation and the human for sentiment or comedy; and periodically they would be distracted by the allurements of grand opera.

If Weber can be said to have had a successor, it was Heinrich Marschner (1795–1861),[26] who first became widely known in 1828 for *Der Vampyr*, an opera now remembered mainly because it was one of Wagner's models for *Der fliegende Holländer* (see especially the ballade in Act III). Marschner's *Templer und Jüdin* ("The Templar and the Jewess," 1829) was adapted from Scott's *Ivanhoe*. His masterpiece, *Hans Heiling* (1833), was on a libretto by Eduard Devrient from a story by Körner, originally intended for Mendelssohn. As the central situation of *Templer und Jüdin* is similar to that of *Lohengrin*, so the figure of Hans Heiling, half man and half earth spirit, in love with a mortal woman, has many points of resemblance to Wagner's Dutchman. Yet in the working out of the story as well as in the music much of the trivial is mingled with the serious. The style for the most part is that of the popular Singspiel, with simple tunes in symmetrical patterns, interspersed with spoken dialogue. Echoes of Weber, Italian opera, and Meyerbeer's *Robert le Diable* are heard. In some respects the music looks ahead to Wagner: the frequent chromatic passing tones in the melody, especially at cadences; the use of modulating sequences; and occasionally a passage of grimly powerful declamation. Many of the choruses are interesting, and the finales of the first and third acts are well constructed. The most original number, and one which shows Marschner's gifts to good advantage, is the melodrama and lied at the beginning of the second scene of Act II.[27] Yet, on the whole, his talent was of second rank, the Biedermeier spirit in music. His later works, in which there are many traces of the fashionable Italian and French opera of the time, contributed nothing to his fame.

Along with the romantic traits of Marschner there lived in German opera a current of sentimental or comic drama, descended from the eighteenth-century Singspiel. A very popular opera was Konradin Kreutzer's (1780–1849)[28] *Nachtlager in Granada* ("The Night-Camp at Granada"), first performed at Vienna in 1834. The libretto, based on

[26] Münzer, *Heinrich Marschner*; G. Fischer, *Musik in Hannover* (2d ed.) and *Marschner-Erinnerungen*; Gaartz, *Die Opern Heinrich Marschners*; Gnirs, *Hans Heiling*.

[27] The melody at the words "Sonst bist du verfallen" is the original of Wagner's death-announcement theme in *Die Walküre*.

[28] Riehl, essay in *Musikalische Charakterköpfe* I.

Friedrich Kind's play of the same title, uses the old reliable motif of the good prince in disguise conferring rewards on humble virtue and innocent young love and offers occasion for romances, hunting choruses, a conspirators' chorus, a prayer, airs and ensembles, all somewhat in the manner of Auber and Donizetti—light, sometimes trifling, but on the whole pretty and pleasing music in a harmless way. A more spirited comic vein was worked by Gustav Albert Lortzing (1801–51) [29] in his most successful work, *Zar und Zimmermann* ("Czar and Carpenter," Leipzig, 1837), and especially in *Der Waffenschmied* ("The Armorer," Vienna, 1846). The latter abounds in humorous situations like those of the older Viennese Singspiel, with a fresh, pleasant, often witty melodic style and some ensembles that recall the spirit of Mozart. Most characteristic, however, are the simple songs in folk idiom, reminiscent of the tunes of J. A. Hiller. With *Der Wildschütz* ("The Poacher," 1842) and even more pronouncedly with *Undine* (1845) Lortzing—who in all these works was his own librettist—ventured on the ground of romantic opera, with its supernatural beings and theme of redemption through love. Lortzing was hardly capable of composing music equal to the emotions and characters of this libretto, but his systematic use of recurring motifs and his powers of musical description (especially the water-sprites' music, first heard in Act II, scene 5) are interesting both in themselves and as predecessors of the music of Wagner's *Ring*. Another of Lortzing's comic operas, *Hans Sachs* (1840), is one of the numerous sources of *Die Meistersinger*.

Other composers of German opera toward the middle of the nineteenth century must be only briefly mentioned. Otto Nicolai's (1810–49) [30] *Lustigen Weiber von Windsor* ("The Merry Wives of Windsor," Berlin, 1849) is a fine comic work in which Italian and German characteristics are happily blended. Its sparkling, cosmopolitan style contrasts with the simple homemade quality of another popular contemporary work, *Martha* (1847) by Friedrich von Flotow (1812–83), [31] a sentimental old-fashioned piece which has inexplicably survived while many better operas have been forgotten. An important younger figure of this period

[29] Biographies by Kruse and Killer; *Gesammelte Briefe*, ed. Kruse; Laue, *Die Operndichtung Lortzings*; Burgmüller, *Die Musen darben.*

[30] *Tagebücher* (ed. B. Schröder, 1892; ed. W. Altmann, 1937); Kruse, *Otto Nicolai; idem*, "Otto Nicolai's italienische Opern."

[31] R. Flotow, *Friedrich von Flotow's Leben von seiner Witwe*; Dent, "A Best-Seller in Opera."

was Peter Cornelius (1824–74),[32] disciple of Liszt and champion of Wagner, a poet and composer who wrote his own librettos. His *Barbier von Bagdad* ("The Barber of Bagdad," Weimar, 1858) is a wholly delightful oriental comedy in a sophisticated musical idiom obviously influenced by Wagner, especially with respect to its harmony and melodic line. The rhythms, deriving in part from oriental verse forms, are particularly varied and interesting—for example, the aria "O holdes Bild" (Act II, scene 2) is in alternate 4/4 and 3/4 measures; five-measure phrases are also common throughout the score. Each of the two acts runs continuously, without marked division into numbers. The orchestra has an important role not only in the formal scheme but also in the providing of many humorous details in the accompaniments. A half-dozen recurring motifs are used systematically. *Der Barbier* is not high comedy like *Die Meistersinger* but a farce, cleverly using every resource of music for farcical purposes (see for example the canonic duet "Wenn zum Gebet" in Act I). The freedom of rhythm, the declamatory melodies, the frequent wide intervals and chromatic harmonies often foreshadow the style of Strauss's *Rosenkavalier*. There is also some parody of Italian opera, especially in the sentimental unison love duet "So mag kein anders Wort erklingen" in the second scene of Act II. (This scene is also an unintentional parody of the love duet in the second act of Tristan, with the Barber filling the role of Brangäne.)

During the 1830s and 1840s it seemed almost as if the Italians had been driven from German opera houses only to be replaced by the French. The works of Herold and Adam were particularly popular, while the equally gifted native composers Marschner and Lortzing were often neglected. The situation was saved by Wagner, who after early experiments in the Italian style and that of French grand opera went on to create a new epoch of national German romantic opera in *Der fliegende Holländer*, *Tannhäuser*, and *Lohengrin*.

[32] Complete editions of Cornelius's literary works (4 vols.) and musical works (5 vols., B&H, 1905–6); biographies by M. Hasse and C. M. Cornelius; Hasse, *Peter Cornelius und sein Barbier von Bagdad*.

# CHAPTER 23

# *WAGNER*[1]

From time to time in the history of music there have been composers whose works summed up the achievement of a whole epoch, making the final synthesis of a style: Palestrina and Bach are the outstanding examples. There have been other composers whose work incorporated not only the end of one style but the beginning of another as well: to this group belong Beethoven and Wagner. Wagner's operas, to and including *Lohengrin*, were the consummation of German romantic opera of the nineteenth century; the later music dramas were in a style which, although retaining many features of what had gone before, nevertheless introduced innovations in both theory and practice. These innovations were not confined to the music but embraced the whole drama, and in working them out Wagner, who perceived all the implications of his ideas and developed them with typical German thoroughness, touched on many issues that were fundamentally involved with nineteenth-century thought. He is the only eminent composer whose writings have been considered important outside the conventional limits of the field of music. For him, indeed, these conventional limits hardly existed; consequently, in order to understand his music, it is necessary to take into account his views on other subjects, including his philosophy of art in general and of the drama in particular. Whether one agrees or disagrees with these views is a question of the same order as whether one likes or dislikes the music: in either case it is desirable to comprehend as well as judge.

[1] Wagner's complete musical works have been published in a Collected Edition by Breitkopf & Härtel. There is as yet no comprehensive bibliography of the enormous Wagner literature. (Oesterlein's *Katalog*, limited to items published during Wagner's lifetime, lists over 10,000 titles.) The primary sources are: Wagner, *Mein Leben*; idem, *Gesammelte Schriften und Dichtungen* (5th ed.); idem, *Briefe in Originalausgaben*; for other principal sources, see Newman's *Life*. The standard

In music, Wagner was for the most part self-taught. During his student days at Leipzig he became acquainted with some of Beethoven's works and heard at the theatre the plays of Schiller and Shakespeare, as well as the operas of Weber and Marschner. He wrote dramas and some instrumental music, including a Symphony in C major which was performed in 1833. During two seasons as chorus trainer at Würzburg (1833–34) he became familiar with many more works of the current opera repertoire and composed his own *Feen* ("The Fairies"), his first completed opera (never performed during Wagner's lifetime). This is a

biography for many years was that of Glasenapp (*Das Leben Richard Wagners*), now superseded by Ernest Newman's *Life of Richard Wagner*. Koch's *Richard Wagner* emphasizes the literary side of Wagner's production; the most popular short German biography is Julius Kapp's (32d ed., 1929); see also W. Jacob, *Taten der Musik*. The "orthodox" Wagner gospel is expounded in the official periodical *Bayreuther Blätter* (from 1878, ed. for many years by Hans von Wolzogen) and in the works of Houston Stewart Chamberlain (*Richard Wagner* and *Das Drama Richard Wagners*. Cf. also his *Grundlagen des neunzehnten Jahrhunderts*). The following books may be found useful: Newman, *The Wagner Operas*; Saitschick, *Götter und Menschen in Richard Wagners Ring*; Mann, "Leiden und Grösse Richard Wagners," in his *Leiden und Grösse der Meister*; A. E. F. Dickinson, *The Musical Design of The Ring*; Hutcheson, *A Musical Guide to the . . . Ring*; Strunk, *Source Readings*, pp. 874–903. Paul Bekker's *Richard Wagner* is diffuse and involved but worth reading for its many insights; a useful new viewpoint is suggested in Joseph Kerman's "Wagner: Thoughts in Season." The most important works dealing specifically with Wagner's music are: Adler, *Richard Wagner, Vorlesungen*; Lorenz, *Das Geheimnis der Form bei Richard Wagner* (4 vols.); Kurth, *Romantische Harmonik und ihre Krise in Wagner's Tristan*; and Westernhagen, *Vom Holländer zum Parsifal*.

A tabular list of Wagner's operas and music dramas is given here:

| TITLE | DATE OF COMPOSITION (incl. scoring) | FIRST PERFORMANCE |
|---|---|---|
| *Die Feen* | 1833 | Munich, 1888 |
| *Das Liebesverbot* | 1835 | Magdeburg, 1836 |
| *Rienzi* | 1838–40 | Dresden, 1842 |
| *Der fliegende Holländer* | 1841 | Dresden, 1843 |
| *Tannhäuser* | 1843–45 | Dresden, 1845 |
| *Lohengrin* | 1846–48 | Weimar, 1850 |
| *Der Ring des Nibelungen* | Poem begun 1848, completed 1852 | First complete performance, Bayreuth, 1876 |
| I. *Das Rheingold* | 1853–54 | Munich, 1869 |
| II. *Die Walküre* | 1854–56 | Munich, 1870 |
| III. *Siegfried* | 1856–57, 1864–65, 1869–71 | Bayreuth, 1876 |
| IV. *Götterdämmerung* | 1869–74 | Bayreuth, 1876 |
| *Tristan und Isolde* | 1857–59 | Munich, 1865 |
| *Die Meistersinger von Nürnberg* | 1862–67 | Munich, 1868 |
| *Parsifal* | 1877–82 | Bayreuth, 1882 |

long work, with the usual subdivision into recitatives, arias, ensembles, and the like. A few traits of the music suggest the later composer of *Rienzi*, but the style on the whole is modeled after Beethoven and Weber. The romantic idiom of the period is handled with great energy, aiming at big theatrical effects by conventional means. There is no technical reason why this opera could not have been performed; it is by no means an inexpert work, only it lacks individuality. Wagner's libretto, based on a fairy tale of Carlo Gozzi, introduces all the fantastic and decorative apparatus of romantic opera in profusion, but without the unifying power of a really significant dramatic idea.

If *Die Feen* may be regarded as an essay in German romantic opera, *Das Liebesverbot* ("The Ban on Love") showed Wagner eagerly assimilating the Italian style. Bellini's *Montecchi e Capuletti* had aroused much enthusiasm at Leipzig in 1834, and Wagner was temporarily in reaction against the alleged heaviness, lack of dramatic life, and unvocal quality of the typical German operas. His libretto for *Das Liebesverbot* was based on Shakespeare's *Measure for Measure*; it is full of comic scenes and has some spoken dialogue. The music is a blend of Auber, Rossini, and Donizetti, with distinct traces of Meyerbeer in the finales, which often seem to strain terribly for effect. The melodies are florid, often with typically Italian cadenzas, and everything is repeated at great length. The best quality of the score is its liveliness and enthusiasm, though even this becomes wearisome after a time. There is not one really distinguished theme in the whole work; the duet in bolero rhythm in the first scene of Act II may be taken as typical of the style (Example 95). Some of the crowd scenes faintly foreshadow the ending of Act II of *Die Meistersinger*; the duet of Isabella and Marianna and the latter's aria in the last act have a sultry erotic quality which looks forward to Richard Strauss. *Das Liebersverbot* was performed only once, and then very badly, at Magdeburg in 1836, with the composer conducting.

From 1837 to 1839 Wagner was music director of the theatre at Riga. Here he began the composition of *Rienzi*, based on Bulwer-Lytton's novel and inspired by a performance of Spontini's *Cortez* which Wagner had witnessed at Berlin in 1836. In the summer of 1839 he went to Paris; the first stage of the trip was the memorable stormy sea voyage to London, the impressions of which later influenced him in the composition of *Der fliegende Holländer* ("The Flying Dutchman"). The two and a half years in Paris were a nightmare of failure, disap-

## Das Liebesverbot, Act II, no. 7

EXAMPLE 95 WAGNER

Ha, welch' ein Tod für Lieb' und Eh — re, ihm weih' ich mei — ne Ju — gend-kraft, für die er-hab(ne)

pointment, and poverty. Even the efforts of Meyerbeer on his behalf did not avail to obtain him a hearing. Yet during this time Wagner completed *Rienzi* and wrote *Der fliegende Holländer*, finishing the latter at the suburb of Meudon in August, 1841. At last *Rienzi* was accepted by the Opera at Dresden, where the first performance took place October 20, 1842. Wagner had come from Paris in the summer to supervise the rehearsals. The success of the work was immediate and overwhelming and led to a demand for *Der fliegende Holländer*, which was produced in January, 1843. A month later Wagner was appointed music director for life of the Dresden Opera.

*Rienzi*, as we have already noted (p. 322), was a grand opera in the fashion of the time, with just enough novelty to make it extremely popular. The reception of *Der fliegende Holländer* was less flattering: in externals this work was less brilliant than *Rienzi*, and its inner dramatic significance went for the most part unperceived. This was not altogether the fault of the audiences, for Wagner himself had not yet perfected his technique. *Der fliegende Holländer* is essentially a German romantic opera in the tradition of *Der Vampyr* or *Hans Heiling* (though without spoken dialogue), and is divided into the customary numbers.

Some of these are quite successful, while others seem mechanical and forced, monotonous in rhythm, and without marked originality of melody or harmony. Wagner took his version of the medieval legend of the Flying Dutchman from a tale by Heinrich Heine, adding features suggested by Marschner's *Vampyr*. As in *Der Freischütz*, nature, animated by supernatural forces, is all-pervasive. This time it is not the forest but the sea : in the storm music, the steersman's song in Act I, and the sailors' choruses in Act III, Wagner set forth with all his power the impressions gathered in the voyage from Riga to London. These portions are not mere musical descriptions of the sea but are filled with symbolic meaning for the human drama. In the story of the redemption of the Dutchman from the curse of immortality by Senta's love Wagner for the first time clearly worked out the idea of salvation through love which became fundamental in his later dramas. It is stated in Senta's Ballad (Act II), the central number of the opera and the one first composed. The ballad, a type of song which in earlier nineteenth-century opera had been as a rule only a set piece, here becomes the pivot of the whole dramatic and musical development, and its traditional two-part form is used to contrast the ideas of curse and salvation. The themes chosen are good examples of Wagner's characteristic procedure of representing basic dramatic ideas by specific musical formulae : the opening motif forming an empty fifth, the stormy chromatics, and the diminished sevenths [2] are set against the calm diatonic major melody of the second section. The ultimate salvation—already prophesied at the end of the overture—is symbolized in the finale of the opera by using the latter theme for an extended plagal cadence in D major. These two themes (or rather theme groups) and their derivatives are used systematically in many other parts of the opera; Wagner has already adopted the device of the reminiscence motif, but has not yet extended it to every portion of the work. The historical interest of *Der fliegende Holländer* lies not so much in this device—which, as we have seen, was not new with Wagner —as in the quality of the themes themselves, in the individuality of their harmonies, and the way they seem to embody the essential dramatic idea, completing its expression and giving it depth and emotional power.

[2] The first motif has an obvious resemblance to the beginning of Beethoven's Ninth Symphony, which Wagner had heard for the first time adequately played by the Paris Conservatoire orchestra under Habeneck. For the orchestration here, as elsewhere in this opera and also in *Tannhäuser*, Wagner had learned much from Berlioz.

Another important number in *Der fliegende Holländer* is the C minor recitative and aria of the Dutchman in Act I ("Die Frist ist um"), ending with his pathetic appeal for death ("Ew'ge Vernichtung, nimm mich auf !") which is echoed mysteriously in E major by the voices of the unseen crew—a momentary shift of tonality made more striking by the immediate, implacable return to C minor in the orchestral coda. The long duet of Senta and the Dutchman in the finale of Act II is the climax of the drama, but its operatic style is an unfortunate lapse into an earlier and less individual musical idiom. Of the remaining numbers it is necessary to mention only the familiar Spinning Song which opens the second act, with the women's voices in A major offering a pleasant contrast to the dark colors of Act I and making an ideal prelude to Senta's Ballad.

In *Tannhäuser* (1845) Wagner aimed to unite the two elements which he had developed separately in *Der fliegende Holländer* and *Rienzi*, to clothe the dramatic idea of redemption in the garments of grand opera. His poem combined materials from a number of different sources, treating of the medieval legend of the knight Tannhäuser, who sojourned with Venus in her magic mountain and later went on a pilgrimage to Rome to obtain absolution, which was refused him: "Sooner will this dry staff blossom than your sins be forgiven," he was told by the Pope. But the staff miraculously blossomed, a sign of God's mercy. To this story Wagner added the episode of the Song Contest and the figure of Elizabeth, through whose pure love and intercession the miracle of salvation was effected. All this is cast in the traditional outlines of an opera with the customary theatrical devices. The division into numbers is still clear, though with more sweep and less rigidity than in the earlier works There are solos (for example, Tannhäuser's song in praise of Venus, Elizabeth's "Dich, teure Halle," her Prayer, Wolfram's song to the Evening Star), ensembles (especially the end of Act II), choruses (for example, the Pilgrims' Choruses for men's voices,[3] a favorite medium in nineteenth-century opera), the Venusberg ballet, and the brilliant crowd scene of the Entrance of the Knights and the Song Contest in Act II. Numbers such as these, treated with Wagner's mastery of stage effect and in a style that audiences could easily understand, assured the success of *Tannhäuser*, though the new work did not arouse enthusiasm equal to that which had greeted *Rienzi*. Yet even

[3] Sopranos and altos are added for climactic effect at the end of Act III.

where *Tannhäuser* is most operatic, it does not sacrifice the drama to outward show. The spectacular scenes are connected with the action and have a serious dramatic purpose; indeed, there are few operas in which form and content are so well balanced.

The portions of *Tannhäuser* that listeners failed to comprehend were just those which were most important in Wagner's estimation, and most significant in view of his later development, namely the recitatives, of which Tannhäuser's narrative of his pilgrimage to Rome (Act III) is the principal example. Here is a long solo containing some of the central incidents of the drama; it is certainly not an aria with regular melody and balanced phrases, but neither is it recitative of the neutral, declamatory type found in earlier operas (and elsewhere in Wagner also). It is a melody strictly molded to the text, a semirealistic declamation of the words combined with expression of their content by means of a flexible line supported by an equally important harmonic structure. In addition to providing the harmony, the orchestra has certain musical motifs which, by reason of their character and their association with the text, are heard as a commentary on the words, or as a further and purely musical expression of their meaning (Example 96). This is the style which came to prevail almost exclusively in Wagner's later works, and to which he gave the name *Sprechgesang*, that is, "speech song." It was not entirely new with Wagner—Weber had done something similar in *Euryanthe*—but he used it so extensively, wielded it so effectively, and built it so firmly into his whole theory of the music drama that he perhaps rightly ranks as its discoverer. To the original singers of *Tannhäuser*, as well as to the audience, it was a mystery. Even the famous soprano Wilhelmine Schröder-Devrient, Wagner's staunch friend from the beginning and one from whom he received much inspiration, confessed that she could not make head or tail of her role of Venus; and the tenor Tichatschek, though equally devoted to the composer, had not the slightest perception of his new dramatic aims. Little by little, however, a small section of the Dresden public began to sympathize; this group—which, significantly, included few professional musicians—was the nucleus of the future Wagner cult.

The essential dramatic idea in *Tannhäuser* is, of course, the opposition of the world of sensual ecstasy and the world of ascetic renunciation, the former represented by Venus and her court, the latter by Elizabeth and the Pilgrims. Both Wagner's expansion of the Venusberg ballet for

400 THE NINETEENTH CENTURY

the disastrous Paris performances of 1861 and his revision of the last finale to include the actual appearance of Venus served to accentuate the contrast between the two basic ideas of the opera. Wagner's music embodies the character of each of these worlds with an imaginative grasp and intensity of utterance which is more remarkable than anything else in the whole score. His greatness as a composer lies just in this power of evoking in the listener's mind such conceptions, in all their emotional depth and complexity, by means of music in which every detail is consciously or unconsciously directed toward the expressive purpose. In pursuit of his aims, Wagner found it necessary to rely more and more on the resources of harmony and instrumental color; as the aria diminished in importance, the orchestra rose correspondingly. This is evident in *Tannhäuser* both in the thematic importance of the accompaniments and in the separate orchestral pieces. The introduction to the third act, depicting Tannhäuser's pilgrimage, is one of those short symphonic poems of which there were to be more in the later works— Siegfried's Rhine Journey in *Götterdämmerung*, for example, or the Good Friday music in *Parsifal*. The overture to *Tannhäuser* is a complete composition in itself, and, like those of *Der fliegende Holländer* or *Die Meistersinger*, a synopsis of the larger dramatic and musical form to follow.

It has been noted [4] that the first six completed operas of Wagner are grouped in pairs, and that within each pair, each member is in many ways complementary to the other. This is especially noticeable with *Tannhäuser* and *Lohengrin*. The latter was composed in the years 1846–48, though not performed until 1850 at Weimar, under Liszt's direction. Its sources, like those of *Tannhäuser*, are found in folklore and Germanic legend, but the treatment now is considerably different. In *Lohengrin* Wagner is less concerned with the tale itself or the historical setting and more with the timeless significance of the events portrayed. The characters, though adequately depicted as human, are at the same time agents or personifications of forces the conflict of which makes the drama. Thus Lohengrin may be said to represent divine love and its longing for reciprocal love and faith from mankind, while Elsa represents human nature incapable of the necessary unquestioning trust. Whatever meaning one may see in the story, the necessity of some interpretation in the sense suggested is unavoidable. In keeping with

[4] See Chamberlain, *Das Drama Richard Wagners.*

this view of the drama, the musical setting of *Lohengrin* is altogether less spectacular than that of *Tannhäuser*; there are no sensational contrasts, and an extraordinary unity of mood prevails throughout. The system of reminiscence motifs is still further developed, not only in extent but also in the changed function of the motifs themselves : they are no longer used simply to recall earlier scenes and actions but to symbolize situations or abstract ideas. For example, the motif which some analysts label "the forbidden question," first sung by Lohengrin as he lays the command on Elsa never to inquire his name or country, is a complete, periodic, eight-measure theme (Example 97). It recurs, in whole or in

### *Lohengrin*, Act I

EXAMPLE 97                                                                            WAGNER

Nie sollst du mich be - fra-gen,    noch Wi - ssens Sor - ge  tra-gen, wo-

- her  ich  kam  der  Fahrt,    noch wie  mein  Nam'  und  Art!

part, wherever throughout the opera the situation touches pointedly on this prohibition : in the introduction to Act II, during the dialogue between Ortrud and Friedrich in the first scene, in the second scene at Ortrud's hypocritical warning to Elsa against the "unknown" knight, at Elsa's sign of doubt in the last scene of the act, and in the closing orchestral cadence; it comes into the duet of Act III, rises to full force as Elsa's fatal question is asked, echoes again at the end of this scene, and is heard once more at Elsa's entrance in the last finale. Other characteristic motifs are used in a similar way. The principle is not yet that of the *Ring*, where the motifs are shorter, essentially harmonic and rhythmic rather than melodic, and employed continuously in a symphonic web; nevertheless, *Lohengrin* carries the practice further than any preceding opera and clearly points the way to Wagner's later style.

From the formal point of view *Lohengrin* has shed many traces of the traditional division into numbers, as well as much of the distinction between aria and recitative. The new free declamation is the normal style in this work, except in a few places like Elsa's "Einsam in trüben Tagen"—and even here the three strophes of the solo are separated by choruses and recitatives—Lohengrin's narrative in Act III, the Bridal Chorus, and the duet following this. The colorful orchestral prelude to Act III is often played as a separate concert number. The prelude to the opera, unlike the overture to *Tannhäuser*, is in one mood and movement, representing (according to Wagner's statement) the descent and return of the Holy Grail, the type of Lohengrin's own mission, as we hear when the same themes and harmonies accompany his narrative in Act III. The A major tonality of the prelude is associated with Lohengrin throughout the opera, just as the key of F-sharp minor is assigned to Ortrud and, as a rule, the flat keys to Elsa. The harmony of *Lohengrin* is remarkably diatonic; there is very little chromaticism of the sort found in the middle section of the Pilgrims' Chorus or the Evening Star aria in *Tannhäuser*. The orchestration likewise contrasts with that of *Tannhäuser*: instead of treating the instruments as a homogeneous group, Wagner by preference divides them into antiphonal choirs, often with the violins subdivided and the wood-wind section expanded so as to make possible a whole chord of three or four tones in a single color. The effect, while less brilliant than in *Tannhäuser*, is at the same time richer and more subtle. Even in the last scene of Act II, showing the dawn of day heralded by trumpet fanfares, and the procession to the minster, the sonority is restrained in comparison with the usual grand-opera treatment of such places.

The skillfully written choruses in *Lohengrin* are an important musical and dramatic factor. For the most part the chorus is treated either as realistically entering into the action, or else as an "articulate spectator" in the manner of Greek tragedy (especially in the second scene of Act I and the finale of Act III). The prominence of the chorus may have been suggested to Wagner by his study of Gluck's *Iphigénie en Aulide*, which he revised for performances at Dresden in 1847.

*Lohengrin* is generally regarded as the last of the German romantic operas. It has many resemblances to Weber's *Euryanthe*, not only in the plot and characters [5] but also in the continuity of the music, the style of declamation, and the use of recurring motifs. It was Wagner's last dramatic composition for five years, or until he began work on the music

[5] The basic plot—the trial of a wife's love—is common to the two works. The character of Elsa corresponds to Euryanthe, Telramund and Ortrud to Lysiart and Eglantine; the figure of the good king is also in both. Act I of *Lohengrin*, as Bekker points out (*Richard Wagner*, chap. 6), was doubtless also influenced by Marschner's *Templer und Jüdin*.

of *Das Rheingold* in 1853.[6] In 1849, as a result of quarrels with his superiors and a multitude of other difficulties climaxing in his active participation in the revolutionary uprising of May of that year, Wagner was obliged to flee from Dresden. He sought refuge at Weimar with Liszt, who aided him to escape to Switzerland. Settled at Zurich, Wagner found leisure to clarify in his own mind the new ideas on music and the theatre which had already been occupying him at Dresden, and of which some intimations may be found in his earlier operas, *Lohengrin* especially. The result of these cogitations was a series of essays, including the important *Oper und Drama* ("Opera and Drama," published in 1851), a systematic account of the philosophy and technical methods by which all his subsequent works were to be governed. A knowledge of *Oper und Drama* is indispensable for anyone who seriously desires to understand these works—the *Ring, Tristan, Die Meistersinger*, and *Parsifal*—even though Wagner's practice is not always consistent with his theories.[7]

The doctrines of *Oper und Drama* are best exemplified in *Der Ring des Nibelungen* ("The Ring of the Nibelungs"), which consists of four consecutive dramas : *Das Rheingold* ("The Rhine Gold"), shorter than the others, and a prelude to them; *Die Walküre* ("The Valkyrie"); *Siegfried*; and *Götterdämmerung* ("The Twilight of the Gods"). Altogether, the composition of the *Ring* occupied twenty years of Wagner's life. Its subject combines two distinct Germanic myth cycles, the story of Siegfried and that of the downfall of the gods. Wagner in 1848 wrote a drama, *Siegfrieds Tod* ("The Death of Siegfried"), which he expected to set to music at once; but as the subject grew in his mind, he felt the need for another drama to precede this, and wrote *Der junge Siegfried* ("Young Siegfried") in 1851. The work expanded still further : *Die Walküre* was required to lead up to *Der junge Siegfried,* and *Das Rheingold* as a general prelude to the whole. These two poems, in this order, were written in 1852, after which *Der junge Siegfried* and *Siegfrieds Tod* were revised as the present *Siegfried* and *Götterdämmerung* respectively, the whole text being completed by the end of 1852.[8] Mean-

[6] The short musical sketches made in 1850 for *Siegfrieds Tod* are similar in style to the *Lohengrin* music. See Newman, *Wagner* II, 159–61.

[7] The English translation of *Oper und Drama* by Edwin Evans is recommended. There is a good summary in G. Abraham, *A Hundred Years of Music.*

[8] On the changes made in the earlier poems, and some resulting inconsistencies in the present text, see Newman, *Wagner* II, chap. 17; on the symbolism, Overhoff, *Richard Wagners germanisch-christlicher Mythos.*

while some sketches for the music had been made; composition was begun in 1853, and by 1857 the setting was completed through the second act of *Siegfried*. After an interim during which he composed *Tristan* and *Die Meistersinger*, Wagner resumed work on the *Ring* in 1865, though *Götterdämmerung* was not finished until nine years later. The first performances of the whole tetralogy took place at Bayreuth in 1876.

The story of the *Ring* is so familiar—or, at least, is so easily accessible in popular books of all sorts, not to mention the scores themselves—that there is no need to recapitulate it here. The material is taken not from history (as in *Rienzi*), or folklore (as in *Die Feen*), or even legend (as in *Der fliegende Holländer* and *Tannhäuser*), but from mythology. The reason is not primarily that the myth is entertaining, but that it is meaningful. According to Wagner the myth presents, in the simplest, most inclusive, and most concentrated form imaginable, the interplay of eternal forces affecting the relation of men to God, to nature, and to each other in society—in other words, living, eternal issues of religious, social, and economic importance, with which it is the duty of art consciously to deal. These issues are set before us in the myth, and consequently in Wagner's *Ring*, by means of symbols, either objects (the Gold, Valhalla, the Sword) or persons (Wotan, Siegfried, Brünnhilde). It is the nature of a symbol to be capable of various interpretations; and although Wagner labored hard, both in the poem itself and in other writings, to make clear his own interpretation of the *Ring*, he did not fully succeed —partly because of some inconsistencies in his thinking and the obscurity of his literary style, but more because the symbols were so ambiguous that it was impossible to make a single definitive explanation of them. Many writers have tried to do so, and have argued vehemently, each according to his own convictions, for or against the doctrines conceived to be embodied in the *Ring*. Still others regard any intentional preaching in art as either of no importance or else downright vicious and inartistic. There is no need at this day to add anything more to the enormous mass of controversial literature about Wagner. It is not within the scope of a book like this to investigate the alleged effects of his teaching, in the *Ring* or elsewhere, on European politics.[9] That he did teach —that his views of art and the theatre impelled him in his operas to

---

[9] An introduction to this subject, with bibliographies, may be found in Viereck's *Metapolitics from the Romantics to Hitler*.

assume the role of prophet as well as musician—is a fact, whether one approves it or not; but all that concerns us here is the consequences of that fact in his art work itself.

It is not easy to dramatize abstractions. In the *Ring*, Wagner felt obliged to introduce some explanatory passages which slow down or interrupt the action of the play—for example, the long dialogue between Wotan and Brünnhilde in the second scene of Act II of *Die Walküre*. For the benefit of opera audiences, who are not particularly interested in metaphysics, these passages are often cut or shortened in performance. The same is true of the many repetitions of the story which occur from time to time, and other apparent digressions. All these matters have their justification, however, in Wagner's theories; moreover, the leisurely pace of the action suggests the tempo of the long medieval epic poems from which the incidents were taken. Another interesting reminiscence of these poetic models is Wagner's employment of *Stabreim*, or alliteration, instead of the more modern device of end rhymes :

> Gab sein Gold mir Macht ohne Mass,
> nun zeug' sein Zauber Tod dem der ihn trägt !
> (As its gold gave me might without measure,
> Now may its magic deal death to him who wears it !)
> *Das Rheingold*, scene 4

The relation of music to drama is one of the subjects on which Wagner discourses in much detail in his writings. The first proposition of *Oper und Drama* is : "The error in opera hitherto consisted in this, that a means of expression (the music) has been made an end, while the end itself (the drama) has been made the means." [10] It does not follow, however, that now poetry is to be made primary and music secondary, but that both are to grow organically out of the necessities of dramatic expression, not being brought together, but existing as two aspects of one and the same thing. Other arts as well (the dance, architecture, painting) are to be included in this union, making the music drama a Gesamtkunstwerk, that is, a composite or total art work. This is not, in Wagner's view, a limitation of any of the arts; on the contrary, only in such a union can the full possibilities of each be realized. The "music of the future," then, will exist not in isolation as heretofore, but as one aspect of the Gesamtkunstwerk, in which situation it will develop new

---

[10] "Oper und Drama," in *Gesammelte Schriften* III, 231 ; cf. J. M. Stein, *Richard Wagner and the Synthesis of the Arts*.

technical and expressive resources and will progress beyond the point to which it has now arrived, a point beyond which is cannot substantially progress in any other way.

This view was the consequence of a typical nineteenth-century philosophy. Wagner regarded the history of music as a process of evolution which must inevitably continue in a certain direction. The theory that the line of progress involved the end of music as a separate art and its absorption into a community of the arts is not without analogy to the communistic and socialistic doctrines of the period, with their emphasis on the absorption of the interests of the individual into those of the community as a whole.[11] It is not surprising that some such view of the future of music should have arisen in the second half of the nineteenth century. It is plain enough to us now that the resources of music—that is, of the kind of music which had been growing up since Beethoven—were approaching their utmost limits at this time, and that these limits were in fact reached in the works of Wagner, Brahms, R. Strauss, and Mahler. It has been the mission of twentieth-century composers to recognize this situation and to create new musical styles, much as the composers of the seventeenth century had to do after the culmination of sixteenth-century polyphony in the works of Palestrina, Byrd, and Lassus. In discerning the approaching end of a musical style, therefore, Wagner was right. His error was in postulating the Gesamtkunstwerk as the only possible road for the future.

Wagner held that music in itself was the immediate expression of feeling, but that it could not designate the particular object toward which feeling was directed. Hence, for him the inner action of the drama existed in the music, while the function of word and gesture was to make definite the outer action.[12] This aesthetic is the theoretical basis of many features of the *Ring* and later works. For example, since the inner action is regarded as being always on a plane of feeling where music is appropriate and necessary, there is no spoken dialogue or simple recitative. Moreover, the inner action (unlike the outer) is continuous; hence the music is continuous. (In this theory, intermissions between the acts and the performance of the *Ring* on four separate evenings instead of all at once can only be regarded as one of Wagner's reluctant concessions to human frailty.) Transitions from one scene to the next are made by means of orchestral interludes when necessary, and within each scene the music has a continuity of which the most obvious technical sign is

[11] Cf. Barzun, *Darwin, Marx, Wagner.*

[12] Cf. Schopenhauer, *Die Welt als Wille und Vorstellung* I, Book III, sec. 52; and Vol. II ("Ergänzungen"), chap. 39.

the avoidance of perfect cadences. Continuity in music, however, is more than avoidance of perfect cadences. It is a result of the musical form as a whole, and since form in Wagner (as in any composer) is partly a function of harmonic procedure, this is an appropriate place to consider these two subjects together.

The statements most frequently made about Wagner's harmony are (1) that it is "full of chromatics" and (2) that the music "continually modulates." Both statements are true but superficial. Much of the chromaticism in the earlier works (for example, in the original version of *Tannhäuser*) is merely an embellishment of the melodic line or occurs incidentally in the course of modulating sequences. Many of the chromatic passages in the *Ring*, such as the magic sleep motif, are found in the midst of long diatonic sections. The impression that Wagner continually modulates is due in part to a short-breathed method of analysis based on a narrow conception of tonality, which tends to see a modulation at every dominant-tonic progression and, preoccupied with such details, overlooks the broader harmonic scheme. A more comprehensive and illuminating view is set forth by Alfred Lorenz in his four studies entitled *Das Geheimnis der Form bei Richard Wagner* ("The Secret of Form in Richard Wagner"). Lorenz, in the enthusiasm of discovery, occasionally strains the facts to make them fit his theory; nevertheless he does succeed in showing that Wagner's music dramas are cast in definite musical forms, and that the formal clarity is evident not only in each work as a whole but also in the constituent sections, down to the smallest. The structure of the music is inseparable from that of the drama, and one of its fundamental elements is the key scheme. *Das Rheingold*, for example, is regarded as a large a–b–a form in D-flat, with an introduction in E-flat (dominant of the dominant); D-flat is also the tonality of the *Ring* as a whole. *Tristan* is likewise in three-part form, Acts I and III corresponding, and Act II being the "b" section—though here the correspondence is one of themes and dramatic action, not of tonality. The three acts of *Die Meistersinger* in the same way make a huge a–a–b form, the first two being equal in length and the third as long as the first two together. These two forms, the *Bogen* (a–b–a, literally "bow") and *Bar* (a–a–b),[13] are frequently exemplified also in the structure of the

---

[13] The Bar, consisting of two *Stollen* (a a) and an *Abgesang* (b), was the favorite form of the German minnesinger. It is well illustrated in both versions of Walther's "Preislied," and explained by Hans Sachs (see *Die Meistersinger*, Act III, sc. 2).

scenes and smaller subdivisions : thus the fifteenth "period" of Act II of *Siegfried* (three measures before "Noch einmal, liebes Vöglein" to change of signature to four sharps "nun sing") is an a–b–a or Bogen in E minor (18+30+21 measures) and the introduction to Act II of *Die Walküre* is a Bar in A minor (introduction, 14 measures; two *Stollen*, 20+19 measures; *Abgesang*, 20 measures). Other form types (strophic, rondo) also appear, and many units are composed of two or more of the basic types in various modifications and combinations.[14] One may not choose to follow Lorenz in every detail, and it would certainly be in order to question some of his interpretations of the basic formal schemes; but taken as a whole, it is impossible in the face of his demonstration not to be convinced of the essential orderliness, at once minute and all-embracing, of the musical cosmos of the *Ring*, as well as of *Tristan, Die Meistersinger*, and *Parsifal*. It is an orderliness not derived at second hand from the text but inhering in the musical structure itself. Was Wagner fully aware of it? One is tempted to think not, since he says almost nothing about it in his writings. Yet whether conscious or un-conscious, the sheer grasp and creation of such huge and complex organisms is a matter for wonder. It may be unnecessary to remark that the fact (if it is a fact) that Wagner's creative processes were largely instinctive or unconscious does not of itself invalidate any analysis of his music. It is no essential part of a composer's business to be aware, in an analytical sense, of everything he is doing.

Within the larger frameworks of order, and subsidiary to them, take place the various harmonic procedures which have given rise to Wagner's reputation : modulations induced by enharmonic changes in chromatically altered chords and forwarded by modulating sequences; the interchangeable use of major and minor modes and the frequency of the mediants and the flat supertonic as goals of modulation; the determination of chord sequences by chromatic progression of individual voices; the presence of "harmonic parentheses" within a section, related to the tonality of the whole as auxiliary notes or appoggiaturas are related to the fundamental harmony of the chord with which they occur; the systematic treatment of sevenths and even ninths as consonant chords; the resolution of dominants to chords other than the tonic; the

[14] Lorenz's system of analysis cannot be adequately illustrated without going into greater detail than is possible here. See his outline of Act I of *Die Walküre* in Abraham, *A Hundred Years of Music*, Part II, and cf. A. E. F. Dickinson, "The Structural Methods of *The Ring*."

combination of melodies in a contrapuntal tissue; and finally, the frequent suspensions and appoggiaturas in the various melodic lines, which contribute as much as any single factor to the peculiar romantic, Wagnerian, "longing" quality of the harmony—a quality heard in perfection in the prelude to *Tristan und Isolde*.

While the musical forms of Wagner's dramas are determined in part by the harmonic structure, a more obvious role is played by the continuous recurrence and variation of a limited number of distinct musical units generally know as leitmotifs or leading motifs. The term "leitmotif" is not Wagner's but he did use the apparently synonymous word *Hauptmotiv* (principal motif). It seems likely that Wagner suggested this word, as well as the system of analyzing his music dramas in terms of motifs, to Heinrich Porges, whose book on *Tristan und Isolde* written in 1866–77 (though not published before 1902) uses this method. The analysis of Wagner's music in terms of leitmotifs was popularized by Hans von Wolzogen, first editor of the *Bayreuther Blätter* and author of many "guides" to the music dramas.[15]

Different analysts distinguish, and variously name, seventy to two hundred leitmotifs in the *Ring*. Each is regarded as the focal point of expression of a certain dramatic idea, with which it remains associated throughout the tetralogy. The clue to the association of motif and idea is to be found at the first appearance of the former; for example, the Valhalla motif is first heard at the opening of the second scene of *Das Rheingold* as the curtain rises to reveal the castle of Valhalla. Here, as usual at the first statement of a motif, Wagner repeats and spins out the phrase so as to impress it on the memory; moreover, there is a premonition of the Valhalla motif at the end of the preceding scene, where its derivation from the Ring motif is obvious. The motifs are short and of pronounced individual character; they are often suggested by a pictorial image (as the fire motifs), or by association (as the trumpet figure for the sword motif), but each aims to convey not merely a picture but also the essence of the idea for which the visible symbol stands. In this capacity the motifs may recur, not simply as musical labels, but whenever the idea recurs or is suggested in the course of the drama, forming a

---

[15] See for example his *Thematischer Leitfaden durch die Musik zu Richard Wagners Festspiel Der Ring des Nibelungen* (1876) and later similar works; further in Newman, *Wagner* III, 382–83; cf. also the references in note 1 on page 392. On the earlier history of recurring themes in opera, see G. F. Schmidt, *Die frühdeutsche Oper* II, 255–80; Bücken, *Der heroische Stil in der Oper, passim.*

symphonic web which corresponds in theory, and generally also in fact, to the dramatic web of the action. The connection between the musical forms so evolved and the dramatic forms is thus complete. The motifs may be contrapuntally combined, or varied, developed, and transformed in accordance with the changing fortunes of the idea they represent. Relationship of ideas may be shown by thematic relationships among the motifs (Example 98), though probably some of the resemblances are

EXAMPLE 98          Motifs from the *Ring*

not intentional. Altogether, the statement, recurrence, variation, development, and transformation of the motifs is analogous to the working out of musical material in a symphony.

Since the inner meaning of the drama is found in music, it follows in Wagner's theory that the orchestra is the basic medium rather than the voices. In his phrase, the words "float like a ship on the sea of orchestral harmony." Only rarely are the leitmotifs sung. As a rule, the voice will make a free counterpoint to the instrumental melody. The voice part, however, is always itself melodic, never merely declamatory as in recitativo secco; its line is so arranged as not only to give the correct declamation but also to reproduce the accent, tempo, and inflections appropriate to each character. Textual repetition is avoided. In theory there are to be no ensembles, especially in the old-fashioned sense where some voices are used only to supply a harmonic background; but this rule Wagner relaxed on occasion, as in the finale of Act II of *Götter-dämmerung* or the quintet in *Die Meistersinger*. Of Wagner's genius as an orchestrator there is no need to speak here. His music is the realization of the full, rich, romantic sound ideal of the nineteenth century. Its peculiar texture is determined in large part by the nature of the melodic lines : long phrased, avoiding periodic cadential points (this in contrast to *Lohengrin* and earlier works), so designed that every note tends to move on without ever quite coming to rest.[16] The full resources of sym-phonic style—counterpoint, orchestral color, and formal structure—are invoked. This in itself was not new in the history of opera, for many earlier composers (for example, Monteverdi in *Orfeo*) had done the same. But Wagner, besides having the immensely developed instru-mental resources of the nineteenth century at his disposal, was con-scious as no earlier composer had been of the drama as the generating force in the whole plan; and he was original in placing the orchestra at the center, with the essential drama going on in the music, while words and gesture furnished only the outer happenings. From this point of view his music dramas may be regarded as symphonic poems the program of which, instead of being printed and read, is explained and acted out by persons on the stage.

Wagner despised "opera," yet his music dramas have been as popu-lar as any operas. What is the source of their appeal? Primarily, of course, the music itself. Yet there are certain other factors which have at different times made for popular success in opera. One of these factors in the nineteenth century was the appeal to national pride, as in some of Weber's and Verdi's works. Such an appeal is indirectly present in most of Wagner's operas insofar as they are founded on Germanic myths or

[16] This is one meaning of Wagner's term "unending melody"; it has other mean-ings as well. See Lorenz, *Geheimnis der Form* I, 61–70; Kurth, *Romantische Har-monik* (2d ed.), Part 7.

legends; but this kind of nationalism is of little importance, since Wagner thought of his dramas as universal, dealing with what he called the "purely human," not limited to Germans in the sense in which *Der Freischütz* was. Even *Die Meistersinger*, for all its reference to "holy German art," is not narrow in its patriotism or jingoistic in spirit.

Another and more general means of popular appeal in opera is stage spectacle. Wagner availed himself of this resource unstintedly, though always maintaining that every one of his effects grew of necessity out of the drama itself. It would be difficult to think of any beguiling, eye-catching, fanciful, sensational device in the whole history of opera from Monteverdi to Meyerbeer which Wagner did not appropriate and use with expert showmanship somewhere in his works. One has only to look at the poem of the *Ring* to see how prominent is this element; it has a large place also in *Parsifal*. In *Tristan* and *Die Meistersinger*, however, it is less in evidence, for these are dramas of human character and as such appeal directly to fundamental human emotions with less need of spectacular stage effects. This quality of direct, human appeal is heard at only a few places in the *Ring*, as in the love scenes of Siegmund and Sieglinde (*Die Walküre*, Act I), of Siegfried and Brünnhilde (*Siegfried*, Act III), or in the scene of Wotan's farewell to Brünnhilde (*Die Walküre*, Act III); and when Wagner, like Wotan in this scene, put aside his concern with godhood to create the truly memorable characters of Walther, Eva, Hans Sachs, Isolde, and Tristan, he created two works that are likely to outlive all the pageantry and symbolism of the *Ring*.

The poem of *Tristan und Isolde* was begun at Zurich in 1857 and the score finished in 1859. It is often regarded as a monument to Wagner's love for Mathilde Wesendonck, the wife of one of his most devoted friends during his years of exile. Newman sensibly points out, however, that this view probably confuses cause and effect, that Wagner did not compose *Tristan* because he was in love with Mathilde, but rather that he was in love because he was composing *Tristan*. Either way, the matter is not important. In 1857–58 Wagner composed five songs to poems by Mathilde; two of these (*Träume* and *Im Treibhaus*) are made up of thematic material used in *Tristan*, and Wagner later described them as "studies" for the opera. *Tristan* was undertaken at a time when there appeared no prospect of ever bringing the *Ring* to performance, and it was Wagner's hope that a less exacting music drama might have rather better prospects of success. But by now his ideas of what consti-

tuted a practicable work had so far outgrown the actual practice of the
theatres that *Tristan* for many years could not be produced. After more
than seventy rehearsals at Vienna in 1862–63 it was abandoned as
impossible. Finally in 1864 the young king Ludwig of Bavaria sum-
moned Wagner to Munich and placed almost unlimited resources at his
disposal. After careful preparation, the first performance took place at
Munich on June 10, 1865, under the direction of Hans von Bülow.

The legend of Tristan and Isolde is probably of Celtic origin. In the
early thirteenth century it was embodied by Gottfried of Strassburg in
a long epic poem, which was Wagner's principal source for his drama.
Wagner's changes consisted in compressing the action, eliminating nonessential personages (for example, the original second Isolde, "of the
white hands"), and simplifying the motives. Some details were doubtless
borrowed from other sources : the extinction of the torch in Act II from
the story of *Hero and Leander*, the dawning of day at the end of the love
scene from Shakespeare's *Romeo and Juliet*, and Tristan's delirium in
Act III from Matthew Arnold's poem; the love duet in the second act
has some points reminiscent of a dialogue between Faust and Helena
in the second part of Goethe's drama and the figure of Brangäne as
watcher was perhaps suggested by Goethe's Lynceus.[17] The prominence
of the motif of death, the yearning for fulfillment of love in release and
annihilation which broods over the whole drama, were at least partly
due to Wagner's absorption in the philosophy of Schopenhauer, with
whose works he had first become acquainted in 1852.[18] But whatever
the contributions of others, *Tristan und Isolde* is Wagner's own. It is
owing to him, and to him alone, that this is now one of the great love
stories, living in the imagination of millions along with the tales of
Romeo and Juliet, Paolo and Francesca, Launcelot and Guinevere.

The peculiar strength of the drama arises from the fact that external
events are simplified to the utmost, so that the action is almost all inner,
and consequently expressed almost wholly in music. The words themselves often melt into music, losing their very character as intelligible
language, nearly superfluous in many places where the plane of expres-

[17] *Faust*, Part II, lines 9372–9418, 11288–11337. These literary derivations are
suggested with some diffidence. The torch episode is found in Méhul's *Mélidor et
Phrosine*; the watcher is a common figure in German medieval love poems. Cf.
Loomis, ed., *The Romance of Tristram and Ysolt by Thomas of Britain*, introduction.
[18] There are echoes here also of Novalis and F. von Schlegel. Cf. Mann, "Leiden
und Grösse Richard Wagners," in his *Leiden und Grösse der Meister*, pp. 130–32.

sion is purely that of the emotions—as, for example, in Isolde's "Liebestod" at the end of Act III. "Every theory was quite forgotten," wrote Wagner; "during the working out I myself became aware how far I had outsoared my system." [19]

The three leading ideas of the drama—love, night, and death—are inseparable, but each one in turn is especially emphasized in each of the three acts. The magic potion of Act I is, in Wagner's version, purely a symbol, figuring forth the moment of realization of a love already existing but unacknowledged. Isolde's extinction of the torch is the symbol of Act II; the ecstatic greeting of the lovers leads into the duet "Descend upon us, night of love," followed by the love-death music with the words "O could we but die thus together, endless, never to awaken!" The climax of the whole scene is in the song of Brangäne, off stage: "Lonely I watch in the night; you that are lost in the dream of love, heed the lonely one's call: sorrow comes with awakening. Beware! O beware! For the night soon passes." Few artists have so poignantly expressed what many human beings have experienced, the unutterably sorrowful realization in the midst of happiness that this moment cannot last. There is a comparable passage in the *Arabian Nights*:

Presently one of them arose and set meat before me and I ate and they ate with me; whilst others warmed water and washed my hands and feet and changed my clothes, and others made ready sherbets and gave us to drink; and all gathered round me being full of joy and gladness at my coming. Then they sat down and conversed with me till night-fall, when five of them arose and laid the trays and spread them with flowers and fragrant herbs and fruits, fresh and dried, and confections in profusion. At last they brought out a fine wine-service with rich old wine; and we sat down to drink and some sang songs and others played the lute and psaltery and recorders and other instruments, and the bowl went merrily round. Hereupon such gladness possessed me that I forgot the sorrows of the world one and all and said, "This is indeed life; O sad that 'tis fleeting." [20]

The doom fated from the beginning is fulfilled. Tristan, reproached by King Mark, mortally wounded by Melot, is carried home to his castle of Kareol and dies as Isolde comes to him bringing Mark's forgiveness. The love-death of Isolde herself brings the tragedy to an end.

Volumes could be, and have been, written about the music of *Tristan und Isolde*. The extreme simplification and condensation of the action,

[19] "Zukunftsmusik," in *Gesammelte Schriften* VII, 119.
[20] *Tale of the Third Kalendar* (Burton's translation).

the reduction of the essential characters to only two, and the treatment of these two as bearers of a single all-dominating mood conduce to unity of musical effect and at the same time permit the greatest possible freedom for development of all the musical elements, unchecked by elaborate paraphernalia or the presence of antimusical factors in the libretto. There are comparatively few leitmotifs, and many of the principal ones are so much alike that it is hard to distinguish and label them clearly. The dominant mood is conveyed in a chromatic style of writing which is no longer either a mere decorative adjunct to, or a deliberate contrast with, a fundamentally diatonic idiom, but which is actually the norm, so much so that the few diatonic motifs are felt as deliberate departures, "specters of day" intruding into the all-prevailing night of the love drama. It is impossible here to enter into a comprehensive examination of the technical aspects of this chromaticism;[21] we can only note that history has shown the "*Tristan* style" to be the classical example of the use of a consistent chromatic technique within the limits of the tonal system of the eighteenth and nineteenth centuries. It was not only the climax of all romantic striving in this direction but also the point of departure for Wagner's own later experiments in *Parsifal*, for the more sophisticated, external, ironic chromaticism of Richard Strauss, and for the twelve-tone system of Schoenberg, the conclusion of the whole style. The power of the *Tristan* chromaticism comes from its being founded in tonality. A feature of it is the ambiguity of the chords, the constant, immanent, felt possibility that almost any chord may resolve in almost any one of a dozen different directions. Yet this very ambiguity could not exist except for underlying tonal relations, the general tendencies of certain chord progressions within the tonal system. The continuous conflict between what *might be*, harmonically, and what actually *is*, makes the music apt at suggesting the inner state of mingled insecurity and passionate longing that pervades the drama. This emotional suggestiveness is accompanied throughout by a luxuriance of purely sensuous effect, a reveling in tone qualities and tone combinations as if for their own sake, evident in both the subdued richness of the orchestration and the whole harmonic fabric.

Such matters as these are felt by even the casual listener to *Tristan und Isolde*. What is less obvious, though it may be dimly sensed, is the

[21] This task has been performed, with great thoroughness and insight, by E. Kurth in his *Romantische Harmonik und ihre Krise in Wagners Tristan*.

complete formal perfection of the work. Here again the reader must be
referred for details to the epoch-making study of Lorenz.[22] The close
correspondence of Acts I and III, with the resulting Bogen form of the
opera as a whole, has already been mentioned. As to the tonality, Lorenz
holds it to be E major—beginning in the subdominant (A minor) and
ending in the dominant (B major). The tonic itself, in this view, is
almost never sounded, this being at the same time an instance of the
persistent avoidance of resolution in the harmony and a symbol of the
nature of the love of Tristan and Isolde which attains its satisfaction only
in the ideal, not the actual world. The only extended E major portion
of the opera is the scene of Tristan's vision of Isolde in Act III. The
complete first theme as announced in the prelude (measures 1–17) recurs
only three times in the course of the opera, once at the climax of each
act: at the drinking of the potion in Act I, after Mark's question near
the end of Act II, and at Tristan's death in Act III; its function is thus
that of a refrain for the whole work. The continuity and formal symmetry, demonstrable in full only by a detailed analysis, are neatly
epitomized by the fact that the opening chromatic motif of the prelude
receives its final resolution in the closing measures of the last act
(Example 99).

*Tristan und Isolde*

EXAMPLE 99    WAGNER
(a) Prelude.    (b) End of Act III

The score of *Tristan* was completed in 1859. After an unhappy
season in Paris, marked by the scandalous rejection of the revised *Tannhäuser* at the Opéra (March, 1861), Wagner lived for a year and a half
in Vienna. With the failure of prospects for performing *Tristan* there,
his fortunes reached their lowest ebb. His dramatic rescue by the enthusiastic King Ludwig of Bavaria brought happier times, but six
months after the successful first performance of *Tristan* Wagner was

[22] *Das Geheimnis der Form,* II.

compelled to leave Munich, owing largely to political jealousies on the part of the king's ministers. He found a home at Hof Triebschen near Lucerne, where he remained from 1866 to 1872. His first wife having died in 1866, he married in 1870 Cosima von Bülow, daughter of Liszt and former wife of Hans von Bülow, the pianist and conductor. Wagner's chief activity in the early years at Triebschen was the composition of *Die Meistersinger*.

*Die Meistersinger von Nürnberg* ("The Mastersinger of Nuremberg") had been sketched in 1845, as a kind of comic pendant to *Tannhäuser*. Toward the end of 1861 Wagner planned the work anew,[23] writing some parts of the music before the words. The score was completed in 1867 and first performed at Munich in the following year. The story has for historical background the Mastersinger Guilds of sixteenth-century Nuremberg and their song contests, bound about with traditional rules and customs. Wagner not only incorporated many of these points but also borrowed several names and characters of real Master-singers, notably Hans Sachs, the cobbler-poet-composer who lived 1494–1576.[24] Likewise of historical interest is Wagner's use of an actual Mastersinger melody (the march theme beginning at measure forty-one of the overture), the parody of the Mastersingers' device of *Blumen* or melodic ornaments (literally "flowers") in Beckmesser's songs, and the paraphrase of a poem by the real Hans Sachs (the chorale "Wach' auf !" in Act III). Yet *Die Meistersinger* is not a museum of antiquities but a living, sympathetic re-creation in nineteenth-century terms of an epoch of German musical history, with the literal details of the past illuminated by reference to an ever timely issue, the conflict between tradition and the creative spirit in art. Tradition is represented by the Mastersingers' Guild; the deadly effect of blind adherence to the rules is satirized in the comic figure of Beckmesser, a transparent disguise for the Viennese critic Eduard Hanslick, whose views and influence had made him one of the most persistent and conspicuous of Wagner's opponents. The impetuous, innovating drive of the young artist, impatient of all restraints, is incarnated in the person of Walther von Stolzing, whose conflict with the

[23] On the differences between the two versions, and some minor inconsistencies in the final draft, see Newman, *Wagner* III, 156–64; the various sources of the play are studied in Roethe, "Zum dramatischen Aufbau der Wagnerschen *Meistersinger.*" Cf. also Rayner, *Wagner and Die Meistersinger*; H. Thompson, *Wagner and Wagenseil.*

[24] Many of Sachs's melodies may be found in *Das Singebuch des Adam Puschmann*, ed. by G. Münzer, 1906.

Mastersingers is finally resolved by the wisdom of Hans Sachs, the artist grown wise through experience. Sachs shows that neither tradition nor novelty can suffice by itself; they are reconcilable by one who understands the living spirit behind all rules of art and hence realizes that the new must constantly learn from the old, the old constantly absorb the new. It is probably not fanciful to suggest that in Walther and Hans Sachs Wagner has drawn idealized portraits of two aspects of himself, and that the views of Sachs represent his own mature philosophy of art, set forth with deep insight and poetic beauty. One feature of this philosophy is the professed reliance on the judgment of "the people" as final arbiter in artistic matters. *Das Volk* was one of Wagner's most beloved abstractions, one which he always carefully distinguished from *das Publikum*. One is sometimes tempted to believe that the distinction in his mind was simply between those who liked Wagner's music dramas and those who preferred Rossini or Meyerbeer : the former comprising all the unspoiled virtues and sound instincts of the race, while the latter were unhealthy, misled, or corrupt. Yet there is fundamental truth in the doctrine of the sovereignty of the people in art which *Die Meistersinger* proclaims, so long as one understands "the people" in the democratic sense of the word, not as a mob but as bearers of a profound, partly unconscious instinct which—in the long run—is apt to perceive and judge rightly.

In the last analysis, however, *Die Meistersinger* is not to be regarded as a treatise on the philosophy of art; its teachings are of little importance in comparison to the drama and music themselves. It is by far the most human, the most easily accessible, of all Wagner's works. It has every requirement of good comedy : the simple love story of Walther and Eva, the charming scenes of David and the apprentices, the broadly comic strokes of Beckmesser's serenade and his ridiculous attempt to steal Walther's song for the contest. Above all is to be noted the character of Hans Sachs, Wagner's greatest dramatic figure, who surveys the whole drama from the standpoint of one who through suffering has attained resignation, having learned to find joy in the happiness of others and the triumph of principles.

It is interesting to note that, with such a play as this, Wagner was led to compose a score that more nearly approaches the traditional outlines of opera than any of his works since *Tannhäuser*. To be sure, the principle of symphonic development of a set of leitmotifs is main-

tained, and there is no return to the old-fashioned recitative; but withal
there is an amount of formalization of which the listener is, perhaps,
hardly aware, since it fits so naturally with the dramatic requirements.
Like the Orpheus legend, the *Meistersinger* story is essentially musical
in conception. Within its framework fall the four "arias" of Walther,
the serenade of Beckmesser, Pogner's "Address," David's song in Act III,
and Sachs's two monologues, as well as the formal overture and the
chorale at the beginning of Act I. Even more operatic, though no less
appropriate, are the apprentices' choruses and the huge final ensemble in
Act I, the comic crowd scene at the end of Act II, and the glorified mass
finale with a ballet and choruses in Act III. Then, too, there is the
quintet in the third act, which is as much pure opera as anything in
Donizetti or Verdi : an interpolated number in closed form (a–b–a) and
a remote key (G-flat), which does not directly further the action and has
only a slight thematic connection with the rest of the work—a number
which, in a word, would be out of place in the strict theoretical form
of the music drama, but is justifiable here on the same grounds that
justify the canonic quartet in *Fidelio* or some of the ensembles of *Don
Giovanni*.[25]

It is a sign of Wagner's versatility that, at the same period of his
life, he could compose two works which differ so much not only in
dramatic plan but also in musical style as do *Die Meistersinger* and
*Tristan*. Both the historical background and the nature of the subject
matter of *Die Meistersinger* are reflected in the diatonic quality of most
of the music, in a certain squareness of rhythmic structure and simplicity
of idiom. The chorales, the many melodies of folklike cast, the fugal
section and the contrapuntal combination of three principal themes in
the overture, as well as the contrapuntal style of the finale and of many
other passages—all seem to contain or suggest the very traits and forms
that have always been most typical of German music. By contrast the
freer, more chromatic individual Wagnerian touch is heard in the love
scenes and the monologues of Hans Sachs. The beautiful orchestral
prelude to the third act is not only the quintessence of the musical style
but also the high point of the drama, the complete, living description of
the noble character of Sachs; there is no better example of music as the
heart of dramatic life, the true carrier of the inner action of the play.

The essentially musical character of the drama in both *Tristan* and

[25] See above, p. 287.

*Die Meistersinger* is shown significantly by the fact that in both these works the musical forms are more clear and comprehensive than anywhere else in Wagner. This is, of course, only another way of saying that in these two works we come as close as possible to the ideally perfect union of music and drama within the Wagnerian system. The form type most prevalent in *Die Meistersinger* is, as we have already mentioned, the Bar, of which five examples should be especially noted : (1) Beckmesser's serenade in Act II is a pedantically correct example of two identical Stollen and an Abgesang, the whole being twice repeated to make a song of three strophes. (2) Walther's first song before the Mastersingers, "Am stillen Herd," is a Bar in which the two Stollen are almost, but not quite, identical. (3) Walther's trial song, "So rief der Lenz," is a more extended Bar with two distinct themes in each Stollen, carried on grimly to the end in spite of the uproar of opposition from his audience. (4) In Walther's dream song, the first version of the Prize Song, the two Stollen are not identical, the second being altered so as to cadence in the dominant. (5) In the final version of the Prize Song the melody is further extended and the differences between the two Stollen are likewise greater though still without loss of the essential felt likeness. In addition to many other instances of Bar form, some shorter and some longer than the above, the opera as a whole exemplifies the same structure : anyone who will take the trouble to compare Acts I and II, either with or without the help of Lorenz's outline,[26] will discover that there is a detailed parallelism of the action, and that furthermore in most cases each scene in the second act is a parody of the corresponding scene in Act I—a relationship already foreshadowed by the overture, in which the themes of the middle section parody those of the first. Acts I and II thus form two Stollen, of which Act III is the Abgesang. The whole opera is rounded off by the thematic and tonal correspondence of the beginning and the ending; Lorenz notes that the entire finale, from the entrance of the Mastersingers on, is an expanded and varied reprise of the overture.[27]

The principal events in Wagner's life after *Die Meistersinger* were the completion of the *Ring*, the removal to Bayreuth in 1872, and the first full performance of the *Ring* at the new theatre there in 1876. *Parsifal*, his last music drama, was composed between 1877 and 1882, and first performed at Bayreuth January 13, 1882, exactly a year and

[26] *Das Geheimnis der Form* III, 11–13.
[27] *Ibid.*, p. 171.

one month before Wagner's death. The sources of the *Parsifal* drama
are even more varied than those of the earlier works. The convergence of
many lines of philosophic thought, the complex and often obscure symbolism of the persons and events, make this the most difficult of all
Wagner's music dramas to comprehend, even though the outer action is
comparatively simple. The legend of the Holy Grail (already touched
upon in *Lohengrin* and some other uncomposed dramatic sketches) is
combined with speculations on the role of suffering in human life, and
the central idea is again that of redemption—this time not through love,
but by the savior Parsifal, the Pure Fool, the one "made wise through
pity." The solemnity of this theme, as well as the use of the Christian
symbol of the Eucharist, justifies the designation of Parsifal as a "religious festival-play," a character carefully maintained in performances in
the present-day opera theatre.

No doubt the complexity of the poem is responsible for the music of
*Parsifal* being less clear in formal outlines than that of either *Tristan* or
*Die Meistersinger*. There is sufficient resemblance between the first and
third acts to delineate a general a–b–a structure, but neither the key
scheme nor other details of the various scenes are as amenable to analysis as in the case of the other two works. The music, like that of *Tannhäuser*, depicts different worlds of thought and feeling in sharpest
possible contrast; but whereas in *Tannhäuser* there were two such
worlds, in *Parsifal* there are three. Least important, being merely a foil
for the other two, is the realm of sensual pleasure exemplified in the
second act: the Magic Garden and the Flower Maidens of Klingsor's
castle, and Kundry as seductress under the power of evil magic. If we
compare the music of these scenes with the ebullient eroticism of the
Venusberg music or the glowing ardors of the *Siegfried* finale, we may
be aware of a slight falling off in Wagner's earlier elemental power, a
trifle of oversophistication in the technical means. Not so, however, in
the first and third acts. Here are opposed and intermingled the worlds of
Amfortas and of the Grail, the agonizing penitent and the mystical
heavenly kingdom of pity and peace. The Amfortas music is of the
utmost intensity of feeling, expressed in richness of orchestral color,
plangency of dissonance, complexity and subtlety of harmonic relationships, and a degree of chromaticism which carries it more than once to
the verge of atonality. The Grail music, on the other hand, is diatonic
and almost churchlike in style. The very opening theme of the prelude

(the Last Supper motif), a single-line melody in free rhythm, is reminiscent of Gregorian chant; the Grail motif is an old Amen formula in use at the Dresden Royal Chapel when Wagner conducted there. One feature of the Grail scenes in *Parsifal* deserves special emphasis, namely the expertness of the choral writing. One does not ordinarily look to opera composers for excellence in a field of composition which has always been chiefly associated with the church, and the peculiar technique of which has not always been grasped by even some of the greatest composers. Wagner's distinguished choral writing in *Lohengrin, Die Meistersinger,* and above all in *Parsifal* is therefore of interest;[28] in particular, the closing scenes of Acts I and III of *Parsifal,* with their fine choral effects and the device of separated choirs, with the high and low voices giving an impression in music of actual space and depth, recall the Venetian composers of the later sixteenth century.

In attempting to estimate the significance of Wagner in the history of opera one must first of all acknowledge the man's unswerving idealism and artistic integrity. However open to criticism some aspects of his personal conduct may have been, as an artist he stood uncompromisingly for what he believed to be right. He fought his long battle with such tenacity that his final success left no alternative for future composers but to acknowledge the power of the Wagnerian ideas and methods, whether by imitation, adaptation, or conscious rebellion. His form of the music drama did not, as he had expected, supersede earlier operatic ideals, but certain features of it were of permanent influence. Chief among these was the principle that lay at the basis of the Gesamtkunstwerk idea, namely, that every detail of a work must be connected with the dramatic purpose and serve to further that purpose. Wagner is to be numbered among those opera composers who have seriously maintained the dignity of drama in their works. In addition, many of his procedures left their mark on the next generation or two of composers, for example, the parallel position of voice and orchestra, the orchestral continuity, and the symphonic treatment of leitmotifs. Other matters, however, were less capable of being imitated. Wagner's use of Nordic mythology as subject matter, and his symbolism, were so individual that most attempts to copy them resulted only in unintended parody. The qualities of his

---

[28] It is not always remembered that Wagner greatly admired the music of Palestrina and had made an arrangement of his *Stabat Mater* for a concert in 1848.

poetry, though appropriate enough in connection with his own music, are not those of the highest literary art. Likewise the structure of aesthetic, economic, historical, and other doctrines by which Wagner sought to give theoretical support to his artistic aims can no longer be defended, though a knowledge of it is none the less valuable for the sake of the light it sheds on his own artistic practice.

In the last analysis, the important thing about Wagner is his music. It would not have been his wish to be remembered primarily as a musician, but the world has so chosen, and the world in this case has probably understood the genius better than he understood himself. The quality of Wagner's music that has been the cause of its great popularity has been equally the cause of the severest attacks upon it by musicians, namely, that it is not pure, absolute, spontaneous music, created for music's sake and existing in a realm governed only by the laws of sound, rhythm, and musical form. Wagner is not, like Bach or Mozart, a musician's musician. There is about him in music, as in literature and philosophy, something of the nature of an amateur, though on a gigantic scale and an intellectual level which make the word seem ridiculous.[29] For him no art was self-sustaining. Music, like poetry and gesture, was but one means to a comprehensive end which can perhaps best be defined as "great theatre." Granted this end (which may or may not be conceived as a limitation), it is hardly possible to deny the adequacy of Wagner's music in relation to it. Not only does the music possess sensuous beauty. It can suggest, depict, characterize a universe of the most diverse objects and ideas. Above all is its power—by whatever aesthetic theory one seeks to explain it—of embodying or evoking feeling, with a purity, fullness, and intensity surely not surpassed in the music of any other composer. Such emotion is justified by the grandiose intellectual conceptions with which it is connected and by the monumental proportions of the musical forms in which it is expressed. In this monumental quality, as well as in the characteristic moods, aspirations, and technical methods of his music, Wagner is fully representative of the time in which he lived.

By 1900 the Wagner cult had reached unbelievable proportions, but since then the tide has ebbed. Neither the modes of feeling he projected, nor the musical idiom in which he spoke, nor the ideas he sought to

---

[29] Mann, *Leiden and Grösse*, p. 104 *et passim*.

propagate by means of his magic arts can evoke now the vehement response they did around the turn of the century. Wagner the man and artist, no longer an object of passionate loyalty or passionate loathing, has become simply one of the great composers of the past. Dusk falls on the gods; their works, for a little while, live after them.

CHAPTER 24

# THE LATER
# NINETEENTH CENTURY

FRANCE.[1] The state of musical taste in Paris (that is to say, in France) from 1840 to 1870 is sufficiently illustrated by three facts : the adoration of Meyerbeer, the neglect of Berlioz, and the craze for Offenbach. The disaster of the Franco-Prussian War was a salutary shock to both public and musicians. The rise of a new school and a new spirit in French music began when the Société Nationale de Musique was founded, with the device *Ars gallica*. Undiscriminating acceptance of incongruous musical styles on the one hand and a frivolous addiction to the trivialities of operetta on the other were succeeded by a strenuous effort to restore in modern terms the great musical individuality which had belonged to France in the sixteenth, seventeenth, and eighteenth centuries. The range of activity was widened. Whereas before 1870 composers had centered nearly all their efforts on opera, now choral, symphonic, and chamber music began to be undertaken; higher standards of musical education were introduced, and a more cultivated and exacting public gradually came into being. This renewal of national musical life made the opera more vital, original, and adventurous. And although the highest rewards of popular success still went to those composers who were able and willing to bend their talents to the public fancy, nevertheless

[1] *Almanach des Spectacles*, Paris, 1874–1913; *Cinquante Ans de musique française*, ed. Rohozinski; Bruneau, *La Musique française*; Rolland, *Musiciens d'aujourd'hui*; Seré, *Musiciens français d'aujourd'hui* (contains excellent bibliographical lists); E. B. Hill, *Modern French Music*; Coeuroy, *La Musique française moderne;* Jullien, *Musiciens d'aujourd'hui*, 2 vols. (1892–94); Tiersot, *Un Demi-siècle de musique française* [1870–1917]; Aubry, *La Musique française d'aujourd'hui*; M. Cooper, "Opera, 1890–1910," in *French Music: From the Death of Berlioz to the Death of Fauré*, chap. v.

the best work found hearing and appreciation; there were no scandals like those of the Second Empire, when *Tannhäuser* was hissed off the stage and *Les Troyens* closed after only twenty-one performances. It is worth remarking that almost every important new operatic work in Paris after 1870 was produced not at the Opéra but at the more enterprising and progressive Opéra-comique. The old distinction between the forms of opera and opéra comique had practically disappeared by the end of the nineteenth century, for the latter had by then largely abandoned the traditional spoken dialogue; so the repertoire of the two theatres contrasted simply as large-scale, established, conventional works in the one, and new, often experimental works in the other—alternating, of course, with the light, operetta-like pieces, which continued to flourish. Composers of serious operas that should have been produced at the Paris Opéra frequently had recourse also to the Théâtre de la Monnaie at Brussels for the first performances; and Monte Carlo was the scene of some notable premières. How little the term "opéra comique" in this period had to do with "comic" opera will be realized by recalling that Bizet's *Carmen*, Delibes's *Lakmé*, Lalo's *Roi d'Ys*, Massenet's *Manon*, Bruneau's *Attacque du moulin*, D'Indy's *Fervaal*, Charpentier's *Louise*, and Debussy's *Pelléas et Mélisande* were all staged at the Théâtre de l'Opéra-comique in Paris.

One of the first new operas of distinction to be produced was Georges Bizet's (1838–75)[2] *Carmen* in 1875. *Carmen* was not altogether a failure at first, but its full success in France did not begin until some eight years after the composer's death. It stands today as the most popular and vital French opera of the later nineteenth century. Its Spanish subject was a reflection of the exotic trend in French music which had begun a generation earlier with David; but more important than this feature was the realism with which scenes and characters were depicted, a realism which the librettists had somewhat toned down from Mérimée's original story (especially with respect to Carmen herself), but which still was strong enough to scandalize Paris in the seventies. The tragic ending of this opéra comique was also a novelty. As to the music, Bizet had formed his style from many sources. Probably the least important feature is the mild Spanish local color evident in such numbers as the Habañera, the Toreador Song, and the seguidilla "Près des remparts de Seville"

---

[2] Biographies by W. Dean (1948) and M. Curtiss (1958); special Bizet number of RdM (November, 1938); Istel, *Bizet und Carmen*.

(Act I). Many of the choruses and ensembles are in characteristic operetta style. Fundamental, however, is the firm, concise, and exact musical expression of every situation in terms of which only a French composer would be capable : the typical Gallic union of economy of material, perfect grasp of means, vivid orchestral color, and an electric vitality and rhythmic verve, together with an objective, cool, yet passionate sensualism. This opera contains some spoken dialogue and is otherwise divided into the conventional arias, ensembles, and other numbers. So far as Bizet was concerned, Wagner's music dramas and theories might never have existed. The occasional repetition of certain motifs is of no more significance in *Carmen* than in Verdi's *Rigoletto* a quarter of a century earlier. The whole structure and aesthetic of *Carmen* was such that Nietzsche, after he had turned against Wagner, might point to it as the ideal opera according to the principles of a properly "Mediterraneanized" European art.[3] It is hard to imagine what was in the minds of those contemporary critics who found the music untuneful, lacking in definite outlines, and overpowered by a too rich orchestration—charges, in a word, of Wagnerianism, such as had been leveled earlier at Gounod. But "Wagnerian" was a convenient word in France at this time for damning anything a critic disliked or could not understand. The styles of Gounod and Bizet do, indeed, have much in common, but the affinity is more apparent in Bizet's earlier operas *Les Pêcheurs de perles* ("The Pearl Fishers," 1863) and *Djamileh* (1872). But these works have less musical individuality and interest than *Carmen*; in fact, the only other compositions of Bizet that compare with this opera are his incidental music to Daudet's play *L'Arlésienne* (1872) and his early Symphony in C (1855).

The slight exotic flavor of *Carmen* and *Les Pêcheurs de perles* is found again in *Lakmé* (1883), the best opera of Léo Delibes (1836–91),[4] which has a Hindu locale and a tragic plot faintly reminiscent of Meyerbeer's *Africaine* and more than faintly foreshadowing Puccini's *Butterfly*. Delibes's music is elegant, graceful, and well orchestrated but lacks the intense quality of Bizet's. In *Lakmé* the oriental perfume is blended with an otherwise conventional idiom. Delibes's amusing and tuneful opéra comique *Le Roi l'a dit* ("The King Said So," 1873) is still remembered; a more serious work, *Jean de Nivelle* (1880), was almost equally

---

[3] "Der Fall Wagner," ¶ 3; "Jenseits von Gut und Böse," Part VIII *passim*.
[4] Biography by H. de Curzon.

successful at first but has not remained in the repertoire. On the whole, Delibes excelled as a composer of ballets, his best works in this form being *La Source* (1866), *Coppélia* (1870), and *Sylvia* (1876).

A more substantial figure than Delibes in French nineteenth-century opera was Ernest Reyer (1823–1909).[5] Reyer belongs with those composers whose music often compels more respect for its intentions than admiration for its actual sound. He had "genius without talent," [6] that is, lofty and ideal conceptions without the technique for realizing them fully in an attractive musical form. This incapacity may have been due in part to his defective early training, but it was also a matter of temperament; as a critic he was a despiser of mere prettiness, a rebel against the superficial judgments of the Paris public,[7] and an early defender of Berlioz and Wagner. Reyer was influenced by the fashionable orientalism in his choice of subjects, as seen in his symphonic ode *Sélam* (1850) and the ballet-pantomime *Sacountala* (1858). His first important operatic work, *La Statue* (1861), is also an oriental story. A similar background is found in his last opera, *Salammbô* (1890), taken with few alterations from Flaubert's novel and treated in an austere oratorio-like style, yet with a grandeur of line recalling the spirit of Berlioz's *Troyens*; the plot in general and the closing scene in particular are reminiscent of Verdi's *Aida*. The most successful of Reyer's operas was *Sigurd* (composed in the 1870s, first performed 1884); the subject is almost identical with that of Wagner's *Siegfried* (Act III) and *Götterdämmerung*, with a touch of *Tannhäuser* in the shape of a seductive ballet, with a wordless chorus of elves, in Act II. But the resemblance to Wagner is only skindeep, even in the libretto: Sigurd talks in the accents of Quinault's Renaud rather than like the great blond lad of the *Ring*; and the rest of the personages likewise somehow seem more Gallic than Teutonic. In the music there is no sign whatever of Wagner; on the contrary, we find the old separate numbers of grand opera, a distinctly periodic melody, and very little chromaticism. There is some recurrence of motifs, but this is not a distinctly Wagnerian trait. The musical style is serious and even has a certain nobility; its model, clearly enough, is *Les Troyens*.

Parisian journalists had been crying "Wolf! wolf!" for years before any serious reflection of Wagner's ideas or musical style became

[5] See his *Notes de musique* and *Quarante Ans de musique*; also biography by De Curzon and the same author's *Légende de Sigurd*.

[6] Alfred Bruneau, quoted in Combarieu, *Histoire* III, 389.

[7] See Lavignac, *Encyclopédie*, Part I, Vol. III, pp. 1727–28.

apparent in French music. The bitterness of the Franco-Prussian War, aggravated by Wagner's silly gibes in his playlet *Eine Kapitulation*, delayed his acceptance still longer. Yet by the early eighties apparently all was forgiven, and Wagner became the rage in Paris for some ten or twelve years.

From 1885 Wagner's work acted directly or indirectly on the whole of artistic thought, even on religious and intellectual thought of the most distinguished people of Paris. . . . Writers not only discussed musical subjects, but judged painting, literature, and philosophy, from a Wagnerian point of view. . . . The whole universe was seen and judged by the thought of Bayreuth.[8]

A remarkable evidence of this enthusiasm was the flourishing periodical *La Revue Wagneriénne* (1885–88), contributors to which included Verlaine, Mallarmé, Huysmans, and practically every other important writer in Paris (Baudelaire had been converted already in 1861). One effect of all this was to introduce the subject of music to many people who would not otherwise have taken an interest in it; another was to stimulate symphonic composition. In opera, the risks involved in the magic garden of Wagnerism were so patent that the composers for the most part withstood temptation, though not always without effort. It is sometimes difficult to decide what is to be called imitation of Wagner and what is simply acceptance of new ideas, such as the abolition of formal separate arias and recitatives. Taken altogether, however, the direct influence of Wagner on French opera, in both literary and musical treatment, is seen most strongly in works by three composers : Chabrier, D'Indy, and Chausson.[9]

Emanuel Chabrier (1841–94) [10] was one of the foremost composers of the new movement in France, as well as a pianist of exceptional ability. At first sight he seems an unlikely person to be an apostle of Wagner, for the pieces by which he is best known (the orchestral rhapsody *España* and the *Bourrée Fantasque*) show him as a composer of typical Gallic vivacity, wit, and rhythmic exuberance. It is these qualities which are uppermost in his first important comic opera, *L'Etoile* ("The Star," 1877),[11] and in his best-known stage work, *Le Roi*

[8] Rolland, *Musicians of Today*, p. 253.

[9] Cf. D'Indy, *Richard Wagner et son influence sur l'art musical français*.

[10] See Hill, *Modern French Music*, chap. IV, and studies by Martineau and Servières.

[11] This work was produced in the United States as *The Merry Monarch* and elswhere under various titles. See Loewenberg, *Annals*.

*malgré lui* ("The King in Spite of Himself," 1887), harmonically one of the most original opéras comiques of this period. But in 1879 Chabrier heard a performance of *Tristan und Isolde* at Munich which made a strong impression on him, reinforced by his experience shortly afterwards in directing rehearsals of *Lohengrin* and *Tristan* for performances at Paris. His opera *Gwendoline* (first performed at Brussels in 1886) is obviously influenced by Wagnerian elements : the libretto brings echoes of *Der fliegende Holländer*, of the Valhalla mythology, and above all of *Tristan*, even to a love duet in the second act and a love-death at the end of the third. The form is a compromise between continuous drama and the older number opera. The music shows more than a trace of Wagner in its systematic use of leitmotifs, chromatics, chords of the seventh and ninth, and the characteristic appoggiaturas and suspensions. However, this must not be taken to mean that it is a mere copy of Wagner's idiom. Chabrier had an individual harmonic style, one quite advanced for his time, as well as a genuine and sometimes profound gift of serious expressiveness. The most interesting portions of *Gwendoline* are the Spinning Song in Act I, which incorporates an air from Moore's *Irish Melodies*, the love duet (strongly reminiscent of *Tristan*), and the orchestral prelude to Act II, the style of which has been well described as one of the links between Wagner and Debussy.[12] The skillful voice writing and the highly poetic orchestration of this opera should also be noted. But the uneven quality of the music as a whole, together with a rather dull and awkwardly proportioned libretto, have worked against its success. In his unfinished opera *Briseïs* (Act I performed 1899) Chabrier demonstrated even more daring harmonies than in *Gwendoline*.

Somewhat similar in subject matter to *Gwendoline*, and likewise tinctured with Wagnerian conceptions, is César Franck's (1822–90)[13] only important opera, *Hulda*, composed in 1882–85 and first performed in 1894. But the most thorough and at the same time the most personal adaptation of Wagner's methods to French opera was brought about by Franck's pupil Vincent d'Indy (1851–1931)[14] in his *Fervaal* (1897) and *L'Etranger* ("The Stranger," 1903). Like Wagner, D'Indy wrote his own

[12] Abraham, *A Hundred Years of Music*.

[13] Biographies by D'Indy and L. Vallas; Van den Borren, *L'Oeuvre dramatique de César Franck*; see also the bio-bibliography by Lynn.

[14] Vallas, *Vincent d'Indy*; also the following special studies : Bréville, *Fervaal*; Calvocoressi, *L'Etranger*; Destranges, *Le Chant de la cloche*; idem, *Fervaal*; idem, *L'Etranger*. See also D'Indy's *Wagner et son influence sur l'art musical français*.

librettos. The background of *Fervaal* is vaguely mythological, and the action in both operas is treated as symbolic of broad moral issues—the conflict between pagan religion and sacrificial love in *Fervaal* and the expiation of unlawful love through death in *L'Etranger*. But whereas Wagner's symbolism is nearly always in practice wielded for theatrical effect, D'Indy's evident purpose is to make art a vehicle for essentially religious teachings and to use every possible artistic means toward this end. The almost medieval combination of this austere ideal with a catholic breadth of resource, welded into unity by superb technical skill, is the clue to D'Indy's style.[15] It explains how he was able to take over many features of Wagner's music dramas without sacrificing his own individuality : pseudo mythology, symbolism, continuity of the music, harmonic sophistication, the symphonic orchestral texture with cyclical recurrence of motifs, free arioso treatment of the voice line, Wagnerian instrumental sonorities, even (in the love music of the first and third acts of *Fervaal*) actual reminiscenes of *Tristan*. Indebtedness to Wagner is much less apparent in *L'Etranger* than in the earlier opera. The strange suggestiveness of the musical landscape in the introduction to Act II of *Fervaal* and the somber, mysterious poetry of the following scene are especially noteworthy. The third scene of Act II of *L'Etranger* is remarkable for imaginative and pictorial power (Example 100). As in his dramatic choral works, *Le Chant de la cloche* ("The Song of the Bell," 1879–83) and *La Légende de St. Christophe* (composed 1908–15), in the operas too D'Indy introduces choral treatments of Gregorian melodies, notably the "Pange lingua" in the transcendently beautiful closing scene of *Fervaal*.[16] That neither of these operas has become popular may be owing in part to the unusual character of their librettos but more to the music, which lacks the simple, salient, easily perceived qualities necessary for success on the stage. One cannot help feeling that, for the theatre, the music has many of the defects of Wagner without the latter's compelling emotional power. Yet *Fervaal* in particular deserves respect as one of the outstanding French operas of the later nineteenth century in the noble tradition of Berlioz's *Troyens*.

The influence of Wagner is still noticeable in *Le Roi Arthus* by Ernest Chausson (1855–99), first performed in 1903. It is a not very

[15] See Rolland, chapter on D'Indy in *Musiciens d'aujourd'hui*.

[16] Cf. also the quotation of the intonation of the "Credo" in Act II, sc. 1 of the same opera; and in the finale of Bruneau's *Messidor* (also 1897), the plainsong passage from the Litany.

## *L'Etranger*, Act II, sc. 3

EXAMPLE 100

D'INDY

*(Example 100 continued)*

successful mixture of old grand-opera formal elements with the new Wagnerian idiom, including the inevitable Tristanesque love duet in Act I. Neither libretto nor music offers any passages of real distinction; indeed, the composer himself regarded *Le Roi Arthus* as only an experiment. This is perhaps the final word for all the attempts by French composers to assimilate Wagner's methods in the nineteenth century, since no consistent or historically important school grew out of them. Along with these experiments the natural line of French lyric opera in descent from Gounod continued to flourish. We now turn our attention to the composers of this distinctively national group.

The first is Camille Saint-Saëns (1835–1921),[17] whose *Princesse jaune* ("The Yellow Princess," 1872) set the fashion for Japanese subjects in comic opera. Saint-Saëns's most famous dramatic work is the biblical *Samson et Dalila* (1877), half opera and half oratorio, like Liszt's *Legende von der heiligen Elisabeth* or D'Indy's *St. Christophe*. Saint-Saëns was not by nature a dramatic composer, but his technical facility and knowledge of many different musical styles enabled him to construct smooth and competent, if not exciting, works in dramatic form. Of his sixteen stage works the most successful (next to *Samson et Dalila*) were *Henri VIII* (1883), *Ascanio* (1890), and the opéra comique *Phryné* (1893). Another composer of conservative national tendency was Edouard Lalo (1823–92) [18] with *Le Roi d'Ys* (1888), based on a Breton legend. The music of this opera is original in style, of remarkable rhythmic vitality, varied in color, and admirably adapted to the stage— qualities that have assured its survival to the present day. Three other French composers of the late nineteenth century should be mentioned in passing, though their work is less important than that of Saint-Saëns or Lalo : Emile Paladilhe (1844–1926; *Patriel*, 1886); Benjamin Godard (1849–95), a composer of facile and pleasing melodies whose *Jocelyn* (1888) was long remembered because of one number, the "Berceuse"; and Isidore De Lara (1858–1935), English by birth and residence but most of whose operas, including the successful *Messaline* (1899), were written to French texts and produced in France.

The outstanding French opera composer of this era was Jules Massenet (1842–1912),[19] an exceptionally productive worker whose

[17] Biographies by Langlois and Chantavoine; see also the composer's own writings, especially *Portraits et souvenirs*; Du Tillet, "A propos du drame lyrique."

[18] Biography by G. Servières.

[19] Biographies by L. Schneider and Bruneau; Massenet, *Mes Souvenirs*.

music is marked by characteristic French traits that we have already noticed in earlier composers such as Monsigny, Auber, Thomas (Massenet's teacher), and Gounod. First among these is the quality of the melody. Massenet's melody is of a highly personal sort : lyrical, tender, penetrating, sweetly sensuous, rounded in contours, exact but never violent in interpreting the text, sentimental, often melancholy, sometimes a little vulgar, and always charming. This melody determines the whole texture. The harmonic background is sketched with delicacy and a fine sense of instrumental color, and every detail of the score shows smooth craftsmanship. With no commitment to particular theories of opera, Wagnerian or otherwise, Massenet within the limits of his own style never hesitated to make use of any new device that had proved effective or popular, so that his works are not free of eclecticism and mirror in their own way most of the successive operatic tendencies of his lifetime. The subjects and their treatment also show the composer's sensitiveness to popular taste. Thus *Le Roi de Lahore* (1877) is an oriental story, *Le Cid* (1885) is in the manner of grand opera, *Esclarmonde* (1889) is Wagnerian, *La Navarraise* (1894) shows the influence of Italian *verismo*, and *Cendrillon* (1899) recalls Humperdinck's *Hänsel und Gretel*; but *Le Jongleur de Notre Dame* (1902) is a miracle play for which there could have been no public demand, but which the composer treated with special affection and thereby produced one of his best operas. The suspicion sometimes arises that Massenet's choice of subjects, as well as his use of certain fashionable musical devices, was motivated by a desire to give his audiences what he knew they wanted rather than by any inner impulsion. But there is no sacrifice of musical individuality in all this; and in the case of a composer whose instincts were so completely of the theatre, who always succeeded in achieving so neatly and spontaneously just the effect he intended, it seems a little ungracious to insist too strongly on an issue of artistic sincerity. Massenet excelled in the musical depiction of passionate love, and most of his best works are notable for their heroines—unforgettable ladies all, of doubtful virtue perhaps, but indubitably alive and vivid. To this gallery belong Salomé in *Hérodiade* (1881), the heroines of *Manon* (1884), *Thaïs* (1894), *Sapho* (1897), and Charlotte in *Werther* (1892). With these works should also be mentioned *Thérèse* (1907), one of the last operas of Massenet to obtain general success.

Massenet traveled the main highway of French tradition in opera and his natural gifts so corresponded to the tastes of his day that success seemed to come almost without effort. Nor was his style without influence, direct or indirect, on later French composers. But he was the last to produce operas so easily. Changing musical idioms and new literary movements had their effect on the next generation, giving its work a less assured, more experimental character. One of these literary movements was that known as "naturalism."

The word "naturalism" and the related word "realism," however useful they may be in the study of literature or the graphic arts, are exceedingly vague when applied to music. Unless they refer to the unimportant practice of imitating everyday sounds by voices or instruments in a musical composition (as, for example, the bleating of sheep in Strauss's *Don Quixote*), it is difficult to see what meaning they can have that is related directly to music itself. What some writers call "realistic" or "naturalistic" music is simply, in effect, a certain kind of program music; the realism is deduced not from the music but from an extra-musical fact (such as a title) about the composition in question. When we speak of realistic or naturalistic opera, therefore, we have reference primarily to the libretto; we mean that the opera presents persons, scenes, events, and conversations that are recognizably similar to the common daily experience of its audience, and that these things are treated seriously, as becomes matters of real moment, not with persiflage or fantasy as in an operetta. It goes without saying that such tendencies in late nineteenth-century opera grew out of earlier tendencies in literature. Thus Bizet's *Carmen*, the first important realistic opera in France and one of the principal sources of the Italian verismo, was based on Mérimée's story. The chief disciples of realism in later nineteenth-century French literature were Guy de Maupassant (1850–93) and Emile Zola (1840–1902). The latter found a musical interpreter in Alfred Bruneau (1857–1934),[20] Massenet's pupil, the librettos of whose principal operas were either adapted from Zola's books or written especially for the composer by Zola himself; to the former group belong *Le Rêve* ("The Dream," 1891) and *L'Attacque du moulin* ("The Attack on the Mill," 1893); to the latter *Messidor* (1897), *L'Ouragan* ("The Hurricane," 1901), and *L'Enfant roi* ("The Child King," 1905). These works were concerned with current social and economic problems, pre-

[20] Boschot, *La Vie et les œuvres d'Alfred Bruneau*; see also Bruneau's own writings.

sented in compact, tense situations with symbolical overtones, and in prose instead of the customary verse. Unfortunately, the rhythm of Zola's prose did not always inspire Bruneau to achieve correspondingly flexible rhythms in the music; the melodic line is declamatory rather than lyrical, but the regular pattern of accentuation indicated by the bar lines becomes monotonous. The music is austere; it is especially apt in the creation of moods through reiterated motifs, but with all its evident sincerity and undoubted dramatic power, the important quality of sensuous charm is often lacking. Nevertheless, Bruneau is significant as a forerunner of some later experiments in harmony and as an independent, healthy force in the growth of modern French opera, counterbalancing to some extent the Wagnerian tendencies of D'Indy and the hedonism of Massenet.

A fuller measure of success in the field of operatic naturalism was granted to another pupil of Massenet, Gustave Charpentier (1860–1956).[21] The "musical novel" *Louise* (1900) is his only important opera, a strange but successful combination of several distinct elements. In scene, characters, and plot *Louise* is realistic; Charpentier, writing his own libretto, has almost gone out of his way to introduce such homely details as a bourgeois family supper, the reading of a newspaper, and a scene in a dressmaking shop; many of the minor personages are obviously taken "from life," and sing in a marked Parisian dialect. The melodramatic closing scene recalls the mood of the Italian verismo composers. Charpentier, like Bruneau, touches occasionally on social questions : the issue of free love, the obligations of children to their parents, the miseries of poverty. But along with realism there is symbolism, especially in the weird figure of the Noctambulist, personification of "the pleasure of Paris." Paris itself is, as Bruneau remarked,[22] the real hero of this opera. Behind the action is the presence of the great city, seductive, mysterious, and fatal, enveloping persons and events in an atmosphere of poetry like that of the forest in Weber's *Freischütz*. Its hymn is the ensemble of street cries, running like a refrain through the first scene of Act II and echoing elsewhere throughout the opera. To realism and symbolism is added yet a third factor : sentiment. The dialogue between Louise and her father in Act I is of a convincing tenderness, while the love music of Act III, with the often-heard "Depuis le jour,"

[21] Delmas, *Gustave Charpentier et le lyrisme français*; Himonet, *Louise*.
[22] *La Musique française,* p. 154.

is not only a fine scene of passion but also one of the few of its kind in late nineteenth-century French opera that never reminds us of *Tristan und Isolde*—or hardly ever. It was the achievement of Charpentier to take all this realism, symbolism, and sentiment, holding together only with difficulty in the libretto itself, and mold them into one powerful whole by means of music. The score reminds one in many ways of Massenet: there is the same spontaneity and abundance of ideas, the same simple and economical texture, obtaining the maximum effect with the smallest apparent effort. The harmonic idiom is more advanced than Massenet's but less daring than Bruneau's. The orchestral music is continuous, serving as background for spoken as well as sung passages, and is organized by recurring motifs. A number of standard operatic devices are cleverly adapted to the libretto: Julien's serenade with accompaniment of a guitar, the ensemble of working girls in Act II (where the tattoo of the sewing machine replaces the whirr of the old romantic spinning wheel), and the ballet-like scene where Louise is crowned as the Muse of Montmartre in Act III. On the whole, it will be seen that when this opera is cited as an example of naturalism the word needs to be taken with some qualifications. In any case, it is not the naturalism that has caused it to survive, for this was but a passing fashion. *Louise* remains in the repertoire for the same reason as other successful operas: because it has melodious and moving music wedded to a libretto that permits the music to operate as an effective partner in the projection of the drama.

Fashions in opera might come and go, but the operetta and kindred forms went their way unperturbed. The line of French light opera, established in the nineteenth century by Auber, Adam, and Offenbach, was continued after 1870 by Charles Lecocq (1832–1918),[23] whose best work was *La Fille de Madame Angot* (1872); Jean-Robert Planquette (1848–1903), whose sentimental and still popular *Cloches de Corneville* ("The Bells of Corneville") came out in 1877; Edmond Audran (1840–1901) with *La Mascotte* (1880); and Louis Varney (1844–1908) with *Les Mousquetaires au couvent* ("The Musketeers in the Convent," 1880). Somewhat later began the long series of popular operas and operettas by André Messager (1853–1929),[24] distinguished conductor and facile composer in a straightforward, attractively melodious vein (*La Basoche*, 1890; *Les P'tites Michu*, 1897; *Monsieur Beaucaire*, 1919). At the beginning of the twentieth century appeared the operettas of Claude Terrasse (1867–1923), including *Le Sire de Vargy* (1903) and *Monsieur de la Palisse* (1904).

[23] Louis Schneider, *Hervé. Charles Lecocq.*
[24] Biographies by Augé-Laribé and H. Février.

ITALY. As Italians in the eighteenth century would have nothing to do with Gluck, so in the nineteenth they cared little for Wagner. It was not until the eighties that even *Lohengrin* began to be accepted. With the exception of Boito, no important out-and-out Wagner disciples appeared in Italy. There was considerable talk about Wagner and considerable skepticism as to the future of Italian opera, but the only result of any consequence was to call forth a vigorous national reaction of which the greatest monument is Verdi's *Otello*. Italian opera was too secure in its tradition and methods, too deeply rooted in the national life, to be susceptible to radical experiments, especially experiments resulting from aesthetic theories of a sort in which Italians were temperamentally uninterested. A mild influence of German romanticism, but hardly more, may be found in a few Italian opera composers of the late nineteenth century. Alfredo Catalani (1854–93) [25] is the most distinguished of this group; his principal operas were *Loreley* (1890; a revision of his *Elda* which had appeared in 1880), *Dejanice* (1883), and *La Wally* (1892). Catalani has a refined melodic style, nearly always free of exaggerated pathos, with interesting harmonies and a good balance of interest between voice and orchestra. Along with traces of Tristanesque chromaticism are experiments in harmony and texture that anticipate some of the favorite devices of Puccini. The robust rhythms are notable, especially in the choruses and dances of *La Wally*. Unfortunately, Catalani appeared at a time when the Italian public was being seduced by Mascagni and Leoncavallo, so that his reserved and aristocratic music was drowned by the bellow of verismo. Some influence of Wagner seems to be present in the harmonies and the important position of the orchestra in the operas of Antonio Smareglia (1854–1929),[26] whose chief work, *Nozze istriane* ("Istrian Wedding"), was performed in 1895; but Smareglia lacked the convincing popular touch in his melodies and his operas were not greatly successful. Alberto Franchetti (1860–1942) has been called "the Meyerbeer of Italy" because of his fondness for massive scenic effects, but his music, on the whole, is undistinguished; his principal operas were *Cristoforo Colombo* (1892) and *Germania* (1902). None of these composers was attracted by the verismo movement of the 1890s, which was the popular trend in Italy at that time.

[25] See biography by C. Gatti and articles by J. W. Klein.
[26] See biographical studies by Nacamuli and A. and M. Smareglia.

The most explosive reaction against Wagner was launched with the performance of *Cavalleria rusticana* ("Rustic Chivalry") by Pietro Mascagni (1863–1945)[27] in 1890 and *I pagliacci* ("The Clowns") by Ruggiero Leoncavallo (1858–1919) two years later. Neither composer was ever able to duplicate the fantastic success these two works achieved, though Mascagni approached it with *L'amico Fritz* (1891) and *Iris* (1898), while Leoncavallo's *Zaza* (1900) became fairly widely known. But *Cavalleria* and *Pagliacci*, now usually given on the same evening as a double bill, are the classics of verismo, or "realism."[28] This typically Italian movement resembles the French naturalism in the use of scenes and characters from common life; but the French naturalists used these materials as a means for the development of more general ideas and feelings, idealizing both scene and music, whereas the goal of the Italian realists was simply to present a vivid, melodramatic plot, to arouse sensation by violent contrasts, to paint a cross section of life without concerning themselves with any general significance the action might have. Verismo is to naturalism what the "shocker" is to the realistic novel, and the music corresponds to this conception. It aims simply and directly at the expression of intense passion through melodic or declamatory phrases of the solo voices, to which the orchestra contributes sensational harmonies. Choral or instrumental interludes serve only to establish a mood which is to be rent asunder in the next scene. Everything is so arranged that the moments of excitement follow one another in swift climactic succession. It cannot be denied that there was plenty of precedent in Donizetti and the earlier works of Verdi for melodramatic situations in opera; but by comparison the action of the veristic operas takes place as in an atmosphere from which the nitrogen has been withdrawn, so that everything burns with a fierce, unnatural flame, and moreover quickly burns out. The brevity of these works is due not so much to concentration as to rapid exhaustion of the material. Much the same is true of the verismo movement as a whole, historically considered. It flared like a meteor across the operatic sky of the 1890s, but by the end of the century it was practically dead, though its influence can occasionally be detected in some later operas.

The leading figure in Italian opera of the late nineteenth and the

---

[27] Studies by De Donno; biography by Jeri (1945); *Mascagni parla* (reminiscences, 1945).

[28] See Rinaldi, *Musica e verismo*.

early twentieth century was Giacomo Puccini (1858–1924),[29] who resembles Massenet in his position of mediator between two eras, as well as in many features of his musical style. Puccini's rise to fame began with his third opera, *Manon Lescaut* (1893), which is less effective dramatically than Massenet's opera on the same subject (1884) but rather superior in musical interest—this despite occasional reminiscences of *Tristan*, which few composers in the nineties seemed able to escape. Puccini's world-wide reputation rests chiefly on his next three works: *La Bohême* (1896), *Tosca* (1900), and *Madama Butterfly* (1904). *La Bohême* is a sentimental opera with dramatic touches of realism, on a libretto adapted from Henri Murger's *Scènes de la vie de Bohême* ("Scenes of Bohemian Life"), which had been dramatized in 1849 under the title *La Vie de Bohême*; *Tosca*, taken from Victorien Sardou's drama of the same name (1887), is "a prolonged orgy of lust and crime" made endurable by the beauty of the music; and *Madama Butterfly* is a tale of love and heartbreak in an exotic Japanese setting. The outstanding musical characteristic of Puccini in all these operas is the "sensuous warmth and melting radiance of the vocal line." [30] It is like Massenet without Massenet's urbanity: naked emotion crying out, and persuading the listener's feeling by its very urgency. For illustrations the reader need only recall the aria "Che gelida manina" and the ensuing duet in the first scene of *La Bohême*, the closing scene of the same work, or the familiar arias "Vissi d'arte" in *Tosca* and "Un bel dì" in *Butterfly*. The history of this type of melody is instructive. It will be remembered that in Verdi we encountered from time to time a melodic phrase of peculiar poignancy which seemed to gather up the whole feeling of a scene in a pure and concentrated moment of expression, such as the "Amami, Alfredo" in *La traviata* (Example 93), the recitative "E tu, come sei pallida" of *Otello* (Example 94), or the kiss motif from the same work. Later composers, perceiving that the high points of effectiveness in Verdi were marked by phrases of this sort, naturally became ambitious to write operas which should consist entirely (or as nearly so as possible) of such melodic high points, just as the verismo composers had tried to write operas consisting entirely of melodramatic shocks. Both

[29] Studies by Carner and Sartori; *Carteggi Pucciniani*, ed. Gara; *Giacomo Puccini* (symposium), ed. Sartori; Ricci, *Puccini interprete di se stesso*. For bibliography, see Marino, "Giacomo Puccini: A Check List."

[30] Carner, *Puccini*, p. 273; the entire section is an excellent analysis of the composer's melodic and general musical style.

tendencies are evidence of satiety of sensation. These melodic phrases in Verdi are of the sort sometimes described as "pregnant"; their effect depends on the prevalence of a less heated manner of expression elsewhere in the opera, so that they stand out by contrast. But in Puccini we have, as an apparent ideal if not always an actuality, what may be called a kind of perpetual pregnancy in the melody, whether this is sung or entrusted to the orchestra as a background for vocal recitative. The musical utterance is kept at high tension, almost without repose, as though it were to be feared that if the audiences were not continually excited they would go to sleep. This tendency toward compression of language, this nervous stretto of musical style, is characteristic of the *fin de siècle* period.

The sort of melody we have been describing runs through all of Puccini's works. In his earliest and latest operas it tends to be organized in balanced phrases, but in those of the middle period it becomes a freer line, often embodying a set of recurring motifs. These motifs of Puccini, admirably dramatic in conception, are used either simply for recalling earlier moments in the opera or, by reiteration, for establishing a mood, but they do not serve as generating themes for musical development.

Puccini's music was enriched by the composer's constant interest in the new harmonic developments of his time; he was always eager to put current discoveries to use in opera. One example of striking harmonic treatment is the series of three major triads (B-flat, A-flat, E-natural) which opens *Tosca* and is associated throughout the opera with the villainous Scarpia (Example 101). The harmonic tension of the augmented fourth outlined by the first and third chords of this progression

*Tosca,* the "Scarpia" chords

PUCCINI

EXAMPLE 101

Andante molto sost.

*tutta forza*
(*8va bassa*)

is by itself sufficient for Puccini's purpose; he has created his atmosphere
with three strokes, and the chord series has no further use but to be repeated intact whenever the dramatic situation requires it. One common
trait of Puccini's, found in all his operas from the early *Edgar* (1889)
down to his last works, is the "side-slipping" of chords (Example 102);

EXAMPLE 102          *Madama Butterfly*, Act II          PUCCINI

doubtless this device was learned from Verdi (compare the passage "Oh!
come è dolce" in the duet at the end of Act I of *Otello*) or Catalani, but
it is based on a practice common in much non-European music and one
going back in Western musical history to medieval organum and faux-
bourdon. Its usual purpose in Puccini is to break a melodic line into a
number of parallel strands, like breaking up a beam of light by a prism
into parallel bands of color. In a sense it is a complementary effect to
that of intensifying a melody by duplication at the unison and octaves—
an effect dear to all Italian composers of the nineteenth century and one
to which Puccini also frequently resorted. Parallel duplication of the
melodic line at the fifth is used to good purpose in the introduction to
scene 3 of *La Bohême* to suggest the bleakness of a cold winter dawn;
at the third and fifth, in the introduction to the second scene of the same
opera, for depicting the lively, crowded street scene (a passage which
may or may not have been in the back of Stravinsky's mind when he
wrote the music for the first scene of *Petrouchka*); and parallelism of
the same sort, extended sometimes to chords of the seventh and ninth
(as with Debussy), is found at many places in the later operas.

   The most original places in Puccini, however, are not dependent
on any single device; take for example the opening scene of Act III of
*Tosca*, with its broad unison melody in the horns, the delicate descending parallel triads over a double pedal in the bass, the Lydian melody of

the shepherd boy, and the faint background of bells, with the veiled, intruding threat of the three Scarpia chords from time to time—an inimitably beautiful and suggestive passage, technically perhaps owing something to both Verdi and Debussy, but nevertheless thoroughly individual.

An important source of color effects in Puccini's music is the use of exotic materials. Exoticism in Puccini was more than a mere borrowing of certain details but rather extended into the very fabric of his melody, harmony, rhythm, and instrumentation.[31] It is naturally most in evidence in the works on oriental subjects, *Madama Butterfly* and *Turandot* (1926). *Turandot*, based on a comedy of the eighteenth-century Carlo Gozzi and completed after Puccini's death by Franco Alfano, shows side by side harmonic experimentation (for example, the bitonality at the opening of Acts I and II), the utmost development of Puccinian lyric melody, and the most brilliant orchestration of any of his operas.

Puccini did not escape the influence of verismo, but the realism of his operas is always tempered by, or blended with, romantic and exotic elements. In *La Bohême*, common scenes and characters are invested with a romantic halo; the repulsive melodrama of *Tosca* is glorified by the music; and the few realistic details in *Madama Butterfly* are unimportant. A less convincing attempt to blend realism and romance is found in *La fanciulla del West* ("The Girl of the Golden West"), taken from a play by David Belasco and first performed at the Metropolitan Opera House in 1910. Though enthusiastically received by the first American audiences, *La fanciulla* did not attain as wide or enduring popularity as the preceding works. The next opera, *La rondine* ("The Swallow," 1917), was even less successful. A return was made, however, with the *trittico*, or triptych, of one-act operas performed at the Metropolitan in December, 1918: *Il tabarro* ("The Cloak"), a veristic melodrama; *Suor Angelica* ("Sister Angelica"), a miracle play; and *Gianni Schicchi*, the most popular of the three, a delightful comedy in the spirit of eighteenth-century opera buffa. Puccini's comic skill, evidenced also in some parts of *La Bohême* and *Turandot*, is here seen at its most spontaneous, incorporating smoothly all the characteristic harmonic devices of his later period. Only the occasional intrusion of sentimental melodies in the old vein breaks the unity of effect.

Puccini was not one of the great composers, but within his own limits

[31] See Carner's essay, with musical examples, "The Exotic Element in Puccini."

—of which he was perfectly aware—he worked honorably and with mastery of his technique. Bill Nye remarked of Wagner's music that it "is better than it sounds"; Puccini's music, on the contrary, often sounds better than it is, owing to the perfect adjustment of means to ends. He had the prime requisite for an opera composer, an instinct for the theatre; to that he added the Italian gift of knowing how to write effectively for singers, an unusually keen ear for new harmonic and instrumental colors, a receptive mind to musical progress, and a poetic imagination excelling in the evocation of dreamlike, fantastic moods. Even *Turandot*, for all its venturesome harmonies, is a romantic work, an escape into the exotic in both the dramatic and the musical sense.

A younger contemporary of Puccini was Umberto Giordano (1867–1948),[32] whose *Andrea Chénier* (1896) is like a rescue opera of the French Revolution period without the rescue; both plot and music show the influence of verismo in the exaggerated emphasis on effect at all costs (Example 103). Apart from its undoubted dramatic qualities, the score offers little of interest; the harmonies are heavy and old-fashioned and there are few notable lyric passages in the voice parts, though some local color is provided by the use of revolutionary songs ("Ça ira," "La Carmagnole," "La Marseillaise"). *Fedora* (1898) and *Siberia* (1903) are in the same style, with Russian instead of French background. In *Madame Sans-Gêne* (New York, 1915) the composer's theatrical talents are applied to a vivacious and tuneful comedy drama. Of Giordano's later operas, *La cena delle beffe* ("The Feast of Jests," 1924), a lurid four-act melodrama, has been the most successful. None of these are of great significance musically; they are the work of a gifted but not profound composer operating within the traditional Italian framework and skillfully adapting it to the current practice of orchestral continuity. A similar but less conspicuous position must be assigned to Francesco Cilèa (1866–1950),[33] who was, incidentally, one of the first Italian composers of this period to have occupied himself much with music in other forms than opera. His *Adriana Lecouvreur* (1902), based on a libretto by Scribe, is an involved drama of the age of Louis XV with expertly contrived music of a lyrical-tragic sort obviously influenced by Puccini, unadventurous harmonically or rhythmically but good theatre and effective for the singers.

---

[32] Biography by Cellamare (1949).
[33] Biography by T. d'Amico (1960); see also Pilati, "Francesco Cilèa."

*Andrea Chénier*, SC. 2

EXAMPLE 103                                                  GIORDANO

GERMANY.[34] Wagner affected the course of lyric drama like a new planet hurled into a solar system. The center of the operatic universe shifted; all the old balances were disturbed; regroupings took place, accompanied by erratic movements. These consequences were least marked in Italy, more so in France, and most of all, naturally, in Germany. Yet even there they did not appear quickly; established traditions —romantic opera in the manner of Marschner and grand opera on the model of Meyerbeer—were still strong. Max Bruch's (1838–1920)[35] *Loreley* (1863), on a libretto originally written for Mendelssohn, was a

[34] General bibliography: Schiedermair, *Die deutsche Oper*; R. Louis, *Die deutsche Musik der Gegenwart* (1909); Istel, "German Opera Since Richard Wagner"; idem, *Die moderne Oper* (2d ed., 1923); *Monographien moderner Musiker*, ed. Segnitz; Moser, *Geschichte der deutschen Musik* III 351–451, *passim*; Kroyer, "Die circumpolare Oper."

[35] Biography by F. Gysi (1922).

romantic opera, conventional in form though with some progressive traits in the musical style; Karl Goldmark's (1830–1915) [36] *Königin von Saba* ("The Queen of Sheba," 1875), one of the favorite German works of the later nineteenth century, is an agreeable but old-fashioned grand opera, complete with set numbers, ballets, pageantry, and some conventional strokes of oriental color. Goldmark had accepted Wagner as far as *Tannhäuser*, but was evidently not acquainted with, or at any rate not at all influenced by, the later style of *Tristan* and the *Ring*.

Some typically Wagnerian subject matter had come into German opera independently of Wagner: thus Karl Mangold (1813–89) had produced a *Tanhäuser* in 1846 and Heinrich Dorn (1804–92) [37] a *Nibelungen* in 1854, both composed without knowledge of Wagner's corresponding works; Dorn's opera, indeed, was seriously regarded for a time as rivaling Wagner's *Ring*. One of the first composers in whom the direct influence of Wagner can be seen was Franz von Holstein (1826–78),[38] poet and composer whose "grand opera" *Der Haideschacht* (1868) was based on Hoffmann's tale *Die Bergwerke zu Falun* ("The Mines at Falun"); but Holstein resented being known as a mere epigone of Wagner and in fact demonstrated considerable independence in his *Hochländer* ("The Highlanders") of 1876, a historical grand opera in the tradition of Meyerbeer, which incidentally uses some Scottish melodies. Wagnerian ideas in subject matter and treatment, use of leitmotifs, importance of the orchestra, and attempted musical continuity—all modified, however, by some compromises with older operatic forms—are evident in *Iwein* (1879) and *Gudrun* (1882) by August Klughardt (1847–1902),[39] in *Gudrun* (1884) by Felix Draeseke (1835–1913),[40] *Kunihild* (also 1884) by Cyrill Kistler (1848–1907), *Wieland der Schmied* (1880, rev. 1894) by Max Zenger (1837–1911), and *Kudrun* (1896) by the Swiss Hans Huber (1852–1921).[41] But some of these composers later managed to shake off the Wagnerian influence and develop along lines more congenial to their own temperaments—Kistler, for example, toward operas of a simple popular style, Zenger (especially in his last opera, *Eros und Psyche*, 1901) toward the classical ideal of Gluck,

[36] Goldmark, *Erinnerungen*; biography by L. Koch.
[37] Dorn, *Aus meinem Leben*; Rauh, *Heinrich Dorn als Opernkomponist*.
[38] Biography by G. Glaser.
[39] Biography by L. Gerlach.
[40] Biography by E. Röder.
[41] Biography by E. Refardt (1944).

and Huber, with moderate success, toward romantic opera (*Die schöne Bellinda*, 1916).

The Wagnerian school toward the end of the century is represented by Felix von Weingartner (1863–1942)[42] with *Sakuntala* (1884), *Genesius* (1892), and the trilogy *Orestes* (1902), as well as many later dramatic works in various styles; Heinrich Zöllner (1854–1941) with *Faust* (1887); and especially August Bungert (1845–1915),[43] whose *Homerische Welt* ("The Homeric World"), consisting of two cycles of six operas in all, was the most ambitious musico-dramatic undertaking since the *Ring* but nevertheless failed to make its way with the public because of appallingly uninteresting music. These composers for the most part followed Wagner in writing their own librettos. Among other Wagnerian works of this period may be mentioned some early operas by other composers who subsequently developed a more personal style: Kienzl's *Urvasi* (1886), Schillings's *Ingwelde* (1894), R. Strauss's *Guntram* (1894), Pfitzner's *Armer Heinrich* (1896), and D'Albert's *Kain* (1900).

The inevitable consequence of all this imitation of Wagner was a reaction. Both public and composers, growing tired of repetitions of a style in which Wagner had already said the final word, were ready for something new, and ways out were sought in three directions: comic opera, popular opera ("Volksoper"), and fairy-tale opera ("Märchenoper"). An outstanding work in the comic genre was *Der Widerspenstigen Zähmung* ("The Taming of the Shrew," 1874) by Hermann Goetz (1840–76),[44] an opera which, like Cornelius's *Barbier von Bagdad*, has never had the wide success it merits by the cleverness of its libretto and the Mozartean humor of its music. A later, more sophisticated school of comic opera, going back for musical inspiration to *Der Barbier* or Wagner's *Meistersinger*, is represented by the celebrated but seldom performed *Corregidor* (1896) of Hugo Wolf (1860–1903).[45] Based on a story by P. A. de Alarcón, *Der Corregidor* is in many respects an inspired attempt to create a gay, original German comic opera "without the gloomy, world-redeeming ghost of a Schopenhaurian philosopher in

[42] See Weingartner's own writings, especially *Lebenserinnerungen* and *Die Lehre von der Wiedergeburt des musikalischen Dramas* (1895).
[43] Biography by M. Chop (1903).
[44] Biographies by Kreuzhage and Kruse.
[45] Biographies by Decsey, Walker, and Von Graedener-Hattingberg; Hellmer, *Der Corregidor*.

the background." [46] This laudable intention was frustrated by Wolf's long-standing admiration for Wagner's music : the orchestra of *Der Corregidor* is as heavily polyphonic as that of *Die Meistersinger*, and the music is full of leitmotifs—a style completely unsuited to Wolf's libretto. Moreover Wolf, like Schubert and Schumann, was not at home in the theatre : his invention seems to have been paralyzed by the requirements of the stage; the music goes from one song to the next like a Liederspiel; neither persons nor situations are adequately characterized. This composer, "who could be so dramatic in the lied, here in the drama remained above all a lyricist." [47] *Der Corregidor*, though not lacking in finely wrought details,[48] was a failure as an opera. Another Spanish subject, from Lope de Vega, was treated by Anton Urspruch (1850–1907) in his comic opera *Das Unmöglichste von allem* ("The Most Impossible of All," 1897), with light parlando dialogue and intricate contrapuntal ensembles derived from the style of Mozart. A more spirited and dramatic composer in this field was the Austrian Emil Nikolaus von Rezniček (1860–1945),[49] whose *Donna Diana* (1894; another Spanish subject) gave promise of a future that was not realized in his next few operas; but with *Ritter Blaubart* ("Knight Bluebeard," 1920), "an eclectic score embodying elements of Italian cantilena style and the technique of French impressionism," [50] he renewed his reputation.

One of the best German comic operas of the late nineteenth century was D'Albert's *Abreise* ("The Departure," 1898), a fine example of swift-moving dialogue with a tuneful, spontaneous, and deftly orchestrated score, somewhat reminiscent of Cornelius. More in the *Meistersinger* idiom were Blech's comic operas *Das war ich* ("That Was I," 1902) and the more ambitious *Versiegelt* ("Sealed," 1908); but these, like Wolf's *Corregidor*, suffered from the music being, as a rule, too heavy and polyphonic for the simple librettos. Two other similar comic operas of this period were Schillings's *Pfeifertag* ("The Parliament of Pipers," 1899) and R. Strauss's *Feuersnot* ("The Fire Famine," 1901),

[46] Letter of Wolf to Grohe, 1890. See Istel, "German Opera Since Wagner," pp. 278–79.

[47] Moser, *Geschichte der deutschen Musik* III, 397.

[48] For instance : the duet "In solchen Abendfeierstunden," Act II; Frasquita's "In dem Schatten meiner Locken" (Act I), a charming song taken from Wolf's earlier *Spanisches Liederbuch*; Luka's monologue (Act III, sc. 3), the most nearly dramatic music in the opera.

[49] Studies by Chop and Specht.

[50] Slonimsky, *Music Since 1900*.

the latter an extraordinary combination of humor, eroticism, and autobiography, with music which shows the composer in transition from his
early Wagnerian style to that of *Salome* and *Elektra*. On the whole,
however, German comic opera of this type in the late nineteenth and the
early twentieth century is disappointing. No unified or generally
accepted tradition was evolved, and individual works of talent remained
isolated experiments which their composers seemed unable to repeat.

It was otherwise with the *Volksoper*. Two works of this class in the
late nineteenth century were Ignaz Brüll's (1846–1907) *Das goldene
Kreuz* ("The Golden Cross," 1875), a pleasant comedy with music
slightly reminiscent of Auber; and the popular *Trompeter von Säck-
ingen* (1884) by the Alsatian Viktor Nessler (1841–90), with men's
choruses, airs, and dances all in a simple, tuneful style. Even more successful was *Der Evangelimann* (1895) by the Austrian Wilhelm Kienzl
(1857–1941).[51] The personage of the "Evangelimann" has no English
equivalent; he is a wandering mendicant who receives alms in return
for reading and telling stories from the Scriptures. Kienzl's appeal is
founded on the application of Wagnerian techniques to nonheroic subjects, but much of his musical material has a distinctly folklike flavor
(Example 104). *Der Evangelimann* is, in fact, a kind of anthology of
popular dance and song types, together with sentimental melodies in the
vein of Nessler and amusing reminiscences of *Lohengrin, Tristan, Die
Meistersinger,* and *Hänsel und Gretel*— all attached to a libretto of the
most flagrantly melodramatic-romantic sort. Its popularity in Germany
and Austria may be judged by the fact that *Der Evangelimann* had over
5,300 performances in the first forty years of its existence. Closely related
to Kienzl's work is that of another Austrian, Julius Bittner (1874–
1939),[52] whose operas (to his own texts) are based on a folklike type of
melody, alternating closed numbers with declamatory passages and combining sentiment with humor. *Die rote Gred* ("Red-headed Gred,"
1907) and *Der Musikant* ("The Musician," 1910) show his characteristic style in purest form; *Der Bergsee* ("The Mountain Lake," 1911) has
curious post-Wagnerian reminiscences. *Das höllisch Gold* ("The Infernal
Gold," 1916), a humorous miracle play, was his most varied and most
popular work. Likewise in the field of people's opera must be noted the

---

[51] Two *Festschriften* (1917, 1937) have been dedicated to Kienzl; see his autobiography and other writings; essay by Morold in Segnitz's *Monographien* III;
selections from the autobiography and letters in *Kienzl-Rosegger*, ed. H. Sittner.

[52] Biography by R. Specht.

*Der Evangelimann,* Act I

EXAMPLE 104

KIENZL

O Zit-ter-bart, o Zit-ter-bart, o Franz Xa-ve-rius Zit-ter-bart! Du

triffst ja nicht den La-den mehr; die Ku-gel ist für dich zu schwer.

Viennese Richard Heuberger (1850–1914) with *Barfüssele* (1905) and the Czech Karel Weis (1862–1944) with *Der polnische Jude* (1901), both works popular in their day. Finally may be mentioned the Viennese operetta, which flourished in the early twentieth century with new hits by Franz Lehár[53] (1870–1948; *Die lustige Witwe,* "The Merry Widow," 1905), Oscar Straus[54] (1870–1954; *Ein Walzertraum,* "A Waltz Dream," 1907; *Der tapfere Soldat,* "The Chocolate Soldier," 1908), and Leo Fall (1873–1925; *Die Dollarprinzessin,* "The Dollar Princess," 1907).

The way of recourse to the *Märchenoper* as a means of escape from wholesale imitation of Wagner—in effect, a return to one kind of subject matter that had been current in the early romantic era—was discovered almost inadvertently. Alexander Ritter (1833–96),[55] a disciple of Liszt and composer of a number of historically important symphonic poems, had produced at Munich in 1885 a fairy-tale opera, *Der faule Hans* ("Lazy Hans"), which, although it had only a moderate success, is of interest as being a forerunner of a most important fairy-tale opera which came out in 1893: Engelbert Humperdinck's (1854–1921)[56] *Hänsel*

[53] Biographies by Czech (1957) and Peteani.
[54] Grun, *Prince of Vienna* (1955).
[55] Biography by Von Hausegger (1907).
[56] Biography by Besch; Kuhlmann, *Stil und Form in der Musik von Humperdincks Hänsel und Gretel.*

*und Gretel.* Humperdinck first wrote this music for a play for his sister's children to perform at home; made into a full opera, it caught the public fancy to such a degree as to start a whole new school in Germany. People turned with relief from the misty depths of mythology to the homely, familiar, enchanted world of the fairy tale, to subjects like those which their grandparents had enjoyed in the days of Marschner and Lortzing. The transition was made easier because Humperdinck kept up an appearance of loyalty to Wagner: the music of *Hänsel und Gretel* is, in fact, a peculiar mixture of German folk melody and Wagnerian polyphony. Perhaps the texture is too complicated for the subject matter, but if this be a fault, it is one easy to forgive in view of the many musical beauties and the heartfelt, simple emotion of the work. The music brings together many qualities rooted in the affections of Germans over generations: the songs and dances of the children, the idyllic forest scenes, just enough of the supernatural (but with a comic touch), and the chorale-like feeling of the "Evening blessing" melody, which recurs in the finale to the words

> When past bearing is our grief,
> God himself will send relief.

Among the many fairy-tale operas in neo-Wagnerian style that followed *Hänsel und Gretel* were Humperdinck's *Königskinder* ("The Royal Children"), first composed in 1898 as incidental music to a play made into an opera ten years later; Zöllner's best opera, *Die versunkene Glocke* ("The Sunken Bell"), in 1899; *Lobetanz* (1898) by Ludwig Thuille (1861–1907),[57] *Illsebill* (1903) by Friedrich Klose (1862–1942),[58] *Rübezahl* (1904) by Hans Sommer (1837–1922),[59] and two works by Humperdinck's pupil Leo Blech (871–1958):[60] *Alpenkönig und Menschenfeind* ("Alpine King and Man's Enemy," 1903; revised in 1917 under the title of *Rappelkopf*) and *Aschenbrödel* ("Cinderella," 1905). Here in varying degrees the post-Wagnerian musical idiom was adapted to popular subjects. To this group of composers belongs also Richard Wagner's son Siegfried Wagner (1869–1930),[61] another pupil of

---

[57] Biography by Munter (1923).          [58] Biography by Knappe (1921).
[59] Biography by E. Valentin (1939).
[60] W. Jacob, ed., *Leo Blech: Ein Brevier* (1931).
[61] See S. Wagner, *Erinnerungen*; letters, ed. Rebois; Glasenapp, *Siegfried Wagner und seine Kunst*; Du Moulin-Eckart, *Wahnfried*; other studies by Pretzsch and Daube. (*Der Bärenhäuter* is untranslatable. The story on which it is based will be found under the title "Des Teufels russiger Bruder" in Grimm, *Kinder- und Haus-Märchen* [Berlin, 1815] II, 100–105.)

Humperdinck, whose *Bärenhäuter* (1899) was the first and best of a long series of fairy-tale operas to his own texts which attempt to combine legend, symbolism, and humor in a popular style. None of the later works, however, attained the lasting success of *Hänsel und Gretel*, which remains the classic example of late nineteenth-century German *Märchenoper* as well as a perennial source of pleasure for children of all ages.

# CHAPTER 25

# NATIONALISM AND OPERA

The nineteenth century saw the rise of independent schools of composition in many countries that had previously been tributary to the chief musical nations of Europe or, like Spain and England, had been for a long time only on the periphery of the main developments. In the growth of musical nationalism opera played a leading part, since the use of characteristic national subjects, often from patriotic motives, stimulated composers to seek an equally characteristic national expression in their music. National operas, as a rule, were not exportable; only exceptionally (as in the case of some Russian operas) did these works make their way into foreign countries. The national schools are important in the history of nineteenth-century opera, however, and it is the purpose of the present chapter to give a survey of their development.

RUSSIA.[1] Native opera began to appear in Russia before the end of the eighteenth century. It had been preceded, as in the countries of western Europe, by various types of drama that used music in incidental

[1] Bibliography: (1) General histories of Russian music: Asaf'ev, *Russkaia muzyka ot nachala XIX stoletiia*; Akademiia Nauk, Institut istorii iskusstv, *Istoriia russkoi muzyki*; Keldysh, *Istoriia russkoi muzyki*, Vols. II and III; Livanova, *Ocherki i materialy po istorii muzykal'noi kultury*; Calvocoressi and Abraham, *Masters of Russian Music*; Abraham, *Studies in Russian Music*; idem, *On Russian Music*. (2) General works on Russian opera: Bernandt, *Slovar' oper*; Cheshikhin, *Istoriia russkoi opery*; Druskin, *Voprosy muzykal'noi dramaturgii opery*; Iarustovskii, *Dramaturgiia russkoi opernoi klassiki*; Asaf'ev, *Izbrannye trudy*; Newmarch, *The Russian Opera*. See also articles in *Sovetskaia muzyka*. (3) For the period before Glinka: Findeisen, *Ocherki po istorii muzyki v Rossii . . . do kontsa XVIII veka*; idem, "The Earliest Russian Operas"; Ginzburg, *Russkii muzykal'nyi teatr 1700–1835*; Rabinovich, *Russkaia opera do Glinki*; Livanova, *Russkaia muzykal'naia kul'tura XVIII veka*; Gozenpud, *Muzykal'nyi teatr v Rosii*; Lehmann, *Russlands Oper und Singspiel in der zweiten Hälfte des 18. Jahrhunderts*; Seaman, "The National Element in Early Russian Opera"; Selden, "Early Roots of Russian Opera"; Mooser, *Opéras . . . joués en Russie durant le 18e siècle*. See also in bibliography, titles under Berkov (1950) and Druskin (1956).

fashion : religious mystery plays, going back to the sixteenth century or earlier, as well as school dramas and court pageants in the seventeenth and eighteenth centuries. When the first public theatre was opened at St. Petersburg in 1703 its offerings consisted for the most part of foreign plays which occasionally used incidental music. The record of Italian opera at the Russian court begins in 1731; under Catherine the Great (reigned 1762–96) St. Petersburg became as much of a cosmopolitan center for opera as London, with Galuppi, Paisiello, Cimarosa, Salieri, and others in residence for varying lengths of time, while many other Italians, as well as the leading composers of the French opéra comique and German Singspiel, were represented in the repertoires. During the last quarter of the century nearly 350 operas had their premieres in Russia, over thirty new ones coming out in the year 1778 alone. Most of the operas by foreign composers that were performed in Russia were sung in the original languages, and even some by Russian composers had foreign-language librettos : thus Dmitri Bortniansky (1751–1825), who during his years of study in Italy had produced Italian operas, after his return to St. Petersburg in 1779 wrote comic operas to French librettos.

Nevertheless, by the 1770s operas with original Russian texts began to appear; musical scores of about thirty such works before 1800 have been preserved, and librettos of forty more. Most of them are comic and some are satirical, while sentimental or fairy-tale elements begin to appear toward the end of the century; the usual form is spoken dialogue alternating with solo airs and ensembles. The plots typically introduce characteristic Russian scenes and persons and the music may draw on popular folk melodies. In one early comic opera entitled *The Miller-Magician, Deceiver and Matchmaker* (Moscow, 1779), all the songs were set to popular tunes, in the manner of the earliest French opéras comiques. More often, however, the composers incorporated folk song into their own more sophisticated style which they had learned from Western examples or training. The leading composer of Russian opera before 1800 was Evstigney Ipatovich Fomin (1761–1800), who produced a half-dozen comic operas at St. Petersburg between 1786 and 1800; his *The Coachmen* (1787) had a score entirely based on folk material and including choruses in which the composer attempted to transcribe the authentic polyphony of Russian folk song.

Russian opera was thus well under way by the end of the eighteenth century. Under Alexander I (reigned 1801–25) the great upsurge of national sentiment, imbued in Russia as elsewhere with the spirit of Byronesque romanticism, wonderfully encouraged the production of national opera. Curiously, one of the principal composers of Russian opera in the early nineteenth century was a versatile Neapolitan, Catterino Cavos (1775–1840), who came to St. Petersburg in 1799 and remained for the rest of his life. He composed, to Russian, French, or Italian texts, over forty operas; among those on Russian themes and in the Russian language were *Ilya the Hero* (1807), *The Firebird* (1822), and *Ivan Susanin* (1815), his best work and one that remained a model of musical nationalism until Glinka's opera on the same subject replaced it twenty years later. Among the native-born composers of the early and middle nineteenth century was Alexey Nikolayevich Verstovsky (1799–1862), whose chief operas, *The Tomb of Askold*[2] (Moscow, 1835) and *Thunder* (Moscow, 1857), held the stage in Russia into the twentieth century.

An important milestone in the history of Russian opera was the performance in 1836 at St. Petersburg of *A Life for the Tsar* (now known under its original title, *Ivan Susanin*) by Mikhail Ivanovich Glinka (1804–57).[3] Although it has sometimes been regarded as the very foundation and source of Russian national opera, *A Life for the Tsar* owed its reputation in this respect more to its plot and its immense and long-continued popularity in Russia than to any consistent, strongly pronounced national qualities in the music, which indeed sounds for the most part as much French or Italian as Russian. Quotations from folk song occur in the opening of Susanin's aria No. 3 and in the accompaniments to Susanin's last two solo passages at the end of Act IV, and the choral theme of the epilogue so took hold on popular fancy as to become almost a second national anthem; but, with few exceptions, melodies such as that of the Bridal Chorus in Act III (Example 105) represent Glinka's nearest approach in this score to a genuinely national idiom. Compensation may be found for the undistinguished quality of much of the music in the clear and varied orchestration, which was a model for all the later Russian nationalists, including Rimsky-Korsakov.

[2] Given at New York in 1869, the first Russian opera in America.

[3] Akademiia Nauk, Institut istorii iskusstv, *Pamiati Glinki, 1857–1957: Issledovaniia i materialy*; Glinka, *Literaturnoe nasledie*; *idem, Zapiski*; see also titles in bibliography under Livanova (1950), Stasov (1953, 1955), Dmitriev (1957), and Protopopov (1961). Biographies in English by Calvocoressi (1911) and Montagu-Nathan (1916).

### A *Life for the Tsar*, Act III

EXAMPLE 105                                        GLINKA

Moreover, in the extensive use of recurring motifs Glinka was far in advance of any opera composer before Wagner. The Polish soldiers, for example, are characterized by themes in the national dance rhythms of polonaise and mazurka, which, first heard in the ball scene of Act II, recur in Act III at the entrance of the Poles, and the mazurka rhythm again at their appearance in Act IV. The quasi-folk-song theme of the opening chorus is used as a leitmotif of Russian heroism, sung by the hero Susanin in Act III as he defies the Polish conspirators; and the opposing national motifs are again contrasted in the orchestral introduction to the epilogue. Susanin's last aria (Act IV) is to a large extent made up of previously heard themes, the recurrences here producing a purposeful dramatic effect. The theme of the final chorus, repeated again and again with cumulative power, has been subtly prepared by two or three statements earlier in the opera. This brilliant epilogue is not only the climax of patriotic emotion but also a fine example of the highly colored mass effects of sound and spectacle so beloved in Russian opera.

Although *A Life for the Tsar* was more popular, the significant musical foundations for the future were laid in Glinka's second and last opera, *Ruslan and Ludmila* (1842). The libretto is a fantastic and incoherent fairy tale adapted from a poem of Pushkin; the music, in spite of some traces of Weber, is more original than that of Glinka's earlier opera, and the musical characterizations more definite. The system of recurring motifs is abandoned; almost the only trace of it is the recurrent descending whole-tone scale associated with the wicked magician Chernomor (Example 106)—said to be the earliest use of the whole-tone scale in European music. At least five distinct styles or procedures characteristic of later Russian music appear in *Ruslan and Ludmila*: (1) the heroic, broad, solemn, declamatory style, with modal suggestions and archaic effect (introduction and song of the Bard, Act I);

EXAMPLE 106    *Ruslan and Ludmila*, Act IV

GLINKA

(2) the Russian lyrical style, with expressive melodic lines of a folkish cast, delicately colored harmony featuring the lowered sixth or raised fifth, and chromatically moving inner voices (Fina's ballad and Ruslan's first aria in Act II); (3) depiction of fantastic occurrences by means of unusual harmonies, such as whole-tone passages or chord progressions pivoting about one note (scene of Ludmila's abduction, toward the end of Act I); (4) oriental atmosphere, sometimes using genuine oriental themes (Persian chorus at opening of Act III), sometimes original melodies (Ratmir's romance, Act V), but always characterized by fanciful arabesque figures in the accompaniment and a languorous harmony and orchestration; (5) the vividly colored choruses and dances, with glittering instrumentation and often daring harmonies (chorus in honor of Lel, finale of Act I; Chernomor's march and following dances,

especially the *lezginka*, finale of Act IV)— models for such scenes in Borodin's *Prince Igor*, Rimsky-Korsakov's *Sadko*, and even Stravinsky's *Sacre du Printemps*.

The first important Russian opera after *Ruslan and Ludmila* was Alexander Sergeyevich Dargomyzhsky's (1813–69) [4] *Russalka* (1856), likewise on a text from Pushkin and somewhat similar in subject to Glinka's work. Musically, however, it was inferior to *Ruslan*; its best feature was the realistic declamation of the recitative, which Dargomyzhsky proceeded to develop to the highest degree in his last opera, *The Stone Guest*. This work (a setting of Pushkin's Don Juan drama) was completed after Dargomyzhsky's death by Cui, orchestrated by Rimsky-Korsakov, and first performed in 1872. It is no masterpiece and never had a popular success, but it was influential on later Russian opera because of the composer's attempt to write the entire work (except for some songs near the beginning of Act II) in a melodic recitative, a vocal line which should be in every detail the equivalent of the words. The result, though accurate in declamation and dramatic in places, lacks sharp characterization or melodic interest, and there is no compensation for the melodic poverty in the orchestral part, which is conceived as accompaniment rather than a continuous symphonic tissue. In his repudiation of set musical forms and his high respect for the words, Dargomyzhsky may have been influenced to a slight degree by Wagner's theories, though there is no trace of Wagner in the musical substance itself. Harmonically, some interest attaches to Dargomyzhsky's use of whole-tone scale fragments as motifs for the Statue and some passages constructed entirely on this scale.

Dargomyzhsky had arrived in his own way at certain features of the Wagnerian music drama; but the most explicit and self-conscious disciple of Wagner in Russia was Alexander Nikolayevich Serov (1820–71). His first opera, *Judith* (1863), shows the composer's admiration for all the methods of grand opera of the Meyerbeer and early Wagner type. In his third and last opera, *The Power of Evil* (completed by N. T. Soloviev and first produced in 1871), Serov aimed "to embody the Wagnerian theories in a music drama written in Russian, on a Russian subject," and to keep "more closely than has yet been done [*sic*] to the forms of Russian popular music, as preserved unchanged in our folk-

[4] See studies by Pekelis (1951) and Serov (1953).

songs." [5] The result, however, was a disappointing hybrid, full of striking but superficial effects. Serov's operas won little regard from musicians but were nevertheless popular enough with the public to remain in the repertoire of Russian opera companies until the First World War.

From about the middle of the nineteenth century, Russian musicians were divided into two groups. In one were the professional, foreign-trained, and officially supported composers who were not primarily interested in musical nationalism but wished to see Russian musical life develop along the same lines as in western Europe, particularly Germany. The head of this school was Anton Rubinstein (1829–94), the famous pianist, founder and first director of the Imperial Conservatory at St. Petersburg. Of Rubinstein's nineteen operas (eight on Russian and eleven on German texts), *The Demon* (1875) had a considerable success both in Russia and abroad. Its libretto strongly recalls Wagner's *Fliegende Holländer*, but the forms are conventional and the musical style is that of pre-Wagnerian romanticism mingled with some oriental elements. Musically more interesting, though less popular, was *The Merchant Kalashnikov* (1880). Rubinstein's biblical operas, or rather stage oratorios (for example, *The Maccabees,* 1875), are remembered now only for a few separate numbers.

The leading composer of the nonnationalist school was Piotr Ilyich Tchaikovsky (1840–93),[6] in whom Slavic temperament and German training were leavened by lyrical genius and a lively appreciation of Italian opera and French ballet. Reckoned by bulk, if not also by musical excellence, Tchaikovsky's achievement is as important in the field of opera as in that of the symphony. After two early works in which he experimented with the then fashionable nationalism—*The Guardsman* (1874) and *Vakula the Smith* (1876; in a revised version as *The Little Slippers,* 1887)—Tchaikovsky produced his masterpiece, *Eugen Onegin*, at Moscow in 1879. In both the libretto (after Pushkin) and the musical style this is an old-fashioned romantic opera, but the music is in Tchaikovsky's happiest vein, with graceful melodies, expressive har-

[5] Quoted in Newmarch, *The Russian Opera*, p. 157.
[6] Iarustovskiĭ, *Opernaia dramaturgiia Chaĭkovskogo*; *Muzykal'noe nasledie Chaĭkovskogo*; biographies in English by Newmarch and E. Evans; *Diaries* in English translation; Abraham, ed., *Tchaikovsky: A Symposium*; Bowen and Von Meck, "*Beloved Friend*"; Zagiba, *Tschaikovskij*; see also titles in bibliography under Al'shvang, Berliand-Chernaia, Iakovlev.

monies, transparent and imaginative orchestration—true and living in expression without the hysterical emotionalism of some of the later symphonic works. The character of the heroine, Tatiana, is delineated with especial sympathy, and that of Onegin himself is scarcely less vivid. The ballet music (particularly the waltz in Act II) is tuneful and charming, as are also the choruses in Act I. Tchaikovsky's next three operas were in a more heavily dramatic style. *The Maid of Orleans* (1881, libretto after Schiller) was less successful than *Mazeppa* (1884, from a poem of Pushkin), which contains two of the composer's finest dramatic moments: the monologue of Kochubey and the extremely pathetic final scene. *The Enchantress* (1887) had such a disappointing reception that Tchaikovsky returned to his more characteristic lyrical style for his last two operatic works: *The Queen of Spades* (1890), his most popular opera next to *Onegin*, and *Iolanthe* (1892). In *The Queen of Spades*, based on a melodramatic tale of Pushkin, Tchaikovsky attained a more nearly perfect balance than in any of his other operas between dramatic declamation, lyrical expressiveness, and divertissement music (see especially the ballets in Act II).

The struggle for Russian national music, begun by Glinka and Dargomyzhsky, was carried on after 1860 by a group of five composers:[7] Balakirev, Cui, Mussorgsky, Borodin, and Rimsky-Korsakov. All were amateurs; only Rimsky-Korsakov—and he only at a comparatively late stage of his career—ever had a thorough conventional technical training in composition. Balakirev wrote no operas. César Antonovich Cui (1835–1918)[8] wrote ten, but most of them are not Russian in subject, none are Russian in musical style, and, with the possible exception of *William Ratcliffe* (1869), they are unimportant from any point of view. The Russian national opera in its highest development, therefore, is the work of the remaining three composers of the "mighty five."

The lack of the usual technical musical education (which meant, at this time, a German conservatory training) had the advantage of turning the nationalist composers to the resources of their own country for dramatic and musical material, and to their own instincts and national traditions for the means of shaping this material into operatic form. These conditions were especially important for Modest Petrovich

[7] Livanova, *Stasov i russkaia klassicheskaia opera*.

[8] Cui, *Izbrannye stat'i* (1952). The composer's *Musique en Russie* (1880) is the source of many errors concerning the Russian national school.

Mussorgsky (1839–81),[9] the most original of the group, who in *Boris Godunov* (St. Petersburg, 1874) created one of the great masterpieces of nineteenth-century opera, a monument of much that is most typical in Russian musical drama and at the same time an absolutely personal, inimitable work. *Boris* was first composed in 1868–69 and rewritten in 1871–72. In 1896 Rimsky-Korsakov prepared a thoroughly revised version, with "corrections" of the harmony, improvements in the orchestration, a different order of scenes, and many cuts; the deleted portions were restored in a second revision (1908), and in this form the opera made its way into the repertoire of all foreign opera houses. After the revolution of 1918 the composer's own score was revived for performances in Russia, and this original version was published in 1928.

The libretto of *Boris Godunov* was prepared by Mussorgsky himself, using as sources Pushkin's drama of the same title and N. M. Karamzin's *History of the Russian Empire*. The character of the half-mad emperor Boris (reigned 1598–1605), especially as sung and acted by Feodor Chaliapin, is one of the most vivid in all opera. An equally potent force in the action is the cruel, anonymous mass of the Russian people—a force visibly present in the mighty crowd scenes but also invisibly working like the relentless pressure of Fate at every step toward the catastrophe of the drama. With grim poetic vision Mussorgsky set this primeval force in the closing scene of the opera [10] over against the figure of the Idiot Boy, who, left alone at the last on a darkened stage, keens his lament: "Weep, ye people; soon the foe shall come, soon the gloom shall fall; woe to our land; weep, Russian folk, weep, hungry folk!" One senses in such scenes the influence of the democratic ideals prevalent in Russia during the sixties and seventies in the period after the liberation of the serfs under Alexander II, ideals so eloquently expounded in the writings of Tolstoy. In comparison to the elemental power of most of Mussorgsky's opera, the love episode (Act III) seems both dramatically and musically a pale diversion—as does most of the love interest in Russian opera generally. In form, *Boris Godunov* is a series of detached scenes rather than a coherently developed plot, thus

[9] Biography by Calvocoressi (1956); Leyda and Bertensson, *The Musorgsky Reader*; Godet, *En Marge de Boris Godounof*; Abraham, "Moussorgsky's *Boris* and Pushkin's"; Hoffmann-Erbrecht, "Grundlagen der Melodiebildung bei Mussorgski"; cf. also Szabolcsi, *Bausteine zu einer Geschichte der Melodie*.

[10] References are to Mussorgsky's 1874 version, piano-vocal score published by J. & W. Chester, Ltd., London, cop. 1926.

illustrating the Russian habit, in both musical and literary creation (compare Tolstoy's *War and Peace*), of complete absorption in the present moment, leaving the total impression to be achieved by the cumulative impact of many separate effects.

A striking feature of Mussorgsky's music is the way in which, in the declamation, the melodic line always manages to convey the emotion of the text in the most direct, compressed, and forcible manner imaginable. Perhaps the best examples of this are the two most familiar scenes of the opera, the last part of Act II (including the "clock scene") and the farewell and death of Boris in Act IV. Here Mussorgsky realized the ideal of dramatic, semimelodic recitative which Glinka had foreshadowed in *Ruslan and Ludmila* and which Dargomyzhsky had sought in *The Stone Guest*. Much of the same gloomy power, though with less violence, is displayed in the monastery scene at the beginning of Act I. A more songful idiom, equally characteristic of the composer, is heard in the first part of the Inn scene (Act I, scene 2). Still more characteristic are the children's songs in the first part of Act II—examples of a psychological insight and musical style in which Mussorgsky is almost unique, and which he had demonstrated in his song cycle *The Nursery* (composed 1870–72). It is to be noted that in all these songs, whether declamatory or lyrical, the melodic line is the guiding factor. It is a style of melody which, with its peculiar intervals (especially the falling fourth at cadences), monotonous reiteration of patterns, irregularity of phrase structure, and archaic, modal basis, has grown most intimately out of Russian folk song. To this melodic line the harmony is generally a mere added support, but it likewise is of a strongly personal type, blended of modal feeling, impressionistic—often childlike—fondness for the mere sound of certain combinations, an unconventional harmonic training, and (one suspects) the happy outcome of improvisation at the piano. While the harmony remains consonant and tonal, nevertheless any effort to analyze a typical passage of Mussorgsky according to textbook principles will show how completely foreign his methods were to the conventional practice of the nineteenth century. Not unrelated to the naïveté of his harmonies is Mussorgsky's reveling in raw, massive color effects. This trait is seen most clearly in the great crowd scene of the coronation, the orchestral introduction of which is also an example of the Russian mannerism of alternating chords pivoting on one common tone (in this case A-flat$^7$ and D$^7$ on the common tone G-flat=F-sharp).

The chorus itself in this scene is built on the same traditional tune that Beethoven used in his second "Razumovsky" Quartet.

Of Mussorgsky's other operas the principal one is *Khovantchina*, a "people's drama" upon which he worked devotedly but spasmodically from 1873 until the end of his life, but which was left unfinished after all; completed and orchestrated by Rimsky-Korsakov, it was performed at St. Petersburg in 1886. Mussorgsky here took for his subject the conflict of the old feudal regime and the sect of the Old Believers with the new Western tendencies in Russia during the first years after the accession of Peter the Great (1689). Both libretto and music are as intensely national as in *Boris*, but the drama moves less vigorously and the musical style in general is less well sustained. Nevertheless the best numbers— including the prelude, the crowd scenes, Shaklovity's aria in Act III, and especially some of the choruses of the Old Believers where Mussorgsky seems to have distilled the very spirit of ancient Russian church style— are equal to anything elsewhere in his works.

Mussorgsky's cardinal aim was realistic expression at all costs : truth before beauty, melodic recitative "*true to life* and not melodic in the classical sense . . . a sort of melody created by [human] speech . . . intelligently justified melody" [11] (Example 107). To this end, he avoided conventional formulae, evolving a style as restrained, economical, and incapable of successful imitation as that of Debussy. By temperament, Mussorgsky was inclined to depict predominantly that side of the Russian character which gives itself over to gloom and mysticism, to the emotions of violence, brutality, and madness which predominate in *Boris Godunov* and *Khovantchina*. A different, though no less normal, aspect of the national personality comes to life in *Prince Igor*, the opera by Alexander Porfirievich Borodin (1833–87) [12] first performed at St. Petersburg in 1890. The libretto is by the composer, after a plan by Stasov; the score, unfinished at Borodin's death, was completed by Glazounov and Rimsky-Korsakov and orchestrated by the latter. The story is taken from a medieval Russian epic (apparently genuine, though long suspected to be an eighteenth-century forgery), but the central plot is of little importance except to give occasion for the many episodic scenes which make up most of the opera. Some of these scenes are comic, others

[11] Letter to Stasov, December 25, 1876 (*The Musorgsky Reader*, p. 353).
[12] Biographies by Dianin (Russian; 2d ed., 1960) and Abraham (English, 1927); Habets, *Borodin and Liszt*.

EXAMPLE 107

Andante

MUSSORGSKY

are love scenes, but a large place is also reserved for spectacle, dances, and choruses (for example, the well-known Polovtsian ballets in Act II). The musical ancestor of *Prince Igor* is Glinka's *Ruslan and Ludmila*, and its principal descendant is Rimsky-Korsakov's *Sadko*. The style of *Prince Igor* is predominantly lyric, with many of the arias in conventional Italian forms; there is some arioso writing, but little dramatic recitative in the manner of Dargomyzhsky. Indeed, the music is not dramatic at all in the sense in which *Boris Godunov* is dramatic; it does not so much embody a drama as present a series of musical tableaux to accompany and complete the stage pictures. In technical details also it is less unconventional than Mussorgsky; the most original portions are the oriental scenes, for which Borodin evolved an idiom partly based on Central Asiatic themes but fundamentally an outgrowth of his eighteen-year-long absorption in the subject and his study of all available musical and historical material. His ancestry (he was the illegitimate son of a Caucasian prince) may also have given him a particular bent toward this style which, with its persistent rhythmic patterns, chromatic intervals, and melodic arabesques, dominates the second and third acts of the opera. *Prince Igor*, like *Boris Godunov*, makes some use of recurring motifs, but a more important source of unity is the derivation, unobtrusive but unmistakable, of many of the themes of Acts II and III from phrases in the melody of the first Polovtsian chorus.[13]

If *Boris Godunov* represents a darkly fanatical aspect of the Russian character and *Prince Igor* a cheerful, hearty one, then the picture is completed by Nikolay Andreyevich Rimsky-Korsakov (1844–1908),[14] whose most characteristic operas reflect a fairy-tale world of fantasy, romance, and innocent humor. This individual musical and dramatic style of Rimsky-Korsakov was not arrived at without some experimentation, and even after it had been achieved, he still continued to experiment. His first two operas, *The Maid of Pskov* (1873), and *May Night* (1880), showed the influence of Dargomyzhsky and Glinka. *The Snow Maiden* (1882) was more spontaneous and original, based on a fairy legend with vaguely symbolic touches. *Mlada* (1892), in which some

---

[13] Abraham, *Studies in Russian Music*, pp. 132–41.

[14] N. A. Rimskiï-Korsakov, *Letopis' moeï muzykal'noï zhizni* (7th ed., 1955); English (from the 5th ed., 1935) as *My Musical Life* (New York, 1942); A. N. Rimskiï-Korsakov, *N. A. Rimskiï-Korsakov: Zhizn' i tvorchestvo*; see other titles in bibliography under Gozenpud (1957), Iastrebtsev, and USSR, Tsentral'nyï gosudarstvennyï literaturnyï arkhiv (1951); Abraham, *Rimsky-Korsakov*.

traces of Wagner may be seen, was adapted from a libretto which was to have been collectively composed by Cui, Mussorgsky, Rimsky-Korsakov, and Borodin twenty years before (this joint undertaking was never completed). *Christmas Eve* (1895) was, like *May Night*, taken from a story by N. V. Gogol (1809–52). Both these works are village tales, with love stories and comic-supernatural additions; the subject of *Christmas Eve* is the same as that of Tchaikovsky's *Vakula the Smith*. In 1898 appeared Rimsky-Korsakov's masterpiece, *Sadko*,[15] an "opera legend," a typical combination of the epic and fantastic in a libretto adapted jointly by the composer and V. I. Bielsky from an eleventh-century legend and drawing much of the musical material from Rimsky-Korsakov's symphonic poem of the same title (1867, with revisions in 1869 and 1891). Then followed several experimental works : *Mozart and Salieri*, *Boyarinya Vera Sheloga* (both 1898), and *The Czar's Bride* (1899), the last a real tragedy with arias and concerted numbers in the old Italian style, "the old operatic convention of the first half of the nineteenth century decked out with Wagnerian leit-motives and Dargomizhskian 'melodic recitative' and mildly flavoured here and there with the Russian folk-idiom." [16] *Czar Saltan* (1900), another fairy tale, returned to distinctive national traits in both libretto and music. *Servilia* (1902) and *Pan Voyevode* (1904) were unsuccessful essays in more dramatic plots with Wagnerian influence in the music. *Kaschey the Immortal* (1902) was also Wagnerian in technique, with declamatory lines and constant use of lietmotifs, as well as in the redemption idea woven into the legendary story; the music represents Rimsky-Korsakov's extreme excursion in the direction of chromaticism and dissonance. The last two operas were, with *Sadko*, the most important : *The Legend of the Invisible City of Kitezh* (1907) and *The Golden Cockerel* (1909). *Kitezh* has been called "the Russian Parsifal" because of its mystical and symbolical story, based on two ancient legends. But beyond an evident aspiration to combine features of pagan pantheism and orthodox Christianity in the figure of the heroine Fevronya, the symbolism is vague and not of fundamental importance. *The Golden Cockerel*, from a humorous-fantastic tale of Pushkin, is more objective and ironic, even satirical, but equally unclear as to the detailed application of its moral.

Other than a gradual growth in complexity of idiom and an in-

[15] See monograph by Tsukkerman (1936).
[16] Abraham, *Studies in Russian Music*, p. 248.

creasing skill in the fabrication of piquant harmonic and coloristic effects, there is little that can be called an evolution in Rimsky-Korsakov's musical style through these fifteen operas—nothing remotely comparable to the change in Wagner from *Die Feen* to *Parsifal*. Rimsky-Korsakov was a lyrical and pictorial composer, resembling Mendelssohn in exquisiteness of detail as well as in the absence of strongly emotional and dramatic qualities. The realism of Mussorgsky was not for him : art, he once said, was "essentially the most enchanting and intoxicating of lies" [17]—a statement that doubtless explains much in his own music. The dramatic force of the last act of *The Maid of Pskov* and the serious musical characterization of Fevronya in *Kitezh* are exceptional in his work; his original, personal contribution lies in another realm.

[He] must be granted the quite peculiar power of evoking a fantastic world entirely his own, half-real, half-supernatural, a world as limited, as distinctive and as delightful as the world of the Grimms' fairy-tales or as Alice's Wonderland. It is a world in which the commonplace and matter-of-fact are inextricably confused with the fantastic, naivete with sophistication, the romantic with the humorous, and beauty with absurdity. He was not its inventor, of course; he owed it in the first place to Pushkin and Gogol. But he gave it a queer touch of his own, linking it with Slavonic antiquity and hinting at pantheistic symbolism, which makes it peculiarly his. And musically, of course, he reigns in it undisputed. He invented the perfect music for such a fantastic world : music insubstantial when it was matched with unreal things, deliciously lyrical when it touched reality, in both cases coloured from the most superb palette musician has ever held.[18]

For Rimsky-Korsakov an opera was primarily a musical rather than a dramatic-literary work; hence the importance of musical design, which frequently dominates both the poetry and the scenic plan (for example, the rondo form in the fourth tableau of *Sadko*). Along with this there is usually a definite association of certain keys with certain moods and, in most of the operas, a consistent use of recurring motifs. These are not, as in Wagner, the material out of which a symphonic fabric is developed but are rather melodic fragments (sometimes only a phrase from a large theme) or even inconspicuous harmonic progressions, woven into the opera in a kind of mosaic pattern; they are as often given to the voices as to the orchestra. In the harmony, two distinct idioms are usually found in each opera : one chromatic, fanciful, cunningly contrived, for the

---

[17] Quoted in Calvocoressi and Abraham, *Masters of Russian Music*, p. 411.
[18] Ibid., p. 422. Quoted by permission of the publisher.

EXAMPLE 108

*Sadko*, sc. 2

RIMSKY-KORSAKOV

*(Example 108 continued)*

imaginary scenes and characters (Example 108); and the other diatonic, solid, often modal, for the "real" world. The vocal parts, as usual in Russian opera, alternate between melodic recitative and closed aria-like forms. In his lyrical melodies, Rimsky-Korsakov owes much to the model of Glinka; his own melodies are elegant and graceful, though marked by certain persistently recurring formulae. An important factor in his style is the extensive use of folk tunes, and of original tunes of folk-song type; the source or inspiration for many of these was his own collection of Russian folk songs, made in 1876. Church melodies are also occasionally used, notably in *Kitezh*. The oriental idiom, however, is much less extensive and less significant in Rimsky-Korsakov's music than in that of either Balakirev or Borodin. Like all Russian opera composers, he excelled in the depiction of crowd scenes, especially in *The Maid of Pskov* (Act II), *Sadko, Kitezh* (Act II and finale), and the humorous ensembles in *May Night, Christmas Eve,* and *Sadko.* Above all, of course, he is distinguished for his mastery of orchestral effects, a virtuosity in the treatment of instrumental color such as few composers in history have equaled.

A number of minor Russian opera composers of the late nineteenth- and early twentieth-century period can be only briefly mentioned. Eduard Napravnik (1839–1916), as conductor of the St. Petersburg Opera from 1869, was influential in bringing out the works of the native school; the most successful of his own operas was *Dubrovsky* (1895). A pupil of Rimsky-Korsakov, but influenced in opera by Tchaikovsky, was Anton Stepanovich Arensky (1861–1906; *Raphael,* 1894). Also under the influence of Tchaikovsky were the operatic works of Sergey Vassilievich Rachmaninov (1873–1943),[19] Alexander Tikhonovich Gretchaninov (1864–1956), and Mikhail Mikhailovich Ippolitov-Ivanov (1859–1935). Sergey Ivanovich Taneyev (1856–1918) produced an *Orestes* trilogy (1895) in severe contrapuntal style with admixtures of Rubinstein and Tchaikovsky. The impressionist movement was reflected in Russian opera in the works of Vladimir Ivanovich Rebikov (1866–1920).

Early composers of opera in the Ukraine [20] were Semyon Stepanovich Gulak-Artemovsky (1813–73), whose *Zaporozhets za Dunayem* ("A

[19] Boelza, *S. V. Rakhmaninov i russkaia opera* (1947).

[20] Arkhymovych, *Ukraïns'ka klasychna opera*; Dovzhenko, *Narysy z istorii ykraïns'koi radians'koi muzyky.* Music in *Ukrainskaia klassicheskaia muzyka* (*Antologiia klassicheskoi muzyki narodov SSSR* [Moscow, Muzgiz, 1955], Vyp. 1).

Cossack Beyond the Danube," 1863), in spoken dialogue with simply harmonized songs and choruses, was long popular; and Pyotor Petrovich Sokalsky (1832–87)[21] with *Mazeppa* (1859), *Maiskaya noch* ("May Night," 1863), and *Obsada Dubno* ("The Siege of Dubno," 1878). The chief creator of Ukrainian national opera was Nikolai Vitalievich Lissenko (1842–1912), who used folk melodies in most of his works. His principal opera was *Taras Bulba* (1890); another work, *Natalka-Poltavka* ("Natalie from Poltava," 1890), was also popular, and he wrote two operas on librettos adapted from Gogol: *Rizdviana Nich* ("Christmas Night," 1882) and *Utoplena* (from "May Night," 1885).[22]

POLAND. The early history of opera in Poland[23] is similar to that in Russia, except that the importation of Italian operas began as early as 1628; the first regular court opera was organized five years later and presented a dozen Italian operas and ballets before 1646. A public opera theatre was constructed at Warsaw in 1724, but the opere serie of Hasse and other Italian composers failed to win a large following; after 1765, however, a repertoire of French opéra comique and Italian opera (sometimes in Polish translation) in the renamed "National Public Theatre" proved more attractive. The influence of an intense national spirit was evident in Polish opera from the 1770s onward. As in Russia, the first operas in Poland on national themes were in the form of spoken dialogue with songs interspersed. The earliest of such works was *Nedza uszczesliwiona* ("Misery Made Happy") by Mathias Kamienski (1734–1821), produced at Warsaw in 1778. Another notable early Polish opera was Jan Stefani's (1746–1829)[24] *Cracovians and Mountaineers* (1794); this remained popular to the end

[21] Biography by Karysheva (1959).

[22] On opera in some of the other nations of the Soviet Union, see Tigranov, *Armianskŭ muzykaľnyĭ teatr* (1960); Kulikovich, *Belaruskaia savetskaia opera* (1957).

[23] Bibliography: (1) General works on the history of Polish music: Jachimecki, *Historia Muzyki polskiej w zarysie*; *idem, Muzyka polska*; Reiss, *Najpiekniejsza ze wsystkich jest muzyka polska*; Opieński, *La Muusikue polonaise*. (2) General histories of opera in Poland: Karasowski, *Rys historyczny opery polskiej*; *Muzyka*, tom 10 ("Opera: Monografia zbiorowa"), ed. M. Gliński; Reiss, *Muzyka w Krakowie w XIX wieku*; Michaowski, *Opery polskie* (catalogue and chronology, 1788–1953); Glowacki, "The History of Polish Opera." (3) On the period before Moniuszko: Bernacki, *Teatr, dramat i muzyka za Stanislawa Augusta*; Zetowski, "Teoria polskiej opery narodowej z końca XVIII i poczatku XIX wieku"; Wierzbicka, *Zróda do historii teatru warszawskiego od roku 1762 do roku 1833*; Opieński, "Les Premiers Opéras polonais"; Golos, "Italian Baroque Opera in Seventeenth-Century Poland."

[24] See in bibliography, articles by Karasowski (1857), Niewiadomski (1931), and Stromenger (1946).

of the nineteenth century and has been revived several times since, while some of its melodies (using Polish dance rhythms) have passed into the realm of national folk song. A prolific if not especially distinguished composer was Joseph Xaver Elsner (1768–1854),[25] Chopin's teacher, whose *King Lokietek* (1818) was a rescue opera with a libretto reminiscent of *Les Deux Journées*. An influential personage in the early nineteenth century was Karol Kurpinski (1785–1857)[26] with *Jadwiga* (1814), a historical opera on an original Polish libretto, and *Zabobon* (1816; also known by an alternative title, *The New Cracovians*), a work in popular style that was quite successful.

The definitive creation of a Polish national school of opera, however, is due to Stanislaw Moniuszko (1819–72),[27] whose famous *Halka*—first produced at Vilna privately in 1847, then publicly in 1854, and in its final version in four acts at Warsaw in 1858—has remained a staple of the Polish opera theatre to this day. Curiously, the music of *Halka* does not sound markedly "Polish," at least to a foreigner. The style is rather that of early nineteenth-century romanticism, remarkable for lyric grace of melody, with expressive but unsensational harmonies and transparent instrumentation; yet *Halka*, for all its disarming naïveté, is not devoid of real dramatic force. The conventional recitative-aria form of Moniuszko's operas is modified by the use of transitional passages and recurring themes. Other works, similar in style to *Halka*, include *The Raftsman* (1858), the comedy *The Countess* (1860), and especially the semicomic opera *The Haunted Manor* (1865), next to *Halka* his best and most popular work and one that makes considerable use of recurring motifs.

Owing to unfavorable political conditions, the promising work begun by Moniuszko did not come to complete fruition in the latter part of the nineteenth century. One of the principal composers in this period was Wladislaw Zelenski (1837–1921)[28] with *Konrad Wallenrod* (1885), a grand opera on a historical subject; *Goplana* (1896), a romantic fairy-tale opera with lyrical melodies and delicate orchestral colors; and *An Old Fairy Tale* (*Stara baśń*, 1907), in which the influence of both Weber

---

[25] Biography by Nowak-Romanowicz (1957).

[26] Biography by Pomorska (1948); Reiss, "Koryfeusz muzyki polskiej."

[27] Biographies by Walicki (1873), Jachimecki (1921), and Opieński (1924); see also articles listed under Karasowski, Poźniak, and Rudziński.

[28] Biographies by Szopski (1928) and Jachimecki (1952); see also Paderewski, "Konrad Wallenrod"; Niewiadomski, "W Zeleński i jego *Goplana*."

and Wagner is conspicuous. Others who came to a greater or lesser degee under the Wagnerian spell were Sigismund Noskowski [29] (1846–1909; *Livia Quintilla*, 1898); Henryk Jarecki (1846–1918; *Powrót taty*, "The Father's Return," 1897); Roman Statkowski (1860–1925), whose *Filenis* (1904) won the prize in an international competition, and whose style in this and his other opera *Maria* (1906) was somewhere between pre-Wagnerian and the music drama; Ignace Jan Paderewski (1860–1941), more celebrated as a pianist than for his one opera, *Manru* (1901);[30] and Miecyslaw Soltys (1863–1929; *Panie Kochanku*, 1924). A new generation of more progressive tendencies began to be heard from after the restoration of Polish independence in 1919.

CZECHOSLOVAKIA.[31] The father of Bohemian music was Bedřich Smetana (1824–84),[32] whose first great success came in 1866 with *The Bartered Bride*. This melodious comic opera, so permeated with the rhythms and spirit of national music, has become famous all over the world. Two other comic operas of Smetana, *The Kiss* (1876) and *The Secret* (1878), showed advances in technical skill and were almost as successful in the composer's own country as *The Bartered Bride*. Smetana's serious operas, especially *Dalibor* (1868) and *Libussa* (composed 1872, performed 1881), were attacked by patriotic critics because of their use of certain procedures associated with Wagner, such as leitmotifs and the declamatory character of the vocal parts. But the alleged Wagnerisms hardly ever penetrated to the substance of the music, which remained stoutly individual. The leader of the next generation of Bohemian composers, Antonin Dvořák (1841–1904),[33] was primarily a symphonic rather than a dramatic musician, though several of his ten operas were successful at Prague. *The Cunning Peasant* (1878) was

[29] Chybiński, "Zygmunt Noskowski."

[30] Essay on *Manru* by Niewiadomski (1901).

[31] Bibliography: (1) General music histories: Hostinský, *Die Musik in Böhmen*; Soubies, *Histoire de la musique en Bohême*; Helfert, *Geschichte der Musik in der tschechoslovakischen Republik*; Nejedlý, *Dějiny opery Národníko divadla*. (2) General works on opera: Teuber, *Geschichte des Prager Theaters*; Hnilička, *Kontury vývoje hudby poklasické v Čechách*; Boelza, *Cheshskaia opernaia klassika*; Hoza, *Opera na Slovensku*. Principal composers before Smetana were: František Skroup (1801–62), František Skuherský (1830–92), Karel Sebor (1845–1903), Karel Bend! (1838–97), and Vilém Blodek (1834–74); for others, see Adler, *Handbuch* II, 925.

[32] Pražák, *Smetanovy zpěvohry*; Nejedlý, *Bedřich Smetana*; idem, *Zpěvohry Smetanovy*; *Smetana in Briefen*; Abraham, "The Genesis of *The Bartered Bride*."

[33] Šourek, *Život a dílo Antonína Dvořáka*; see also studies in English by Fischl (ed.), Robertson, and Šourek; Clapham, "The Operas of Antonín Dvořák."

inspired by Smetana's *Bartered Bride*. *The Devil and Kate* (1899) was Dvořák's most popular work in the comic style. In serious opera, he underwent the influence first of Meyerbeer and then of Wagner; the height of his achievement in this field was attained in a late work, *Rusalka* (1901), the libretto of which was well adapted to his lyrical powers. A third figure in Bohemian music was Zdenko Fibich (1850–1900),[34] a prolific composer who, more internationally minded than either Smetana or Dvořák, came fully under the influence of romanticism and the Wagnerian music drama. He was noted especially for the classical trilogy *Hippodameia* (1890–91), set entirely as a melodrama—that is, orchestral music accompanying or alternating with a spoken text—a form established by the eighteenth-century Bohemian composer Georg Benda. Fibich's best opera was *Sarka* (1897), based on a story from Czech mythology.

Other composers of this generation were Adalbert Hřimalý (1842–1908; *The Enchanted Prince*, 1872), Joseph Nešvera (1842–1914; *Woodland Air*, 1897), and Hanuš Trneček (1858–1914).

An important Bohemian composer of the late nineteenth century was Joseph Bohuslav Foerster (1859–1951),[35] whose most successful operas were *Eva* (1889) and *Jessika* (1905). Four pupils of Fibich also made their mark in Bohemian opera: Karel Kovařovic (1862–1920; *On the Old Bleaching Ground*, 1901), Karel Weis (1862–1944), Antonín Horák (1875–1910), and Otakar Ostrčil (1879–1935; *The Bud*, 1911). An influential composer and teacher was Vitězlav Novák (1870–1949),[36] with four operas of which the most important was *The Imp of Zvikov* (1915).

HUNGARY. The founder of opera in Hungary[37] was Ferenc Erkel (1810–93), whose *Hunyady László* (1844) holds the same position in its

---

[34] Rektorys, ed., *Zdeněk Fibich*.

[35] See *J. B. Foerster: Jeho životní pouť a tvorba* (1949); Foerster, *Der Pilger* (memoirs, first publ. in Czech, 1947).

[36] Stěpán, *Novák a Suk*; see also Newmarch, "New Works in Czechoslovakia" (1931).

[37] Bibliography: Eősze, *Az opera útja* (Budapest, 1960), pp. 465–96; Abrányi, *Erkel Ferenc élete és müködése*; Bónis, *Mosonyi Mihály*; articles in the series *Zenetudományi tanulmányok*, Vol. II, 1954 (*Erkel Ferenc és Bartók Béla emlékére*), on Erkel by I. Barna (pp. 175–218) and J. Maróthy (pp. 25–174); Vol. IV, 1955 (*A magyar zene történetéből*), on Erkel by Barna (pp. 211–72; continuation of the essay in Vol. II); and Vol. IX, 1961 (*Az opera történetéből*), on Erkel by Somfai (pp. 81–158) and on Mosonyi by Bónis (pp. 169–96; also in German: "Die ungarischen Opern M. Mosonyi's," *Studia musicologica* II [1962] 139–88).

country as do *A Life for the Tsar* in Russia and *Halka* in Poland; and Erkel's other operas were almost equally popular, especially *Bánk-Ban* (1861). Another important national composer was Mihály Mosonyi (1814–70), whose chief opera, *Szép Ilonka* ("Fair Ilonka"), was pro-_ duced in 1861. Others of the early nationalist group were Andreas Bartay (1798–1856), whose *Csel* ("The Trick," 1839) was the first original Hungarian comic opera; and August von Adelburg (1830–73), with the successful opera *Zrinyi* in 1868. Later nationalists included Jenö Hubay (1858–1937), a celebrated violinist and prolific composer whose principal opera, *A Cremonai hegedis* ("The Violin Maker of Cremona," 1894), is still given; and Ede Poldini (1869–1957) with the comic opera *A csavargó és királylány* ("The Vagabond and the Princess," 1903). The works of Odön Mihalovich (1842–1929) were Germanic and Wagnerian in musical style, even when on Hungarian librettos (*Toldi szerelme*, "Toldi's Love," 1893), and a pronounced flavor of German romanticism is heard in the operas of Géza Zichy (1849–1924),[38] whose most ambitious undertaking was a trilogy on the life of Rákóczi (produced at Budapest 1905–12). A similarly international romantic style is characteristic of the music of the noted pianist-composer Ernst von Dohnányi (1877–1960) in his opera *A Vajda tornya* ("The Tower of the Voyvod"), produced at Budapest in 1922.

The principal opera composers of Rumania were: Liubicz Skibinski (*Verfel cu Dor*, 1879); Edoardo Caudella (1841–1923; *Petru Raresch*, 1900); Georg Kosmovici (*Marioara*, 1904); Theodor von Flondor (d. 1908; *Mosúl Ciorkârlan*, 1901): Sabin Dragoi (b. 1894); a pupil of Dvořák and Janáček, with sophisticated modern use of Rumanian folk song in *Napasta* (1928); and Georges Enesco (1881–1955), with one opera, *Oedipe* (Paris, 1936).

Croatian opera is represented by Vatroslav Lisinski (1819–54; *Ljubav i Zloba*, 1846); Ivan Zajc (Giovanni von Zaytz, 1831–1914; *Nikola Subič Zrinski*, 1876); Franz Vilhar (1852–1928; *Smiljana*, 1897); Peter Konjović (b. 1882; *Koštana*, 1931); Krešimir Baranović (b. 1894; *Striženo-Košeno*, 1932); and Jakov Gotovac (b. 1895; *Morana*, 1930).

In Serbia the only opera composers of importance were Davorin Jenko (1835–1914),[39] whose many works for the theatre include the first Serbian comic opera, *Vračara* ("The Enchantress," 1882); and Alexander Savine (1881–1949; *Xenia*, 1919). Bulgarian opera has two composers: Georgi Atanasov (1881–1931), a pupil of Mascagni (*Borislav*, 1911), and Pantcho

[38] Autobiography (*Aus meinem Leben*).
[39] Cvetko, *Davorin Jenko: Doba, življenje, delo*.

Vladigerov (b. 1899), with the nationalist opera *Tsar Kaloyan* (1936). A nationalist of Greece was Manolis Kalomiris (1883–1962), whose *Protomastoros* ("The Master Builder," 1916) was the first opera by a Greek on a Greek subject; his later works include *Mother's Ring* (1917) and a festival opera with choruses on a historical subject, *Constantine Paleologos*—the last Byzantine emperor, who ruled from 1448 to 1453—first performed in the theatre of Herod Atticus at Athens in the summer of 1962.

The first Turkish operas, *Tas Babek* and *Kerem*, by Ahmed Adnan Saygun (b. 1907), were produced at Ankara in 1934 and 1957 respectively.

GERMANIC, SCANDINAVIAN, AND BALTIC COUNTRIES. On the whole, opera found no very congenial ground in these countries, but there are sporadic examples, of which some of the most important will be mentioned.

· The earliest Dutch opera, *De triomferende min* ("Love's Triumph") by Carolus Hacquart (*ca.* 1649-*ca.* 1730), was published in 1680, but its first performance took place only in 1920 at Arnhem. During the nineteenth century, when the Netherlands was largely under the musical domination of Germany, a few national operas were produced. Among composers of this period [40] were Richard Hol (1825–1904; *Floris V*, 1892); Cornelis van der Linden (1839–1918; *Leiden ontzet*, "The Relief of Leiden," 1893); Henri Brandts-Buys (1850–1905; *Albrecht Beiling*, 1881); Karl Dibbern (b. 1855; *Odja*, 1901); Emile van Brucken-Fock (1857–1944; *Seleneia*, 1895); Cornelis Dopper (1870–1939; *Het Eerekruis*, "The Cross of Honor," 1903); and Charles Grelinger (b. 1873), with the successful opera *Op Hoop van Zegen* ("On Board the 'Hope of Blessing,'" 1907). Jan Brandts-Buys (1868–1933) was more German than Dutch (*Die drei Schneider*, Dresden, 1916), but national traits appeared in the realistic-satiric operas of Hol's pupil Johan Wagenaar (1862–1941); his *Doge van Venetie* (1904) and *De Cid* (1916) are serious operas.

Flemish [41] opera composers of the nineteenth and early twentieth centuries were : Joseph Mertens (1834–1901; *De zwaarte Kapitein*, 1877); Peter Benoit (1834–1901; *Le Roi des Aulnes*, 1859; *Isa*, 1867); Jan Blockx (1851–1912;[42] *De Herbergprinses*, 1896; *De Bruid der Zee*, 1901); Paul Gilson (1865–1942; *Prinses Zonneschijn*, 1903); and Auguste de Boeck (1865–1937; *La Route d'Emeraude*, 1921).

Denmark, like Holland, has been to a large extent a musical province of Germany. The German composer Franz Gläser (1798–1861) wrote three operas to Danish texts. The earliest national opera composers were Johan

---

[40] Reeser, *Een Eeuw nederlandse Muziek*; Bottenheim, *De Opera in Nederland*; Dresden, *Het Muziekleven in Nederland sinds 1880*.

[41] Closson, ed., *La Musique en Belgique*; Corbet, ed., *De vlaamse Muziek sedert Benoit*.

[42] Biography by Frank Blockx (1943).

Hartmann (1805–1900; *Liden Kirsten*, 1846); Henrik Rung (1807–71; *Stormen paa København*, 1845); Siegfried Saloman (1816–99; *Diamant-korset*, 1847); and Peter Arnold Heise (1830–79; *Drot og Marsk*, 1878). Four operas by Peter Erasmus Lange-Müller (1850–1926) were produced at Copenhagen (*Spanske Studenter*, 1883). One of the most successful Danish comic operas was Carl August Nielsen's (1865–1931)[43] *Maskarade* (1906). The most prolific Danish opera composer was August Enna (1860–1939; *Hexen*, 1892; *The Match Girl*, 1897).

The first Norwegian opera [44] was *A Mountain Adventure* by Waldemar Thrane (1790–1828), which was published by 1824 but not performed on the stage until 1850. Twenty years later came *Junkeren og Flubergrosen* ("The Knight and the Fluberg Sprite") by Martin Andreas Udbye (1820–99), and in 1894 the first of Johannes Haarklou's (1847–1925) five operas, *Fra gamle Dage* ("Of Olden Days"). Ole Olsen (1850–1927) wrote four operas, of which *Lajla* was performed at Christiania in 1908. Gerhard Schjelderup (1859–1933), though of Norwegian birth, composed most of his operas to German texts; the same is true of Sigwardt Aspestrand (1856–1941). Catherinus Elling (1858–1942) wrote one opera, *Kosakkerne* (1897).

Sweden from the seventeenth century had been in touch with the general development of opera in Europe.[45] Italian, French, and German subjects and musical styles, as might be expected, dominated Swedish opera houses in the late eighteenth and early nineteenth centuries. The earliest attempt at a Swedish historical subject was made by Carl Stenborg with *Konung Gustaf Adolphs Jagt* ("King Gustavus Adolphus's Hunting Party") in 1777, a "comedy mingled with songs," imitated from Collet's *opéra comique La Partie de chasse de Henri IV*, part of which had been used by Weisse and Hiller for their popular Singspiel *Die Jagd* in 1770.[46] The first grand opera in Swedish was *Thetis och Pelée* (1773), by the Italian composer Francesco Antonio Uttini (1723–95). Swedish opera composers in the early and middle nineteenth century included Franz Berwald (1796–1868),[47] J. N. Ahlström (1805–57), Adolf Lindblad (1891–78), and Johan August Södermann (1832–76). Some German composers in this period also occasionally wrote operas to Swedish texts. A more definitely national type of Swedish opera, using native legends and folk melodies, appeared toward the end of the nineteenth century with the works of Ivar Hallström (1826–1901; *Den Bergtagna*, "The Mountain Ghost," 1874). Nationalism was temporarily pushed aside by the desire to emulate the Wagnerian music drama, as in the earlier operas of Andreas

[43] Biographies of Nielsen by T. Meyer and L. Dolleris.
[44] Kindem, *Den norske Operas Historie*; Benestad, *Waldemar Thrane*.
[45] See Moberg, "Essais d'opéras en Suède," in *Mélanges de musicologie*, pp 123–32; Engländer, *Joseph Martin Kraus*; Sundström, "Franz Berwalds Operor."
[46] See Lindström, "Vårt första nationella Sångspel."
[47] Biography by R. Layton (1957).

Hallén (1846–1925; *Harald Viking*, Leipzig, 1881), though more independent traits are evident in his *Waldemar's Treasure*, written for the opening of the new Stockholm Opera in 1899. A Wagner propagandist in Sweden was Richard Henneberg (1853–1925), who wrote a comic opera, *Drottningen's Pilgrimage*, in 1882. A combination of the Wagner style with national melodies is found in the operas of Wilhelm Stenhammar (1871–1927; *Tirfing*, 1898; *Das Fest auf Solhaug*, Stuttgart, 1899). A more decisive step toward national opera, though still on a Wagnerian basis, was *Arnjlot* (1910), by Olof Wilhelm Peterson-Berger (1867–1942).[48] Natanaël Berg (1879–1957) and Kurt Atterberg (b. 1887) were distinguished chiefly in the field of the symphony, though both produced operas. A notable opera composer of their generation was Ture Rangström (1884–1947; *Kronbruden*, "The Crown Bride"; Stuttgart, 1919, and in Swedish at Stockholm from 1922; based on Strindberg's drama).

In Finland there was no national opera before the twentieth century. *Kung Carls Jakt* ("King Charles's Hunting Party") by Fredrik Pacius (1809–91), performed at Helsinki in 1852 and sometimes called the "first Finnish opera," was by a German-born composer and on a Swedish text.[49] The first opera composed to Finnish words was Oskar Merikanto's (1868–1924)[50] *Pohjan Neiti* ("The Maid of Bothnia"), performed at Viipuri in 1908. Merikanto's subsequent works (*Elinan Surma*, "Elina's Death," 1910; *Regina von Emmeritz*, 1920) were somewhat influenced by Italian verismo methods. Other composers of this period were Erkki Gustaf Melartin (1875–1937; *Aino*, 1909) and Selim Palmgren (1878–1951; *Daniel Hjort*, 1910, on a Swedish text). A more distinctly national style, with folk melodies and recitative rhythms adapted to the Finnish language, was exemplified by Armas Launis (1884–1959; *Seitsemän veljestä*, "The Seven Brothers," 1913; *Kullervo*, 1917). Another Finnish folk-song scholar, Ilmari Krohn (1867–1960), produced the opera *Tuhotulva* ("The Deluge") at Helsinki in 1928. Important Finnish operas by Leevi Madetoja (1887–1947), a pupil of D'Indy, are *Pohjalaisia* ("The East Bothnians," 1924) and *Juha* (1935).

A few national operas were produced in the smaller Baltic states after the First World War. In Latvia an opera company was organized at Riga in 1919. National composers include Alfreds Kalnins (1879–1951; *Banuta*, 1920; *Dzimtenes Atmoda*, "The Nation's Awakening," 1933, a historical opera); Jāzeps Mediņš (1877–1947; *Vaidelote*, "The Virgin," 1927); Jānis Mediņš (b. 1890; *Uguns un Nakts*, "Fire and Night," 1921); and Jānis Kalnins (b. 1904; *Hamlet*, 1936). A Lithuanian opera house was opened at Kaunas toward the end of 1920 and the first Lithuanian opera, *Birute*, by Petrauskas Miskas, was performed in 1921. Another Lithuanian composer is Jurgio Karnavičius (b. 1885; *Grazina*, 1933). Estonian operas

[48] Biography by Carlberg (1950).
[49] See Loewenberg, *Annals*.
[50] Biography by Suomalainen (1950).

have been composed by Arthur Lemba (b. 1885; *Armastus ja Surm*, "Love and Death," Tallinn, 1931; *Elga*, 1934).

JAPAN. The development of modern opera in Japan [51] (as distinct from that nation's traditional musical-dramatic forms, the *nō* and *kabuki*) followed a course similar in many respects to that in the countries of eastern Europe. Apparently the first Western opera to be staged in Japan was Gounod's *Faust* (Act I only) at Tokyo in 1894. Gluck's *Orfeo*, in Japanese translation and with a Japanese cast, was heard at Tokyo in 1903. The first opera by a Japanese composer was *Hagoromo* ("Magic Clothes of an Angel," 1906), based on a national legend and set to music by Kōsuke Komatsu (b. 1884). Subsequent composers aimed to amalgamate the tradition of Japanese musical drama with that of Western opera. Representative works in this line are: *Kurofune* ("Black Ships," 1940) by Kōsaku Yamada (b. 1886); *Yūzuru* ("Crane of Twilight") by Ikuma Dan (b. 1924), first produced at Tokyo in 1952 and known in the West from performances at Zurich in 1957; and *Shuzenji-monogatari* ("A Tale at Shuzenji"; Tokyo, 1954, and Los Angeles, 1962) by Osamu Shimizu (b. 1911). The libretto of *Kurofune* uses a national historical subject; that of *Yūzuru* is based on a national folk tale, while *Shuzenji-monogatari* simply takes over a *kabuki* drama without altering so much as a word. In these and other modern operas, national subjects—and to a certain extent also national musical materials—are blended with various Western musical styles from Puccini to the most advanced contemporary idioms.

SPAIN, PORTUGAL, AND LATIN AMERICA. [52] With the disappearance of the old tonadilla in the first half of the nineteenth century, Spanish national opera went into an eclipse from which it did not emerge until about 1850. The first signs of reaction against the reign of Italian opera and French opéra comique in Spanish theatres appeared in the works of a resident Italian composer, Basilio Basili, who in the late thirties and early forties brought out at Madrid a number of comic operas in Span-

[51] For the information here presented I am indebted to the courtesy of Professor Kōzo Hattori of the University of Arts, Tokyo.

[52] See Chase, *The Music of Spain*, for a survey of this subject, with bibliographies. Further consult: Lavignac, *Encyclopédie*, Part I, Vol. IV, pp. 2290–2351, 2470–84; Salazar, *La música contemporánea en España*; music dictionaries of Saldoni and Pedrell and the "Espasa" encyclopedia; Trend, *A Picture of Modern Spain*; Peña y Goñi, *La ópera española*; Subirá, *Historia y anecdotario del Teatro Real*; idem, *El Teatro del Real Palacio*; Muñoz, *Historia de la zarzuela*. See also titles under early Spanish opera (above, p. 268).

ish. The first of these (1837) was labeled a *zarzuela-comedia*, thus reviving the ancient Spanish designation. Within a decade the new zarzuela was flourishing, in a form derived from the eighteenth-century tonadilla, using music of a light, popular, national style with admixture of some French and Italian elements. Many of the early librettos were from French sources—an instance of the influence which France has constantly exerted on the growth of national Spanish music. The leading composer of this first period of the revival was Francisco Asenjo Barbieri (1823–94), who produced over seventy zarzuelas between 1850 and 1880, including the classic work of this type, *Pan y toros* ("Bread and Bulls," 1864). This and other zarzuelas of Barbieri were long popular and have been influential on the development of national music in both Spain and South America. The principal contemporaries of Barbieri were Rafael José María Hernándo (1822–88), Joaquín Gaztambide (1822–70), Cristóbal Oudrid y Segura (1829–77), and Emilio Arrieta y Corera (1823–94).

Two distinct types of zarzuela developed at Madrid, corresponding to the two types of French opéra comique that evolved during the nineteenth century. On the one hand was the *genero chico*—comic, popular, informal, often quite ephemeral pieces in one act, which were produced in immense numbers throughout the century and indeed have continued up to the present day. The other type was the *zarzuela grande*, usually in three acts, which might be on a serious subject and even in some cases approach the scale and style of grand opera. Most composers of the later nineteenth century wrote zarzuelas of both kinds. Some of the most popular works of the genero chico were *La gran vía* ("The Great Road," 1886) by Federico Chueca (1846–1908), in collaboration with Joaquín Valverde (1846–1910); *La viejecita* ("The Old Woman," 1897) by Manuel Fernández-Caballero (1835–1906); *La bruja* ("The Witch," 1887) and *La revoltosa* ("The Revolutionary Girl," 1897) by Ruperto Chapí y Lorente (1851–1909); and above all *La verbena de la paloma* ("The Festival of Our Lady of the Dove," 1894) by Tomas Bretón y Hernández (1850–1923).[53]

Along with the rise of the popular zarzuela came a growing desire for a national serious opera in Spain. Spanish composers of the earlier nineteenth century had rarely used Spanish texts or national subjects, and their music seldom had anything differentiating it from the contempo-

[53] Biography by Salcedo.

rary Italian style. A solitary early crusader for Spanish opera was Joaquín Espín y Guillén (1812–81), one act of whose *Padilla, o el Asedio de Medina* ("Padilla; or, The Siege of Medina") was performed at Madrid in 1845. Later in the century, however, the zarzuela composers interested themselves in the task of creating a more permanent and artistic form of national lyric drama than could be made of the pieces in the genero chico to which they owed their popular success. Barbieri had definite ideas on the subject; Arrieta, who had composed a number of Italian operas, expanded his two-act zarzuela *Marina* into a three-act Spanish opera with recitatives (1871). Chapí wrote several serious zarzuelas (*La tempestad*, "The Storm," 1882; *Curro Vargas*, 1898) as well as operas (*Margarita la Tornera*, 1909), but his genius was for the comic rather than the serious. Bretón, who had also written Italian operas, composed a Spanish opera, *La Dolores*, in 1895. Still another composer of this period was Emilio Serrano y Ruiz (1850–1939), with the operas *Irene de Otranto* in 1891 and *Gonzalo de Cordoba* (to his own text) in 1898.

The honorable title of "father of modern Spanish music" belongs to Felipe Pedrell (1841–1922),[54] distinguished scholar, composer of operas and symphonic and choral works, and teacher or mentor of most of the Spanish composers of the following generation. Pedrell combined a deep feeling for the qualities of Spanish folk song and the great Spanish music of the past with a romantic-mystical temperament which led him frequently into paths where the general public could not follow. He was a greater idealist than composer, and his beneficent influence on Spanish music is out of all proportion to the very slight outward success of his own works. He was dubbed "the Spanish Wagner"; his most successful opera, *La Celestina* (1904), was called "the Spanish *Tristan*." These expressions exaggerate the resemblance of his work to Wagner's. That there was some influence is unquestionable, but the examples of Glinka, Mussorgsky, and the other Russian opera composers were at least equally potent. As a matter of fact, if comparisons must be made, the composer whom Pedrell most closely resembles is D'Indy. The likeness is one of both temperament and musical style : each was irresistibly drawn into the orbit of Wagner; each, being an ardent nationalist and an artist of high ethical purpose, adapted the technique of the music

[54] Studies by Tebaldini, Curzon, and Istel; Pedrell, *Jornadas de arte*; catalogue by Reiff.

drama for his own aims; and each succeeded in being individual in spite of this debt. D'Indy was a better technician than Pedrell and was more at home in the realm of purely musical expression; Pedrell, on the other hand, drew his musical idiom from more varied sources.

The most important of Pedrell's ten operas is *Los Pirineos* ("The Pyrenees"), a trilogy in three acts with prologue, composed to a Catalan text of Victor Balaguer in 1890–91 and first performed in Italian translation at Barcelona in 1902.[55] The poem offers a number of effective

EXAMPLE 109 *Los Pirineos*, Act II

scenes, but on the whole its nature is more that of an epic than of a dramatic work. Pedrell's setting is unified by the use of leitmotifs. An idea of his style may be gained from Example 109, part of the Funeral March in the second act. The orchestra has a much less conspicuous posi-

[55] *Los Pireneos* is itself the first opera of a larger trilogy, of which *La Celestina* is the second number; the third, *Raymond Lully*, was not completed.

tion than in Wagner, and the voice parts are nearly always melodic. An important proportion of the score is given to set pieces, which appear in great variety. The composer's scholarly conscience is shown in his evident care to reproduce as authentically as possible the oriental idiom in the solos of the heroine, "Moon-Ray"; the scene of the Love Court in Act I offers modern adaptations of trouvère and troubadour art forms— *tenso, lai,* and *sirventes.* There are quotations from plainsong and from sixteenth-century Spanish church composers, and the excellent choral writing throughout the opera should be especially mentioned. The prologue in particular should make a very effective concert number for a choral society.

It is too much to claim that Pedrell is to be numbered among the greatest opera composers. His dramatic sense often failed him. Too many pages of *Les Pirineos* are thin in inspiration, repetitious, and lacking in rhythmic vitality and variety. But, out of a sincere artist's soul, enough moments of greatness have emerged to make this work an honor to its composer and country and to entitle it to at least an occasional performance, even if in a shortened version.

The national spirit which Pedrell did so much to inspire achieved world-wide recognition in the piano music of two of his pupils, Isaac Albéniz (1860–1909) [56] and Enrique Granados (1867–1916).[57] Both these composers essayed opera, but without important results. Albéniz, apparently under a mistaken notion of his own gifts, and also instigated by a wealthy English patron who fancied himself a dramatic author, devoted several years to writing operas in a heavy, pseudo-Wagnerian style but finally obtained a moderate success with a comic work, *Pepita Jiménez* (1896). Granados, like many of his contemporaries, was interested in trying to re-create the spirit of Madrid as typified in Goya, and the music of his principal opera, *Goyescas* (New York, 1916), was expanded from a series of piano pieces of the same title. The plot of this opera has a strong tinge of Italian verismo.

In addition to his influence on what may be called the main stream of modern Spanish opera, Pedrell is also the founder of the regional school of Catalonia. The leading figure in this school is Jaime Pahissa (b. 1880), with *La presó de Lleida* ("The Prison of Lérida," 1906; rewritten in 1928 as the three-act opera *La Princesa Margarida*) and *Gala Placidia* (1913).

[56] Laplane, *Albeniz*; Collet, *Albeniz et Granados.*
[57] Studies by Boladeres Ibern and Subirá.

Other Catalan composers are Enric Morera [58] (1865–1942; *Emporium,* 1906), Juan Lamote de Grignon (1872–1949; *Hesperia,* 1907), and Joan Manén (b. 1883; *Acté,* 1903). Independent regional development is characteristic of Spanish music, but the only extensive regional opera outside Catalonia is found in the Basque country. The oustanding composer here was José María Usandizaga (1887–1915) with the nationalistic *Mendi-Mendyian* (1910) and the successful Puccinian melodramatic opera *Las golondrinas* ("The Swallows," 1914). Another Basque composer is Jesús Guridi (b. 1886), whose national folk opera *Mirentxu* (1910) was followed in 1920 by a more ambitious work with some Wagnerian traits, *Amaya,* and a successful zarzuela, *El Caserio* ("The Hamlet"), in 1926.

The early history of dramatic music in Portugal [59] is similar to that of Spain, except that there was no distinct national form of as great importance as the tonadilla. The first opera in Portuguese was *La vida do grande D. Quixote de la Mancha* (1733) by Antonio José da Silva (1705–39), an isolated attempt which led to nothing. Italian opera came to Portugal as early as 1682, but its flourishing period began only about 1720. Of the Portuguese composers who devoted themselves to writing in the Italian style, the chief was Marcos Antonio Portugal (1762–1830), whose thirty-five operas were widely performed in Europe in the late eighteenth and early nineteenth centuries. He was also the composer of twenty-one comic operas to Portuguese texts. Italian and French opera continued to dominate the Portuguese stage throughout the nineteenth century; Miguel Pereira's (1843–1901) opera *Eurico* (1870), with Italian text arranged from a Portuguese novel, is typical of this tendency. Native composers only occasionally adopted their own language or musical idiom, except for comic pieces. In this genre, however, there were successful works by Antonio Luiz Miró (d. 1853; *A marqueza,* 1848); Guilherme Cossoul (1828–80; *A cisterna do diablo,* "The Devii's Cistern," 1850); Francisco Alves Rente (1851–91; *Verde gaio,* "Light Yellow," 1876); and Domingo Cyriaco de Cardoso (1846–1900; *O burro do Senhor Alcaide,* "The Mayor's Donkey," 1891). An outstanding nationalist composer was Alfredo Keil (1850–1907), of whose serious Portuguese operas *Serrana* (1899) was most frequently performed. The principal later composer of operas in Portugal was Rui Coelho (b. 1891; *Belkiss,* 1938).

[58] Biography by Iglesias.

[59] Bibliography: Luper, "The Music of Portugal," in Chase, *Music of Spain,* chap. XVIII; Vieira, *Diccionario biographico de musicos portuguezes;* Fonseco Benevides, *O real theatro de S. Carlos de Lisboa;* Lavignac, *Encyclopédie,* Part I, Vol. IV, pp. 2422–35, 2447–57.

Opera in Latin America [60] has been for the most part an offshoot of Italian and Spanish opera. In the colonial period the missionaries promoted plays with music, and at larger centers (for example, Lima) there were performances of the works of Calderón and other Spanish dramatists with music. The earliest extant opera in the New World seems to have been *La purpúra de la rosa* by Tomás de Torrejón y Velasco, performed at Lima in 1701. An Italian opera, *La Partenope*, with music by Manuel Zumaya, was produced at Mexico City in 1711. A few tonadillas were brought from Spain to the American colonies in the eighteenth century, but regular seasons of opera did not begin before the second quarter of the nineteenth century. Brazil had a national opera company from 1857, and the most famous Latin American opera composer of the nineteenth century, Antonio Carlos Gomes (1836–96),[61] was a Brazilian who studied in Italy and produced at Milan in 1870 his masterpiece, *Il Guarnay*, a work still given in Brazil and Italy. Although Gomes chose national subjects for some of his operas and endeavored also to introduce national elements in his music, he was too strongly inclined to the Italian style to be entirely successful. A like inclination is evident in the music of Henrique Eulalio Gurjão (1833–85), whose best-known opera was *Idalia* (1881). Leopoldo Miguez (1850–1902) was influenced by Wagner in *Os Saldunes* (1901). Even the so-called nationalist composer Alberto Nepomuceno (1864–1920) did not develop an independent musical style in his operas.

[60] Chase, *A Guide to the Music of Latin America*, 2d ed. (1962); publications of the Pan American Union, Washington, D.C. Periodicals: *Handbook of Latin American Studies*; *Boletín latino-americano de música*; *Rivista brasileira de música*; special number of RM, February-March, 1940 ("La Musique dans les pays latins"). Slonimsky, *Music of Latin America*; Chase, *The Music of Spain*; *idem*, articles with bibliographies in *Harvard Dictionary of Music* (by countries); Alfredo Fiorda Kelley, *Cronología de las óperas . . . etc. cantados en Buenos Aires* [1825–1933]; Acquarone, *História de la música brasileira*; Corrêa de Azevedo, *150 anos de música no Brasil (1800–1950)*; Ayesterán, *Crónica de una temporada musical en el Montevideo de 1830*; Abascal Brunet, *Apuntes para la historia del teatro en Chile*; Abascal Brunet and Pereira Salas, *Pepe Vila* [1861–1936]: *La zarzuela chica en Chile*; Pereira Salas, *História de la música en Chile*; Salas and Feo Calcaño, *Sesquicentenario de la opera en Caracas . . . ciento años de opera 1808–1958*; R. Stevenson, "Opera Beginnings in the New World"; *idem*, *The Music of Peru*; Sixto Prieto, "El Perú en la música escénica" (bibliography of scores and librettos of operas, ballets, etc., the subjects of which relate to Peru); Saldívar, *História de la música en México*; Stevenson, *Music in Mexico*; Romero, *La ópera en Yucatán*; Maria y Campos, *Una temporada de opera italiana en Oaxaca* [1874–75]; Tolón and González, *Operas cubanas y sus autores*; Sáez, *El teatro en Puerto Rico*.

[61] Studies by Seidl, Marchant, and Andrade; Corrêa de Azevedo, "Carlos Gomes"; biography by Gomes Vaz de Carvalho (3d ed., 1946).

In Argentina the Italian influence was even stronger, though national subjects were occasionally used, as in *La indígena* (1862) by Vinceslao Fumi (1823–80) and in *Pampa* (1897) and *Yupansky* (1899) by Arturo Berutti (1862–1938). Justin Clérice (1863–1908), a native of Argentina, won recognition in Europe for his French comic operas and ballets.

Early Mexican composers of Italian operas were Luis Baca (1826–55), Cenobio Paniagua (1821–82; *Catalina di Guisa*, 1864), and Melesio Morales (1838–1908), whose principal works were *Ildegonda* (1866), *Cleopatra* (1891), and *Anita*, a one-act opera in verismo style (never performed). German romanticism is characteristic of the music of Ricardo Castro (1864–1907) in *La Légende de Rudel*, though national themes had appeared in his earlier *Atzimba*. A distinguished national opera on an Aztec subject, using popular melodies, was *Guatimotzín* (1871) by Aniceto Ortega (1823–75). A recent national historical opera in Mexico was *Tata Vasco* by Miguel Bernal Jiménez (b. 1910), presented at Morelia in 1941, which includes many choral scenes and draws musical material from diverse sources including Gregorian chant and Indian melodies.[62]

Most of the favorite Spanish zarzuelas were brought to the New World and inspired similar works by local composers in all Latin American countries. Thus the Venezuelan José Angel Montero (1839–81) produced fifteen zarzuelas as well as an opera, *Virginia* (1873). In Colombia, zarzuelas and similar pieces were composed by Juan Crisóstomo Osorio y Ricaurte (1863–87) and Santos Cifuentes (1870–1932); in Mexico there was a popular comic opera, *Keofar* (1893), by Felipe Villanueva (1862–93). Other Latin American opera composers in this period were: in Colombia, Augusto Azzali (*Lhidiac*, 1893) and José María Ponce de León (1846–82; *Ester*; *Florinda*); in Peru, Daniel Alomias Robles (1871–1942; *Illa-Cori*) and Teodoro Valcárcel (1900–1942; *Suray-Surita*, ballet opera); in Chile, Eleodoro Ortíz de Zarate (1865–1953; *La fioraia di Lugano*, 1895, with Italian text); and in Cuba, Eduardo Sanches de Fuentes (1874–1944; *Dolorosa*, 1910; *Kabelia*, 1942).[63]

The twentieth-century national musical renaissance in Latin

---

[62] See Stevenson, *Music in Mexico*, chap. IV and pp. 262–64; Barros Sierra, "*Tata Vasco* y su partitura."

[63] See Chase, "Some Notes on Afro-Cuban Music and Dancing."

America did not bring forth operas comparable in either number or importance to the music produced in other forms. In Argentina, where there was more native opera than anywhere else, the Italian influence was still predominant. This is especially the case with Ettore Panizza (b. 1875), whose works include *Il fidanzato del mare* ("The Bridegroom of the Sea," 1897), *Medio evo latino* (1900; three one-act operas, each placed in a different Latin country and a different medieval century), *Aurora* (1908, commissioned for the opening of the new Teatro Colón at Buenos Aires), and *Bisanzio* (1939). Alfredo Schiuma's (b. 1885) Italian opera *Tabaré* (1925), closely patterned after Verdi's *Forza del destino*, was very successful; another highly praised work of Schiuma is *Las Vírgenes del sol* (1939).[64] A more definitely national group is represented by Felipe Boero (1884–1958) with his folk opera *El matrero* ("The Rogue," 1929). Others in this group are Pascal de Rogatis (b. 1881; *Huémac*, 1916; *La novia del hereje*, "The Heretic's Bride," 1935), Raul Espoile (b. 1889; *La ciudad roja*, "The Red City," 1938), and Enrique Casella (b. 1891; *La tapera*, "The Ruin").

In Brazil the new nationalism was evident in the works of Oscar Lorenzo Fernandez (1897–1948; *Malazarte*, 1941), Francisco Mignone (b. 1897), and Comargo Guarnieri (b. 1907; one-act comic opera *Pedro Malazarte*, 1942). Heitor Villa-Lobos (1887–1959), the most famous of recent South American composers, wrote four operas but only one (*Izaht*, composed 1912–14) was ever performed—in 1940 in a concert version and in 1958 at Rio de Janeiro on the stage.

THE BRITISH ISLES [65] AND THE UNITED STATES. Little need be added to what has already been written about English opera in the nineteenth century.[66] It was a time when serious opera was universally understood to mean Italian opera, that "exotic and irrational entertainment" which the British had been patronizing ever since the days of Dr. Johnson.[67] Almost the only English musical stage works to have any success at all in the nineteenth century were those of the light variety, by such composers as Balfe, Wallace, Benedict, and (later) Sullivan. The Carl Rosa Opera Company, beginning in 1875, commissioned a few English works, including some from Arthur Goring Thomas (1850–92), whose *Esmeralda*

[64] Ferrari Nicolay, "En torno a *Las Vírgenes*."
[65] Walker, *History of Music in England*; E. W. White, *The Rise of English Opera*.
[66] See above, p. 338.
[67] Cf. Mapleson, *Memoirs*; Carlyle, "The Opera."

and *Nadeshda* were given at London in 1883 and 1885 respectively. The current vogue for Wagner—signalized by the establishment of a London branch of the Wagner Society which published a periodical entitled *Meister* from 1888 to 1895, and furthered by the circumstance that most of the leading English composers of the generation of the 1840s and 1850s received their training in Germany—was reflected in the numerous English operas on national historical or "Nordic" legendary subjects and in a musical style obviously inspired from Bayreuth. Perhaps the most zealous English disciple of Wagner was Frederick Corder (1852–1932; *Nordisca*, 1887, and *Ossian*, 1905). Sullivan's *Ivanhoe* made a great stir at its first production in 1891 but has fortunately long since disappeared from the stage. Other operas of a German-romantic cast were produced in England (and in some instances also in Germany) by Sir Frederic Cowen (1852–1935),[68] Sir Alexander Campbell Mackenzie (1847–1935), and Sir Charles Villiers Stanford (1852–1924).[69] Cowen's *Pauline* (1876) was commissioned by the Carl Rosa company; his *Thorgrim* and two others of similar titles were produced at London in the 1890s. Mackenzie's *Colomba*, first heard at London in 1883, was later produced in Germany; his most successful opera was *The Cricket on the Hearth*, composed around 1900 and first performed in 1914. Stanford attempted to create an English *Meistersinger* in *The Canterbury Pilgrims* (1884), but was better known for his comic opera *Shamus O'Brien* (1896); his *Much Ado about Nothing* made a favorable impression at its first performance in 1901 and was revived in 1935.

The revival of Celtic literature in the late nineteenth and early twentieth centuries led to a number of operas on Celtic legends. Most notable among these was Josef Holbrooke's (1878–1958) [70] mythological Welsh trilogy *The Cauldron of Anwen*, broadly conceived along Wagnerian lines and written in a neoromantic musical style strongly influenced by Wagner. Welsh subjects also attracted Joseph Parry (1841–1903), Granville Bantock (1868–1946; *Caedmar*, 1892; *The Seal Woman*, 1924), and George Lloyd (b. 1913). Scottish stories or legends were used by Hamish MacCunn (1868–1916) in *Jeanie Deans* (from Scott's *Heart of Midlothian*; performed at Edinburgh in 1894)

---

[68] See his memoirs, *My Art and My Friends*.

[69] On Stanford, see Fuller-Maitland, *The Music of Parry and Stanford*, chap. 9, and biography by H. P. Greene.

[70] Biography by G. Lowe (1920); see also the symposium *Josef Holbrooke* (1937).

and *Diarmid* (London, 1897), as well as in *Quentin Durward* by Alick Maclean (Newcastle-on-Tyne, 1920); and Irish subjects appear with Robert O'Dwyer's (1862–1949) *Eithne*, on a Gaelic text (Dublin, 1910), and Geoffrey Palmer's (b. 1882) *Sruth na Maoile* ("The Sea of Moyle"; Dublin, 1923).

English operetta and light opera of this period were represented by Alfred Cellier (1844–91); Edward Soloman (1853–95); George H. Clutsam (1866–1951); Sidney Jones (1861–1946; *The Geisha*, 1896); Sir Edward German (1862–1936; *Merrie England*, 1902); Ivan Caryll (1861–1921; *The Duchess of Dantzic*, 1903); Edward Naylor (1867–1934; *The Angelus*, 1909); and Hubert Bath (1883–1945; *Bubbles*, 1923). Later comic operas by English composers were Lord Berners's (1883–1950) *Carosse du Saint-Sacrement* (Paris, 1921) and Arthur Benjamin's (1893–1960) *The Devil Take Her* (1932)—both witty one-act pieces in a fluent modern style.

The early history of opera in the United States [71] is similar to that in the other nations of the Western Hemisphere. It begins in colonial times with the importation of comic operas from Europe (in this case English ballad opera instead of the Spanish zarzuela); during the nineteenth and early twentieth centuries fashion favors successively Italian opera, French grand opera, or German music drama. Tentative and unsuccessful efforts are made by native composers to imitate the musical style currently in vogue, sometimes applying it to "American" subjects, the Indians and the Puritan colonists being the two commonest sources of material for librettos. Prizes are offered and awarded; new operas by American composers are produced with fanfare, given a few performances, then shelved and forgotten. A few experimental works on a small scale are produced, but the American public shows little interest in them, preferring to hear *Il barbiere di Siviglia*, *Il Trovatore*, *Les Huguenots*, or *Die Walküre* in sumptuous settings and sung by expensive foreign stars. In a word, American opera remains, until well into the twentieth century, simply a longed-for but unrealized ideal.

It is possible that the first opera performance in the United States took place as early as 1703, but the earliest date which can yet be substantiated is 1735, when *Flora; or, Hob in the Well*, a ballad opera, was presented at Charleston, South Carolina. *The Beggar's Opera* and

[71] General bibliography: *Dictionary of American Biography*; histories of American music by Ritter (to 1880), Howard, and Chase; Hipsher, *American Opera*; Ewen, *Complete Book of the American Musical Theater*; memoirs by Mapleson, Gatti-Casazza; other studies by Mattfeld, Kolodin, Moore, Carson, Gagey, R. Davis.

several similar works were played in New York in 1750–51, and a like
repertoire was heard in Annapolis and Upper Marlborough, Maryland,
in 1752. In the same year ballad operas were given at Williamsburg,
Virginia. Philadelphia followed two years later. All during the latter
half of the eighteenth century there were seasons of opera, fairly regularly at New York and sporadically at other places; the total number
in proportion to the population was actually greater than at any period
since. Most of the works so presented were English comic operas (Shield,
Storace, Dibdin, and others), but there were also a few French opéras
comiques (Grétry, Monsigny, Philidor), usually in translation and with
the music more or less extensively altered and adapted by English and
American arrangers, besides many pantomimes and ballets. French
opera, both grand and comic, flourished at New Orleans from 1791
until the Civil War and even afterwards. The first season of regular
Italian opera in New York was in 1825. From that time on, the uneven
career of foreign opera in the United States becomes too complicated to
follow here even in outline, the more since our chief concern is not with
"opera in America" but "American opera."

The known American operas of the eighteenth century have been
thoroughly studied by Oscar G. T. Sonneck.[72] Many of these were of the
type of *The Beggar's Opera*, with characters and dialects appropriate
to the American locale. Toward the end of the century there were
imitations and adaptations of popular plays, such as *The Archers* (1796),
with music by the English-born composer Benjamin Carr (1768–1831),
inspired by Schiller's *Tell*; in 1797 there was a melodrama, *Ariadne
Abandoned,* possibly imitated from Benda. Still other "operas" were
on patriotic themes, with battle scenes and allegorical tableaux. None of
these pieces had continuous music; most, in fact, were merely plays with
incidental songs. The composers (or arrangers) included Francis Hopkinson (1737–91; *The Temple of Minerva*, 1781), James Hewitt (1770–
1827; *Tammany*, 1794), and Victor Pelissier, a native of France who
came to America around 1792 and produced several plays with music,
among them *Edwin and Angelina; or, The Banditti* at New York in
1796. In 1808 an "operatic melo-drame" by J. N. Barker entitled *The*

---

[72] "Early American Operas," in his *Miscellaneous Studies*, pp. 16–92. See also
Sonneck's *Bibliography of Early Secular American Music*; *Early Concert Life in
America*; *Early Opera in America*; and further, Wegelin, *Micah Hawkins*; idem,
*Early American Plays*; Seilhamer, *History of the American Theatre*; Mates, *The
American Musical Stage before 1800*.

*Indian Princess* was performed at Philadelphia; like the earlier examples mentioned, this was a play (the first extant one on the popular story of Pocahontas and Captain John Smith) with extensive musical numbers composed by John Bray (1782–1822), including descriptive instrumental pieces, songs, and choruses.[73] A similar work, *The Enterprise*, with music by Arthur Clifton (b. *ca.* 1784), was given at Baltimore in 1822.[74] These are but two examples of many such homemade semi-operatic entertainments that dot the history of the American stage in the early part of the nineteenth century.

The first publicly performed opera with continuous music by a native American composer was *Leonora* by William Henry Fry (1813–64),[75] given at Philadelphia in 1845 and in a revised version at New York in 1858—a work of considerable competence and musical interest, modeled on the styles of Donizetti and Meyerbeer. Fry's next opera, *Notre-Dame de Paris*, was given at Philadelphia in 1864. Another American composer of this period was George Frederick Bristow (1825–98), whose *Rip Van Winkle* (New York, 1855) was arranged from Irving's tale with added love scenes and other episodes. This opera has some spoken dialogue; the music is conventional and undistinguished, a lame imitation of the fashionable European light-opera style.

Of the many German-descended or German-trained American composers in the later nineteenth century, the most important in the field of opera was Walter Damrosch (1862–1950),[76] whose first success with *The Scarlet Letter* (1896) was hardly equaled by his two later works, *Cyrano* (1913) and *The Man without a Country* (1937). Damrosch's music is pleasantly put together and technically well fashioned, but does not depart from the style of late nineteenth-century German romanticism. A rather more original score, though one still strongly suggestive of Wagner, is John Knowles Paine's (1839–1906) *Azara*, published in 1901 but performed only in concert version (1907). The operas of George Whitefield Chadwick (1854–1931)[77] attracted little attention outside his native Boston, but those of his pupils Converse, Hadley, and Parker (see below, p. 533) were more widely recognized.

[73] See Hitchcock, "An Early American Melodrama."
[74] Gettel, "Arthur Clifton's *Enterprise*."
[75] Biography by W. T. Upton (1954).
[76] Autobiography, *My Musical Life.*
[77] Yellin, "The Life and Operatic Works of George Whitefield Chadwick."

Dependence of American composers on foreign (usually German) models in the nineteenth century, and lack of any sustained movement toward a national musical style, are painfully illustrated in the operas above mentioned and those of lesser composers of the same period. Two early opera composers of German birth were Eduard de Sobolewski (1808–72; *Mohega*, Milwaukee, 1859) and Johann Heinrich Bonawitz (1839–1917; *Ostrolenka*, Philadelphia, 1875). With this group may also be listed the Americans Frederick Grant Gleason (1848–1903; *Otho Visconti*, Chicago, 1907) and Louis Adolphe Coerne (1870–1922), of whose three operas only *Zenobia* was ever performed (at Bremen, 1905; the first opera by an American composer to be staged in Europe). To the same generation as Coerne belong Arthur Finley Nevin (1871–1943; *Poia*, Berlin, 1910; *The Daughter of the Forest*, Chicago, 1918), Joseph Carl Breil (1870–1926; *The Legend*, New York, 1919), and John Adam Hugo (1873–1945; *The Temple Dancer*, New York, 1919).

American operetta and comic opera may be traced from the works of the German-born Julius Eichberg (1824–93; *The Doctor of Alcantara*, Boston, 1862) through Dudley Buck (1839–1909; *Deseret*, New York, 1880), Edgar Stillman Kelley (1857–1944; *Puritania*, Boston, 1892), and John Philip Sousa (1854–1932; *El Capitan*, Boston, 1896) to Reginald De Koven (1859–1920; *Robin Hood*, Chicago, 1890) and Victor Herbert (1859–1924; *Babes in Toyland*, 1903). Both De Koven and Herbert attempted grand opera, but without much success (De Koven's *The Canterbury Pilgrims*, New York, 1917, and *Rip van Winkle*, Chicago, 1920; Herbert's *Natoma*, Philadelphia, 1911, and *Madeleine*, New York, 1914).

In light opera and musical comedy [78] after the First World War the two leading figures were Jerome Kern (1885–1945; *Sally*, 1920) and George Gershwin (1898–1937; [79] *Of Thee I Sing*, 1931). Each of these composers has written one distinguished work in more serious style: Kern's *Show Boat* (1927) and Gershwin's *Porgy and Bess* (1935); both works have become practically American folk operas. Notable musical comedies of later vintage were Rodgers and Hammerstein's *Oklahoma!* (1943) and *South Pacific* (1949) and Lerner and Loewe's *My Fair Lady* (1956; from Shaw's *Pygmalion*).

[78] C. Smith, *Musical Comedy in America*; S. Green, *The World of Musical Comedy*.
[79] Biographies by Armitage and Ewen; Durham, *Du Bose Heyward*.

PART 5

# THE
# TWENTIETH
# CENTURY

# CHAPTER 26

# OLD BOTTLES AND
# NEW WINE

The most radical influence on musical style in the first fifteen years of the present century was impressionism, which originated in France with Debussy and made itself felt nearly everywhere gradually from 1900 on. Another source of change was the development of the post-Wagnerian late romantic style in Germany and Austria, evident in Mahler, early Schoenberg, and Richard Strauss. A third set of influences came from composers who carried on with the national movements already begun in the nineteenth century. The effects of these forces appeared in varying degrees and combinations, but underlying all change was the conservative power of tradition, still inescapable and still respected: progress, not revolution, was the ruling ideal, and even "advanced" experiments soon slipped into the central current of evolution without causing too much disturbance.

IMPRESSIONISM AND THE FRENCH SCENE. The most important French opera of the early twentieth century was *Pelléas et Mélisande* by Claude Debussy (1862–1918),[1] on a text by Maurice Maeterlinck. It is Debussy's only work for the stage, with the exception of the miracle drama *Le Martyre de Saint-Sébastien* (1911, based on D'Annunzio's play) and an early cantata, *L'Enfant prodigue*, which has sometimes been given in operatic form. The first sketches for *Pelléas et Mélisande* are dated 1893, and Debussy revised the score continually. The first performance took place at the Opéra-Comique on April 30, 1902—

---

[1] Biographies by Vallas and Lockspeiser; Debussy's essays, published under the title *Monsieur Croche, anti-dilettante*; studies of *Pelléas et Mélisande* by Gilman, Maurice Emmanuel, and Van Ackere.

"one of the three or four red-letter days in the history of our lyric stage," as Romain Rolland said.[2]

It is customary, and in the main correct, to regard *Pelléas et Mélisande* as a monument to French operatic reaction from Wagner; but this opera is at the same time a focal point of French dramatic music, gathering up many essential national traits and giving them exceptionally clear and perfect expression, though colored by the individual genius of Debussy. The personal qualities of the music are so salient that they tend to usurp attention, and it is therefore well to emphasize that *Pelléas* is characteristic not only of Debussy but also of France.

Four things have marked French opera from the beginning of its history. First is the belief that an opera is fundamentally a drama in words to which music has been added; from this doctrine comes the insistence on clear and realistic declamation of the text. Both the contemporary admiration for Lully's recitative and Rousseau's later objections to it as "mannered" came from the same interest in the text as basic to the drama and hence to the opera. In no other country has so much attention been given to this issue. The flourishing of the opéra comique with its spoken dialogue was a constant witness that the French were willing to do without music rather than let it interfere with the understanding of the words. *Pelléas et Mélisande* conforms to this ideal. It is one of the rare instances of a long play, not expressly made for music, being turned into an opera with practically no rearranging.[3] In most places the music is no more than an iridescent veil covering the text : the orchestral background is shadowy, evanescent, almost a suggestion of sound rather than sound itself; and the voice part, with its independence of the bar line, narrow range, small intervals, and frequent chanting on one tone, adheres as closely as possible to the melody of French speech. Only in a few places, as in Mélisande's song at the beginning of Act III or in the love duet in Act IV, scene 4, does the melody become really lyric. How typical this narrow melodic line is of French music may be realized by comparing the contours of French folk-song melodies with those of German or English folk songs, the

---

[2] *Musiciens d'aujourd'hui*, essay on Debussy.

[3] The following scenes in the play are omitted in the opera : Act I, sc. 1; Act II, sc. 4; Act III, sc. 1; and Act V, sc. 1. There are many other small omissions ranging from a single phrase to a dozen lines, and numerous alterations in wording. Some words have been added : see especially Act III, sc. 1 of the opera.

instrumental themes of Saint-Saëns or César Franck with those of a German like Richard Strauss, or French nineteenth-century recitative in general with the wide-ranging arioso of Verdi or Wagner. The use of the Wagnerian type of melody with French words, such as we find in the operas of Chabrier and D'Indy (and, to a lesser extent, in Bruneau and Charpentier), was soon felt to be unnatural. In the return to a more natural declamation and in the damping of orchestral sonorities, therefore, Debussy was in accord not only with the traditional French practice but with an even more ancient ideal, that of the early Florentine founders of opera, Peri, Caccini, and Gagliano.

The second historical feature of French opera is its tendency to center the musical interest not in the continuous orchestra or in the solo aria but in the divertissements, that is, interludes in the action where music might be enjoyed without the attention being divided by the necessity of following the drama at the same time. In early French opera and through the nineteenth century the common form of divertissement was the ballet with choruses. There are no ballets in *Pelléas*, and only one quite brief chorus, but the function of the divertissement is fulfilled by the orchestral preludes and the interludes which are played for changes of scene. Here, and here only, music has the foreground and the full symphonic resources are employed. But the interludes are not independent of the action; rather, they resume in wordless and concentrated form what has just passed and by gradual transition prepare for what is to come. Thus Debussy combines the Lullian form of opera with the nineteenth-century practice of treating every detail as a means toward the central dramatic purpose.

Still another constant feature of French opera has been the deliberate choice of measured, objective, well-proportioned, and rational dramatic actions. The French have not been misled, except momentarily, either by the desire to be forceful at any cost or by the attractions of metaphysical speculation. Not that French opera is as direct and uninhibited in its approach as the Italian; but the French prefer to suggest a hidden meaning by subtle juxtaposition of facts, trusting to stimulate the imagination rather than overwhelm it with exhaustive details, as Wagner tends to do. Now the quintessence of this indirect, suggestive method in literature is found in the movement known as symbolism, of which Maeterlinck's five-act drama *Pelléas et Mélisande* (1892) is an outstanding example. The story is purposely vague and seems slight indeed when reduced to a bare summary. But the whole effect is in the manner, not the matter. As Edmund Gosse has said :

Maeterlinck is exclusively occupied in revealing, or indicating, the mystery which lies, only just out of sight, beneath the surface of ordinary life. In order to produce this effect of the mysterious he aims at an extreme simplicity of diction, and a symbolism so realistic as to be almost bare. He allows life itself to astonish us by its strangeness, by its inexplicable elements. Many of his plays are really highly pathetic records of unseen emotion; they are occupied with the spiritual adventures of souls, and the ordinary facts of time and space have no influence upon the movements of the characters. We know not who these orphan princesses, these blind persons, these pale Arthurian knights, these aged guardians of desolate castles, may be; we are not informed whence they come, nor whither they go; there is nothing concrete or circumstantial about them. Their life is intense and consistent, but it is wholly of a spiritual character; they are mysterious with the mystery of the movements of a soul.[4]

Debussy's music perfectly supports the mysterious, spiritual character of the drama, doing everything by understatement and whispered suggestion. The full orchestra is hardly ever heard outside the interludes. Instrumental doubling is avoided; solo timbres and small combinations are the rule, while the strings are often muted and divided. There are only four fortissimos in the whole score. Debussy's almost excessive "genius for good taste"[5] is apparent if we contrast the wild greeting of the lovers in the second act of *Tristan* with the meeting of Pelléas and Mélisande in Act IV (Example 110), or the touching scene of Mélisande's death in Act V with Isolde's Liebstod.

However, soft music is not of necessity better than loud music; restraint is of no artistic value unless we are made aware that there is something to be restrained. And here we come to the fourth and last quality characteristic of French opera, which Debussy carries to the ultimate degree, namely a capacity for the appreciation of the most refined and complex sensory stimuli. In the quality of its acceptances as well as of its refusals, French opera has always tended to be aristocratic. The style of musical impressionism which *Pelléas et Mélisande* exemplifies is essentially one of aristocratic sensualism, treating sounds as of primary value for themselves irrespective of accepted grammatical forms, and creating moods by reiterated minute impacts of motifs,

[4] "Maeterlinck," in *Encyclopædia Britannica* (11th ed.) XVII, 299a. Quoted by permission.
[5] Rolland, *Musiciens d'aujourd'hui.*

*Pelléas et Mélisande*, Act IV, sc. 4

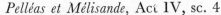

EXAMPLE 110

DEBUSSY

harmonies, and timbres. These elements in *Pelléas* sounded so completely unprecedented in themselves, and so completely detached from the familiar system of musical progressions, that audiences were at first bewildered; but they soon learned to associate the musical moods with those of the poetry and discovered a marvellous correspondence between the two. For as Maeterlinck's drama moved in a realm outside ordinary time and space, so Debussy's music moved in a realm outside the then known tonal system; lacking any strong formal associations within the field of music itself, his harmonies were irresistibly attracted to the similarly free images of the poet. Never was a happier marriage of music and verse. The technical methods of Debussy are familiar to all students of music and may be only briefly indicated here.[6] Modal, whole-tone, or pentatonic melodies and harmonies suggest the far-off, dreamlike character of the play. The free enchainment of seventh and ninth chords, often in organum-like parallel movement, and the blurring of tonality by complex harmonic relationships are also typical. Certain motifs recur and are transformed and harmonically varied, but they are not treated in the continuous symphonic manner of Wagner. D'Indy has well expressed their function by the term "pivot themes."[7]

[6] See further M. Emmanuel, *Pelléas et Mélisande*, pp. 97–114 *et passim*.
[7] *Richard Wagner et son influence sur l'art musical français*, p. 81.

The influence of Wagner on Debussy is felt chiefly in a negative fashion, that is, by the care Debussy took to avoid writing like Wagner. In those days it was not easy. Debussy complained of his first draft of the duet in Act IV that "the ghost of old Klingsor, alias R. Wagner, keeps peeping out." [8] But the final score cannot be said to owe anything to Wagner beyond the orchestral continuity, the use of recurring motifs, and the exclusion of all merely ornamental details; in technique, idiom, feeling, and declamation it is Debussy's own. Whatever he had learned from *Tristan* or from Mussorgsky's *Boris Godunov*, from Massenet, Grieg, or from oriental music had been completely assimilated. So peculiarly was the musical style fitted to Maeterlinck's drama that it is no wonder Debussy was never able to find another suitable libretto. *Pelléas et Mélisande*, like *Fidelio*, remains an isolated masterpiece of its composer in the field of opera.

The next notable French opera of the twentieth century was Paul Dukas's (1865–1935) [9] *Ariane et Barbe-Bleue* ("Ariadne and Blue-beard," 1907)—like *Pelléas*, the composer's only opera and likewise on a symbolist drama by Maeterlinck. The influence of Debussy is apparent in the declamation and in some details of the harmony, but the recitative is less supple and poetic than Debussy's. The orchestration is sonorous, using the brasses with brilliant effect, and the musical style on the whole is anything but impressionistic. Dukas was a composer of great technical attainment whose strong point was the development of ideas in large symphonic forms. Unfortunately, his themes are too often undistinguished in themselves, and their development marked less by inspiration than by system and perseverance; for example, the constant practice of repeating the exposition of a theme immediately in a new key (compare the exposition in the first movement of César Franck's symphony) becomes almost a mannerism. Dukas's harmony is subtle, but here again one sometimes feels the absence of any compelling musical or dramatic reason for some of his complicated chord progressions. Another defect is the excessive reliance on the augmented triad in association with the whole-tone scale, a device which has lost the attraction of novelty since 1907. So much must be stated by way of negative criticism of *Ariane et Barbe-Bleue*; on the other hand, its many excellences must be empha-

---

[8] Letter to Chausson, quoted in Abraham, *A Hundred Years of Music*, p. 278.
[9] Studies by Samazeuilh and Favre; special Dukas number of RM, May–June, 1936.

sized. The work is less an opera than a huge symphony with the addition of choruses (essential to the drama, not mere embellishments) and solo voices. Cyclical recurrence and transformation of themes are used to create an architectural structure of grand proportions. The large coda that forms the end of Act III is particularly impressive, summing up with Beethovenian finality all the principal themes of the opera and rounding off the whole with the theme which was first heard in the opening measures of the prelude to Act I. Among the many fine details of the score is the song of the "five daughters of Orlamonde," a folk-songlike melody from which many of the motifs of the opera are derived (Example 111). Altogether, *Ariane et Barbe-Bleue* is the most important French lyric drama of the early twentieth century next to *Pelléas et Mélisande*—important, that is, if measured in terms of artistic qualities rather than popular following. It is none the less significant musically for lacking those traits that made the success of Massenet and Charpentier.

Several more operas of this period merit special mention, each being in its own way a distinctive contribution. Déodat de Séverac's (1873–1921) [10] *Cœur du moulin* ("The Heart of the Mill," 1909), a simple and poignant love story in a pastoral setting, has a musical score in which the influence of Debussy is modified by an original gift for direct, spontaneous expression and a charming regional flavor of southern France, evident especially in the choruses. Although its individual features were acclaimed by critics, *Le Cœur du moulin* has not had any popular success. Better known are the two operas of Maurice Ravel (1875–1937).[11] *L'Heure espagnole* ("The Spanish Hour," 1911), a one-act opera buffa based on the comedy of Franc-Nohain, is a tour de force of rhythm and orchestration, varied and witty in declamation, with a libretto in which the art of the *double-entendre* is carried to a height worthy of Favart. The vocal lines are suggestive of Richard Strauss, while under them the orchestra carries on a suite of Spanish dances ending with a mock-grand "scena and habañera." The scene being laid in a clockmaker's shop gives occasion for many charming and clever sound effects, among which the cuckoo motif is, of course, prominent. The strength of this opera is in just those qualities which Dukas's *Ariane*

[10] Biography by B. Selva (1930).
[11] Roland-Manuel, *Maurice Ravel et son œuvre dramatique*; special numbers of RM (April, 1925; December, 1938).

EXAMPLE 111

DUKAS

lacks, namely piquant details and a sense of lightness, gaiety, and improvisation. Ravel's "lyrical fantasy" *L'Enfant et les sortilèges* ("The Child and the Sorceries"), on a libretto by Colette, was first performed at Monte Carlo in 1925. It is a charming score, one worthy of the composer of *Ma Mère l'Oye*, lighter in texture than *L'Heure espagnole* but equally rich in ingenious orchestral and vocal effects.

Le Pays ("The Country," 1912), by J. Guy Ropartz (1864–1955),[12] is a soundly dramatic and well-proportioned score with symphonic treatment of the orchestra, original in inspiration and evidencing the sound classical training its composer received from César Franck. One can detect in it a modified Wagnerianism in the melody and harmony, as well as the then fashionable obsession with the sound of the augmented fifth chord. A special position must be assigned to the operas of Gabriel-Urbain Fauré (1845–1924),[13] the most important of which are *Prométhée* (1900) and *Pénélope* (1913). The latter particularly is a beautiful example of the composer's exquisite harmonic style, which lends to the classical subject matter an appropriate atmosphere of repose and remoteness, evoking the feeling of the antique world as no more common idiom could. From the viewpoint of theatrical effectiveness, *Pénélope* is perhaps too refined; the slow tempo of the action (in Acts I and II especially) emphasizes the statuesque quality which is both the greatest musical beauty and the most serious dramatic weakness of this opera.

In sum, the dominant tendency of late nineteenth- and early twentieth-century French opera was idealistic; the noble, if somewhat vague, striving of *Fervaal* and *L'Etranger*, the mood of meditation on destiny in *Pelléas* and *Ariane*, the naïve religious faith of *Le Jongleur de Notre Dame*, the moral earnestness of *Le Cœur du moulin* and *Le Pays*, the serene, contemplative beauty of *Pénélope*—all show this. Even the so-called naturalistic operas of Bruneau and Charpentier used realism largely as a means of calling forth idealistic sentiment. Thus motivated, composers sought to bring into the theatre the finest and most comprehensive resources of a highly developed musical art—resources enriched after 1900 by the new techniques of impressionism—aspiring toward universality of expression, freely using any and all means to which they found themselves attracted. Viewed from a later age, theirs seems an

[12] Biographies by Lamy (1948) and Kornprobst (1949).
[13] Biographies by Koechlin and N. Suckling; special number of RM (October, 1922).

art of leisure and luxury, such as is possible only in a time of prosperity and peace. But leisure gave time for the unfolding of ideals, while luxury provided the material means for their realization on a scale which we have not seen since and probably shall not in the near future.

Among the minor composers of serious opera in this period were Gabriel Pierné (1863–1937; *La Fille de Tabarin*, 1901), Alexandre Georges (1850–1938; *Charlotte Corday*, 1901), Xavier Leroux (1863–1919; *La Reine Fiamette*, 1903, influenced by Puccini and Massenet; *Le Chemineau*, 1907), Henri Février (1875–1957; *Monna Vanna*, 1909), and Jean Noguès (1875–1932), whose *Quo Vadis* (1909) is a mild blend of Massenet and Fauré. Distinguished especially for works in a lighter vein were the Venezuelan-French Reynaldo Hahn (1875–1947; *La Carmélite*, 1902) and Camille Erlanger (1863–1919; *Le Juif polonais*, 1900; *Aphrodite*, 1906). More individual in style was Raoul Laparra (1876–1943) with his operas on Spanish subjects, the most popular being *La Habanera* (1908) and *L'Illustre Fregona* (1931). The music of Ernest Bloch's (1880–1959) *Macbeth* (1910), strongly influenced by Debussy, has declamatory vocal lines, much parallelism in the orchestral texture, and a monotonously constant use of the augmented 5–7 chord, which seems to have fascinated opera composers of this period as much as the diminished seventh had fascinated their predecessors a hundred years earlier. *Macbeth* was severely criticized on account of its "modernistic" harmonies and rhythms and soon dropped out of the repertoire, but has been occasionally revived. Sylvio Lazzari (1857–1944) with *La Lépreuse* (1912) and Louis Aubert (b. 1877) with *La Forêt bleue* (Geneva, 1913) had no great success, but Henri Rabaud's (1873–1949) oriental opéra comique *Mârouf, savetier de Caire* ("Marouf, Cobbler of Cairo," 1914), a witty, brilliantly scored work, has become a favorite both in Paris and abroad. It is undoubtedly one of the finest modern comic operas, a worthy descendant of the long French line of works in this style and on similar subjects. Another oriental opera was Gabriel Dupont's (1878–1914) *Antar*, finished in 1914 but not performed until 1921. The Belgian Albert Dupuis (b. 1877; *La Passion*, Monte Carlo, 1916) in his operas reverted to the style of Massenet.

It must be remembered that throughout the period we have been considering the semidramatic form of the ballet occupied much of the attention of French composers. Lalo's *Namouna* (1882) never received the recognition it merited, but in the early twentieth century the performances of such works as Florent Schmitt's mimodrama *La Tragédie de Salomé* (1907), Ravel's *Daphnis et Chloé* (1912), and Stravinsky's *Firebird, Petrouchka*, and *The Ceremonial of Spring* (1910, 1911, and 1913 respectively) were important musical events.

**Impressionism made its mark in Germany with Franz Schreker**

(1878–1934),[14] whose first opera, *Der ferne Klang* ("The Distant Tone"), was composed in 1903–9, though not performed until 1912. The first notable feature of Schreker's music is the harmony, which basically is like that of Debussy (seventh and ninth chords as consonant units; free use, singly or in combination, of chromatic alteration, pedal points, and organum-like parallel progressions; treatment of sensuous effect as an end in itself). But it is the Debussy of *L'Après-midi*, the *Nocturnes*, and *La Mer* rather than of the subdued *Pelléas et Mélisande* who is Schreker's model. His texture is exceedingly full, often having complicated decorative rhythmic motifs within the beat, or making use of several separated tone masses (as in the opening of Act II of *Der ferne Klang*). All this is, of course, supported by an orchestration of corresponding richness, in which harps, muted strings and horns, glissandi, tremolos, and similar effects are prominent. The feeling of tone impressions (*Klang*) in Schreker's operas is so strong as to lead naturally to a symbolism in which sounds become the embodiment of ideal, mystic forces. There are other signs of the late romantic period as well: occasional Straussian storm and stress in the harmony, reminiscences of Verdi in a melodic line, and traces of Puccini's declamation and orchestral treatment.

The whole, nevertheless, is not mere patchwork but an original and very effective theatrical style which made Schreker, during the years of the First World War and the decade after, one of the most highly regarded opera composers in Germany. His librettos (written by himself) have been criticized for awkwardness of language and for their preoccupation with sex in exaggerated, pathological forms. *Die Gezeichneten* ("The Stigmatized Ones," 1918), a Renaissance subject, has this feature to an extreme degree. His chief work, *Der Schatzgräber* ("The Treasure Digger," 1920), shows a tendency toward more triadic harmony, with much parallelism, and a somewhat less complicated texture. The leitmotif system is much less prominent here than in his earlier works, and in *Irrelohe* (1924) it is abandoned altogether. Meanwhile *Das Spielwerk und die Prinzessin* ("The Playthings and the Princess"), considerably revised in 1920 from the original version of 1913, experimented with pandiatonicism and other new harmonic devices.

THE ITALIAN TRADITIONS. Opera in Italy during the early 1900s

[14] Studies by Bekker, Kapp, and R. S. Hoffmann; also numerous articles in *Anbruch* (see especially Jahrg. II, VI, X).

continued without any noticeable break along the lines already drawn before the turn of the century. The leading composer at this time was Puccini, whose work has already been dealt with.[15] Along with the passing of the fashion for verismo, more and more Italian composers began to take interest in other forms of composition as well as opera, and to become more susceptible to the influence of current tendencies from abroad. It was a period of internationalism, even a certain amount of eclecticism. After Wagner came Strauss, Debussy, and Stravinsky in turn to stamp their impress, more or less distinctly, on Italian composers. Interest was aroused in symphonic and chamber music, as evidenced in the output of such men as Giuseppe Martucci (1856–1909) and Giovanni Sgambati (1841–1914), while an important renewal of church music was led by Don Lorenzo Perosi (1872–1956) and Enrico Bossi (1861–1925).

Aside from the opera composers already mentioned, three names deserve particular notice in the early twentieth-century period. A quite popular figure was the German-Italian Ermanno Wolf-Ferrari (1876–1948),[16] whose special talent was for comedy on librettos either adapted from the eighteenth-century Goldoni or of a similar type. These include *Le donne curiose* ("The Curious Ladies," Munich, 1903) and *Il segreto di Susanna* ("The Secret of Suzanne," Munich, 1909), his most famous work. His only tragic opera, an experiment with some of the methods of verismo, was *I gioielli della Madonna* ("The Jewels of the Madonna," Berlin, 1911), a work strongly suggestive of Donizetti with modern trimmings in harmony and rhythm. The Serenade in Act II, perhaps the best-known number in the opera, is a good illustration of the vivacity and rather superficial harmonic cleverness of the style. One of the last composers of the verismo school, whose work is full of the old traditional Italian opera devices, was Mascagni's pupil Riccardo Zandonai (1883–1944);[17] his most important opera is *Francesca da Rimini* (1914), based on D'Annunzio's tragedy of the same name, a smoothly contrived score with a pleasant tincture of late romantic harmony.

The decline of verismo and the effort to combine some of its features with the neoromantic or exotic type of opera found in Puccini, Giordano, and others is one symptom of a new spirit in Italian musical life.

[15] See above, pp. 441–45.
[16] Biographies by De Rensis and Grisson; Pfannkuch, "Das Opernschaffen Ermanno Wolf-Ferraris."
[17] Bonajuti Tarquini, *Riccardo Zandonai, nel ricordo dei suoi intimi.*

Particular evidence is found in the operas of Italo Montemezzi (1875–1952),[18] especially *L'amore dei tre rè* ("The Love of the Three Kings," 1913) and *La nave* ("The Ship," 1918), where the influence of both Wagner and Debussy is blended with a native Italian lyricism to produce music sound in workmanship, rich in instrumental color, conservative in idiom though not merely imitative, and of enduring beauty. *L'amore dei tre rè* is one of the best Italian tragic operas since Verdi's *Otello*. Notable is the refinement of style : chromaticism is handled with intelligence and restraint, intensifying the expression of feeling by the very refusal to dwell on obvious tricks of theatrical effect. There are memorable moments of classic breadth, as at the end of the love duet in Act II (Example 112). The voice line is an admirable adjustment of vocal melody to a continuous symphonic texture; recurring motifs and a carefully worked out key scheme make a formal whole of satisfying proportions. Altogether this opera, with its night-shrouded castle, its lovers swooning in sensual ecstasy, and the tragic figure of the blind Archibaldo, with its music which seems from beginning to end one low cry of voluptuous pain, of delicately scented agony and hopeless fatalism, is an appropriate work with which to close our contemplation of the course of Italian opera at the end of the romantic period : the ripe fruit of a dying age, the sunset of a long and glorious day.

Some less well-known Italian composers of opera in the twentieth century may be mentioned here. Ottorino Respighi (1879–1936),[19] especially noted for his symphonic poems, wrote a number of operas in a neoromantic idiom strongly influenced by impressionism : the comic colorful *Belfagor* (1923), *La campana sommersa* ("The Sunken Bell," 1927), the spectacular biblical ballet *Belkis* (1930), the mystery play *Maria Egiziaca* (1932), and *La fiamma* ("The Flame," 1934), with a sumptuous orchestral texture. Riccardo Pick-Mangiagalli (1882–1949) had some operas performed successfully at Rome, and his *Ospite inatteso* ("The Unexpected Guest," 1931) was the first opera to have a world premiere by radio. The operas of Felice Lattuada (1882–1962) were conventional in the main. Operas by Mario Castelnuovo-Tedesco (b. 1895) include *La mandragola* (1926) and some later works in miniature style. Adriano Lualdi (b. 1885) wrote his most popular opera, *La figlia del rè* ("The King's Daughter"), in 1922. One of the most prolific Italian composers was Lodovico Rocca (b. 1895), whose works include *Il dibuc* (1934) and *L'uragano* (1952).

[18] Tretti and Fiumi, eds., *Omaggio a Italo Montemezzi.*
[19] Biography by E. Respighi (1954).

EXAMPLE 112    *·L'amore dei tre rè*, Act II    MONTEMEZZI

While the Wagnerian movement found some echo in Italy, the influence of verismo in turn was felt in Germany. Its methods are evident in *Tiefland* ("The Lowlands," 1903) by Eugen d'Albert (1864–1932),[20] first produced at Prague in 1903, the most successful of this composer's twenty operas. *Tiefland* is a brutally realistic drama in an effective musical setting that combines Italian-style recitative with Wagnerian harmonies and recurrent motifs in the manner of Puccini. Another popular veristic opera in Germany was *Mona Lisa* (1915) by Max von Schillings (1868–1933),[21] murder and melodrama against a Renaissance background, with a modern frame of prologue and epilogue; the music lies strongly under the influence of Puccini in melody and instrumentation and apparently also of early Debussy in the harmony, and there is some tendency toward separate musical numbers instead of the symphonic continuity of Von Schillings's earlier operas, although recurring motifs are still present. Still another German opera of the realist school was Wolfgang von Waltershausen's (1882–1954)[22] *Oberst Chabert* (1912), written in a nonmelodic declamatory style with the dramatic situations underlined by rapidly fluctuating harmonies in which the constant alternation of two triads at the interval of an augmented fourth has the effect of a persistently recurring motif.

POST-WAGNER AND ANTI-WAGNER IN GERMAN OPERA. A certain eclectic tendency, not unlike that found in Italy, is manifest in German opera of the early twentieth century. The influences of impressionism and verismo already noted in the work of some German composers are combined with other features inherited from the post-Wagnerian and late romantic style. Representative of a more purely German tradition—though explicitly conservative and romantic—was Hans Pfitzner (1869–1949),[23] in whose works a musical language deriving fundamentally from Wagner came to be modified by more diatonic melody, asceticism of feeling, long dwelling on mystical, subjective moods, and frequently

[20] E. Schmitz, "Eugen d'Albert als Opernkomponist."
[21] Biography by W. Raupp.
[22] See Waltershausen's writings on music, listed in the bibliography; Sailer, "Waltershausen und die Oper."
[23] Biographies and studies by Dent, Abendroth (1935; the basic biography), Valentin, Müller-Blattau, Rutz; Riezler, *Hans Pfitzner und die deutsche Bühne*; Halusa, "Pfitzners musikdramatisches Schaffen"; Bahle, *Hans Pfitzner und der geniale Mensch*; studies of separate operas by R. Louis (*Die Rose vom Liebesgarten*, 1901), Hirtler, and Berrsche (*Der arme Heinrich*). See also Pfitzner's writings listed in the bibliography.

dissonant contrapuntal texture with long-breathed melodic lines
(Example 113). Pfitzner's *Armer Heinrich* of 1896 had a pronounced

*Palestrina*, Prelude

EXAMPLE 113

PFITZNER

success, surpassed only by that of his masterpiece, the "musical legend"
*Palestrina* in 1917. The latter is a version of Baini's romantic but un-
founded story of the way Palestrina "rescued" polyphonic church music
by composing his "Pope Marcellus" Mass for the Council of Trent;

musical motifs from the Mass are incorporated in Pfitzner's score. It does not require any great penetration to perceive that Pfitzner (who in this one instance was his own librettist) has treated the legend with reference to his own position as defender of the ancient, good tradition of music against the modernists and Philistines. This implication, not unrelated to the dramatic idea of Wagner's *Meistersinger*, was doubtless responsible in part for the favor *Palestrina* enjoyed for a time with the German public, a favor which died out after a couple of decades and which never found much echo in other countries. A more advanced harmonic style and partial return to the form of separate numbers was apparent in Pfitzner's later opera, *Das Herz* ("The Heart," 1931).

Contemporary with Pfitzner was the Viennese Alexander von Zemlinsky (1872–1942);[24] of the six operas of his that were produced between 1897 and 1933 the most successful was *Es war einmal* ("Once upon a Time," 1900), but his influence has also been felt through the work of two of his distinguished pupils, Arnold Schoenberg and Erich Korngold. Another Viennese composer of this generation was Franz Schmidt (1874–1939),[25] a pupil of Bruckner and esteemed in Austria as a symphonist, who had some success with the first of his two operas, *Notre Dame* (composed 1902–4, first performed 1914). Other contemporaries whose work for the theatre was mostly conservative in musical style include : Paul Graener (1872–1944; *Friedemann Bach*, 1931), Max Ettinger (1874–1951; *Frühlings Erwachen,* 1928), Joseph Haas[26] (1879–1960; *Tobias Wunderlich,* 1937), Julius Weismann (1879–1950; *Leonce und Lena,* 1925), Walter Braunfels (1882–1954; *Die Vögel,* 1920), and Paul von Klenau (1883–1946; *Rembrandt van Rijn,* 1937).

A solitary and enigmatic figure in music of the early twentieth century was Ferruccio Busoni (1866–1924).[27] Of mixed German and Italian ancestry, one of the foremost concert pianists of his day, a scholar and philosopher, he reminds one of an artist of the Renaissance in the breadth of his outlook. His aesthetic views, which involved rejection of Wagner and adherence to the operatic ideals of Mozart, made him an important early protagonist of the neoclassic movement. His first opera, *Die Brautwahl* ("The Bridal Choice," 1912), revives the classical principle of set numbers, though the libretto and music still retain many

[24] See special number of *Der Auftakt* (Prague, 1921).
[25] Biography by A. Liess (1951).
[26] Biography by K. Laux (1954).
[27] Biographies by Dent (1933), Guerrini (1944), and Giazotto (1947); Bekker, *Klang und Eros*; Gatti, "The Stage Works of Ferruccio Busoni"; writings of Busoni and "Nota bio-bibliografica."

romantic traits. The one-act *Arlecchino* (1917) is an ironical comedy making use of the old commedia dell' arte masks and including some spoken dialogue. The score of *Turandot* (two acts; first performed on the same program with *Arlecchino*) was arranged from earlier incidental music to Gozzi's play. *Doktor Faust*, completed by Busoni's disciple Philipp Jarnach and produced posthumously in 1925, is the composer's principal opera and one of the most significant musical treatments of this subject in the twentieth century. Busoni (here as always his own librettist) went back not to Goethe but to the medieval version of the Faust legend, adapting it to his own mystical and symbolical intentions. The score is cast in large musical forms, skillfully using both conventional set numbers and complex polyphony, the whole worked out with uncompromising idealism and making exceptional demands on an audience's attention. It may be true, as Professor Dent has said, that "one cannot apply to *Doctor Faust* the ordinary standards of operatic criticism. It moves on a plane of spiritual experience far beyond that of even the greatest of musical works for the stage";[28] but, like many another high plane of "spiritual experience," this one is sometimes dull for outsiders. Despite moments of dramatic force and musical beauty, the general style of *Doktor Faust* is so compressed, so complex in both its dramatic and harmonic implications, and so rooted fundamentally in the late German romantic sound-world that the opera is unlikely ever to become a permanent work in the repertoire.

We have traced hitherto the different movements in Germany that may be understood as being, in one way or another, attempts to break away from the potent spell of Wagner : in the fairy-tale opera, by the choice of a different kind of subject matter while retaining to varying degrees the Wagnerian idiom, the technique of leitmotifs, and the general idea of the Gesamtkunstwerk; in the Volksoper, by radical simplicity of both subject matter and music; in the "realistic" operas of D'Albert and others, by returning to dramas of uncomplicated human passion without metaphysical implications in a musical style influenced by the methods of Italian verismo; and in the operas of some other composers (notably Schreker), by infusing into the Wagnerian form some of the methods of French impressionism. After the first decade of the twentieth century there becomes evident a rather general antiromantic

[28] *Ferruccio Busoni*, p. 304.

tendency, evidenced by changing ideals as to both the form and the content of opera : in form, a movement of return to the eighteenth-century principle of separate musical numbers, with the device of recurring motifs playing only a subordinate role (as in the later works of Von Schillings, Pfitzner, and Schreker); in content, by a return to purely human drama—historical or other—and a musical idiom emphasizing melody, clarity of texture, basically diatonic harmony, and formal structure governed by purely musical principles. This general neoclassic tendency is of course subject to all sorts of exceptions and modifications in individual cases, and after 1920 it finds itself in competition with more radical movements which it will be our business to describe in the next chapter; nevertheless, it persists until well along in the twentieth century. Its chief representative is Richard Strauss (1864–1949),[29] whose work is an epitome of the movement from post-Wagner to anti-Wagner in Germany.

Strauss had already produced two operas—*Guntram* (1894) and *Feuersnot* (1901)—and most of his symphonic poems before he attracted the horrified attention of the entire operatic world with *Salome* in 1905. Oscar Wilde's drama, originally written in French, translated into German by Hedwig Lachmann, and then considerably compressed and revised by Strauss himself, formed the libretto. Its peculiar blend of oriental, sensuous, decadent luxuriance was perfectly captured in the music, which describes the necrophilic ecstasy of Salome as vividly as Wagner had once described the agonies of the suffering Amfortas. The final scene of *Salome* was one of the first—perhaps the very first—in which the suggestive power of music had been successfully applied to such a subject, yet it is only one instance of Strauss's amazing skill in musical characterization. Formally, *Salome* is in the Wagnerian style : the orchestra is dominant, the music is continuous throughout the one act, there is a system of leitmotifs, the texture is uniformly thick and polyphonic, the rhythms are nonperiodic, and the voice parts are mostly of an arioso character. Strauss's mastery of orchestral effect, the individuality and variety of his instrumental coloring, are as evident in the operas as in the symphonic poems. His harmony, which sounded so daring and dissonant at the turn of the century, is no longer novel, but

[29] Bibliography: Krause, *Richard Strauss: Gestalt und Werk*; Trenner, ed., *Richard Strauss: Dokumente seines Lebens und Schaffens*; R. Strauss, *Betrachtungen und Erinnerungen*; correspondence (see bibliography); Schuh, *Über Opern von Richard Strauss*.

just for this reason we can now better appreciate how appropriate it is for the dramatic purposes. Technically it may be regarded as a continuation of Wagner, with progressions generally conditioned by chromatic voice leading but less bound up with romantic expressiveness, more remote and sudden in its modulations, and much more dissonant. It it a kind of harmony which assumes a familiarity with Wagner on the listener's part, and which as it were telescopes the characteristic Wagner progressions in a manner analogous to the treatment of a fugue subject in stretto. (We have already noticed a similar evolution from the Verdi melodic style in Puccini's operas.) The melodies in *Salome* are of two sorts : either declamatory, with many unusual intervals rising out of the harmonic progressions, or else long-sustained, impassioned outpourings, marked by a very wide range and wide leaps. Strauss has managed to combine the characteristics of the music drama with the striking dramatic quality of Italian verismo and also to introduce some features of grand opera (for example, the Dance of the Seven Veils).

The characteristics of *Salome* are pushed even further in *Elektra* (1909), the first opera Strauss wrote in collaboration with his principal librettist, the Austrian poet and dramatist Hugo von Hofmannsthal (1874–1929). In *Elektra* the central passion is the heroine's insane thirst for vengeance on the murderers of her father, and here again Strauss has matched the somber horrors of the libretto with music of fearful dissonance, lurid melodramatic power, and a harmonic idiom in which for long stretches polytonality is the normal state. Perhaps the most noticeable feature of the score is the contrast between this dissonant idiom and the occasional stretches of lush, late-romantic sentimentality, with cloying sevenths, ninths, chromatic alterations, and suspensions. Whatever the composer's intentions may have been, these portions give the final dreadful touch of spiritual abnormality to the whole action; they are like something familiar suddenly seen in a ghastly, strange light.

With *Der Rosenkavalier* ("The Rose-Bearer," 1911), a "comedy for music," Strauss and Hofmannsthal achieved an enduring success not equaled by any of their other joint creations. This romantic comedy of Viennese life around the time of Maria Theresa—the mid-eighteenth century—forms a perfect libretto, with humor, farce, sentiment, swiftly moving action, variety of scenes, and superb characterizations. The music is as varied as the drama. In some portions it is no less complex (though considerably less dissonant) than that of *Salome* and *Elektra*.

The erotic quality of the love music in the first part of Act I is equal to Strauss's best in this vein. For the most part, however, the style of *Der Rosenkavalier* is more simple and tuneful than that of his earlier operas. The famous waltzes are anachronistic; the waltzes of Schubert, Lanner, and J. Strauss, which these imitate, were not, of course, a feature of eighteenth-century Vienna. But this is of little importance, and it is still less important that Strauss has seen fit to decorate the waltz themes with some of his own harmonic twists. The best musical characterizations are those of the Princess, a figure of mingled humor, wisdom, and pathos, and her country cousin Baron Ochs, a type of comic boor drawn, at Strauss's insistence, rather more coarsely than Hofmannsthal would have preferred. Sophie and Octavian, the young lovers, are by comparison colorless; their music is that of situations and sentiment rather than of personalities, and any possible realism in their relationship is prevented by making Octavian's part a *Hosenrolle*, a "trouser role"— that is, a man's part sung by a woman, like Mozart's Cherubino. The scene of their first meeting and the presentation of the silver rose thus moves in an atmosphere of ideal, magical, passionless beauty, unsurpassed anywhere in the whole realm of opera. It is remarkable that here Strauss writes in an almost purely diatonic idiom, even emphasizing the triads by outlining them in the melodies; one of the composer's happiest inspirations, the theme of the silver rose (high, dissonant appoggiatura triads with celesta, flutes, harps, and three solo violins), tinkles against this background.

The ensembles of *Der Rosenkavalier* are virtuoso creations, particularly the scene of the levee in Act I: a dissolution and at the same time an apotheosis of the eighteenth-century opera buffa ensemble, bringing together all the elements of this form in seeming confusion and yet with a curious illusion of realism; the introduction of a stylized Italian tenor aria, a veritable interpolated number in this scene, is accomplished in the spirit of sporting with the formal technique. The first two-thirds of Act III forms another long ensemble of broad farcical nature with elements of the old Viennese popular theatre, laid on musically with a rather heavy hand, but of an irresistible comic dash which can only be compared to the ending of the second act of *Die Meistersinger* or the finale of *Falstaff*. After all this hurly-burly follows one of those transformations of mood which are so characteristic of *Der Rosenkavalier*. The trio for three soprano voices (Sophie, the Princess,

Octavian) is another superlative number, a melting baroque texture of long-spun, interweaving lines above simple diatonic harmonies. The long decrescendo continues : the last song is a duet in G major, two strophes of a lyric melody in thirds and sixths, in the style of the old German Singspiel. The themes of the silver rose and the lovers' first meeting sound once more. The opera closes with a pantomime of the Princess's little Negro pageboy, to the same music which was heard at his first appearance near the beginning of Act I. This masterly finale was largely shaped by Strauss's requirements. Hofmannsthal at one time feared it would be feeble in effect, but Strauss wrote : "It is at the conclusion that a musician, if he has any ideas at all, can achieve his best and supreme effects—so you may safely leave this for me to judge . . . from the Baron's exit onwards, I'll *guarantee* that, provided you undertake to guarantee the rest of the work." [30]

*Der Rosenkavalier* was hardly finished before Strausss and Hofmannsthal were at work on their next collaborative effort, *Ariadne auf Naxos* (1912), designed as a pendant to a German version of Molière's *Bourgeois Gentilhomme*. This one-act piece is a profoundly poetic, sensitive treatment of the myth of Ariadne and Bacchus, in form and spirit suggesting the pastorales and ballets of Lully and Molière, which were likewise usually enclosed within a comedy;[31] and like those models, it introduces comic-satirical elements through personages borrowed from the Italian commedia dell' arte. Strauss's music continues the trend toward diatonicism and simplicity already evident in *Der Rosenkavalier*; harmonically, it starts from the point which the composer had reached in the silver-rose scene of the earlier opera and becomes progressively less and less chromatic. The trio in scene 3 for three sopranos is similar to the trio in the last act of *Der Rosenkavalier* and is likewise followed by a simple folklike song. A new element is the light, swift, parlando style of the comic scenes and of the prologue, which was added in 1916 when *Ariadne* was taken out of its original setting in the Molière play. One role, that of Zerbinetta, is especially written for a high coloratura soprano. The leitmotif technique is used to a slight extent, but the

[30] Letter of September 12(?), 1910. Quoted by permission from E. Oser's translation in *A Working Friendship*, pp. 67–68.

[31] The analogy will be seen most clearly by comparison with the following works of Molière: *La Princesse d'Elide* (1664), *Psyché* (a *tragédie–ballet*, 1671), the pastorale in *La Comtesse d'Escarbagnas* (1671), and the pastoral *intermèdes* in *Georges Dandin* (1668) and *Le Malade imaginaire* (1673), music by M. A. Charpentier.

orchestra (only thirty-six players) is subordinated to the voices, and there is a distinct tendency toward division into separate numbers.

*Ariadne auf Naxos* was the definitive stage of Strauss's conversion to a Mozartean style, an intimate opera in which the musical idiom is refined to classic purity in comparison with the earlier works. From this point on, Strauss remained musically conservative. He had summed up in his own career the transition from Wagnerian music drama to the new anti-Wagnerian opera. But the flame of inspiration no longer burned quite so steadily; moreover, Strauss's later operas, while no less perfect in construction and technical realization than his earlier ones, fell coldly on the ears of a changed postwar world, a world which could only hear his music as something out of a vanished and irrecoverable past. This historical misfortune has deprived the opera-going public, especially outside Germany, of acquaintance with some works that well deserve to be better known.

One of these is *Die Frau ohne Schatten* ("The Woman without a Shadow"), composed during the years of the First World War on a libretto by Hofmannsthal based on one of his prose tales, and first performed at Vienna in 1919. *Die Frau ohne Schatten* is a weightily symbolic drama with a complex score of grandiose proportions, embodying contrasting musical styles and rich in orchestral effects. On a more intimate scale is *Intermezzo* (1924), a "middle-class comedy with symphonic interludes" on a libretto by the composer in an autobiographical vein reminiscent of the *Sinfonia domestica*, and a real virtuoso piece for the soprano. With *Die ägyptische Helena* (1928, revised version 1933) Strauss and Hofmannsthal returned, not altogether successfully, to the realm of mythology. The best of their postwar operas was the "lyrical comedy" *Arabella*, similar in atmosphere and general sound to *Der Rosenkavalier*, with a plot verging on operetta but handled with delicacy and spontaneous lyric warmth, a happy blending of Strauss's full orchestral sonorities and fine details of chamber music style. *Die schweigsame Frau* ("The Silent Woman," 1935), on a libretto by Stefan Zweig after Ben Jonson, is a comedy including some spoken dialogue, recitatives, lyric passages, and many ensembles, with a few musical quotations from older composers and Strauss himself. *Friedenstag* ("Day of Peace," 1938) is an exceptional one-act work in subject, style, and spirit. Its author, Josef Gregor, also delivered the librettos of Strauss's next two operas, both on mythological themes: *Daphne* (1938), a "bucolic tragedy," and *Die Liebe der Danae* ("The Love of Danae"), a "merry mythological tale" composed in 1938–40 but not performed until 1952.

Strauss's last opera, *Capriccio* (1942), is a one-act "conversation piece for music" on a libretto by Clemens Krauss—"no work for the public, only a fine dish for connoisseurs," the composer said. With only a pretext of a plot, *Capriccio* revolves about a discussion (which never reaches a positive conclusion) of certain "theoretical questions of art," especially the relation of words, music, and staging in opera; yet for all the lack of dramatic movement, the personages are no mere shadows, but fully drawn human characters. The scene is laid in Paris at the time of the Gluck-Piccinni quarrel, which gives Strauss occasion to quote now and then a musical phrase from operas by these two composers. *Capriccio* completes a cycle which *Ariadne* began. Appropriately to its period, the score is of a stylized rococo quality and is held throughout in the mood of chamber music. A full orchestra is required but is used for the most part only in small combinations; the sonority of the string sextet, first heard in the introduction, runs like a thread through the opera. The words are made to come clearly through the polyphonic orchestral texture,[32] being conveyed in lifelike dialogue and broadly designed ensembles; the principal aria, a number of central importance in the score, is a lyrical setting of a sonnet translated from Ronsard's *Continuation des Amours* (Paris, 1555; see Example 114). Altogether, *Capriccio* must be regarded as among the very best of Strauss's operas, the musical testament of an artist in the matured wisdom of age: in this, as in other respects, a worthy companion to Verdi's *Falstaff*.

OTHER COUNTRIES. The sources of the main stream of operatic production in the early part of the twentieth century were still the three countries Italy, France, and Germany. At the same time, the nationalist movement continued more or less vigorously in other lands, although as time went on the earlier marked national quality of the music tended to become somewhat overlaid by foreign elements and thus more nearly approach a common international style. In addition, a few composers of this period brought out operas which, while not distinctively national or otherwise outstanding, deserve to be at least mentioned.

The two principal Polish opera composers of the early twentieth century were Ludomir Różycki (1883–1953) and Karol Szymanowski

---

[32] Always an important consideration with Strauss; cf. his prefaces to this opera and *Intermezzo*.

EXAMPLE 114

R. STRAUSS

*(Example 114 continued)*

(1882–1937).[33] Różycki, though regarded in Poland as a nationalist composer, had absorbed Western influences from Germany. His works include *Eros and Psyche* (1917), the comic opera *Casanova* (1923), *Beatrice Cenci* (1927), and *Madame Walewska* (composed 1945), as well as a successful ballet, *Pan Twardowski* (1921). Szymanowski, the leading Polish composer of this period, worked primarily in symphonic and choral forms and wrote only two operas. *Hagith* (composed 1912–14) was influenced in subject matter and construction by Strauss's *Elektra* and in harmony largely by the music of Ravel. Particularly important is Szymanowski's *Król Roger* ("King Roger," 1926), a monumental dramatic work on a libretto somewhat similar to Schreker's *Der ferne Klang*. The music is harmonically rich in a neoimpressionistic idiom, with national influences in the melody; the solo lines range freely from declamatory-arioso phrases to ample melodic arches. The choral writing is particularly effective; some of the choral sonorities are derived from Russian Church style, with full texture, doubling of the parts, and parallel movement of the voices (Example 115). The ballets in Act II introduce oriental motifs.

A group of composers who for the most part came to recognition only after the establishment of Polish independence in 1919 includes Henryk Melcer (1869–1928; *Marja*, 1904); Emil Mlynarski (1870-1935; *Summer Night*, 1924); Henryk Opienski (1870–1942; *Jacob the Lutenist*, 1927); Tadeusz Joteyko (1872–1932; *Zygmund August*, 1925); Felix Nowowiejski (1877–1946; *Baltic Legend*, 1924);[34] and Adam Tadeusz Wieniawski (1879–1950; *Megae*, 1912).

The most famous Hungarian opera of the twentieth century is *Duke Bluebeard's Castle* by Béla Bartók (1881–1945),[35] composed in 1911 and first performed at Budapest in 1918—"the first genuinely Hungarian and at the same time modern opera." [36] The libretto by Béla Balász, inspired by Maeterlinck's version of the ancient tale and first published in 1910 as a "mystery play," involves only two characters and

[33] On Różycki, see biography by Wieniawski; also articles by Chybiński and Różycki in bibliography. The standard biography of Szymanowski is by Łobaczewska (1950); other biographies by Jachimecki (1927) and Golachowski (1956); see also in bibliography articles by Jachimecki and Iwaszkiewicz.

[34] Kamienski, "Legenda bałtyku."

[35] Biographies by H. Stevens and S. Moreux; *Béla Bartók: A Memorial Review*; Kroó, *Bartók Béla szinpadi müvei* (the chapter on *Duke Bluebeard's Castle*, in English translation, appeared in *Studia Musicologica* I [1961] 251–340); Lendvai, "A kékszakállu herceg vára" (important musical analysis).

[36] Kroó, "Duke Bluebeard's Castle," p. 340.

EXAMPLE 115

SZYMANOWSKI

(*Example 115 continued*)

(Example 115 continued)

contains hardly any external action; the inner, symbolic drama proceeds with the opening, one after another, of the seven doors that give on the hall of Blubeard's castle. Bartók's music, like Debussy's for *Pelléas*, seems a perfect and inimitable embodiment of the mysterious text. The music flows unbrokenly throughout the single act, its continuity emphasized by recurrence of "pivot" motifs and themes. The orchestral color and harmony, impressionistic in essence but stamped everywhere with Bartók's individuality, supports a vocal line consisting for the most part of irregular declamatory phrases whose melodic and rhythmic outlines derive from Hungarian folk song (Example 116).

Equally imbued with Hungarian national feeling though far less radical in musical idiom than *Bluebeard* are the stage works of Zoltán Kodály (b. 1882),[37] which combine spoken dialogue with songs and choruses either borrowed from or composed in the style of folk music : *Háry János* (1926), on the adventures of a comic character from national folklore; the ballad opera *Székely fonó* ("The Spinning-Room," 1932, revised from the original version of 1924); and *Czinka Panna*, composed for a national centennial celebration and produced at Budapest in 1948.

A notable figure in Spanish opera of the early twentieth century was Manuel de Falla (1876–1946)[38] although, like Szymanowski, Bartók, and Kodály, he worked mainly in other forms of composition. His principal opera is the charming little marionette piece *El retablo di Maese Pedro* ("Master Peter's Puppet Show," 1923), for three singing parts and an orchestra of twenty-five players, on an episode from *Don Quixote*, using a boy soprano as narrator and in a musical style that cleverly combines archaic features with modern harmonies in an austere but appropriate texture. Falla's earlier opera, *La vida breve* ("Life Is Short"), composed in 1905 and first performed in 1913, is less notable for its dramatic qualities than for the ballets in Act II; Falla's other ballets, *El amor brujo* and *El sombrero de tres picos*, are important works in this form.

During the last twenty years of his life Falla was continually occupied with what he intended to be his masterwork, *La Atlántida*. Although this vast "scenic cantata" was left unfinished, the music was put together from the composer's sketches by his devoted pupil Ernesto Halffter (b. 1905); it is as yet uncertain how much of the music as published is

---

[37] Biography by Eősze.
[38] Biography by Pahissa; V. S. Viu, "The Mystery of . . . *La Atlántida.*"

EXAMPLE 116

BARTÓK

(*Example 116 continued*)

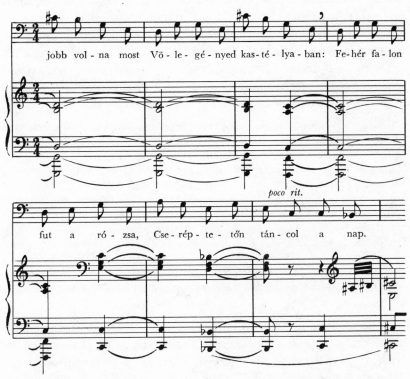

jobb vol - na   most   Vö - le - gé - nyed kas - té - lya - ban:   Fe-hér fa - lon

fut   a   ró - zsa,   Cse - rép - te - tőn   tán - col   a   nap.

actually the work of Falla and how much that of Halffter. Portions of *La Atlántida* were performed in public for the first time, without staging, at Barcelona on November 24, 1961. The first stage production (with the words in Italian translation) took place at La Scala on June 18, 1962, and a concert version (incomplete) was given at New York on September 29 and 30, 1962.

The text of *La Atlántida* is taken from an epic poem (1878) by Mossén Jacinto Verdaguer. Within a framework of half-pagan, half-Christian mythology it ranges from the remote geological past over the legendary history of the Spanish peninsula, recounting the exploits of Hercules, the Gardens of the Hesperides, the opening of the Straits of Gibraltar, the destruction of Atlantis, the founding of Cadiz and Barcelona, and culminating with a prophetic vision of Columbus's voyages and the establishment of a Spanish empire in America. In form as well as in some aspects of the subject, the work is reminiscent of Milhaud's *Christophe Colomb. Atlántida* is a monumental combination of oratorio and opera, some three hours in length, requiring for full performance a narrator, a dozen soloists, two choruses, and a huge orchestra. The music has extraordinary variety and breadth; the style in general is markedly different from that of Falla's earlier works and has an austere, archaic grandeur (especially in the many choral portions) that recalls the spirit of the great sixteenth-century Spanish church composers.

Some other continental European composers of opera in the first part of the twentieth century will be briefly noticed here. In Spain, the disciples of Pedrell include Angel Barrios (b. 1882) and Conrado del Campo y Zabaleta (1879–1953) with a jointly composed opera, *El Avapiés* (1919; the title is the name of a quarter in Madrid), and Amadeo Vives (1871–1932), composer of the "lyric eclogue" *Maruxa* (1914) and the popular comic opera *Doña Francisquita* (1923). Joaquín Turina (1882–1949) composed the operas *Margot* (1914) and *Jardín de oriente* (1923). A notable composer of Holland was Willem Pijper (1894–1947), whose only completed opera, *Halewijn*, was given at Amsterdam in 1933. In Switzerland Othmar Schoeck (1886–1957), distinguished especially as a writer of songs, produced a number of operas, the most successful of which was *Penthesilea* (1927).

The situation in England in the early part of the twentieth century is interesting because of the contrast between the work of continentally oriented composers and the efforts of others to create a viable opera of distinctly English character. To the former group belongs the only (so far) successful woman opera composer, Dame Ethel Smyth (1858–1944).[39] Following two early operas brought out in Germany, her principal stage work, *The Wreckers*, written originally on a French libretto, was produced in a German translation (as *Strandrecht*) at Leipzig in 1906 and finally played in English at London in 1909; it has been revived there with success since 1939. Her next opera was a comedy, *The Boatswain's Mate*, which had a fair success in England; two further one-act operas appeared in 1923 and 1925.

A virtual expatriate was Frederick Delius (1862–1934);[40] born in England of German parentage, he lived most of his life abroad—first in Florida, then for a period of study in Leipzig, and from 1888 in France.

[39] Biography by C. St. John (1959); see also the composer's own writings, especially her memoirs (*Impressions That Remained*); Capell, "Dame Ethel Smyth's Operas at Covent Garden" (1923).

[40] Biography by Heseltine; Hutchings, "Delius's Operas."

Three of his six operas came to performance, all first in Germany. The best known of them, *A Village Romeo and Juliet* (1907), might from the story almost have been entitled "A Village Tristan and Isolde." It is full of lovely music in a late romantic style—rich in texture, chromatic, with long expressive lines for the solo voices and some fine choral scenes. Celtic folk-song idiom is apparent in some places, for example in Vreli's song at the opening of scene 4; the familiar orchestral selection *The Walk to the Paradise Garden* (from the end of scene 5) is typical of the style.

Among other early twentieth-century composers of serious opera in English were John Edmund Barkworth (1858–1921; *Romeo and Juliet*, 1916) and Ernest Bryson (1867–1942; *The Leper's Flute*, 1926). Philip Napier Miles (1865–1935),[41] active promoter of opera in England, composed *Westward Ho!* (1913) and *Markheim* (1924). Well constructed and worked out though conservative in musical style were the operas of Nicholas Comyn Gatty (1874–1946): *Greysteel* (1906), *Duke or Devil* (1909), the romantic Shakespearean *Tempest* (1920), and the charming fairy opera *Prince Ferelon* (1921). Sir Eugene Goossens (1893–1958) had some success with his two operas on texts by Arnold Bennett: *Judith* (1929) and *Don Juan de Mañera* (1937). Others in this period were Sir Donald Francis Tovey (1875–1940; *The Bride of Dionysus*, 1932), Colin Macleod Campbell (1890–1953; *Thais and Talmaae*, 1921), and Lawrance Arthur Collingwood (b. 1887; *Macbeth*, 1934). The only one of Albert Coates's (1882–1953) three operas to be produced in England was *Pickwick* (1936).

About 1908 Rutland Boughton (1878–1960),[42] an ardent disciple of Wagner's theories and himself a composer of frankly romantic tendencies, conceived the idea of founding an English equivalent of Bayreuth. One outcome of this project was the establishment of the Glastonbury Festival in 1914 and the production there in 1916 of Boughton's *The Round Table*, designed to be the first music drama in an Arthurian tetralogy. (*The Birth of Arthur*, the prologue, had been heard earlier, with a piano substituting for the orchestra.) Boughton completed the tetralogy, but only the second number (*The Lily Maid*) was performed, in 1934, and the entire cycle still awaits production.

[41] Colles, "Philip Napier Miles."
[42] See Boughton's own writings listed in bibliography; Hurd, *Immortal Hour*; Antcliffe, "A British School of Music-Drama."

Meanwhile, the composer had achieved an unexpected success with a less ambitious but appealing opera, *The Immortal Hour* (1914).

The two leading English composers of the early twentieth century, Gustav Holst (1874–1934)[43] and Ralph Vaughan Williams (1872–1958),[44] made significant contributions to opera. Holst's *Savitri* (composed 1908, performed 1916) is a chamber opera of exquisite tenderness and simple emotion, in a musical style that suggests the Eastern setting of the story without attempting literal imitation of Hindu melodies; it contains some beautiful writing for women's chorus. Holst's principal opera, the one-act comedy *The Perfect Fool*, had successful performances at Covent Garden in 1923; the music shows the composer fully emancipated from the neo-Wagnerian tendencies of his earlier dramatic works. *At the Boar's Head* (1925) is a Shakespearean intermezzo with words from *Henry IV*, a jolly work made up largely of traditional English tunes, somewhat in the manner of ballad opera. The influence of these works is not to be reckoned so much by their outward success as by the fact that they represent the serious, original, and uncompromising efforts of a first-rank English composer in the restricted and rather thankless field of native opera. Much the same may be said of Vaughan Williams's dramatic works. *The Shepherds of the Delectable Mountains*, a pastoral episode after Bunyan, has been frequently revived in England since its first performance in 1922. *Hugh the Drover; or, Love in the Stocks* (1924) is a ballad-type opera with continuous music, containing allusions to a number of traditional tunes without direct quotation, and as thoroughly English in spirit as anything of Gilbert and Sullivan. *Sir John in Love* (1929), based on Shakespeare's *Merry Wives of Windsor*, is the composer's biggest work for the stage (four acts); the music is similar to that of *Hugh the Drover*, but more highly developed both formally and harmonically—a truly English *Falstaff* not unworthy of comparison with Verdi's Italian one. The Gilbert and Sullivan tradition lives on in *The Poisoned Kiss* (1936), a tuneful comic opera with spoken dialogue. *Riders to the Sea* (1937) is a restrained but moving setting (in one act) of Synge's play, the vocal parts in flexibly declaimed melodies and the harmonies in neomodal style with much parallel chord progression, the whole having a subdued

[43] Biography by Imogen Holst; *idem, The Music of Gustav Holst.*
[44] Howes, *The Music of Ralph Vaughan Williams;* see also Gordon, "Folklore in Modern English Opera."

intensity of feeling that accords well with the peculiar atmosphere of the drama.

German influences were still preponderant in American music at the beginning of the twentieth century, but by this time composers were more thoroughly trained, more ambitious, versatile, and productive, and were speaking a more authoritative musical language. Nevertheless it is worth remarking that neither of the two leading figures in this generation, Charles Martin Loeffler and Edward MacDowell, wrote an opera. The principal composers who did write for the theatre were three pupils of Chadwick : Frederick Shepherd Converse (1871–1940), Henry Hadley (1871–1937),[45] and Horatio Parker (1863–1919).[46] Converse's *The Pipe of Desire* (Boston, 1906) was the first American opera to be presented at the Metropolitan (1910)—a pleasant, tuneful score showing some influence of impressionism. Another opera, *The Sacrifice*, was given at Boston in 1911. Hadley's chief successes, in a sound conservative style, were *Azora, Daughter of Montezuma* (Chicago, 1917) and *Cleopatra's Night* (New York, 1920).

Parker's two prize-winning operas, *Mona* (New York, 1912) and *Fairyland* (Los Angeles, 1915), are regarded by many as significant American operas that have been unjustly ignored. The neglect is certainly not due to any technical shortcomings in the scores, which are sound in craftsmanship, large in conception, distinguished in musical ideas, and well planned for theatrical effect. But the librettos are sadly old-fashioned : *Mona*, a sufficiently good drama in essence, is markedly in the romantic style of its day, with a scene laid in ancient Britain and the whole obviously owing much to *Tristan und Isolde*. *Fairyland* is one of those combinations of whimsy, symbolism, and vague pantheistic aspiration such as are found in the fairy operas of Rimsky-Korsakov or in Converse's *Pipe of Desire*; and Parker's music is likewise typical of the late romantic period. *Mona* is a slightly modernized *Tristan*, with the same sort of continuous symphonic structure, system of leitmotifs, opulent harmony, chromatic melody, and avoidance of cadences that characterize its model; *Fairyland* is somewhat lighter in texture and more diatonic in harmony—Wagner leavened by a dash of

---

[45] See biography by Boardman and monograph by Berthoud.
[46] Chadwick, *Horatio Parker*; D. S. Smith, "A Study of Horatio Parker"; memoir by Semler.

late Strauss. Musically, the gravest accusation that can be made against either opera is that the same things had been said before; and it may be regretted that these works had the misfortune to come at a moment when tastes in musical matters were on the verge of radical change.

Of later American operas in conservative style, designed for full-scale production, the most successful were two by Deems Taylor (b. 1885):[47] *The King's Henchman* (New York, 1927) and *Peter Ibbetson* (New York, 1931), smooth, expert works in a mild late-romantic style with modern trimmings, well molded to the taste of that large majority of the opera-going public who are pleased with expressive melodies and sensuous harmonies that pleasantly stimulate without disturbing. Other American operas at the Metropolitan have been less enthusiastically received—for example, Richard Hageman's (b. 1882) *Caponsacchi* (1937, after a first performance in German translation at Freiburg in 1932). Among American operas that have been produced under respectable auspices and gone their way without leaving a mark may be mentioned Ernest Carter's (1866–1953) *The White Bird* (Chicago, 1924) and John Laurence Seymour's (b. 1893) prize-winning *In the Pasha's Garden* (New York, 1935).[48]

National scenes and subjects, as might be expected, have been frequently tried. Charles Wakefield Cadman's (1881–1946) *The Robin Woman (Shanewis)*, given at the Metropolitan in 1918, uses a number of authentic Indian tunes and has an attractive, if superficial, melodic vein, but is slight in substance and awkward in dramatic details. The same composer's *A Witch of Salem* (Chicago, 1926) had a fair number of performances. An important American historical opera was *Merry Mount* by Howard Hanson (b. 1896),[49] commissioned by the Metropolitan and produced there in 1934. The score incorporates many ballets and choruses in a wild, implausible story of Puritan New England. It may be the extravagance of the libretto which has interfered with the full success of *Merry Mount*, or it may be a somewhat stiff, oratorio-like, undramatic quality and the generally static harmonic and melodic style of much of the music. Yet there is considerable variety of idiom: the

[47] See study by J. T. Howard.
[48] For fuller lists see Hipsher, *American Opera*; Howard, *Our Contemporary Composers*.
[49] See study by Tuthill (1936).

love strains of Bradford's aria "Rise up, my love" with the following duet, and the "Walpurgisnacht" ballets in Act II are particularly remarkable; and the work as a whole is able, serious, and uncompromising—a compliment of the sort that opera audiences do not always seem to appreciate.

# CHAPTER 27

# TRADITION AND RENEWAL: THE RECENT PAST[1]

Of all musical forms, opera is the most immediately sensitive to changes in political, economic, social, and general cultural conditions. Its very nature as a complex and costly public spectacle largely dependent on official patronage or private subsidy makes it especially vulnerable to political dictates and economic vicissitudes: its subject matter reflects, positively or negatively, current human preoccupations; its form, content, and idiom are all affected by changing ideals of dramatic and musical style. Two world wars, a world-wide economic depression, and the emergence of political systems committed to strict control of art in the interest of the state have been the salient external factors in the first half of the twentieth century. Widespread emigration of authors and composers in the 1930s affected the development of opera in the United States and elsewhere. The passionately felt need of the artist to come to grips in contemporary terms with contemporary issues stimulated new uses of traditional techniques and experiments with new dramatic and musical means. Technological developments also played a part: radio, television, and the long-playing phonograph record immensely increased

[1] General bibliography: K. H. Wörner, *Neue Musik in der Entscheidung*; Collaer, *La Musique moderne*; Slonimsky, *Music Since 1900*; Machlis, *Introduction to Contemporary Music*; *Oper im XX. Jahrhundert* (*Musik der Zeit*, Heft 6); *Opera Annual*, ed. H. Rosenthal (1954 and following years). See also bibliography, including articles in current periodicals and the section "Current Chronicle" in MQ (April, 1948, and following issues). On opera in the United States, see especially the files of *Opera News* (1936+) and *American Composers Alliance Bulletin* (1938, 1952+); Heinsheimer, "Opera in America Today" (MQ, 1951).

the actual and potential audience, bringing the traditional repertoire and style of opera within everyone's reach and making it possible, to some extent at least, for the public to become acquainted with newer developments. As a result opera has become of interest to a larger number of people than ever before in its history. Free pursuit of the new, together with an enlarged and diverse public, accounts for an unprecedented diversity of operatic styles in our time—the "polyphonic" or "many-voiced century," as one writer has called it.[2]

As in all periods, the subject matter of twentieth-century opera has been drawn variously from imagined dramatic interactions of human personalities, from history, myth, legend, or folklore, or from the circumstances of contemporary life; treatment has been serious or light, earnest or satirical or playful, as of timeless significance or as applicable peculiarly to the present moment. The aims have been equally varied : mere amusement or entertainment (whether of a general public or of special groups, as for example opera for children); instruction and conversion —that is, propaganda; comedy with contemporary social application; or high tragedy in the Aristotelian sense: "the imitation of an action that is serious and also, as having magnitude, complete in itself . . . with incidents arousing pity and fear, wherewith to accomplish its catharsis of such emotions" [3]—this kind of drama, inviting the audience as it does to contemplate heroic greatness of deed or character, being in some instances more or less overtly directed toward confirmation of religious faith.

We may recall that the twentieth century inherited, along with the timeless and unchanging line of light or "entertainment" opera, two fundamentally contrasting conceptions of serious musical drama. Stated in simplest terms, these were : (1) the Wagnerian drama of ideas, with personages primarily symbolical and with music in a continuous orchestral texture organized by means of leitmotifs, the vocal lines being of declamatory or arioso character; and (2) the Verdian drama of typical human beings in psychological interaction, with music in the form of distinct numbers connected by recitatives and a texture of emotionally expressive vocal melody sustained by orchestral accompaniment. By and large, composers at the beginning of the twentieth century adhered to one or the other of these two basic conceptions, even if with compromises

[2] K. Honolka, *Das vielstimmige Jahrhundert* (1960).
[3] Aristotle, *Poetics*, chap. vi (1449b20), Bywater's translation.

or modifications : Strauss in *Salome* and *Electra* (and later in *Die Frau
ohne Schatten*) was in the line of descent from Wagner, as was essentially
also Debussy in *Pelléas et Mélisande* despite its un-Wagnerian harmonies
and dynamics; on the other hand, Puccini and the composers of the
verismo school descended (in both senses of the word) from Verdi. Meanwhile, a new conception was growing up, or rather an old one was being
revived : the eighteenth-century classical idea of an opera as primarily
a musical entity, with poetry "the obedient daughter of music," as
Mozart had expressed it. This new-old conception involved, as a rule,
the use of distinct musical numbers in definite form, objectivity of
expression, and a tendency to let the music develop in its own way,
following the dramatic action in broad lines but not attempting to
mirror it in detail. This conception of opera, an early example of which
is Strauss's *Ariadne*, has influenced many twentieth-century composers
—Falla, Ravel and most of the French, some Germans (notably Hindemith), and Stravinsky, especially in *The Rake's Progress*.

One development that attracted much attention in the 1920s and
1930s was the opera of social protest, conspicuous first in Germany and
later in the United States. To be sure, the theme of social protest had
occurred in opera before, but now it became explicit and central instead
of only incidental.

Another phenomenon of the period since 1920 has been the tendency
to combine the traditional form of opera with certain features of the
oratorio, such as a narrator or a contemplative or didactic chorus. Introduction of oratorio-like elements has occurred typically in large-scale
works on historical or legendary subjects, such as Stravinsky's *Oedipus
rex*, Milhaud's *Christophe Colomb*, Hindemith's *Mathis der Maler*,
Egk's *Columbus*, Schoenberg's *Moses und Aron*, and Orff's *Antigonae*.
A like infiltration of oratorio or cantata technique is found in some stage
works of smaller scale, such as Falla's *Retablo de Maese Pedro*, Vaughan
Williams's *Pilgrim's Progress*, and Britten's *Rape of Lucretia*. Forerunners of the opera-oratorio may be found in Wagner's *Parsifal* and
Pfitzner's *Palestrina*, but the combination is especially characteristic of
the mid-twentieth century.

Likewise characteristic of this period is the importance of ballet,
especially ballet with dramatic elements (Bartók, Stravinsky, Prokofiev)
and the incorporation of choreographic (often also choral) spectacle in
opera (as in many of the works mentioned above), or even a fusion of

opera and ballet as in Casella's "choreographic comedy" *La giara*
(1924) or Henze's *Boulevard Solitude* (1952). Still another feature of
the twentieth century is the unprecedented extent to which composers
have worked in smaller forms—"chamber" or "workshop" opera,
requiring few performers, sometimes written specifically for amateurs
or for children. This movement, the result of special conditions, has
been particularly prominent in England and the United States, but is
not by any means confined to those countries. Finally may be mentioned
the rise of opera for the new media of radio and television and the
writing of incidental music for films as well as for stage plays.

No single one of the typical twentieth-century operatic phenomena
(except for the use of radio or television) can be called completely "new."
What is new, as has already been said, is the unprecedented diversity of
operatic styles existing in one and the same period. In part, of course,
that diversity is an illusion caused by our nearness to events, our lack of
historical perspective; but even discounting this (insofar as possible) the
diversity remains. We shall try to cope with it by making a division into
six general headings (determined chiefly by considerations of musical
style) and mentioning some representative works under each. But the
reader must be warned at the outset that our categories have been
selected only for convenience in ordering the material and do not claim
to be rigid or mutually exclusive. Some composers and some works might
equally well be placed under a different heading or under more than
one. Above all, denominations like traditional, popular, national, progressive, experimental, and the like imply no judgment as to aesthetic
value : there are, of course, better and worse works within each category;
but no one category is inherently or necessarily superior to another.

## 1. THE TRADITION

Despite many well-publicized experiments and new departures, a
large proportion of operas produced after 1920—including some of the
best as well as most popular works of this period—kept recognizably
close to traditional forms and subjects and avoided any radical departure
from accepted musical styles. In the favorable environment of Italy the
tradition was carried on by Franco Alfano (1876–1954),[4] the choice of

---

[4] *Cinquanta anni di opera e balletto in Italia* (1954); Gatti, "Franco Alfano";
*idem*, "Recent Italian Operas"; Della Corte, *Ritratto di Franco Alfano*.

whom to complete the unfinished score of Puccini's *Turandot* was symbolical of his intermediary position in the history of Italian opera. Alfano had become known as early as 1904 for his *Risurrezione* ("Resurrection"); his most significant later works were *La leggenda di Sakuntala* (1921), a heavily tragic work of grand-opera proportions, and the one-act neo-Puccinian lyrical comedy *Madonna Imperia* (1927), whose vocal lines, alternating smoothly between melodic phrases and a lively, expressive arioso, are supported by luscious harmonies in impressionistic orchestral colors—a perfect match for the refinedly voluptuous text. Alfano's *L'ultimo Lord* (1930), a vivacious comic work, and *Il dottor Antonio* (1949) continued in the same essentially conservative style.

The operas of Ildebrando Pizzetti (b. 1880)[5] are somewhat less conservative in their harmonies than those of Alfano. They have a continuous full-bodied orchestral texture in a mosaic of recurring motifs, are primarily lyrical in expression with flexible speechlike vocal melodies, and are characterized by extensive dramatic use of choruses in a sensitive polyphonic style inspired by classical Italian models. The most important of Pizzetti's early operas, and one of his best scores, was *Fedra* (1915), on a text by Gabriele D'Annunzio. A group of works to his own librettos comprised *Debora e Jaele* (1922), *Fra Gherardo* (1928), and *Lo straniero* ("The Stranger," 1930). Pizzetti's later operas include *Orséolo* (1935), *Vanna Lupa* (1949), *Ifigenia* (first given in radio broadcast, 1950), *Cagliostro* (1953), *La figlia di Iorio*, a "pastoral tragedy" by D'Annunzio (1954), and *Assassinio nella cattedrale* ("Murder in the Cathedral," 1958), based on a translation of T. S. Eliot's play.

In France, conditions after the First World War were less favorable than in Italy for new serious operas in styles so closely related to tradition as were those of Alfano and Pizzetti. Paris, the principal and virtually the only important operatic center, readily accepted new pieces in the lighter forms, but the public for serious opera either remained content with the standard old repertoire or centered its attention on composers of distinctly "modern" tendencies. Thus a quite exceptional event was the production in 1939 of Henri Sauguet's (b. 1901) *Chartreuse de Parme*, a work conforming in every external detail to the pattern of nineteenth-century singers' opera and couched in a simple—though far

[5] Biography by Gatti; La Morgia, ed., *La città dannunziana di Ildebrando Pizzetti*.

from unsophisticated—musical idiom that might have traced its lineage from Satie.

One of the outstanding French operas of the mid-twentieth century was *Les Dialogues des Carmélites* by Francis Poulenc (1899–1963),[6] performed at Milan in January, 1957, and at Paris in June of the same year. In contrast to the composer's earlier satirical, surrealist comic opera *Les Mamelles de Tirésias* ("The Breasts of Tiresias," 1947) and his later tense monodrama *La Voix humaine* ("The Human Voice," 1959), the *Carmélites* presents no ostentatiously novel features either in subject, form, or musical idiom. The theme of its libretto—written by Georges Bernanos after a novella by Gertrude von Le Fort—is the conquest of fear by divine grace. The central personage is a timorous young Carmelite nun caught in the religious persecutions under the Reign of Terror; the drama, developed with fine psychological perception and excellent balance between inner and outer action, had obvious and terrible implications for conditions in France in the 1940s, but its topical features are less important than its universal significance. The latter is powerfully communicated by Poulenc's music, selflessly devoted to the text and bound with it in a union no less perfect than that which Debussy had accomplished in *Pelléas*. These two operas are alike furthermore in the way they achieve profoundly dramatic results through restraint in the use of resources. Like Debussy, Poulenc connects the scenes within each act by means of instrumental interludes and makes unobtrusive use of recurring themes. The vocal solo lines, cast for the most part in quasi-melodic declamation (see Example 117), are kept in clear relief above the continuous, ever-changing, but always lucid and evocative orchestral sonorities. The chorus, used only sparingly throughout most of the opera, comes into the foreground at the dramatic, moving final scene. Altogether, *Les Dialogues des Carmélites* takes a worthy and, one may hope, a permanently honored place in the history of French opera.

In the German-speaking countries the composer who probably best represents the continuing central tradition in opera is an Austrian, Gottfried von Einem (b. 1918).[7] In his music often piercing harmonic

[6] Hell, *Francis Poulenc*; Poulenc, *Entretiens avec Claude Rostand*; *idem*, "Comment j'ai composé les *Dialogues des Carmélites*"; La Maestre, "Francis Poulenc und seine Bernanos-Oper."

[7] Rutz, *Neue Oper: Gottfried Einem und seine Oper Dantons Tod*; Von Einem, "*Der Prozess*"; Graf, "*Der Prozess* von Gottfried von Einem"; analysis of *Der Prozess* by W. Reich in MQ XL (1954) 62–76.

EXAMPLE 117

POULENC

com - me l'en - fant de la vieil - les - se, et aus-

si la plus ha - sar - dé - e, la plus me - na - cé - e.

Pour dé - tour - ner cet - te me - na - ce, j'au - rais bien don-

-né ma pau - vre vi - e,

dissonances and sharp variegated rhythms are contained within an essentially tonal and romantic framework of expression with singable melodic lines, the whole enlivened by original thematic ideas and handled with a natural flair for stage effect. Von Einem's output for the theatre hitherto includes, in addition to ballets, the two operas *Dantons Tod* ("The Death of Danton," 1947), on a libretto adapted from Georg Büchner's drama, an immediately appealing work especially notable for its tumultuous crowd scenes, and *Der Prozess* ("The Trial," 1953), based on Franz Kafka's novel, a score in which each scene constitutes a musical unit with its own characteristic rhythms, its own singing (or speaking) style, instrumental color, and formal pattern.

Another opera composer to be noted here is Werner Egk (b. 1901), like Von Einem primarily a musician of the theatre. His *Columbus*, originally written for radio broadcast in 1933 and frequently performed since on German stages in a revised version, is a rather static combination of opera and epic; a later and possibly better mixture of these elements is found in *Irische Legende* (1955). Most memorable of Egk's operas is *Peer Gynt* (1938), a straightforward human drama with a musical score of considerable variety, color, and melodic interest. Rudolf Wagner-Régeny (b. 1903) is known chiefly through *Der Günstling* ("The Favorite," 1935) and *Die Bürger von Calais* ("The Citizens of Calais," 1939). A favorite composer in Switzerland is Heinrich Sutermeister (b. 1910), who combines a pleasing melodic style with good feeling for the theatre, exemplified in the tragic operas *Romeo und Julia* (1940) and *Raskolnikoff* (1948; after Dostoyevsky), as well as in various short works of lighter character, written for the radio and later revised for regular theatre performance.

In England and the United States the ultraconservative style in opera has been illustrated in mid-century by two competent large-scale works, both launched under favorable official auspices: *Troilus and Cressida* (London, 1954) by Sir William Walton (b. 1902) [8] and *Vanessa* (New York, 1958) by Samuel Barber (b. 1910). More varied and adventurous, though still not involving any radical break with tradition, has been the work of two composers whose interest centers largely in the musical theatre: Benjamin Britten (b. 1913) [9] in England and Gian

---

[8] Reizenstein, "Walton's *Troilus and Cressida.*"

[9] D. Mitchell and H. Keller, eds., *Benjamin Britten*; E. W. White, *Benjamin Britten*; *Benjamin Britten: Das Opernwerk (Musik der Zeit*, Heft 11, 1955); Britten and others, *The Rape of Lucretia: A Symposium*; numerous articles in *Tempo* and other periodicals (see bibliography).

Carlo Menotti (b. 1911) in the United States. Significantly, a considerable proportion of their output has been in the form of chamber opera.

Britten's most important large operas are *Peter Grimes* (1945) and *A Midsummer Night's Dream* (1960). The former is an admirably constructed drama, with music in separate numbers linked by orchestral interludes and a few recurring themes, in an idiom permeated with the spirit of English folk song while unobtrusively incorporating individual traits of color, rhythm, and harmony. An outstanding feature is the sensitive declamation of the text; the expertly handled choral sonorities play an important part in creating the stark dramatic atmosphere of the work. *Peter Grimes* seems to be well established in the repertoire. *A Midsummer Night's Dream* is a less successful score despite some beautiful numbers—the duets in Act I, the comic rehearsal of the rustics in the first scene of Act II, and the ensemble for six boys at the end of the same act, for example. But some mannerisms, such as glissandi in the double-basses and ostinato techniques generally, are overworked, and a certain monotony of effect results from the prevailing color of high voices; in particular, the countertenor role of Oberon is dramatically unconvincing. Britten's operas for smaller performing groups include the tragic *Rape of Lucretia* (1946), which uses a commentative "chorus" consisting of two solo voices; the comic *Albert Herring* (1947); and an unusual work, *The Turn of the Screw* (1954), a dramatization of Henry James's tale with music in the form of fourteen variations on a tone row —which, however, is treated as a theme rather than by the usual twelve-tone techniques of construction and moreover is so conceived and harmonized as to produce an effect not far removed from conventional tonality. The music successfully captures the supernatural mood of the story, but the dramatic material is perhaps too subtle to be effectively projected in the theatre. Wholly delightful are Britten's operas for children, *The Little Sweep* (1949) and *Noye's Fludde* (1958). All in all, there can be no question as to Britten's signal importance in contemporary English opera or his significance as an original, skillful, and idealistic composer adapting himself without sacrifice of integrity to the practical conditions of his place and time.

Other British composers of opera are: Arthur Benjamin (1893–1960; *A Tale of Two Cities*, 1953); Alan Dudley Bush (b. 1900; *Wat Tyler*, 1952); Lennox Berkeley (b. 1903; *Nelson*, 1951); and Michael Tippett (b.

1905), whose *Midsummer Marriage* (1955) is a significant and original work.

Menotti is a born theatre composer of the order of Puccini and the verismo school. His musical style is eclectic, drawing upon heterogeneous elements with a single eye to dramatic effect, of which he is an unerring master. He writes his own librettos. Conspicuous among his many successful works for the stage are *The Medium* (1946), an unashamed melodrama perfectly matched by equally melodramatic music; a short comic opera, *The Telephone* (1947); and *The Consul* (1950), a compelling treatment of the tragedy of homeless persons in an indifferent world. *Amahl and the Night Visitors*, originally produced on television in 1951, is on the way to becoming a popular classic. It is not necessary to make extravagant claims for Menotti's musical originality in order to recognize that he is one of the very few serious opera composers on the contemporary American scene who thoroughly understand the requirements of the theatre and are making a consistent, sincere attempt to reach the large opera-loving public; his success is a testimonial to the continuing validity of a long and respectable operatic tradition.

Another well-established American composer of serious opera is Douglas Moore (b. 1893). In *The Devil and Daniel Webster* (1939) and later in *Giants in the Earth* (1951) and *The Ballad of Baby Doe* (1956), Moore combined distinctively American subject matter and musical idiom with good theatrical craftsmanship. More recent works are *Gallantry*, a "soap opera" (1958), and *The Wings of the Dove* (1961).

The marked rise of local opera groups, both amateur and professional, and the generally increased opportunities for performance of new works in the United States have encouraged the production of operas by American composers, especially since the end of the Second World War. Undoubtedly the most flourishing branch of the musical theatre in this country is still musical comedy, and no work has yet risen to challenge the secure place of *Porgy and Bess* in the history of American opera. Among the more or less successful newer works outside the musical comedy class may be listed : *The Warrior* (1947) and *The Veil* (1950) by Bernard Rogers (b. 1893); *The Trial of Lucullus* (1947) by Roger Sessions (b. 1896); *The Tender Land* (1954) by Aaron Copland (b. 1900); *The Mighty Casey* (1953) by William Schuman (b. 1910); *The Ruby* (1955) and *The Trial at Rouen* (1956) by Norman Dello Joio (b. 1913); *The Crucible* (1961) by Robert Ward (b. 1917); *Good Soldier Schweik* (1958) by the talented American-born Czech composer Robert Kurka (1921–57); *The Wife of Martin Guerre*

(1956) by William Bergsma (b. 1921); *The Jumping Frog of Calaveras County* (1950) by Lukas Foss (b. 1922); *Susannah* (1955) and *Wuthering Heights* (1959) by Carlisle Floyd (b. 1926); [10] and operas by Hugo Weisgall (b. 1912), including *The Tenor* (1952), *The Stronger* (1952), and *Six Characters in Search of an Author* (1959, after Pirandello).[11]

## 2. COMIC OPERA

"Comic opera," in the twentieth century as in earlier periods, is a designation embracing many different types. At one end of the scale are frankly popular works—musical comedies, operettas, and the like— that seek to entertain a large public by means of (1) music in a style familiar enough to be enjoyed without much effort or close attention but containing some novelty in details; and (2) a dramatic content uncompli- cated, superficial (in the sense of carrying no "message"), humorous or sentimental or both, and possibly enlivened by reference to current foibles or topics in the news. Other kinds of comic opera may be dis- tinguished by music in a more advanced style, greater sophistication of plot and subtlety of characterization, or evidence of some aim (for example, satire) in addition to that of entertainment. Most successful writers of light popular works produce nothing of significance outside that special field. Examples of more sophisticated kinds of comic opera, however, have come from nearly every composer for the theatre in the present century, including some who are equally competent in the "serious" realm—Alfano, Poulenc, Britten, and Menotti, for instance, as we have already seen.

Among the composers of comic opera in France during the interwar years were Charles Levadé (1869–1948; *La Rôtisserie de la Reine Pédauque*, 1920; *La Peau de Chagrin*, 1929), Marcel Samuel-Rousseau (1882–1955; *Le Bon Roi Dagobert*, 1927), and especially Jacques Ibert (1890–1962). Ibert's *Angélique* (1927) is a one-act farce with spoken dialogue, the music scintillating and epigrammatic, using polytonal chords, dance rhythms, and conventional melodies dressed up with dissonant harmonies—a twentieth-century revival of the old spirit of the Paris vaudevilles. Later operatic works of Ibert include *Le Roi d'Yvetot* (1930), *L'Aiglon* and *Les Petites Cardinal* (1937 and 1938, both in collaboration with Honegger), and a radio opera, *Barbe-Bleue* (1943). Other notable French comic operas were Sauguet's *Le Plumet*

---

[10] See articles by Eyer and Sabin.
[11] Rochberg, "Hugo Weisgall."

*du colonel* (1924), Milhaud's three "opéras minutes" (1927), and Honegger's *Les Adventures du Roi Pausole* (1930).

The comic spirit in French opera was characterized by a peculiar national combination of sophistication and spontaneity. In Germany and Italy it was more typically connected with self-consciously "advanced" musical and literary movements. One conspicuous "hit" in Germany was *Jonny spielt auf* ("Johnny Strikes Up," 1927) by Ernst Krenek (b. 1900) [12]—a combination of fantasy and gross realism set to exuberant rhythms and catchy tunes in jazz style with just enough dissonance to give the impression of daring "modernism." Considerable variety of mood was achieved within this general idiom, from the gaudily vulgar strains of a restaurant orchestra to romantic expressiveness and the final apotheosis of Johnny, the Negro band leader, symbol of the vigorous optimistic new world "conquering Europe with the dance." Krenek intended *Jonny* to be taken seriously, but audiences for the most part regarded it as a comedy or satire, and—whether or not owing to this misunderstanding—it had a brilliant though short-lived success.

The comic operas of Paul Hindemith (1895–1963) [13] well illustrate the satirical tendencies fashionable in Germany during the late 1920s. *Hin und Zurück* ("There and Back," 1927) is a one-act tour de force in which the second half reverses the action of the first, so that at the end the situation is exactly the same as at the beginning; the music correspondingly reverses the order of its themes and movements, though without going into the intricacies of strict retrograde canon. The work is scored for an orchestra of seven wind instruments and two pianos; the music, in various styles by turns but unified in effect nevertheless, is decidedly clever and successful in performance. *Neues vom Tage* (1929; revised 1954), the last opera of Hindemith to be produced in Germany before the war, is a longer work, a witty revue about a married couple who, through their efforts to obtain evidence for a divorce, become "the news of the day," with characters so firmly established in the minds of their public that they no longer have any right of private action and cannot even drop their divorce proceedings although they wish to. On this plot are strung several amusing episodes, including a chorus of stenographers to the rhythmic accompaniment of clacking typewriters and a bathroom scene. The music, like most of Hindemith's in this

[12] See the composer's books *Music Here and Now* and *Zur Sprache gebracht.*
[13] Biography by H. Strobel (3d ed., 1948); Hindemith, *A Composer's World.*

period, is linear in texture and strongly rhythmic, well suited to the lively action. There is, of course, a jazz scene, and the final chorus is a fugue. One of Hindemith's most charming stage works is a children's opera, *Wir bauen eine Stadt* ("We Build a Town"), in straightforward simple melodic style, first performed at Oxford in 1931.

Comedy on contemporary subject matter was not a prominent feature of Italian opera under the Fascist government. Composers rather sought material in the safe and distant past, producing such works as the *Tre commedie goldoniane* (1926) of G. F. Malipiero (b. 1882),[14] three short comedies after Goldoni in concentrated musical settings, for the most part in lively *parlando* recitative over continuous orchestra; and *La donna serpente* (1932) by Alfredo Casella (1883–1947),[15] based on a tale by Carlo Gozzi. These are excellent examples of the Italian neoclassical movement, which also inspired the subjects and musical treatment of some other operas by the same two composers—for example, Malipiero's trilogy *L'Orfeide* (1925), his operas *Antonio e Cleopatra* (1938) and *Ecuba* (1941), and Casella's *Favola d'Orfeo* (1932).

Comic operas of a more robust and popular character were appearing around this time in Czechoslovakia. *Schwanda the Bagpiper* by Jaromir Weinberger (b. 1896), first performed at Prague in 1927, is doubtless the most widely known of these. Boshuslav Martinů (1890–1959),[16] a native of Czechoslovakia who from 1923 lived in Paris and later in the United States, has been heard mainly in symphonic and chamber compositions; but he also wrote twelve operas, including *Comedy on the Bridge* (1937) and others both comic and serious which still remain little known.

More recent comic operas by some of the composers above mentioned include Sauguet's *La Gageure imprévue* ("The Unexpected Wager," 1944) and G. F. Malipiero's *I capricci di Callot* ("The Caprices of Callot," 1942) and *Venere prigionera* ("Venus Imprisoned," 1957). Interesting experiments in form as well as in subject matter and musical idiom have been tried by younger composers since the 1940s. Particular mention may be made of Riccardo Malipiero (b. 1914; nephew of G. F.

---

[14] Bontempelli, *Gian Francesco Malipiero*; Gatti, ed., *L'opera di Gian Francesco Malipiero*.

[15] D'Amico and Gatti, eds., *Alfredo Casella*; see also the composer's memoirs, *I segreti della giara*.

[16] Safránek, "Bohuslav Martinů und das musikalische Theater."

Malipiero) [17] in Italy, with *Minnie la candida* (1942), *La donna è mobile* ("Woman Is Fickle," 1954), and a bitterly satirical television opera, *Battono alla porta* ("They Beat on the Door," 1961), which introduces electronic effects. Equally adventurous works, in different directions, have appeared in other countries. Comic opera, being by nature less subject than serious opera to the drag of tradition, continues in the twentieth century to be what it has always been, a congenial soil for the sprouting of new ideas.

## 3. POLITICAL OPERA

In the seventeenth and eighteenth centuries operas were used in schools for teaching moral and religious doctrines; in the twentieth century in like manner operas were used for teaching left-wing political doctrines. In both cases the method was to clothe the teachings in easily understood, popularly accessible music. The principal twentieth-century examples stemmed from the "epic theatre" movement in Germany, headed by Bertolt Brecht (1898–1956).[18] Foremost among them were two settings of Brecht's librettos by Kurt Weill (1900–1950): *Die Dreigroschenoper* ("The Threepenny Opera," 1928) and *Aufstieg und Fall der Stadt Mahogonny* ("The Rise and Fall of the City of Mahogany," 1927; extended version, 1930), both of which remain popular in spite of political changes that have made many parts of their original librettos outdated. (A revised "Americanized" text for *The Threepenny Opera* was provided by Marc Blitzstein in 1952.) Similar in political aim were Weill's school opera *Der Jasager* ("The One Who Consents," 1930) and a larger work, *Die Bürgschaft* ("The Surety," 1932), his last opera to be presented in Germany before the coming of the Nazi regime. Weill later had a second career in the United States as composer of operas and musical comedies, including *Knickerbocker Holiday* (1938), *Street Scene* (1947), and the "folk opera" *Down in the Valley* (1938).

Other works of Brecht in musical settings were *Die Massnahme* (1930) with music by Hanns Eisler (1898–1962) and *Das Verhör des Lukullus* ("The Trial of Lucullus") by Paul Dessau (b. 1894), first given in East Germany in 1951 and revived after 1959. Conspicuous among

[17] Sartori, *Riccardo Malipiero.*

[18] See, in addition to Brecht's own writings: Shumacher, *Die dramatischen Versuche Bertolt Brechts*; Hartung, "Zur epischen Oper Brechts und Weills"; Drew, "Topicality and the Universal"; articles in *The Score*, No. 23 (July, 1958).

recent politically slanted works was *Intoleranza 1960* by the Italian composer Luigi Nono (b. 1924), first performed at Venice in 1961. It is a "scenic action" on a libretto which, while incorporating Communist quotations and slogans, is nevertheless conceived as a protest against authoritarianism rather than as party-line propaganda; the music, typically for Nono, effectively uses various novel sound effects and is in an "advanced" style markedly incongruous with the officially sponsored ideals of Moscow.

Satire of less doctrinaire stripe flourished in some of the early stage works of Krenek : *Der Sprung über den Schatten* ("The Leap over the Shadow," 1924), a farce operetta of variegated musical styles; *Zwingburg* ("Dungeon Castle," 1924); and three short pieces from 1928, including *Schwergewicht* ("Heavyweight"), a satire on the glorification of prominent athletes.

The opera of social protest with music in popular style reechoed in the United States, chiefly with Marc Blitzstein's (b. 1905) *The Cradle Will Rock* (1937), in which spoken dialogue alternates with recitatives and songs in a cultured and clever jazz idiom. Blitzstein's *No for an Answer* (1941) is similar in aim and general musical style, though with a wider range of expression, and includes some fine choral portions.

The political right produced no important operatic propaganda, with the possible exception of a couple of works from Italy. Casella's *Il deserto tentato* ("The Conquest of the Desert," 1937), a "mystery in one act" inspired by Mussolini's Ethiopian adventure, aimed to reflect the "poetic exaltation of the civilizing mission of a great nation" in music of rather simple oratorio-like style with massive choral sections. Malipiero's *Giulio Cesare* (1936), based on Shakespeare's play, was also conceived at least in part as a gesture of acclaim to Mussolini.

## 4. SOVIET RUSSIA[19] AND EASTERN EUROPE

In the Soviet Union the all-reaching power of the state has been exerted, especially since about 1930, in favor of certain kinds of music and opera. This influence, together with the manner in which the

[19] Bibliography : *Sovetskaia opera: Sbornik kriticheskikh statei* (1953); Kulikovich, *Sovetskaia opera na sluzhbe partii i pravitel'stva* (1955); articles in *Sovetskaia muzyka, passim*; Abraham, *Eight Soviet Composers*; Laux, *Die Musik in Russland und der Sowjetunion (II. Teil)*; Moisenco, *Realist Music*; Olkhovsky, *Music under the Soviets*; Polyakova, *Soviet Music*.

musical life of the country is organized, has tended to produce a body of Soviet music cut off from, and apparently largely indifferent to, the various contemporary "advanced" currents in western Europe and the Americas. The officially accepted ideals require, among other things, that music should be treated as the possession of the entire people and not only of a musical elite; that its material should be sought in, or shaped by, the music of the people of its own country or region; that it should emphasize melody and be written in a style not too difficult for general comprehension; that it should be "optimistic" in spirit and that its subject matter—where a text is involved—should affirm socialist ideals. This policy naturally encouraged production of a great many symphonic poems, ballets, choruses, and operas distinguished rather for massive size and sound political intentions than for musical vitality. On the other hand, official policy aimed to stimulate the development of popular and especially of regional musical life within the Soviet Union and thus to enrich the musical language of the country from genuine Eastern folkloristic sources. Among the many non-Russian national operas performed since 1930 may be mentioned: Reinhold Glière's (1875–1956) *Shah-Senem* (1934), based on Caucasian legends and including musical elements from Caucasian and Iranian sources; Sergey Vassilenko's (1872–1956) *Buran* (1939), with colors and rhythms derived from national Uzbek music; operas in the Tatar language by Nazib Zhiganov (b. 1911), particularly *Jalil* (1957); *Aïchurek* (1939) by Aldylas Moldybaev (b. 1906), based on a Kirghizian epic poem and using national melodies; and operas by two leading composers from the Ukraine, Boris Liatoshinsky (b. 1895; *Schors,* 1938) and Y. S. Meitus (b. 1903; *The Young Guard,* 1950).

A work long regarded as a model for Soviet opera was *The Quiet Don* by Ivan Dzerzhinsky (b. 1909), first performed at Leningrad in 1935 and subsequently with great success all over the country. This work appears to hold a position in the history of Soviet opera comparable to that of Moniuszko's *Halka* in Poland or Erkel's *Hunyady László* in Hungary: its patriotic subject is treated in accordance with Dzerzhinsky's conviction that "everything that is lived by the people" can be expressed in opera but that this must be done "in artistically generalized, typified figures, avoiding the pitfalls of naturalism";[20] the music is

[20] Symposium on Soviet opera in *Sovetskaia muzyka* (May, 1939), quoted in Abraham, *Eight Soviet Composers,* p. 82.

technically naïve, simple in texture, predominantly lyric, containing many melodies that suggest folk song without actual citation, and having a few "modern" touches of harmony and rhythm. A similar work, once even more highly regarded by Soviet critics, was Dzerzhinsky's second opera, *Virgin Soil Upturned* (1937). Dzerzhinsky was representative of a trend in the 1930s toward the "song opera," of which one of the best examples was *Into the Storm* (1939) by Tikhon Khrennikov (b. 1913). The "song opera" as a type, however, was subject to certain inherent weaknesses, principally the lack of clear, individual characterization through recitatives and ensembles and the general absence of sharply defined dramatic contrasts.

Stalin's pointed approval of *The Quiet Don* was timed so as to coincide with a blast of official wrath at *Lady Macbeth of Mtzensk* by Dmitri Shostakovich (b. 1906).[21] When this opera was first presented at Moscow in 1934 it won praise at home and soon made its way abroad; two years later, an article in *Pravda* denounced it as "confusion instead of natural human music," unmelodic, fidgety, and neurasthenic, and moreover bad in that it tried to present a wicked and degenerate heroine as a sympathetic character. It is hard to say how much of the story, in Shostakovich's treatment, was intended as satire and how much as mere pornography and perversion. The music is brutal, lusty, vivid in the suggestion of cruelty and horror, full of driving rhythm and willful dissonance. As in other works of his early period, Shostakovich excels in two idioms : a nervously energetic presto, thin textured, tonally erratic, and rhythmically irregular; and a long-spun adagio, mounting with clashing contrapuntal lines to sonorous climaxes. There are some fine choral scenes (particularly in the last act), and some of the aria melodies are related to folk-song idiom, though the solo lines for the most part are declamatory and interwoven with the orchestral texture.

Needless to say, *Lady Macbeth* promptly disappeared from the Soviet theatres. The early wholesale condemnation of the opera gave way to a more discriminating evaluation by later Soviet critics, especially since a marked change in Shostakovich's style was signalized in his Fifth Symphony (1937)—a change that mirrored the transition from the revolutionary and experimental period in Soviet music to a period of stricter control under party directives. Similar but less acute crises of policy occurred afterwards, notably in 1948 when criticism of V. I. Muradeli's

[21] Biographies by Martynov and Rabinovich (1959).

(b. 1908) opera *The Great Friendship* caused it to be withdrawn and brought forth an official decree warning against "formalism" and "anti-popular" tendencies in Soviet music.[22] Objections were made also to K. Dankevich's (b. 1905) historical opera *Bogdan Khmelnitzky* when it came out in 1951, but a new version two years later was more favorably received. The decree was rescinded in 1958, and Shostakovich's revision of *Lady Macbeth*, under the title *Katerina Izmailova*, was staged in 1962. The new version made few changes in the libretto; when the opera was given at London in 1963 (its first performance in the West) critical opinion of the musical revisions was generally favorable.

Other notable operas by Soviet composers are Dzerzhinsky's *Fate of a Man* (1962), Khrennikov's *Mother* (1958, based on a novel by M. Gorky), Dmitry Kabalevsky's (b. 1904) *The Family of Taras* (1947, after B. Gorbatov's story *The Unvanquished*), and Y. A. Shaporin's (b. 1889) *The Decembrists* (1953).

The outstanding name among the composers of Soviet Russia, however, is that of Sergey Prokofiev (1891–1953).[23] Neither his life nor his music can be called typical for a Soviet composer : from 1918 to 1933 he lived abroad, chiefly at Paris; an early opera, *The Gambler*, composed in 1915–17, was first performed (in a revised version) at Brussels in 1929. *The Love for Three Oranges* (Chicago, 1921) has a merrily lunatic plot based on a fantastic tale by Gozzi, well suited to Prokofiev's sharp rhythmic style of this period and to his talents for humor and grotesquerie. Choruses, external to the action, intervene capriciously; the solo parts make a mosaic of detached phrases over sparse but colorful orchestration; the only extended tunes are the well-known orchestral March and Scherzo.

Prokofiev's next opera was *The Flaming Angel* (composed 1919–27; concert performance 1954; first stage performance, Venice, 1955). Another fantastic libretto—this time a tragedy, laid in Germany of the sixteenth century, full of superstition, evil magic, ecstatic visions, hallucination, and horror—gave occasion for a complex but theatrically effective score, with arioso vocal lines over rather heavy orchestral

---

[22] A translation of the statement issued by the Central Committee of the Communist Party is printed in Olkhovsky, *Music under the Soviets*, pp. 280–85.

[23] *Autobiography* (2d ed., 1961); Nest'ev, *Prokof'ev* (1957; English translation, 1960); R. Jahn, "Vom *Spieler* zur *Erzählung vom wahren Menschen.*" See also articles by D. Mitchell (on *The Love for Three Oranges*) and Swarsenski (on *The Flaming Angel*).

accompaniment and some impressive choral scenes forming the climax of the last act. *The Flaming Angel*, being sadly deficient in optimistic proletarian spirit, has been welcomed only in the decadent West.

Returned to Russia, Prokofiev began the long and difficult process of adapting his earlier pungent, ironic, often dissonant style to the requirements of his own country. He busied himself with ballets and other semidramatic compositions (including *Lieutenant Kije*, the "symphonic tale" *Peter and the Wolf*, and the cantata *Alexander Nevsky*) and finally a new opera, *Semyon Kotko* (1940), based on scenes from the life of a hero of the Revolution of 1918. Here the composer's typical declamatory prose style was relieved by some tuneful episodes, but both libretto (written, as usual, by Prokofiev himself) and music were adversely criticized; *Semyon* was soon withdrawn, but was revived in a concert performance in 1957 and on the stage at Perm and Leningrad in 1960. Another opera on a contemporary subject, *The Story of a Real Man*, was withdrawn after a private performance in 1948; its first public performance occurred at Moscow in 1960.

More successful was the comic opera *The Duenna*,[24] composed in 1939–40, performed at Leningrad in 1946, and revived at Moscow in 1959. The libretto, adapted from Sheridan's play, gave Prokofiev ample scope for comedy and satire as well as for lyrical expression, providing likewise "an opportunity to introduce many formal vocal numbers—serenades, ariettas, duets, quartets and large ensembles—without interrupting the action." [25] These "formal vocal numbers" are scattered throughout the score; many of them alternate kaleidoscopically with fragments of dialogue in short tuneful phrases or strict recitative, all held together by a continuous pulsatile accompaniment with countermelodies and mildly dissonant harmonies. The whole spirit and structure of the work, as well as the plot and characters, make it a charming modern descendant of the classical *opera buffa*.

In 1955 at Leningrad occurred the premiere of Prokofiev's operatic masterpiece, *War and Peace*. Based on Tolstoy's novel and composed largely under the patriotic emotions of the war years (a partial performance of the first version took place in 1946), this is a historical grand opera of heroic proportions, consisting in its final form of thirteen scenes and a choral prologue. The epic range of incidents and emotions

---

[24] The Russian title is *Betrothal in a Monastery*.
[25] The composer, quoted in Nest'ev (1960), p. 323.

EXAMPLE 118     *War and Peace*, ACT I, SC. 1          PROKOFIEV

is matched by music of corresponding variety and convincing dramatic power. As in his previous operas, Prokofiev makes some use of recurrent themes as a unifying device, and in the vocal writing maintains a balance between flexible declamation and lyrical closed forms, both solo and ensemble (see Example 118). Choruses naturally contribute to the grandeur of the whole, though not so conspicuously as to overshadow the individual characters. The score is particularly rich in expressive (not sentimental) melodies, and the distinctly national character of the melodic writing is unmistakable; the harmonic style is tonal, prevailingly diatonic and consonant, but with a quality of originality that reminds one of Mussorgsky. More than any of his other works for the theatre, *War and Peace* places Prokofiev in the great tradition of Russian opera : profoundly national in inspiration and musical style but also profoundly human and therefore transcending national limitations.

Leoš Janáček (1854–1928),[26] the leading composer in Czechoslovakia in the first quarter of the twentieth century, may be called a nationalist in the sense that all his operas were written to texts in his own language and his melodic idiom was one that grew organically out of the rhythms and inflections of national speech and folk song. But his style, particularly in the late works, was so individual and his genius for dramatic characterization so exceptional as to make him a figure of more than national importance. His most famous opera, *Jenufa* (Czech title : *Her Foster Daughter*), produced at Brno in 1904 but ignored elsewhere until after the performance at Prague in 1916, already has passages showing distinctive shapes and concise rhythms rising out of speech intonation, along with expansive melodies of a more conventionally romantic sort. Greater concentration of both drama and music is found in the beautifully poetic, moving *Katya Kabanova* (1921)—a work equally remarkable for sensitive characterizations, fine orchestral colorings, and an indescribable poignancy of expression in the melodic outlines (see Example 119)—one of the masterpieces of twentieth-century opera.

Tender and strange, blended of humor and pity, is *The Sly Vixen*

[26] J. Vogel, *Leoš Janáček, dramatik*; idem, *Leoš Janáček: Leben und Werk*; Brod, *Leoš Janáček*; Holländer, "Leoš Janáček in seinen Opern"; Racek, "Der Dramatiker Janáček"; Shawe-Taylor, "The Operas of Leoš Janáček." Published correspondence : in Czech, Prague, 1950, 1951; in German and English translations, 1955 (see bibliography).

EXAMPLE 119    *Katya Kabanova*, Act III

JANÁČEK

Vzpo - me - nu si, jak ke mně ho - vo - řil?

Jak mne li - to - val?    Nev - zpó - me - nu!

Ach, ty no - ci, jak jsou mi tě - žké!

*(Example 119 continued)*

Všichni jdou spat tak leh - ce, i já jdu! A - le

*cresc.*

*f*

**Più mosso** *f*

jak bych se do mo - hy - ly kla - dla. Ta

*sfz*

hrů - za po tmě!

*sfz*

*sfz*

Ně - ja - ký hluk!

*sfz* *rit.*

Fl.

*ff*

Vla.

*rit.*

*(Example 119 continued)*

(1924), a work which may be regarded as complementary to *Katya* and is even more original in style—this despite some impressionistic influences in the harmony and orchestration. *The Makropulos Case* (1926) shows Janáček on the way to the final stage of his style, reached in the *Glagolitic Mass* of 1927 and the opera *The House of the Dead*, composed in 1928 and first performed in 1930. *The House of the Dead* has no plot, properly speaking; its scenes are taken from Dostoyevsky's memoirs of his prison life in Siberia. The music is intensely concentrated, stark, primitive, violent, with rough harmonies and raw orchestral colors—a grim finale for a composer whose four greatest operas were all written after the age of sixty-five.

Other Czechoslovak composers of opera include Otakar Zich (1879–1934; *Guilt*, 1922); Rudolf Karel (1880–1945), the last pupil of Dvořák (*Godmother's Death*, 1933); Jaroslav Křička (b. 1882; *White Ghost*, 1929); Alois Haba (b. 1893; *Die Mutter*, 1931, and later operas using quartertones); and Eugen Suchon (b. 1908; *The Whirlpool*, 1949).[27]

The leading Polish opera composer of the mid-twentieth century is Tadeusz Szeligowsky (b. 1896), whose *Bunt Żakow* ("The Revolt of the

[27] Clapham, "*The Whirlpool.*"

Zaks") [28] was produced at Warsaw in 1951 and shortly thereafter at other Polish cities and at Moscow. Its plot is based on an occurrence at the University of Cracow in 1549: the "Zaks"—students of peasant birth who received their education in return for performing menial duties—rebelled because of ill treatment and left the university and the town in a body. A love story and some comic episodes are added to make up the libretto, but the main emphasis is on the stirring choral scenes. Szeligowsky's music, though harmonically conservative, is very well adapted to the requirements of the theatre. Many of the tunes and rhythms have a definite national folk character; in keeping with the historical background are some stylized or literal references to Polish poetry and music of the sixteenth century.

## 5. THE NEW LINES

The music of most of the operas considered hitherto in this chapter has been "conservative" in the sense of being attached to a continuing tradition—introducing new elements of course, but not too abruptly, and not being especially concerned with any fundamental change in the established musical order. But the first half of the twentieth century was —or at any rate so it appears to us now—anything but conservative in music. The composers whose names dominate that period were innovators, many of them self-consciously so, and some to such a degree as to be quite incomprehensible to the vast majority of the music-consuming public. To be sure, most of their music sounds less radical to us than it did to their immediate contemporaries; but the gap between the twentieth-century composer and the public is still wide, and nowhere wider, probably, than in opera. In the eighteenth century everyone wanted to hear new operas; now most people prefer to hear old ones. The only radically new opera of the last fifty years to come anywhere near general public acceptance is Berg's *Wozzeck*, which dates from 1925.

Roughly speaking, the development of Western musical style since 1915 may be summarized as follows : A period lasting until about 1930 was marked by diverse experiments with all the elements of composition, including rhythm but especially looking toward either a radical extension of the classical concept of tonality or the complete transcendence of that concept. After about 1930 two main directions are discernible : (1) Reconciliation with tonality in a modern musical idiom, moderation of

[28] Lissa, "Pierwsza opera w Polsce Ludowej. (*Bunt żaków*)."

extreme dissonance, maintenance of communication, and in general some degree of attachment to tradition. The composers who followed this direction sought inspiration largely from preromantic Western art music. (2) Replacement of tonality by other systems of order, typically some form of organization stemming from principles developed by Schoenberg in the 1920s. Composers who followed this direction generally retained some elements of traditional music, though in the more extreme manifestations connection with the past, as well as the idea of music as a sensuous language of communication, seems to have disappeared. Of course the two tendencies which we have thus artificially distinguished interacted in practice and moreover were accompanied by various experiments in timbre, rhythm, and form and by occasional exotic influences. Most recently, the rise of electronic music has opened a completely new field, one whose special possibilities for opera have barely begun to be explored.

The combination of drama and choreography, so typical in the history of French opera, is illustrated in an important opera-ballet, *Padmâvati* by Albert Roussel (1869–1937),[29] produced at Paris in 1923. *Padmâvati* is a large work, scenically splendid, with fascinating rhythms and beautiful choral writing. Roussel's complex, highly refined harmonic style incorporates Hindu scales and melodic formulas so perfectly as to make the exotic quality an inherent part of the music, not a mere external adornment. In the same way, within a smaller framework, Roussel uses Greek scales in the one-act lyric opera *La Naissance de la lyre* (1925), on a libretto adapted by Théodore Reinach from Sophocles' *Ichneutai*.

A major composer of French opera was the Swiss Arthur Honegger (1892–1955),[30] whose output includes many ballets and much music for films as well as operas. *Judith* (1926), rewritten as an opera from the incidental music to René Morax's biblical drama produced in 1925, has the characteristic traits of Honegger's style at this period: fervid declamatory phrases in incisive rhythms over percussive harmonies the progressions of which are actuated by contrapuntal, chromatically moving lines generally in contrary motion, with much use of ostinato figures. The chorus functions chiefly as a background for the soloists'

[29] Special issue of RM (1929); biography by Basil Deane (1961).
[30] Biographies by Delannoy and Tappolet.

singing, except in the last scene, with its strong closing fugue "Gloire au dieu tout puissant Jehovah des armées." Honegger's *Antigone* (1927), to a text by Jean Cocteau "freely adapted from Sophocles," is a concentrated, continuous symphonic setting of the drama without word repetitions, arias, ballets, or any other diversionary matter. The vocal lines are constantly in a type of recitative analogous to that of Lully (that is, deriving its pace, accent, and contour immediately and in detail from the words), but of course much more varied in rhythm and melodic pattern than Lully's. An unusual feature of the declamation is the placing of first syllables on the accented beat instead of treating them in the usual way as anacruses, resulting in a singular vehemence of expression (Example 120). The orchestral part is dissonant and percussive;

*Antigone*, sc. 4

EXAMPLE 120                                                         HONEGGER

the effect is altogether stark, quite in keeping with the grim, swift-moving text.

Honegger is especially notable as a composer of the typical twentieth-century combination form of opera-oratorio. His *King David* (1921) is a work of this type, as are also, in different ways, the "stage oratorio" *Cris du monde* (1931) and the "dramatic legend" *Nicolas de Flue* (1941). Most important in this category, however, is *Jeanne d'Arc au bûcher* (1938), on a text by Paul Claudel. As in all his serious dramatic works, Honegger here is concerned with basic social and moral conflicts of man in the modern world, dramatized in historic-legendary characters of heroic stature. Like a medieval cathedral, *Jeanne d'Arc* unites sacred and secular, great and small, ascetic and sensuous, the solemn and the grotesque, profundity and naïveté, in one vast structure of poetic and musical architecture : solos, choruses, and ballets, Gregorian chants, dance tunes, medieval and modern folk songs, mingle in the complex, highly colored, music of Honegger; five speaking and five solo parts, a mixed chorus, and a children's chorus are required in addition to a full orchestra.

A minor but far from negligible French opera composer was Honegger's pupil Marcel Delannoy (1898–1962), whose most successful stage work, *Le Poirier de Misère* ("Misère's Peartree," 1927), is a "Flemish legend" set to music in the restless, dissonant style of the time.

The dramatic works of Darius Milhaud (b. 1892),[31] most prolific of all twentieth-century French composers, divide naturally into three groups: (1) opera-oratorios: a trilogy, *Orestie* (composed 1913–24), consisting of the operas *Agamemnon* (1927), *Les Choéphores* ("The Libation-Bearers"; 1919 in concert form, 1935 on the stage), and *Les Euménides* (1927); *Christophe Colomb* (1930); and *David* (1954). (2) Short operas, surrealistic, ironic, comic, or satirical, all composed 1924–26: *Les Malheurs d'Orphée* (1926); the opéra-bouffe *Esther de Carpentras* (1938); *Le Pauvre Matelot* (1927); three "opéras minutes," each ten to fifteen minutes long: *L'Enlèvement d'Europe* (1927), *L'Abandon d'Ariane* (1928), and *La Délivrance de Thésée* (1928); and *Fiesta* (1958). (3) The heroic operas *Maximilien* (1932), *Médée* (1939), and *Bolivar* (1950). To the foregoing may be added an early opera, *La Brebis égarée* ("The Lost Lamb"; composed 1910–15, performed 1923), the scenic cantata *La Sagesse* (1945), and the mystery play *Le Jeu de Robin et Marion* (1951), besides ballets and incidental music to plays.

*Le Pauvre Matelot*, Milhaud's first big success, is a setting of a short three-act play by Jean Cocteau about a sailor who, returning home rich after an absence of many years, decides to test his wife's fidelity by telling her he is a rich friend of her husband who, he says, is about to return home in utter poverty; the wife, not recognizing him, murders the supposed stranger in order to get his money for her husband. The peculiar unreality of Cocteau's text is heightened by Milhaud's music, which is in a half-serious, ironic manner, constantly tuneful with sophisticated dissonant harmonies (see Example 121). Similar musical procedures, in a more mocking spirit, are evident in the three *opéras minutes*, parodies of Greek myths in the fashion of the old Théâtre de la Foire. *Esther de Carpentras*, a modern, lightly satirical version of the biblical Esther

---

[31] Studies by Collaer and G. Beck; Milhaud, *Notes sans musique*; Rostand, "The Operas of Darius Milhaud."

Example 121

*Le Pauvre Matelot*, Act II

Milhaud

Animé ♩ = 112

*Sa femme*      *le Matelot*

En - trez.     Je

(sempre con 8va)

viens, je viens, Ma - da - me, vous ap-por-ter des nou-vel-les...

F.      le M.

De mon é - poux...    De votre é-poux, en vé-ri - té, des nou-vel-les, Ma-

*mp*

*(Example 121 continued)*

da - me, de votre é - poux.    Il est mort....Non, Madame, il

vit,    je l'ai vu,    voi - lá    trois se - mai    - nes.

story, is especially remarkable for the comic ensembles of Act I and the vivid crowd scenes of Act II.

Of the operas of the *Orestie* trilogy (the dramas of Aeschylus in translation by Paul Claudel) only *Les Euménides* is set entirely to music. All three include massive choral portions, constantly polytonal in a dissonant texture of blended ostinato figures; extremely sonorous and effective are the places in *Les Choéphores* where the chorus instead of singing speaks in powerful rhythmic measures sustained by a large battery of percussion.

Similar technical procedures mark *Christophe Colomb*. Its two acts and twenty-seven scenes call for ten principal soloists, thirty-five other solo parts, three speaking parts, a chorus, and an orchestra reinforced by a special percussion section. Claudel's drama is conceived in epic-allegorical form, with a Narrator and other external personages, presented in a series of tableaux which are explained, commented on, and connected by choral and spoken interludes with percussion accompaniment. The mystical interpretation of Christopher Columbus is always at the forefront as the various scenes in his career unfold. The climax of Act I is the scene of the mutiny on board Columbus's ship; this act ends with a gigantic setting (in Latin) of the Sanctus. Part II finally takes us back to the Inn at Valladolid, the exact point at which the action began after the prologue, and there is an epilogue ending with a choral Alleluia.

Much of the music is in planar polytonal harmony, that is, with free dissonance arising from superposing motifs (often chord streams) in different tonalities, though as a rule no one motif is completely in a single key. The usual method of construction, except in the longest scenes, is to introduce one theme, establish it by ostinato-like repetition, then add successively one, two, or more themes, each of which is also usually treated in ostinato fashion. Of course the various planes of harmony are kept distinct to some degree by contrasting timbres; and there is compensation for the static harmonic effect produced by constant complex dissonance in the variety and vitality of Milhaud's rhythmic patterns as well as in the monumental impression produced by this type of musical construction. Moreover, when the long-continued dissonance finally resolves to a simple chord at the end of a section, the intensity of the resolution is magnified. An example of this is the mutiny scene in Act I, where after a climax of four tonalities in the chorus and four in the orchestra (a total of seven different keys at once, one being reduplicated); the whole resolves on a closing climactic triad of B-flat major.

Milhaud applied similar techniques to *Maximilien*, a historical opera based on a drama by Franz Werfel. Here, however, the degree of stylization surpasses that of any previous works : action, melodies, rhythms, all are ritualistic; even church hymns and military marches are indicated in formal, antirealistic outline as parts of a tonal design rather than representations of actual happenings. But in *Médée* there is less of the monumental, less dissonance, more lyricism, and more interest in the individual figures of the drama. The restrained dramatic force of the scene of the preparation of the enchantments is remarkable. Most expressive are the slow, melismatic, long lines in the soprano role of the suffering Creusa, innocent victim of Medea's cruelty. *Bolivar*, with *Christophe Colomb* and *Maximilien*, completes a trilogy of operas on Latin American subjects; like *Médée*, it concentrates on characterizing the persons of the drama, and continues the composer's gradual trend away from the revolutionary character of his earlier works. *David* was commissioned to celebrate the 3,000th anniversary of Jerusalem as the capital of David's kingdom; its music seems like a final summing-up of Milhaud's operatic development, a synthesis in which all elements of his style appear, now transfigured and calm within the broad framework of this festival opera-oratorio.

Hindemith, like Milhaud, began as an iconoclast and later modified his style, softening harmonic asperities and clarifying tonal relationships. Several large works of his dating from the 1920s were issued later in revised versions which incorporated such changes. Among them was the opera *Cardillac* [32] (1926; revised 1952), on an excellent tragic libretto by Ferdinand Lyon. No opera of this period more clearly exemplifies the classical principle of separate musical numbers; each number, moreover, is constructed according to purely musical laws, the themes being straightforwardly developed in the manner of a concerto, undeflected by any attempt to illustrate mere details of the text : music and drama run parallel but without interpenetration. The "absolute," instrumental character of the music is reinforced by the prevailing texture, highly rhythmic and contrapuntal; the voice is treated in the late baroque manner as one melodic line among concertizing instruments. In addition to this characteristic linear style, two other idioms are occasionally used : a kind of accompanied recitative in which the vocal declamation is set against a single rhapsodic line in the orchestra; and a quieter, chordal, neoromantic style which foreshadows some aspects of Hindemith's later development (for example, the recitative and aria "Die Zeit vergeht" in Act I, scene 2). The chorus writing is vigorous, idiomatic, and effective, especially in the closing scene.

*Mathis der Maler* ("Matthias the Painter," 1938) is an opera-oratorio with a libretto by the composer on the subject of Matthias Grünewald, the sixteenth-century German painter—a long, complex work holding much the same position in Hindemith's dramatic production as *Christophe Colomb* in Milhaud's and embracing a great variety of musical styles, among which suggestions of medieval modality are prominent. The most familiar portions of *Mathis* are those arranged by the composer as an orchestral suite, which is frequently heard in concert programs.

[32] Willms, *Führer zur Oper Cardillac.*

The neobaroque trend in Hindemith's music culminates in *Die Harmonie der Welt* ("The Harmony of the Universe," 1957).[33] Like *Mathis*, this is an opera-oratorio, but on an even greater scale : there are eleven solo roles in addition to choruses, and a full orchestra is supplemented by a second orchestra on the stage; many of the sets require a divided stage. Each of the fourteen scenes in the five acts represents an episode in the life and philosophy of the astronomer Johannes Kepler, the title of whose treatise *Harmonices mundi* (1619) Hindemith adopted for his opera. The drama of *Mathis der Maler* had dealt with the position of the artist in society; *Die Harmonie der Welt* was conceived rather as an exemplification of Hindemith's views— going back to medieval teachings—of the order in a work of music as being symbolical of an all-embracing order in the physical and spiritual universe. Consequently, the events and characters have a symbolic function as well as a dramatic one, and this entails both a certain static quality in the development of the drama and an occasional impression that some of the persons are more like allegorical figures than real human beings. This monumental, oratorio-like character of *Die Harmonie der Welt*, in addition to the enormous resources required for its presentation, will doubtless prevent it from ever becoming fixed in the operatic repertoire—which is a misfortune. A richly polyphonic orchestral texture is the basis of the musical structure. As in many twentieth-century operas, classical instrumental forms play a large role in the musical development. Examples are : the "scherzo" in 7/8 time in Act II; the "variations on an old war song" in Act V; and especially the closing scene, reminiscent of the grandiose finales in baroque opera, which introduces the earth, sun, and planets (each represented by the personage who was its mystical incarnation in the drama) in a magnificent apotheosis, to a sonorous, orchestral-choral passacaglia on a theme made up of the following tones :

Tones of passacaglia theme from *Die Harmonie der Welt*

EXAMPLE 122                                          HINDEMITH

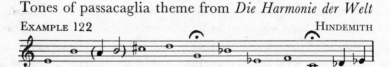

Another important work of the opera-oratorio type was Igor

[33] Briner, "Eine Bekenntnisoper Paul Hindemith."

Stravinsky's (b. 1882) [34] *Oedipus rex* ("Oedipus the King"), performed first in concert form in 1927 and the next year on the stage. Its Latin text is a translation of Cocteau's French version of Sophocles. *Oedipus rex* is more oratorio than opera : all the "action" is narrated between the several "scenes," which consist of stark, blocklike solo and choral numbers that magically convey the feeling of the ancient tragedy, antique, impersonal, yet eternally significant. An earlier one-act opera of Stravinsky, *Mavra* (1922), is a short comic piece, stylized almost to the point of burlesque, with puppetlike characters, the action running from beginning to end as it were in a single breath of swift song over continuous music, eccentrically rhythmic and brilliantly scored for a small group of solo instruments.

Stravinsky's only full-length opera is *The Rake's Progress* (1951), on a libretto by W. H. Auden and Chester Kallman, inspired by Hogarth's prints of the same title. This work, like everything else of Stravinsky's, has been so much written about that little need be said here. It is the most thorough example in modern times of a return to classical opera. Not only does it consist of separate solo (or ensemble) vocal numbers with accompaniment by a small orchestra; its whole texture, the harmonic and melodic idiom of the music itself, are neo-Mozartean. A harpsichord accompanies the recitatives; there is a closing "moral," as in *Don Giovanni*; and the mingled tone of spoofing and sentiment throughout is reminiscent of *Figaro* or *Così fan tutte*. Part of the charm of *The Rake's Progress*, of course, comes from our being kept constantly aware that its eighteenth-century costume is a disguise which only half conceals the sophisticated complexity of the drama and music—a mask which can be enjoyed for its own inanimate beauty but which at the same time shields the oversensitive spectator from direct contact with the emotions of laughter and pity, thereby allowing him to enjoy those emotions behind an unmoving mask of his own. But the disguise is forgotten when we come to the dialogue between Tom and Nick in Act III and the pathetic closing scenes in Bedlam, including Anne's tender farewell lullaby (Example 123).

[34] Wade, "A Selected Bibliography of Igor Stravinsky"; Stravinsky, *Poetics*; *idem, Memories and Commentaries*; Stravinsky and Craft, *Conversations*; *idem, Expositions and Developments*; Ramuz, *Souvenirs*; Vlad, *Strawinsky*; Morton, "Stravinsky," in *Encyclopédie de musique* (Fasquelle, 1961); Stravinsky, "On *Oedipus rex*"; Goldovsky, "*Mavra*"; articles on *The Rake's Progress* by White, C. Mason, Schuh, Kerman, Craft, and D. Cooke.

## The Rake's Progress, Act III

EXAMPLE 123

STRAVINSKY

Gent - ly, lit - tle boat, A - cross the o - cean float, the

crys - tal waves di - vi - ding: the sun ___ in the west Is go - ing to rest

Glide, glide, glide, to - ward the is - lands of the Blest.

We turn now to some operas based on an aesthetic of drama and a musical style fundamentally different from those so far considered. The expressionist movement in the early part of the twentieth century was reflected in opera most clearly in the works of Arnold Schoenberg (1874–1951) [35] and his pupil, Alban Berg (1885–1935). [36] Schoenberg's *Erwartung* ("Expectation") and *Die glückliche Hand* ("The Lucky Hand") were composed in 1909 and 1913 respectively, though not performed until 1924. Both call for a large orchestra, usually subdivided with only a few instruments playing at one time, and both are in the dissonant, thick Schoenbergian harmonic style of the prewar period. The voice lines are wide in range, with large, ultraexpressive intervals, occasionally going over into *Sprechstimme*—that is, a kind of vocal utterance halfway between speaking and singing, with exactly notated rhythm but only approximately notated pitch. Both dramas are essentially subjective, the outward scenery and action being symbolical; both are, in scale, rather cantatas than operas. *Erwartung* is a monodrama : a woman seeking her lover finds only his dead body, over which she sings a long monologue, a modernistic Liebestod. *Die glückliche Hand* has three soloists with a chorus of twelve voices, and uses colors symbolically in scenery, costumes, and lighting. Schoenberg's later one-act comic opera, *Von Heute auf Morgen* ("From Today until Tomorrow," 1930), is completely in the twelve-tone technique, with distinct recitatives and arias, thus following the general trend of the postwar period toward the number opera. Of the three works, *Erwartung* is the most successful; in both dramatic technique and musical style it may be regarded as a foretaste of Berg's *Wozzeck*.

Schoenberg's one large work for the theatre is *Moses und Aron*, of which he wrote the entire libretto and had composed the music of the first two acts by 1932 (only a few sketches exist for the music of Act III); a radio performance was given in 1954 and the first stage performance in 1957. *Moses und Aron* is an opera-oratorio in which Schoenberg has

---

[35] Biography by Stuckenschmidt; Wörner, *Gotteswort und Magie*; *idem*, "Arnold Schoenberg and the Theater"; Keller, "Schoenberg's *Moses and Aron*"; Babbitt, "An Introduction to the Music [of *Moses und Aron*]," in brochure accompanying the recording of the opera Columbia K3L–241; Keller, "Schoenberg's Comic Opera [*Von Heute auf Morgen*]."

[36] Biographies and studies by Reich and Redlich; Leibowitz, "Alban Berg et l'essence de l'opéra"; Reich, "A Guide to *Wozzeck*"; Kerman, "Terror and Self-Pity"; Jouve, *Wozzeck ou le nouvel opéra*; Perle, "The Music of *Lulu*"; *idem*, "*Lulu*: The Formal Design."

taken the biblical material for dramatic presentation of the tragic abyss (tragic, because unbridgeable by good will) that lies between wisdom and action : Moses, the philosopher-lawgiver, cannot communicate his vision; Aron, the man of action, can only misunderstand and falsify it. Schoenberg's profound drama is united to a musical score of fearful difficulty (he himself doubted whether a performance would actually be possible), towering in conception, masterly in realization, and of overwhelming dramatic effect. Within the unity imposed by consistent use of a single tone row is endless variety of expression and sound, from the (symbolical) Sprechstimme of Moses' role to the gorgeous oriental colors and wild dance rhythms in the scene of the worship of the Golden Calf. *Moses und Aron*, though unfinished—and its very incompleteness may also be symbolic—is one of the great works of twentieth-century opera, and one that will remain significant for many generations.

In contrast to the oratorio-like character of so many contemporary operas, those of Berg are pure theatre. *Wozzeck*, composed between 1914 and 1922 and first performed at Berlin in 1925, is based on a "dramatic fragment" by Georg Büchner (1813–37), the original twenty-five scenes being reduced by Berg to fifteen and grouped in three acts of five scenes each. Wozzeck, the hero, is a representative of what he himself calls "Wir arme Leut' " ("We poor folk"), tormented by circumstances, suffering but unconscious of guilt, finally murdering his mistress and drowning himself, driven always by forces he never thinks of questioning or resisting. Despite the date of Büchner's drama, *Wozzeck* is thoroughly typical of the postwar period in Germany; its atmosphere seems as though infected by the morbid, bitter, neurotic mood of that time. Yet it is not merely topical : Wozzeck is a universal figure, symbol of the oppressed and, in a larger sense, of man in his naked helplessness before blind powers that care nothing about his fate. Since the expressionist technique makes every external object a projection of Wozzeck's own soul, the scenes, characters, and events of the opera have an unearthly quality, like a nightmarish puppet show; and Berg's music belongs to this nightmare world as surely as Debussy's belongs to the dream world of *Pelléas et Mélisande*. The harmonic style of *Wozzeck* is in most places atonal, full of strange, wonderful color effects (for example, the scene of Wozzeck's suicide) and distorted reminiscences of the normal "waking" world (for example, the "folk song" in Act I, the caricature of the *Rosenkavalier* waltzes in Act II). The vocal lines, mostly in sharply pointed declamation with abrupt wide intervals, alternate between ordinary speech, Sprechstimme, and song. There are a few recurring motifs, notably Wozzeck's "Wir arme Leut'" (see Example 124), but

EXAMPLE 124    *Wozzeck*, Act I, sc. 1

BERG

the chief means of unity is the organization of each act and scene in set musical forms derived from classical patterns. But these patterns reveal themselves only on analysis; it is no part of the composer's intention that the auditor should perceive them, unless subliminally. Sometimes they have a direct dramatic function: there is a grim fitness, for example, in the choice of the learned passacaglia form for the scene (Act I, scene 4) where Wozzeck submits himself to a doctor as a subject for scientific experiments. The scenes within each act are connected by orchestral interludes; the longest of these, in Act III, recapitulates the themes of the entire drama in climax before leading into the brief coda-like final scene. *Wozzeck* provoked a riot at the first performance; now that the sound of the music has become more familiar, it has come to be generally recognized not only as a powerful drama in music but also as one of the few really successful operas in a fully modern style.

Berg's second opera, *Lulu*, was completed in substance before the composer's death, but the orchestration had been finished only through the first two acts and a small part of the third. The first two acts, and two fragments of the third, were performed in 1937 and there have been frequent revivals since. The libretto is taken, with some cuts, from two plays by Frank Wedekind. The central personage, Lulu, is conceived as the incarnation of the "primal woman-spirit," and the drama is concerned with the fatal effects of her attraction for various lovers, finally ending with her own doom. Although externally occupied with the most realistic details, the work is not essentially realistic but rather expressionistic, sometimes grotesquely and extravagantly so. As drama, the subject is too specialized to have the same elemental human appeal that *Wozzeck* has; and it is probably this defect, as much as the notorious complexity of the music, that has kept *Lulu* from becoming as popular as Berg's earlier opera. Notwithstanding the complexity, however, *Lulu* is marvellously effective in the theatre. The changing flow of the drama and the intensity of its emotional expression are always controlled by the composer's intellectual power in wielding musical forms. Certain motifs, harmonies, tone series, and combinations are associated with particular characters and scenes. The opera is not, as has often been stated, based throughout on a single tone row, but its felt musical unity is the result of interconnections among the different formal elements. Such subtle relationships are no more consciously grasped by the audience than are the comparable relationships in *Wozzeck*; but the formal unity and the dramatic import of both works can be sensed in the theatre without a knowledge of their technical construction.

Within the general orbit of the Schoenbergian musical style was *Alkestis* (1924) by Egon Wellesz (b. 1885),[37] a one-act setting of a text by Hofmannsthal (after Euripides) in a series of broad tableux in a rather austere, monolithic idiom. The important position of the chorus in this work was even more emphasized in Wellesz's *Die Bakchantinnen*

[37] Beer, "Egon Wellesz und die Oper"; Redlich, "Egon Wellesz."

(1931). Likewise of the same Central European school were two operas of Ernst Krenek : *Das Leben des Orest* ("The Life of Orestes," 1930), a half-satirical treatment of the Orestes myth cycle; and the large historical opera *Karl V* (1938), Krenek's most important work for the theatre, remarkable for nobility of style well suited to the grandeur of the subject. Krenek's *Pallas Athene weint* ("Pallas Athene Weeps," 1955) presents scenes of the war between Athens and Sparta with application to the modern issue of how to defend freedom without succumbing to tyranny; the music is based on an adaptation of the twelve-tone technique. A somewhat similar technique is used in *The Bell Tower* (Urbana, 1957), an expertly wrought, dramatically and musically satisfying setting of a libretto by the composer based on the story by Herman Melville.

Since 1940 an increasing number of composers in every country have adopted some form of twelve-tone technique, either using it as the basis of all their writing or blending or combining it with other techniques and styles. The leading composer of this school in Germany, Wolfgang Fortner (b. 1907), is distinguished for symphonic and choral works as well as operas; his principal opera is *Die Bluthochzeit* ("Blood Wedding," 1957), a melodious, clean-textured setting of García Lorca's tragedy *Bodas de sangre*.

Among many other composers in postwar Germany, two have attracted particular notice for their operas. The Swiss-born Rolf Liebermann (b. 1910)[38] in *Lenore 40/45* (1952) and *Penelope* (1954) has juxtaposed contrasting musical styles for novel treatment, half realistic and half fantastic-satirical, of contemporary subject matter. His *School for Wives* (1955) is a witty modern version, with music in tonal style, of Molière's comedy. Hans Werner Henze (b. 1926) in *Boulevard Solitude* (1952) presented a realistic adaptation of the *Manon Lescaut* story in which each of the separate scenes is accompanied by a stylized modern dance. Henze, one of the most active younger German composers for the theatre, next produced *Ein Landarzt* ("A Country Doctor," 1953), based on Kafka's story, with music in a style deriving from Berg's *Lulu*; and *König Hirsch* ("King Stag," 1956), a fairy-tale opera with a long, elaborate, and variegated score. *Der Prinz von Homburg* (1960), adapted from Kleist's drama, is a full-scale grand opera with choruses, but its carefully constructed music fails to avoid monotony.

[38] R. Klein, "Rolf Liebermann als dramatischer Komponist"; Glanville-Hicks, "Some Reflections on Opera."

One of the most successful strict applications of twelve-tone technique to opera is heard in *Il prigionero* ("The Prisoner," 1950) by Luigi Dallapiccola (b. 1904) [39]—successful, because the technical method is perfectly absorbed into the musical content : gradations of dissonance, all the subtle sonorities, function for expressive ends, and the solo parts are conceived, in the good Italian tradition, as singing human voices rather than abstract contrapuntal lines. Four soloists, a large orchestra (including saxophones, vibraphone, and other "extra" wood winds and percussion), with brass, bells, and organ and large and small choruses onstage, make up the performing forces. There are four scenes, with a prologue and two choral interludes on Latin liturgical texts. The drama centers around the condition of a Prisoner tortured by hope, "the ultimate torture," but destined never in this world to escape; this Prisoner (nameless, like all the other characters) is the type of modern man. Dallapiccola's thought was occupied with the same theme of imprisonment and escape in his *Canti di prigionia* ("Songs of the Prison," 1941) and *Canti di liberazione* ("Songs of Liberation," 1955). The music of *Il prigionero* makes use at times of fixed forms, and often approaches the effect of conventional tonality (especially in the second choral interlude). An idea of the style can be obtained from a portion of the second "ricercare" from scene 3, based on a recurrent motif associated with the ironic word "fratello" ("brother") by which his jailers always address the Prisoner (Example 125).

## 6. SOME EXPERIMENTS

In the course of the general tendency toward sophistication or massiveness in opera music of the 1930s, a move in the opposite direction, toward radical simplification, was undertaken by Carl Orff (b. 1895).[40] The resulting works aroused more comment, favorable or otherwise, than any other operas of the time—to begin with, because none were operas in the traditional sense of the word, and none were so called in their titles. The *Carmina burana* (1937), *Catulli carmina* (1943), and *Trionfo di Afrodite* (1953) are essentially combinations of cantata and

---

[39] Vlad, "Dallapiccola 1948–1955"; Nathan, "The Twelve-Tone Compositions of Luigi Dallapiccola"; Dallapiccola, "The Genesis of the *Canti di prigionia*."

[40] Liess, *Carl Orff*; Kiekert, *Die musikalische Form in den Werken Carl Orff's*; Helm, "Carl Orff"; W. Keller, *Karl Orff's Antigonae*; Stäblein, "Schöpferische Tonalität."

EXAMPLE 125    *Il prigionero*, SC. 3

DALLAPICCOLA

ballet; so also, but in a different manner and with greater use of spoken dialogue, are *Die Bernauerin* (1947) and *Astutuli* (1953). More like operas in the ordinary sense are *Der Mond* ("The Moon," 1939) and *Die Kluge* ("The Wise Woman," 1943), though it would perhaps be more accurate to designate these as "folk-plays with music." The typical idiom in *Die Kluge* is a narrow-ranged, strongly accented melody with many repeated notes and with the phrases reiterated over and over in ostinato fashion; this melody is accompanied by the simplest possible harmonies, statically persistent, from a small orchestra with emphasis on percussion instruments and percussive rhythmic sound.

This type of percussive-ostinato background, with still further simplification of harmony and melody, is applied to a totally different kind of dramatic material in Orff's two operas *Antigonae* (1949) and *Oedipus der Tyrann* (1959), both settings of Hölderlin's translations from Sophocles. In these, there are five gradations of vocal delivery for both soloists and chorus: (1) ordinary speech; (2) rhythmic semi-speech (similar to Berg's Sprechstimme); (3) a form of stylized speech consisting of rhythmic chanting centered on one tone but punctuated by melodic deflections to nearby tones or occasional wide leaps; (4) the same, but expanding into a longer quasi-melodic chant; and (5) a combination of (3) or (4) with sweeping stepwise fast impassioned melismatic outbursts, characteristically placed at the beginning of a phrase (Example 126). The voices may be either unaccompanied or accompanied by ostinato rhythmic patterns in many different combinations of percussion, either without fixed pitch or in static harmonies. The chorus constantly participates in the action and each scene is in a clearly outlined musical form. No description can do more than suggest the unique effects produced by the composer's peculiar choice of means. Music, reduced nearly to the primal elements of rhythm and single tones, enters into a union with language that conjures up for the imagination a far-off mythical stage in the history of human speech when word and tone were still one and unseparated. The variety of sounds and the varying degrees of dramatic tension that Orff manages to achieve within his self-imposed musical limitations are remarkable; nevertheless, the very intensity of the idiom tends to limit the length of time within which it can be effective, and for this reason perhaps *Oedipus*, being shorter than *Antigonae*, is the more successful of the two works.

EXAMPLE 126     *Oedipus der Tyrann*     ORFF

Orff's is certainly the most significant "experiment" in the musical theatre of the twentieth century. Some others that have attracted attention, but that have not—or not yet—led to any important consequences, include the two operas on texts of Gertrude Stein composed by Virgil Thomson (b. 1896):[41] *Four Saints in Three Acts* (1934) and

[41] Hoover and Cage, *Virgil Thomson*; Helm, "Virgil Thomson's *Four Saints in Three Acts.*"

EXAMPLE 127

JANÁČEK

Jak je les di - vu - krás - ný!

Až ru - sal - ky přij - dou za - se do - mů,

do svých let ních si - del,

*(Example 127 continued)*

*(Example 127 continued)*

sl - zet poh - nu - tím    nad    shle - dá - ním!

*The Mother of Us All* (1947), both in a sophisticatedly simple musical style with sensitive word-setting; Max Brand's [42] *Maschinist Hopkins* (1929), climax in opera of the "motoristic" era of the 1920s, an expressionistic work with mechanical sound effects, dissonant percussive harmonies, and some numbers in jazz style; and Louis Gruenberg's (b. 1884) *The Emperor Jones* (1933), based on Eugene O'Neill's play and exploiting a neoprimitive orchestra with drum rhythms and choral interludes. A momentary sensation in Europe was George Antheil's (1900–1959) satirical jazz opera *Transatlantic* (1930). More recent novelties were Boris Blacher's (b. 1903) *Abstract Opera No. 1* (Frankfurt, 1953), on a text of meaningless syllables with music in lightly satirical vein; and *Aniara* (1959), by the Swedish composer Karl-Birger Blomdahl (b. 1916), in which the characteristic unearthly sound of

[42] Brand, " 'Mechanische' Musik und das Problem der Oper"; articles in *Signale für die musikalische Welt*, 1929, 1930.

electronic music is applied to a drama on a space ship out of control, falling endlessly into the interstellar depths.

Here our survey of the history of opera ends. It is sad to think that so much beauty lies buried in the silence of the past, that all these things which so mightily pleased our forefathers have become old things of yesterday. The operas of the past can live now, with their movement and color and sound, for the most part only in our imagination, as we are able to cast ourselves back for a moment to the times when they were part of the life of men now passed away, "faded into impalpability through death, through absence, through change of manners." [43] But earth remains and ancient beauty comes again in new forms. "Here in these woods," sings Janáček's Forester (see Example 127), "life renews itself, and the nightingales return with each returning Spring to find their nests, and Love . . . always the same : where then was parting, now is meeting." [44]

[43] Joyce's *Ulysses*, ninth episode.
[44] Paraphrase of Max Brod's German version of Janáček's text.

# BIBLIOGRAPHY

❀

## I

## BIBLIOGRAPHIES, LEXICONS, GUIDES, HISTORIES, COLLECTED ESSAYS, AND OTHER GENERAL WORKS

Abbiati, Franco. Storia della musica. Milan, A. Garzanti, 1953–54. 5 vols.

Aber, Adolf. Die Musik im Schauspiel, Geschichtliches und Aesthetisches. Leipzig, M. Beck, 1926.

Abert, Anna Amalie. Die Oper : Von den Anfangen bis zum Beginn des 19. Jahrhunderts. Cologne, 1953.

—— "Wort und Ton," in Gesellschaft für Musikforschung: Bericht über den internationalen . . . Kongress Hamburg 1956 (Kassel, [etc.] Bärenreiter, 1957) 43–46.

Abert, Anna Amalie, and Hans Ehinger. "Oper," MGG X, 1–75.

Abert, Hermann. Gesammelte Schriften und Vorträge. Halle an der Saale, M. Niemeyer, 1929.

—— Grundprobleme der Operngeschichte. Leipzig, B&H, 1926.

Abry, Emile. Histoire illustrée de la littérature française . . . par E. Abry, C. Audic, P. Crouzet. Paris, Didier, 1935. New ed.

Ademollo, Alessandro. Bibliografia della cronistoria teatrale italiana. Milan, Ricordi, 1888.

Adler, Guido. Handbuch der Musikgeschichte unter Mitwirkung von Fachgenossen. Frankfurt/M., Frankfurter Verlags-Anstalt, 1924.

Albinati, Giuseppe. Piccolo dizionario di opere teatrali, oratori, cantati, ecc. Milan, Ricordi, 1913.

Altmann, Wilhelm. Führer durch die einaktigen Opern, Operetten und Singspiele des Verlages Ed. Bote und G. Bock. Berlin, Bote & Bock, 1919.

—— Katalog der seit 1861 in den Handel gekommenen theatralischen Musik (Opern, Operetten, Possen, Musik zu Schauspielen, usw) : Ein musikbibliographischer Versuch. Wolfenbüttel, Verlag für musikalische Kultur und Wissenschaft, 1935.

Ambros, August Wilhelm. Geschichte der Musik, Band IV. Leipzig, Leuchart, 1909. 3d ed., rev. and enl. by Hugo Leichtentritt.

Andeutungen zur Geschichte der Oper. Marienwerder, A. Baumann, 1845. "Besonderer Abdruck aus dem ersten Hefte des Archivs für vaterländische Interessen pro 1845."

Appia, Adolphe. Die Musik und die Inscenierung : Aus dem Französischen übersetzt. Munich, Bruckmann, 1899.

Apthorp, William Foster. The Opera Past and Present. London, John Murray, 1901.

Arnals, Alexander d'. Der Operndarsteller : Lehrgang zur musikalischen Darstellung in der Oper. Berlin, Bote & Bock, [1932].

Arundell, Dennis. "Operatic Ignorance," PMA LI (1924–25) 73–96.

Associazione dei musicologi italiana. Bolletino : Catalogo delle opere musicali sino ai primi decenni del secolo XIX, Parma, 1910–11.
Catalogues of music collections by cities, under each city by libraries, under each library by forms and media, e.g., "opere teatrali."

Aubin, Léon. Le Drame lyrique : Histoire de la musique dramatique en France. [Tours, Edition de l' "Echo littéraire et artistique"], 1908.

Auden, W. H. "Quelques réflexions sur la musique et sur l'opéra," in Encyclopédie de la musique (Paris, Fasquelle, [cop. 1958]) I, 93–100.

—— "Some Reflections on Opera as a Medium," Tempo No. 2 (Summer, 1951) 6–10.

Austin, Cecil. "Cinema Music," M&L V (1924) 177–91.

Balanchine, George. Balanchine's Complete Stories of the Great Ballets. Edited by Francis Mason. Garden City, N.Y., Doubleday & Co., 1954.

Barrenechea, Maríano Antonío. Historia estética de la música, con dos estudios mas sobre consideraciones historicas y tecnicas acerca del canto y la obra maestra del teatro melodramatico. Buenos Aires, Editorial Claridad, 1941.

Bauer, Rudolf. Oper und Operette : Ein Führer durch die Welt der Musikbühne. Berlin, Deutsche Buch-Gemeinschaft, [1959].

Bekker, Paul. Klang und Eros. Stuttgart and Berlin, Deutsche Verlags-Anstalt, 1922.

—— Kritische Zeitbilder. Berlin, Schuster & Loeffler, 1921.

—— Das Operntheater. Leipzig, Quelle & Meyer, 1931.

—— Wandlungen der Oper. Zurich and Leipzig, Orell Füssli, [1934]. Translated as : The Changing Opera. [New York], W. W. Norton, [1935].

Beloch, Julius. "La populazione d'Italia nei secoli XVI, XVII e XVIII," Bulletin de l'Institut international de statistique III (1888) 1–42.

Bernet Kempers, Karel P. De Italiaansche Opera, haar Ontstaan en Ontwikkeling van Peri tot Puccini. Amsterdam, H. J. Paris, 1929.

Bertrand, Paul. "Pure Music and Dramatic Music," MQ IX (1923) 545–55.

Bethléem, Abbé L., and others. Les Opéras, les opéras-comiques et les opérettes. Paris, Editions de la Revue des lectures, 1926.

Biancolli, Louis, and Robert Bagar, eds. The Victor Book of Operas. New York, Simon & Schuster, 1953. Newly rev. ed.

Bie, Oskar. Die Oper. Berlin, S. Fischer, 1913.

Biehle, Herbert. Musikgeschichte der Stadt Bautzen. Berlin Dissertation, 1923.

Blaze de Bury, Yetta. "The French Opera," *Nineteenth Century* (1890) No. 2, 39–53.

Böhme, Franz Magnus. Geschichte des Tanzes in Deutschland. Leipzig, B&H, 1886. 2 vols.

Boll, André. La Grande Pitié du théâtre lyrique. Paris, Editions France Empire, 1946.

Bollert, Werner. Aufsätze zur Musikgeschichte. Bottrop, Postberg, 1938.

Bologna. Liceo musicale. Biblioteca. Catalogo della biblioteca del Liceo musicale di Bologna, compilato da Gaetano Gaspari. Bologna, Libreria romagnoli dell' acqua, 1890–1905. 4 vols.

Bonaccorsi, Alfredo. "L'opera in musica," RMI XXXVI (1929) 594–99.

Bonaventura, Arnaldo. L'opera italiana. Florence, Novissima enciclopedia monografia illustrata, [1928].

—— Saggio storico sul teatro musicale italiano. Leghorn, R. Giusti, 1913.

Boston Public Library. Allen A. Brown Collection. A Catalogue of the Allen A. Brown Collection of Books Relating to the Stage. Boston, 1919.

—— Catalogue of the Allen A. Brown Collection of Music. Boston, 1910–16. 4 vols.

Botstiber, Hugo. Geschichte der Ouvertüre und der freien Orchesterformen. Leipzig, B&H, 1913.

Brandl, Willy. Der Weg der Oper. Stuttgart, Curt E. Schwab, 1949.

British Museum. Department of Manuscripts. Catalogue of Manuscript Music in the British Museum, by Augustus Hughes-Hughes. London, 1906–9. 3 vols.

—— Department of Printed Books. Catalogue of Printed Music Published between 1487 and 1800 Now in the British Museum, by W. Barclay Squire. [London], 1912. 2 vols. The Second Supplement (1940) lists all acquisitions from 1912 to 1940 and makes corrections of the 1912 catalogue.

—— Department of Printed Books. King's Music Library. Catalogue of the King's Music Library, by William Barclay Squire. London, 1927–29. 3 vols.

Brockway, Wallace, and Herbert Weinstock. The Opera : A History of Its Creation and Performance, 1600–1941. New York, Simon & Schuster, 1941. 2d ed. : New York, Pantheon, 1962.

Bruneau, Alfred. La Musique française : Rapport sur la musique en France du XIIIe au XXe siècles; la musique à Paris en 1900. Paris, E. Fasquelle, 1901.

Brussels. Bibliothèque royale de Belgique. Catalogue de la bibliothèque de F. J. Fétis acquise par l'état belge. Ghent, J. S. Van Doosselaere; Brussels, C. Muquardt : Paris, Firmin-Didot, 1877.

—— Conservatoire royal de musique. Bibliothèque. Catalogue de la bibliothèque du Conservatoire royal de musique de Bruxelles . . . par Alfred Wotquenne. Brussels, J.-J. Coosemans, 1898– . 4 vols. Annexe[s]

I, Brussels, O. Schepens, 1901, contains : Libretti d'opéras et d'oratorios italiens du XVIIe siècle.

Bücken, Ernst. Der heroische Stil in der Oper. Leipzig, Kistner & Siegel, 1924.

Bulthaupt, Heinrich Alfred. Dramaturgie der Oper. Leipzig, B&H, 1887. 2 vols.

Burian, Karel Vladimir. Die Oper : Ihre Geschichte in Wort und Bild. [Prague], Artia, 1961.

Bustico, Guido. Bibliografia delle storie e cronistorie dei teatri italiani. Milan, Bollettino bibliografico musicale, 1929.

Cambridge University. Fitzwilliam Museum. Library. Catalogue of the Music in the Fitzwilliam Museum, Cambridge, by J. A. Fuller-Maitland. London, C. J. Clay, 1893.

Canal, Pietro. Dalla musica in Mantova. Venice, Presso la segreteria del R. Istituto, 1881.

Capell, Richard. Opera. London, E. Benn, [1930].

Capri, Antonio. Il melodramma dalle origini ai nostri giorni. Modena, Guanda, 1938.

Carducci, Edgardo. "The Tenor Voice in Europe," M&L XI (1930) 318–23.

Challis, Bennett. "The Techniques of Operatic Acting," MQ XIII (1927) 630–45.

Chavarri, Eduardo López. Historia de la música. Barcelona, Imprenta elzeviriana, 1929. 3d ed.

Cheney, Sheldon. The Theatre. New York, Longmans, Green, 1929.

Child, Harold. "Some Thoughts on Opera Libretto," M&L II (1921) 244–53.

Chouquet, Gustave. Histoire de la musique dramatique en France. Paris, Firmin-Didot, 1873.

Chrysander, Friedrich. "Ueber die Unsittlichkeiten in unseren Operntexten," AMZ XIV (1879) 257–59, 273–74, 305–8.

Clément, Félix. Dictionnaire des opéras (dictionnaire lyrique), rev. et mis à jour par Arthur Pougin. Paris, Larousse, [1905].

Closson, Hermann. Musique et drame. Brussels, [Institut national belge de radiodiffusion], 1939.

Combarieu, Jules. Histoire de la musique. Paris, A. Colin, 1920. 3d ed. 3 vols.

—— "Histoire du théâtre lyrique." RHCM VII (1907) 581–97; VIII (1908) 1–594 *passim;* IX (1909) *passim;* X (1910) *passim.*

Cone, Edward T. "Music : A View from Delft," MQ XLVII (1961) 439–53.

Corbet, August. Het Muziekdrama in de XVIe en XVIIe Eeuwen in Italie gezien in het Licht van H. Wölfflin's *Kunstgeschichtliche Grundbegriffen:* Ein Bijdrage tot de Theorie van het Parallelisme in de Kunst. Antwerp, De Sikkel, 1936.

Covent Garden Opera Series. London, Boosey & Hawkes, 1947(?)– .

Cross, Milton. Complete Stories of the Great Operas. Garden City, N.Y., Doubleday & Co., 1955.

Crowell's Handbook of World Opera. Compiled by Frank Ledlie Moore. New York, Thomas Y. Crowell Co., [1961].

Curzon, Henri de. L'Evolution lyrique au théâtre dans les differents pays : Tableau chronologique. Paris, Fortin, 1908.

Czech, Stan. Das Operettenbuch. Stuttgart, Muth, 1960. 4th ed.

Czerny, Peter, ed. Opernbuch. Berlin, Henschelverlag, [1961]. 5th ed.

Damerini, Adelmo, and Gino Roncaglia, eds. Musicisti della scuola emiliano. Siena, Accademia Musicale Chigiana, 1956.

Dassori, Carlo. Opere e operisti (dizionario lirico 1541–1902) : Elenco nominativo universale dei maestri compositori di opere teatrali, col prospetto cronologico dei lori principali lavori e catalogo alfabetico generale delle opere . . . coll' indicazione di data e di luogo della prima rappresentazione, avuto speciale reguardo al repertorio italiano. Genoa, R. Istituto sordomuti, 1903.

Davey, Henry. History of English Music. London, Curwen, [1921]. 2d ed., revised.

Decugis, Nicole, and Suzanne Reymond. Le Décor de théâtre en France du moyen âge à 1925. Paris, Compagnie Française des Arts Graphiques, 1953.

Deditius, Annemarie. Theorien über die Verbindung von Poesie und Musik. Liegnitz, Seyffarth, 1918.

Della Corte, Andrea. Drammi per musica dal Rinuccini allo Zeno. Turin, Unione Tipografico-Editrice Torinese, [1958]. 2 vols.

—— Il libretto e il melodramma. Turin, A. Viretto, [1951].

—— La "poesia per musica" ed il libretto d'opera. Introduzione a una storia dell' opera. Turin, Gheroni, 1950.

—— "Questioni melodrammaliturgiche in un saggio sul libretto," Collectanea historiae musicae II (1956) 127–34.

—— Tre secoli di opera italiana. Turin, Arione, [1938].

Denkmäler des Theaters : Inszenierung, Dekoration, Kostüm des Theaters. Vienna, Nationalbibliothek; Munich, R. Piper, [1925?–30]. In twelve parts; plates (some colored) in portfolios, with explanatory text laid in. Also published as : Monumenta scenica : The Art of the Theatre. London, Batsford, 1925–31.

Dent, Edward J. "The Nomenclature of Opera," M&L XXV (1944) 132–40, 213–26.

—— Opera. New York, Penguin Books, [1940].

—— "The Translation of Operas," PMA LXI (1934–35) 81–104.

Dilla, Geraldine P. "Music Drama : An Art Form in Four Dimensions," MQ X (1924) 492–99.

Doisy, Marcel. Musique et drame. Paris, A. Flament, [1949].

Dubech, Lucien, J. de Montbrial, and Hélène Horn-Monval. Histoire générale illustrée du théâtre. Paris, Librairie de France, 1931–34. 5 vols.

Dumesnil, René. Histoire illustré du théâtre lyrique. Paris, Plon, [1953].

—— L'Opéra et l'opéra-comique. Paris, Presses Universitaires de France, 1947. 2d ed.

Edwards, [Henry] Sutherland. History of the Opera from Monteverdi to Donizetti. London, W. H. Allen, 1862. 2d ed.

Eichborn, Hermann. Die Trompete in alter und neuer Zeit. Leipzig, B&H, 1881.

Einstein, Alfred. Essays on Music. New York, W. W. Norton, [1956].

—— "German Opera, Past and Present," MMus XI, No. 2 (January–February, 1934) 65–72.

—— "The Mortality of Opera," M&L XXII (1941) 358–66.

Elson, Arthur. A Critical History of Opera : Giving an Account of the Rise and Progress of the Different Schools, with a Description of the Master Works in Each. Boston, L. C. Page, 1901.

Elson, Louis C. "Atrocities and Humors of Opera," MQ VI (1920) 206–13.

Enciclopedia della spettacolo. Rome, Casa Editrice Le Machere, 1954–  . 5 vols. to 1960.

Euting, Ernst. Zur Geschichte der Blasinstrumente im 16. und 17. Jahrhundert. Berlin, A. Schulze, 1899.

Ewen, David. Encyclopedia of the Opera. New York, A. A. Wyn, [1955].

Falconi, Dino, and Angelo Frattini. Guida alla rivista e all' operetta. Milan, Academia, [1953].

Ferand, Ernst. Die Improvisation in der Musik. Zurich, Rhein-Verlag, [1938].

Fink, Gottfried Wilhelm. Wesen und Geschichte der Oper : Ein Handbuch für alle Freunde der Tonkunst. Leipzig, G. Wigand, 1838.

Foss, Hubert J. The Heritage of Music. Vol. III. London, Oxford University Press, 1951.

Frankenfelder, August. Historische Elemente in der Oper und ihre ästhetische Bedeutung. Würzburg, Becker, 1896.

Freedley, George, and John A. Reeves. A History of the Theatre. New York, Crown Publishers, [1941].

Fürst, Leonhard. Der musikalische Ausdruck der Körperbewegung in der Opernmusik. Miesbach, Mayr, 1932.

Galli, Amintore. Estetica della musica ossia del bello nella musica sacra, teatrale, e da concerto in ordine alla sua storia. Turin, Bocca, 1899.

Galloway, W. Johnson. The Operatic Problem. London, Long, 1902.

Gavazzeni, Gianandrea. La morte dell' opera. [Milan], Meridiana, [1954].

—— La musica e il teatro. [Pisa], Nistri-Lischi, [1954].

—— "La poesia dell' opera in musica," RassM XI (1938) 137–62.

Gedenkschrift für Hermann Abert. Halle an der Saale, M. Niemeyer, 1928.

Geisenheyner, Max. Kulturgeschichte des Theaters : Volk und Drama. Berlin, Safari-Verlag, 1951.

Gilder, Rosamond, and George Freedley. Theatre Collections in Libraries and Museums : An International Handbook. New York, Theatre Arts, 1936.

Ginisty, Paul. Le Melodrama. Paris, L. Michaud, [1910].

Gloggner, Carl. "Oper und Gesangskunst," *Musikalisches Wochenblatt* I (1870) 65–67, 81–82, 97–98, 113–14.

Goddard, Joseph. The Rise and Development of Opera. London, W. Reeves, 1912.

Götze, Willibald. Studien zur Formbildung der Oper. Frankfurt/M., Brönner, 1935.

Goldschmidt, Hugo. "Zur Geschichte der Arien- und Symphonie-Formen," MfMg XXXIII (1901) 61–70.

Goode, Gerald. The Book of Ballets. New York, Crown Publishers, [1939].

Grand-Carteret, John. "Les Titres illustrés et l'image au service de la musique," RMI V (1898) 1–63, 225–80; VI (1899) 289–329; IX (1902) 557–635; XI (1904) 1–23, 191–227.

Grégoir, Edouard. Des Gloires de l'opéra et la musique à Paris. Brussels, Schott, 1878. 3 vols.

—— Littérature musicale. Brussels, Schott, 1872–76. 4 vols.

—— Panthéon musical populaire. Brussels, Schott, 1876–77. 6 vols.

Gregor, Hans. Die Welt der Oper—die Oper der Welt. Berlin, Bote & Bock, [1931].

Gregor, Joseph. Kulturgeschichte der Oper : Ihre Verbindung mit dem Leben, den Werken des Geistes und der Politik. Vienna, Gallus Verlag; Zurich, Scientia Verlag, [1950]. 2d ed.

—— Weltgeschichte des Theaters. [Zurich], Phaidon, [1933].

Griggs, John C. "The Influence of Comedy upon Operatic Form," MQ III (1917) 552–61.

Grove, Sir George. Dictionary of Music and Musicians. Edited by Eric Blom. London, Macmillan, 1954. 5th ed. 9 vols. Supplementary Volume. New York, St. Martin's Press, 1961.

Grün, Bernard. Kulturgeschichte der Operette. Munich, Langen, Müller, [1961].

Gundry, Inglis. "The Nature of Opera as a Composite Art," PMA LXXIII (1946–47) 25–33.

Haas, Robert M. Afführungspraxis der Musik. Wildpark-Potsdam, Athenaion, [1931].

Hagemann, Carl. Oper und Szene : Aufsätze zur Regie des musikalischen Dramas. Berlin, Schuster & Loeffler, 1905.

Hansemann, Marlise. Der Klavier-Auszug von den Anfängen bis Weber. Borna, Meyen, 1943.

Hartnoll, Phyllis, ed. The Oxford Companion to the Theatre. London, New York, Oxford University Press, 1957. 2d ed. See especially the articles "Incidental Music" (E. Blom) and "Opera" (A. Loewenberg).

Hatton, A. P. "Personality in Opera," M&L XII (1931) 164–69.

Hausswald, Günter. Das neue Opernbuch. Berlin, Henschelverlag, 1957. 7th ed.

Haweis, Hugh Reginald. Music and Morals. New York, Harper, 1872.

Hédouin, Pierre. Mosaique : Peintres—musiciens— . . . à partir du 15e siècle jusqu'à nos jours. Paris, Heugel, 1856.

Heinrich, Viktor. Komik und Humor in der Musik. Vienna Dissertation, 1931.

Heseltine, Philip. "The Scope of Opera," M&L I (1920) 230–33.

Hirsch, Franz. Die Oper und der Literaturgeist : Ein Wort zu Operntextreform. Leipzig, Voigt, 1868.

Hirsch, Paul. Katalog der Musikbibliothek Paul Hirsch . . . Band II: Opern-Partituren. Berlin, Breslauer, 1930.

Hope-Wallace, Philip. A Picture History of Opera. New York, Macmillan, [1959].

Horowicz, Bronislaw. Le Théâtre d'opera : Histoire—réalisations scéniques —possibilités. Paris, Editions de Flore, 1946.

Hostomská, Anna. Opera. Prague, Státní nakladatelství krásné literatury, hubdy a umění, 1958. 3d ed.

Howes, Frank. A Key to Opera. London and Glasgow, Blackie, [1939].

—— "Professor Wellesz on Opera," M&L XV (1934) 120–27.

Hussey, Dyneley. Euridice; or, The Nature of Opera. London, K. Paul, 1929.

—— Some Composers of Opera. London, New York, Toronto, Oxford University Press, 1952.

Istel, Edgar. Das Buch der Oper. Berlin, M. Hesse, [1920]. 2d ed.

—— Die komische Oper : Eine historisch-ästhetische Studie. Stuttgart, C. Grüninger, [1906].

—— Das Libretto : Wesen, Aufbau und Wirkung des Opernbuchs. Berlin and Leipzig, Schuster & Loeffler, 1914. Translated (revised) as : The Art of Writing Opera Librettos. New York, G. Schirmer, [1922].

—— Revolution und Oper. Regensburg, G. Bosse, 1919.

Jansen, Lothar. Studien zur Entwicklungsgeschichte der Oper in Italien, Frankreich, und Deutschland. Bonn Dissertation, 1914.

Junk, Victor. Die Bedeutung der Schlusskadenz im Musikdrama. Leipzig, L. Doblinger, [1926].

Kapp, Julius. Das Opernbuch : Eine Geschichte der Oper und ein musikalisch-dramatischer Führer. Leipzig, Hesse & Becker Verlag, 1941. New ed.

Karstädt, Georg. "Zur Geschichte des Zinken und seiner Verwendung in der Musik des 16.–18. Jahrhunderts," AfMf II (1937) 385–432.

Keller, Otto. Die Operette in ihrer geschichtlichen Entwicklung. Vienna, Stein-Verlag, 1926.

Keppler, Philip, Jr. "Some Comments on Musical Quotation," MQ XLII (1956) 473–85.

Kerman, Joseph. Opera as Drama. New York, Alfred A. Knopf, 1956.

Kinsky, Georg. [Geschichte der Musik in Bildern.] A History of Music in Pictures. London, J. M. Dent, [1937].

Kirby, Percival R. "The Kettle-drums : An Historical Survey," M&L IX (1928) 34–43.

Klein, Herman. The Golden Age of Opera. London, George Routledge, 1933.

Klob, Karl Maria. Die Oper von Gluck bis Wagner. Ulm, H. Kerler, 1913.

Kobbé, Gustav. Kobbé's Complete Opera Book. Edited and revised by the Earl of Harewood. New York, G. P. Putnam's Sons, [1954].

Köhler, Louis. Die Melodie der Sprache in ihrer Anwendung besonders auf das Lied und die Oper. Leipzig, Weber, 1853.

Krause, Ernst. Briefe über die Oper : Die Erneuerung der Musikbühne. [Dresden], VVB Verlag, Dresdner Verlag, [1951].

—— Oper von A–Z : Ein Handbuch. Leipzig, B&H, 1961.

Kraussold, Max. Geist und Stoff der Operndichtung : Eine Dramaturgie in Umrissen. Leipzig, Strache, 1931.

Krehbiel, Henry Edward. A Book of Operas. New York, Macmillan, 1928. 2 vols. in one, combining "A Book of Operas" and "A Second Book of Operas."

[Kretzschmar, Hermann.] Festschrift Hermann Kretzschmar zum 70. Geburtstag. Leipzig, Peters, 1918.

—— "Für und gegen die Oper," JMP XX (1913) 59–70.

—— Gesammelte Aufsätze über Musik und anderes. Leipzig, F. W. Grunow, 1910–[11]. 2 vols.

—— Geschichte der Oper. Leipzig, B&H, 1919.

—— Geschichte des neuen deutschen Liedes. I. Teil : von Albert bis Zelter. Leipzig, B&H, 1911.

Krieger, Ludwig. Die sozialische Lage der Theatermusiker. Heidelberg, Schulze, 1913.

Kunath, Martin. "Die Charakterologie der stimmlichen Einheiten in der Oper," ZfMw VIII (1925–26) 403–10.

—— Die Oper als literarische Form. Leipzig Dissertation, 1925.

Lajarte, Théodore de. Bibliothèque musicale du théâtre de l'opéra. Paris, Librairie des bibliophiles, 1878. 2 vols.

—— Curiosités de l'opéra. Paris, Calmann Lévy, 1883.

La Laurencie, Lionel de. Inventaire critique du fonds Blancheton de la Bibliothèque du Conservatoire de Paris. Paris, E. Droz, 1930–31. 2 vols.

Lang, Paul Henry. Music in Western Civilization. New York, W. W. Norton, [1941].

Lavignac, Alexandre Jean Albert, ed. Encyclopédie de la musique et Dictionnaire du Conservatoire. Première Partie : Histoire de la musique. Paris, Delagrave, 1913–22. 5 vols.

Leibowitz, René. Histoire de l'opéra. [Paris], Buchet-Chastel, Corrêa, [1957].

Leichtentritt, Hugo. Music, History, and Ideas. Cambridge, Mass., Harvard University Press, 1938.

Leti, Giuseppe, and Louis Lachat. L'Esotérisme à la scène : La Flûte enchantée, Parsifal, Faust. Annecy, L. Dépollier, 1935.

Lindner, Ernst Otto. Zur Tonkunst : Abhandlungen. Berlin, I. Guttentag, 1864.

Loewenberg, Alfred, compiler. Annals of Opera, 1597–1940 : Compiled from the Original Sources. Geneva, Societas Bibliographica, [1955]. 2d ed. 2 vols.

López Chavarri. See Chavarri, Eduardo López.

Loschelder, Josef. Die Oper als Kunstform. Vienna, A. Schroll, [1941].

Luciani, Sebastiano Arturo. La rinascità del dramma : Saggio sul teatro di musica. Rome, Ausonia, 1922.

MacFarren, Sir George Alexander. "The Lyrical Drama," PMA VI (1880) 125–40.

McSpadden, Joseph W. Operas and Musical Comedies. New York, Thomas Y. Crowell Co., [1954]. Enlarged ed.

Madrid. Biblioteca nacional. Departamento de manuscritos. Catálogo de las piezas de teatro. Madrid, Blass, 1934–35. 2 vols.

Manferrari, Umberto. Dizionario universale delle opere melodrammatiche. Florence, Sansoni Antiquariato, 1954–55. 3 vols.

Manners, Charles. "The Financial Problems of National Opera," M&L VII (1926) 93–105.

Mantzius, Karl. A History of Theatrical Art in Ancient and Modern Times. London, Duckworth, 1903–21. 6 vols.

Martens, Frederick Herman. A Thousand and One Nights of Opera. New York, D. Appleton, [1926].

Matthews, Brander. "The Conventions of the Music Drama," MQ V (1919) 255–63.

Mayer, Anton. Die Oper : Eine Anleitung zu ihrem Verständnis. Berlin, K. Wolff, [1935].

Mayer, Ernesto Rodolfo. "Verso quali mète è diretta l' 'opera'?" RMI XLII (1938) 363–67.

Maylender, Michele. Storia delle accademie d'Italia. Bologna, L. Cappelli, [1926–30]. 5 vols.

Mayor, A. Hyatt, Mercedes Viale, A. della Corte, and A. G. Bragaglia. Tempi e aspetti della scenografia. [Turin, Edizioni Radio Italiani, 1954.]

Mengelberg, Curt Rudolf. "Das Musikdrama als Kunstform," Die Musik XIII (1913–14) 288–99.

Mercure de France. Paris. 1672–1820.

Mila, Massimo. "Il concetto di musica drammatica," RassM IV (1931) 98–106.

Monaldi, Gino. Cantanti evirati celebri del teatro italiano. Rome, Ausonia, 1920.

Moser, Hans Joachim. Geschichte der deutschen Musik. Stuttgart and Berlin, J. G. Cotta, 1920–24. 3 vols.

Die Musik in Geschichte und Gegenwart. Edited by Friedrich Blume. Kassel & Basel, Bärenreiter, 1949–

Musik und Bild : Festschrift Max Seiffert. Kassel, Bärenreiter, 1938.

Napoli-Signorelli, Pietro. Storia critica dei teatri antichi e moderni. Naples, V. Orsino, 1787–90. 6 vols. A later ed., 1813, 10 vols.

Navarra, Ugo. Nel tricentenario del teatro lirico 1637–1937 : Grande inchiesta particolare sulle condizioni odierne della scena melodrammatica. Milan, Alba, 1937.

Neitzel, Otto. Der Führer durch die Oper des Theaters der Gegenwart. Leipzig, A. G. Liebeskind, 1890–98. 3 vols.

Newman, Ernest. More Stories of Famous Operas. New York, Alfred A. Knopf, 1943.

—— Seventeen Famous Operas. New York, Alfred A. Knopf, 1955.

—— Stories of the Great Operas and Their Composers. New York, Garden City Publishing Company, [1928]. 3 vols. in one.

New York Public Library. The Development of Scenic Art and Stage Machinery : A List of References in the New York Public Library. New York, 1920.

—— Stage Scenery : A List of References to Illustrations Since 1900 in the New York Public Library. Compiled by William Burt Gamble. New York, [New York Public Library] 1917.

Nicoll, Allardyce. The Development of the Theatre. New York, Harcourt, Brace, 1958. 4th ed.

—— A History of English Drama, 1660–1900. Cambridge, The University Press, 1952–59. 6 vols.

Niecks, Frederick. "Historical Sketch of the Overture," SIMG VII (1905–6) 386–90.

Ollone, Max d'. Le Théâtre lyrique et le public. Paris & Geneva, La Palatine, [1955].

O'Neill, Norman. "Music to Stage Plays," PMA XXXVII (1911) 85–102.

"Opera," in Enciclopedia universal ilustrada europea-americana ("Espasa") XXI, 1297–1300; XXXIX, 1360–94.

Pankratova, V. A., ed. Opernye libretto : Kratkoe izlozhenie soderzhaniia oper. Moscow, Gos. muz. izd-vo, 1962.

Pannain, Guido. L'Opera e le opere ed altri scritti di letteratura musicale. Milan, Edizioni Curci, 1958.

Paoli, Domenico de. L'opera italiana dalle origini all' opera verista. Rome, Studium, [1955].

Paris. Bibliothèque nationale. Département des imprimés. Catalogue du fonds de musique de la Bibliothèque nationale, par J. Ecorcheville. Paris, 1910–14. 8 vols.

—— Conservatoire national de musique et de déclamation. Bibliothèque. Catalogue bibliographique . . . avec notices et reproductions musicales des principaux ouvrages de la réserve, par J. B. Weckerlin. Paris, Firmin-Didot, 1885.

Pastor, Ludwig, Freiherr von. The History of the Popes, from the Close of the Middle Ages. Vols. 29, 30, 31. London, Kegan Paul, 1938–40.

Peltz, Mary Ellis. The Metropolitan Opera Guide. New York, The Modern Library, [1939].

Percival, Robert. "Can Opera Be Made to Pay?" M&L VII (1926) 114–19.

[Pereira Peixoto d'Almeida Carvalhaes, Manoel.] Catálogo da importante biblioteca que pertencen ao . . . erudito e bibliofilo ilustre Manuel de Carvalhaes . . . organisado par Augusta Sâ da Costa. Lisbon, 1928.

Petit, Henri. "Défense de l'opéra-comique," L'Information musicale II (1942) Nos. 76 and 77.

Petzoldt, Richard. Die Oper in ihrer Zeit. Leipzig, VEB B&H, 1956.

Peyser, Herbert F. "Some Observations on Translation," MQ VIII (1922) 353–71.

Pizzetti, Ildebrando. Musica e dramma. Rome, Edizioni della Bussola, [1945].

Pols, André M. Trilogie van de Hartstocht: Don Giovanni, Tristan en Eroos, Pelléas. Antwerp, Die Poorte, 1952.

Polyphonie. Premier cahier (1947–48): Le Théâtre musical.

Prod'homme, Jacques Gabriel. "Etat alphabétique sommaire des archives de l'opéra," RdM XIV (1933) 193–205.

—— L'Opéra (1669–1925). Paris, Delagrave, 1925.

—— "Two Hundred and Fifty Years of the Opéra (1669–1919)," MQ V (1919) 513–37.

Pulver, Jeffrey. "The Intermezzi of the Opera," PMA XLIII (1916–17) 139–63.

Raabe, Peter. Kulturwille im deutschen Musikleben. Regensburg, G. Bosse, [1936].

Rabich, Ernst. Die Entwicklung der Oper. Langensalza, Beyer, 1926.

Radford, Maisie. "A Comparative Study of Indigenous Forms of Opera," M&L VII (1926) 106–13.

Reclams Opern- und Operettenführer. Stuttgart, Reclam-Verlag, [1956].

Refardt, Edgar. Verzeichnis der Aufsätze zur Musik in den nichtmusikalischen Zeitschriften der Universitätsbibliothek Basel abgeschlossen auf den 1. Januar 1924. Leipzig, B&H, 1925.

Renner, Hans. Die Wunderwelt der Oper: Der grosse Führer durch die Oper und die klassische Operette. Berlin, Vier Falken Verlag, [1938].

Riemann, Hugo. Handbuch der Musikgeschichte. 2d ed. Leipzig, B&H, 1919–22. 2 vols. in 5 parts.

—— Opern-Handbuch: Repertorium der dramatisch-musikalischen Litteratur. Leipzig, H. Seemann Nachfolger, [published in parts; 1881–1900?].

Rinaldi, Mario. L'opera in musica: Saggio estetico. Rome, "Novissima," [1934].

Rolandi, Ulderigo. Il libretto per musica attraverso i tempi. Rome, Edizioni dell' Ateneo, 1951.

Rolland, Romain. "Les Maîtres de l'opéra : Recueil de musique inédite du XVIIe et du XVIIIe siècle," RHCM III (1903) 40–41, 178–79.

—— Musiciens d'autrefois. Paris, Hachette, 1924. 9th ed. Translated as : Some Musicians of Former Days. London, K. Paul, 1915.

Roncaglia, Gino. Invito all' opera. Milan, Tarantola, 1954. 2d ed.

Rosenfeld, Paul. Discoveries of a Music Critic. New York, Harcourt, Brace, [1936].

Ross, Anne, ed. The Opera Directory. New York, Sterling Publishing Co., 1961.

Rossi-Doria, Gastone. "Opera," in Enciclopedia italiana XXV (1935) 390–404.

Rubsamen, Walter. "Political and Ideological Censorship of Opera," in Papers of the American Musicological Society, Annual Meeting, 1941 ... Edited by Gustave Reese (Printed by the Society [cop. 1946]) 30–42.

Sadler's Wells Opera Books. London, John Lane, 1945– .

Salvioli, Giovanni. Bibliografia universale del teatro drammatico italiano. Volume primo. Venice, [1894–]1903. A-Czarina only; no more published.

Sauerlandt, Max. Die Musik in fünf Jahrhunderten der europäischen Malerei etwa 1450 bis etwa 1850. Leipzig, Langewiesche Verlag, 1922.

Schaal, Richard. "Die vor 1801 gedruckten Libretti des Theatermuseums München," Mf X (1957) 388–96, 487–97; XI (1958) 54–69, 168–77, 321–36, 462–77; XII (1959) 60–75, 161–77, 299–306, 454–61; XIII (1960) 38–46, 164–72, 299–306, 441–48; XIV (1961) 36–43, 166–83.

Schering, Arnold. Aufführungspraxis alter Musik. Leipzig, Quelle & Meyer, 1931.

—— Geschichte des Instrumentalkonzerts. Leipzig, B&H, 1927, 2d ed.

—— Geschichte des Oratoriums. Leipzig, B&H, [1911].

—— Musikgeschichte Leipzigs. Leipzig, Kistner & Siegel, 1926. 3 vols.

Schiedermair, Ludwig. "Ueber den Stand der Operngeschichte," in International Music Society, Second Congress Report (Leipzig, B&H, 1907) 212–16.

Schladebach, Julius. "Geschichte der Oper bis auf Gluck," Die Wissenschaft im 19. Jahrhundert I (1856) 361.

Schletterer, Hans Michael. Die Entstehung der Oper. Nördlingen, C. H. Beck, 1873.

—— Zur Geschichte dramatischer Musik und Poesie in Deutschland. Augsburg, Schlosser, 1863.

Schmitz, Eugen. Geschichte der weltlichen Solo–Kantate. Leipzig, B&H, 1914.

Scholz, János, ed. Baroque and Romantic Stage Design. New York, Beechhurst Press, [1955]. New ed.

Schünemann, Georg. Geschichte der deutschen Schulmusik. Leipzig, Kistner & Siegel, 1928.

Schuré, Edouard. Le Drame musicale. Paris, Didier, 1886. 2 vols.

Schwanbeck, Gisela. Bibliographie der deutschsprachigen Hochschulschriften zur Theaterwissenschaft von 1885 bis 1952. Berlin, Gesellschaft für Theatergeschichte, 1956.

Scuola veneziana, La (secoli XVI–XVIII), note e documenti. Siena, Libreria editrice Ticci, 1941.

Sear, H. G. "Operatic Mortality," M&L XXI (1940) 60–74.

Searle, Humphrey. Ballet Music: An Introduction. London, Cassell, [1958].

Sedwick, B. Frank. "Opera Errors," JAMS VII (1954) 48–51.

Seltsam, William H., compiler. Metropolitan Opera Annals : A Chronicle of Artists and Performances. New York, H. W. Wilson Co., in Association with the Metropolitan Opera Guild, Inc., 1947.

Serov, Aleksandr Nikolaevich. Aufsätze zur Musikgeschichte. Berlin, Aufbau-Verlag, 1955.

Skraup, Siegmund. Die Oper als lebendiges Theater. Berlin, Henschel-Verlag, 1956. 3d ed.

Small, Herbert F. "On Opera," MQ IV (1918) 37–49.

Solvay, Lucien. L'Evolution théatrale. Brussels and Paris, G. van Oest, 1922. 2 vols.

Sonneck, Oscar George Theodore. Miscellaneous Studies in the History of Music. New York, Macmillan, 1921. Contains "Caractacus Not Arne's Caractacus," "Ciampi's Bertoldo, Bertoldino e Cacasenno and Favart's Ninette à la cour: A Contribution to the History of the Pasticcio," "A Description of Alessandro Striggio and Francesco Corteggia's Intermedi : Psyche and Amor, 1565," "Early American Opera," and "A Preface."

—— "Noch etwas über Opernlexika," Die Musik XIII (1913–14) Qt. 4, 140–43.

—— See also United States Library of Congress.

Statisticus [pseud.]. "Notes sur l'histoire de l'Opéra," RHCM III (1903) 277–79.

Steger, Hellmuth, and Karl Howe. Operettenführer, von Offenbach bis zum Musical. Frankfurt/M., Hamburg, Fischer, 1958.

Steidel, Max. Oper und Drama. Karlsruhe, G. Braun, 1923.

Stieger, Franz. "Opernkomponistinnen," Die Musik XIII (1913–14) Qt. 4, 270–71.

Storck, Karl G. L. Das Opernbuch : Ein Führer durch den Spielplan der deutschen Opernbühnen. Stuttgart, Muth, [1949]. 45th ed.

[Strangways, A. H. Fox.] "Opera and the Musician," M&L XIII (1932) 119–25.

Streatfeild, Richard Alexander. The Opera. London, G. Routledge, 1925. 5th ed.

Struck, Gustav. "Die Wende zur Literatur-Oper : Zur 50 Wiederkehr der *Salome*-Uraufführung," M IX (1955) 589–94.

Strunk, Oliver, ed. Source Readings in Music History. New York, W. W. Norton, 1950.

Szabolcsi, Bence, and Dénes Bartha, eds. Az opera történetéből. Budapest, Akadémiai Kiadó, 1961. Series : Zenetudományi tanulmányok, IX.

Ternant, Andrew de. "French Opera Libretti," M&L XI (1930) 172–76.

Theatrical Designs from the Baroque through Neo-Classicism : Unpublished Material from American Private Collections. New York, H. Bittner, 1940. 3 vols.

Thrane, Carl. Danske Komponister. Copenhagen, Forlagsbureaunet, 1875.

Tiersot, Julien. "Lettres de musiciens écrites en francais du XVe au XXe siècle," RMI XVII (1910)–XXI (1914); XXIII (1916); XXIX (1922)–XXX (1923); XXXIII (1926)–XXXIV (1927); XXXVI (1929)–XXXVIII (1931), *passim*.

Tiraboschi, Girolamo. Storia della letteratura italiana. Rome, L. P. Salvioni, 1782–97. 10 vols.

Tittmann, Julius. Kleine Schriften zur deutschen Literatur und Kulturgeschichte. Göttingen, Dieterischen Buchhandlung, 1847.

Tommasini, Vincenzo. "Del drama lirico," RMI XXXIX (1932) 73–113.

Tonelli, Luigi. Il teatro italiano dalle origini ai giorni nostri. Milan, Modernissima, 1924.

Torrefranca, Fausto. "L'officina dell' opera," RassM III (1930) 136–46.

—— "Opera as a 'Spectacle for the Eye,' " MQ I (1915) 436–52.

Touchard-Lafosse, G. Chroniques secrètes et galantes de l'opéra depuis 1667 jusqu'en 1845. Paris, Lachapelle, 1846. 4 vols.

Tovey, Donald Francis. Essays in Musical Analysis, III : The Concerto. London, Oxford University Press, 1936.

Towers, John. Dictionary-Catalogue of Operas and Operettas Which Have Been Performed on the Public Stage. Morgantown, W. Va., Acme, [1910].

Toye, Francis. "Is Musical Reservation Justifiable?" MQ I (1915) 118–28.

Turin. Biblioteca civica. Sezione teatrale. [Letteratura drammatica. Turin, G. B. Vassallo, 1912, 1911. 2 vols.]

United States Library of Congress. Division of Music. Catalogue of Opera Librettos Printed before 1800. Prepared by Oscar George Theodore Sonneck. Washington, Government Printing Office, 1914. 2 vols.

—— Dramatic Music (Class M 1500, 1510, 1520) : Catalogue of Full Scores. Compiled by E. G. T. Sonneck. Washington, Government Printing Office, 1908.

Upton, George Putnam. The Standard Light Operas. Chicago, A. C. McClurg, 1902.

—— The Standard Operas. Chicago, A. C. McClurg, 1928. New ed.

Vaillat, Léandre. Ballets de l'Opéra de Paris (ballets dans les opéras—

nouveaux ballets). Paris, Compagnie Française des Arts Graphiques, 1947.

Valentin, Erich. "Dichtung und Oper : Eine Untersuchung des Stilproblems der Oper," AfMf III (1938) 138–79.

Vatielli, Francesco. "Operisti-librettisti dei secoli XVII e XVIII," RMI XLIII (1939) 1–16, 315–32, 605–21.

Vetter, Walther. Mythos—Melos—Musica : Ausgewählte Aufsätze zur Musikgeschichte. Leipzig, Deutscher Verlag für Musik, 1957.

Vogel, Emil. Bibliothek der gedruckten weltlichen Vokalmusik Italiens aus den Jahren 1500–1700. Berlin, A. Haack, 1892. New ed. (A. Einstein) serially in MLA Notes, 2d ser. II, No. 3 (June, 1945) to V, No. 4 (September, 1948).

Walker, Ernest. A History of Music in England. 3d ed., revised by J. A. Westrup. Oxford, Clarendon Press, 1952.

Weigl, Bruno. Die Geschichte des Walzers nebst einem Anhang über die moderne Operette. Langensalza, Beyer, 1910.

Wellesz, Egon. Essays on Opera. Translated . . . by Patricia Kean. London, Dennis Dobson, [1950].

Westrup, Jack A. "The Nature of Recitative," Proceedings of the British Academy XLII (1956) 27–43.

Wichmann, Heinz. Der neue Opernführer, mit einem Anhang, Klassische Operetten. Berlin, P. Franke, 1943.

Wiese, Berthold. Geschichte der italienischen Litteratur. Leipzig and Vienna, Bibliographisches Institut, [1898–]1899. Fourth to fifteenth centuries by Wiese; sixteenth century to present by E. Pèrcopo.

Wolff, Hellmuth Christian. "Orpheus als Opernthema," Musica XV (1961) 423–25.

Wossidlo, Walter. Opern-Bibliothek : Populärer Führer durch Poesie und Musik. Leipzig, Rühle & Wendling, [1919?].

Zenetudományi tanulmányok. Series of collections of musicological essays; Budapest, Hungarian Academy of Sciences, 1953–62. 10 vols., each with separate title. Articles on the history of opera in Vol. II (Erkel Ferenc és Bartók Béla emlékére, 1954); Vol. IV (A magyar zene történetéből, 1955); Vol. V (Mozart emlékére, 1957); and Vol. IX (Az opera történetéből, 1961).

Zingel, Hans Joachim. "Studien zur Geschichte des Harfenspiels in klassischer und romantischer Zeit," AfMf II (1937) 455–65.

Zopff, Hermann. Grundzüge einer Theorie der Oper. Leipzig, Arnold, 1868.

# II

## MUSIC AND DRAMA TO THE END OF THE SIXTEENTH CENTURY

Adam de la Halle. Le Jeu de Robin et de Marion. Précédé du Jeu du Pèlerin. Edité par Kenneth Varty. [Transcriptions musicales d'Eric Hill.] London, Harrap, [1960].

—— Œuvres complètes du trouvère Adam de la Halle, poésies et musique: Publiées . . . par E. de Coussemaker. Paris, A. Durand & Pedone-Lauriel, 1872.

Alaleona, Domenico. "Su Emilio de' Cavalieri," *La nouva musica*, Nos. 113–14 (1905) 35–38, 47–50.

Albrecht, Otto E. Four Latin Plays of St. Nicholas from the 12th Century Fleury Play-Book : Text and Commentary, with a Study of the Music of the Plays, and of the Sources and Iconography of the Legends. Philadelphia, University of Pennsylvania Press; London, Oxford University Press, 1935.

Anglès, Higini. La música a Catalunya fins al segle XIII. Barcelona, Institut d'Estudis Catalans : Biblioteca de Catalunya, 1935.

Anthon, Carl Gustav. Music and Musicians in Northern Italy during the Sixteenth Century. Harvard Dissertation, 1943.

Anticlo, ——. "Gli spiriti della musica nella tragedia greca," RMI XX (1913) 821–87.

Aristotle. Aristotle's Treatise on Poetry. Translated . . . by Thomas Twining. London, Payne and Son [etc.], 1789.

Augé-Chiquet, Mathieu. La Vie, les idées et l'œuvre de Baïf. Paris [etc.], Edouard Privat Hachette, 1909.

Bacot, Jacques, tr. and ed. Représentations théâtrales dans les monastères du Tibet : Trois mystères tibetains. Paris, Bossard, 1921.

Ballard, William J. The Sources, Development and Culmination of the Dramatic Madrigal. Ann Arbor, University Microfilms, 1958.

Bartholomaeis, Vincenzo de, ed. Laude drammatiche e rappresentazioni sacre. Florence, Le Monnier, 1943. 3 vols.

Bartsch, Karl. Romances et pastourelles françaises des XIIe et XIIIe siècles. Leipzig, F. Vogel, 1870.

Becherini, Bianca. "La musica nelle 'Sacre rappresentazioni' Fiorentine," RMI LIII (1951) 193–241.

Bohn, [Emil?]. "Theophilus : Niederdeutsches Schauspiel aus einer Handschrift des 15. Jahrhunderts," MfMg IX (1877) 3–4. Music, pp. 24–25.

Bonaventura, Arnoldo. "Le maggiolate," RMI XXIV (1917) 272–99.

Bonfantini, Mario, ed. Le sacre rappresentazioni italiane : Raccolta di testi dal secolo XIII al secolo XVI. [Milan], Bompiani, [1942].

Bowles, Edmund A. "The Role of Musical Instruments in Medieval Sacred Drama," MQ XLV (1959) 67–84.

Brandsetter, Renward. "Musik und Gesang beiden Luzerner Osterspielen," *Der Geschichtsfreund* XL (1885) 145–68.

Brinkmann, Hennig. Zum Ursprung des liturgischen Spieles. Bonn, F. Cohen, 1929.

Brown, Howard Mayer. Music in the French Secular Theater, 1400–1550. Cambridge, Mass., Harvard University Press, 1963.

Brownlow, Jane. "The Bardi Coterie," PMA XXII (1896) 111–27.

Bukofzer, Manfred. "The *Book of the Courtier* on Music," MTNA XXXVIII (1944) 230–35.

Burckhardt, Jakob. The Civilization of the Period of the Renaissance in Italy. London, C. K. Paul, 1878. 2 vols.

Camillucci, Guido. "*L'Amfiparnaso,* comedia harmonica," RMI LIII (1951) 42–60.

Casella, Alfredo, ed. La favola di Orfeo, opera in un atto di Messer Angelo Ambrogini detto "Poliziano." Milan, Carisch, [1934].

Castiglione, Baldassare, conte. Il libro del cortegiano. Florence, Heredi di Philippo di Giunta, 1528. Translated by Thomas Hoby as : The Courtier. [New York], The National Alumni, [1907].

Chailley, Jacques. "Le Drame liturgique médiéval à St.-Martial de Limoges," Revue d'histoire du théâtre VII (1955) 127–44.

—— "La Nature musicale du *Jeu de Robin et Marion,*" in *Mélanges d'histoire du théâtre du moyen-âge et de la renaissance, offerts à Gustave Cohen* . . . (Paris, Librairie Nizet, 1950) 111–17.

Chambers, E. K. The Medieval Stage. London, Oxford University Press, 1903. 2 vols.

Chrysander, Friedrich. "Ludovico Zacconi als Lehrer des Kunstgesanges," VfMw VII (1891) 337–96; IX (1893) 249–310; X (1894) 531–67.

Civita, A. Ottavio Rinuccini e il sorgere del melodramma in Italia. Mantua, Manuzio, 1900.

Clément, Félix. "Liturgie, musique et drama du moyen âge," *Annales archéologiques* VII (1847) 303–20; VIII (1848) 36–48, 77–87, 304–11; IX (1849) 27–40, 162–74; X (1850) 154–60; XI (1851) 6–15.

Cohen, Gustave. Histoire de la mise en scène dans le théâtre réligieux français du moyen âge. Paris, Champion, 1926. New ed.

Cohen, Gustave, ed. Anthologie du drame liturgique en France au moyen-âge : Textes originaux accompagnés de traductions. Paris, Les Editions du Cerf, 1955.

—— Recueil de farces françaises inédites du XVe siècle. Cambridge, Mass., Mediæval Academy of America, 1949.

Colomb de Batines. Bibliografia delle antiche rappresentazioni italiane sacre e profane, stampate nei secoli XV e XVI. Florence, Società tip., 1852. Additions by E. Narducci in Il bibliofilo III (1882) 73–74, 87–88.

Comte, Charles, and Paul Laumonier. "Ronsard et les musiciens du XVIe siècle," Revue d'histoire littéraire de la France VII (1900) 341–81.

Corbin, Solange. "Le Manuscrit 201 d'Orléans : Drames liturgiques dits de Fleury," Romania LXXIV (1953) 1–43.

Coussemaker, Edmond de. Drames liturgiques du moyen âge. Rennes, H. Vatar, 1860; Paris, Lib. archéologique de V. Didron, 1861.

Crocker, Eunice. The Instrumental Ensemble Canzona. Radcliffe Dissertation, 1943.

D'Ancona, Alessandro. Origini del teatro italiano. Turin, E. Loescher, 1891. 2d ed. 2 vols.

—— Sacre rappresentazioni dei secoli XIV, XV e XVI. Florence, Successori Le Monnier, 1872. 3 vols.

Dent, Edward J. "The *Amfiparnaso* of Orazio Vecchi," MMR XXXVI (1906) 50–52, 74–75.

—— "Notes on the *Amfiparnaso* of Orazio Vecchi," SIMG XII (1910–11) 330–47.

De Vito, M. S. L'origine del dramma liturgico. Milan, Dante Alighieri, [1939?].

Donovan, Richard B. The Liturgical Drama in Medieval Spain. Toronto, Pontifical Institute of Musical Studies, 1958.

"Early Elizabethan Stage Music," MA I (1909–10) 30–40; IV (1912–13) 112–17.

Einstein, Alfred. "Firenze prima della monodia," RassM VII (1934) 253.

—— "The Greghesca and the Giustiniana of the Sixteenth Century," *Journal of Renaissance and Baroque Music* I (1946) 19–32.

—— The Italian Madrigal. Princeton, Princeton University Press, 1949. 3 vols.

—— "Die mehrstimmige weltliche Musik von 1450–1600," in Adler, *Handbuch der Musikgeschichte* (Frankfurt/M., Frankfurter Verlags-Anstalt, 1924) 358–73.

[Eitner, Robert.] "Die Quellen zur Entstehung der Oper," MfMg XIII (1881) 10–15, 21–28.

Ellinwood, Leonard. "The *Conductus*," MQ XXVII (1941) 165–204.

Engel, Hans. "Nochmals die Intermedien von Florenz 1589," in *Festschrift Max Schneider zum 80. Geburtstage* (Leipzig, Deutscher Verlag für Musik, [1955]) 71–86.

Fano, Fabio, ed. La camerata fiorentina : Vincenzo Galilei. Milan, Ricordi, 1934. (Istituzioni e monumenti dell' arte musicale italiana, Vol. IV.)

Flecha, Mateo. Las Ensaladas (Praga, 1581). Transcripción y estudio por Higinio Anglès. . . . Barcelona, Diputación Provincial de Barcelona : Biblioteca Central, 1954.

Flemming, Willi. Geschichte des Jesuitentheaters in den Landen deutscher Zunge. Berlin, Gesellschaft für Theatergeschichte, 1923.

Frati, Lodovico. "Musica e balli alla corte dei Pico della Mirandola," RMI XXV (1918) 249–58.

—— "Torquato Tasso in musica," RMI XXX (1923) 389–400.

Fremy, Edouard. Origines de l'Académie française : L'Académie des derniers Valois. Paris, E. Leroux, [1887].

Frere, Walter Howard, ed. The Winchester Troper, from Mss. of the Xth and XIth Centuries, with Other Documents Illustrating the History of Tropes in England and France. London, [Printed for the Henry Bradshaw Society by Harrison and Sons], 1894.

Galilei, Vincenzo. Dialogo della musica antica, et della moderna. Fiorenza, G. Marescotti, 1581. Facsimile reprint, Rome, R. Accademia d'Italia, 1934.

[Galluzzi, Riguccio.] Istoria del granducato di Toscana sotto il governo della casa Medici. Florence, Stamperia di R. del Vivo, 1781. 5 vols. New ed., Florence, 1822. 11 vols.

Gandolfi, Riccardo. "Appunti di storia musicale : Cristofano Malvezzi— Emilio de' Cavalieri," *Rassegna nazionale* XV (November, 1893) 297– 306.

Gautier, Léon. Histoire de la poésie liturgique au moyen âge : Les tropes. Paris, V. Palmé, 1886.

Gégou, Fabienne. "Fragments de drame liturgique (?) découvert dans le manuscrit La Vallière de la Bibliothèque Nationale," RdM XLV (1960) 76–83.

Gérold, Théodore. La Musique au moyen âge. Paris, Champion, 1932.

Ghisi, Federico. Alle fonti della monodia : Due nuovi brani della *Dafne*; il *Fuggilotio musicale* di G. Caccini. Milan, Bocca, 1940.

—— "Un Aspect inédit des intermèdes de 1589 à la cour medicéenne et le développement de courses masquées et des ballets équestres durant les premières décades du XVIIe siècle," in *Les Fêtes de la Renaissance* (Paris, Centre National de la Recherche Scientifique, 1956) 145–52.

—— I canti carnascialeschi nelle fonti musicali del XV e XVI secolo. Florence-Rome, L. S. Olschki, 1937.

—— "An Early 17th Century MS with Unpublished Italian Monodic Music by Peri, Caccini, and Marco da Gagliano," *Acta musicologica* XX (1948) 46–60.

—— Feste musicali della Firenze Medicea. Florence, Vallecchi, 1939.

Glareanus, Henricus. Dodecachordon. Leipzig, B&H, 1888. Translated and transcribed by Peter Bohn. Originally published 1547.

Goldschmidt, Hugo. "Verzierungen, Veränderungen und Passaggien im 16. und 17. Jahrhundert," MfMg XXIII (1891) 111–26.

Greenberg, Noah, ed. The Play of Daniel [Br. Mus. Egerton 2615]. New York, Oxford University Press, 1959.

Greulich, Martin. Beiträge zur Geschichte des Streichinstrumentenspiels im 16. Jahrhundert. Saalfeld, Günther, [1934?].

Guy, Henri. Bibliographie critique du trouvère Adan de la Hale. Paris, A. Fontemoing, [1900].

—— Essai sur la vie et les œuvres littéraires du trouvère Adan de le Hale. Paris, Hachette, 1898.

Hamilton, Edith. "The Greek Chorus, Fifteen or Fifty?" *Theatre Arts Monthly* XVII (1933) 459.

Handschin, Jacques. "Das Weinachts-Mysterium von Rouen als musikgeschichtliche Quelle," *Acta musicologica* VII (1935) 97–110.

Hartmann, Arnold, Jr. "Battista Guarini and *Il pastor fido*," MQ XXXIX (1953) 415–25.

Henderson, William James. Some Forerunners of the Italian Opera. London, John Murray, 1911.

Hoepffner, Ernest. "Les Intermèdes musicaux dans le *Jeu provençal de*

*Sainte Agnès,*" in *Mélanges d'histoire du théâtre du moyen-âge et de la renaissance, offerts à Gustave Cohen* ... (Paris, Librairie Nizet, 1950) 97–104.

Hoffmann von Fallersleben, August Heinrich. In dulci jubilo . . . ein Beitrag zur Geschichte der deutschen Poesie. Hanover, C. Rümpler, 1854.

Hol, Joan C. "*L'Amfiparnaso e Le veglie di Siena,*" RMI XL (1936) 3–22.

—— "Horatio Vecchi et l'évolution créatrice," in *Gedenkboek Dr. D. F. Scheurleer* (The Hague, Nijhoff, 1925) 159–67.

—— Horatio Vecchi's weltliche Werke. Leipzig, Heitz, 1934.

—— "*Le veglie di Siena* de Horatio Vecchi," RMI XLIII (1939) 17–34.

"*Hortus musarum* de Pierre Phalèse, deuxième partie (1553)," in *Chansons au luth et airs de cour français du XVIe siècle* (Paris, E. Droz, 1934).

Hughes, Dom Anselm, ed. Early Medieval Music up to 1300. London, New York, Toronto, Oxford University Press, 1954. (NOHM, Vol. II.)

Ingegneri, Angelo. Della poesia rappresentativa e del modo di rappresentare le favole sceniche. Ferrara, V. Baldini, 1598.

Jeppesen, Knud, ed. Die Mehrstimmige italienische Laude um 1500. Leipzig, B&H; Copenhagen, Levin & Munksgaard, 1935.

Jubinal, Achille, ed. Mystères inédits du quinzième siècle. Paris, Téchener, 1837. 2 vols.

Kaff, Ludwig. Mittelalterliche Oster- und Passionsspiele aus Oberösterreich im Spiegel musikwissenschaftlicher Betrachtung. Linz, Oberösterreich Landesverlag, in Komm., 1956.

Kinkeldey, Otto. "Luzzasco Luzzaschi's Solo-Madrigale mit Klavierbegleitung," SIMG IX (1907–8) 538–65.

—— Orgel und Klavier in der Musik des 16. Jahrhunderts. Leipzig, B&H, 1910.

Kirby, Percival R. "A 13th Century Ballad Opera," M&L XI (1930) 163–71.

Kretzenbacher, Leopold. Frühbarockes Weihnachtsspiel in Kärnten und Steiermark : Klagenfurter und Grazer Weihnachtsspieltexte des frühen 17. Jahrhundert als kulturhistorische Denkmäler der Gegenreformation in Innerösterreich. Klagenfurt, Geschichtsverein für Kärnten, 1952.

Krieg, Eduard. Das lateinische Osterspiel von Tours. [With Anhang : "Das lateinische Osterspiel aus der Handschrift 927 (Ff. 1–8) der Stadtbibliothek von Tours."] Würzburg, Triltsch, 1956.

Kroyer, Theodor. Anfänge der Chromatik im italienischen Madrigal des XVI. Jahrhunderts. Leipzig, B&H, 1902.

Kühl, Gustav. "Die Bordesholmer Marienklage, herausgegeben und eingeleitet," *Jahrbuch des Vereins für niederdeutsche Sprachforschung* XXIV (1898) 1–75 and Musikbeilage of 14 pages.

Kuhn, Max. Die Verzierungskunst in der Gesangs-Musik des 16.–17. Jahrhunderts (1535–1650). Leipzig, B&H, 1902.

Lach, Robert. "Das mittelaltleriche Musikdrama im Spiegel der Kunstge-schichte," in *Festschrift Adolph Koczirz* (Vienna, Strache, [1930]) 17–20.

Lacroix, Paul. Ballets et mascarades de cour, de Henri III à Louis XIV (1581–1652). Geneva, J. Gay, 1868–70. 6 vols.

Landi, Antonio. Il commodo, commedia d'Antonio Landi con i suoi inter-medi [etc.]. Florence, I. Giunti, 1566. The intermedi are by G. B. Strozzi the elder. Earlier ed. 1539.

Lavoix, Henri. "Les Opéras madrigalesques," *Revue et gazette musicale* XLIV (1877) 307–9, 323–24, 331–32.

Lebègue, Raymond. Le Mystère des Actes des Apôtres. Paris, Champion, 1929.

—— "Les Représentations dramatiques à la cour des Valois," in *Les Fêtes de la Renaissance* (Paris, Centre National de la Recherche Scientifique, 1956) 85–91.

Liliencron, Rochus, Freiherr von. "Die Chorgesänge des lateinischen-deutschen Schuldramas im 16. Jahrhundert," VfMw VI (1890) 309–87.

Lipphardt, Walther. Die Weisen der lateinischen Osterspiele des 12. und 13. Jahrhunderts. Kassel, Bärenreiter, [1948].

Liuzzi, Fernando. "Drammi musicali dei secoli XI–XIV," *Studi medievali, nuova serie* III (1930) 82–109.

—— "L'espressione musicale nel dramma liturgico," *Studi medievali, nuova serie* II (1929) 74–109.

Lozzi, C. "La musica e specialmente il melodramma alla Corte Medicea," RMI IX (1902) 297–338.

Lucianus Samosatensis. Lucian; with an English Translation by A. M. Harmon. London, W. Heinemann; New York, Macmillan, 1913–36. Contains "On the Dance," V, 209–89.

Lupo, Bettina. "Scene e persone musicale dell' *Amfiparnaso*," RassM XI (1938) 445–59.

Marsan, Jules. La Pastorale dramatique en France à la fin du XVIe et au commencement du XVIIe siècle. Paris, Hachette, 1905.

Martin, Henriette. "La 'Camerata' du Comte Bardi et la musique floren-tine du XVIe siècle," RdM XIII (1932) 63–74, 152–61, 227–34; XIV (1933) 92–100, 141–51.

Modena. Accademia di Scienze, Lettere ed Arti in Modena. Orazio Vecchi, precursore del melodramma (1550–1605) nel IV centenario della nascità. Contributi di studio raccolti dalla Accademia di Scienze, Lettere ed Arti di Modena. Modena, 1950.

Mone, Franz Joseph, ed. Altdeutsche Schauspiele. Quedlinburg and Leip-zig, G. Basse, 1841.

—— Schauspiele des Mittelalters. Karlsruhe, C. Macklot, 1846. 2 vols.

Morphy, G., compiler. Les Luthistes espagnoles du XVIe siècle. Leipzig, B&H, 1902. 2 vols.

Mountford, J. F. "Greek Music in the Papyri and Inscriptions," in J.

Powell and E. Barber, *New Chapters in the History of Greek Literature,* *Second Series* (London, Oxford University Press, 1929) 146–83.

Musique et poésie au XVIe siècle. Paris. Editions du Centre National de la Recherche Scientifique, [1954].

Nagel, Willibald. "Die Chöre aus *Philargyrus* von Petrus Dasypodius," MfMg XXI (1889) 109–12.

—— "Die Musik in den schweitzerischen Dramen des 16. Jahrhunderts," MfMg XXII (1890) 67–83.

Neri, Achille. "Gli intermezzi del *Pastor fido,*" *Giornale storico della letteratura italiana* XI (1888) 405–15.

Nolhac, Pierre, and Angelo Solerti. Il viaggio in Italia di Enrico III, re di Francia, e le feste a Venezia, Ferrara, Mantova, e Torino. Turin, L. Roux, 1890.

Orel, Alfred. "Die Weisen im 'Wiener-Passionsspiel' aus dem 13. Jahrhundert," *Mitteilungen des Vereins für Geschichte der Stadt Wien* VI (1926) 72–95.

Palisca, Claude V. "Girolamo Mei : Mentor to the Florentine Camerata," MQ XL (1954) 1–20.

—— "Vincenzo Galilei and Some Links between 'Pseudo-Monody' and Monody," MQ XLVI (1960) 344–60.

Palisca, Claude V., ed. Girolamo Mei (1519–1594) : Letters on Ancient and Modern Music to Vincenzo Galilei and Giovanni Bardi. A Study with Annotated Texts. [Rome], American Institute of Musicology, 1960.

Pedrell, Felipe. "*La Festa d'Elche* ou le drame lyrique liturgique La Mort et l'assomption de la Vierge," SIMG II (1900–1901) 203–52.

Perinello, C. "L' *Amfiparnaso* di Horatio Vecchi," RMI XLI (1937) 1–23.

Phalèse. *See* Hortus musarum.

Pirrotta, Nino. "Temperaments and Tendencies in the Florentine Camerata," MQ XL (1954) 169–89. Originally published in Italian in *Le manifestazioni culturali dell' Accademia Nazionale di Santa Cecilia.* Rome, 1953.

—— "Tragédie et comédie dans la 'Camerata fiorentina,'" in *Musique et poésie au XVIe siècle* (Paris, Editions du Centre National de la Recherche Scientifique, 1954) 287–97.

Poliziano, Angelo Ambrogini, known as. Le stanze, l'Orfeo e le rime. Florence, G. Barbèra, 1863.

—— Orfeo. *See* Casella, Alfredo.

Prunières, Henry. "Ronsard et les fêtes de cour," RM V (May, 1924) 27–44.

Quittard, Henri. "L' *Hortus musarum* de 1552–53 et les arrangements de pièces polyphoniques pour voix seule et luth," SIMG VIII (1906–7) 254–85.

—— "Le Théorbe comme instrument d'accompagnement," *Bulletin français de la SIM.* (1910) 221–37, 362–84.

Reese, Gustave. Music in the Middle Ages. New York, W. W. Norton, [1940].

—— Music in the Renaissance. New York, W. W. Norton, 1954.

Refardt, Edgar. "Die Musik der Basler Volksschauspiele des 16. Jahrhunderts," AfMw III (1921) 199.

Reinach, Théodore. La Musique grècque. Paris, Payot, 1926.

Rolandi, Ulderico. "Didascalie sceniche in un libretto dell' *Euridice* del Rinuccini (1600)," RMI XXXIII (1926) 21–27.

Rolland, Romain. "Les Origines de l'opéra et les travaux de M. Angelo Solerti," RHCM III (1903) 127–29, 280–82.

Roncaglia, Gino. "Gli elementi precursori del melodramma nell' opera di Orazio Vecchi : Attuazioni e limiti," RMI LV (1953) 251–56.

—— "Orazio Vecchi, precursore drammatico ed umorista," RMI LI (1949) 265–73.

Ronga, Luigi. "Lettura storica dell' *Amfiparnaso*," RassM XXIII (1953) 101–15.

[Rossi, Bastiano de'.] Descrizione dell' apparato e degli intermedi fatti per la commedia rappresentata in Firenze nelle nozze de' serenissimi Don Ferdinando Medici, e Madama Cristina di Loreno, gran duchi di Toscana. Florence, A. Padouani, 1589.

Rothschild, James, Baron de, ed. Le Mistère du Viel Testament. Paris, Firmin-Didot, 1878–91. 6 vols.

Rubsamen, Walter. Literary Sources of Secular Music in Italy (ca. 1500). Berkeley and Los Angeles, University of California Press, 1943.

Sachs, Curt. Die Musik der Antike. Potsdam, Athenaion, [1928].

Sacre rappresentazioni nel manoscritto 201 della Bibliothèque municipale di Orléans. Ed. fototipica. Testi e musiche trascritti e commentati da Giampiero Tintori. Precede uno studio di Raffaello Monterosso. Cremona, Athenaeum Cremonense, 1958.

Schering, Arnold. "Zur Geschichte des begleiteten Sologesangs im 16. Jahrhundert," ZIMG XIII (1911–12) 190–96.

Schlitzer, Franco. "A Letter from Cesti to Salvator Rosa," MMR LXXXIV (1954) 150–52.

Schneider, Max. Die Anfänge des Basso Continuo und seiner Bezifferung. Leipzig, B&H, 1918.

—— "Zur Geschichte des begleiteten Sologesangs," *Festschrift Hermann Kretzschmar zum 70. Geburtstage überreicht von Kollegen, Schülern, und Freunden* (Leipzig, C. F. Peters, 1918) 138–40.

Schoenemann, Otto. "Der Sündenfall und Marienklage : Zwei niederdeutsche Schauspiele," MfMg VII (1875) 129–39, 145–57.

Schrade, Leo. "Les Fêtes du mariage de Francesco dei Medici et de Bianca Cappello [1579]," in Les Fêtes de la Renaissance (Paris, Editions du Centre National de la Recherche Scientifique, 1956) 107–31.

—— La Représentation d' Edipo Tiranno au Teatro Olimpico (Vicenze

1585). Paris, Editions du Centre National de la Recherche Scientifique, 1960.

Schuler, Ernst August. Die Musik der Osterfeiern, Osterspiele und Passionen des Mittelalters. Kassel & Basel, Bärenreiter, [1951].

Schwietering, Julius. "Ueber den liturgischen Ursprung des mittelalterlichen geistlichen Spiels," *Zeitschrift für deutsche Altertum* LXII (1925) 1–20.

Sievers, Heinrich. Die lateinischen liturgischen Osterspiele der Stiftskirche St. Blasien zu Braunschweig. Wolfenbüttel, Georg Kallmeyer, 1936.

Silbert, Doris. "Francesca Caccini, Called La Cecchina," MQ XXXII (1946) 50–62.

Smits van Waesberghe, Jos. "A Dutch Easter Play," MD VII (1953) 15–37.

—— Muziek en drama in de Middeleeuwen. Amsterdam, Bigot & Van Rossum, 1942.

Smoldon, William L. "The Easter Sepulchre Music-Drama," M&L XXVII (1946) 1–17.

—— "Medieval Church Drama and the Use of Musical Instruments," *The Musical Times* CIII, No. 1438 (December, 1962) 836–40.

—— "The Music of the Medieval Church Drama," MQ XLVIII (1962) 476–97.

Solerti, Angelo. Gli albori del melodramma. Milan; R. Sandron, [1905]. 3 vols.

—— "Laura Guidiccioni ed Emilio de' Cavalieri : I primi tentativi del melodramma," RMI IX (1902) 797–829.

—— "Precedenti del melodramma," RMI X (1903) 207–33, 466–84.

—— "Primi saggi del melodramma giocoso," RMI XII (1905) 814–38; XIII (1906) 91–112.

—— Vita di Torquato Tasso. Turin, Rome, E. Loescher, 1895. 3 vols.

Solerti, Angelo, ed. Ferrara e la corte Estense nella seconda metà del secolo decimosesto : I discorsi di Annibale Romei, gentiluomo ferrarese. Città di Castello, S. Lapi, 1891.

Solerti, Angelo, compiler and ed. Le origini del melodramma : Testimonianze dei contemporanei. Turin, Fratelli Bocca, 1903.

Sonneck, Oscar George Theodore. "A Description of Alessandro Striggio and Francesco Corteccia's Intermedi *Psyche and Amore*, 1565," MA III (1911) 40.

Sternfeld, Frederick W. "Le Symbolisme musical dans quelques pièces de Shakespeare présentées à la cour d'Angleterre," in *Les Fêtes de la Renaissance* (Paris, Editions du Centre National de la Recherche Scientifique, 1956) 319–33.

Stevens, John. "Music in Mediæval Drama," PMA LXXXIV (1957–58) 81–95.

Stratman, Carl J. Bibliography of Medieval Drama. Berkeley and Los Angeles, University of California Press, 1954.

Symonds, John Addington. The Renaissance in Italy : Italian Literature. New York, Henry Holt, 1882. 2 vols.

Tasso, Torquato. Opere. Pisa, Capuro, 1821–32. 33 vols.

Teatro italiano antico. Milan, 1808–12. 10 vols.

Thomas, L. P. "Les Strophes et la composition du Sponsus," *Romania* LV (1929) 45–112.

—— "La Versification et les leçons douteuses du Sponsus," *Romania* LIII (1927) 43–81.

Tiby, Ottavio. La musica bizantina, teoria e storia. Milan, Fratelli Bocca, 1938.

Tiersot, Julien. "Ronsard et la musique de son temps," SIMG IV (1902–3) 70–142.

Tirabassi, M. A. "Introduction à l'étude de la parabole des vierges sages et des vierges folles," *Annales de la Société R. d' archéologie de Bruxelles* XXXII (1926) 15.

Toffani, Giuseppe, ed. Storia letteraria d'Italia : Il Cinquecento. Milan, Vallardi, 1929. 3d ed.

Trend, John Brande. "The Mystery of Elche," M&L I (1920) 145–57.

Turrini, G. "De Vlaamsche Componist Giovanni Nasco te Verona (1547–1551)," *Tijdschrift der Vereeniging voor Nederl. Muziekgeschiedenis* XIV, No. 3 (1935) 132–59; XV, No. 2 (1937) 84–93. Also in Italian, *Note d'archivio* XIV (1937) 180–225.

Tutti i trionfi, carri, mascherate, o Cante carnascialeschi andati per Firenze dal tempo del magnifico Lorenzo de' Medici fino all' anno 1559. Cosmopoli [i.e., Lucca], 1750. 2d ed.

Ursprung, Otto. "Das Sponsus-Spiel," AfMf III (1938) 80–95, 180–92.

Vecchi, Giuseppe. Uffici drammatici padovani. Florence, L. S. Olschki, 1954.

Vecchi, Orazio. *L'Amfiparnaso*. Trascrizione e interpretazione di Bonaventura Somma. Rome, De Santis, [1953].

Vicentino, Nicola. L'antica musica ridotta alla moderna prattica. Rome, A. Barre, 1555.

Walker, D. P. "Musical Humanism in the 16th and Early 17th Centuries," MR II (1941) 1–13, 111–21, 220–27, 288–308; III (1942) 55–71.

—— Der musikalische Humanismus in 16. und frühen 17. Jahrhunderts. Kassel & Basel, Bärenreiter, 1949.

—— "La Musique des intermèdes florentins de 1589 et l'humanisme," in *Les Fêtes de la Renaissance* (Paris, Editions du Centre National de la Recherche Scientifique, 1956) 133–44.

Weakland, Rembert. "The Rhythmic Modes and Medieval Latin Drama," JAMS XIV (1961) 131–46.

Wessely, Carl. Antike Reste griechischer Musik. [Vienna, 1891.]

Yates, Frances A. "Dramatic Religious Processions in Paris in the Late Sixteenth Century," *Annales musicologiques* II (1954) 215–70.

—— The French Academies of the Sixteenth Century. [London], Warburg Institute, University of London, 1947.

—— "Poésie et musique pour les magnificences du mariage du Duc de Joyeuse, Paris, 1581," in *Musique et poésie au XVIe siècle* (Paris, Editions du Centre National de la Recherche Scientifique, 1954) 248.

Young, Karl. The Drama of the Medieval Church. Oxford, Clarendon Press, 1933. 2 vols.

Zarlino, Gioseffo. Le istituzioni harmoniche. Venetia, [Pietro da Fino?], 1558.

# III

## *SEVENTEENTH CENTURY*

Abert, Anna Amalie. Claudio Monteverdi und das musikalische Drama. Lippstadt, Kistner & Siegel, 1954.

—— "Schauspiel und Opernlibretto im italienischen Barock," Mf II (1949) 133–41.

Adel, Kurt. Das Jesuitendrama in Oesterreich. Vienna, Bergland-Verlag, [1957].

Ademollo, Alessandro. La bell' Adriana ed altre virtuose del suo tempo alla corte di Mantova : Contributo de documenti per la storia della musica in Italia nel primo quarto del Seicento. Città di Castello, Lapi, 1888.

—— I primi fasti del teatro di via della Pergola in Firenze (1657–1661). Milan, Ricordi, [etc., 1885].

—— I teatri di Roma nel secolo decimosettimo. Rome, L. Pasqualucci, 1888.

Adler, Guido. "Einleitung [to Cesti's *Pomo d'oro*]," DTOe, Jahrg. III, Part 2 (1896) v–xxvi.

—— "Die Kaiser Ferdinand III., Leopold I., Joseph I. und Karl VI. als Tonsetzer und Förderer der Musik," VfMw VIII (1892) 252–74.

Alaleona, Domenico. Studi su la storia dell' oratorio musicale in Italia. Turin, Bocca, 1908.

Aldrich, Putnam C. The Principal Agréments of the Seventeenth and Eighteenth Centuries : A Study in Musical Ornamentation. Harvard Dissertation, 1942.

Allacci, Leone. Drammaturgia . . . accresciuta e continuata fino all' anno MDCCLV. Venice, G. Pasquali, 1755. First published Rome, 1666.

Allam, Edward. "Alessandro Stradella," PMA LXXX (1954) 29–42.

Amour, L. Maurice. "Les Musiciens de Corneille, 1650–1699," RdM XXXVII (1955) 43–75.

Apel, Willi. "Anent a Ritornello in Monteverdi's *Orfeo*," MD V (1951) 213–22.

Arger, Jane. Les Agréments et le rhythme : Leur représentation graphique dans la musique vocale française du XVIIe siècle. Paris, Rouàrt, Lerolle, [pref. 1917].

Arger, Jane. "Le Rôle expressif des 'agréments' dans l'école vocale française de 1680 à 1760," RdM I (1917–19) 215–26.

Arnheim, Amalie. "Ein Beitrag zur Geschichte des einstimmigen weltlichen Kunstliedes in Frankreich im 17. Jahrhundert," SIMG X (1908–9) 399–421.

Arnold, Frank T. The Art of Accompaniment from a Thorough-Bass as Practiced in the XVIIth and XVIIIth Centuries. London, Oxford University Press, 1931.

Arundell, Dennis. The Critic at the Opera. London, Benn, 1957.

—— Henry Purcell. London, Oxford University Press, 1927.

Bannard, Yorke. "Music of the Commonwealth," M&L III (1922) 394–401.

Barclay Squire. See Squire, W. Barclay.

Barthélemy, Maurice. André Campra, sa vie et son oeuvre (1660–1744). Paris, Picard, 1957.

—— "La Musique dramatique à Versailles de 1660 à 1715," XVIIe siècle No. 34 (March, 1957) 7–18.

—— "Les Opéras de Marin Marais," RBM VII (1953) 136–46.

—— "L'Orchestre et l'orchestration des oeuvres de Campra," RM No. sp. 226 (1955) 97–104.

Bartmuss, Arwed Waldemar. Die Hamburger Barockoper und ihre Bedeutung für die Entwicklung der deutschen Dichtung und der deutschen Bühne. Jena Dissertation, 1925.

Bauer, Anton. Opern und Operetten in Wien : Verzeichnis ihrer Erstaufführungen in der Zeit von 1629 bis zur Gegenwart. Graz, Cologne, Vienna, Hermann Böhlaus Nachfolge, 1955.

Baxter, William Hubbard, Jr. Agostino Steffani : A Study of the Man and His Work. University of Rochester Dissertation, 1957. 2 vols.

Beare, Mary. The German Popular Play Atis and the Venetian Opera : A Study of the Conversion of Operas into Popular Plays, 1675–1722. Cambridge, University Press, 1938.

Beaujoyeulx, Baltasar de. Balet comique de la royne, faict aux nopces de Monsieur le Duc de Ioyeuse & madamoyselle de Vaudemont sa soeur. Paris, LeRoy, Ballard & Patisson, 1682.

Becker, Heinz. "[Review of :] Hellmuth Christian Wolff : Die Barockoper in Hamburg (1678–1738)," Mf XIII (1960) 211–14.

Benham, Evelyn. "A Musical Monopolist [J. B. Lully]," M&L IX (1928) 249–54.

Benvenuti, Giacomo. "Il manoscritto veneziano della Incoronazione di Poppea," RMI XLI (1937) 176–84.

Berend, Fritz. Nicolaus Adam Strungk. Hanover, E. Homann, [1915].

Bergmans, Paul. "Une Collection de livrets d'opéras italiens (1669–1710)," SIMG XII (1910–11) 221–34.

Bernhard, Christoph. Die Kompositionslehre Heinrich Schützens in der

Fassung seines Schülers Christoph Bernhard. Edited with an introduction by J. M. Müller-Blattau. Leipzig, B&H, 1926.

Bertolotti, Antonio. Artisti francesi in Roma nei secoli XV, XVI e XVII. Mantua, Mondovi, 1894.

—— Musici alla corte dei Gonzaga in Mantova dal secolo XV al XVII: Notizie e documenti raccolti negli Archivi Mantovani. Milan, Ricordi, [1890].

Bicknell, Joan Colleen. Interdependence of Word and Tone in the Dramatic Music of Henry Purcell. Stanford University Dissertation, 1960.

Bittrich, Gerhard. Ein deutsches Opernballett des siebzehnten Jahrhunderts : Ein Beitrag zur Frühgeschichte der deutschen Oper. Leipzig, Frommhold & Wendler, 1931.

Blaze, [François Henri Joseph], called Castil-Blaze. L'Académie impériale de musique . . . de 1645 à 1855. Paris, Castil-Blaze, 1855.

—— Chapelle-musique des rois de France. Paris, Paulin, 1832.

—— De l'opéra en France. Paris, Janet et Cotelle, 1820.

—— L'Opéra-Italien de 1548 à 1856. Paris, Castil-Blaze, 1856.

Blümml, Emil Karl, and Gustav Gugitz. Alt-Wiener Thespiskarren : Die Frühzeit der Wiener Vorstadtbühnen. Vienna, A. Schroll, 1925.

Böhme, Erdmann Werner. "Die frühdeutsche Oper in Altenburg," *Jahrbuch der Theaterfreunde für Altenburg und Umkreis* (1930) 53 ff.

—— Die frühdeutsche Oper in Thüringen. Stadtroda in Thuringia, Richter, 1931.

—— Musik und Oper am Hofe Christians von Sachsen-Eisenberg (1677–1707). Stadtroda in Thuringia, Richter, [1930]. First published in *Mitteilungen des Geschichts- und Altertumsvereins zu Eisenberg in Thüringen*, 41. und 42. Heft (8. Band, 1. und 2. Heft, 1930).

—— "Zur Vorgeschichte der Barockoper in Altenburg," *Jahrbuch der Theaterfreunde für Altenburg und Umkreis* (1931).

Böttger, Friedrich. Die "Comédie-Ballet" von Molière-Lully. Berlin, Funk, 1931.

Boislisle, Arthur Michel de. "Les Débuts de l'opéra français à Paris," *Mémoires de la Société de l'histoire de Paris* II (1876) 172 ff.

Bonaventura, Arnaldo. "Una celebre cantante livornese del Settecento," *Musica d'oggi* VI (1924) 255–58.

Borcherdt, Hans Heinrich. "Beiträge zur Geschichte der Oper und des Schauspiels in Schlesien bis zum Jahre 1740," *Zeitschrift für die Geschichte Schlesiens* XLIII (1909) 217 ff.

Borrel, Eugène. L'Interprétation de la musique française (de Lully à la révolution). Paris, F. Alcan, 1924.

—— "L'Interprétation de l'ancien récitatif français," RdM XII (1931) 13–21.

—— Jean-Baptiste Lully : Le cadre, la vie, la personnalité, le rayonnement, les oeuvres, bibliographie. Paris, La Colombe, 1949.

Borrel, Eugène. "Les Notes inégales dans l'ancienne musique française," RdM XII (1931) 278–89.

—— "Remarques sur l'histoire de la musique au théâtre en France au XVIIe siècle," RdM XXXIX (1957) 56–60.

Borren, Charles van den. *Il ritorno d'Ulisse in patria* du Claudio Monteverdi. Brussels, Weissenbruch, 1925.

Bowden, William R. The English Dramatic Lyric, 1603–42 : A Study in Stuart Dramatic Technique. New Haven, Yale University Press, 1951.

Bragaglia, Anton Giulio. "Celebrazioni Marchigiane : Giacomo Torelli da Fano," *Il giornale di politica e di letteratura* X (1934) 331–62; XI (1935) 69–80.

Bricqueville, Eugène de. Le Livret d'opéra français de Lully à Gluck. Brussels, 1888.

Briganti, Francesco. Gio. Andrea Angelini-Bontempi (1624–1705) musicista, letterato, architetto : Perugia-Dresda. Florence, L.S. Olschki, 1956.

Bukofzer, Manfred F. Music in the Baroque Era. New York, W. W. Norton, 1947.

Caccini, Giulio. Le nuove musiche : Riproduzione dell' edizione dell' 1601. Rome, Raccolte Claudio Monteverdi (R. Mezzetti), 1930.

Calmus, Georgy. "Drei satirisch-kritische Aufsätze von Addison über die italienische Oper in England," SIMG IX (1907–8) 131–45, 448.

Cametti, Alberto. "Alcuni documenti inediti su la vita di Luigi Rossi," SIMG XIV (1912–13) 1–26.

—— Christina di Svezia, l'arte musicale e gli spettacoli teatrali in Roma. Rome, Tipografia Romano Mezzetti, 1931.

—— Il teatro di Tordinona, poi di Apollo. Tivoli, A. Chicca, 1939.

Capri, Antonio. Il Seicento musicale in Europa. Milan, Hoepli, 1933.

Carfagno, Simon A. The Life and Dramatic Music of Stefano Landi with a Transliteration and Orchestration of the Opera *Sant' Alessio*. University of California, Los Angeles Dissertation, 1960. 2 vols. in 4.

Carlez, Jules. Pierre et Thomas Corneille librettistes. N.p., n.d.

—— La *Sémiramis* de Destouches. Caen, H. Delesques, 1892.

Castil-Blaze. *See* Blaze.

Catelani, Angelo. Delle opere di Alessandro Stradella esistente nel l'archivio musicale della R. Biblioteca Palatina di Modena. Modena, C. Vincenzi, 1866.

Cavalli, Francesco. Venti arie tratte dai drami musicali di Francesco Cavalli. Vienna-Trieste, Verlag Schmiedel (Mozarthaus), 1909.

Celani, Enrico. "Canzoni musicale del secolo XVII," RMI XII (1905) 109–50.

Champigneulle, Bernard. "L'Influence de Lully hors de France," RM XXII (February–March, 1946) 26–35.

Chevaillier, Lucien. "Le Récit chez Monteverdi," RHCM X (1910) 284–94.

Chrysander, Friedrich. "Eine englische Serenata von J. Sigismund Kusser um 1710," AMZ XIV (1879) 408–12, 417–22.

—— "Die Feier des zweihundertjährigen Bestandes der Oper in Hamburg," AMZ XIII (1878) 113–15, 129–32, 145–48.

—— "Geschichte der Braunschweig-Wolfenbüttelschen Capelle und Oper vom XVI. bis zum XVIII. Jahrhundert," *Jahrbücher für musikalische Wissenschaft* I (1863) 147–286.

—— ["Geschichte der Hamburger Oper"], AMZ XII–XV (1877–80):
  "Die erste Periode," AMZ XII (1877) 369–486 *passim*
  "Die zweite Periode," AMZ XIII (1878) 289–442 *passim*
  ". . . unter . . . J. S. Kusser 1693–1696," AMZ XIV (1879) 385–408 *passim*
  ". . . vom Abgange Kusser's bis zum Tode Schott's," AMZ XIV (1879) 433–534 *passim*
  ". . . unter der Direction von Reinhard Keiser (1703–1706)," AMZ XV (1880) 17–87 *passim*.

Clark, George Norman. The Seventeenth Century. Oxford, Clarendon Press, 1929.

Clarke, Henry Leland. "Cambert, Lully, and Blow." Unpublished essay.

—— Dr. John Blow (1649–1708), Last Composer of an Era. Harvard Dissertation, 1947.

Collaer, Paul. "L'orchestra di Claudio Monteverdi," *Musica* II (Florence, 1943) 86–104.

[Conti, Armand de Bourbon, prince de.] Traité de la comédie et des spectacles selon la tradition de l'église, tirée des conciles & des saints pères. Paris, L. Billaine, 1669.

Coradini, Francesco. Antonio Maria Abbatini e d. Lorenzo Abbatini: Notizie biografiche. Arezzo, Scuola tipografica aretina, 1922.

—— "P. Antonio Cesti: Nuove notizie biografiche," RMI XXX (1923) 371–88.

Coryate, Thomas. Coryat's Crudities . . . New York, Macmillan, 1905. Originally published 1611.

Cousser, Jean Sigismond. Composition de musique, suivant la méthode françoise . . . Stoutgard, 1684.

Crocioni, Giovanni. L'Alidoro o dei primordi del melodramma. Bologna, L. Parma, 1938.

Crussard, Claude. "Marc-Antoine Charpentier théoricien," RdM XXVII (2e–3e trimestre 1945) 49–68.

—— Un Musicien français oublié, Marc-Antoine Charpentier. Paris, Floury, 1945.

Cummings, William H. "Matthew Locke, Composer for the Church and Theatre," SIMG XIII (1911–12) 120–26.

Cutts, John. "Le Rôle de la musique dans les masques de Ben Jonson et notammement dans *Oberon* (1610–1611)," in *Les Fêtes de la Renaissance* (Paris, Editions du Centre National de la Recherche Scientifique, 1956) 285–303.

Davari, Stefano. "Notizie biografiche del distinto maestro di musica

Claudio Monteverdi," *Atti e memorie della R. Accademia Virgiliana di Mantova* X (1884–85) 79–183.

De Angelis, Alberto. "Il teatro farnese di Parma," RMI XLIII (1939) 364–82.

Dedekind, Constantin Christian. Heilige Arbeit über Freud und Leid der alten und neuen Zeit in Music-bekwehmen Schau-Spielen (9) ahngewendet. Dresden, 1676.

—— Neue geistliche Schauspiele (5) bekwehmet zur Musik. [Dresden], 1670.

Deierkauf-Holsboer, S. Wilma. Le Théâtre du Marais. II : Le Berceau de L'Opéra et de la Comédie-française, 1648–1673. Paris, Nizet, 1958.

DeLage, Joseph O., Jr. The Overture in Seventeenth-Century Italian Opera. Ann Arbor, University Microfilms, 1961.

Della Corte, Andrea. "*La forza d'amor paterno* di Alessandro Stradella," *Musica d'oggi* XIII (1931) 389–94.

—— "Tragico e comico nell' opera veneziana della seconda parte del Seicento," RassM XI (1938) 325–33.

Demarquez, Suzanne. Purcell: La Vie, l'oeuvre, discographie. Paris, La Colombe, [1951].

Demuth, Norman. "A Musical Backwater," MQ XL (1954) 533–47.

Denizard, Marie. "La Famille française de Lully," MM VIII, No. 5 (1912) 1–14.

Dent, Edward J. "The Baroque Opera," MA I (1909–10) 93–107.

—— Foundations of English Opera. Cambridge (England), University Press, 1928.

—— "Italian Chamber Cantatas," MA II (1911) 142–53, 185–99.

—— "The Musical Interpretation of Shakespeare on the Modern Stage," MQ II (1916) 523–37.

De' Paoli, Domenico. Claudio Monteverdi. Milan, Hoepli, 1945.

De Rensis, Raffaello. Ercole Bernabei. Rome, tip. Sociale, 1920.

—— "Un musicista diplomatico del Settecento : Agostino Steffani," *Musica d'oggi* III, No. 5 (May, 1921) 129–32.

"Documents historiques : Les origines de l'opéra en France," RHCM VIII (1908) 562–64.

Doebner, Richard, ed. Briefe der Königin Sophie Charlotte von Preussen und der Kurfürstin Sophie von Hannover an hannoversche Diplomaten. Leipzig, S. Hirzel, 1905.

Doni, Giovanni Battista. Compendio del trattato de' generi de' modi della mvsica. Rome, A. Fei, 1635.
Abstract of a larger work which was never published. Portions of this work are quoted in Solerti's *Origini* under the title "Trattato della musica scenica."

—— Lyra Barberina ΑΜΦΙΧΟΡΔΟΣ : Accedunt eiusdem opera, pleaque nondum edita ad veterem musicam illustrandam pertinentia. Florentiae typis Caesareis, 1763. 2 vols.

Ducharte, Pierre-Louis. La Commedia dell' arte et ses enfants. Paris, Editions d' "Art et Industrie," 1955.

Du Gérard, N. B. Tables alphabetique & chronologique de pieces representées sur l'ancien Theatre italien, depuis son etablissement jusqu'en 1697. Paris, Prault, 1750.

Dupré, Henri. Purcell. Paris, Alcan, 1927. Translated, New York, Alfred A. Knopf, 1928.

Ecorcheville, Jules. "Corneille et la musique," Courrier musical IX (1906) 405–12, 438–49. Also separate : Paris, Fortin, 1906.

—— De Lulli à Rameau, 1690–1730 : L'esthétique musicale. Paris, Fortin, 1906.

—— "Lully gentilhomme et sa descendance," MM VII, No. 5 (1911) 1–19; No. 6, pp. 1–27; No. 7, pp. 36–52.

Ehrichs, Alfred. Giulio Caccini. Leipzig, Hesse & Becker, 1908.

Einstein, Alfred. "Agostino Steffani," Kirchenmusikalisches Jahrbuch XXIII (1910) 1–36.

—— "Agostino Steffani," Neue Musik-Zeitung XLIX (1928) 316–19.

—— "Ein Bericht über den Turiner Mordanfall auf Alessandro Stradella," in Festschrift Adolf Sandberger (Munich, Zierfuss, 1918) 135–37.

Eitner, Robert. "Johann Philipp Krieger," MfMg XXIX (1897) 114–17.

Eitner, Robert, ed. "Das älteste bekannte deutsche Singspiel, Seelewig, von S. G. Staden, 1644," MfMg XIII (1881) 53–147.

Engelke, Bernhard. Musik und Musiker am Gottorfer Hofe. Band 1. Die Zeit der englischen Komödianten (1590–1627). Breslau, Hirt, 1930.

Engländer, Richard. "Il Paride in musica (1662) di G. A. Bontempi," Note d'archivio XVII (1940) 39–53.

—— "Zur Frage der Dafne (1671) von G. A. Bontempi und M. G. Peranda," Acta musicologica XIII (1941) 59–77.

Enzinger, Moriz. Die Entwicklung des Wiener Theaters vom 16. zum 19. Jahrhundert. Berlin, Gesellschaft für Theatergeschichte, 1918–19. 2 vols.

Eppelsheim, Jürgen. Das Orchester in den Werken Jean-Baptiste Lullys. Tutzing, H. Schneider, 1961.

Epstein, Peter. "Dichtung und Musik in Monteverdi's Lamento d'Arianna," ZfMw X (1927–28) 216–22.

—— "Zur Rhythmisierung eines Ritornells von Monteverdi," AfMw VIII (1926) 416–19.

Evans, Herbert Arthur, ed. English Masques. London, Glasgow, Blackie & Son, 1897.

Evans, Willa McClung. Ben Jonson and Elizabethan Music. Lancaster, Pa., Lancaster Press, 1929.

Evelyn, John. Diary. London, J. M. Dent, 1907. 2 vols.

Fassini, Sesto. "Gli albori del melodramma italiano a Londra," Giornale storico della letteratura italiana LX (1912) 340–76.

Fellerer, Karl Gustav. Beiträge zur Musikgeschichte Freisings. Freising, Freising. Tagbl., 1926.

Fetting, Hugo. Die Geschichte der Deutschen Staatsoper. Berlin, Henschel, 1955.

Finney, Gretchen Ludke. "Chorus in *Samson Agonistes*," *Publications of the Modern Language Association of America* LVIII (1943) 649–64.

—— "*Comus*, Dramma per Musica," *Studies in Philology* XXXVII (1940) 483–500; also separate.

Flemming, Willi, ed. Die Oper. Leipzig, Reclam, 1933.

Flood, W. H. Grattan. "Quelques Précisions nouvelles sur Cambert et Grabu à Londres," RM IX (August, 1928) 351–61.

Florence, Italy. R. Istituto musicale. Atti dell' accademia del R. Istituto musicale di Firenze, Anno XXXIII : Commemorazione della riforma melodrammatica. Florence, Galletti e Cocci, 1895.

Fogaccia, Piero. Giovanni Legrenzi. Bergamo, Edizioni Orobiche, [1954].

Forsyth, Cecil. Music and Nationalism : A Study of English Opera. London, Macmillan, 1911.

Fortune, Nigel. "Italian Secular Monody from 1600 to 1635 : An Introductory Survey," MQ XXXIX (1953) 171–95.

—— "Italian 17th-Century Singing," M&L XXXV (1954) 206–19.

Frati, Lodovico. "Per la storia della musica in Bologna nel secolo XVII," RMI XXXII (1925) 544–65.

Freund, Hans, and Wilhelm Reinking. Musikalisches Theater in Hamburg: Versuch über die Dramaturgie der Oper. Hamburg, Hans Christians, 1938.

Friess, Hermann. 300 Jahr Münchener Oper. [Munich, im Auftrag der Intendanz der Bayerischen Staatsoper, s.d.]

Fürstenau, Moritz. "Die Oper *Antiope* und die Bestellungen des Kurfürstlich Sächsischen Vicekapellmeisters Nicolaus Adam Strunck und des Hofpoeten Stefano Pallavicini," MfMg XIII (1881) 1–6.

—— "Eine theologische Zeitschrift des 17. Jahrhunderts über Castraten und Oper : Johann Samuel Adami," *Musikalisches Wochenblatt* I (1870) 241–43.

—— Zur Geschichte der Musik und des Theaters am Hofe zu Dresden. Dresden, R. Kuntze, 1861–62. 2 parts.

Gaspari, Gaetano. "Dei musicisti Bolognesi al XVII secolo e delle loro opere a stampa," *Atti e memorie della R. R. Deputazione di storia patria per le provincie dell' Emilia, Nuova serie* III (1878) 1–24.

Gastoué, Amadée. "Les Notes inédites du Marquis de Paulmy sur les oeuvres lyriques françaises (1655–1775)," RdM Série spéciale, No. 1 (1943) 1–7.

Geffcken, Johannes. "Die ältesten Hamburgischen Opern," *Zeitschrift des Vereines für Hamburgische Geschichte* III (1851) 34–55.

Gentili, Alberto. "Alessandro Stradella," in *Miscellanea della Facoltà di*

*Lettere e Filosofia, Serie Prima* (Turin, R. Università di Torino, 1936) 155–76.

Gérold, Théodore. L'Art du chant en France au XVIIe siècle. Strasbourg, G. Fischbach, 1921.

Ghisi, Federico. Del *Fuggilotio musicale* di Giulio Romano (Caccini): Saggio critico. Rome, De Santis, 1934.

Ghislanzoni, Alberto. Luigi Rossi (Aloysius de Rubeis), biografia e analisi delle composizioni. Milan-Rome, Fratelli Bocca, [cop. 1954].

Giazotto, Remo. Il melodramma a Genova nei secoli 17 & 18 : Con gli elenchi completi dei titoli, dei musicisti, dei poeti e degli attori di quei componomenti rappresentati fra il 1652 e il 1771 ai teatre detti "Del Falcone" e "Da S. Agostino." Genoa, A cura dell' ente del Teatro Carlo Felice, 1941.

—— Vita di Alessandro Stradella. [Milan], Curci, [1962]. 2 vols.

Goldschmidt, Hugo. "Cavalli als dramatischer Komponist," MfMg XXV (1893) 45–48, 53–58, 61–111.

—— "Claudio Monteverdi's Oper : *Il ritorno d'Ulisse in patria*," SIMG IX (1907–8) 570–92.

—— "Francesco Provenzale als Dramatiker," SIMG VII (1905–6) 608–34.

—— "Die Instrumentalbegleitung der italienischen Musikdramen in der ersten Hälfte des XVII. Jahrhunderts," MfMg XXVII (1895) 52–62.

—— Die italienische Gesangsmethode des XVII. Jahrhunderts und ihre Bedeutung für die Gegenwart. Breslau, Schlesische Buchdruckerei, 1890. 2d ed., Breslau, S. Schottlaender, 1892.

—— Die Lehre von der vokalen Ornamentik, erster Band : Das 17. und 18. Jahrhundert bis in die Zeit Glucks. Charlottenburg, P. Lehsten, 1907.

—— "Monteverdi's *Ritorno d'Ulisse*," SIMG IV (1902–3) 671–76.

—— Studien zur Geschichte der italienischen Oper im 17. Jahrhundert. Leipzig, B&H, 1901–4. 2 vols. Review by R. Rolland, RHCM II (1902) 20–29.

Gołos, Jerzy. "Italian Baroque Opera in Seventeenth-Century Poland," *The Polish Review* VIII, No. 2 (Spring, 1963) 67–75.

Gombosi, Otto. "Some Musical Aspects of the English Court Masque," JAMS I, No. 3 (1948) 3–19.

Grattan Flood. *See* Flood, William Henry Grattan.

Gray, Alan. "Purcell's Dramatic Music," PMA XLIII (1916–17) 51–62.

Groppo, Antonio. Catalogo di tutti i drammi per musica recitati ne' teatri di Venezia dall' anno 1637 sin all' anno presente 1745. Venice, A. Groppo, [1745?].

Gros, Etienne. Philippe Quinault. Paris, E. Champion, 1926.

Grout, Donald Jay. "The Chorus in Early Opera," in *Festschrift Friedrich Blume* (Kassel, Bärenreiter, 1963) [151]–161.

—— "German Baroque Opera," MQ XXXII (1946) 574–87.

—— "The Music of the Italian Theatre at Paris, 1682–1697," in *Papers of the American Musicological Society, Annual Meeting, 1941 ... Edited by Gustave Reese* (Printed by the Society [cop. 1946]) 158–70.

Grout, Donald Jay. "Seventeenth Century Parodies of French Opera," MQ XXVII (1941) 211–19, 514–26.

—— "Some Forerunners of the Lully Opera," M&L XXII (1941) 1–25.

Haar, James. "Astral Music in Seventeenth-Century Nuremberg: The *Tugendsterne* of Harsdörffer and Staden," MD XVI (1962) 175–89.

Haas, Robert M. "Beitrag zur Geschichte der Oper in Prag und Dresden," *Neues Archiv für Sächsische Geschichte und Altertumskunde* XXXVII (1916) 68–96.

—— "Gioseppe Zamponis *Ulisse nell' isola di Circe,*" ZfMw III (1920–21) 385–405.

—— Die Musik des Barocks. Potsdam, Athenaion, [1934].

—— "Zur Neuausgabe von Claudio Monteverdis *Il ritorno d'Ulisse in Patria,*" SzMw IX (1922) 3–42.

Hadamowsky, Franz. Barocktheater am Wiener Kaiserhof: Mit einem Spielplan (1625–1740). Vienna, Sexl, 1955. Reprinted from *Jahrbuch der Gesellschaft für Wiener Theaterforschung,* 1951–52.

Hampe, Theodor. Die Entwicklung des Theaterwesens in Nürnberg von der 2. Hälfte des 15. Jahrhunderts bis 1806. Nuremberg, J. L. Schrag, 1900.

[Harsdörffer, Georg Philipp.] Frauenzimmer Gesprechspiele so bey ehrund tugendliebenden Gesellschaften mit nutzlicher Ergetzlichkeit beliebet und geübet werden mögen. Nuremberg, W. Endtern, 1643–57. 8 vols.

Hartmann, Fritz. Sechs Bücher Braunschweigischer Theatergeschichte. Wolfenbüttel, J. Zwissler, 1905.

[Hawkins, John?] Memoirs of the Life of Sig. Agostino Steffani. [London? 17—.]

Herford, Charles. "Jonson," in *Dictionary of National Biography* X (1917) 1069–79.

Hess, Heinz. Zur Geschichte des musikalischen Dramas im Seicento: Die Opern Alessandro Stradellas. Leipzig, B&H, 1906.

Heuss, Alfred. Die Instrumental-Stücke des *Orfeo* und die venetianischen Opern-Sinfonien. Leipzig, B&H, 1903. (Both parts of this work were published independently in SIMG IV.)

Hjelmborg, Bjørn. "Aspects of the Aria in the Early Operas of Francesco Cavalli," in *Natalicia musicologica Knud Jeppesen* (Copenhagen, W. Hansen, 1962) 173–98.

—— "Une Partition de Cavalli," *Acta musicologica* XVI–XVII (1944–45) 39–54.

Holland, A. K. Henry Purcell: The English Musical Tradition. London, Penguin Books, 1949.

Holst, Imogen. Henry Purcell: The Story of His Life and Work. London, Boosey & Hawkes, 1961.

Holst, Imogen, ed. Henry Purcell, 1659–1695 : Essays on His Music. London, Oxford University Press, 1959.

Huber, Wolfgang. Das Textbuch der frühdeutschen Oper : Untersuchung über literarische Voraussetzung, stoffliche Grundlagen und Quellen. Munich Dissertation, 1957.

[Hunold, Christian Friedrich.] Die allerneueste Art, zur reinen und galanten Poesie zu gelangen. Hamburg, G. Liebernickel, 1707.

—— "Gesellschaftliche Verhältnisse in der Oper zu Anfang des achtzehnten Jahrhunderts," AMZ [New Series] XV (1880) 753–58, 769–73, 785–90.

—— Theatralische, galante und geistliche Gedichte. Hamburg, G. Liebernickel, 1706.

Ingram, R. W. "Operatic Tendencies in Stuart Drama," MQ XLIV (1958) 489–502.

Jander, Owen H. A Catalogue of the Manuscripts of Compositions by Alessandro Stradella Found in European and American Libraries. Wellesley, Mass., Wellesley College, 1962. Rev. ed.

Kellner, Altman. Musikgeschichte des Stiftes Kremsmünster. Kassel & Basel, Bärenreiter, 1956.

Kiesewetter, R[aphael] G[eorg], Edler von Wiesenbrunn. Schicksale und Beschaffenheit des weltlichen Gesanges. Leipzig, B&H, 1841.

Klages, Richard. Johann Wolfgang Franck. Hamburg, 1937.

Kleefeld, Wilhelm. "Hessens Beziehungen zur alten deutschen Oper," Vom Rhein: Monatsschrift des Altertumsvereins für die Stadt Worms IV (1905) 15.

—— "Das Orchester der Hamburger Oper 1678–1738," SIMG I (1899–1900) 219–89.

Klein, Herman. "The Vienna Hofoper," M&L XIV (1933) 239–46.

Köchel, Ludwig, Ritter von. Johann Josef Fux. Vienna, A. Hölder, 1872.

—— Die kaiserliche Hofmusikkapelle in Wien von 1543 bis 1867. Vienna, Beck, 1869.

Kramer, Margarete. Beiträge zu einer Geschichte des Affektenbegriffes in der Musik von 1550–1700. Halle Dissertation, 1924.

Kreidler, Walter. Heinrich Schütz und der Stile concitato von Claudio Monteverdi. Kassel, Bärenreiter, 1934.

Křenek, Ernst. "Zur musikalischen Bearbeitung von Monteverdis Poppea," SchwM LXXVI (1936) 545–55.

Kretzschmar, Hermann. "Beiträge zur Geschichte der venetianischen Oper," JMP XIV (1907) 71–81; XVII (1910) 61–71; XVIII (1911) 49–61.

—— "Einige Bemerkungen über den Vortrag alter Musik," JMP VII (1900) 53–68.

—— "Monteverdi's Incoronazione di Poppea," VfMw X (1894) 483–530.

—— "Die venetianische Oper und die Werke Cavalli's und Cesti's," VfMw VIII (1892) 1–76.

Kutscher, Artur. Vom Salzburger Barocktheater zu den Salzburger Fest-spielen. Düsseldorf, Pflugscher-Verlag, 1939.

La Laurencie, Lionel de. "André Campra, musicien profane : Notes bio-graphiques," *Année musicale* III (1913) 153–205.

—— "Une Convention commerciale entre Lully, Quinault et Ballard en 1680," RdM II (1920–21) 176–82.

—— Les Créateurs de l'opéra français. Paris, F. Alcan, 1930. New ed.

—— Lully. Paris, F. Alcan, 1911.

—— "Notes sur la jeunesse d'André Campra," SIMG X (1908–9) 159–258. Also separate : Leipzig, B&H, 1909.

—— "L'Opéra français au XVIIe siècle : La musique," RM VI (January, 1925) 26–43.

—— "Un Opéra inédit de M.-A. Charpentier : *La Descente d'Orphée aux enfers*," RdM X (1929) 184–93.

—— "L'*Orfeo nell' inferni* d'André Campra," RdM IX (1928) 129–33.

—— "Les Pastorales en musique au XVIIe siècle en France avant Lully et leur influence sur l'opéra," in *International Musical Society, 4th Congress Report* (London, Novello, 1912) 139–46.

Lang, Paul Henry. The Literary Aspects of the History of the Opera in France. Cornell Dissertation, 1935.

La Roche, Charles. Antonio Bertali als Opern- und Oratorienkomponist. Vienna Dissertation, 1919.

La Tour, Georges Imbart de. "La Mise en scène d' *Hippolyte et Aricie*," MM IV (1908) 247–71.

Lawrence, William John. The Elizabethan Playhouse and Other Studies. Philadelphia, J. B. Lippincott, 1912.

—— "The English Theatre Orchestra: Its Rise and Early Characteristics," MQ III (1917) 9–27.

—— "Foreign Singers and Musicians at the Court of Charles II," MQ IX (1923) 217–25.

—— "Notes on a Collection of Masque Music," M&L III (1922) 49–58.

[Le Cerf de la Viéville, Jean Laurent, seigneur de Freneuse.] Comparaison de la musique italienne et de la musique françoise. Brussels, F. Foppens, 1704–6. 3 vols. Also forms Vols. 2–4 of Jacques Bonnet's Histoire de la musique et de ses effets. Amsterdam, J. Royer, 17—.

[Leclercq, Louis.] Les Décors, les costumes, et la mise en scène au XVIIe siècle, 1615–1680, par Ludovic Celler [pseud.]. Paris, Liepmannssohn & Dufour, 1869.

Leichtentritt, Hugo. "On the Prologue in Early Opera," MTNA XXXI (1936) 292–99.

Lengl, Georg. Die Genesis der Oper. Munich, Mössl, 1936.

[Le Prévost d'Exmes, François.] Lully, musicien. [Paris, 1779.]

LeRoux, Maurice. Claudio Monteverdi. [Paris], Editions du Coudrier, [1951].

Levinson, André. "Notes sur le ballet au XVIIe siècle : Les danseurs de Lully," RM VI (January, 1925) 44–55.

Lieboldt, J. "Der Verbleib der alten Hamburger Operndekoration *Der Tempel Salomonis*," *Mitteilungen des Vereins für Hamburgische Geschichte* XIII (1890) 128–29.

[Limojon de St. Didier, Alexandre Toussaint.] La Ville et la république de Venise. Paris, G. de Luyne, 1680. Translated as : The City and Republick of Venice. London, C. Brome, 1699.

Lindner, Ernst Otto. Die erste stehende deutsche Oper. Berlin, Schlesinger, 1855. 2 vols.

Liuzzi, Fernando. I musicisti in Francia. Vol. I : Dalle origini al secolo XVII. Rome, Edizioni d'Arte Dansei, 1946.

Loschelder, Josef. "Aus Düsseldorfs italienischer Zeit : Römische Quellen zu Agostino Steffanis Leben," in Karl Gustav Fellerer, ed., *Beiträge zur Musikgeschichte der Stadt Düsseldorf* (Cologne & Krefeld, Staufen-Verlag, 1952) 17–53.

Lote, Georges. "La Déclamation du vers français à la fin du XVIIe siècle," *Revue de phonétique* II (1912) 313–63.

Lugli, A. Il melodramma, l'ultima geniale creazione del rinascimento. Milan, A. Ballardi, 1921.

Lully et l'opéra français. RM, numéro spécial, Vol. VI (January, 1925).

McManaway, J. G. "Songs and Masques in *The Tempest*," in *Luttrell Society Reprints*, No. 14 (1953) 71–96.

McMullen, Edward Wallace. The Earliest Operatic Adaptations of Shakespeare. Columbia Dissertation (A.M.), 1939.

Maione, Italo. "Tasso-Monteverdi : *Il combattimento di Tancredi e Clorinda*," RassM III (1930) 206–15.

Malipiero, Gian Francesco. Claudio Monteverdi. Milan, Treves, 1929.

—— "Claudio Monteverdi of Cremona," MQ XVIII (1932) 383–96.

Manifold, John Streeter. The Music in English Drama from Shakespeare to Purcell. London, Rockliff, [1956].

Mantica, Francesco, ed. Prime fioriture del melodramma italiano. Rome, Casa editrice Claudio Monteverdi, 1912–30. 2 vols.

Mariani, Valerio. "Ricordando Sabbatini e Torelli scenografi marchigiani," *Rassegna Marchigiana* XII (1934) 193–207.

Mark, Jeffrey. "Dryden and the Beginnings of Opera in England," M&L V (1924) 247–52.

—— "The Jonsonian Masque," M&L III (1922) 358–71.

Masson, Paul-Marie. "*Les Fêtes vénitiennes* de Campra," RdM XIII (1932) 127–46, 214–26.

—— "Lullistes et Ramistes," *L'Anée musicale* I (1911) 187–211.

Maugars, André. "Response faite à un curieux sur le sentiment de la musique d'Italie, écrite à Rome le premier octobre 1639 . . . in deutscher Uebersetzung mitgetheilt von W. J. von Wasialewski," MfMg X (1878) 1–9, 17–23.

Maxton, Willy. Johann Theile. Tübingen Dissertation, 1927.

Meer, J. H. van der. Johann Josef Fux als Opernkomponist. Bilthoven, A. B. Creyghton, 1961. 3 vols. plus music supplement.

Menantes, pseud. See Hunold, Christian Friedrich.

Ménestrier, Claude François. Des Ballets anciens et modernes. Paris, R. Guignard, 1682.

Menke, Werner. Das Vokalwerk Georg Philipp Telemanns : Uberlieferung und Zeitfolge. Kassel, Bärenreiter, 1942.

Mercure françois, Le. Paris, J. Richer, 1612–48. 25 vols.

Mersenne, Marin. Harmonie universelle. Paris, S. Cramoisy, 1636–37.

Mielsch, Rudolf. "Dafne, die erste deutsche Oper," Die Musik XIX (May, 1927) 586–91.

Mies, Paul. "Ueber die Behandlung der Frage im 17. und 18. Jahrhundert," ZfMw IV (1921–22) 286–304.

Mila, Massimo. "Jacopo Peri," RassM VI (1933) 214–27.

Moberg, Carl Allan. "Un Compositeur oublié de l'école de Lully : Jean Desfontaines," RdM X (1929) 5–9.

Molmenti, P[ompeo] G[herardo]. La storia di Venezia nella vita privata dalle origini alla caduta della repubblica. Bergamo, Istituto italiano d'arti grafiche, 1905–8. 3 vols.

Monaldi, Gino. I teatri di Roma negli ultimi tre secoli. Naples, R. Ricciardi, 1928.

[Monteverdi, Claudio.] See special number of RassM II (October, 1929).

Moore, Robert Etheridge. Henry Purcell and the Restoration Theatre. London, Heinemann, [1961].

—— "The Music to Macbeth," MQ XLVII (1961) 22–40.

Morgan [Sydney (Owenson)], Lady. The Life and Times of Salvator Rosa. London, 1824. 2 vols.

Muffat, Georg. Suavioris harmoniae instrumentalis hyporchematicae florilegium I. Augustae Vindelicorum, Typis Jacobi Koppmayr, 1695. Reprinted in DTOe, Vol. 2.

—— Florilegium secundum. Passovii, Typis Georgij Adam Höller, 1698. Reprinted in DTOe, Vol. 4.

Nagel, Willibald. "Daniel Purcell," MfMg XXX (1898) 47–53.

Nagler, A. M. "Lullys Opernbühne," in Kleine Schriften der Gesellschaft für Theatergeschichte, Heft 17 (Berlin, 1960) 9–26.

Narciss, Georg Adolf. Studien zu den Frauenzimmergesprächspielen Georg Philipp Harsdörfers. Leipzig, H. Eichblatt, 1928.

Naylor, Edward Woodall. "Music and Shakespeare," MA I (1909–10) 129–48.

—— Shakespeare and Music. London, J. M. Dent, [1931].

Nef, Karl. Zur Geschichte der deutschen Instrumentalmusik in der 2. Hälfte des 17. Jahrhunderts. Leipzig, B&H, 1902.

—— "Zur Instrumentation im 17. Jahrhundert," JMP XXXV (1929) 33–42.

Neisser, Arthur. *Servio Tullio,* eine Oper aus dem Jahre 1685 von Agostino Steffani. Leipzig, C. G. Röder, 1902.

Nettl, Paul. "Beitrag zur Geschichte des deutschen Singballets," ZfMw VI (1923–24) 608–20.

—— "Exzerpte aus der Raudnitzer Textbüchersammlung," SzMw VII (1920) 143–44.

—— "Zur Geschichte der kaiserlichen Hofkapelle von 1636–1680," SzMw XVI (1929) 70–85; XVII (1930) 95–104; XVIII (1931) 23–35; XIX (1932) 33–40.

Neuhaus, Max. "Antonio Draghi," SzMw I (1913) 104–92.

Neumann, Friedrich-Heinrich. Die Aesthetik des Rezitativs : Zur Theorie des Rezitativs im 17. und 18. Jahrhundert. Strasbourg, Heitz, 1962.

Nicoll, Allardyce. "Italian Opera in England : The First Five Years," *Anglia* XLVI (1922) 257–81.

Nietan, Hanns. Die Buffoszenen der spätvenezianischen Oper (1680 bis 1710). Halle Dissertation, 1925.

Noack, Friedrich. "Die Musik zu der molièreschen Komödie *Monsieur de Pourceaugnac* von Jean Baptiste de Lully," in *Festschrift für Johannes Wolf* (Berlin, Breslauer, 1929) 139–47.

Nodot, ——. "Le Triomphe de Lully aux Champs-Elysées," RM VI (January, 1925) 89–106. First printing of Bibliothèque de l'Arsenal MS 6.542, pp. 260 ff.

Norman, Gertrude. A Consideration of Seicento Opera with Particular Reference to the Rise of the Neapolitan School. Columbia Dissertation (A. M.), 1937.

Noyes, Robert Gale. Ben Jonson on the English Stage, 1660–1776. Cambridge, Mass., Harvard University Press, 1935.

—— "Contemporary Musical Settings of the Songs in Restoration Dramatic Operas," *Harvard Studies and Notes in Philology and Literature* XX (1938) 99–121.

Nuitter. *See* Truinet.

Nungezer, Edwin. Dictionary of Actors and Other Persons Associated with the Public Representations of Plays in England before 1642. New Haven, Yale University Press; London, Oxford University Press, 1929.

Oliver, A. Richard. "Molière's Contribution to the Lyric Stage," MQ XXXIII (1947) 350–64.

O'Neill, Norman. "Music to Stage Plays in England," SIMG XIII (1911–12) 321–28.

Opel, Julius Otto. "Die erste Jahrzehnte der Oper in Leipzig," *Neues Archiv für sächsische Geschichte und Altertumskunde* V (1884) 116–141.

Osthoff, Wolfgang. Das dramatische Spätwerk Claudio Monteverdis. Tutzing, Hans Schneider, 1960.

—— "Neue Beobachtungen zu Quellen und Geschichte von Monteverdis *Incoronazione di Poppea,*" Mf XI (1958) 129–38.

Osthoff, Wolfgang. "Die venezianische und neapolitanische Fassung von Monteverdis *Incoronazione di Poppea*," *Acta musicologica* XXVI (1954) 88–113.

—— "Zu den Quellen von Monteverdis *Ritorno di Ulisse in Patria*," *Studien zur Musikwissenschaft*, XXIII (1956) 67–78.

Ottzen, Curt. Telemann als Opernkomponist. Berlin, E. Ebering, 1902. 2 vols. See review by Oskar Fleischer, ZIMG III, 497.

Pannain, Guido. "Studi monteverdiani," RassM XXVIII (1958) 7–15, 97–108, 187–95, 281–92; XXIX (1959) 42–50, 95–105, 234–46, 310–21; XXX (1960) 24–32, 230–40, 312–24; XXXI (1961) 14–26.

Paoli, Domenico de. Monteverdi. Milan, Hoepli, 1945.

Paoli, Rodolfo. "Difesa del primo melodramma," RassM XX (1950) 93–100.

Parry, Sir C[harles] Hubert H[astings]. The Music of the Seventeenth Century. London, Oxford University Press, 1938. 2d ed. (OHM, Vol. III.)

—— "The Significance of Monteverde," PMA XLII (1915–16) 51–67.

Passuth, Laszlo. Monteverdi : Der Roman eines grossen Musikers. Vienna-Berlin-Stuttgart, Paul Neff Verlag, 1959.

Pepys, Samuel. The Diary of Samuel Pepys. London, G. Bell; New York, Harcourt, Brace, 1924–26. 8 vols.

Perrault, Charles. Les Hommes illustres qui ont paru en France pendant ce siècle. Paris. A. Dezallier, 1696.

Piccioli, Giuseppe. Composizioni di antichi autori bolognesi. Bologna, Bongiovanni, 1933.

Pirchan, Emil, Alexander Witeschnik, and Otto Fritz. 300 Jahre Wiener Operntheater : Werk und Werden. Vienna, Fortuna Verlag, [1953].

Pirro, André. Schütz. Paris, F. Alcan, 1913.

Pirrotta, Nino. " 'Commedia dell' Arte' and Opera," MQ XLI (1955) 305–24.

Policastro, Guglielmo. "Musica e teatro nel Seicento nella provincia di Catania," RMI LV (1953) 109–48.

—— "I teatri dell '600 in Catania," RMI LIV (1952) 207–17, 316–28.

Pougin, Arthur. "L'Orchestre de Lully," *Le Ménestrel* LXII (1896) 44–45, 59–60, 67–68, 76, 83–84, 91–92, 99–100.

—— "Les Origines de l'opéra français : Cambert et Lully," *Revue d'art dramatique* Année 6, tome XXI (1891) 129–55.

—— Les Vrais Créateurs de l'opéra français, Perrin et Cambert. Paris, Charvay, 1881.

Prendergast, Arthur H. "The Masque of the Seventeenth Century," PMA XXIII (1897) 113–31.

Pribram, Alfred Francis. Materialen zur Geschichte der Preise und Löhne in Oesterreich. Band I. Vienna, C. Ueberreuter, 1938.

Prod'homme, Jacques Gabriel. "The Economic Status of Musicians in France until the French Revolution," MQ XVI (1930) 83–100.

—— "Pierre Corneille et l'opéra français," ZIMG VII (1905–6) 416–21.

Prota-Giurleo, U. Francesco Cirillo e l'introduzione del melodramma a Napoli. Grumo Nevano, A cura del Comune, 1952.

Prunières, Henry. "L'Académie royale de musique et de danse," RM VI (January, 1925) 3–25.

—— Le Ballet de cour en France avant Benserade et Lully. Paris, H. Laurens, 1914.

—— Cavalli et l'opéra vénitien au XVIIIe siècle. Paris, Rieder, [1931].

—— Claudio Monteverdi. Paris, F. Alcan, 1924.

—— "De l'interpretation des agréments du chant aux XVIIe et XVIIIe siècles," RM XIII (May, 1932) 329–44.

—— "Jean de Cambefort," Année musicale II (1912) 205–26.

—— "La Jeunesse de Lully (1632–62)," MM V (1909) 234–42, 329–53.

—— "Lecerf de la Viéville et l'esthétique musicale classique au XVIIe siècle," MM IV (1908) 619–54.

—— "Lettres et autographes de Lully," MM VIII (1912) 19–20.

—— "I libretti dell' opera veneziana nel secolo XVII," RassM III (1930) 441–48.

—— Lully. Paris, H. Laurens, 1909.

—— "Lully and the Académie de Musique et de Danse," MQ XI (1925) 528–46.

—— "Lully, fils de meunier," MM VIII (1912) 57–61.

—— "Monteverdi's Venetian Operas," MQ X (1924) 178–92.

—— "Les Musiciens du Cardinal Antonio Barberini," in Mélanges de musicologie (Paris, Droz, 1933) 117–22.

—— "Notes sur la vie de Luigi Rossi (1598–1653)," SIMG XII (1910–11) 12–16.

—— "Notes sur les origines de l'ouverture française," SIMG XII (1910–11) 565–85.

—— "Notes sur une partition faussement attribuée à Cavalli : L'Eritrea (1686)," RMI XXVII (1920) 267–73.

—— L'Opéra italien en France avant Lulli. Paris, E. Champion, 1913. Review by R. Rolland, MM X, No. 5 (1914) 6–15.

—— "Les Premières Ballets de Lully," RM XII (June, 1931) 1–17.

—— "Recherches sur les années de jeunesse de J. B. Lully," RMI XVII (1910) 646–54.

—— "Les Représentations du Palazzo l'Atlante à Rome (1642) d'après des documents inédits," SIMG XIV (1912–13) 218–26.

—— La Vie et l'œuvre de Claudio Monteverdi. Paris, Librairie de France, 1926. 2d ed., 1931. Translated as : Monteverdi : His Life and Works. London, J. M. Dent, 1926.

—— La Vie illustre et libertine de Jean-Baptiste Lully. Paris, Plon-Nourrit, [1929].

Purcell's The Fairy Queen, as Presented at the Royal Opera House, Covent Garden : A Photographic Record by Edward Mandinian with Preface to the Original Text, a Preface by Prof. E. J. Dent, and Articles by Constant Lambert and Michael Ayrton. London, John Lehmann, 1948.

Pure, Michel de. Idée des spectacles anciens et nouveaux. Paris, M. Brunet, 1668.

Quinault, Philippe. Théâtre. Paris, Compagnie des Libraires, 1739. 5 vols.

Quittard, Henri. "L'Orchestre de l' *Orfeo*," RHCM VII (1907) 380–89, 412–18.

Radet, Edmond. Lully, homme d'affaires, propriétaire et musicien. Paris, L. Allison, [1891].

Rau, Carl August. Loreto Vittori. Munich, Verlag für moderne Musik, [1916].

Redlich, Hans Ferdinand. Claudio Monteverdi, Leben und Werk. Olten, Verlag Otto Walter AG, 1949. Translated as : Claudio Monteverdi : Life and Works. London, New York, Toronto, Oxford University Press, 1952.

—— "Monteverdi-Renaissance," *Atlantis* VIII (1936) 768.

—— "Notationsprobleme in Cl. Monteverdis *Incoronazione di Poppea*," *Acta musicologica* X (1938) 129–32.

—— "Sull' edizione moderna delle opere di Claudio Monteverdi," RassM VIII (1935) 23–41.

—— "Zur Bearbeitung von Monteverdis *Orfeo*," SchwM LXXVI (1936) 37–42, 74–80.

Reiner, Stuart. "Collaboration in *Chi soffre speri*," MR XXII (1961) 265–82.

Rendell, E. D. "Some Notes on Purcell's Dramatic Music, with Especial Reference to the *Fairy Queen*," M&L I (1920) 135–44.

Reuter, Fritz. "Die Entwicklung der Leipziger, insbesondere italienischen Oper bis zum siebenjährigen Krieg," ZfMw V (1922–23) 1–16.

—— Die Geschichte der deutschen Oper in Leipzig am Ende des 17. und am Anfang des 18. Jahrhunderts (1693–1720). Leipzig Dissertation, 1923.

Reyher, Paul. Les Masques anglais. Paris, Hachette, 1909.

Ricci, Corrado. Vita barocca. Milan, L. F. Cogliati, 1904.

Ricci, Vittorio. "Un melodramma ignoto della prima metà del '600 : *Celio di Baccio Baglioni e di Niccolò Sapiti*," RMI XXXII (1925) 51–79.

Richard, Pierre. "Stradella et les Contarini : Episode des moeurs vénitiennes au XVIIe siècle," *Le Ménestrel* XXXII (1864–65), XXXIII (1865–66), *passim*.

Riedel, Emil. Schuldrama und Theater. Hamburg, L. Voss, 1885.

Riemann, Hugo. "*Basso ostinato* und *Basso* quasi *ostinato:* Eine Anregung," in *Festschrift Liliencron* (Leipzig, B&H, 1910) 193–202.

Ritscher, Hugo. Die musikalische Deklamation in Lully's Opernrezitativen. Berlin Dissertation, 1925.

Ritter, A. G. "Die musikalischen Chöre des Chr. Th. Walliser zur Tragödie *Andromeda*," MfMg I (1869) 134–41.

Rokseth, Yvonne. "Antonia Bembo, Composer to Louis XIV," MQ XXIII (1937) 147–67.

Rolandi, Ulderico. "*Il Ciclope:* Dramma harmonica con musica di D. Lorenzo Ratti (Roma : 1628)," *Note d'archivio* X (1933) 253–60.

Rolland, Romain. "Notes sur l' *Orfeo* de Luigi Rossi et sur les musiciens italiens à Paris, sous Mazarin," RHCM I (1901) 225–36, 363–72.

—— "L'Opéra populaire à Venise : Francesco Cavalli," MM II, No. 1 (1906) 61–70, 151–60.

—— Les Origines du théâtre lyrique moderne : Histoire de l'opéra en Europe avant Lully et Scarlatti. Paris, E. Thorin, 1895. New ed. Paris, E. de Boccard, 1931.

—— "La Première Représentation du *San Alessio* de Stefano Landi en 1632, à Rome, d'après le journal manuscrit de Jean Jacques Bouchard," RHCM II (1902) 29–36, 74–75.

—— "La Représentation d' *Orféo* à Paris et l'opposition religieuse et politique à l'opéra," RHCM I (1901) 10–17.

Rommel, Otto. Die Alt-Wiener Volkskomödie : Ihre Geschichte vom barocken Welt-Theater bis zum Tode Nestroys. Vienna, Schroll, [1952].

Roncaglia, Gino. Le composizioni di Alessandro Stradella esistenti presso la R. Biblioteca Estense di Modena. Milan, Bocca, 1942.

—— La rivoluzione musicale italiana (secolo XVII). Milan, G. Bolla, 1928.

—— "Il *Trespolo tutore* di Alessandro Stradella, 'la prima opera buffa,'" RMI LVI (1954) 326–32.

R[onga], L[uigi]. "Su Monteverdi e sull' opera italiana del Seicento," RMI LVII (1955) 140–50.

Rotondi, Joseph E. Literary and Musical Aspects of Roman Opera, 1600–1650. Ann Arbor, University Microfilms, 1959.

Rudhart, Franz Michael. Geschichte der Oper am Hofe zu München . . . Erster Theil : Die italienische Oper von 1654–1787. Freising, F. Datterer, 1865.

Sabbatini, Nicola. Pratica di fabricar scene, e machine ne' teatri. Ravenna, Pietro de Paoli, 1638. New ed. German ed. as : Anleitung Dekorationen und Theatermaschinen herzustellen. Weimar, Gesellschaft· der Bibliophilen, 1926. Ed. by Willi Flemming.

Sachs, Curt. "Die Ansbacher Hofkapelle unter Markgraf Johann Friedrich (1672–86)," SIMG XI (1909–10) 105–37.

[Salvioli, Giovanni.] I teatri musicali di Venezia nel secolo XVII. Milan, Ricordi, [1879].

Salza, Abd-el-kader. "Drammi inediti di Giulio Rospigliosi," RMI XIV (1907) 473–508.

Sandberger, Adolf. "Beziehungen der Königin Christine von Schweden zur italienischen Oper und Musik, insbesondere zu M. A. Cesti : Mit einem Anhang über Cestis Innsbrucker Aufenthalt," *Bulletin de la Société union musicologique* V (1925) 121–73.

Sandberger, Adolf. "Zur Geschichte der Oper in Nürnberg in der 2. Hälfte des 17. und zu Anfang des 18. Jahrhunderts," AfMw I (1918) 84–107.

——— "Zur venezianischen Oper," JMP XXXI (1924) 61–70; XXXII (1925) 53–63.

Sartori, Claudio. Monteverdi. Brescia, La Scuola, 1953.

Savaron, Jean. Traitté contre les masques. Paris, Perier, 1611. 3d ed.

Saviotti, Alfredo. "Feste e spettacoli nel Seicento," Giornale storico della letteratura italiana XLI (1903) 542–77.

Schering, Arnold. "Zur Geschichte des italienischen Oratoriums im 17. Jahrhundert," JMP X (1903) 31–44.

Scheurleer, D. F. "Ein Marionetten-Theater te Amsterdam 1696," Tijdschrift der Vereeniging voor Noord Nederlands Muziekgeschiedenis IX, No. 3 (1912) 147–53.

Schiedermair, Ludwig. "Die Anfänge der Münchener Oper," SIMG V (1903–4) 442–68.

——— "Briefe Johann Philipp Käfers," in Festschrift Adolf Sandberger (Munich, Zierfuss, 1918) 121–28.

——— Die deutsche Oper : Grundzüge ihres Werdens und Wesens. Bonn, Berlin, Ferd. Dümmlers Verlag, 1943. 3d ed.

——— "Die Oper an den badischen Höfen des 17. und 18. Jahrhunderts," SIMG XIV (1912–13) 191–207, 369–449, 510–50.

Schild, M. Die Musikdramen Ottavio Rinuccinis. Würzburg, Mayr, 1933.

Schletterer, Hans Michael. Vorgeschichte und erste Versuche der französischen Oper. Berlin, R. Damköhler, 1885. (Vol. III of his Studien zur Geschichte der französischen Musik.)

Schlitzer, Franco. Intorno alla Dori di Antonio Cesti. Florence, Edizioni Sansoni Antiquariato, 1957.

Schmidt, Günther. Die Musik am Hofe der Markgrafen von Brandenburg-Ansbach vom ausgehenden Mittelalter bis 1806. Kassel, Bärenreiter, 1956.

Schmidt, Gustav Friedrich. "Die älteste deutsche Oper in Leipzig am Ende des 17. und Anfang des 18. Jahrhunderts," in Festschrift Adolf Sandberger (Munich, Zierfuss, 1918) 209–57.

——— Die frühdeutsche Oper und die musikdramatische Kunst Georg Caspar Schürmann's. Regensburg, G. Bosse, 1933. 2 vols.

——— "Johann Wolfgang Francks Singspiel Die drey Töchter Cecrops," AfMf IV (1939) 257–316.

——— Neue Beiträge zur Geschichte der Musik und des Theaters am Herzoglichen Hofe zu Braunschweig-Wolfenbüttel. Munich, W. Berntheisel, 1929.

——— "Zur Geschichte, Dramaturgie und Statistik der frühdeutschen Oper (1627–1750)," ZfMw V (1922–23) 582–97, 642–65; VI (1923–24) 129–57, 496–530.

Schmidt, Immanuel. "Ueber Ben Jonson's Maskenspiele," Archiv für das Studium der neueren Sprachen XXVII (1860) 55–90.

Schmitz, Arnold. "Monodien der Kölner Jesuiten aus der ersten Hälfte des 17. Jahrhunderts," ZfMw IV (1921–22) 266–85.

Schmitz, Eugen. "Antonio Brunelli als Monodist," ZIMG XI (1909–10) 383–86.

—— "Zur Frühgeschichte der lyrischen Monodie Italiens im 17. Jahrhundert," JMP XVIII (1911) 35–48.

—— "Zur Geschichte des italienischen Continuo-Madrigals im 17. Jahrhundert," SIMG XI (1909–10) 509–28.

—— "Zur musikgeschichtlichen Bedeutung der Harsdörfferschen 'Frauenzimmergesprächspiele,' " in Festschrift . . . Liliencron (Leipzig, B&H, 1910) 254–77.

Schneider, Constantin. "Franz Heinrich von Biber als Opernkomponist," AfMw VIII (1926) 281–347.

Schneider, Louis. Un Précurseur de la musique italienne aux XVIe et XVIIe siècles : Claudio Monteverdi. Paris, Perrin, 1921.

Das Schönbrunner Schlosstheater : Beiträge. Vienna, Bundesministerium für Unterricht im H. Baur-Verlag, 1947.

Scholes, Percy. The Puritans and Music in England and New England. London, Oxford University Press, 1934.

Scholz, Hans. Johann Sigismund Kusser. Leipzig, Röder, 1911.

Schrade, Leo. Monteverdi, Creator of Modern Music. New York, W. W. Norton, 1950.

Schreiber, Irmtraud. Dichtung und Musik der deutschen Opernarien 1680–1700. Bottrop i. W., Postberg, 1934.

Schulze, Walter. Die Quellen der Hamburger Oper (1678–1738). Hamburg-Oldenburg, G. Stalling, 1938.

Settecento italiano, Il. Milan-Rome, Bestetti & Tumminelli, 1932. 2 vols.

Sietz, Reinhold. Henry Purcell, Zeit—Leben—Werk. Leipzig, B&H, 1955.

Silin, Charles I. Benserade and His Ballets de Cour. Baltimore, Johns Hopkins Press, 1940.

Sittard, Josef. Zur Geschichte der Musik und des Theaters am württembergischen Hofe. Stuttgart, W. Kohlhammer, 1890–91. 2 vols.

Solerti, Angelo. "Un balletto musicato da Claudio Monteverdi," RMI XI (1904) 24–34.

—— "Feste musicale alla Corte di Savoia nella prima metà del secolo XVII," RMI XI (1904) 675–724.

—— "Lettere inedite sulla musica di Pietro della Valle a G.B. Doni ed una veglia drammatica-musicale del medesimo," RMI XII (1905) 271–338.

—— Musica, ballo e drammatica alla corte Medicea dal 1600 al 1637. Florence, R. Bemporad, 1905.

—— "I rappresentazioni musicali di Venezia dal 1571 al 1605," RMI IX (1902) 503–58.

—— "Un viaggio in Francia di Giulio Caccini," RMI X (1903) 707–11.

Sonneck, Oscar George Theodore. "*Dafne*, the First Opera," SIMG XV (1913–14) 102–10.

Speer, Daniel. Grund-richtiger, kurtz, leicht und nöthiger Unterricht der musikalischen Kunst. Ulm, G. W. Kühnen, 1687.

Spink, Ian. "Playford's 'Directions for Singing after the Italian Manner,' " MMR LXXXIX (1959) 130–35.

Spitz, Charlotte. "Eine anonyme italienische Oper um die Wende des 17. zum 18. Jahrhundert," ZfMw II (1919–20) 232–35.

—— "Die Entwickelung des 'stilo recitativo,' " AfMw III (1921) 237–44.

Squire, William Barclay. "J. W. Franck in England," MA III (1911–12) 181–90.

—— "The Music of Shadwell's *Tempest*," MQ VII (1921) 565–78.

—— "An Opera under Innocent X," in *Gedenkboek . . . Scheurleer* (The Hague, Nijhoff, 1925) 65–71.

—— "Purcell's Dramatic Music," SIMG V (1903–4) 489–564.

Stanley, Albert Augustus. "Cesti's *Il Pomo d'Oro*," MTNA I (1906) 139–49.

Stefan, Paul. Die Wiener Oper : Ihre Geschichte von den Anfängen bis in der neueste Zeit. Vienna, Augartenverlag, 1932.

Stenhouse, May. The Character of the Opera Libretto according to Quinault. Columbia Dissertation (A.M.), 1920.

Storz, Walter. Der Aufbau der Tänze in den Opern und Balletts Lully's vom musikalischen Standpunkte aus betrachtet. Göttingen, Dieterischen Universitäts-Buchdruckerei, 1928.

Swalin, Benjamin F. "Purcell's Masque in *Timon of Athens*," in *Papers of the American Musicological Society, Annual Meeting, 1941 . . . Edited by Gustave Reese* (Printed by the Society [cop. 1946]) 112–24.

Swanepoel, Pieter. Das dramatische Schaffen Henry Purcells. Vienna Dissertation, 1926.

Taubert, Otto. "*Daphne*, das erste deutsche Operntextbuch," in *Programm des Gymnasiums zu Torgau* (Torgau, Fr. Lebinsky, 1879).

Tessier, André. "Berain, créateur du pays d'opéra," RM VI (January, 1925) 56–73.

—— "Les Deux Styles de Monteverdi," RM III, No. 8 (June, 1922) 223–54.

—— "Giacomo Torelli a Parigi e la messa in scena delle *Nozze di Peleo e Teti* di Carlo Caproli," RassM I (1928) 573–90.

—— "*L'Orontée* de Lorenzani et l'*Orontea* du Padre Cesti," RM IX, No. 8 (1928) 169–86.

—— "Quelques notes sur Jean Desfontaines," RdM X (1929) 9–16.

—— "Robert Cambert à Londres," RM IV (December, 1927) 101–22.

Teutsche Arien, welche auf dem Kayserlich-privilegierten Wienerischen Theatro in unterschiedlich producirten Comoedien, deren Titeln hier jedesmahl beygerucket, gesungen worden : Codex MS 12706–12709 der Wiener Nationalbibliothek. Vienna, E. Strache, 1930.

Thorp, Willard, ed. Songs from the Restoration Theatre. Princeton, Princeton University Press, 1934.

Tiby, Ottavio. L'incoronazione di Poppea di Claudio Monteverdi. Florence, A. Vallechi, 1937.

Tiersot, Julien. "Les Choeurs d' Esther de Moreau," RHCM III (1903) 35–40.

—— "La Musique des comédies de Molière à la Comédie-française," livre, [1922].

—— "La Musique des comédies de Molière à la Comédie-française," RdM VI (1922) 20–28.

Tintelnot, Hans. Die Entwicklungsgeschichte der barocken Bühnendekoration in ihren Wechselbeziehungen zur bildenden Kunst. Berlin, Mann, 1938.

Tirabassi, Antonio. "The Oldest Opera : Belli's Orfeo Dolente," MQ XXV (1939) 26–33.

Toni, Alceo. "Sul basso continuo e l'interpretazione della musica antica," RMI XXVI (1919) 229–64.

Torchi, Luigi. "L'accompagnamento degli istrumenti nei melodrammi italiani della prima metà del Seicento," RMI I (1894) 7–38; II (1895) 666–71.

—— "Canzoni ed arie italiane ad una voce nel secolo XVII," RMI I (1894) 581–656.

Torrefranca, Fausto. "Il 'grande stregone' Giacomo Torelli e la scenografia del Seicento," Scenario III (1934) 473–80.

—— "La prima opera francese in Italia? (l'Armida di Lulli, Roma 1690)," in Festschrift für Johannes Wolf (Berlin, Breslauer, 1929) 191–97.

Torri, Luigi. "Il primo melodramma a Torino," RMI XXVI (1919) 1–35.

Trenkle, J. B. "Ueber süddeutsche geistliche Schulkomödien," Freiburger Diöcesan-archiv II (1866) 131–76.

[Truinet, Charles Louis Etienne, and A. E. Roquet (Thoinan).] Les Origines de l'opéra français. Paris, Plon-Nourrit, 1886.

Tufts, George. "Ballad Opera : A List and Some Notes," MA IV (1912–13) 61–86.

Untersteiner, Alfredo. "Agostino Steffani," RMI XIV (1907) 509–34.

Ursprung, Otto. "Ueber die Aufführung von Monteverdis Combattimento und von Peris Euridice durch das musikwissenschaftliche Seminar der Universität München," ZfMw XVI (1934) 188–90.

Vallas, Léon. Un Siècle de musique et de théâtre à Lyon (1688–1789). Lyon, P. Masson, 1932.

Vogel, Emil. "Claudio Monteverdi : Leben, Werken im Lichte der zeitgenössischen Kritik," VfMw III (1887) 315–450.

—— "Marco da Gagliano," VfMw V (1889) 396–442, 509–68.

Wagner, Rudolf. "Beiträge zur Lebensgeschichte Johann Philipp Kriegers und seines Schülers Nikolaus Deinl," ZfMw VIII (1925–26) 146–60.

Wallaschek, Richard. Das K. k. Hofoperntheater. Vienna, Gesellschaft für vervielfältigende Kunst, 1909.

Waltershausen, Hermann Wolfgang Karl Sartorius, Freiherr (von). *Orpheus und Eurydike:* Eine operndramaturgische Studie. Munich, Drei Masken, 1923.

Ward, Charles. "*The Tempest:* A Restoration Opera," *ELH Journal of English Literary History* XIII, No. 2 (June, 1946) 119–30.

Weaver, Robert Lamar. Florentine Comic Operas of the Seventeenth Century. Ann Arbor, University Microfilms, 1958.

—— "Sixteenth-Century Instrumentation," MQ XLVII (1961) 363–78.

Weilen, Alexander von. Geschichte des Wiener Theaterwesens von den ältesten Zeiten bis zu den Anfängen der Hoftheater. Vienna, Gesellschaft für vervielfältigende Kunst, 1899.

——Zur Wiener Theatergeschichte : Die vom Jahre 1629 bis zum Jahre 1740 am Wiener Hofe zur Aufführung gelangten Werke theatralischen Charakters und Oratorien. Vienna, A. Hölder, 1901.
An important supplement to Köchel's *Kaiserliche Hofmusikkapelle;* see corrections in Nettl, "Exzerpte aus der Raudnitzer Textbüchersammlung," SzMw VII (1920) 143–44.

Wellesz, Egon. "Die Aussetzung des Basso Continuo in der italienischen Oper," in *International Musical Society, Fourth Congress Report* (London, Novello, 1912) 282–85.

—— Der Beginn des musikalischen Barock und die Anfänge der Oper in Wien. Vienna and Leipzig, Wiener literarische Anstalt, 1922.

—— "Cavalli und der Stil der venetianischen Oper von 1640–1660," SzMw I (1913).

—— "Einige handschriftliche Libretti aus der Frühzeit der Wiener Oper," ZfMw I (1918–19) 278–81.

—— "Die Opern und Oratorien in Wien von 1660–1708," SzMw VI (1919) 5–138.

—— "Zwei Studien zur Geschichte der Oper im 17. Jahrhundert," SIMG XV (1913) 124–54.

Werckmeister, Andreas. Der edlen Music-Kunst Würde, Gebrauch und Missbrauch. Frankfurt, Calvisius, 1691.

Werner, Arno. "Briefe von J. W. Franck, die Hamburger Oper betreffend," SIMG VII (1905–6) 125–28.

Werner, Theodor Wilhelm. "Agostino Steffanis Operntheater in Hannover," AfMf III (1938) 65–79.

Westrup, Jack Allan. "The Cadence in Baroque Recitative," in *Natalicia musicologica Knud Jeppesen* (Copenhagen, W. Hansen, 1962) 243–52.

—— "Monteverdi and the Orchestra," M&L XXI (1940) 230–45.

—— "Monteverdi's *Lamento d'Arianna*," MR I (1940) 144–54.

—— "The Originality of Monteverde," PMA LX (1933–34) 1–25.

—— Purcell. London, J. M. Dent; New York, E. P. Dutton, [1937]. New York, Pellegrini & Cudahy, 1949.

—— "Two First Performances : Monteverdi's *Orfeo* and Mozart's *La Clemenza di Tito*," M&L XXXIX (1958) 327–35.

White, Eric Walter. The Rise of English Opera. London, John Lehmann, 1951.

Wiedemann, Carla. Leben und Wirken des Johann Philipp Förtsch, 1652–1732. Kassel & Basel, Bärenreiter, 1955.

Wiel, Taddeo. I codici musicali contariniani del secolo XVII nella R. Biblioteca di S. Marco in Venezia. Venice, F. Ongania, 1888.

—— "Francesco Cavalli," MA IV (1912–13) 1–19.

Wiley, W. L. The Early Public Theatre in France. Cambridge, Mass., Harvard University Press, 1960.

Winterfeld, Carl von. Johannes Gabrieli und sein Zeitalter. Berlin, Schlesinger, 1834. 3 vols.

Witeschnik, Alexander. Wiener Opernkunst : Von den Anfängen bis zu Karajan. Vienna, Buchgemeinschaft Donauland, [1961].

Wolff, Hellmuth Christian. Die Barockoper in Hamburg (1678–1738). Wolfenbüttel, Möseler, 1957. 2 vols.

—— Die venezianische Oper in der zweiten Hälfte des 17. Jahrhunderts. Berlin, Elsner, 1937.

Worsthorne, Simon Towneley. "Some Early Venetian Opera Productions," M&L XXX (1949) 146–51.

—— Venetian Opera in the Seventeenth Century. Oxford, Clarendon Press, 1954.

—— "Venetian Theatres : 1637–1700," M&L XXIX (1948) 263–75.

Wotquenne, Alfred. Etude bibliographique sur le compositeur napolitain Luigi Rossi. Brussels, Coosemans, 1909.

Zelle, Friedrich. Johann Philipp Förtsch. Berlin, R. Gaertner, 1893.

—— Johann Theile und Nikolaus Adam Strungk. Berlin, R. Gaertner, 1891.

—— Johann Wolfgang Franck. Berlin, R. Gaertner, 1889.

Zenger, Max. Geschichte der Münchner Oper. Munich, Verlag für praktische Kunstwissenschaft, Dr. F. X. Weizinger & Co., 1923.

Zucker, Paul. Die Theaterdekoration des Barok. Berlin, R. Kaemmerer, 1925.

## IV

### *EIGHTEENTH CENTURY*

Abert, Anna Amalie. Christoph Willibald Gluck. Munich, Bong, [1960].

—— "Der Geschmackswandel auf der Opernbühne, am Alkestis-Stoff dargestellt," Mf VI (1953) 214–35.

Abert, Hermann. "Die dramatische Musik," in *Herzog Karl Eugen von Württemberg und seine Zeit* I (Esslingen a. N., 1907) 555–611.

—— "Glucks Alkestis im Stuttgarter Landestheater," ZfMw VI (1923–24) 353–61.

Abert, Hermann. "Gluck und unsere Zeit," *Die Musik* XIII (1913–14) Qt. 4, 3–9.

—— "Händel als Dramatiker," in *Haendelfestspiele* (*Göttingen, 1922*). Göttingen, Turm-Verlag, 1922.

—— "Herzog Karl von Württemberg und die Musik," in *Süddeutsche Monatshefte* V (1908) Band 1, 548–54.

—— "Johann Christian Bach's italienische Opern und ihr Einfluss auf Mozart," ZfMw I (1918–19) 313–28.

—— "Mozart and Gluck." M&L X (1929) 256–65.

—— Niccolo Jommelli als Opernkomponist, mit einer Biographie. Halle an der Saale, M. Niemeyer, 1908.

—— W. A. Mozart. Neubearb. und erweiterte Ausg. von Otto Jahns *Mozart*, hrsg. von Anna Amalie Abert. Leipzig, B&H, 1956. 7th ed. 2 vols.

—— "Zur Geschichte der Oper in Württemberg," in *III. Kongress der Internationalen Musikgesellschaft . . . Bericht* (Vienna, Artaria; Leipzig, B&H, 1909) 186–93.

Abraham, Gerald. "The Operas," in *The Mozart Companion*, ed. H. C. Robbins Landon and Donald Mitchell (London, Rockliff; New York, Oxford University Press, [1956]) 283–323.

Abraham, Gerald, ed. Handel: A Symposium. London, New York, Toronto, Oxford University Press, 1954.

Achenwall, Max. Studien über die komische Oper in Frankreich im 18. Jahrhundert und ihre Beziehungen zu Molière. Eilenburg, Offenhauer, 1912.

Adimari, Lodovico. "Satira quarta: Contro alcuni vizi delle donne, e particolamente contro le cantatrice," in *Satire del marchese Lodovico Adimari* (London, Si vende in Livorno presso T. Masi e comp., 1788) 183–253.

Ahnell, Emil Gustave. The Concept of Tonality in the Operas of Jean-Philippe Rameau. Ann Arbor, University Microfilms, 1957.

Albert, Maurice. Les Théâtres de la foire (1660–1789). Paris, Hachette, 1900.

—— Les Théâtres des boulevards (1789–1848). [Paris?], Lecène et Oudin, 1902.

Alfieri, Pietro. Notizie biografiche di Niccolò Jommelli di Aversa. Rome, Tip. delle belle arte, 1845.

Algarotti, Francesco, conte. Saggio sopra l'opera in musica. Leghorn, Coltellini, 1763.

Allorto, Riccardo. "Stefano Arteaga e *Le rivoluzioni del teatro musicale italiano*," RMI LII (1950) 124–47.

Altmann, Charlotte. Der französische Einfluss auf die Textbücher der klassischen Wiener Operette. Vienna Dissertation, 1935.

Anderson, Emily, ed. The Letters of Mozart and His Family Chronologically Arranged, Translated and Edited with an Introduction, Notes and Indices . . . with Extracts from the Letters of Constanze Mozart to

Johann Antoñ André Translated and Edited by C. B. Oldman. London, Macmillan, 1938. 3 vols., paged continuously.

Anecdotes dramatiques : Contenant toutes les pièces de théâtre . . . joués à Paris . . . jusqu'à l'année 1775. Paris, Duchesne, 1775. 3 vols.

Anheisser, Siegfried. Für den deutschen Mozart. Emsdetten i. Westf., H. & J. Lechte, 1938.

—— "Die unbekannte Urfassung von Mozarts *Figaro*," ZfMw XV (1932–33) 301–17.

Arend, Max. "Gluck, der Reformator des Tanzes," *Die Musik* XIII (1913–14) Qt. 4, 16–22.

—— Gluck, eine Biographie. Berlin, Schuster & Loeffler, 1921.

—— "Die Ouvertüren zu Glucks *Cythère assiégée*," ZfMw IV (1921–22) 94–95.

—— "Die unter Gluck's Mitwirkung, verschollene älteste deutsche Übersetzung der *Iphigenia auf Tauris*," ZIMG VII (1905–6) 261–67.

Armitage-Smith, J. N. A. "The Plot of *The Magic Flute*," M&L XXXV (1954) 36–39.

Arnaldi, Enea, conte. Idea di un teatro nelle principali sue parte simile a' teatri antichi. Vicenza, A. Veronese, 1762.

Arnheim, Amalie. *"Le Devin du village* von Jean-Jacques Rousseau und die Parodie *Les Amours de Bastien et Bastienne*," SIMG IV (1902–3) 686–727.

Arnoldson, Mrs. Louise Parkinson. Sedaine et les musiciens de son temps. Paris, l'Entente linotypiste, 1934.

Arteaga, Stefano. Le rivoluzioni del teatro musicale italiano, dalla sua origine fino al presente. Venice, C. Palese, 1785. 2d ed. 3 vols.

Asenjo y Barbieri, Francisco. Cancionero musical de los siglos XV y XVI. Madrid, Tip. de los huérfanos, [1890].

Aubignac, François Hédelin, abbé d'. La Pratique du théâtre. Amsterdam, J. F. Bernard, 1715. New ed. Alger, J. Carbonel, 1927.

Auriac, Eugène d'. Théâtre de la foire : Recueil de pièces représentées aux foires St.-Germain et St.-Laurent, précédé d'une essai historique sur les spectacles forains. Paris, Garnier frères, 1878.

Babbitt, Irving. Rousseau and Romanticism. Boston and New York, Houghton Mifflin, 1919.

Babcock, Robert W. "Francis Coleman's 'Register of Operas,' 1712–1734," M&L XXIV (1943) 155–58. Supplemented and corrected in a letter by O. E. Deutsch, *ibid*. XXV (1944) 126.

Bacher, Otto. "Die deutschen Erstaufführungen von Mozarts *Don Giovanni*," *Jahrbuch des Freien deutschen Hochstifts Frankfurt a. M.* (1926) 338–79. Also separately reprinted.

—— "Ein Frankfurter Szene zu Glucks *Don Juan*," ZfMw VII (1924–25) 570–74.

—— "Frankfurts musikalische Bühnengeschichte im 18. Jahrhundert.

Theil I. Die Zeit der Wandertruppen (1700–1786)," *Archiv für Frankfurts Geschichte und Kunst* (1925) 133–206.

Bacher, Otto. Die Geschichte der Frankfurter Oper im 18. Jahrhundert. Frankfurt/M., Englert und Schlosser, 1926.

—— "Ein Mozartfund," ZfMw VIII (1925–26) 226–30.

—— "Zur Geschichte der Oper auf Frankfurter Boden im 18. Jahrhundert," ZfMw VIII (1925–26) 93–102.

Barberet, Vincent. Lesage et le théâtre de la foire. Nancy, 1887.

Barberio, Francesco. "Disavventure di Paisiello," RMI XXIII (1916) 534–58.

—— "Giovanni Paisiello tra le ire di un copista e di un innovatore," RMI XXII (1915) 301–18.

—— "Lettere inedite di Paisiello [1792–1812]," RMI XXIV (1917) 173–88.

—— "I primi dieci anni di vita artistica di Paisiello," RMI XXIX (1922) 264–76.

Barbieri, Francisco. *See* Asenjo y Barbieri.

Barclay Squire. *See* Squire, William Barclay.

Bardi-Poswiansky, Benno. Der tolle Kapellmeister : Heitere Oper in 3 Akten mit Benutzung Reinhard Keiserscher Melodien. Textbuch. Berlin, Revo-Verlag, [1929].

Baroni, Jole Maria. "La lirica musicale di Pietro Metastasio," RMI XII (1905) 383–406.

Bartha, Dénes, and László Somfai. Haydn als Opernkapellmeister : Die Haydn-Dokumente der Esterházy-Opernsammlung. Mainz, Schott's Söhne, 1960.

Bateson, F. W. English Comic Drama, 1700–1750. Oxford, Clarendon Press, 1929.

Bauer, Anton. Das Theater in der Josefstadt zu Wien. Vienna and Munich, Manutiuspresse, 1957.

Beau, A. Eduard. "Die Musik im Werk des Gil Vicente," *Volkstum und Kultur der Romanen* IX (1936) 177–201.

Beaulieu, Henri. Les Théâtres du boulevard de Crime . . . de Nicolet à Déjazet (1752–1862). Paris, H. Daragon, 1905.

Beaumarchais, Pierre Augustin, Caron de. Théâtre : Lettres relatives à son théâtre. Texte établi et annoté par Maurice Allem et Paul-Courant. [Paris, Librairie Gallimard, 1957.]

Beck, Paul. "Oberschwäbische Volkstheater im 18. Jahrhundert," *Alemannia* XX (1892) 73–97.

Beer, Otto Fritz. Mozart und das Wiener Singspiel. Vienna Dissertation, 1932.

Behrend, William. "Weyse und Kuhlau : Studie zur Geschichte der dänischen Musik," *Die Musik* III, No. 22 (1904) 272–86.

Bekker, Paul. "Glucks *Alkeste* auf der Bühne," ZfMw I (1918–19) 193–96.

Bellaigue, Camille. "Les Epoques de la musique : L'opéra-comique," *Revue des deux mondes* (1905) No. 5, 177–210.

—— "Les Epoques de la musique : L'opéra mélodique—Mozart," *Revue des deux mondes* (1901) No. 6, 885–907.

—— "Les Epoques de la musique : L'opéra récitatif," *Revue des deux mondes* (1900) No. 6, 608–38.

Belluci la Salandra, Mario. Opere teatrali serie e buffe di Nicolò Piccinni. Rome, Edizioni Psalterium, 1935. For corrections, etc., see *Note d'archivio* XIII (1936) 55–58.

—— Saggio cronologico delle opere teatrali di Gaetano Latilla. Bari, 1935. Separate from *"Japigia," Rivista di arch., storica e arte*.

—— Triade musicale bitontina: . . . Logroscino, Traetta, Planelli. Bitonto, A. Amendolagene, 1935.

[Benjamin, Lewis Saul.] Life and Letters of John Gay . . . by Lewis Melville [pseud.]. London, D. O'Connor, 1921.

Benn, Frederick Christopher. Mozart on the Stage. London, Ernest Benn Ltd., 1946.

Bérard, Jean Antoine. L'Art du chant. Paris, Dessait & Saillant, 1755.

Berger, Arthur V. *"The Beggar's Opera,* the Burlesque, and Italian Opera," M&L XVII (1936) 93–105.

Berthier, Paul. Réflexions sur l'art et la vie de Jean-Philippe Rameau, 1683–1764. Paris, Picard et Cie., 1957.

Beyle, Henri. Vies de Haydn, de Mozart et de Métastase. Paris, H. Champion, 1914. Text established and annotated by Daniel Muller, preface by Romain Rolland.

Bitter, Christof. Wandlungen in den Inszenierungsformen des *Don Giovanni* von 1787 bis 1928 : Zur Problematik des musikalischen Theaters in Deutschland. Regensburg, G. Bosse, 1961.

Bitter, Karl Hermann. Mozart's *Don Juan* und Gluck's *Iphigenia in Tauris:* Ein Versuch neuer Uebersetzungen. Berlin, F. Schneider, 1866.

Blom, Eric. "The Problem of *Don Giovanni,*" M&L XIII (1932) 381–90.

Blondel, S. "Les Castrats," *La Chronique musicale* IX (1875) 241–50.

Boas, Hans. "Lorenzo da Ponte als Wiener Theaterdichter," SIMG XV (1913–14) 325–38.

[Bobillier, Marie.] "Grétry, sa vie et ses œuvres," in *Mémoires couronnés et autres mémoires publiés par l'Académie royale . . . de Belgique,* Tome XXXVI, 1884.

Bötcher, Elmar. Goethes Singspiele *Erwin und Elmire* und *Claudine von Villa Bella* und die "opera buffa." Marburg, Elwert, 1912.

Bollert, Werner. Die Buffoopern Baldassare Galuppis. Bottrop, Postberg, 1935.

—— "Giuseppe Petrosellini quale librettista di opere," RMI XLIII (1939) 531–38.

—— "Tre opere di Galuppi, Haydn e Paisiello sul' *Mondo della luna* di Goldoni," *Musica d'oggi* XXI (1939) 265–70.

Bolte, Johannes. Die Singspiele der englischen Komödianten und ihrer Nachfolger in Deutschland, Holland und Skandinavia. Hamburg and Leipzig, L. Voss, 1893.

Bonnet, George Edgar. Philidor et l'évolution de la musique française au XVIIIe siècle. Paris, Delagrave, 1921.

[Bonnet, Jacques.] Histoire de la musique, et de ses effets. Paris, J. Cochart, 1715.

Borcherdt, Hans Heinrich. "Geschichte der italienischen Oper in Breslau," *Zeitschrift für die Geschichte Schlesiens* XLIV (1910) 18 ff.

Borland, John E. "French Opera before 1750," PMA XXXIII (1907) 133–57.

Borrel, Eugène. "Notes sur l'orchestration de l'opéra *Jephte* de Montéclair (1733) et de la symphonie des *Elémens* de J. F. Rebel (1737)," RM No. sp. 226 (1955) 105–16.

—— "Un Paradoxe musical au XVIIIe siècle," in *Mélanges de musicologie* (Paris, Droz, 1933) 217–21.

Borren, Charles van den. Alessandro Scarlatti et l'esthétique de l'opéra napolitain. Paris, Editions de la Renaissance d'occident, 1921.

—— "Roma centro musicale del Settecento," RMI XXXI (1924) 69–71.

Bourdelot, Pierre. *See* Bonnet, Jacques.

Boyer, Noël. La Guerre des bouffons et la musique française (1752–1754) suivi de : Le Mal des chèvres. . . . Paris, Les Editions de la Nouvelle France, [1945].

Bragard, Roger. *"Li Voyedje di Tchaufontaine,"* in *Mélanges Ernest Closson* (Brussels, Société Belge de Musicologie, 1948) 48–59.

Braun, Lisbeth. "Die Balletkomposition von Joseph Starzer," SzMw XIII (1926) 38–56.

Breitholtz, Lennart. Studier i operan *Gustaf Wasa*. Uppsala, Lundequistska Bokhandeln, [1954].

Brenet, Michel, pseud. *See* Bobillier, Marie.

Breydert, Frédéric M. Le Génie créateur de W. A. Mozart : Essai sur l'instauration musicale des personnages dans *Les Noces de Figaro, Don Juan, La Flute enchantée*. Paris, Editions Alsatia, 1956.

Briquet, Marie. "L'Alceste de E.-J. Floquet," *Mélanges d'histoire et d'esthétique musicales offerts à Paul-Marie Masson* II (Paris, 1955) 19–29.

Brosses, Charles de. Lettres familières sur l'Italie. Paris, Firmin-Didot, 1931.

Brown, John. Letters on the Italian Opera. London, T. Cadell, 1791. 2d ed.

Brück, Paul. "Glucks *Orpheus und Euridike*," AfMw VII (1925) 436–76.

Brückner, Fritz. Georg Benda und das deutsche Singspiel. Leipzig, B&H, 1904. Also SIMG V (1903–4) 571–621.

—— "Zum Thema 'Georg Benda und das Monodram,' " SIMG VI (1904–5) 496–500.

Brüggemann, Fritz. Bänkelgesang und Singspiel vor Goethe. Leipzig, Reclam, 1937.

Bruger, Hans. Glucks dramatische Instrumentationskunst und ihre geschichtlichen Grundlagen. Teil 1 : Glucks italienischen Werke (einschliesslich der Wiener Reformopern). Heidelberg Dissertation, 1922.

Brukner, Fr. Die Zauberflöte: Unbekannte Handschriften und seltene Drucke aus der Frühzeit Mozarts Oper. Vienna, Gilhofer & Rauschburg, 1934.

Bruyère, André. "Les Muses galantes," RM No. 218 (1952) 5–31.

Bruyr, José. Grétry. Paris, Rieder, [1931].

Burney, Charles. A General History of Music from the Earliest Ages to the Present Period. London, Printed for the Author, 1776. Also : 2d ed., with critical and historical notes by Frank Mercer. London, Foulis; New York, Harcourt, Brace, 1935.

—— Memoirs of the Life and Writings of the Abate Metastasio; in Which Are Incorporated Translations of His Principal Letters. London, G. G. and J. Robinson, 1796. 3 vols.

—— The Present State of Music in France and Italy. London, T. Becket, 1771.

—— The Present State of Music in Germany, the Netherlands, and United Provinces. London, T. Becket, 1773. 2 vols.

Burt, Nathaniel. "Opera in Arcadia," MQ XLI (1955) 145–70.

Burton, Humphrey. "Les Académies de musique en France au XVIIIe siècle," RdM XXXVII (1955) 122–47.

Busi, Leonida. Benedetto Marcello. Bologna, N. Zanichelli, 1884.

Bustico, Guido. "Gli spettacoli musicali al 'Teatro Novo' di Novara (1779–1873)," RMI XXV (1918) 84–103, 202–48; "Nuovo contributo," RMI XXVI (1919) 615–52.

—— Pier Alessandro Guglielmi, musicista. Massa, Medici, 1898.

Cahn-Speyer, Rudolf. Franz Seydelmann als dramatischer Komponist. Leipzig, B&H, 1909.

Callegari, Matelda. "Il melodramma e Pietro Metastasio," RMI XXVI (1919) 518–44; XXVII (1920) 31–59, 458–76.

Calmus, Georgy. "Die Beggar's Opera von Gay und Pepusch," SIMG VIII (1906–7) 286–335.

—— Die ersten deutschen Singspiele von Standfuss und Hiller. Leipzig, B&H, 1908.

—— Zwei Opernburlesken aus der Rokokozeit. Berlin, Liepmannssohn, 1912. Contents : Télémaque (Lesage), The Beggar's Opera (Gay and Pepusch).

Cametti, Alberto. "Critiche e satire teatrali romane del '700," RMI IX (1902) 1–35.

—— "Leonardo Vinci e i suoi drammi in musica al Teatro delle Dame 1724–30," Musica d'oggi VI (1924) 297–99.

Cametti, Alberto. "Saggio cronologico delle opere teatrali (1754–1794) di Nicolò Piccinni," RMI VIII (1901) 75–100.

Campardon, Emile. L'Académie royale de musique au XVIIIe siècle. Paris, Berger-Levrault, 1884. 2 vols.

—— Les Comédiens du roi de la troupe italienne. Paris, Berger-Levrault, 1880. 2 vols.

—— Les Spectacles des foires . . . depuis 1595 jusqu'à 1791. Paris, Berger-Levrault, 1877. 2 vols.

Cannon, Beekman C. Johann Mattheson, Spectator in Music. New Haven, Yale University Press, 1947.

Capri, Antonio. Il Settecento musicale in Europa. Milan, Hoepli, 1936.

Carey, Clive. "The Problem of Don Giovanni Again," M&L XIV (1933) 30–35.

Carlez, Jules. Un Opéra biblique au XVIIIe siècle. Caen, Le Blanc-Hardel, 1879.

Carmena y Millán, Luis. Crónica de la ópera italiana en Madrid desde el año 1738 hasta nuestros dias. Madrid, M. Minuesa de los Rios, 1878.

Carmody, Francis J. Le Repertoire de l'opéra-comique en vaudevilles de 1708 à 1764. Berkeley, California, University of California Press, 1933.

Carreras y Bulbena, José Rafael. Domenech Terradellas. Barcelona, F. X. Altés, 1908.

Carroll, Charles Michael. François-André Danican-Philidor : His Life and Dramatic Art. Ann Arbor, University Microfilms, 1960. 2 vols.

Casavola, Franco. Tommaso Traetta di Bitonto (1727–1779) : La vita e le opere. Bari, Società di Storia Patria per la Puglia, 1957.

Celani, Enrico. "Musica e musicisti in Roma (1750–1850)," RMI XVIII (1911) 1–63; XX (1913) 33–88.

Cesari, Gaetano, and others. Antonio Bartolomeo Bruni, musicista cuneese (1751–1821). Turin, S. Lattes, 1931.

Chailly, Luciano. Il matrimonio segreto, guida musicale. [Milan], Istituto d'Alta Cultura, [1949].

Chantavoine, Jean. Mozart dans Mozart. Paris, Desclée de Brouwer, [1948].

Chatfield-Taylor, H. C. Goldoni : A Biography. New York, Duffield, 1913.

Chrysander, Friedrich. "Adonis: Oper von Reinhard Keiser," AMZ XIII (1878) 65–70, 81–87, 97–101.

—— "Der erste Entwurf der Bassarie 'Nasce al bosco' in Händel's Oper Ezio (1732)," AMZ XIV (1879) 641–46.

—— G. F. Händel. Leipzig, B&H, 1858–67. 3 vols.

—— "Mattheson's Verzeichniss Hamburgischer Opern von 1678 bis 1728, gedruckt im Musikalischen Patrioten, mit seinen handschriftlichen Fortsetzungen bis 1751, nebst Zusätzen und Berichtigungen," AMZ XII (1877) 198–282, passim.

—— "Musik und Theater in Mecklenburg," Archiv für Landeskunde in *den Grossherzogthümern Mecklenburg* IV (1854) 105–25, 258–80, 346–79.

—— "Neue Beiträge zur mecklenburgischen Musikgeschichte," *Archiv für Landeskunde in den Grossherzogthümern Mecklenburg* VI (1856) 666–82.

—— "Die Oper *Don Giovanni* von Gazzaniga und von Mozart," VfMw IV (1888) 351–435.

—— "Reinhard Keiser," in *Allgemeine deutsche Biographie* XV (1882) 540–51.

[Cimarosa, Domenico.] Per il bicentenario della nascità di Domenico Cimarosa. Aversa, A cura del Comitato per le Celebrazioni, 1949. Contains "Annali delle opere," pp. 73–148 by F. Schlitzer and other essays.

Clercx, Suzanne. Grétry, 1741–1813. Brussels, Editions La Renaissance du Livre, [1944].

Clive, Geoffrey. "The Demonic in Mozart," M&L XXXVII (1956) 1–13.

Cohen, Hermann. Die dramatische Idee in Mozarts Operntexten. Berlin, Cassirer, 1916.

Combarieu, Jules. "J.-J. Rousseau et le mélodrame," RHCM I (1901) 273–77.

—— "L'Opéra-comique d'hier et d'aujourd'hui," (RHCM VII (1907) 549–63.

Confalonieri, Giulio. "Nota su *Varrone e Perrica* di Alessandro Scarlatti," *Accademia musicale chigiana* XIV (1957) 39–49.

Conrad, Leopold. Mozarts Dramaturgie der Oper. Würzburg, Triltsch, 1943.

[Contant d'Orville, André Guillaume.] Histoire de l'opéra bouffon. Amsterdam and Paris, Grangé, 1768. 2 vols.

Cooper, Martin. Gluck. New York, Oxford University Press, 1935.

—— Opéra comique. New York, Chanticleer Press, [1949].

Coopersmith, J[acob] M[aurice]. [1.] An Investigation of Georg Friedrich Händel's Orchestral Style. [2.] A Thematic Index of the Printed Works of Händel. Harvard Dissertation, 1932. 12 vols.

—— "The Libretto of Handel's *Jupiter in Argos*," M&L XVII (1936) 289–96.

Corder, Frederick. "The Works of Sir Henry Bishop," MQ IV (1918) 78–97.

Cortese, Nino. "Un' autobiografia inedita di Giovanni Paisiello," RassM III (1930) 123–35. Following is Paisiello's autobiography.

Cotarelo y Mori, Emilio. Historia de la zarzuela o sea El drama lírico en España, desde su origen a fines del siglo XIX. Madrid, Tipografía de Archivos, 1934.

—— Orígenes y establecimento de la ópera en España hasta 1800. Madrid, Tip. de la "Revista de arch.," [etc.], 1917.

Cotarelo y Mori, Emilio, ed. Colección de entremeses, loas, bailes, jácaras y mojingangas desde fines del siglo XVI á medíados del XVII. Madrid, Bailly-Baillière, 1911.

Croce, Benedetto. I teatri di Napoli, secolo XV–XVIII. Naples, L. Pierro, 1891. New ed., 1916.

Crowder, C. Fairfax. "Neglected Treasures in Handel's Operas," M&L II (1921) 135–48.

Cucuel, Georges. Les Créateurs de l'opéra-comique français. Paris, F. Alcan, 1914.

—— "La Critique musicale dans les 'revues' du XVIIIe siècle," L'Année musicale II (1912) 127–203.

—— "Giacomo Casanova e la musica," RMI XXXVI (1929) 446–65.

—— "Notes sur la comédie italienne de 1717 à 1789," SIMG XV (1913–14) 154–66.

—— "Les Opéras de Gluck dans les parodies du XVIIIe siècle," RM III (1922) No. 5, 201–21; No. 6, 51–68.

—— "Sources et documents pour servir à l'histoire de l'opéra-comique en France," L'Année musicale III (1913) 247–82.

Cummings, William H. "The Lord Chamberlain and Opera in London, 1700 to 1741," PMA XL (1914) 37–72.

Curiel, Carlo Leone. Il teatro S. Pietro di Trieste, 1690–1801. [Milan], Archetipographia di Milano, 1937.

Curzon, Henri de. Grétry. Paris, Laurens, [1907].

Dacier, Emile. "Les Caractères de la danse: Histoire d'un divertissement pendant la première moitié du XVIIIe siècle," RHCM V (1905) 324–35, 365–67.

—— "Une Danseuse française à Londres au début du XVIIIe siècle," MM III (1907) 437–63, 746–65.

—— "L'Opéra au XVIIIe siècle : Les premières représentations du Dardanus de Rameau," RHCM III (1903) 163–73.

Dahms, Walter. "The 'Gallant' Style of Music," MQ XI (1925) 356–72.

Dahnk-Baroffio, Emilie. "Nicola Hayms Anteil an Händels Rodelinde-Libretto," Mf VII (1954) 295–300.

Dallapiccola, Luigi. "Notes on the Statue Scene in Don Giovanni," Music Survey III (1950) 89–97.

Damerini, Adelmo. "Un precursore italiano di Gluck : Tommaso Traetta," Il pianoforte (July, 1927).

—— "Tommaso Traetta : Cenni biografici," Bollettino bibliografico musicale II (July, 1927) 1–13.

D'Angeli, Andrea. Benedetto Marcello, vita e opere. Milan, Fratelli Bocca, 1940.

—— Commemorazione di Gio. Batta. Pergolesi. Padua, L. Penada, 1936.

Da Ponte, Lorenzo. Memorie. New York, Lorenzo e Carlo Da Ponte, 1823. 2 vols. Translated, with introduction and notes, by L. A. Sheppard, Boston, Houghton Mifflin, 1929. Translated by Elisabeth Abbott, edited and annotated by Arthur Livingston, Philadelphia, J. B. Lippincott, 1929. Other editions : Bari, G. Laterza, 1918 (Italian); Paris, Henri Jonquières, 1931 (French; includes previously unpublished letters to Casanova; preface and notes by Raoul Vèze).

—— Storia compendiosa della vita di Lorenzo Da Ponte scritta di lui medesimo. New York, Riley, 1807.

D'Arienzo, Nicola. "Le origini dell' opera comica," RMI II (1895) 597–628; IV (1897) 421–59; VI (1899) 473–95; VII (1900) 1–33.

Dean, Winton. Handel's Dramatic Oratorios and Masques. London, New York, Oxford University Press, 1959.

—— "The Libretto of The Secret Marriage," Music Survey III (1950) 33–38.

De Angelis, Alberto. Il teatro Alibert o delle Dame nella Roma papale. Tivoli, A. Chicca, [1951].

De' Calsabigi, Ranieri. "Dissertazione . . . su le poesie drammatiche del Sig. Abate Pietro Metastasio," in Poesie del Signor Abate Pietro Metastasio (Paris, Vedova Quillan, 1755–69) I, xix–cciv.

—— Risposta . . . alla critica ragionatissima delle poesie drammatiche del C. de' Calsabigi, fatta del baccelliere D. Stefan Arteaga. Venice, Curti, 1790.

Decker, Herbert. Dramaturgie und Szene der Zauberflöte. Regensburg, G. Bosse, [1950].

De Dominicis, Giulia. "Romà centro musicale nel Settecento," RMI XXX (1923) 511–28.

Degey, Maurice. Les Echos imprévus de la mort de Grétry. Liége, Editions de la Vie wallonne, 1938.

Della Corte, Andrea. "Appunti sull' estetica musicale di Pietro Metastasio," RMI XXVIII (1921) 94–119.

—— Baldassare Galuppi : Profilo critico. Siena, 1948.

—— "Cimarosa nel '99 e nella fortuna postuma," RassM IX (1936) 280–83.

—— Figuras y motivas de lo opera bufa italiano. Buenos Aires, La revista de musica, 1928.

—— Gluck e i suoi tempi. Florence, G. C. Sansoni, 1948.

—— "Nel II centenario della morte di Pergolesi : Il geloso schernito e Il maestro di musica," RassM IX (1936) 202–8.

—— "Notizie di Gaetano Pugnani musicista torinese (1731–1798)," Rassegna mensile municipale "Torino" (1931) 26–39.

—— L'opera comica italiana nel 1700. Bari, G. Laterza, 1923. 2 vols.

—— Paisiello : Con una tavola tematica. L'estetica musicale di P. Metastasio. Turin, Fratelli Bocca, 1922.

—— Piccinni (Settecento italiano) : Con frammenti musicali inediti e due ritratti. Bari, G. Laterza, 1928.

—— "Tetide in Sciro, l'opera di Domenico Scarlatti ritrovata," RassM XXVII (1957) 281–89.

—— Tutto il teatro di Mozart. [Turin], Edizioni Radio Italiana, [1957].

Della Corte, Andrea, ed. Canto e bel canto (Tosi e Mancini). Turin, G. B. Paravia, [1933].

Della Torre, Arnaldo. Saggio di una bibliografia delle opere intorno a Carlo Goldoni (1793–1907). Florence, Alfani e Venturi, 1908.

Demarquez, Suzanne. "Un Voyageur français et la musique italienne au XVIIIe siècle," RM, numéro spécial, "La Musique dans les pays Latins" (February–March, 1940) 125–33.

De Napoli, Giuseppe. "Niccolò Piccinni nel secondo centenario della nascità," RMI XXXV (1928) 209–18.

Dennis, John. An Essay on the Opera's after the Italian Manner, Which Are About to Be Established on the English Stage : With Some Reflections on the Damage Which They May Bring to the Publick.... London, J. Nutt, 1706.

Dent, Edward J. Alessandro Scarlatti : His Life and Works. New Impression, with Preface and Additional Notes by Frank Walker. London, Edward Arnold, [1960]. First published 1905.

—— "Alessandro Scarlatti," PMA XXX (1904) 75–90.

—— "Emanuel Schikaneder," M&L XXXVII (1956) 14–21.

—— "Ensembles and Finales in 18th Century Italian Opera," SIMG XI (1909–10) 543–69; XII (1910–11) 112–38.

—— "Giuseppe Maria Buini," SIMG XIII (1911–12) 329–36.

—— Handel. London, Duckworth, [1934].

—— "Handel on the Stage," M&L XVI (1935) 174–87.

—— "Italian Opera in the Eighteenth Century, and Its Influence on the Music of the Classical Period," SIMG XIV (1912–13) 500–509.

—— "Leonardo Leo," SIMG VIII (1906–7) 550–66.

—— Mozart's Operas : A Critical Study. London, Chatto & Windus; New York, McBride, Nast, 1913. 2d ed., New York, Oxford University Press, 1947.

—— Mozart's Opera The Magic Flute: Its History and Interpretation. Cambridge, W. Heffer, 1911.

—— "Notes on Leonardo Vinci," MA IV (1912–13) 193–201.

—— "The Operas of Alessandro Scarlatti," SIMG IV (1902–3) 143–56.

—— "A Pastoral Opera [La fede riconosciuta, 1710] by Alessandro Scarlatti," MR XII (1951) 7–14.

De' Paoli, Domenico. "Diane ed Endimione di Alessandro Scarlatti," RassM XIII (1940) 139–46.

De Rensis, Raffaello. Musica italiana in Francia : La riforma intitolata a Gluck. Rome, Casa editrice "Musica," 1916.

Desastre, Jean. Carlo Broschi : Kuriose Abenteuer eines Sopranisten. Zurich, Bürdecke & Herwig, 1903.

[Desboulmiers, Jean Auguste Julien.] Histoire anecdotique et raisonée du théâtre italien, depuis son rétablissement en France jusqu'à l'année 1769. Paris, Lacombe, 1769. 7 vols.

—— Histoire du théâtre de l'opéra-comique. Paris, Lacombe, 1769. 2 vols.

Desessarts, Nicolas Toussaint Lemoyne. Les Trois Théâtres de Paris, ou abrégé historique de l'établissement de la Comédie Françoise, de la Comédie Italienne & de l'Opéra. Paris, Lacombe, 1777.

Desnoiresterres, Gustave. Gluck et Piccinni, 1774–1800. Paris, Didier, 1875. 2d ed.

Deutsch, Otto Erich. Das Freihaustheater auf der Wieden, 1787–1801. Vienna-Leipzig, Deutsche Verlag für Jugend und Volk Gesellschaft, [1937].

—— Handel : A Documentary Biography. London, A. & C. Black; New York, W. W. Norton, 1955.

—— Mozart und die Wiener Logen : Zur Geschichte seiner Freimaurer-Kompositionen. Vienna, Wiener Freimaurer-Zeitung, 1932.

Diderot, Denis. Le Neveu de Rameau : Satyre publiée pour la première fois sur le manuscrit original autographe. Paris, Plon, Nourrit, 1891.

Dietz, Max. Geschichte des musikalischen Dramas in Frankreich während der Revolution bis zum Directorium (1787 bis 1795). Vienna, Groscher & Blaha, 1885. 2d ed., Leipzig, B&H, 1893.

Di Giacomo, Salvatore. Il conservatorio dei poveri di Gesu Cristo e quello di S. M. di Loreto. Palermo, Sandron, 1928.

—— Il conservatorio di Sant' Onofrio a Capuana e quello di S. M. della Pietà dei Turchini. Naples, Sandron, 1924.

[Ditters] von Dittersdorf, Karl. Karl von Dittersdorfs Lebensbeschreibung : Seinem Sohne in die Feder diktiert. Leipzig, B&H, 1801. Translated as: The Autobiography of Karl von Dittersdorf. London, R. Bentley, 1896. Modern German editions : Leipzig, Reclam, 1909 (Istel); Regensburg, G. Bosse, [ca. 1940] (E. Schmitz); Leipzig, Staackmann, 1940 (Loets).

Donath, Gustav. "Florian Gassmann als Opernkomponist," SzMw II (1914) 34–211.

Doran, John. "Mann" and Manners at the Court of Florence, 1740–1786 : Founded on the Letters of Horace Mann to Horace Walpole. London, R. Bentley, 1876. 2 vols.

Downes, Edward O. D. "The Neapolitan Tradition in Opera," in International Musicological Society, Report of the Eighth Congress, New York 1961 (Kassel, [etc.], Bärenreiter, 1961) I, 277–84.

—— The Operas of Johann Christian Bach as a Reflection of the Dominant Trends in Opera Seria 1750–1780. Harvard Dissertation, 1958.

—— "Secco Recitative in Early Classical Opera Seria (1720–80)," JAMS XIV (1961) 50–69.

Draper, John W. Eighteenth Century English Aesthetics : A Bibliography. Heidelberg, C. Winter, 1931.

Druilhe, Paule. Monsigny. Paris, La Colombe, [1955].

DuBos, Jean Baptiste. Critical Reflections on Poetry, Painting and Music. London, J. Nourse, 1748. 3 vols. Translated from the French 5th ed. Originally published anonymously, Paris, 1719.

Ducannès-Duval, G. "L'Opéra à Bordeaux en 1784," RdM XXI (1937) 82–83.

Dumesnil, René. Le Don Juan de Mozart. Paris, Editions musicales de la librairie de France, 1927; Paris, Editions d'histoire et d'art, Plon, [1955].

—— "Le Livret et les personnages de Don Giovanni," RM No. 4 (February, 1927) 118–28.

Ebert, Alfred. Attilio Ariosti in Berlin (1697–1703). Leipzig, Giesecke & Devrient, 1905.

Eckermann, Johann Peter. Gespräche mit Goethe. Berlin, Bong, [1916]. 2 vols.

Edgar, Clifford B. "Mozart's Early Efforts in Opera," PMA XXXII (1906) 45–58.

—— "A Résumé of Mozart's Early Operas," ZIMG VII (1905–6) 460–64.

Einstein, Alfred. "Concerning Some Recitatives in Don Giovanni," M&L XIX (1938) 417–25.

—— "Das erste Libretto des Don Giovanni," Acta musicologica IX (1937) 149–50.

—— "The First Performance of Mozart's Entführung in London," MR VII (1946) 154–60.

—— Gluck. London, Dent; New York, E. P. Dutton, [1936].

—— Gluck : Sein Leben, seine Werke. Zurich & Stuttgart, Pan-Verlag, [1954]. English translation : London, J. M. Dent & Son; New York, E. P. Dutton & Co., [1954].

—— "Mozart e Tarchi : Un episodio della storia delle Nozze di Figaro," RassM VIII (1935) 269–72.

—— "Mozart et l'opéra-bouffe à Salzburg," RdM XXI (1937) 1–4.

—— Mozart, His Character, His Work. New York and London, Oxford University Press, 1945.

—— "Ein Schüler Gluck's," Acta musicologica X (1938) 48–50.

—— "Die Text-Vorlage zu Mozart's Zaide," Acta musicologica VIII (1936) 30–37.

—— "Eine unbekannte Arie der Marcelline," ZfMw XIII (1930–31) 200–205.

Eisenschmidt, Joachim. Die szenische Darstellung der Opern Georg Friedrich Händels auf der Londoner Bühne seiner Zeit. Wolfenbüttel and Berlin, Kallmeyer, 1940.

Eitner, Robert. "Benedetto Marcello," MfMg XXIII (1891) 187–94, 197–211.

—— "Die deutsche komische Oper," MfMg XXIV (1892) 37–92.

—— "Der Generalbass des 18. Jahrhunderts," MfMg XII (1880) 151–54.

Ellinger, Georg. "Händel's Admet und seine Quelle," VfMw I (1885) 201–24.

Engel, Carl. "A Note on Domenico Cimarosa's Il matrimonio segreto," MQ XXXIII (1947) 201–6.

Engel, Gustav. "Eine mathematisch-harmonische Analyse des *Don Giovanni* von Mozart*,*" VfMw III (1887) 491–560.

Engel, Hans. "Die Finali der Mozartschen Opern," *Mozart-Jahrbuch 1954* (1955) 113–34.

—— "Richard Wagners Stellung zu Mozart," in *Festschrift Wilhelm Fischer* (Innsbruck, 1956) 39–48.

Engelke, Bernhard. "Aus den entscheidenden Entwicklungsjahren der Opéra-comique," in *Festschrift Arnold Schering* (Berlin, A. Glas, 1937) 51–60.

Engländer, Richard. "Domenico Fischietti als Buffokomponist in Dresden," ZfMw II (1919–20) 321–52, 399–442.

—— "Dresden und die deutsche Oper im letzten Drittel des 18. Jahrhunderts," ZfMw III (1920–21) 1–21.

—— "Das Ende der *opera seria* in Dresden : Naumanns *Clemenza di Tito* 1769," *Neues Archiv für Sächsische Geschichte und Altertumskunde* XXXIX (1918) 311–29.

—— "Glucks *Cinesi* und *Orfano della China*," *Gluck-Jahrbuch* I (1913) 54–81.

—— "Gluck und der Norden," *Acta musicologica* XXIV (1952) 62–83.

—— Johann Gottlieb Naumann als Opernkomponist. Leipzig, B&H, 1922.

—— Joseph Martin Kraus und die Gustavianische Oper. Uppsala, Almqvist & Wiksell; Leipzig, O. Harrassowitz, [1943].

—— "Die Opern Joseph Schusters," ZfMw X (1927–28) 257–91.

—— "The Sketches for *The Magic Flute* at Upsala," MQ XXVII (1941) 343–55.

—— "Zur Musikgeschichte Dresdens gegen 1800," ZfMw IV (1921–22) 199–241.

—— "Zur Psychologie des Gustavianischen Opernrepertoires," in *Natalicia musicologica Knud Jeppesen* (Copenhagen, W. Hansen, 1962) 267–82.

Epstein, Th. Don Giovanni von Mozart. Frankfurt/M., Offenbach/M., Andre, 1870.

Fabbri, Mario. Alessandro Scarlatti e il principe Ferdinando de' Medici. Florence, L. S. Olschki, 1961.

Färber, Sigfrid. Das Regensburger Fürstlich Thurn und Taxissche Hoftheater und seine Oper 1760–1786. [Regensburg], Pustet, 1936.

Fassini, Sesto. "Il melodramma italiano a Londra ai tempi del Rolli," RMI XIX (1912) 35–74, 575–636.

—— Il melodramma italiano a Londra nella prima metà del Settecento. Turin, Bocca, 1914.

Faustini-Fasini, Eugenio. "Gli astri maggiori del 'bel canto' Napoletano," *Note d'archivio* XII (1935) 297–316.

—— "Documenti paisielliani inediti," *Note d'archivio* XIII (1936) 105–27.

—— G. B. Pergolesi attraverso i suoi biografi e le sue opere. Milan, Ricordi, 1900.

Faustini-Fasini, Eugenio. "Leonardo Leo e la sua famiglia," *Note d'archivio* XIV (1937) 11–18.

—— Opere teatrali, oratori e cantate di Giovanni Paisiello (1764–1808): Saggio storico-cronologico. Bari, Laterza, 1940.

Favart, Charles Simon. Mémoires et correspondances littéraires, dramatiques et anecdotiques. Paris, L. Collin, 1808. 3 vols.

—— Théâtre. Paris, DuChesne, 1763–[77]. 10 vols.

Fedeli, Vito. "Dal *Cavaliere Ergasto* alla *Molinarella*," RMI XVIII (1911) 357–81.

—— "*La Molinarella* di Piccinni," SIMG XIII (1911–12) 302–21, 507.

—— "Un' opera sconosciuta di Pergolesi?" SIMG XII (1910–11) 139–50.

Fehr, Max. Apostolo Zeno, 1668–1750, und seine Reform des Operntextes. Zurich, A. Tschopp, 1912.

—— "Pergolesi und Zeno," SIMG XV (1913–14) 166–68.

—— "Zeno, Pergolesi und Jommelli," ZfMw I (1918–19) 281–87.

Fellerer, Karl Gustav. "Max von Droste-Hülshoff," AfMf II (1937) 160–72.

—— "Mozart und Händel," *Mozart-Jahrbuch 1953* (1954) 47–55.

Fellmann, Hans Georg. Die Böhmsche Theatergruppe und ihre Zeit. Leipzig, L. Voss, 1928.

Fellowes, E. H. "The Philidor Manuscripts," M&L XII (1931) 116–29.

Festschrift zur Händel-Ehrung der Deutschen Demokratischen Republik 1959. Leipzig, Deutsche Verlag für Musik, [1959].

Fischer, Georg. Musik in Hannover. Hanover, Hahn, 1903. 2d enlarged edition of his Opern und Concerte im Hoftheater zu Hannover bis 1866.

Fischer, Wilhelm. " 'Der, welcher wandelt diese Strasse voll beschwerden,' " *Mozart-Jahrbuch 1950* (1951) 41–48.

—— "Piccinni, Gluck und Mozart," *Mozart-Jahrbuch 1953* (1954) 9–14.

Fiske, Roger. "The Operas of Stephen Storace," PMA LXXXVI (1959–60) 29–44.

—— "A Score for *The Duenna*," M&L XLII (1961) 132–41.

Fitzlyon, April. The Libertine Librettist : A Biography of Mozart's Librettist Lorenzo da Ponte. London, J. Calder, [1955].

Flögel, Bruno. "Studien zur Arientechnik in den Opern Händels," *Händel-Jahrbuch* II (1929) 50–156.

Flood, W. H. Grattan. "The *Beggar's Opera* and Its Composers," M&L III (1922) 402–6.

Florimo, Francesco. La scuola musicale di Napoli e i suoi conservatori. Naples, V. Morano, 1880–82. 4 vols. 2d ed.

Flower, Newman. George Frideric Handel : His Personality and His Times. New and revised ed. London, Cassell, 1959.

Fondi, Enrico. La vita e l'opera letteraria del musicista Benedetto Marcello. Rome, W. Modes, 1909.

Font, Auguste. Favart, l'opéra-comique et la comédie-vaudeville aux XVIIe et XVIIIe siècles. Paris, Fischbacher, 1894.

Fontana, Francesco. "Vita di Benedetto Marcello," in *Estro poetico-armonico parafrasi sopra le primi venticinque salmi, poesia di Girolamo*

*Asconio Giustiniani, musica di Benedetto Marcello* (Venice, Sebastiano Valle, 1803), I, 1–48.

Franklin, Benjamin. "The Ephemera : An Emblem of Human Life," in *The Writings of Benjamin Franklin*, edited by Albert Henry Smith (New York, Macmillan, 1907) VII, 206–9.

Frati, Lodovico. "Antonio Bernacchi e la sua scuola di canto," RMI XXIX (1922) 443–91.

—— "Attilio Ottavio Ariosti," RMI XXXIII (1926) 551–57.

——. "Un impresario teatrale del Settecento e la sua biblioteca," RMI XVIII (1911) 64–84.

—— "Metastasio e Farinelli," RMI XX (1913) 1–30.

—— "Musicisti e cantanti bolognesi del Settecento," RMI XXI (1914) 189–202.

—— "Satire di musicisti," RMI XXII (1915) 560–66.

Freisauff, Rudolf von. Mozart's *Don Juan*, 1787–1887. Salzburg, H. Kerber, 1887.

Friedländer, Max. Das deutsche Lied im 18. Jahrhundert. Stuttgart and Berlin, Cotta, 1902. 3 parts in 2 vols.

Friedrich, Götz. Die humanistische Idee der *Zauberflöte* : Ein Beitrag zur Dramaturgie der Oper. Hrsg. vom Ministerium für Kultur, Hauptabteilung künstlerische Lehranstalten. Dresden, VEB Verlag der Kunst, 1954.

Fuchs, Albert. "Wieland et l'esthétique de l'opéra," *Revue de littérature comparée* X (1930) 608–33.

Fuchs, Marianne. Die Entwicklung des Finales in der italienischen Opera Buffa vor Mozart. Vienna Dissertation, 1932.

Fürstenau, Moritz. "Maria Antonia Walpurgis, Kurfürstin von Sachsen: Eine biografische Skizze," MfMg XI (1879) 167–81.

—— "Zur Don Juan-Literatur," MfMg II (1870) 41–47.

Fuller-Maitland, John Alexander. The Age of Bach and Handel. Oxford, Clarendon Press, 1902. 2d ed., London, Oxford University Press, 1931. (OHM, Vol. IV.)

Gagey, Edmond M. Ballad Opera. New York, Columbia University Press, 1937.

Gardien, Jacques. Jean-Philippe Rameau. Paris, La Colombe, 1949.

Gastoué, Amadée. "Gossec et Gluck à l'opéra de Paris : Le ballet final d'*Iphigénie en Tauride*," RDM XVI (1935) 87–99.

—— "Nicolò Piccinni et ses opéras à Paris," *Note d'archivio* XIII (1936) 52–54.

Gay, John. The Beggar's Opera. London, De la Mare Press, 1905.

Gaye, Phoebe Fenwick. John Gay : His Place in the 18th Century. London, Collins, 1938.

Geiringer, Karl. The Bach Family : Seven Generations of Creative Genius. New York, Oxford University Press, 1954.

—— Haydn : A Creative Life in Music. New York, W. W. Norton, 1946.

Geiringer, Karl. "Haydn as an Opera Composer," PMA LXVI (1939–40) 23–30.

—— Joseph Haydn : Der schöpferische Werdegang eines Meisters der Klassik. Mainz, B. Schott's Söhne, 1959.

Genest, Emile. L'Opéra-comique connu et inconnu. Paris, Fischbacher, 1925.

Gentili, Alberto. "La raccolta Mauro Foà nella Biblioteca Nazionale di Torino," RMI XXXIV (1927) 356–68.

Georges, Horst. Das Klangsymbol des Todes im dramatischen Werk Mozarts. Wolfenbüttel-Berlin, G. Kallmeyer, 1937.

—— "Mozart—oder : Die Zeitlosigkeit der Oper," Hamburger Jahrbuch für Theater und Musik 1951, 77–83.

Georgiades, Thrasybulos. "Aus der Musiksprache des Mozart-Theaters," Mozart-Jahrbuch 1950 (1951) 76–98.

Gerber, Rudolf. Christoph Willibald Gluck. Potsdam, Athenaion, [1950].

—— Der Operntypus Johann Adolf Hasses und seine textlichen Grundlage. Leipzig, Kistner & Siegel, 1925.

Geulette, Thomas Simon. Notes et souvenirs sur le théâtre-italien au XVIIIe siècle. Paris, E. Praz, 1938.

Gherardi, Evaristo, compiler. Le Théâtre italien de Gherardi. Amsterdam, M. C. le Cene, 1721. 6 vols. 5th ed.

Giazotto, Remo. "Apostolo Zeno [,] Pietro Metastasio e la critica del Settecento," RMI XLVIII (1946) 324–60; XLIX (1947) 46–56; L (1948) 39–65, 248–58; LI (1949) 43–66, 130–61.

—— Poesia melodrammatica e pensiero critico nel Settecento. Milan, Fratelli Bocca, [1952].

Giraldi, Romolo. Giovanni Battista Pergolese. Rome, Laziale, 1936.

Girdlestone, Cuthbert. Jean-Philippe Rameau : His Life and Work. London, Cassel & Co., [1957].

Gluck, Christoph Willibald, Ritter von. Collected Correspondence and Papers. Edited by Hedwig and E. H. Mueller von Asow, translated by Stewart Thomson. London, Barrie and Rockliff, [1962].

—— "Correspondance inédite," MM X, No. 11 (1914) 1–16.

—— "Vier Gluck-Briefe," Die Musik XIII (1913–14) Qt. 4, 10–15.

Gluck-Jahrbuch. Jahrgang I–IV (1913, 1915, 1917, 1918). Leipzig, B&H. Ed. by H. Abert.

Gmeyner, Alice. Die Opern M. A. Caldaras. Vienna Dissertation, 1935.

Die Göttinger Händel-Festspiele (Festschrift). Göttingen, Göttinger Händelgesellschaft, 1953.

Goldoni, Carlo. Mémoires. Paris, Veuve Duchesne, 1787. 3 vols. Translated as : Memoirs of Goldoni. London, H. Colburn, 1814. 2 vols.

Goldschmidt, Hugo. "Das Cembalo im Orchester der italienischen Oper der zweiten Hälfte des 18. Jahrhunderts," in Festschrift Liliencron (Leipzig, B&H, 1910) 87–92.

—— Die Musikästhetik des 18. Jahrhunderts und ihre Beziehungen zu seinen Kunstschaffen. Zurich, Rascher, 1915. *See also* review by A. Schering, ZfMw I (1918–19) 298–308.

—— "Die Reform der italienischen Oper des 18. Jahrhunderts und ihre Beziehungen zur musikalischen Aesthetik," in *III. Kongress der Internationalen Musikgesellschaft . . . Bericht* (Vienna, Artaria; Leipzig, B&H, 1909) 196–207.

Gómez, Julio. "Don Blas de Laserna : Un capítolo de la historia del teatro lirico español," *Archivo y museo al ayuntamicuto de Madrid* (1925–26).

Gonzales Ruiz, Nicolas. La caramba (vida alegre y muerte ejemplar de una tonadillera del siglo XVIII). [Madrid, Ediciones Morata, 1944.]

Gottsched, Johann Christoph. Nöthiger Vorrath zur Geschichte der deutschen dramatischen Dichtkunst oder Verzeichniss aller deutschen Trauer- Lust- und Sing-Spiele, die im Druck erschienen von 1450 bis zur Hälfte des jetzigen Jahrhunderts. Leipzig, J. M. Teubner, 1757–65. 2 vols.

—— Versuch einer kritischen Dichtkunst vor die Deutschen. Leipzig, B. C. Breitkopf, 1730. 2d ed., 1737.

Goudar, Ange. Le Brigandage de la musique italienne. 1777.

[Goudar, Mme. Sara.] De Venise, remarques sur la musique & la danse. Venice, C. Palese, 1773.

Gounod, Charles François. Mozart's *Don Giovanni:* A Commentary. London, R. Cocks, 1895. Translated from the 3d French ed.

Grannis, Valleria Belt. Dramatic Parody in Eighteenth Century France. New York, Institute of French Studies, 1931.

Grasberger, Franz. "Zur Symbolik der *Zauberflöte*," in *Bericht über den internationalen musikwissenschaftlichen Kongress Wien, Mozartjahr 1956* (Graz, Böhlaus, 1958) 249–52.

Grattan Flood. *See* Flood, William Henry Grattan.

Graves, Richard. "The Comic Operas of Stephen Storace," *The Musical Times* XCV (October, 1954).

—— "English Comic Opera : 1760–1800," MMR LXXXVII (1957) 208–15.

Greither, Aloys. Die sieben grossen Opern Mozarts : Versuche über das Verhältnis der Texte zur Musik. Heidelberg, Verlag Lambert Schneider, 1956.

Grétry, André Ernest Modeste. Mémoires, ou essais sur la musique. Paris, Imprimerie de la république, [1797]. 3 vols. First published 1789.

—— Oeuvres complètes : Réflexions d'un solitaire. Brussels-Paris, Von Oest, 1919–22. 4 vols.

Grimm, Friedrich Melchior, Freiherr von. Correspondance littéraire, philosophique et critique. Paris, Garnier, 1877–82. 16 vols. Contains "Lettre sur Omphale," XVI, 287–309.

—— Le Petit Prophète de Boemischbroda. Paris, 1753.

—— "Poëme lyrique," in *Encyclopédie ou Dictionnaire raisonné . .* (Neuchâtel, S. Faulche, 1765) XII, 822–36.

[Grosley, Pierre Jean.] New Observations on Italy and Its Inhabitants. London, L. Davis & C. Reymers, 1769. 2 vols.

Grout, Donald J. The Origins of the Opéra-comique. Harvard Dissertation, 1939.

Grüel, C. Aufschlüsse über die Bedeutung des angeblich Schikaneder'schen Textes zu Mozart's *Zauberflöte*. Magdeburg, Creutz, 1868.

Güttler, Hermann. Königsbergs Musikkultur im 18. Jahrhundert. Kassel, Bärenreiter, [1929].

Guiet, René. L'Evolution d'un genre : Le livret d'opéra en France de Gluck à la révolution (1774–1793). Northampton, Mass., Smith College, Dept. of Modern Languages, 1936.

Guingené, Pierre Louis. Notice sur la vie et les ouvrages de Nicolas Piccini. Paris, Panckoucke, [1801].

Haas, Robert M. Gluck und Durazzo im Burgtheater. Zurich, Amalthea, 1925.

—— "Josse de Villeneuves Brief über den Mechanismus der italienischen Oper von 1756," ZfMw VII (1924–25) 129–63.

—— "Die Musik in der Wiener deutscher Stegreifkomödie," SzMw XII (1925) 1–64.

—— "Teutsche Comedie Arien," ZfMw III (1920–21) 405–15.

—— "Die Wiener Ballet-Pantomime im 18. Jahrhundert und Glucks *Don Juan*," SzMw X (1923) 3–36.

—— "Der Wiener Bühnentanz von 1740 bis 1767," JMP XLIV (1937) 77–93.

—— "Wiener deutsche Parodieopern um 1730," ZfMw VIII (1925–26) 201–25.

—— Die Wiener Oper. Vienna-Budapest, Eligius, 1926.

—— Wolfgang Amadeus Mozart. Potsdam, Akademische Verlagsgesellschaft Athenaion, 1950. 2d ed.

Haberl, Franz X. "Johann Mattheson : Biographische Skizze," *Caecilien Kalender* (1885) 53–60.

Haböck, Franz. Die Gesangskunst der Kastraten : Erster Notenbuch A. Die Kunst des Cavaliere Carlo Broschi Farinelli. B. Farinellis berühmte Arien. Vienna, Universal, [1923].

—— Die Kastraten und ihre Gesangskunst. Stuttgart, Deutsche Verlags-Anstalt, 1927.

Händel-Festspiele . . . 1922 : Veranstaltet vom Universitätsbund. Göttingen, W. H. Lange, 1922.

Händel-Jahrbuch. Leipzig, B&H, 1928–.

Hagen, Oskar. "Die Bearbeitung der Händelschen *Rodelinde* und ihre Uraufführung am 26. Juni 1920 in Göttingen," ZfMw II (1919–20) 725–32.

Halle. Stadtarchiv. Georg Friedrich Händel, Abstammung und Jugendwelt. Halle, Gebauer-Schwetschke, 1935.

Hamilton, Mrs. Mary (Neal). Music in Eighteenth Century Spain. Urbana, The University of Illinois, 1937.

Harich, J. "Das Repertoire des Opernkapellmeisters Joseph Haydn in Esterháza (1780–1790)," The Haydn Yearbook I (1962) 9–110.

Hastings, Margaret. "Gluck's Alceste," M&L XXXVI (1955) 41–54.

Hauger, George. "William Shield," M&L XXXI (1950) 337–42.

Hawkins, John. A General History of the Science and Practice of Music. London, T. Payne, 1776. 5 vols.

Hédouin, Pierre. Richard Coeur-de-Lion de Grétry. Boulogne, Birlé-Morel, 1842.

Heger, Theodore E. The Function and Type of Music in the English Dramatic Theater of the Early 18th Century. Michigan A.M. Dissertation, 1939.

Heinichen, Johann David. Der General-Bass in der Composition. Dresden, bey dem Autor, 1728. A revised ed. of his Neu erfundene und gründliche Anweisung (Hamburg, B. Schiller, 1711).

Heinse, Wilhelm. Hildegard von Hohenthal. Berlin, Vossischen Buchhandlung, 1795–96. 3 vols.

Helfert, W. "Zur Geschichte des Wiener Singspiels," ZfMw V (1922–23) 194–209.

Henderson, William James. "A Note on Floridity," MQ II (1916) 339–48.

Heriot, Angus. The Castrati in Opera. London, Secker & Warburg, 1956.

Heulhard, Arthur. La Foire Saint-Laurent : Son histoire et ses spectacles. Paris, A. Lemerre, 1878.

—— Jean Monnet. Paris, A. Lemerre, 1884.

Heuss, Alfred. "Carl Heinrich Graun's Montezuma," ZIMG VI (1904–5) 71–75.

—— "Das dämonische Element in Mozarts Werken," ZIMG VII (1906) 175–86.

—— "Gluck als Musikdramatiker," ZIMG XV (1913–14) 274–91.

—— "Graun's Montezuma und seine Herausgabe durch Albert Mayer-Reinach," MfMg XXXVII (1905) 67–71.

—— "Mozarts Idomeneo als Quelle für Don Giovanni and Die Zauberflöte," ZfMw XIII (1930–31) 177–99.

—— "Zu Umlauf's Singspiel : Die Bergknappen," ZIMG XIII (1911–12) 164–71.

Hiller, Johann Adam. Johann Adam Hiller. Leipzig. C. F. W. Siegel, [1915].

Hiltebrandt, Philipp. Preussen und die römische Kurie. Berlin, Bath, 1910. Vol. I : Die vorfriderizianische Zeit (1625–1740).

Hinrichsen, Max, ed. Ninth Music Book, Containing John Gay and the Ballad Opera [The Beggar's Opera] by Geoffrey Handley-Taylor and Frank Granville Barker. . . . London & New York, Hinrichsen Edition, [1957].

Hirsch, R. Mozart's *Schauspieldirektor:* Musikalische Reminiscenzen. Leipzig, Matthis, 1859.

Hirschberg, Eugen. Die Enzyklopädisten und die französische Oper im 18. Jahrhundert. Leipzig, B&H, 1903. *See also* review by A. Heuss, ZIMG V (1903–4) 280–87.

Hirschfeld, Robert. "Mozart's *Zaide* in der Wiener Hofoper," ZIMG IV (1902–3) 66–71.

Hirzel, Bruno. "Operatic Italy in 1770—by an Eyewitness," MTNA V (1910) 219–31.

Hitzig, Wilhelm. Georg Friedrich Händel, 1685–1759 : Sein Leben in Bildern. Leipzig, Bibliographisches Institut, [1935].

Hocquard, Jean Victor. "III. Le Pensée dramatique de Mozart," in *La Pensée de Mozart* (Paris, Editions du Seuil, [1958]) 341–566.

Hodermann, Richard. Georg Benda. Coburg, H. Wechsung, 1895.

—— Geschichte des Gothaischen Hoftheaters 1725–1779. Hamburg, L. Voss, 1894.

Höffding, Harold. Jean Jacques Rousseau and His Philosophy. New Haven, Yale University Press; London, Oxford University Press, 1930. Translated from the 2d Danish ed.

Högg, Margarete. Die Gesangskunst der Faustina Hasse und das Sängerinnenwesen ihrer Zeit in Deutschland. Königsbrück i. Sa., Pabst, 1931.

Hoffman, Ernst Theodor Amadeus. "Don Giovanni : A Marvelous Adventure Which Befell a Traveling Enthusiast." Translated by Abram Loft. MQ XXXI (1945) 504–16.

Hoffmann von Fallersleben, August Heinrich. Unsere volkstümlichen Lieder. Leipzig, W. Engelmann, 1900. 4th ed.

Holl, Karl. Carl Ditters von Dittersdorfs Opern für das wiederhergestellte Johannisberger Theater. Heidelberg, C. Winter, 1913.

Holmes, William C. "Pamela Transformed," MQ XXXVIII (1952) 581–94.

Holzer, Ludmilla. "Die komische Opern Glucks," SzMw XIII (1926) 3–37.

Hopkinson, Cecil. A Bibliography of the Works of C. W. von Gluck, 1714–1787. London, Printed for the Author, 1959.

Hucke, Helmuth. "Die beiden Fassungen der Oper *Didone abbandonata* von Domenico Sarri," in *Gesellschaft für Musikforschung: Bericht über den internationalen . . . Kongress Hamburg 1956* (Kassel, [etc.], Bärenreiter, 1957) 113–17.

—— "La *Didona abbandonata* di Domenico Sarri nella stesura del 1724 e nella revisione di 1730," *Gazzetta musicale di Napoli* (1956) No. 11–12.

—— "Die neapolitanische Tradition in der Oper," in *International Musicological Society, Report of the Eighth Congress, New York 1961* (Kassel, [etc.], Bärenreiter, 1961) I, 253–77.

Hueber, Kurt. "Gli ultimi anni di Giovanni Bononcini : Notizie e documenti inediti," *Atti e memorie della Accademia di Scienze, Lettere e Arti di Modena*, Ser. 5, XII (1954) 3–21.

Hughes, Charles W. "John Christopher Pepusch," MQ XXXI (1945) 54–70.

Hughes, Spike [i.e., Patrick Cairns Hughes]. Famous Mozart Operas : An Analytical Guide for the Opera-Goer and Armchair Listener. London, Hale, 1957.

Hussey, Dyneley. "Casanova and *Don Giovanni*," M&L VIII (1927) 470–72.

Hutchings, A. J. B. "The Unexpected in Mozart," M&L XX (1939) 21–31.

Iacuzzi, Alfred. The European Vogue of Favart : The Diffusion of the Opéra-Comique. New York, Institute of French Studies, 1932.

Irving, William Henry. John Gay, Favorite of Poets. Durham, N.C., Duke University Press, 1940.

Iselin, Isaak. Pariser Tagebuch 1752. Basel, Benno Schwabe, 1919.

Istel, Edgar. "Einiges über Georg Benda's 'akkompagnierte' Monodramen," SIMG VI (1904–5) 179–82.

—— Die Entstehung des deutschen Melodramas. Berlin, Schuster & Loeffler, 1906.

—— "Gluck's Dramaturgy," MQ XVII (1931) 227–33.

—— "Mozart's *Magic Flute* and Freemasonry," MQ XIII (1927) 510–27.

—— Studien zur Geschichte des Melodrams. I. Jean Jacques Rousseau als Komponist seiner lyrischen Szene *Pygmalion*. Leipzig, B&H, 1901. Continued in *Annals de la Société Jean Jacques Rousseau* I (1905) 141–72; II (1906); III (1907) 119–55.

Jacobs, Reginald. Covent Garden, Its Romance and History. London, Simpkin, 1913.

Jäger, Erich. "Gluck und Goethe," *Die Musik* XIII (1913–14) Qt. 4, 131–39.

Jahn, Otto. W. A. Mozart. Translated as : Life of Mozart. London, Novello, Ewer, 1882. 3 vols. (From the 2d German ed., 1867.) *See also* Abert, Hermann.

Jansen, Albert. Jean-Jacques Rousseau als Musiker. Berlin, Reimer, 1884.

Janz, Curt Paul. "Kierkegaard und das Musikalische, dargestellt an seiner Auffassung von Mozarts *Don Juan*," Mf X (1957) 364–81.

Japy, André. L'Opéra royal de Versailles. [Versailles], Comité National pour la Sauvegarde du Château de Versailles, 1958.

Jenny, Ernst. "Das alte Basler Theater auf dem Blömlein," *Basler Jahrbuch* (1908) 1–68.

Jersild, Jorgen. "Le Ballet d'action italien du 18e siècle au Danemark," *Acta musicologica* XIV (1942) 74–93.

Johnson, Harold Edgar. Iphigenia in Tauris as the Subject for French Opera. Cornell A.M. Thesis, 1939.

Jouve, Pierre Jean. Le Don Juan de Mozart. Freiburg, Librairie de l'Université, 1942. Translated as : Mozart's Don Juan. London, Stuart, 1957.

Jullien, Adolphe. La Cour et l'opéra sous Louis XVI. Paris, Didier, 1878.

—— La Ville et la cour au XVIIIe siècle. Paris, E. Rouveyre, 1881.

Jungk, Klaus. Tonbildliches und Tonsymbolisches in Mozarts Opern. Berlin, Triltsch & Huther, 1938.

Junk, Victor. Goethe's Fortsetzung der *Zauberflöte*. Berlin, Duncker, 1899.

Junker, Hermann. "Zwei 'Griselda'-Opern," in *Festschrift Adolf Sandberger* (Munich, Zierfuss, 1918) 51–64.

Kaestner, Erwin. Das Opernproblem und seine Lösung bei Mozart. Jena, Neuenhahn, 1932.

Kaestner, Rudolf. Johann Heinrich Rolle. Kassel, Bärenreiter, 1932.

Kalbeck, Max. "Zu Scheidemantels Don *Juan*-Uebersetzung," *Die Musik* XIII (1913–14) Qt. 4, 67–72.

Kapp, Julius. Geschichte der Staatsoper Berlin. Berlin, M. Hesse, 1937. New ed., 1942.

—— 185 Jahre Staatsoper. Berlin, Atlantic-Verlag, 1928.

—— 200 Jahre Staatsoper im Bild. Berlin, M. Hesse, 1942.

Kaul, Oskar. Geschichte der Würzburger Hofmusik im 18. Jahrhundert. Würzburg, Becker, 1924.

—— "Die musikdramatischen Werke des Würzburgischen Hofkapellmeisters Georg Franz Wassmuth," ZfMw VII (1924–25) 390–408, 478–500.

Keller, Hans. "The *Entführung*'s 'Vaudeville,'" MR XVII (1956) 304–13.

Keller, Otto. "Gluck-Bibliographie," *Die Musik* XIII (1913–14) Qt. 4, 23–37, 85–91.

—— Wolfgang Amadeus Mozart: Bibliographie und Ikonographie. Berlin, Gebrüder Paetel, 1927.

Kelly, Michael. Reminiscences of the King's Theatre. London, H. Colburn, 1826. 2 vols.

Kerchove, Arnold de. "Méditations sur le Don Juan de Mozart," *Cahiers du sud* XLIII (1956) No. 336.

Kidson, Frank. *The Beggar's Opera*, Its Predecessors and Successors. Cambridge, The University Press, 1922.

Kierkegaard, Søren. Either/Or, a Fragment of Life . . . Volume One, translated by David F. Swenson and Lillian Marvin Swenson. Princeton, Princeton University Press; London, Humphrey Milford, Oxford University Press, 1944.
Contains: "The Immediate Stages of the Erotic or The Musical Erotic," pp. 35–110.

Killer, Hermann. Die Tenorpartien in Mozarts Opern. Kassel, Bärenreiter, 1929.

King, Alexander Hyatt. Mozart in Retrospect: Studies in Criticism and Bibliography. London, New York, Toronto, Oxford University Press, 1955.

Kinsky, Georg. "Glucks Reisen nach Paris," ZfMw VIII (1925–26) 551–66.

Kirby, F. E. "Herder and Opera," JAMS XV (1962) 316–29.

Kirkpatrick, Ralph. Domenico Scarlatti. Princeton, Princeton University Press, 1953.

Kisch, Eve. "Rameau and Rousseau," M&L XXII (1941) 97–114.

Kitzig, Berthold. "Briefe Carl Heinrich Grauns," ZfMw IX (1926–27) 385–405.

Kleefeld, Wilhelm. Landgraf Ernst Ludwig von Hessen-Darmstadt und die deutsche Oper. Berlin, Hofmann, 1904.

Klein, Rudolf. "Die Tonarten des Don Giovanni," OeM XI (1956) 259–60.

Kling, H. "Caron de Beaumarchais et la musique," RMI VII (1900) 673–97.

Klob, Karl Maria. Beiträge zur Geschichte der deutschen komischen Oper. Berlin, "Harmonie," [1903].

Kloiber, Rudolf. Die dramatischen Ballette von Christian Cannabich. Munich Dissertation, 1927.

Knapp, J. Merrill. "A Forgotten Chapter in English Eighteenth-Century Opera," M&L XLII (1961) 4–16.

—— "Handel, the Royal Academy of Music, and Its First Opera Season in London (1720)," MQ XLV (1959) 145–67.

Köchel, Ludwig, Ritter von. Chronologisch-thematisches Verzeichnis sämtlicher Tonwerke Wolfgang Amade Mozarts. Ann Arbor, J. W. Edwards, 1947. 3d ed., revised and with a Supplement by Alfred Einstein.

Komorzyński, Egon von. Emmanuel Schikaneder. Berlin, B. Behr, 1901.

—— Emmanuel Schikaneder: Ein Beitrag zur Geschichte des deutschen Theaters. Vienna, Doblinger, [1951].

—— Mozart: Sendung und Schicksal. Vienna, Kremayr & Scheriau, [1955]. 2d ed.

—— Pamina, Mozarts letzte Liebe. Berlin, Max Hesse, [1941].

—— "Streit um den Text der Zauberflöte," Alt-Wiener Kalender (1922) 79–105.

—— "Das Urbild der Zauberflöte," Mozart-Jahrbuch 1952 (1953) 101–9.

—— "Die Zauberflöte: Entstehung und Bedeutung des Kunstwerks," Neues Mozart-Jahrbuch I (1941) 147–74.

—— "Die Zauberflöte und Dschinnistan," Mozart-Jahrbuch 1954 (1955) 177–94.

—— "Zauberflöte und Oberon," Mozart-Jahrbuch 1953 (1954) 150–61.

Krause, Christian Gottfried. Abhandlung von der musikalischen Poesie. Berlin, J. F. Voss, 1752.

Krauss, Rudolf. Das Stuttgarter Hoftheater von den ältesten Zeiten bis zur Gegenwart. Stuttgart, J. B. Metzler, 1908.

—— "Das Theater," in Herzog Karl Eugen von Württemberg und seine Zeit (Esslingen a. N., 1907) I, 481–554.

Krebs, Carl. Dittersdorfiana. Berlin, Gebrüder Paetel, 1900.

Krehbiel, Henry. Music and Manners in the Classical Period. New York, Scribner, 1899.

Kretzschmar, Hermann. "Allgemeines und Besonderes zur Affektenlehre," JMP XVIII (1911) 63–77; XIX (1912) 65–78.

Kretzschmar, Hermann. "Aus Deutschlands italienischer Zeit," JMP VIII (1901) 45–61.

—— "Die *Correspondance littéraire* als musikgeschichtliche Quelle," JMP X (1903) 77–92; also in his *Gesammelte Aufsätze* II, 210–25.

—— "Hasse über Mozart," ZIMG III (1901–2) 263–65.

—— "Mozart in der Geschichte der Oper," JMP XII (1905) 53–71.

—— "Zum Verständnis Glucks," JMP X (1903) 61–76.

—— "Zwei Opern Nicolo Logroscinos," JMP XV (1908) 47–68.

Krogh, Torben Thorberg. "Reinhard Keiser in Kopenhagen," in *Musikwissenschaftliche Beiträge: Festschrift für Johannes Wolf* (Berlin, Breslauer, 1929).

—— Zur Geschichte des dänischen Singspiels im 18. Jahrhundert. Copenhagen, Levin & Munksgaard, 1924.

Krone, Walter. Wenzel Müller. Berlin, Ebering, 1906.

Kufferath, Maurice. *La Flûte enchantée* de Mozart. Paris, Fischbacher, 1914.

Kurth, Ernst. "Die Jugendopern Glucks bis *Orfeo*," SzMw I (1913) 193–277.

Lach, Robert. "Sebastian Sailers *Schöpfung* in der Musik," *Akademie der Wissenschaften in Wien, Denkschriften*, 60. Band, 1. Abhandlung (1917).

Lafont du Cujala. "Réflexions sur l'état actuel de la musique dramatique en France," *Mercure de France* (February, 1782) 38–44.

Lalande, Joseph Jérôme Lefrançais de. Voyage d'un françois en Italie, fait dans les années 1765 & 1766. A Venise, et se trouve à Paris chez Desaint, 1769. 8 vols.

La Laurencie, Lionel de. "Deux Imitateurs français des bouffons : Blavet et Dauvergne," *Année musicale* II (1912) 65–125.

—— "Un Emule de Lully : Pierre Gautier de Marseille," SIMG XIII (1911–12) 39–69, 400.

—— "La Grande Saison italienne de 1752 : Les bouffons," MM VIII, No. 6 (1912) 18–33; Nos. 7–8, pp. 13–22. Also separate as : Les Bouffons (1752–1754). Paris, Publications de la Revue SIM, 1912.

—— "Leclair; une assertion de Fétis; Jean-Marie Leclair l'ainé à l'orchestre de l'Opéra," RHCM IV (1904) 496–503.

—— "Un Musicien dramatique du XVIIIe siècle français : Pierre Guedron," RMI XXIX (1922) 445–72.

—— "Un Musicien italien en France à la fin du XVIIIe siècle," RdM XII (1931) 268–77.

—— Orphée de Gluck : Etude et analyse. Paris, Mellottée, 1934.

—— "Quelques documents sur Jean-Philippe Rameau et sa famille," MM III (1907) 541–614.

—— Rameau, biographie critique. Paris, Laurens, [1908].

—— "Rameau et les clarinettes," MM IX, No. 2 (1913) 27–28.

—— "Rameau et son gendre," MM VII, No. 2 (1911) 12–23.

Laloy, Louis. "Les Idées de Jean-Philippe Rameau sur la musique," MM III (1907) 1144–59.

Landon, H. C. Robbins. "Haydn's Marionette Operas," *The Haydn Year-book* I (1962) 111–97.

Lang, Paul Henry. "Handel—Churchman or Dramatist?" in *Festschrift Friedrich Blume* (Kassel, Bärenreiter, 1963) [214]–220.

—— "Haydn and the Opera," MQ XVIII (1932) 274–81.

Langlois, Rose-Marie. L'Opéra de Versailles. Paris, P. Horay, 1958.

[Lardin, Jules.] *Zémire et Azor* par Grétry : Quelques questions à propos de la nouvelle falsification de cet opéra. Paris, Moëssard et Jousset, 1846.

La Rotella, Pasquale. Niccolo Piccinni. Bari, Cressati, 1928.

Larsen, Jens Peter. Die Haydn-Ueberlieferungen. Copenhagen, Munks-gaard, 1939.

La Salandra. *See* Belluci La Salandra.

Lauppert, Albert von. Die Musikästhetik Wilhelm Heinses : Zugleich eine Quellenstudie zur Hildegard von Hohenthal. Greifswald, J. Abel, 1912.

Lawner, George. Form and Drama in the Operas of Joseph Haydn. University of Chicago Dissertation, 1959.

Lawrence, William John. "Early Irish Ballad Opera and Comic Opera," MQ VIII (1922) 397–412.

—— "The Early Years of the First English Opera House," MQ VII (1921) 104–17.

—— "Marionette Operas," MQ X (1924) 236–43.

[Le Blond, Gaspard Michel, ed.] Mémoires pour servir à l'histoire de la révolution opérée dans la musique par M. le Chevalier Gluck. Naples and Paris, Bailly, 1781.

Leclerc, Hélène. "*Les Indes galantes* (1735–1952) : Les sources de l'opéra-ballet, l'exotisme orientalisant, les conditions matérielles du spectacle," *Revue d'histoire du théâtre* V (1953) 259–85.

Lee, Vernon, pseud. *See* Paget, Violet.

Leerink, Hans. Joseph Haydn : Een Leven vol Muziek. Amsterdam, A. & G. Strengholt, [1949].

Lehner, Walter. "Franz Xaver Süssmayr als Opernkomponist," SzMw XVIII (1931) 66–96.

Leichtentritt, Hugo. Händel. Stuttgart-Berlin, Deutsche Verlags-Anstalt, 1924.

—— "Handel's Harmonic Art," MQ XXI (1935) 208–23.

—— Reinhard Keiser in seinen Opern. Berlin, Tessarotypie-Actien-Gesellschaft, 1901.

Leist, Friedrich. "Geschichte des Theaters in Bamberg bis zum Jahre 1862," *Berichte des historischen Vereins zu Bamberg* LV (1893) 1–283.

Lejeune, Caroline. "Opera in the Eighteenth Century," PMA XLIX (1922–23) 1–20.

Lenzewsky, Gustav. "Friedrich der Grosse als Komponist des Singspiels *Il Re Pastore*," *Schriften des Vereins für die Geschichte Berlins* XXIX (1912) 20.

Leo, Giacomo. Leonardo Leo, celebre musicista del secolo XVIII, ed il suo omonimo Leonardo Leo di Corrado : Nota storica. Naples, Cozzo-lino, 1901.

Leo, Giacomo. Leonardo Leo . . . e le sue opere musicali. Naples, Melfi & Joele, 1905.

[Léris, Antoine de.] Dictionnaire portatif des théâtres. Paris, C. A. Jom-bert, 1754. Another ed., 1763.

Lert, Ernst. Mozart auf dem Theater. Berlin, Schuster & Loeffler, 1918.

Le Sage, Alain René. Le Théâtre de la foire ou l'Opéra-comique. Paris, P. Gandouin, 1724–37. 10 vols.

Leux, Irmgard. Christian Gottlob Neefe. Leipzig, Kistner & Siegel, 1925.

—— "Ueber die 'verschollene' Händel-Oper *Hermann von Balcke*," AfMw VIII (1926) 441–51.

Levallois, Andrée, and Anne Souriau. "Caractérologie musicale (les per-sonnages du *Don Juan* de Mozart)," *Revue d'esthétique* VII (1954) 157–82.

Levarie, Siegmund. Mozart's *Le Nozze di Figaro* : A Critical Analysis. Chicago, University of Chicago Press, 1952.

Lincoln, Stoddard. "The First Setting of Congreve's *Semele*," M&L XLIV (1963) 103–17.

Livermore, Ann Lapraik. "*The Magic Flute* and Calderón," M&L XXXVI (1955) 7–16.

—— "The Spanish Dramatists and Their Use of Music," M&L XXV (1944) 140–49.

Livingston, Arthur. Lorenzo da Ponte in America. Philadelphia, Lippin-cott, 1930.

Lockwood, Elisabeth M. "Some Old-Fashioned Music," M&L XII (1931) 262–70.

Loehner, Ermanno von. "Carlo Goldoni e le sue memorie," *Archivio veneto* XXIII (1881) 45–65; XXIV (1882) 5–27.

Loewenberg, Alfred. "*Bastien and Bastienne* Once More," M&L XXV (1924) 176–81.

—— "Gluck's *Orfeo* on the Stage," MQ XXVI (1940) 311–39.

—— "Lorenzo da Ponte in London," MR IV (1943) 171–89.

—— "Paisiello's and Rossini's *Barbiere di Siviglia*," M&L XX (1939) 157–67.

Loft, Abram. "The Comic Servant in Mozart's Operas," MQ XXXII (1946) 376–89.

The London Stage, 1660–1800. Carbondale, Southern Illinois University Press, 1960–62. Part II : 1700–29, ed. by Emmett L. Avery, 2 vols. Part III : 1729–47, ed. by Arthur H. Scouten, 2 vols. Part IV : 1747–76, ed. by George W. Stone, 3 vols.

Long des Clavières, P. "Lettres inédites de A. E. M. Grétry," RMI XXI (1914) 699–727.

—— "Les *Réflexions d'un solitaire* par A. E. M. Grétry," RMI XXVI (1919) 565–614.

Lorenz, Alfred Ottokar. Alessandro Scarlatti's Jugendoper. Augsburg, Benno Filser, 1927. 2 vols.

—— "Alessandro Scarlattis Opern und Wien," ZfMw IX (1926–27) 86–89.

—— "Das Finale in Mozarts Meisteropern," Die Musik XIX (June, 1927) 621–32.

Lowens, Irving. "The Touch-Stone (1728) : A Neglected View of London Opera," MQ XLV (1959) 325–42.

Lozzi, C. "Brigida Banti, regina del teatro lirico nel secolo XVIII," RMI XI (1904) 64–76.

Luciani, Sebastiano Arturo. "Domenico Scarlatti," RassM XI (1938) 460–72; XII (1939) 20–31, 61–74.

Lüthge, Kurt. Die deutsche Spieloper. Brunswick, W. Piepenschneider, 1924.

Luin, E. J. "Giovanni Ferrandini e l'apertura del Teatro Residenziale a Monaco nel 1745," RMI XXXIX (1932) 561–66.

—— "Mozarts Opern in Skandinavien," in Bericht über den internationalen musikwissenschaftlichen Kongress Wien, Mozartjahr 1956 (Graz, Böhlaus, 1958) 387–96.

Lutze, G. Aus Sonderhausens Vergangenheit. III. Band. Sonderhausen, Fr. Aug. Eupel, 1919.

Mably, Gabriel Bonnot de. Lettres à Madame la Marquise de P . . . sur l'opéra. Paris, Didot, 1741.

McClure, Theron Reading. A Reconstruction of Theatrical and Musical Practice in the Production of Italian Opera in the Eighteenth Century. Ann Arbor, University Microfilms, 1956.

Maddalena, E. "Libretti del Goldoni e d'altri," RMI VII (1900) 739–45.

Magni-Dufflocq, Enrico. "Domenico Cimarosa, note biografiche," Bollettino bibliografico musicale V (1930) 5–15.

Maier, Johann Christoph. Beschreibung von Venedig. Leipzig, J. A. Barth, 1795. 4 vols. 2d ed.

[Mainwaring, John.] Memoirs of the Life of the Late George Frederic Handel. London, R. & J. Dodsley, 1760.

Malherbe, Charles Théodore. "Un Précurseur de Gluck : Le comte Algarotti," RHCM II (1902) 369–74, 414–23.

Malignon, Jean. Rameau. [Paris], Editions du Seuil, [1960].

[Marcello, Benedetto.] Il teatro alla moda, osia metodo sicuro, e facile per ben comporre, & esequire l'Opere Italiane in Musica all' uso moderno. [Venice], Borghi di Belisania per A. Licante, [ca. 1720]. Among the numerous later editions the following may be cited : Venice, Tip. dell' Ancora, 1887; Milan, Bottega di Poesia, 1927; French translation ("Le Théâtre à la mode au XVIIIe siècle") Paris, Fischbacher, 1890; German translation ("Das Theater nach der Mode") Munich and Berlin, G. Müller, [1917]; English translation : MQ XXXIV (1948) 371–403; XXXV (1949) 85–105.

Marchesan, Angelo. Della vita e delle opere di Lorenzo Da Ponte. Treviso, Turazza, 1900.

Marmontel, Jean François. Elémens de littérature. [Paris, Née de la Rochelle], 1787. 6 vols.

Marpurg, Friedrich Wilhelm. Anleitung zur Musik überhaupt und zur Singkunst besonders. Berlin, A. Wever, 1763.

—— Historisch-kritische Beiträge zur Aufnahme der Musik. Berlin, G. A. Lange, 1754–62. 5 vols.

Martens, Heinrich. Das Melodram. Berlin, Vieweg, 1932. (Music.)

Martienssen, C. A. "Holger Danske, Oper von Fr. L. Ae. Kunzen," ZIMG XIII (1911–12) 225–32.

Marx, Adolf Bernhard. Gluck und die Oper. Berlin, O. Janke, 1863. 2 vols.

Mason, James Frederick. The Melodrama in France from the Revolution to the Beginning of Romantic Drama. Johns Hopkins Dissertation, 1911. Chapter I published : Baltimore, J. H. Furst, 1912.

Masson, Paul-Marie. "Les Deux Versions du Dardanus de Rameau," Acta musicologica XXVI (1954) 36–48.

—— "Les Idées de Rousseau sur la musique," SIM Revue musical VIII, No. 6 (1912), 1–17; Nos. 7–8, pp. 23–32.

—— "La Lettre sur Omphale (1752)," RdM XXVII (1945) 1–19.

—— "Musique italienne et musique française," RMI XIX (1912) 519–45.

—— L'Opéra de Rameau. Paris, Laurens, 1930.

—— "Rameau and Wagner," MQ XXV (1939) 466–78.

Mattei, Saverio. Memorie per servire alla vita di Metastasio. Colle, A. M. Martini, 1785.

Mattheson, [Johann]. Grundlage einer Ehrenpforte. Hamburg, In Verlegung des Verfassers, 1740. New ed., Berlin, L. Liepmannssohn, 1910.

—— Mithridat, wider den Gift einer welschen Satyre, genannt : La musica. Hamburg, Geissler, 1749.

—— Der musikalische Patriot. Hamburg, 1728.

—— Das neu-eröffnete Orchestre. Hamburg, B. Schillers Wittwe, 1713.

—— Die neueste Untersuchung der Singspiele. Hamburg, C. Herold, 1744.

—— Der vollkommene Capellmeister. Hamburg, C. Herold, 1739.

Maurer, Julius. Anton Schweitzer als dramatischer Komponist. Leipzig, B&H, 1912.

Mayer-Reinach, Albert. "Carl Heinrich Graun als Opernkomponist," SIMG I (1899–1900) 446–529.

—— "Zur Herausgabe des Montezuma von Carl Heinrich Graun in den Denkmälern deutscher Tonkunst," MfMg XXXVII (1905) 20–31.

Meinardus, Ludwig. "Johann Mattheson und seine Verdienste um die deutsche Tonkunst," in Waldersee, Sammlung musikalischer Vorträge (Leipzig, B&H, 1879–98) I, 215–72.

Meissner, August Gottlieb. Bruchstücke zur Biographie J. G. Naumann's. Prague, K. Barth, 1803–4. 2 vols.

Melville, Lewis, pseud. *See* Benjamin, Lewis Saul.

Mennicke, Karl. Hasse und die Brüder Graun als Sinfoniker. Leipzig, B&H, 1906.

—— "Johann Adolph Hasse : Eine biographische Skizze," SIMG V (1903–4) 230–44, 469–75.

Merbach, Paul Alfred. "Das Repertoire der Hamburger Oper 1718–1750," AfMw VI (1924) 354–72.

Merlo, Johann. "Zur Geschichte des Kölner Theaters im 18. und 19. Jahrhundert," *Annalen des historischen Vereins für den Niederrhein* L (1890) 145–219.

Metastasio, Pietro. Dramas and Other Poems. Translated from the Italian by John Hoole. London, Otridge, 1800.

—— Lettere. Florence, Della rosa, 1787–89. 4 vols.

—— Lettere disperse e inedite, Vol. I. Bologna, N. Zanichelli, 1883.

—— Opere. Padua, G. Foglierini, 1811–12. 17 vols.

—— *See also* Burney, *Memoirs*.

Meyer, Ralph. Die Behandlung des Rezitatives in Glucks italienischen Reformopern. Leipzig, B&H, 1919.

Migot, Georges. Jean-Philippe Rameau et le génie de la musique française. Paris, Delagrave, 1930.

Milizia, Francesco. Trattato completo, formale e materiale del teatro. Venice, Pasquali, 1794.

Minor, Jakob. Christian Felix Weisse. Innsbruck, Wagner, 1880.

Mirow, Franz. Zwischenaktsmusik und Bühnenmusik des deutschen Theaters in der klassischen Zeit. Berlin, Gesellschaft für Theatergeschichte, 1927.

Misson, Maximilien. A New Voyage to Italy. London, R. Bonwicke, 1714. 2 vols.

Mitjana y Gordón, Rafael. Histoire du développement du théâtre dramatique et musical en Espagne des origines au commencement du XIXe siècle. Uppsala, Almqvist & Wiksell, 1906.

Mizler [von Kolof], Lorenz [Christoph]. Neu eröffnete musikalische Bibliothek. Leipzig, Im Verlag des Verfassers, 1739–54. 4 vols.

Mohr, Albert Richard. Frankfurter Theaterleben im 18. Jahrhundert. Frankfurt/M., W. Kramer, 1940.

Moller, Johannes. Cimbria literata. Havniae, G. E. Kisel, 1744. 3 vols.

Mondolfi, A. "Cimarosa copista di Handel," *Gazzetta musicale di Napoli* (1956) No. 7–8.

Mondolfi, Anna, and Helmut Hucke. "Neapel," in MGG IX, 1307–42.

Monnet, Jean. Mémoires. Paris, Louis-Michaud, [1884].

Monnier, Philippe. Venise au XVIIIe siècle. Paris, Perrin, 1907. Translated as : Venice in the Eighteenth Century. London, Chatto & Windus, 1910.

Montagu, Lady Mary [Pierrepont] Wortley. The Letters and Works of Lady Mary Wortley Montagu, London, Bickers, [1861]. 2 vols.

—— Letters to and from Pope. In Alexander Pope, *Works* (London, Longman, 1847) VII, 27–119.

Mooser, R. Aloys. "Un Musicien espagnol en Russie à la fin du XVIIIe siècle," RMI XL (1936) 432–49.

Morenz, Siegfried. *Die Zauberflöte:* Eine Studie zum Lebenszusammenhang Aegypten—Antike—Abendland. Münster & Cologne, Böhlau-Verlag, 1952.

Mortari, Virgilio. "L' *Oca del Cairo* di W. A. Mozart," RMI XL (1936) 477–81.

Moser, Hans Joachim. Christoph Willibald Gluck. Stuttgart, Cotta, 1940.

[Mozart, Wolfgang.] Ausstellung die Zauberflöte : Mozarthaus, Katalog. Salzburg, Mozarteum, 1928.

Mozart : Briefe und Aufzeichnungen. Gesamtausgabe, hrsg. von der Internationale Stiftung Mozarteum, Salzburg; gesammelt und erläutert von Wilhelm A. Bauer und Otto Erich Deutsch. Band I : 1755–1776. Kassel, [etc.], Bärenreiter, 1962.

Mozart, die Dokumente seines Lebens. Gesammelt und erläutert von Otto Erich Deutsch. In : Mozart, *Neue Ausgabe sämtlicher Werke*, Serie 10, Werkgruppe 34. Kassel, Bärenreiter, 1955.

Mozart in Italia : I viaggi, a cura di Guglielmo Barblan, con scritti di G. Barblan [and others]. Le lettere, a cura di Andrea della Corte. [Milan], Ricordi, [1956].

Mozart-Jahrbuch, ed. Abert. Munich, Drei Masken, 1923–29. 3 vols. (suspended 1925–28).

—— hrsg. von der Internationalen Stiftung Mozarteum. Salzburg, 1951– . Articles relevant to opera will be found separately listed under the following authors : Engel, Fellerer, Fischer, Georgiades, Komorzynski, Orel, Schmid, and Zingerle.

Mozart operái. Budapest, 1956.

Mozart und seine Welt in zeitgenössischen Bildern. In : Mozart, *Neue Ausgabe sämtlicher Werke*, Serie 10, Werkgruppe 32. Kassel, Bärenreiter, 1955.

Müller, Erich H. "Isaak Iselins *Pariser Tagebuch* als musikgeschichtliche Quelle," ZfMw VII (1924–25) 545–52.

Müller-Blattau, Joseph M. Georg Friedrich Händel : Der Wille zur Vollendung. Mainz, Schott, [1959].

—— "Gluck und die deutsche Dichtung," JMP XLV (1938) 30–52.

Müller-Hartmann, Robert. "Wieland's and Gluck's Versions of the *Alkestis*," *Journal of the Warburg Institute* II (October, 1938) 176–77.

Muratori, Lodovico Antonio. Della perfetta poesia italiana, spiegata e dimostrata con varie osservazioni. Venice, S. Colete, 1724. Contains: Lib. III, Cap. V (Vol. II, pp. 30–45) "De' difetti, che possono osservarsi ne' moderni Drammi." Refutation of Muratori's criticisms is undertaken by Johann Mattheson in his *Nueste Untersuchung der Singspiele*.

Musatti, Cesare. "Drammi musicali di Goldoni e d' altri tratti dalle sue commedie," *Ateneo Veneto* XXI (1898) 51–60. Also separate : Venice, Fratelli Visentini, 1898.

Myers, Robert Manson. "Mrs. Delany : An Eighteenth-Century Handelian," MQ XXXII (1946) 12–36.

Nagel, Willibald. "Deutsche Musiker des 18. Jahrhunderts im Verkehr mit J. Fr. A. v. Uffenbach," SIMG XIII (1911–12) 69–106.

—— "Das Leben Christoph Graupner's," SIMG X (1908–9) 568–612.

Negri, Francesco. La vita di Apostolo Zeno. Venice, Alvisopoli, 1816.

Nettl, Paul. "Casanova and Music," MQ XV (1929) 212–32.

—— "An English Musician at the Court of Charles VI," MQ XXVIII (1942) 318–28.

—— Mozart and Masonry. New York, Philosophical Library, [1957].

—— "Mozart, Casanova, Don Giovanni," SchwM XCVI (1956) 60–65.

—— Musik und Freimaurerei : Mozart und die königliche Kunst. [Esslingen], Bechtle Verlag, [1956].

Neues Mozart-Jahrbuch : Im Auftrage des Zentralinstituts für Mozartforschung am Mozarteum Salzburg, hrsg. von Erich Valentin. Regensburg, G. Bosse, 1941–43. 3 Jahrgänge.

Newman, Ernest. Gluck and the Opera. London, B. Dobell, 1895.

Nicolai, Paul. Der Ariadne-Stoff in der Entwicklungsgeschichte der deutschen Oper. Viersen, J. H. Meyer, 1919.

Niggli, Arnold. "Faustina Bordoni-Hasse," in Waldersee, *Sammlung musikalischer Vorträge* (Leipzig, B&H, 1879–98) II, 261–318.

Nin [y Castellano], J[oachin]. Sept Chansons picaresques espagnoles anciennes, librement harmonisées et précédées d'une étude sur les classiques espagnols du chant. Paris, M. Eschig, 1926.

—— Septs Chants lyriques espagnols anciens, librement harmonisés et précédés d'une étude sur les classiques espagnols du chant. Paris, M. Eschig, 1926.

Noack, Friedrich. "Die Opern von Christoph Graupner in Darmstadt," in *Bericht über den I. Musikwissenschaftlichen Kongress der Deutschen Musikgesellschaft* (Leipzig, B&H, 1926) 252–59.

Nohl, Ludwig. Die Zauberflöte: Betrachtungen über Bedeutung der dramatischen Musik in der Geschichte des menschlichen Geistes. Frankfurt/M., Schneider, 1862.

Nouveau Théâtre italien, Le. Paris, Briasson, 1733–1753. New ed.

Nowak, Leopold. Joseph Haydn : Leben, Bedeutung und Werk. Zurich, Leipzig, Vienna, Amalthea-Verlag, [1959]. 2d ed.

Nuovo, Antonio. Tommaso Traetta. Bitonto, A. Amendolagine, 1938.

Oliver, Alfred Richard. The Encyclopedists as Critics of Music. New York, Columbia University Press, 1947.

Olivier, Jean Jacques (pseud.). Les Comédiens français dans les cours d'Allemagne au XVIIIe siècle. Paris, Société française d'imprimerie et de libraire, 1901-5. Series 1-4.

Orel, Alfred. Goethe als Operndirektor. Bregenz, E. Russ, 1949.

—— "Die Legende um Mozarts Bastien und Bastienne," SchwM No. 91 (1951) 137-43.

—— "Mozart auf Goethes Bühne," Mozart-Jahrbuch 1953 (1954) 85-94.

"Origen y progressos de las tonadillas que se cantan en los Coliseos de esta Corte," Memorial literario, instructivo y curioso de la corte de Madrid XII (1787) 169-80.

[Origny, Abraham Jean Baptiste Antoine d'.] Annales du théâtre-italien. Paris, Duchesne, 1788. 3 vols.

Orlandini, Giuseppe. "Domenico Cimarosa e la musica nella seconda civiltà latina," Rivista bolognese II [?] (1868) 933-47, 1005-24.

[Paget, Violet.] Studies of the Eighteenth Century in Italy. London, W. Satchell, 1880. "By Vernon Lee" (pseud.).

Pahlen, Kurt. Das Rezitativ bei Mozart. Vienna Dissertation, 1929.

Paisiello, Cavalier Giovanni. "Saggio del corso dei travagli musicali del cavaliere Giovanni Paisiello," RassM III (1930) 124-35.

[Parfaict, François.] Dictionnaire des théâtres de Paris. Paris, Lambert, 1756. 7 vols.

—— Histoire de l'ancien théâtre italien depuis son origine en France, jusqu'à sa suppression en l'année 1697. Paris, Lambert, 1753.

—— Mémoires pour servir à l'histoire des spectacles de la foire. Paris, Briasson, 1743.

Parini, Giuseppe. "La evirazione (La musica) [Ode]," in Le odi, il giorno e poesie minore, con note di Guido Mazzoni (Florence, Barbèra, 1947) 50-57.

Parisini, G. Musica e balli in Faenza nel 1745. Faenza, Lega, 1935.

Parodies du nouveau théâtre italien . . . avec les airs gravés, Les. Paris, Briasson, 1738. New ed.

Parolari, Cornelio. "Giambattista Velluti," RMI XXXIX (1932) 263-98.

Pascazio, Nicola. L'uomo Piccini e la querelle célèbre. Bari, Laterza, 1951.

Pastore, Giuseppe A. Leonardo Leo. Galatina (Lecce), Editore Pajano, 1957.

Pauly, Reinhard G. "Alessandro Scarlatti's Tigrane," M&L XXXV (1954) 339-46.

—— "Benedetto Marcello's Satire on Early 18th-Century Opera," MQ XXXIV (1948) 222-33.

Paumgartner, Bernhard. "Die beiden Fassungen des Idomeneo: Ein Beitrag zur Dramaturgie Mozarts," M IX (1955) 423-29.

—— Mozart. Freiburg & Zurich, Atlantis-Verlag, [1958]. 5th ed.

Pavan, Giuseppe. Contributo alla storia del teatro musicale; il dramma più musicato; l'Artaserse del Metastasio. Cittadella, Tip. Sociale, 1917.

Pearce, Charles E. "Polly Peachum" : The Story of Polly and The Beggar's Opera. London, S. Paul, [1923].

Pedrell, Felipe. "L'Eglogue *La Forêt sans amour* de Lope de Vega, et la musique et les musiciens du théâtre de Calderón," SIMG XI (1909–10) 55–104.

—— Teatro lírico español anterior al siglo XIX. La Coruña, Berea, [1897–]1898. 5 vols.

Peiser, Karl. Johann Adam Hiller. Leipzig, Gebrüder Hug, 1894.

Pelicelli, Nestore. "Musicisti in Parma nel secolo XVIII : La musica alla corte di Parma nel 1700," *Note d'archivio* XI (1934); XII (1935) 27–42, 82–92.

Pellisson, Maurice. Les Comédies-ballets de Molière. Paris, Hachette, 1914.

Pfeiffer, Konrad. Von Mozarts göttlichem Genius : Eine Kunstbetrachtung auf der Grundlage der Schopenhauerschen Philosophie. Berlin, Verlag Walter de Gruyter & Co., 1956. 3d ed.

Pierre, Constant. Les Hymnes et chansons de la révolution : Aperçu général et catalogue avec notes historiques, analytiques et bibliographiques. Paris, Imprimerie nationale, 1904.

Pincherle, Marc. "Antonio Vivaldi : Essai biographique," RdM XI (1930) 161–70, 265–81.

—— Vivaldi. Paris, Editions Le Bon Plaisir, Librairie Plon, [1955]. Translated as : Vivaldi : Genius of the Baroque. New York, W. W. Norton, [1957].

Piovano, Francesco. "A propos d'une recente biographie de Léonard Leo," SIMG VIII (1906–7) 70–95, 336.

—— "Baldassare Galuppi : Note bio-bibliografiche," RMI XIII (1906) 676–726; XIV (1907) 333–65; XV (1908) 233–74.

—— "Elenco cronologico delle opere (1757–1802) di Pietro Guglielmi," RMI XII (1905) 407–46.

—— "Notizie storico-bibliografiche sulle opere di Pietro Guglielmi (Guglielmini) con appendice su Pietro Guglielmi," RMI XVI (1909) 243–70, 475–505, 785–820; XVII (1910) 59–90, 376–414, 554–89, 822–77. This is about the son, Pietro Carlo Guglielmi, 1763–1817.

—— "Un Opéra inconnu de Gluck," SIMG IX (1907–8) 231–81, 448.

Pirro, André. Descartes et la musique. Paris, Fischbacher, 1907.

Pirrotta, Nino. "Falsirena e la più antica delle cavatine," *Collectanea historiae musicae* II (1957) 355–66.

Pistorelli, L. "Due melodrammi inediti di Apostolo Zeno," RMI III (1896) 261–74.

—— "I melodrammi giocosi del Casti," RMI II (1895) 36–56, 449–72; IV (1897) 631–71.

Piton, Alexis. "Les Origines du mélodrame français à la fin du XVIIIe siècle," *Revue d'histoire littéraire* (1911) 256–96.

Planelli, Antonio. Dell' opera in musica. Naples, D. Campo, 1772.

Plümicke, Carl Martin. Entwurf einer Theatergeschichte von Berlin. Berlin and Stettin, F. Nicolai, 1781.

Pohl, Karl Ferdinand. Joseph Haydn. Leipzig, B&H, 1878–1927. 3 vols. in 2.

Poladian, Sirvart. Handel as an Opera Composer. Ann Arbor, University Microfilms, 1958.

Polko, Elise. Die Bettler-Oper. Hanover, Rümpler, 1863. 3 vols.

Pompeati, Arturo. "Il Parini e la musica," RMI XXXVI (1929) 556–74.

Potter, John. The Theatrical Review; or, New Companion to the Playhouse; Containing a Critical and Historical Account of Every Tragedy, Comedy, Opera, Farce &c Exhibited at the Theatres during the Last Season. London, S. Crowder, 1772. 2 vols.

Pougin, Arthur. "Bernardo Mengozzi," RMI XXV (1918) 176–201, 323–44.

—— Un Directeur d'opéra au dix-huitième siècle; l'opéra sous l'ancien régime; l'opéra sous la révolution. Paris, Fischbacher, 1914.

—— Jean-Jacques Rousseau musicien. Paris, Fischbacher, 1901.

—— Madame Favart, étude théâtrale, 1727–1772. Paris, Fischbacher, 1912.

—— Molière et l'opéra-comique. Paris, J. Baur, 1882.

—— Monsigny et son temps. Paris, Fischbacher, 1908.

—— Musiciens français du XVIIIe siècle : Dezèdes. Paris, N. Chaix, 1862.

—— L'Opéra-comique pendant la révolution de 1788 à 1801. Paris, A. Savine, 1891.

Powers, Harold S. "Il Serse trasformato," MQ XLVII (1961) 481–92; XLVIII (1962) 73–92.

Preibisch, Walter. "Quellenstudien zu Mozart's Entführung aus dem Serail: Ein Beitrag zur Geschichte der Türkenoper," SIMG X (1908–9) 430–76.

Prochazka, R. Mozart in Prag. Prague, G. Neugebauer, 1899.

Prod'homme, Jacques Gabriel. "Austro-German Musicians in France in the Eighteenth Century," MQ XV (1929) 171–95.

—— "Les Dernières Représentations du Devin du village (mai–juin 1829)," RM VII (August, 1926) 118–25.

—— "Deux Collaborateurs italiens de Gluck : Raniero de Calzabigi e Giuseppe D'Affligio," RMI XXIII (1916) 33–65, 201–18.

—— "A French Maecenas of the Time of Louis XV : M. de la Pouplinière," MQ X (1924) 511–31.

—— Gluck. Paris, Société d'Editions Françaises et Internationales, 1948.

—— "Gluck's French Collaborators," MQ III (1917) 249–71.

—— "Lettres de Gluck et à propos de Gluck (1776–1787)," ZIMG XIII (1911–12) 257–65.

—— "Marie Fel (1713–1794)," SIMG IV (1902–3) 485–518.

—— "La Musique à Paris de 1753 à 1757, d'après un manuscrit de la Bibliothèque de Munich," SIMG VI (1904–5) 568–87.

—— "Notes sur deux librettistes français de Gluck : Du Roullet et Moline (d'après des documents inédits)," ZIMG VII (1905–6) 12–15.

—— "*Le Page inconstant*: Ballet anacréontique . . . sur la musique de Mozart," RdM XVI (1935) 205–12.

—— "A Pastel by La Tour : Marie Fel," MQ IX (1923) 482–507.

—— "Pierre de Jélyotte (1713–1797)," SIMG III (1901–2) 686–717.

—— "Rosalie Levasseur, Ambassadress of Opera," MQ II (1916) 210–43.

Prota-Giurleo, Ulisse. Alessandro Scarlatti, "il Palermitano" (la patria & la famiglia). Naples, L'autore, 1926.

—— La grande orchestra del Teatro S. Carlo nel Settecento (da documenti inediti). Naples, L'autore, 1927.

—— Musicanti napoletani alla corte di Portogallo nel 700. Naples, Elzevira, 1925.

—— Nicola Logroscino, "il dio dell' opera buffa." Naples, L'autore, 1927.

—— "Sacchini fra Piccinisti e Gluckisti," *Gazzetta musicale di Napoli* (1957) Nos. 4 and 5.

Provenzal, Dino. La vita e le opere di Lodovico Adimari. Rocca S. Casciano, L. Cappelli, 1902.

Prunières, Henry. "Défense et illustration de l'Opéra-comique," RM XIV (November, 1933) 243–47.

Pupino-Carbonelli, Giuseppe. Paisiello. Naples, Tocco, 1908.

Puttman, Max. "Zur Geschichte der deutschen komischen Oper von ihren Anfängen bis Dittersdorf," *Die Musik* III (1903–4) Qt. 4, 334–49, 416–28.

Quadrio, Francesco Saverio, abate. Della storia e della ragione d'ogni poesia. Bologna, F. Pisarri, 1739–49. 4 vols.

Quantz, Johann Joachim. Versuch einer Anweisung die Flöte traversiere zu spielen. Leipzig, C. F. Kahnt, 1906. Originally published Berlin, J. F. Voss, 1752.

Quittard, Henri. "Les Années de jeunesse de J. P. Rameau," RHCM II (1902) 61–63, 100–14, 152–70, 208–18.

—— "*Le Bucheron*, opéra comique de Philidor," RHCM VII (1907) 421–24.

—— "*Ernelinde*, de Philidor," RHCM VII (1907) 469–74.

—— "La Première Comédie française en musique," *Bulletin français de la SIM* IV (1908) 378–96, 497–537.

—— "*Le Sorcier*, opéra comique de Philidor," RHCM VII (1907) 537–41.

Raab, Leopold. Wenzel Müller. Boden bei Wien, Verein der N.-Oe. Landesfreunde in Boden, 1928.

Rabany, Charles. Carlo Goldoni : Le théâtre et la vie en Italie au XVIIIe siècle. Paris, Berger-Levrault, 1896.

Raccolta di melodrammi giocosi scritti nel secolo XVIII. Milan, Soc. tip. dei classici italiani, 1826.

Raccolta di melodrammi serj scritti nel secolo XVIII. Milan, Soc. tip. dei classici italiani, 1822. 2 vols.

Radiciotti, Giuseppe. "L'arte di G. B. Pergolesi," RMI XVII (1910) 916–25.

—— Pergolesi. Milan, Fratelli Treves, [1935]. German edition : Giovanni Battista Pergolesi : Leben und Werk. [Enlarged and rev. by Antoine E. Cherbuliez.] Zurich, Pan-Verlag, [1954].

Raeburn, Christopher. "*Figaro* in Wien," OeM XII (1957) 273–77.

—— "Die textlichen Quellen des *Schauspieldirektors*," OeM XIII (1958) 4–10.

—— "Das Zeitmass in Mozarts Opern," OeM XII (1957) 329–33.

Raeburn, Michael, and Christopher Raeburn. "Mozart Manuscripts in Florence," M&L XL (1959) 334–40.

Raeli, V. "The Bi-Centenary of Tommaso Traetta," *The Chesterian* VIII (1926–27) 217–23.

—— "Tommaso Traetta," *Rivista nazionale di musica* (March, 1927).

[Raguenet, François.] Défense du parallèle des Italiens et des François en ce qui regarde la musique et l'opéra. Paris, C. Barben, 1705.

—— Paralele des Italiens et des François en ce qui regarde la musique et les opéras. Paris, J. Moreau, 1602 [i.e., 1702]. Translated as : A Comparison between the French and Italian Musick and Opera's . . . to Which Is Added a Critical Discourse upon Opera's in England. London, W. Lewis, 1709. German translation with notes in Mattheson's *Critica Musica* (Hamburg, 1722).

Rauber, A. Die Don Juan Sage im Lichte biologischer Forschung. Leipzig, Georgi, 1898.

Redlich, Hans F. "Handel's *Agrippina* (1709): Problems of a Practical Edition," MR XII (1951) 15–23.

—— "*L'oca del Cairo*," MR II (1941) 122–31.

Reichardt, Johann Friedrich. Ueber die deutsche comische Oper. Hamburg, C. E. Bohn, 1774.

Reichel, Eugen. "Gottsched und Johann Adolph Scheibe," SIMG II (1900–1901) 654–68.

Reiff, A. "Die Anfänge der Oper in Spanien, mit Textproben," *Spanien, Zeitschrift für Auslandskunde* Jahrgang I, Heft 3 (1919).

Reimers, Dagmar. Geschichte des Rigaer deutschen Theaters von 1782–1822. Poznan, A. Meyer, 1942.

[Rémond de Saintmard, Toussaint.] Reflexions sur l'opéra. The Hague, J. Neaulme, 1741.

"Revue der Revueen : Zum 200. Geburtstag von Chr. W. Gluck," *Die Musik* XIII (1913–14) Qt. 4, 223–27, 276–78.

Riccoboni, Luigi. Reflexions historiques et critiques sur les differens théâtres de l'Europe. Paris, J. Guérin, 1738.

Richebourg, Louisette. Contribution à l'histoire de la "Querelle des Bouffons." Paris, Nizet, 1937.

Riedinger, Lothar. "Karl von Dittersdorf als Opernkomponist," SzMw II (1914) 212–349.

Riess, Otto. "Johann Abraham Peter Schulz' Leben," SIMG XV (1913–14) 169–270.

Rinaldi, Mario. Antonio Vivaldi. Milan, Istituto d'alta cultura, [1943].

Rivalta, Camillo. Giuseppe Sarti. Faenza, F. Lega, 1928.

Roberti, Giuseppe. "La musica in Italia nel secolo XVIII secondo le impressioni di viaggiatori stranieri," RMI VII (1900) 698–729; VIII (1901) 519–59.

Robinson, Percy. Handel and His Orbit. London, Sheratt & Hughes, 1908.

—— "Handel up to 1720 : A New Chronology," M&L XX (1939) 55–63.

Rockstro, William Smyth. The Life of George Frederick Handel. London, Macmillan, 1883.

Rogers, Francis. "Handel and Five Prima Donnas," MQ XXIX (1943) 214–24.

—— "The Male Soprano," MQ V (1919) 413–25.

—— "Sophie Arnould (1740–1803)," MQ VI (1920) 57–61.

Rognoni, Luigi. Un' opera incompiuta di Mozart : L' oca del Cairo; a proposito di una ricostruzione. Milan, Bocca, 1937.

Rolandi, Ulderico. Il librettista del Matrimonio segreto: Giovanni Bertati. Trieste, C. Reali, 1926.

Rolland, Romain. "L'Autobiographie d'un illustre oublié : Telemann," in Voyage musical au pays du passé (Paris, Eduard-Joseph, 1919).

—— "Le Dernier Opéra de Gluck : Echo et Narcisse (1779)," RHCM III (1903) 212–15.

—— "Gluck, une révolution dramatique," Revue de Paris (1904) No. 3, 736–72.

—— Haendel. [New ed.] Paris, Michel, [1951].

—— "Métastase, précurseur de Gluck," MM VIII, No. 4 (1912) 1–10.

Roncaglia, Gino. Il melodioso Settecento italiano. Milan, Hoepli, 1935. Contains examples of music by Galuppi, Paisiello, Cimarosa, A. M. Bononcini, and T. Giordani.

Ronga, Luigi. "Scarlatti fra due epoche," Musicista VII (1940) 57–61.

Rosa, Salvator. "La musica," in Mattheson, Mithridat (Hamburg, Geissler, 1749) i–lvi, with German translation.

Roscoe, P. C. "Arne and The Guardian Outwitted," M&L XXIV (1943) 237–45.

Rosenfeld, Ernst. Johann Baptist Schenk als Opernkomponist. Vienna Dissertation, 1921.

Rosenthal, Harold. Two Centuries of Opera at Covent Garden. London, Putnam, 1958.

Rosenthal, Karl. "Ueber Volksformen bei Mozart : Ein Beitrag zur Entwicklung der Vokalformen von 1760 bis 1790," SzMw XIV (1927) 5–32.

Ross, Erwin. Deutsche und italienische Gesangsmethode : Erläutert auf Grund ihrer geschichtlichen Gegensätzlichkeit im achtzehnten Jahrhundert. Kassel, Bärenreiter, 1928.

Rossell, Denton. The Formal Construction of Mozart's Operatic Ensembles and Finales. Ann Arbor, University Microfilms, 1956. 2 vols.

Roth, Hermann. "Händels Ballettmusiken," *Neue Musik-Zeitung* XLIX (1928) 245–52.

—— "Händels Ballettoper *Ariodante*: Zur deutscher Uraufführung," ZfMw IX (1926–27) 159–67.

—— "Zur Karlsruher Einrichtung von Händels *Tamerlan*," ZfMw V (1922–23) 380–82.

Rousseau, Jean Jacques. Dictionnaire de musique. Amsterdam, M. M. Rey, 1768. Vol. II, Amsterdam, M. M. Rey, 1779. Translated as : A Complete Dictionary of Music. London, J. Murray, 1779.

—— Lettre à Mr. d'Alembert sur les spectacles. Ed. critique par Max Fuchs. Geneva, Droz; Lille, Giard, 1948.

—— Œuvres complètes. Paris, P. Dupont, 1823–26. 25 vols. Contains "Confessions," Vols. 14–16; writings on music, Vols. 11–13.

Roustan, Marius. Les Philosophes et la société française au XVIIIe siècle. Paris, Hachette, 1911.

Rowell, Lewis E., Jr. Four Operas of Antonio Vivaldi. University of Rochester Dissertation, 1958.

Rubsamen, Walter. "Mr. Seedo, Ballad Opera, and the Singspiel," in *Miscelánea en homenaje a Mons. Higinio Anglés* (Barcelona, Consejo Superior de Investigaciones Científicas, 1958–61) II, 776–809. Also separate.

Rückert, Heinz. "Das musikalische Theater ruft nach Händel," *Händel-Jahrbuch* VIII (1956) 57–61.

Russo, Joseph Louis. Lorenzo da Ponte, Poet and Adventurer. New York, Columbia University Press, 1922.

Russo, Luigi. Metastasio. Bari, G. Laterza, 1921.

Sacchi, Giovenale. Vita del cavaliere Don Carlo Broschi. Vinegia, Coleti, 1784.

Sachs, Curt. Musik und Oper am kurbrandenburgischen Hofe. Berlin, J. Bard, 1910.

Sage, Jack. "Calderón e la música teatral," *Bulletin hispanique* LVIII (1956) 275–300.

Saint-Evremond, Charles de Marguetel de St. Denis, Seigneur de. Œuvres meslées. London, Tonson, 1709. 3 vols. 2d ed. Contains "Sur les opera," II, 214–22; "Les Opera, comedie," II, 223–92; "A Monsieur Lulli," III, 106–7.

Saint-Foix, Georges de. "Autour de Paisiello," RMI XLVIII (1946) 243–50.

—— "La Conclusion de l'ouverture de *Don Juan*," RdM V (1924) 169–72.

—— "Le Livret de *Così fan tutte*," RdM XI (1930) 43–97.

—— "Les Maîtres de l'opéra bouffe dans la musique de chambre à Londres," RMI XXXI (1924) 507–26.

—— "Sammartini et les chanteurs de son temps," RMI XLIII (1939) 357–63.

—— "Le Théâtre à Salzbourg en 1779–80," RdM XVI (1935) 193–204.

Salazar, Adolfo. Juan del Encina y la música en el primitivo teatro español. Mexico, D.F., 1940. (Bóletin de musicologia y folklore, January, 1940.)

—— La música en el primitivo teatro español, anterior a Lope de Vega y Calderón. México, A. Salazar, [1942?].

Samson, Ingrid. "Paisiello—La bella Molinara," NZfM CXX (1959) 368–71.

Sandberger, Adolf. "Tommaso Traëtta," DTB XIV, No. 1 (1913) xii–xc.

Saracino, Emanuele. Tommaso Traetta (cenni biografico-artistici). Bitonto, A. Amendolagine, [pref. 1954].

Scarlatti, Gli : Alessandro, Francesco, Pietro, Domenico, Giuseppe; note e documenti sulla vita e sulle opere. Siena, Ticci Poligrafico, 1940.

Schatz, Albert. "Giovanni Bertati," VfMw V (1889) 231–71.

Scheibe, Johann Adolf. Critischer Musikus. Leipzig, B. C. Breitkopf, 1745. New ed.

Schenk, Erich. Wolfgang Amadeus Mozart : Eine Biographie. Zurich, Amalthea Verlag, [1955]. Translated as : Mozart and His Times. New York, Alfred A. Knopf, 1959.

Schenk, Johann Baptist. ["Autobiographische Skizze"], SzMw XI (1924) 75–85.

Scherillo, Michele. L'opera buffa napoletana durante il Settecento : Storia letteraria. [Milan], R. Sandron, [1917]. 2d ed. First published as : Storia letteraria dell' opera buffa napolitana dalle origini al principio del secolo XIX. Naples, R. Università, 1883.

—— "La prima commedia musicale a Venezia," Giornale storico della letteratura italiana I (1883) 230–59.

Schering, Arnold. "Zwei Singspiele des Sperontes," ZfMw VII (1924–25) 214–20.

Schiedermair, Ludwig. Bayreuther Festspiel im Zeitalter des Absolutismus. Leipzig, C. F. Kahnt, 1908.

—— "Zur Geschichte der frühdeutschen Oper," JMP XVII (1910) 29–43.

Schiedermair, Ludwig, ed. Die Briefe W. A. Mozarts und seiner Familie. Munich, G. Müller, 1914.

Schletterer, Hans Michael. Das deutsche Singspiel von seinen ersten Anfängen bis auf die neueste Zeit. Leipzig, B&H, [1863?].

—— "Giovanni Battista Pergolesi," in Waldersee, Sammlung musikalischer Vorträge (Leipzig, B&H, 1879–98) II, 139–78.

—— "Die Opernhäuser Neapels," MfMg XIV (1882) 175–81, 183–89; XV (1883) 12–19.

Schlitzer, Franco. Antonio Sacchini : Schede e appunti per una sua storia teatrale. Siena, [Ticci], 1955.

—— Cimarosa. Milan, Ricciardi, 1950.

Schlitzer, Franco. Goethe e Cimarosa, con un' appendice di note bio-bibliografiche : In occasione della VII Settimana Musicale (16–22 settembre 1950). Siena, Ticci, 1950.

Schlitzer, Franco, ed. Tommaso Traetta, Leonardo Leo, Vincenzo Bellini: Notizie e documenti raccolti in occasione della "IX Settimana Musicale Senese" 16–22 settembre 1952. Siena, Ticci, 1952.

Schmid, Anton. Christoph Willibald Ritter von Gluck. Leipzig, F. Fleischer, 1854.

Schmid, Ernst Fritz. "Mozart und Monsigny," Mozart-Jahrbuch 1957 (1958) 57–62.

Schmid, Johan Jacob von. Die Zauberflöte: Beschouwingen over Mozart's Opera; een Bijdrage tot de Cultuurgeschiedenis en de Geesteswetenschappen. Assen, Van Gorcum, 1956.

Schmid, Otto. Die Heimstätten der sächsischen Landestheater. Dresden, A. Waldheim, [19—?].

—— Das sächsische Königshaus in selbstschöpferischer musikalischer Bethätigung (Musik am sächsischen Hofe). Leipzig, B&H, 1900.

Schmidt, Heinrich. Johann Mattheson, ein Förderer der deutschen Tonkunst, im Lichte seiner Werke. Leipzig, B&H, 1897.

Schmitz, Eugen. "Formgesetze in Mozarts Zauberflöte," in Festschrift Max Schneider zum 80. Geburtstage (Leipzig, Deutscher Verlag für Musik, [1955]) 209–14.

—— "Zu Mozarts Bastien und Bastienne," Hochland IX, No. 2 (1912) 607–11.

Schneider, Constantin. "Die Oratorien und Schuldramen Anton Cajetan Adlgassers," SzMw XVIII (1931).

Schneider, Ludwig. Geschichte der Oper und des königlichen Opernhauses in Berlin. Berlin, Duncker & Humblot, 1852.

Schneider, Max. "Die Begleitung des Secco-Rezitativs um 1750," Gluck-Jahrbuch III (1917) 88–107.

Schnerich, Alfred. "Wie sahen die ersten Vorstellungen von Mozart's Don Juan aus?" ZIMG XII (1910–11) 101–8.

Schramm, Erich. "Goethe und Diderots Dialog Rameaus Neffe," ZfMw XVI (1934) 294–307.

Schütze, Johann Friedrich. Hamburgische Theatergeschichte. Hamburg, J. P. Treder, 1794.

Schuh, Willi. "Il Flauto magico," in Festschrift Friedrich Blume (Kassel, Bärenreiter, 1963) [327]–339.

—— "Über einige frühe Textbücher zur Zauberflöte," in Bericht über den internationalen musikwissenschaftlichen Kongress Wien, Mozartjahr 1956 (Graz, Böhlaus, 1958) 571–78.

Schultz, William Eben. Gay's Beggar's Opera: Its Content, History, and Influence. New Haven, Yale University Press, 1923.

—— "The Music of the Beggar's Opera in Print, 1728–1923," MTNA XIX (1934) 87–99.

Schwan, Wilhelm Bernhard. Die opernästhetischen Theorien der deutschen klassischen Dichter. Bonn Dissertation, 1928.

Schwartz, Rudolf. "Zur Geschichte der liederlosen Zeit in Deutschland," JMP XX (1913) 13–27.

Schwarz, Max. "Johann Christian Bach," SIMG II (1900–1901) 401–54.

Scudo, Pierre. Le Chevalier Sarti. Paris, Hachette, 1857. (Previously in Revue des deux mondes, 1854–56.)

—— "Pergolèse et La serva padrona," Revue des deux mondes XXXII, No. 41 (September 1, 1862) 226–30.

Sear, H. G. "Charles Dibdin : 1745–1814," M&L XXVI (1945) 61–65.

Segnitz, Eugen. Goethe und die Oper in Weimar. Langensalza, Beyer, 1908.

Seiffert, Max. "J.A.P. Schultz' 'dänische' Oper," AfMw I (1918–19) 422–23.

—— "Zur Biographie Joh. Adolph Hasse's," SIMG VII (1905–6) 129–31.

Seligmann, Herbert Wolff. Beiträge zur Geschichte der Bühne der opera seria. Bonn Dissertation, 1924.

Serauky, Walter. "Das Ballett in G. F. Händels Opern," Händel-Jahrbuch VIII (1956) 91–112.

—— Georg Friedrich Händel : Sein Leben, sein Werk. Band 3 : [Von Händels innerer Neuorientierung bis zum Abschluss der Samson (1736–1743)] and Band 4 : [Von Händels Semele bis zum Abschluss des Judas Makkabäus (1743–1746)]. Leipzig, Deutscher Verlag für Musik, 1956–58.

Sharp, Geoffrey. "Don Giovanni: Some Observations," MR IV (1943) 45–52.

Sherwin, Oscar. Mr. Gay : Being a Picture of the Life and Times of the Author of the Beggar's Opera. New York, John Day, 1929.

Siegmund-Schultze, Walther. Georg Friedrich Händel : Leben und Werk. Leipzig, Deutscher Verlag für Musik, 1954.

—— "Der Gesangsstil der Händel-Oper," MuG IX (1959) 137–41.

Siena Settimane Musicali. B. Galuppi detto "Il Buranello" (1706–1785): Note e documenti, raccolti in occasione della settimana celebrativa, (20–26 settembre 1948). Siena, Ticci, 1948.

Sievers, Heinrich. 250 Jahre Braunschweigisches Staatstheater, 1690–1940. Brunswick, Appelhans, 1941.

Silva, G. Silvestri. Illustri musicisti calabresi : Leonardo Vinci. Genoa, Tip. Nazionale, [1935].

Simon, Alicja. "Grétry au Théâtre national de Varsovie," in International Society for Musical Research, First Congress, Report (Burnham, Plainsong and Medieval Music Society, [1930]).

Sittard, Josef. "Reinhard Keiser in Württemberg," MfMg XVIII (1886) 3–12.

Smith, William C. Concerning Handel, His Life and Works : Essays. London, Cassell, [1948].

Smith, William C., compiler. The Italian Opera and Contemporary Ballet in London, 1789–1820 : A Record of Performances and Players with Reports from the Journals of the Time. London, Society for Theatre Research, [1955].

Solar Quintes, Nicolás A. "Nuevas aportaciones a la biografía de Carlos Broschi (Farinelli)," *Anuario musical* III (1948) 187–204.

—— "Nuevos documentos para la biografía del compositor Sebastián Durón," *Anuario musical* X (1955) 137–62.

Soleinne, Martineau de. Bibliothèque dramatique. Paris, Administration de l'Alliance des arts, 1843–45. 7 vols. See also : Tableau générale du catalogue (Paris, Administration de l'Alliance des arts, 1845); and Table des pièces du théâtre décrites dans le catalogue . . . par Charles Brunet publiée par Henri de Rothschild (Paris, D. Morgand, 1914).

Somerset, H. V. F. "Giovanni Paisiello," M&L XVIII (1937) 20–35.

—— "Jean Jacques Rousseau as a Musician," M&L XVII (1936) 37–46, 218–24.

Sommer, Hans. "Die Oper *Ludwig der Fromme* von Georg Caspar Schürmann," MfMg XIV (1882) 48–51, 53–55.

—— "Zur Schürmann'schen Oper *Ludovicus Pius*," MfMg XXIV (1892) 137–39.

Sondheimer, Robert. "Gluck in Paris," ZfMw V (1922–23) 165–75.

Sonette, Jean Jacques, pseud. *See* Goudar, Ange.

Sonneck, Oscar George Theodore. "Ciampi's *Bertoldo, Bertoldino e Cacasenno* and Favart's *Ninette à la cour*," SIMG XII (1911) 525–64.

—— "Die drei Fassungen des Hasse'schen *Artaserse*," SIMG XIV (1912–13) 226–42.

—— "Foot-note to the Bibliographical History of Grétry's Operas," in *Gedenkboek . . . Scheurleer* (The Hague, Nijhoff, 1925) 321–36.

—— "*Il Giocatore,*" MA IV (1912–13) 160–74.

—— "La nuova rappresentazione del *D. Giovanni* di Mozart a Monaco," RMI III (1896) 741–55.

Sooper, Frances O. "The Music of Dittersdorf," M&L XI (1930) 141–45.

Specht, Richard. Das Wiener Operntheater : Von Dingelstedt bis Schalk und Strauss. Vienna, P. Knepler, 1919.

Spectator, The (London, 1711–1714). London and Toronto, J. M. Dent, 1919–26. 4 vols.

Speziale, G. "Ancora per Paisiello," RassM IV (1931) 1–16.

Spinelli, Alessandro Giuseppe. Bibliografia goldoniana. Milan, Dumolard, 1884.

Spitta, Philipp. Johann Sebastian Bach. Leipzig, B&H, 1930. 4th ed. 2 vols.

—— "Rinaldo di Capua," VfMw III (1877) 92–121.

Spitz, Charlotte. Antonio Lotti in seiner Bedeutung als Opernkomponist. Borna–Leipzig, Noske, 1918.

—— "Die Opern *Ottone* von G. F. Händel (London 1722) und *Teofane* von A. Lotti (Dresden 1719) : Ein Stilvergleich," in *Festschrift Adolf Sandberger* (Munich, Zierfuss, 1918) 265–71.

Squire, William Barclay. "Gluck's London Operas," MQ I (1915) 397–409.

—— "An Index of Tunes in the Ballad-Operas," MA II (1910–11) 1–17.

Stählin, Karl. Aus den Papieren Jacob von Stählins. Königsberg, Ost-Europa-Verlag, 1926.

Stauder, Wilhelm. "Johann André : Ein Beitrag zur Geschichte des deutschen Singspiels," AfMf I (1936) 318–60. Also separate : Leipzig, B&H, 1936.

Stefan, Paul. Die Zauberflöte: Herkunft, Bedeutung, Geheimnis. Vienna, Reichner, 1937.

Steglich, Rudolf. "Das deutsche Händelfest in Leipzig," ZfMw VII (1924–25) 587–92.

—— "Göttinger Händelfestspiele 1924," Zeitschrift für Musik XCI (1924) 496–98.

—— "Göttinger Händel-Opern Festspiele 1927," Zeitschrift für Musik XCIV (1927) 424–26.

—— "Das Händelfest in Münster (2. bis 5. Dezember 1926)," ZfMw IX (1926–27) 290–93.

—— "Die Händel-Opern-Festspiele in Göttingen," ZfMw III (1920–21) 615–20.

—— "Händels Oper Rodelinde und ihre neue Göttinger Bühnenfassung," ZfMw III (1920–21) 518–34.

—— "Händels Saul in szenischer Darstellung," Zeitschrift für Musik XC (1923) Heft XVII, 15–17.

—— "Händels Xerxes und die Göttinger Händel-Opern-Festspiele 1924," ZfMw VII (1924–25) 21–33.

—— "Händel und die Gegenwart," Zeitschrift für Musik XCII (1925) 333–38.

—— "Die neue Händel-Opern-Bewegung," Händel-Jahrbuch I (1928) 71–158.

—— "Schütz und Händel," Zeitschrift für Musik LXXXIX (1922) 478–80.

—— "Ueber die gegenwärtige Krise der Händelpflege," ZfMw X (1927–28) 632–41.

Steinitzer, Max. Zur Entwicklungsgeschichte des Melodrams und Mimodrams. Leipzig, C. F. W. Siegel, [1919].

Stendhal, pseud. See Beyle, Henri.

Stephenson, Kurt. Hamburgische Oper zwischen Barock und Romantik. Hamburg, J. P. Toth, [1948].

Sternfeld, Frederick W. "The Melodic Sources of Mozart's Most Popular Lied," MQ XLII (1956) 213–22.

Stier, Ernst. "Georg Caspar Schürmann," Die Musik III, No. 2 (1903–4) 107–11.

Strasser, Stefan. "Susanna und die Gräfin," ZfMw X (1927–28) 208–16.

Streatfeild, Richard Alexander. Handel. New York, John Lane, 1909.

Streatfeild, Richard Alexander. "Handel, Rolli, and Italian Opera in London in the Eighteenth Century," MQ III (1917) 428–45.

Strüver, Paul. Die cantata da camera Alessandro Scarlattis. Munich Dissertation, 1924.

Stubenrauch, Herbert, Wilhelm Herrmann, and Claus Helmut Drese. 175 Jahre Nationaltheater Mannheim : Dokumente zur Theatergeschichte, zusammengestellt und erläutert. Mannheim, Nationaltheater, 1954.

Subirá, José. El compositor Iriarte (1750–1791) y el cultivo español del melólogo (melodrama). Madrid, Consejo Superior de Investigaciones Científicas, Instituto Español de Musicología, 1949–50. 2 vols.

—— El gremio de representates españoles y la Cofradia de Nuestra Señora de la Novena. Madrid, Consejo Superior de Investigaciones Científicas, Instituto de Estudios Madrileños, 1960.

—— Historia de la música teatral en España. Barcelona, Editorial Labor, 1945.

—— "Les Influences françaises dans la tonadilla madrilène du XVIIIe siècle," in Mélanges de musicologie (Paris, Droz, 1933) 209–16.

—— Los maestros de la tonadilla escénica. Barcelona, Editorial Labor, 1933.

—— "Un manuscrito musical de principios del siglo XVIII : Contribución a la musica teatral española," Anuario musical IV (1949) 181–91.

—— La música en la casa de Alba. Madrid, ["Sucesores de Rivadeneyra"], 1927.

—— El operista español d. Juan Hidalgo. Madrid, Bermejo, 1934.

—— La participación musical en el antiguo teatro español. Barcelona, Diputación provincial, 1930.

—— "Le Style dans la musique théâtrale espagnole," Acta musicologica IV (1932) 67–75.

—— La tonadilla escénica. Madrid, Tipografía de archivos, 1928–30. 3 vols.

—— Tonadillas teatrales inéditas. Madrid, Tipografía de archivos, 1932.

Supplément aux parodies du théâtre italien. Paris, Duchesne, 1765. New ed.

Szabolcsi, Bence. "Exoticisms in Mozart," M&L XXXVII (1956) 323–32.

—— "Mozart et la comédie populaire," in Studia musicologica I (Budapest, Hungarian Academy of Sciences, 1961) 65–91. Originally published in Hungarian (Budapest, 1957).

Szametz, Ralph. Hat Mozart eine Psychose durchgemacht? Frankfurt Dissertation, 1936.

Tanner, Richard. Johann David Heinichen als dramatischer Komponist. Leipzig, B&H, 1916.

Taut, Kurt. "Verzeichnis des Schrifttums über Georg Friedrich Händel," Händel-Jahrbuch VI (1933).

Taylor, Eric. "William Boyce and the Theatre," MR XIV (1953) 275–87.

Taylor, Sedley. The Indebtedness of Handel to the Works by Other Composers : A Presentation of Evidence. Cambridge, University Press, 1906.

Teneo, Martial. "Les Chefs-d'œuvre du chevalier Gluck à l'Opéra de Paris," RHCM VIII (1908) 109–16.

—— "La Détresse de Niccola Piccinni," RHCM VIII (1908) 237–44, 279–81.

—— "Un Spectacle à la cour en 1763," MM I (1905) 480–86.

Tenschert, Roland. Christoph Willibald Gluck, der grosse Reformator der Oper. Olten & Freiburg i Br., O. Walter AG., [1951].

—— Mozart : Ein Leben für die Oper. Vienna, Frick, 1941.

—— "Die Ouvertüren Mozarts," Mozart-Jahrbuch II (1924).

Terry, Charles Stanford. Johann Christian Bach. London, Oxford University Press, 1929.

Theater-Kalendar auf das Jahr . . . (Reichard). Gotha, Vols. 1–25, 1775–1800.

Thouret, Georg. "Einzug der Musen und Grazien in die Mark," Hohenzollern-Jahrbuch IV (1900) 192–230.

Thrane, Carl. "Sarti in Kopenhagen," SIMG III (1901–2) 528–38.

Tibaldi Chiesa, Mary. Cimarosa e il suo tempo. [Milan], A. Garzanti, [1939].

Tiersot, Julien. "Etude sur Don Juan de Mozart," Le Ménestrel LXII (1896) 399–411 passim; LXIII (1897) 1–139 passim.

—— "Etude sur Orphée de Gluck," Le Ménestrel LXII (1896) 273–386 passim.

—— "Gluck and the Encyclopædists," MQ XVI (1930) 336–57.

—— Histoire de la chanson populaire en France. Paris, Plon, Nourrit, 1889.

—— Jean-Jacques Rousseau. Paris, Alcan, 1912.

—— "La Musique de J.-J. Rousseau," MM VIII, No. 6 (1912) 34–56.

—— "Rameau," MQ XIV (1928) 77–107.

—— "L'ultima opera di Gluck, Eco e Narciso," RMI IX (1902) 264–96.

Tintori, Giampiero. L'opera napoletana. [Milan, Ricordi, 1958.]

Titon du Tillet, [Evrard]. Le Parnasse françois. Paris, J. B. Coignard, 1732–[43]. 2 vols., paged continuously.

Tommasini, Oreste. "Pietro Metastasio e lo svolgimento del melodramma italiano," in Scritti di storia e critica (Rome, E. Loescher, 1891) 153–222.

Tosi, Pietro Francesco. Opinioni de' cantori antichi, e moderni, o sieno Osservazioni sopra il canto figurato. [Bologna, L. dalla Volpe, 1723.] Translated as : Observations on the Florid Song; or, Sentiments on the Ancient and Modern Singers. London, J. Wilcox, 1742. Later English editions : 1743, 1906, 1926.

Tottmann, Albert. Mozart's Zauberflöte. Langensalza, Beyer, 1908. Makes use of C. Grüel's "Aufschlüsse über die Bedeutung des angeblich Schikanederschen Textes zu Mozart's Zauberflöte," Magdeburg, 1868.

Tovey, Donald Francis. "Christopher Willibald Gluck (1714–1787) and the Musical Revolution of the Eighteenth Century," in *The Heritage of Music*, ed. Hubert J. Foss (London, Oxford University Press, 1934) II, 69–117.

Tutenberg, Fritz. "Die *opera-buffa* Sinfonie und ihre Beziehungen zur klassischen Sinfonie," AfMw VIII (1926–27) 452–72.

"Ueber das Rezitativ," *Bibliothek der schönen Wissenschaften* XI, No. 2 (1764) 209; XII, No. 1 (1765) 1; XII, No. 2 (1765) 217.

Uffenbach, Johann Friedrich von. Pharasmen : Ein Singspiel. Berlin, O. Elsner, 1930.

Uhlenbruch, Fritz. Herforder Musikleben bis zur Mitte des 18. Jahrhunderts. Münster Dissertation, 1926.

Ujfalussy, J. "Intonation, Charakterbildung und Typengestaltung in Mozarts Werken," in *Studia musicologica* I (Budapest, Hungarian Academy of Sciences, 1961) 93–145. Originally published in Hungarian (Budapest, 1957).

Ulibishev, Aleksandr Dmitrievich. Mozart's Opern : Kritische Erläuterungen. Leipzig, B&H, 1848. Originally in French.

Ursprung, Otto. "*Celos* usw., Text von Calderón, Musik von Hidalgo,— die älteste erhaltene spanische Oper," in *Festschrift Arnold Schering* (Berlin, A. Glas, 1937) 223–40.

Valdrighi, Luigi Francesco, conte. I Bononcini da Modena. Modena. G. T. Vincenzi, 1882.

Valentin, Erich. Georg Philipp Telemann. Burg b.M., A. Hopfer, [1931].

Vallas, Léon. "Jacques-Simon Mangot," RdM V (1924) 123–26.

Van Vechten, Carl. "Notes on Gluck's *Armide*," MQ III (1917) 539–47.

Vatielli, Francesco. "Le opere comiche di G. B. Martini," RMI XL (1936) 450–76.

—— "Riflessi della lotta Gluckista in Italia," RMI XXI (1914) 639–72.

Veen, J. van der. Le Mélodrame musical de Rousseau au romantisme : Ses aspects historiques et stylistiques. The Hague, Martinus Nijhoff, 1955.

Vené, Ruggero. "The Origin of *Opera Buffa*," MQ XXI (1935) 33–38.

Verlet, Pierre. "L'Opéra de Versailles," *Revue d'histoire du théâtre* IX (1957) 133–54.

Vetter, Walther. Die Arie bei Gluck. Leipzig Dissertation, 1921.

—— "Deutschland und das Formgefühl Italiens : Betrachtungen über die Metastasianische Oper," *Deutsches Jahrbuch der Musikwissenschaft* V (1960) 7–37.

—— "Georg Christoph Wagenseil als Vorläufer . . . Glucks," ZfMw VIII (1925–26) 385–402.

—— "Gluck's Entwicklung zum Opernreformation," AfMw VI (1924) 165–212.

—— "Glucks Stellung zur tragédie lyrique und opéra comique," ZfMw VII (1924–25) 321–55.

—— "Gluck und seine italienischen Zeitgenossen," ZfMw VII (1924–25) 609–46.

—— "Italienische Opernkomponisten um Georg Christoph Wagenseil," in *Festschrift Friedrich Blume* (Kassel, Bärenreiter, 1963) [363]–374.

—— "Mozart im Weltbild Richard Wagners," in *Bericht über den internationalen musikwissenschaftlichen Kongress Wien, Mozartjahr 1956* (Graz, Böhlaus, 1958) 657–60.

—— "Stilkritische Bemerkungen zur Arienmelodik in Glucks *Orfeo*," ZfMw IV (1921–22) 27–49.

—— "Zur Entwicklungsgeschichte der opera seria um 1750 in Wien," ZfMw XIV (1931–32) 2–28.

Villarosa, Carlo Antonio de Rosa, marchese de. Memorie dei compositori di musica del regno di Napoli. Naples, Stamperia reale, 1840.

[Villeneuve, Josse de.] Lettre sur le méchanisme de l'opéra italien. Ni Guelfe, ni Gibelin; ni Wigh, ni Thoris. Paris, Duchesne; Florence and Paris, Lambert, 1756. German translation by R. Haas, ZfMw VII (1924–25) 129–63. *See also* Bédarida, Henri. "L'Opéra italien jugé par un amateur français en 1756," in *Mélanges de musicologie* (Paris, Droz, 1933) 185–200.

Viollier, Renée. "Les Divertissements de J.-J. Mouret pour la 'Comédie italienne' à Paris," RdM XXIII (1939) 65–71.

—— Jean-Joseph Mouret, le musicien des grâces, 1682–1738. Paris, Librairie Floury, 1950.

—— "Un Opéra-ballet au XVIIIe siècle: *Les Festes ou le triomphe de Thalie*," RdM XVI (1935) 78–86.

Vitale, Roberto. Domenico Cimarosa. Aversa, Noviello, 1929.

Vivaldi, Antonio; note e documenti sulla vita e sulle opere. Rome, Sansaini, 1939.

Voigt, F. A. "Reinhard Keiser," VfMw VI (1890) 151–203.

Volbach, Fritz. Die Praxis der Händel-Aufführung, 2. Theil: Das Händel-Orchester . . . I. Das Streichorchester. Charlottenburg, "Gutenberg," 1899.

Volkmann, Hans. "Domenico Terradellas," ZIMG XIII (1911–12) 306–9.

Walker, Frank. "*Orazio:* The History of a Pasticcio," MQ XXXVIII (1952) 369–83.

—— "Pergolesi Legends," MMR LXXXII (1952) 144–48, 180–83.

—— "Some Notes on the Scarlattis," MR XII (1951) 185–203.

Walter, Friedrich. Geschichte des Theaters und der Musik am kurpfälzischen Hofe. Leipzig, B&H, 1898.

Waltershausen, Hermann Wolfgang Karl Sartorius, Freiherr (von). *Die Zauberflöte:* Eine operndramaturgische Studie. Munich, H. Bruckmann, 1920.

Weckerlin, Jean Baptiste. L'Ancienne Chanson populaire en France. Paris, Garnier, 1887.

Weichlein, William J. A Comparative Study of Five Musical Settings of

Metastasio's Libretto of *La Clemenza di Tito*. Ann Arbor, University Microfilms, 1957. 2 vols.

Weil, Rudolf. Das Berliner Theaterpublikum unter A. W. Ifflands Direktion (1746–1814). Berlin, Gesellschaft für Theatergeschichte, 1932.

Wellesz, Egon. "Ein Bühnenfestspiel aus dem 17. Jahrhundert," *Die Musik* LII (1914) Qt. 4, pp. 191–217.

—— "*Don Giovanni* and the 'dramma giocoso,'" MR IV (1943) 121–26.

—— "Francesco Algarotti und seine Stellung zur Musik," SIMG XV (1913–14) 427–39.

—— "Giuseppe Bonno," SIMG XI (1909–10) 395–442.

Welti, Heinrich. "Gluck und Calsabigi," VfMw VII (1891) 26–42.

Wendschuh, Ludwig. Ueber Jos. Haydns Opern. [Halle a. S.], 1896.

Werner, Arno. "Sachsen-Thüringen in der Musikgeschichte," AfMw IV (1922) 322–35.

—— Städtische und fürstliche Musikpflege in Weissenfels bis zum Ende des 18. Jahrhunderts. Leipzig, B&H, 1911.

Werner, Eric. "Leading or Symbolic Formulas in *The Magic Flute*," MR XVIII (1957) 286–93.

Werner, Theodor Wilhelm. "Zum Neudruck von G. Ph. Telemanns *Pimpinone* in den Reichsdenkmalen," AfMf (1936) 361–65.

Westerman, Gerhart von. Giovanni Porta als Opernkomponist. Munich Dissertation, 1921.

Wiel, Taddeo. I teatri musicali di Venezia nel Settecento. Venice, Visentini, 1897.

Wieland, Christoph Martin. Sämmtliche Werke, 26. Band : Singspiele und Abhandlungen. Leipzig, G. J. Göschen, 1796. Contains : "Versuch über das Deutsche Singspiel" (pp. 229–67, 323–42); "Ueber einige ältere Deutsche Singspiele, die den Nahmen Alceste führen" (pp. 269–320).

Winckelmann, Johann Joachim. Sämtliche Werke. Donauöschingen, Im Verlage deutscher Classiker, 1825–29. 12 vols. Contains "Gedanken über die Nachahmung der griechischen Werke in der Malerei und Bildhauerkunst," I, 1–58; "Geschichte der Kunst des Alterthums," III–VI.

Winesanker, Michael. "Musico-Dramatic Criticism of English Comic Opera, 1750–1800," JAMS II (1949) 87–96.

—— The Record of English Musical Drama, 1750–1800. Cornell Dissertation, 1944.

Winterfeld, Carl von. *Alceste*, 1674, 1726, 1769, 1776, von Lulli, Händel und Gluck. Berlin, Bote & Bock, 1851.

Wirth, Helmut. "Johann Christian (Jean Chrétien) Bach," RIdM n.s. No. 8 (Autumn, 1950) 133–42.

—— Joseph Haydn als Dramatiker. Wolfenbüttel, Kallmeyer, 1940.

—— "The Operas of Joseph Haydn before *Orfeo*," in *Joseph Haydn, Orfeo ed Euridice . . . Analytical Notes* (Boston, Haydn Society, [1951]) 12–48.

Wörner, Karl. "Die Pflege Glucks an der Berliner Oper von 1795–1841," ZfMw XIII (1930–31) 206–16.

Wolff, Hellmuth Christian. *Agrippina:* Eine italienische Jugendoper von Georg Friedrich Händel. Wolfenbüttel, Kallmeyer, 1943.

—— Die Händel-Oper auf der modernen Bühne: Ein Beitrag zu Geschichte und Praxis der Opern-Bearbeitung und -Inszenierung in der Zeit von 1920 bis 1956. Leipzig, Deutscher Verlag für Musik, 1957.

Wolzogen, Alfred von. Ueber die scenische Darstellung von Mozart's *Don Giovanni.* Breslau, Leuckart, 1860.

Wortsmann, Stephan. Die deutsche Gluckliteratur. Nuremberg, Karl Koch, 1914.

Wotquenne, Alfred. Alphabetisches Verzeichnis der Stücke in Versen aus den dramatischen Werken von Zeno, Metastasio und Goldoni. Leipzig, B&H, 1905.

—— "Baldassare Galuppi (1706–1785): Etude bibliographique sur ses œuvres dramatiques," RMI VI (1899) 561–79.

—— Catalogue thématique des œuvres de Chr. W. v. Gluck. Leipzig, B&H, 1904. Ergänzung und Nachträge . . . Leipzig, Reinecke, 1911, ed. by Josef Liebeskind. "Ergänzungen und Berichtigungen," *Die Musik* XIII (1913–14), Qt. 1, 288–89, by Max Arend.

Wright, Edward. Some Observations Made in Travelling through France, Italy &c in the Years 1720, 1721, and 1722. London, T. Ward and E. Wicksteed, 1730. 2 vols.

Wyndham, Henry Saxe. The Annals of Covent Garden Theatre from 1732–1897. London, Chatto & Windus, 1906. 2 vols.

Wyzewa, Teodor de. W. A. Mozart: Sa vie musicale et son œuvre de l'enfance à la pleine maturité. Paris, Desclée, [1937]. G. de Saint-Foix is joint author of Vols. I and II and sole author of Vol. III.

Wyzewa, Teodor de, and Georges de Saint-Foix. W.-A. Mozart, sa vie musicale et son œuvre. Paris, Desclée, de Brouwer et Cie., 1912–46. 5 vols.

Yorke-Long, Alan. Music at Court: Four Eighteenth-Century Studies. London, Weidenfeld & Nicolson, [1954].

Zabala, Arturo. La opera en la vida valenciana del siglo XVIII. Valencia, Instituto de literatura y estudios filológicos, 1960.

Zeller, Bernhard. Das recitativo accompagnato in den Opern Johann Adolf Hasses. Halle a. S., Hohmann, 1911.

Zelter, Carl Friedrich. "Ein Aufsatz . . . über Georg Benda und seine Oper *Romeo und Julie,*" AMZ XIV (1879) 645–49.

Zeno, Apostolo. Lettere. Venice, F. Sansoni, 1785. 6 vols.

—— Poesie drammatiche. Orleans, Couret de Villeneuve, 1785–86. 11 vols.

[Zille, Moritz Alexander.] *Die Zauberflöte:* Text-Erläuterung für alle Verehrer Mozarts. Leipzig, T. Lissner, 1866.

Zingerle, Hans. "Musik- und Textform in Opernarien Mozarts," *Mozart-Jahrbuch 1953* (1954) 112–15.

Zuckerkandel, Viktor. Prinzipien und Methoden der Instrumentation in Mozarts dramatischen Werken. Vienna Dissertation, 1927.

## V

## NINETEENTH CENTURY

### A. GENERAL

Abbiati, Franco. Giuseppe Verdi. Milan, Ricordi, 1959. 4 vols.

Abert, Hermann. "Robert Schumann's *Genoveva*," ZIMG XI (1909–10) 277–89.

Abraham, Gerald. "The Best of Spontini," M&L XXIII (1942) 163–71.

—— "*The Flying Dutchman:* Original Version," M&L XX (1939) 412–19.

—— A Hundred Years of Music. London, Duckworth, 1949. 2d ed.

—— "The Leitmotif since Wagner," M&L VI (1925) 175–90.

—— "Nietzsche's Attitude to Wagner: A Fresh View," M&L XIII (1932) 64–74.

—— "Weber as Novelist and Critic," MQ XX (1934) 27–38.

Abraham, Gerald, ed. The Music of Schubert. New York, W. W. Norton, 1947.

—— Schumann: A Symposium. London, New York, Toronto, Oxford University Press, 1952.

Adam, Adolphe. Derniers souvenirs d'un musicien. Paris, Michel Levy frères, 1859.

—— Souvenirs d'un musicien . . . précédés de notes biographiques écrites par lui-même. Paris, Calmann-Lévy, 1884.

Adami, Giuseppe. Il romanzo della vita di Giacomo Puccini. Milan-Rome, Rizzoli, 1944. 3d ed.

Adler, Guido. "*Euryanthe* in neuer Einrichtung [von Gustav Mahler]," ZIMG V (1903–4) 269–75.

—— Richard Wagner, Vorlesungen gehalten an der Universität zu Wien. Munich, Drei Masken Verlag, 1923. 2d ed. (first publ. 1904).

Adorno, Theodor Wiesengrund. Versuch über Wagner. Berlin & Frankfurt/M., Suhrkamp, [1952].

Alberti, C. E. R. Ludwig van Beethoven als dramatischer Tondichter. Stettin, 1859.

Almanach des Spectacles. Paris, Nos. 1–43, 1874–1913.

Altmann, Wilhelm. "Lortzing als dramaturgischer Lehrer," *Die Musik* XIII (1913–14) Qt. 4, 157–58.

—— "Meyerbeer-Forschungen: Archivalische Beiträge aus der Registratur der Generalintendantur der Königlichen Schauspiele zu Berlin," SIMG IV (1902–3) 519–34.

—— "Spontini an der Berliner Oper : Eine archivalische Studie," SIMG IV (1902–3) 244–92.

Amico, Tomasino d'. Francesco Cilèa. Milan, Curci, [1960].

Anheisser, Siegfried. "Das Vorspiel zu *Tristan und Isolde* und seine Motivik," ZfMw III (1921) 257–304.

Annen, Josef. Le versioni italiane rappresentate delle opere di Riccardo Wagner. Muralto-Locarno, Tipografia Moderna Pax, [1943].

Antonini, G. "Un episodio emotivo di Gaetano Donizetti," RMI VII (1900) 518–35.

Appia, Adolphe. La Mise en scène du drame Wagnérien. Paris, L. Chailley, 1895.

Arnaudiès, Fernand. Histoire de l'opéra d'Alger : Episodes de la vie théâtrale algéroise, 1830–1940. Algiers, V. Heintz, [1941].

Atti del primo Congresso Internazionale di Studi Spontiniani. Jesi-Maiolati-Fabriano-Ancona, 6–9 settembre 1951. Relazioni, communicazioni, verbali. Fabriano, Arti Grafiche "Gentile," 1954.

Augé de Lassus, Lucien. Boieldieu . . . : Biographie critique illustrée. Paris, H. Laurens, [1908].

Augé-Laribé, Michel. Messager, musicien de théâtre. Paris, La Colombe, [1951].

Bacchelli, Riccardo. Rossini e esperienze rossiniane. Milan, Mondadori, 1959.

Bätz, Rüdiger. Schauspielmusiken zu Goethes *Faust*. Leipzig Dissertation, 1924.

Bagge, Selmar. "Robert Schumann und seine *Faust*-Scenen," in Waldersee, *Sammlung musikalischer Vorträge* (Leipzig, Graf, 1879) I, 121–40.

Baily, Leslie. The Gilbert & Sullivan Book. London, Cassell & Co., 1956; New York, Coward-McCann, 1957. Revised ed.

"Le Ballet au XIXe siècle," RM II (December, 1921; numéro special) 97–231.

Ballo, Ferdinando. Arrigo Boito. Turin, Edizioni Arione, [1938].

Barblan, Guglielmo. L'opera di Donizetti nell' età romantica. Bergamo, Edizione del Centenario a cura della Banca Mutua Popolare, 1948.

Bardi-Poswiansky, Benno. Flotow als Opernkomponist. Königsberg Dissertation, 1924.

Barford, Peter T. "The Way of Unity : A Study of *Tristan und Isolde*," MR XX (1959) 253–63.

Barini, Giorgio. "Noterelle Belliniane," RMI IX (1902) 62–71.

Barraud, Henry. Hector Berlioz. [Paris], Costard, [1955].

Barrett, William. Balfe : His Life and Work. London, Remington, 1882.

Barricelli, Jean-Pierre, and Leo Weinstein. Ernest Chausson : The Composer's Life and Works. Norman, University of Oklahoma Press, [1955].

Barry, C. A. "Introductory to the Study of Wagner's Comic Opera Die *Meistersinger von Nürnberg*," PMA VII (March 7, 1881) 74–97.

Barzun, Jacques. Berlioz and the Romantic Century. Boston, Little, Brown, 1950. 2 vols.

—— Darwin, Marx, Wagner : Critique of a Heritage. Boston, Little, Brown, 1941. 2d ed. : Garden City, N.Y., Doubleday & Co., 1958.

Batka, Richard. Die alt-italienische Aria : Ida Isori und ihre Kunst des Bel-Canto. Vienna, H. Heller, 1912.

—— Die moderne Oper. Prague, Verlag der Lese- und Redehalle der deutschen Studenten in Prag, 1902.

Bauer, Anton. 150 Jahre Theater an der Wien. Leipzig, Vienna, Amalthea-Verlag, [1952].

Baumann, Ken C. The Change of Style in Verdi's Operatic Work in the Interlude between Aida and Otello. Cornell A.M. Thesis, 1945.

Beaufils, Marcel. Wagner et le wagnérisme. Paris, Ed. Aubier, 1946.

Becker, Heinz. Der Fall Heine-Meyerbeer : neue Dokumente revidieren ein Geschichtsurteil. Berlin, W. de Gruyter, 1958.

—— "Meyerbeers Beziehungen zu Louis Spohr," Mf X (1957) 479–86.

—— "Meyerbeers Ergänzungsarbeit an Webers nachgelassener Oper Die drei Pintos," Mf VII (1954) 300–12.

Becker, Heinz, ed. See Meyerbeer.

Becker, Marta. "Der Einfluss der Philosophie Schellings auf Richard Wagner," ZfMw XIX (1931–32) 433–47.

Beckers, Paul. Die nachwagner'sche Oper bis zum Ausgang des 19. Jahrhunderts im Spiegel der Münchener Presse. Bielefeld, Beyer & Hausknecht, 1936.

Beethoven, Ludwig van. Ludwig van Beethoven : Ein Bekenntnis mit Briefen und Zeitdocumenten. [Hrsg. von Heinz Freiberger.] [Berlin], Verlag der Nation, [1951].

Beetz, Wilhelm. Das Wiener Opernhaus 1869 bis 1945. [Zurich], The Central European Times Verlag, [1949].

Bekker, Paul. Wagner : Das Leben im Werke. Stuttgart, Deutsche Verlags-Anstalt, 1924. Translated as : Richard Wagner : His Life in His Works. New York, W. W. Norton, [1931].

Belardinelli, Alessandro, ed. Documenti Spontiniani inedite. Raccolti, tradotti e annotati. Florence, Ed. Sansoni Antiquariato, 1955. 2 vols.

Bellaigue, Camille. "Les Epoques de la musique: Le grand opéra français," Revue des deux mondes (1906) No. 5, 612–49.

Bellasis, Edward. Cherubini : Memorials Illustrative of His Life. London, Burns & Oates, 1874.

Bellini, Vincenzo. Epistolario, a cura di Luisa Cambi. Verona, Mondadori, 1943.

Berl, Paul. Die Opern Giuseppe Verdis in ihrer Instrumentation. Vienna Dissertation, 1931.

Berlioz, Hector. A Travers Chants : Etudes musicales. Paris, Michel Lévy, 1872. 2d ed.

—— Les Grotesques de la musique. Paris, A. Bourdilliat, 1854.

—— Mémoires. Paris, Michel Lévy, 1870. Translated as : Memoirs of Hector Berlioz. New York, Tudor, [1935]. Annotated and the translation revised by Ernest Newman.

—— Les Musiciens et la musique. Paris, Calmann-Lévy, [1903]. A selection of articles from the *Journal des débats*, 1835–63.

—— New Letters of Berlioz, 1830–1868. With Introduction, Notes and English Translation by Jacques Barzun. New York, Columbia University Press, 1954.

—— Les Soirées de l'orchestre. Paris, Michel Lévy, 1852. Translated as : Evenings in the Orchestra. New York and London, Alfred A. Knopf, 1924.

Besch, Otto. Engelbert Humperdinck. Leipzig, B&H, 1914.

Beyle, Henri. Vie de Rossini, suivi des notes d'un dilettante. Paris, E. Champion, 1922. Preface and annotations by Henry Prunières. Translated as : Memoirs of Rossini. London, T. Hookham, 1824.

Biedenfeld, [Ferdinand, Freiherr von]. Die komische Oper der Italiener, der Franzosen und der Deutschen. Leipzig, Weigl, 1848.

Bienenfeld, Elso. "Verdi and Schiller," MQ XVII (1931) 204–8.

Billeci, A. *La Bohème* di Giacomo Puccini : Studio critico. Palermo, Vesca, 1931.

Bitter, K[arl] H[ermann]. Die Reform der Oper durch Gluck und R. Wagner's Kunstwerk der Zukunft. Brunswick, F. Vieweg, 1884. Critical review by H. Kretzschmar, VfMw I (1885) 227–34.

[Bizet, Georges.] *See* RdM XXII (November, 1938), special number devoted to Bizet.

Bizet, René. Une Heure de musique avec Oscar Straus. Paris, Editions cosmopolites, 1930.

Blum, Klaus. "Bemerkungen Anton Reichas zur Aufführungspraxis der Oper," Mf VII (1954) 429–40.

Bohe, Walter. Die Wiener Presse in der Kriegszeit der Oper. Würzburg, Triltsch, 1933. Published also with the title : Wagner im Spiegel der Wiener Presse.

Boïto, Arrigo. Lettere. Rome, Società editrice "Novissima," [1932].

—— "Pensieri critici giovanili," RMI XXXI (1924) 161–98.

—— Tutti gli scritti, a curo di Piero Nardi. [Milan], A. Mondadori, [1942].

Bollert, Werner. "Hugo Wolfs *Corregidor*," *Musica* XIV (1960) 143–47.

Bonaccorsi, Alfredo. Giacomo Puccini e i suoi antenati musicali. Milan, Curci, [1950].

—— "La sinfonia del *Barbiere* prima del *Barbiere*," RassM XXIV (1954) 210–19.

Bonafé, Félix. Rossini et son oeuvre. [Conférence prononcée à la Fondation Rossini, à Paris, le 25 juin 1955.] Le Puy-en-Velay, Editions la Main de Bronze, 1955.

Bonaventura, Arnaldo. Giacomo Puccini. Leghorn, [1925].

—— Verdi. Paris, F. Alcan, 1923.

Bonavia, Ferrucio. Verdi. London, Oxford University Press, 1930.

Bonnefon, Paul. "Les Métamorphoses d'un opéra (lettres inédites d'Eugène Scribe)," *Revue des deux mondes* (1917) No. 5, 877–99.

Boromé, Joseph A. "Bellini and *Beatrice di Tenda*," M&L XLII (1961) 319–35.

Borrelli, E. "Il Wort-Ton-Drama," RassM VII (1934) 333–43, 433–36.

Borren, Charles van den. L'Oeuvre dramatique de César Franck : *Hulda* et *Ghiselle*. Brussels, Schott Frères, 1907.

Borriello, A. Mito, poesia e musica nel *Mefistofele* di Arrigo Boito, con prefazione di V. Gui. Naples, Guida, [1950].

Boschot, Adolphe. "A propos du centenaire de *La Damnation de Faust*," RM XXII (February–March, 1946) 11–14.

—— Le Faust de Berlioz : Etude sur la *Damnation de Faust* et sur l'âme romantique. Paris, Librairie Plon, 1945.

—— Hector Berlioz, une vie romantique. Paris, Plon, [1951]. Edition définitive.

––— L'Histoire d'un romantique : Hector Berlioz. I. La Jeunesse d'un romantique . . . 1803–1831. Paris, Plon-Nourrit, 1906. New ed., rev. et cor. [1946]. II. Un Romantique sous Louis-Philippe . . . 1831–1842. Paris, Plon-Nourrit, 1908. Ed. rev. et cor. 1948. III. Le Crépuscule d'un romantique . . . 1842–1869. Paris, Plon-Nourrit, 1913. Ed. rev. et cor. [1950].

—— "Sur Gluck et Wagner," *Revue politique et littéraire* XXXVII (1900) 19–23.

—— La Vie et les œuvres de Alfred Bruneau. Paris, Fasquelle, [1937].

Bossi, Lea. Donizetti. Brescia, Ed. La Scuola, 1956.

Botti, Ferruccio. Giuseppe Verdi. Alba, Istituto Missionario Pia Società S. Paolo, [1941].

Boucher, Maurice. Les Idées politiques de Richard Wagner. Paris, Aubier, 1948. Translated as : The Political Concepts of Richard Wagner. New York, M & H Publications, [1950].

Bouvet, Charles. Spontini. Paris, Rieder, [1930].

Brancour, René. Félicien David. Paris, H. Laurens, [190–].

—— Méhul. Paris, H. Laurens, [1912].

Braunstein, Josef. Beethovens Leonore-Ouvertüren : Eine historisch-stilkritische Untersuchung. Leipzig, B&H, 1927.

—— "Gibt es zwei Fassungen von der Ouvertüre Leonore Nr. 2?" ZfMw IX (1926–27) 349–60.

Brenon, Algernon. "Giuseppe Verdi," MQ II (1916) 130–62.

Bréville, Pierre de, and H. Gauthier-Villars. *Fervaal:* Etude thématique et analytique. Paris, A. Durand, 1897.

Brindejont-Offenbach, Jacques. Offenbach, mon grand-père. Paris, Plon, 1940.

Brion, Marcel. Schumann et l'âme romantique. Paris, A. Michel, [1954].

Brockt, Johannes. "Verdi's Operatic Choruses," M&L XX (1939) 309–12.

Brown, Maurice J. E. Schubert : A Critical Biography. London, Macmillan & Co.; New York, St. Martin's Press, 1958.

Bruneau, Alfred. Massenet. Paris, Delagrave, 1934.

—— Musiques d'hier et de demain. Paris, Bibliothèque Charpentier, 1900.

Brunswick, Mark. "Beethoven's Tribute to Mozart in *Fidelio*," MQ XXXI (1945) 29–32.

Brusa, Filippo. "Il *Nerone* di Arrigo Boito," RMI XXXI (1924) 392–443.

Burgmüller, Herbert. Die Musen darben : Ein Lebensbild Albert Lortzings. Düsseldorf, Progress-Verlag, [1956].

Buschkötter, Wilhelm. "Jean François Le Sueur : Eine Biographie," SIMG XIV (1912–13) 58–154.

Bustico, Guido. "Un librettista antiromantico (Angelo Anelli)," RMI XXVIII (1921) 53–81.

—— "Saggio di una bibliografia di libretti musicali di Felice Romani," RMI XIV (1907) 229–84.

—— "Saverio Mercadante a Novara," RMI XXVIII (1921) 361–96.

Butler, E. M. The Fortunes of Faust. Cambridge, The University Press, 1952.

Calvocoressi, Michel D. Vincent d'Indy, *L'Etranger:* Le poème, analyse thématique de la partition. Paris, Editions du Courrier musical, [1903].

Cametti, Alberto. "Donizetti a Roma : Con lettere e documenti inediti," RMI XI (1904) 761–88; XII (1905) 1–39, 515–54, 689–713; XIII (1906) 50–90, 522–45, 616–55; XIV (1907) 301–32.

—— "Il *Guglielmo Tell* e le sue prime rappresentazioni in Italia," RMI VI (1899) 580–92.

—— La musica teatrale a Roma cento anni fa : Il *Corsaro* di Pacini. Rome, Mezzetti, 1931.

—— La musica teatrale a Roma cento anni fa : Olivo e Pasquale di Donizetti. Rome, A. Manuzio, 1928.

—— Un poeta melodrammatico romano . . . Jacopo Ferretti. Milan, Ricordi, [1898].

Cantillon, Arthur. Essai sur les symboles de la tétralogie wagnerienne. Mons, Imprimerie générale, 1911.

Canudo, Ricciotto. "L'Esthétique de Verdi et la culture musicale italienne," MM III (1907) 719–37.

Capri, Antonio. Musica e musicisti d'Europa dal 1800 al 1938. Milan, Hoepli, 1939. 2d ed.

—— Verdi, uomo e artista. Milan, Ed. ufficio concerti, 1939.

Carlez, Jules. Catel. Caen, H. Delesques, 1894.

—— Grimm et la musique de son temps. Caen, Le Blanc-Hardel, 1872.

—— L'Œuvre d'Auber. Caen, Le Blanc-Hardel, 1874.

—— Pacini et l'opéra italien. Caen, H. Delesques, 1888.

Carlyle, Thomas. "The Opera," in *Critical and Miscellaneous Essays* (New York, Scribner, 1904) IV, 397–403.

Carner, Mosco. "The Exotic Element in Puccini," MQ XXII (1936) 45–67.

—— Puccini : A Critical Biography. London, Duckworth, 1958; New York, Alfred A. Knopf, 1959.

—— "Puccini's Early Operas," M&L XIX (1938) 295–307.

Cattini, Umberto. "Note sul *Roberto Devereux* de Gaetano Donizetti," *Ricordiana* III (1957) 478–88.

Cauchie, Maurice. "The High Lights of French *Opéra Comique*," MQ XXV (1939) 306–12.

Cellamare, Daniele. Mascagni e la *Cavalleria* visti da Cerignola. Rome, Filli Palombi, 1941.

—— Umberto Giordano : La vita e le opere. [Milan], Garzanti, [1949].

Cenzato, Giovanni. Itinerari verdiani : La semplicità di una vita grande di opere, luminosa di gloria. Milan, Casa Editrice Ceschina, [1955]. 2d ed.

Chamberlain, Houston Stewart. Das Drama Richard Wagners. Leipzig, B&H, 1921. 6th ed. First published 1892. Translated as : The Wagnerian Drama. London and New York, John Lane, 1915.

—— Die Grundlagen des neunzehnten Jahrhunderts. Munich, F. Bruckmann, 1912. 10th ed. First published 1900. Translated as : Foundations of the Nineteenth Century. Munich, F. Bruckmann, 1911.

—— Richard Wagner. Munich, F. Bruckmann, [1936]. 9th ed. First published 1896. English translation : London, Dent, 1900.

Chantavoine, Jean. Camille Saint-Saëns. Paris, Richard-Masse, 1947.

Chantavoine, Jean, and Jean Gaudefroy-Demombynes. Le Romantisme dans la musique européenne. Paris, A. Michel, 1955.

Cherbuliez, Antoine Elisée Adolphe. Giuseppe Verdi : Leben und Werk. Rüschliken-Zurich, Albert Müller Verlag, 1949.

Chop, Max. August Bungert. Leipzig, H. Seemann Nachfolger, 1903.

—— E. N. v. Reznicek. Vienna, Leipzig, Universal-Edition, [1920].

Chorley, Henry F. Music and Manners in France and Germany. London, Longmans, 1844.

—— Thirty Years' Musical Recollections. New York, Alfred A. Knopf, 1926.

Chrysander, Friedrich. "Spontini nach Mitteilungen von Caroline Bauer und H. Marschner," AMZ XIV (1879) 259–64, 274–80, 289–93.

—— ". . . über Wagners Tannhäuser," ZIMG V (1903–4) 208–19.

Cinquante Ans de musique française de 1874 à 1925. Paris, Librairie de France, [1925]. Ed. by L. Rohozinski.

Coeuroy, André. La Tosca de Puccini. Paris, Mellottée, [1922?].

—— "Wagner et le ballet," RM II (December, 1921) 206–13.

—— Weber. Paris, Denoël, 1953. New ed.

Collet, Henri. Samson et Dalila de C. Saint-Saëns. Paris. Mellottée, [1922].

Colling, Alfred. César Franck, ou le concert spirituel. Paris, R. Julliard, [1951].

Colombani, A. L'opera italiana nel secolo XIX. Milan, Ed. Corriere della Sera, 1900.

Colson, J. B. Manuel dramatique. Bordeaux, chez l'auteur, 1817.

Commons, Jeremy. "[Donizetti's] *Emilia di Liverpool*," M&L XL (1959) 207–28.

Cone, Edward T. "The Old Man's Toys : Verdi's Last Operas," *Perspectives USA*, No. 6 (Winter, 1954) 114–33.

Confalonieri, Giulio. Prigionia di un artista. (Il romanzo di Luigi Cherubini.) [Milan], Genio, [1948]. 2 vols.

Cooley, William Julius, Jr. Music in the Life and Works of Franz Grillparzer. Ann Arbor, University Microfilms, 1954.

Cooper, Martin. "Charles Gounod and His Influence on French Music," M&L XXI (1940) 50–59.

—— French Music : From the Death of Berlioz to the Death of Fauré. London, Oxford University Press, 1951.

—— Georges Bizet. London and New York, Oxford University Press, 1938.

Cornelissen, Thilo. C. M. v. Webers *Freischütz* als Beispiel einer Opernbehandlung. Berlin, Matthiesen, 1940.

Cornelius, Carl Maria. Peter Cornelius, der Wort- und Tondichter. Regensburg, G. Bosse, [1925].

Cornelius, Peter. Literarische Werke. Leipzig, B&H, 1904–5. 4 vols.

Cornet, J. Die Oper in Deutschland und das Theater der Neuzeit. Hamburg, O. Meissner, 1849.

Cortolezis, Fritz. "Gedanken über eine stilgerechte Aufführung des *Fidelio*," *Neues Beethoven Jahrbuch* III (1926) 93–102.

Costa, Alessandro. "Schopenhauer e Wagner," RMI XXXIX (1932) 1–12.

Crosten, William L. French Grand Opera : An Art and a Business. New York, King's Crown Press, 1948.

Curtiss, Mina. Bizet and His World. New York, Alfred A. Knopf, 1958.

—— "Fromental Halévy," MQ XXXIX (1953) 196–214.

—— "Gounod Before *Faust*," MQ XXXVIII (1952) 48–67.

—— "Unpublished Letters by Georges Bizet," MQ XXXVI (1950) 375–409.

Curzon, Henri de. Ernest Reyer. Paris, Perrin, 1924.

—— La Légende de Sigurd. Paris, Fischbacher, [1889].

—— Léo Delibes, Paris, G. Legouix, 1926.

—— "L'Opéra en 1843 : Mémoire du directeur Léon Pillet," RdM II (1920–21) 223–33.

—— "Les Opéras-comiques de Boieldieu," RM XIV (November, 1933) 249–63.

Czech, Stan. Franz Lehár : Weg und Werk. Berlin, Werk-Verlag, 1942.

—— Schön ist die Welt : Franz Lehárs Leben und Werk. Berlin, Argon-Verlag, [1957].

Daffner, Hugo. Friedrich Nietzsches Rundglossen zu Bizets *Carmen*. Regensburg, Bosse. 1938.

·Damerini, Adelmo. Amilcare Ponchielli. Turin, Edizioni Arione, [1940].

Dandelot, Arthur. Evolution de la musique de théâtre depuis Meyerbeer jusqu'à nos jours. Paris, Flammarion, 1927.

Daninger, Josef G. Sage und Märchen im Musikdrama : Eine ästhetische Untersuchung an der Sagen- und Märchenoper des 19. Jahrhunderts. Prague, Hoffmanns Witwe, 1916.

Daube, Otto. Siegfried Wagner und die Märchenoper. Leipzig, Deutscher Theater-Verlag, M. Schleppegrell, [1936].

Dauriac, Lionel. "Herbert Spencer et Meyerbeer," ZIMG V (1903–4) 103–9.

—— Meyerbeer. Paris, Alcan, 1913.

—— "Un Problème d'esthétique Wagnérienne," MM IV (1908) 50–55.

Dean, Winton. Bizet. London, J. M. Dent & Sons, Ltd., 1948.

—— "Bizet's Self-Borrowings," M&L XLI (1960) 238–44.

—— "*Carmen:* An Attempt at a True Evaluation," MR VII (1946) 209–20.

—— "An Unfinished Opera by Bizet," M&L XXVIII (1947) 347–63.

De Angelis, Alberto. "Cantanti italiani del secolo XIX : Erminia e Giuseppe Frezzolini," RMI XXXII (1925) 438–54.

Decaux, Alain. Offenbach, roi du second empire. [Paris], P. Amiot, [1958].

Decsey, Ernst. Franz Lehár. Munich, Drei Masken-Verlag, 1930. 2d ed.

—— Hugo Wolf. Berlin, Schuster & Loeffler, [1919]. 3d–6th ed., revised.

—— Johann Strauss. Stuttgart, Berlin, Deutsche Verlags-Anstalt, 1922.

—— Johann Strauss : Ein wiener Buch. Vienna, Paul Neff Verlag, 1948.

De Donno, Alfredo. Mascagni nel 900 musicale. Rome, Casa del libro, [1935].

—— Modernità di Mascagni. Rome, Pinciana, 1931.

De Eisner-Eisenhof, A. "Giuseppe Weigl : Una biografia," RMI XI (1904) 459–83.

Della Corte, Andrea. "La drammaturgia nella *Semiramide* di Rossini," RassM XI (1938) 1–6.

—— Un Italiano all' estero, Antonio Salieri. Turin, G. B. Paravia, [1936].

Delmas, Marc. Gustave Charpentier et le lyrisme français. Paris, Delagrave, 1931.

Demuth, Norman. César Franck. London, Dennis Dobson Ltd.; New York, Philosophical Library, 1949.

De Napoli, Giuseppe de. Amilcare Ponchielli (1834–1886) : La vita, le opera, l'epistolario . . . Cremona, Società Editoriale "Cremona Nuova," 1936.

—— La triade melodrammatica altamurana : Giacomo Tritto, 1733–1824; Vincenzo Lavigna, 1776–1836; Saverio Mercadante, 1795–1870. Milan, Rosio e Fabe, 1932.

Dent, Edward J. "A Best-Seller in Opera [Flotow's *Martha*]," M&L XXII (1941) 139–54.

—— "Italian Opera in London," PMA LXXI (1944–45) 19–42.

—— The Rise of the Romantic Opera. (The Messenger Lectures at Cornell University, 1937–38.) Typescript, 256 pp.

—— "The Romantic Spirit in Music," PMA LIX (1932–33) 85–102.

—— "Translating *Trovatore*," M&L XX (1939) 7–20.

De Rensis, Raffaello. Primo Riccitelli : *I compagnacci;* guida attraverso la commedia e la musica. Milan, Bottega di poesia, 1923.

Destranges, Etienne. *Le Chant de la cloche*, de Vincent d'Indy : Etude analytique. Paris, Tresse et Stock, 1890.

—— *L'Etranger* de M. Vincent d'Indy : Etude analytique et thématique. Paris, Fischbacher, 1904.

—— L'Evolution musicale chez Verdi : *Aida—Othello—Falstaff*. Paris, Fischbacher, 1895.

—— *Fervaal* de Vincent d'Indy : Etude thématique et analytique. Paris, A. Durand, 1896.

—— *Messidor* d'A. Bruneau : Etude analytique et critique. Paris, Fischbacher, 1897.

—— L'Œuvre théâtral de Meyerbeer : Etude critique. Paris, Fischbacher, 1893.

—— *L'Ouragan* d'Alfred Bruneau : Etude analytique et thématique. Paris, Fischbacher, 1902.

—— *Le Rêve* d'Alfred Bruneau : Etude thématique et analytique. Paris, Fischbacher, 1896.

Deutsch, Otto Erich. "*Hoffmann* in Wien," OeM XIII (1958) 16–20.

—— Schubert, a Documentary Biography. Translated by Eric Blom. London, J. M. Dent & Sons, [n.d.].

—— Schubert : Thematic Catalogue of All His Works. New York, W. W. Norton, [1950].

Dickinson, Alan Edgar Frederic. "Berlioz and *The Trojans*. Part I : Forward from Beethoven," *Tempo*, No. 48 (Summer, 1958) 24–28.

—— The Musical Design of *The Ring*. London, Oxford University Press, 1926.

—— "The Structural Methods of *The Ring*," MMR LXXXIV (1954) 87–92, 124–29.

Donati Petteni, Giuliano. Donizetti. Milan, Fratelli Treves, 1930.

Donington, Robert. Wagner's *Ring* and Its Symbols : The Music and the Myth. London, Faber & Faber, [1963].

Dorn, Heinrich. Aus meinem Leben. Berlin, B. Behr, 1870–86. 7 vols.

—— Gesetzgebung und Operntext (eine Schrift für Männer) : Zeitgemässe Betrachtungen. Berlin, Schlesinger, 1879.

Dünnebeil, Hans, ed. Carl Maria von Weber, ein Brevier. Berlin, AFAS-Musikverlag, 1949.

Dünnebeil, Hans, ed. Schrifttum über Carl Maria von Weber mit Schall-plattenverzeichnis. Berlin, Bote und Bock, 1957. 4th ed.

Dufrane, Louis. Gossec. Paris, Fischbacher, 1927.

Duhamel, Raoul. "Eugène Delacroix et la musique," RMI XLIII (1939) 35–54, 333–56.

—— "Ferdinand Herold," RM XIV (November, 1933) 278–90.

—— "Quelques Maîtres de l'opéra-comique au XIXe siècle," RM XIV (November, 1933) 291–302.

Du Moulin-Eckart, Richard Maria Ferdinand. Wahnfried. Leipzig, Kistner & Siegel, 1925.

Dunhill, Thomas F. Sullivan's Comic Operas : A Critical Appreciation. New York, Oxford University Press; London, Edw. Arnold, 1928.

Du Tillet, Jacques. "A propos du drame lyrique : Une lettre de M. Camille Saint-Saëns," Revue politique et littéraire (July 3, 1897) 27–30.

Edwards, Henry Sutherland. The Life of Rossini. London, Hurst & Blackett, 1869.

—— Rossini and His School. New York, Scribner & Welford, 1881.

Egert, Paul. Peter Cornelius. Berlin, B. Hahnefeld, [ca. 1940].

Ehinger, Hans. E. T. A. Hoffmann als Musiker und Musikschriftsteller. Olten & Cologne, Walter, [1954].

Ehrenhaus, Martin. Die Operndichtung der deutschen Romantik : Ein Beitrag zur Geschichte der deutschen Oper. Einleitung und I. Teil. Breslau, F. Hirt, 1911.

Ehrhard, Auguste. "La Danse à l'opéra en 1834 : Les débuts de Fanny Elssler," Bulletin de la société des amis de l'université de Lyon XIX (1906) 61–81.

Einstein, Alfred. Music in the Romantic Era. New York, W.W. Norton, 1947.

—— "Richard Wagners Liebesverbot: Zur Aufführung am Münchner National-Theater (24. März 1923)," ZfMw V (1922–23) 382–86.

—— "Vincenzo Bellini," M&L XVI (1935) 325–32.

Ellis, William Ashton. "Cyrill Kistner and Kunihild," The Meister VI (1893) 64–79.

—— "Richard Wagner's Prose," PMA XIX (1892) 13–33.

Engel, Carl. "Die Wagnerdämmerung," MQ XIV (1928) 438–55.

Engel, Hans. "Über Richard Wagners Oper 'Das Liebesverbot,'" in Festschrift Friedrich Blume (Kassel, Bärenreiter, 1963) [80]–91.

—— "Versuche einer Sinndeutung von Richard Wagners Ring des Nibelungen," Mf X (1957) 225–41.

—— "Wagner und Spontini," AfMw XII (1955) 167–77.

Engelfred, Abele, "Hulda . . . di Cesare Franck," RMI II (1895) 312–23.

Engländer, Richard. "Paërs Leonora und Beethovens Fidelio," Neues Beethoven Jahrbuch IV (1930) 118–32.

—— "The Struggle between German and Italian Opera at the Time of Weber," MQ XXXI (1945) 479–91.

Engler, Günther. Verdis Anschauung vom Wesen der Oper. Breslau, Stenzel, 1938.

Eösze, László. Az opera útja. Budapest, Zenemükiadó Vállalat, 1960.

Ernst, Alfred. "Les Motifs du Héros dans l'œuvre de R. Wagner," RMI I (1894) 657–77.

—— L'Œuvre dramatique de Berlioz. Paris, Levy, 1884.

—— "Thaïs . . . de J. Massenet," RMI I (1894) 296–306.

Esbert, C. L. R. "Hans Sachs," M&L XVII (1936) 59–61.

Eschweiler, Hans-Georg. Klara Ziegler : Ein Beitrag zur Theatergeschichte des 19. Jahrhunderts. Rostock Dissertation, 1935.

Ettler, Carl. "Bibliographie des œuvres de Meyerbeer," RHCM IV (1904) 436–44.

Faller, H. Die Gesangskoloratur in Rossinis Opern und ihre Ausführung. Berlin, Triltsch & Huther, 1935.

Fano, Fabio. "Norma nella storia del melodramma italiano," RassM VIII (1935) 315–26.

Favre, Georges. "L'Amitié de deux musiciens Boieldieu et Cherubini," RM XXII (1946) 217–25.

—— Boieldieu : Sa vie—son œuvre. Paris, Droz, 1944–45. 2 vols.

Fehr, Max. Richard Wagners Schweitzer Zeit. Aarau and Leipzig/Aarau and Frankfurt/M., H. R. Sauerländer, [1934–53]. 2 vols.

Fellerer, Karl Gustav. "Verdi und Wagner," Studi italiani III (1959) 46–55.

Ferchault, Guy. Faust : Une legende et ses musiciens. Paris, Larousse, [1948].

Ferrari, A. Rodigino; le convenienze teatrali; analisi della condizione presente del teatro musicale italiano. Milan, Redaelli, 1843.

Ferrarini, Mario. Parma teatrale ottocentesca. Parma, Casanova, [1946].

Février, Henry. André Messager : Mon maître, mon ami. Paris, Amiot-Dumont, 1948.

Filippi, Joseph de. Parallèle des principaux théâtres modernes de l'Europe et des machines théâtrales françaises, allemandes et anglaises. Paris, Lévy, 1870. 2 vols.

Fischer, Georg. Marschner-Erinnerungen. Hanover and Leipzig, Hahn, 1918.

Fleischer, Oskar. "Napoleon Bonaparte's Musikpolitik," ZIMG III (1901–2) 431–40.

Floch, Siegfried. Die Oper seit Richard Wagner. Cologne, Fulda, 1904.

Flood, W. H. Grattan. William Vincent Wallace : A Memoir. Waterford, "The Waterford News," 1912.

Flotow, Rosa. Friedrich von Flotow's Leben von seiner Witwe. Leipzig, B&H, 1892.

Foerster-Nietzsche, Elizabeth. "Wagner and Nietzsche : The Beginning and End of Their Friendship," MQ IV (1918) 466–89.

Fondi, Enrico. "Il sentimento musicale di Vittorio Alfieri," RMI XI (1904) 484-99.

Fouque, Octave. "Le Sueur comme prédécesseur de Berlioz," in Les Révolutionnaires de la musique (Paris, Calmann-Lévy, 1882) 1-183.

Fraccaroli, Arnaldo. Bellini. Verona, A. Mondadori, 1945.

—— Donizetti. Milan, A. Mondadori, 1945.

—— Giacomo Puccini si confida e racconta. [Milan], Ricordi, [1957].

—— Rossini. Milan, Casa Editrice Mondadori, 1944. 4th ed.

—— La vita di Giacomo Puccini. Milan, Ricordi, 1925.

Fragapane, Paolo. Spontini. [Bologna], Sansoni, [1954].

Fraguier, Marguerite-Marie de. Vincent d'Indy : Souvenirs d'une élève. Paris, Jean Naert, 1933.

"The Freischütz in London, 1824," ZIMG XI (1909-10) 251-54.

Frensdorf, Victor Egon. Peter Winter als Opernkomponist. Erlangen, Junge, 1908.

Friedländer, Max. "Deutsche Dichtung in Beethovens Musik," JMP XIX (1912) 25-48.

Friedrich, Gerhard. Die deutsche und italienische Gestaltung des Falstaff-Stoffes in der Oper. Habelschwerdt, Groeger, 1941.

Friedrich, Julius. Claus Schall als dramatischer Komponist. Herchenbach, Wanne-Eickel, 1930.

Fries, Othmar. Richard Wagner und die deutsche Romantik : Versuch einer Einordnung. Zurich, Atlantis-Verlag, [1952].

Fröhlich, Willi. Jean Paul's Beziehungen zur Musik. Frankfurt Dissertation, 1922.

Frost, Henry F. "Some Remarks on Richard Wagner's Music Drama Tristan und Isolde," PMA VIII (1882) 147-67.

Gaartz, Hans. Die Opern Heinrich Marschners. Leipzig, B&H, 1912.

Gál, Hans. "A Deleted Episode in Verdi's Falstaff," MR II (1941) 266-72.

Gallini, Natale. "Inediti donizettiani," RMI LV (1953) 257-75.

Gallusser, Rita. Verdis Frauengestalten. Zurich Dissertation, 1936.

Gandolfi, Riccardo. "Cinque lettere inedite di Giuseppe Verdi," RMI XX (1913) 168-72.

Gatti, Carlo. Catalani : La vita e le opere. [Milan], Garzanti, [1953].

—— Verdi. [Milan], Arnoldo Mondadori Editore, [1951]. "Nuova [i.e., 3d] edizione riveduta," [1953]. Translated as : Verdi, the Man and His Music. New York, G. P. Putnam's Sons, [1955].

Gatti, Guido Maria. Le Barbier de Seville de Rossini : Etude historique et critique, analyse musicale. Paris, P. Mellottée, [1924?].

—— "Boito's Nero," MQ X (1924) 596-621.

—— "The Works of Giacomo Puccini," MQ XIV (1928) 16-34.

Gaudier, Charles. Carmen de Bizet : Etude historique et critique, analyse musicale. Paris, P. Mellottée, [1922].

Gautier, Théophile. Les Beautés de l'opéra. Paris, Soulié, 1845.

—— Histoire de l'art dramatique en France depuis vingt-cinq ans. Paris, Magnin, Blanchard, 1858–59. 6 vols.

Gavazzeni, Gianandrea. "Donizetti e l' *Elisir d'amore*," RassM VI (1933) 44–50.

Geddo, Angelo. Donizetti (l'uomo, le musiche). Bergamo, Edizioni della Rotonda, [1956].

George, André. *Tristan et Isolde* de Richard Wagner : Etude historique et critique, analyse musicale. Paris, Mellottée, [1929].

Gerigk, Herbert. "Das alte und das neue Bild Rossinis," ZfMw XVI (1934) 26–32.

Gerlach, L. August Klughardt, sein Leben und seine Werke. Leipzig, Hug, 1902.

Ghislanzoni, Alberto. Gaspare Spontini : Studio storico-critico. Rome, Edizioni dell' Ateneo, 1951.

Giani, Romualdo. "Il *Nerone* di Arrigo Boito," RMI VIII (1901) 861–1006.

Gianoli, Luigi. Verdi. Brescia, La Scuola, [1951].

Gilman, Lawrence. Wagner's Operas. New York, Toronto, Farrar & Rhinehart, [1937].

Girardon, Renée. "Le Don Chabrier à la Bibliothèque Nationale," RdM XXVIIe année, Tome XXIV, nouv. sér. 75–76 (3e–4e trimestre 1945) 69–87; XXVIIIe année, nouv. sér. 77–78 (1e–2e trimestre 1946) 22–28.

Glasenapp, Carl Friedrich. Das Leben Richard Wagners. Leipzig, B&H, 1904–11. 6 vols. 4th ed. Translated as : The Life of Richard Wagner. London, Paul, Trench & Trübner, 1900–1908. 6 vols.

—— Siegfried Wagner und seine Kunst. Leipzig, B&H, 1911.

—— Siegfried Wagner und seine Kunst. Neue Folge. I. Schwartz-schwanenreich (Leipzig, B&H, 1913); II. Sonnenflammen (Leipzig, B&H, 1919).

—— Versuch einer thematischen Analyse der Musik zu Siegfried Wagner's *Kobold*. Leipzig, M. Brockhaus, 1904.

Glaser, G. Franz von Holstein, ein Dichterkomponist des 19. Jahrhunderts. Leipzig Dissertation, 1930.

Gnirs, Anton. Hans Heiling. Carlsbad, Heinich, 1931.

Goldberg, Isaac. The Story of Gilbert and Sullivan. New York, Simon & Schuster, 1928.

Goldmark, Karl. Erinnerungen aus meinem Leben. Vienna, Rikola, 1922. Translated as : Notes from the Life of a Viennese Composer. New York, A. and C. Boni, 1927.

Goldschmit-Jentner, Rudolf Karl. "Wagner und Nietzsche," in *Die Begegnung mit dem Genius: Darstellungen und Betrachtungen.* (Hamburg, Christian Wegner Verlag, [1946].)

Gorer, R. "Weber and the Romantic Movement," M&L XVII (1936) 13–24.

Goslich, Siegfried. Beiträge zur Geschichte der deutschen romantischen

Oper zwischen Spohrs *Faust* und Wagners *Lohengrin*. Leipzig, Kistner & Siegel, 1937.

Gounod, Charles François. Autobiographical Reminiscences, with Family Letters and Notes on Music. London, W. Heinemann, 1896.

—— Mémoires d'un artiste. Paris, Calmann Lévy, 1896. 5th ed. Translated as : Memoirs of an Artist. New York, Rand, McNally, 1895.

Graedener-Hattingberg, Magda von. Hugo Wolf. Vienna, E. Wancura, 1953.

Graf, Herbert. Richard Wagner als Regisseur. Vienna Dissertation, 1925.

Gramisch, Lore. Die Erscheinungsformen des melodramatischen Stils im 19. Jahrhundert. Vienna Dissertation, 1936.

Grattan Flood. *See* Flood, William Henry Grattan.

Gray, Cecil. "Pietro Raimondi," MR I (1940) 25–35.

—— "Vincenzo Bellini," M&L VII (1926) 49–62.

Greeff, Paul. E. T. A. Hoffmann als Musiker und Musikschriftsteller. [Cologne & Krefeld], Staufen-Verlag, 1948.

Grégoir, Edouard. Bibliothèque musicale populaire. Brussels, Schott, 1877–79. 3 vols.

Griepenkerl, Wolfgang Robert. Die Oper der Gegenwart. Leipzig, Hinrich, 1847.

Grosheim, Georg Christoph. Selbstbiographie. Hamburg, Kassel, F. Settnick, 1925.

Gross, Rolf. Joseph Hartmann Stuntz als Opernkomponist. Würzburg, Triltsch, 1936.

Grovlez, Gabriel. "Jacques Offenbach : A Centennial Sketch," MQ V (1919) 329–37.

Grun, Bernard. Prince of Vienna : The Life, the Times and the Melodies of Oscar Straus. London, W. H. Allen, 1955.

Gysi, Fritz. Max Bruch. Zurich, Orell Füssli, [1922].

Haas, Robert M. "Zur Wiener Balletpantomime um den *Prometheus*," *Neues Beethoven Jahrbuch* II (1925) 84–103.

Hadamowsky, Franz Heinz Otto. Die Wiener Operette : Ihre Theater- und Wirkungsgeschichte. Vienna, Bellaria Verlag, 1947.

Hadow, Sir William Henry. Studies in Modern Music, Second Series. New York, Macmillan, [1923]. 10th ed.

Hänsler, Rolf. Peter Lindpainter als Opernkomponist. Stuttgart-Caunstadt, Kirchoff, [1930].

Halévy, François. Derniers Souvenirs et portraits. Paris, M. Lévy, 1863.

—— Souvenirs et portraits. Paris, M. Lévy, 1861.

Hanslick, Eduard. Die moderne Oper : Kritiken und Studien. Berlin, A. Hofmann, 1875. This is also the title of a series of books by Hanslick, the respective subtitles and dates of which are as follows : I. Die moderne Oper, 1875; II. Musikalische Stationen, 1880; III. Aus dem Opernleben der Gegenwart, 1884; IV. Musikalische Skizzenbuch, 1888; V. Musikalisches und Litterarisches, 1889; VI. Aus dem Tagebuche eines

Musikers, 1892; VII. Fünf Jahre Musik (1891–1895), 1896; VIII. Am Ende des Jahrhunderts (1895–1899), 1899; IX. Aus neuer und neuester Zeit, 1900.

—— Vom Musikalisch-Schönen : Ein Beitrag zur Revision der Aesthetik der Tonkunst. Leipzig, R. Weigel, 1854.

Hardy, Joseph. Rodolphe Kreutzer : Sa jeunesse à Versailles. Paris, Fischbacher, 1910.

Hasse, Max. Der Dichtermusiker Peter Cornelius. Leipzig, B&H, 1922–23. 2 vols.

—— Peter Cornelius und sein *Barbier von Bagdad*. Leipzig, B&H, 1904.

Hasselberg, Felix. *Der Freischütz:* Friedrich Kinds Operndichtung und ihre Quellen. Berlin, Dom Verlag, 1921.

Hausegger, Siegmund von. Alexander Ritter : Ein Bild seines Characters und Schaffens. Berlin, Marquardt, [1907].

Hausswald, Günther, ed. Carl Maria von Weber : Eine Gedenkschrift. Dresden, VVV Dresden Verlag, 1951.

Hédouin, Pierre. Gossec, sa vie et ses ouvrages. Paris, Prignet, 1852.

Heinemann, Franz. "Schillers *Wilhelm Tell* in der Musikgeschichte des 19. Jahrhunderts," *Zeitschrift für Bücherfreunde* XI, No. 2 (1907) 321–38.

Hellberg (-Kupfer), Geerd. Richard Wagner als Regisseur. Berlin, Gesellschaft für Theatergeschichte, 1942.

Hellmer, Elmund, ed. *Der Corregidor* von Hugo Wolf. Vienna, Hugo Wolf Verein; Berlin, S. Fischer, 1900.

Hellouin, Frédéric. Gossec et la musique française à la fin du XVIIIe siècle. Paris, A. Charles, 1903.

—— Un Musicien oublié : Catel. Paris, Fischbacher, 1910.

Henseler, Anton. Jakob Offenbach. Berlin-Schöneberg, M. Hesse, 1930.

Hernried, Robert. "Hugo Wolf's *Corregidor* at Mannheim," MQ XXVI (1940) 19–30.

—— "Hugo Wolfs 'Four Operas,'" MQ XXXI (1945) 89–100.

Herre, Max. Franz Danzi : Ein Beitrag zur Geschichte der deutschen Oper. Munich Dissertation, 1930.

Herzfeld, Friedrich. Königsfreundschaft : Ludwig II. und Richard Wagner. Leipzig, Goldmann, [1939].

Hess, Willy. Beethovens Oper *Fidelio* und ihre drei Fassungen. Zurich, Atlantis Verlag, [1953].

—— "Die künstlerische Dreieinheit in Wagners Tondramen : Einige 'unzeitgemässe' Betrachtungen im Geiste Richard Wagners," Mf XI (1958) 293–306.

Heuberger, Richard. Im Foyer : Gesammelte Essays über das Opernrepertoire der Gegenwart. Leipzig, H. Seemann, 1901.

—— Musikalische Skizzen. Leipzig, H. Seemann, 1901.

Heuss, Alfred. "Verdi als melodischer Charakteristiker," ZIMG XV (1913–14) 63–72.

Hey, Julius. Richard Wagner als Vortragsmeister 1864–1876 : Erinnerungen. Leipzig, B&H, 1911.

Heyden, Otto. Das Kölner Theaterwesen im 19. Jahrhundert. Emsdetten, Lechte, 1939.

Himonet, André. Lohengrin . . . étude historique et critique, analyse musicale. Paris, Mellottée, [1925].

—— Louise de Charpentier : Etude historique et critique, analyse musicale. Paris, Mellottée, [1922].

Hirsch, Hans. Richard Wagner und das deutsche Mittelalter. Vienna, R. M. Rohrer, 1944.

Hirschfeld, Robert. "Oper in Wien [1857–1900]," ZIMG I (1899–1900) 264–67.

Hirt, Giulio C. "Autografi di G. Rossini," RMI II (1895) 23–35.

Hirzel, Bruno. "Der Text Wagner's Liebesverbot nach der Handschrift in Washington," SIMG XIII (1911–12) 348–82.

Hodik, Fritz. Das Horn bei Richard Wagner. Innsbruck Dissertation, 1937.

Hoechst, Coit Roscoe. Faust in Music. Gettysburg, Pa., Gettysburg Compiler Print, 1916.

Hoffmann, Ernst Theodor Amadeus. Sämtliche Werke. Leipzig, M. Hesse, 1900. 15 vols.

—— Musikalische Novellen und Aufsätze : Vollständige Gesamtausgabe, hrsg. von Dr. Edgar Istel. Regensburg, G. Bosse, [1921?]. 2 vols.

Hogarth, George. Memoirs of the Musical Drama. London, R. Bentley, 1838. 2 vols. New ed. as : Memoirs of the Opera in Italy, France, Germany, and England. London, R. Bentley, 1851. 2 vols.

Hohenemser, R. Luigi Cherubini. Leipzig, B&H, 1913.

Holde, Artur. "A Little-Known Letter by Berlioz and Unpublished Letters by Cherubini, Leoncavallo, and Hugo Wolf," MQ XXXVII (1951) 340–53.

Hollinrake, Roger. "Nietzsche, Wagner and Ernest Newman," M&L XLI (1960) 245–55.

Hoover, Kathleen O'Donnell. "Gustave Charpentier," MQ XXV (1939) 334–50.

—— "Verdi's Rocester," MQ XXVIII (1942) 505–13.

Hughes, Gervase. Composers of Operetta. London, Macmillan, 1962.

—— The Music of Arthur Sullivan. London, Macmillan & Co.; New York, St. Martin's Press, 1960.

Hussey, Dyneley. "Beethoven as a Composer of Opera," M&L VIII (1927) 243–52.

—— Verdi. London, J. M. Dent, 1948.

Hutcheson, Ernest. A Musical Guide to the Richard Wagner Ring of the Nibelung. New York, Simon & Schuster, 1940.

Indy, Vincent d'. César Franck. Paris, F. Alcan, 1906. Translated : New York, John Lane, 1910.

—— Richard Wagner et son influence sur l'art musical français. Paris, Delagrave, 1930.

Irvine, David. *Parsifal* and Wagner's Christianity. London, H. Grevel, 1899.

Istel, Edgar. "Act IV of *Les Huguenots*," MQ XXII (1936) 87–97.

—— "Beethoven's *Leonora* and *Fidelio*," MQ VII (1921) 226–51.

—— Bizet und *Carmen*. Stuttgart, J. Engelhorn, 1927.

—— Die Blütezeit der musikalischen Romantik in Deutschland. Leipzig, B. G. Teubner, 1909. 2d ed., 1921.

—— "Fünf Briefe Spohrs an Marschner," in *Festschrift . . . Liliencron* (Leipzig, B&H, 1910) 110–15.

—— "A Genetic Study of the *Aida* Libretto," MQ III (1917) 34–52.

—— "German Opera Since Richard Wagner," MQ I (1915) 260–90.

—— "Hermann Goetz," ZIMG III (1901–2) 177–88.

—— Das Kunstwerk Richard Wagners. Leipzig, B. G. Teubner, 1918.

—— "Meyerbeer's Way to Mastership," MQ XII (1926) 72–109.

—— Die moderne Oper vom Tode Wagners bis zum Weltkrieg. Leipzig, B. G. Teubner, 1915. 2d ed., 1923.

—— "The *Othello* of Verdi and Shakespeare," MQ II (1916) 375–86.

—— "Peter Cornelius," MQ XX (1934) 334–43.

—— "Rossini : A Study," MQ IX (1923) 401–22.

Jacob, Heinrich Eduard. Johann Strauss, Father and Son. [New York], Greystone Press, 1940.

—— Johann Strauss und das neunzehnte Jahrhundert. Amsterdam, Querido Verlag, 1937.

Jacob, Walter. Taten der Musik : Richard Wagner und sein Werk. Regensburg, Bosse, [1952].

Jacob, Walter, ed. Leo Blech : Ein Brevier. Hamburg-Leipzig, Prisman-Verlag, [1931].

Jacobsohn, Fritz. Hans Gregors komische Oper, 1905–1911. Berlin, Oester-held, [1911].

Jähns, Friedrich Wilhelm. Carl Maria von Weber in seinen Werken: Chronologisch-Thematische Verzeichniss seiner sämmtlichen Compositionen . . . Berlin, Lienau, 1891.

Janowitzer, Erwin. Peter Cornelius als Opernkomponist. Vienna Dissertation, 1921.

Jaspert, Werner. Johann Strauss. Berlin, Werk Verlag, [1939].

Jean-Aubry, G. "A Romantic Dilettante : Emile Deschamps (1791–1871)," M&L XX (1939) 250–65.

Jensen, Wilhelm. Spontini als Opernkomponist. Berlin Dissertation, 1920.

Jeri, Alfredo. Mascagni : Quindici opere, mille episodi. Cernusco sul Naviglio, Grazanti, 1945. 3d ed.

Jones, Arthur E. The Choruses in the Operas of Richard Wagner : A Study of Massed Vocal Ensemble in Music Drama. Ann Arbor, University Microfilms, 1957.

Jouvin, B[enoît Jean Baptiste]. Hérold, sa vie et ses œuvres. Paris, Au Ménestrel, Heugel, 1868.

Jullien, Adolphe. "Ambroise Thomas," RMI III (1896) 358–66.

—— "A Propos de la mort de Charles Gounod," RMI I (1894) 60–67.

—— "Hector Berlioz," RMI I (1894) 454–82.

—— Hector Berlioz, sa vie et ses œuvres. Paris, Librairie de l'Art, 1888.

—— Musiciens d'aujourd'hui. Paris, Librairie de l'Art, 1892–94. 2 vols.

Kalbeck, Max. Opern-Abende. Berlin, "Harmonie," 1898.

Kapp, Julius. Carl Maria von Weber. Berlin, M. Hesse, 1944. 15th ed.

—— Meyerbeer. Berlin, Schuster & Loeffler, [1920]. 8th ed., 1930.

—— Richard Wagner. Berlin, M. Hesse, 1929. 32d ed.

—— Richard Wagner und die Berliner Oper. Berlin-Schöneberg, M. Hesse, 1933.

—— Richard Wagner und die Frauen. Berlin-Halensee, M. Hesse, [1951]. Translated as : The Loves of Richard Wagner. London, W. H. Allen, 1951.

Karsten, Werner. "Harmonische Analyse des Tristan-Akkordes," SchwM XCI (1951) 291–96.

Kastner, Emerich. Bibliotheca Beethoveniana : Versuch einer Beethoven-Bibliographie. Leipzig, B&H, 1913.

—— Die dramatischen Werke R. Wagner's : Chronologisches Verzeichnis der ersten Aufführungen. Leipzig, B&H, 1899. 2d ed.

Keller, Otto. Franz von Suppé. Leipzig, R. Wöpke, 1905.

—— Karl Goldmark. Leipzig, H. Seemann, [1901].

Kenney, Charles Lamb. A Memoir of Michael William Balfe. London, Tinsley, 1875.

Kerman, Joseph. "Verdi's Otello, or Shakespeare Explained," The Hudson Review VI (1953–54) 266–77.

—— "Wagner : Thoughts in Season," The Hudson Review XIII (1960–61) 329–49.

Keys, A. C. "Schiller and Italian Opera," M&L XLI (1960) 223–37.

Kienzl, Wilhelm. Meine Lebenswanderung. Stuttgart, J. Engelhorn, 1926.

Kienzl-Rosegger : Wilhelm Kienzls Lebenswanderung im Auszug . . . . Briefwechsel mit Peter Rosegger. Ed. by Hans Sittner. Zurich & Vienna, Amalthea-Verlag, [1953].

Killer, Hermann. Albert Lortzing. Potsdam, Athenaion, 1938.

Kirby, Percival R. "Washington Irving, Barham Livius and Weber," M&L XXXI (1950) 133–47.

—— "Weber's Operas in London, 1824–1826," MQ XXXII (1946) 333–53.

Klein, John W. "Alfredo Catalani," MQ XXIII (1937) 287–94.

—— "Alfredo Catalani : 1854–93," M&L XXXV (1954) 40–44.

—— "Bizet and Wagner," M&L XXVIII (1947) 50–62.

—— "Bizet's Early Operas," M&L XVIII (1937) 169–75.

—— "Boito and His Two Operas," M&L VII (1926) 73–80.

—— "Catalani and His Operas," MMR LXXXVIII (1958) 67–69, 101–7.

—— "Meyerbeer's Strangest Opera," MMR LXXXIX (1959) 221–26.

—— "Nietzsche and Bizet," MQ XI (1925) 482–505.

—— "Verdi and Boito," MQ XIV (1928) 158–71.

—— "Verdi's Italian Contemporaries and Successors," M&L XV (1934) 37–45.

—— "Wagner and His Operatic Contemporaries," M&L IX (1928) 59–66.

Kling, H. "Goethe et Berlioz," RMI XII (1905) 714–32.

—— "Helmine de Chézy," RMI XIV (1907) 25–39.

Klob, Karl Maria. Die komische Oper seit Lortzing. Berlin, "Harmonie," [1905].

Knappe, Heinrich. Friedrich Klose. Munich, Drei Masken, 1921.

Knopf, Kurt. Die romantische Struktur des Denkens Richard Wagners. Jena, G. Neuenhahn, 1932.

Knudsen, Hans. "Das Posener Theater unter Franz Wallner," Zeitschrift der historischen Gesellschaft für die Provinz Posen XXVI (1911) 225–42.

[Koch, Lajos.] Karl Goldmark. Budapest, Hauptstädtische Hausdruckerei, 1930.

Koch, Max. Richard Wagner. Berlin, E. Hofmann, 1907–18. 3 vols.

Kohut, Adolph. Auber. Leipzig, Reclam, 1895.

Komorzyński, Egon von. "Lortzings Waffenschmied und seine Tradition," Euphorion VIII (1901) 340–50.

Kracauer, Siegfried. Orpheus in Paris. New York, Alfred A. Knopf, 1938. First published as : Jacques Offenbach und das Paris seiner Zeit. Amsterdam, de Lange, 1937.

Kralik, Heinrich. Das Opernhaus am Ring. Vienna, Brüder Rosenbaum, [1955]. Translated as : The Vienna Opera House. Vienna, Verlag Brüder Rosenbaum; [London, Methuen & Co.], [1955].

Kraus, Ludwig. Das deutsche Liederspiel in den Jahren 1800–1830. Halle Dissertation, 1921.

Kretzschmar, Hermann. "Giuseppe Verdi," JMP XX (1913) 43–58.

—— "Die musikgeschichtliche Bedeutung Simon Mayrs," JMP XI (1904) 27–41.

—— "Peter Cornelius," in Waldersee, Sammlung musikalischer Vorträge (Leipzig, B&H, 1879–98) II, 225–60.

—— "Ueber das Wesen, das Wachsen und Wirken Richard Wagners," JMP XIX (1912) 49–64.

—— "Ueber die Bedeutung von Cherubinis Ouvertüren und Hauptopern für die Gegenwart," JMP XIII (1906) 75–91.

Kreuzhage, Eduard. Hermann Goetz. Leipzig, B&H, 1916.

Krienitz, Willy. Richard Wagner's Feen. Munich, G. Müller, 1910.

Krohn, Ilmari. "Puccini : Butterfly," in Gedenkboek D. F. Scheurleer (The Hague, Nijhoff, 1925) 181–90.

Kroll, Erwin. Carl Maria von Weber. Potsdam, Athenaion, [1934].

Kroll, Erwin. Ernst Theodor Amadeus Hoffmann. Leipzig, B&H, 1923.

Krott, Rudolfine. Die Singspiele Schuberts. Vienna Dissertation, 1921.

Kroyer, Theodor. "Die circumpolare Oper," JMP XXVI (1919) 16–33.

Krüger, Viktor. Die Entwicklung Carl Maria von Webers in seinen Jugendopern *Abu Hassan* und *Silvana*. Vienna Dissertation, 1907.

Krüger-Riebow, Joachim. "Albert Lortzing als politischer Freiheitssänger,"
MuG I (1951) 10–15.

Kruse, Georg Richard. Albert Lortzing. Berlin, "Harmonie," 1899.

—— Hermann Goetz. Leipzig, Reclam, [1920].

—— "Meyerbeers Jugendopern," ZfMw I (1918–19) 399–413.

—— Otto Nicolai. Berlin, Verlag "Berlin-Wien," [1911].

—— "Otto Nicolai's italienische Opern," SIMG XII (1910–11) 267–96.

Kuckuk, Ludwig. Peter Winter als deutscher Opernkomponist. Heidelberg
Dissertation, 1924.

Kufferath, Maurice. "*Fervaal* . . . di V. d'Indy," RMI IV (1897) 313–27.

—— *Fidelio* de L. van Beethoven. Paris, Fischbacher, 1913.

Kuhlmann, Hans. Stil und Form in der Musik von Humperdincks Oper
*Hänsel und Gretel*. Borna-Leipzig, Universitätsverlag von Robert Noske,
1930.

Kurth, Ernst. Romantische Harmonik und ihre Krise in Wagners *Tristan*.
Berlin, M. Hesse, 1923. 2d ed.

Kuznitzky, Hans. "Weber und Spontini in der musikalischen Anschauung
von E. T. A. Hoffmann," ZfMw X (1927–28) 292–99.

Lafontaine, H. C. de. "Richard Wagner," PMA XVI (1890) 63–78.

La Laurencie, Lionel de. "Les Débuts de Viotti comme directeur de l'opéra
en 1819," RdM V (1924) 110–22.

Laloy, Louis. "Le Drame musical moderne," MM I (1905) 8–16, 75–84,
169–77, 233–50.

Lamm, Max. Beiträge zur Entwicklung des musikalischen Motivs in den
Tondramen Richard Wagners. Vienna Dissertation, 1932.

Lamy, Félix. Jean-François le Sueur. Paris, Fischbacher, 1912.

Landestheater Hannover: 100 Jahre Opernhaus, 1852–1952. Hanover,
Städtisches Verkehrs- und Presseamt; Landestheater Hannover, 1952.

Landormy, Paul Charles René. Bizet. [Paris], Gallimard, [1950].

—— *Faust* de Gounod. Paris, P. Mellottée, [1922].

—— *Faust*, de Gounod : Etude et analyse. Paris, Mellottée, 1944.

—— Gounod. Paris, Gallimard, 1942.

—— La Musique française de Franck à Debussy. Paris, Gallimard, [1943].

—— La Musique française de la Marseillaise à la mort de Berlioz. Paris,
Gallimard, 1944.

—— "Vincent d'Indy," MQ XVIII (1932) 507–18.

Langlois, Jacques. Camille Saint-Saëns. Moulins, Crépin-Leblond, 1934.

Larousse, Pierre. Grand dictionnaire universel du XIXe siècle. Paris, 1874.
15 vols. and 2 supplements.

Laue, Hellmuth. Die Operndichtung Lortzings. Bonn am Rhein, L. Röhr-
scheid, 1932.

Lavignac, Albert. Le Voyage artistique à Bayreuth. Paris, C. Delagrave,
1900. 4th ed. Translated as : The Music Dramas of Richard Wagner and
His Festival Theatre in Bayreuth. New York, Dodd, Mead, 1904. New
French edition : [1951].

Lavoix, H[enri], *fils.* Histoire de l'instrumentation depuis le seizième siècle
jusqu'à nos jours. Paris, Firmin-Didot, 1878.

Lehmann, Lilly. Studien zu *Fidelio.* Leipzig, B&H, 1904.

Leib, Walter. Joseph Huber : Beitrag zur Geschichte der circumpolaren
Oper. Heidelberg Dissertation, 1923.

Leibowitz, René. "Fidelio ou l'amour de l'opéra," *Les Temps modernes* X
(1955) 1505–17.

Leichtentritt, Hugo. "Schubert's Early Operas," MQ XIV (1928) 620–38.

Leo, Sophie Augustine. "Musical Life in Paris (1817–1848)," MQ XVII
(1931) 259–71, 389–403.

Leoni, Carlo. Dell' arte e del teatro nuovo di Padova: Racconto anecdotico.
Padua, Sacchetto, 1873.

Leroy, L. Archier. Wagner's Music Drama of *The Ring.* London, N.
Douglas, [1925].

Lespês, Léo. Les Mystères du grand-opéra. Paris, Maresq, 1843.

Levi, Vito. "Un grande operista italiano (Antonio Smareglia, 1854–1929),"
RMI XXXVI (1929) 600–15.

Lippman, Edward Arthur. "The Esthetic Theories of Richard Wagner,"
MQ XLIV (1958) 209–20.

Liszt, Franz. Dramaturgische Blätter, I. Abtheilung. Essays über musikalische Bühnenwerke . . . Leipzig, B&H, 1881.

—— Gesammelte Schriften. Leipzig, B&H, 1880–83. 6 vols.
Vol. III, Parts 1 and 2 are the "Dramaturgische Blätter."

Loisel, Joseph. *Manon* de Massenet : Etude historique et critique, analyse
musicale. Paris, Mellottée, [1922].

Longyear, Rey Morgan. Daniel-François-Esprit Auber (1782–1871): A
Chapter in French Opéra Comique. Ann Arbor, University Microfilms,
1957.

—— " 'Le Livret bien fait' : The Opéra Comique Librettos of Eugène
Scribe," *The Southern Quarterly* I (1963) 169–92.

—— "*La Muette de Portici,*" MR XIX (1958) 37–46.

—— "Notes on the Rescue Opera," MQ XLV (1959) 49–66.

Loomis, Roger Sherman, ed. The Romance of Tristram and Ysolt by
Thomas of Britain. New York, Columbia University Press, 1931. Rev. ed.

Loos, Paul Arthur. Richard Wagner : Vollendung und Tragik der deutschen Romantik. Bern, Francke, [1952].

Lorenz, Alfred Ottokar. Das Geheimnis der Form bei Richard Wagner.
Berlin, M. Hesse, 1924–33. 4 vols.

Lortzing, Gustav Albert. Gesammelte Briefe. Regensburg, Gustav-Bosse Verlag, [1913]. 3d ed., 1947.

Loschelder, Josef. Das Todesproblem in Verdis Opernschaffen. Stuttgart, Deutsche Verlagsanstalt, 1938.

Lothar, Rudolf, [and Julius Stern]. 50 Jahre Hoftheater : Geschichte der beiden Wiener Hoftheater unter der Regierungszeit des Kaisers Franz Josef I. Vienna, Steyermühl, [1898].

Lualdi, Adriano. "Arrigo Boito, un' anima," RMI XXV (1918) 524–49.

Ludwig II, King of Bavaria. König Ludwig II. und Richard Wagner: Briefwechsel . . . . Karlsruhe i. B., G. Braun, [1936–39]. 5 vols.

Lütge, Wilhelm. "Zu Beethovens Leonoren-Ouvertüre Nr. 2," ZfMw IX (1926–27) 235–36.

Lusson, A. L. Projet d'un théâtre d'opéra définitif pour la ville de Paris en remplacement de l'opéra provisoire. Paris, Gratiot, 1846.

Lynn, Thelma. César Franck : A Bio-bibliography. New York, 1934. Typescript. Available at the New York Public Library.

Lyon, Raymond, and Louis Saguer. Les Contes d'Hoffmann: Etude et analyse. Paris, Editions Mellottée, 1948.

Macchetta, Mrs. Blanche Roosevelt (Tucker). Verdi : Milan and Othello . . . by Blanche Roosevelt. London, Ward & Downey, 1887.

MacCormack, Gilson. "Weber in Paris," M&L IX (1928) 240–48.

Maecklenburg, Albert. "Der Fall Spontini-Weber," ZfMw VI (1923–24) 449–65.

—— "Verdi and Manzoni," MQ XVII (1931) 209–18.

Magnani, Giuseppe. Antonio Salieri. [Legnano], Edito a cura del commune di Legnano e di un comitato cittadino, 1934.

Maione, Italo. Il dramma di Wagner. Naples, Libr. Scientifica, 1959. 2d ed.

Maisch, W. Puccinis musikalische Formgebung, untersucht an der Oper La Bohême. Neustadt a. d. Aisch, Schmidt, 1934.

Malherbe, Charles Théodore. Auber : Biographie critique. Paris, H. Laurens, [1911].

——"Le Centenaire de Donizetti et l'exposition de Bergamo," RMI IV (1897) 707–29.

Malherbe, Henry. Carmen. Paris, Michel, [1951].

Mandalari, M. T. "Gradi della evoluzione drammatica nel Ballo in Maschera di Verdi," RassM XII (1931) 277–87.

Mann, Thomas. Altes und Neues : Kleine Prosa aus 6 Jahrzehnten. Frankfurt/M., S. Fischer Verlag, 1953. Contains : "Briefe Richard Wagners," 575–86; "Wagner und kein Ende," 787–89.

—— Leiden und Grösse der Meister. Berlin, S. Fischer, 1935. A condensed English translation of the essay on Wagner in this volume is found in Mann's Freud, Goethe, Wagner (New York, Alfred A. Knopf, 1937).

Manschunger, Kurt. Ferdinand Kauer. Vienna Dissertation, 1929.

Mapleson, James Henry. The Mapleson Memoirs, 1848–1888. London, Remington, 1888. 2d ed. 2 vols.

Marcello, ——. "La prima rappresentazione del *Guglielmo Tell* a Parigi," RMI XVI (1909) 664–70.

Marek, George R. Puccini, a Biography. New York, Simon & Schuster, 1951.

Mariani, Renato. "L'ultimo Puccini," RassM IX (1936) 133–40.

Marino, Samuel J. "Giacomo Puccini : A Check List of Works by and about the Composer," *Bulletin of the New York Public Library* LIX, No. 2 (February, 1955) 62–81.

Marix-Spire, Thérèse. "Gounod and His First Interpreter, Pauline Viardot," MQ XXXI (1945) 193–211, 299–317.

Martens, Frederick H. "Music Mirrors of the Second Empire," MQ XVI (1930) 415–34, 563–87.

Martersteig, Max. Das deutsche Theater im 19. Jahrhundert. Leipzig, B&H, 1924.

Mascagni, Pietro. Mascagni parla : Appunti per le memorie di un grande musicista. Rome, De Carlo, [1945].

Massenet, Jules. Mes Souvenirs. Paris, P. Lafitte, [1912]. Translated as: My Recollections. Boston, Small, Maynard, [1919].

Mayer, Ludwig K. "Eine Vorwebersche 'Preciosa'-Musik," AfMf I (1936) 223–27.

Mayerhofer, Gottfried. Abermals vom Freischützen : Der Münchener *Freischütze* von 1812 [by Franz Xavier von Caspar]. Regensburg, Bosse, 1959.

Medicus, Lotte. Die Koloratur in der italienischen Oper des 19. Jahrhunderts. Zurich, Wetzikon & Rüti, 1939.

Merbach, Paul Alfred. "Briefwechsel zwischen Eduard Devrient und Julius Rietz," AfMw III (1921) 321–60.

—— "Parodien und Nachwirkungen von Webers *Freischütz*," ZfM II (1919–20) 642–55.

Merlo, G. M. "L'arte di Arrigo Boito e il valore di *Nerone*," RassM VIII (1935) 126–32.

Meyerbeer, Giacomo. Briefwechsel und Tagebücher . . . herausgegeben und kommentiert von Heinz Becker. Band I : Bis 1824. Berlin, de Gruyter, [1960].

Mila, Massimo. Giuseppe Verdi. Bari, Laterza, 1958.

—— Il melodramma di Verdi. Bari, G. Laterza, 1933.

—— "Verdi als Politiker," *Melos* XVIII (1951) 73–78.

Miragoli, Livia. Il melodramma italiano nell' Ottocento. Rome, P. Maglione & C. Strini, [1924].

Misch, Ludwig. "*Fidelio* als ethisches Bekenntnis," in *Beethoven-Studien* (Berlin, de Gruyter, 1950) 143–49.

Monaldi, Gino. "A proposito del centenario di Vincenzo Bellini," RMI IX (1902) 72–78.

—— Verdi : La vita, le opere. Milan, Bocca, 1951.

—— Vincenzo Bellini. Milan, Sonzogno, [1935].

Mondolfi, A. "Appunti donizettiani : Il Belisario," Gazzetta musicale di Napoli (1957) Nos. 1 and 2.

—— "Appunti donizettiani : L'Assedio di Calais," Gazzetta musicale di Napoli (1957) No 4.

—— "Appunti donizettiani : Pia de' Tolomei e Poliuto," Gazzetta musicale di Napoli (1957) No. 6.

Monographien moderner Musiker, ed. E. Segnitz. Leipzig, C. F. Kahnt, 1906–9. 3 vols.

Monterosso, Raffaello. La musica nel risorgimento. Milan, F. Vallardi, 1948.

Moos, Paul. Richard Wagner als Aesthetiker. Berlin and Leipzig, Schuster & Loeffler, 1906.

Mosel, Ignaz Franz, Edler von. Ueber das Leben und die Werke des Anton Salieri. Vienna, J. B. Wallishausser, 1827.

—— Versuch einer Aesthetik des dramatischen Tonsatzes. Vienna, A. Strauss, 1813. New ed., Munich, Lewy, 1910, with introduction and notes by Eugen Schmidt.

Moser, Hans Joachim. Carl Maria von Weber : Leben und Werk. Leipzig, VEB B&H, 1955. 2d ed.

—— "Giuseppe Verdi," RassM XII (1939) 149–58.

—— "Kleine Beiträge zu Beethovens Liedern und Bühnenwerken," Neues Beethoven Jahrbuch II (1925) 43–65.

Moser, Max. Richard Wagner in der englischen Literatur des 19. Jahrhunderts. Bern, Stämpfli, 1938.

Moss, Arthur, and Evalyn Marvel. Cancan and Barcarolle : The Life and Times of Jacques Offenbach. New York, Exposition Press, [cop. 1954].

Moutoz, A. Rossini et son Guillaume Tell. Paris, A. Pilon, 1872.

Münzer, G. Heinrich Marschner. Berlin, "Harmonie," 1901.

Munter, Friedrich. Ludwig Thuille. Munich, Drei Masken, 1923

Nacamuli, Guido Davide. Discorso commemorativo su Antonio Smareglia. Trieste, Giuliana, 1930.

Nardi, Piero. Vita di Arrigo Boito. Milan, Casa Editrice Mondadori, 1944. 2d ed.

Nathan, Hans. Das Rezitativ der Frühopern Richard Wagners. Berlin, Dobrin, 1934.

Naylor, Bernard. "Albert Lortzing," PMA LVIII (1931–32) 1–13.

Naylor, Edward Woodall. "Verdi and Wagner," PMA XX (1893) 1–10.

Neretti, Luigi. L'importanza civile della nostra opera in musica. Florence, Tipografia cooperativa, 1902.

Neues Beethoven Jahrbuch. Augsburg, B. Filser, 1924– . Articles relevant to opera will be found separately listed under the names of the following authors : Cortolezis, Engländer, Haas, Moser, Schiedermair, Unger, Wallner, Waltershausen.

Neumann, Alfred Robert. The Evolution of the Concept Gesamtkunstwerk in German Romanticism. Ann Arbor, University Microfilms, 1951.

Neumann, Egon. Die Operetten von Johann Strauss. Vienna Dissertation, 1919.

Newman, Ernest. Hugo Wolf. London, Methuen, [1907].

—— The Life of Richard Wagner. New York, Alfred A. Knopf, 1933–46. 4 vols.

—— The Wagner Operas. New York, Alfred A. Knopf, 1949.

Nicolai, Otto. Tagebücher. Edited, with biographical notes, by B. Schröder. Leipzig, B&H, 1892. New ed. by Wilhelm Altmann. Regensburg, G. Bosse, 1937.

Nietzsche, Friedrich. Gesammelte Werke. Munich, Musarion, 1920–29. 23 vols. Contains : "Die Geburt der Tragödie," Vol. 3; "Jenseits von Gut und Böse," Vol. 15; "Der Fall Wagner," "Nietzsche contra Wagner," Vol. 17.

Niggli, Arnold. "Giacomo Meyerbeer," in Waldersee, Sammlung musikalischer Vorträge (Leipzig, B&H, 1879–98) V, 287–324.

Nohl, Walther. "Beethovens Opernpläne," Musik XXXI, No. 11 (August, 1939) 741–47.

Nordau, Max. Entartung. Berlin, Duncker, 1893. 2 vols. Translated as : Degeneration. New York, D. Appleton, 1895.

Notarnicola, Biagio. Saverio Mercadante, biografia critica nel 150° dalla nascità (1795–1945). Rome, [Tipi della Poliglotta], 1945.

—— Saverio Mercadante nella gloria e nella luce. Rome, Editrice "Diplomatica," 1948–49.

Nowak, Leopold. "Beethovens Fidelio und die österreichischen Militärsignale," OeM X (1955) 373–75.

Oberdorfer, Aldo. Giuseppe Verdi. [Milan], Mondadori, 1949.

Odendahl, Laurenz. Friedrich Heinrich Himmel. Bonn, P. Rost, 1917.

The Meister : The Quarterly Journal of the London Branch of the Wagner Society. London, George Redway, 1888–94. 7 vols.

Oesterlein, Nikolaus. Katalog einer Wagner-Bibliothek. Leipzig, B&H, 1882–95. 4 vols.

Oesterreicher, Rudolf. Emmerich Kálmán : Der Weg eines Komponisten. Zurich, Leipzig, Vienna, Amalthea Verlag, [1954].

Offenbach, Jacques. Offenbach en Amérique : Notes d'un musicien en voyage. Paris, Calmann Lévy, 1877. English translation : Orpheus in America. Bloomington, Indiana University Press, [1957].

Ollone, Max d'. "Gounod et l'opéra-comique," RM XIV (November, 1933) 303–8.

"L'Opéra-comique au XIXe siècle," RM XIV (November, 1933) 241–312.

Orsini, Giovanni. Pietro Mascagni e il suo Nerone. Milan, A.&G. Carisch, 1935.

Ortigue, Joseph Louis d'. Le Balcon de l'opéra. Paris, Renduel, 1833.

—— De l'école musicale italienne. Paris, Au dépot central des meilleures productions de la presse, 1839. Second edition in 1840 entitled : Du théâtre-italien et son influence sur le goût musical français.

Overhoff, Kurt. Richard Wagners germanisch-christlicher Mythos : Einführungen in den Ring des Nibelungen und Parsifal. Dinkelsbühl/ Mittelfranken, Kronos-Verlag, [1955].

Pagani, Severino. Alfredo Catalani : Ombre e luci nella sua vita e nella sua arte. Milan, Casa Editrice Ceschina, 1957.

Pagano, Luigi. "Arrigo Boito : L' artista," RMI XXXI (1924) 199–234.

Palmer, John. "Gesture and Scenery in Modern Opera," MQ II (1916) 314–30.

Pannain, Guido. Ottocento musicale italiano : Saggi e note. Milan, Curci, [1952].

—— "Rossini nel Guglielmo Tell," RMI XXXI (1924) 473–506.

—— "Saggio sulla musica a Napoli nel secolo XIX," RMI XXXV (1928) 198–208; 331–42; XXXVI (1929) 197–210; XXXVII (1930) 231–42; XXXVIII (1931) 193–206; XXXIX (1932) 51–72.

—— "Vincenzo Bellini," RassM VIII (1935) 1–13, 100–110, 174–88, 237–44.

Pardo Pimentel, Nicolas. La opera italiana. Madrid, Aguado, 1851.

Parker, Douglas C. Bizet. London, Routledge & Kegan Paul, 1951. 2d ed.

—— "A View of Giacomo Puccini," MQ III (1917) 509–16.

Pastura, Francesco. Bellini secondo la storia. Parma, U. Guanda, 1959.

—— "Due frammenti della Beatrice di Tenda di Bellini," RassM VIII (1935) 327–34.

—— Vincenzo Bellini. Turin, Società Editrice Internazionale, 1959.

Paulig, Hans. Peter Cornelius und sein Barbier von Bagdad: Ein stilkritischer Vergleich der Originalpartitur mit der Bearbeitung von Felix Mottl. Cologne Dissertation, 1923.

Pearson, Hesketh. Gilbert and Sullivan : A Biography. New York, Harper, 1935.

Pelicelli, Nestore. "Musicisti in Parma dal 1800 al 1860," Note d'archivio XII (1935) 213–22, 317–63; XIII (1936) 180–97.

Pereira Peixoto d'Almeida Carvalhaes, Manoel. Inês de Castro : Na opera e na choregraphia italianas. Lisbon, Castro Irmão, 1908, 1915. 2 vols.

Perrino, Marcello. Nouvelle Methode de chant . . . précédé . . . de la vie de Benedetto Marcello . . . d'une notice sur les usages du théâtre en Italie. Paris, Ebrard, 1839. Originally published as : Osservazioni sul canto. Naples, Stampa reale, 1810.

Peteani, Maria von. Franz Lehar : Seine Musik, sein Leben. Vienna, London, Glocken Verlag, 1950.

Peterson-Berger, Olof Wilhelm. "The Life Problem in Wagner's Dramas," MQ II (1916) 658–68.

—— Richard Wagner als Kulturerscheinung. Leipzig, B&H, 1917. Review by R. Hohenemser, ZfMw I, 683–84.

—— "The Wagnerian Culture Synthesis," MQ VII (1921) 45–56.

Peyser, Herbert F. "*Tristan*, First-Hand," MQ XI (1925) 418–36.

Pfordten, Hermann, Freiherr von der. Carl Maria von Weber. Leipzig, Quelle & Meyer, [1918].

Pilati, Mario. "Francesco Cilèa," *Bollettino bibliografico musicale* VII, No. 6 (June, 1932) 5–13. Followed by unsigned "Bibliografia delle opere musicali di Francesco Cilèa," 14–16.

Pinetti, Gian Battista. Teatro Donizetti (già Riccardi); la stagione d'opera alla fiera d'agosto; cronistoria illustrata dal 1784 al 1936. Bergamo, Sesa, 1937.

Pirker, Max. *Die Zauberflöte*. Vienna, Wiener literarischer Anstalt, 1920.

Pizzetti, Ildebrando. "L'arte di Verdi : Spiriti e forme," RassM X (1937) 201–6.

—— "Contrappunto e armonia nell' opera di G. Verdi," RassM XXI (1951) 189–200.

—— "Il Faust della leggenda, del poemo e del dramma musicale," RMI XIII (1906) 1–49.

—— La musica di Vincenzo Bellini. Florence, La Voce, [1915?]. Also in his *La musica italiana dell' Ottocento*, 149–228.

—— La musica italiana dell' Ottocento. Turin, Edizioni Palatine, [1947].

Pizzetti, Ildebrando, ed. Vincenzo Bellini. Milan, Fratelli Treves, [1936]. Rev. ed. : Milan, Garzanti, 1940.

Pohl, Richard. "Richard Wagner," in Waldersee, *Sammlung musikalischer Vorträge* (Leipzig, B&H, 1879–98) V, 121–98.

Policastro, Guglielmo. Vincenzo Bellini. Catania, Studio editoriale moderno, 1935.

Pompée, Hélène. Peppino ou enfance et jeunesse de Giuseppe Verdi. Paris, Corrêa, [1940].

Pompei, Edoardo. Pietro Mascagni. Rome, Editrice nazionale, 1912.

Pougin, Arthur. Adolphe Adam. Paris, G. Charpentier, 1877.

—— Auber : Ses commencements, les origines de sa carrière. Paris, Pottier de Lalaine, 1873.

—— Boieldieu. Paris, Charpentier, 1875.

—— "Les Dernières Années de Spontini," RMI XXIX (1922) 54–80, 236–63.

—— F. Halévy, écrivain. Paris, A. Clauden, 1865.

—— "Gounod écrivain," RMI XVII (1910) 590–627; XVIII (1911) 747–68; XIX (1912) 239–85, 637–95; XX (1913) 453–86, 792–820.

—— Herold. Paris, H. Laurens, [1906].

—— "Massenet," RMI XIX (1912) 916–85.

—— Méhul. Paris, Fischbacher, 1893. 2d ed.

—— "Notice sur Méhul par Cherubini," RMI XVI (1909) 750–71.

Pougin, Arthur. "La première Salle Favart et l'opéra-comique 1801–1838," *Le Ménestrel* LX (1894) and LXI (1895), *passim*.

—— William-Vincent Wallace. Paris, A. Ikelmer, 1866.

Pourtalès, Guy de. Wagner : Histoire d'un artiste. Paris, Gallimard, 1942. New ed.

Presser, Diether. "Die Opernbearbeitung des 19. Jahrhunderts," AfMw XII (1955) 228–38.

Pretzsch, Paul. Die Kunst Siegfried Wagners. Leipzig, B&H, 1919.

Prod'homme, Jacques Gabriel. "Les Deux *Benvenuto Cellini* de Berlioz," SIMG XIV (1912–13) 449–60.

—— François-Joseph Gossec, 1734–1829 : La vie, les oeuvres, l'homme et l'artiste. Paris, La Colombe, 1949.

—— Gounod. Paris, Delagrave, [1911]. 2 vols.

—— "*Léonore ou l'amour conjugal*, de Bouilly et Gaveaux," SIMG VII (1905–6) 636–39.

—— "Lettres de G. Verdi à Léon Escudier," *Bulletin de la Société union musicologique* V (1925) 7–28.

—— "Lettres inédites de G. Verdi à Léon Escudier," RMI XXXV (1928) 1–28, 171–97, 519–52.

—— "Miscellaneous Letters by Charles Gounod," MQ IV (1918) 630–53.

—— "Rossini and His Works in France," MQ XVII (1931) 110–37.

—— "Une Source française de l' *Anneau du Nibelung*," RdM XXI (1942) 2–7.

—— "Spontini et Ch. Gounod," ZIMG XI (1909–10) 325–28.

—— "Unpublished Letters from Verdi to Camille du Locle," MQ VII (1921) 73–103.

—— "Wagner and the Paris Opéra : Unpublished Letters (February–March, 1861)," MQ I (1915) 216–31.

—— "Wagner, Berlioz and Monsieur Scribe : Two Collaborations That Miscarried," MQ XII (1926) 359–75.

—— "The Works of Weber in France (1824–1926)," MQ XIV (1928) 366–86.

"Prospetto cronologico delle opere di Gaetano Donizetti," RMI IV (1897) 736–43.

Prunières, Henry. "Stendhal and Rossini," MQ VII (1921) 133–55.

Puccini, Giacomo. Carteggi pucciniani. A cura di Eugenio Gara. [Milan], Ricordi, [1958].

—— Epistolario. Milan, A. Mondadori, 1928. Translated as : Letters of Giacomo Puccini. Philadelphia and London, J. B. Lippincott, 1931.

Pültz, Wilhelm. Die Geburt der deutschen Oper : Roman um Carl Maria v. Weber. Leipzig, v. Hase & Koehler, [1939].

Pugliati, Salvatore. Chopin e Bellini. Messina, Editrice Universitaria, [1952].

Rabich, Franz. Richard Wagner und die Zeit. Langensalza, Beyer, 1925.

Radiciotti, Giuseppe. "Due lettere inedite di G. Rossini e la sua definitiva partenza da Bologna," RMI XXXII (1925) 206–12.

—— "La famosa lettera al Cicognara non fu scritta dal Rossini," RMI XXX (1923) 401–7.

—— Gioacchino Rossini. Tivoli, A. Chicca, 1927. 3 vols.

—— "Primi anni e studi di Gioacchino Rossini," RMI XXIV (1917) 145–72, 418–48.

—— "Il *Signor Bruschino* ed il *Tancredi* di G. Rossini," RMI XXVII (1920) 231–66.

Radius, Emilio. Verdi vivo. Milan, Bompiani, 1951.

Raff, Joachim. Die Wagnerfrage. Brunswick, Vieweg, 1854.

Raimund, Ferdinand. Die Gesänge der Märchendramen in den urspringlichen Vertonungen. Vienna, A. Schrall, 1924. (Vol. VI of his collected works.)

Rauh, Adam. Heinrich Dorn als Opernkomponist. Neustadt a. d. Aisch, Schmidt, 1939.

Rayner, Robert Macey. Wagner and *Die Meistersinger*. London, Oxford University Press, 1940.

Rebois, Henri. La Renaissance de Bayreuth de Richard Wagner à son fils Siegfried. Paris, Fischbacher, 1933.

Refardt, Edgar. Hans Huber : Leben und Werk eines Schweizer Musikers. Zurich, Atlantis-Verlag, [1944].

Regli, Francesco. Dizionario biografico dei più celebri poeti ed artisti melodrammatici . . . in Italia dal 1800 al 1860. Turin, E. Dalmazzo, 1860.

Reiber, Kurt. Volk und Oper : Das Volkstümliche in der deutschen romantischen Oper. Würzburg, Triltsch, 1942.

Reich, Willi. "Dokument eines Gesprächs : (Zur Wiener Erstaufführung von Wolfs *Corregidor*)," *Musica* XIV (1960) 148–50.

Reicha, Antoine. Art du compositeur dramatique. Paris, A. Farrenc, 1832. 2 vols.

Reina, Calcedonio. Il cigno catanese : Bellini. Catania, "Etna," 1935.

Reipschläger, Erich. Schubaur, Danzi und Poissl als Opernkomponisten. Berlin-Mariendorf, H. Wegner, 1911.

Rellstab, Ludwig. "Die Gestaltung der Oper seit Mozart," *Die Wissenschaft im 19. Jahrhundert* II (1856) 361.

Rensis, Raffaello de. Arrigo Boito. Florence, Sansoni, 1942.

Revue Wagnérienne. Paris, 1885–88.

Reyer, i.e., Louis Etienne Ernest Rey. Notes de musique. Paris, Charpentier, 1875. 2d ed.

—— Quarante Ans de musique. Paris, Calmann Lévy, [1909].

Ricca, Vincenzo. Il centenario della *Norma:* Vincenzo Bellini. Catania, N. Gianotta, 1932.

Ricci, Luigi. Puccini interprete di se stesso. [Milan], Ricordi, [1954].

Ricci des Ferres-Cancani, Gabriella. Francesco Morlacchi (1784–1841): Un maestro italiano alla corte di Sassonia. Florence, Olschki, 1958.

Riedel, Fridolin. Richard Wagner : *Der Ring des Nibelungen*. Leipzig, Max Beck, 1942. 3d ed.

Rieger, Erwin. Offenbach und seine Wiener Schule. Vienna, Wiener literarischer Anstalt, 1920.

Riehl, Wilhelm Heinrich. Musikalische Charakterköpfe. Stuttgart, Cotta, 1899. 2 vols.

—— Zur Geschichte der romantischen Oper. Berlin, Weltgeist-Bücher, [1928].

Rinaldi, Mario. Musica e verismo. Rome, Fratelli de Santis, [1932].

—— "Valori drammatici e musicali del *Simon Boccanegra* di Verdi," RassM VIII (1935) 42–53.

—— Verdi critico : I suoi giudizi, la sua estetica. Rome, Ergo, 1951.

Rinuccini, Giovanni Battista. Sulla musica e sulla poesia melodrammatica italiana del secolo XIX. Lucca, L. Guidotti, 1843.

Robert, Paul-Louis. "Correspondance de Boieldieu," RMI XIX (1912) 75–107; XXII (1915) 520–59.

Röder, Erich. Felix Draeseke : Der Lebens- und Leidensweg eines deutschen Meisters. Dresden, W. Limpert, [1932–37]. 2 vols.

Roethe, Gustav. "Zum dramatischen Aufbau der Wagnerschen *Meistersinger*," *Akademie der Wissenschaften, Berlin: Sitzungsberichte* (Jahrgang 1919) 673–708.

Rogers, Francis. "Adolphe Nourrit," MQ XXV (1939) 11–25.

—— "Victor Maurel," MQ XII (1926) 580–601.

Rognoni, Luigi. Rossini : Con un' appendice comprendente lettere, documenti, testimonianze. [Modena], Guanda, [1956].

Rolandi, Ulderico. Quattro poeti ed un compositore alle prese . . . per un libretto d'opera (*Il bravo* di S. Mercadante). Rome, A. Marchesi, 1931.

Rolland, Romain. "*L'Etranger* de Vincent d'Indy," RMI XI (1904) 129–39.

Roncaglia, Gino. "L'abbozzo del *Rigoletto* di Verdi," RMI XLVIII (1946) 112–29.

—— L'ascensione creatrice di Giuseppe Verdi. [Florence], Sansoni, [1951].

—— L'Otello di Giuseppe Verdi. Florence, Fussi, [1946].

—— Rossini, l'olimpico. Milan, Fratelli Bocca, [1953]. 2d ed.

—— "Il 'temo-cardine' nell' opera di Giuseppe Verdi," RMI XLVII (1943) 220–29.

—— "Vincenzo Bellini, il musicista, quale appare dal suo epistolario," RMI L (1948) 159–77.

Roosevelt, Blanche. *See* Macchetta.

[Rossini, Gioacchino.] Articles in *La Rassegna musicale* XXIV, No. 3 (July–September, 1954).

Rossmayer, Richard. Konradin Kreutzer als dramatischer Komponist. Vienna Dissertation, 1928.

Royer, Louis. Bibliographie stendhalienne. Paris, Champion, 1931.

Rubsamen, Walter H. "Music and Politics in the 'Risorgimento,'" *Italian Quarterly* V (1961–62) 100–120.

Rühlmann, Franz. Richard Wagner und die deutsche Opernbuehne. Kiel Dissertation, 1925.

Rusca, Paolo. "Studi critici sul *Tristano e Isotta*," RMI XIX (1912) 286–314.

—— "Il *Tannhäuser* nella vita e nell' arte di Riccardo Wagner," RMI XXI (1914) 675–98.

Sachs, Curt. "The Road to Major," MQ XXIX (1943).

Sachs, Edwin O., and E. A. E. Woodrow. Modern Opera Houses and Theatres. London, B. T. Batsford, 1896–98. 3 vols.

St. John-Brenon, Algernon. "Giuseppe Verdi," MQ II (1916) 130–62.

Saint-Saëns, Charles Camille. Portraits et souvenirs. Paris, Société d'édition artistique, [1900]. Translated as : Musical Memoirs. Boston, Small, Maynard, [1919].

Saitschick, Robert. Götter und Menschen in Richard Wagners *Ring des Nibelungen:* Eine Lebensdeutung. Tübingen, Katzmann, [1957]. 3d ed.

Salburg, Edith, Gräfin. Ludwig Spohr. Leipzig, Koehler & Amelang, [1936].

Salerno, F. Le donne Pucciniane. Palermo, A. Trimarchi, 1929.

[Salvioli, Giovanni.] Saggio bibliografico relativo ai melodrammi di Felice Romani [per] Luigi Lianovosani [pseud.]. Milan, Ricordi, [1878].

[——] Serie cronologica delle opere teatrali, cantate, ed oratori del maestro Giovanni Comm. Pacini. Milan, Ricordi, 1875.

Sandberger, Adolf. "Rossiniana," ZIMG IX (1907–8) 336–45.

—— "Zu den literarischen Quellen von Richard Wagners *Tannhäuser*," in *Gedenkboek . . . Scheurleer* (The Hague, Nijhoff, 1925) 267–69.

Sanders, Ernest. "*Oberon* and *Zar und Zimmermann*," MQ XL (1954) 521–32.

Santi, Piero. "Senso comune e vocalità nel melodramma pucciniano," RassM XXVIII (1958) 109–21.

Sartori, Claudio. "Franco Faccio e venti anni di spettacoli di fiera al Teatro Grande di Brescia," RMI XLII (1938) 64–77, 188–203, 350–62.

—— Puccini. [Milan], Nuova Accademia Editrice, [1958].

—— "Lo *Zeffiretto* di Angelo Tarchi," RMI LVI (1954) 233–40.

Sartori, Claudio, ed. Giacomo Puccini. Milan, Ricordi, 1959.

Sassi, Ramualdo. "Lettere inedite di Gaspare Spontini," *Note d'archivio* XII (1935) 165–83.

Saussine, Henri de. "L'Harmonie Bellinienne," RMI XXVII (1920) 477–82.

Schäfer, Karl. Das Opernschaffen Siegfried Wagners. Vienna Dissertation, 1936.

Schall, Heinrich. Beiträge zur Entwicklungsgeschichte der Oper mit besonderer Berücksichtigung der deutschen in neuerer Zeit. Bonn, J. Bach, 1898.

Schemann, Ludwig. Cherubini. Stuttgart, Deutsche Verlags-Anstalt, 1925.

Schemann, Ludwig. "Cherubinis dramatisches Erstlingsschaffen," *Die Musik* XVII (June, 1925) 641–47.

Schenk, Erich. Johann Strauss. Potsdam, Athenaion, 1940.

Schiedermair, Ludwig. "Eine Autobiographie Pietro Generalis," in *Festschrift Liliencron* (Leipzig, B&H, 1910) 250–53.

—— Beiträge zur Geschichte der Oper um die Wende des 18. und 19. Jahrhunderts. Leipzig, B&H, 1907–10. 2 vols.

—— "Briefe . . . an Simon Mayr," SIMG VIII (1906–7) 615–29.

—— "*I sensali del teatro*," SIMG VI (1904–5) 589–94.

—— "Ueber Beethovens *Leonore*," ZIMG VIII (1906–7) 115–26.

—— "Ein unbekannter Opernentwurf für Beethoven," *Neues Beethoven Jahrbuch* VII (1937) 32–36.

Schletterer, Hans Michael. "Ludwig Spohr," in Waldersee, *Sammlung musikalischer Vorträge* (Leipzig, B&H, 1879–98) III, 127–62.

Schlitzer, Franco. "Curiosità epistolari inedite nella vita teatrale di G. Donizetti," RMI L (1948) 273–83.

—— L'eredità de Gaetano Donizetti: Da carteggi e documenti del l'archivio dell' Accademia Chigiana. Siena, Ticci, 1954.

—— Frammenti biografici di Gaspare Spontini con lettere inedite. Siena, [Tip. Ticci], 1955. 2 vols.

—— Inediti verdiani nell' archivio dell' Accademia Chigiana. Siena, Ticci, 1953.

—— Mondo teatrale dell' Ottocento: Episodi, testimonianze, musiche e lettere inedite. Naples, F. Fiorentino, [1954].

—— L'ultima pagina della vita di Gaetano Donizetti, da un carteggio inedito dell' Accademia Chigiana. Siena, [Ticci], 1953.

Schmid, Otto. Carl Maria von Weber und seine Opern in Dresden. [Dresden?, Selbstverlag des Verfassers, 1922.]

—— Richard Wagner: Gedanken über seine Ideale und seine Sendung. Langensalza, Beyer, 1920.

Schmidt, Friedrich. Das Musikleben der bürgerlichen Gesellschaft Leipzigs im Vormärz (1815–1848). Langensalza, Beyer, 1912.

Schmidt, Leopold. Zur Geschichte der Märchenoper. Halle an der Saale, O. Hendel, 1895.

Schmidt, Ludwig. "Briefe von und über Carl Maria von Weber," ZIMG III (1901–2) 93–99.

Schmieder, Wolfgang. "Lortzing privat: Drei unveröffentlichte Briefe des Meisters," M V (1951) 7–12.

Schmitz, Eugen. "Louis Spohr's Jugendoper *Alruna*," ZIMG XIII (1911–12) 293–99.

—— "Zur Geschichte des Leitmotivs in der romantischen Oper," *Hochland* IV, No. 2 (1907) 329–43.

Schnapp, Friedrich. "E. T. A. Hoffmanns letzte Oper," SchwM LXXXVIII (1948) 339–45.

—— "Robert Schumann's Plan for a Tristan-Opera," MQ X (1924) 485–91.

Schneider, Louis. Hervé. Charles Lecocq. Paris, Perrin, 1924.

—— Massenet. Paris, L. Carteret, 1908. Revised ed., without illustrations and documents, Paris, Charpentier, 1926.

—— Offenbach. Paris, Perrin, 1923.

Schnoor, Hans. Weber auf dem Welttheater : Ein Freischützbuch. Dresden, Deutscher Literatur-Verlag Otto Melchert, 1942.

—— Weber : Gestalt und Schöpfung. Dresden, VEB Verlag der Kunst, 1953.

Scholes, Percy A. The Mirror of Music, 1844–1944 : A Century of Musical Life in Britain as Reflected in the Pages of the Musical Times. London, Novello & Co., Ltd., and Oxford University Press, 1947. 2 vols.

Scholz, Hans. "Hektor Berlioz zum 50. Todestage," ZfMw I (1918–19) 328–51.

Schopenhauer, Arthur. Sämmtliche Werke. Leipzig, Brockhaus, 1922–23. 6 vols.

Schubert, Karl. Spontinis italienische Schule. Strasbourg, Heitz, [1932].

Schünemann, Georg. "Mendelssohns Jugendopern," ZfMw V (1922–23) 506–45.

—— "Eine neue Tristan-Handschrift zu Richard Wagners 125. Geburtstag," AfMf III (1938) 129–37.

Schuller, Kenneth Gustave. Verismo Opera and the Verists. Washington University Dissertation, 1960.

Segnitz, Eugen. "Anselmo Feuerbach e Riccardo Wagner," RMI XIII (1906) 437–50.

—— "La musica nel romanticismo tedesco," RMI XV (1908) 500–18.

Selden, Margery Stomne. "Napoleon and Cherubini," JAMS VIII (1955) 110–15.

—— See also Stomne, Margery.

Serafin, Tullio, and Alceo Toni. Stile, tradizioni e convenzioni del melodramma italiano del Settecento e dell' Ottocento. [Milan], Ricordi, [1958].

Serauky, Walter. "Die Todesverkündigungsszene in Richard Wagners Walküre als musikalisch-geistige Achse des Werkes," Mf XII (1959) 143–51.

Servières, Georges. La Musique française moderne. Paris, G. Havard, 1897.

—— "Le 'Wagnerisme' de C. Saint-Saëns," RMI XXX (1923) 223–44.

Shaw, George Bernard. The Perfect Wagnerite. New York, Brentano's, 1909.

Shedlock, J. S. "The Correspondence between Wagner and Liszt," PMA XIV (1888) 119–43.

Simon, James. Faust in der Musik. Leipzig, C. F. W. Siegel, [1906].

Sincero, Dino. "Da Tannhäuser a Parsifal," RMI XXI (1914) 122–26.

Sittard, Josef. "Gioachimo Antonio Rossini," in Waldersee, *Sammlung musikalischer Vorträge* (Leipzig, B&H, 1879–98) IV, 385–433.

Slanina, Ernst Alfred. Die Sakralszenen der deutschen Oper des frühen 19. Jahrhunderts. Bochum-Langendreer, Pöppinghaus, 1935.

Slawik, Friedrich. Die Jugendopern Richard Wagners und ihre Beziehungen zu den späteren Meisterwerken. Vienna Dissertation, 1928.

Smareglia, Ariberto. Vita ed arte di Antonio Smareglia. [Lugano, C. Mazzuconi, 1932.]

Smareglia, Mario, compiler. Antonio Smareglia nella storia del teatro melodrammatico italiano dell' Ottocento attraverso critiche e scritti raccolti da Mario Smareglia. Pola, Smareglia, [1934].

Solar Quintes, Nicolás A. "Saverio Mercadante en España y Portugal," *Anuario musical* VII (1952) 201–8.

Somiglio, Carlo. "Del teatro reale d'opera in Monaco di Baviera e del suo repertorio," RMI V (1898) 721–53.

Sonneck, Oscar George Theodore. "Heinrich Heine's Musical Feuilletons," MQ VIII (1923) 119–59, 273–95, 435–68.

Soubies, Albert. Histoire de l'opéra-comique : La seconde Salle Favart, 1840–[1887]. Paris, E. Flammarion, 1892–93. 2 vols.

—— Histoire du théâtre-lyrique, 1851–1870. Paris, Fischbacher, 1899.

—— Le Théâtre-italien de 1801 à 1913. Paris, Fischbacher, 1913.

Soubies, Albert, and Henri de Curzon. Documents inédits sur le *Faust* de Gounod. Paris, Fischbacher, 1912.

Specht, Richard. E. N. v. Reznicek. Leipzig, E. P. Tal, 1923.

—— Giacomo Puccini. Berlin-Schöneberg, M. Hesse, [1931]. English translation : New York, Alfred A. Knopf, 1933.

—— Julius Bittner. Munich, Drei Masken, 1921.

Spencer, H. "Meyerbeer," RMI X (1903) 126–28.

Spinner, Leopold. Das Rezitativ in der romantischen Oper bis Wagner. Vienna Dissertation, 1931.

Spitta, Philipp. "Die älteste Faust-Oper und Goethe's Stellung zur Musik," in his *Zur Musik* (Berlin, Paetel, 1892) 199–234.

—— "Jessonda," in his *Zur Musik* (Berlin, Paetel, 1892) 237–66.

Spohr, Louis. Louis Spohr's Selbstbiographie. Kassel and Göttingen, Wigand, 1860–61. 2 vols. English translation : London, Reeves & Turner, 1878. New German ed. : Kassel & Basel, Bärenreiter, 1954–55. 2 vols.

Spontini, G. "Lettere inedite," *Note d'archivio* IX (1932) 23–40.

Stebbins, Lucy Poate, and Richard Poate Stebbins. Enchanted Wanderer: The Life of Carl Maria von Weber. New York, G. P. Putnam, [1940].

Stefan, Paul. Das neue Haus : Ein Halbjahrhundert Wiener-Opernspiel und was voranging. Vienna and Leipzig, E. Strache, 1919.

Stefan-Gruenfeldt, Paul. Georges Bizet. Zurich, Atlantis-Verlag, [1952].

Stefani, Giuseppe. Verdi e Trieste. Trieste, Il Comune, 1951.

Steglich, Rudolf. "Das melodische Hauptmotiv in Beethovens *Fidelio*," AfMw IX (1952) 51–67.

Steigman, B. M. " 'Nicht mehr Tristan,' " MQ VII (1921) 57–67.

Stein, Jack M. Richard Wagner and the Synthesis of the Arts. Detroit, Wayne State University Press, 1960.

Stein, Leon. The Racial Thinking of Richard Wagner. New York, Philosophical Library, [1950].

Stendhal, pseud. *See* Beyle, Henri.

Stier-Somlo, Helene. Das Grimmsche Märchen als Text für Opern und Spiele. Berlin and Leipzig, de Gruyter, 1926.

Stock, · Richard Wilhelm. Richard Wagner und seine Meistersinger. Nuremberg, Verlag Karl Ulrich & Co., 1938.

Stomne, Margery. The French Operas of Luigi Cherubini. Yale Dissertation, 1951.

Stoullig, E. Les Annales du théâtre et de la musique. Paris, Ollendorf, 1899.

Strecker, Ludwig. Richard Wagner als Verlagsgefährte : Eine Darstellung mit Briefen und Dokumenten. Mainz, B. Schott's Söhne, 1951.

Strelitzer, Hugo. Meyerbeers deutsche Jugend-Opern. Münster Dissertation, 1922.

Strobel, Heinrich. "Die Opern von E. N. Méhul," ZfMw VI (1923–24) 362–402.

Strobel, Otto. Richard Wagner. Leben und Schaffen. Eine Zeittafel. Bayreuth, Verlag der Festspielleitung, 1952.

Sullivan, Herbert, and Newman Flower. Sir Arthur Sullivan : His Life, Letters & Diaries. London, Cassell & Co., [1950]. New and rev. ed.

Tabanelli, Nicola. "Oriani e la musica," RMI XLII (1938) 325–43, 495–505.

Tebaldini, Giovanni. "Giuseppe Persiani e Fanny Tacchinardi : Memorie ed appunti," RMI XII (1905) 579–91.

Teneo, Martial. "Le Chevalier de Malte ou la reine de Chypre," ZIMG VIII (1906–7) 352–54.

—— "Jacques Offenbach d'après des documents inédits," MM VII, No. 12 (1911) 1–35.

—— "Jacques Offenbach : His Centenary," MQ VI (1920) 98–117.

—— "Pierre Montan Berton," RHCM VIII (1908) 389–97, 416–24, 493.

Thayer, Alexander Wheelock. The Life of Ludwig van Beethoven. Ed. by H. E. Krehbiel. New York, The Beethoven Association, [1921].

Thiess, Frank. Puccini : Versuch einer Psychologie seiner Musik. Vienna, P. Zsolnay, 1947.

Thomas of Britain. The Romance of Tristram and Ysolt. *See* Loomis, Roger Sherman, ed.

Thomas, Eugen. Die Instrumentation der *Meistersinger von Nürnberg* von Richard Wagner. Vienna, Universal, [1907]. 2 vols. 2d ed.

Thompson, Herbert. Wagner and Wagenseil. London, Oxford University Press, 1927.

Thompson, Oscar. "If Beethoven Had Written *Faust*," MQ X (1924) 13–20.

Tiersot, Julien. "Auber," RM XIV (November, 1933) 265–78.

—— "Bizet and Spanish Music," MQ XIII (1927) 566–81.

—— "Charles Gounod : A Centennial Tribute," MQ IV (1918) 409–39.

—— Un Demi-siècle de musique française. Paris, Alcan, 1918.

—— "Gounod's Letters," MQ V (1919) 40–61.

—— "Hector Berlioz and Richard Wagner," MQ III (1917) 453–92.

Till, Theodor. Die Entwicklung der musikalischen Form in Richard Wagners Opern und Musikdramen, von der Ouvertüre (Vorspiel) und deren Funktionsvertretern aus betrachtet. Vienna Dissertation, 1930.

Tommasini, Vincenzo. "L'opera di Riccardo Wagner e la sua importanza nella storia dell' arte e delle cultura," RMI IX (1902) 113–47, 422–41, 694–716.

Torchi, Luigi. "*Consuelo* di A. Rendano," RMI X (1903) 564–80.

—— "*Germania*, dramma lirico in un prologo, due quadri ed un epilogo di Luigi Illica. Musica di Alberto Franchetti," RMI IX (1902) 377–421.

—— "*Guglielmo Ratcliff* . . . di Pietro Mascagni," RMI II (1895) 287–311.

—— "*Iris* . . . di Pietro Mascagni," RMI VI (1899) 71–118.

—— "*Oceana* di A. Smareglia," RMI X (1903) 309–66.

—— "L'opera di Giuseppe Verdi e i suoi caratteri principali," RMI VIII (1901) 279–325.

—— "R. Schumann e le sue 'Scene tratte dal *Faust* di Goethe,'" RMI II (1895) 381–419, 629–65.

—— "The Realistic Italian Operas," in *Famous Composers and Their Works, New Series* (Boston, J. B. Millet, [1900]) I, 183.

—— "Studi di orchestrazione : L' *Anello del Nibelunge* di Riccardo Wagner," RMI XX (1913) 347–53; XXI (1914) 509–12, 768–75.

—— "*Tosca*, di G. Puccini," RMI VII (1900) 78–114.

Torrefranca, Fausto. "Arrigo Boito," MQ VI (1920) 532–52.

Torri, Luigi. "Saggio di bibliografia verdiana," RMI VIII (1901) 379–407.

Tovey, Donald Francis. "Dungeon Scene from *Fidelio*," in *Essays in Musical Analysis. V : Vocal Music* (London, Oxford University Press, 1937) 185–93.

Toye, Francis. Giuseppe Verdi. London, W. Heinemann; New York, Alfred A. Knopf, 1931.

—— Rossini : A Study in Tragi-Comedy. London, Barker, [1954]. New ed.

—— "Verdi," PMA LVI (1929–30) 37–53.

Unger, Max. "Beethoven und das Wiener Hoftheater im Jahre 1807," *Neues Beethoven Jahrbuch* II (1925) 76–83.

—— Ein Faustopernplan Beethovens und Goethes. Regensburg, G. Bosse, [1952].

Unterholzner, Ludwig. Giuseppe Verdis Opern-typus. Hanover, A. Madsack, [1933].

Vajro, Massimiliano. Arrigo Boito. Brescia, La Scuola, [1955].

Valentin, Caroline. " 'Ach wie ist's möglich dann' von H. von Chézy und seine erste Melodie," in Festschrift Liliencron (Leipzig, B&H, 1910) 358–86.

Valentin, Erich. Hans Sommer : Weg, Werk und Tat eines deutschen Meisters. Brunswick, H. Litolff, 1939.

Vallas, Léon. "The Discovery of Musical Germany by Vincent d'Indy in 1873," MQ XXV (1939) 176–94.

—— La Véritable Histoire de César Franck (1822–1890). Paris, Flammarion, [1955]. Translated as : César Franck. London, Harrap; New York, Oxford University Press, 1951.

—— Vincent d'Indy. Paris, Editions Albin Michel, [1946–50]. 2 vols.

Van Vechten, Carl. "Back to Delibes," MQ VIII (1922) 605–10.

—— "Shall We Realize Wagner's Ideals?" MQ II (1916) 387–401.

Vautier, Gabriel. "Le Jury de lecture et l'opéra sous la restauration," RHCM X (1910) 13–25, 44–49, 75–78.

Verdi : Bolletino quadrimestrale dell' Istituto di Studi Verdiani. Parma-Busseto. Vol. I (1960). Articles on Un ballo in maschera, with bibliography.

[Verdi, Giuseppe.] Comitato nazionale per le onoranze a Giuseppe Verdi nel cinquantenario della morte. Mostra degli autografi musicali di Giuseppe Verdi. Ridotto del Teatro alla Scala. [Milan, Unione Tipografica, 1951.]

—— I copialettere. [Milan, Stucchi Ceretti, 1913.] Ed. by G. Cesari and A. Luzio, preface by M. Scherillo.

[——] Giuseppe Verdi. Scritti di S. A. M. Bottenheim, Matteo Glinski, Augusto Hermet, Dyneley Hussey, Pierre Petit, Ulderico Rolandi, Franco Schlitzer, Bence Szabolcsi, Albert van der Linden, Frank Walker; raccolti in occasione delle Celebrazione Verdiane . . . 1951. Siena, Ticci, [Printed for the Accademia Musicale Chigiana], 1951.

Viardot-Garcia, Pauline. "Pauline Viardot-Garcia to Julius Rietz (Letters of Friendship)," MQ I (1915) 350–80, 526–59; II (1916) 32–60.

Vetter, Walther. "Richard Wagner und die Griechen," Mf VI (1953) 111–26.

Vienna. Internationale Ausstellung für Musik- und Theaterwesen, 1892. Fach-Katalog der Abtheilung des Königreiches Italien. Vienna, [J. N. Vernoy], 1892.

Viereck, Peter. Metapolitics from the Romantics to Hitler. New York, Alfred A. Knopf, 1941.

Viotta, H. A. "Richard Wagner's verhouding tot die muziekgeschiedenis," in Gedenkboek . . . Scheurleer (The Hague, Nijhoff, 1925) 359–65.

Visetti, Albert. "Tendencies on the Operatic Stage in the Nineteenth Century," PMA XXII (1896) 141–51.

Vittadini, Stefano. Il primo libretto del *Mefistofele* di Arrigo Boito. Milan, Gli amici del museo teatrale alla scala, 1938.

Vlad, Roman. "Anticipazioni nel linguaggio armonico verdiano," RassM XXI (1951) 237–46.

Wagner, Richard. Briefe in Originalausgaben. Leipzig, B&H, [1911–13]. 17 vols.

—— Gesammelte Schriften und Dichtungen. Leipzig, B&H, n.d. 12 vols. 5th ed.

—— Letters : The Burrell Collection, Edited with Notes by John N. Burk. New York, Macmillan, 1950. See also review by Thomas Mann in his *Altes und Neues* (Frankfurt/M., S. Fischer Verlag, 1953) 575–86.

—— Mein Leben : Volks-Ausgabe. Munich, Bruckmann, 1914.

—— Opera and Drama. New York, C. Scribner; London, W. Reeves, [1913]. Translated by Edwin Evans.

Wagner, Siegfried. Erinnerungen. Stuttgart, J. Engelhorn, 1923.

Wahl, Eduard. Nicolo Isouard. Munich, C. Wolf, 1906.

Wahle, Werner. Richard Wagners szenische Visionen und ihre Ausführung im Bühnenbild. Munich Dissertation, 1937.

Waldersee, Paul. "Robert Schumann's *Manfred*," in Waldersee, *Sammlung musikalischer Vorträge* (Leipzig, B&H, 1879–98) II, 1–20.

Walker, Frank. "Donizetti, Verdi and Mme. Appiani," M&L XXXII (1951) 1–18.

—— Hugo Wolf, a Biography. London, Dent, [1951]; New York, Alfred A. Knopf, 1952.

—— "The Librettist of *Don Pasquale*," MMR LXXXVIII (1958) 219–23.

—— The Man Verdi. New York, Alfred A. Knopf, 1962.

—— "Mercadante and Verdi," M&L XXXIII (1952) 311–21; XXXIV (1953) 33–38.

—— "Verdi's Ideas on the Production of His Shakespearean Operas," PMA LXXVI (1951) 11–21.

Wallner, Bertha Antonia. "Fidelio in Gotik und Barock," *Neues Beethoven-Jahrbuch* X (1942) 78–103.

Waltershausen, Hermann Wolfgang Karl Sartorius, Freiherr (von). Der Freischütz : Ein Versuch über die musikalische Romantik. Munich, Bruckmann, 1920.

—— Das Siegfried-Idyll, oder, Die Rückkehr zur Natur. Munich, H. Bruckmann, 1920.

—— "Zur Dramaturgie des *Fidelio*," Neues Beethoven Jahrbuch I (1924) 142–58.

Wassermann, Rudolf. Ludwig Spohr als Opernkomponist. Munich, Huber, 1909.

Weber, Carl Maria, Freiherr von. Sämtliche Schriften, ed. Georg Kaiser. Berlin and Leipzig, Schuster & Loeffler, 1908.

Weber, Max Maria von. Carl Maria von Weber. Leipzig, E. Keil, 1864–66. 3 vols.

Weingartner, Felix. Bayreuth (1876–1896). Leipzig, B&H, 1904.

—— Lebenserinnerungen. Zurich and Leipzig, Orell Füssli, [1928–29]. 2 vols. Translated as : Buffets and Rewards. London, Hutchinson, [1937].

—— Die Lehre von der Wiedergeburt des musikalischen Dramas. Kiel and Leipzig, Lipsius & Fischer, 1895.

Weinstock, Herbert. Donizetti and the World of Opera in Italy, Paris, and Vienna in the First Half of the Nineteenth Century. New York, Pantheon Books, [1963].

Weissmann, Adolph. "Richard Wagner : Constructive and Destructive," MQ XI (1925) 138–56.

Werfel, Franz. Verdi : Roman der Oper. Berlin, Zsolnay, [1924]. Translated as : Verdi : A Novel of the Opera. New York, Simon & Schuster, 1926.

—— Verdi : The Man in His Letters. New York, L. B. Fischer, [1942]. Edited by Franz Werfel and Paul Stefan, translated by Edward Downes.

Werneck-Brueggemann, Fritz. Ueber E. T. A. Hoffmanns Oper *Aurora:* Anlässlich der 3. Funk-Aufführung. Rudolstadt, Edda-Verlag, 1936.

Westernhagen, Curt von. Richard Wagner : Sein Werk, sein Wesen, sein Welt. [Zurich], Atlantis-Verlag, [1956].

—— Vom Holländer zum Parsifal : Neue Wagner-Studien. [Freiburg i. Br. and Zurich], Atlantis-Verlag, [1962].

White, Terence. "The Last Scene of Götterdämmerung : A New Production," M&L XVII (1936) 62–64.

Wiessner, Georg Gustav. Richard Wagner, der Theater-Reformer vom Werden des deutschen Nationaltheaters im Geiste des Jahres 1848. Emsdetten (Westf.), Lechte, 1951.

Williamson, Audrey. Gilbert & Sullivan Opera : A New Assessment. London, Rockliff, 1955. 2d ed.

Wimmersdorf, W. Oper oder Drama? Die Notwendigkeit des Niederganges der Oper. Rostock i. M., C. J. E. Volckmann, 1905.

Winternitz, Giorgio F. "I cimeli belliniani della R. Academia Filarmonica di Bologna," RMI XL (1936) 104–18.

Wirth, Helmut. "Natur und Märchen in Webers *Oberon,* Mendelssohns *Ein Sommernachtstraum* und Nicolais *Die lustigen Weiber von Windsor,*" in *Festschrift Friedrich Blume* (Kassel, Bärenreiter, 1963) [389]–397.

Wörner, Karl. "Beiträge zur Geschichte des Leitmotivs in der Oper [Teil I]," ZfMw XIV (1931–32) 151–72.

—— Beiträge zur Geschichte des Leitmotivs in der Oper (Teil 2, 3). Bayreuth, Ellwanger, 1932.

—— Robert Schumann. [Zurich], Atlantis-Verlag, [1949].

Wolzogen, Alfred von. Ueber Theater und Musik : Historisch-kritische Studien. Breslau, Trewendt, 1860.

—— "Wagners *Siegfried,*" in Waldersee, *Sammlung musikalischer Vorträge* (Leipzig, B&H, 1879–98) I, 59–80.

Wolzogen und Neuhaus, Hans Paul, Freiherr von. Lebensbilder. Regensburg, Bosse, [1923].

—— Thematischer Leitfaden durch die Musik zu Richard Wagners Festspiel *Der Ring des Nibelungen*. Leipzig, E. Schloemp, 1876.

Würz, Anton. Franz Lachner als dramatischer Komponist. Munich, Knorr & Hirth, 1928.

Zademack, Franz. Die Meistersinger von Nürnberg : Richard Wagners Dichtung und ihre Quellen. Berlin, Dom-Verlag, 1921.

Zadig (pseud.?). "Ludovic Halévy," *Revue politique et littéraire* (1899) No. 2, p. 705.

Zambiasi, G. "Le date (a proposito de G. Verdi) : Bibliografia," RMI VIII (1901) 408–12.

Zavadini, Guido. Donizetti : Vita, musiche, epistolario. Bergamo, Istituto Italiano d'Arti Grafiche, 1948.

Zoref, Fritz. Wesen und Entwicklung des musikalischen Erinnerungsgedankens in der deutschen romantischen Oper. Vienna Dissertation, 1919.

Zur Nedden, Otto. Die Opern und Oratorien Felix Draesekes. Marburg Dissertation, 1926.

# VI

## *NINETEETH CENTURY*

### B. NATIONALISM

Abascal Brunet, Manuel. Apuntes para la historia del teatro en Chile : La zarzuela grande. Santiago de Chile, Imprenta universitaria, 1940–51. 2 vols.

Abascal Brunet, Manuel, and Eugenio Pereira Salas. Pepe Vila : La Zarzuela chica en Chile. Santiago de Chile, Imprenta universitaria, 1952.

Abraham, Gerald. Borodin, the Composer and His Music. London, Wm. Reeves, [1927].

—— "The Genesis of *The Bartered Bride*," M&L XXVIII (1947) 36–49.

—— "Moussorgsky's *Boris* and Pushkin's," M&L XXVI (1945) 31–38.

—— On Russian Music. New York, Scribner, 1939.

—— "*Prince Igor:* An Experiment in Lyrical Opera," MQ XVII (1931) 74–83.

—— Rimsky-Korsakov. London, Gerald Duckworth, [1949].

—— Studies in Russian Music. New York, Scribner, 1936.

—— *See also* Calvocoressi.

Abraham, Gerald, ed. Tchaikovsky : A Symposium. London, Lindsay Drummond, 1945.

Ábrányi, Kormél. Erkel Ferenc élete és müködése. Budapest, 1895.

Acquarone, Francisco. História da música brasileira. Rio de Janeiro, Editora Paulo de Azevedo Ltda., [n. d.].

Adaiewsky, E. "Glinka : Etudes analytiques," RMI XI (1904) 725–60; XVII (1910) 113–29.

Adorján, Andor. "L'Opérette hongroise," *Revue de Hongrie* VI (1910) 269–80.

Akademiia Nauk SSSR. Institut istorii iskusstv. Istoriia russkoĭ sovetskoĭ muzyki. Moscow, Muzgiz, 1956–59. 3 vols.; vol. 4 in preparation.

—— Institut istorii iskusstv. Pamiati Glinki, 1857–1957 : Issledovaniia i materialy. Moscow, Akademiia Nauk, 1958.

Alarcón, Esperanza. "La ópera en México, sus comienzos y los mexicanos autores de óperas," *Boletín del instituto mexicano de musicología y folklore* I (1940) 5–9.

Almeida, Renato. História da música brasileira. Rio de Janeiro, F. Briguiet, 1942. 2d ed.

Al'shvang, Arnol'd Aleksandrovich. P. I. Chaĭkovskiĭ. Moscow, Gos. muzykal'noe izd-vo, 1959.

Andrade, Mário de. Carlos Gomez. Rio de Janeiro, Pongetti, 1939.

Arkhymovych, Lidiia Borysivna. Ukraïns'ka klasychna opera. Kiev, Derzh. vyd-vo obrazotvorchoho mystetstva i muzychnoï lit-ry, 1957.

Armitage, Merle. George Gershwin, Man and Legend. New York, Duell, Sloan & Pearce, [1958].

Asaf'ev, Boris Vladimirovich. Izbrannye trudy. Moscow, Akademiia Nauk SSSR, 1952–54. 5 vols. (Vol. 1 : Glinka; Vol. 2 : Tchaikovsky, Rubinstein, Rachmaninov, Dargomyshsky, Serov, . . . ; Vol. 3 : The "Mighty Five"; Vol. 4 : On Russian Musical Culture; Vol. 5 : On Soviet Music.)

—— Russkaia muzyka ot nachala XIX stoletiia. Moscow-Leningrad, Akademiia Nauk SSSR, 1930. Translated as : Russian Music from the Beginning of the 19th Century. Ann Arbor, J. W. Edwards, [1953].

Ayesterán, Lauro. Crónica de una temporada musical en el Montevideo de 1830. Montevideo, Ediciones Ceibo, 1943.

Badalbeĭli, Afrasiiab. Azerbaĭdzhanskiĭ gosudarstvennyĭ ordena Lenina teatr opery i baleta im. M. F. Akhundova : Kratkiĭ ocherk. Moscow, 1959.

Barros Sierra, José. "*Tata Vasco* y su partitura," *Romance* II, No. 23 (April [1941]).

Batka, Richard. Aus der Opernwelt : Prager Kritiken und Skizzen. Munich, Callwey, 1907.

Béha, Paul-Emile. "De l'inédit sur l'édition originale de *Boris Godounof*," SchwM XCVIII (1958) 200–202.

Beliaev, Viktor Mikhaĭlovich. Musorgsky's *Boris Godunov* and Its New Version. London, Oxford University Press, 1928.

Benestad, Finn. Waldemar Thrane : En Pionér i norsk Musikliv. Oslo, Universitetsforlag, 1961.

Berkov, Pavel Naumovich, ed. Russkaia komediia i komicheskaia opera XVIII veka. Moscow, Iskusstvo, 1950.

Berliand-Chernaia, E. S. Pushkin i Chaĭkovskiĭ. [Moscow], Muzgiz, 1950.

Bernacki, Ludwik. Teatr, dramat i muzyka za Stanisława Augusta. Lvov, Zakład Narodowy imienia Ossolińskich, 1925. 2 vols.

Bernandt, Grigoriĭ Borisovich. Slovar' oper. Moscow, Sovetskiĭ Kompozitor, 1962.

Bernstein, Nikolaĭ Davidovich. Russland's Theater und Musik zur Zeit Peters des Grossen. Riga, Giżycki; Leipzig, Pabst, [1904].

Bertensson, Serge. "Ludmila Ivanovna Shestakova—Handmaid to Russian Music," MQ XXXI (1945) 331–38.

Bilbao, José. Teatro Real : Recuerdos de las cinco temporadas del empresario Arana. Madrid, Editorial Norma, 1936.

Blockx, Frank. Jan Blockx, 1851–1912. Brussels, Uitgeversmij. A. Manteau, [1943].

Boelza, Igor' Fedorovich. Cheshskaia opernaia klassika. Moscow, Iskusstvo, 1951.

Boelza, Igor' Fedorovich, ed. S. V. Rakhmaninov i russkaia opera : Sbornik stateĭ. Moscow, Vserossiĭskoe Teatral'noe Obshchestvo, 1947.

Boladeres Ibern, Guillermo de. Enrique Granados. Barcelona, Editorial Arte y letras, [1921].

Bónis, Ferenc. Mosonyi Mihály. Budapest, 1960.

Borren, Charles van den. Peter Benoit. Antwerp, De Nederlandsche Boekhandel, 1943.

Bosch, Mariano. Historia de la ópera en Buenos Aires. Buenos Aires, El Comercio, 1905.

Bottenheim, S. A. M. De Opera in Nederland. Amsterdam, P. N. Van Kampen & Zoon, 1946.

Bowen, Catherine D. Free Artist. New York, Random House, [1939].

Bowen, Catherine D., and Barbara von Meck. "Beloved Friend." New York, Random House, 1937.

Brabec, Ernst. Richard Wagner und Friedrich Smetana. Prague Dissertation, 1937.

Braga, Theophilo. Historia do theatro portuguez [Vol. III] : A baixa comedia e a opera, secolo XVIII. Oporto, Impr. portugueza-editora, 1870–71.

Braudo, Evgeniĭ Maksimovich. "Concerts, Opera, Ballet in Russia Today," MMus X, No. 4 (May–June, 1933) 213–19.

—— "The Russian Panorama," MMus X, No. 2 (January–February, 1933) 79–86.

Bravo, F. Suarez. "La Musique à Barcelone : Los Pireneos de F. Pedrell," ZIMG III (1901–2) 231–39.

Brazil. Ministerio da educação e saude. Relação das opéras de autores brasileiros por Luiz Heitor Corrêa de Azevedo. Rio de Janeiro, Serviço gráfico do Ministerio da educação e saude, 1938.

Broeckx, Jan L. Lodewijk Mortelmans. Antwerp, Uitgeversmij. N. v. Standaard-Boekhandel, 1945.

Calvocoressi, Michel D. "Boris Goudonov," MM IV (1908) 61–78.

—— Glinka. Paris, H. Laurens, [1911?].

—— "Le Mariage, par Moussorgsky," MM IV (1908) 1284–90.

—— Modest Mussorgsky : His Life and Works. Fair Lawn, N.J., Essential Books, 1956.

—— "Moussorgsky's Musical Style," MQ XVIII (1932) 530–46.

—— "L'orchestrazione autentica dal *Boris Godunof*," RassM I (1928) 633–39.

—— "La vera *Kovanscina* di Mussorgski," RassM V (1932) 166–75.

—— "Il vero e completo *Boris Godunof*," RassM I (1928) 217–25.

Calvocoressi, Michel D., and Gerald Abraham. Masters of Russian Music. New York, Alfred A. Knopf, 1936.

Carlberg, Bertil. Peterson-Berger. Stockholm, Bonnier, [1950].

Carlsen, Irina Margaret. A Russian Opera Reader. Vancouver, B.C., [Dept. of Slavonic Studies, University of British Columbia], 1956.

Carson, Wm. G. B. St. Louis Goes to the Opera, 1837–1941. St. Louis, The Missouri Historical Society, 1946.

Cernicchiaro, Vincenzo. Storia della musica nel Brasile dai tempi coloniali sino ai nostri giorni. Milan, Fratelli Riccioni, 1926.

Chaĭkovskiĭ, Modest Il'ich. The Life and Letters of Peter Ilich Tchaikovsky. London, J. Lane, 1906. Ed. from the Russian by Rosa Newmarch.

Chaĭkovskiĭ, Petr Il'ich. Diaries : Translated from the Russian with Notes by Wladimir Lakond [pseud.]. New York, W. W. Norton, 1945.

Chase, Gilbert. America's Music, from the Pilgrims to the Present. New York, Toronto, London, McGraw-Hill Book Co., [1954].

—— A Guide to the Music of Latin America, 2d ed., revised and enlarged. Washington, Pan American Union, 1962.

—— The Music of Spain. New York, Dover Publications, [1958]. 2d ed.

—— "Origins of the Lyric Theater in Spain," MQ XXV (1939) 292–305.

—— "Some Notes on Afro-Cuban Music and Dancing," *Inter-American Monthly* I, No. 8 (December, 1942) 32–33.

Cheshikhin, Vsevolod. Istoriia russkoĭ opery (1674–1903). St. Petersburg, Jurgenson, 1905.

Chybiński, A. "Zygmunt Noskowski," *Przegląd Powszechny* CIV (1909) 130–36.

Clapham, John. "The Operas of Antonín Dvořák," PMA LXXXIV (1957–58) 55–69.

Closson, Ernest, and Charles Van den Borren, eds. La Musique en Belgique du Moyen Age à nos jours. Brussels, La Renaissance du Livre, [1950].

Collet, Henri. Albeniz et Granados. Paris, Librairie Plon, 1948. New ed.

Cooper, Martin. Russian Opera. London, Max Parrish & Co., [1951].

Corbet, August, ed. De vlaamse Muziek sedert Benoit. Met de medewerking van F. van der Mueren, [and others]. Antwerp, Vlaams Economisch Verbond, 1951.

Corrêa de Azevedo, L. H. "Carlos Gomes : Sua verdadeira posição no quadro da ópera italiana no sec. XIX e na evolução da musica brasileira," *Boletin latino-americano de música* III (1937) 83–87.

Corrêa de Azevedo, L. H. 150 anos de música no Brasil (1800–1950). Rio de Janeiro, Libraria José Olympio, 1956.

Cowen, Sir Frederic Hymen. My Art and My Friends. London, E. Arnold, 1913.

Cui, César. Izbrannye stat'i. Leningrad, Gos. muzykal'noe izd-vo, 1952.

—— La Musique en Russie. Paris, Fischbacher, 1880.

Curzon, Henri de. Felipe Pedrell et *Les Pyrénées*. Paris, Fischbacher, 1902.

Cvetko, Dragotin. Davorin Jenko : Doba, življenje, delo. Ljubljana, Slovenski knjižni zavod, 1955.

Czerwiński, B. "Henryk Jarecki," EMTA (1886) 31–32, 34–37.

Dale, William H. A Study of the Musico-Psychological Dramas of Vladimir Ivanovich Rebikov. University of Southern California Dissertation, 1955.

Damrosch, Walter. My Musical Life. New York, Scribner, 1923.

David, Ernest. Les Opéras du juif Antonio José da Silva. Paris, A. Wittersheim, 1880.

Davis, Ronald L. A History of Resident Opera in the American West. Ann Arbor, University Microfilms, 1961.

Dianin, Sergeĭ Aleksandrovich. Borodin : Zhizneopisanie, materialy i dokumenty. Moscow, Gos. muzykal'noe izd-vo, 1960. 2d ed.

Dieckmann, Karin. *Die Braut von Messina* auf der Bühne im Wandel der Zeit. Helsingfors Dissertation, 1935.

Dmitriev, A. N. Muzykal'naia dramaturgiia orkestra M. I. Glinki. Leningrad, 1957.

Dobronić, A. "A Study of Jugoslav Music," MQ XII (1926) 56–71.

Dolleris, Ludwig. Carl Nielsen, en Musikografi. Odense, Fyns Boghandels Forlag, 1949.

Dovzhenko, Valerian D. Narysy z istorii ukraïns'koï radians'koï muzyky. Kiev, Derzh. vid-vo obrazotvorchoho mystetstva i muz. lit-ry URSR, 1957. Vol. I.

Dresden, Sem. Het Muziekleven in Nederland sinds 1880. Amsterdam, Uitgeversmaatschappij "Elsevier," 1923.

Druskin, Mikhail Semenovich. Ocherki po istorii russkoĭ muzyki, 1790–1825. Leningrad, Gos. muzykal'noe izd-vo, 1956.

—— Voprosy muzykal'noĭ dramaturgii opery. Leningrad, Gos. muzykal'noe izd-vo, 1952.

Durham, Frank. DuBose Heyward : The Man Who Wrote Porgy. Columbia, University of South Carolina Press, 1954.

Elson, Louis C. The History of American Music. New York, Macmillan, 1925. Revised to 1925 by Arthur Elson.

Engländer, Richard. "Die Gustavianische Oper," AfMw XVI (1959) 314–27.

Evans, Edwin. Tchaikovsky. New York, Pellegrini & Cudahy, 1949.

Ewen, David. Complete Book of the American Musical Theater : A Guide to More Than 300 Productions of the American Musical Theater from *The Black Crook* (1866) to the Present, with Plot, Production History, Stars, Composers, Librettists, and Lyricists. New York, Henry Holt & Co., [1959]. Rev. ed.

—— A Journey to Greatness : The Life and Music of George Gershwin. New York, Henry Holt & Co., [1956].

Fédorov, V. "Le Voyage de M. I. Glinka en Italie," *Collectanea historiae musicae* II (1957) 179–92.

Ferrari Nicolay, Mauricio. "En torno a *Las Vírgenes del Sol,* la nueva opera argentina," *Estudios* (Buenos Aires) Año 29, tomo 62 (1939) 29–46.

Fétis, Edouard. Les Musiciens belges, tome premier. Brussels, Ajamar, n.d.

Findeisen, Nikolaĭ Fedorovich. "The Earliest Russian Operas," MQ XIX (1933) 331–40.

—— "Die Entwicklung der Tonkunst in Russland in der ersten Hälfte des 19. Jahrhunderts," SIMG II (1900–1901) 279–302.

—— Ocherki po istorii muzyki v Rossii . . . do kontsa XVIII veka. Moscow, Leningrad, Gosudarstvennoe izdatel'stvo, Muzsektor, 1928–29.

—— "Die Oper in Russland," ZIMG I (1899–1900) 367–75.

Fiorda Kelly, Alfredo. Cronología de las óperas, dramas líricos, oratorios, himnos, etc. cantados en Buenos Aires. Buenos Aires, Riera, 1934.

Fischl, Viktor, ed. Antonín Dvořák, His Achievement. London, L. Drummond, [1943].

Foerster, Josef Bohuslav. Der Pilger : Erinnerungen eines Musikers. Einleitende Studie und Auswahl für die deutsche Ausgabe von F. Pala. Prague, Artia, 1955.

[——] J. B. Foerster : Jeho životní pouť a tvorba, 1859–1949. [Prague], Orbis, [1949].

Fonseco Benevides, Francisco da. O real theatro de S. Carlos de Lisboa, desde a sua funação em 1793 até á actualidade. Lisbon, Castro Irmão, [1883].

Fuller-Maitland, John Alexander. The Music of Parry and Stanford. Cambridge, W. Heffer, 1934.

Gagey, Edmond McAdoo. The San Francisco Stage : A History. New York, Columbia University Press, 1950.

Galindo, Miguel. Nociones de historia de la música mejicana, tomo 1. Colima, Tip. de "El dragón," 1933.

Gettel, William D. "Arthur Clifton's *Enterprise,*" JAMS II (1949) 23–35.

Gettemann, H. "*Sniégourotchka* opéra de M. Rimsky-Korsakoff," RHCM VIII (1908) 137–43, 179–87, 213–16.

Gilse van der Pals, Nikolai van. N. A. Rimsky-Korssakow : Opernschaffen nebst Skizze über Leben und Wirken. Paris-Leipzig, W. Bessel, 1929.

Ginzburg, Semen L'vovich, ed. Russkiĭ muzykal'nyĭ teatr 1700–1835. Moscow, "Iskusstvo," 1941.

Glinka, Mikhail Ivanovich. Literaturnoe nasledie. [Leningrad], Gos. muzykal'noe izd-vo, 1952–53. 2 vols.

—— Zapiski. Leningrad, Gos. muzykal'noe izd-vo, 1953.

Glowacki, John M. The History of Polish Opera. Boston University Dissertation, 1952.

Goddard, Scott. "Editions of *Boris Goudonov*," M&L X (1929) 278–86.

Godet, Robert. En Marge de *Boris Godounof:* Notes sur les documents iconographiques de l'édition Chester. Paris, F. Alcan, 1926.

Gomes Vaz de Carvalho, Itala. Vida de Carlos Gomes. Rio de Janeiro, A. Noite, 1946. 3d ed.

Gozenpud, Abram Akimovich. Muzykal'nyĭ teatr v Rossii : Ot istokov do Glinki. Leningrad, Gos. muzykal'noe izd-vo, 1959.

—— N. A. Rimskiĭ-Korsakov : Temy i idei ego opernogo tvorchestva. Moscow, Gos. muzykal'noe izd-vo, 1957.

Graf, Herbert. The Opera and Its Future in America. New York, W. W. Norton, [1941].

—— Producing Opera for America. Zurich, New York, Atlantis Books, [1961].

Green, Stanley. The World of Musical Comedy : The Story of the American Musical Stage as Told through the Careers of Its Foremost Composers and Lyricists. New York, Ziff-Davis, [1960].

Greene, Harry Plunket. Charles Villiers Stanford. London, E. Arnold, [1935].

Habets, Alfred. Alexandre Borodine, d'après la biographie et la correspondance publiées par M. Wladimir Stassof. Paris, Fischbacher, 1893. Translated as : Borodin and Liszt. London, Digby, Long, [1895].

Hackett, Karleton. "The Possibilities of Opera in America," MTNA IV (1909) 52–60.

Handbook of Latin American Studies. Cambridge, Mass., Harvard University Press, 1936–.

Harászti, Emil. La Musique hongroise. Paris, Laurens, 1933.

Hebanowski, S. "Trzydziestolecie opery Poznanskiej," *Kronika miasta Poznania* (1949) 201–18.

Helfert, Vladimír. Geschichte der Musik in der tschechoslovakischen Republik. Prague, Orbis-Verlag, 1936.

Hipsher, Edward E. American Opera and Its Composers. Philadelphia, T. Presser, [1927].

Hitchcock, H. Wiley. "An Early American Melodrama : *The Indian Princess* of J. N. Barker and John Bray," *MLA Notes*, 2d ser., XII, No. 3 (1954–55) 375–88.

Hnilička, Alois. Kontury vývoje hudby poklasické v Čechách. Prague, 1935.

Hoffmann-Erbrecht, Lothar. "Grundlagen der Melodiebildung bei Mussorgski," in *Bericht über den internationalen musikwissenschaft-*

*lichen Kongress Bamberg 1953* (Kassel & Basel, Bärenreiter, [1954]) 262–66.

Hoffmeister, Karel. Antonín Dvořák. London, John Lane, 1928. Ed. and translated by Rosa Newmarch.

Hofmann, Rostislav. Moussorgski. Paris, Editions du Coudrier, [1952].

—— Rimski-Korsakov : Sa vie, son oeuvre. Paris, Flammarion, 1958.

—— Un Siècle d'opéra russe (de Glinka à Stravinsky). Paris, Corrêa, [1946].

Holbrooke, Josef. Contemporary British Composers. London, C. Palmer, [1925].

[——] Josef Holbrooke : Various Appreciations by Many Authors. London, R. Carte & Co., 1937.

Hostinský, Otakar. Die Musik in Böhmen. Vienna, Hof- u. Staatsdruckerei, 1894.

Howard, John Tasker. "The Hewitt Family in America," MQ XVII (1931) 25–39.

—— Our American Music : Three Hundred Years of It. With Supplementary Chapters by James Lyons. New York, Thomas Y. Crowell Co., [1954]. 3d ed.

—— Studies of Contemporary American Composers : Deems Taylor. New York, J. Fischer, 1927.

Hoza, Stefan. Opera na Slovensku. Martin, Osveta, 1953–54. 2 vols.

Hussey, Dyneley. "Nationalism and Opera," M&L VII (1926) 3–16.

Huygens, Constantijn. Correspondance et œuvre musical. Leiden, W. J. A. Jonckbloet, 1882.

Iakovlev, Vasiliĭ Vasil'evich. Pushkin i muzyka. Moscow, Gos. muzykal'noe izd-vo, 1949.

Iarustovskiĭ, B. M. Dramaturgiia russkoĭ opernoĭ klassiki. Moscow, Muzgiz, 1953. Translated as : Die Dramaturgie der klassischen russischen Oper. Berlin, Henschelverlag, 1957.

—— Opernaia dramaturgiia Chaĭkovskogo. Moscow, Gos. muz. izd-vo, 1947.

Iastrebtsev, Vasiliĭ Vasil'evich. Nikolaĭ Andreevich Rimskiĭ-Korsakov : Vospominaniia, 1886–1908. [Leningrad, Gos. muzykal'noe izd-vo, 1959.]

Iglesias, Ignasi. Enric Morera : Estudi biografie. Barcelona, Artis, [1921].

Inch, Herbert Reynolds. A Bibliography of Glinka. [New York, 1935.] Typewritten; available in the Music Division of the New York Public Library.

Istel, Edgar. "Felipe Pedrell," MQ XI (1925) 164–91.

—— "Isaac Albeniz," MQ XV (1929) 117–48.

Jachimecki, Zdzisław. "Dwie opery polskie o Napoleonie," *Muzyka* (1929) No. 1, 5–13.

—— Historia muzyki polskiej w zarysie. Warsaw, Gebethner i Wolff, [1920].

Jachimecki, Zdzisław. Muzyka polska w rozwoju historycznym. Cracow, S. Kamiński, [1948–51]. 2 vols.

—— "Stanislaus Moniuszko," MQ XIV (1928) 54–62.

—— Stanisław Moniuszko. Warsáw, Gebethner i Wolff, [1921].

—— Władysław Żeleński. Cracow, Polskie Wyd. Muzyczne, 1952.

Kann-Novikova, E. M. I. Glinka. Moscow, Muzgiz, 1950–55. 3 vols.

Karasowski, Maurycy. "Jan Stefani," Ruch Muzyczny (1857) 210–14; 217–19, 226–29, 237–39.

—— "Moniuszko jako kompozytor dramatyczny," Biblioteka Warszawska (1861) vol. 82 (i.e., vol. 2 of n.[3]s. [1861–65], vol. II of 1861), 261–81.

—— Rys historyczny opery polskiej, poprzedzony szczegółowym poglądem na dzieje muzyki dramatycznej powszechnej. Warsaw, M. Glúcksberg, 1859.

—— "Rys historyczny opery polskiej z końca epoki panowania Stanisława Augusta aż do dni naszych," Biblioteka Warszawska (1858) vol. 70 (i.e., vol. 6 of n.[2]s., vol. II of 1858), 94–122, 276–312.

Karysheva, T. P. P. Sokal's'kiï : Narys pro zhyttia i tvorchist'. Kiev, Derzh. vid-vo obrazotvorchoho mystetstva i muzychnoï lit-ri URSR, 1959.

Keefer, Lubov. "Opera in the Soviet," MLA Notes, 2d ser., II, No. 2 (March, 1945) 110–17.

Keeton, A. E. "Elgar's Music for The Starlight Express," M&L XXVI (1945) 43–46.

Keldysh, Iurii Vsevoldovich. Istoriia russkoï muzyki. Moscow, Muzgiz, 1947, 1954. Vols. 2 and 3.

Kelly, Alfredo. See Fiorda Kelly, Alfredo.

Kindem, Ingeborg Eckhoff. Den norske Operas Historie. Oslo, E. G. Mortensen, 1941.

Kleczyński, J. "Opera polska przed i po Halce," EMTA (1885) 224–25.

Klein, Herman. "Albéniz's Opera Pepita Jiménez," The Musical Times LIX (March, 1918) 116–17.

Kling, H. "Le Centenaire d'un compositeur suisse célèbre : Louis Niedermeyer," RMI IX (1902) 830–59.

Kolodin, Irving. The Story of the Metropolitan Opera, 1883–1950 : A Candid History. New York, Alfred A. Knopf, 1953.

Kulikovich, Mikola. Belaruskaia savetskaia opera. Munich, 1957.

Lange, Francisco Curt. "Leon Ribeiro," Boletin latino-americano de musica III (1937) 519–36.

Laplane, Gabriel. Albeniz : Sa vie, son oeuvre. [n.p.], Editions du Milieu du Monde, [1956].

Latoszewski, Z. "Opera w Polsce pryedrozbiorowej," Wiadomości Muzyczne (1925) 45–47; Muzyk Wojskowy (1926) No. 3.

Layton, Robert. Berwald. London, publ. under the auspices of the Anglo-Swedish Literary Foundation [by] Blond, [1959].

Lehmann, Dieter. Russlands Oper und Singspiel in der zweiten Hälfte des 18. Jahrhunderts. Leipzig, B&H, 1958.

Leonard, Richard Anthony. A History of Russian Music. London, Jarrolds, [1956].

Leyda, Jay, and Sergei Bertensson, eds. The Musorgsky Reader : The Life of Modeste Petrovich Musorgsky in Letters and Documents. New York, W. W. Norton, 1947.

Lindström, Sven. "Vårt första nationalla Sångspel," STM XXIV (1942) 68–83.

Livanova, Tamara Nikolaevna. Ocherki i materialy po istorii ruskoĭ muzykal'noĭ kultury. Moscow, "Iskusstvo," 1938.

—— Russkaia muzykal'naia kul'tura XVIII veka v ee sviaziakh s literaturoĭ, teatrom i bytom. Moscow, Gos. muzykal'noe izd-vo, 1952–53. 2 vols.

—— Stasov i russkaia klassicheskaia opera. Moscow, Gos. muzykal'noe izd-vo, 1957.

Livanova, Tamara Nikolaevna, ed. M. I. Glinka : Sbornik materialov i stateĭ. Moscow, Gos. muzykal'noe izd-vo, 1950.

Lloyd-Jones, David. "[Borodin's] The Bogatyrs: Russia's First Operetta," MMR LXXXIX (1959) 123–30.

Loëb, Harry Brunswick. "The Opera in New Orleans," Louisiana Historical Society, Proceedings and Reports IX (1916) 29–41.

Loft, Abram, translator. "Excerpts from the Memoirs of J. W. Tomaschek," MQ XXXII (1946) 244–64.

Lowe, George. Josef Holbrooke and His Work. London, K. Paul [etc.]; New York, E. P. Dutton, 1920.

Lualdi, Adriano. "Il Principe Igor de Borodine," RMI XXIII (1916) 115–39.

Maine, Basil. "Don Juan de Mañara: Goossens' New Opera," The Chesterian XVI (1935–36) 5–10.

Marchant, Annie d'Armond. "Carlos Gomes, Great Brazilian Composer," Bulletin of the Pan American Union LXX (1936) 767–76.

Maria y Campos, Armando de. Una temporada de opera italiana en Oaxaca. Mexico, Ediciones populaires, 1939.

Martineau, René. Emmanuel Chabrier. Paris, Dorbon, [1910].

Mates, Julian. The American Musical Stage before 1800. New Brunswick, Rutgers University Press, [cop. 1962].

Mattfeld, Julius. A Hundred Years of Grand Opera in New York, 1825–1925 : A Record of Performances. New York, The New York Public Library, 1927.

Mayer-Serra, Otto. Panorama de la música mexicana desde la independencia hasta la actualidad. [México], El Colegio de México, [1941].

Mellers, Wilfrid. "Music, Theatre and Commerce : A Note on Gershwin, Menotti and Marc Blitzstein," The Score No. 12 (June, 1955) 69–76.

Meyer, Torben. Carl Nielsen, Kunstneren og Mennesket : En Biografi. Gennemgang af Vaerkerne : Frede Shanford Petersen. Copenhagen, Nyt Nordisk Forlag, 1947–48. 2 vols.

Michałowski, Kornel. Opery Polski. [Cracow], Polskie Wydawnictwo Muzycne, [1954].

Mitjana y Gordón, Rafael. "La Musique en Espagne," in Lavignac, *Encyclopédie de la musique* (Paris, Delagrave, 1920) Part I, Vol. IV, 1913–2351.

Moberg, Carl Allan. "Essais d'opéras en Suède, sous Charles XII," in *Mélanges de musicologie* (Paris, Droz, 1933) 123–32.

Montagu-Nathan, Montagu. Glinka. London, Constable, 1916.

—— A History of Russian Music. London, W. Reeves, [1914]. 2d ed., 1918.

—— Moussorgsky. London, Constable, 1916.

—— "The Origin of *The Golden Cockerel*," MR XV (1954) 33–38.

—— Rimsky-Korsakof. London, Constable, 1916.

Moore, Edward C. Forty Years of Opera in Chicago. New York, H. Liveright, 1930.

Mooser, Robert Aloys. Annales de la musique et des musiciens en Russie au XVIIIe siècle. Geneva, Mont-Blanc, 1948–51. 3 vols.

—— Contribution à l'histoire de le musique russe : L'Opéra-comique français en Russie au XVIIIe siècle. Geneva, L'auteur, 1932.

—— "Un Musicien espagnol en Russie à la fin du XVIIIe siècle [Martin i Soler]," RMI XL (1936) 432–49.

—— L'Opéra-comique français en Russie au XVIIIe siècle. Geneva-Monaco, Editions René Kistner, 1954. 2d ed.

—— Opéras, intermezzos, ballets, cantates, oratorios joués en Russie durant le 18e siècle. Avec l'indication des oeuvres de compositeurs russes parues en Occident, à la même époque. Essai d'un répertoire alphabétique et chronologique. Geneva, R. Kistner; Monaco, Union Européene d'Editions, 1955. 2d ed.

Morgan, James O. French Comic Opera in New York, 1855–1890. Ann Arbor, University Microfilms, 1959.

Moscow. Gosudarstvennaia konservatoriia. Kafedra istorii russkoĭ muzyki. Istoriia russkoĭ muzyki. Moscow, Gos. muzykal'noe izd-vo, 1957–60. 3 vols.

Muñoz, Matilde. Historia de la zarzuela y el género chico. Madrid, Editorial Tesoro, [1946].

Muzyka : Monografje muzyczne. Warsaw, [1934]. Mateusz Gliński, ed. Tom 10 (incorrectly called tom 9), also called rok 11, nr. 8–9.

Muzykal'noe nasledie Chaĭkovskogo : Iz istorii ego proizvedeniĭ. Moscow, Akademiia Nauk SSSR, 1958.

Nejedlý, Zdeněk. Bedřich Smetana. [Prague], Orbis, 1950–54. 2d ed. 7 vols.

—— Dějiny opery Národního divadla. [Prague], Práce, 1949. 2d ed.

—— Frederick Smetana. London, G. Bles, [1924].

—— J. B. Foerster. Prague, M. Urbánek, 1910.

—— Zpěvohry Smetanovy. Prague, Státní nakl. politické literatury, 1954. 2d ed.

Newmarch, Rosa. The Music of Czechoslovakia. London, Oxford University Press, 1942.

—— The Russian Opera. New York, E. P. Dutton, [1914].

—— Tchaikovsky, His Life and Works. New York, J. Lane, 1900.

—— "Tchaikovsky's Early Lyrical Operas," ZIMG VI (1904–5) 29–34.

Niewiadomski, S. "*Manru* [of Paderewski]," *Biblioteka Warszawska* (1901) vol. 243 (i.e., vol. 143 of n.[4]s., vol. III of 1901) 87–104.

—— "O pierwszej muzyce do *Fausta* i o jej twórcy Antonim [-ie?] Radziwille," *Muzyka* (1929) Nos. 3–4.

—— "W. Zeleński i jego *Goplana*," EMTA (1897) 64.

—— "Z przeszłošci opery polskiej," *Muzyka* (1931) 65–68.

Nilsson, Kurt. Die Rimsky-Korssakoffsche Bearbeitung des *Boris Godunoff* von Mussorgskii als Objekt der vergleichenden Musikwissenschaft. Münster, Buschmann, 1937.

Nosek, Vladimir. The Spirit of Bohemia : A Survey of Czechoslovak History, Music, and Literature. London, G. Allen & Unwin, [1926].

Noskowski, W. "*Damy i huzary* Łucjana Kamieńskiego," *Muzyka Polska* (1938) No. 10, 452–55.

Nowak-Romanowicz, Alina. Jósef Elsner. Cracow, Polskie Wydawn. Muzyczne, [1957].

Opieński, Henryk. La Musique polonaise. Paris, Gebethner & Wolff, 1929.

—— "Les Premiers Opéras polonais considérés dans leur rapports avec la musique de Chopin," RdM X (1929) 92–98.

—— Stanisław Moniuszko, życie i dzieła. Lvov-Poznan, Nakładem Wydawn. Polskiego, 1924.

Paderewski, I. J. "*Konrad Wallenrod*," *Tygodnik Illustrowany* I (1885) 175–76.

Panov, Petŭr. "Der nationale Stil N. A. Rimsky-Korsakows," AfMw VIII (1926) 78–117.

Paris, Luis. Museo-archivo teatral (Madrid) : Catálogo provisional. Madrid, Yagües, 1932.

Patterson, Frank. "Fifty Years of Opera in America," MTNA XXIII (1928) 176–85.

Pedrell, Felipe. Cancionero musical popular español. Valls, E. Castells, [1918–22]. 4 vols.

—— Jornadas de arte (1841–1891). Paris, Ollendorf, 1911.

—— "La Musique indigène dans le théâtre espagnol du XVIIe siècle," SIMG V (1903) 46–90.

—— Orientaciones (1892–1902) : Continuaciò de Jornadas de arte. Paris, Ollendorf, 1911.

—— Por nuestra música : Algunas observaciones sobre la magna cuestión de una escuela lírico nacional. Barcelona, Heurich, 1891.

Pekelis, Mikhail Samoĭlovich. Dargomyzhskiĭ i narodnaia pesnia. Moscow, Muzgiz, 1951.

Pekelis, Mikhail Samoïlovich, ed. Istoriia russkoĭ muzyki. Moscow, Muzgiz, 1940. Vol. II.

Peña y Goñi, Antonio. La ópera española y la música dramática en España en el siglo XIX. Madrid, El Liberal, 1881.

Pereira Peixoto d'Almeida Carvalhaes, Manoel. Marcos Portugal na sua musica dramatica. Lisbon, Castro Irmão, 1910.

Pereira Salas, Eugenio. História de la música en Chile (1850–1900). [Santiago], Universidad de Chile, 1957.

——— See also Abascal Brunet.

Peterson-Berger, Olof Wilhelm. Peterson-Berger Recensioner : Glimtar och Skuggor ur Stockholms musik Värld 1896–1923. Stockholm, Ahlén & Åkerlund, 1923.

Pisk, Paul A. "Lazare Saminsky," The Chesterian XX (1938–39) 74–78.

Poliński, A. Pierwszi tworcy oper polskich," Kurjer Warszawski (1905) No. 1.

Pols, André M. Vijftig Jaar vlaamsche Opera. Antwerp, Drukkerij Pierre Dirix, [1943].

Pomorska, Hanna. Karol Kurpiński. [Warsaw], Czytelnik, 1948.

Poźniak, W. "Niezrealizowane projekty operowe Moniuszki," Kwartalnik Muzyczny (1948) Nos. 21–22, 234–51.

——— "Opera polska przed Moniuszka : Szkic historyczny," Muzyka (1951) No. 12 (21), 30–37.

Pražák, Přemysl. Smetanovy zpěvohry. Prague, Za svobodu, 1948. 4 vols.

Prod'homme, Jacques Gabriel. "Chabrier in His Letters," MQ XXI (1935) 451–65.

Protopopov, Vladimir Vasil'evich. Ivan Susanin Glinki : Muzykal'no-tvorcheskoe issledovanie. Moscow, Izd-vo Akademii Nauk SSSR, 1961.

——— Opernoe tvorchestvo Chaĭkovskogo. Moscow, Akademiia Nauk SSSR, 1957.

Rabinovich, Aleksandr Semenovich. Russkaia opera do Glinki. [Moscow], Muzgiz, 1948.

Raux Deledicque, Michel. Albéniz, su vida inquieta y ardorosa. [Buenos Aires], Ediciones Peuser, [1950].

Reeser, Eduard. Een Eeuw nederlandse Muziek [1815–1915]. Amsterdam, Querido, 1950.

Reiff, A. "Ein Katalog zu den Werken von Felipe Pedrell," AfMw III (1921) 86–97.

Reiss, J[ósef]. W[ładysław]. "Koryfeusz muzyki polskiej, Karol Kurpiński," Wiedza i Życie (1949) 1061–69.

——— Muzyka w Krakowie w XIX wieku. Cracow, W. L. Anczyc, 1931.

——— Najpiękniejsza ze wszystkich jest muzyka polska. Cracow, T. Gieszczykiewicz, 1946; Warsaw, Polskie Wydawnictwo Muzyczne, [1958].

Rektorys, Artuš, ed. Zdeněk Fibich : Sborník dokumentů a studií o jeho životé a díle. [Prague], Orbis, 1951–52. 2 vols.

Richter, Carl Ludwig. Zdenko Fibich. Prague, F. A. Urbánek, 1900.

Riesemann, Oskar von. Monographien zur russischen Musik. Munich, Drei Masken, 1923–26. 2 vols. Vol. II, Modest Petrowitsch Mussorgski, translated as : Moussorgsky. New York, Tudor, 1935.

Rimskiĭ-Korsakov, Andreĭ Nikolaevich. N. A. Rimskiĭ-Korsakov : Zhizn' i tvorchestvo. Moscow, Ogiz-Muzgiz, 1933–46. 5 vols.

Rimskiĭ-Korsakov, Nikolaĭ Andreevich. Letopis' moeĭ muzykal'noĭ zhizni. Moscow, Gos. muzykal'noe izd-vo, 1955. 7th ed. English translation of 5th ed. (1935) as : My Musical Life. New York, Alfred A. Knopf, 1942.

—— My Musical Life. New York, Alfred A. Knopf, 1923. Translated from the revised second Russian edition.

[——] USSR, Tsentral'nyĭ gosudarstvennyĭ literaturnyĭ arkhiv. N. A. Rimskiĭ-Korsakov : Sbornik dokumentov. Moscow, Gos. muzykal'noe izd-vo, 1951.

Ritter, Frédéric Louis. Music in America. New York, Scribner, 1883.

Robertson, Alec. Dvořák. New York, Pellegrini & Cudahy, 1949.

Rogers, Francis. "America's First Grand Opera Season," MQ I (1915) 93–101.

—— "Henriette Sontag in New York," MQ XXVIII (1942) 100–104.

Rogge, Hendrik Cornelis. "De Opera te Amsterdam," Oud Holland V (1887) 177, 241–62.

—— "De Opvoeringen van Mozarts Don Juan in Nederland," Tijdschrift der Vereeniging voor Noord-Nederlands Muziekgeschiedenis II (1887) 237–77.

Romero, Jésus C. La ópera en Yucatán. Mexico, Ediciones "Guion de América," 1947.

Rubinstein, Anton. Erinnerungen aus fünfzig Jahren, 1839–1889. Leipzig, B. Senff, 1895. Translated from the Russian.

Rudziński, Witold. "Szkice Moniuszkowskie. IV. Śpiewak domowy," Muzyka (1952) No. 9/10 (30–31) 65–76.

Sabaneev, Leonid Leonidovitch. Geschichte der russischen Musik. Leipzig, B&H, 1926.

—— Modern Russian Composers. Translated by Joffe. New York, International Publishers, [1927].

Sáez, Antonia. El teatro en Puerto Rico (notas para su historia). [San Juan], Editorial Universitaria, Universidad de Puerto Rico, 1950.

Salas, Carlos, and Eduardo Feo Calcaño. Sesquicentenario de la opera en Caracas : Relato histórico de ciento años de opera 1808–1958. Caracas, Tip. Vargas, 1960.

Salazar, Adolfo. La música contemporánea en España. Madrid, Ediciones La Nave, [1930].

Salcedo, Angel S. Tomás Bretón. Madrid, Imprenta clásica española, 1924.

Saldívar, Gabriel. História de la música en México (épocas precortesiana y colonial). Mexico, "Cvltvra," 1934.

Saldoni, Baltasar. Diccionario biográfico-bibliográfico de efemérides de músicos españoles. Madrid, D. Antonio Perez Dubrull, 1868–81. 4 vols.

Sanders, Paul F. Moderne nederlandsche Componisten. The Hague, Kruseman, [1930].

Saunders, William. "The American Opera," M&L XIII (1932) 147–55.

—— "National Opera, Comparatively Considered," MQ XIII (1927) 72–84.

Seaman, Gerald. "The National Element in Early Russian Opera, 1779–1800," M&L XLII (1961) 252–62.

Seidl, Roberto. Carlos Gomes. Rio de Janeiro, [Imprensa moderna], 1935.

Seilhamer, George Overcash. History of the American Theatre. Philadelphia, Globe Printing House, 1888–91. 3 vols.

Selden, Margery Stomne. "Early Roots of Russian Opera," JAMS XV (1962) 206–11; see also ibid. XVI (1963) 257–60.

Seroff, Victor I. The Mighty Five. New York, Allen, Towne and Heath, [1948].

—— Rachmaninoff. New York, Simon & Schuster, 1950.

Serov, Aleksandr Nikolaevich. Rusalka, opera A. S. Dargomyzhskogo. Moscow, Gos. muzykal'noe izd-vo, 1953.

Servières, Georges. Emmanuel Chabrier. Paris, F. Alcan, 1912.

Shaw, George Bernard. London Music in 1888–89 as Heard by Corno di Bassetto. New York, Dodd, Mead, 1937.

Silva, Lafayette. Historia do teatro brasileiro. Rio de Janeiro, Ministério da educaçiõ e saude, 1938.

Sincero, Dino. "Boris Godounow al teatro Alla Scala di Milano," RMI XVI (1909) 385–94.

Sixto Prieto, Juan. "El Perú en la música escénica," Fenix No. 9 (1953) 278–351.

Skilton, Charles Sanford. "American Opera," MTNA XX (1925) 112–18.

Slonimsky, Nicolas. Music of Latin America. New York, Thomas Y. Crowell, 1945.

Smetana, Bedřich. Smetana in Briefen und Erinnerungen. Hrsg. und eingeleitet von František Bartoš. Prague, Artia, 1954. English translation : Letters and Reminiscences. Prague, Artia, [1955].

Smith, Cecil. Musical Comedy in America. New York, Theatre Arts Books, [1950].

Solvay, Lucien. Notice sur Jean Blockx. Brussels, Hayez, 1920.

Sonneck, Oscar George Theodore. A Bibliography of Early Secular American Music (Eighteenth Century). Washington, D.C., The Library of Congress, Music Division, 1945.

—— Early Concert Life in America. Leipzig, B&H, 1907.

—— Early Opera in America. New York, G. Schirmer, [1915].

—— Francis Hopkinson, the First American Poet-Composer. Washington, D.C., Printed for the Author by H. L. McQueen, 1905.

Soriano Fuertes, Mariano. História de la música española. Madrid, Martin y Salazar; Barcelona, Narciso Ramírez, 1856–59. 4 vols.

Soubies, Albert. Histoire de la musique en Bohême. Paris, E. Flammarion, 1898.

Šourek, Otakar. Antonín Dvořák : His Life and Works. Prague, Orbis, 1952; New York, Philosophical Library, [1954].

—— Život a dílo Antonína Dvořáka. Prague, Hudební matice umělecké besedy, 1922–33. 4 vols.

Sovetskaia muzyka. [Moscow], Gos. muzykal'noe izd-vo, 1933–

Stals, Georgs. Das lettische Ballett der Rigaer Oper. Riga, Kadilis, 1943.

Stasov, Vladimir Vasil'evich. Izbrannye stat'i o M. I. Glinke. Moscow, Gos. muzykal'noe izd-vo, 1955.

—— Mikhail Ivanovich Glinka. Moscow, Gos. muzykal'noe izd-vo, 1953.

—— Russkiia i inostrannyia opery ispolniavshiasia na Imperatorskikh Teatrakh v Rosii v XVIII-m'i XIX-m stoletiiakh. St. Petersburg, 1898.

—— Sobranie sochinenii. Vols. 1–3 (works of 1847–86) : St. Petersburg, M. M. Stasiulevich, 1894. Vol. 4 (works of 1886–1904) published separately in 1905.

Stefan, Paul. Anton Dvořák. New York, Greystone, [1941]. Translated and rearranged from the German edition, which was based on the authoritative four-volume biography by Otakar Šourek.

Steigman, B. M. "The Great American Opera," M&L VI (1925) 359–67.

Štěpán, Václav. Novák a Suk. Prague, Hudební matice umělecké besedy, 1945.

Stevenson, Robert. Music in Mexico, a Historical Survey. New York, Thomas Y. Crowell Co., [1952].

—— The Music of Peru : Aboriginal and Viceroyal Epochs. Washington, Pan American Union, [1960].

—— "Opera Beginnings in the New World," MQ XLV (1959) 8–25.

Streatfeild, Richard Alexander. Musiciens anglais contemporains. Paris, Editions du temps présent, 1913.

Stromenger, K. "Jan Stefani," Łódź Teatralna (1946–47) No. 3, 15–19.

Subirá, José. Enrique Granados. Madrid, [Z. Ascasíbar], 1926.

—— Historia y anecdotario del Teatro Real. Madrid, Editorial Plus Ultra, [1949].

—— El Teatro del Real Palacio (1849–1851), con un bosquejo preliminar sobre la música palatina desde Felipe V hasta Isabel II. Madrid, Consejo Superior de Investigaciones Científicas, Instituto Español de Musicología, 1950.

Sundström, Einar. "Franz Berwalds Operor," STM XXIX (1947) 16–62.

Suomalainen, Yrjö. Oskar Merikanto : Suomen kotien jäveltäjä. Helsinki, Kustannusosakeyhtiö Otava, [1950].

Swan, Alfred J. "Moussorgsky and Modern Music," MQ XI (1925) 271–80.

Szabolcsi, Bence. Bausteine zu einer Geschichte der Melodie. Budapest, Corviva, [1959].

Szabolcsi, Bence, ed. Az opera történetéből. Budapest, Akadémiai Kiadó, 1961.

Szopski, Felicjan. Władysław Żeleński. Warsaw, Gebethner i Wolff, [1928].

Szyfman, Arnold. "Problem opery polskiej," Muzyka (1951) No. 9 (18), 18–21.

Tebaldini, Giovanni. "Felipe Pedrell ed il dramma lirico spagnuolo," RMI IV (1897) 267–98, 494–524. Also separate : Turin, Bocca, 1897.

Teuber, Oscar. Geschichte des Prager Theaters. Prague, Haase, 1883–87. 3 vols.

Theatro comico portuguez, ou Collecção das operas portuguezas, que se representárão na casa do theatro público do Bairro Alto di Lisboa. Lisbon, S. T. Ferreira, 1787–92. 4 vols.

Thomson, Virgil. "George Gershwin," MMus XIII, No. 1 (November–December, 1935) 13–19.

—— "Most Melodious Tears," MMus XI, No. 1 (November–December, 1933) 13–17.

Tigranov, Georgiĭ. Armianskiĭ muzykal'nyĭ teatr. Erevan, Armianskoe gos. izd-vo, 1956, 1960. 2 vols. Vol. II has imprint : Erevan, Aipetrat, 1960.

Törnblom, Folke H. "Opera [in Sweden]," Theatre Arts XXIV (1940) 597–600.

Tolón, Edwin T., and Jorge A. González. Operas cubanas y sus autores. Havana, [Imprenta Ucar, García], 1943.

Trend, John Brande. A Picture of Modern Spain. New York, Houghton Mifflin, 1921.

Trilogia Los Pireneos y la critica, La. Barcelona, Oliva, 1901.

Trocki, Ladislas von. Die Entwickelung der Oper in Polen. Leipzig, Voigt, 1867.

Tsukkerman, Viktor Abramovich. Sadko: Opera-bylina N. A. Rimskogo-Korsakovo. Moscow, Muzgiz, 1936.

Tutenberg, Fritz. "Moderne schwedische Musik und Musiker im Umriss, II : Die schwedische Oper," Zeitschrift für Musik CVI (1939) 930–34.

Upton, William Treat. "Max and Agathe vs. Rodolph and Agnes, et al.," MLA Notes, 2d ser., IV, No. 2 (March, 1947) 217–24.

—— "Secular Music in the United States 150 Years Ago," in Papers of the American Musicological Society, Annual Meeting, 1941 . . . Edited by Gustave Reese (Printed by the Society [cop. 1946]) 105–11.

—— William Henry Fry : American Journalist and Composer-Critic. New York, Thomas Y. Crowell Co., 1954.

USSR. Tsentral'nyĭ gosudarstvennyĭ literaturnyĭ arkhiv. N. A. Rimskiĭ-Korsakov : Sbornik dokumentov. Moscow, Gos. muzykal'noe izd-vo, 1951.

Vieira, Ernesto. Diccionario biographico de musicos portuguezes : Historia e bibliographia da musica em Portugal. Lisbon, M. Moreira & Pinheiro, 1900. 2 vols.

Villalba, L. "La cuestión de la ópera española : Carta abierta," *La Ciudad de Dios* XXXIII, No. 2 (1913) 204–11.

Virella Cassañes, Francisco. La ópera en Barcelona. Barcelona, Redondo y Zumetra, 1888.

Virgilio, Rudolph. Development of Italian Opera in New York. New York, Italian Library of Information, 1938.

Walicki, Aleksandr. Stanisław Moniuszko. Warsaw, Nakład autora, Skład główny w księgarni Gebethnera i Wolffa, 1873.

Walsh, T. J. Opera in Old Dublin, 1819–1839. [Wexford, Ireland], Wexford Festival, 1952.

Waters, Edward N. Victor Herbert : A Life in Music. New York, Macmillan Co., 1955.

Wegelin, Oscar. Early American Plays, 1714–1830. New York, The Dunlap Society, 1900.

—— Micah Hawkins and the Saw-Mill : A Sketch of the First Successful American Opera and Its Author. New York, privately printed, 1917.

White, Richard Grant. "Opera in New York," *Century Magazine* I (1881) 686–703, 865–82; II (1882) 31–43, 193–210.

Wierzbicka, Karyna. Źródła do historii teatru warszawskiego od roku 1762 do roku 1833. Wrocław, Zakład narodowy imienia Ossolińskich, 1951. Cz. 1.

Wilson, Charles. "The Two Versions of *Goyescas*," MMR LXXXI (1951) 203–7.

Winkelmann, Johann. Josef Myslivecek als Opernkomponist. Vienna Dissertation, 1905.

Winter, Marian Hannah. "American Theatrical Dancing from 1750–1800," MQ XXIV (1938) 58–73.

Yellin, Victor. The Life and Operatic Works of George Whitefield Chadwick. Harvard Dissertation, 1957.

Zagiba, Franz. Tschaikovskij : Leben und Werk. Zurich, Leipzig, Vienna, Amalthea-Verlag, [1953].

Zawiłowski, Konrad. Stanislaus Moniuszko. Vienna Dissertation, 1902.

Zetlin, Mikhail. The Five : The Evolution of the Russian School of Music. New York, International Universities Press, [cop. 1959].

Zetowski, S. "Teoria polskiej opery narodowej z końca XVIII i początku XIX wieku," *Muzyka Polska* (1937) 274–80.

Zichy, Géza. Aus meinem Leben. Stuttgart, Deutsche Verlags-Anstalt, 1911–13. 2 vols.

Zurita, Marciano. Historia del género chico. Madrid, Prensa popular, 1920.

# VII

## *TWENTIETH CENTURY*

Abendroth, Walter. Hans Pfitzner. Munich, A. Lagen & G. Müller, 1935.

Abert, Anna Amalie. "Stefan Zweigs Bedeutung für das Alterswerk von Richard Strauss," in *Festschrift Friedrich Blume* (Kassel, Bärenreiter, 1963) [7]–15.

Abraham, Gerald. Eight Soviet Composers. London, New York, Toronto, Oxford University Press, [1943].

Ackere, Jules van. Maurice Ravel. [Brussels], Elsevier, [1957].

—— *Pelléas et Mélisande*, ou la recontre miraculeuse d'une poésie et d'une musique. Brussels, Librairie Encyclopédique, 1952.

Almanach der deutschen Musikbücherei auf das Jahr 1924/25. Regensburg, Gustav Bosse, 1924.

Altmann, Wilhelm. "Ur- und Erstaufführungen von Opernwerken auf deutschen Bühnen in den letzten Spielzeiten 1899/1900 bis 1924/25," in *Jahrbuch der Universal-Edition* (1926).

American Composers Alliance Bulletin. New York, 1938, 1952–  .

Amico, Fedele d', and Guido M. Gatti, eds. Alfredo Casella. [Collected essays by various authors.] [Milan], Ricordi, [1958].

Annuario del teatro lirico italiano, 1940–  . [Milan], Edizioni Corbaccio, [1940–    ].

Antcliffe, Herbert. "A British School of Music-Drama : The Work of Rutland Boughton," MQ IV (1918) 117–27.

Antheil, George. "Opera—a Way Out," MMus XI, No. 2 (January–February, 1934) 89–94.

—— "Wanted—Opera by and for Americans," MMus VII, No. 4 (June–July, 1930) 11–16.

Archibald, Bruce. "Ulysses in Tone," *Opera News* XXIII, No. 19 (March 9, 1959) 12–13, 28.

Armitage, Merle, ed. Arnold Schoenberg. New York, G. Schirmer, 1937.

—— ed. Igor Stravinsky : Articles and Critiques. New York, G. Schirmer, 1936.

Arnold, Denis. "Strauss and Wilde's *Salome*," MMR LXXXIX (1959) 44–49.

Arundell, Dennis. "Arthur Benjamin's Operas," *Tempo* No. 15 (Spring, 1950) 15–18.

Aubry, Georges Jean. La Musique française d'aujourd'hui. Paris, Perrin, 1916. Translated as : French Music of Today. London, K. Paul [etc.], 1919.

Babbitt, Milton. "An Introduction to the Music [of Schoenberg's *Moses und Aron*]," in brochure accompanying the recording of the opera: Columbia K 3 L –241.

Bachmann, Claus-Henning. "Oper in entzauberter Welt," *Musica* XIV (1960) 75–80.

Bahle, Julius. Hans Pfitzner und der geniale Mensch : Eine psychologische Kulturkritik. Constance, C. Weller, [1949].

Barblan, Guglielmo. *"L'oro,* ultima opera di Pizzetti alla 'Scala,' " RMI XLIX (1947) 57–68.

Barlow, Samuel. "Blitzstein's Answer," MMus XVIII, No. 2 (January–February, 1941) 81–83.

Bauer, Marion. "Darius Milhaud," MQ XXVIII (1942) 139–59.

Beck, Georges. Darius Milhaud. (Etude suivie du catalogue chronologique complet de son oeuvre.) Paris, Heugel & Cie., 1949.

—— Darius Milhaud; catalogue chronologique complet de son oeuvre (supplément) : oeuvres composées de novembre 1949 à avril 1956. Paris, Heugel et Cie., [1956?].

Beecham, Sir Thomas. Frederick Delius. New York, Alfred A. Knopf, 1960.

Beer, Otto Fritz. "Egon Wellesz und die Oper," *Die Musik* XXIII (1931) 909–12.

Bekker, Paul. Franz Schreker : Studie zur Kritik der modernen Oper. Berlin, Schuster & Loeffler, 1919.

—— Das Musikdrama der Gegenwart. Stuttgart, Strecker & Schröder, 1909.

—— Neue Musik. Berlin, E. Reiss, 1920. 5th ed.

—— "The Opera Walks New Paths," MQ XXI (1935) 266–78.

Béla Bartók : A Memorial Review including Articles on His Life and Works, Reprinted from Tempo, the Quarterly Review of Contemporary Music; a Chronological Listing of Works [and] Bartók on Records. New York, Boosey & Hawkes, [1950].

Benjamin Britten : Das Opernwerk. Bonn, Boosey & Hawkes, [1955].

Bennett, Howard G. "Opera in Modern Germany," MTNA XXIX (1934) 65–73.

Berg, Alban. "A Word about *Wozzek,*" MMus V, No. 1 (November–December, 1927) 22–24.

Bernet Kempers, Karel Philippus. Inleiding tot de Opera *Halewijn* van Willem Pijper. Rotterdam, Brusse, [1948?].

Berrsche, Alexander. Kurze Einführung in Hans Pfitzners Musikdrama *Der arme Heinrich.* Leipzig, [1910].

Berthoud, Paul B. The Musical Works of Dr. Henry Hadley. New York, National Association for American Composers and Conductors, 1942.

Bibliographie für Theatergeschichte 1905–1910, bearbeitet von Paul Alfred Merbach. Berlin, Selbstverlag der Gesellschaft für Theatregeschichte, 1913.

Bie, Oscar. "Stand der Oper," *Die Neue Rundschau* XLIII, No. 2 (July–December, 1932) 124–31.

Bitter, Werner. Die deutsche komische Oper der Gegenwart : Studien zu ihrer Entwicklung. Leipzig, Kistner & Siegel, 1932.

Blaukopf, Kurt. "Autobiographische Elemente in Alban Bergs *Wozzeck*," OeM IX (1954) 155–58.

Blitzstein, Marc. *"Hin und Zurück* in Philadelphia," MMus V, No. 4 (May–June, 1928) 34–36.

—— "On *Mahagonny*," *The Score* No. 23 (July, 1958) 11–13.

—— "The Phenomenon of Stravinsky," MQ XXI (1935) 330–47.

Boardman, Herbert Russell. Henry Hadley, Ambassador of Harmony. Emory University, Georgia, Banner Press, [1932].

Boll, André. Marcel Delannoy. Paris, Ventadour, [1957].

—— "Marcel Delannoy, musicien de théâtre," RM XXV, No. 209 (1949) 22–29.

Bonajuti Tarquini, Vittoria. Riccardo Zandonai, nel ricordo dei suoi intimi. Milan, Ricordi, 1951.

Bontempelli, Massimo. Gian Francesco Malipiero. Milan, Bompiani, [1942].

Boughton, Rutland. The Death and Resurrection of the Music Festival. London, W. Reeves, [1913].

—— The Glastonbury Festival Movement. London, [Somerset Press], 1922. Reprinted from *Somerset and the Drama* [by S. R. Littlewood and others].

—— Music Drama of the Future : *Uther and Igraine*, Choral Drama . . . with Essays by the Collaborators. London, W. Reeves, 1911.

—— "A National Music Drama : The Glastonbury Festival," PMA XLIV (1917–18) 19–35.

Brand, Max. " 'Mechanische' Musik und das Problem der Oper," *Musik-blätter des Anbruch* VIII (1926) 356–59.

Brecht, Bertolt. "Two Essays," *The Score* No. 23 (July, 1958) 14–26.

Bréville, Pierre de. Un Grand Musicien français : Marie-Joseph Erb, sa vie et son oeuvre. Strasbourg, F. X. Le Roux, 1948.

Briner, Andres. "Eine Bekenntnisoper Paul Hindemith : Zu seiner oper *Die Harmonie der Welt*," SchwM XCIX (1959) 1–5, 50–56.

Britten, Benjamin, and others. The Rape of Lucretia: A Symposium by Benjamin Britten, Eric Crozier, John Piper, Henry Boys. London, John Lane, 1948.

Brod, Max. Leoš Janáček. Vienna, [etc.], Universal Edition, [1956].

Bruneau, Alfred. La Vie et les œuvres de Gabriel Fauré. Paris, Charpentier & Fasquelle, 1925.

Burkhard, Willy. "Zu meiner Oper *Die schwarze Spinne*," M III (1949) 126–28.

Busne, Henry de. *"Ariane et Barbe-bleue* de M. Paul Dukas," MM III (1907) 465–71.

Busoni, Ferruccio. Entwurf einer neuen Aesthetik der Tonkunst. Leipzig, Insel-Verlag, [19—]. Translated as : Sketch of a New Esthetic of Music. New York, G. Schirmer, 1911.

[——] "Nota bio-bibliografica su Ferruccio Busoni," RassM XIII (1940) 82–88.

—— Über die Möglichkeiten der Oper und über die Partitur des *Doktor Faust*. Leipzig, B&H, 1926.

—— Von der Einheit der Musik. Berlin, M. Hesse, [1923].

—— Wesen und Einheit der Musik. Revidiert, ergänzt und mit Nachwort versammelt von J. Herrmann. Berlin, Wunsiedel, Hesse, 1956. Translated as : The Essence of Music and Other Papers. London, Rockliff, 1957.

Busser, Henri. De *Pelléas* aux *Indes galantes*, de la flûte au tambour. Paris, A. Fayard, [1955]. 4th ed.

Campogalliani, Ettore. Luigi Ferrari-Trecate operista : Tema e variazioni. Verona, Edizioni di "Vita Veronese," 1955.

Canudo, Ricciotto. "Le Drame musical contemporain," MM III (1907) 1185–92; IV (1908) 56–60.

Capell, Richard. "Dame Ethel Smyth's Operas at Covent Garden," MMR LIII (1923) 197–98.

Casella, Alfredo. I segreti della giara. Florence, Sansoni, 1941. Translated as : Music in My Time. Norman, University of Oklahoma Press, [1955].

Cecil, George. "Impressions of Opera in France," MQ VII (1921) 314–30.

—— "Monte Carlo : Opéra de Luxe," MQ IX (1923) 65–71.

Chadwick, George. Horatio Parker. New Haven, Yale University Press, 1921.

Chailley, Jacques. "Le Symbolisme des thèmes dans *Pelléas et Mélisande*," *L'Information musicale*, No. 64, 2e année (April 3, 1942) 889–90.

Challis, Bennett. "Opera Publics of Europe : Impressions and Reminiscences," MQ XII (1926) 564–79.

Cherbuliez, Antoine-Elisée. "Kleine Monographie der Schweizer Oper," M I (1947) 96–99.

Chybiński, A. "L. Różycki jako twórca dramatu muzycznego *Bolesław Śmiały*," *Młoda Muzyka* (1909) No. 7–8.

Cinquanta anni di opera e balletto in Italia. [A cura di Guido M. Gatti.] Rome, Carlo Bestetti, Edizioni d'Arte, [1954].

Clapham, John. "*The Whirlpool:* A Slovak Opera," MR XIX (1958) 47–51.

Coeuroy, André. La Musique française moderne. Paris, Delagrave, 1922.

Cohen, Alex. "Ernest Bloch's *Macbeth*," M&L XIX (1938) 143–48.

Collaer, Paul. Darius Milhaud. Paris, Richard-Masse, Editeurs, 1947.

—— La Musique moderne, 1905–1955. Paris-Brussels, Elsevier, 1955.

Colles, H. C. "Philip Napier Miles," M&L XVII (1936) 357–67.

Cooke, Deryck. "*The Rake* and the 18th Century," *The Musical Times* CIII (1962) 20–23.

Copland, Aaron. Our New Music. New York, Whittlesey, [1941].

Corrodi, Hans. Othmar Schoeck : Bild eines Schaffens. Frauenfeld, Huber, [1956]. 3d ed.

—— "Othmar Schoeck's *Massimilla Doni*," M&L XVIII (1937) 391–97.

Cortese, Louis. Alfredo Casella. Genoa, Orfini, [1935].

Craft, Robert. "Reflections on *The Rake's Progress*," *The Score* No. 9 (September, 1954) 24–30.

Crozier, Eric. "Foreword to *Albert Herring*," *Tempo* No. 4 (Summer, 1947) 10–14.

Dallapiccola, Luigi. "The Genesis of the *Canti di prigionia* and *Il prigioniero:* An Autobiographical Fragment," MQ XXXIX (1953) 355–72.

Danckert, Werner. Claude Debussy. Berlin, de Gruyter, 1950.

Deane, Basil. Albert Roussel. London, Barrie and Rockliff, [1961].

De Angelis, Alberto. "Musica e musicisti nell' opera di G. d'Annunzio," RMI XLIII (1939) 275–301.

Debussy, Claude. Monsieur Croche, anti-dilettante. Paris, Dorbon-aîné, 1921.

Delannoy, Marcel. Honegger. Paris, Flore, P. Horay, [1953].

Della Corte, Andrea. "*The Rake's Progress* di I. Strawinsky," RMI LIII (1951) 262–68.

—— Rittrato di Franco Alfano. Turin, G. B. Paravia, [1935].

Demuth, Norman. Albert Roussel. [London], United Music Publishers, [n.d.].

Dent, Edward J. "Busoni's *Doctor Faust*," M&L VII (1926) 196–208.

—— Ferrucio Busoni: A Biography. London, Oxford University Press, 1933.

—— "Hans Pfitzner," M&L IV (1923) 119–32.

De' Paoli, Domenico. "Italy's New Music of the Theatre," MMus VIII, No. 1 (November–December, 1930) 21–26.

—— "*Orfeo* and *Pelléas*," M&L XX (1939) 381–98.

—— "Pizzetti's *Fra Gherardo*," MMus VI, No. 2 (January–February, 1929) 39–42.

De Rensis, Raffaello. Ermanno Wolf-Ferrari, la sua vita d'artista. Milan, Fratelli Treves, 1937.

—— Ottorino Respighi. Turin, Paravia, [1935].

Desderi, Ettore. "Le tendenze attuali della musica: Il teatro," RMI XXXVIII (1931) 247–77.

D'Estrade-Guerra, O. "Les Manuscrits de *Pelléas et Mélisande*," RM No. sp. 235 (1957) 5–24.

Deutsch, Max. "*Phèdre*, de Marcel Mihalovici," RIdM No. 12 (Spring, 1952) 66–74.

Dickinson, A. E. F. "Round about *The Midsummer Marriage*," M&L XXXVII (1956) 50–60.

Dioli, Arrigo, and Maria Fernanda Nobili. La vita e l'arte di Amilcare Zanella. Bergamo, Edizioni Orobiche, [1941].

Drew, David. "Brecht versus Opera," *The Score* No. 23 (July, 1958) 7–10.

—— "Topicality and the Universal: The Strange Case of Weill's *Die Bürgschaft*," M&L XXIX (1958) 242–55.

Du Bled, Victor. "Le Ballet de l'opéra," RM II (December, 1921) 191–205.

[Dukas, Paul.] RM numéro spécial (May–June, 1936) contains articles on Dukas's operas.

Dumesnil, Maurice. Claude Debussy, Master of Dreams. New York, Ives Washburn, [1940].

—— "Gabriel Dupont, Musician of Normandy," MQ XXX (1944) 441–47.

Egk, Werner. "Irische Legende," OeM X (1955) 125–30.

—— Musik, Wort, Bild. Texte und Anmerkungen : Betrachtungen und Gedanken. Munich, A. Langen, G. Müller, [1960].

Einem, Gottfried von. "Der Prozess," OeM VIII (1953) 198–200.

Einstein, Alfred. "L'opera tedesca d'oggi," RassM V (1932) 26–37.

Emmanuel, Maurice. Pelléas et Mélisande de Debussy : Etude et analyse. Paris, Mellottée, [1925?]. New ed., 1950.

Engelfred, Abele. "Enoch Arden di Riccardo Strauss," RMI VI (1899) 176–84.

Eősze, László. Kodály Zoltán, élete és munkássága. Budapest, Zeneműkiadó Vállalat, 1956. In English : Zoltan Kodaly, His Life and Work. London, Collet, 1962.

Epstein, Peter. "Paul Hindemiths Theatermusik," Die Musik XXIII (May, 1931) 582–87.

Erhardt, Otto. "The Later Operatic Works of Richard Strauss," Tempo No. 12 (Summer, 1949) 23–31.

—— Richard Strauss : Leben, Wirken, Schaffen. Olten & Freiburg i. B., O. Walter AG., [1953].

Evans, Peter. "Britten's New Opera [A Midsummer Night's Dream] : A Preview," Tempo No. 53–54 (1960) 34–48.

Everett, Horace. "Notes on The Tender Land," Tempo No. 31 (Spring, 1954) 13–16.

Eyer, Ronald. "Carlisle Floyd's Susannah," Tempo No. 42 (Winter, 1956–57) 7–11.

Fähnrich, Hermann. "Das 'Mozart-Wagner-Element' im Schaffen von Richard Strauss," SchwM LXXXIX (1959) 311–16.

—— "Richard Strauss über das Verhältnis von Dichtung und Musik (Wort und Ton) in seinem Opernschaffen," Mf XIV (1961) 22–35.

Falle, G. "Canadian Opera," Canadian Forum XXXVI (1956) 206–7.

[Fauré, Gabriel Urbain.] See RM, numéro spécial (October, 1922).

[——] "Gabriel Fauré : Note biografiche," Bollettino bibliografico musicale V, No. 3 (March, 1930) 5–[17].

—— Lettres intimes. Présentées par Philippe Fauré-Fremiet. Paris, La Colombe, [1951].

Fauré-Frémiet, Philippe. Gabriel Fauré. Nouvelle éd., suivie de Réflexions sur la confiance Fauréenne et de Notes sur l'interprétation des oeuvres. Paris, A. Michel, [1957].

Favre, Georges. Paul Dukas : Sa vie, son oeuvre. Paris, La Colombe, [1948].

Ferchault, Guy. "A propos de Mélisande," *L'Information musicale*, No. 60, 2e année (March 7, 1942) 819–21; No. 62, 2e année (March 20, 1942) 874.

Fickler, August. "Oper und Operette in Rundfunk und Fernsehen 1957," NZfM CXIX (1958) 282–88.

Finck, Henry T. Richard Strauss. Boston, Little, Brown, 1917.

Foerster, Lilian A. "*Peter Grimes* in Score and Performance," *Musicology* I (1947) 221–41.

Forneberg, Erich. "Das Volkslied als expressionistisches Symbol in Alban Bergs *Wozzeck*," NZfM CXX (1959) 261–65.

Fortner, Wolfgang. "Bluthochzeit nach Federico Garcia Lora," *Melos* XXIV (1957) 71–73.

Gardner, John. "*The Duenna* [by Roberto Gerhard] (1945–47)," *The Score* No. 17 (September, 1956) 20–26.

Gatti, Guido Maria. "Franco Alfano," MQ IX (1923) 556–77.

—— "Gabriele D'Annunzio and the Italian Opera Composers," MQ X (1924) 263–88.

—— Ildebrando Pizzetti. Turin, G. B. Paravia, [1934]; 2d ed., Milan, Ricordi, [1955]. English translation : London, Dennis Dobson, 1951.

—— "Ildebrando Pizzetti," MQ IX (1923) 96–121, 271–86.

—— "Malipiero and Pirandello at the Opera," MMus XI, No. 4 (May–June, 1934) 213–16.

——Musicisti moderni d'Italia e di fuori. Bologna, Pizzi, 1920.

—— "Opernkomponist Ferruccio Busoni," *Melos* XXV (1958) 189–94.

—— "Recent Italian Operas," MQ XXIII (1937) 77–88.

—— "The Stage Works of Ferruccio Busoni," MQ XX (1934) 267–77.

—— Il Teatro alla Scala rinnovato : Le prime quattro stagioni. Milan, Fratelli Treves, 1926.

—— "Two *Macbeths:* Verdi—Bloch," MQ XII (1926) 22–31.

Gatti, Guido M., ed. L'opera di Gian Francesco Malipiero : Saggi di scrittori italiani e stranieri ... seguiti dal catalogo delle opere con annotazioni dell' autore e da ricordi e pensieri dello stesso. [Bologna], Edizioni di Treviso, 1952.

Gatti-Casazza, Giulio. Memories of the Opera. New York, Charles Scribner's Sons, 1941.

Gavazzeni, Gianandrea. Altri studi pizzettiani. Bergamo, Stamperia Conti, [1956].

—— "Karol Szymanowski e il *Re Ruggero*," RassM X (1937) 409–15.

—— Tre studi su Pizzetti. Como, E. Cavalleri, 1937.

George, André. Arthur Honegger. Paris, C. Aveline, 1926.

Giazotto, Remo. Busoni : La vita nell' opera. [Milan], Genio, [1947].

Gilman, Lawrence. Aspects of Modern Opera. London, John Lane; New York, Dodd, Mead, 1924.

—— Debussy's *Pelléas et Mélisande*, a Guide to the Opera. New York, G. Schirmer, 1907.

Glanville-Hicks, P[eggy]. "Some Reflections on Opera : Rolf Liebermann, a Man of the Theatre," *American Composers Alliance Bulletin* VI, No. 4 (1957) 12–15, 22.

"*Gloriana:* A Synopsis," *Tempo* No. 28 (Summer, 1953) 8–13.

Golachowski, Stanisław. Karol Szymanowski. [Wyd. 1 Cracow], Polskie Wydawnictwo Muzyczne, [1956].

Goldovsky, Boris. "*Mavra*, a Lyric Masterpiece," *Chrysalis* IV (1951) 3–4.

Goléa, Antoine. Pelléas et Mélisande : Analyse poétique et musicale. Paris, [Impr. du Château-Rouge], 1952.

Gordon, Diane Kestin. Folklore in Modern English Opera. University of California, Los Angeles Dissertation, 1959. 2 vols.

Goslich, Siegfried. "Das Wandbild : Othmar Schoeck und Ferruccio Busoni," M XI (1957) 322–25.

Graf, Max. "*Der Prozess* von Gottfried von Einem," OeM VIII (1953) 259–64.

Gregor, Joseph. Richard Strauss. Munich, R. Piper, [1939].

—— "Typen der Regie der Oper im 20. Jahrhundert," in *Bericht über den internationalen musikwissenschaftlichen Kongress Wien, Mozartjahr 1956* (Graz, Böhlaus, 1958), 253–60.

Grisson, Alexandra Carola. Ermanno Wolf-Ferrari. Regensburg, Bosse, 1941; 2d ed., Zurich, Amalthea-Verlag, [1958].

Guerrini, Guido. Ferruccio Busoni : La vita, la figura, l'opera. Florence, Casa Editrice Monsalvato, 1944.

Gui, Vittorio. "Arlecchino," RassM XIII (1940) 30–37.

Gutman, Hans. "*Mahagonny* and Other Novelties," MMus VII, No. 4 (June–July, 1930) 32–36.

—— "Tabloid Hindemith," MMus VII, No. 1 (December; 1929–January, 1930) 34–37.

Hall, Raymond. "The *Macbeth* of Bloch," MMus XV, No. 4 (May–June, 1938) 209–15.

Halusa, Karl. Hans Pfitzners musikdramatisches Schaffen. Vienna Dissertation, 1929.

Hamburg, Nordwestdeutscher Rundfunk. Zur Uraufführung von Arnold Schönbergs nachgelassener Oper *Moses und Aron* : Die Uraufführung fand am 12. März 1954 in der Hamburger Musikhalle statt. [Hamburg, 1954(?).]

Hammerschmidt, Wolfgang. 10 Jahre Komische Oper. (Berlin 1947–1957.) Berlin, Komische Oper, [1958].

Handschin, Jacques. Igor Stravinsky. Zurich and Leipzig, Hug, 1933.

Harászti, Emil. Béla Bartók, His Life and Works. Paris, The Lyrebird Press, [1938].

—— "Le Problème du Leit-motiv," RM IV (August, 1923) 35–37.

Harcourt, Eugène d'. La Musique actuelle en Allemagne et Autriche-Hongrie. Paris, Durdilly, [1908].

—— La Musique actuelle en Italie. Paris, Durdilly, [1907].

Harth, Walther. "Oper zwischen Montage und Breitwand," Melos XXIV (1957) 4–8.

Hartung, Günther. "Zur epischen Oper Brechts und Weills," Wissenschaftliche Zeitschrift des Martin-Luther-Universität Halle-Wittenberg VIII (1959) 659–73.

Hausswald, Günter. "Antiker Mythos bei Richard Strauss," M XII (1958) 323–26.

Heinsheimer, H. W. "Opera in America Today," MQ XXXVII (1951) 315–29.

—— "Die Umgestaltung des Operntheaters in Deutschland," Anbruch XV (August–September, 1933) 107–13.

Hell, Henri. Francis Poulenc, musicien français. Paris, Plon, [1958]. English translation : London, Calder, [1959].

Helm, Everett. "Carl Orff," MQ XLI (1955) 285–304.

—— "Virgil Thomson's Four Saints in Three Acts," MR XV (1954) 127–32.

Henze, Hans Werner. "Neue Aspekte in der Musik," NZfM CXXI (1960) 3–9.

[Heseltine, Philip.] Frederick Delius. Reprinted with Additions, Annotations and Comments by Hubert Foss. New York, Oxford University Press, 1952.

Hill, Edward Burlingame. Modern French Music. Boston and New York, Houghton Mifflin, 1924.

Hill, Richard S. "Concert Life in Berlin, Season 1943–44," MLA Notes, 2d ser. I, No. 3 (June, 1944) 13–33.

—— "Schoenberg's Tone-Rows and the Tonal System of the Future," MQ XXII (1936) 14–37.

Hindemith, Paul. A Composer's World : Horizons and Limitations. Cambridge, Mass., Harvard University Press, 1952.

Hirtler, Franz. Hans Pfitzners Armer Heinrich in seiner Stellung zur Musik des ausgehenden 19. Jahrhunderts. Würzburg, K. Triltsch, 1940.

Hoérée, Arthur. Albert Roussel. Paris, Rieder, 1938.

Hoffman, Rudolf Stephan. Franz Schreker. Leipzig, E. P. Tal, 1921.

Hofmannsthal, Hugo von. "Ce que nous avons voulu en écrivant Ariane à Naxos et Le Bourgeois Gentilhomme," MM VIII, Nos. 9–10 (1912) 1–3.

Hohlfeld, Charlotte. "Wieder eine neue Oper : Kolumbus von Karl-Rudi Griesbach," MuG IX (1959) 80–82.

Holländer, Hans. "Hugo von Hofmannsthal als Opernlibrettist," Zeitschrift für Musik XCVI (1929) 551–54.

—— "Leoš Janáček and His Operas," MQ XV (1929) 29–36.

—— "Leoš Janáček in seinen Opern," NZfM CXIX (1958) 425–27.

—— "The Music of Leos Janacek—Its Origin in Folklore," MQ XLI (1955) 171–76.

Holst, Imogen. "Britten's *Let's Make an Opera!*," *Tempo* No. 18 (Winter, 1950–51) 12–16.

—— Gustav Holst. London, Oxford University Press, 1938.

—— The Music of Ralph Vaughan Williams. London, New York, To- University Press, 1951.

Honolka, Kurt. Das vielstimmige Jahrhundert : Musik in unserer Zeit. Stuttgart, Cotta, [1960].

Hoover, Kathleen O'Donnell, and John Cage. Virgil Thomson : His Life and Music. New York, Thomas Yoseloff, [1959].

Howard, John Tasker. Our Contemporary Composers : American Music in the Twentieth Century. New York, Thomas Y. Crowell Co., 1941.

Howes, Frank. The Dramatic Works of Ralph Vaughan Williams. London, Oxford University Press, 1937.

—— The Music of Ralph Vaughan Williams. London, New York, Toronto, Oxford University Press, 1954.

Hübner, O. Richard Strauss und das Musikdrama. Leipzig, [Pabst], 1910. 2d ed.

Hurd, Michael. Immortal Hour, the Life and Period of Rutland Boughton. London, Routledge and Kegan Paul, [1962].

Husssey, Dyneley. "Walton's *Troilus and Cressida*," M&L XXXVI (1955) 139–45.

Hutchings, Arthur. "Delius's Operas," *Tempo* No. 26 (Winter, 1952–53) 22–29.

Huth, Arno. "Forbidden Opus—Protestant," MMus XVI, No. 1 (November–December, 1938) 38–41.

Inghelbrecht, Germaine, and D. E. Inghelbrecht. Claude Debussy. [Paris], Costard, [1953].

Internationale Richard-Strauss-Gesellschaft, *Mitteilungen*. Berlin, No. 1– (October, 1952– ).

Istel, Edgar. "For a Reversion to Opera," MQ X (1924) 405–37.

Iwaszkiewicz, J. "Dzieje *Króla Rogera*," *Muzyka* (1926) 271–72.

Jachimecki, Zdzisław. Karol Szymanowski. Cracow, Skład gł. w Księgarni Jagiellońskiej (Druk. "Czasu"), 1927.

—— "Karol Szymanowski," MQ VIII (1922) 23–37.

—— "Karol Szymanowski," *Slavonic and East European Review* XVII (July, 1938) 174–85.

—— "Operetka Karola Szymanowskiego," *Muzyka* (1952) Nos. 3–4 (24–25), 27–39.

Jahn, Renate. "Vom *Spieler* zur *Erzählung vom wahren Menschen*," MuG XI (1961) 232–38.

Janáček, Leoš. Korespondence Leoše Janáčka s libretisty Výletů Broučkových. Prague, Hudebni Matice, 1950.

Janáček, Leoš. Korespondence Leoše Janáčka s Marié Calmou a MUDr. Frant. Veselým. Prague, Orbis, 1951.

—— Leoš Janáček in Briefen und Erinnerungen, ausgewählt, mit Beiträgen und Anmerkungen versehen von Bohumír Štědroň. [Prague], Artia, [1955]. Translated as : Letters and Reminiscences. Prague, Artia, 1955.

Jardillier, Robert. Pelléas. Paris, C. Aveline, 1927.

Jones, John Kester. The Elektra of Strauss : The Relation of the Music to the Drama. University of California, Berkeley A.M. Thesis, 1955.

Jouve, Pierre Jean, and Michel Fano. Wozzeck ou le nouvel opéra. Paris, Plon, [1953].

Kalisch, Alfred. "Impressions of Strauss's Elektra," ZIMG X (1908–9) 198–202.

Kamieński, Ł. "[Nowowiejski's] Legenda Bałtyku," Muzyka (1924) No. 2, 64–68.

Kamiński, M. Ludomir Rózycki, the Jubilee Concert : Biographical Notes. Katowice, 1951.

Kapp, Julius. Franz Schreker. Munich, Drei Masken, 1921.

—— Die Staatsoper Berlin 1919 bis 1925. Stuttgart, Deutsche Verlags-Anstalt, [1925].

Keller, Hans. "Britten and Mozart," M&L XXIX (1948) 17–30.

—— "Britten's Beggar's Opera," Tempo No. 10 (Winter, 1948–49) 7–13.

—— "Schoenberg's Comic Opera [Von Heute auf Morgen]," The Score No. 23 (July, 1958) 27–36.

—— "Schoenberg's Moses and Aron," The Score No. 21 (October, 1957) 30–45.

Keller, Wilhelm. Karl Orff's Antigonae: Versuch einer Einführung. Mainz, Schott, [1950].

Kerman, Joseph. "Grimes and Lucretia," The Hudson Review II (1949–50) 277–84.

—— "Opera à la mode. [Stravinsky's The Rake's Progress]," The Hudson Review VI (1953–54) 560–77.

—— "Terror and Self-Pity : Alban Berg's Wozzeck," The Hudson Review V (1952–53) 409–19.

Kiekert, Ingeborg. Die musikalische Form in den Werken Carl Orff's. Regensburg, Gustav-Bosse Verlag, 1957.

Klebe, Giselher. "Meine Oper Alkmene," Melos XXVIII (1961) 272–75.

—— "Uber meine Oper Die Räuber," Melos XXIV (1957) 73–76.

Klein, John W. "Delius as a Musical Dramatist," MR XXII (1961) 294–301.

—— "Some Reflexions on Gloriana," Tempo No. 29 (Autumn, 1953) 16–21.

—— "Wozzeck—a Summing-up," M&L XLIV (1963) 132–39.

Klein, Rudolf. "Frank Martins erste Oper [Der Sturm]," OeM XI (1956) 50–56.

—— "Molière auf der Opernbühne : Zur Salzburger Uraufführung von Liebermanns *Schule der Frauen*," OeM XII (1957) 151–54.

—— "Rolf Liebermann als dramatischer Komponist," *Melos* XXI (1954) 275–80.

—— "Rolf Liebermanns Opera semiseria *Penelope*," SchwM XCIV (1954) 271–76.

—— "Style et technique musicale de l'opéra *La Tempête* de Frank Martin," SchwM XCVI (1956) 240–44.

Koechlin, Charles Louis Eugène. Gabriel Fauré : Avec citations musicales dans le texte. Paris, Plon, [1949]. New ed.

Koegler, Horst. "Opernkomponisten heute : Eine Rundfrage des Internationalen Theaterinstituts der UNESCO," *Melos* XX (1953) 316–18.

Korngold, Julius. Deutsches Opernschaffen der Gegenwart. Vienna, Rikola, 1922.

—— Die romanische Oper der Gegenwart. Vienna, Rikola, 1922.

Kornprobst, Louis. J. Guy Ropartz : Etude biographique et musicale. Strasbourg, Editions Musicales d'Alsace, [1949].

Krause, Ernst. "*Penelope* und der neue Kurs," MuG V (1955) 125–27.

—— Richard Strauss : Gestalt und Werk. Leipzig, B&H, 1955.

Krenek, Ernst. Music Here and Now. New York, W. W. Norton, [1939]. Originally in German, 1937.

—— "The New Music and Today's Theatre," MMus XIV, No. 4 (May–June, 1937) 200–203.

—— "Opera between the Wars," MMus XX, No. 2 (January–February, 1943) 102–111.

—— "Problemi di stile nell' opera," RassM VII (1934) 199–202.

—— Selbstdarstellung. Zurich, Atlantis-Verlag, [1948].

—— Zur Sprache gebracht : Essays über Musik. Munich, Langen/ Müller, [1958].

Krieger, Erhard. "Heinrich Kaminski's Drama *Jürg Jenatsch*," *Zeitschrift für Musik* C (1933) 992–95.

Kroó, György. Bartók Béla szinpadi müvei. Budapest, 1962.

Krüger, Karl Joachim. Hugo von Hofmannsthal und Richard Strauss. Berlin, Junker und Dünnhaupt, 1935.

Kulikovich, Mikola. Sovetskaia opera na sluzhbe partii i pravitel'stva. Munich, 1955.

Labroca, Mario. "The Rebirth of Italian Opera," MMus IV, No. 4 (May–June, 1927) 8–14.

La Maestre, André Espiau de. "Francis Poulenc und seine Bernanos-Oper," OeM XIV (1959) 4–9.

—— "Milhauds *Christophe Colomb*," OeM XII (1957) 9–12.

La Morgia, Manlio, ed. La città dannunziana di Ildebrando Pizzetti : Saggi e note. [Pescara, Comitato Centrale Abruzzese per le Onoranze a I. Pizzetti; Milan, Ricordi], 1958.

Lamy, Fernand. J. Guy Ropartz : L'homme et l'œuvre. Paris, Durand et Cie., [1948].

Landormy, Paul Charles René. "Gabriel Fauré," MQ XVII (1931) 293–301.

—— "Maurice Ravel," MQ XXV (1939) 430–41.

Landowski, Marcel. Honegger. [Paris], Editions du Seuil, [1957].

Landowski, Wanda Alice L. Maurice Ravel : Sa vie, son oeuvre. Paris, Les Editions Ouvrières, [1950].

Lang, Paul Henry. "Background Music for *Mein Kampf*," *Saturday Review of Literature* XXVIII, No. 3 (January 20, 1945) 5–9.

Laux, Karl. Joseph Haas. Berlin, Henschelverlag, 1954.

—— Die Musik in Russland und der Sowjetunion. Berlin, Henschelverlag, 1958.

—— "Oper aus Ost und West," MuG IX (1959) 153–58.

Leibowitz, René. "Alban Berg et l'essence de l'opéra : Réflexions sur la musique dramatique 'sub una specie,' " *L'Arche* No. 13, 3e année (February, 1946) 130–34; No. 13, 4e année (March, 1946) 158–66.

—— "Renaissance de l'opéra," *Les Temps modernes* XII, No. 134 (1957) 1599–1607.

Lendvai, Ernö. "A kékszakállu herceg vára," *Magyar Zene* I (1961) 339–87.

Lepel, Felix von. Die Dresdner Oper als Weltkulturstätte. Dresden, Spohr, 1942.

—— Max von Schillings und seine Oper *Mona Lisa:* Ein Ruhmesblatt für die Städtische Oper in Berlin-Charlottenburg. Berlin-Charlottenburg, Selbstverlag, 1954.

Lesznai, Lajos. Béla Bartók, sein Leben—seine Werke. Leipzig, Deutscher Verlag für Musik, 1961.

Lewinski, Wolf-Eberhard von. "Der Dramatiker Giselher Klebe," *Melos* XXVIII (1961) 4–7.

Liess, Andreas. Carl Orff : Idee und Werk. [Zurich], Atlantis-Verlag, [1955].

—— Franz Schmidt, Leben und Schaffen. Graz, H. Böhlaus Nachf., 1951.

—— "Die musiké techné Carl Orffs," M IX (1955) 305–9.

Lindner, Dolf. Richard Strauss/Joseph Gregor : *Die Liebe der Danae;* Herkunft, Inhalt und Gestaltung eines Opernwerkes. Vienna, Oesterreichischer Diana Verlag, [1952].

Lissa, Z. "Pierwsza opera w Polsce Ludowej. (*Bunt żaków*)," *Muzyka* (1951) No. 10 (19), 3–29.

List, Kurt. "*Lulu*, after the Premiere," MMus XV, No. 1 (November–December, 1937) 8–12.

Łobaczewska, Stefanja. Karol Szymanowski : Życie i twórczość. Cracow, Polskie Wydawnictwo Muzyczne, [1950].

Lockspeiser, Edward. Debussy. New York, Pellegrini & Cudahy, 1949 [i.e., 1952]. 3rd ed.

—— "Musorgsky and Debussy," MQ XXIII (1937) 421–27.

Lopatnikoff, Nikolai. "*Christophe Colomb* [by Milhaud]," MMus VII, No. 4 (June–July, 1930) 36–38.

Louis, Rudolf. Die deutsche Musik der Gegenwart. Munich, G. Müller, 1909. 3d ed., 1912.

—— Hans Pfitzners *Die Rose vom Liebesgarten*. Munich, C. A. Seyfried, 1904.

Lualdi, Adriano. "Claudio Debussy, la sua arte e la sua parabola," RMI XXV (1918) 271–305.

McCredie, Andrew. "Contemporary Swedish Opera," *Sweden in Music* (*Musikrevy International*) XV (1960) No. 3 extra, 34–38.

Machlis, Joseph. Introduction to Contemporary Music. New York, W. W. Norton, [1961].

Maclean, Charles. "*La Princesse Osra* [by Herbert Bunning] and *Der Wald* [by Ethel Smyth]," ZIMG III (1901–2) 482–88.

Malipiero, Gian Francesco. "Orchestra e orchestrazione," RMI XXIII (1916) 559–69; XXIV (1917) 89–114.

Mann, Thomas. Pfitzners *Palestrina*. Berlin, S. Fischer, 1919.

Manuel, Roland. See Roland-Manuel.

Marangoni, Guido, and Carlo Vanbianchi. "La Scala," studie e ricerche : Note storiche e statistiche (1906–20). Bergamo, Istituto italiano d'arti grafiche, 1922.

Martynov, Ivan I. Dmitri Shostakovich, the Man and His Work. New York, Philosophical Library, [cop. 1947]. Trans. from the Russian by T. Guralsky.

Mason, Colin. "Stravinsky's Opera [*The Rake's Progress*]," M&L XXXIII (1952) 1–9.

Mason, Ronald. "Herman Melville and *Billy Budd*," *Tempo* No. 21 (Autumn, 1951) 6–8.

Mathis, Alfred. "Stefan Zweig as Librettist and Richard Strauss," M&L XXV (1944) 163–76, 226–45.

Matthes, Wilhelm. "Paul von Klenau," *Blätter der Staatsoper* XX (1940) 5–14.

Mila, Massimo. "Ascoltando *La figlia de Jorio* di Pizzetti," RassM XXV (1955) 103–7.

—— "*Il prigioniero* di L. Dallapiccola," RassM XX (1950) 303–11.

—— "*The Turn of the Screw*," *The Score* No. 10 (December, 1954) 73–76.

Milhaud, Darius. Notes sans musique. Paris, Juilliard, 1949. Translated as : Notes without Music : An Autobiography. London, Dennis Dobson, 1952. American edition with final chapter especially written for it : New York, Alfred A. Knopf, 1953.

Milner, Anthony. "*Billy Budd*," *The Score* No. 6 (May, 1952) 59–61.

Mitchell, Donald. "The Character of Lulu," MR XV (1954) 268–74.

Mitchell, Donald. "Prokofieff's *Three Oranges:* A Note on Its Musical-Dramatic Organisation," *Tempo* No. 41 (Autumn, 1956) 20–24.

—— "*The Turn of the Screw:* A Note on Its Thematic Organization," MMR LXXXV (1955) 95–100.

Mitchell, Donald, and Hans Keller, eds. Benjamin Britten : A Commentary on His Works, from a Group of Specialists. London, Rockliff, [1952].

Moisenco, Rena. Realist Music : 25 Soviet Composers. London, Meridian Books, 1949.

Moreux, Serge. Béla Bartók. Paris, Richard-Masse, 1955. Rev. ed.

Morton, Lawrence. "Stravinsky," in *Encyclopédie de la musique* III (Paris, Fasquelle, 1961) 740–52.

Müller-Blattau, Joseph. Hans Pfitzner. Potsdam, Athenaion, 1940.

Muller, Daniel. Leoš Janáček. Paris, Rieder, [1930].

Murrill, Herbert. "*The Rake's Progress*," *The Score* No. 6 (May, 1952) 55–58.

Nathan, Hans. "The Twelve-Tone Compositions of Luigi Dallapiccola," MQ XLIV (1958) 289–310.

Nest'ev, Izrail' Vladimirovich. Prokof'ev. Moscow, Gos muzykal'noe izd-vo, 1957. English translation : Stanford, California, Stanford University Press, 1960.

Nest'ev, Izrail' Vladimirovich, ed. Sergeĭ Prokof'ev, 1953–1963 : Stat'i i materialy. Moscow, Sovetskiĭ Kompozitor, 1962.

Newman, Ernest. Richard Strauss. London and New York, J. Lane, 1908.

Newmarch, Rosa. "New Works in Czechoslovakia : Janáček and Novák," *The Chesterian* XII (July, 1931) 213–19.

Oboussier, Robert. "Randbemerkungen zu meiner Oper *Amphitryon*," M IV (1950) 458–60.

Oeser, Fritz. "Janáčeks Oper *Schicksal*," M XII (1958) 586–92.

Ohrmann, Fritz. "Max Brands Oper *Maschinist Hopkins*," *Signale für die musikalische Welt* LXXXVIII (1930) 395–99.

Oláh, Gustav. "Bartók and the Theatre," *Tempo* No. 14 (Winter, 1949–50) 4–8. Reprinted in *Béla Bartók: A Memorial Review*, 54–60.

Olkhovsky, Audrey. Music under the Soviets : The Agony of an Art. New York, F. A. Praeger, 1955.

Olsen, Derrick. "Souvenirs et réflexions d'un interprète à propos de la création de *Léonore 40–45*," SchwM XCIV (1954) 277–78.

Opera Annual. Edited by Harold Rosenthal. London, John Calder, 1954– .

"Opera As It Is—and May Be," general title of several articles in M&L IV (1923) 85 ff.

Opera News. New York, Metropolitan Opera Guild, [December] 1936– .

Oper im Bild : Ein Querschnitt durch das deutsche Opernschaffen seit 1945. Berlin-Halensee, M. Hesse, [1961].

Oper im XX. Jahrhundert. Bonn, Boosey & Hawkes, [1954].

Oper in neuer Gestalt. *Musica* XIII (April, 1959) No. 4.

Orel, Alfred. "Ein unbekanntes Szenar zu Hans Pfitzners *Palestrina*," SchwM LXXXIX (1949) 132–38.

Osthoff, Helmuth. "Mozarts Einfluss auf Richard Strauss," SchwM XCVIII (1958) 409–17.

Othmar Schoeck im Wort : Äusserungen des Komponisten mit einer Auswahl zeitgenössischer Bekenntnisse. St. Gall, Tschudy, 1957.

Pagano, Luigi. "*Dèbora e Jaéle* di Ildebrando Pizzetti," RMI XXX (1923) 47–108.

Pahissa, Jaime. Vida y obra de Manuel de Falla. Buenos Aires, Ricordi Americana, 1947. Translated as : Manuel de Falla, His Life and Works. London, Museum Press, [1954].

Pahlen, Kurt. Manuel de Falla und die Musik in Spanien. Olten & Freiburg i. B., Walter, [1953].

Pannain, Guido. "Il *Dottor Faust*," RassM XIII (1940) 20–29.

Parente, Alfredo. "Note sull' estetica musicale contemporanea in Italia," RassM III (1930) 289–310.

Perle, George. "*Lulu:* The Formal Design," JAMS XVII (1964) 179–92.

—— "The Music of *Lulu:* A New Analysis," JAMS XII (1959) 185–200. Corrections : *ibid*. XIV (1961) 96.

Petzet, Walter. "*Maschinist Hopkins*," *Signale für die musikalische Welt* LXXXVII (1929) 1363–65.

Peyser, Herbert F. "Some Fallacies of Modern Anti-Wagnerism," MQ XII (1926) 175–89.

Pfannkuch, Wilhelm. Das Opernschaffen Ermanno Wolf-Ferraris. Kiel Dissertation, 1952.

Pfitzner, Hans Erich. Gesammelte Schriften. Augsburg, B. Filser, 1926. 3 vols.

—— Reden, Schriften, Briefe. Unveröffenlichtes und bisher Verstreutes. Hrsg. von Walter Abendroth. [Berlin-Frohnau & Neuwied/Rhein], Luchterhand, [1955].

—— Vom musikalischen Drama : Gesammelte Aufsätze. Munich and Leipzig, Süddeutsche Monatshefte, 1915.

Pincherle, Marc. Albert Roussel. Geneva, Kister, [1957].

Pintacuda, Salvatore. Renzo Bossi. Milan, M. Gastaldi, 1955.

Pisk, Paul A. "Schönberg's Twelve-Tone Opera," MMus VII, No. 3 (April–May, 1930) 18–21.

Pizzetti, Ildebrando, "*Ariadne et Barbebleue* . . . de Paul Dukas," RMI XV (1908) 73–112.

—— "*Pelléas et Mélisande* . . . Debussy," RMI XV (1908) 350–63.

Plomer, William. "Notes on the Libretto of *Gloriana*," *Tempo* No. 28 (Summer, 1953) 5–7.

Pollatschek, Walter. Hofmannsthal und die Bühne. Frankfurt Dissertation, 1924.

Polyakova, Lyudmila. Soviet Music. Moscow, Foreign Languages Publishing House, [1961].

Ponz de Leon, Giuseppe. "Il dramma lirico nell' arte di Pizzetti," RMI XLIII (1939) 539–44.

Porter, Andrew. "Britten's *Billy Budd*," M&L XXXIII (1952) 111–18.

—— "Britten's *Gloriana*," M&L XXXIV (1953) 277–87.

Poulenc, Francis. "Comment j'ai composé les *Dialogues des Carmélites*," *L'Opéra de Paris* No. XIV (1957?) 15–17.

—— Entretiens avec Claude Rostand. Paris, R. Julliard, [1954].

Pound, Ezra Loomis. Antheil and the Treatise of Harmony. Chicago, P. Covici, 1927.

Previtali, F. "*Turandot* [Busoni]," RassM XIII (1940) 38–46.

Prod'homme, Jacques Gabriel. "The Recent Fiftieth Anniversary of the 'New Opera,'" MQ XII (1926) 13–21.

Prokof'ev, Sergeï Sergeevich. Autobiography, Articles, Reminiscences. [Compiled, edited, and annotated by S. Shlifstein; translated by Rose Prokofieva.] Moscow, Foreign Languages Publishing House, [1959?]. Translation of : S. S. Prokof'ev : Materialy, documenty, vospominaniia. Moscow, Gos. muzykal'noe izd-vo, 1956. 2d ed., 1961.

—— "The War Years," MQ XXX (1944) 421–27.

Prunières, Henry. "Honegger's *Judith*," MMus III, No. 4 (May–June, 1926) 30–33.

Raabe, Peter. Die Musik im dritten Reich. Regensburg, G. Bosse, [1935].

Rabinovich, D. Dmitry Shostakovich, Composer. Moscow, Foreign Languages Publishing House, 1959.

Racek, Jan. "Der Dramatiker Janáček," *Deutsches Jahrbuch der Musikwissenschaft* V (1961) 39–57.

——Leoš Janáček. Leipzig, Reclam, [1962?].

Ramuz, Charles Ferdinand. Souvenirs sur Igor Stravinsky. Paris, Gallimard, Editions de la Nouvelle Revue Française, [1929].

La Rassegna Musicale XXXII, Nos. 2, 3, 4 (1962). (Special number containing articles and bibliographies on opera in the twentieth century.)

Raupp, Wilhelm. Eugen d'Albert. Leipzig, Koehler & Amelang, [1930].

—— Max von Schillings. Hamburg, Hanseatische Verlagsanstalt, [1935].

[Ravel, Maurice.] *See* the two special issues of RM : April, 1925; December, 1938.

Rebatet, Lucien. "L'Enregistrement de *Pelléas et Mélisande*," *L'Information musicale* II (1942) No. 54.

Redlich, Hans Ferdinand. Alban Berg : The Man and His Music. London, Calder; New York, Abelard-Schuman, [1957].

—— Alban Berg : Versuch einer Würdigung. Vienna, Universal Edition, 1957.

—— "Egon Wellesz," MQ XXVI (1940) 65–75.

—— "A New Welsh Folk Opera [Parrott's *The Black Ram*]," M&L XXXVII (1956) 101–6.

—— "The Significance of Britten's Operatic Style," *Music Survey* II (1950) 240–45.

—— "Unveröffentlichte Briefe Alban Bergs an Arnold Schönberg," in *Festschrift Friedrich Blume* (Kassel, Bärenreiter, 1963) [272]–280.

Reich, Willi. Alban Berg. Vienna, H. Reichner, [1937].

—— "Alban Berg's *Lulu*," MQ XXII (1936) 383–401.

—— "Alban Bergs Oper *Lulu*," *Melos* XIX (1952) 337–42.

—— A Guide to Alban Berg's *Wozzek*. [New York, League of Composers, 1931.]

—— "A Guide to *Wozzeck*," MQ XXXVIII (1952) 1–21.

——"*Lulu*—the Text and Music," MMus XII, No. 3 (March–April, 1935) 103–11.

—— "Paul Hindemith," MQ XVII (1931) 486–96.

Reizenstein, Franz. "Walton's *Troilus and Cressida*," *Tempo* No. 34 (Winter, 1954–55) 16–27.

Respighi, Elsa. Ottorino Respighi: Dati biografici ordinati. [Milan], Ricordi, [1954].

Richard Strauss Jahrbuch. Bonn, 1954–1959/60. 2 vols.

Riemer, Otto, "Johannes Driessler als Opernkomponist," M VI (1952) 398–406.

Riesenfeld, Paul. "Die Romantik der neuen Sachlichkeit," *Signale für die musikalische Welt* LXXXVII (1929) 1075–78.

Riezler, Walter. Hans Pfitzner und die deutsche Bühne. Munich, Piper, 1917.

—— "Neue Horizonte: Bemerkungen zu Carl Orffs *Antigonae*," in *Gestalt und Gedanke, ein Jahrbuch* ([Munich], Oldenbourg, [1951]) 103–16.

Rimkus, Günter. "*Der arme Konrad:* Eine Oper von Jean Kurt Forest," MuG IX (1959) 198–202.

Rinaldi, Mario. Lo *Straniero* de Ildebrando Pizzetti. Florence, Casa Editrice Monsalvato, 1943.

Rochberg, George. "Hugo Weisgall," *American Composers Alliance Bulletin* VII, No. 2 (1958) 2–7.

Röttger, Heinz. Das Formproblem bei Richard Strauss. Berlin, Junker & Dünnhaupt, 1937.

Roland-Manuel. Manuel de Falla, "Cahiers d'art," 1930.

—— Maurice Ravel. London, Dennis Dobson, 1947.

—— Maurice Ravel et son œuvre dramatique. Paris, Librairie de France, 1928.

Rolland, Romain. Musiciens d'aujourd'hui. Paris, Hachette, 1912. 5th ed. Translated as: Musicians of Today. New York, Holt, 1915. 2d ed.

Roseberry, Eric. "The Music of *Noye's Fludde*," *Tempo* No. 49 (Autumn, 1958) 2–11.

Rosenzweig, Alfred. Zur Entwicklungsgeschichte des Strauss'schen Musikdramas. Vienna Dissertation, 1923.

Rossi-Doria, Gastone. "Il teatro musicale di G. F. Malipiero," RassM II (1929) 354–64.

Rostand, Claude. La Musique française contemporaine. Paris, Presses Universitaires, 1952. Translated as : French Music Today. New York, Merlin Press, [1957].

—— "The Operas of Darius Milhaud," Tempo No. 19 (Spring, 1951) 23–28.

Roth, Ernst, ed. Richard Strauss, Bühnenwerke : Dokumente der Uraufführungen. Stage Works, Documents of the First Performances. London, Boosey & Hawkes, 1954.

Rózycki, L. "Dzieje Erosa i Psyche," Muzyka (1930) No. 2, 82–85.

—— "Kilka słów o mojej Beatrix Cenci," Muzyka (1927) 69–70.

—— "O mojej operze Casanova," Muzyka (1925) 129–30.

Rutz, Hans. Hans Pfitzner : Musik zwischen den Zeiten. [Vienna], Humboldt-Verlag, [1949].

—— Neue Oper : Gottfried Einem und seine Oper Dantons Tod. Vienna, Universal Edition, [1947].

—— "Strawinsky und die Zukunft der Oper : Versuch einer geschichtlichen Perspektive," OeM VII (1952) 213–18.

Sabaneev, Leonid Leonidovitch. "Remarks on the Leitmotif," M&L XIII (1932) 200–206.

Sabin, Robert. "Carlisle Floyd's Wuthering Heights," Tempo No. 59 (Autumn, 1961) 23–26.

Šafránek, Miloš. Bohuslav Martinů, the Man and His Music. New York, Alfred A. Knopf, 1944.

—— "Bohuslav Martinů und das musikalische Theater," Musica XIII (1959) 550–54.

Sailer, Rudolf. Waltershausen und die Oper. Cologne Dissertation, 1957.

Saint-Cyr, Mario. Musicisti italiani contemporanei . . . prima serie. Rome, De Santis, [1932?].

St. John, Christopher. Ethel Smyth : A Biography. With Additional Chapters by V. Sackville-West and Kathleen Dale. [London, New York, Toronto], Longmans, Green & Co., [1959].

Salazar, Adolfo. La música moderna : Las corrientes directrices en el arte musical contemporáneo. Buenos Aires, Editorial Losada, 1944. Translated as : Music in Our Time : Trends in Music Since the Romantic Era. New York, W. W. Norton, 1946.

Samazeuilh, Gustave. Paul Dukas. Paris, A. Durand, 1913.

Saminsky, Lazare. "Jürg Jenatch," MMus VII, No. 1 (December, 1929–January, 1930) 37–39.

—— "More about Faustus," MMus V, No. 1 (November–December, 1927) 38–39.

—— Music of Our Day. New York, T. Y. Crowell, [1939]. New ed.

"Sampiero Corso et Henri Tomasi," RM No. 230 (1956).

Sargent, Winthrop. "Orlando in Mount Kisco" [Gian Carlo Menotti], *The New Yorker* XXXIX, No. 11 (May 4, 1963) 49 ff.

Sartori, Claudio. Riccardo Malipiero. Milan, Edizioni Suvini Zerboni, 1957. In English.

Schaal, Richard. Hugo Kaun : Leben und Werk (1863–1932). Ein Beitrag zur Musik der Jahrhundertwende. Regensburg, J. Habbel, [1946?].

Schaeffner, André. Igor Stravinsky. Paris, Rieder, [1931].

Schloezer, Boris Fedorovich. Igor Stravinsky. Paris, C. Aveline, 1929.

—— "The Operatic Paradox," MMus IV, No. 1 (November–December, 1926) 3–8.

Schmitz, Eugen. "Eugen d'Albert als Opernkomponist," *Hochland* VI, No. 2 (1909) 464–71.

—— Richard Strauss als Musikdramatiker. Munich, Lewy, 1907.

Schreiber, Flora Rheta, and Vincent Persichetti. William Schuman. New York, G. Schirmer, [1954].

Schuch, Friedrich von. Richard Strauss, Ernst von Schuch und Dresdens Oper. Dresden, Verlag der Kunst in Arbeitsgemeinschaft mit dem Dresdner Verlag, [1952].

Schuh, Willi. Das Bühnenwerk von Richard Strauss in den unter Mitwirkung des Komponisten geschaffenen letzten Münchner Inszenierungen : Ein Bildwerk. . . . Zurich, Atlantis-Verlag; London & New York, Boosey & Hawkes, 1954.

—— Othmar Schoeck. Zurich, Hug, [1934].

—— "*Tristan und Isolde* im Leben und Wirken Richard Strauss," in *Bayreuther Festspielbuch, 1952.*

—— Über Opern von Richard Strauss. (Kritiken und Essays, Band I.) Zurich, Atlantis-Verlag, [1947].

—— Von Neuer Musik. Zurich, Freiburg i. B., Atlantis-Verlag, [1955].

—— "Zur Harmonik Igor Strawinskys unter besonderer Berücksichtigung von *The Rake's Progress,*" in *Internationaler Musik-Kongress Wien 1952, Bericht* (Vienna, Österreichischer Bundesverlag, 1953) 127–34.

Schumacher, Ernst. Die dramatischen Versuche Bertolt Brechts, 1918–1933. Berlin, Rütten & Loening, 1955.

Schwerké, I. "Paul Dukas : A Brief Appreciation," MQ XIV (1928) 403–12.

Seldes, Gilbert. "Delight in the Theatre," MMus XI, No. 3 (March–April, 1934) 138–41.

—— "Jazz Opera or Ballet?" MMus III, No. 2 (January–February, 1926) 10–16.

Selva, Blanche. Déodat de Séverac. Paris, Delagrave, 1930.

Semler, Isabel Parker. Horatio Parker : A Memoir for His Grandchildren Compiled from Letters and Papers. New York, G. P. Putnam's Sons, 1942.

Seré, Octave. Musiciens français d'aujourd'hui. Paris, Mercure de France, 1911.

Seroff, Victor I. Debussy : Musician of France. New York, G. P. Putnam's Sons, [1956].

—— Dmitri Shostakovitch. New York, Alfred A. Knopf, 1943.

Servières, Georges. Edouard Lalo. Paris, H. Laurens, [1925].

—— Gabriel Fauré. Paris, H. Laurens, 1930.

Shawe-Taylor, Desmond. "The Operas of Leoš Janáček," PMA LXXXV (1958–59) 49–64.

Shlifstein, S. "On War and Peace," MMus XX, No. 3 (March–April, 1943) 185–87.

Shostakovich, Dmitrii. "My Opera, Lady Macbeth of Mtzensk," MMus XII, No. 1 (November–December, 1934) 23–30.

Slonimsky, Nicolas. Music Since 1900. New York, Coleman-Ross Co., Inc., 1949. 3d ed.

—— "Sergei Prokofiev : His Status in Soviet Music," American Quarterly on the Soviet Union II, No. 1 (1939) 37–44.

Smith, David Stanley. "A Study of Horatio Parker," MQ XVI (1930) 153–69.

Smith, Julia Frances. Aaron Copland, His Work and Contribution to American Music. New York, E. P. Dutton, 1955.

Smyth, Dame Ethel. Impressions That Remained : Memoirs. New York, Alfred A. Knopf, 1946. First published London, New York [etc.], Longmans, Green, 1919. 2 vols.

Sovetskaia opera : Sbornik kriticheskikh statei. Moscow, Gos. muzykal'noe izd-vo, 1953.

Die sowjetische Musik im Aufstieg : Eine Sammlung von Aufsätzen. Hrsg. vom Sowj. Komponistenverband d. UdSSR Red. Kollegium, E. A. Groschewa. Halle-Saale, Mitteldeutscher Verlag, 1952.

Specht, Richard. Richard Strauss, Die Frau ohne Schatten: Thematische Einführung. Berlin, Fürstner, 1919.

—— Richard Strauss und sein Werk. Leipzig, P. Tal, 1921. 2 vols.

Squire, W. H. Haddon. "The Aesthetic Hypothesis and The Rape of Lucretia," Tempo, New ser., No. 1 (September, 1946) 1–9.

Stäblein, Bruno. "Schöpferische Tonalität : Zum Grossaufbau von Orffs Antigonae," M VI (1952) 145–48.

Stefan, Paul. "Schoenberg's Operas," MMus II, No. 1 (January, 1925) 12–15.

—— "Schönberg's Operas," MMus VII, No. 1 (December, 1929–January, 1930) 24–28.

Stein, Erwin. "The Turn of the Screw and Its Musical Idiom," Tempo No. 34 (Winter, 1954–55) 6–14.

Stephan, Rudolf. "Zur jüngsten Geschichte des Melodrams," AfMw XVII (1960) 183–92.

Sternfeld, Frederick W. "Some Russian Folk Songs in Stravinsky's Petrouchka," MLA Notes, 2d ser. II, No. 2 (March, 1945) 95–107.

Stevens, Halsey. The Life and Music of Béla Bartók. New York, Oxford University Press, 1953.

Strauss, Franz, ed. Richard Strauss Briefwechsel mit Hugo von Hofmannsthal. Vienna, Zsolnay, 1926. Translated as: Correspondence between Richard Strauss and Hugo von Hofmannsthal, 1907-1918. New York, Alfred A. Knopf, 1927.

Strauss, Richard. "The Artistic Testament of Richard Strauss. Translated and with an Introduction by Alfred Mann," MQ XXXVI (1950) 1-8.

—— Betrachtungen und Erinnerungen. Zurich, Atlantis-Verlag, [1957]. 2d ed.

[——] Richard Strauss et Romain Rolland: Correspondance, fragments de journal. Paris, A. Michel, [1951].

Strauss, Richard, and Hugo von Hofmannsthal. Briefwechsel. Gesamtausgabe. Hrsg. von Franz Strauss und Alice Strauss, bearb. von Willi Schuh. 2d ed. Translated as: A Working Friendship: The Correspondence between Richard Strauss and Hugo von Hofmannsthal. New York, Random House, [1961].

Strauss, Richard, and Joseph Gregor. Briefwechsel, 1934-1949: Im Auftrag der Wiener Philharmoniker, hrsg. von Roland Tenschert. Salzburg, O. Müller, [1955].

Strauss, Richard, and Stefan Zweig. Briefwechsel. [Hrsg. von Willi Schuh.] [Frankfurt/M.], S. Fischer, 1957.

Stravinsky, Igor Fedorovich. Chroniques de ma vie. Paris, Denoël & Steele, [1935]. Translated as: Chronicles of My Life. London, V. Gollancz, 1936.

—— Memories and Commentaries. Garden City, N.Y., Doubleday, 1960.

—— "On Oedipus Rex," Encounter XVIII (1962) 29-35.

—— Poetics. New York, Vintage, 1956.

—— Poétique musicale sous forme de six leçons. Cambridge, Mass., Harvard University Press, 1942.

—— See RM, numéro spécial (May-June, 1939).

Stravinsky, Igor, and Robert Craft. Conversations with Igor Stravinsky. Garden City, N.Y., Doubleday, 1959.

—— Expositions and Developments. Garden City, N.Y., Doubleday, 1962.

Strobel, Heinrich. Paul Hindemith. Mainz, B. Schott's Söhne, [1948]. 3d ed.

—— "The Rake's Example," Melos XIX (1952) 7-9.

Stuart, Charles. "Katya Kabanova Reconsidered," MR XII (1951) 289-95.

Stuckenschmidt, Hans Heinz. Arnold Schönberg. Zurich & Freiburg i. B., Atlantis-Verlag, [1951]. 2d ed., 1957. English translation: New York, Grove Press, [1959].

—— "Ernst Křenek," MMus XVI, No. 1 (November-December, 1938) 41-44.

—— "Hellenic Jazz," MMus VII, No. 3 (April-May, 1930) 22-25.

Stuckenschmidt, Hans Heinz. "Opera in Germany Today," MMus XIII, No. 1 (November–December, 1935) 32–37.

—— "Rede über Busonis *Doktor Faust*," SchwM XCVI (1956) 3–9.

Suckling, Norman. Fauré. London, Dent, 1946.

Swarsenski, Hans. "Sergeii Prokofieff : *The Flaming Angel*," *Tempo* No. 39 (Spring, 1956) 16–27.

Szabolcsi, Bence, and Dénes Bartha, eds. Bartók Béla emlékére. Budapest, Akadémiai Kiadó, 1962. Series : Zenetudományi tanulmányok, X.

Tappolet, Willy. Arthur Honegger. Zurich, Atlantis-Verlag, [1954].

Tebaldini, Giovanni. "Telepatia musicale : A proposito dell' *Elettra* di Richard Strauss," RMI XVI (1909) 400–412.

Tenschert, Roland. "*Die Frau ohne Schatten:* Ihre Stellung und Bedeutung innerhalb von Richard Strauss' Opernschaffen," OeM VIII (1953) 139–43.

—— "A 'Gay Myth' : The Story of *Die Liebe der Danae*," *Tempo* No. 24 (Summer, 1952) 5–11.

—— "Die Kadenzbehandlung bei Richard Strauss," ZfMw VIII (1925–26) 161–82.

—— "Richard Strauss' Opernfassung der deutschen Übersetzung von Oscar Wildes *Salome*," *Richard Strauss Jahrbuch* (1959–60) 99–106.

—— Richard Strauss und Wien : Eine Wesensverwandtschaft. Vienna, Verlag Brüder Hollinek, 1949.

—— "Das Sonett in Richard Strauss' Oper *Capriccio*," SchwM XCVIII (1958) 1–5.

——"Versuch einer Typologie der Richard Strausschen Melodik," ZfMw XVI (1934) 274–93.

Thomas, Juan Maria. Manuel de Falla en la isla. [n.p.], Ediciones Capella Classica, [n.d.].

Thompson, Oscar. Debussy, Man and Artist. New York, Dodd, Mead, 1937.

—— "Fly-Wheel Opera," MMus VII, No. 1 (December, 1929–January, 1930) 39–42.

Thompson, Randall. "George Antheil," MMus VIII, No. 4 (May–June, 1931) 17–27.

Thomson, Virgil. The Musical Scene. New York, Alfred A. Knopf, 1945.

—— The State of Music. New York, W. Morrow, 1939.

Tiersot, Julien. "Edouard Lalo," MQ XI (1925) 8–35.

Tolksdorf, Cäcilie. John Gays *Beggar's Opera* und Bert Brechts *Dreigroschenoper*. Rheinberg, Rhl., Sattler & Koss, 1934.

Torchi, Luigi. "L'esito del concorso Sonzogno : Le tre opere rappresentate al 'Teatro Lirico' di Milano," RMI XI (1904) 516–49.

—— "*Ghismonda*, opera in tre atti di Eugenio D'Albert," RMI III (1896) 526–61.

—— "*Salome* di Riccardo Strauss," RMI XIV (1907) 113–56.

—— "*La vita nuova* di E. Wolf-Ferrari," RMI X (1903) 712–36.

Torrefranca, Fausto. "La nuova opera di Riccardo Strauss," RMI XIX (1912) 986–1031.

—— "*Il Rosencavalier* di R. Strauss," RMI XVIII (1911) 147–79.

—— "R. Strauss e l' *Elektra*," RMI XVI (1909) 335–84.

Trenner, Franz, ed. Richard Strauss : Dokumente seines Lebens und Schaffens. Munich, Verlag C. H. Beck, [1954].

Tretti, Luigi, and Leonello Fiumi, eds. Omaggio a Italo Montemezzi. Verona, Tip. Ghidini e Fiorini, [1952].

Tuthill, Burnet C. "Howard Hanson," MQ XXII (1936) 140–53.

Vaillat, Léandre. La Danse à l'Opéra de Paris. Paris, Amiot-Dumont, [1951].

Valentin, Erich. Hans Pfitzner. Regensburg, G. Bosse, 1939.

Vallas, Léon. Claude Debussy et son temps. Paris, F. Alcan, 1932; Paris, A. Michel, [1958]. Translated as : Claude Debussy, His Life and Works. London, Oxford University Press, 1933.

Veress, Sandor. "*Bluebeard's Castle,*" *Tempo* No. 13 (Autumn, 1949) 32–37; No. 14 (Winter, 1949–50) 25–35. Reprinted in *Béla Bartók: A Memorial Review*, 36–53.

Viu, Vicente Salas. "The Mystery of Manel de Falla's *La Atlántida,*" *Inter-American Music Bulletin* No. 33 (January, 1963) 1–6.

Vlad, Roman. "Dallapiccola 1948–1955," *The Score* No. 15 (March, 1956) 39–52.

—— Strawinsky. [Turin], Giulio Einaudi, 1958. English translation : London, New York, Oxford University Press, 1960.

Vogel, Jaroslav. Leoš Janáček, dramatik. Prague, Nákl. Hudební matice Umělecké besedy, 1948.

—— Leoš Janáček : Leben und Werk. Prague, Artia, [cop. 1958].

Vogel, Werner. Thematisches Verzeichnis der Werke von Othmar Schoeck. Zurich, Atlantis-Verlag, 1956.

Wachten, Edmund. "Der einheitliche Grundzug der Straussschen Formgestaltung," ZfMw XVI (1934) 257–74.

Wade, Carroll D. "A Selected Bibliography of Igor Stravinsky," MQ XLVIII (1962) 372–84.

Warlock, Peter, pseud. *See* Heseltine.

Weissmann, Adolph. "Germany's Latest Music Dramas," MMus IV, No. 4 (May–June, 1927) 20–26.

Wellesz, Egon. "Hofmannsthal and Strauss," M&L XXXIII (1952) 239–42.

—— "The Return to the Stage," MMus IV, No. 1 (November–December, 1926) 19–24.

Werba, Erik. "Musik der freien Entscheidung : Werner Egks *Irische Legende,*" OeM X (1955) 231–36.

Werker, Gerard. "Oper *Katja Kabanowa* van Leos Janacek," *Mens en Melodie* XIV (1959) 178–82.

Westphal, Kurt. Die moderne Musik. Leipzig and Berlin, B. G. Teubner, 1928.

Westphal, Kurt. "Das musikdramatische Prinzip bei Richard Strauss," *Die Musik* (September, 1927) 859–64.

White, Eric Walter. Benjamin Britten : A Sketch of His Life and Works. London, Boosey & Hawkes, 1948. New ed., 1954.

—— *"The Rake's Progress," Tempo* No. 20 (Summer, 1951) 10–18.

White, John S. The Salome Motive. New York, Eloquent Press Corp., N. Morgillo, n.d. [*ca.* 1947].

Wieke, Johannes. "Paul Kurzbachs Oper *Thyl Claas,*" MuG VIII (1958) 626–28.

Wieniawski, Adam. Ludomir Różycki. Warsaw, Gebethner i Wolff, [1928].

Wiesengrund-Adorno, Theodor. "Transatlantic," MMus VII, No. 4 (June–July, 1930) 38–41.

Willms, Franz. Führer zur Oper *Cardillac* von Paul Hindemith. Mainz, B. Schott, [1926].

—— "Paul Hindemith : Ein Versuch," *Von neuer Musik* I (1925) 78–123.

Witherspoon, Herbert. "Grand Opera and Its Immediate Problems," MTNA XXVII (1932) 148–49.

Wörner, Karl H. "Arnold Schoenberg and the Theater," MQ XLVIII (1962) 444–60.

—— "Egk and Orff : Representatives of Contemporary German Opera," MR XIV (1953) 186–204.

—— Gotteswort und Magie : Die Oper *Moses und Aron* von Arnold Schönberg. Heidelberg, Schneider, 1959.

—— "Katjas Tod, die Schlussszene der Oper *Katja Kabanowa* von Leoš Janáček," SchwM XCIV (1959) 91–96.

—— Neue Musik in der Entscheidung. Mainz, B. Schott's Söhne, [1956]. 2d ed.

[Wolf-Ferrari, Ermanno.] *See* special number of *Zeitschrift für Musik* CVIII, No. 1 (January, 1941).

Wolff, Stéphane. Un demi-siècle d'opéra comique (1900–1950). [Paris], A. Bonne, [1953].

Young, Percy M. Vaughan Williams. London, Dennis Dobson, 1953.

# MODERN EDITIONS
## OF OPERAS OR EXCERPTS FROM OPERAS COMPOSED BEFORE *1800*
### Including Pre-operatic Works of the Sixteenth Century

## ABBREVIATIONS

| | |
|---|---|
| *B&H* | Breitkopf & Härtel |
| *C.E.* | Collected Edition (Gesamtausgabe) |
| *C.F.* | *Les Chefs d'œuvre classiques de l'opéra français* (Leipzig, B&H, 1880) |
| *DdT* | *Denkmäler deutscher Tonkunst* (Leipzig, B&H, 1892–1931) |
| *DTB* | *Denkmäler deutscher Tonkunst : Denkmäler der Tonkunst in Bayern* (Braunschweig, H. Litolff's Verlag, 1900–1938) |
| *DTOe* | *Denkmäler der Tonkunst in Oesterreich* (Vienna, Artaria, 1894–  ) |
| *EDM* | *Das Erbe Deutscher Musik.* Erste Reihe, Reichsdenkmale (Leipzig, B&H, 1935–  ) |
| *EP* | R. Eitner, ed., *Publikationen älterer praktischer und theoretischer Musikwerke, vorzugsweise des XV. und XVI. Jahrhunderts* (Berlin, Bahn; Leipzig, B&H, 1873–1905) |
| *HAM* | Archibald T. Davison and Willi Apel, eds., *Historical Anthology of Music* (Cambridge, Mass., Harvard, 1950) II |
| *JF* | Knud Jeppesen, ed., *La Flora, arie &c. antiche italiane* (Copenhagen, Hansen, 1949) 3 vols. |
| *LAM* | Ludwig Landshoff, ed., *Alte Meister des Bel Canto* (Frankfurt, New York, C. F. Peters, 1912–27) 5 vols. |
| *MM* | Carl Parrish and John F. Ohl, eds., *Masterpieces of Music before 1750* (New York, Norton, 1951) |

OHM　　*The Oxford History of Music.* 2d edition (London, Oxford, 1929–38)

RB　　Hugo Riemann, ed., *Musikgeschichte in Beispielen* (Leipzig, B&H, 1921)

SB　　Arnold Schering, ed., *Geschichte der Musik in Beispielen* (Leipzig, B&H, 1931; reprint, New York, Broude Bros., 1950)

SCA　　*Smith College Archives* (Northampton, Mass., Smith College, 1933–　　)

TEM　　Carl Parrish, ed., *A Treasury of Early Music* (New York, Norton, 1958)

## SHORT TITLES (see also bibliography)

Abert: Anna Amalie Abert, ed., *Die Oper von den Anfängen bis zum Beginn des 19. Jahrhunderts* (Cologne, A. Volk, 1953)

Bücken: Ernst Bücken, *Die Musik des Rokokos und der Klassik* (Wildpark-Potsdam, Akademische Verlagsgesellschaft Athenaion, 1927)

Burney: Charles Burney, *A General History of Music from the Earliest Ages to the Present Period* (London, Printed for the Author, 1776)

Bush: Geoffrey Bush, ed., *Songs from the Ballad Operas* (London, Elkin; New York, Galaxy, 1956) 3 vols.

*I classici*: *I classici della musica italiana.* Raccolta diretta da Gabriele d'Annunzio (Milan, Società Anonima Notari La Santa, 1919–21) 36 vols.

—— (Milan, Istituto Editorale Italiano, 1918–20) 307 Quaderni.

Deldevez: Edouard Deldevez, ed., *Fondation de l'opéra en France* (Paris, Richault, *ca.* 1875)

Della Corte: Andrea della Corte, ed., *Piccola antologia settecentesca* (Milan, Ricordi, 1925)

Delsarte: François Delsarte, ed., *Archives du chant* (Paris, Choudens, ca. 1900) 7 vols.

Einstein: Alfred Einstein, *A Short History of Music* (New York, Knopf, 1947), supplement of music examples

Gevaert: François Auguste Gevaert, *Les Gloires d'Italie* (Paris, Heugel, 1868) 2 vols.

Goldschmidt: Hugo Goldschmidt, *Studien zur Geschichte der italienischen Oper im 17. Jahrhundert* (Leipzig, B&H, 1901–4) 2 vols.

Krehbiel: Henry E. Krehbiel, ed., *Voices from the Golden Age of Bel Canto* (New York, G. Schirmer, 1910)

Leichtentritt: Hugo Leichtentritt, ed., *Deutsche Hausmusik aus vier Jahrhunderten* (Berlin, Hesse, 1905)

Mantica: Francesco Mantica, ed., *Prime fioriture del melodramma Italiano* (Rome, Casa editrice Claudio Monteverdi, 1912–30) 2 vols.

Mortari: Francesco Cavalli, *Tre frammenti di opere.* Elaborazione di Virgilio Mortari (Milan, Carisch, 1942)

*Musica Britannica* (London, Stainer and Bell, 1951–　　)

*Nagels Musik Archiv* (Hanover, Adolph Nagel, 1927–　　)

Prosnak: Jan Prosnak, *Kultura muzyczna Warszawy XVIII w.* (Cracow, Polskie Wydawn. Muzyczne, 1955) 2 vols.

Prunières: Henry Prunières, *Maîtres du chant* (Paris, Heugel, [1924–27]) 6 vols. in one

Riemann: Hugo Riemann, *Handbuch der Musikgeschichte* (Leipzig, B&H, 1919–22) 2 vols. in 5 parts

Sabol: A. J. Sabol, ed., *Songs and Dances for the Stuart Masque* (Providence, R.I., Brown University Press, 1959)

Sondheimer: Robert Sondheimer, ed., *Werke aus dem 18. Jahrhundert* (Berlin-Basel, Edition Bernoulli, 1922–39) 52 Hefte

Torchi: Luigi Torchi, ed., *L'arte musicale in Italia* (Milan, Ricordi, 1897–1908?)

Wolff BoHg: Hellmuth C. Wolff, *Die Barockoper in Hamburg, 1678–1738* (Wolfenbüttel, Möseler, 1957) 2 vols.

Wolff DBa: Hellmuth C. Wolff, ed., *Deutsche Barockarien* (Kassel, Bärenreiter, n.d.) 2 vols.

Worsthorne: S. Towneley Worsthorne, *Venetian Opera in the 17th Century* (Oxford, Clarendon, 1954)

Zanon: Maffeo Zanon, *30 Arie Antiche* (Milan, Ricordi, 1922)


Abbatini, Antonio (1597–1680)
*La comica del cielo* : LAM I
*Dal male il bene* : see Marazzoli

Aranaz, Pedro (1742–1821)
*La maja limonera* : Subirá, *Tonadilla escénica* III

Ariosti, Attilio (1666–*ca.* 1740)
*Lucio vero* : LAM II

Arne, Thomas Augustine (1710–78)
*Achilles in Petticoats* : Bush
*Alfred* : *Three Songs*, ed. A. Carse (London, Augener, 1928)
*Artaxerxes* : Overture, ed. G. Warrack (London, Hawkes and Son, *ca.* 1941)
*Comus* : *Musica Britannica* III; Dances, ed. Whittaker (London, Oxford, 1938)
*The Guardian Outwitted* : Bush
*The Judgment of Paris* : Overture, ed. A. Carse (London, Augener, 1939)

Bach, Johann Christian (1735–82)
*Amadis des Gaules* : Geiringer, *Music of the Bach Family* (New York, 1954)
*Carattaco* : LAM II

Banchieri, Adriano (1568–1634)
*Il festino nella sera* : complete, ed. B. Somma, De Santis (Rome, 1939); ed. F. Vatielli, *I classici* I (Quad. 1–3); translation, *The Animals Improvise Counterpoint* (New York, 1937)
*La pazzia senile* : ed. Torchi IV; ed. F. Vatielli, *I classici* I (Quad. 1–3)
*La saviezza giovanile* : ed. R. Allorto, *Le Chant du Monde* (Milan, 1956)

Beaulieu, Lambert de
 *Circe, ou le Ballet comique de la reine* : complete, ed. J. B. Weckerlin,
    C.F.; Deldevez
Benda, Georg (1722–95)
 *Ariadne auf Naxos* : complete, ed. Einstein (Leipzig, C. W. F. Siegel,
    1920)
 *Der Jahrmarkt* : complete, ed. Th. W. Werner, DdT 64; complete,
    newly ed. and rev. H. J. Moser, DdT, Neuauflage, 64 (1959)
Bernasconi, Andrea (1706–84)
 *Adriano* : Krehbiel
Bianchi, Francesco (1752–1810)
 *L'orfano della China* : Krehbiel; Della Corte
 *La villanella rapita* : Della Corte
Blow, John (1649–1708)
 *Venus and Adonis* : complete, ed. G. P. E. Arkwright, Old English
    Edition, No. 25 (London, J. Williams, 1902); complete, ed. A. Lewis
    (Paris, Oiseau-Lyre, 1939); HAM 243
Bononcini, Giovanni Battista (1670–1747)
 *Astianatte* : HAM 262
 *Erminia* : LAM I
 *Mario fuggitivo* : LAM I
 *Polifemo* : complete, ed. Gerd Kärnbach (Berlin, Fürstner, 1938)
Bontempi, Giovanni Andrea Angelini (1624–1705)
 *Dafne* : RB 105; Engländer, "Zur Frage der *Dafne*," *Acta musicologica*
    XIII (1941) 61 ff.
 *Il Paride* : Burney *History*, Book IV
Bustos, Mariano
 *La Necedad* : Subirá, *Tonadilla escénica* III
Caccini, Francesca (1588–*ca.* 1640)
 *La liberazione di Ruggiero* : complete, ed. Doris Silbert, SCA VII
    (1945); LAM I; Goldschmidt I, 174–79
Caccini, Giulio (*ca.* 1546–1618)
 *Euridice* : EP X; RB
 *Le nuove musiche* : Facsimile, ed. Mantica, *Prime fioriture* II; *I classici*
    IV (Quad. 9–12); Deldevez; SB 172, 173; HAM 184; JF I, III;
    Prunières, III
Caldara, Antonio (1670–1736)
 *La costanza in amor vince l'inganno* : LAM II
 *Dafne* : DTOe 91
Cambert, Robert (*ca.* 1628–77)
 *Les Peines et les plaisirs d'amour* : complete, C.F.
 *Pomone* : complete, C.F.; SB 222; HAM 223; Deldevez
Campra, André (1660–1744)
 *L'Europe galante* : complete, C.F.
 *Les Festes vénitiennes* : complete, C.F.; SB 261; TEM 45

*Iphigénie en Tauride* : Deldevez
*Tancrède* : complete, C.F.
Carnicer, Ramón (1789–1855)
  *Los maestros de la Raboso* : Subirá, *Tonadilla escénica* III
Castel, José
  *La gitanilla en el coliseo* : Subirá, *Tonadilla escénica* III
Cavalieri, Emilio de (*ca.* 1550–1602)
  *Rappresentazione di anima e di corpo* : Facsimile, ed. Mantica, *Prime fioriture* I; *I classici* X (Quad. 35–36); SB 169; HAM 183; OHM III; TEM 37; Deldevez; ed. Fr. Vatielli (Leipzig, 1906); ed. G. Tebaldini (1915); ed. E. Gubitosi (Milan and New York, Ricordi, *ca.* 1956); Goldschmidt I, 153–54
Cavalli, Francesco (1602–76)
  *Alcibiade* : SIMG, Jg. 2 (1900); Goldschmidt I, 389–90
  *Elena rapita da Teseo* : JF III
  *Ercole amante* : HAM 206; Mortari
  *Erismena* : JF III
  *Eritrea* : Deldevez
  *Giasone* : Prologue and Act I, EP XII; JF III; RB 101; SB 201; Mortari
  *Le nozze di Teti e Peleo* : Goldschmidt I, 391–402
  *Ormindo* : Sinfonia, SIMG, Jg. 4 (1903); SB 200
  *Serse* : HAM 206
  See also : *Venti arie tratte dai drammi musicali di Francesco Cavalli*, ed. Zanon (Vienna-Trieste, Vlg. Schmiedel, 1909)
Cesti, Pietro Antonio (1623–69)
  *Argia* : SB 203
  *Le Disgrazie d'amore* : EP XII
  *La Dori* : EP XII; OHM III; RB 103; Wolff, BoHg II
  *La magnanimità d'Alessandro* : EP XII
  *l'Orontea* : Gevaert; LAM I
  *Il pomo d'oro* : Acts I, II, IV only, DTOe III$^2$, IV$^2$; SB 202; HAM 221
  *Semiramide* : EP XII
Charpentier, Marc-Antoine (1634–1704)
  C.E. : *Oeuvres*, ed. G. Lambert (Paris, Editions de la Lyre d'Or, 1948–53) 15 vols.
  *La Couronne de fleurs* : ed. H. Busser (Paris, 1907)
  *Le Malade imaginaire* : ed. Saint-Saëns (Paris, Durand, 1894); first intermedio, ed. J. Tiersot (Paris, Heugel, 1925)
  *Médée* : Three airs, ed. Guy-Lambert (Paris, Éditions de la Lyre d'Or, 1950–51)
Cimarosa, Domenico (1749–1801)
  *Le astuzie femminili* : ed. Respighi (Milan, Ricordi, n.d.)
  *Convito* : Zanon
  *Credulo* : Zanon
  *Le donne rivali* : Zanon

*Giannina e Bernardone* : ed. Respighi (Milan, Ricordi, n.d.); ed. F. d'Arcais (Milan, Ricordi, 1870?)

*Il matrimonio segreto* : (Leipzig, Peters, 1871); (Mainz, Schott, n.d.)

*I traci amanti* : Della Corte

*La vergine del sole* : LAM II

Colasse, Pascal (1649–1709)

*Les Saisons* (with Lully) : complete, C.F.; Delsarte

*Thétis et Pélée* : complete, C.F.

Conti, Francesco (1681–1732)

*Griselda* : SB 274

Cornacchioli, Giacinto (17th century)

*Diana schernita* : Goldschmidt I, 185–87

Corteccia, Francesco (16th century)

Intermedi of 1539 : SB 99

Cousser, Johann Sigismund

See Kusser, Johann Sigismund

Della Viola, Alfonso

*Il Sacrificio d'Abramo* : Solerti, "Precedenti del melodramma"; Solerti, *Gli albori*

Destouches, André-Cardinal (1672–1749)

*Les Eléments* : complete, C.F.; Prunières VI

*Issé* : complete, C.F.

*Omphale* : complete, C.F.

See also Lacôme, ed. *Les Fondateurs de l'opéra français* (Paris, Enoch, 1878)

Dibdin, Charles (1754–1814)

*Lionel and Clarissa* : ed. A. Reynolds (London, Elkin, 1926)

*The Quaker* : ed. F. Pascal (1904)

Dittersdorf, Karl Ditters von (1739–99)

*Der Betrug durch Aberglauben* (Leipzig, Peters, n.d.)

*Doktor und Apotheker* : complete, ed. Kleinmichel in Senff's *Opernbibliothek*; ed. E. Fischer and F. Gessner (Berlin, R. Birnbach, *ca.* 1943); ed. H. Burkhard (Vienna, Universal, 1935); HAM 305; Abert

*Hieronymus Knicker* : Kleinmichel in Senff's *Opernbibliothek*

Draghi, Giovanni Baptista (1657–1712)

*Creso* : Wolff, BoHg II

*La pazienza di Socrate* : SB 226

*Psiche* : RB 116

See also Neuhaus, "Antonio Draghi," SzMw I (1913) 104–92

Duni, Egidio Romoaldo (1709–75)

*La Clochette* : Delsarte VI

*La Fée Urgèle* : Delsarte VI

*Les Moissonneurs* : Delsarte VI

Durante, Francesco (1684–1755)

*Arlecchino* : ed. G. L. Tocchi (Milan, Carisch, 1937)

Esteve y Grimau, Pablo (d. 1794)
*El desvalido* : Pedrell, *Cancionero* IV
*Garrido enfermo y su testamento* : Subirá, *Tonadilla escénica* III
*El juicio del año* : Subirá, *Tonadilla escénica* III; Subirá, *Maestros* I
*Los novios y la maja* : Pedrell, *Cancionero* IV
*El pretendiente* : Pedrell, *Cancionero* IV
*Los signos del año* : Subirá, *Inéditas*

Ferandiere, Fernando
*La consulta* : Subirá, *Tonadilla escénica* III; Subirá, *Maestros* I

Flecha, Mateo (1530–1604)
*Las ensaladas* (1581) : ed. H. Anglès (Barcelona, Diputación Provincial, 1954)

Förtsch, Johann Philipp (1652–1732)
See Zelle, *J. P. Förtsch*; Wolff, BoHg II

Franck, Johann Wolfgang (1644–*ca.* 1710)
*Die drey Töchter Cecrops* : complete, EDM II (DTB XXXVIII)
See also Zelle, *J. W. Franck*; Wolff, BoHg II

Fux, Johann Josef (1660–1741)
C.E., Serie V—Opern (Kassel, Bärenreiter, 1962–   )
*Costanza e fortezza* : complete, ed. E. Wellesz, DTOe 34–35 (Jg. XVII); incomplete, ed. G. Smith, SCA II; SB 272
*La decima fatica d'Hercole* : aria in A. Liess, *Wiener Barockmusik* (Vienna, 1946)

Gabrieli, Andrea (*ca.* 1510–86)
*Edipo tiranno* : ed. L. Schrade (Paris, 1960)

Gabrieli, Domenico (*ca.* 1640–90)
*Clearco in Negroponte* : LAM III
*Flavio Cuniberto* : LAM III

Gagliano, Marco da (*ca.* 1575–1642)
*Dafne* : incomplete, EP X; SB 175; RB 69; Einstein 24; Krehbiel
*La Flora* : Goldschmidt I, 180–84; LAM I
See also Krehbiel

Galuppi, Baldassare (1706–85)
*Adriano in Siria* : Krehbiel
*Il filosofo di campagna* : complete, ed. V. Mortari (Milan, Carisch, 1938); complete, ed. Wolf-Ferrari (Milan, Ricordi, *ca.* 1954); HAM 285; *I classici* XIII (Quad. 54–58); Zanon
*L'inimico delle donne* : Gevaert

Galván, Ventura
*Los vagamundos y ciegos fingidos* : Subriá, *Tonadilla escénica* III; Subirá, *Maestros* II

García, Manuel
*El majo y la maja* : Subirá, *Tonadilla escénica* III

Gassmann, Florian Leopold (1729–74)

   *La contessina* : DTOe, XLII–XLIV (Jg. 21¹)

   See Donath, "Gassmann als Opernkomponist," SzMw II (1914) 34–211

Gluck, Christoph Willibald (1714–87)

   C.E. : *Werke*, ed. Pelletan and others (Leipzig, B&H, 1873–96); contains *Alceste, Armida, Echo und Narziss, Iphigenie in Aulis, Iphigenie auf Tauris, Orpheus und Euridice; Sämtliche Werke*, ed. R. Gerber (Kassel and Basel, Bärenreiter–Vlg., 1951– )

   *Armide* : SB 313

   *Don Juan* : complete, ed. A. Einstein, DTOe 82 (Jg. XXX²)

   *L'innocenza giustificata* : complete, ed. A. Einstein, DTOe 60 (Jg. XLIV)

   *Iphigénie en Tauride* : complete, ed. H. Abert (Leipzig, Eulenburg, 1927); Einstein 39

   *Le nozze d'Ercole e d'Ebe* : complete, ed. H. Abert, DTB 14²

   *Orfeo ed Euridice* : complete, DTOe 44a (Jg. XXI²); HAM 292

   *La Rencontre imprévue* : complete (Leipzig, B&H, 1923; Paris, Legouix, 1923); as *Die Pilger von Mecca* (Leipzig, Gluckgesellschaft, 1931); Abert

   *Il trionfo di Clelia* : LAM II

Grabu, Louis

   *Albion and Albanius* : Dent, *Foundations*

Graun, Karl Heinrich (1704–59)

   *Montezuma* : complete, ed. A. Meyer-Reinach, DdT 15; ed. H. J. Moser, DdT, Neuauflage, 15; HAM 282

Graupner, Christoph (1683–1760)

   See Wolff BoHg II

Grétry, André Ernest Modeste (1741–1813)

   C.E. : *Collection complète des oeuvres de Grétry* (Leipzig, B&H, 1884–1923) 44 vols. in 39

   *La Caravane du Caire* : complete, C.F.

   *Céphale et Procris* : complete, C.F.

   *Les Deux Avares* : ed. R. Kleinmichel (Vienna, Universal, 1911)

   *Richard Coeur-de-Lion* : HAM 306

Guerrero, Antonio

   *Los señores fingidos* : Subirá, *Tonadilla escénica* III

Guglielmi, Pietro (1728–1804)

   *I finti amori* : Della Corte

   *L'inganno amoroso* : Della Corte

Handel, George Frideric (1685–1759)

   C.E. : *Georg Friedrich Händels Werke*. Herausgegeben von Friedrich Chrysander (Leipzig, B&H, 1858–94, 1902); *Hallische Händel-Ausgabe* . . . Herausgegeben von Max Schneider und Rudolf Steglich (Kassel, Bärenreiter–Vlg., 1955—)

   *Alcina* : JF I, III

*Rinaldo* : SB 278; JF I, III; MM 44
*Serse* : JF I, II
*Tamerlano* : JF II, III
Hasse, Johann Adolph (1699–1783)
   *Arminio* : complete, EDM 27–28; Abert
   *Euristeo* : LAM II; A. Schering, *Perlen alter Kammermusik* (Leipzig,
      C. F. Kahnt Nachf.)
   *Leucippo* : Bücken
   *Piramo e Tisbe* : Bücken
   See also Otto Schmid, *Musik am sächsischen Hofe* I, II
Haydn, Franz Joseph (1732–1809)
   C.E. : Hrsg. vom Joseph-Haydn-Institut, Cologne (Munich-Duisberg,
      G. Henle, 1958—)
   *L'infedeltà delusa* : ed. H. C. Robbins Landon (Salzburg, Haydn-Mozart
      Presse, 1961)
   *Lo speziale* : German translation, *Der Apotheker*, ed. R. Hirschfeld
      Vienna, Universal, 19??)
Heubel, Johann Georg
   *Triumph der Freundschaft* : DTOe 64 (Jg. XXXIII[1])
Hidalgo, Juan (*ca.* 1600–1685)
   *Celos aun del aire matan* : ed. Subirá (Barcelona, Biblioteca de Cata-
      lunya, 1933)
   *Empezo la noche toda* : Pedrell, *Teatro* III
   *Ni amor se libra de amor* : Pedrell, *Cancionero* IV
   See also Pedrell, *Teatro* IV, V
Hiller, Johann Adam (1728–1804)
   *Der Erntekranz* : SB 309b
   *Die Jagd* : complete, ed. Kleinmichel (Leipzig, Senff, 1890); complete,
      ed. Lortzing (Leipzig, 1904)
   *Die Liebe auf dem Lande* : M. Friedlaender, *Das deutsche Lied im 18.
   Jahrhundert* (Stuttgart and Berlin, Cotta, 1902)
   *Lisuart und Dariolette* : HAM 301
   *Die verwandelten Weiber* : Friedlaender (see above, *Die Liebe*)
Holzbauer, Ignaz (1711–83)
   *Günther von Schwarzburg* : complete, ed. H. Kretzschmar, DdT 8–9
      (1902); complete, ed. H. J. Moser, DdT, Neuauflage, 8–9 (1957)
Huber, Josef Karl
   *Etwas wider Vermuten* : DTOe 64 (Jg. XXXIII[1])
Intermedi of 1589
   *Les Fêtes de Florence (1589), Vol. I. Musique des Intermèdes de "La
   Pellegrina,"* ed. D. P. Walker (Paris, Editions du Centre national de la
      recherche scientifique, 1963)
Jommelli, Niccolò (1714–74)
   *Fetonte* : complete, ed. H. Abert, DdT 32–33 (1907); complete, rev. and
      ed. H. J. Moser, DdT, Neuauflage, 32–33

Joseph I, Holy Roman Emperor (1678–1711)
> See G. Adler, *Musikalische Werke der Kaiser Ferdinand III, Leopold I, und Joseph I* (Vienna, Artaria, 1892–93) II

Kamieński, Mathias (1734–1821)
> See Prosnak, supplement

Keiser, Reinhard (1674–1739)
> *Adonis* : HAM 267; RB 197
>
> *Croesus* : complete, ed. M. Schneider, DdT 37–38 (1912); complete, rev. and ed. H. J. Moser, DdT, Neuauflage, 37–38 (1958); SB 269; TEM 46; Leichtentritt
>
> *La forza della virtù* : SB 268
>
> *L'inganno fedele* : incomplete, ed. M. Schneider, DdT 37–38 (1912); incomplete, rev. and ed. H. J. Moser, DdT, Neuauflage, 37–38; RB 127; Leichtentritt
>
> *Der lächerliche Prinz Jodelet*; EP XVIII (Jg. 21–22)
>
> *Octavia* : Handel, C.E., ed. Chrysander, Supplement, VI
>
> *Pomona* : E. O. Lindner, *Die erste stehende deutsche Oper* II
>
> See also R. Eitner in MfMg XVI (1883), supplement; H. Unger, ed., *Althamburgische Opernsuiten . . .* (Berlin, Bote und Bock, 1933); Wolff, BoHg II

Krieger, Johann Philipp (1649–1725)
> *Flora* : SB 236b
>
> *Procris* : SB 236a
>
> See also H. J. Moser, ed., *Vierundzwanzig Lieder und Arien* (Nagels Musik Archiv, 174–75)

Kurz, Joseph Felix (1715–86)
> *Der auf das neue begeisterte und beliebte Bernardon* : DTOe 64 (Jg. XXXIII[1])
>
> *Bernardon auf der Gelseninsel* : DTOe 64
>
> *Die glückliche Verbindung des Bernardon* : DTOe 64

Kusser, Johann Sigismund (1660–1727)
> *Erindo* : incomplete, ed. H. Osthoff, *Das Erbe deutscher Musik, Landschaftsdenkmale, Schleswig-Holstein*, 3; SB 250

Landi, Stefano (*ca.* 1581–1650)
> *La morte d'Orfeo* : Goldschmidt I, 188–201
>
> *Il Sant' Alessio* : Goldschmidt I, 202–57; HAM 208, 209; Riemann II, Part 2, 255–61; Torchi V

Lanier, Nicolas (1588–1666)
> *Luminalia* : OHM III, 200
>
> See also Sabol

Laserna, Blas de (1741–1816)
> *El majo y la italiana fingida* : Subirá, *Tonadilla escénica* III
>
> *El trueque de los amantes* : Subirá, *Inéditas*
>
> See also Nin, *Sept Chansons picaresques* and *Sept Chants lyriques*; Pedrell, *Cancionero* IV; Pedrell, *Teatro lírico* II

Latilla, Gaetano (1711–91)
*Siroë* : Krehbiel
See also Prunières I
Lawes, Henry (1596–1662)
*Comus* : ed. E. H. Visiak (Bloomsbury, Nonesuch Press, 1937); Sabol;
HAM 204
*The Triumphs of the Prince d'Amour* : Sabol
Legrenzi, Giovanni (1626–90)
*Eteocle e Polinice* : RB 106–7
*Il Giustino* : SB 231
*Totila* : ed. G. Tebaldini (Milan, Ricordi, 1937); Wolff, *Die venezian-
ische Oper*; Heuss . . . *die venetianischen Opern-Sinfonien*; ed.
Prunières, RM Supplément I, July, 1923; OHM III, 177
Leo, Leonardo (1694–1744)
*Amor vuol sollerenze* : Sondheimer 46–47
*Olimpiade* : LAM II
*S. Elena al Calvario* : Sondheimer 46–47
See also Marx, *Gluck und die Oper*, No. 3; Gevaert I, II; Prunières I;
Zanon
Leopold I, Holy Roman Emperor (reigned 1658–1705)
See G. Adler, *Musikalische Werke der Kaiser Ferdinand III, Leopold I,
und Joseph I* (Vienna, Artaria, 1892–93) II
Linley, Thomas, Sr. (1733–95)
*The Duenna* : complete, ed. A. Reynolds (London, Boosey and Co.,
1925); Bush
Locke, Matthew (*ca.* 1630–77)
*Cupid and Death* : complete, ed. Dent, *Musica Britannica* II; OHM
III, 213–18; Dent, *Foundations*
*Macbeth* (incidental music) : Dent, *Foundations*
*Psyche* : OHM III, 291–93; Dent, *Foundations*
*The Tempest* (incidental music) : complete, ed. W. G. Whittaker (Lon-
don, Oxford, 1934); OHM III, 289–90
Löhner, Johann (1645–1705)
*Theseus* : Sandberger, "Zur Geschichte der Oper in Nürnberg," AfMw
I (1918) 84–107; same ed. (Munich, Drei Masken Vlg., 1921)
*Triumphierende Treue* : Sandberger, see above
Lotti, Antonio (1667–1740)
*Alessandro Severo* : SB 270
*Ascanio* : Schmid, *Musik am sächsischen Hofe* I
See also Gevaert
Lully, Jean-Baptiste (1632–87)
C.E. : *Oeuvres complètes de J.-B. Lully . . . publiées sous la direction de
Henry Prunières* . . . (Paris, Editions de la Revue musicale, 1930–39)
10 vols. (Contains the following operas : *Alceste, Amadis de Gaule,
Cadmus et Hermione*)

*Alceste* : complete, ed. Prunières, C.F.; HAM 224, 225

*Armide et Renaud* : EP XIV; complete, C.F.; ed. R. Lalande (Paris, H. Lemoine, *ca.* 1957); SB 234; MM 36

*Isis* : complete, C.F.; Abert

*Persée* : complete, C.F.; SB 232

*Roland* : SB 233

In addition to the above, C.F. contains the following complete editions: *Atys, Bellérophon, Cadmus et Hermione, Phaëton, Proserpine, Psyché, Les Saisons* (finished by Colasse), *Thésée*

Majo, Gian Francesco di (1732–70)

*Alessandro* : Bücken 115

*Ifigenia in Tauride* : LAM II

See also Marx, *Gluck und die Oper*, Musical Supplement Nos. 5 and 6

Malvezzi, Christoforo (1547–97)

Intermedi of 1589 (with Marenzio, Cavalieri, *et al.*) : Goldschmidt I, 374–80

Marais, Marin (1656–1728)

*Semele* : suite, ed. L. Boulay (Paris, Sofirad, 1958)

Marazzoli, Marco (*ca.* 1602–62)

*Chi soffre, speri* : Goldschmidt I, 312–24

*Dal male il bene* : Goldschmidt I, 325–48

See also L. Torri, *Quattro arie tratte da melodrammi italiani del secolo XVII* (Padua, Zanibon, n.d.); LAM III

Marcello, Benedetto (1686–1739)

*Arianna* : ed. O. Chilesotti, *Biblioteca di rarità musicale* (Milan, Ricordi, 1884–1915) 4; LAM II

Marcolini, Juan

*Naranjera, petimetre y extranjero* : Subirà, *Tonadilla escénica* III

Marenzio, Luca (1553–99)

Intermedi of 1589 (with Cavalieri, Malvezzi, *et al.*) : Schneider, *Die Anfänge des Basso Continuo*, pp. 116–57

Mattheson, Johann (1681–1764)

See Wolff BoHg; Wolff DBa I

Mayberg, Johann Wilhelm (18th century)

*Der Kaufmann zu London* : DTOe 64 (Jg XXXIII[1])

Mazzocchi, Domenico (1592–1665)

*La catena d'Adone* : Goldschmidt I, 155–73; LAM I; Prunières III

Mazzocchi, Virgilio (1597–1646)

*Chi soffre, speri* : see Marazzoli

See also Torchi V

Melani, Jacopo (1623–76)

*Il girello* : LAM I

*La Tancia, overo il podestà di Colognole* : Goldschmidt I, 349–73; *Atti dell' Accademia del R. Istituto musicale di Firenze, Anno XXXIII* (1895) Supplement 3; Riemann II, Part 2, 240 ff.

Misón, Luis (d. 1766)
Los ciegos : Subirá, Inéditas
Una mesonera y un arriero : Subirá, Maestros I; Subirá, Tonadilla escénica III
Los jardineros : ed. M. N. Hamilton, in Music in Eighteenth Century Spain
Monsigny, Pierre-Alexandre (1729–1817)
Le Déserteur : complete (Paris, A. Leduc, No. 5204)
See Delsarte VI
Monteverdi, Claudio (1567–1643)
C.E. : Tutte le opere. Nuovamente date in luce da G. Francesco Malipiero (Asola, G. F. Malipiero; Vienna, Universal, 1926–42) 16 vols.
Arianna (Lament) : SB 177; JF II; Prunières III
Il ballo delle ingrate : ed. D. Stevens (London, Schott; New York, Associated, 1960); Torchi VI
Il combattimento di Tancredi e di Clorinda : I classici XIX
L'incoronazione di Poppea : complete, Goldschmidt II; ed. Ghedini (Milan, Ricordi, 1953); Abert; RB 91, 92
Orfeo : facsimile of 1609 edition, ed. A. Sandberger (Augsburg, 1927); SB 176; HAM 187; MM 31
Il ritorno d'Ulisse in patria : complete, ed. R. Haas, DTOe 57 (Jg. XXIX¹); SB 178; Prunières III
This list supplements the list of editions in Grove's Dictionary, 5th ed. (1954) V, 846–47. See also Die Musik in Geschichte und Gegenwart IX, 528–29
Moral, Pablo del
La ópera casera : Subirá, Tonadilla escénica III
La tia burlada : Subirá, Inéditas
Mouret, Jean-Joseph (1682–1738)
Triomphe des sens : Prunières VI
Mozart, Wolfgang Amadeus (1756–91)
C.E. : Werke. Hrsg. von J. Brahms, F. Espagne, [et al.] (Leipzig, B&H, 1876–86); idem, reprinted (Ann Arbor, Mich., J. W. Edwards, 1951–56); Neue Ausgabe sämtlicher Werke. . . . hrsg. von der Internationalen Stiftung Mozarteum Salzburg (Kassel, Bärenreiter, 1955—)
Müller, Wenzel (1767–1835)
Die Schwestern von Prag : ed. R. Kleinmichel (Leipzig, Senff, 1890); ed. Czarniawski (Vienna, Universal, 1935)
Naumann, Johann Gottlieb (1741–1801)
Medea : Sondheimer, 30/31
Protesilao : Sondheimer, 30/31
Paisiello, Giovanni (1740–1816)
Il barbiere di Siviglia : full score (Milan, Ricordi, 1868); piano-vocal score (Milan, Ricordi, ca. 1879, 1903)
Nina : I classici XX (Quad. 80–81)

*La bella molinara* (*Die schöne Müllerin*) : complete (Leipzig, Senff, 1890); Della Corte

*La serva padrona* : Della Corte

*Socrate immaginario* : complete, ed. G. Barini (Florence, 1939)

Pallavicino, Carlo (1630–88)

*L'amazone corsara* : Heuss, . . . *die ventianischen Opern- Sinfonien*

*Le amazoni nelle isole fortunate* : Goldschmidt I, 403 f.; Worsthorne

*Antiope* : RB 120; Riemann II, Part 2, 469 f.

*Diocletiano* : SB 224; Wolff BoHg II

*Gallieno* : Worsthorne

*Gerusalemme liberata* : complete, ed. H. Abert, DdT 55; rev. and ed., H. J. Moser, DdT, Neuauflage, 55

*Messalina* : Wolff, *Die venezianische Oper*, Anhang, No. 67

Palomino, José

*El canapé* : Subirá, *Tonadilla escénica* III

Pepusch, John Christopher (1667–1752)

*The Beggar's Opera* : facsimile of 1729 edition (Larchmont, N.Y., Argonaut, 1961); complete, ed. F. Austin (London, Boosey and Co., 1920); SB 281; HAM 264; for a complete list of modern editions see *Die Musik in Geschichte und Gegenwart* X, 1029–30

Peranda, Marco Giuseppe (*ca.* 1600–1675)

See Bontempi, *Dafne*

Pergolesi, Giovanni Battista (1710–36)

C.E. : *Opera omnia*, ed. F. Caffarelli (Rome, Gli amici della musica da camera, 1939–42); *idem*, republished by Bärenreiter (Kassel, 1943)

*Lo frate 'nnammorato* : Della Corte

*Olimpiade* : LAM II; Gevaert; Krehbiel

*La serva padrona* : complete, ed. K. Geiringer (Vienna, Universal, 1953); *I classici* XXIII (Quad. 89–90); HAM 287; Einstein 36

Peri, Jacopo (1561–1633)

*Dafne* : Ghisi, *Alle fonti della monodia* (Milan, 1940); Schneider, *Die Anfänge*, 109

*Euridice* : facsimile (Rome, R. Accademia d'Italia, 1934); Torchi VI; *I classici* XXIV (Quad. 95–96); SB 171; HAM 182; RB 56; Deldevez

*Flora* (with Gagliano) : see Gagliano, *Flora*

*La sole lusinghiera* : Solerti, *Gli albori* (1904)

Pez, Johann Christoph (1664–1716)

*Trajano* : ed. B. A. Wallner, DTB 27–28

Philidor, François-André Danican (1726–95)

*Ernelinde* : complete, C.F.

*Le Maréchal ferrant* : Delsarte VI

*Sancho Pança* : Delsarte VI; Prunières VI

*Le Sorcier* : Delsarte VI

*Tom Jones* : Delsarte VI

Piccinni, Niccolò (1728–1800)

*Alessandro nelle Indie* : LAM II; Gevaert; Zanon

*La buona figliuola*: *I classici musicali italiani* (Milan, 1941–43) 7; Eistein 31; Della Corte

*Le contadine bizzarre* : Della Corte

*Didon* : complete, C.F.

*Le Faux Lord* : HAM 300

*La molinarella* : Della Corte

*Roland* : complete, C.F.

*Le vicende della sorte* : Della Corte

*La villeggiatura* : Della Corte

Porpora, Nicola (1686–1768)

See Zanon

Provenzale, Francesco (1627–1704)

*Il schiavo di sua moglie*: HAM 222

*La stellidaura vendicata* : LAM I

See also Rolland, *Histoire de l'opéra en Europe*, Supplement

Purcell, Henry (*ca.* 1659–95)

C.E. : *Works*. Published by the Purcell Society (London, Novello, Ewer and Co., 1878–1928; 1958?–    )

*Dido and Aeneas* : complete, ed. Dent (London, Oxford, 1925); HAM 255

*King Arthur* : SB 247

Quagliati, Paolo (*ca.* 1555–1628)

*Il carro di fedeltà d'amore* : ed. V. Gotwals and P. Keppler (1957) SCA 13

Rameau, Jean-Philippe (1683–1764)

C.E. : *Oeuvres complètes*. Publiées sous la direction de C. Saint-Saëns (Paris, A. Durand, 1896–1924); contains *Castor et Pollux, Dardanus, Les Festes d'Hébé ou les talents lyriques* (opéra-ballet), *Hippolyte et Aricie, Les Indes galantes* (opéra-ballet), *Platée* (comédie lyrique), *Zaïs* (pastorale héroique), *Zoroastre*

*Castor et Pollux* : SB 296, 297a; MM 41

*Dardanus* : SB 297b; HAM 277

*Le Temple de la gloire* : HAM 276

See also C.F.—contains editions of all works noted above in the C.E. except *Zaïs*

Reichardt, Johann Friedrich (1752–1814)

See H. J. Moser, *Alte Meister des deutschen Liedes* (Leipzig, Peters, 1912) 28, 29

Rinaldo da Capua (fl. 1737–78)

*Vologeso* : Krehbiel

*La zingara* : Della Corte

Rosales, Antonio

*El recitado* : Subirá, *Tonadilla escénica* III; Subirá, *Maestros* II

Rossi, Luigi (*ca.* 1598–1653)
    *Orfeo* : Goldschmidt I, 295–311; SB 199; Prunières III
    *Il palazzo incantato* : Goldschmidt I, 385–88; LAM I; SIMG, Jg. 1
        (1900) 56–59
Rossi, Michelangelo (fl. 1620–60)
    *Erminia sul Giordano* : Goldschmidt I, 258–72; Prunières III; H.
        Botstiber, *Geschichte der Ouvertüre*, Beilage 2.
Rousseau, Jean-Jacques (1712–78)
    *Le Devin du village* : HAM 291
Sacchini, Antonio (1730–86)
    *Chimène ou Le Cid* : complete, C.F.
    *Montezuma* : Gevaert
    *Oedipe à Colone* : Delsarte III
    *Renaud* : complete, C.F.
    *Tamerlano* : Zanon
Salieri, Antonio (1750–1825)
    *Les Danaïdes* : complete, ed. G. Lefèvre, C.F.
    *La grotta di Trofonio* : Della Corte
    *Tarare* : complete, C.F.; *Kleine Harlekinade, komisches Intermezzo aus
        der Oper Axur, König von Ormus* [German title of *Tarare*], ed. F.
        Schröder (Mainz, Schott, 1951)
Sarri, Domenico (1679–1744)
    *Didone abbandonata* : LAM II
    *Vespasiano* : Zanon
Sarti, Giuseppe (1729–1802)
    *Armida e Rinaldo* : *A Giuseppe Sarti nel 2° centenario di sua nascità
        (1729–1929)* (Faenza, Soc. tipografica faentina, 1929)
    *Fra due litiganti il terzo gode* : Della Corte
    See also Gevaert
Sartorio, Antonio (*ca.* 1620–81)
    *Adelaide* : SB 223; *Nagels Musik Archiv* 141
Scarlatti, Alessandro (1660–1725)
    *La caduta de decem viri* : TEM 44; Bücken 38 f.
    *Il Clearco in Negroponte* : LAM III
    *La donna ancora è fedele* : LAM III
    *Eraclea* : Haas, *Die Musik des Barocks*, 297 f.
    *Griselda* : SB 259; HAM 259
    *Gl'inganni felici* : SB 258
    *La Rosaura* : EP XIV; RB 119; Krehbiel
    *Il trionfo dell' onore* : ed. V. Mortari (Milan, Carisch, 1941)
    See also Dent, *Scarlatti*
Schenk, Johann (1753–1836)
    *Der Dorfbarbier* : ed. R. Haas (1927) DTOe 66 (Jg. XXXIV); ed. R.
        Kleinmichel (Vienna, Universal, 1914)
    *Le nymphe di Rheno* : EDM 44

Schiassi, Gaetano Maria (d. 1754)
*Alessandro nell' Indie* : Krehbiel
Schürmann, Georg Caspar (*ca.* 1672–1751)
*Die getreue Alceste* : Abert
*Heinrich der Vogler* : MfMg XVII (1885) Beilage, 148–60
*Ludwig der Fromme* : incomplete, EP XVII; SB 293
Staden, Sigmund Theophil (1607–55)
*Seelewig* : Eitner, MfMg XIII (1881)
Standfuss, J. C. (d. 1756?)
*Die verwandelten Weiber* : SB 309a
Steffani, Agostino (1654–1728)
*Alarico* : DTB 11 $^2$
*Henrico Leone* : ed. Th. Werner, *Musikalische Denkwürdigkeiten* (Hanover, 1926) I; LAM III; HAM 244; *Nagels Musik Archiv* 141
*Niobe* : RB 117
*Orlando generoso* : Einstein 30
*Tassilone* : ed. G. Croll, *Denkmäler Rheinischer Musik* (Kassel, Bärenreiter, 1958)
See also DTB 6$^2$, 12$^1$
Storace, Stephen (1763–96)
*No Song, No Supper* : ed. R. Fiske (1959) *Musica Britannica* XVI
*The Siege of Belgrad* : Thouret, *Musik am preussischen Hofe* (Leipzig, B&H, 1892–97) 9
Stradella, Alessandro (1644–82)
*Il Corispero* : HAM 241
*Il Floridoro* : LAM I
*La forza d'amor paterno* : ed. Gentili (Milan, Ricordi, 1930)
*Giasone* : aria from an intermezzo, LAM III
*Orazio* : JF I
See also Deldevez
Striggio, Alessandro (*ca.* 1535–*ca.* 1595)
*Il cicalamento delle donne al bucato* : ed. E. Mucci (Rome, de Santis, 1947)
Strungk, Nikolaus Adam (1640–1700)
*Esther* : Wolff BoHg II
Telemann, Georg Philipp (1681–1767)
*Pimpinone* : ed. Th. Werner (1936), EDM 6; rev. and ed. W. Bergmann (1955), EDM 6; SB 266
Terradellas, Domingo (1713–51)
*Mérope* : ed. R. Gerhard (Barcelona, Diputación Provincial : Biblioteca Central, 1951); SB 298
See also Carreras y Bulbena, *Domenech Terradellas*
Theatrical chansons, 15th and 16th centuries
*Theatrical Chansons of the Fifteenth and Early Sixteenth Centuries,* ed.

Howard Mayer Brown (Cambridge, Mass., Harvard University Press, 1963)

Theile, Johann (1646–1724)
 *Orontes* : Wolf BoHg II

Torelli, Gaspare
 *I fidi amanti* : Torchi IV

Traetta, Tommaso (1727–79)
 See DTB 14¹, 17

Umlauf, Ignaz (1746–96)
 *Die Bergknappen* : ed. R. Haas (1911) DTOe 36 (Jg. XVIII ¹)

Valledor, Jacinto
 See Subirá, *Tonadilla escénica* III

Vecchi, Orazio (1550–1605)
 *Amfiparnaso* : EP XXVI; Torchi IV; ed. C. Perinello (Milan, 1938); SB 164

Vinci, Leonardo (1690–1730)
 *Artaserse* : Zanon
 See also Gevaert; Bücken 36

Vitali, Filippo (ca. 1600–1653)
 See JF II, III; Gevaert

Vittori, Loreto (1604–70)
 *La Galatea* : Goldschmidt I, 273–94

Vivaldi, Antonio (?1678–1741)
 See Prunières I

Ziani, Marc' Antonio (1653–1715)
 See Heuss, . . . *die venetianischen Opern-Sinfonien*

# SOURCES OF EXAMPLES
# AND TRANSLATIONS

1. Coussemaker, ed. *Oeuvres complètes du trouvère Adam de la Halle.*
   Translation: Robin: Yes, and you shall be my love, you shall have
   my belt, my purse, and my buckle. Shepherdess, sweet girl, give me
   your rosary. Marion: Gladly, my sweet friend.
2. *Ballet comique de la reine* (1582) p. 31.
3. Schneider, *Die Anfänge des Basso Continuo*, pp. 147–48.
   Translation: Rejoice, ye mortal throng, happily and gladly rejoice
   at such a gift, and with music and song allay the fatigue of your toil.
4. Solerti, *Gli albori del melodramma.*
   Translation: Thou with heavenward-pointing horns fixed in thy
   broad and spacious forehead: O Lycian Pan!
5. *L'Euridice composta in musica in stile rappresentativo da Giulio
   Caccini Romano* (Florence, G. Marescotti, 1600), p. 15.
   Translation: And raising her eyes toward heaven, her lovely face
   pale and colorless, all her great beauty remained immobile, frozen.
6. Kretzschmar, *Geschichte der Oper*, p. 38. Realization omitted.
   Translation: Alas! How my heart turns cold in my breast with
   horror and pity; O miserable beauty, how in an instant, ah! thou
   art brought low.
7. Caccini, *L'Euridice*, 1600.
   Translation: To song, to dance, to the shade, to the flower-decked
   meadows, to the happy streams run singing, O shepherds, on this
   blessed day.
8. *La Dafne di Marco da Gagliano . . . rappresentata in Mantova*
   (Florence, G. Marescotti, 1608), pp. 3–4.
   Translation: If a heart can find mercy above in the golden cloisters,
   hear our lamentations and prayers, O monarch and king of Heaven.
9. *L'Orfeo favola in musica da Claudio Monteverdi rappresentata in
   Mantova l'anno 1607 & novamente data in luce* (Venice, R.
   Amadino, 1609), p. 1.
10. Monteverdi, C.E. XI, 31. Note values halved, bar lines twice as
    frequent.
    Translation: Remember, O shady thickets, my long and bitter
    torments.

11. Monteverdi, *Orfeo*, facsimile of first ed. Figures in brackets correspond to Malipiero's realization, C.E. XI, 59.
Translation : Messenger : To you I come, Orpheus, unhappy messenger of most unhappy and baneful news. Thy lovely Euridice— Orpheus : Alas, what do I hear? Messenger : Thy beloved wife is dead. Orpheus : Alas !

12. Monteverdi, *Orfeo*, facsimile of first ed. Last two accidentals under bass notes correspond to Malipiero's realization, C.E. XI, 61.
Translation : Calling to thee, Orpheus ! Orpheus ! after a deep sigh she breathed her last in my arms and I remained, my heart filled with pity and horror.

13. *La catena d'Adone posta in musica da Domenico Mazzocchi* (Venice, A. Vincenti, 1627), p. 23. Rome, Bibl. Santa Cecilia, G.C.S. 2. C.6
Translation : The breeze smiles to the fair sky of your divine countenance, and amid dances and songs is revealed to you a smiling new heaven, a new earth, and a new world.

14. *Il S. Alessio, dramma musicale . . . posto in musica da Stefano Landi Romano* (Rome, P. Masotti, 1634), p. 107.
Translation : Brief shall be the delay; rest and take hope. And when thou art come to the last hour, do not fear death. Contemplate the dark pass, full of hope to all who have suffered pain.

15. *Il S. Alessio . . .* , p. 1.

16. *Il S. Alessio . . .* , pp. 1–2.

17. *La Galatea, dramma del Cav.ᵉ Loreto Vittori da Spoleti, dal medesimo posto in musica* (Rome, V. Bianchi, 1639), pp. 112–13.
Translation : Weep, O fields and flowers, for the vanished splendors; and thou, O earth, wrap thy breast in a dark mantle and sadly keep company to our plaints.

18. Rossi, *Orfeo* (Rome, Biblioteca Apostolica Vaticana, MS Chigi Q. V 58, f. 189).
Translation : Kill me, O sorrows : and while I go with desperate pace amidst these savage rocks seeking how I may die, to you more than to a serpent or a wild beast is due that despicable glory. Kill me : since death knew that Euridice alone was my life, and he does not remember that I still live. Kill me, O sorrows.

19. Mazzocchi, *Chi soffre, speri* (Rome, Biblioteca Apostolica Vaticana, MS Barb. lat. 4376, ff. 49ᵛ–50).
Translation : Let each one follow his pleasure, as long as I may live happily on this shady bank where my father, near to death, promised me (may the prophecy be true !) an unexpected outcome of fortunate happenings.

20. Abbatini, *Dal male il bene* (Rome, Biblioteca Apostolica Vaticana, MS Barb. lat. 4376, ff. 49ᵛ–50).
Translation : What is the good of searching forever so anxiously to

know what others do? Of fretting my brain in my own craze to understand what may be outside of this and that?

21. Montervedi, C.E. XIII, 80–81. Realization omitted.
Translation : Seneca : Reason is the ruler of man and gods. Nero : You—you—you drive me to frenzy!

22. Monteverdi C.E. XIII, 136. Signature changed from one flat; flat omitted under bass C in measures 1, 4, 8.
Translation : When I am with you my heart beats, when you are away I am dull; I long for and constantly think about your beauty.

23. Monteverdi, C.E. XIII, 85–86. Realization omitted.
Translation : O my adored one, still in my arms I held thee. Poppea, I hardly breathe; I gaze upon thy lips and, gazing, recover with my eyes the fiery spirit which, embracing thee, O dear one, I diffused into thee.

24. Cavalli, *Egisto* (Venice, Biblioteca Nazionale di San Marco, MS It. IV–411, ff. 84–85ᵛ). Time values halved; original time signature C$\frac{3}{2}$, no accidentals in signature.
Translation : Rejoice with me, beloved trees; resound with glad harmonies, ye songsters; Lidio returns and leaves Clori.

25. Cavalli, *Egisto* (Venice, Biblioteca Nazionale di San Marco, MS It. IV–411, f. 50ᵛ). Time values halved; original signature $\frac{3}{2}$. Bar lines added before measures 5, 9, 16.
Translation : Weep, sorrowing eyes, and let the fountain and river weep to my tearful plaint.

26. Cavalli, *Giasone* (Venice, Biblioteca Nazionale di San Marco, MS It. IV–363, ff. 58ᵛ–59). Original time signature $\frac{3}{2}$; time values halved.
Translation : Open to me the creaking hinges of the magic cave and admit me among the shades of the black abode.

27. Venice, Biblioteca Nazionale di San Marco, MS It. IV–41, ff. 30–30ᵛ.
Translation : If perfidious Love pierce thee with his arrows . . .

28. DTOe VI, 108. Continuo omitted.
Translation : These are the tricks used by madmen and mountebanks.

29. Venice, Biblioteca Nazionale di San Marco, MS It. IV–41, f. 33ᵛ.
Translation : The sweet sighs and afflictions are precious to me.

30. Rolland, *Histoire de l'opéra en Europe*, Supplément musical, p. 9. Reduced from four staves.
Translation : Let me die, cruel stars.

31. H. Hess, *Die Opern Alessandro Stradellas*, pp. 88–89. Introduction omitted (six measures of two parts over continuo).
Translation : What are you thinking of, my heart? Your beloved is lost, and lost is all hope of ever having him back.

32. DdT LV, 102. Bass and realization omitted.
Translation : Victory! victory! etc.

33. DdT LV, 74. Realization and German text (translation) omitted.
Translation : Cruel lady, you laugh at me but I shall laugh at you.
I shall pray to Jupiter that he someday burn with his lightnings the
one who has outraged me.

34. DTB XII$^2$, 119–20. Condensed from five staves; realization omitted.
Translation : Cease, O fate, to make me suffer.

35. DTB XII$^2$, 159. Accompaniment (three-part strings) omitted.
Translation : I tremble, and mortal cold runs through my veins.

36. DTB XII$^2$, 163–64. Condensed from five staves; realization omitted.
Translation : The trumpet calls me here.

37. MfMg XIII (1881).
Translation : Ah, omnipotent God, worker of miracles, who has led
me mercifully through many a plight ! Neither in misery nor in happiness would I know what to do without you.

38. Franck, *Cara Mustapha*; H. C. Wolff, *Die Barockoper in Hamburg*
(Möseler Verlag, Wolfenbüttel and Zurich) II, 40–41.
Translation : Parting, sad parting, forever; ah, how my heart is torn
by suffering, all too heavy.

39. *Das Erbe deutscher Musik*, ser. 2, II, 147. Realization omitted.
Translation : When one has achieved his goal he should not let any
misgivings trouble his happiness, which will be gone before he knows
it.

40. Kusser, *Erindo*; H. C. Wolff, *Die Barockoper in Hamburg* II, 68–69.
Translation : Thus, in this longed-for sanctuary, may remembrance
and pledge both flourish together.

41. SB ex. 232. Accompaniment omitted.
Translation : O death, come and put an end to my sad lot.

42A. *Atys, Tragédie mise en musique par Monsieur de Lully* . . . A Paris,
Par Christopher Ballard . . . M.DC.LXXXIX, pp. 58–59.
Translation : When danger is pleasant, how can one be fearful of it?
Is it so wrong to love overmuch that which we find lovable?

42B. *Atys, Tragédie mise en musique par Monsieur de Lully* . . . , 2d ed.,
Oeuvre VI, [Paris] Christopher Ballard . . . M.DCCXX, pp. 42–43.

43. Lully, *Amadis*. Prunières ed. *Opéras* III, 95–96. Condensed from
five staves; flat added before last bass note of measure 8.
Translation : Thick woods, redouble your shade; you will never be
dark enough, you will never conceal deeply enough my unhappy
love.

44. Lully, *Phaëton* (1683).

45. *Old English Edition* XXV, 110. Slurs omitted.

46. *Old English Edition* XXV, 21. Reduced from three staves; realization omitted.

47. *Old English Edition* XXV, 130–31. Realization omitted.

48. Purcell, C.E. XXVI, 41.

49. Purcell, C.E. IX, 17–18. Reduced from four staves; realization omitted.

50. Purcell, C.E. XIX, 49. Reduced from two staves; realization omitted.

51. Händel, C.E. Supplement VI, 104. Reduced from four staves; names of instruments changed from "violino e flauto dolce"; "(Bassi)" changed to "[Continuo]."
Translation : Babble not so loud, O crystal-silver brook.

52. Händel, C. E. Supplement VI, 26.
Translation : Ormena ! Ormena, thou settest me on fire !

53. DdT XXXVII/XXXVIII, 38. Reduced from five staves; realization omitted; stage direction translated.
Translation : . . . and lovest no other?

54. DdT XXXVII/XXXVIII, 202. Reduced from five staves.
Translation : Gods, show pity.

55. Händel, C. E. LVII, 72. Accompaniment omitted.
Translation : Let the world fall.

56. Händel, C.E. LXVIII, 82–83. Recitative reduced from five staves, aria from six staves.
Translation : (Recitative) What do I hear? O God ! Cleopatra will yet die. Vile soul, when wilt thou depart? But still ! To avenge myself I shall have . . . . (Aria) If you do not feel pity for me, just Heaven, I shall die.

57. Rameau, C.E. X, *Appendice*, p. 26.
Translation : Mournful spot, where everything breathes shame and sorrow; dark and cruel realm of despair.

58. A. Scarlatti, *Mitridate Eupatore* (Library of Congress M 1500 .S28M5 case. f. 45–46ᵛ).
Translation : Kind Gods of our fathers, graciously hear my sorrow; as you favored with your help the undertakings of my ancestors, give strength to him who is preparing to punish a traitor.

59. Dent, *Alessandro Scarlatti*, p. 110. Realization omitted; figure and accidentals in brackets correspond to Dent's realization.
Translation : O vain hope ! O broken faith ! O brief, alluring, dolorous, impious happiness ! From whom now can I seek aid or consolation? In heaven, on the sea or the earth, in the abyss? Ah! Mithridates is dead !

60. Händel, C.E. XCII. Three string parts omitted; ornamented version of melody by Dr. Putnam Aldrich.
Translation : Never was shade of plant so dear, precious, and kindly.

61. Haas, *Aufführungspraxis*, p. 186. Signature changed from two flats.
Translation : . . . explains the cruelty of fate.

62. Vinci, *Artaserse* (Library of Congress M 1500 .V6A6), pp. 17 ff.
Translation : The wave of the sea bathes the valley and the mountain, goes by in the river, is imprisoned in the fountain, murmurs and groans always until it returns to the sea.

63. Pergolesi, *L'Olimpiade* (MS copy, Library of Congress M 1500 .P42O6 case).
Translation : While you sleep, Love increases the pleasure of your dreams with the thought of my pleasure.

64. Gerber, *Der Operntypus Hasses*, pp. 77–78. Slurs added, other slight changes in notation.
Translation : I will be silent if you desire it, but you are wronging my faithfulness if you call me betrayer.

65. DdT XV, 166. Accompaniment reduced from four staves.
Translation : Without regret I leave a greatness which I have known to be all too fragile and fleeting, and which I have possessed without being overcome by pride. A great and strong soul should always be ready to quit those goods from which death one day will separate him. But thou, O faithful wife !

66. DTB XIV¹, 146–47. Accompaniment (first and second violins, viola, continuo) omitted; realization and reduction omitted.
Translation : Do not weep for my misfortunes, do not be distressed at my torments.

67. DTB XIV², 144. Accompaniment (four string parts) omitted.
Translation : As your beautiful flame is lighted in your natal star, so will it shine resplendent.

68. DTOe LX, 46–47. Reduced from nine staves.

69. *I classici della musica italiana* XXIII, Quaderno 89–90, p. 11.
Translation : And yes and no, and no and yes, and here and there, and up and down—now enough of this : let's have an end of it !

70. *I classici della musica italiana* XX, Quaderno 80, pp. 6–7. Reduced from three staves.
Translation : But if Lindoro comes, then, ah ! then all is joy, all is well. When I shall see my love . . .

71. *Théâtre de la Foire*, Vol. I.

72. Monsigny, *Le Déserteur*. Piano-vocal score, Paris, Alphonse Leduc, no. A.L. 5204, pp. 10–11.
Translation : Can one give pain to the one he loves? Why try to annoy him? It is just like being spiteful toward oneself.

73. Grétry, C.E. I, 43–44. Orchestra parts condensed from seven staves.
Translation : O Richard, O my king ! All the world abandons you; only I in all the earth am concerned about you; I alone want to break your chains, and all the rest abandon you.

74. *The Beggar's Opera*, 2d ed. (1728), p. [45]. Repeat marks after first double bar omitted to conform with text.

75. Hiller, *Die Jagd* (Leipzig, 1772).
Translation : O, that his heart loved me as my heart loves him !

76. Dittersdorf, *Das rote Käppchen*. MS Vienna Nationalbibliothek.
Translation : 1. Why, in a word, does Mr. Schulz stay at home and not appear at today's meal? 2. I thank you for the food and drink,

when drunken men fall off their chairs. (Refrain) It might go bad with the women, but if one stays at home nothing can happen.

77. Subirá, *La tonadilla escénica* III, [16–17].
Translation : Let us go to the market, my dear.

78. Cherubini, *Lodoïska* (Paris, s.d. [1791?]), pp. 180–83.
Translation : Alas, in this cruel refuge, there was enough of my misfortune. . . . the end of the woes which I have suffered.

79. Cherubini, *Les Deux Journées*. Piano-vocal score, Universal Ed. 3157, p. 14. Text underlaid from another ed., Braunschweig, Meyer, [before 1862].
Translation : Good Frenchman, may God reward you; a good deed is never in vain.

80. Spontini, *Fernand Cortez*. Leipzig, Hofmeister, plate no. 1135, p. 282. Condensed from three staves.
Translation : Sorrowful presentiments, you do not deceive me; my fate is decided.

81. Auber, *La Muette de Portici*. Novello piano-vocal score, p. 137.
Translation : Holy love for our country, give us boldness and pride; to my country I owe life and it owes me liberty.

82. Meyerbeer, *L'Africaine*. Edition Peters No. 2773, piano-vocal score, p. 127. Reduced from three staves; indication of instruments omitted.
Translation : How pale she is ! What cold runs in my veins !

83. Berlioz, *Les Troyens*. Piano-vocal score, Choudens, p. 420. Names of instruments translated; flat added before bass D in measure 11; first eighth rest added in measure 15.
Translation : Farewell, proud city, which generous striving has so quickly built and made to flourish; my loving sister, follower in all my wanderings; farewell, my people, farewell !

84. Boieldieu, *Jean de Paris*. Piano-vocal score, Brussels, E. Loweryns, s.d., [ca. 1830?], pp. 60–61.
Translation : Remain faithful to Glory, cherish the beauty of ladies : that is the way to act like a true French cavalier.

86. Translation : Return, my protectress, help your poor servant; turn from me the rigor of a fate whose caprice I fear.

87. Herold, *Le Pré aux clercs*. Piano score, Paris, Léon Grus, plate no. 1746, pp. 72–73.

88. Mercadante, *La Vestale*. Piano-vocal score, [183–?] plate no. v. 12212 v, pp. 155–62.
Translation : Vestal & chorus : Through my being courses the horrid cold of death; surely a God whom the Tiber abhors today gave a sign in Heaven; he has crushed a father's heart, has changed joy into lamentation, glad songs of triumph into silence and terror.
Emilia : Chaste goddess, if our love is such a horrible crime, let one victim be enough to satisfy your anger; I pray for the hero : O save Decio's life and give me a hundred fearful and terrible deaths.

Decio : She did not know that I had penetrated this sanctuary forbidden to all men. I profaned the place sacred to the goddess. If heaven demands vengeance, if it awaits a victim, cut off this head, still girt with laurels.

89. Rossini, *Tancredi*. Piano-vocal score, Paris, Launer, plate no. 3237, pp. 50–51.

90. Donizetti, *Linda di Chamounix*. Piano-vocal score, Paris, Schonenberger, s.d. [184–?] plate no. S–975, p. 157.
Translation : If our love is so hateful to men, let us break the hard tie of this bitter life : in Heaven above our struggle will be ended.

91. Bellini, *La sonnambula*. Novello octavo piano-vocal score.
Translation : Ah, I will not look upon thee, O flower so soon withered; thou hast passed away even as love, which endured but a single day.

92. Verdi, *Ernani*. Piano-vocal score, Novello, plate no. 8063, pp. 174–75. Condensed from six staves.
Translation : So thou didst laugh, Lion of Castile, and every mountain of Iberia; every glad echo produced a great roar as once against the oppressing Moor.

93. Verdi, *La Traviata*. Piano-vocal score, G. Schirmer, p. 108.
Translation : Love me, Alfredo, love me as I love you.

94. Verdi, *Otello*. Piano-vocal score, Ricordi, plate no. 52105, p. 361.
Translation : And thou, how pale thou art! and motionless, and mute, and lovely, blessed creature born under an evil star.

95. Wagner, *Das Liebesverbot*. Piano-vocal score. B&H, plate no. E. B. 4520, p. 396.
Translation : Ah, what a death for love and honor; to it I dedicate my youthful strength.

96. Wagner, *Tannhäuser*. Eulenburg small score, plate no. E.E. 4850, pp. 648–49. Reduced from six staves.
Translation : With fervor in my heart such as no sinner has ever felt, I sought the road to Rome.

97. Wagner, *Lohengrin*. B&H, plate no. 25700, p. 140.
Translation : Never shalt thou ask me, never trouble to know whence I came, nor my name and state.

100. D'Indy, *L'Etranger*. Piano-vocal score, Durand (1902), pp. 149–50. Some notes enharmonically altered.
Translation : O sea ! Sinister sea, seductive in thy raging.

101. Puccini, *Tosca*. Piano-vocal score, G. Ricordi & Co., plate no. q 109916 q, p. 1. By kind permission of G. Ricordi & Co., Milan.

102. Puccini, *Madama Butterfly*. Piano score, Ricordi, plate no. 110001, p. 123.

103. Giordano, *Andrea Chénier*. Piano-vocal score, Sonzogno (1896), plate no. 929, pp. 88–89.

Translation : I have often heard her say with her ardent voice :
have faith in love, Chénier ! thou art loved !

104. Kienzl, *Der Evangelimann*. Bote & Bock, piano-vocal score (1894),
plate no. 14035, pp. 66–67. Upper staff of accompaniment omitted.
Translation : You're not hitting anything any more. The bowling
ball is too heavy for you.

105. Glinka, *A Life for the Tsar*. Piano-vocal score, Moscow, n.d., p. 212.
Alto voice and accompaniment omitted.

106. Glinka, *Ruslan and Ludmila*. Piano-vocal score, Moscow, P. Jurgenson, s.d., plate no. 30087, pp. 269–70.

107. Mussorgsky, *Boris Godunov*. Piano-vocal score, London, J. & W.
Chester, plate no. J.W.C. 9722, p. 154. Reproduced by permission
of J. & W. Chester, Ltd., London.
Translation : Phew ! Give me air ! This suffocates my soul ! I felt
blood surging upward to my face, then down again like a torrent.
O conscience, thou art cruel, merciless thy vengeance !

108. Rimsky-Korsakov, *Sadko*. Piano-vocal score, Leipzig, M. P. Balaieff,
[1906?] plate no. 1434–1643, pp. 82–83.
Translation : Come out from the blue sea, come out to the green
fields; come out, prophetic sisters.

109. Pedrell, *Los Pirineos*. Piano-vocal score, J. B. Pujol, plate no. P.25C.,
pp. 239–40. Time signature, tempo mark, and first "pp" inserted
from previous directions.

110. Debussy, *Pelléas et Mélisande*. Piano-vocal score, Durand (1907),
p. 236.
Translation : Mélisande : Pelléas ! Pelléas : Mélisande ! Is it thou,
Mélisande ? Mélisande : Yes. Pelléas : Come here.

111. Dukas, *Ariane et Barbe-Bleue*. Piano-vocal score, Durand (1906),
pp. 72–74. Reduced from three or five staves to show only essential
harmonic outline; recitatives (two soloists) omitted.
Translation : The five daughters of Orlamonde (the black fairy is
dead) have sought the gates, have lighted their five lamps, have
opened the towers, have traversed three hundred rooms without
finding daylight, have opened a well . . .

112. Montemezzi, *L'amore dei tre re*. Piano-vocal score, Ricordi, plate no.
114651, pp. 126–27. Reduced from four staves; first two measures
notated with signature of three flats instead of three sharps.
Translation : Take, take her; there thou art, Fiora.

113. Pfitzner, *Palestrina*. Piano-vocal score cop. 1916 by Adolph Fürstner
(A.7403, 7415, 7418F), p. 5.

114. Richard Strauss, *Capriccio*. Piano-vocal score, Boosey & Hawkes,
plate no. 8453, pp. 80–81. Copyright 1942 by Richard Strauss. Reprinted by permission of Boosey & Hawkes Inc., Sole Agents.
Translation of Pierre de Ronsard's Sonnet XXVIII from his *Continuation des Amours* (Paris, 1555). Pierre de Ronsard, *Oeuvres*

*complètes,* Vol. VII, ed. Paul Laumonier (Paris, Droz, 1934), pp. 145–46.

Je ne saurois aimer autre que vous,
Non, Dame, non, je ne saurois le faire:
Autre que vous ne me sauroit complaire,
Et fust Venus descendue entre nous.
  Vos yeus me sont si gracieus & dous,
Que d'un seul clin ils me peuvent defaire,
D'un autre clin tout soudain me refaire,
Me faisant vivre ou mourir en deux cous.
  Quand je serois cinq cens mille ans en vie,
Autre que vous, ma mignonne m'amie,
Ne me feroit amoureus devenir.
  Il me faudroit refaire d'autres venes,
Les miennes sont de vostre amour si plenes,
Qu'un autre amour n'y sauroit plus tenir.

115. Szymanowski, *König Roger.* Piano-vocal score, Universal Ed., plate no. U.E. 7750, pp. 23–26. Used by permission of Universal Editions, A.G., Vienna.
Translation: See, there he is! There he comes! Seize the wretch, kill the blasphemer, stone him, stone him!

116. Bartók, *Herzog Blaubarts Burg.* Piano-vocal score, Universal Ed., plate no. U.E. 7026, p. 11. Copyright 1921 by Universal Edition. Renewed 1948. Copyright and renewal assigned to Boosey & Hawkes Inc. Reprinted by permission.
Translation: The walls are wet! What moisture is this on my hands? Do the rocks and dungeons weep?—Ah, Judith, better were the bright days of our betrothal, when white walls enclosed the garden of roses and sunshine gilded the gables.

117. Poulenc, *Les Dialogues des Carmélites.* Piano-vocal score, Ricordi, plate no. R.1471, pp. 80–81. By kind permission of G. Ricordi & Co., Milan.
Translation: . . . like the child of one's old age, and also the most risky, the most threatened. To turn away this threat I would gladly have given my poor life.

118. Prokofiev, *War and Peace* (Moscow, 1958, plate no. M 26793$^a$), pp. 77–79.
Translation: . . . when from the gold-drenched hills the herds are flocking down to the river, and the clamor of their lowing thunders melodiously across the waters; and, his nets hauled in, the fisherman in his boat is shore-bound, sailing alone, framed by bushes . . .

119. Janáček, *Katja Kabanowa.* Piano-vocal score, Universal Ed., plate no. U.E. 7103, pp. 143–45. Used by permission of Universal Editions, A.G., Vienna.
Translation: How kindly my Boris spoke to me, how tenderly! I

know no more. The nights are full of terror; everyone goes to rest, but for me it is like sinking into the grave. This fear of the dark! And such a noise!—That is like singing!

120. Honegger, *Antigone*. Piano-vocal score, Senart, plate no. EMS7297, pp. 51–52.
Translation : Neither does justice impose laws of this sort, and I did not believe that your decree could make the caprice of a man prevail over the rule of the immortals, over the laws which are not written.

121. Milhaud, *Le Pauvre Matelot*. Piano-vocal score, Paris, Heugel, [no plate no.] pp. 38–40.
Translation : His wife : Come in! The sailor : I come to bring you news, Madame. His wife : Of my husband? The sailor : Yes, indeed, Madame, news of your husband. His wife : He is dead . . . The sailor : No, Madame, he is alive, I saw him three weeks ago.

122. Hindemith, *Die Harmonie der Welt*. Piano-vocal score, Mainz, B. Schott's Söhne, ed. no. 4925.

123. Stravinsky, *The Rake's Progress*. Piano-vocal score, Boosey & Hawkes, plate no. B&H 17088, p. 222. Copyright 1949, 1950, 1951 by Boosey & Hawkes Inc. Reprinted by permission.

124. Berg, *Wozzeck*. Universal Ed., plate nos. U.E. 7379/U.E. 121000, p. 29. Used by permission of Universal Editions, A.G., Vienna.
Translation : We poor folk! See, Captain : money, money! Those who have no money!

125. Dallapiccola, *Il Prigionero*. Piano-vocal score, S. Zerboni, plate no. S. 4464 Z., pp. 61–62. By kind permission of Edizioni Suvini Zerboni, Milan.
Translation : I cannot control [myself]. Surprised here, at night, I could not avoid renewed, atrocious sufferings. What to do? Return to my dark cell and wait still, always in vain?

126. Orff, *Oedipus der Tyrann*. Piano-vocal score, Mainz, B. Schott's Söhne, ed. no. 4996, p. 234. © 1959 by B. Schott's Soehne, Mainz. Reprinted by permission of the original copyright owners and their U.S. representatives, Associated Music Publishers, Inc., New York.
Translation : Perish the man, whoe'er he was, that loosed me from the cruel fetters on my feet and rescued me from death and saved my life, conferring no kindness thereby! For had I then died, I had not been so sore a woe to my friends or mine own self. (Chorus :) I too could have wished it thus. (E. P. Coleridge's translation)

127. Janáček, *Das schlaue Füchslein*. Piano-vocal score, Universal Ed., plate no. U.E. 7564, pp. 176–78. Used by permission of Universal Editions, A.G., Vienna.

# INDEX

Numbers in italic type under titles or names of persons represent
entries of special importance